Warman's
GLASS
3RD EDITION

EDITED BY ELLEN T. SCHROY

Published by

**krause
publications**

700 E. State Street • Iola, WI 54990-0001
Telephone: 715/445-2214

Please call or write for our free catalog.
Our toll-free number to place an order or obtain a free catalog is 800-258-0929
or please use our regular business telephone 715-445-2214
for editorial comment and further information.

Library of Congress Catalog Number: 98-84636
ISBN: 0-87341-649-X

Printed in the United States of America

Photos on the front cover are, top left: Cambridge Glass, dresser compact, #681, light cutting,
emerald with Peach-blow rose knob, $210; top right: Morgantown Glass, Rawsthorne, #33, jug, Anna Rose, Peacock Optic,
reeded handle, 48 oz, $195; bottom right: Carnival glass, Poppy Show, Northwood, plate, green, 9" d, $3,000; center: Fostoria Glass,
Fairfax, #2375, oil, Azure, ftd, #283 Kasmir plate etching, $185; bottom left: Carnival Glass, vase, Tornado, pastel green tornado centers, $2,100.
Photos at bottom right and left are courtesy of Mickey Reichel Auction Center. The other photos are courtesy of the late Jerry Gallagher.

Photos featured on the back cover are: Carnival Glass, Hattie, Imperial, chop plate,
amber, 10-1/2" d, $3,850 (photo courtesy of Albrecht Auction: and Fire King cup and saucer, Alice pattern, Jade-ite, $12.
Pictured on the spine is an Orrefors vase, Gunnar Wennerberg, 1909, Kosta Boda, Sweden (photo courtesy of Kosta Boda).

ACKNOWLEDGMENTS

As I finish this edition of *Warman's Glass*, the sweet smell of peonies fills my office. The pretty spring flowers are held in a pretty vase that is a yard-sale find. Part of the fun and excitement of writing *Warman's*, whether this edition, or the general price guides, is using the antiques and collectibles I've grown to treasure. But, there are more important things to treasure, those being family and friends who encourage and offer support while a new edition is being credited. To Jeffrey, Mark, Linda, Brian, Mom and Dad, Janet, Tracy, neighbors Jocelyn and her husband Harry, and Mary, I've got to add a whole new list of cyber friends. This new support team includes Marie, Dorothy, Jerry, Larry, Michael, Woody, Sam, Judy, Kathy, Anne, and Connie, plus others. From tangible offerings, such as baby-bottle prices to expert advice on pricing and the weekly bouts of humor we share, this group of friends means a lot. From the cookies offered over the fence, to the words of "you can do this" and hugs, real and cyber, the energy is found to keep researching, writing, and exploring.

This edition probably represents more cyber exploration than any other I've done. Daily readings of postings from WWW.CGA and DGShopper Online have taught me many things, from how to discern colors of carnival glass to what types of patterns to watch for in Depression era glassware. I greatly enjoy visiting Angela Bowey's Glass Museum On-Line, (http://www.glass.co.nz). My list of bookmarks reads like a "who's who" of the cyber glassworld. E-mail has connected me to pattern glass experts and led me to other experts and manufacturers, such as Orrefors Kosta Boda. You will see many more internet references in the individual category introductions, leading along these exciting paths.

Real life support also includes the friendly faces at many auction houses, antiques shows, flea markets, and malls. I can't begin to list all of you, those who offer smiles, hand shakes, assistance of all kinds. Through our discussions, I find I am constantly learning and being challenged to discover more. I have always loved the research and information gathering aspects of my career, and through the help of many, I continue to enjoy this fascinating marketplace. I've had great cooperation from auction houses, both large and small, in the form of catalogs, prices realized, press releases, newsletters, and photographs, all of which are appreciated.

Associates at Krause Publications in Iola, Wisconsin, are the best! To Jon Brecka, Pat Klug, Kris Manty, and the other 399 employees, a heart felt thank you for your fine efforts. The professional attitude each brings to this book is appreciated. As I write this section in late April 1998, I have no idea to whom I owe these thanks, since many hands will help create the edition you are holding. However, I am confident that this edition will be one *we are all proud of*. From the editors to the production staff to the sales staff and all the others, *thank you.*

Some new categories have been added, like Buttons. Other categories have been rearranged to make the listings easier to read or understand. Some categories have been lengthened to reflect their strong presence in the marketplace. Others are diminished to show the fact that they are not quite as popular in the 1990s. All are now given to you, the reader, the collector, the dealer, the appraiser, the student. Enjoy! I'm off to find more glassware to research, to read about, to ponder over, as I continue to learn about glassware, as well as all kinds of antiques and collectibles.

Ellen Louise Tischbein Schroy
P.O. Box 392
Quakertown, PA 18951-1119
e-mail: Schroy@voicenet.com

INTRODUCTION

Warman's Glass offers antiques and collectibles collectors and dealers information about all the major glass-collecting categories in one book. As part of Warman's Encyclopedia of Antiques and Collectibles series, *Warman's Glass* gives readers a wealth of information, as well as hundreds of listings, photographs, marks, and illustrations, all relating to the colorful world of glass collecting. It also serves as a companion to *Warman's Antiques and Collectibles Price Guide.*

Warman's Glass includes listings from the antiques marketplace, collectibles marketplace, and studio art of contemporary craftsmen. Because this is a "Warman's" book, you will find detailed information relating to the history to glass type and/or company, reference books, collectors' clubs, and tips to spotting reproductions. Of course, the listings are as detailed as possible. Careful attention has been given to listing correct pattern names, colors, sizes, and other pertinent details.

Warman's Glass covers individual companies, such as Fostoria and Morgantown, as well as the general glass categories such as Depression Glass and Pattern Glass. Since *Warman's Glass* is a price guide, it cannot list every pattern or piece made. Warman's is continually increasing the glass coverage in the Warman price guides as more knowledge and references are found. For more than forty years, Warman guides have been the leaders in the antiques and collectibles field, a tradition this and subsequent editions will continue.

History

Historians date early examples of glassware back as far as the third century B.C. These early combinations of sand and ash were probably the results of accidental mixing at the edges of a fire.

The first real attempts at glassmaking are not well documented, but examples of early utilitarian pieces, such as bottles and bowls, have survived. The Egyptians used glass objects and were very fond of small beads and pieces, which they used as decorations. Because of the great pyramids, historians have carefully documented glassware pieces.

As human civilization developed and spread throughout the world, it became more necessary to preserve and transport foods. Glass bottles and jars, made from local raw materials, were the answer. The color variations found allow modern science to evaluate the type of sand and other minerals that were available to the glassblowers.

As the technologies for glassblowing and later mass production evolved, so did its uses. Utilitarian objects were followed by the production of window panes and soon decorative objects. The scientific use of glass led to advances in many fields. We really don't think when using a Corningware container out of the freezer and putting it directly into the microwave that it is really made of glass and that the ability to use glass in this fashion developed only recently. Glass was first used for storage, and only later for cooking. Modern kitchens now include glass as stove tops in addition to the utilitarian and decorative glassware we have come to take almost for granted. Who knows what kind of developments will occur as glass manufacturers look to the next century!

Glassblowers and manufacturers are credited with many patents for glass techniques, as well as manufacturing advances. However, the real credit for attracting collectors to glass must be given to those who continually strived to develop new colors and shapes. By adding certain minerals and chemicals, glass changes colors and can become stronger or weaker. Certain combinations, such as those Findlay used for his beautiful onyx ware, created stunning pieces, but the glass was very brittle so that few examples survive.

Antique and collectible glassware is like precious jewels. Glassware is available in every color and hue of the rainbow. Like precious stones, glassware can be engraved, carved, etched, and made into wonderful creations. European glassmakers created masterpieces by engraving crystal objects with detailed portraits and other types of decoration. Cameo glass examples of Gallé and Daum Nancy factories were blown and feature carved layers of different colors, much the same way cameo jewelry brooches are created by carving shells. Etched intaglio designs grace cut glass, as well as later mass-produced pieces made by such companies as Imperial and Fostoria.

Crystal clear glassware was the objective of early blowers as they tried to experiment with different combinations. Cut glass decorators demanded high quality clear leaded glass for their creations.

Gemlike colors of rich deep blues, amethyst, emerald greens, and blood reds can be found throughout the ages of glass collecting. Experimental color combinations to artists such as Louis Tiffany and Frederick Carder at Steuben resulted in the iridescent hues of Favrile and Aurene glass. Cambridge and Heisey produced vivid translucent colors, like Heatherbloom and Alexandrite.

Glassware has always been manufactured to appeal to the woman's eye. Brides choose their trousseau and table settings today just as they did in past generations. Specialized serving pieces, such as berry bowls, cheese domes, and pickle castors were the glories of the past. Today's brides are able to choose from hundreds of crystal patterns, but do not have access to the wide variety of firms of their grandmothers' and great grandmothers' eras. Today's bride may serve berries from a standard round bowl, while her great grandmother served berries from a peach-blow basket, in a silver plated holder, into delicate, matching sauce dishes.

Care and storing tips

Glass is easy to care for and store. Most glass was produced for utilitarian purposes. Those lovely sauce bowls were really made for everyday use. Manufacturers designed their glass for heavy use while appealing to the eye, and many objects were mass produced. The survival rate is high.

Today's collectors can often purchase mint or fine condition examples of most glass, provided they are willing to pay the price. Pieces that show aging, e.g., some gilding removed by washing, are also desirable, since it may be proof of authenticity.

Glassware can be repaired using modern techniques that produce amazing results. Edges with chips can be ground. The price is lower, but not significantly. Most importantly, the glass is available for re-use. It's beauty can continue to be appreciated.

Take care when purchasing glassware. Examine each piece carefully. Look and feel for wear and imperfections. After purchase, make certain to wrap each piece separately in several layers. Glass can shatter when dropped, but also when exposed to changes in temperature. If you purchase a wonderful piece, carry it around for several hours, and suddenly go out into the cold air, beware. Don't unwrap the glass! Allow it to adjust gradually to the colder temperatures. Likewise, when you take it back indoors, gently unwrap the piece and allow it to come to room temperature before adding it to your collection. Never wash it until it's temperature matches that of the environment.

During the summer, care should be taken to gradually cool glass. Storing a newly acquired treasure in a car trunk for hours is fine. Just do not take it into the house and wash it immediately in cold water. Milk glass of the post-World War II era is especially vulnerable to changes in temperatures.

Today, we know that exposing colorless flint glassware to strong sunlight may cause it to chemically react and develop a purple hue. The popular decorating idea of the 1920s through the 1950s of placing shelves of glass in window frames has proven disastrous for many pieces of glass. What our modern home environment will do to glassware is still not clearly established. Colored glassware hues do not appear to fade, but owners are well advised to use caution if they have strong lighting in their display cabinets.

Most antique and collectible glassware should never see the inside of a dishwasher. The temperatures are too severe and the water pressures too great. Gently hand washing glassware protects the pieces and gives collectors an opportunity to study their collections. Learn the feel of your glassware: remember how heavy it feels, and how sharp the cuttings or patterns feel. This knowledge will help you spot reproductions and copycats.

When storing antique and collectible glassware, make sure the storage area is sturdy. Shelves should be well secured. Periodically check that glass objects are not moving slightly because of normal vibrations. Objects should not touch one another; place pieces of packing materials between stacked objects. Even more precautions should be taken in earthquake-prone areas. It is a good idea to gently remove stoppers from cruets, decanters, etc. periodically to make sure they haven't become stuck. There are many commercial cleaners available to remove interior stains. When trying one of these products, start with the minimum suggested by the manufacturer and proceed with caution and gentle pressure. Never use harsh chemicals on hand-painted pieces, gold trim, iridized finishes, or things that appear very delicate. Once enamel, gilt, or paint is removed, the price of the piece is diminished.

Glass collectors should maintain an inventory of their collections. This will allow them to have a better idea of what their collection contains, its value, etc. When preparing an inventory, write a detailed description of each piece, what history you might know, the purchase price, dealers' names and addresses, date, any reference books, etc. Some collectors also photograph their items, giving them an instant identification guide to their collections.

Organization of the book

Listings: Objects are listed alphabetically by category, beginning with ABC Plates and ending with Whimsies. If you have trouble identifying the category to which your glassware belongs, use the extensive index in the back of the book. It will guide you to the proper category.

We have made the listings descriptive enough so that specific objects can be identified. We also emphasize items that are actively being sold in the marketplace. Some harder-to-find objects are included to demonstrate market spread—useful information worth considering when you have not traded actively in a category recently. A few categories in this book also appear in *Warman's Antiques and Collectibles Price Guide*, *Warman's Americana and Collectibles*, and *Warman's Depression Glass*. The listings in *Warman's Glass* expand on these two volumes, creating a new companion volume for the general dealer or specialized collector.

History: Collectors and dealers enhance their appreciation of objects by knowing something about their history. We present a capsule history for each category. In many cases, this history contains collecting hints or other useful information. Collectors are encouraged to continue to learn and share their knowledge about their specific interests. Research of the past decades by such people as Ruth Webb Lee, George and Helen McKearin, Alice Metz, and E. McCamley Belknap has been treasured and enhanced by modern researches such as Regis and Mary Ferson and Jerry Gallagher, as well as the late William Heacock and Hazel Weatherman.

References: Books are listed in most categories to help you learn more about the objects. Included are author, title, publisher, and date of publication or most recent edition. If a book has been published by a small firm or individual, we have indicated (published by author). Beginning with this edition, the address from which to obtain these hard-to-locate sources is included when possible.

Many of the books included in the lists are hard to find. The antiques and collectibles field is blessed with a dedicated core of book dealers who stock these specialized publications. You will find them at flea markets and antiques shows and through their advertisements in trade publications. Books go out of print quickly, yet many books printed over 25 years ago remain the standard work in a category. Used book dealers often can locate many of these valuable reference sources. Many dealers publish annual or semi-annual catalogs. Ask to be put on their mailing lists. The Internet now also offers a wonderful source for finding out-of-print glass books.

Periodicals: The newsletter or bulletin of a collectors' club usually provides the concentrated focus sought by specialty collectors and dealers. However, there are publications, not associated with collectors' clubs, about which collectors and dealers should be aware. These are listed in their appropriate category introductions.

In the antique and collectible glass field, there are several general periodicals, as well as specialized periodicals, to which the glass collector should subscribe:

Antique Bottle & Glass Collector, P.O. Box 187, East Greenville, PA 18041

Antique Trader Weekly, P.O. Box 1050, Dubuque, IA 52001; http://www.csmonline.com

AntiqueWeek, P.O. Box 90, Knightstown, IN 46148; http://www.antiqueweek.com

Antiques & Collecting, 1006 South Michigan Avenue, Chicago, IL 60605

Glass Collector's Digest, P.O. Box 553, Marietta, OH 45750-0553

Maine Antique Digest, P.O. Box 358, Waldoboro, ME 04572; http://www.maineantiquedigest.com

The Daze, Depression Glass Daze, Inc., 10271 State Rd, Box 57, Otisville, MI 48463-0057

Space does not permit listing all the national and regional publications in the antiques and collectibles field. The above is a sampling. A check with your local library will bring many other publications to your attention.

Collectors' Clubs: Collectors' clubs add vitality to the antiques and collectibles field. Their publications and conventions produce knowledge which often cannot be found elsewhere. Many of these clubs are short-lived; others are so strong that they have regional and local chapters.

Museums: The best way to study a specific field is to see as many documented examples as possible. For this reason, we have listed museums where significant collections in that category are on display. Special attention must be directed to the complex of museums which make up the Smithsonian Institution in Washington, D.C. Premiere collections of glassware are available for study at several major museums, including the Chrysler Museum in Norfolk, Va.; the Corning Museum of Glass, Corning, N.Y.; and the Toledo Museum Art Museum, Toledo, Ohio.

Reproductions: Reproductions are a major concern to all collectors and dealers. Throughout this edition, notes and information will alert you to known reproductions and keys to recognizing them. Most reproductions are unmarked; the newness of their appearance is often the best clue to uncovering them. The information is designed to serve as a reminder of past reproductions and prevent you from buying them, believing them to be period.

We strongly recommend subscribing to *Antique & Collectors Reproduction News*, a monthly newsletter that reports on past and present reproductions, copycats, fantasies, and fakes. Send $32 for twelve issues to: ACRN, P.O. Box 12130, Des Moines, IA 50312-9403.

Reproductions are only one aspect of the problem; outright fakes are another. Unscrupulous manufacturers make fantasy items which never existed., e.g., the Eyewinker pattern never included a goblet. Reproduction Eyewinker goblets can easily be found.

Paper labels are now being reproduced and placed on period glassware, as well as reproductions. This statement is made to make you aware of, and to question, each piece you purchase. Is the piece the proper color, shape, density? Does the label appear original; does it show signs of age that are consistent with a piece of glassware from this time period? Questions, questions, and more questions are often a collector's constant companion, but can lead to a sense of satisfaction.

Marks: Antique and collectible glass may have manufacturers' marks. Unfortunately, most types of glass are unmarked. It was very difficult to include a mark in a mold. Certain marks, like Heisey's "H" in a diamond, are very small and can be difficult to find. Some of the acid-etched glass marks are also difficult to identify. Careful study of pieces is necessary. Don't be afraid to ask dealers to show you where a piece is marked. Paper labels may have become lost over the years. The dates given on the marks included in this volume are often approximate. Several manufacturers, like Imperial Glass, used several different marks. Therefore, marks should be considered as clues, just as style, color, and other characteristics can lead to the discovery of the maker and date of manufacture.

Price notes

In assigning prices, we assume the object is in very good condition. If otherwise, we note this in our description. It would be ideal to suggest that mint, or unused, examples of all objects exist. The reality is that objects from the past were used. Because of this, some normal wear must be expected.

Whenever possible, we have tried to provide a broad listing of prices within a category so you have a "feel" for the market. We emphasize the middle range of prices within a category, while also listing some objects of high and low value to show market spread.

We do not use ranges because they tend to confuse rather than help the collector and dealer. How do you determine if your object is at the high or low end of the range? There is a high degree of flexibility in pricing in the antiques field. If you want to set ranges, add or subtract 10 percent from our prices.

One of the hardest variants with which to deal is the regional fluctuations of prices, as well as the type of market, be it an auction or flea market. We have tried to strike a balance. Know your region and subject before investing heavily. If the best buys for cameo glass are in Montreal or

Toronto, then be prepared to go there if you want to save money or add choice pieces to your collection. Research and patience are key factors to building a collection of merit. Another pricing segment of glassware are the traditional reference books. Referred to as "book price," collectors should consider this like the prices found as "list prices" on new cars. It's a place to start negotiating.

Another factor that affects prices is a sale by a leading dealer or private collector. We temper both dealer and auction house figures.

Price research

Everyone asks, "Where do you get our prices?"

They come from many sources.

First, we rely on auctions. Auction houses and auctioneers do not always command the highest prices. If they did, why do so many dealers buy from them? The key to understanding auction prices is to know when a price is high or low in the range. We think we do this and do it well. This third edition of *Warman's Glass* represents a concentrated effort to contact more regional auction houses, both large and small. The cooperation has been outstanding and has resulted in an ever-growing pool of auction prices and trends to help us determine the most up-to-date auction prices.

Second, we work closely with dealers. We screen our contacts to make certain they have full knowledge of the market. Dealers make their living from selling antiques; they cannot afford to have a price guide which is not in touch with the market.

Collectors work closely with us. They are specialists whose devotion to research and accurate information is inspiring. Generally, they are not dealers. Whenever we have asked them for help, they have responded willingly and admirably.

Warman's Glass is designed to be a buyer's guide suggesting what you would have to pay to purchase an object on the open market from a dealer or collector. It is not a seller's guide to prices. People frequently make this mistake. In doing so, they deceive themselves. If you have an object listed in this book and wish to sell it to a dealer, you should expect to receive approximately 50 percent of the listed value. If the object will not resell quickly, expect to receive even less.

STATE OF THE MARKET

Investing in glassware offers opportunities to spend anywhere from a few dollars to hundreds of thousands of dollars. A new piece of Westmoreland glassware might be added to a collection for about $10 or less, while a choice piece of cameo glass can cost thousands of dollars. Collectors often specialize in a specific pattern or type of glass to provide definition and restraint to their collections.

Current glass-collecting opportunities reflect new areas of interest, as well as strongly established older categories. Collectors are continually offered a new rainbow of colors and objects. Original boxes are treasured; documentation and advertisements are saved and studied; labels are never removed. Collectors of 18th, 19th, and early 20th century glass face different challenges: who made the piece, how was it used, when was it made?

Specialized antiques and collectibles shows concentrating primarily on glass are doing well in the late 1990s. Dealers continue to offer high-quality glassware. More specialized shows, such as cut glass shows and Depression glass shows, are drawing more and more collectors. These specialized shows feature a larger variety of patterns and pieces than found at a general show. These shows expand a collector's horizons. For example, a Depression glass show includes not only the patterns defined as Depression glass, like Moderntone, but also fine glassware produced by Heisey, Cambridge, Fostoria, and others. Specialized shows are a wonderful place to experience the myriad of colors available, learn about the shapes, and see the wealth of sizes produced.

General antiques shows try to present a balanced approach. Promoters actively try to include dealers representing the broad market. You will find dealers offering art glass, cut glass, Depression glass, and pattern glass. General line dealers also offer some glassware items.

Flea markets and antique malls are like general antiques shows in that they try to appeal to the broad marketplace. Both of these venues can be great places to spend hours searching for examples to add to collections.

Overall, prices for glassware are remaining stable. Some of the high-end art glasses, like Tiffany and Steuben, have suffered slightly due to reproductions and examples of lesser quality that have been signed later by unscrupulous characters. However, even with this identification problem, the major auction houses continue to be able to do well with stunning examples. Some of the hand-produced glassware produced in America, such as Morgantown, Fostoria, and Tiffin, are showing steady increases in their prices. Many collectors are choosing to invest in these types of glasswares, enjoying their aesthetic designs, clarity, or color. Another area that is showing an increased interest by collectors is studio art glass. Unique pieces are now entering the secondary market and establishing some exciting prices. The one aspect of the glassware market that has fallen on hard times is the area of damaged pieces. Little tolerance is now made for broken, chipped, or damaged pieces. Collectors should strive for the best example they can find.

Glassware dealers continue to maintain large inventories. It is not unusual for a dealer to work closely with collectors and other dealers to supply patterns or items currently in demand. It always pays to ask a dealer if they have any other examples in their inventories. It is this type of customer service that makes glass dealers a special group in the field of antiques.

The Internet and World Wide Web of antiques and collector dealers are making an impact on the world of collecting. By connecting to this fascinating world, collectors can now purchase almost any type of glassware. Whether it's from a cyber mall, shop, web site, or auction, purchases can be made easily. The ability to shop at any hour of the day or night, in the comfort of one's home, will let collectors increase their spending. Dealers are learning the importance of this message and many are going on-line to service this expanding market. This is an area where accurate descriptions are highly desirable; digital images may offer exciting views. However, just like the real world, it's up to the buyer to decide how many dollars to spend and if the descriptions are accurate. And, just as in the real world, the cyber world offers excellent resources for finding out-of-print books, like Robert Eaton's *Eaton's Glass Books on the Web* (http://glassbooks.com). For people interested in Carnival Glass, there is an on-line collector's club, WWW.CGA at http://www.woodsland.com. Collectors who specialize in Depression Glass can subscribe to an on-line magazine, DG Shopper, http://www.dgshopper.com. Both of these sites offer articles, chat rooms, vendors, and auctions, as well as reference areas filled with images and interesting information. What is hard to describe is the amount of knowledge that one can gleam from participating in these kinds of websites. It certainly offers collectors a way to contact more experienced collectors and ask questions about color, manufacturers, care, etc. One of the most fascinating aspects of the Internet is that it is always expanding, giving collectors new areas to explore.

AUCTION HOUSES

The following auction houses cooperate with Warman's by providing catalogs of their auctions and price lists. This information is used to prepare *Warman's Antiques and Collectibles Price Guide*, volumes in the Warman's Encyclopedia of Antiques and Collectibles. This support is truly appreciated.

Albrecht & Cooper Auction Services
3884 Saginaw Rd
Vassar, MI 48768
(517) 823-8835

Sanford Alderfer Auction Company
501 Fairgrounds Rd
Hatfield, PA 19440
(215) 393-3000
web site: http://www.alderfer
  company.com

Andre Ammelounx
The Stein Auction Company
P.O. Box 136
Palantine, IL 60078
(847) 991-5927

Apple Tree Auction Center
1616 W. Church St.
Newark, OH 43055
(614) 344-4282

Arthur Auctioneering
RD 2, P.O. Box 155
Hughesville, PA 17737
(717) 584-3697

Aston Macek Auctioneers &
  Appraisers
2825 Country Club Rd
Endwell, NY 13760-3349
(607) 785-6598

Auction Team Köln
Jane Herz
6731 Ashley Court
Sarasota, FL 34241
(941) 925-0385

Auction Team Köln
Postfach 501168 D 5000
Köln 50, W. Germany

Bailey's Antiques
102 E Main St.
Homer, MI 49245
(517) 568-4014

Bill Bertoia Auctions
1881 Spring Rd
Vineland, NJ 08360
(609) 692-1881

Biders Antiques Inc.
241 S Union St.
Lawrence, MA 01843
(508) 688-4347

Butterfield, Butterfield & Dunning
7601 Sunset Blvd.
Los Angeles, CA 90046
(213) 850-7500

220 San Bruno Ave.
San Francisco, CA 94103
(415) 861-7500

755 Church Road
Elgin, IL 60123
(847) 741-3483

C. C. Auction Gallery
416 Court
Clay Center, KS 67432
(913) 632-6021

W. E. Channing & Co., Inc.
53 Old Santa Fe Trail
Santa Fe, NM 87501
(505) 988-1078

Chicago Art Galleries
5039 Oakton St.
Skokie, IL 60077
(847) 677-6080

Christie's
502 Park Ave.
New York, NY 10022
(212) 546-1000
web site: http://www.sirius.com/
  ~christie/

Christie's East
219 E. 67th St.
New York, NY 10021
(212) 606-0400

Cincinnati Art Galleries
635 Main St.
Cincinnati, OH 45202
(513) 381-2128

Mike Clum, Inc.
P.O. Box 2
Rushville, OH 43150
(614) 536-9220

Cohasco Inc.
Postal 821
Yonkers, NY 10702
(914) 476-8500

Samuel J. Cottonne
15 Genesee St.
Mt. Morris, NY 14510
(716) 583-3119

Craftsman Auctions
1485 W. Housatoric
Pittsfield MA 02101
(413) 448-8922

Dargate Auction Galleries
5607 Baum Blvd.
Pittsburgh, PA 15206
(412) 362-3558
web site: http://www.dargate.com

DeWolfe & Wood
P.O. Box 425
Alfred, ME 04002
(207) 490-5572

Marlin G. Denlinger
RR3, Box 3775
Morrisville, VT 05661
(802) 888-2775

Dixie Sporting Collectibles
1206 Rama Rd.
Charlotte, NC 28211
(704) 364-2900
web site: http://www.sportauction

William Doyle Galleries, Inc.
175 E 87th St.
New York, NY 10128
(212) 427-2730
web site: http://www.doyle
  galleries.com

Dunbar Gallery
76 Haven St.
Milford, MA 01757
(508) 634-8697

Early Auction Co.
123 Main St.
Milford, OH 45150
(513) 831-4833

Fain & Co.
P.O. Box 1330
Grants Pass, OR 97526
(888) 324-6726

Ken Farmer Realty & Auction Co.
105A Harrison St.
Radford, VA 24141
(703) 639-0939
web site: http://kenfarmer.com

Flomaton Antique Auction
207 Palafox St.
Flomaton, AL 36441
(334) 296-3059

William A. Fox Auctions Inc.
676 Morris Ave.
Springfield, NJ 07081
(201) 467-2366

Freeman\Fine Arts Co. of
    Philadelphia, Inc.
1808 Chestnut St.
Philadelphia, PA 19103
(215) 563-9275

Garth's Auction, Inc.
2690 Stratford Rd.
P.O. Box 369
Delaware, OH 43015
(614) 362-4771

Green Valley Auction Inc.
Route 2, Box 434
Mt. Crawford, VA 22841
(540) 434-4260

Guerney's
136 E. 73rd St.
New York, NY 10021
(212) 794-2280

Hake's Americana & Collectibles
P.O. Box 1444
York, PA 17405
(717) 848-1333

Gene Harris Antique Auction
    Center, Inc.
203 South 18th Ave.
P.O. Box 476
Marshalltown, IA 50158
(515) 752-0600

Norman C. Heckler & Company
Bradford Corner Rd.
Woodstock Valley, CT 06282
(203) 974-1634

High Noon
9929 Venice Blvd.
Los Angeles, CA 90034
(310) 202-9010

Leslie Hindman, Inc.
215 W. Ohio St.
Chicago, IL 60610
(312) 670-0010

Michael Ivankovich Auction Co.
P.O. Box 2458
Doylestown, PA 18901
(215) 345-6094

Jackson's Auctioneers &
    Appraisers
2229 Lincoln St.
Cedar Falls, IA 50613
(319) 277-2256
e-mail: jacksons@corenet.net

James D. Julia Inc.
Rt. 201 Skowhegan Rd.
P.O. Box 830
Fairfield, ME 04937
(207) 453-7125

La Rue Auction Service
201 S. Miller St.,
Sweet Springs, MO 65351
(816) 335-4538

Leonard's Auction Company
1631 State Rd.
Duncannon, PA 17020
(717) 957-3324

Joy Luke
The Gallery
300 E. Grove St.
Bloomington, IL 61701
(309) 828-5533

Mapes Auctioneers & Appraisers
1729 Vestal Pkwy
Vestal, NY 13850
(607) 754-9193

Martin Auctioneers Inc.
P.O. Box 477
Intercourse, PA 17534
(717) 768-8108

McMasters Doll Auctions
P.O. Box 1755
Cambridge, OH 43725
(614) 432-4419

Metropolitan Book Auction
123 W. 18th St., 4th Floor
New York, NY 10011
(212) 929-7099

Wm. Frost Mobley
P.O. Box 10
Schoharie, NY 12157
(518) 295-7978

William Morford
RD #2
Cazenovia, NY 13035
(315) 662-7625

New England Auction Gallery
P.O. Box 2273
W. Peabody, MA 01960
(508) 535-3140

New Hampshire Book Auctions
P.O. Box 460
92 Woodbury Rd.
Weare, NH 03281
(603) 529-7432

Norton Auctioneers of Michigan
Inc.
50 West Pearl at Monroe
Coldwater, MI 49036
(517) 279-9063

Old Barn Auction
10040 St. Rt. 224 West
Findlay, OH 45840
(419) 422-8531
web site: http://www.oldbarn.com

Richard Opfer Auctioneering Inc.
1919 Greenspring Dr.
Timonium, MD 21093
(410) 252-5035

Pacific Book Auction Galleries
133 Kerney St., 4th Floor
San Francisco, CA 94108
(415) 989-2665
web site: http://www.nbn.
    com/~pba/

Pettigrew Auction Company
1645 S. Tejon St.
Colorado Springs, CO 80906
(719) 633-7963

Phillips Fine Art Auctions
406 E. 79th St.
New York, NY 10021
(212) 570-4830

Pleasant Valley Auction Hall
P.O. Box 1739, South Ave.,
Pleasant Valley, NY 12569
(914) 831-0200
website: www.auction
    web.com/aar-ny
e-mail: Hikertwo@aol.com

Postcards International
2321 Whitney Ave., Suite 102
P.O. Box 5398
Hamden, CT 06518
(203) 248-6621
web site: http://www.csmonline.
    com/postcardsint/

Poster Auctions International
601 W. 26th St.
New York, NY 10001
(212) 787-4000

Provenance
P.O. Box 3487
Wallington, NJ 07057
(201) 779-8725

David Rago Auctions, Inc.
333 S. Main St.
Lambertville, NJ 08530
(609) 397-9374

Lloyd Ralston Toys
173 Post Rd.
Fairfield, CT 06432
(203) 255-1233

Mickey Reichel Auctioneer
1440 Ashley Rd.
Boonville MO 65233
(816) 882-5292

Sandy Rosnick Auctions
15 Front St.
Salem, MA 01970
(508) 741-1130

Thomas Schmidt
7099 McKean Rd.
Ypsilanti, MI 48197
(313) 485-8606

Seeck Auctions
P.O. Box 377
Mason City, IA 50402
(515) 424-1116
website: www.willowtree.com/
~seeckauctions

L. H. Selman Ltd.
761 Chestnut St.
Santa Cruz, CA 95060
(408) 427-1177
web site: http://www.selman.com

Sentry Auction
113 School St.
Apollo, PA 15613
(412) 478-1989

Robert W. Skinner Inc.
Bolton Gallery
357 Main St.
Bolton, MA 01740
(508) 779-6241

Skinner, Inc.
The Heritage on the Garden
63 Park Plaza
Boston, MA 02116
(617) 350-5429

C. G. Sloan & Company Inc.
4920 Wyaconda Rd.
North Bethesda, MD 20852
(301) 468-4911
web site: http://www.cgsloan.com

Smith & Jones, Inc., Auctions
12 Clark Lane
Sudbury, MA 01776
(508) 443-5517

Smith House Toy Sales
26 Adlington Rd.
Eliot, ME 03903
(207) 439-4614

R. M. Smythe & Co.
26 Broadway
New York, NY 10004-1710

Sotheby's
1334 York Ave.
New York, NY 10021
(212) 606-7000
web site: http://www.sothebys.com

Southern Folk Pottery Collectors
Society
1828 N. Howard Mill Rd.
Robbins, NC 27325
(910) 464-3961

Stanton's Auctioneers
P.O. Box 146
144 S. Main St.
Vermontville, MI 49096
(517) 726-0181

Stout Auctions
11 W. Third St.
Williamsport, IN 47993-1119
(765) 764-6901

Michael Strawser
200 N. Main St., P.O. Box 332
Wolcottville, IN 46795
(219) 854-2859

Swann Galleries Inc.
104 E. 25th St.
New York, NY 10010
(212) 254-4710

Swartz Auction Services
2404 N. Mattis Ave.
Champaign, IL 61826-7166
(217) 357-0197
web site: http://www/Swartz
Auction.com

Theriault's
P.O. Box 151
Annapolis, MD 21401
(301) 224-3655

Toy Scouts
137 Casterton Ave.
Akron, OH 44303
(216) 836-0668
e-mail: toyscout@salamander.net

Treadway Gallery, Inc.
2029 Madison Rd.
Cincinnati, OH 45208
(513) 321-6742
web site: http://www.a3c2net.
com/treadwaygallery

Victorian Images
P.O. Box 284
Marlton, NJ 08053
(609) 985-7711

Victorian Lady
P.O. Box 424
Waxhaw, NC 28173
(704) 843-4467

Vintage Cover Story
P.O. Box 975
Burlington, NC 27215
(919) 584-6900

Bruce and Vicki Waasdorp
P.O. Box 434
10931 Main St.
Clarence, NY 14031
(716) 759-2361

Web Wilson Antiques
P.O. Box 506
Portsmouth, RI 02871
1-800-508-0022

Winter Associates
21 Cooke St. Box 823
Plainville, CT 06062
(203) 793-0288

Wolf's Auctioneers
1239 W. 6th St.
Cleveland, OH 44113
(614) 362-4711

Woody Auction
Douglass, KS 67039
(316) 746-2694

ABBREVIATIONS

The following are standard abbreviations which we have used throughout this edition of *Warman's*.

ABP=American Brilliant Period
adv = advertising
ah = applied handle
C = century
c = circa
circ = circular
cov = cover
d = diameter or depth
dec = decorated
DQ = Diamond Quilted
ed = edition
emb = embossed
ext. = exterior
ftd = footed
gal = gallon
ground = background
h = height
hp = hand painted
hs = high standard
illus = illustrated, illustration
imp = impressed
int. = interior
irid = iridescent
IVT = inverted thumbprint
j = jewels
K = karat
l = length
lb = pound

ll = lower left
lr = lower right
ls = low standard
mfg = manufactured
MIB = mint in box
MOP = mother-of-pearl
NE = New England
No. = number
opal = opalescent
orig = original
os = orig stopper
oz = ounce
pat = patent
pcs = pieces
pgs = pages
PUG = printed under the glaze
pr = pair
pt = pint
qt = quart
rect = rectangular
sgd = signed
sngl = single
SP = silver plated
SS = Sterling silver
sq = square
w = width
yg = yellow gold
# = numbered

ABC PLATES

History: The majority of early ABC plates were manufactured in England and imported into the United States. They achieved their greatest popularity from 1780 to 1860. American glassware manufacturers were eager to have glass ABC plates compete in the marketplace. Glass examples could offer another dimension by embossing and/or stippling. The alphabet letters which often surround the rim helped teach a child in the days before formal schooling was available to all.

Glass ABC plates are found in pressed patterns in clear and a wide rainbow of colors. Some designs were based on nursery rhymes, while others reflect the events of the times, like the assassination of President Garfield.

References: Mildred L. and Joseph P. Chalala, *A Collector's Guide to ABC Plates, Mugs and Things*, Pridemark Press, 1980; Doris Anderson Lechler, *Children's Glass Dishes, China and Furniture, Volume II,* Collector Books, 1986, 1990 value update; Irene and Ralph Lindsey, *ABC Plates & Mugs,* Collector Books, 1997; Noel Riley, *Gifts for Good Children*, Richard Dennis Publications, 1991.

Collector's Circle: ABC Plate/Mug Collectors, 67 Stevens Ave., Old Bridge, NJ 08857.

6" d
Barley pattern, colorless	45.00
Cane pattern, alphabet on stippled rim, colorless	48.00
Christmas Eve, Santa on chimney, colorless	75.00
Deer and Tree pattern, colorless	50.00
Ding Dong Bell, colorless	75.00
Dog, standing on grass, tree in center, colorless	70.00
Dog's head center, colorless	45.00
Duck, amber	45.00
Elephant with howdah, three waving Brownies, Ripley & Co., colorless	135.00
Floral bouquet with bow, colorless	50.00
Hen and chicks, colorless	45.00
Jumbo, emb alphabet border	95.00
Little Bo Peep, center scene, raised alphabet border	50.00
Plain center, colorless, white scalloped edge	65.00
President Garfield, profile bust center, colorless, frosted alphabet border	60.00
Starburst pattern, alphabet border, scalloped rim, New Martinsville, colorless	40.00
Star Medallion pattern, colorless	40.00
Thousand Eye pattern, blue	70.00
Thousand Eye pattern, vaseline	65.00
Young Girl, portrait, colorless	65.00
Westward Ho pattern	60.00

6-1/4" d, colorless and frosted
Christmas Morning, frosted center, stippled alphabet border	175.00
Rabbit in cabbage patch, frosted center, stippled alphabet border	65.00

6-3/4" d
Independence Hall, 1776-1876, colorless and frosted	145.00

7" d
Centennial Exhibition, 1776-1876, American eagle center, colorless	110.00
Clock face center, Arabic and Roman numerals, alphabet center, frosted and colorless	75.00
Easter Greetings, alphabet border with gilt letters, floral center, beaded edge, milk glass	45.00
Emma, girl's head in center, beaded rim, Higbee bee mark, colorless	90.00
Plain center, emb alphabet border, beaded rim, milk glass	55.00
Stork, marigold carnival glass	65.00

7-3/4" d
Arabic and Roman numerals, colorless	50.00

8" d
Frosted Stork, flake	125.00

ADVERTISING

History: Advertising on glass began with early bottles. Other types of containers, from pickle jars to whiskey bottles, can be found engraved, etched, painted, and labeled. Early manufacturers often used illustrations of the product so that even an illiterate buyer could identify a product. The country store of years past was filled with glass jars which contained advertising and slogans.

Another popular way of advertising was a giveaway or premium. Many types of glassware articles were given away by merchants, manufacturers, and salesmen. Carnival glass was popular with the advertiser because it was durable and it was equally popular with the housewife because it was pretty. Today, carnival glass advertising plates and other forms command a high price.

Usually a collector does not think of glass as a medium when considering advertising collectibles. However, the variety of colors, shapes, and sizes, makes an interesting collection. Many bottles and other types of glass containers have been replaced by plastic containers and the former brown, green, and cobalt blue containers have become collectible.

References: Art Anderson, *Casinos and Their Ashtrays,* 1994, printed by author (P.O. Box 4103, Flint, MI 48504); Barbara Edmonson, *Old Advertising Spirits Glasses,* Maverick Publications, 1988; Ted Hake, *Hake's Guide to Advertising Collectibles*, Wallace-Homestead, 1992; Bill and Pauline Hogan, *Charlton Standard Catalogue of Canadian Country Store Collectables*, Charlton Press, 1996; Ray Klug, *Antique Advertising Encyclopedia*, Vol. 1 (1978, 1993 value update) and Vol. 2 (1985), L-W Promotions; Mary Jane Lamphier, *Zany Characters of the Ad World*, Collector Books, 1995; Patricia McDaniel, *Drugstore Collectibles*, Wallace-Homestead, 1994; Tom Morrison, *More Root Beer Advertising & Collectibles,* Schiffer Publishing, 1997.

Collectors' Circle: Antique Advertising Assoc. of America, P.O. Box 1121, Morton Grove, IL 60053; National Assoc. of Paper and Advertising Collectibles, P.O. Box 500, Mount Joy, PA 17552.

Ashtray
Baker's Cocoa	90.00
Barber Supplies, William Marvy, clear, red, white, and blue adv, 5" d	15.00
B. F. Goodrich Vogue Heels, heel shaped, red, white, and blue adv, 3-1/2" x 2-1/4", 1940s	35.00
Chesterfield, MIB	20.00
Coon Chicken Inn, clear, black bell hop, c1930, 4" d	45.00
Dobbs Hats, dark amethyst, hat shape	30.00
Firestone Tire, yellow tire, colorless glass insert, 3-13/16" d	50.00

Goodrich Tire, green, tire shape 40.00
Goodyear, amber, tire shape 35.00
Grant's Scotch Whiskey, cobalt blue 15.00
Grapette Soda, milk glass...35.00
J. S. Hoskins Lumber Co., Baltimore, MD, blue lettering,
    white ground...25.00
Levy's Jewish Rye Bread, milk glass, Art Deco shape, illus of
    black boy eating bread 75.00
Macbeth Evans, pink...15.00
Reno Cal-Neva, Capri blue, red and white design,
    3-1/2" d 6.50
Royal Caribbean Cruise Lines, colorless, octagonal, blue
    crown and anchor logo, 4" d 15.00
Bank
    Charles Chaplin, 3-3/4" h, Geo Borgfeldt & Co., painted fig-
        ure standing next to barrel slotted on lid, name emb on
        base..220.00
    Elsie the Cow, colorless cased to white int., milk bottle
        shape, Save for a Rainy Day, 4-1/2" h.....................25.00
    Esso, clear, emb "Watch Savings Grow" 15.00
    Laurel Federal, colorless...12.00
    Lincoln Bank, colorless, bottle shape, orig top hat, paper
        label, 9" h...50.00
    Pittsburgh Paints, colorless, log cabin shape, pa-2 per
        label...45.00
Basket, marigold carnival glass, John H. Brand Furniture
    Co., Wilmington, DE 90.00
Beer Glass, ftd, Moerlein's Brewery, etched band, National La-
    ger Beer, Good Luck molded in glass, 6-1/4" h.......65.00
Bottle, Old Tub Whiskey, moon shining black boy,
    1930s 120.00
Bowl
    Citizens Mutual Trust, Wheeling, 1924, Chinese red,
        Northwood 95.00
    Horlacher, Peacock tail pattern, purple carnival glass 85.00
    Issac Benesch, purple carnival glass, Millersburg mark,
        6-1/4" d 175.00
    Sterling Furniture Co., purple carnival glass...............245.00
Bread Plate, Pioneer Flower Mill, San Antonio, clear.........50.00
Calling Card Tray, carnival glass
    Fern Brand Chocolates, amethyst, two turned up sides,
        6-1/2" d 700.00
    Fern Brand Chocolates, purple, two turned up sides,
        6-1/4" d 175.00
    Issac Benesch, Holly Whirl pattern, marigold 125.00
Candy Jar, cov, Schrafft's Chocolates, 6" sq, Massachusetts
    pattern 35.00
Champagne Glass, cranberry, Compliments of Frederick Bary
    Co., trumpet shape, 22" h......................................175.00
Clock, McCord Motor Gaskets, metal and glass...............95.00
Counter Plate, El Producto..25.00
Decanter, Belle of Kentucky, colorless crystal, ribbed, gold let-
    ters, orig stopper 100.00
Dish, marigold carnival glass, "Compliments of Pacific Coast
    Mail Order House, Los Angeles, CA".....................700.00
Dispenser
    Hunter's Root Beer, milk glass 50.00
    Radium Vitalizer, vaseline body, emb letters, cylindrical,
        metal spigot and lid, 10" x 16" 425.00
Display Case, counter top, colorless
    Dr. West's Toothbrush...375.00
    Tootsie Rolls, Pure Delicious Chocolate Candy..........350.00
Eye Cup, Optrex Safe Guards Sight, 5" h Optrex bottle with eye
    cup, cobalt blue, bottom of bottle emb "Optrex" 48.00
Factices, large perfume display bottle
    Ellen Tracey, 11" h..225.00

Lisson, 13-1/2" h...225.00
Pavlova, 12" h...200.00
Romeo Gigli, 17" h..250.00
Sharper Image, 12" h, cobalt blue 200.00
Hat, carnival glass
    Horlacher, Peacock Tail pattern, green 90.00
    Miller's Furniture, Harrisburg, basketweave, marigold....95.00
Ice Cream Dish, Borden's, illus of Elsie the Cow..............20.00
Jar, emb
    Adam's Pure Chewing Gum, colorless, sq, thumbprint design
        on stopper, etched label, 11" h...............................145.00
    Beich's Candy, colorless, emb lettering, 10" h 60.00
    Bob's Big Boy Restaurant, colorless, Bob's 1985 Collector
        Series...30.00
    Buffalo Peanuts , colorless, orig top 125.00
    Candy Bros. Manufacturing Co., St. Louis, colorless, 4 lb
        size 75.00
    Cavalier Boot Cream, colorless...................................10.00
    Chico's Peanuts, colorless, tin litho lid and base........275.00
    Compressed Lozenges, H. K. Mulford Co., Phila and Chica-
        go, brown, sq, metal screw top, c1880, 11-1/2" h....85.00
    Dr. Stevens Cough Drops, colorless, paper label 65.00
    Faultless Wonder Nipples, amber, round, frosted glass nip-
        ple shaped cov, emb label, 13" h.............................800.00
    Kiss-Me Chewing Gum, American Chicle Co., colorless, sq,
        chamfered corners, glass stopper, flanged lip, emb "Kiss-
        Me," paper label..450.00
    La Palina Cigars, round, knob finial on cov, emb and paper
        labels, 7" h, 6" d 75.00
    Lutted's S. P. Cough Drops, colorless, chimney finial on roof
        cov, emb shingle, log, and window designs, emb label
        and "Genuine Has J.L. Stamped On Each Drop," ftd,
        7" h...425.00
    Peerless Hardware Soap, colorless, spherical, metal threaded
        lid, canted, red stencil-style label on raised band..... 145.00
    Planter's Peanuts, colorless, barrel shape, peanut finial on
        cov, emb lettering, staves, and Mr. Peanut characters,
        12" h, 8-1/2" d 225.00
    Rexall Drug, colorless, spherical, emb script label, no cov,
        4-1/2" h, 5" d 150.00
    Swift's Toilet Soap, semi ovoid, glass cov, emb label ...175.00
Lamp Shade, ceiling type, Pittsburgh Ice Cream, red and black
    lettering, "We Serve The Cream of Pittsburgh," milk glass
    base, 1917 patent 325.00
Marbles, Drakes Cakes, Play The Game, Be Fair, Don't Cheat,
    Don't Play on the Street, mesh bag full of 15 machine
    made glass marbles, late 1940s 20.00
Measuring Cup, Lenkerbrok Farms, Inc., colorless, red letters,
    Pyrex, 8 oz 10.00
Mug
    Compliments for...Elling...Harrisburg, PA, Fisherman's pat-
        tern, Dugan carnival glass, multicolored, letters partially
        readable 200.00
    Golden Knight Saving Soap, colorless, emb letters 25.00
    Lease Savers, Customer Quencher, Thermo-Serv 5.00
Paperweight
    American Card Clothing Co., Worcester, MA, 1882,
        colorless..25.00
    American Glass & Construction Co., Rochester, NY, glass
        reinforced with wire, rect, 3" x 4-1/2" 20.00
    Bell Telephone, bell shape, cobalt blue......................50.00
    Canton, OH, Centennial, 1909, ruby stained, 4-1/4" x 2-3/4" x
        3/4" h...45.00
    Columbia National Bank...20.00
    Elgin Watches 35.00
    Golden Pheasant Gunpowder, multicolored................40.00

Independent Press Room, Los Angeles, colorless, rect... 20.00
Leeson & Co., Boston, Linen Thread Importers, colorless, black and white illus, 4-1/8" l 50.00
Lehigh Sewer Pipe & Tile Co., Ft. Dodge, IA, colorless, 4" l..20.00
Macbeth-Evans Glass Co., Pittsburgh, PA, rect 25.00
New York Telephone Bell System, bell shape, cobalt blue 95.00
Old Bridgeport Double Copper Distilled Pure Rye Whiskey, Brownsville, PA, colorless, 3" d 35.00
Radekar Lumber Co., men working logs, multicolored scene, milk glass..50.00
Wurtz Auto Garage, Degenhart....................................40.00

Perfume Bottle
California Perfume Bottle, NY, violet scent, orig label...45.00
Le Golliwogg, de Vigney, Paris, colorless frosted body, painted label, black puff wig, stopper with figural Golliwogg head, 3-1/2" h....................................95.00
Lightners Jockey Club, label under glass, glass stopper 315.00
Lucky Lindy Perfume, Nipoli Co., colorless, 1927 ....30.00
Owl Drug Co., Oil of Sweet Almond, orig label, 1 oz, cork top 5.00

Plate, carnival glass
Brazier Candies, purple, hand grip, 6" d 250.00
Campbell & Beesley Co., purple...................................450.00
Davidson Chocolate Society, purple, 6-1/4" d 245.00
Eagle Furniture, purple...245.00
Eat Paradise Soda Candies, Season's Greetings, purple, 6" d 200.00
Fern Brand Chocolates, amethyst, 6" d 1,100.00
Fern Brand Chocolates, purple, 6" d...........................225.00
Greengard Furniture Co., purple.................................600.00
Old Rose Distillery, Grape and Cable pattern, green, stippled, 9" d...265.00
Roods Chocolate, Pueblo, purple................................750.00
Spector's Department Store, Heart and Vine pattern, marigold, 9" d..325.00
Utah Liquor Co., hand grip, 6" d 300.00
We Use Brocker's, purple, 7" d 500.00

Plate, carnival glass, 6" d, Fern Brand Chocolates, amethyst, $1,100. Photo courtesy of Mickey Reichel Auction Center.

Plate, pressed glass, Massachusetts, Schrafft's Chocolate adv..75.00
Pomade Jar, F. B. Strouse, NY, clambroth, figural bear, 3-3/4" h 375.00

Salt and Pepper Shakers, pr
Chef Boy Ar Dee, white, Hazel Atlas............................60.00
General Electric, milk glass, refrigerator shape............35.00
Pepsi Cola, colorless, bottle shape..............................45.00

Seltzer Bottle
Barrett & Co. Mineral Water Ashton U Lyne, 6-1/2" h, dark forest green, emb name.............................35.00
J & B Jewsbury & Brown Manchester, light cobalt blue, acid etched name on front set in star, chrome top 100.00

Shoe
Cobalt blue, gold lettering "St. Paul Furnishing Company, Widows and Orphans Protected"..............................75.00
Orange, Albert E. Lee Jeweler & Optometrist, Enterprise, Alabama, 1920s, 4-1/2" l................................35.00

Sign
Imperial Glass, 6" x 3-1/4" 300.00
La Senorite, La Camille, reverse painted on glass, red letters with white outlines, black ground, back light assembly... 250.00

Slide, used in movie theater, black background
Heinz Ketchup, child standing next to giant ketchup bottle..35.00
It Might Happen To You! Fire Might Turn A Garage Into A Grave Yard, Is Your Car Insured. See this agency of the Hartford Fire Insurance Co., colored fire disaster scene, Manhattan Slide & Film Co. 25.00
Money Gets Away Easily, The Only Safe Plan Is To Carry a Check Book & Keep Your Money in the Bushton State Bank, US Slide Co. 20.00
The New Way Buy From The Sunshine Display Rack The Quality Biscuits of the World Kept Clean and Fresh Under Glass Covers, Advertising Slide Co. 22.00
There's Only 2 Kinds of Ice Cream, Finnin's Café, ice cream freezer with flowers, U.S. Slide Co., Kansas City 20.00
Tom Mix, My Kriss Kross (razor) Kit Is My Best Pal, Edward F. Keller, Kansas City 50.00
Use Snow Bell Flour, winter scene with church on hill top, US Slide Co. 20.00

Tray
Houze Glass Co., Point Marion, PA, Season's Greetings, smoke ground, red reindeer, white snowflakes and lettering, 4-3/4" x 3-3/4" 15.00
Teaberry Gum, amber..110.00

Tumbler
Clark's Teaberry Gum, vaseline 45.00
Columbia Steamship, red and yellow logo, 1957, 5" h ...30.00
Drink Ferro-Phos, colorless, etched, 4-1/4" h...............35.00
Elsie, Borden's, Bicentennial, 1976, set of 6................90.00
Olsen's Big New Store, etched "Christmas Greetings, 1901" 45.00
Uneeda Milk Biscuit, chocolate slag, Indiana Tumbler and Goblet Co., small base chip.................................90.00
Wash Board, child size, Caroline Washboard, 2 in 1 Junior, colorless 45.00
Whiskey Dispenser, Ask for Sanderson's Whiskey, colorless, etched, 15-1/2" h...................................475.00

Whiskey Shot Glass, colorless
Always Good, Dan's Rye, Brown & Daniel, Chicago, IL....25.00
Big Horn Whiskey, Taylor & Williams Distillery, Louisville, KY, c1900..20.00
Blue Rye, John Barth Co., Milwaukee, IL, c1898..........30.00
John Spengler, Wholesale Liquors, Kansas City, MO ..12.00
Lititz Springs, Straight Rye Whiskey, John C. Horting, Lititz, PA..30.00

The Blochdale, Pennsylvania Pure White Whiskey, 1912...20.00
Top Knot Whiskey, partridge, cut and polished...........40.00
White Swan Distilling Co., Indianapolis, IN, c1915 ....15.00
Wishing You Luck, Sterling Tavern, Mike and Florence, 2nd
    & G St., Eureka, CA..35.00

AGATA GLASS

History: Agata glass was invented in 1887 by Joseph Locke of the New England Glass Company, Cambridge, Massachusetts.

Agata glass was produced by coating a piece of peachblow glass with metallic stain, spattering the surface with alcohol, and firing. The resulting high-gloss, mottled finish looked like oil droplets floating on a watery surface. Shading usually ranged from opaque pink to dark rose, although pieces in a pastel opaque green also exist. A few pieces have been found in a satin finish.

Reference: Kenneth Wilson, *American Glass 1760-1930: The Toledo Museum of Art, Volume I, Volume II*, Hudson Hills Press and The Toledo Museum of Art, 1994.

Bowl
    4" d, green opaque body, mottled border with scalloped
        gold tracery 650.00
    5-1/4" d, 2-1/2" h, ten ruffled rim, shaded rose pink, all over
        blue and gold oil spots..550.00
    5-1/4" d, 3" h, ruffled, peachblow opaque body, all over
        bright blue staining spots.....................................750.00
    5-3/8" d, deep rose, crimped rim 700.00
    8" d, 4" h, green opaque body, staining and gold trim..1,150.00
Celery Vase
    6-1/2" h, scalloped sq top, opaque pink shading to deep
        rose body, glossy finish...725.00
    7" h, sq, fluted top 625.00
Creamer, opaque pink shading to rose body, applied
    handle...1,200.00
Cruet, 6" h, pale green opaque bulbous body, random oil spot
    dec, applied handle, acid finish, orig faceted dark green
    stopper 600.00
Finger Bowl
    4-1/2" d, ruffled rim, opaque pink shading to rose body, pro-
        nounced mottling, deep pink lining........................800.00
    5-1/4" d, 2-5/8" h, crushed raspberry shading to creamy pink,
        all over gold mottling, blue accents 995.00
Juice Tumbler, 3-3/4" h, opaque pink shading to rose body,
    mottling, deep pink lining 825.00
Lemonade Tumbler, 1-5/8" d base, 2-1/2" d top, 5-1/8" h, New
    England peachblow shading, pronounced mottling, gold
    tracery 1,250.00
Pitcher, 6-3/8" h, crimped rim, opaque pink shading to rose
    body, pronounced mottling, deep pink lining 1,750.00
Plate, 6-5/8" d, opaque pink shading to rose body, ribbon candy
    fluted rim...875.00
Punch Cup, 3" d, 2-3/4" h, deep color, oily spots with blue high-
    lights, applied handle with mottling.........................625.00
Salt Shaker, delicate shading of pink to rose 625.00
Snuff Bottle, 2-3/4" h, opaque pink shading to rose body, carne-
    lian stopper..250.00
Spittoon, 5-3/8" d, 2-3/4" h, squatty round body, ruffled and
    scalloped rim...600.00
Spooner
    3-3/4" h, green opaque body, mottled upper band and nar-
        row gold band 950.00

Juice Tumbler, 3-3/4", $800.

4-1/2" h, 2-1/2" w, sq top, wild rose peachblow ground, small
    areas of wear 400.00
Toothpick Holder, 2-1/4" h, flared, green opaque, orig blue oil
    spots, green trim 795.00
Tumbler
    Green opaque ground, gold border, profuse intense
        mottling..750.00
    Peachblow ground 3-3/4" h, deep metallic stain obscures
        most of ground, satin finish 950.00
    Peachblow ground, 3-7/8" h, gold tracery, bold black
        splotches 785.00
Vase
    4-1/4" h, quatraform, opaque pink shading to rose body,
        pinched sides, ruffled scalloped rim......................725.00
    4-1/2" h, quatraform, flared rim, opaque pink shading to
        deep rose body, random oil spot dec....................900.00
    4-5/8" h, ruffled, four deep dimples, rose-pink, consistent
        overall gold veining 1,380.00
    5" h, 6" w, round, acid cut peachblow, four way scalloped
        top, good mineral staining...................................2,900.00
    7-1/4" h, baluster, opaque pink shading to deep rose body,
        random oil spot dec, satin finish 1,650.00
    8" h, lily, shiny surface, crimson peachblow ground, large
        black splotches 1,085.00
    8" h, bulbous stick form, deep wild rose shaded color, gold
        and blue spotting 1,955.00
Whiskey Taster, 2-5/8" h, opaque pink shading to rose body,
    acid finish 750.00

AKRO AGATE GLASS

History: The Akro Agate Co. was formed in 1911, primarily to produce marbles. In 1914, the owners moved from near Akron, Ohio, to Clarks-burg, West Virginia, where they opened a large factory. They continued to profitably produce marbles until after the Depression. In 1930,

1932–48

the competition in the marble business became too intense, and Akro Agate Co. decided to diversify.

Two of their most successful products were the floral ware lines and children's dishes, first made in 1935. The children's dishes were very popular until after World War II when metal dishes captured the market.

The Akro Agate Co. also made special containers for cosmetics firms, such the Jean Vivaudou Co. and Pick Wick bath salts (packaged in the Mexicali cigarette jar). Operations continued successfully until 1948. The factory, a victim of imports and the increased use of metal and plastic, was sold to the Clarksburg Glass Co. in 1951.

Akro Agate glass is a thick-walled type of glass. Many patterns were made in fired-on, opaque, solid, transparent, and marbleized colors. Colors include black, blue, cobalt blue, cream, green, pumpkin, white, and yellow. Marbleized combinations are limitless, and unusual combinations command the highest prices. An example of an unusual color combination is called "Lemonade and Oxblood" and is usually found in children's dishes. The yellow background has blood red streaks, and while it is striking in appearance, the name might not be popular with today's mothers.

The Akro Agate Company bought Westite molds after the Westite factory burned in 1936. Westite was known for production of household-type fixtures, as well as flower pots, creamers, etc. Westite was made in several colors, but a brown and white marbleized combination was most prevalent, followed by a marbleized green and white combination. The Akro Agate Co. began production using these molds and its own striking color combinations.

Many Akro Agate pieces are marked "Made in USA" and often include a mold number. Some pieces also have a small crow in the mark. Westite pieces are marked with a "W" inside a diamond shape.

References: Gene Florence, *Collectors Encyclopedia of Akro Agate Glassware*, revised ed., Collector Books, 1975, 1992 value update; Roger and Claudia Hardy, *Complete Line of the Akro Agate*, published by author, 1992.

Collectors' Clubs: Akro Agate Art Assoc., P.O. Box 758, Salem, NH 03079; Akro Agate Collector's Club, 10 Bailey St., Clarksburg, WV 26301.

Reproduction Alert: Pieces currently reproduced are not marked "Made In USA" and are missing the mold number and crow.

Apple, cov, pumpkin..175.00
Ashtray
    2-7/8" sq, blue and red marble 12.00
    2-7/8" sq, blue marble.................................8.00
    2-7/8" sq, red marble..................................8.00
    4" x 2-7/8" sq, red marble...........................8.00
    4" w, blue, Hotel Lincoln............................75.00
    4-1/2" w, hexagon, blue and white...............35.00
Basket, two handles, orange and white............35.00
Bell
    Light blue, 5-1/4" h 60.00
    Pumpkin, 5-1/4" h 50.00
Bowl
    5" d, emb leaves, white opaque, orange marbleized
      swirls..35.00

    6" d, cream opaque, brown marbleized swirls, Westite ... 25.00
Children's Play Dishes, small unless otherwise noted
Bowl
    Octagonal, white 10.00
    Stacked Disc and Panel, large, green 18.00
Cereal Bowl
    Concentric Ring, blue, large 25.00
    Interior Panel, green, transparent, large 15.00
    Octagonal, rope handle, cream, large..........11.00
    Stacked Disk Interior Panel, blue, transparent, large ...45.00
    Cigarette Holder, gray and white 15.00
Creamer
    Chiquita, cobalt blue, baked-on....................9.00
    Interior Panel, blue, opaque, large...............42.50
    Octagonal
      Blue, large 15.00
      Sky blue, large, open handle 22.50
    Stacked Disk
      Green, opaque 8.00
      Pink...22.50
      Stippled Band, green, transparent, 1-1/4" h............25.00
Creamer and Sugar
    Chiquita, cobalt blue 20.00
    Interior Panel, turquoise..............................50.00
    J Pressman, cobalt blue, baked-on 12.00
    Octagonal, closed handle, medium blue, white lid, large.. 38.00
    Stacked Disk
      Medium blue..12.00
      Pink...45.00
    Stacked Disk Interior Panel, turquoise 50.00
Cup
    Chiquita
      Cobalt Blue, transparent 13.00
      Green, opaque 6.50
    Concentric Rib, green, opaque....................4.50
    Concentric Ring
      Green, opaque 7.00
      Periwinkle..30.00
      Rose, large 35.00
    Interior Panel
      Blue, medium 6.00
      Pumpkin...35.00
    J Pressman, lavender.................................30.00
    Octagonal
      Dark green, closed handle, large............6.00
      Green, closed handle, 2-1/4", large 8.00
      Green, open handle 10.00
    Plain Jane..14.00
    Stacked Disk
      Dark blue, opaque................................12.00
      Green, opaque 5.00
      Light blue, opaque 12.00
    Stacked Disk Interior Panel
      Blue, transparent, large 40.00
      Pumpkin...35.00
    Stippled Band
      Green, large 20.00
      Topaz, 1-1/4" h 20.00
Cup and Saucer
    Chiquita
      Cobalt blue, transparent........................18.00
      Green Opaque 7.00
    Concentric Ring, azure trans-optic, 1-1/4" h.....30.00
    Interior Panel
      Green and white marble.........................35.00
      Pumpkin opaque 30.00

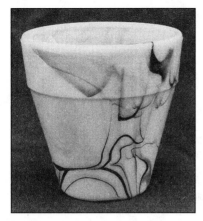

Flower Pot, 5-1/4" d, 5-1/4" h, brown swirls, white ground, Westite, $17.50.

Stacked Disk Interior Panel, green and white marble...35.00
Stippled Band
Amber, large..20.00
Azure..42.00
Cobalt Blue, large...35.00
Topaz...28.00
Demitasse Cup, J Pressman
Green...9.75
Pink..30.00
Demitasse Saucer, J Pressman, green.............................8.00
Flower Pot
1-1/2" h, opaque green...7.50
2-1/4" h, ribbed, green and white.........................9.00
2-1/2" h, Banded Dark, aqua................................6.00
2-1/2" h, Stack Disk
Green and white..11.00
Orange and white..15.00
3-1/2" h, Ribs and Flutes, cream..........................5.00
4" h, Stacked Disk, green and white....................22.00
5-1/4" h, white opaque, brown marbleized swirls,
Westite..17.50
5-1/2" h, scalloped top, blue................................30.00
Lamp
12" h, brown and blue marble, 4" d black octagonal top,
Globe Spec Co..75.00
13" h, green and brown marble, round 5-1/4" d ribbed base,
Houzex...95.00
Marbles, Chinese Checkers, orig box of 60...................125.00
Match Holder, gun shape, white opaque, green marbleized
swirls..15.00
Mexicalli Hat, blue and white..20.00
Mexicalli Jar, orange and white.......................................40.00
Mortar and Pestle, white, hand painted flowers.............12.00
Pitcher
Interior Panel, green, transparent.......................30.00
Octagonal, light blue, 2-7/8" h............................25.00
Stacked Disk, green, opaque...............................10.00
Stacked Disk and Panel, blue, transparent.........50.00
Stippled Band, green, transparent.......................15.00
Planter
Chiquita, green, oval, 6" h.....................................5.00
Graduated Dark, black, scalloped, emb company name and
address, 3" h..35.00
Rect, wire cart holder, orange and white.............35.00
Plate
Concentric Rib, opaque
Green..2.50
Yellow...3.00
Concentric Ring
Dark blue..5.00

Light blue..5.00
J Pressman, 3-3/4" d, green, baked-on.................4.00
Interior Panel
Azure blue, large..10.00
Green transparent, 4-1/2" d, large......................5.00
Medium blue, large..13.00
Octagonal
Blue, large..10.00
Green, opaque, large...4.00
Lime..5.00
Oxblood, marbleized, 4-1/4" d.............................13.00
Stacked Disk, green opaque, 3-1/4" d...................4.00
Stacked Disk Interior Panel, blue, transparent, large...18.00
Stippled Band
Green, transparent, 4-1/4" d.................................6.00
Topaz, large..9.00
Powder Jar
Colonial Lady, white...60.00
Scottie Dog, blue opaque.....................................75.00
Saucer
Chiquita, green opaque..2.00
Concentric Rib, yellow...2.50
Concentric Ring
Green, opaque..3.00
Ivory..3.00
Pink...4.00
White...2.00
Yellow..3.00
Interior Panel
Azure Blue, large..7.00
Green transparent...3.00
Medium blue, large..8.00
Octagonal
Pink, dark...6.00
White, large..10.00
Stacked Disk Interior Panel, blue, transparent, large...15.00
Stippled Band, green, transparent, 2-3/4" d..........3.00
Set
Chiquita, green opaque, 6 pcs.............................70.00
Interior Panel, jadite, 21 pcs..............................335.00
Interior Panel, yellow, opaque, white teapot lid, large, 21 pc
set...350.00
Little American Maid, Octagonal, large size, 4 light green 4-
1/4" plates, 4 yellow 3-1/2" plates, 4 ivory 3-3/8" bowls, 4
pumpkin cups, 4 white saucers, light blue teapot and cov,
light blue creamer, ivory cover for sugar, (sugar bowl
missing), orig box, 21 pcs...............................275.00
Octagonal, opaque green and white, 23 pcs.......145.00
Stippled Band, transparent amber, 17 pcs..........215.00
Stippled Band, transparent azure blue, large size,
17 pcs...470.00
Stippled Band, transparent green, 17 pcs...........225.00
Sugar
Chiquita, cobalt blue, transparent.........................9.00
Interior Panel, lemonade and oxblood.................40.00
Octagonal, white opaque, orange marbleized......10.00
Stacked Disk, white..6.00

Marble, 5/8" d, Popeye Corkscrew, 1930-35, $60.

Stacked Disk Interior Panel
    Blue, medium 15.00
    Cobalt Blue...30.00
Teapot, cov
    Chiquita
        Cobalt blue transparent.........................32.00
        Green opaque 16.00
    Concentric Rib Opaque, cobalt blue, white lid 42.00
    Interior Panel
        Green, white lid, large 42.00
        Medium blue, blue lid, large..................50.00
    Octagonal
        Bright blue, white lid, open handle...........24.00
        Medium blue, green lid, large, open handle 20.00
        Raised Daisy, blue 60.00
    Stacked Disk
        Green...12.00
        Medium blue..14.00
        Pink..17.00
        Pumpkin, beige lid..................................25.00
    Stacked Disk Interior Panel
        Blue, transparent, large......................85.00
        Green with white 45.00
    Stippled Band
        Amber, large..50.00
        Azure 90.00
Teapot, open
    Chiquita, green, opaque 8.00
    Concentric Rib, light blue, opaque 8.00
    Interior Panel
        Green, luster..10.00
        Green, transparent, large.......................15.00
        Oxblood marble......................................28.00
        Pink, opaque 9.75
    J Pressman, cobalt blue, baked-on 8.75
    Octagonal, turquoise, large 15.00
    Oxblood, marble..28.00
    Stacked Disk, medium blue 7.00
Tumbler, 2" h
    Stacked Disk, white..6.00
    Stacked Disk Interior Panel
        Blue, transparent....................................20.00
        Green, transparent 10.00
Vase
    2-3/8" h, red, white, green streaks 5.00
    3-1/4" h, cornucopia, multicolored 15.00
    3-1/4" h, urn shape, white opaque, orange marbleized swirls,
        ftd 9.00
    3-3/4" h, green, marble, smooth top...........18.00
    4-1/4" h, lily, marble.....................................15.00
    4-5/8" h, Jean Vivaudou Co., white opaque, blue marbleized
        swirls, emb handles..............................12.00
    6-1/4" h, tab handle, marbled........................35.00
    8" h, Ribs and Flutes, cobalt blue 35.00
    8-3/4" h, Seven Darts, pumpkin...................35.00
Water Set
    Octagonal, open handle, blue pitcher, dark green
        tumbler 65.00
    Stippled Band, green, pitcher and six tumblers 105.00

AMBERINA GLASS

1883

History: Joseph Locke developed Amberina glass in 1883 for the New England Glass Works. "Amberina," a trade name, describes a transparent glass which shades from deep ruby to amber. It was made by adding powdered gold to the ingredients for an amber-glass batch. A portion of the glass was reheated later to produce the shading effect. Usually it was the bottom which was reheated to form the deep red; however, reverse examples have been found. Locke's July 24, 1883 patent described the base as an amber glass containing gold and further claimed that ruby, violet, a greenish, or bluish tint may be developed during the process.

Most early Amberina is flint-quality glass, blown or pattern molded. Patterns include Diamond Quilted, Daisy and Button, Venetian Diamond, Diamond and Star, and Thumbprint.

In addition to the New England Glass Works, the Mount Washington Glass Co. of New Bedford, Massachusetts, copied the glass in the 1880s and sold it at first under the Amberina trade name and later as "Rose Amber." It is difficult to distinguish pieces from these two New England factories. Boston and Sandwich Glass Works never produced the glass.

Amberina glass also was made in the 1890s by several Midwest factories, among which was Hobbs, Brockunier & Co. Trade names included "Ruby Amber Ware" and "Watermelon." The Midwest glass shaded from cranberry to amber, and the color resulted from the application of a thin flashing of cranberry to the reheated portion. This created a sharp demarcation between the two colors. This less-expensive version was the death knell for the New England variety.

In 1884, Edward D. Libbey was given the use of the trade name "Amberina" by the New England Glass Works. Production took place during 1900, but ceased shortly thereafter. In the 1920s, Edward Libbey renewed production at his Toledo, Ohio, plant for a short period. The glass was of high quality. Amberina from this era is marked "Libbey" in script on the pontil. A round paper label with the company logo may also be found.

References: Gary Baker et al., *Wheeling Glass 1829-1939*, Oglebay Institute, 1994 (distributed by Antique Publications); Neila and Tom Bredehoft, *Hobbs, Brockunier & Co. Glass*, Collector Books, 1997; George P. and Helen McKearin, *American Glass,* reprint, Crown Publishers, 1941, 1948; John A. Shuman III, *The Collector's Encyclopedia of American Art Glass,* Collector Books, 1988, 1994 value update; Kenneth Wilson, *American Glass 1760-1930*, 2 vols., Hudson Hill Press and The Toledo Museum of Art, 1994.

Reproduction Alert: Reproductions abound. Flashed pieces of amberina have invaded the market. Care should be taken when examining a piece to detect scratches and other defects. True amberina glass may shade in color but will be consistent. Modern reproductions lack the deep coloration and subtle shading of the originals.

Additional Listings: Libbey, Hobbs, Brockunier, Mount Washington.

Basket
    6" h, 5" w, enameled white daisies, int. ribbed design,
        applied amber handle 225.00
    7" h, applied amber wishbone dec, loop handle, attributed to
        New England Glass Works 1,300.00

8" h, 5" w, rose bowl shape, enameled white, blue, and gold floral dec, deep amberina coloration, applied amber-green handle 200.00

8-1/2" h, 8" w, swirled ribbed design, irid finish to base and handle, applied clear loop handle 150.00

12-1/2" h, 5" w, Swirl pattern, egg-shaped, applied amber glass prunts, tall amber feet, inverted wishbone handle..... 275.00

15" h, 10" w, Swirl pattern, gold rose dec, fence design, elaborate gold floral design, applied feet, applied amber rigaree handle 350.00

Berry Set, 9" sq master bowl, ten 4-7/8" sq individual bowls, Daisy and Button pattern, minor edge roughness, small flakes, some color variation, assembled 11 pc set 110.00

Beverage Set, Optic Diamond Quilted pattern, 7" h pitcher, 3 punch cups, 2 tumblers, New England Glass Works 825.00

Bonbon, 7" d, 1-1/2" h, wavy six pointed 1-1/2" w rim, fuchsia shading to pale amber, sgd "Libbey" 625.00

Bowl

4-1/4" h, 8-3/4" d, Optic Diamond Quilted pattern, stand-up color...585.00

4-1/2" d, 2-1/4" h, tricorn, fuchsia shading to amber, Venetian Diamond design...325.00

7" d, applied vaseline ribbon edge, pinched feet, attributed to New England...225.00

7-1/2" d, Diamond Quilted pattern, rolled over scalloped edge 195.00

9" d, six pinched corners, alternating panels of rib and diamond points, ground pontil 200.00

9" w, square, Daisy and Button pattern.......................250.00

Butter dish, cov, 7" d, 5" h, Inverted Thumbprint pattern top, amber knob, amber Daisy and Button type pattern base..... 300.00

Butter Pat, 2-3/4" d, Daisy and Button pattern, sq, notched corners, pr 250.00

Carafe, 7-1/8" h, Inverted Thumbprint pattern, reversed color, swirled neck 175.00

Celery Boat, 14" l, 5" w, 2-1/2" h, Daisy and Button pattern, Hobbs, Brockunier & Co., minute roughness on bow 750.00

Celery Vase, 6-1/2" h

Diamond Optic pattern...375.00

Inverted Thumbprint pattern 145.00

Optic Expanded Diamond pattern, New England Glass Works...345.00

Centerpiece, 14" l, canoe, Daisy and Button pattern, Hobbs, Brockunier & Co. 950.00

Compote, 8-3/4" d, Inverted Thumbprint pattern..............350.00

Cordial, 4-1/2" h, trumpet shape....................................225.00

Cracker Jar, cov

5" h, 5-1/2" w, Joseph Locke, New England Glass Works, cov missing 550.00

8" h, 5-3/4" d, Inverted Thumbprint pattern, barrel shape, rare glass cov, applied amber knob finial, attributed to Hobbs, Brockunier & Co., c. 1885 ....785.00

Creamer and Sugar, 4-1/2" h, Diamond Quilted pattern, crimped top, amber reeded handles 650.00

Cruet

5-1/2" h, Inverted Thumbprint pattern, fuchsia trefoil spout, neck, and shoulder, orig stopper, Mt. Washington.... 435.00

5-3/4" h, 4" d, Inverted Thumbprint pattern, deep amber shading to cranberry red, replaced stopper..........145.00

6-3/4" h, 3" d, applied amber handle, orig amber cut faceted stopper, attributed to New England Glass Works 275.00

Decanter

Optic Diamond Quilted pattern, solid amber faceted stopper, 12" h 485.00

Reverse Inverted Thumbprint pattern, ground and polished pontil..125.00

Dish, leaf shape, ftd, pressed, Gillander 1,200.00

Finger Bowl, fluted, fuchsia to amber 375.00

Finger Bowl and Underplate, 5" x 2-1/2" h bowl, 6-3/4" d underplate, reverse amberina, Inverted Thumbprint pattern, applied and fire-on enamel blossoms, thistles, Queen Anne's lace, cattails, and ferns, gold rim 575.00

Hair Receiver, 4-1/2" d, 2" h, two pc, deep fuchsia shading to amber, partial Libbey label 1,750.00

Ice Cream Plate, 5-1/2" sq, Daisy and Button pattern, Hobbs, Brockunier & Co. 95.00

Juice Tumbler, 3-3/4" h, 2-1/2" d, applied reeded amber handle, slight ribbing, tapered body, New England Glass Works..395.00

Lamp, Lincoln Drape, Aladdin 800.00

Lemonade Tumbler, 5-1/4" h, Swirl pattern, gold dec, applied handle..250.00

Marmalade, cov, 5-1/4" h, Inverted Thumbprint pattern, white metal cov, Mt. Washington 250.00

Parfait, 6-1/2" h, Swirl pattern, gold leaf and bud dec 295.00

Pickle Castor Insert, 4-1/4" h, 4" d, Inverted Thumbprint pattern, Mt. Washington... 425.00

Pitcher

4-1/2" h, sq top, Inverted Thumbprint pattern, applied amber reeded handle..325.00

5" h, Daisy and Button pattern, Hobbs, Brockunier & Co...425.00

6-3/4" h, 4" w, Inverted Thumbprint pattern, ruffled rim, applied amber loop handle 195.00

8" h, 5" d, amberina-opalescent, clear reeded handle, ruffled top, wide flange petticoat shape...........................650.00

8-1/4" h, 6" w, ruffled, melon ribbed form, Inverted Thumbprint pattern, applied amber glass loop handle.....325.00

10" h, 4-3/4" d, Optic Diamond Quilted pattern, applied amber handle, ground pontil.....................................235.00

Posy Pot, 3" d, applied wishbone feet, berry pontil 300.00

Punch Cup

2-1/2" h, applied reeded amber handle, slight ribbing, tapered body, attributed to Mt. Washington 245.00

2-1/2" h, 3-1/2" w, Diamond Quilted pattern, applied reeded amber handle, good coloration to two-thirds of rounded body, set of 5...325.00

Ramekin and Underplate, 4-1/4" d, 2-1/4" h, slightly ribbed 250.00

Rose Bowl, 5-1/2" d, 5-1/2" h, Diamond Quilted pattern, deep color, pinched tricorn rim, applied amber reeded shell feet, attributed to New England Glass Works 550.00

Salt Shaker, elongated Baby Thumbprint pattern, orig top... 150.00

Sauce, Daisy and Button pattern 40.00

Spooner

4-1/2" h, Inverted Thumbprint pattern, New England Glass Works...100.00

Punch Cup, Inverted Thumbprint pattern, colorless reeded handle, $150.

5" h, Diamond Quilted pattern, pinched scalloped top .. 150.00
Sugar Bowl, cov, 4-1/4" h, Inverted Thumbprint pattern, New England Glass Works 375.00
Sugar Shaker, 4" h, globular, Inverted Thumbprint pattern, emb floral and butterfly lid...425.00
Syrup Pitcher
  Hobnail pattern, orig pewter top std "Pat. Jan 29 84," Hobbs, Brockunier & Co., 3 hobs chipped.........................300.00
  Inverted Thumbprint pattern, 5-5/8" h, New England Glass Works, fuchsia to amber with rosy tint, silver plate fitting, slight in the making internal air-trap in glass collar ... 750.00
Toothpick Holder
  Baby Inverted Thumbprint pattern
    Square top, 2-1/4" h, 1-1/2" w.................................295.00
    Tricorn 275.00
  Inverted Thumbprint, pedestal base, NTHCS #82......235.00
  Optic Diamond Quilted pattern, sq
    2-3/8" h 295.00
    2-1/2" h, shape #28, Mt. Washington 285.00
  Venetian Diamond, Libbey......................................200.00
Tumbler, Optic, reverse amberina.................................140.00
Vase
  4-5/8" h, 6" d, deep fuchsia color, shape #3013, flowerform, six petal like scallops, sgd "Amberina" above "Libbey" in circle...1,250.00
  5-3/4" h, lily, elongated blossom, brilliant fuchsia shading to Alexandrite blue to amber foot, New England, int. stain... 500.00
  6-3/4" h, roll down lip, optic diamond body 300.00
  7" h, cylindrical, Inverted Thumbprint pattern, Midwestern type coloration, ruffled rim......................................165.00
  7" h, lily, ribbed body, applied amber feet, attributed to New England Glass Works 395.00
  7-1/2" h, 11-1/4" l, fan shape, swirled and ribbed, applied amber rigaree edge and wishbone feet, pastoral landscape scene dec highlighted with gold edge, minor loss to painting 195.00
  10" h, lily, fuchsia highlights 675.00
  10" h, 5-1/8" d, cylindrical, Swirl pattern, enameled pink and white flowers, green leaves, gold trim, attributed to New England Glass Works..350.00
  10-1/2" h, swagged and ruffled lip, snake form entwined around neck, heavy enameled goldfinches perched on thistle blossoms, attributed to Le Gras, c1890.......595.00
  11" h, shape #3006, lily, Libbey signature in pontil.....875.00
  11-1/4" h, shape #3004, sgd "Libbey" 1,200.00
  12" h, trumpet, ribbed body, attributed to New England Glass Works 350.00
  12-1/4" h, 3-1/4" d, swirled calla lily shape, cranberry shading to golden amber foot, amber applied spiral trim............ 165.00
  15" h, lily shape, deep red shading to amber, large lily top, flint, c1880 ....825.00
  23" h, trumpet, ribbed body, knobbed stem, raised circular base, attributed to New England Glass Works ...1,250.00
Whimsey, hat, 3-1/4" d, 2-3/8" h, Expanded Diamond pattern, ground pontil 175.00
Whiskey Taster
  2-1/2" h, Diamond Quilted pattern, deep coloration ...125.00
  2-3/4" h, Baby Diamond Quilted pattern, deep fuchsia to deep amber, minor surface scratches......................50.00

AMBERINA GLASS, PLATED

History: The New England Glass Company, Cambridge, Massachusetts, first made Plated Amberina in 1886; Edward Libbey patented the process for the company in 1889.

Plated Amberina was made by taking a gather of chartreuse or cream opalescent glass, dipping it in Amberina, and working the two, often utilizing a mold. The finished product had a deep amber to deep ruby red shading, a fiery opalescent lining, and often vertical ribbing for enhancement. Bases are usually yellow gold. Handles are generally applied plain amber pieces. Designs range from simple forms to complex pieces with collars, feet, gilding, and etching.

Edward Libbey's patent used an opalescent glass which was plated with a gold ruby. The pieces also have a vertical ribbed effect, and a wide range of items were made, including creamers, finger bowls, lemonade tumblers, punch cups, toothpick holders, and vases.

A cased Wheeling glass of similar appearance had an opaque white lining but is not opalescent and does not have a ribbed body.

The New England Glass Company used paper labels which read "N. E. Glass Co. 1886 Aurora." However, these labels were used infrequently and are rarely found.

References: Gary Baker et al., *Wheeling Glass 1829-1939*, Oglebay Institute, 1994 (distributed by Antique Publications); George P. and Helen McKearin, *American Glass,* reprint, Crown Publishers, 1941, 1948; John A. Shuman III, *The Collector's Encyclopedia of American Art Glass,* Collector Books, 1988, 1994 value update; Kenneth Wilson, *American Glass 1760-1930,* 2 vols., Hudson Hill Press and The Toledo Museum of Art, 1994.

Reproduction Alert: Examples with rough pontils, inferior linings, and even runny, blurry colors, are appearing on the market.

Bowl
  8" w, border of deep dark mahogany, 12 vertical stripes alternating with 12 vertical opalescent fuchsia stripes, off-white casing 7,500.00
  8" w, 3-1/2" h, raised ruffled rim, twelve-ribbed body, fuchsia-red shaded to amber, cased to opal white interior.........4,315.00
Celery Vase, vertical ribbing..2,750.00
Cream Pitcher, 2-3/4" h, 3-1/2" w, bulbous, vertical ribbing, raspberry shading two-thirds down to golden amber base, elaborate strap handle, deep oil spots dec 1,950.00
Cruet, 6-3/4" h, faceted amber stopper 3,200.00

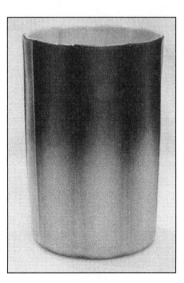

Tumbler, 3-3/4" h, $1,950.

Lamp Shade, 14" d, hanging, swirled, ribbed 4,750.00
Milk Pitcher, applied amber handle, orig "Aurora" label...7,500.00
Parfait, vertical ribbing, applied amber handle, c1886.....1,500.00
Pitcher, 6-1/2" h, vertical ribbing, applied amber handle ...4,500.00
Punch Cup, vertical ribs, applied handle 1,500.00
Salt Shaker, vertical ribs, orig top 1,200.00
Spooner, 4" h, vertical ribbing, ground pontil 2,000.00
Syrup Pitcher, vertical ribbing, orig top, applied amber
    handle..5,600.00
Tumbler, 9 optic ribs, fuchsia top shading to butter
    cream 1,750.00
Vase
   3-1/4" h, bulbous, vertical ribbing, bluish-white lining... 2,500.00
   6-1/4" h, flared cylinder, twelve ribs, deep fuchsia shading to
    amber, cased in opal white, thin walls 4,025.00
   7-1/4" h, lily shape, raspberry red shading to bright amber,
    opal white casing 2,750.00

ANIMAL COLLECTIBLES

History: The representation of animals in fine arts, decorative arts, and on utilitarian products dates back to antiquity. Some religions endowed certain animals with mystical properties. Authors throughout written history used human characteristics when portraying animals. It did not take glass manufacturers long to realize that there was a ready market for glass novelties. In the early 19th century, walking sticks and witch balls were two dominate forms. As the century ended, glass-covered dishes with an animal theme were very popular.

In the years between World Wars I and II, glass manufacturers such as Fostoria Glass Co. and A. H. Heisey & Co. created a number of glass animal figures for the novelty and decorative-accessory markets. In the 1950s and early 1960s, a second glass-animal craze swept America, led by companies such as Duncan & Miller and New Martinsville-Viking Glass Co. A third craze struck in the early 1980s when companies such as Boyd Crystal Art Glass, Guernsey Glass, Pisello Art Glass, and Summit Art Glass began offering the same animal figure in a wide variety of collectible glass colors, with some colors in limited production.

There are two major approaches to glass animal collecting: (a) animal type; and (b) manufacturer. Most collectors concentrate on one or more manufacturers, grouping their collections accordingly.

References: Marbena Jean Fyke, *Collectible Cats*, Book I (1993, 1995 value update), Book II (1996), Collector Books; Lee Garmon and Dick Spencer, *Glass Animals of the Depression Era*, Collector Books, 1993; Everett Grist, *Covered Animal Dishes*, Collector Books, 1988, 1993 value update; Frank L. Hahn and Paul Kikeli, *Collector's Guide to Heisey and Heisey By Imperial Glass Animals*, Golden Era Publications, 1991; Todd Holmes, *Boyd Glass Workbook*, published by author, 1992; Evelyn Zemel, *American Glass Animals A to Z*, A to Z Productions, 1978.

Periodicals: *Boyd Crystal Art Glass Newsletter*, P.O. Box 127, 1203 Morton Ave., Cambridge, OH 43725; *Jody & Darrell's Glass Collectibles Newsletter*, P.O. Box 180833, Arlington, TX 76096; *The Glass Animal Bulletin*, P.O. Box 143, North Liberty, IA 52317-0143.

Collectors' Clubs: Boyd Art Glass Collectors Guild, P.O. Box 52, Hatboro, PA 19040; Canine Collectibles Club of America, Suite 314, 736 N. Western Ave., Lake Forest, IL 60045; Cat Collectors, 33161 Wendy Dr., Sterling Heights, MI 48310; Folk Art Society of America, P.O. Box 17041, Richmond, VA 23226; Frog Pond, P.O. Box 193, Beech Grove, IN 46107; Squirrel Lovers Club, 318 W. Fremont Ave., Elmhurst, IL 60126; Wee Scots, Inc., P.O. Box 1512, Columbus, IN 47202.

Note: Prices for glass animal figures are for the colorless variety unless otherwise noted.

Angelfish, Heisey 125.00
Bear, Mirror Images, ruby
   Baby..60.00
   Mama...80.00
Bear, Mosser Glass Co., solid, sitting
   Autumn Amber 45.00
   Tawny 12.00
Bear, New Martinsville
   Baby..50.00
   Mama...150.00
   Papa, crystal 200.00
   Papa, satinized..225.00
Bird, Lalique, frosted colorless, pr, 4" h........................ 125.00
Bird, Murano, purple, lavender, gold, 21-1/2" l.............. 850.00
Boar, Baccarat, silver label, round seal, etched mark, 4-1/2" w,
   3-1/2" h 150.00
Bridge Hound, Cambridge
   Amber..45.00
   Crown Tuscan 55.00
   Emerald 50.00
Bull, Heisey by Imperial
   Amber..900.00
   Black...750.00
Bulldog, Co-Operative Flint.. 125.00
Bunny, New Martinsville, head up 60.00
Butterfly, Westmoreland
   Crystal, 4-1/2" 45.00
   Light blue, small 22.50
   Pink, small 20.00
   Smoke, small 20.00
Camel, L. E. Smith
   Amber..70.00
   Cobalt Blue..95.00
   Colorless 50.00
Cat, Baccarat, Egyptian, 6-1/4" h................................. 225.00
Cat, Mosser Glass Co., sitting, 3" h
   Chocolate 7.50
   Heirloom Pink 7.50
   Violet D'Orr 10.00
Cat, Tiffin, Sassie Suzie, milk glass.............................. 300.00
Chanticleer, Fostoria 215.00
Chick, New Martinsville, orange/red 65.00
Colt, Fostoria
   Lying down, 2-7/8"..30.00
   Standing 50.00
Colt, Heisey by Imperial, standing................................. 85.00
Doe, Fostoria, blue, 4-1/2" h.. 40.00
Dog, Baccarat, pointer, silver label, round seal, etched mark,
   7" l 150.00
Dog, Baccarat, sitting, silver label, round seal, etched mark,
   4" w, 4-1/4" h... 150.00
Dog, Boyd Crystal Art Glass, Skippy, sitting Crown Tuscan... 12.00
   Pippin Green 10.00

Dog, Cambridge, bridge pencil, amber, 1-7/8" 22.00
Dog, L. E. Smith, Scottie, 5" h
    Black...60.00
    White milk glass...85.00
Dolphin, Baccarat, blue, silver label, round etched seal,
    6-1/4" l..185.00
Donkey, Duncan Miller...120.00
Dove, Duncan Miller...120.00
Duck, Baccarat, amethyst, 2-1/2" w, 2-1/2" h...............65.00
Duck, Boyd Crystal Art Glass, Debbie, introduced July 1981
    English Yew...6.00
    Snow...7.00
Duck, Fostoria, Mama, frosted amber, 4" h 35.00
Duck, Viking, amber, orig label...................................45.00
Ducklings, Baccarat, pr, frosted................................125.00
Ducklings, Boyd's Crystal Art Glass, introduced September
    1981
    Furr Green...5.00
    Golden Delight 4.00
Duckling, Fostoria, frosted amber, head back. 2-1/2" h 35.00
Elephant, Co-Operative Flint
    Amber...85.00
    Crystal, 13" h, minor damage...........................300.00
    Green, 7" h, flower frog back 250.00
    Pink, 7" h, flower frog back...............................200.00
    Pink, 13" h, tusks repaired...............................400.00
Elephant, Fostoria
    Black...95.00
    Colorless 65.00
Fawn, Tiffin, flower floater
    Citron green..325.00
    Cobalt blue...500.00
Flying Mare, cobalt blue...750.00
Frog, Baccarat, acid stamped mark
    Crystal and green...95.00
    Solid green...100.00
Frog, Co-Operative Flint, pink....................................200.00
Giraffe, Heisey...300.00
Goose, Duncan Miller, bluish cast..............................210.00
Goose, Heisey, wings up...85.00
Goose, Paden City, blue...125.00
Hen, Boyd's Crystal Art Glass, vaseline, 5" 45.00
Hen, Kanawa, blue slag, covered dish..........................95.00
Hen, New Martinsville 45.00
Heron, Duncan...150.00
Horse, Baccarat, stylized Art Deco, rearing, one black, other
    colorless, 9" h, mkd, one with orig paper label, price for
    pr...320.00
Horse, Fostoria, #2564, rearing 45.00
Horse, L. E. Smith, bookends, pr.................................48.00
Horse, Paden City, sun turned color............................150.00
Koala Bear in Tree, Baccarat, artist sgd "R Riget," silver label,
    round seal, etched mark, 5" w, 5" h..................200.00
Mermaid, Fostoria 200.00
Monkey, Baccarat, silver label, round seal, etched mark, 2" w,
    3" h...150.00
Mouse, Pee Gee Glass Co., boy and girl mouth, 3" h
    White Delight..14.00
    Wild Cherry...16.00
Ox, Baccarat, red label, round seal, etched mark, 4" w,
    2-1/2" h...150.00
Owl, Viking, amber, 3" h..60.00
Panther, Indiana
    Amber...225.00
    Blue 200.00
Pelican, Baccarat, solid, acid stamped mark.................75.00

Pelican, Fostoria...65.00
Pelican, New Martinsville..95.00
Penguin, Fostoria..75.00
Pheasant, Paden City, blue
    Chinese 150.00
    Head turned..150.00
Pheasant, Tiffin
    Copen blue, male and female pr, paperweight bases... 800.00
    Crystal, controlled bubbles, single 325.00
Pig, New Martinsville
    Mama...325.00
    Piglet..60.00
Piranha..125.00
Polar Bear, Fostoria...75.00
Polar Bear, Paden City...65.00
Police Dog, Mirror Image, ruby....................................75.00
Pony, Boyd Crystal Art Glass, Joey, introduced March 1980
    Candy Swirl...18.00
    Chocolate 30.00
    Persimmon..27.50
Pony, Imperial, Heisey mold
    Caramel slag...40.00
    Crystal, c1964..48.00
Pony, Paden City, 11-1/2"
    Blue...125.00
    Crystal..75.00
Porpoise, New Martinsville...475.00
Rabbit, Baccarat, black, 4" w, 2" h.............................90.00
Rabbit, New Martinsville, mama 325.00
Ring Neck Pheasant, Heisey 185.00
Robin, Westmoreland, 5-1/8"
    Crystal 20.00
    Pink...24.00
    Red...30.00
    Smoke...24.00
Rocking Horse, Guernsey Glass Co., Rocky, reproduction of
    1915 Cambridge candy container, 4-1/4" l, 13" h
    Carousel slag..15.00
    Holly Berry..12.00
Rooster, Baccarat, silver label, round seal, etched mark, 3-1/4"
    w, 4-1/4" h..150.00
Rooster, Heisey, fighting stance, 8-1/2" h....................165.00
Rooster, Lalique, frosted and colorless, pr, 8" h, some
    damage 275.00
Rooster, L. E. Smith, 8-1/2" h, amber 50.00
Rooster, Paden City
    Barn Yard, blue..200.00
    Chanticleer, blue..175.00
    Elegant, blue..200.00
    Head down, blue...200.00
Seahorse, Fostoria 175.00
Seal, Mirror Images, baby, ruby 75.00
Seal, New Martinsville
    Black, tall handle holder....................................650.00
    Crystal, large, with ball......................................60.00
Shark, Baccarat 115.00
Star Fish, New Martinsville, 6-1/5" l 40.00
Swallow, Baccarat, silver label, round seal, etched mark,
    6-1/2" w, 2" h...150.00
Swan, Cambridge, 7" x 5" 30.00
Swan, Duncan Miller
    3", orig paper label..85.00
    4-3/4"...85.00
    7-1/2", ruby...42.00
Swan, L. E. Smith, 8-1/2" h, cobalt blue.........................65.00

Ad showing the ultimate in aquariums! Crockery and Glass Journal, September 1931.

Swordfish, Duncan Miller
  Blue Opalescent...425.00
  Colorless 275.00
Thrush, Haley...25.00
Tiger, Heisey Club
  Blue Ice 50.00
  Cobalt Blue...95.00
  Yellow Mist 50.00
Tiger, Heisey by Imperial
  Black 65.00
  Caramel Slag...100.00
  Jade 95.00
  Nut Brown..325.00
  Yellow..325.00
Tiger, New Martinsville
  Head down...195.00
  Head up 85.00
Turtle, L. G. Wright, amber...............................85.00
Turtle, Viking, green, orig label.........................30.00
Turtle, Westmoreland, cigarette box................45.00
Walrus, 10-1/2" l, 5-3/4" h, Murano, attributed to Salviati, solid lattimo white in topaz, shaded to colorless overall surround, applied tusks, eyes, and ears.....................175.00

Whale, Pilgrim, orig labels, purchased at New York World's Fair, 1964, MIB.........................45.00
Whale, Vetreria Cendeses Corroso, humpback, aquamarine glass, turquoise blue lips and eyes, etched overall and splotched with metallic oxides to produce corroded effect, base incised "Cenedeses Murano 97V" and "Talberto" 1,380.00
Wolfhound, Mirror Image, ruby carnival 150.00
Wren, Westmoreland, 2-1/2"
  Light blue 22.50
  Pink 20.00
  Pink Mist...22.50

ARCHITECTURAL ELEMENTS

History: Architectural elements, many of which are hand-crafted, are those items which have been removed or salvaged from buildings, ships, or gardens. Windows, ornaments, and newel post finials are examples of architectural elements found in glass. Part of their desirability is due to the fact that it would be extremely costly to duplicate the items today.

The current trends of preservation and recycling of architectural elements has led to the establishment and growth of organized salvage operations that specialize in removal and resale of elements. Special auctions are now held to sell architectural elements from churches, mansions, office buildings, etc. Today's decorators often design an entire room around one architectural element, such as a Victorian marble bar or mural, or use several as key accent pieces.

References: Ronald S. Barlow (comp.), *Victorian Houseware, Hardware and Kitchenware*, Windmill Publishing, 1991; Len Blumin, *Victorian Decorative Art*, available from ADCA (P.O. Box 126, Eola, IL 60519), n.d.; Maude Eastwood wrote several books about doorknobs which are available from P.O. Box 126, Eola, IL 60519; Constance M Greiff, *Early Victorian*, Abbeville Press, 1995; Philip G. Knobloch, *A Treasure of Fine Construction Design*, Astragal Press, 1995; James Massey and Shirley Maxwell, *Arts & Crafts*, Abbeville Press, 1995; *Ornamental French Hardware Designs*, Dover Publications, 1995; Ernest Rettelbusch, *Handbook of Historic Ornament from Ancient Times to Biedermeier*, Dover Publications, 1996; Edward Shaw, *Modern Architect* (reprint), Dover Publications, 1996; *Turn of the Century Doors, Windows and Decorative Millwork*, Dover Publications, 1995 reprint; Stanley Shuler, *Architectural Details from Old New England Homes,* Schiffer Publishing, 1997; Margaret and Kenn Whitmeyer, *Bedroom & Bathroom Glassware of the Depression Years,* Collector Books, 1990, 1992 value update; Kenneth Wilson, *American Glass 1760-1930*, 2 vols., Hudson Hill Press and The Toledo Museum of Art, 1994; Web Wilson, *Great Glass in American Architecture,* E. P. Dutton, New York, 1986.

Periodicals: *American Bungalow*, P.O. Box 756, Sierra Madre, CA 91204; *Glass Art Magazine,* P.O. Box 260377, Highlands Ranch, CO 80126-0377; *Glass Patterns Quar-*

terly, P.O. Box 131, Westport, KY 40077; *Stained Glass,* P.O. Box 22642, Kansas City, MO 64113; *The Historic Traveler Newsletter,* Allan Mann Communications, 14519 Greenleaf St., Sherman Oaks, CA 91403-3770; *The Old House Journal,* Dovetale Publishers, 2 Main St.,. Gloucester, MA 01930-5726; *Traditional Building,* 69A 7th Ave., Brooklyn, NY 11217-3618; *Victorian Homes Sourcebook,* Victorian Homes, P.O. Box 61, Millers Falls, MA 01349.

Collector's Club: Antique Doorknob Collectors of America, Inc., P.O. Box 126, Eola, IL 60519.

Museums: Chrysler Museum, Norfolk, VA; Corning Museum of Glass, Corning, NY; National Center for the Study of Frank Lloyd Wright, P.O. Box 444, Ann Arbor, MI, 48106; University of Connecticut, William Benton Museum of Art, Storrs, CT.

Cabinet Knob
   Floral emb, center hole to accommodate screw.............5.00
   Hexagonal, geometric, metal screw, large
      Amber...5.00
      Black..8.00
      Crystal..4.00
      Green...5.00
      Milk glass...5.00
      Pink..5.00
   Hexagonal, geometric, metal screw, medium
      Amber...5.00
      Black..8.00
      Crystal..4.00
      Green...5.00
      Lavender...9.00
      Milk glass...5.00
      Pink..5.00
   Hexagonal, geometric, metal screw, small
      Amber...5.00
      Black..8.00
      Blue..6.00
      Crystal..4.00
      Green...5.00
      Milk glass...5.00
      Pink..5.00
   Onion shape, flush mounted, jadite.........................10.00
   Round, flush mounted or center metal screw, medium
      Amber...8.00
      Black..10.00
      Crystal..4.00
      Green...5.00
   Milk glass...6.00
   Pink..5.00
Clothes Hook, short hook, pink, c1930.....................10.00
Curtain Tiebacks, pr
Amberina, orig pewter shanks, New England Glass
   Works..165.00
Depression Glass, crystal, feather, 7" l.......................5.00
Depression Glass, green, flat, floral, 3-1/2" d............20.00
Mercury Glass, grape dec, 2-1/2" d...........................50.00
Opalescent Glass, large petaled flowers, orig pewter
   shanks, attributed to Sandwich...........................125.00
Doorbell Pull, cut glass, tapered shank, 1-3/4" d........55.00
Door Knobs, pr, glass knob, metal mountings and shaft
   Amber, deep color, octagonal....................................80.00
   Crystal, oval, cut design..40.00
   Jadite, hexagonal...115.00
   Topaz, center design, hexagonal..............................85.00

Doors, pr, 89" h, 21" w, stained and painted glass, finches
   and flowers, Renaissance style fretwork borer, French,
   20th C...2,750.00
Drawer Pull, anchor, center flush mounted
   Amber...9.00
   Crystal..5.00
   Green...8.00
   Milk glass..9.00
   Pink..8.00
Drawer Pull, bar, double, crystal, Depression-era...........10.00
Drawer Pull, round or faceted ends, metal screws
   Amber...15.00
   Blue..18.00
   Crystal..10.00
   Green...12.00
   Lavender...20.00
   Milk glass..15.00
   Pink..18.00
Fish Bowl, 35-1/2" h, 13" d clear round glass bowl, painted iron
   frame of three half mermaid and half female figures rising
   from base, highlighted by gold trim, three sockets to illu-
   minate fish bowl, small bruise on lower rim of fish bowl,
   Victorian...1,380.00
Hand Towel Holder, double clear glass rods, metal mounting
   bracket
   Blue..40.00
   Jadite...35.00
   Milk glass, white...15.00
   Pink..35.00
Lightning Rod Ball, America, 1870-1920
   4" d, chestnut form, deep ruby red, sheared mouths, no met-
     al collars..190.00
   4-3/8" d, emb moon and star design, ball form, ruby red,
     sheared mouths, acceptable collar ship, no metal
     collars...210.00
   4-1/2" d, Electra, round ball, emb lettering, cobalt blue,
     ground mouths, no metal collars...........................160.00
   4-1/2" d, Electra, round ball, emb lettering, ruby red, ground
     mouths, no metal collars, acceptable collar chip..180.00
   4-1/2" d, plain ball, gold mercury, ground mouth, metal
     "Kretzer Brand/Trademark" collars.......................110.00
   4-1/2" d, plain ball, orange milk glass, sheared collared
     mouths, no metal collars.....................................325.00
   4-5/8" d, Electra, emb lettering, cone form, ruby red, sheared
     collared mouth, no metal collars...........................230.00
   5" d, quilt raised diamond glass ball, gold mercury, sheared
     mouth, metal "Kretzer Brand/Trademark" collars...275.00
   5" d, quilt flattened diamond glass ball, grayish green, ground
     threaded mouth, some mouth chips, 1/2" crack........90.00

Lightning Rod Ball, ball shape, emb moon and star design, ruby red, sheared mouth, 4-3/8" d, collar chip, America, 1870-1920, $210. Photo courtesy of Norman C. Heckler and Co.

5" d, quilt raised diamond glass ball, ruby red, sheared collared mouth with molded threads, no metal collars 230.00

5" d, quilt raised diamond glass ball, silver mercury, sheared mouth, metal "Kretzer Brand/Trademark" collars...275.00

Newel Post Knob

6-1/2" h, double cut overlay, white cut to cranberry, stars and circle dec, several small nicks 625.00

8-1/4" h, pressed glass, electric blue, hobbed pineapple form, brass base, c1840-60 .... 200.00

Panel, 4" sq, American Luxfer Prism Co., Chicago, designed by Frank Lloyd Wright, designed based on flower composed of circles and squares, 12 pc set 920.00

Soap Dish, wall mounted, transparent blue, c1940 .... 12.00

Toilet Paper Holder, colorless glass arms, glass rod 18.00

Toothbrush Holder, wall mounted, opaque blue glass, slots for five toothbrushes, central well for toothpaste tube 20.00

Towel Bar

Colorless glass, one piece, curved ends, mounting brackets

Blue 35.00

Jadite 25.00

Milk glass 15.00

Jadite glass holders, colorless glass towel rod 20.00

Pink glass, faceted balls, colorless glass towel rod 15.00

Window, leaded and stained

13-1/4" h, 30-1/2" h, Gothic interlocking arch motif, etched design inside arched sections, beveled orig frame 300.00

18" d, 29-1/2" h, attributed to Belcher Mosaic Glass Co., passion flower, pink ribbon, and rose bud against variegated amber ground, opalescent roundels, sea green and reddish umber frame of mosaic glass, unsigned 2,875.00

19" x 15", blue, amber, and colorless segments arranged symmetrically in broad leaf canes, centrally hand painted with bird and floral motif, conserved in wood frames, frame la-

beled "Frederick Crowninshield/43W 18th St, New York, NY," removed from Barnes Building, Beacon Hill, Boston, built 1891, one panel cracked, pr.............................865.00

22-1/4" w x 40-3/4" h, and 18-1/4" w x 22-1/4" h, attributed to Donald McDonald, large floral blooms and leaves, deep green olive green, yellow, and brown, amber and apple green border, unsigned, matched pr.................2,875.00

27-1/2" w, 29" h, Tiffany, central tiny white blossoms radiating toward large mottled brown and white pebbled blossoms, pink and green stamens, amber glass surround, geometric green glass border 20,000.00

33" w, 31-1/2" h, large massive stag elk, full set of horns, standing in landscape of shrubs and hills, deep cobalt blue over crystal, overlay, acid cut, 19th C 3,000.00

34" w, 39" h, arched, jeweled navy border framing abstract amber and white mosaic, faceted circles, arched wooden frame, 1900 ....500.00

36" w, 36" h, blue grapes, green leaves, blue scrolls, opal red ribbon, amber ground, blue pane border, orig wood frame 600.00

38" d, 16" d, skylight alcove, mosaic dome, semi-circular lavender and opalescent amber segments interspersed with diamond spacers, progressive lappet design, reinforced with leading, mounted in wood frame surrounded by wood balls, frame labeled "Frederick Crowninshield/43W 18th St, New York, NY," removed from Barnes Building, Beacon Hill, Boston, built 1891 ....2,875.00

44-1/2" w, 21-1/2" h, Tiffany, central monogram medallion of orig company "Louis C. Tiffany and Associated Artists," multicolored floral rectilinear panel with ripple glass and jewels, aqua-blue mottled glass border, mounted in window frame, 1878-82, removed from Bishop's House and Chancery Office, Burlington, VT 3,500.00

BACCARAT GLASS

History: The Sainte-Anne glassworks at Baccarat in Voges, France, was founded in 1764 and produced utilitarian soda glass. In 1816, Aime-Gabriel d'Artiques purchased the glassworks, and a Royal Warrant was issued in 1817 for the opening of Verrerie de Vonâoche éa Baccarat. The firm concentrated on lead-crystal glass products. In 1824, a limited company was created.

From 1823 to 1857, Baccarat and Saint-Louis glassworks had a commercial agreement and used the same outlets. No merger occurred. Baccarat began the production of paperweights in 1846. In the late 19th century, the firm achieved an international reputation for cut-glass table services, chandeliers, display vases, centerpieces, and sculptures. Products eventually included all forms of glassware. The firm is still active today.

Reference: Jean-Louis Curtis, *Baccarat*, Harry N. Abrams, 1992; Paul Jokelson and Dena Tarshis, *Baccarat Paperweights and Related Glass*, Paperweight Press, 1990 (distributed by Charles E. Tuttle Co.).

Additional Listings: Paperweights.

Manufacturer/Distributor: Baccarat Inc., 36 Mayfield Ave., Edison, NY 08837-3821.

Ashtray, 4-1/2" d, Pinwheel, sgd 85.00
Atomizer, 5" h, 3-1/2" l, oval, etched crystal body, metal chrome top, marked 90.00
Biscuit Jar, cov, 6" h, crystal, etched ground, cranberry flowers, leaves, and vines, marked inside lid 600.00
Bookends, pr, 12" h, crystal, serpentine tube on molded rocky form base, etched "Baccarat, France"...................150.00
Bowl
    5-1/2" d, cameo, colorless etched leaf ground, carved chartreuse floral dec.....................................100.00
    5-1/2" d, cov, teardrop finial.......................................225.00
    8" d, Rose Tiente, scalloped, ftd, sgd.........................115.00
    14" d, 3-1/2" h, wide flattened rim, narrow knopped foot, etched "Baccarat, France".....................................500.00
Box, cov, 2-3/4" d, 2-1/4" h, white airplane design on sides, etched mark 125.00
Brandy Snifter, crystal, gilded foliate cartouche, monogrammed "N," set of 12 ....275.00
Calling Card Holder, 5-1/2" h, opaline, fan shape, pedestal base, relief butterflies, trees, and flowers, sgd 195.00
Candelabra, pr, crystal, 32" h, four light, diamond cut baluster standard, four scrolling candle arms terminating in urn form sockets, etched glass globes hung with prisms.....2,000.00
Candlesticks, pr
    9" h, Swirled...225.00
    10-3/4" h, Eiffel Tower pattern, Rose Tiente 225.00
    14-1/2" h, baluster form, crystal, spiral, dome base, 19th C 245.00
Celery Tray, 9-1/2" l, 3-1/2" w, Rose Tiente 45.00
Champagne Bucket, 9-1/4" h, tapering cylinder, rect stop fluted molded sides, stamped "Baccarat, France" 400.00
Chandelier, 42" h, 29" w, 12 scrolling candle arms, foliate crown surmounting figures, prisms..............................12,365.00
Cigar Lighter, Rose Tiente, SP top....................................150.00
Cologne Bottle
    5-1/2" h, Rose Tiente, Diamond Point Swirl, orig stopper 125.00
    7" h, crystal, frosted rosette ground, gold floral swags and bows, cut faceted stopper, pr 335.00

Crystal Ball, 6-1/2" h, solid glass sphere, conforming separate sq holder, labeled and stamped, modern............. 290.00
Dealer's Sign, crystal 110.00
Decanter, conforming orig stopper
    9-3/4" h, Rose Tiente 125.00
    14" h, crystal, amphora style, lightly ribbed, collared stem, domed foot, acid stamped mark 260.00
Decanter Set, decanter and 6 cordials, Rose Tiente Swirl .. 500.00
Dresser Jar, cov, 2-1/2" h, 4-1/2" w, cranberry cut to green base, finely textured bark-like ground, finely cut tiny flowers and leaves, irregular border bands, gold checkerboard type pattern, mkd in pontil, monogrammed lid marked "Sterling" 2,350.00
Epergne, 10-3/4" h, four cranberry overlay cut to clear vases, gilt metal holder...550.00
Fairy Lamp, 3-7/8" h, shaded white to clear 275.00
Figure
    3" h, 3-1/4" h, bear's head, crystal, silver label, etched mark 220.00
    3-1/2" h, 4-3/4" l, Sphinx, silver label, round etched mark 150.00
    6" h, angel playing horn, colorless 50.00
    10" h, obelisk 425.00
Finger Bowl
    4-3/4" d, 6-3/4" d underplate, ruby ground, gold medallions and flowers dec......................................350.00
    5" d, panel cut, set of 8 ....700.00
Goblet
    Perfection pattern...40.00
    Vintage pattern, cone shaped amber bowl, etched grape design, cut stem and base, 6 pc set.....................125.00
Jar, cov
    6" h, 3-3/4" d, sapphire blue, Swirl, mkd 95.00
    7" d, cameo cut, gilt metal mounts, imp "Baccarat" ...350.00
Jewelry Box, cov, 4" d, 2-3/4" h, hinged lid, Button and Bow pattern, sapphire blue, brass fittings.........................145.00
Mustard Jar, cov, 3" d, 5" h, Rose Tiente, Swirl 85.00
Paperweight, sulfide

Paperweight, sulphide of Pope Pius XII, ruby ground, sgd, $165.

Bonaparte, 1974, limited edition, spiraled single overlay, orig box...60.00
Henry, Patrick, 1977, limited edition, spiraled single overlay, orig box 65.00
Hoover, 1971, limited edition, spiraled single overlay, orig box...60.00
Jackson, 1972, limited edition, spiraled single overlay, orig box...60.00
Truman, 1973, limited edition, spiraled single overlay, orig box...60.00
Zodiac, Libra, c1955...165.00
Perfume Bottle, black, Art Deco style, D'Orsay 225.00
Pitcher, 9-1/4" h, Rose Tiente, Helical Twist pattern 295.00
Rose Bowl
    3" d, cranberry, lace enamel dec................................155.00
    5-1/2" h, 2-1/4" d opening, Cuir, round seal mark 400.00
Stemware
    47 pc set, rounded cuts on bowl, baluster stem, hexagonal foot, 6 water goblets, 10 saucer champagnes, 3 large wines, 7 smaller wines, 10 sherries, 11 cordials 650.00
    49 pc set, rounded cuts on bowl, inverted baluster stem, circular foot, 10 water goblets, 13 saucer champagnes with open stem, 12 sherries, 14 wines..........................700.00
Sweetmeat Jar, cov, cranberry colored strawberries, blossoms, and leaves, cut back to clear ground of ferns, silver plated cover and handle, sgd 350.00
Toasting Goblet, 7" h, #340103, pr 150.00
Toothpick Holder, 2-1/2" h, Rose Tiente 225.00
Tumbler, 3-1/2" h, Rose Tiente...5.00
Tumble-Up, carafe and tumbler, Rose Tiente, Swirl pattern 350.00
Vase
    6-1/8" h, cobalt blue, white lace dec...........................250.00
    9-1/4" h, ovoid, crystal, large thumbprint design, acid stamped mark 200.00
    10-1/4" h, inverted bell form, five etched urns with tall scrolling branches, printed factory mark, 20th C 800.00
    12" h, expanding circular section on short foot, opaline, pale yellow enameled hummingbird, butterfly, and summer blossoms, border of pink thistle blossoms and gilt leaves, mkd "Baccarat le 26 Septembre 1860"..............1,000.00
Wash Bowl and Pitcher, Rose Tiente Swirl 800.00
Wine, 7" h, green cut to colorless, 11 pc set 850.00

BARBER BOTTLES

History: Barber bottles, colorful glass bottles found on shelves and counters in barber shops, held the liquids barbers used daily. A specific liquid was kept in a specific bottle, which the barber knew by color, design, or lettering. Some barber bottles indicated the name of the product, like "Bay Rum," while others were more decorative. The bulk liquids were kept in utilitarian containers under the counter or in a storage room.

Barber bottles are found in many types of glass—art glass with various decorations, pattern glass, and commercially prepared and labeled bottles.

References: Ronald S. Barlow, *The Vanishing American Barber Shop*, Windmill Publishing, 1992; *Barbershop Collectibles*, L-W Book Sales, 1996; Keith E. Estep, *Shaving Mug & Barber Bottle Book*, Schiffer Publishing, 1995; Richard Holiner, *Collecting Barber Bottles*, Collector Books, 1986; Ralph & Terry Kovel, *Kovels' Bottles Price List*, 10th ed., Crown Publishers, 1996; Philip L. Krumholz, *Value*

Guide for Barberiana & Shaving Collectibles, Ad Libs Publishing Co., 1989; John Odell, *Digger Odell's Official Antique Bottle and Glass Collector Magazine Price Guide Series*, Vol. 1, published by author (1910 Shawhan Rd., Morrow, OH 45152), 1995; Michael Polak, *Bottles, Identification and Price Guide, 2nd Edition,* Avon Books, 1997.

Note: Prices are for bottles without original stoppers unless otherwise noted.

Advertising
    Koken's Quinine Tonic for the Hair, 7-1/2" h, clear, label under glass...195.00
    Lucky tiger, red, green, yellow, black, and gilt label under glass, emb on reverse...85.00
    Vegederma, cylindrical, bulbous, long neck, amethyst, white enamel dec of bust of woman with long flower hair, tooled mouth, pontil scar, 8" h...130.00
Amber, Hobb's Hobnail 250.00
Amethyst
    6-3/4" h, white enameled flowers, orange dot pattern, pontil 95.00
    8" h, cylindrical, bulbous body, long neck, white and orange floral dec, sheared mouth, pontil scar....................90.00
    8" h, Mary Gregory type dec, white enameled child and flowers, 8" h..250.00
    8" h, white enameled daisies, round pontil 165.00
Art Glass, cylindrical, bulbous body, long bulbous neck, amethyst and light yellow amber mottled design, all over pink irid, ground mouth, smooth base, 7-1/4" h 325.00
Blue, horizontal brown band design, applied white enamel floral pattern, sheared lip, exposed pontil, 8" h 115.00
Canary, Hobnail pattern, three pouring rings, round lip, smooth base, 7-1/4" h 85.00
Clambroth, emb "Water" in red letters across front, porcelain stopper, 8" h 50.00
Cobalt Blue
    Bell shape, raised white and orange enameled flowers, sheared lip, exposed pontil, 8-1/2" h.....................125.00
    Cylindrical, bulbous body, long neck, white enamel, traces of gold dec, tooled mouth, pontil scar, 7-1/4" h 100.00
Colorless, ribbed, dec band around center, gold trim, raised enamel dot pattern, pontil, 6-1/2" h 75.00

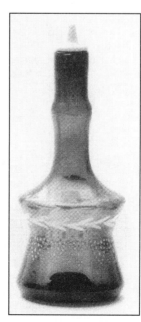

Emerald Green, cylindrical, corset waisted form, long neck, white enamel and gilt dec, sheared mouth, pontil scar, white porcelain stopper, American, 1870-1920, 7-1/2" h, some int. residue, $400. Photo courtesy of Norman C. Heckler and Co.

Crackle, cranberry, swirl...220.00
Cranberry, rings of hobnails on neck, 6-3/4" h 175.00
Cut Glass, hobstar base, pewter top, 5" h..........................90.00
Electric Blue, cylindrical corset waisted form, long neck, opalescent wandering vine dec, tooled mouth, smooth base, 7-1/2" h 210.00
Emerald Green
    7-1/2" h, cylindrical corset waisted form, long neck, white enamel and gilt dec, sheared mouth, pontil scar, some int. residue...400.00
    7-1/2" h, cylindrical modified corset waisted form, long neck, lighter green enamel and floral gilt dec, tooled mouth, pontil scar...275.00
    8-1/2" h, cylindrical bell form, long neck, orange and white enameled floral dec, sheared mouth, pontil scar, some int. haze, 8-1/2" h......................................210.00
Iridescent, Loetz type, crackled green over cobalt blue, blown, ground pontil, c1900, 7-1/2" h 250.00
Latticino, cylindrical, bulbous, long neck, clear frosted glass, white, red, and pale green vertical stripes, tooled mouth, pontil scar, 8-1/4" h...200.00
Lime Green, Amethyst, cylindrical, bulbous bodies, long necks, profuse floral gilt dec, tooled mouth, pontil scar, 8" h, matched pr..350.00
Lime Green, satin glass, classical bird claw grasping ball, ground mouth, smooth base, 7" h, pr.....................100.00
Milk Glass
Bay Rum, hand painted pink and white flowers, green leaves, pastel ground, rolled lip, pontil, 9".......................150.00
    Witch Hazel, painted letters and flowers, 9" h............115.00
Opalescent
    Coin Spot pattern, blue 300.00
    Coin Spot pattern, cranberry, 7-1/2" h 180.00
    Daisy and Fern pattern, cranberry, cylindrical segmented melon body, long neck, tooled mouth, smooth base, 7-5/8" h, some minor int. residue.............................120.00
    Fern pattern, cranberry, sq, long neck, tooled mouth, smooth base, 8-1/4" h 325.00
    Seaweed, pattern cranberry, bulbous 465.00
    Spanish Lace pattern, electric blue ground, sq, long neck, tooled mouth, smooth base, 7-7/8" h, pr 250.00
    Stars and Stripes pattern, cranberry, pale blue, tooled mouth, smooth base, 7-1/4" h, pr 600.00
    Stripes pattern, cranberry, cylindrical segmented melon form, long neck, tooled mouth, smooth base, 7-1/4" h........ 180.00
    Waffle pattern, light blue, rolled lip, 9-1/4" h 125.00
Sapphire Blue
    Enameled white and yellow daisies, green leaves, 8-5/8" h 125.00
    Mary Gregory type dec, white enamel dec of girl playing tennis, cylindrical bulbous form, long neck, tooled mouth, pontil scar, 8" h..150.00
Spatter
    Cranberry ground, opalescent white mottling, sq, long neck, tooled mouth, smooth base, 8-1/2" h.......................160.00
    Light blue and white, polished mouth and base, 8-1/4" h 200.00

BASKETS

History: Glass baskets have been made by glassblowers for centuries. Their popularity led to wonderful creations of art glass with thorny handles, as well as plain baskets with simple designs. Cut glass baskets have often enjoyed a special place because of their beauty.

Pressed glass patterns often also included a basket form to match the compotes and stemware lines.

Unlike their popular natural material counterpart, glass baskets were not made for gathering eggs or going to market, but for holding delicate candies, potpourri, or flowers. Special baskets were made to hold sugar or jelly, while others were made to hold spoons. Small baskets were often included on an elegantly decorated table to hold salt of almonds at each place setting. Larger, usually more ornate baskets were used as centerpieces to hold fruit and/or flowers. Truly elegant table decorations were treasured and often special pieces were used only for specific functions. One served pickles from pickle castors, almonds from baskets, and so on.

Manufacturers of glass baskets include Heisey, Cambridge, Tiffany, and other well-known names. Examples are found in almost every color and generally have applied fixed handles.

Reference: John Mebane, *Collecting Bride Baskets and Other Glass Fancies*, Wallace-Homestead, 1976.

4-1/2" h, Massachusetts pattern, U.S. Glass Co., colorless, applied colorless handle 65.00
4-1/2" h, 3-3/4" w, satin, mother of pearl, Herringbone pattern, deep pink ruffled edge, pink shaded ground, white int., applied colorless thorn handle............................. 450.00
5" h, Octagon, Heisey, flamingo 90.00
5" h, 5-1/2" w, Czechoslovakia, pink, applied black handle .. 75.00
5-1/2" h, Czechoslovakia, blue hobnail, black and clear trim and handle.. 75.00
5-1/2" d, 8" h, cut glass, Berlyn pattern, Quaker City Glass Co., applied twisted handle, three step pedestal base, American Brilliant period 375.00
6" h, 4-3/4" d, spatter, pink, brown, and white spatter, white int., ruffled edge, applied colorless thorny handle 175.00
6" h, 6" w, star shape, sapphire blue, white pattern, applied blue thorn handle, c1890 .... 225.00
6" h, 7" w, pale blue int. shading to white, opaque white ext., ten rows of hobnails, applied amber edge, applied amber thorn handle; Victorian 110.00
6-1/2" d, cut glass, intaglio floral cutting, applied twisted handle American Brilliant period 150.00
6-1/2" h, 5" w, Czechoslovakia, opaque blue, black trim, enameled daisies, roses, and butterfly, applied clear handle...... 80.00
6-1/2" h, 5" w, Czechoslovakia, opaque green, white casing, applied black rim and handle.................................... 70.00
6-1/2" h, 5" w, Czechoslovakia, red, blue, and yellow spatter cased with orange, applied clear handle................ 85.00
6-1/2" h, 5" w, Czechoslovakia, tomato red, black trim, clear handle.. 70.00
6-1/2" h, 5-1/2" w, Czechoslovakia, brilliant orange, black trim, crystal thorn handle.. 100.00
6-1/2" h, 7" l, deep brown and green, yellow and white ground, white ext., ruffled edge, applied crystal edge, rope twisted handle, c1890 .... 195.00
6-1/2" h, 7" l, blown hobnail, 12 rows of hobnails, sky-blue int., white ext., applied amber edge and thorn handle ...265.00
6-1/2" h, 9-1/2" l, 8" w, pink opalescent body, overshot vaseline twisted handle, blown-out hobnails on ruffled edges, c1890.. 324.00
6-3/4" h, creamy opaque body, applied pink flowers, applied vaseline twist handle 200.00
6-3/4" h, 5" d, Hobnail pattern, yellow opaque body, crimped edge, applied colorless thorn handle 195.00

Heisey, vertical grooved base, colorless, $90.

7" h, Fenton, Rose Overlay, ruffled 75.00

7" h, Hobnail pattern, white body, rose int. 95.00

7" h, Portland pattern, Portland Glass Co., colorless, applied colorless pressed leafy handle 90.00

7" h, Reverse 44 pattern, U.S. Glass Co., colorless, gold trim applied reeded handle 125.00

7" h, 6" w, Czechoslovakia, green spangle with mice flecks, cased in white, applied black trim and handle 95.00

7" h, 6-3/4" l, 5-3/4" w, vaseline opalescent, Diamond Quilted pattern, applied pink flowers and colorless leaves, applied colorless twisted thorn handle........................200.00

7" h, 7-1/2" w, Czechoslovakia, blue, red and white spatter on green spatter ground, black trim and handle 95.00

7" h, 9" w, brilliant chartreuse ext., lined in shocking pink, pulled and pinched in middle, applied clear fan center handle, applied clear ruffled feet 100.00

7-1/4" h, 5-1/4" d, orange, colorless rigaree, applied crystal leaves, applied colorless handle............................175.00

7-1/2" h, Cabbage Leaf, pink overlay, yellow int., applied colorless thorn handle 190.00

7-1/2" h, 4-3/4" d, pink candy stripe swirl overlay, white lining, ruffled edge, applied colorless twisted thorn handle ...175.00

7-1/2" h, 5" w, brilliant pink-purple int., deep brown spatter, applied crystal casing, unusual gather in thorn handle 70.00

7-1/2" h, 5-1/4" w, oxblood red and opaline swirled body, gold aventurine splotches, gold enamel dec, thick crystal casing, crystal handle 285.00

7-1/2" h, 5-1/2" w, shaded green, textured diamond quilted pattern body, swirl top, U-shaped square thorn handle 125.00

7-1/2" h, 8" l, deep mahogany red to cherry red to pale yellow, white lining, tightly crimped edge, twisted clear rope handle, c1890..265.00

7-3/4" h, 7" w, satin, mother of pearl, diamond quilted pattern body, deep gold, melon ribbed body, sq crimped top, sq spatter handle, Mt. Washington, c1880 ....795.00

8" d, creamy opaque body, rose lining, amber edged ruffled rim, twist handle 185.00

8" h, 6" d, Diamond Quilted pattern, opalescent vaseline shading to pink, applied pink handle.............................165.00

8" h, 6-1/2" w, brilliant yellow and white spatter, pulled down tightly crimped edge, applied sapphire blue handle in V-shape, applied blue leaf feet, slight amount of roughage to one foot, one thorn on handle chipped..............100.00

8" h, 8-1/2" w, deep mahogany shading to red to pale green, solid opaque white casing, applied crystal edge, applied crystal rope handle, Victorian................................125.00

8" h, 11" d, cut glass, Harvard pattern, hobstars and prisms, American Brilliant period 475.00

8-1/2" h, caramel shading to apricot, colorless edge, applied colorless thorn handle 275.00

8-1/2" h, New Martinsville, Janice, crystal, red handle 90.00

8-1/2" h, Stevens and Williams, opaque white, pink scallops, applied colorless handle 250.00

8-1/2" h, Tiffin, paneled transparent sky blue 85.00

8-3/4" h, 5" d, opalescent light vaseline, green edge, thorny nubs, applied colorless handle 195.00

8-3/4" h, 7-1/2" w, pot shaped crystal body, deep pink handle with white latticino stripes, 3 matching feet.......... 850.00

9" h, peachblow, amber ruffle, petal feet, applied amber thorn handle...195.00

9" h, 5" w, bright yellow ext., tomato red int., three swirled blown out balls, pulled down basket shape, twisted thorn handle, Victorian...175.00

9" h, 5-1/2" w, apricot to pink opalescent, pedestal rose bowl shape, vertical ribbed int., applied colorless leaves, stems, and vines, applied twisted thorn handle, c1880 ......275.00

9" h, 6" w, pale pink shading to white ext., brilliant yellow int., cabbage rose design, applied twisted thorn handle, Victorian...125.00

9" h, 6-1/2" w, Czechoslovakia, pink satin, green satin twisted handle..100.00

9" h, 7" w, deep pink int., clear casing, mottled pink, purple, and brown swirl effect, wide border of enameled and painted dec done in Turkish manner, applied pale custard handle 225.00

9-1/2" h, 5-1/2" l, green, delicate etched flowers and stems, ruffled rim, applied handle 60.00

10" h, Czechoslovakia, brilliant orange, blue and white enameled daisy, gold trim, black edge, black handle... 115.00

10" h, Imperial, Twisted Optic, vaseline......................... 110.00

10" h, Snail pattern, George Duncan & Sons, clear, pewter handle, cake type...115.00

10" h, 7-1/2" w, Czechoslovakia, pink, applied black rim and handle.. 95.00

10" h, 7-1/2" w, Czechoslovakia, pink, pink spatter, applied vaseline flowers and leaves, clear applied handle ... 115.00

10-1/4" h, Czechoslovakia, vaseline and yellow stripes, overlaid red, white, blue, yellow, orange millefiori type pattern, clear twist handle 115.00

10-1/2" h, 6" d, Czechoslovakia, acid finished clear body, ruffled, applied green leaves, two red cherries, green acid twist handle 125.00

10-1/2" h, 7" w, pink over opaque creamy white ground, applied amber edge, applied amber feet, melon ribbed body, tall loop amber handle, Victorian 90.00

10-1/2" h, 11" w, melon-ribbed base, blue cased opalescent, robin's egg blue shading to crystal, crossed crystal handle, two rows of blown hobnails, c1890 .... 375.00

11" h, Cleo pattern, Cambridge, amber, two side handles45.00

11" h, 11" w, turquoise blue shading to clear crystal, opalescent int., three rows of hobnails, melon shaped body, applied cross V-shaped handle 125.00

11-1/4" h, 8-1/2" w, colorless, jeweled rose cut, engraved, sgd "Heisey," shape #458... 250.00

11-1/2" h, Illinois pattern, colorless, applied colorless handle 110.00

11-1/2" h, 7-1/2" d, green satin, applied crystal and yellow rose flower, crystal thorn handle 110.00

11-1/2" h, 8-1/4" w, colorless, floral enamel dec, gold trim, sgd "Heisey".. 95.00

11-3/4" h, 8-1/4" l, colorless, engraved bird on branch with leaves, sgd "Heisey" 300.00

12" h, Cabbage Rose pattern, colorless, applied colorless handle..115.00

12" h, 6-1/2" h, emerald green, engraved floral and bow, sterling silver base, sgd "Hawkes," slight dent to weighted base 150.00

12" h, 8-1/4" l, plain sides, painted green ground, white enamel beads along top and bottom, white enameled monogram, sgd "Heisey"...200.00

12" h, 15" l, Broken Column pattern, colorless, applied colorless handle..125.00

13" h, 11" w, deep pink int. over pale cream white ext., three rows of hobnails on edge, applied amber edge, four applied amber feet, applied amber thorn cross-form handle, Victorian..200.00

15" h, 11" d, white ext., deep pink int., melon rib shape, heavily crimped and ruffled, four applied frosted thorn feet, applied frosted crossed V-shaped handle, Victorian..............300.00

15-1/2" h, 8" w, colorless, wide panel pattern, enameled deep blue and red flowers, green leaves, sgd "Heisey" 135.00

19" h, 12" w, blue aurene, purple highlights, ruffled, applied loop handle, inscribed "Aurene, 455" 5,250.00

Biscuit Jars

History: The biscuit or cracker jar was the forerunner of the cookie jar. Biscuit jars were made of various materials by leading glass manufacturers of the late 19th and early 20th centuries.

Bristol Glass

6" h, 4-5/8" d, light gray body, enameled white, pink, and blue flowers, green leaves, gold stems, SP rim, cov, and handle..145.00

6-1/2" h, allover enameled pink, blue, white, and yellow floral dec, green leaves, SP top, rim, and handle...........125.00

6-1/2" h, 5-1/4" d, satin finish, opaque beige ground, pink roses, gold leaves, gray foliage, SP top, rim, and handle 195.00

Cased Glass, 6-1/4" h, blue, enameled pink roses and green leaves, SP top, rim and handle 145.00

Cranberry Glass, 9" h, 6-1/4" d, two applied clear ring handles, applied clear feet and flower prunt pontil, ribbed finial knob...195.00

Crown Milano

6" h, 5-1/2" d, barrel shape, pale yellow ground shades to creamy white, deep pink apple blossoms, green leaves, gray-green branches, SP Pairpoint lid and collar, "P" in diamond logo emb in floral motif...............................695.00

6-1/2" h, pseudo Burmese coloration, painted acorns and oak leaves, quadruple plate mkd "M.W."...............445.00

Loetz Type, 6-1/2" h, translucent white mother-of-pearl irid green raindrop spatter, melon swirls, SP lid, rim, and handle..225.00

Mt. Washington, 8-1/2" h, colorless ground, tapering body, molded in scrolls, gold highlights, gold single petal blossoms each framed by elaborate gold feather scrolls, small side cartouches of colorless glass framed by fancy gold scrolls, lid sgd "MM 4425," collar, flame finial, and bail with worn gilt finish 1,500.00

New England Glass Works, melon ribbed, pink floral dec, lid and bail missing 60.00

Opalescent, 7-3/4" h, William and Mary pattern, English...875.00

Opalware

9" h, pink shaded, polychrome scene of castle, hand painted stylized florals, quadruple plate lid and frame 275.00

10" h, 8" d, pale purple ground, red and purple lilacs, resilvered fittings..320.00

Opaque, 9" h, glossy pink, quilted diamond pattern, small hairline in outer layer, quadruple plate lid and frame 110.00

Pairpoint, 9-1/2" h, burnt orange, floral dec, blown-out floral base, sgd 350.00

Pigeon Blood, 7" h, melon rib shape, resilvered frame and lid 425.00

Pomona, 10-1/2" h, 5-1/2" w, first ground, acanthus leaf design, excellent staining, applied wishbone base, crack in base..200.00

Satin Glass, 7-1/4" h, pink, molded shell base, enameled floral dec, SP lid and handle 315.00

Vaseline Glass, 7" h, threaded, SP rim, lid, and handle.....160.00

Wave Crest, 9" h, yellow roses, molded multicolored swirl ground, incised floral and leaf dec on lid, mkd "Quadruple Plate" 400.00

BLACK GLASS

History: Black glass was one of the colors made during early glass productions as far back as 1600. These early bottles had a thick body and were primarily used for fermenting liquids, where the glass walls had to withstand the pressures of the fermenting ale or wine. The Bohemians developed an opaque black glass which they used as a base for gold matte decorations, often of an Oriental style. Other European glassware manufacturers, as well as the English, produced black glass items; however, its popularity was always limited.

American production of black glass dates back to Deming Jarvis when he was at the Boston and Sandwich Glass Co. about 1865. His ingredients included manganese and powdered charcoal. While developing glass with greater strengths and other desirable properties, glass-blowers noticed that the more manganese they added, the darker the purple glass became. Some early "black" glass pieces may actually be very dark purple or even very dark green. Other 19th century glasshouses, like Atterbury, Dalzell, and Gilmore, produced lamps, bottles, and other items of black glass.

In 1915, Westmoreland Specialty Co. introduced a black glass line and this "new" color was quickly copied by Duncan and Miller, as well as Northwood, Fenton, and Cambridge. Fostoria was one of the last of the major manufacturers to get involved when it began production in 1924, and by that time, demand was beginning to wane. The United States Glass Co. became the leading exponent of black glass during the 1920s and continued to hold this lead until around 1926.

Popularity of black glass rose again in 1928 with the introduction of black stemmed wares. Morgantown Glass Works led the way, quickly followed by Fostoria and Central Glass Works. Black tableware sets were introduced during this period. Shapes reflected the design attitudes of the times, and square plates and square-footed stemware created a bold statement.

By 1932, demand began to drop off again, as it did for most handmade glass. Cambridge continued its ebony line until 1939. Raw ingredient shortages caused by World War II seriously affected the colored glassware industry, and almost no black glass was produced again until 1949, when Westmoreland issued black variety items. Again, some of the major glass makers, Fostoria, Cambridge, and Viking, entered the field. Smaller manufacturers like Boyd and Degenhart also joined the marketplace. A large percentage of the black glass offered in today's marketplace comes from the last surge, which lasted into the mid-1950s.

References: Margaret James, *Black Glass, An Illustrated Price Guide*, Collector Books, 1981; Marlena Toohey, *A Collector's Guide To Black Glass*, Antique Publications, 1988.

Ashtray, 4" d, Hazel Atlas, 1930-36
    Cloverleaf pattern, match holder center 65.00
    Square...10.00
Basket
    5" h, emb, basketweave bands, two handles 50.00
    7" h, crystal handle, Cambridge..................................130.00
Batter Set, batter jug and syrup, colorless body, black cover
    and tray, Paden City, 1936..75.00
Berry Bowl, Ribbon pattern, Hazel Atlas, c1930.................25.00
Bookends, pr
    Horse, L. E. Smith, 1950s..60.00
    Scottie, frosted, made by Imperial for National Cambridge
        Collectors, Inc. 50.00
Bowl
    6-1/2" d, Victory pattern, Diamond Glass Ware Co.......30.00
    7-1/2" d, Alternating Flute and Panel, Imperial, c1930....42.00
    10" d, Deerwood pattern, U.S. Glass, ftd....................100.00
Bud Vase, Blossom Time, Cambridge, 10" h, gold encrusted
    dec 325.00
Butter Dish, cov, Heisey, rect 110.00
Cake Plate
    Black Forest pattern, Paden City, 2" h pedestal 85.00
    Mt. Pleasant, L. E. Smith Glass Co., 10" d, low, ftd.......30.00
Candelabra, Decagon, Cambridge, #638, 3 lite................72.50
Candleholder
    2-1/2" h, Deerwood pattern, U.S. Glass 110.00
    3" h, Oak Leaf pattern, Fostoria....................................90.00
    3" h, Victory pattern, Diamond Glass Ware Co. 95.00
    4" h, opaque, wafer foot, three knobs on stem, etched "Italia," Venini paper label 125.00
    6" h, frog, bright finish, Tiffin......................................185.00
    9-1/2" h, Doric, Cambridge, pr 160.00
Candy Dish, cov, Ovide pattern, Hazel Atlas, 1930-35 .....40.00
Celery Tray
    Lodestar pattern, Heisey...50.00
    Viking, clear swan handle, oval.....................................60.00
Cereal Bowl
    4-7/8" h, Orchid pattern, Paden City, early 1930s.........35.00

Fruit Bowl, Mt. Pleasant, scalloped, $40.

    5" d, Diamond Quilted pattern, Imperial, early 1930s ...15.00
Cigarette Box, cov, 4-3/8" l, Flower Garden with Butterflies pattern,
    U.S. Glass, late 1920s...125.00
Compote
    Co-Operative Glass Co., 6-1/2" d, c1924.....................35.00
    Blossom Time, Cambridge, gold encrusted dec 225.00
    Flower Garden with Butterflies pattern, U.S. Glass, 7" h, late
        1920s...175.00
    Veined Onyx, L. E. Smith, 5" h, ftd 35.00
Console Bowl
    Autumn pattern, McKee, 8-1/2" d 40.00
    Enameled dec 50.00
Console Set, Fostoria, #2402, Deco bowl, pr candleholders..70.00
Cookie Jar, cov, Amy, L. E. Smith Glass Co. 95.00
Cordial Decanter, 12 oz, ball shape, applied colorless handle,
    orig colorless stopper, Cambridge, Farber Bros. metal
    holder, c1933 .... 95.00
Creamer
    Cloverleaf pattern, Hazel Atlas, 1930-36 ....20.00
    Deerwood pattern, U.S. Glass 60.00
    Diamond Quilted pattern, Imperial, early 1930s 15.00
    Mt. Pleasant, L. E. Smith Glass Co................................20.00
    Victory pattern, Diamond Glass Ware Co. 45.00
Cream Soup Bowl, 4-3/4" d, Diamond Quilted pattern, Imperial,
    early 1930s 15.00
Cup and Saucer
    Cloverleaf pattern, Hazel Atlas, 1930-36 ....20.00
    Diamond Quilted pattern, Imperial, early 1930s 20.00
    Mt. Pleasant, L. E. Smith Glass Co................................20.00
    Victory pattern, Diamond Glass Ware Co.......................45.00
Fern Bowl, Greek Key, 4-1/4" h, L. E. Smith..................... 25.00
Floor Vase, 28-1/2" h, raised bulbous oval body, polished rim,
    flared at base, American 500.00
Ice Bucket
    Diamond Quilted pattern, Imperial, early 1930s 85.00
    Tally Ho pattern, Cambridge, Farber Bros. chromium plated
        frame and handle, c1935 ....95.00
Mayonnaise, silver dec, L. E. Smith 15.00
Nappy
    4-1/2" d, Dawn, Heisey...35.00
    5-1/2" d, Diamond Quilted pattern, Imperial, early 1930s.. 25.00
Nut Bowl, 5-3/4" d, handle, Mt. Pleasant, L. E. Smith Glass
    Co...25.00
Pitcher, Gloria, oval, some wear to silver, Cambridge.... 950.00
Place Card Holder, 2-1/2" h, Fostoria 30.00
Plate
    6" d, Cloverleaf pattern, Hazel Atlas, 1930-36 ....15.00

Candleholder, Fostoria, 4" h, $35.

7" d, "V"-shaped open handles......................................12.00
8" d, Diamond Quilted pattern, Imperial, early 1930s...18.00
8" d, Victory pattern, Diamond Glass Ware Co............28.50
8-1/2" d, gold edge 10.00
10-1/2" d, grill, Cloverleaf pattern, Hazel Atlas, 1930-36 ..25.00
Relish, 2-part, Lodestar, Heisey.......................................65.00
Salt Shaker, sterling silver floral dec...............................15.00
Sandwich Server, center handle
    Co-Operative Flint 35.00
    Diamond Quilted pattern, Imperial, early 1930s 45.00
    Flower Garden with Butterflies pattern, U.S. Glass, late
        1920s...115.00
    Mt. Pleasant, L. E. Smith Glass Co., 12" d 40.00
Sherbet
    Cloverleaf pattern, Hazel Atlas, 1930-36 ....20.00
    Diamond Quilted pattern, Imperial, early 1930s 20.00
    Mt. Pleasant, L. E. Smith Glass Co..............................20.00
    Victory pattern, Diamond Glass Ware Co. 25.00
Snack Plate, 8-1/4" sq plate with cup indent, cup, Mt. Pleasant,
    L. E. Smith Glass Co..20.00
Soap Dish, Westite..45.00
Sugar, cov
    Cloverleaf pattern, Hazel Atlas, 1930-36 ....25.00
    Deerwood pattern, U.S. Glass 60.00
    Diamond Quilted pattern, Imperial, early 1930s 20.00
    Mt. Pleasant, L. E. Smith Glass Co..............................22.00
    Victory pattern, Diamond Glass Ware Co. 45.00
Sweet Pea Vase, 7" h, 8-1/2" d, Cambridge, c1922...........55.00
Tumbler
    Fern, 12 oz, ftd, Fostoria 35.00
    Town and Country, Heisey...40.00
Urn, 7" h, 2 handles, Dancing Girls, L. E. Smith 40.00
Vase
    6" h, #1250, Everglades, Cambridge..........................225.00
    7" h, Diagonal Star Bad, Eagle Glass Co., c1898.........35.00
    7-1/2" h, Pyramid, ftd...24.00
    7-3/4" h, flared top, silver deposit dec, Diamond Glass Ware
        Co., c1939...50.00
    8" h, Tut, Fostoria..65.00
    10" h, Black Forest pattern, Paden City 95.00
    10" h, Utopia...195.00
    10-1/2" h, floral dec, satin, Tiffin................................115.00
    12" h, Deerwood pattern, U.S. Glass 120.00

BLENKO

History: Blenko Glass Co., located in Milton, West Virginia, was founded in 1922 by British glassmaker William J. Blenko. He originally made stained glass for church windows, but since 1929 has made decorative household glass and glass building slabs. Blenko provided the blown faceted windows for the Art Force Academy Chapel in Colorado Springs, Colorado.

After 1929

Blenko glassware is handmade and only marked with paper labels. Tall pieces, ranging from 18 to 28 inches, are specialties of this manufacturer. Another specialty is crackle glass. Vibrant colors and heavy walls are predominate with the clean modern lines of most pieces.

Today, visitors to the Milton, West Virginia, factory can enjoy tours and visit the factory outlet.

Periodical: *Antique Notes Newsletter,* P.O. Box 67, Milton, WV 22541-0067.

Manufacturer: Blenko Glass Visitor Center Museum and Wholesale Outlet, P.O. Box 67, Milton, WV 22541-0067.

Additional Listings: Crackle Glass.

Ashtray, freeform
    Amethyst, 8" l..15.00
    Green, 1951 ....9.00
Bowl
    3" d, 4" h, amber, scalloped edge................................10.00
    6-1/4" d, tangerine, turned in edge 12.00
    6-1/2" d, amber, scalloped edge, heavy base.............17.50
Compote
    5-3/4" d, 6" h, red bowl shades to gold, gold stem and
        foot 20.00
    10" d, 5-1/2" h, amber, scalloped edge 25.00
Creamer, red, applied colorless handle 20.00
Decanter
    10" h, amethyst, orig amethyst stopper........................35.00
    13" h, hand blown, tear drop stopper 85.00
    15-1/2" h, 6" h pointed stopper, colorless, hand blown ...30.00
    19-1/4" h, 7" d base, 12" l stopper, amberina crackle body,
        bell shape, hand blown, pontil mark 160.00
Hour Glass, 19" h, colorless body, wood case 45.00
Paperweight, snowman, red top hat................................. 25.00
Pitcher
    4-1/4" h, electric blue crackle body, frilled top, applied color-
        less handle 25.00
    6-1/2" h, colorless bulbous body, applied colorless
        handle 20.00
Tankard, 9" h, gold body, applied colorless handle 25.00
Vase
    4" h, 4" w, emerald green crackle body, double pinched top,
        hand blown...35.00
    7-3/4" h, 6-1/2" w at top, Rosette, colorless crackle body, four
        applied rosettes, hand blown, pontil scar 90.00
    8" h, 9" d, crimped, ftd, colorless body, c1950 ....150.00
    8-1/2" h, Florette pattern, flared, colorless 35.00
    9-1/4" h, 6-1/2" w, fluted, hand blown, emerald green crackle
        body, pontil scar..95.00
    11" h, 6" w, rose colorless crackle body, waisted cylinder,
        hand blown, c1950..125.00
    25" h, avocado crackle body, tapered neck, scalloped
        edge 40.00
Water Set, 10" h dark amber pitcher, random small indentations
    on body, six 6" h tumblers 72.00

BLOWN THREE MOLD

History: The Jamestown colony in Virginia introduced glassmaking to America. The artisans used a "free-blown" method.

Blowing molten glass into molds was not introduced into America until the early 1800s. Blown three-mold glass used a pre-designed mold that consisted of two, three, or more hinged parts. The glassmaker placed a quantity of molten glass on the tip of a rod or tube, inserted it into the mold, blew air into the tube, waited until the glass cooled, and removed the finished product. The three-part mold is the most common and lends its name to this entire category.

The impressed decorations on blown-mold glass usually are reversed, i.e., what is raised or convex on the outside will be concave on the inside. This is useful in identifying the blown form.

By 1850, American-made glassware was relatively common. Increased demand led to large factories and the creation of a technology, which eliminated the smaller companies.

Collectors should be aware that reproductions of blown mold glass are offered widely in the marketplace. Some reproductions are specially produced for museums and gift shops. While many are marked, most are not. Modern artists have kept the craft of blown molded glassware alive, and collectors should learn to recognize the characteristics of new glass.

References: George S. and Helen McKearin, *American Glass*, reprint, Crown Publishers, 1941, 1948; Kenneth Wilson, *American Glass 1760-1930: The Toledo Museum of Art, Volume I, Volume II*, Hudson Hills Press and The Toledo Museum of Art, 1994.

Collectors' Club: The National American Glass Club, Ltd., 7417 Allison St., Hyattsville, MD 10784.

Museums: Corning Museum of Glass, Corning, NY; Sandwich Glass Museum, Sandwich, MA.

Additional Listings: Early American Glass and Stiegel-Type.

Basket
 3-1/2" h, 3-1/8" d, cobalt blue, plain base, traces of gold dec on ribs, solid applied handle, pontil 125.00
 4-1/2" h, 4" d, colorless, rayed base, solid applied handle, pontil scar...300.00
Bird Cage Fountain, 5-1/4" h, colorless, ground mouth, pontil scar, McKearin GI-12 ....50.00
Bottle, 7-1/4" h, olive green, McKearin GIII-16.................330.00
Bowl, colorless
 4-1/4" d, 1-3/4" h, outward folded rim, straight sided, sixteen diamond base, pontil.................................215.00
 5" d, rounded sides, outward folded rim, rayed base, pontil scar..200.00
 5-3/8" d, folded rim, twelve diamond base, pontil scar, McKearin GII-6...125.00
 6" d, 1-3/4" h, outward folded rim, straight slanting sides, sixteen diamond base, pontil.......................140.00
 6-1/4" d, folded rim, twelve diamond base, pontil scar...200.00
 6-3/8" d, 5-3/4" h, folded rim, sixteen diamond base, ftd, pontil, tilts to one side, McKearin GII-18 ....4,800.00
Carafe, 9-1/4" h, dark yellow amber, rayed base, deep pontil scar...2,400.00
Celery Vase, colorless, Pittsburgh, McKearin GV-21 ......650.00
Cordial, 2-7/8" h, colorless, ringed base, pontil, heavy circular foot, freehand formed, McKearinGII-18 ....550.00
Creamer
 3-1/4" h, colorless, formed mouth and spout, ringed base, applied solid handle with curled end 375.00
 3-1/2" h, colorless, applied handle.............................125.00
 4-3/8" h, brilliant sapphire blue, ftd, applied round base, applied solid handle, fine curled ending, flared mouth, tooled rim, ringed base with pontil, Boston & Sandwich, c1820, McKearin GI-29 ....2,400.00
 7-1/2" h, colorless, applied handle, small rim chip, check at base of handle...120.00
Cruet
 5-3/8" h, colorless, plain base, formed pouring lip, pontil, McKearin GII-28 ....150.00
 7-3/4" h, cobalt blue, scroll scale pattern, ribbed base, pontil, applied handle, French 265.00

Cup Plate, 3-7/8" d, folded rim, rayed base, pontil scar, three McKearin labels, ex-collection George McKearin and TMR Culbertson, McKearin GII-1 ....600.00
Decanter
 McKearin GII-6, 8-1/2" h, light sea green, Kent-Ohio pattern...2,415.00
 McKearin GIV-7, 10" h, colorless, arch and fern design, snake medallion, minor chips, mold imperfections 165.00
 McKearin GII-18, 8" h, colorless, 3 applied rings, replaced wheel stopper...110.00
 McKearin GII-19, 8-1/4" h, colorless, replaced wheel stopper 115.00
 McKearin GIII-15, colorless, flared mouth, period stopper, pontil scar, quart, attributed to Keene Marlboro Street Glassworks, Keene, NH, 1820-40 ....120.00
 McKearin GIII-16, colorless, flared mouth, period stopper, pontil scar, pint, attributed to Keene Marlboro Street Glassworks, Keene, NH, 1820-40 ....230.00
 McKearin GIII-16, yellowish olive, sheared mouth, pontil scar, pint, Keene Marlboro Street Glassworks, Keene, NH, 1820-40, some light abrasions......................350.00
 McKearin GIII-19, colorless, flared mouth, period stopper, pontil scar, quart, applied crimped snake trailing, attributed to Keene Marlboro Street Glassworks, Keene, NH, 1820-40 ....550.00
 McKearin GIII-20, colorless, flared mouth, pontil scar, pint, attributed to Keene Marlboro Street Glassworks, Keene, NH, 1820-40, no stopper...110.00
 McKearin Plate 5, #2, similar to, unlisted Baroque type pattern, sapphire blue, flared mouth, pontil scar, quart, French, 19th C...350.00
Dish, colorless
 5" d, outward rolled rim, pontil scar, McKearin GIII-21 ... 130.00
 5-1/4" d, McKearin GII-16......................................65.00
 5-1/2" d, McKearin GII-18......................................50.00
 6-3/8" d, folded rim, rayed base, iron pontil..................90.00
Flask, 5-1/4" h, colorless, arch and diamond pattern, sheared mouth, pontil, Continental.....................................300.00
Flip Glass, colorless
 5-1/2" h, McKearin GII-18......................................165.00
 5-5/8" h, 4-5/8" h, eighteen diamond base..................135.00

Decanter, Keene Marlboro Street Glassworks, Keene, NH, 1820-40, yellowish olive, sheared mouth, pontil scar, pint, McKearin GIII-16, some light int. haze, $350. Photo courtesy of Norman C. Heckler and Co.

6" h, McKearin GII-18 ....125.00

Hat

2-1/8" h, colorless, fifteen diamond base, pontil, folded
rim 275.00

2-1/4" h, colorless, swirled rayed base, pontil, folded
rim 125.00

2-5/8" h, 2-1/4" d, sapphire blue, folded rim, ringed and pontil
base...850.00

Ink Bottle, 2-1/4" d, deep olive green, McKearin GII-2 ....195.00

Inkwell

1-7/8" h, 2-3/4" d, amber, drum shape, faint ringed base,
pontil scar 125.00

2" h, 2-5/8" d, olive green, McKearin GII-18.................125.00

Lamp

4" h, 3" d, peg, colorless, heavy applied solid pegs, period
tin matching double burners, short factory ground neck,
McKearin GII-18, pr...1,450.00

6-1/2" h, colorless, double paw pressed base, orig brass collar,
mkd "BTM font/Mt. Vernon Works," McKearin GI-30.. 800.00

Miniature Decanter, colorless

2-5/8" h, McKearin GIII-12......................................165.00

3-1/2" h, ground upper rim, McKearin GIII-12.............125.00

Mustard

3-7/8" h, colorless, flanged lip, iron pontil 50.00

4-1/4" h, colorless, pontil, cork stopper, orig paper label,
McKearin GI-15 ....85.00

5" h, colorless, clear sheared ball finial, flanged, folded lip,
pontil, orig matching cov 125.00

5-1/4" h, colorless, plain base, pontil, orig pressed finial finish, hollow blown cov, McKearin GI-24 ....90.00

Pan, 1-1/2" h, 5" d, colorless, McKearin GI-6...................185.00

Pitcher, colorless

7" h, base of handle reglued, McKearin GIII-5.............145.00

8-1/2" h, tool mark at lower part of applied handle 250.00

10-3/4" h, McKearin GV-17.....................................420.00

Plate, 5-3/8" d, colorless, folded rim, plain base, pontil...150.00

Salt, master

Basket shape, colorless..120.00

Galleried rim, rayed base, sapphire blue, 2-1/2" h ..1,600.00

Hollow stem and base, colorless, pontil 575.00

Rayed and ringed base, purple blue, pontil, 2-1/4" h...750.00

Salt Shaker, colorless

4-5/8" h, pontil base, orig metal cap 75.00

5" h, sheared lip, orig metal cap and pontil 75.00

Sugar, 2-1/2" h, 5" d, brilliant sapphire blue, rolled flanged lip,
solid applied base with pontil attributed to Boston &
Sandwich, c1820, McKearin GI-29 ....3,250.00

Toddy Plate, 4-1/4" d, colorless, folded rim, rayed base,
pontil...265.00

Toilet Water Bottle

5-3/4" h, cobalt blue, tam-o-shanter cap.....................300.00

6-5/8" h, yellow green, tapering ovoid, plain base, pontil, orig
matching stopper, McKearin GI-3, type II..........2,650.00

6-3/4" h, deep sapphire blue, tooled flared mouth, period
tam-o-shanter stopper, pontil scar, some light int. residue
near base 180.00

6-3/4" h, violet, flared lip, smooth base, period tam-o-shanter
stopper 650.00

Tumbler, colorless

3-3/8" h, barrel form, tooled rim, pontil scar, attributed to
Keene Marlboro Glassworks, Keene, NH, 1820-40, McK-
earin GIII-14..190.00

4-5/8" h, sheared rim, pontil scar, unlisted, similar to McK-
earin GV-5 ....110.00

5-5/8" h, sheared rim, pontil scar, attributed to Boston and
Sandwich, McKearin GII-18 ....130.00

6-1/4" h, McKearin GII-19...155.00

Vase, 9" h, colorless, engraved flowers, leaves, and berries,
McKearin GV-21 ....7,500.00

Vinegar Bottle, 6-3/4" h, cobalt blue, ribbed, orig stopper, McK-
earin GI-7 ....285.00

Whiskey Taster, colorless

1-5/8" h, ringed base, pontil 200.00

2-3/8" h, applied handle, McKearin GII-18.................285.00

BOHEMIAN GLASS

History: The once-independent country of Bohemia, now a part of the Czech Republic, produced a variety of fine glassware: etched, cut, overlay, and colored. Glass production has been recorded there as early as the 14th and 15th centuries. Wheel-cutting techniques were practiced in the 16th century. By the mid-19th century, coal replaced wood as fuel and many new factories sprang up. Beautiful examples of exquisite cutting and engraved portraits were skillfully crafted. Bohemian glassware first appeared in America in the early 1820s and continues to be exported to the U.S. today.

Bohemia is known for its "flashed" glass that was produced in the familiar ruby color, as well as in amber, green, blue, and black. Common patterns include Deer and Castle, Deer and Pine Tree, and Vintage.

Most of the Bohemian glass encountered in today's market is from 1875 to 1900 period. Bohemian glassware was carried around the world by travelers and salesmen. Engravers often decorated pieces to fill the demand of this ground of eager buyers and tailored their decorations to fit the tastes and desires of the buyers. Bohemian-type glass also was made in England, Switzerland, and Germany.

References: Brigitte Klesse and Hans Mayr, *European Glass from 1500-1800, The Ernesto Wolf Collection*, Kremayr & Scheriau, 1987; Sylvia Petrova and Jean-Luc Olivie (eds.), *Bohemian Glass*, Abrams, 1990; Robert and Deborah Truitt, *Collectible Bohemian Glass*, R & D Glass, 1995; Kenneth Wilson, *American Glass 1760-1930: The Toledo Museum of Art, Volume I, Volume II,* Hudson Hills Press and The Toledo Museum of Art, 1994.

Reproduction Alert.

Beaker

4-1/2" h, blue and white overlay, arched panels with gilt ivy
and stylized foliage on oval white overlay, flaring base,
mid-19th C 225.00

4-1/2" h, blue and white overlay, multicolored spring floral
bouquet on oval white overlay, gilt foliate, arched panels,
mid- to late-19th C 250.00

4-1/2" h, colorless, continuous scene of hunters in landscape, band of flowering branches 350.00

4-5/8" h, waisted cylindrical, multicolored enameled morning glories between cut roundels, pink overlay, white
ground..600.00

4-3/4" h, green flashed, circular and oval cut windows, multicolored enameled flowers, gilt lines 220.00

4-3/4" h, white overlay, multicolored enameled peasant girl,
oval cartouche edged with gilt ivy, loose bouquet of flowers on reverse...450.00

5" h, pink flashed opaque, cut stylized leaves and drapery,
enamel and gilt flowering branches, flaring base, late-
19th C 475.00

Bowl, ftd, ten panels, shaped top, leaf and grape design, 3-1/8" d, 2" h, $35.

5-18" h, blue and white overlay, rect panel engraved with stag landscape, oval roundels, named scenes, gilt highlights, late 19th C.....................................300.00

5-1/4" h, white on amethyst overlay, quatrefoil and circular cut windows, painted trailing roses........................250.00

5-1/2" h, amber and ruby flashed, alternating panels engraved with cornucopia, flowers, beehive, and urn, cut panels, scalloped foot...225.00

5-1/2" h, amber flashed, engraved, animals and building, C scroll panels, flared foot, c1860..............................125.00

5-3/4" h, flared, colorless, all over pattern of cut circles each containing finely painted ornately blue, and yellow flowers, flashed amber yellow around each circle with black tracery, amber flashed pedestal, black flashed circular base, c1880..950.00

Bonbonniere and Undertray, cov, 10-1/2" h, all over painted floral garland dec, pear form finial..........................1,400.00

Bottle, 12-1/4" h, blue cut to clear, frosted leaf dec.........450.00

Bowl

3" d, 1-3/4" h, Lityalin, three rows of honeycomb cutting, mottled brown, designed to simulate polished agate, Frederich Eggerman, c1935...395.00

6-1/2" d, 5-1/2" h, cov, translucent crystal ground, studio enameled gold, red, blue, and green foliate elements, delicate black outline, dec repeated on cov and base, in the manner of Steinschonau..................................635.00

12-1/2" d, double cut overlay, cobalt blue cut to clear ... 265.00

Box, cov, domed lid, ruby flashed

3-1/2" d, Vintage pattern, engraved clear and frosted grape clusters and vines, gilt brass fittings.......................165.00

3-3/4" d, engraved clear and frosted buildings, scrolling foliate bands, brass fittings...185.00

Bud Vase, 7-1/2" h, shaded green to pink stem, applied petal ribbon, three blown-out spherical bulbs................135.00

Butter Dish, cov, enameled white cut to red, floral and figural cartouches on gilt foliate dec ground.....................700.00

Castor Set, 18" h, three ruby cut to colorless bottles, matching steeple-shaped stoppers, silver plated metal holder........350.00

Celery Tray, ruby flashed, Deer and Castle pattern, clear and frosted...110.00

Center Bowl

9" d, 11-1/2" h, ribbed and ruffled green irid bowl, elaborate metal base with three cherubs playing flutes.........525.00

9-1/2" d, 3-3/4" h, transparent citron-green encasing seven dark red centered purple-aubergine pad blossoms with trailing stems, attributed to Harbach......................325.00

Cologne Bottle, 5" h, cobalt blue, tiered body dec, white and gold flowers and scrolls 175.00

Compote

7" d, amber flashed, cut leaf and floral dec, green band at top, pedestal base 125.00

7-3/4" h, enameled white cut to red, floral and figural cartouches on gilt foliate dec ground.........................800.00

9-1/2" d, 6-1/2" h, amber flashed, Deer and Castle pattern, engraved, clear and frosted animals, castle, and trees 195.00

Condiment Set, Deer and Tree, amber flashed.............285.00

Console Set, 10" d bowl, ruby flashed, cut back jumping stag and cartouche, matching candlesticks.................275.00

Cream Pitcher and Sugar, 3-1/4" h x 3-1/4" d cream pitcher, 2-1/4" h x 3-1/2" sugar, Schwarzlot, three hollow bun feet on each, pitcher dec by country scene of well-dressed couple, nobleman with walking stick, wandering troubadour playing mandolin, sugar dec with panoramic rustic scene, including three peasants, villages, and castles, both sigh Lobmeyer signature................................1,500.00

Cruet

Amber cut to clear, floral arrangement intaglio carved on ruby flashed ground of three oval panels with carved frames of floral swags, five cut-to-clear panels at neck, three embellished with gold scrolls, all edged in brilliant gold, sixteen decorative panels edged in gold, base and stopper both sgd "4"................................750.00

Iridescent purple over amber, applied threading, polished pontil..110.00

Decanter

8-1/4" h, octagonal, triple ringed neck, windows engraved with names scenes of Pague on alternating pink and blue flashed areas, yellow flashed ground, enameled black foliage..950.00

14-3/4" h, octagonal, clear with greenish tint, engraved forest and deer scene, orig stopper..............................100.00

15-1/2" h, ruby cut to clear, geese dec, cut stopper ..150.00

Decanter Set

14" h x 4-1/4" w decanter, six 5" h x 2" goblets, ruby cut to clear, ovoid body, cut indentations on slender neck, pinwheel and other cuttings 225.00

16-1/4" h decanter, four 6-3/4" h goblets, cased ruby red, long neck with elongated cut panels with gilt edge, gilt tracery on ruby panels, border of twelve semi-circles at top and bottom, six multicolored painted circular cartouches with flowers, gilt tracery, pointed stopper with six cut elongated petal shapes with gilt dec, long stemmed goblets with found bowl with ruby red border, cut border of semi-circles, gilt tracery, cut six-sided stem, c1880..........1,850.00

Dresser Bottle, 9-1/4" h, emerald green, gold leaf dec, pr..225.00

Flip Glass, 6" h, 6" d, colorless, cut, engraved forest scene with fox and birds 125.00

Goblet

5" h, amber overlay, cut and frosted forest scenes, early 20th C 95.00

5-1/2" h, ruby flashed, engraved stag, rocky landscape, enameled stylized foliage and flowers, flaring base...........220.00

6-1/4" h, Annagelb, hexagonal bowl, raised enameled bosses, gilt named scenes, conforming knop and petal base 425.00

6-3/4" h, white and cranberry overlay, thistle form bowl, six teardrop panels alternately enameled with floral bouquets and cut with blocks of diamonds, faceted knob and spreading scalloped foot, gilt trim........................600.00

7" h, ruby cut to clear, stag and foliate dec, 12 pc set ... 750.00

7" h, white ground, fruit and floral dec, 12 pc set 950.00

8-1/2" h, amethyst cut to clear, early 20th C 40.00

Jar, cov

5" h, colorless crystal body overlaid in bright orange, cut facets in geometric motif, applied faceted finials, pr 230.00

6" h, quatraform, green, maroon-red threading, metal rim, swing bail handle and cover 250.00

7" h, barrel shape, bands of clear engraving, red satin discs, barrel finial..165.00

Jug, 8-1/4" h, dark olive green spherical body, irid pulled feather silvery luster, applied offset twisted basket handle, raised pedestal foot, berry prunt at pontil..........1,265.00

Lamp, 25" h, candlestick type, amber overlay, cut and frosted foliate panels, pr..................................500.00

Mantle Lusters, 12-1/2" h, 6-1/2" w, deep cobalt blue overlay, opaque white cut away, gold trim, pr.....................250.00

Mug, 6" h, ruby flashed, engraved castle and trees, applied clear handle, sgd "Volmer, 1893" 95.00

Nappy, 5" d, colorless shading to amber, enameled daisy dec, applied ring handle 50.00

Perfume Bottle, 7" h, ruby flashed, Deer and Castle, clear and frosted, gold dec 120.00

Pokal, cov, 21-1/2" h, amber cut to colorless, 19th C 500.00

Powder Box, 4-1/4" d, round, straight sides, flat top, ruby flashed, etched cov with leaping stag, forest setting, landscape and birds on sides, clear base 120.00

Punch Set, 11" h, 11-1/2" d tray, curved oval bow, undertray, frosted clear glass, red glass jewels as centers of gold enameled swags and medallions, bowl elaborately engraved, dated 1875 and relating to Carl Buschbeck........................345.00

Rose Bowl, 7" d, 4" h, green irid, molded swirled organic elements, trifid pewter base rim..................................245.00

Scent Bottle, 10" h, 5" d, cased cobalt blue, finely cut, gilt and beige floral and foliage dec on top two tiers, gilt and beige baskets and roses on base tier, gilt and beige floral and foliage dec on matching stopper, star cut bottom, pointed stopper, c1840 ....1,800.00

Spill Vase, 6-3/8" h, overlay, cut white to cranberry, 19th C, very minor chips, pr 420.00

Stein

4-1/2" h, 2-3/4" d, ruby flashed, engraved dog and deer in forest, "Souvenir de Luchon" on front, pewter mounts 250.00

6-1/2" h, 3" d, ruby flashed, engraved cathedral panels, leaves, and scrolls, pewter mounts, ruby inset lid 320.00

Sugar Shaker, ruby flashed, Bird and Castle pattern, clear and forted 90.00

Teapot, 11" w, cranberry cut to clear, panels of flowers, gilt spout and handle 220.00

Tray, 8-1/2" l, 2" h, oblong colorless body, pedestal foot, gold and turquoise dec, J & L Lobmeyer mark at center..........575.00

Tumbler

4" h, colorless, each dec with costumed boy and girl in different outdoor setting, J & L Lobmeyer mark on base, 8 pc set..1,100.00

4" h, ruby flashed, cut design, gold dec, 4 pc set 150.00

4-1/4" h, colorless, leaded, enameled German inscription, florals, heart, two hands shaking, dated 1727, pontil scar..550.00

Urn, 7" h, 3-1/8" w at top, colorless glass over layer of vaseline and black flash, engraved border at top, three engraved oval panels with wheat design between them, one panel with girl with watering can in garden, other with house and trees, third with church and trees, black pedestal base with engraved diamond design, oval petal design on foot, c1880 .... 1,475.00

Vase

4" h, brilliant cobalt blue body, irid blue oil-spot dec, three applied bright blue finger handles, polished pontil......750.00

5" h, green irid double bulbed body, vertical stripes interspersed with round spots, all over irid, molded base, top rim smoothed..345.00

5-1/4" h, brilliant cobalt blue irid oval body, copper overlay cut in Secessionist motif, smooth base 425.00

5-1/4" h, colorless ground, seven tooled scallops at rim, yellow and maroon swirls, irid dec, attributed to Kralik.......375.00

5-1/4" h, mold blown pinched fishbowl sphere, faintly opal persuasion crackled as water, enamel painted fish, water lilies, aquatic plants, attributed to Moser 345.00

5-3/4" h, lemon yellow oval body, green irid pulled feather motif, polished pontil 1,035.00

6" h, colorless pinched oval, flared and folded rim, brick red, white, and burgundy spots, foliate etching on int. surface..500.00

6" h, six ruffle rim, conical body, applied pedestal foot, gold irid int., amber spotted surface, polished base 290.00

6-3/4" h, amber etched to clear, deer and forest dec..... 135.00

7-3/8" h, ruby etched to clear, deer and architecture, foliate and abstract dec, price for pr 950.00

7-1/2" h, 4-1/2" w, pinched and pulled in top, swirled body, red ground, purple irid 100.00

8-3/4" h, striated blue, green, burgundy-red oval cased to opal body lined in turquoise blue, gilt enamel medallions centered by red glass jewels 320.00

9-1/4" h, trumpet form, ruby cut to clear, all over rose and foliate dec..75.00

9-1/4" h, 3-1/2" d, ovoid body, slender neck, widening at top, white overlay cut to ruby, gold dec on center panels, painted floral sprays on white ground, painted florals circling near top and bottom 150.00

9-1/2" h, burgundy red oval body cased with opal white, gilded scroll and swag dec, opal, green, and turquoise glass beaded highlights 435.00

9-1/2" h, satin finish, enameled medallion of roses.....115.00

9-3/4" h, 4-3/4" w at top, trumpet shape, cased cranberry, scalloped eight-section cut top edge, ivory and gold enameled intertwined scroll design around top and base in each section, eight cut to clear elongated arches extend from top to base, notched and scalloped base, c1840 .... 1,275.00

10" h, brilliant cobalt blue body, irid blue oil-spot motif, applied ribbed bright blue handles, polished pontil 865.00

10" h, irid red and amber, concentric loops, ground rims, pr..350.00

10-1/2" h, irid smooth rose red surface, tapered vessel with four integrated solid supports, polished pontil.......490.00

10-1/2" h, ocean wave design, variegated red paperweight ground..175.00

11" h, overlay, gold enameled white cut to cranberry, elongated windows 275.00

11-1/4" h, ftd, ruby etched to colorless, foliate dec, wear, chips..50.00

12" h, mold blown apple green double-bulbed body, lower half enhanced by spotted red dec, polished top rim, Czechoslovakian-style...175.00

13" h, flared quatraform tooled rim, bulbous pinched base, irid dark red body, pulled green and white dec, polished pontil..450.00

17-1/2" h, stick, ice blue, multicolored enameled florals, pr 200.00

Whiskey Glass, 3-1/4" h, clear, engraved, early 19th C, pr 250.00

BOTTLES

History: Cosmetic bottles held special creams, oils, and cosmetics designed to enhance the beauty of the user.

Some also claimed, especially on their colorful labels, to cure or provide relief from common ailments.

A number of household items, e.g., cleaning fluids and polishes, required glass storage containers. Many are collected for their fine lithographed labels. Others are collected because of the rainbow of colors in which they were manufactured.

Baby and nursing bottles, used to feed the young and sickly, were a great help to the housewife because of their graduated measure markings, replaceable nipples, and the ease with which they could be cleaned, sterilized, and reused.

Bitters, a "remedy" made from natural herbs and other mixtures with an alcohol base, often was viewed as the universal cure-all. The names given to various bitter mixtures were imaginative, though the bitters seldom cured what their makers claimed. The manufacturers of bitters needed a way to sell and advertise their products. They designed bottles in many shapes, sizes, and colors to attract the buyer. During the Civil War a tax was levied on alcoholic beverages. Since bitters were identified as medicines, they were exempt from this tax. The alcoholic content was never mentioned. In 1907, when the Pure Foods Regulations went into effect, "an honest statement of content on every label" put most of the manufacturers out of business.

Medicine bottles contained "medicines" of all kinds, from bitters and elixirs to snakebite remedies to serious medicines. These small bottles make very interesting collectibles as their claims rival the best of today's Madison Avenue advertising executives.

Milk bottles have been a favorite with collectors for many years. Some specialize in a particular type of milk bottle, i.e., cream top, while others devote their collection to bottles from a specific geographic area. Milk bottles are being reproduced. Most, by use of blank bottles, then being processed with color slogans, designs, and fictitious farms. Reproduction Elsie the Borden's popular cow, Hopalong Cassidy, and Disney characters have crept into the market. The process has improved and some are virtually undetectable, except to the serious collector. A low price for a very unusual bottle may be a tip off.

Mineral water bottles contained water from a natural spring. Spring water was favored by health-conscious people between the 1850s and 1900s.

Soda Bottles, beer bottles, and other popular drink bottles carried our favorite beverages from the manufacturers to the stores' or the distributors' shelves. Painted labels and a myriad of colors attract today's collectors.

References: Joseph K. Baldwin, *Collector's Guide To Patent and Proprietary Medicine Bottles of the Nineteenth Century,* Thomas Nelson, 1973; William E. Covill, *Ink bottles and Ink Wells,* William s. Sullwold Publishing, 1971; Jeffrey L. Giarde, *Glass Milk Bottles: Their Makers and Marks,* printed by author; Ralph & Terry Kovel, *Kovels' Bottles Price List,* 10th ed., Crown Publishers, 1996; Donald E. Lord, *California Milks,* published by author; Peck and Audie Markota, *Western Blob Top Soda and Mineral Bottles,* 2nd ed., published by authors, 1994; George S. and Helen McKearin, *American Glass,* reprint, Crown Publishers, 1941, 1948; John Odell, *Digger Odell's Official Antique*

Bottle and Glass Collector Magazine Price Guide Series, Vols. 1 through 8, published by author (1910 Shawhan Rd., Morrow, OH 45152), 1995; Diane Ostrander, *Guide to American Nursing Bottles,* 1984, revised ed. by American Collectors of Infant Feeders, 1992; Michael Polak, *Bottles, Identification and Price Guide, 2nd Edition,* Avon Books, 1997; Carlyn Ring, *For Bitters Only,* published by author 203 Kensington Rd., Hampton Falls, NH 03844), 1980; Dick Roller (comp.), *Indiana Glass Factories Notes,* Acorn Press, 1994; Carlo and Dorothy Sellari, *The Standard Old Bottle Price Guide,* 1989, 1997 value update, Collector Books; J. H. Thompson, *Bitters Bottles,* Century House, 1947; John Tutton, *Udder Delightful, Udder Fantastic, and Udderly Beautiful,* published by author (Rt. 4, Box 929, Front Royal, VA 22630); Richard Watson, *Bitters Bottles,* Thomas Nelson and Sons, 1965; Kenneth Wilson, *American Glass 1760-1930: The Toledo Museum of Art, Volume I, Volume II*, Hudson Hills Press and The Toledo Museum of Art, 1994.

Periodicals: *Antique Bottle and Glass Collector,* P.O. Box 180, East Greenville, PA 18041; *Antique Bottle Collecting Magazine,* 4 Lower Clifton Hill, Clifton, Bristol B58 England; *Bitters Report,* P.O. Box 1253, Bunnell, FL 32110; *Bottles & Bygones,* 30 Brabant Rd., Cheadle Hulme, Cheadle, Cheshire Sk8 7AU, U.K., *British Bottle Review,* B. B. R. Publishing, P.O. Box 310, Richmond, Surrey TW9 1FS, U.K., *Canadian Bottle and Stoneware Collector,* P.O. Box 310, Ontario L1C 3Li Canada; *Hawaii Bottle Museum News,* P.O. Box 25152, Honolulu, HI 96825; *Miniature Bottle Collector,* P.O. Box 2161, Pals Verdes Peninsula, CA 90274-8161; *The Bitters Report,* P.O. Box 1253, Bunnell, FL 32110.

Collectors' Clubs: American Collectors of Infant Feeders, 5161 W. 59th St., Indianapolis, IN 46254-1107; Antique Bottle & Collectibles Club, P.O. Box 1061, Verdi, NV 89439; Antique Bottle Club of Northern Illinois, P.O. Box 571, Lake Geneva, WI 53147; Antique Bottle Collectors of North Florida, P.O. Box 14796, Jacksonville, FL 32238; Apple Valley Bottle Collectors Club, 3015 Northwestern Pike, Winchester, VA 22603-3825; Baltimore Antique Bottle Club, P.O. Box 36061, Towson, MD 21286-6061; Delmarva Antique Bottle Club, 57 Lakewood Dr., Lewes, DE 19958; Del-Val Miniature Bottle Club, 57104 Del Aire Landing Rd., Philadelphia, PA 19114; Early Tennessee Bottle & Collectibles Society, 4521 Jones Rd., Knoxville, TN 37918-7722; Empire State Bottle Collectors Assoc., 22 Paris Rd., New Hartford, NY 13413; Federation of Historical Bottle Collectors, Inc., 88 Sweetbriar Branch, Longwood, FL 32750-2783; First Chicago Bottle Club, P.O. Box A3382, Chicago, IL 60690; Forks of the Delaware Bottle Collectors Assoc., P.O. Box 693, Easton, PA 18042; 49'er Historical Bottle Club, P.O. Box 1570; Cedar Ridge, CA 95924; Genessee Valley Bottle Collectors Assoc., P.O. Box 7528, Rochester, NY 14615; Great Lakes Miniature Bottle Club, 19745 Woodmont, Harper Woods, MI 48225-1873; Gulf Coast Bottle & Jar Club, P.O. Box 1754; Pasadena, TX 77501; Historical Bottle Diggers of Virginia, 1176 South Dogwood Dr., Harrisburg, VA 22801; Hudson Valley Antique Bottle Club, 6 Columbus Ave., Cornwall on Hudson, NY, 12520; Huron Valley Antique Bottle & Insulator Club, 2475 W Walton Blvd., Waterford, MI 48329-4435; Jersey Shore Bottle Club, P.O. Box 995, Toms River, NY 08754; Las

Vegas Antique Bottle & Collectibles Club, 3901 E. Stewart #16; Las Vegas, NV 89110-3152; Lilliputian Bottle Club, 54 Village Circle, Manhattan Beach, CA 90266-7222; Middle Tennessee Bottle & Collector's Club, 1750 Keyes Rd., Greenbrier, TN 37073; Midwest Antique Fruit Jar & Bottle Club, P.O. Box 38, Flat Rock, IN 47234-5660; Mini Bottle Club, 47 Burradon Rd., Burradon Northumberland N323 7NF U.K., M-T Bottle Collectors Assoc., Inc., P.O. Box 1581 DeLand, FL 32721; National Assoc. of Milk Bottle Collectors, Inc., 4 Ox Bow Rd., Westport, CT 06880-2602; New England Antique Bottle Club, 120 Commonwealth Rd., Lynn, MA 01904; New Jersey Antique Bottle Collectors Assoc., 117 Lincoln Place, Waldwick, NJ 07463-2114; Pennsylvania Bottle Collector's Assoc., 251 Eastland Ave., York, PA 17402-1105; Pittsburgh Antique Bottle Club, RD 3, Box 280, Indiana, PA 15701; Potomac Bottle Club, 8411 Porter Lane, Alexandria, VA 22380-2140; Richmond Area Bottle Collectors, 2801 Battery Ave., Richmond, VA 23228; San Bernardino County Historical Bottle and Collectible Club, P.O. Box 6759, San Bernardino, CA 92412; San Jose Antique Bottle Collectors Assoc., P.O. Box 5432, San Jose, CA 95159; Sarasota-Manatee Antique Bottle Collectors Assoc., P.O. Box 3105; Sarasota, FL 34230-3105; Somers Antique Bottle Club, P.O. Box 373, Somers, CT 06071;Western New York Miniature Liquor Bottle Club, P.O. Box 182, Cheektowaga, NY 14225-0182; Yankee Bottle Club, P.O. Box 702, Keene, NH 03431.

Museums: Billings Farm Museum, Woodstock, VT; Hawaii Bottle Museum, Honolulu, HI; National Bottle Museum, Ballston Spa, NY; National Bottle Museum, Richmond, Surrey, England; Old Bottle Museum, Salem, NJ; Southwest Dairy Museum, Arlington, TX.

Baby and Nursing

Acme, clear, lay-down, emb 65.00
Baby's Delight 45.00
Brockway Glass #862 ....10.00
Bunny, Anchor Hocking 16.00
Bunny, Hazel Atlas 15.50
Cala Nurser, oval, clear, emb, ring on neck, 7-1/8" h 8.00
Cat, Anchor Hocking 25.00
Cats and Kittens, enamel dec with oz measurements..21.50
Comfy, bottle with orig nipple 15.00
Dominion Glass Co., Canada, 8 oz, narrow mouth, orig filled with Vanilla Extract from Pure Standard Products, orig label, nursery rhyme, "I had a little hobby horse," imp image of little boy riding rocking horse, 1940s 15.00
Dr. Pepper 12.00
Embossed baby, late 1940s 10.00
Empire Nursing Bottle, bent neck, 6-1/2" h 50.00
Evenflo, 4 oz, black plastic ring, flat cap, rubber nipple orig cardboard sleeve, paper adv flyer, date 1956 on sleeve..... 12.00
Fire King, sapphire blue
    4 oz...20.00
    8 oz...60.00
    Binky's Nip Cap..210.00
    Steri-Seal Nipple Cover, colorless, emb on cover ...25.00
Fred Flintstone, 1977...5.00
Griptight, banana shape, hole at both ends, colorless, emb name...25.00
Hailwoods Graduated Feeding Bottle, aqua, applied top, flattened bladder shape, 2" neck, markings up to 8 oz on back, front emb with name, 7" h.............................75.00
Happy Baby 9.00

Hygeia, adv on panels 15.00
Hygienic Feeder, emb, open on both ends 30.00
Little Folk 36.00
Manx Feeding Bottle, bulbous, clear, tooled sq collar, emb "Patent July 4, 1876," 3" h.....................................200.00
Marguerite Feeding Bottle, inside screw, daisy on top 35.00
Mother's Comfort, clear, turtle type............................25.00
Nonpareil Nurser, aqua, 5-1/2" h................................20.00
Nursery Rhyme, enameled Jack and Jill......................15.00
Ovale Nurser, Non-Rolling, Whitall Tatum & Co., 6 oz, applied lip, narrow mouth..10.00
Pepsi, adv, 1994 limited edition 4.00
Plain, 4 oz, "K" inside shield mark 16.00
Pottstown, PA, dairy giveaway, set of five bottles, each enameled with nursery rhyme, one with bank top, other with plastic closure, nipple, yellow and blue congratulations box, never used 25.00
Pyrex
    4 oz, narrow mouth, orig cardboard sleeve 12.00
    8 oz, air vent feature, six-sided, narrow top, pink and blue graphics, orig box 20.00
7-Up, adv 2.00
Sure Feed Ltd. Carfidd, flat turtle shape, long neck, colorless, emb on top...40.00
Sweet Babee Nurser, colorless, emb "Easy Clean, Pat'd May 3, 1910" 15.00
Teddy's Pet, Peaceful Nights, colorless, emb, turtle shape, 4 oz..70.00
The Hygienic Feeder, banana shape, hole at both ends, colorless, emb name..25.00
Tuffy Kap, nipple cov, colorless, emb "Tuffy KAP U.S.A." around cap, "B" in circle on flat top 10.00
Vitaflo, OH 3.25

Beer

Augusta Brewing Co., Augusta, CA, aqua, painted label, 7" h..15.00
Buffalo Brewing Co., Sacramento, CA, emb buffalo jumping through horse head, amber, blob top, 12" h.............20.00
Callie & Co. Limited, emb dog's head, St. Helens below center, dark green, ring-type blob top, 8-1/4" h..............20.00
Central Brand Extra Lager Beer, aqua, paper label, 9-1/2" h...8.00
Chattachoochee Brewing Co., Brownsville, AL, aqua, emb, 9-1/2" h...10.00
Cock n' Bull Ginger Beer, painted label, crow top, 7" h....6.00
Cumberland Brew Co., Cumberland, MD, amber.........10.00
Excelsior, aqua, 9-1/4" h..18.00
Germania Brewing Co., aqua, emb, 7-1/2" h 15.00
Grand Price Beer, Gulf Brewing Co., Houston, colorless, crown top, paper label, 9" h....................................10.00
Hand Brew Co., Pawtucket, RI, aqua............................15.00
Iroquois, Buffalo, emb Indian's head, amber................12.00
McCormick Brewery, Boston, 1897, colorless 12.00
National Brewing Co., Baltimore, amber, emb eagle, blob top..20.00
Piel Bros., East New York Brewery, fancy emb logo, aqua..20.00
Rolling Rock Extra Pale, blue and white label, green bottle, unopened...18.50
Royal Ruby, ABM, 9-1/2" h...25.00
Schlitz Brewing Co., amber, painted label, 9-1/2" h 10.00
Southern Brewing Co., green, paper label, 9-1/2" h.......4.00

Beverage

A Merry Christmas/Corking Good Stuff/Happy New Year, bald headed man sealing bottle mkd "1891 Rye," colorless with brown, yellow, blue and flesh tone colored label under glass, ground mouth, screw threads, metal cap, smooth base, half pint..700.00

Arny & Shinn, Georgetown, D. C., "This Bottle Is Never Sold," soda water, squat cylindrical, yellow ground, applied heavy collared mouth, smooth base, half pint, professionally cleaned 150.00

Bay Rum, 11-1/4" h, amethyst, blown molded, paneled body, partial label, burst bubble, mold imperfections 375.00

Cole & Southey Washington DC, soda water, squat cylindrical, aquamarine, applied sloping collared mouth with ring, smooth base, half pint, professionally cleaned........110.00

Drink Howel's Original Orange-Julep, 12" h, cylindrical, colorless, white, gold, red, and yellow orange label under glass, sheared mouth, metal cap, smooth base, America, 1880-90 ....125.00

Grapette, 1946 ....10.00

J. M. Roseberry & Co., Alexandria, VA, eagle wreath and shield, soda water, attributed to Baltimore Glass Works, Baltimore, MD, 1845-60, squat cylindrical form, yellowish green, applied sloping collared mouth, iron pontil mark, half pint, overall ext. wear, 3/8" flat chip.................800.00

M. Flanagan Petersburg, Va., Philadelphia XXX Porter & Ale, squat cylindrical, green with olive tone, heavy applied collared mouth, iron pontil mark, half pint, overall ext. wear 230.00

Steinke & Kornahrens/Soda Water/Return This Bottle/Charleston SC, America, 1845-60, octagonal, cobalt blue, applied sloping collared mouth, iron pontil mark, oversize half pint, 7-3/4" h, professionally cleaned to orig luster, some remaining scratches....................................650.00

W. H. Buck Norfolk VA, soda water, squat cylindrical, deep green, applied heavy collard mouth, iron pontil mark, half pint, some ext. wear and scratches 240.00

Bitters

A. S. Hopkins Union Stomach Bitters, greenish-yellow, applied tapered collar lip, smooth base, 9-1/4" h 265.00

Alpine Herb Bitters, amber, sq, smooth base, tooled lip, 9-5/8" h 175.00

Baker's Orange Grove Bitters, yellowish-amber, smooth base, applied mouth, 90-1/2" h 185.00

Bell's Cocktail Bitters, Jas. M. Bell & Co., New York, amber, applied ring, smooth base, 10-1/2" h 450.00

Ben Franklin, America, 1840-60, tapered barrel form, light blue green, applied collared mouth with ring, pontil scar, 10" h...3,280.00

Brown's Celebrated Indian Herb Bitters/Patented Feb. 11, 1868, figural Indian maiden, emb, golden amber, ground lip, smooth base, 12-1/4" h...................................350.00

Bourbon Whiskey Bitters, barrel shape, cherry puce, applied sq collar, smooth base, 9-3/4" h..............................500.00

Caldwell's Herb Bitters/The Great Tonic, triangular, beveled and lattice work panels, yellowish-amber, applied tapered lip, iron pontil 400.00

Cannon's Dyspeptic Bitters, America, 1860-90, sq, beveled corners, emb with cannon balls and ramrods, three full panels with emb cannon barrels, golden amber, applied sloping collared mouth, smooth base, 10" h, 3/4" bruise and repair to top of mouth, some int. residue 3,250.00

Cherry Cordial Bitters, America, 1870-90, sq, beveled corners and indented panels, light yellow amber, tooled sloping collared mouth with ring, smooth base, 8-7/8" h roughness to do manufacturer's tool 140.00

Chestnut, freeblown, New England, 1780-30
4-7/8" h, light yellow with olive tone, sheared mouth, applied collar, pontil scar 300.00

5-1/8" h, yellow olive, sheared mouth, applied round collar, pontil scar....................................210.00

5-3/4" h, light yellow, sheared mouth, applied rim, pontil scar....................................140.00

6-1/4" h, light olive yellow, sheared mouth, narrow applied round collar, pontil scar....................................220.00

7-1/8" h, medium yellow olive, short applied sloping collared mouth, pontil scar....................................170.00

8" h, yellow olive, applied sloping collared mouth with ring, pontil scar....................................190.00

8-1/2" h, light to medium olive yellow, sheared mouth applied ring, pontil scar....................................250.00

10-1/4" h, yellow green, olive tone, sheared mouth, applied rim, pontil scar, some minor ext. wear......325.00

Clarke's Vegetable Sherry Wine Bitters, aqua, smooth base, applied mouth, 14" h 575.00

Drake's Plantation Bitters, puce, Arabesque design, tapered lip, smooth base, 9-3/4" h....................................295.00

Dr. A. S. Hopkins Union Stomach Bitters, F. S. Amodon, Sole Prop., Hartford, Conn., USA, sq amber bottle, orig neck seal 98-percent orig graphic front label, 95-percent rear label, orig contents, 9-1/2" h....................................240.00

Dr. Bell's Blood Purifying Bitters The Great English Remedy, America, 1860-90, rect, indented panels, bright golden yellow, applied sq collared mouth, smooth base, 9-1/2" h 140.00

Dr. Loew's Celebrated Stomach Bitters & Nerve Tonic, green, smooth base, tooled lip, 9-1/4" h 150.00

Dr. Petzold's Genuine German Bitters Incpt 1862, medium amber, colorful graphic front label, oval, 10-1/2" h 950.00

Dr. Porter's Medicated Stomach Bitters......................75.00

Dr. Walkinshaw's Curative Bitters, Batavia, NY, sq amber bottle, 90-percent orig label, orig contents, 10" h 315.00

Godfrey's Celebrated Cordial Bitters, NY, aqua, pontil, applied mouth, 10" h....................................1,225.00

Goff's Bitters, H on bottom, amber and colorless, 5-3/4" h 25.00

Greeley's Bourbon Bitters, America, 1860-80, barrel shape, applied sq collared mouth, smooth base
Apricot puce, 9-1/8" h, shallow 3/8" burst bubble on top barrel ring 180.00
Copper puce, 9-1/4" h, shallow 1/4" flake on side of flanged mouth....................................120.00
Gray topaz, 9-1/8" h, one slightly ground spot.......190.00
Root beer brown with puce overtones, 9-1/8" h, pinhead sized bruise on top corner of mouth...................230.00
Smoky gray-brown, 9-1/4" h 225.00

Hall's Bitters, America, 1860-80, barrel form, light yellow amber, applied sq collared mouth, smooth base, 9-1/8" h.... 230.00

Hasterlik's Celebrated Stomach Biters, sq amber, 98-percent front label with eagle, shield, and flags, 9-1/4" h 55.00

Herkules Bitter, America, 1870-90, globular, two flattened label panels, emerald green, tooled mouth with ring, smooth base, 7-1/4" h....................................2,000.00

H. H. Warner & Co./Tippecanoe, American, 1860-80, cylindrical, yellow amber with olive tone, tooled mushroom mouth, smooth base, 8-3/4" h....................................170.00

Hibernia Bitters, amber, sq, smooth base, tooled lip, 9-1/4" h 125.00

Holtzermann's Patent Stomach Bitters, amber, complete label, 9-1/2" h....................................425.00

Hops & Malt Bitters, golden amber, tapered collar lip, smooth base, 9-1/8" h 250.00

I. Newton's Jaundice Butters, Norwich VT, 1940-60, rect, wide beveled corners, deep aquamarine, tooled flared mouth, pontil scar, 6-7/8" h....................................700.00

J. C.& Co., molded pineapple form, deep golden amber, blown molded, 19th C, 8-1/2" h.................460.00

John Moffit, Phoenix Bitters, NY, olive amber, eight sided, round collar pontil, 6-3/8" h 2,500.00

John Root's Bitters/1834/Buffalo, N.Y., rect, beveled corners, recessed panels, cabin type roof, bluish green, applied sloping collared mouth with ring, smooth base, 10" h, 3" crack in one shoulder............................190.00

Johnson's Calisaya Bitters, Burlington VT, 1870-90, sq, beveled corners, indented panels

    Golden yellow, 10" h..............................120.00

    Yellow amber, applied sloping collared mouth with ring, smooth base, 10" h, two shallow partial burst bubbles on shoulder......................................210.00

Kelly's Old Cabin Bitters, cabin shape, amber, sloping collar lip, smooth base, 9" h...........................725.00

Keystone Bitters, barrel shape, golden amber, applied tapered collar, sq lip, smooth base, 9-3/4" h 175.00

McKeever's Army Bitters, amber, sloping collared lip, smooth base, 10-5/8" h.........................1,700.00

Mist of the Morning Sole Agents Barnett & Lumley, golden amber, sloping collar lip, smooth base, 9-3/4" h....300.00

National Bitters, corn cob shape, puce amber, applied ring lip, smooth base, 12-5/8" h...................350.00

Old Homestead Wild Cherry Bitters, America, 1860-90, tall house form, yellow amber, applied sloping collared mouth, smooth base, 9-1/2" h, crudely applied lip has air under some of natural folds, sand grain above door 150.00

Old Sachem Bitters and Wigwam Tonic, America, 1840-60, barrel form, applied sq collared mouth, pontil scar

    Aquamarine, yellow striation above and to right of word Sachem, 10" h, pinhead size flake on top of mouth 4,750.00

    Deep plum amethyst, 9" h, minor ext. scratches....550.00

    Golden amber, 9-1/4" h 600.00

    Olive yellow, 9-1/4" h.............................1,700.00

    Puce copper, 9-1/4" h, three pinhead sized flakes at top corner of mouth 375.00

Red Jacket Bitters, Monheimer & Co., sq, amber, tooled lip, smooth base, 9-1/2" h...............................100.00

Schroeder's Bitters, Louisville, KY, amber, tooled lip, smooth base, 11-3/4" h 350.00

Simon's Centennial Bitters, George Washington bust shape, aqua, applied mouth, smooth base, 9-1/8" h 650.00

Sir Robert, Edgar's English Life Bitters-G E Graves Proprietor Rutland Vt. USA, American, 1860-80, sq, beveled corners, yellow amber, applied sloping collared mouth, smooth base, 8-1/2" h, 1/4" shallow burst bubble 170.00

S. T. Drake's Plantation Bitters, figural, America, 1860-80, sq tall log cabin form, applied sloping collared mouth, smooth base

    Apricot puce, five log type, 9-3/4" h........................275.00

    Strawberry puce, five log type, 9-3/4" h.................220.00

    Yellow with olive tone, four log type, 10-1/4" h.......350.00

Suffolk Bitters, Philbrook & Tucker, Boston, pig shape, amber, applied mouth, smooth base, 10-1/8" l 600.00

Sunny Castle Stomach Bitters, Jos. Dudenhoefer, Milwaukee, sq, amber, tooled lip, smooth base, 9" h........125.00

Tippecanoe, Warner & Co., amber, applied mushroom lip, 9" h...95.00

Traveller's Bitters, America, 1834-70, man standing with cane, oval, amber, 10-1/2" h 265.00

Warner's Safe Tonic Bitters, America, 1870-90, oval, golden yellow, tooled double collared mouth, smooth base, 7-3/8" h, some minor ext. high point wear 650.00

William Allen's Congress Bitters, America, 1860-80, rect, in-

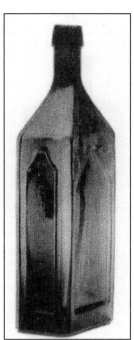

William Allen's Congress Bitters, America, 1860-80, rect, indented panels, yellow amber with olive tone, applied sloping collared mouth, smooth base, 10-1/8" h, $1,700. Photo courtesy of Norman C. Heckler and Co.

dented panels, applied sloping collared mouth, smooth base, 10-1/8" h

    Aquamarine...200.00

    Yellow amber with olive tone 1,700.00

Zingan Bitters, amber, applied mouth, smooth base, 11-7/8" h 150.00

Cosmetic

Boswell & Warner's Colorific, rect, cobalt blue, indented panels, tooled sq lip, c1880, 5-1/2" h.....................85.00

De Vry's Dandero-Off Hair Tonic, colorless, paper label, 6-1/2" h 15.00

Edwards Harlene Astol Hair Colour Restorer, three sunken panels, cobalt blue, 7" h..........................55.00

Ferd. Muhlens Inc., New York No. 4711 Bath Salts, orig label...20.00

Harrisons Hair Colour Restorer, Amber, Reading, sunken panel, emb on front, 6" h 18.00

Hind's Honey and Almond Cream, 5-1/2" h 7.50

Hyacinthia Toilet hair Dressing, rect, aqua, crude applied lip, open pontil, 6" h.......................................25.00

Kickapoo Sage Hair Tonic, cylindrical, cobalt blue, tooled mouth, matching stopper, smooth base, 5" h 160.00

Kranks Cold Cream, milk glass, 2-3/4" h.........................6.50

Mrs. S. A. Allens World's Hair Restorer, amber, rect, three sunken panels, emb name and "London" on base, 7 h...... 30.00

Pompeian Massage Cream, amethyst, 2-3/4" h..............9.00

Prichard & Constance, London & New York, Tonic Bath Crystals, orig label 20.00

The Mexican Hair Renewer, rounded shoulder, rect emb on edges, cobalt blue, 7" h 35.00

Violet Dulce Vanishing Cream, eight panels, 2-1/2" h.....7.50

Demijohn

10-7/8" h, New England, freeblown, cylindrical, yellowish amber, applied sloping collared mouth, pontil scar 50.00

14-1/4" h, America, 1860-80, emb monogram on shoulder and "Trademark" and logo of carboy on base, cylindrical, apple green, applied sloping collared mouth, smooth base, 1/8" irid bruise on base................................120.00

17-3/8" h, America, 1860-80, cylindrical, four piece mold, light sapphire blue, applied sloping collared mouth, smooth base, 1/2" flat chip under applied mouth, shallow 1/4" open bubble near base....................................220.00

Figural

Ballet Dancer, 12" h, milk glass, pink and brown paint dec highlights, sheared mouth, removable head as closure, pontil scar, attributed to America, 1860-90............525.00

Barrel Form, 4-7/8" h, yellow olive green, fancy rigaree trailing around body, two sleigh runner feet serve as base, each emb with repeating sunburst motif, tooled mouth, pontil scar, Europe, 18th C.......................................450.00

Bear, 10-5/8" h, dense yellow amber, sheared mouth, applied face, Russia, 1860-80, flat chip on back.......400.00

Big Stick, Teddy Roosevelt's, 7-1/2" h, golden amber, sheared mouth, smooth base, flat flake at mouth...................170.00

Bull, John, 11-3/4" h, bright orange amber, tooled mouth, smooth base, attributed to England, 1870-1900,...160.00

Cherub Holding Medallion, 11-1/8" h, blue opaque milk glass, sq collared mouth, ground pontil scar, attributed to America, 1860-90 .... 120.00

Chinaman, 5-3/4" h, seated form, milk glass, ground mouth, orig painted metal atomizer head, smooth base, America, 1860-90 ....120.00

Fish, 11-1/2" h, "Doctor Fisch's Bitters," golden amber, applied small round collared mouth, smooth base, America, 1860-80, some ext. highpoint wear, burst bubble on base..160.00

Garfield, James, President, 8" h, colorless glass bust set in turned wood base, ground mouth, smooth base, America, 1880-1900 ....80.00

Indian Maiden, 12-1/4" h, "Brown's Celebrated Indian Herb Bitters," yellow amber, inward rolled mouth, smooth base, America, 1860-80 ....600.00

Pig, Suffolk Bitters, America, 1860-90, shaded yellow amber, applied double collared mouth, smooth base, 10-1/8" l, minor ext. high point wear 750.00

Pineapple, 8-3/4" h, "W & Co./N.Y.," America, 1845-60, brilliant yellow green with strong olive tone, applied double collard mouth, iron pontil mark, 8" meandering crack through body 425.00

Shoe, dark amethyst, ground mouth, smooth base 125.00

Washington, George, 10" h, "Simon's Centennial Bitters," aquamarine, applied double collared mouth, smooth base, America, 1860-80..650.00

Food

Baking Powder, Eddy's, tin top 12.00

Banana Flavoring, Herberlings, paper label, 8" h 10.00

Blueberry, 11" h, 10 lobed flutes, medium green, tooled rolled collared mouth..160.00

Candy, Prices Patent Candie Company, England, 1840-60, rect wedge form, cobalt blue, applied sloping collared mouth with ring, pontil scar, 7" h 350.00

Catsup
   Curtis Brothers, colorless, blue label 12.00
   Cuyuga County Tomato Catsup, aqua, swirl design, 10" h..65.00
   Quickshank, paper label 5.00

Celery Salt, 8" h, Crown Celery Salt, Horton Cato & Co., Detroit, yellow amber, smooth base, ground lip, orig shaker type cap 175.00

Extract
   Baker's Flavoring Extracts, 4-3/4" h, aqua, sq ring lip ...15.00

John Bull, English, 1870-1900, bright orange amber, tooled mouth, smooth base, 11-3/4" h, $160. Photo courtesy of Norman C. Heckler and Co.

L. C. Extract, label, orig box 180.00

Ginger, Sanford's orig label 12.00

Honey, Land of Lakes, honeycomb, metal cap 8.00

Horseradish
   As You Like It, pottery, clamp 25.00
   Heinz Nobel & Co., emb, two anchors, horse head on lid, 1873, 5" h...275.00

Lemonade, G. Foster Clark & Co., Eiffel Tower, 2-3/4" h.. 10.00

Lemon Extract, Louis & Company................................10.00

Lime Juice
   10-1/4" h, arrow motif, olive amber, smooth base, applied mouth..85.00
   13" h, tapered cylinder, blob top, overall emb lime foliage, emb "L. Rose & Co."...35.00

Malted Milk, Horlick's Malted Milk, Racine, half pint.....20.00

Olive, Chef, 5" h...5.00

Peanut Butter, 5" h, Bennett Hubba 20.00

Pepper Sauce, 8" h, S & P Pat. Appl. For, teal blue, smooth base, tooled lip..50.00

Pickle, cathedral, America, 1845-80, sq, beveled corners
   10-5/8" h, 4 fancy cathedral arch designs, medium green, tooled rolled mouth, smooth base 650.00
   11-1/2" h, 3 fancy cathedral designs, greenish-aqua, tooled rolled mouth, smooth base 150.00
   11-3/4" h, 4 different fancy cathedral arch designs, protruding irregular panels, aquamarine, tooled sq mouth, iron pontil mark 170.00

Snuff, freeblown, rect, wide beveled corners, olive green, sheared mouth, pontil scar, attributed to New England, 1800-30, 4-1/2" h 130.00

Vinegar, jug shape
   Weso Biko Co. Cider Vinegar.................................45.00
   Whitehouse, 10" h...20.00

Household

Ammonia
   Golden Key, paper label, 8" h 5.00
   Parson's, aqua, 1882...20.00

Blueing, Jennings, aqua, blob top, 7" h 8.00

Cleaning, Lysol
    4" h, amber 22.00
    4-1/2" h, colorless, Lysol London on base 18.00
    5" h, jug, yellow amber, Lysol on front, Boots All British on
        back 24.00
    6" h, amber, Lysol London on base.........................20.00
    6-1/2" h, jug, amber, Lysol Boots All British around
        shoulder 20.00
    6-1/2" h, jug, black, applied top, c1914 ....60.00
    7" h, jug, amber, round, name in script on front.......24.00
Gin
    8-3/4" h, tapered, yellow olive, applied mushroom mouth,
        tubular pontil scar, Netherlands, 1780-1830 ....50.00
    9-1/4" h, tapered, yellow olive, applied mushroom mouth,
        pontil scar, Netherlands, 1780-1830 ....50.00
    9-7/8" h, tapered, yellow olive, flared wide mouth opening
        to 2-1/8" d, pontil scar, Netherlands, 1780-1830, trans-
        formed into wide mouth preserve jar.................275.00
    10" h, London Jockey/Clubhouse/Gin, America, 1860-80,
        sq, beveled corners, brilliant deep yellow green, applied
        sloping collared mouth with ring, smooth base 700.00
Glue, Bull Dog Brand Liquid Glue, aqua, ring collar,
    3-1/2" 6.50
Oil, Standard Oil Co., colorless, orig label, 6" h............7.50
Polish
    Alma Polish, aqua, name emb on shoulder, mkd "M & Go"
        on base, 5" h..8.00
    EZ Stove Polish, aqua, 6" h 15.00
    Gordon's Chafola Furniture Polish, emb, open
        pontil 150.00
    Osborn's Liquid Polish, cylindrical, yellow olive, inward
        rolled mouth, tubular pontil scar, American, 1840-60,
        3-5/8" h...475.00
    Sewing Machine Oil, Sperm Brand, clear, 5-1/2" h....5.00
    Shoe Polish, Everett & Barron Co., oval, clear, 4-3/4" ..5.00

Ink

Bell
    2-1/2" h, aqua 10.00
    3-1/2" h, "M" emb on body, colorless......................35.00
Boat
    Cobalt blue, shear top..28.00
    Dark green, emb "M" on both sides, 2" h.................20.00
    Moss green, sear top, two pen rests, 2-1/2" h..........30.00
Cylindrical
    2" h, cobalt blue, ringed neck 28.00
    4-1/4" h, Waterman's, colorless, paper label with bottle of ink,
        wooden bullet shaped case, orig paper label..........10.00
    5-1/2" h, ice blue, 2 rings at bottom, 2 at top, 1-1/2" neck
        with pour lip 30.00
    5-5/8" h, America, 1840-60, "Harrison's Columbia Ink,"
        cobalt blue, applied flared mouth, pontil scar, 3" crack,
        mouth roughness, C #764 ....140.00
    6" h, Hyde London, cobalt blue, emb, 1-1/2" neck with
        pour lip...60.00
Figural, America, 1860-90
    2" h, house, domed offset neck for, emb architectural fea-
        tures of front door and 4 windows, colorless, sheared
        mouth, smooth base, Carter's Ink, some remaining int.
        ink residue, C #614...650.00
    2" h, locomotive, aquamarine, ground mouth, smooth
        base, C #715 ....800.00
    2-3/8" h, log cabin, rect, colorless, tooled sq collared
        mouth, smooth base, pinhead sized hole in one base
        corner, some int. haze, C #680 ....190.00

2-5/8" h, house, 1-1/2 story cottage form, full label on re-
    verse "Bank of Writing Fluid, Manuf by the Senate Ink
    Co. Philadelphia," aquamarine, tooled sq collared
    mouth, smooth base, small area of label slightly faded,
    C #682 ....300.00
3-1/8" h, rect log cabin, colorless, ground mouth, smooth
    base, 1/8" bruise on int. of mouth, possibly done at
    manufacture...375.00
Hexagonal, 9-7/8" h, America, 1900-20, "Carter," cathedral
    panels, colorless with pale yellow cast, machined mouth,
    smooth base, similar to C #820..............................700.00
Inverted Concial
    2-3/8" h, Stoddard, NH, 1846-1860, deep yellow-olive,
        sheared mouth, pontil scar, pinhead flake on mouth
        edge, C #15 ....170.00
    2-1/2" h, America, 1840-60, medium cobalt blue, tooled
        mouth, tubular pontil scar, C #23 ....800.00
    2-1/2" h, America, 1840-60, "Woods/Black Ink/Portland,"
        aquamarine, inward rolled mouth, pontil scar, C #12,
        unearthed with some remaining stain................170.00
Master
    5-1/2" h, cobalt blue, sq, pour lip, emb on side "Hyde
        London," cleared 60.00
    6" h, cobalt blue, round, pour spout, emb "Hyde
        London" 85.00
    8-1/2" h, aqua, 2" neck, crude applied pour lip, some
        bubbles...40.00
    10-1/2" h, eighteen sides, cobalt blue......................95.00
Octagonal
    Aqua, cut away base to lay on side 20.00
    G. H. Gilbert Co., West Brookfield, MA, orig label ...150.00
    Harrison's Columbian Ink, light green......................60.00
    Laughlin's And Bushfield Wheeling Va., 2-7/8" h, aquama-
        rine, inward rolled mouth, pontil scar 300.00
    Light forest green with slight amber swirls, burst top,
        3-1/2" h..18.00
Square, Temple London, emb top, one pen rest, aqua24.00
Teakettle, sapphire blue, long curved spout, orig metal cap,
    2" h, C #1257 ....500.00
Tent
    Aqua, ribbing goes from neck to base, single pen rest on
        side, 2-1/2" h...55.00

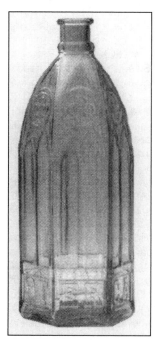

**Carter Master, hexagonal, cathedral
panels, colorless with pale yellowish cast, machined mouth, smooth
base, America, 1900-20, 9-7/8" h,
$700. Photo courtesy of Norman C.
Heckler and Co.**

Light cornflower blue, ribbing from bottom of neck to base, single pen rest 85.00

Triangular, Derby's All British, emb, aqua, sheared lip 30.00

Umbrella, America, 1840-60

2-1/8" h, twelve-sided, sapphire blue, inward rolled mouth, pontil, scar, C #182, professionally cleaned 950.00

2-1/4" h, New England, 1840-60, octagonal, golden amber, sheared mouth, C #145.............................160.00

2-3/8" h, octagonal, sapphire blue, inward rolled mouth, pontil, scar, C #141 ....700.00

2-5/8" h, octagonal, lime green, labeled "Williams/Black/Empire/Ink/New York," tooled mouth, smooth base, label 95-percent intact, C #173...160.00

2-5/8" h, octagonal, sapphire blue, inward rolled mouth, pontil, scar, C #129 ....950.00

2-5/8" h, octagonal, yellow, inward rolled mouth, pontil, scar, C #129 ....1,200.00

Medicine

A. B. L. Myers, AM Rock Rose, New Haven, America, 1845-60, rect, beveled corners, indented panels, brilliant rich blue, applied heavy collared mouth, iron pontil mark, 9-3/8" h, some int. stain near base, open shallow burst bubble 1,100.00

Alexander's Silameau, America, 1840-60, violin form, bulbous neck, sapphire blue, applied sq collared mouth, pontil scar, 6-1/8" h, professionally cleaned, some remaining residue 425.00

American Expectorant, America, 1840-60, octagonal, greenish aquamarine, outward rolled mouth, pontil scar, 5-7/8" h 425.00

Arthurs Renovating Syrup, A. A., American, 1845-60, sq, narrow beveled corners, medium blue green, applied sloping collared mouth, iron pontil mark, 9" h 950.00

Bennetts Hyssop Cure Stockport, rect, aqua, sunken panel, 5-1/2" h..30.00

Black Swamp Syrup, colorless, light staining on orig label, orig contents, 7" h...50.00

Booth & Sedgwick's London Cordial Gin, American, 1845-60, sq, beveled corners, deep blue green, applied sloping collared mouth with ring, iron pontil mark, 9-3/4" h 375.00

Brants Indian Balsam, America, 1840-60, octagonal, aquamarine, applied sloping collared mouth, pontil scar, 6-3/4" h 150.00

C. Hemistreet & Co., Troy, N.Y., America, 1840-60, octagonal, medium to deep sapphire blue, applied double collared mouth, pontil scar, 6-3/4" h, minor ext. haze 180.00

C. W. Roback, MD, Dr. Roback Swedish Remedy, America, 1840-60, octagonal, bright aquamarine, applied sq collared mouth, pontil scar, 6" h.................................160.00

Dan Patch White Liniment, colorless, complete wrap around label, orig contents, box, 7" h.................................280.00

Davis & Miller Druggist, Baltimore, attributed to Baltimore Glass Works, Baltimore, MD, 1845-60, cylindrical, brilliant sapphire blue, applied sq collared mouth, iron pontil, mark, 3" d, 7-1/2" h 1,800.00

Dr. Bowman's Indian Ointment, America, 1840-60, octagonal, aquamarine, applied sloping collared mouth, pontil scar, 6" h...275.00

Dr. Davis's Compound Syrup Of Wild Cherry And Tar, America, 1840-60, octagonal, indented panels, greenish aquamarine, applied sloping collared mouth, pontil scar, 6-5/8" h, 1/4" chip under mouth 40.00

Dr. Henley's Celery, Beef and Iron, C B & I Extract Co., America, 1884-94, amber, tooled top, smooth base, 9-1/4" h .. 120.00

Dr. J. a. Sherman's Rupture Curative Compound, America,

1870-80, rect, indented panels, cobalt blue, blue triations, tooled, applied sq collar, smooth base, 8-1/4" h 1,000.00

Dr. J. Webster's Cerevisa Angelica Duplex (coat of arms), America, 1840-60, rect, beveled corners, brilliant medium yellowish green, applied sloping collared mouth with ring, pontil scar, 7-1/8" l, some light int. stain on shoulders 1,300.00

Dr. McMunn's Elixir of Opium, round aqua, orig inside paper wrapper, bottle emb "Opium," 4-1/2" h 140.00

Dr. Roback Swedish Remedy, C. W. Roback, MD, America, 1840-60, octagonal, bright aquamarine, applied sq collared mouth, pontil scar, 4-1/2" h 140.00

Dr. Rookes Rheumatic Lixile, dense cobalt blue, slope shouldered rect, double collar, three sunken panels, 5" h... 50.00

Dr. Seymour's Balsam of Wild Cherry & Comfrey, America, 1840-60, octagonal, aquamarine, applied sloping collared mouth, pontil scar, 6-1/2" h 475.00

Dutchers Dead Shot For Bed Bugs St. Albans VT, America, 1840-60, rect, narrow beveled corners, aquamarine, applied sq collared mouth, pontil scar, 5" h...............400.00

E. A. Buckhout's Dutch Liniment, Prepared At Mechanicsville, Saratoga Co. NY, rect, beveled corners, figure of standing Dutch man, tooled mouth, pontil scar, 4-5/8" h 400.00

Elipizone A Safe Cure For Fits & Epilepsy H. C. Root London, aqua, rect, emb front panel, 6-1/2" h.......................55.00

From The Laboratory of G. W. Merchant, Chemist, Lockport, N. Y., attributed to Lockport Glass Works, Lockport, NY, 1840-60, rect, chamfered corners, deep yellowish green, applied sloping collard mouth, tubular pontil scar, 5-1/2" h..500.00

Granular Citrate of Magnesia, kite with letter inside, ring top, cobalt blue, 8" h...35.00

G. W. House Clemens Indian Tonic, ring top, aqua, 5" h 100.00

Hayman's Balsam of Horehound, ice blue, emb on front panel, 5" h..20.00

Hunt's Liniment Prepared By G. E. Stanton, Sing Sing, N.Y., rect, wide beveled corners, bright yellow green, inward rolled mouth, pontil scar, 4-1/2" h.......................2,000.00

Iceland Balsam For Pulmonary Consumption, Iceland Balsam, America, 1830-50, rect, beveled corners, emb on 3 sides, yellow olive, short applied sloping collared mouth, pontil scar, 6-1/2" h, professionally cleaned, light emb lettering 5,500.00

I. L. St. John's Cough Syrup, America, 1840-60, octagonal, brilliant aquamarine, applied sloping collared mouth, pontil scar, 6-1/4" h...140.00

I. Newport's Panacea Purifier Of The Blood Nerwich, VT, attributed to Stoddard Glasshouse, Stoddard, NH, 1846-60, cylindrical, indented emb panels, yellow olive, applied sloping collared mouth with ring, iron pontil ring, 7-3/8 h, shall chip on sloping collar 1,900.00

J. L. Leavitt, Boston, attributed to Stoddard Glasshouse, Stoddard, NH, 1846-60, cylindrical, yellow olive, applied sloping collard mouth with ring, iron pontil mark, 8-1/8" h...... 275.00

Jones & Elmes Veterinary Surgeons London, 9" l, 3" neck, oval, dark cornflower blue, c1896 ....50.00

Kimball's Anodyne Toothache Drops, Troy, NH, olive green, three pc mold, cylinder, pontil scarred base, 9" h ...425.00

L. P. Dodge Rheumatic Liniment Newburg, America, 1840-60, rect, beveled corners, light golden amber, applied sloping collared mouth, pontil scar, 6" h, appears to have been cleaned 750.00

Manchester Wilds Gout & Rheumatic Mixture, aqua, two sunken panels, 6" h 18.00

Monk's Old Bourbon Whiskey For Medicinal Purposes, America, 1845-60, sq, beveled corners, brilliant yellow olive, applied sloping collared mouth, iron pontil mark, 8-1/4" h.... 1,100.00

O. K. Plantation, triangular, amber, 11" h....................200.00

Pine Tree Tar Cordial, Phila, tree and patent 1959 on one panel, L. Q. G. Wisharts on other, blob top, green, 8" h.........60.00

Pinkstones Curechiline Cures Cattle Diseases, shoulder with Curechiline, emb front panel, aqua, 7-1/2" h............30.00

Radium Radia, colorless, colorful graphic label wraps around 3 sides, orig contents, 5-1/4" h...................210.00

Roshoton & Aspinwall, New York, Compound Chlorine Tooth Wash, golden olive, flared top, pontil, 6" h.............250.00

Rushton Clark & Co., Chemist's New York, aqua, applied top, open pontil, 9-1/2" h.........................100.00

Sanderson's Blood Renovator Milton VT, America, 1840-60, oval, aquamarine, applied sq collared mouth, pontil scar, 8-1/8""h, very minor ext. high point wear................650.00

Security Rheumatic Liniment, colorless, colorful graphic label wraps around 3 sides, orig contents, orig box (top missing), 7-1/2" h 325.00

Shaker Anodyne, NTH, Enfield, NH, aqua, front and rear labels, orig contents, 4" h............................250.00

Shaker Digestive Cordial/AJ White New York, aqua, orig front and rear labels, orig contents, 5-1/2" h..........110.00

Smith's Anodyne Cough Drops Montpelier, America, 1840-60, rect, beveled corners, aquamarine, applied sloping collared mouth, pontil scar, 5-7/8" l.......................140.00

Smith's Green Mountain Renovator, attributed to Stoddard Glasshouse, Stoddard, NH, 1846-1850, rect, wide beveled corners, yellow olive amber, applied double collared mouth, iron pontil mark, 6-3/4" h.........................1,300.00

Sun Drug Co., Los Angeles, CA, America, 1890-1905, light amber, tooled top, smooth base, winged mortar and pestle motif, 5-3/4" h.....................................175.00

Swaim's Panacea Philada, America, 1840-60, cylindrical, indented panels, bright grayish green, applied sloping collared mouth with ring, pontil scar, 7-1/2" h, minor ext. wear..400.00

The Calqueur, Quehen & Smith, pillar with sunken panels on 4 sides, cobalt blue...............................30.00

Thorn's Hop & Burdock Tonic, yellow, 6-3/8" h............40.00

Turner's Balsam, eight sided, aqua, 4-7/8" h.................65.00

True Daff's Elixir, England, 1830-50, rect, beveled edges, yellow green, applied ring lip, bail pontil base, 4-7/8" h........360.00

Use Pritchard's Teething Powders, aqua, rect, emb front panel, 3-1/2" l 12.00

Vaughn's Vegetable Lithontriptic Mixture, aqua, 8" h ...125.00

Warner's London Diabetes Cure, yellow apricot, strong embossing, 1 pint...350.00

Warner's Safe Cure, London

    Olive green, pint...90.00

    Red amber, strong embossing, half pint.................50.00

    Very light yellow, pint.....................................48.00

    Yellow amber, heavy embossing, half pink.............45.00

Web's Cathartic A No. 1 Tonic, amber, 9-1/2" h..........60.00

Whitwell's Liquid Improved Opodeloc, cylindrical, colorless, emb, sloping flanged lip, pontil, two part mold, 4-5/8" h...110.00

Winans Bros. (Indian) Indian Cure for the Blood, orig contents, -1/2" h.......................................525.00

Wyeth's Sage Sulphur Compound, orig label..............20.00

Milk

Abbots, pint, emb cottage cheese jar............................8.00

Alta Crest Farm, Spencer, MA, quart, round, green glass, emb cow's head...1,000.00

Blue Bell Farms, Irvington, NJ, quart, round, orange pyro, Cop-the Cream.......................................140.00

Borden, in script above Elsie, quart, squat, red pyro ...18.00

Swaim's Panacea Philada, America, 1840-60, cylindrical, with indented panels, bright grayish green, applied sloping collared mouth with ring, pontil scar, 7-1/2" h, some minor ext. wear, $400. Photo courtesy of Norman C. Heckler and Co.

Borden's Condensed Milk, quart, Borden Eagle trademark, clear, emb, tin top.....................................100.00

Borden's, half pint, emb "$.03 deposit," cottage cheese jar...8.00

Brookfield Dairy, Hellertown, PA, half pint, round, emb baby top 55.00

Capital Dairy, North Dartmouth, MA, quart, round, clear, emb capital dome emb on front slug plate......................15.00

Cream Top, generic, quart, sq, dish of ice cream, green/orange 15.00

Crowley's, As good as any better'n some try fresh churned buttermilk, quart, picture of lady, cow, and churn, red pyro 25.00

Dairylea, quart, square, red

    Hopalong Cassidy, black pyro.............................75.00

    Miss Dairylea, picture of fruit and vegetables..........15.00

Dykes' Dairy, Youngsville, PA, our milk for your health, man, woman, 2 children, quart, round, red pyro............18.00

Emmadine Farms, quart, toothache square, orange/black pyro 85.00

Empire State Dairy Co., Brooklyn, half pint, round, emb, state seal in frame...10.00

Firestone Farms, Columbiana, OH, one half pint, round, clear, emb, Firestone emblem emb in slug plate.....25.00

Fiske, Rumford, RI, qt, round, emb, cream top............15.00

Florida Store Bottle, $.03, quart, picture of state of Florida, round, emb...22.00

Gettysburg Ice and Storage Co., Gettysburg, PA, quart, round, clear, emb name.................................12.00

Hankin Dairy, 515 3rd Avenue, Brooklyn, quart, clear, emb, tin top..55.00

Hoods, quart, round, cow in framed log, red pyro........12.00

Ingles Dairy, Manchester, NH, Every man's family should have the very best, quart, woman holding child, orange/green pyro.......................................30.00

Jon Alm Dairy, Norwich, NY, quart, sq, tall, picture of girl holding glass, red/blue/orange/brown pyro............30.00

Maple Farms, Brattleboro, VT, quart, sq, amber............8.00

Model Farms, Milford, PA, half pint, round, emb in slug plate, Raw Milk..12.00

Mohawk Farms, Staten Island, NY, quart, large Indian in headdress, round, emb................................40.00

Newport Dairy, quart, squat, round, emb 10.00

Old Homestead Products, quart, stippled glass, picture of log cabin...40.00

One Quart Liquid Brighton Place Dairy Rochester, N. Y., quart, cylindrical, yellow green, machined mouth, smooth base...550.00

Orange County Milk Association, quart, clear emb, keystone in slug plate, tin top..125.00

Palmerton Sanitary Dairy, Palmerton, PA, quart, sq, emb, cream top 12.00

Palm Mead, The City of Palms, quart, palm tree, green pyro...25.00

Saranac Inn Dairy, quart, clear, emb............................30.00

Sheffield Farms, Slawson Decker, NY, quart, logo, round, emb 8.00

State University of New York, Cobleskill, college seal, quart, sq, tall..25.00

Universal Store Bottle, 5-cent deposit, quart, round, emb ...8.00

University of Connecticut, Storrs, CT, one half pint, round, clear, emb name 8.00

Warner Bros., quart, sq, Bugs Bunny with milk carriers, red/back pyro, modern...10.00

White Springs Farm Dairy, Geneva, quart, orange pyro... 12.00

Winona Dairy, Lebanon, NH, for Safety Milk For Health Milk in a Bottle, quart, red pyro.......................................20.00

WW Schultz Sunnyside Farm, Port Jervis in slug plate, round, emb 12.00

Yasgar Farms, Bethel, NY, 25th Anniversary 1994 (Woodstock), quart, sq, brown/yellow pyro 45.00

Mineral or Spring Water

Alburgh A. Spring, VT, cylindrical, apricot amber, applied sloping collared mouth with ring, smooth base, quart, rare with misspelling 1,000.00

Alburgh A. Spring, VT, cylindrical, golden yellow, applied sloping collared mouth with ring, smooth base, quart......800.00

Artesian Water, round, golden chocolate amber, twelve paneled base, iron pontil, 1850-60, pint........................450.00

B. R. Lippincott & Co., Stockton Superior, Mineral Water, Union Glass Works, 1852-58, cobalt blue, applied top, iron pontil, 7-3/8" h...450.00

Buffalo Mineral Water Springs Natures, Materia Medica Trade Mark, yellow, lady sitting on stool, 10-1/2" h.............125.00

Caladonia Spring Wheelock VT, cylindrical, golden amber, applied sloping collared mouth with ring, smooth base, quart 130.00

Chalybeate Water Of The American Spa Spring Co., N. J., cylindrical, light to medium blue green, olive green slag striation I neck, applied heavy collared mouth, smooth base, pint...400.00

Champlain Spring, Alkaline Chalybeate, Highgate, VT, cylindrical, emerald green, applied sloping collared mouth with ring, smooth base, quart.................................200.00

Chase & Co. Mineral Water, San Francisco, CA, green, applied top, iron pontil, 7-3/8" h 60.00

Clarke & Co., New York, America, 1840-60, cylindrical, olive amber, applied sloping collared mouth with ring pontil scar, quart 170.00

D. A. Knowlton, Saratoga, NY, America, 1960-80, high shouldered cylinder, olive green, applied sloping collared mouth with ring, smooth base, quart......................100.00

Gettysburg Katalysine Water, yellow olive, applied sloping collared mouth with ring, smooth base, quart........200.00

Guilford Mineral Sprig Water, Guilford VT, cylindrical, yellow-olive, applied sloping collard mouth with ring, smooth base, quart 475.00

G. W. Weston & Co., Saratoga, NY, America, 1840-60, cylindrical, yellow olive, applied sloping collared mouth with ring, pontil scar, pint, 1" vertical body crack on reverse.... 375.00

Hopkins Chalybeate Baltimore, attributed to Baltimore Glass Works, Baltimore, MD, 1845-60, cylindrical, applied double collared mouth, iron pontil mark, pint
Dense amber (black)..130.00
Medium yellow green 140.00

John Clarke, New York, America, 1960-80, cylindrical, dark olive amber, applied sloping collared mouth with ring, smooth base, quart, some ext. high point wear, 1/8" pot-stone bruise...50.00

Lancaster Glass Works, round, sapphire blue, applied blob top, iron pontil, 1850-60, 7" h 120.00

Lynch & Clarke, New York, America, 1840-60, cylindrical, yellowish olive, applied sloping collared mouth with ring, pontil scar, pint..275.00

Lynde & Putnam, Mineral Waters, San Francisco Cala, Union Glass Works, Philada, teal blue, applied top, iron pontil, 7-1/2" h...100.00

Middletown Healing Springs, Grays & Clark, Middletown, VT, cylindrical, yellow apricot amber, applied sloping collared mouth with ring, smooth base, quart..........1,200.00

Mill's Seltzer Springs, aqua, applied top, smooth base, 7-1/2" h...85.00

Missiquoi, A. Springs, cylindrical, apricot amber, applied sloping collared mouth with ring, smooth base, quart 150.00

M. T. Crawford/Springfield-Superior Mineral Water, Union Glass Works, Philadelphia, PA, 1845-60, squat cylindrical form, mug base, cobalt blue, heavy applied collared mouth, iron pontil mark, half pint, some int. stain, 1/2" bruise on top of mouth 160.00

Round Lake Mineral Water, red amber, 9-1/4" h.........750.00

Rutherford's Premium Mineral Water, ground pontil, dark olive, 7-1/2" h...60.00

San Francisco Glass Works, tapered neck, blob top, sea green, 6-7/8" h..15.00

Saratoga Highrock Spring (fancy rock) Saratoga, NY, America, 1860-80, cylindrical, bright medium green, applied sloping collared mouth with ring, smooth base, pint, 1/2" shallow chip on mouth...850.00

Saratoga Red Spring, America, 1860-80, cylindrical, emerald green, applied sloping collared mouth with ring, smooth base, pint, orig mineral water contents 90.00

Lynch & Clarke/New York, America, 1840-60, cylindrical, yellowish olive, applied sloping collared mouth with ring, pontil scar, pint, $275. Photo courtesy of Norman C. Heckler and Co.

Saratoga Seltzer Water, cylindrical, teal blue-green, applied ring lip, c1890, 7-1/2" h 85.00
Saratoga (star) Springs, cylindrical, applied sloping collared mouth with ring, smooth base, quart
    Dark olive green 300.00
    Emerald green 275.00
    Olive amber 200.00
Vermont Spring, Saxe & Co., Sheldon, VT, cylindrical, citron, applied sloping collared mouth with ring, smooth base, quart 600.00
Veronica Mineral Water, amber, sq...........................10.00
Vichy Water/Hanbury Smith/N.Y., America, 1860-90, cylindrical, brilliant medium blue green, applied sloping collared mouth, smooth base, pint..100.00

Miniature, freeblown, America, 1780-1830

2-3/4" h, globular, yellow amber with olive tone, inward rolled mouth, pontil scar...1,200.00
3-1/2" h, flattened chestnut, light yellow green, sheared mouth, applied string rim, pontil scar, some int. base stain 400.00
3-3/4" h, demijohn, light blue green, sheared mouth, applied string rim, pontil scar...400.00

Poison

Ammonia around shoulder, three sets of ribbing, Poisonous then ribbing and Not To Be taken, 6-1/2" h, cylinder 4.00
Bottled By Jeyes, 7" l, dark straw-amber, oval, ribbing down front with name 12.00
Bowker's Pyrox Poison, colorless...........................30.00
British Household Ammonia, Poisonous Not To Be Taken, 6-1/2" h, aqua, name around neck, panel with emb lettering 20.00
Burdalls Manufacturing Chemists Sheffield Not To Be Taken Internally, 6" l oval, aqua, row of ribbing each side of lettering..22.00
Carbolic Acid, 3 oz, cobalt blue, hexagonal, flat back ...48.00
Chloroform, 5-3/4" h, green, ribbed, label, 1900...........80.00
Clark's Ammonia, aqua, offset neck, 8" h 55.00
Coffin
    3" h, irregular hexagonal, emerald green, glass stopper, ribbed 30.00
    3-1/2" h, cobalt blue, emb, 1890 ....100.00
Cylindrical, crosshatch dec, cobalt blue, flared mouth with stopper, smooth base, 6-1/4" h 250.00
Diamond Antiseptics, 10-3/4" h, triangular shape, golden amber, emb..385.00
Figural, skull, America, 1880-1900, cobalt blue, tooled mouth, smooth base
    2-7/8" h, small hole in nose area 475.00
    4-1/8" h...1,800.00
Foultsons Crescent, 5" h, cobalt blue, sunken ribbed front panel, Not To Be Taken and ribbing on side 65.00
Hobnail, 3-1/2" h, cobalt blue..40.00
Ikey Einstein Poison, rect, ring top, colorless, 3-3/4" h 25.00
Killgerm Disinfectant, oval, aqua, front panel with "Poisonous Not To Be Taken" 6-1/2" l 25.00
Kill Pest Non Poisonous Disinfectant, 5" h, aqua, hexagonal, emb lettering on three panels 20.00
Imperial Fluid Co. Poison, 1 gallon, colorless 95.00
J Wilson Bonsetter, light cobalt blue, rect....................65.00
Lysol, 3-1/4" h, cylindrical, amber, emb "Not To Be Taken" 12.00
McDonalds Steam System, 5-1/2" h, aqua, Poisonous across shoulder..20.00

Melvin & Badger Apothecaries, Boston, Mass, irregular form, cobalt blue, tooled sq mouth, smooth base, 6-1/4" h.. 140.00
Mercury Bichloride, 2-11/16" h, rect, amber 18.00
Norwich Coffin, 3-3/8" h, amber, emb, tooled lip 95.00
Not To Be Taken, cobalt blue, hexagon
    3" h..10.00
    5" H..14.00
Not To Be Taken Gordon Grand Lysol, 5" h, amber jug shape, emb around neck, cross hatching on 2 sides 32.00
Owl Drug Co., 3-3/8" h, cobalt blue, owl sitting on mortar.. 70.00
Plumber Drug Co., 7-1/2" h, cobalt blue, lattice and diamond pattern 90.00
Poison
    3" h, hexagonal, cobalt blue....................................16.00
    3-1/2" h, hexagonal, ribbed, cobalt blue 20.00
Poisonous
    2-1/2" h, cobalt blue, emb lettering around neck, ribbing down front, cleaned..30.00
    4" h, colorless, cylinder, emb lettering on front, ribbing on two sides, sheared lip.......................................15.00
    6-1/2" h, formed lip, colorless...............................22.00
    6-1/2" h, aqua, row of bumps, two lines on each side... 40.00
Poisonous Not To Be Taken
    3" h, dark cobalt blue, hexagon 15.00
    3-1/2" h, cobalt blue, cylinder, Poison on back base, ribbing down front...48.00
    5" h, cobalt blue, hexagon....................................20.00
    6-1/2" h oval, aqua, emb on front panel 20.00
    6-1/2" h oval, aqua, emb on front panel with ribbing, lip chip 10.00
    7" h, hexagon, aqua, formed lip, Poison on one panel, emb down front..35.00
    8" h, oval, cobalt blue, emb on front panel, cleaned ... 40.00
    11-1/2" h, whiskey shaped, green, long neck 50.00
Poisonous Not To Be Taken J. Salmon & Co., oval, aqua 32.00
Sano Bolic Disinfectant, 6" h, aqua, cylinder, sheared top 20.00
Sulpholine, 4" h, rect, colorless 10.00
Thretipene Disinfectant, 9" h, amber, emb Poison around cylinder shaped shoulder, central ribbing of 9 panels, tapers to base, professionally cleaned 225.00
Tinct Gelsem Poison and Hydrag Subchlor Poison, 5-1/2" h, green ribbed cylinder, orig label in rect panel, pr....150.00
Tinct Iodine, 3" h, amber, skull and crossbones 45.00

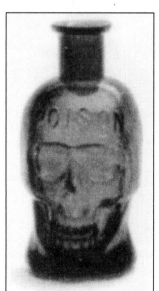

Skull, America, 1880-1900, cobalt blue, tooled mouth, smooth base, 4-1/8" h, $1,800. Photo courtesy of Norman C. Heckler and Co.

Towle's Chlorodyne, 4-1/2" h, colorless 40.00
Trioloids Poison, triangular, blue, c1900, 3-5/16" h.......25.00
USA Hospital Dept., Acetate Potassa, 6-1/2" h, cylindrical, aqua 65.00
Vapo Cresolene Co., 4" h, sq, bumps on 2 panels, cobalt blue...48.00
Victory Chemical Co., Quick Deal Insecticide, 148 Fairmount Ave., Phila, PA, 8 oz, colorless, 7" h.........................15.00

Sarsaparilla

Brown's Sarsaparilla, aqua 12.00
Bull's Extract of Sarsaparilla, beveled corners, 7" l.....400.00
Compound Extract of Sarsaparilla, amber, gallon......140.00
Dalton's Sarsaparilla and Nerve Tonic, blue label........40.00
Dr. Beldings Wild Cherry Sarsaparilla, Dr. Belding Medicine Co., Minneapolis, MN, aqua, complete label, orig contents, orig fancy box (top missing), 9-1/4" h...........180.00
Dr. Guysott's Compound Extract of Yellow Dock and Sarsaparilla, peacock green, sloping lip, iron pontil, 9" h 1,350.00
Dr. Ira Belding's, Honduras Sarsaparilla, colorless, 10-1/2" h 30.00
Dr. Townsend's Sarsaparilla, olive green, pontil...........85.00
Foley's Sarsaparilla 20.00
Guysott's Yellow Dock & Sarsaparilla 40.00
Lancaster Glassworks, barrel, golden amber.............125.00
Sand's Genuine, rect, aqua 95.00
Sawyers Eclipse, aqua...35.00
Skoda's Sarsaparilla, amber 25.00
Wetherell's, aqua..45.00

Soda

Alter & Wilson Manuf, light green applied top, 7" h 20.00
Arny & Shinn/Georgetown, D.C.-A. & S./This Bottle Is/Never Sold, squat cylindrical, blue green, applied sloping collared mouth with ring, smooth base, half pint 140.00
Bacon's Soda Works, light green, blob top, 7" h 9.00
Bryant's Root Beer, This Bottle Makes Five Gallons, amber, applied top, 4-1/2" h 5.00
C. A. Cole/Bottler No. 118/N. Howard St. Balt., squat cylindrical form, yellow olive applied sloping collared mouth with ring, iron pontil mark, oversized half pint, 7-1/2" h, some ext. wear and scratches.......................................850.00
Cape Arco Soda Works, Marshfield, OR, round, light green, applied top, 7" h 10.00
C. Cleminson/Soda & Mineral Water/Troy, NY, squat cylindrical, teal blue, heavy applied sloping collared mouth, iron pontil mark, half pint, 3/8" narrow flat flake on mouth 140.00
Deadwood, SD, blob top...125.00
Dearborn/83/ed Ave. NY, Cream Soda, squat cylindrical form, deep aquamarine, heavy applied sloping collared mouth, smooth base, quarter pint or less, 5-3/4" h, professionally cleaned..130.00
Deamer Grass Valley, aqua, blob top, 7-1/4" hg 7.50
Dr. Pepper, Colorado..18.00
English Soda, light green, applied top, 8" h..................18.00
Fizz, Southern State Siphon Bottling Co., golden amber, 11" h...17.50
Hawaiian Soda Works, aqua, emb, 7-1/2" h....................9.00
Hippo Size Soda Water, clear, crown top, 10" h 6.50
Jackson's Napa Soda, crown cap, 7-1/4" h....................7.50
James Ray/Savannah/Geo.-Gingerale, Hutchinson Soda Water, tall cylinder, cobalt blue, heavy tooled collared mouth, smooth base, 7-3/4" h, professionally cleaned 170.00
Los Angeles Soda Works, aqua, 8" h..............................5.00
Mendocin Bottling Works, A L Reynolds, light green, 7" h ...8.00

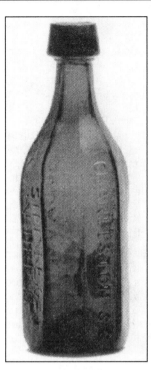

Steinke & Kornahrens Soda Water Return This Bottle Charleston, SC, 1845-60, octagonal, cobalt blue, applied sloping collared mouth, iron pontil mark, oversized half pint, 7-3/4" h, professionally cleaned, $650. Photo courtesy of Norman C. Heckler and Co.

Mission Dry Sparkling, black 9-3/4" h 4.00
Nevada City Soda works, ETR Powell, aqua, applied top, 7" h...9.00
Orange Crush Co., Pat'd July 20, 1926, light green, 9" h....4.00
Perrier, clear, bowling pin shape, paper label, 8-1/2" h....3.00
Rapid City Bottling Works, light green, crown cap, 8" h......5.00
Ross' Royal Belfast Ginger Gale, green, diamond shape, paper label, 10" h 7.50
Sandahl Beverages, clear, 8" h.......................................5.00
Scott & Gilbert Co., San Francisco, brown, crown top, 10" h...6.00
Solano Soda Works, aqua, 8" h.......................................6.00
Tahoe Soda Springs Natural Mineral Water, light green, 7-1/2" h..10.00
Union Glass Works, dark blue, blob top 20.00
Williams Bros., San Jose, CA...8.00
Williamstown/NJ Soda, squat cylindrical form, light bluish green, heavy applied sloping collared mouth, iron pontil mark, half pint, ext. wear and scratches, int. stain.....75.00

Utility

3-5/8" h, freeblown, flattened chestnut form, short neck, bright green, sheared mouth, pontil scar, American, 1800-30..300.00
7-7/8" h, freeblown, rect, chamfered corners, dark olive amber, applied sloping collared mouth with ring, pontil scar, America, 1800-30, ext. wear 275.00
9-1/4" h, freeblown, globular, golden amber, heavy applied mouth, pontil scar, attributed to Midwest America, 1800-30, some int. stain 230.00

Whiskey

A. M. Bininger & Co., No. 19 Broad St., New York, c1860-80, cylindrical, applied handle, yellowish-olive green, applied double collared mouth, smooth base, 7-7/8" h ...1,400.00
Arch Cowan Mason & Co. Leith, applied green, rect shape, blob top, emb front panel, 8" h.................................40.00
Bininger's Regular, 19 Broad St., New York, 1840-50, clock shape, deep gold amber, applied double collared mouth, pontil scar, 5-7/8" h...300.00

Bininger's Travelers Guide, A. M. Bininger & Co., No. 19 Broad St., NY, 1860-80, teardrop form, golden amber, applied double collared mouth, smooth base, 6-3/4" h 200.00

C. A. Richards & Co., 18 & 20 Kilby St, Boston, Mass, 1860-90, sq, beveled corners, applied sloping collared mouth m, smooth base, yellow amber, slug plate address, 9-1/2" h 90.00

C. A. Richards & Co., 99 Washington St., Boston, Mass, 1860-80, sq, beveled corners, applied sloping collared mouth, smooth base
　Blood amber, 9-3/8" h...130.00
　Dark olive green shading to dense black near base, partial orig label "Golden Sheaf Whiskey," 9-1/2" h 150.00
　Deep yellow olive, 9-5/8" h, 1/8" flake off side of mouth 80.00
　Reddish amber, 9-3/8" h...130.00
　Yellow amber with olive tone, 9-5/8" h....................120.00
　Yellow amber with reddish tone, backwards "n," 9-3/8" h...100.00
　Yellow green, 9-1/2" h, 3/8" potstone......................550.00

Caspers Whiskey, Made by Honest North Carolina People, 1870-90, cylindrical, paneled shoulder, cobalt blue, tooled sloping collared mouth with ring, smooth base, 11-3/4" h 325.00

Chestnut Grove Whiskey, 1840-60, flattened chestnut form, applied handle, golden amber, applied mouth with ring, pontil scar, 9" h..110.00

E. G. Booz's Old Cabin Whiskey, Whitney Glass Works, Glassboro, NJ, 1860-80, cabin form, golden amber, applied sloping collared mouth, smooth base, qt, McKearin GVII-4, 3/8" x 1" shallow vertical chip has been replaced on sloping collar mouth 650.00

Freeblown Jug, applied handle, America, 1840-60
　6-1/8" h, pear form, red amber, applied sloping collared mouth, pontil scar...220.00
　8" h, cylindrical corseted form, golden amber, applied double collared mouth, pontil scar....................350.00
　8" h, flattened chestnut, golden amber, applied mouth with ring, pontil scar, 8" h 475.00

Griffith Hyatt & Co., Baltimore, 1840-80, globular, flattened label panels, applied handle, golden amber with olive tone, applied sq collared mouth, pontil scar, 7" h.............375.00

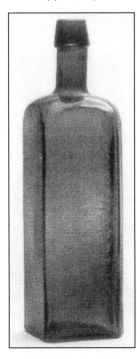

C. A. Richards & Co., 99 Washington St. Boston, Mass, 1860-1880, sq with beveled corners, yellow amber with olive tone, applied sloping collared mouth, smooth base, 9-5/8" h, $120. Photo courtesy of Norman C. Heckler and Co.

H. Pharazyn/Phila/Right Secured, 1860-80, Indian Warrior form, brilliant light yellow amber, inward rolled mouth, smooth base, 12-1/2" h, incomplete mouth with roughness, some minor int. residue 800.00

Lancaster Glassworks, Lancaster, NY, 1860-80, barrel, puce amber, applied double collared mouth, smooth base, 9-5/8" h 180.00

Old Continental Whiskey, yellow amber, 9-1/4" h 650.00

Ridgeway Straight Corn Whiskey, miniature, stoneware.. 50.00

Weeks Glass Works, Stoddard, NH, 1860-70, emb base, cylindrical, yellow amber with olive tone, applied sloping collared mouth with ring, smooth base, 11-1/2" h, retains cork and some int. residue...................................200.00

Wine

5" h, 4-1/2" d w,"CP./1697," England, c1697, sealed, squat onion form, dark olive green, sheared mouth, string rim, pontil scar, some minor ext. wear, shallow chips............9,000.00

8-1/2" h, 3-3/4" d, Alloa Glass Works, Scotland, 1830-60, cylindrical, three piece mold, deep yellow olive, applied sloping collared mouth, pontil scar 325.00

9" h, 5-1/2" w, shaft and globe, England, c1660, bulbous, long tapering neck, olive green, sheared mouth, applied string rim, pontil scar, unearthed, some stain and encrustation, some fissures in glass 3,000.00

9-1/2" h, dark olive, seal reads "Inner Temple," c1845, London 60.00

11-1/2" h, black, three piece mold, pontil base, seal reads "A.S.C.R.," for All Souls Common Room, All Souls College 130.00

13" h, olive amber, cylinder, huge tube pontil, deep kick-up, French, c1780 ....100.00

BREAD PLATES

History: Beginning in the mid-1880s, special trays or platters were made for serving bread and rolls. Designated "bread plates" by collectors, these small trays or platters can be found in porcelain, glass (especially pattern glass), and metals.

Bread plates often were part of a china or glass set. However, many glass companies made special plates which honored national heroes, commemorated historical or special events, offered a moral maxim, or supported a religious attitude. The subject matter appears either horizontally or vertically. Most of these plates are oval and 10 inches in length.

Reference: Anna Maude Stuart, *Bread Plates and Platters*, published by author, 1965.

Additional Listings: Pattern Glass.

Mottos, pressed glass, colorless

Be Industrious, handles, oval..50.00

Faith, Hope, and Charity, plain center, emb "Patd Nov 23, 1875" 45.00

Give Us this Day, round, rosette center and border 65.00

Rock of Ages, 12-7/8" l..175.00

Rock of Ages, milk glass center.................................125.00

Waste Not Want Not...35.00

Pattern glass, (colorless unless otherwise noted)

Actress, Miss Nielson..80.00

Last Supper, Frosted Grape Leaf pattern border, 10-7/8" x 7", $75.

Aurora, ruby stained, large center star, 10" d	50.00
Baltimore, 12-1/2" d	70.00
Basketweave, amber	45.00
Beaded Grape, sq	35.00
Beaded Loop	35.00
Butterfly & Fan	40.00
Canadian, 10" d	45.00
Continental, 11-3/4" l	90.00
Crying Baby, frog on plate, 13" d	100.00
Cupid and Venus, amber	85.00
Cupid and Venus, colorless	40.00
Cupid's Hunt	90.00
Daisy and Button, apple green, 13" l	65.00
Deer and Pine Tree, amber	110.00
Double Vine	50.00
Egyptian, Cleopatra center	60.00
Fern	40.00
Finecut and Panel, amber	45.00
Garden of Eden, 9-1/4" x 12-1/2"	45.00
Good Luck	45.00
Grace	60.00
Grapes, motto	55.00
Horseshoe, double horseshoe handles, 14" l, 10" w	70.00
Iowa, motto	80.00
Lion, lion handles, motto, amber	135.00
Lion Oval, lion handles, frosted	110.00
Minerva	60.00
Moon and Star, rect	48.00
One Hundred and One, farm implement center, 11" d	85.00
Palmette, 9" d	45.00
Polar Bear, frosted	165.00
Princess Feather, 9" d	55.00
Psyche and Cupid	60.00
Roman Rosette, 9" x 11"	55.00
Royal Lady, vaseline	130.00
Scroll and Dark	30.00
Scroll and Flowers, 12" d	40.00
St. Bernard, frosted	125.00
Swan with Flowers	60.00
Tennessee, colored jewels	75.00
Three Graces	50.00
US Coin, frosted coins	325.00
Westward Ho, frosted, oval	200.00
Wheat & Barley, milk glass	65.00

Rabbit Series, Iowa City

Dog Cart Overturned	110.00
Dog Chasing Rabbit	110.00
Frosted center	110.00

Souvenir and commemorative

Garfield Drape, We Mourn, 11-1/2" d	55.00
Liberty and Freedom	65.00
Liberty Bell, signers, hairline in handle	75.00
Old State House, sapphire blue	185.00
Railroad	90.00
Three Presidents, frosted center	95.00
Train	75.00
U. S. Grant	60.00
Virginia Dare	135.00
William J. Bryan, milk glass	45.00

BRIDE'S BASKETS

History: Bride's Baskets are one of the wonderful types of antiques that have evolved into an exciting collecting area from rather plain beginnings. The term "Bride's Basket" was first used around 1920. Until that time, the bowls were described by their makers for their intended use, e.g., berry or fruit bowls. The practice of serving berries and cream was popular from the end of the 18th century into the beginning of the 19th century. Berry sets consisting of a master bowl and matching serving bowls were necessities of a household. Berry bowls were made in most glass types of the period, including vividly colored glass, cut glass, and even pressed glass. By adding a metal frame, or standard, usually with a bail handle, a simple berry bowl became a basket. Ornate silverplated holders enhanced the beauty of the glassware and were added by companies such as Pairpoint and Wilcox. These bowls were a popular wedding gift in the 1880-1920 era, hence, the name "bride's basket."

The name "bride's basket" is now well-known, and although not as popular now as in the post World War I period, bride's baskets are still collected. Art glass bowls with original silverplated holders can command high prices.

Over the years, bowls and bases became separated and married pieces resulted. If the base has been lost, the bowl should be sold separately.

Reference: John Mebane, *Collecting Bride's Baskets and Other Glass Fancies*, Wallace-Homestead, 1976.

Reproduction Alert: The glass bowls have been reproduced.

Note: Items listed below have a silver-plated holder unless otherwise noted.

7-1/2" d, 3-3/4" h, rich pink ext. with opalescent stripes, gold lustered int., sq ruffled edge, Monet Stumpf, Patin ... 125.00

8" d, blue cased glass shading to white bowl, enameled dec, Victorian ... 100.00

8" d, 2-1/8" h, bowl only, satin overlay, shaded pink, clear edging on base, gold and silver sanded flowers and leaves dec, ruffled, off-white lining, ground pontil ... 155.00

8" d, 10-1/2" h, Loetz-type glass, irid blue, and purple, recessed indentations, ruffled, ground pontil, ftd metal stand ... 345.00

8" d, 10-1/2" h, sq crimped edge bowl, white cased to rose-red, cameo cut winged griffins, floral bouquets and swags, fitted SP metal frame with leaf and berry embellished handle, Mt. Washington Glass Co. bowl, frame mkd "Pairpoint" ... 825.00

8-1/4" w, sq, cased, deep rose and white ext., whit int., dragon, floral, and leaf dec, ruffled edge, Mt. Washington.........675.00

8-1/2" d, 14-1/2" h, heavenly blue satin glass shading to pale white, diamond quilted design, pie crust crimped edge, orig fancy silver plated holder, Mt. Washington 400.00

9" d, Peachblow, shiny finish bowl, applied amber rim, SP Wilcox holder...215.00

9" d, 12" h, Mt. Washington, Rose Amber, Coin Spot pattern, deep color, fancy silver plated Pairpoint stand......875.00

9-1/4" d, blue opalescent, crimped rim, reticulated SP holder mkd "Wallingford, Biggins & Rodgers Co."............225.00

9-1/4" d, Peachblow, yellow flowers dec, orig SP holder 225.00

9-3/8" d, cased, shaded pink int. with gold floral dec, clear ruffled rim, whit ext. 110.00

9-1/2" d, MOP satin, Diamond Quilted pattern, deep blue shading to pale blue int., blue shading to white ext., applied frosted crimped edge, Mt. Washington..................600.00

9-1/2" d, pigeon blood, enamel floral dec, SP holder 225.00

9-3/4" d, 2-3/4" h, 3" d, base, bowl only, shaded pink overlay, ruffled edge, white underside, colored enameled flowers and foliage dec, clear and opaque ribbon applied edge.......220.00

9-3/4" d, 11" h, off-white ext., shaded rose int., crystal ruffled edge, Rogers & Bros. SP basket with two small hands, chains, fruit design on holder................................300.00

9-7/8" d, 3" h, 3-3/4" base, bowl only, peachblow, glossy finish, deep pink shading to pale 250.00

10" d, 2-1/2" h, deep rose shading to pink satin bowl, ruffled, enameled floral dec...225.00

10" d, 11" h, Vasa Murrhina, outer amber layer, center layer with hundreds of cream colored spots, random toffee colored spots, dark veins, gold mica flakes, mulberry pink lining, crossed rod thorn handles 635.00

10" w, sq, custard, melon ribbed, enameled daisies, applied rubena crystal rim, twisted and beaded handle, ftd, emb SP frame, mkd "Wilcox"..450.00

10-3/8" h, spangle, multicolored, ruby, cranberry, and green, ivory and yellow base, silver flecks, bowl only.......125.00

10-1/2" d, Hobnail, pink, enameled flowers, ruffled rim, reticulated SP frame..250.00

10-1/2" h, colorless frosted bowl, overlaid in pink crystal, etched acorn and oak leaf dec, gilt metal frame with basket handles, Victorian...250.00

10-1/2" d, 10-3/4" h, MOP satin, Diamond Quilted pattern, deep pink shading to pale pink to off-white, Mt. Washington rectangular form bowl, applied frosted edge, orig fancy silver plated Victorian "Manhattan Silver Company," holder has been resilvered...400.00

10-1/2" d, 12-1/2" h, oval satin bow, blue int., white ext., pleated rim, applied frosted ribbon edge, ornate ftd Forbes frame 250.00

10-3/4" d, 3-1/2" h, bowl only
  Overlay, heavenly blue, enameled white flowers, green leaves, white underside, ruffled 215.00
  Satin, shaded purple, white underside, dainty purple and white flowers, lacy foliage dec 225.00

11" d, cased, pink ext., peachblow int., gold stylized flowers, ornate SP holder with aquatic marine life motif, mkd "Pairpoint Mfg. Co." 825.00

11" d, 10-1/2" h, white and vaseline bowl, all over floral enamel dec, fancy silver plated frame, sgd "Meriden," minor handle restoration...300.00

11" d, 11-1/2" h, tricorn Crown Milano bowl, six large pansies, pale purple and orange tracery medallions, pale yellow int., orig tricorn ftd Pairpoint stand 3,000.00

11" d, 15-1/2" h, satin, deep rose, enamel swan and floral dec, heavy bronze holder with birds perched on top 425.00

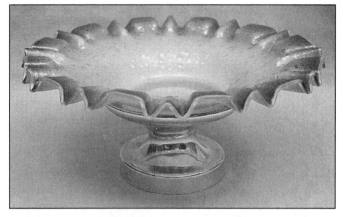

Cased, pink interior with spattered rose dec, purple rim, silver plated pedestal rim, $150.00

11-1/8" d, 3-3/4" h, bowl only, satin, brown shaded to cream overlay, raised dots, dainty gold and silver flowers and leaves dec, ruffled.. 250.00

11-3/8" d, 3-1/4" h, 2-7/8" d base, bowl only, maroon shaded to cream overlay, fancy leaf edges with circle and slot emb designs, dainty enameled pink flowers, gold leaves, white underside 215.00

11-1/2" h, sapphire blue bowl, applied ruffled rim, gold tracery and courting scene dec, ornate ftd Meriden stand 325.00

11-1/2" d, 3-5/8" h, bowl only, shaded green overlay satin, ruffled emb lattice edge, white underside................. 210.00

11-1/2" d, 12" h, dark red satin glass shaded to cream, ruffled and crimped rim, SP stand................................... 275.00

11-1/2" d, 13-1/2" h, ruffled white shading to pink to raspberry bowl, cased in white, plum dec, gold ranches, hanging ferns, gold dotted florals, ornate double handled silver frame, figural flowers on handle and base............ 400.00

13" d, 12" h, brilliant yellow cased jack-in-the-pulpit type bowl, heavily ruffled edge, blown out with enameled orange and green dec, metal holder with bronze finish, featuring leaves, berries, vines, and large bird sitting on branch, Victorian.. 500.00

13" l, 12-1/2" h, oval satin bowl, shaded raspberry ext., brilliant turquoise int., tightly ruffed pleated and fold-in edge, rect shape, white and gold enameled floral leaf and berry dec on ornate ftd rope handled silver plated orig frame 650.00

13-1/2" h, robin's egg blue shaded to white, scalloped rim, applied frosted ribbon, frosted Optic Petal pattern, SP base with engraved griffins, butterflies, and bees on sides, full figural swan inside, figural lilies and berries on handle, mkd "Reed & Barton" 300.00

14" d, satin, rose pink, scalloped, rippled, ribbed, and swirled, lacy allover enamel and gold flower pattern, figural SP base with hummingbird, sgd "Eagle & Co.".......... 1,200.00

14" l, oval yellow-green bowl, cased in pink, encrusted gold flowers, brass flower-form stand, minor wear from stand.........385.00

BRISTOL GLASS

History: Bristol glass is a designation given to a semi-opaque glass, usually decorated with enamel and cased with another color.

Initially, the term referred only to glass made in Bristol, England, in the 17th and 18th centuries. By the Victorian era, firms on the Continent and in America were copying the glass and its forms.

Glass forms commonly found in Bristol glass include cologne bottles, perfume bottles, scent bottles, decanters, finger bowls, and all types of small covered boxes.

Biscuit Jar, cov
   5" d, 7-1/2" h, apple green body, enameled green and yellow flowers and plants, SP rim, cov, handle, and base, figural strawberry finial 195.00
   6-1/2" h, white, brown leaves and white flowers 165.00
Bowl
   Colorless, cinched, ruffled, crimped, hp......................65.00
   Light blue, Cupid playing mandolin, gold trim..............40.00
Box, cov
   1-5/8" l, 1" h, turquoise body, gold dec.......................110.00
   2-1/2" d, round, hinged, Cupid on lid, purple floral dec .. 150.00
   5-3/4" l, 3-5/8" h, egg shape, white body, pink, cream, blue, and yellow flowers 225.00
Cake Stand, celadon green, enameled herons in flight, gold trim..135.00
Candlesticks, pr, 7" h, soft green, gold band 75.00
Compote, fluted, white body, hand painted cat scene, metal base..95.00
Condiment Set, cov mustard pot, pepper shaker with orig lid, open salt, milk white, pink and blue flowers and green leaves dec, 4-1/4" x 5-3/4" SP holder 175.00
Creamer and Sugar, cov, white body, multicolored floral dec 65.00
Cruet, 6-3/4" h, enameled floral dec 50.00
Decanter
   8-3/8" h, gray, encrusted floral engraving, butterflies, gilt trim, vase-like stopper 60.00
   9-1/4" h, 3-1/2" d, apple green body, reeded gold trimmed green handles, matching stopper 120.00
   11-1/4" h, 3-1/2" d, white body, green and brown leaves and ferns, blue flowers with gold trim, matching stopper.. 125.00
   11-1/2" h, ruffled stopper, enameled flowers and butterfly 75.00
Dresser Set, two cologne bottles, cov powder jar, white, gilt butterflies dec, clear stoppers.......................................75.00
Egg Cup, white body, gold bands....................................25.00
Ewer
   4-1/2" h, 2-3/4" d, turquoise, enameled pink flowers, white and green leaves, yellow scrolls, gold trim, applied turquoise handles, pr...190.00
   6-3/8" h, 2-5/8" d, pink ground, fancy gold designs, bands, and leaves, applied handle with gold trim 135.00
Finger Bowl, 4-3/8" d, blue, faceted sides, early 20th C, 8 pc set...500.00
Goblet, 10-3/4" h, pedestal base, opaque blue ground, polychrome enamel floral dec, gilt trim...........................95.00
Hatpin Holder, 6-1/8" h, ftd, blue, enameled jewels, gold dec 100.00
Lamp
   13-1/4" h, blue body, enameled white egret, multicolored flowers and foliage, brass oil fittings, black base...........300.00
   27" h, glass globe and body, molded in high relief foliate and cherub's head dec, polychrome enameled floral reserves, brass mounts, Victorian, electrified 475.00
Mantle Vase, 11" h, painted transfer scene of boy with poodle, large hand painted florals, 19th C, pr 150.00
Miniature Lamp, 10" h, 4-3/4" d, white shaded to soft blue, dainty enameled orange flowers, green leaves, sq ruffled shade, base with matching flowers, brown flying bird, applied opalescent shell feet, orig burner and chimney.......885.00
Mug, 5" h, white, eagle and "Liberty"................................375.00
Patch Box, 1" h, 1-1/4" d, hinged, soft pink ground, enameled brown and white bird...100.00
Perfume Bottle
   3-1/4" h, squatty, blue, gold band, white enameled flowers and leaves, matching stopper..............................100.00

   3-7/8" h, hourglass shape, opaque blue, silver mounted cap 175.00
Pitcher
   2-1/4" h, 3-1/4" d, turquoise body, gold band, enameled yellow flowers and leaves, applied turquoise handle ...65.00
   8-1/4" h, light green body, enameled bird and flowers, applied clear handle 95.00
Plate, 14-1/2" d, white body, hand painted, lavender and ochre French lilacs, green leaves 80.00
Puff Box, cov, round, blue, gold dec 35.00
Ring Box, cov, 1-3/4" h, 1-3/4" d, turquoise body, gold flowers and leaves 50.00
Rose Bowl, 3-1/2" d, shaded blue, crimped edge............65.00
Salt, 2-3/4" d, light gray body, enameled herons and foliage, SP rim and handle 48.00
Sugar Shaker, 4-3/4" h, white, hp flowers 60.00
Sweetmeat Jar
   3" d, 5-1/2" h, deep pink, enameled flying duck, leaves, blue flower dec, white lining, SP rim, lid, and bail handle... 110.00
   4-1/2" d, 5-1/2" h, floral garlands and butterflies dec, SP top and bail handle..125.00
Tumbler, 6-3/4" h, 2-3/4" d, turquoise body, gold and white rope garlands, gold foot 72.00
Urn, 18" h, pink, boy and girl with lamp 550.00
Vase
   4" h, caramel acid finish, hand painted scenic and floral dec, remnants of French retailer's label 50.00
   8" h, 2-3/4" w, Fireglow, beige ground, white flowers, green and gold leaves, worn gold accents, matched pr 100.00
   8-1/2" h, light pink shading to dark pink, hp enameled design 65.00
   8-1/2" h, white body, enameled floral and leaf dec, ruffled top, ram's head handles...75.00
   9" h, white body, portrait of young boy and girl, facing pr 165.00
   9-3/8" h, white body, hand painted, flowers, gold trim, raised enameling, pr 150.00
   10" h, blue body, cut-out base, enameled floral dec, pr .. 120.00
   13" h, 6" d, shaded pastel yellow ground, red and purple poppies and white daisies, tapered cylinder 100.00
   14" h, coach and horses, scrolls dec...........................100.00
   17" h, 7" w, white body, American cattle scene, artist sgd, pr 250.00

Vase, blue, white floral dec, green foliage, ruffled rim, $85.

BRYCE BROTHERS COMPANY

History: Bryce Brothers Company was located in Mt. Pleasant, Pennsylvania. It was incorporated in 1896 and manufactured hand-blown stemware for hotel use, as well as home use. Their designs included etched, engraved, and decorated table wares. Accessory items such as baskets and vases were added. Colored glasswares were added in the early 1920s and reflected popular colors of the times, including amber, amberosa, amethyst, blue, canary, green, and ruby. Some iridescent shades were also made. During the late 1920s, dark blue, light blue, and pink were added to the lines. Aurene colored wares and black wares were added in the 1930s. Colored stems were used with crystal to create interesting color combinations. In 1965, Bryce Brothers Company was bought by Lenox Corporation.

Reference: Hazel Marie Weatherman, *Colored Glassware of the Depression Era, Book 2,* Glassbooks, Inc., 1982.

Periodical: *The Daze,* Box 57, Otisville, MI 48463.

Cocktail, Ringmont, 3 oz
    Cobalt blue..20.00
    Colorless 15.00
Cordial
    Aquarius, flared, satin stem, amethyst..........................30.00
    Delhi, #846, 3-1/2" h, colorless....................................24.00
    Ringmount, colorless..10.00
    St. Moritz, azure bowl, colorless stem...........................20.00
    #435 etch, 3-1/8" h, colorless......................................22.00
    #854, colorless 18.00
Dessert, Silhouette, Carulean Aqua, designed for Eva
    Zeisel 15.00
Goblet
    Amethyst bowl, colorless pyramid stem 30.00
    Aquarius, ruby bowl, colorless stem 25.00
    Carleton, colorless 15.00
    El Rancho, emerald green, 12 oz..................................12.00
    Iced Tea Tumbler, ftd
    El Rancho, dark pink 10.00
    Tempo, dark green...28.00
Juice Tumbler, ftd, Modern, smoke 10.00
Sherbet
    Carleton, colorless 15.00
    El Rancho, emerald green, 6 oz....................................10.00
    Modern, smoke 10.00
    Tempo, dark green...20.00
Tumbler
    El Rancho, yellow, ftd, 5-1/2" h....................................15.00
    Future, Carulean Aqua, ftd 10.00
    Tempo, dark green...25.00
Tumbler Set, eight 6" h ftd tumblers, colorless, green stem, etch
    S15 ....185.00
Vase, El Rancho, burgundy, thumbprint..............................55.00
Water Set, seven #355 6-1/2" h goblets, colorless, green stem,
    etch S15 ....165.00
Whiskey Set, eight 3" h ftd glasses, colorless, green stem, etch
    S15 ....100.00
Wine Set, six #355 4-3/8" h wines, colorless, green stem, etch
    S15 ....165.00

BURMESE GLASS

History: Burmese glass is a translucent art glass originated by Frederick Shirley and manufactured by the Mt.

Washington Glass Co., New Bedford, Massachusetts, from 1885 to c1891.

Burmese glass colors shade from a soft lemon to a salmon pink. Uranium was used to attain the yellow color, and gold was added to the batch so that on reheating, one end turned pink. Upon reheating again, the edges would revert to the yellow coloring. A yellow top edge is a common indicator that the glassworker reheated the piece at least twice. The blending of the colors was so gradual that it is difficult to determine where one color ends and the other begins.

Although some of the glass has a glossy surface, most pieces were acid finished, resulting in a velvet-type finish. The majority of the items were free blown, but some were blown molded in a ribbed, hobnail, or diamond-quilted design. Glass finishing techniques resulted in ruffled edges, turned down rims, and even included the application of stems, leaves, and flowers. Hand-painted enameled decorations include insects, fish, birds, Egyptian motifs, flowers, leaves, and poetic verses. Artists such as Albert Steffin, Frank Guba, Adolf Frederick, and Timothy Canty often signed their works. Paper labels were also used to mark Burmese objects.

American-made Burmese is quite thin and, therefore, is fragile, and brittle. English Burmese was made by Thos. Webb & Sons. Out of deference to Queen Victoria, they called their wares "Queen's Burmese."

References: John A. Shuman, III, *The Collector's Encyclopedia of American Art Glass*, Collector Books, 1988, 1994 value update; Kenneth Wilson, *American Glass 1760-1930: The Toledo Museum of Art, Volume I, Volume II,* Hudson Hills Press and the Toledo Museum of Art, 1994.

Collectors Club: Mount Washington Art Glass Society, P.O. Box 24094, Fort Worth, TX 76124-1094.

Reproduction Alert: Reproductions abound in almost every form. Since uranium can no longer be used, some of the reproductions are easy to spot. In the 1950s, Gunderson produced many pieces in imitation of Burmese.

Museums: New Bedford Glass Museum, New Bedford, MA; The Chrysler Museum, Norfolk, VA; The Corning Museum of Glass, Corning, NY; Sandwich Glass Museum, Sandwich, MA; The Toledo Museum of Art, Toledo, OH.

Gundersen

Basket, 8" h, 5" w, matte finish, applied twisted Burmese rope
    handle..300.00
Hat, 3" h, 4" w brim, Diamond Quilted pattern 375.00
Plate, 9" d, acid finish..650.00
Toothpick Holder...135.00
Vase, 9-1/2" h, Tappan, acid finish 375.00

Mount Washington

Basket, 5-1/2" h, 6" w, very pale yellow shading to deep pink,
    applied frosted loop handle 300.00
Bon Bon
    1-1/2" h, 5-1/4" l, satin finish, rect, bulged-out optic ribbed
    sides, turned in edges.....................................285.00
    2" h, 5-1/4" l, 4-1/2" w, smooth satin finish, rectangular
    bowl, bulged-out optic ribbed sides with turned-in
    edges..285.00

2-3/8" h, 6-1/2" l 4-3/4" w, shiny finish, three applied lemon-yellow prunts, applied handle, heart-shaped rim .. 950.00

Bowl

    5" l, 4-1/2" w, 2" h, rect, thin walls, c1880 .... 425.00

    7-1/4" d, 6" h, 6 ruffled top, 3 pulled edge, 3 applied shell feet, large applied berry over pontil 1,100.00

    12" d, glossy, fluted rim, ten pinched corners 300.00

Chalice, 8-3/4" h, matte finish, 1890s 1,800.00

Cider Pitcher, 6-3/4" h, minor heat check in handle 385.00

Compote, 7"d, 4" h, glossy, ruffled top, baluster stem 330.00

Creamer, 2-5/8" h, enameled vinate dec, ruffled rim 275.00

Cruet

    6" h, salmon shading to white, blue flowers, green leaves and vines 2,950.00

    6-1/8" h, 3-3/4" w, bulbous base, vertical ribbing, acid finish, delicate pink shading two-thirds way down, dainty handle, orig stopper 500.00

Demitasse Cup and Saucer, 2-3/8" h cup, 4-5/8" d saucer, orig paper label on saucer 585.00

Dish, 5" d, 3/4" h, shiny finish, deep color 185.00

Ewer, 6" h, 2-1/2" d base, long spout, loop handle, applied base, deep color, acid finish, c1880 .... 950.00

Ice Cream Bowl, 9" d 2-3/4" h, deep salmon pink shading to bright yellow, satin finish 950.00

Jack in the Pulpit Vase, 6-1/2" h, 3" w top, ruffled, matte finish 425.00

Lamp, 19-1/2" h, 10" d shade, fine pink to yellow shaded ground, Frank Guba hand painted ducks in bright natural colors, three ducks on shade, two on font, fitted with orig Burmese chimney, gilt metal fluid mounts, electrified 11,500.00

Lamp Shade, 5" l, gas light type

    Acid Finish 250.00

    Satin Finish 300.00

Lemonade Set, 7" h x 9" w Egyptian style pitcher, six 4" tumblers, c1880 .... 2,250.00

Milk Pitcher, 7-1/4" h, 4" w, tankard, applied loop handle, matte finish 950.00

Mustard Pot, 4-1/2" h, barrel shape, vertical ribbed body, shiny finish, bail handle, metal collar, hinged lid ... 375.00

Pin Jar, cov, 2-3/4" h, 4" d, unfired finish, tomato shape, melon ribbed, shaded green ground, large purple and white chrysanthemums, green leaves, fancy SP cov 275.00

Pitcher

    5-1/4" h, 3-1/4" w, acid finish, petticoat shape, deep color, applied loop handle 875.00

    9" h, tankard, rural scene and florals, Longfellow verse 3,500.00

Rose Jar, cov

    5" h, 2-1/2" d, petticoat shape, wild rose dec, deep salmon pink shading to yellow, period gold dec cov and metal insert 1,610.00

    5-1/4" h, floral dec 400.00

Salt and Pepper Shakers, pr, 4" h, vertical ribbed body, acid finish, distinct pink coloration half way, orig two part lids 300.00

Sugar Bowl, cov, 4-1/2" w, 3-1/2" h, wishbone feet, matte finish, berry prunt over pontil 750.00

Sugar Shaker, 4-1/2" h, 4" w, painted shaded salmon colored ground, enameled blue and white small flowers done in the manner of Timothy Canty, unfired, orig cover 400.00

Syrup Pitcher

    6" h, pansy dec, silver plated collar and lid, emb florals and winged insects 3,750.00

    6-1/2" h, 3" w, bulbous egg form, enameled purple and yellow spider mums, green and brown leaves, applied sq handle, period fancy SP cov 4,025.00

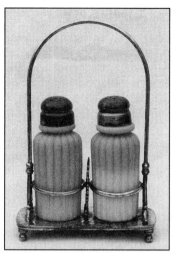

Salt and pepper shakers, pr, silver plated Tufts holder, 7-1/2" h, 4-3/4" w, $600.

Toothpick Holder

    2-1/2" h, tricorn folded in top, light blue blossoms with bright yellow centers, color blush on lower half of body, shape #4 .... 585.00

    2-3/4" h, 3" w, matte finish, sq mouth, bulbous base .. 325.00

    3" h, 3" w, , sq mouth, bulbous base, 7 pine cones, needles, and branches 675.00

Tumbler, 3-3/4" h, 2-3/4" d

    Acid finish, painted and enameled English ivy dec .. 395.00

    Pastel salmon shading to a creamy-yellow 285.00

    Matte finish 175.00

    Shiny finish, egg-shell thin satin body 375.00

Vase

    3" h, 3-1/2" d, bulbous base, yellow enameled daisy and leaves dec 850.00

    5-1/2" h, gourd, flared rim, acid finish 550.00

    5-3/4" h, very pale pink to yellow body, white flowers with yellow centers 600.00

    6" h, bulbous, c1880 .... 350.00

    7" h, 4" w, double gourd, matte finish, deep salmon pink shading to yellow 500.00

    7" h, lily, delicate blush to the mouth of the "lily," refired yellow rim 285.00

    8" h, Queen's Design, #145 gourd shape, stylized floral dec, multicolored enamel blossoms and buds 2,950.00

    8" h, double gourd, turquoise forget-me-knots and peach colored roses 1,250.00

Vase, inverted bell shape, flared scalloped and pinched rim, pedestal base with scalloped rim, acid finish, 4" h, $450.

8-1/2" h, 3-1/2" w base, gourd, matte finish............425.00

8-1/2" h, 3-1/2" w base, gourd, multicolored prunous dec, shades of pale blue and brown, leaves, and stems, 35 white enameled beads on rim, slightly worn 850.00

8-1/2" h, 4-1/2" w, double gourd, deep colors........425.00

8-3/4" h, 5" w, double gourd, matte finish...............435.00

9-3/4" h, lily, unpolished pontil................................750.00

10" h, lily, tricorn trumpet, pink rim shading to yellow base...400.00

10" h, stick, acid finish, scattered sprays of pansies in natural colors.. 440.00

10-1/4" h, 5-1/2" w at shoulder, 5-1/4" neck, gourd shape, acid finish 750.00

11" h, 6" d, white daisies, lemon-yellow ground, No. 146..1,750.00

11-1/2" h, 6-1/2" w, gourd, deep salmon pink to yellow, gold, brown, green, tan, and rust bamboo dec 1,875.00

12" h, ibis in flight, pyramids, palm tree, and sand dunes, rosy-pink blush, drilled 3/8" hole in base........2,750.00

12" h, 6-3/4" w, bulbous stick, Queen's pattern, 3 large open blossoms, 7 buds, enameled white, yellow, blue, green, and gold, c1880..................................3,950.00

12-1/4" h, lily, gross finish.................................875.00

12-1/4" h, lily, matte finish................................750.00

12-3/4" h, glossy finish.....................................875.00

14" h, lily, deep salmon pink shading to brilliant yellow, matte finish, irregular shaped base...................875.00

15" h, lily, brilliant yellow to deep salmon pink, matte finish 950.00

23-1/2" h, trumpet shape, c1890.........................1,400.00

Whiskey Taster, 2-3/4" h, acid finish, Diamond Quilted pattern 175.00

Pairpoint

Hat, 1-1/4" h, shiny finish, c1930.................................450.00

Jack in the Pulpit Vase, 5-1/4" h, 6-3/4" w at crown, deep salmon to brilliant yellow, glossy finish, c1920.......575.00

Vase, 10" h, 5" d, trumpet, scalloped top, deep color, shiny finish, c1920 ....650.00

Webb

Bowl, 6-1/4" d, 3-3/4" h, floral dec, applied colorless rim, mkd "Thos Webb" 1,200.00

Candle Cup Holder, 1-3/4" h, 4-1/4" d, clear glass candle cup, orig unused candle, holder sgd "S. Clarke Patent Trade Mark Fairy," clear glass cup sgd "S. Clarke Trade Mark Fairy," candle imp "Sam Clarke's New Patent Trade Fairy Mark" 850.00

Charger, 10" d, shallow, disk shape 365.00

Creamer and Sugar, 4-1/2" h creamer, 2-1/2" h open sugar, acid finish, wishbone feet, berry pontil, professional repair to one foot on creamer 935.00

Cruet

6-1/2" h, three striking chrysanthemum blossoms, two white and one yellow, coral colored detail stripes mushroom stopper, signed "88" in enamel..............2,950.00

7" h, shiny finish, mushroom stopper, each rib has hint of pink, refired buttery yellow tip of spout 1,250.00

Epergne, 11" h, Queen's, gilt metal center arrangement supports two crimped bowls, central shat, delicate matching floral motif, sgd bowls and metalwork, fairy lamp candle shades and holders missing 2,300.00

Fairy Lamp

3-3/4" h, pyramid, Burmese shade, unsigned clear glass base...145.00

4" h, pyramid, pressed glass base has molded-in "S. Clarke Fairy Pyramid" and dancing fairy logo signature .. 335.00

4" h, oval pink to yellow top, ruffled and crimped bowl, colorless Clarkes holder, orig candle................815.00

5-1/2" h, 5-3/4" w, Cricklite, short crimped skirt flares out from the top of the bowl-shaped base, impressed signature "Thos. Webb & Sons Queens Burmeseware Patented," clear glass candle cup is signed, "S Clarke Fairy Trade Mark Patent," unused wax candle 950.00

6" h, 7-1/2" d spreading, skirt-like, pleated base, two acid etched signatures, "Thos Webb & Sons Queen's Burmeseware Patented" and "S. Clarke's Fairy Patent Trade Mark," clear glass candle cup signed, "Clarke's Criklite Trade Mark"..950.00

18-1/2" h overall, 3-1/2" h acid finished Burmese shades, colorless pressed Clarke inserts, mounted on silver double arm reeded column with stem base, pr.......... 470.00

Jar, cov, 3" h, 2-5/8" d, acid finish, rich coloring, brown leaves, blue and white enameled flowers, star shaped top...300.00

Perfume Bottle, 5" l, flattened elongated oval teardrop, blossom laden branch, blue butterfly, silver screw rim and cap stamped "CM" with hallmarks, cap dented 865.00

Relish Dish, 3" h, 5-3/4" d, 6-1/2" h, 8" w, two hat shaped bowls, pastel yellow crown, shading to blushed rolled rim, three butterflies and dragonfly dec on each, flattened brim with brilliant golden laden bittersweet blossoms, SP tray, figural cala lily on handle of SP handle 1,500.00

Rose Bowl, 3-1/4" h, prunus blossom dec, sq top 285.00

Salt, 2-3/4" d, acid finish, bittersweet colored blossoms, gold branches 450.00

Scent Bottle, 4-7/8 l, 1-1/4" w at shoulder, lay down type, shading from blush at shoulder to soft yellow point, mistletoe leaves, white berries dec, sterling screw on top hallmarked "CM," rampant lion, "N" and anchor 1,400.00

Sweetmeat Jar, cov, 7" h, acid finish, cylindrical, bittersweet and gold foliage, SP collar, lid, and bail handle, sgd.........300.00

Toothpick Holder, shiny, soft peach blush fading to buttery-yellow, eggshell-thin body.....................................435.00

Vase

3-1/2" h, petal top, deep salmon to yellow, matte finish 250.00

3-1/2" h, petal top, deep color, large green leaves, red berries, matte finish 475.00

6" h, white, front has line-drawn, sepia-colored decoration in Chinoiserie motif depicting oriental man after releasing arrow from bow striking goose in mid air, reverse side is continuation of scene, elaborate border encircling shoulder 950.00

8" h, gourd shape, roses and forget-me-nots, three lovely peach-colored rose blossoms cling to leafed branch which swirl down rim, around body and down to the base, entwining strands of turquoise-colored forget-me-not blossoms, double gourd shaped 1,250.00

8-1/2" h, 4" d, acid finish, red buds, green and brown leaves, yellow wafer foot....................................750.00

11" h, 6" d base, white daisies with distinctive yellow-dot centers..1,750.00

14" h, 7" d, bulbous, deep color dec with two monkeys frolicking among bamboo stalks, gold highlighting and trim...13,225.00

23-1/2" h, circa 1890 ....1,250.00

White, faint blush of color on collar and shoulder, golden bird flying toward golden moon decoration, swags of stylized golden bamboo, branches of baby-blue blossoms, Chinoiserie motif 750.00

Whiskey Taster, 2-3/4" tall, molded-in elongated diamond quilted design..285.00

BUTTONS

History: Buttons are objects used to hold articles of clothing in a desired place. In the 18th century, buttons were worn basically by men as status symbols and a sign of wealth. During the peak of this period, it was not unusual to find complete sets of 24 buttons on one coat. While these status symbol buttons were primarily made of metals, glass buttons were made for more practical uses. Because buttons became highly decorative accessories, they soon can be found in wonderful colors and shapes in glass, as well as many other types of materials.

Buttons are collected according to age, material, and subject matter. The National Button Society, founded in 1939, has designated 1918 as the dividing line between old and modern buttons. Shanks and backmarks are important keys to determine the age of buttons. It is the older buttons which attract the most attention of collectors.

Glass buttons are a specialized collecting area. Many of the glass buttons are considered miniature works of art as they are hand made. The term "lampwork" refers to the fact that the glass is worked by a flame of a lamp. After the glass is brought to a melting point, it is worked to a proper consistency by the button maker. The button maker holds a steel rod called a mandrel in one hand, the glass rod to be heated in the other hand. After the rod has been softened in the flame, it is wound around the mandrel. Hence lampwork is also known as "wound glass." Sometimes intricate designs are created with paperweight type canes which the glass button maker also heats and works over the flame. The glass glob is then pressed into a mold and while the glass is still hot, the shank is inserted. When the shank is twisted and causes tiny swirls in the back, it is called a "swirl back." Skilled glass workers can create long stringers of glass which they twist together to form latticino decorations or pull into feather type decorations. Other glass buttons have small pieces of gold or silver foil inserted into the molten glass, creating a unique cased button.

The examples listed below are a very brief sampling of the millions of buttons available to collectors.

References: There are many excellent button books available to collectors. Some of the standard reference books which have information regarding glass buttons are: Clinton E. Arsenault, *Button, Button, Carnival Glass, Iridescent Black Amethyst and Lustre, Book I;* Ruth Miller Clark, *Carnival of Iridescent Luster Buttons, 1986; Book II, 1992* (2100 Dawn Dr., Georgetown, TX 78628); *Book III* (Alan G. Perry, 7614 McKenry St., Houston, TX 77087-3834), 1997; Jane O. Dinkins, *Sketchbook of Little Carnival Glass Buttons,* (1100 Ridgeley Dr., Houston, TX 77055) 1996; Fink & Ditzler, *Buttons, The Collector's Guide To Selecting, Restoring and Enjoying New & Vintage Buttons, 1993;* Edith M. Fuoss and Nora O. Jones, *Black Glass Buttons,* 1945 (reprint by New Leaf Publishers); Edith M. Fuoss and Caroline Smith, *Black Glass Buttons, Return Engagement,* 1952; Elizabeth Hughes and Marion Lester, *The Big Book of Buttons,* 1981 (reprint by New Leaf Publishers); Sibylle Jargstorf, *Baubles, Buttons, and Beads: The Heritage of Bohemia,* Schiffer, 1991; Florence Zacharie Nicholls, *Button Handbook, with Three Supplements, 1943-1949,*(reprints by New Leaf Publishers).

Periodical: *Button Bytes,* http://www.tias.com/articles/buttons. An Internet magazine devoted to Buttons.

Collectors' Clubs: Buckeye State Button Society, 251 Pfeiffer Ave., Akron, OH 44312-4137; Denton Button Club, 500 El Paseo, Denton, TX 76205-8502; National Button Society, 2733 Juno Place, Apt. 4, Akron, OH 44313-4137; Pioneer Button Club, 102 Frederick St., Oshawa, Ontario L1G 2B3 Canada; The Button Club, P.O. Box 2274, Seal Beach, CA 90740.

Museum: Button Bytes, http://www.tias.com/museum/clothing buttons.html.

Aurora Borealis, colorless glass with metallic coating, self shank with thread groove, 1950s, 1/2" 2.00
Black
    Gold luster, fabric-look, self shank, mkd "Le Mode," 1950s, 7/8" l 4.00
    Silver luster, petal look, self shank with threaded groove, mkd "Le Chic," 1950s, 13/16"...........................4.00
    Triangular faceted surface, metal 4 way shank 7.00
Bow, figural, transparent pink, blue, red, or yellow
    Large size...2.00
    Medium size 1.50
    Small size 1.00
Carnival Glass, purple, reference to R. Clark's iridized button book
    Bird dog, 3/4" d, Clark #107 ....11.00
    Buckle & Scrolls, 5/8" d, Clark #941 ....10.00
    Buckle & Scrolls, 7/8" d, Clark #941 ....14.00
    Feathered Spokes, 5/8" d, Clark #1038 ....10.00
    Lazy Wheel, 5/8" d, Clark #432 ....12.00
    Man in the Moon, 5/8" d, Clark #20 ....14.00
    Mr. Fox, 3/4" d, Clark #130...14.00
    Paisley Wheel, 5/8" d, Clark #1144 ....10.00
    Plumes, 5/8" d, Clark #732 ....11.00
    Rosette, 5/8" d, Clark #1171...10.00
    Star & Jewels, 5/8" d, Clark #1205 ....11.00
    Trellis & Spray, 9/16" d, Clark #760..............................5.50
    Windmill, 5/8" d, Clark #451 ....14.00
Charm String, amber, gold Victorian design, bright lavender luster, 1/2" d.. 2.00
Colorless with Gold Trim
    Lacy pattern, self shank, 3/4" d.....................................3.00
    Sunburst pattern, self shank, mkd "Le Chic," 1/2" d 1.50
    Swirled pattern, self shank with thread groove, 1/2".......2.00
Czechoslovakian, diminutive
    Cobalt blue, inlaid ribbons of light green glass, multicolored foil, 4-2ay metal box shank, 3/8" d 5.00
    Floral bouquet, set of 12 ....2.00
    Golden, domed top, decorative molded edge painted gold, self shank, 3/8" d 2.00
Green
    Art Deco, 4 way shank, 11-1/6" d, pr 1.50
    Art Deco, silver colored line design, self shank, 1930s, 1-1/4" 4.00
    Domed, 3/8" silver lustered molded floral band with red painted flowers, self shank, 11/16" d........................4.00
    Multi-sided...2.00
    Oval, transparent, 1" l, set of 5 ....1.50
    Rhinestone center, six sided body, self shank, pr 1.50
Hand Faceted Ball, clear yellow, swirl back, metal loop shank, c1900, 7/16" d 5.00

Green, 3/8" silver lustered molded floral and, red painted flowers, self shank, 11/16" dome, $4.

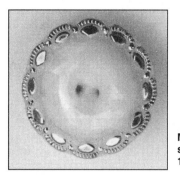

Moonglow, white, gold trim along scalloped edge, shelf shank, 1950s, 7/8" d, $7.

Hand Painted, white ground, hand painted molded flowers, gold paint edge, self shank, mkd "Le Mode" 3.00

Luster

    Silver and gold luster, milk glass ground, La Mode, set of 14...6.00

    Silver, faceted black glass, crescent moon encircling raised earth, sun rays streaming out from behind earth, birdcage shank...7.00

Moonglow

    Black with red, colorless glass molded with plants and flowers, back mark is straight line with angled line at both ends, self shank, 1/2" 5.00

    Fuchsia, smooth dome, internal gold specks, self shank, sgd "B. G. E." (Bailey, Green, and Elger), 3/8" d 2.00

    Green flower, gold trim, 1/2"..2.00

    Green, gold trim, self shank, slightly less than 3/8" d 2.00

    Pale blue, delicate gold trimmed rim, self shank, 1/2" 3.00

    White, gold trim along scalloped edge, self shank, 1950s, 7/8" l..7.00

    White, gold trim, four lobed, self shank, 1/2" d 2.00

Paperweight, complicated millefiori by John Gooderham, white base, 8 flower canes, center small red, white, and blue cane, brass wire shank, sgd with "J" cane on back, 5/8" d, 1/2" h..20.00

Pink

    Loop shank, brass collet, steel back 2.00

    Self shank, 5/16" d, set of 3..2.00

Self shank, looks like coiled yarn, 1-1/16" d, mkd "Costumakers" 3.00

Red, multi-lobed, six lobes separated by painted black lines, black center, self shank with thread groove, 1/2" d .. 2.00

Reverse Painted on Glass, 1-1/2" d, green ground, black scrolled lines, purple stripes, copper frame, iron back, heavy brass shank, 18th C................................... 200.00

Rhinestone, hand made, 3/8" center stone, 50 smaller rhinestones, all prong set, twisted double-rope edge, wire loop shank, rhodium setting, 1-1/2" d.............................. 15.00

Spangle, red, tan painted trim, 1940s, 3/4" 2.00

Venetian, modern, made in Italy, metal shank

    Gold foil center, clear ground 5.00

    Turquoise blue ground, goldstone swirled feathers border design...5.00

    Wound, black ground, small red flower with green leaves, gold swirl dec 5.00

    Wound, clear ground, small red flower with green leaves, gold swirl dec 5.00

White, silver question mark dec... 2.00

Green, Art Deco style, silver colored line design, self shank, 1930s, 1-1/4" d, $4.

Hand Painted, white, molded flowers, gold painted edge, self shank, mkd "Le Mode," 1/2" d, $3.

CAMBRIDGE GLASS

History: Cambridge Glass Company, Cambridge, Ohio, was incorporated in 1901. Initially, the company made clear tableware, later expanding into colored, etched, and engraved glass. More than 40 different hues were produced in blown and pressed glass.

The Cambridge, Ohio, area was a successful location because a good supply of natural gas and silicon sand were available. The area was also rich in talent because of the National Glass Company, which had brought Arthur J. Bennett to manage its new factory. Under his supervision, National Glass produced the first piece of crystal glassware, a water pitcher, in May of 1902. When the company developed financial difficulties in 1907, Mr. Bennett recognized its potential and refinanced the company. By 1910, the company had expanded and opened another plant in Byesville, Ohio. It continued operations until 1917, when it closed and all employees were transferred to the plant at Cambridge. With the addition of these talented employees and new capital investments, the Cambridge Glass Company grew. All products were handmade. More than 5,000 molds were used to create the complete line of patterns offered.

One of the distinctive characteristics of Cambridge glassware is the jewel-like colors. Transparent colors include: amber, amethyst, apple green, Carmen (brilliant ruby red), cinnamon, crystal, Dianthus (light transparent pink), Eleanor Krystol (gold tint), Heather bloom (delicate orchid), LaRosa (light pastel pink), Mandarin Gold (very light gold yellow), mocha, Moonlight (pastel blue), peach-blo (light pink), pistachio (pastel green), Ritz Blue, (bright blue), Royal Blue, Smoke and Willow Blue. Opaque colors include: Azure Blue (dark blue), Blue Milk (light blue), Coral (fleshlike orange-pink), Crown Tucson (fleshlike pink), Ebony (satin finish black), Ebony (black), Heliotrope (purple), Ivory (light cream), Jade (blue-green), Milk (white), Opal (pearly), Pearl Green (glossy green), Pomona Turquoise, and Violet (light purple). Shaded transparent colors include: Amberina, Mardi Gras, (crystal body with assorted color flecks), Rubina, (later called sunset), Tomato (yellow-green at top, blending to red and yellow-green at base), and Varitone (Moonlight, LaRosa, Mocha, and Pistachio).

Five different marks were used during the production years, but not every piece was marked. A paper sticker was used from 1935-1954.

The National Cambridge Collectors, Inc. deserves a great deal of credit for the work it does. Incorporated in 1973, it is a nonprofit educational organization devoted to the preservation and collection of Cambridge Glass company wares. It established a permanent museum in 1982. This group also published excellent reference books, which contain patterns, etchings, and even color comparisons.

The plant closed in 1954. Some of the molds were later sold to the Imperial Glass Company, Bellaire, Ohio.

References: Tom and Neila Bredehoft, *Fifty Years of Collectible Glass, 1920-1970*, Antique Trader Books, 1997; Gene Florence, *Elegant Glassware of the Depression Era, 7th Edition*, Collector Books, 1997; ——, *Very Rare Glassware of the Depression Years, 5th Series*, Collector Books, 1996; National Cambridge Collectors, Inc., *Cambridge Glass Co., Cambridge, Ohio* (reprint of 1930 catalog and supplements through 1934), Collector Books, 1976, 1997 value update; ——, *Cambridge Glass Co., Cambridge, Ohio, 1949 through 1953* (catalog reprint), Collector Books, 1976, 1996 value update; ——, *Colors in Cambridge Glass*, Collector Books, 1984, 1993 value update; ——, *Miami Valley Ohio Study Group, Etchings by Cambridge*, Volume I, 1997; Naomi L. Over, *Ruby Glass of the 20th Century*, Antique Publications, 1990, 1993-94 value update; Bill and Phyllis Smith, *Cambridge Glass 1927-1929* (1986) and *Identification Guide to Cambridge Glass 1927-1929* (updated prices 1996), published by authors (4003 Old Columbus Rd., Springfield, OH 45502).

Periodical: *Cambridge Crystal Ball* Newsletter, P.O. Box 416, Cambridge, OH; *The Daze*, P.O. Box 57, Otisville, MI 48463.

Collectors' Club: National Cambridge Collectors, Inc., P.O. Box 416, Cambridge, OH 43725.

Museums: Cambridge Glass Museum, Cambridge, OH; Museum of the National Cambridge Collectors, Inc., Cambridge, OH.

Miscellaneous Patterns and Etchings

Ashtray
    Shell, #34, 3 toed, orig label
        Mandarian gold 15.00
        Moonlight blue..15.00
    Stack Away, 4 ashtrays, blue, green, pink, and yellow, wood
        base..55.00
Basket
    Hunt's Scene, pink, 11" h 215.00
    #119, amber, crystal handle 75.00
Bookends, pr, crystal
    Eagle, crystal...135.00
    Scotties..150.00
Bowl, 10" d, Flying Nude, Crown Tuscan....................... 250.00
Bridge Hound, #1371
    Ebony 85.00
    Peachblow...60.00
    Pistachio...75.00
Butter Dish, cov, Gadroon, crystal................................. 45.00
Candlesticks, pr
    Calla Lily, emerald..60.00
    Cascade, #400, crystal, 1-lite 47.50
    Dolphin, double, Crown Tuscan..................................250.00
    Everglades, 2-lite, moonlight #3.................................325.00
    Gadroon, ram's head, 4-1/2" h, cobalt opalescent 150.00
    Statuesque, 8-1/4" h, Crown Tuscan..........................200.00
Candy Dish, cov, Seashell, #110, 6" h, ftd, Willow Blue........ 300.00
Cheese and Cracker, Lorna... 35.00
Cigarette Box, cov
    Crown Tuscan 55.00
    #616, small...25.00
Cigarette Holder with Place Card Holder, #3400/114,
    amethyst 50.00
Cocktail, Statuesque, #3100/9, 3 oz
    Forest green, crystal stem..80.00
    Gold Krystol, Crown Tuscan stem.............................125.00

Comport
    Honeycomb, 9" d, 4-3/4" h, ftd, rubina 150.00
    Krome Kraft, 71/2" h, cutout grape motif, amethyst 55.00
    Statuesque, holding shell with Charleton design, gold trim,
        Crown Tuscan 275.00
Condiment Set, Pristine, crystal, 5 pc 98.50
Cordial
    Magnolia..75.00
    Regency, Stradivari, 1 oz...68.00
Cornucopia, #702, Crown Tuscan......................................55.00
Creamer, Martha Washington, amber, clear stick handle 15.00
Creamer and Sugar, Cascade, #400, emerald green 35.00
Cream Soup, Willow Blue, #3400/55, orig liner.................25.00
Cup and Saucer, Martha Washington, amber 12.00
Decanter
    #1321, cobalt blue, 28 oz...230.00
    #84482, Nautilus, crystal...45.00
Finger Bowl, Adam, yellow..25.00
Flower Center, Seashell, #110, crystal
    #42, 8"...250.00
    #44...200.00
Flower Frog
    Bashful Charlotte
        6" h, crystal..95.00
        6" h, green..225.00
        6" h, Mandarian gold 250.00
        6" h, moonlight blue...650.00
        6" h, pink..225.00
        11" h, crystal satin...360.00
        11" h, moonlight blue..600.00
        11" h, moonlight blue satin 775.00
    Blue Jay, 5-1/2" h
        Crystal 120.00
        Green..365.00
        Moonlight blue..200.00
    Draped Lady, 8-1/2" h
        Amber...190.00
        Blue..260.00
        Crown Tuscan...1,850.00
        Crystal, frosted, ribbed base...................................75.00
        Dark pink..150.00
        Emerald, light...300.00
        Frosted green...150.00
        Gold Krystol...275.00
        Green..160.00
        Honey, oval base..495.00
        Light pink..160.00
        Midnight blue..325.00
        Moonlight blue, satin 450.00
        Yellow...180.00
    Draped Lady, 13-1/2" h
        Moonlight blue...850.00
        Peachblow...550.00
        Pink...180.00
    Eagle, 5-5/8" h
        Crystal 350.00
        Pink...365.00
    Heron
        9" h, crystal, fluted base..120.00
        12" h, crystal, smooth base......................................20.00
    Mandolin Lady, 9" h, bend back, green.....................310.00
    Nude, 6-1/2" h, 3-1/4" d, clear....................................95.00
    Rose Lady, 9" h
        Amber...260.00
        Custard, #1 base..1,600.00
        Crystal 300.00

Green..250.00
    Mocha, tall base...275.00
    Peachblow..275.00
    Pink...250.00
Seagull, crystal..65.00
Turtle, 3-1/2" x 5-1/2", #1042, crystal............................175.00
Two Kids, 9" h
    Crystal 155.00
    Honey, oval base..5,235.00
    Light emerald green 250.00
    Moonlight blue...1,200.00
    Pink, frosted..550.00
French Dressing Bottle, Martha Washington, crystal........ 75.00
Goblet
    Aurora, #1066, Carmen red, 6-1/4" h, 11 oz 30.00
    Cascade, #400, crystal 15.00
    Heirloom, crystal, 9 oz..17.50
    Heatherbloom, #3111, 10 oz...45.00
    Imperial Hunt, #3085, pink..55.00
    Magnolia...25.00
    Regency, Stradivari, 10 oz..28.00
Ice Bucket, Chrysanthemum, pink, silver handle 85.00
Iced Tea Tumbler, Lexington, #7966, trumpet, 12 oz,
    ftd 17.50
Ivy Ball, #1236
    Crown Tuscan, Charleton roses dec...........................250.00
    Royal blue...85.00
Jug
    Minerva...300.00
    Optic, #3400, ball shape, Heatherbloom 450.00
Lamp
    Geisha Girl, amber...350.00
    Geisha Girl, light emerald 400.00
    Martha Washington, crystal, 9", electric, portable 95.00
Muddler, rooster, crystal 25.00
Oyster Cocktail, #1066 Aurora, 3-7/8" h, 5 oz, royal blue 28.00
Pitcher, #3900/114, Lexington, cut 65.00
Plate
    Crown Tuscan, 7" d..45.00
    Martha Washington, amber, lunch 12.00
Punch Bowl Set, crystal
    No. 3200, bowl, ten cups 190.00
    Swan, bowl and twelve cups....................................2,200.00
Punch Cup, swan handle 24.00
Salad Plate, Cascade, #400, 6-1/2" d 10.00
Salt and Pepper Shakers, pr, Daffodil, #360, chrome lid 80.00
Seafood Cocktail, Seashell, #110, Crown Tuscan,
    4-1/2" oz... 95.00
Sherbet
    Aurora, #1066, 4-1/2" h, 7 oz, forest green 18.00
    Carmine, crystal...17.00
    Daffodil, #3779, 6 oz, low...24.00
    Imperial Hunt, #3085, tall, pink 40.00
    Regency, Stradivari, low 12.00
Sugar, Martha Washington, crystal................................... 17.50
Swan
    3", Style #1
        Amber...85.00
        Crown Tuscan 60.00
        Crystal...28.00
        Forest Green...200.00
        Gold Crystal..40.00
        Royal Blue 125.00
    3", Style #3, red...110.00
    4-1/2", Style #1, crystal frost, red and black enamel.....350.00
    4-1/2", Style #3, milk glass 95.00

6-1/2", Style #3
  Forest Green...95.00
  Milk Glass...250.00
  Red...325.00
7", crystal, sgd..33.00
8-1/2", Style #1, gold crystal..........................450.00
8-1/2", Style #3
  Forest Green...125.00
  Milk Glass...300.00
  Red...325.00
Torchiere
  #3500/88, Gadroon, forest green top, crystal stem and
    foot...65.00
  #3500/90, crystal, ashtray foot......................48.00
  #3500/90, Royal Blue, ashtray foot 85.00
Tray, #3500/112, 3-part, 15"............................38.50
Tumbler
  Adam, yellow, ftd.......................................25.00
  Carmine, crystal, 12 oz...............................25.00
  Daffodil, #3779, 9 oz, low............................28.00
Urn, 8" h, Crown Tuscan 140.00
Vase
  Everglades, 10-1/2" h, moonlight blue.........350.00
  Flying Nude, Crown Tuscan, hp roses and violets dec,
    creamy pink molded shell bowl held by nude woman, 9" h,
    12" l 175.00
  Hunt's Scene, #797, 8" h, flip, amber, gold edge 400.00
  Nautilus, 7" h, Crown Tuscan, ftd................67.50
  Songbird and Butterfly, #402, 12" h, blue ...375.00
  Songbird and Butterfly, #402, 12" h, pink ...275.00
  Tall Flat Panel, swung, 19-1/4" h, sgd 105.00
Water Set, Gyro Optic, moonlight blue, pitcher, 6 tumblers..250.00
Wine, #1066 Aurora, 4-11/16" h, 3 oz, optic, moonlight blue ..35.00

Patterns and Etchings

Apple Blossom Line #3400, 1930s. Made in amber, blue, dark
  green, light green, pink, and yellow.
  Basket, crystal, 7".....................................475.00
  Bon Bon, #3400/1180, 5-1/4" d, blue 60.00
  Bowl, #3400/2, low, ftd, yellow....................65.00
  Bowl, #3400/1240, oval, yellow....................75.00
  Bowl, 10" d, #3400/1185, green..................145.00
  Bowl, 12" d, 4 toes, #3400/4
    Crystal 90.00
    Green, gold edge...................................130.00
  Butter, cov, #3400/52, pink 500.00
  Candlesticks, pr, #3400/646, pink 110.00
  Celery/Relish
    4-part, #3500/142, crystal 65.00
    5-part, yellow...90.00
  Champagne, yellow 25.00
  Cheese and Cracker, #3400/6, yellow..........65.00
  Cheese Comport, amber.............................50.00
  Cocktail, crystal...14.00
  Cocktail Shaker, #3400/78, crystal, no stopper 95.00
  Comport, 4 toes, #3400, yellow....................60.00
  Compote, 7", #14, yellow.............................85.00
  Console Bowl
    #3400/4, yellow.......................................45.00
    #3400/5, rolled edge, yellow 45.00
  Creamer and Sugar, #3400/68
    Crystal 35.00
    Yellow 60.00
  Cup and Saucer, #3400
    Crystal 25.00
    Yellow 22.00

Apple Blossom etch,
goblet, orig labels, $35.

Finger Bowl, #3130, yellow 95.00
Goblet, #3130, crystal 25.00
Gravy Liner, #1091, yellow............................95.00
Ice Bucket, green.......................................100.00
Jug, #3400/100 76 oz, crystal 390.00
Juice Tumbler, #3130, ftd, green...................30.00
Martini Pitcher, #1408, 60 oz, crystal 1,200.00
Mayonnaise, 3 pc, yellow..............................65.00
Pickle Tray, 9" l, #3400/59, yellow 70.00
Pitcher, #1205, yellow 395.00
Plate
  6" d, #3400, crystal 10.00
  6" d, #3400, yellow......................................8.00
  6" d, #3400/1181, handle, green 42.50
  7-1/2" d, #3400, tea, crystal.......................14.00
  8-1/2" d, #3400, pink 20.00
  8-1/2" d, #3400, yellow 20.00
  9-1/2" d, #3400, yellow 75.00
Relish
  #1083, 2-part, blue 145.00
  #3400/91, 8" d, 3 handle 60.00
  #3400/120, 5-part, yellow 55.00
Server, center handle
  Amber..30.00
  Yellow 40.00
Sherbet, #3130, sherbet...............................20.00
Table Center, 12", #3400/5, crystal 130.00
Tumbler
  5 oz, ftd, yellow...25.00
  9 oz, ftd
    Crystal..14.00
    Yellow 28.00
  #3025, 10 oz, ftd, crystal, black foot 45.00
  #3130, 12 oz, ftd, yellow............................40.00
  12 oz, mushroom shape, crystal 25.00
Whiskey, ftd, 2 oz
  Crystal 30.00
  Green..85.00
  Yellow 65.00
Wine, #3130, green......................................85.00

Blossom Time Etching. Made on crystal and some colors.

Bell, crystal...90.00
Bon Bon, 6" d, 2 handles, crystal...................................25.00
Bud Vase, #274, 10" h, black, gold encrusted............325.00
Cake plate, two handles, crystal...................................40.00
Candy, cov, Martha blank, crystal 95.00
Cheese and Cracker Set, Martha blank, crystal 85.00
Compote, black and gold 225.00
Hat, crystal 300.00
Ice Bucket, crystal......................................125.00
Salt and Pepper Shakers, pr, crystal 50.00

Candlelight Etching 1940s-50s. Made on crystal and Crown Tuscan with gold decoration. Prices listed below for crystal.

Bowl, 12" d, ftd, #3400/4 ....130.00
Cheese, ftd, #3400.......................................70.00
Cordial, cut..225.00
Juice Tumbler, ftd, 5 oz, #3114.................................38.50
Mayonnaise, 2 pc set, gold edge, #3400/11 ....130.00

Caprice Extensive pattern from 1940s-1957. Made in amber, amethyst, cobalt blue, crystal, emerald green, Mandarian gold, moonlight blue, (blue), pink, pistachio, and white milk glass. Some pieces have satinized panels and are referred to as Alpine. Reproductions have been made by Summit Art Glass, which now owns several molds (shown with an asterisk below).

Ashtray, #34, Alpine 27.50
Banana Bowl, blue 400.00
Basket
    #146, crystal, 4", 2 handles, sq 24.00
    #153, blue...60.00
Bon Bon
    #147, blue..50.00
    #154, sq, 2 handles, 6" 48.00
Bowl
    #51, blue...300.00
    #52, 9" d, blue 300.00
    #58, blue...360.00
    #60, 11" d, deep, ruffled, blue, silver overlay.........350.00
    #61, 12-1/2", 4 ftd, Alpine 125.00
    #66, 13" d, ftd, crimped, Alpine 175.00
    #66, ftd, ruffled, blue 200.00
Bridge Set
    Cloverleaf, #173, blue*.................................95.00
    Club, #170, Alpine*...................................125.00
    Diamond, #171, crystal 40.00
    Heart, #169, crystal* 45.00
    Spade, #172, blue*.....................................110.00
    Spade, #172, crystal*..................................40.00
Bubble, #256, 4" d, enamel flowers, blue 400.00
Butter Dish, #52, quarter pound, crystal*....................225.00
Candlestick
    #67, 2-1/2" h, crystal, pr 35.00
    #69, 2-lite, crystal, pr............................300.00
    #70, Alpine, pr 225.00
    #70, blue, pr 160.00
    #638, 3-lite, keyhole, blue, pr 230.00
    #647, 2-lite, keyhole, blue, pr 190.00
    #1338, 3-lite, blue, pr 250.00
    #1577, 5-lite, crystal 260.00
Candy Dish, cov, 3 ftd
    Alpine 130.00
    Pink...230.00
Celery
    #103, blue..330.00
    #126, 4-part, blue.....................................460.00
Champagne, tall, #300, blue....................................42.50

Cheese Stand, blue...600.00
Cigarette Box, cov, crystal 50.00
Cigarette Holder
    #204, blue...60.00
    #205, 2-1/4", blue.....................................75.00
Claret, blue...200.00
Coaster, #20, 5-1/2" d
    Blue...30.00
    Crystal..15.00
    Pink..40.00
Cocktail, #300, blown
    Blue...30.00
    Crystal..20.00
Comport, #136, tall, 6" d
    Crystal..48.00
    Pink...170.00
Condiment Set, #109, 5 pc, blue 550.00
Cordial, #300, blown
    Blue..120.00
    Crystal..50.00
Creamer and Sugar, tray
    Blue, individual size*..................................60.00
    Blue, medium size*....................................70.00
    Blue, large size*.......................................90.00
    Crystal, individual size* 40.00
Cruet, #101, Alpine*...175.00
Cup and Saucer
    Blue...48.00
    Crystal..20.00
    Mandarin gold 36.00
Decanter Set, #187 35 oz ball shaped decanter, five #188 2 oz tumblers, amethyst.. 560.00
Finger Bowl, liner, pressed, #16, blue 140.00
Fruit Bowl
    #18, 5" d, flat, blue..................................130.00
    #19, 5" d, ruffled, blue..............................140.00
Fruit Saucer, crimped, blue, 5" d 90.00
Goblet
    #1, amber, thick, blown............................500.00
    #1, amethyst, thick, blown........................350.00
    #300, blue...40.00
    #300, crystal, 7-3/4" h, 9 oz.....................25.00
Ice Bucket
    Alpine Blue 300.00
    Crystal, orig tongs 60.00
Iced Tea Tumbler
    #301, blown, crystal 18.00
    #310, flat, 12 oz, blue..............................120.00
    #310, flat, 12 oz, crystal 37.50
Ivy Ball, #232, 5" d
    Blue..350.00
    Crystal...130.00
Jelly
    #135, 7", crimped, blue 75.00
    #144, 4", 2 handles, blue..........................32.50
Jug, ball, 80 oz
    Alpine Blue 500.00
    Blue..350.00
    Crystal...150.00
Juice Tumbler, #300, 5 oz, ftd
    Blue...45.00
    Crystal..14.00
Juice Tumbler, #310, 5 oz, flat, blue.........................125.00
Lemon Plate, #152, 6" d
    Blue...15.00
    Pink..50.00

Mayonnaise
    #106, 2 pc, blue* 160.00
    #111, 3 pc, blue 330.00
Nut Bowl, #93, 2-1/2"
    Blue 45.00
    Crystal 18.00
Oil and Vinegar Set, #99, 3 pc
    Blue 260.00
    Crystal 130.00
Old Fashioned tumbler, #310, blue 125.00
Oyster Cocktail, #300, crystal 20.00
Parfait, #300, 5 oz
    Blue 300.00
    Pink 170.00
Pitcher, Doulton, amber 2,200.00
Plate
    6" d, crystal 10.00
    6-1/2" d, blue 42.50
    7" d, crystal, dinner 45.00
    7-1/2" d, blue 40.00
    7-1/2" d, crystal 20.00
    8" d, handle, #131, blue 40.00
    8-1/2" d, blue 45.00
    8-1/2" d, crystal 14.00
    8-1/2" d, Mandarin gold 30.00
    9-1/2" d, dinner, #24, crystal* 50.00
    14" d, #28, Alpine 120.00
Platter, crystal, 14" l, ftd 30.00
Relish
    #122, 3-part, crystal 30.00
    #124, 3-part, Alpine, 8-1/2" l* 70.00
    #124, 3-part, crystal, 8-1/2" l* 24.00
    #126, 4-part, blue* 430.00
    #199, 2-part, crystal 30.00
Rose Bowl, 5" d, crystal 60.00
Salad Bowl
    #49, 8" d, blue 270.00
    #57, 10" d, blue 290.00
    #80, 13" d, cupped, pink 500.00
Salt and Pepper Shakers, pr, #96, flat, blue* 125.00
Sandwich Set, 4 cups, saucers, 8-1/2" plates, creamer and
    sugar, 12" d 4 ftd plate, amber 350.00
Saucer, Mandarin gold 5.00
Sherbet, #300, 6 oz
    Blue 32.00
    Crystal 13.00
Sugar, #133, blue 110.00
Tumbler
    #11, 5 oz, ftd, blue 45.00
    #11, 5 oz, ftd, crystal 14.00
    #12, 3 oz, blue 100.00
    #180, 5 oz, barrel, blue 40.00
    #184, 12 oz, blue 45.00
    #188, 2 oz, blue* 55.00
    #188, 2 oz, Mandarin gold 35.00
    #300, 2-1/2 oz, ftd, blue, rare 300.00
    #300, 10 oz, ftd, crystal 20.00
    #300/2, 12 oz, ftd
        Blue 40.00
        Crystal 22.00
Vase
    #239, 8-1/8" h, amber 190.00
    #239, 8-5/8" h, cobalt blue 290.00
    #242, 6" h, amber 125.00
    #243, 8" h, cobalt blue 400.00
    #245, 5-1/2" h, plain top, crystal 130.00
    #249, 3-1/2" h, ruffled, blue 430.00

    #340, 9-1/2" h, ruffled, blue 800.00
    #344, 4-1/2" h, straight top, blue 225.00
    #345, 5-1/2" h, ruffled, blue 240.00
Whiskey, #300, 2-1/2 oz
    Blue 225.00
    Emerald green 50.00
Wine
    #6, blue, thick* 195.00
    #6, crystal, thick* 35.00
    #300, 2-1/2 oz, blue 80.00
    #300, 2-1/2 oz, crystal 27.50

Chantilly. Late 1940s-50s etching. Made only in crystal.
Bowl
    5-1/2" d, sterling base 70.00
    10" d, divided, sterling base 90.00
    10-1/2" d, Martha blank 100.00
    11-1/2" d, #3900/28 ....65.00
    11-1/2" d, 2 handle, #3900/45 ....120.00
    12-1/2" d, #430 ....65.00
    13" d, 4 toes, 3400/160 ....100.00
Butter, cov, #3400/52 ....200.00
Candlesticks, pr 200.00
Candy, cov, #313, sterling knob 225.00
Celery, Martha blank 65.00
Champagne, #3600, 6" h, 7 oz 35.00
Cheese and Cracker, 13-1/2" d, #3900/34 ....240.00
Cocktail, #3600 ....35.00
Cocktail Icer, crystal 58.00
Cocktail Shaker, glass lid 150.00
Comport, #3900/136, 5-1/2" h 65.00
Cordial, #3625, 4-3/4" h, 1 oz, crystal 65.00
Cordial Decanter, #3400/156, sterling base 260.00
Creamer and Sugar
    #138, sterling base 85.00
    #252 Martha blank 55.00
Cruet, straight top, handle, matching tray 150.00
Cup and Saucer, #3900/17 ....36.00
Decanter, #1321 ....600.00
Dressing Bottle, silver base 150.00
Goblet
    #3600 ....40.00
    #3625 ....45.00
Iced Tea Tumbler, ftd, #3625 ....38.00
Jug, 20 oz, #3900/117 ....250.00
Juice Tumbler, #3600 ....35.00
Marmalade, glass cov 75.00
Mayonnaise, #3900/111, 2 pc 60.00
Oil Cruet, 4 oz 95.00
Pitcher
    20 oz, sterling base 300.00
    76 oz, #3900/115, ice lip 275.00
    86 oz, #1561, ice lip, gold rim 245.00
Plate, #3900/24, dinner 75.00
Relish
    #324, Martha blank, 2-part, 2 handle 38.00
    #324, Martha blank, 3-part 68.00
    #3400/90, 2-part, 6" d, handle 35.00
    #3500, 3-part, handle 70.00
Salad Plate, 7" d, blown, #131 ....150.00
Shaker, #3400, handle 27.50
Sherbet, #3625, tall 22.00
Sherry, #7966 ....85.00
Sherry Decanter, #1321 ....400.00
Tumbler, #3625, ftd, 6-1/2" h, 10 oz 36.00
Wine
    #3600 ....42.00
    #3625 ....48.00

CAMBRIDGE Introduces

—The 3011 Figured Stem Line

as above.   This comes in various color combinations with foot in crystal.

Patent has been applied for on this outstanding and beautiful line.

Tell our advertisers you saw it in THE CROCKERY AND GLASS JOURNAL

Ad, Crockery and Glass Journal, September 1931, showing the #3011 Figure Line.

Cleo. Introduced in 1930. Made in amber, blue, crystal, green, pink and yellow.

Basket, 2 handles, 7", light blue................................40.00
Berry Bowl, crystal...55.00
Bon Bon, 2 handles, crystal.................................60.00
Bowl, 10" d, w/handles, pink...............................110.00
Candlesticks, pr, #627, 4" h, pink........................95.00
Celery, crystal...95.00
Cereal Bowl, crystal..85.00
Cocktail, #3077, pink...75.00
Console Bowl, 12" d, Decagon, pink.....................95.00
Creamer and Sugar, lightning bolt......................110.00
Cup, pink..30.00
Cup and Saucer, crystal......................................42.00
Fruit Bowl, ftd, large, crystal..............................100.00
Goblet, #3077, pink...65.00
Gravy and Liner, double, #917, pink....................350.00
Iced Tea Tumbler, flat, pink.................................95.00
Ice Pail, #851, yellow...170.00
Pitcher, crystal, no lid..500.00
Plate, dinner, blue, Decagon..............................100.00
Powder Box, cov...500.00
Seafood Icer, liner, underplate, green, gold trim........125.00
Sherbet, #3077, pink, low....................................38.00
Tumbler, flat, pink...42.00
Vegetable Bowl, 9-1/2" l
    Crystal..195.00
    Pink..130.00

Decagon made 1930s-40s. Made in amber, black, moonlight blue, green, pink, red, and Ritz blue (cobalt blue).

Bouillon, ftd
    Moonlight blue..20.00
    Ritz blue..22.00
Bowl
    5-1/2" d, cupped, deep, green..........................55.00
    6" d, ftd, green...24.00
    6-3/4" d, flat rim, green....................................24.00
    8-1/2" d, #971, handle
        Amber..37.50
        Pink..45.00
    12" d, flat, moonlight blue.................................75.00
    13" d, #754, green...110.00
Candelabra, #638, 3-lite, black............................72.50
Candlesticks, pr
    #627, 4" h, black..55.00
    #646, 5" h, moonlight blue................................45.00
Candy, cov, #864, moonlight blue........................120.00
Celery, green..37.50
Champagne, saucer, 5-1/2", #3077, Ritz blue.........20.00
Cheese and Cracker, moonlight blue.....................65.00
Club Plate, 10" d, pink..45.00
    Cocktail, 4-1/2" h, #3077
    Moonlight blue..25.00
    Ritz blue..15.00
Creamer, #867
    Green..25.00
    Moonlight blue..32.50
    Ritz blue..25.00
Creamer and Sugar, flat bottom
    Moonlight blue..35.00
    Ritz blue..18.00
Cream Soup, orig liner
    Green..35.00
    Moonlight blue..30.00
    Pink..32.50
Cruet, #193, 6 oz, moonlight blue........................195.00

Cup and Saucer
    Moonlight blue..14.00
    Pink..7.00
Fruit Bowl, 5-1/2" d, pink......................................5.50
Goblet, #3077, 9 oz
    Amber..20.00
    Amethyst..35.00
    Moonlight blue..25.00
    Ritz blue..35.00
Guest Set, #488, 22 oz jug, lid, tray, and tumbler, pink...160.00
Ice Bucket
    Amber..40.00
    Pink..85.00
Juice Tumbler, 5 oz, ftd, moonlight blue.................25.00
Mayonnaise, ftd, handle, ladle, moonlight blue.......75.00
Muffin Tray, 11-1/2", moonlight blue.....................35.00
Nut, ftd, 2-1/2", green...30.00
Oil Bottle, stopper, #197, 6 oz, pink.....................75.00
Oil & Vinegar Tray, #619, handle, pink..................40.00
Pickle Tray, #1082, 9"
    Amber..22.50
    Green..35.00
Pitcher, #937, 68 oz, ice lip, pink.........................95.00
Plate
    6" d, pink...10.00
    8" d, moonlight blue..15.00
    8" d, ftd, pink...15.00
    8-1/2" d, amber..8.00
    8-1/2" d, green...18.50
    9" d, moonlight blue..60.00
Platter, 12-1/2" l, oval, moonlight blue..................75.00
Relish, #1067, 2-part, 9"
    Amber..22.50
    Green..35.00
Salad Dressing Bottle
    #1261, ftd, amber...120.00
    #1263, amber...110.00
Salt and Pepper Shakers, pr, moonlight blue..........85.00
Salt Shaker, Ritz blue..40.00
Sandwich Tray, amber...30.00
Server, center handle
    Green..27.50
    Moonlight blue..45.00
    Pink..40.00
Sherbet
    #3077, amber, low..12.00
    #3077, moonlight blue, low...............................20.00
    #3077, pink, low...18.00
    #3120, moonlight blue, tall...............................16.00
Shrimp Cocktail, liner, #968, amber......................25.00
Soup Bowl, #808, flat rim
    Green..75.00
    Moonlight blue..80.00
Sugar Bowl, flat, pink..7.00
Sugar Pail, #1169, pink..65.00
Sugar Shaker, #813, pink...................................165.00
Syrup, cov, #175, pink..125.00
Tray, 11-1/2" d, handle, amber.............................30.00
Tumbler, ftd
    3-1/2" h, amber..10.00
    3 oz, ftd, Ritz blue..30.00
    5 oz, moonlight blue..10.00
    8 oz, ftd, moonlight blue..................................12.00
    12 oz, ftd, moonlight blue................................20.00
Wine, #3077
    Moonlight blue..35.00

Pink..18.00
Ritz blue..40.00

Diane 1934-1950s etching. Made on amber, blue, Crown Tuscan, crystal, crystal with gold encrusted dec, emerald green, Heatherbloom, some pink, some red, and yellow.

Bobeches, pr, crystal......................................100.00
Bon Bon, crystal, 8-1/2"...................................25.00
Bon Bon Plate, #3900/131, 8" d, 2 handles, crystal......48.00
Bowl
    12" d, #3400, crystal, gold encrusted.......110.00
    12" d, #3400/4, red, wear to gold.........350.00
    12" d, #3900/62, 3 ftd, crystal..............60.00
Candlesticks, pr, #627, crystal.........................85.00
Candy Dish, cov, #3500/57, 3-part, crystal.........85.00
Cigar Holder, ashtray foot, #1337, crystal, gold
    encrusted...350.00
Claret, #3122, amber.......................................50.00
Cocktail, #3122, crystal, 3 oz...........................35.00
Cocktail Shaker, glass lid, crystal..................150.00
Console Bowl, #3400 line, center ftd, pink.......800.00
Cordial, #1066, crystal....................................95.00
Cordial Pitcher, #3400/119, 12 oz, tilt, crystal........250.00
Corn Dish, crystal..40.00
Demitasse Cup and Saucer, crystal................145.00
Goblet, crystal...25.00
Iced Tea Tumbler, 15 oz, 5-1/2", flat, crystal........60.00
Jug, ball, crystal...225.00
Juice Tumbler
    Amber, #3122.................................45.00
    Crystal, ftd.......................................15.00
Marmalade, cov, #147, crystal.......................195.00
Pitcher, Doulton, crystal................................500.00
Plate, #3400, crystal
    6" d, 2 handles...............................32.50
    8" d...16.50
    10-1/2" d..135.00
Plate, #3900, 8" d, crystal..............................16.50
Relish
    #393, 5-part, crystal........................60.00
    #862, 4-part center handle, crystal........110.00
    #3400/91, 3-part, 8" d, ftd, pink........90.00
Salt and Pepper Shakers, pr, crystal...............95.00
Sandwich Server, center handle, crystal.........180.00
Sherbet, #3122, low
    Amber...32.00
    Crystal..24.00
Sherry, #7966, 2 oz, crystal...........................75.00
Tumbler, crystal
    #3122, 10 oz, flat............................65.00
    #3900/118, 5 oz..............................75.00
Vase, 12" h, keyhole, crystal.........................110.00
Wine, 2-1/2 oz, crystal...................................30.00

Elaine Line #1402. Made 1934-1950s. Made only in crystal.
Ball Jug, #3400..275.00
Bitters Bottle, loose tube.............................275.00
Bud Vase
    6" h...55.00
    10" h...55.00
Candlesticks, pr
    #1338, 3-lite..................................165.00
    #3500/94, 2-lite, ram's head............350.00
    #3500/154, 3-lite...........................350.00
Candy, cov...150.00
Claret, #3121...40.00
Cocktail, #3500..42.50

Compote
    #3500/36, 6"...................................60.00
    #300/37, tall, 2 handle....................175.00
Corn Dish...75.00
Creamer and Sugar, #1402/33.......................65.00
Crescent Salad..195.00
Goblet, water
    #3121...40.00
    #3500, short bowl...........................55.00
Iced Tea Tumbler, ftd, #3500.........................40.00
Ice Pail, #1402/52, Tally-Ho, chrome handle, tons......145.00
Icer and liner..80.00
Jug, #3400/38, 80 oz....................................245.00
Juice Tumbler, ftd
    #3035..32.50
    #3121..35.00
Mayonnaise Bowl, 6" d, ftd, handle, #3500/59......80.00
Nappy, 5" d, handle......................................50.00
Nut, #3400/71, 4 ftd......................................60.00
Oil Bottle, #3400/69, 6 oz............................110.00
Pitcher, #3400/141.......................................275.00
Plate
    6-1/2" d...7.50
    8" d...18.00
    10-1/2" d..75.00
    14" d, #3900/166...........................100.00
Relish
    #1402/91, 3-part, 8" l.....................70.00
    #3400/67, 5-part, 12" l....................75.00
    #3500/61, 3-part.............................45.00
    #3500/67, 6 pc inserts....................185.00
    #3500/71, 3-part, center handle........125.00
Salt and Pepper Shakers, pr, #3900/17, ftd......70.00
Sherbet, #3121, tall......................................24.00
Tumbler, #3121, 10 oz..................................25.00
Wine, #3500...60.00
Wine Bottle, stopper...................................1,600.00

Farber Brothers
Cocktail, 6" h, chrome base
    Amber...22.00
    Amethyst...25.00
Cocktail Set, 2 amber, 2 green, 2 smoke, 6 pc set......60.00
Compote
    5-1/2" h, 5-1/4" d, royal blue insert......75.00
    7-1/2" h, Krome Kraft base, amethyst......45.00
    7-1/2" h, Krome Kraft base, cobalt blue......50.00
    7-1/2" h, Krome Kraft base, green......45.00
    7-1/2" h, Lotus, Krome Kraft base, frosted crystal....45.00
Cordial, chrome base
    Amber...20.00
    Amethyst...24.00
Cordial Decanter, #3400/119, forest green......75.00
Cordial Set, 7 pc, chrome plate......................55.00
Decanter
    #113-3, amethyst.............................85.00
    #3400, amethyst, 24 oz....................75.00
Jug, ball, amber, 4 oz....................................25.00
Marmalade, cov, Krome Kraft lid and base
    Amber...35.00
    Amethyst...35.00
Mustard, cov, cobalt blue...............................50.00
Oil and Vinegar Set, 3 oz, amethyst, #5453......40.00
Relish, #3500
    2-part, Gadroon, chrome base, amber......20.00
    2-part, Gadroon, chrome base, crystal......30.00
    2-part, Gadroon, chrome base, green......45.00
    3-part, chrome base, green.................50.00

4-part, 7-1/4" d, chrome base, amethyst...............60.00
4-part, 7-1/4" d, chrome base, crystal....................40.00
4-part, 7-1/4" d, chrome base, green.....................50.00
Salt and Pepper Shakers, pr
    Amber, ball shaped, Krome Kraft base...................35.00
    Amethyst..40.00
Sugar Bowl, cov, cobalt blue, Krome Kraft lid and base ... 55.00
Tumbler, #3400, cobalt blue, 6 oz, 3-1/2" h...................7.50
Wine, amethyst, Duchess Filigree chrome base...........20.00

Mt. Vernon Tableware line. Made late 1920s-40s. Made in amber, Carmen, crystal, emerald green, Heatherbloom, light green, Royal blue, and violet.
Candlesticks, pr, dolphin
    Green..225.00
    Milk Glass..350.00
Cocktail, crystal...9.00
Comport, 6-1/2", Heatherbloom 85.00
Cup, crystal...6.00
Decanter, 40 oz, milk glass.....................................150.00
Mug, cobalt blue, handle...60.00
Pitcher, forest green..300.00
Relish, crystal, 5-part..35.00
Sherbet, low, crystal...7.00
Tumbler, 9 oz, barrel, crystal 15.00

Nude, 3011 Line
Ashtray, moonlight blue 800.00
Brandy
    Crystal 200.00
    Pistachio...145.00
Champagne
    Carmen 175.00
    Pink..650.00
Cigarette Holder
    Crystal, ashtray foot.......................................700.00
    Crystal, frosted 850.00
Claret, Carmen...175.00
Cocktail, crystal...200.00
Compote
    Shell...295.00
    Short, Carmen 660.00
    Tall, Carmen 730.00
    Tall, Moonstone 430.00
    Tall, Pistachio 1,250.00
Cordial, crystal...680.00
Goblet, banquet
    Carmen 700.00
    Ritz Blue 650.00
Goblet, table
    Carmen 250.00
    Smoke, crackle 760.00
Ivy Ball, crystal..500.00
Mint Dish, crystal...760.00
Sauterne, topaz...375.00
Seashell, tall, emerald green....................................600.00
Wine
    Amber...325.00
    Amethyst...300.00

Portia Etching made from 1932 to early 1950s. Made in amber, crystal, crystal with gold encrusted dec, green, Heatherbloom, and yellow. Prices shown are for crystal, (except where noted,) colors would be somewhat higher.
Ashtray, 14" d, 3500/97, sq 45.00
Bowl, #3400/1240, oval, ftd......................................110.00
Candle Bobeches, pr 125.00
Celery Tray, #1402/94, 12" l 70.00
Cocktail
    #3121...32.50

#3130...24.00
Cocktail Icer, 2 pc 75.00
Cocktail Shaker, #3400/175 ....165.00
Cordial
    #1355...125.00
    #3121...32.50
Corn Dish, crystal...50.00
Cornucopia, double candlesticks, pr 230.00
Cranberry Dish, #3400/49, 3-1/2" d 48.00
Cup, #3400...35.00
Cup and Saucer
    #3400...42.50
    #3900/17...38.00
Decanter
    #1321, 28 oz...350.00
    #3400/113...300.00
Finger Bowl, 5" d..55.00
Goblet, #1066...35.00
Ice Bucket..225.00
Jug, ball, gold trim..250.00
Martini Pitcher, orig plunger, #1408, 60 oz 1,500.00
Oil and Vinegar Bottle...375.00
Oyster Cocktail, #3109..40.00
Parfait, #3121..95.00
Pitcher, ball, yellow, gold etched 180.00
Plate
    #3400, 8" d..17.50
    #3500, 6"...14.50
Relish
    #1402/91, 3-part, 8" d round, Tally Ho 58.00
    #3400/200, 3-part..55.00
    #3500/65, 4-part, 12" d...................................55.00
    #3900/124, 2-part, 7".....................................48.00
Seafood, icer and liner..80.00
Sherbet, #3121...25.00
Sherry, #796, 2 oz
    Crystal 50.00
    Crystal, gold encrusted 60.00
Tankard Pitcher...500.00
Tumbler, #3400/38, 12 oz 45.00
Vase, small, gold etched..40.00
Wine, #3121 ....50.00

Rose Point Etching made from 1936 to 1953. Made on crystal, some pieces have gold trim, some have sterling silver trim, others are gold encrusted. A few examples are known on a Crown Tuscan base. Prices listed are for crystal, unless otherwise noted.
Ashtray, 5 pc set 385.00
Basket, #3500/55
    Square...65.00
    Square, set in sterling silver sgd base 295.00
Berry Bowl...125.00
Bobeches...75.00
Bon Bon
    #3400/201...195.00
    #3400/202, ftd..195.00
    #3400/204...195.00
Bowl
    #993, 12-1/2" d...155.00
    #1359, 10" d, ruffled......................................165.00
    #1359, 10-1/2" d..135.00
    #1398, 13" d...275.00
    #3400/4, 12" d, ftd, crystal..............................130.00
    #3400/48, 11" d, 4 ftd, fancy edge 350.00
    #3400/1185, 10" d, 2 handles...........................140.00

#3500/21, 12-1/2" d, ftd, handle, oval 400.00
#3900, 11" d, ftd, handle 125.00
Brandy, #3121, low, repaired..............................75.00
Bud Vase
#274, 10" h, gold encrusted 165.00
#6004, 6" h...95.00
#6004, 6" h, gold encrusted 155.00
Butter Dish, cov, #3900/52, quarter pound................750.00
Café Parfait, #3121, 5 oz...............................125.00
Cake Stand, 3400/35..48.00
Canapé Set, #693/3000, 2 pc, sterling rim 500.00
Candelabra, pr
#496, 2 light, with hurricane globes 800.00
#1268, with bobeches 425.00
Candlestick
#647, keyhole, pr.....................................160.00
#1338, pr..230.00
#3121 with bobeches, single 250.00
#3400/646, 1-lite, 5", pr..............................130.00
#3400/647, 2-lite, pr..................................190.00
#3500, ram's head, pr 300.00
#3500/74, ram's head, pr 280.00
#3900, 2-lite, pr 190.00
#3900/67, 6", pr......................................185.00
Candy Dish, cov
#3500...230.00
#3500/57, 3-part, gold trim..............................135.00
Celery Tray, #3900/120.....................................65.00
Champagne
#3121, tall..32.50
#3500...40.00
Cheese Comport, #3400, gold trim.........................50.00
Cigarette Holder
#1066, oval, ashtray foot 500.00
#1337...295.00
Cocktail, #3121, 6" h, 3 oz................................35.00
Cocktail Icer, #968, 4-1/2" h, 2 pc........................80.00
Cocktail Shaker, crystal..................................275.00
Comport
#3500, 6"..60.00
#3900/136, 5-1/2" 125.00
Console Bowl
#3400/4, flared, gold encrusted 165.00
#3400/97, oval 225.00
Console Set, 12" d #3400/12 bowl, pr of #3400/647 candle-
sticks, Crown Tuscan, gold dec............................700.00
Cordial
#3121...80.00
#7966...175.00
Cordial Decanter, #1320, 40 oz...........................950.00
Corn Relish, #447..95.00
Cracker Plate, #3400/6, 11-1/2" d, 2 handle 75.00
Creamer and Sugar
#3500/14...70.00
#3900...50.00
Cruet, stopper, 6 oz 125.00
French Salad Dressing Bottle, #1263 ....700.00
Goblet, #3121, 10 oz.......................................45.00
Hurricane, Martha base, gold encrusted, pr..............900.00
Ice Bucket, #3400/851, gold encrusted....................300.00
Ice Tea Tumbler
#3121...50.00
#3500...50.00
Lamp, Crown Tuscan 1,275.00
Jug, ball
#3400...400.00

#3900/115, 76 oz...450.00
#3900/118, 32 oz...600.00
Juice Tumbler, #3121, 5 oz.................................42.50
Lazy Susan...400.00
Marmalade, #157, 7 oz, sterling lid......................230.00
Martini Pitcher, crystal, small...........................700.00
Mayonnaise, #3900/19, ftd, spoon.........................100.00
Mustard, #151, 3 oz, sterling lid........................160.00
Oyster Cocktail, #3121, 4-1/2" h, 4 oz.....................45.00
Parfait
#3121...120.00
#3500...125.00
Pickle, #3900/123, ftd, 7".................................65.00
Pitcher
#3400/100..450.00
#3400/141, Doulton 500.00
Plate
#3400, 5" d, handle 50.00
#3400, 6" d...20.00
#3400, 7" d...22.50
#3400, 8-1/2" d..25.00
#3400, 10-1/2" d.......................................170.00
#3500, 8-1/2" d..25.00
#3500/39, 12" d, ftd....................................190.00
#3900, 8" d...25.00
#3900/131, 8" d, 2 handles, ftd 95.00
Relish
#394, 2-part, 10" l....................................95.00
#394, 5-part...170.00
#3400/90, 2-part, 6" d, handle...........................55.00
#3500/60, 2-part, 5-1/2" l..............................30.00
#3500/62, 4-part, 2 handle..............................125.00
#3500/64, 10" l.......................................130.00
#3500/67, 6-part, 12" l, gold encrusted..................600.00
#3500/68, 2-part, 5-1/2"...............................60.00
#3500/71, 3-part, center handle, gold encrusted 245.00
#3500/87, 4-part, 10" d, handle 100.00
#3500/97, 14" l, oval..................................125.00
#3500/152, 4-part, 11" l, 2 handle 200.00
#14032, 3-part, 8" d, handle.............................190.00
Salad Dressing Bowl, #1402/133, twin......................95.00
Salt and Pepper Shakers, pr
#1177, worn chrome tops, #837 center handle tray.... 85.00
#1468, egg shape 195.00
#3400/76, Gloria, glass stops, etched bases.........165.00
#3400/77, plastic tops.................................70.00
Server, #3400/10, center handle..........................155.00
Sherbet, crystal, 7 oz....................................24.00
Sherry Decanter, #1321, 28 oz............................650.00
Shrimp Cocktail, liner, #3900.............................90.00
Shot Glass, #3400/92, 2 oz................................140.00
Torte Plate
13" d, 3 ftd...95.00
14" d, ftd, gold encrusted..............................145.00
14-1/2" d, #3900/167 ....160.00
Tray, #3400/59, 9" 110.00
Tumbler
#3121, 2-1/2 oz, ftd....................................85.00
#3121, 9 oz...40.00
#3121, 10 oz, ftd......................................50.00
#3121, 12 oz, ftd......................................35.00
#3400/38, 5 oz..135.00
#3400/38, 12 oz, mushroom.............................95.00
#3400/92, 2-1/2 oz.....................................175.00
#3500...55.00
Urn, cov, small 850.00

Vase

    #278, Crown Tuscan, gold encrusted, 11" h..........475.00
    #279, 13"...500.00
    #797, flip..300.00
    #1237, key, 10"...135.00
    #1309, 5"...200.00
    #1430, 8"...450.00
    #1528, 10 oz..375.00
    #3400/103, Crown Tuscan, gold encrusted,
        6-1/2" h..350.00
    #6004, 12"...150.00
    8" h, flip..250.00

Wine

    #3121..75.00
    #3500, 2-1/2 oz, short...125.00

Tally Ho Tableware pattern made in amber, amethyst, cobalt blue, crystal, crystal with gold trim, forest green, and Carmen red.

Bowl, 12-1/8", flat rim, Carmen red 75.00
Champagne, 6-1/2", #1402, amethyst.........................30.00
Cheese and Cracker, gold trim...................................60.00
Claret, 4-1/2 oz, red 45.00
Cocktail, cobalt blue 35.00
Cocktail Shaker, cobalt blue 40.00
Comport, #1402/100, 5" h, forest green, crystal stem and
    foot..60.00
Cordial, Carmen red, thick...65.00
Cup and Saucer, cobalt blue..55.00
Decanter Set, decanter, stopper, 6 handled 2-1/2 oz tumblers,
    amethyst...185.00

Goblet

    Luncheon, Carmen red 30.00
    Water, 10 oz, Carmen red 35.00

Ice Bucket, cobalt blue 175.00

Pitcher

    Amethyst, 88 oz...200.00
    Crystal, metal spout and lid.................................105.00

Plate, 9", red 20.00
Platter, 14" l, handle, cobalt blue 75.00
Punch Bowl Set, bowl and 8 mugs, Carmen red 800.00
Punch Cup, crystal, red handle 12.00
Relish, 3-part, 8-1/4" l, handle, cobalt blue..................25.00
Sugar, cobalt blue...55.00
Tankard, amber...95.00

Tumbler

    9 oz, flat, moonlight blue 18.00
    10 oz, flat, Carmen red..20.00

Wildflower Etching made 1940s to 1950s. Made mainly on crystal, some with gold trim, some gold encrusted, some other color pieces made. Prices listed below crystal, unless noted otherwise.

Ball Jug, #3400 ....300.00
Basket, 6" h, 2 handles, sq, #3500/55........................55.00
Bon Bon, 5-1/2" d, 2 handles, #3400/1179 ....40.00

Bowl

    10" d, 2 handles, #3400/1185.............................95.00
    10" d, crystal, gold krystol, matching 12-1/2" d plate,
        sgd..375.00
    11" d 85.00

Bud Vase, 10" h, pink...200.00
Butter, cov, #3400/52...200.00

Candlestick

    #638, 3-lite..80.00
    #646, 1-lite, pr 75.00
    #3900/72, 2-lite, pr..145.00
    #3900/72, 2-lite, pr, gold encrusted....................165.00

Candy Dish, cov

    #3400, 3-part, 8" d..95.00
    #3400/9, 4 ftd..180.00
    #3500/57, 3-part, 8" d...150.00

Celery and Relish

    #3400/67, 5-part, 12" l...55.00
    #3500/64, 3-part, 10" l, 2 handles, gold trim 75.00

Celery Service, #397...60.00

Champagne, #3121, 6-1/2" h, 6 oz

    Crystal..40.00
    Gold trim..50.00

Cheese and Cracker Set, gold encrusted 95.00
Claret, 4-1/2 oz...42.00
Cocktail, #3121, 6" h...32.00

Comport

    #3400/6..37.50
    #3500/148, 6"...60.00

Cordial, #3121, 5-1/4" h, 1 oz.....................................65.00
Dresser Compact, pink..250.00
Finger Bowl...85.00
Goblet, #3121, 8-1/4" h...48.00
Hurricane Lamps, #1604...500.00
Iced Tea Tumbler, #3121, ftd, 12 oz............................45.00
Juice Tumbler, #3121, ftd 35.00

Mayonnaise, #3900/129, 3 pc

    Crystal..140.00
    Pink..165.00

Pickle, 9"..48.00
Pitcher, #3900/117, 20 oz 450.00

Plate

    #3400/35, 11" d, 2 handles, gold trim 120.00
    #3400/1181, 6" d, 2 handles................................35.00
    #3400/1186, 12-1/2" d, 2 handles, gold trim 100.00
    #3900/166, 14-1/4" d, gold trim 130.00

Oyster Cocktail...38.00

Relish

    3-part, 6-1/2" d, gold rim 60.00
    5-part, 10" l..95.00

Salt Shaker, #3400, ftd...30.00
Sherbet, #3121, gold trim..20.00
Sweet Pea Vase, 3-3/4" h, green.................................300.00
Torte Plate, #3900/65, 14" d 85.00
Tumbler, #3121, 10 oz...45.00

Vase

    10" h, keyhole 65.00
    12" h, flip..800.00

Wine, #3121, 3-1/2" h..55.00

CAMEO GLASS

History: Cameo glass is a form of cased glass. A shell of glass was prepared; then one or more layers of glass of a different color(s) was faced to the first. A design was then cut through the outer layer(s) leaving the inner layer(s) exposed.

1921

This type of art glass originated in Alexandria, Egypt between 100 and 200 A.D. The oldest and most famous example of cameo glass is the Barberini or Portland vase, found near Rome in 1582. It contained the ashes of Emperor Alexander Serverus, who was assassinated in 235 A.D.

Emile Gallé is probably one of the best-known cameo glass artists. He established a factory at Nancy, France, in 1884. Although much of the glass bears his signature, he was primarily the designer. Assistants did the actual work on many pieces, even signing Gallé's name. Glass made after his death in 1904 has a star before the name Gallé. Other makers of French cameo glass include D'Argental, Daum Nancy, LeGras, and Delatte. The French cameo glassmakers produced some of the most beautiful examples found in today's antique glass marketplace.

English cameo pieces do not have as many layers of glass (colors) and cuttings as do French pieces. The outer layer is usually white, and cuttings are very fine and delicate. Most pieces are not signed. The best-known makers are Thomas Webb & Son and Stevens and Williams.

Marks: A star before the name Gallé on a piece by that company indicates that it was made after Gallé's death in 1904.

References: Victor Arwas, *Glass Art Nouveau to Art Deco*, Rizzoli International Publications, 1977; Alastair Duncan and George DeBartha, *Glass by Gallé*, Harry N. Abrams, 1984; Ray and Lee Grover, *English Cameo Glass*, Crown Publishers, 1980; Tim Newark, *Emile Galle,* The Apple Press, 1989; Albert C. Revi, *Nineteenth Century Glass*, reprint, Schiffer Publishing, 1981; John A. Shuman, III, *Collector's Encyclopedia of American Art Glass*, Collector Books, 1988, 1994 value update; Wolf Ueker, *Art Nouveau and Art Deco Lamps and Candlesticks,* Abbeville Press, 1986; Kenneth Wilson, *American Glass 1760-1930: The Toledo Museum of Art, Volume I, Volume II,* Hudson Hills Press and The Toledo Museum of Art, 1994.

Additional Listings: See Daum Nancy, and Galle, as well are other makers.

American

Gillander American Glass Co., attributed to
    Lamp Shade, 4-1/2" h, 3-7/8" fitter ring, crimped rim, flared cased body, minor rim chips
        Blue, white blackberry design 250.00

Webb, vase, blue ground, white dec, etched "Thomas Webb & Sons" in banner, 6" h, $3,200.

    Pink, three birds among blossoms 250.00
Vase, 4" h, overlaid in white, cameo etched morning glory blossoms, buds, and leafy vines, shaded blue cased to white oval body 825.00
Harrach, vase, 8" h, 4" d, bright white carved daffodils, leaves, and stems, frosted and green ground 950.00
Honesdale Glass, vase, 12" h, green etched to clear, gold dec trim 1,295.00
Mount Washington
    Bowl, 8" d, 4" h, sq, ruffled edge, two winged Griffins holding up scroll and spray of flowers design, blue over white ground 1,475.00
    Lamp
        17" h, 10" d shade, fluid font and shade composed of opal white opaque glass overlaid in bright rose pink, acid etched butterflies, ribbons, and bouquets centering cameo portrait medallions in classical manner, mounted on silverplated metal fittings, imp "Pairpoint Mfg. Co 3013," electrified 3,105.00
        21" h, 10" d shade, brilliant deep yellow over white, base figural woman with basket of flowers, matching floral design on shade, fancy brass base and font, orig chimney 8,500.00
        24" h, deep rose over white, portrait of woman dec on shade and base, silver-plated fittings 7,500.00

English

Florentine Art, cruet, 6-1/2" h, ruby-red body, textured white enamel meadowland scene, Meadowlark on tall plant stalk, smaller scene on reverse, white rim, trefoil spout, clear frosted handle, teardrop shaped stopper, pontil mark sgd "59" 750.00
Stevens and Williams
    Bowl, 6-1/4" d, 4" h, ftd, cased yellow ground, carved seaweed, applied glass prunt.....................................250.00
    Decanter, 15-1/2" h, citron yellow and colorless ground, sapphire blue overlay, wheel cut and engraved cactus rose blossoms on spiked leaf-forms, matching teardrop stopper 1,265.00
    Lamp, 8" h, yellow ground, red fuchsias and leaves, sgd 2,750.00
    Vase
        4-1/4" h, flared du Barry rose oval, overlaid in white, etched wild geranium plant and grasses, linear borders 850.00
        4-1/4" h, 3-1/4" w, pale blue ground, dainty carved leaves, single large butterfly, band of white beaded cutting at throat, base fully sgd "Stevens & Williams Art Glass, Stourbridge" 1,250.00
        4-1/2" h, broad bright blue oval, overlaid in opaque white glass, cameo etched and cut clusters of cherries on leafy boughs, circular mark on base "Stevens & Williams Art Glass Stourbridge" 1,265.00
        6-1/4" h, Rose du Barry, lush pink rose oval body, etched with white six-petaled blossoms and buds, intricate leaves, butterfly at reverse, linear border.......1,610.00
        9" h, double bulbed gourd shape, reverse colored, du Barry rose over white cased to colorless, cameo etched exotic pink blossoms, circular mark on base "Stevens & Williams Stourbridge"...................2,185.00
        9" h, flared elongated neck, bulbed body, dusky rose overlaid in white, etched overall in passion flowers motif, elaborate top and medial borders, tiny chip under base edge 2,000.00
Unknown Maker
    Cologne Bottle, 6" h, 4-1/4" w, ball shaped, matte yellow,

highly detailed white carved flowers, leaves, and fern font, monogrammed silver screw-on cap, some denting to top 900.00

Marmalade Jar, cov, 5-1/4" h, carved white flowers and leaves, medium blue ground, notch in lid for spoon 1,650.00

Perfume Bottle, 5-1/2" h, 4-3/4" h, citron yellow ground, white carving of flowers, leaves, vines, and buds, carved butterfly, three applied frosted feet, sterling repoussé cover..1,550.00

Plaque, 5-1/2" l, 3-1/2" w, citron yellow, five white carved carnation flowers, leaf...1,275.00

Scent Bottle, 2" h, 1-3/4" d, ball shaped, white cameo carved morning glories, clear frosted ground, chartreuse lining, orig collar and screw-on cap with English hallmarks 950.00

Sweetmeat Jar, cov, 3" h, 4-3/4" d, frosted deep cranberry ground, carved opaque white apple blossoms and leaves, silver plated top, rim, and handle 1,100.00

Vase
3-1/8" h, frosted yellow oval body cased to white, crimson red overlay, cameo etched and cut various plants and grasses below double border design 1,725.00

3-3/4" h, 3" h, carved fuchsia flowers and leaves, lime green triple carved cameo band........................650.00

4-1/8" h, bright sapphire blue ground, white layer, cameo etched single blossoming branch, notched border 850.00

5-1/4" h, cornflower blue oval body, etched white overlay in blossom motif, goldenrod on reverse, spiked border 850.00

7" h, 5" w, corset shape, cranberry, white overlay, carved sprays of sweet peas, leaves, branches, butterfly in flight 1,750.00

Webb
Bowl and Undertray, 5-1/8" d bowl, 6" d underplate, brilliant red layered in sapphire blue, overlaid in white, cameo etched floral design and butterflies, plate with central medallion, each pc stamped "Thomas Webb & Sons/Cameo" 1,380.00

Cologne Bottle
4-3/4" h, white over yellow sphere, intricately etched recumbent fuchsia with elaborate borders above and below, butterfly at center, mounted with silver rim, hinged ball cover, English hallmarks, tiny glass chip on butterfly..980.00

5" h, square blue body, four panels of white overlaid cameo carved and etched blossoms, silver ball cover, damage at two corners, small chips, some cover dents 490.00

5" h, square yellow body, four panels of white overlaid cameo carved and etched blossoms, screw-on silver cover, several chips to white dec, cov dents 520.00

5-1/2" h, brilliant red oval body, layered in white, cameo carved and etched blossoming leafy vines, stylized border, repeated on conical silver hallmarked screw top, base with semicircular mark "Thomas Webb & Sons" 1,500.00

Cup and Saucer, handleless, 2-3/4" h, 5" d, cranberry over crystal, prunous blossom carving, leaves, and branches, 10 blossoms on cup with large butterfly and 25 buds 550.00

Decanter, 9-1/2" h, bulbous, yellow bottle cased with white over bright red layer, cameo etched blossoming leafy vines, applied glass handle attached metal chain to decanter, silver rim, hinged floral motif cap, imp "sterling" and English hallmarks 3,000.00

Perfume Bottle
3-3/4" l, flattened teardrop shape, bright blue, etched forget-me-nots all around, two butterflies on shoulder,

one chip on surface flower, wear to gilt metal screw cap..435.00

5-1/2" l, 2-3/4" w, sq, citron yellow, white overlay, allover carved wild roses, leaves, and buds, orig silver spring-hinge cov 2,750.00

Posey Pot, 2" h, squatty bulbous form, crimson red ground, white morning glory vines, butterfly in flight 865.00

Scent Bottle, 4" l, flattened teardrop shape, sapphire blue, white ferns and grasses dec, butterfly at side, gilt metal hinged cover 920.00

Vase
3-1/4" h, double bulbed shape, bright crimson red body, white overlay, cameo etched passion flower motif, pendant leafy vine above and on reverse, late "Webb" on base..700.00

3-1/4" h, red oval body, layered in white, cameo etched wild geraniums, spike-leafed stems on reverse, dec borders 980.00

4-1/8" h, flared oval, crimson layered in white, cameo etched all around in stylized Asian influence foliate dec..1,050.00

4-1/4" h, flaring yellow baluster form, double linear borders framing naturalistic blossoming plant 425.00

4-1/2" h, bulbous pastel yellow body, white layer cameo etched as dahlia plant on front, maidenhair fern on back, linear borders 490.00

4-1/2" h, pale raison color oval body, layered in white cameo, leafy bough and delicate blossom clusters etched around shoulder, linear border above.................575.00

5" h, flared oval, bright yellow-green overlaid in white, cameo etched rosa rigosa blossom and bud, flying butterfly on back...500.00

5" h, tricolor, bright citron yellow-green oval body, layered in white over red, cameo etched intricate rose blossom, thorny branch, single butterfly on reverse, linear border 1,100.00

5-1/2" h, flared bulbous red oval body, layered white and cameo etched five detailed seashells, various seaweed clusters, base mkd "Thomas Webb & Sons/Cameo" 2,645.00

5-5/8" h, tricolor, baluster, frosted colorless cased to white int., layered in white over Webb red, cameo etched trumpet blossom and buds pendant from linear border 700.00

5-3/4" h, raised rim, bright red oval body, layered in white, six cameo cut trumpet blossoms on decumbent leafy vine, repeating feather border........................1,500.00

7" h, flared red oval body, white layer cameo etched rose blossoms, buds, leaves, and thorned branches, reverse with delicate blossoming bough, linear borders.. 1,840.00

7" h, simulated ivory bulbous body, cameo etched ivy above berries on leafy vines, motif enhanced by sepia coloration, semicircular mark on base "Thos. Webb & Sons" 815.00

7-1/4" h, gourd form, transparent green body, solid applied top stem as handle, three oval aperture openings cut into body, white layered and cameo etched fruit and leaf laden branches, unsgd, chipped, small annealing crack at stem end 3,250.00

7-1/2" h, 6-1/2" w, pillow, brilliant blue, white cameo wild rose dec, two large roses, 12 leaves, large butterfly in flight, full signature 2,750.00

8-3/4" h, lily, flared colorless ground, transparent red overlay, acid etched four stylized repeating blossoms, Webb cartouche at lower edge 1,100.00

9" h, Old Ivory, double gourd body, scenes with warriors on horseback, half-man half-animal figures, bird-serpents, kings and queen, all in elaborate frames, floral backgrounds, orig circular mark on base "Thomas Webb & Sons Cameo," George Woodall design 23,000.00

9-3/4" h, tricolor, broad citron yellow oval body, overlaid in bright Webb red and opal white, cameo etched and carved blossoms on leafy stems, wild grasses at sides, stepped and angular borders, base circular mark "Thos. Webb & Sons. Cameo" 4,600.00

10" h, Old Ivory, six floral designed cartouches set among bamboo leaves and stalks, applied scale covered handles at each side, intricate borders above and below, semicircular mark "Thomas Webb & Sons," design attributed to George Woodall 3,000.00

French

Arsall

Vase

5" h, flared, pink mottled yellow overlaid ground, green layer etched as decumbent blossoms, buds, and leafy stems, sgd "Arsall" in design 325.00

16-1/4" h, flared rim, large frosted pink-white oval body, layered in orange and sienna, etched realistic iris blossoms, spiked leaves, side sgd "Arsall" 1,575.00

Burgun and Schverer

Vase

7-1/4" h, urn form, three handled, translucent fiery amber etched and painted body, medallion cartouches of regional ethnic costumed people, elaborate B & S mark on base 6,900.00

7-3/4" h, frosted gray oval shaded to purple-amethyst, overlaid in purple-amethyst, etched and carved blossoming leafy plants, some martele background, fitted with dec silvered metal foot, glass base inscribed with BS & Co. thistle and cross mark, two side chips at lower side 345.00

9-1/4" h, translucent yellow-green oval body, internally swirled in burgundy and green, overlaid in amethyst and green, etched and carved iris blossoms and leaves, stars, and martele in background, base mkd with BS & Co elaborate thistle and cross mark 7,760.00

Charder

Vase

8-1/4" h, ftd bulbous shape, blue cameo foliate design, cameo sgd "Charder" 500.00

15" h, gourd shape, white ground, orange cameo stylized flowers, cameo sgd "Charder" 800.00

Chouvenin, vase, satin ground, brown overlay cut as wind blown trees, enameled details, yellow highlights, cameo sgd "Chevenin" 550.00

Crystallerie D'Art, vase, 13" h, creamy opal white oval, bright forest green over pastel green layers, etched stylized Art Deco blossoms and leaves, sgd and mkd on base "0. 31 of 100 exemplaries" 880.00

D'Argental

Atomizer, 4" h, cylindrical amber perfume bottle, green and brown overlay, etched landscape of leafy trees, wild geese in flight, sgd "D'Argental" on side, gilt metal fittings mkd "Le Parisien Made in France," "BTE, S.G.D.G." 825.00

Box, cov, 6-7/8" d, compressed spherical form, yellow ground, mauve overlay, cameo carved roses, lid, with central knob, sgd in cameo 1,200.00

Center Bowl, 8-3/4" d, double conical contour, wide everted mouth, frosted ground, cameo cut orchid blossoms and leaves, sgd in cameo "D'Argental" with cross de Lorraine, c1900 .... 2,400.00

D'Argental, vase, riverscape scene viewed through leafy trees, 13" h, $1,540. Photo courtesy of Jackson's Auctioneers & Appraisers.

Perfume Bottle, 5-1/4" h, lime green ground, light and dark burgundy overlay, cameo carved flowers, buds, and leaves, carved signature, gold washed metal top sgd "Le Parisien" 1,200.00

Vase

5" h, frosted oval, mauve and purple-black overlay, etched spring snowdrops, blossoms, and buds, silver rim wrap, side sgd "D'Argental (cross)" 520.00

6-3/4" h, frosted pastel green oval body, overlaid in gray-black, etched blossoms, pods, and leafy poppy plants, side sgd "D'Argental (cross)" 435.00

9-3/4" h, fiery amber oval body, layered in maroon and brown, cameo etched pendant blossoming trumpet vine, lower side sgd "D'Argental," some int. bubbles in glass 1,035.00

10" h, fiery opalescent amber oval body, overlaid in burgundy-red and maroon, etched overall in expansive landscape with distant buildings and castle beyond, lower edge sgd "D'Argental" 1,150.00

11-1/2" h, opal white oval body, overlaid in green and gray, etched shaded levels of riverside scene, tall leafy foreground trees, sgd "D'Argental" in cameo in lower scene 1,725.00

13-3/4" h, opalescent yellow and maroon ground, lake and village showing through birch lined marsh, slight iridescence, cameo sgd "D. Argental" 1,600.00

Daum Nancy

Basket, 6" h, 6-1/2" d, green shaded to clear textured ground, sprays of enamel leaf, branch, and berry design, handle with matching cut cameo pattern, sgd "Daum Nancy" with cross of Lorraine, possible internal fracture in bowl 350.00

Bowl

2-1/2" h, mottled brilliant purple and yellow ground, ext. carved cameo dec of deep blue and bright red grape leaves and vines, int. with bunch of purple grapes, sgd 1,600.00

4-3/4" d, deep blue grape pods, autumn color leaves and vines, mottled yellow, pink, and amethyst ground, quad fold trim, cameo sgd 900.00

Box, cov

3-1/2" d, 2-3/4" h, brilliant yellow and clear mottled ground, green, yellow, and red floral and leaf dec, sgd..1,550.00

4-3/4" d, 2-3/4" h, green grapes and leaves, tan ground 500.00

Bud Vase, 10" h, flared elongated neck, bulbed yellow body layered in green, mottled bright pink, etched stylized leafy design, pedestal foot sgd "Daum (cross) Nancy" 1,150.00

Cologne Bottle

4" h, deeply carved red poppies and green leaves, pink ground, vertical lines, gold rim and stopper with dragonflies, sgd, cross mark 5,000.00

7-1/2" h, amethyst ground, iris floral cutting, "Parfum de Vertus," gilt highlights, base sgd "Daum Nancy".... 1,450.00

Cream Pitcher, 3" h, 2-1/2" d, enamel and cameo, flattened shape, brilliant orange poppy dec, green leaves, stems, and buds, textured opalescent apricot ground, gold trim, sgd "Daum Nancy"...2,150.00

Dish, 6-1/4" d, 3-1/4" h, tricorn, mottled green, amber, and colorless, padded white trumpet blossoms, green leafy vines, rim sgd "Daum Nancy (cross) 1875" 750.00

Ewer, 12" h, colorless frosted oval body, overlaid in bright rose-red, deeply etched as convolvulus blossoms, matching flowers and dec o silver foot, handle, rim, and hinged cov, imp hallmarks and "sterling," glass base sgd in gold "Daum (cross) Nancy"............................4,900.00

Flask, 5-3/4" h, 1-1/2" w, turquoise blue shading to clear, textured ground, cameo and enameled mistletoe dec, gold washed metal, orig stopper, orig leather bound carrying case, sgd..2,100.00

Ice Bucket, 5-1/2" h, 5-1/4" w, shaded green to clear, elaborate scroll and floral cameo dec, gold paint, fancy bronze rim and handle, sgd "Daum Nancy" 1,350.00

Jar, cov, 3" h, 2-3/4" w, deep amethyst colored glass, cased in crystal, cameo cut flowers, leaves, and vines, enameled and gilded, sgd "Daum Nancy" 600.00

Miniature Vase, enamel and cameo dec, sgd

1" h, 2" w, pillow shape, pale yellow and clear frosted round, naturalistic landscape in browns, blue, and green, sgd "Daum"...1,100.00

1-1/8" h, 2" l, pillow shape, brilliant orange yellow ground, trees and snow winter landscape, sgd 1,200.00

1-3/4" h, landscape with birch trees, leaves, branches, and green grass, pale opalescent white ground, sgd...1,200.00

1-3/4" h, 1-1/4" w, tropical island scene, shades of gray, purple and soft peach, palm trees and oasis, sgd "Daum" 900.00

2" h, pale yellow and pink ground, yellow flowers, green leaves and stems, sgd "Daum Nancy"...........1,100.00

2" h, winter scene, various trees, snowy landscape, sgd...1,000.00

2" h, 1-1/2" w, landscape of trees and leaves in green and yellow, sgd...1,200.00

2-1/2" h, rain scene, frosted clear ground, trees and foliage, sgd "Daum Nancy"...............................1,600.00

3" h, scenic, green trees, blue and purple landscape sgd "Daum Nancy".......................................1,100.00

Salt, open, enameled and cameo

1-1/8" h, 2" w, summer landscape, trees and plants, clear frosted ground, enameled green, brown, purple, and yellow, sgd...900.00

1-1/8" x 2-1/8" w, pale vaseline opalescent ground, single layer cutting of flowers, leaves, and stems, gold dec, sgd "Daum Nancy"......................................1,200.00

1-3/4" h, 2" w, double handles, landscape dec with branches, boughs, and cones 1,250.00

2-1/2" h, 3-1/2" l, ftd, green ground, cut leaves and vines, gold dec, sgd "Daum Nancy" 650.00

2-1/2" h, 3-1/2" l, pale opalescent vaseline ground, cameo cut leaves and vines, gold enameled dec, sgd "Daum Nancy"...850.00

Tumbler, 3-1/2" h, colorless textured ground, acid cut and enameled mistletoe, gilt highlights, side engraved "1 May 1910," bottom engraved "Daum Nancy".................275.00

Vase

3-1/2" h, 3" w, olive green ground, rough textured finish, gold leaf and vine dec, "Je mours ou je n attache" carved below neck, sgd in gold under base.....350.00

4-1/2" h, frosted opalescent red, yellow, and green rainbow ground, enameled thistle cut florals, cameo sgd "Daum Nancy" 800.00

4-1/2" h, oval bud, fiery opalescent amber with red striations, etched thistle pods and thorny stems, enameled burgundy-red, sgd "Daum Nancy (cross)" at side.......... 815.00

4-1/2" h, 2" d, slightly opalescent frosted ground, textured background, wild rose cutting, irregular gold rim, sgd... 450.00

5" h, 3-1/2" w, pale pink and yellow opalescent ground, carved and dec leaves and strawberry dec, applied silver repoussé base 450.00

6-1/4" h, 6-1/2" d, colorless spherical body, deep red pedestal foot, emerald green transparent body, etched over al with six repeating thistles in arched foliate frame, sgd in motif "Daum Nancy (cross)"........980.00

6-3/4" h, 3-1/2" w at shoulder, enamel and cameo, textured acid finish clear ground, mottled pale yellow and pink, heavily carved Shasta daisy flowers, enameled with yellow, gold, tan, and brown, dark green leaves veined in yellow, green and yellow textured base, sgd, dripped as lamp base 700.00

7-1/4" h, diamond shaped colorless body, cased bright pink, gilt enhanced fleur-de-lis dec, base inscribed "Daum (cross) Nancy" 520.00

9-3/4" h, 5-1/2" d, highly textured ground, large pink parrot tulips and leaves, sgd 1,200.00

10-1/4" h, ftd baluster, frosted apricot ground, overlaid in pine green, etched trees and lake scene, sgd in cameo "Daum Nancy" 1,600.00

11-1/2" h, mold blown, woodland scene, dark green foliage, peering village, mottled orange and yellow sky, sgd on bottom 10,200.00

13-1/4" h, 4-1/2" w, deep emerald green, carved fleur-de-lis dec with gold, textured and sculptured ground, sgd...250.00

13-1/2"h, 2-1/2" w, cameo floral design of pale yellow marsh flower, multicolored leaves, spatter of pale pink and yellow shading to brilliant green and brown ground, sgd 4,100.00

17-1/2" h, flared rim, elongated bulbed colorless cylinder, overlaid in vitrified autumn orange and yellow colors, etched leaves and seed pods above and below, base incised "Daum Nancy (cross)" 2,100.00

Degue

Vase

6" h, 5" w, pink mottled on clear ground, heavily textured surface, Art Deco cutting, sgd 650.00

14" h, frosted ground, red shading to blue cameo tulips, etched "Degue Made in France".......................700.00

17-1/2" h, ftd oviform, pink to purple cameo foliate design, hand etched "Degue".......................................800.00

Delatte, vase, 10" h, mottled white and colorless satin ground, amethyst iris cutting, cameo sgd "Delatte Nancy"..........600.00

De Vez

Rose Bowl, 3-1/2" d, cobalt blue foliated trees and mountains, pink to yellow sky and water, scalloped rim, sgd 500.00

Vase

5-3/4" h, landscape with mountains, waterfront, trees, and vines, shades of pink and green 750.00

6" h, flared hyacinth form, pink opal layered in pastel yellow and blue, etched genre river scene with three cows wading before a watching cloaked figure, trees, blossoms above, cameo sgd "de Vez" 1,035.00

6" h, maroon and fiery amber oval body, cameo etched cottages, mother and child under tall trees, sgd "De Vez" at side, polished rim..................................980.00

6-1/4" h, fiery amber and maroon oval, river-front vista, sgd "De Vez" in cameo 990.00

6-1/4" h, opaque cream colored oval, layered in rose-red and maroon, cameo etched poppy blossoms, seed pods, leafy stems, sgd "De Vez" at lower edge............1,380.00

8" h, tubular, three color scenic brown castle and trees, blue mountains, frosted ground, sgd 1,400.00

9" h, pink and maroon, rose blossom border and riverside mountain, sgd "De Vez" in cameo 850.00

9-1/4" h, 3" w, landscape with three sailboats, mountains, and buildings, sgd...1,200.00

12" h, 7" w, pale pink and blue ground, bright green cameo carvings of five large birds, scenic landscape, sgd..1,650.00

Galle

Bowl, 5" l, 2-1/2" h, oval, flared mottled green gray oval, cased to pink, layered with mauve, acid etched stylized leafy plants, sgd "Galle" at side..............................635.00

Bud Vase, 4-3/4" h, 1" d, frosted ground, pink poppy, sgd, slight flake at rim 550.00

Ceiling Shade, Plaffonier, 11-1/2" d, 6-1/2" d, conical flared shale, frosted shades of green and gray layered in burgundy red-maroon over green, cameo cut and etched buds and blossoms, leafy stems around rim, sgd "Galle" at side in motif, three gilt metal chains and ceiling mount..........3,220.00

Lamp Base, 9" h, yellow ground, amethyst florals and buds, cameo sgd "Galle" 450.00

Lamp, boudoir, 10-1/2" h, 10" d conical flared shade, oval base, colorless glass cased to fiery yellow, layered in dark maroon under burnt umber, cameo etched and cut as exotic blossoms and leafy stems, sgd "Galle" on shade and base, two circular "Galle/Nancy/Paris" paper labels on base..8,625.00

Perfume Lamp, 7-1/4" h, 4" d, yellow frosted ground, deep rose cyclamen dec, six large open blossoms, five buds, numerous leaves and stems, sgd 1,350.00

Toothpick Holder, 2-1/2" h, chartreuse and medium green seed pods and leafy branches, frosted and orange ground, sgd..500.00

Vase

3-1/2" h, 3-1/4" d, glossy cranberry red, shaded yellow and crystal frosted ground, currants, leaves, and branches dec, sgd 650.00

4-1/4" h, bright frosted red oval body layered in aubergine-black, etched as wild geranium blossoms and leafy stems, sgd "Galle" on motif, collar ridge for atomizer 435.00

4-5/8" h, slightly flattened colorless oval, overlaid in amethyst shaded to purple, etched clematis blossom and leafy vine, glossy fire polished surface, base incised "Galle/depose" 1,265.00

5" h, 3-1/2" w, pale pink and peach ground, lavender and green floral dec, star signature 700.00

5-5/8" h, flared rim and pedestal foot, fiery yellow oval ground, overlaid in rose red, etched delicate leafy stems and berries, sgd "Galle" in motif..........1,500.00

5-3/4" h, flattened oval, elliptical rim, amethyst and green layers, cameo etched with raised center blossoms, leafy vines, sgd "Galle" at side, two small chips to stems 490.00

6-1/2" h, elongated neck on flattened banjo shaped oval, fiery yellow layered in rose red, etched berry laden leafy branches, sgd "Galle" at side.................1,380.00

7-1/2" h, colorless satin ground, yellow-orange base, overlaid with cranberry, cut berries, cameo sgd "Galle," rim ground 770.00

8" h, bulbed frosted colorless oval, pinched quatraform, burnt sienna amber etched spider mums, petals, and "Galle" at reverse...1,265.00

8" h, olive green over colorless glass cased to bright orange, acid-etched water lilies and water grasses, sgd "Galle" on side..1,380.00

8-1/4" h, flattened bulbous body, elongated neck, cased pink layered in amethyst and green, cameo etched wisteria clusters and leafy stems, sgd "Galle" on side 920.00

8-3/4" h, bud, trumpet form, fiery amber layered in blue and purple, cameo etched and cut wild rose blossoms and buds, leaf border below, sgd "Galle" in design 1,380.00

10-1/2" h, 5-1/2" w, blue mountains, frosted pale pink and clear ground, deep brown landscape design, sgd..3,900.00

11" h, bud, tall flattened bottle-form, amethyst overlay, cameo etched blossoms, bud, and vines, sgd "Galle" on back...1,150.00

12" h, ruffled rim, elongated colorless cylinder, overlaid in orange-amber, cameo etched poppy blossoms, fire polished shiny surface, side sgd in vertical Oriental-style, applied tooled camphor foot.................1,150.00

12" h, trumpet, elongated neck with flared rim, bulbous frosted gray body overlaid in burnt sienna orange, etched poppy pods, blossoms, and leafy stems, reverse sgd "(star) Galle" 1,265.00

12-1/2" h, frosted colorless translucent oval body, overlaid in amethyst purple, etched iris blossoms, buds, and spiked leaves, fire polished all over, partial martele background, sgd "Galle" at lower side....2,300.00

13" h, flattened oval, colorless shaded to blue body, layered in bright pink and olive green, cameo etched and cut decumbent bleeding heart blossoms and leafy stems, sgd "Galle" in design on side 5,175.00

13-1/4" h, large conical frosted colorless body, layered in pale green and dark green, cameo cut and carved as tall iris blossoms and spike leaves, Oriental-style, "Galle" vertically on one spike, four tiny leaf edge chips 1,380.00

15" h, 6-1/4" w, 2" d mouth, ovoid bulbous base, elongated tapered neck, slightly flaring mouth, green, blue, and white over clear frosted ground, pale peach int., floral cutting, sgd......................................4,000.00

16" h, flared trumpet-form oval, frosted pale blue and colorless glass layered in amethyst and mauve green, cameo etched hydrangea blossom clusters, leafy stems, sgd "Galle" in design on reverse........2,645.00

Heckert, Fritz

Vase

3-1/4" h, frosted ground, pale cranberry floral and leaf dec, sgd 350.00

3-1/4" h, 2-1/2" w, frosted clear and yellow ground, amethyst floral leaf and branch pattern, sgd 800.00

Legras

Bowl

2-3/4" h, cameo etched colorless body, quatraform rim, enameled sunset snow scene, side sgd "Legras" 375.00

3" h, cameo etched colorless body, enameled stylized grape arbor border, side sgd "Legras" 350.00

4-3/4" l, 1-3/4" h, frosted colorless shaped oval, scenic dec of shepherd and flock of sheep among mountainous landscape, enameled natural colors, sgd "Legras" at end, rim roughness.......................................175.00

Vase

7-1/2" h, satin ground with yellow opalescent highlights, light green, dark green, and amethyst floral cuttings of leaves and florals, cameo sgd "Legras" 2,100.00

8-1/2" h, frosted colorless oval body, etched and dec in pink and maroon enameled flowering branches, mid mkd "Legras," stamped by retailed "Ovington New York/France"...575.00

8-3/4" h, scalloped oval shape, landscape scene, green, brown, peach, and frosty white, chips 50.00

12-1/4" h, flared rim, frosted colorless oval, etched maroon enameled stylized Art Deco swags, geometric dec, side sgd in cameo "Legras".......................575.00

12-1/2" h, elongated bulbous fiery opalescent amber body, overlaid in white and green, cameo etched deep leaf and seed pod motif, lower edge sgd in cameo "Legras"...825.00

14-1/4" h, elongated white flecked pink oval body, etched with three maroon enameled Art Deco stylized fountains with arching water sprays, side sgd in cameo "Legras"...635.00

15-1/2" h, angular oval yellow and brown on white within colorless glass body, three repeating etched Art Deco foliate elements, mahogany brown enameling, side inscribed "Legras"...1,150.00

22" h, raised rim, bulbed cornelian beige-pink oval body, etched seaweeds, aquatic plants, and creatures, enameled dark red and green highlights, side sgd in cameo "Legras"...1,725.00

Le Verre Francais

Bowl; 9" d, 7" h, bulbous, bright orange frosted ground, overlaid in tortoiseshell brown, etched and polished stylized repeating geometric elements, sgd "Charder" at side, "LeVerre Francais" below.......................................920.00

Lamp Shade, 5-1/2" h, 3" d fitter ring, double bulbed red on mottled yellow and turquoise blue ground, butterfly cutting, rim inscribed "Le Verre Francais, France" 1,100.00

Perfume Lamp Night Light Base, 3-1/4" h, cased red to yellow, overlaid in tortoiseshell brown, etched stylized blossoms, rim inscribed "Le Verre Francais," fitted with metal light cap...375.00

Punch Bowl, 12" h, 14-1/2" w, large pedestal bowl, textured ground, acid finish, gray, pink, and green, cameo cut pattern of horse chestnut burrs in mottled browns and rust tortoise shell colors, pedestal base of mottled dark purple, sgd on base 1,600.00

Vase

3-3/4" h, mottled yellow amber body, overlaid in red shaded to olive green, etched foliate design, platform base sgd "Le Verre Francais" 550.00

5-3/4" h, 4-1/4" w, acid finish, shading from clear at shoulder to dark purple, purple wafer base, carved daisy design, sgd..850.00

7-1/2" h, raised rim on ovoid frosted body, tortoiseshell brown overlay, etched as three foliate repeating elements, sgd "Le Verre Francais" on foot.............690.00

10" h, 14" w, bulbous, mottled brilliant yellow, orange, brown and green ground, large cut border of three Art Deco style flowers, three additional cut cameo bands, sgd "La Verre Francais" 450.00

11-1/2" h, trumpet, flared mottled amethyst cone, green etched and cut leaf dec, applied colorless foot with pink, blue, white cane twist within 980.00

11-3/4" h, ftd oval, yellow speckled orange layered in tango red shaded to aubergine foot, etched stylized Art Deco blossoms and dots, disk sgd "Le Verre Francais," base sgd "France" 1,380.00

15-3/4" h, swelled oval, mottled pink, white, and orange layered in lavender and aubergine, etched and polished stylized rose blossoms on thorny stems, mkd "Charder" at side, "Le Verre Francais" on foot, "France/Ovington" on base 1,100.00

16" h, elongated ftd oval, bright mottled orange ground, overlaid in spotted tortoiseshell brown, etched and polished with three tall beetles below and between Art Deco border, striped candy cane mark at one side, other side mkd "Le Verre Francais"................1,150.00

16-1/2" h, elongated ftd oval, bright mottled orange, overlaid in spotted tortoiseshell brown, etched and polished with three tall beetles below and between Art Deco border, striped candy cane mark, sgd "Le Verre Francais" on foot...1,500.00

17-1/2 h, mottled yellow and colorless ground, shaded red toned iris dec, flattened bulbous foot, script engraved "Le Verre Francais" 1,430.00

19" h, mottled yellow vasiform overlaid in orange, etched in five repeats of pendent berries above and below Art Deco borders, 1/2" inch signature cane twist embedded at lower edge 1,725.00

21-1/2" h, mottled orange-amber bulbed oval body, purple-lavender blue overlay, etched as grapes on whirling grapevines, foot inscribed "Le Verre Francais," colored cane embedded below 2,100.00

21-3/4" h, elongated flared orange and yellow oval body, overlaid in mottled tortoiseshell brown to aubergine foot,

Michele, vase, rain scene dec, fiery orange, red, and yellow, 12" h, $1,100. Photo courtesy of Jackson's Auctioneers & Appraisers.

stylized Moroccan Poppy blossoms and seed pods, leafy border, foot sgd "Le Verre Francais" 1,500.00

22" h, floral oval, transparent orange layered in mottled aubergine, blue-white spots, etched and polished convoluted leaf and vine elements, striped candy cane at edge, "Le Verre Francais" on foot 1,380.00

Michel

Lamp, 17" h, 8" d domed shade, frosted yellow ground overlaid in red, etched mountainous landscape as seen through arcade of columns, baluster base, cameo sgd "Michel" 5,000.00

Vase

10-1/4" h, 5-1/4" d, orange and yellow, deep blue overlay, carved sailing ship on one side, lighthouse on obverse, flower border..1,400.00

12-1/4" h, yellow ground, overlaid in burgundy and reddish brown rain scene with trees, cameo sgd "Michel"..1,100.00

Mueller Freres

Lamp, 14-3/4" h, domed cameo shade, mottled orange body, brown overlay, carved leaves and berries on vines with tendrils, sgd in cameo, openwork wrought iron four arm base, curling vine motif 4,000.00

Vase

4-7/8" h, frosted yellow-gray oval, red and maroon overlay, etched cyclamen blossoms, buds, and turning leaves, side sgd in cameo "Muller Fres Luneville" 750.00

5" h, 4" w, squatty, bleeding hearts and leaves, orange and yellow acid spatter ground, sgd "Mueller Fres Luneville" 1,200.00

5-1/4" h, fiery amber oval body, overlaid in orange, olive green, and black, etched trumpet-shaped blossoms, buds, and spiked leaves, sgd "Muller Fres Luneville," small chip to one leaf..575.00

5-1/4" h, 5" w, brilliant orange and black, landscape design, sgd..600.00

5-1/4" h, 5-1/2" w, deep maroon, cranberry finely carved peony, pale yellow opalescent ground 1,800.00

6" h, 3" w, mottled pale green, blue, brown, and orange ground, five sailboats, green and brown painted landscape, sgd "Mueller Fres Luneville"................1,800.00

6-1/4" h, 6-1/4" w, scenic, blue mountains and trees, mottled white and pale pink ground, sgd.............1,100.00

8-3/4" h, oviform, rounded neck, frosted yellow ground, overlaid in burgundy, etched sheep, shepherd, and trees, lake scene, cameo sgd "Muller Freres Luneville"..1,200.00

9-1/2" h, burnt orange ground, tree lined lake in silhouette, three figures picking fruit, another playing a musical instrument, sgd in cameo "Muller Fres Luneville".... 990.00

10" h, oval trumpet opal white body, green overlay etched and martele wheel-cut poppy pods and blossoms, base inscribed "Muller Croismare pres Nancy"..........2,300.00

11-1/2" h, 3-1/2" w, glossy surface, green iris dec, white and green shaded ground, sgd 1,500.00

13-1/2" h, red ground, overlaid in black, cut forest with deer at lake's edge, mkd "Muller Fres Luneville" 2,200.00

21" h, tapered, bun feet, mottled cream, deep yellow and blue ground, overlaid in blue, etched Oriental poppies and foliage, cameo sgd "Muller Freres Luneville" 5,600.00

Richard

Bowl, 6" l, 2-3/4" h, brilliant cased poppy red, brown overlay, acid-etched stylized foliate motif, sgd "Richard" at side..460.00

Vase

4" h, powder blue ground, overlaid in amethyst, floral cuttings, cameo sgd "Richard" 550.00

Richard, vase, black and orange, 13" h, $2,310. Photo courtesy of Jackson's Auctioneers & Appraisers.

4-1/4" h, orange ground, overlaid in cobalt blue, cut florals, cameo sgd "Richard" 275.00

7-1/4" h, yellow cased oval, layered in brown, cameo etched mountainous village waterfront scene, applied brown-black handles at each side, sgd "Richard" at side 825.00

13-1/4" h, striking orange ground, overlaid in deep cobalt blue, mountain lake, fir tree, and castle silhouette, cameo sgd "Richard" 2,325.00

13-1/2" h, 8" w, landscape with mountain and lake, trees, castle and bridge, brilliant bright orange, deep cobalt blue cameo overlay, sgd 3,000.00

Wine, 7-3/4" h, cobalt blue scenic water and sailboats, frosted ground, notched stem......................................400.00

Velez, vase, 8-1/2" h, ftd, tapered, deep cranberry shaded sky silhouettes autumn green trees and woodland grasses, pale green hills and trees along river bank, sgd "Velez" 1,100.00

CAMPHOR GLASS

History: Camphor glass derives its name from its color. Most pieces have a cloudy white appearance, similar to gum camphor; others have a pale tint. Camphor glass is made by treating the glass with hydrofluoric acid vapors.

Other similar types of opaque glassware exist and there is confusion between camphor, clambroth, Bristol, and opaline. All are made using similar manufacturing techniques and have similar characteristics. Today, terms such as camphor and clambroth are giving way to opaline or opaque. Perhaps these names are not quite as descriptive, but they are more meaningful to modern collectors.

Biscuit Jar, cov, white body, brass fittings 65.00
Bookends, pr, 7" h, horse heads, white body 85.00
Bottle, 6-1/2" h, orig stopper 40.00
Bowl
7-1/2" d, 3-1/2" h, white body, flared, scalloped rim, ftd ... 85.00
10" d, fluted rim, polished pontil.................................125.00
Box, cov, 5" d, hinged, enameled holly spray 75.00
Candlesticks, pr, 7" h, hp roses 75.00

Powder Jar, green, dog finial, 4-1/2" h, 4-1/2" w, $45.

Creamer, Wild Rose and Bowknot, white body, rose trim 40.00
Cruet, hp enameled roses, orig stopper............................45.00
Goblet, 7" h, butterscotch bowl, gold dec, blue ring, red
    jewels...90.00
Hair Receiver, white body, gold scroll dec.........................50.00
Lemonade Set, pitcher, eight tumblers, white body, applied
    white handle 165.00
Mustard, cov, Wild Rose and Bowknot, white body, rose
    trim..45.00
Perfume Bottle, 8-1/2" h, pinch type, mushroom cap 50.00
Place Card Holder, 3-3/4" h, ftd 35.00
Plate
    6-1/2" d, Easter Greeting..30.00
    7-1/4" d, hp owl 40.00
Powder Jar, cov, sq, blue body, bird finial, c1920 ....65.00
Ring Tree, 4-1/2" h, white body...20.00
Rose Bowl, hp violets, green leaves 50.00
Salt and Pepper Shakers, pr, Swirl pattern, blue, orig tops.... 45.00
Scent Bottle, 8" h, white body, gold scrolling dec 50.00
Sugar Shaker, 3-1/2" h, tinted yellow ground, pressed leaf dec,
    silver plated top...55.00
Toothpick Holder, bucket shape.......................................30.00
Vase
    8" h, fan shape, clear leaf design and trim 85.00
    10-1/2" h, Grecian shape, double handles, clear base ... 120.00

CANDLEWICK

History: Candlewick, Imperial Glass Corporation's No. 400 pattern, introduced in 1936, was made continuously until October 1982 when Imperial declared bankruptcy. In 1984, Imperial was sold to Lancaster-Colony Corporation and Consolidated Stores International, Inc. Imperial's assets, including inventory, molds, buildings, and equipment, were liquidated in 1985. Imperial's Candlewick molds were bought by various groups, companies, and individuals.

At the liquidation sale, the buildings and site were purchased by Anna Maroon of Maroon Enterprises, Bridgeport, Ohio, with the intent of developing the site into a tourist attraction, Imperial Plaza. The Imperial glass outlet, The Hay Shed, the Bellaire Museum, and a few small businesses moved into the building, but the project failed, and the Imperial building deteriorated and was demolished in July 1995.

The Hay Shed outlet relocated to a building near the Imperial site and operates as a consignment shop for Imperial and other glass. At its 1996 convention, the National Impe-rial Glass Collector's Society started a drive to establish an Imperial museum and preserve the heritage of glassmaking that took place at Imperial for more than 80 years.

Candlewick is characterized by the crystal-drop beading used around the edges of many pieces; around the bases of tumblers, shakers, and other items; in the stems of glasses, compotes, and cake and cheese stands; on the handles of cups, pitchers, bowls, and serving pieces; on stoppers and finials; and on the handles of ladles, forks, and spoons. The beading is small on some pieces, larger and heavier on others.

A large variety of pieces was produced in the Candlewick pattern. More than 650 items and sets are known. Shapes include round, oval, oblong, heart, and square. Imperial added or discontinued items as popularity and demand warranted. The largest assortment of pieces and sets were made during the late 1940s and early 1950s.

Candlewick was produced mostly in crystal. Viennese Blue (pale blue, 1937-1938), Ritz Blue (cobalt, 1938-1941), and Ruby Red (red, 1937-1941) were made. Amber, black, emerald green, lavender, pink, and light yellow pieces also have been found. From 1977 to 1980, four items of 3400 Candlewick stemware were made in solid-color Ultra Blue, Nut Brown, Verde Green, and Sunshine Yellow. Solid-black stemware was made on an experimental basis at the same time.

Other decorations on Candlewick include silver overlay, gold encrustations, cuttings, etchings, and hand-painted designs. Pieces have been found with fired-on gold, red, blue, and green beading. Blanks, i.e., plain pieces, were sold to many companies which decorated them with cuttings, hand paintings, and silver overlay, or fitted them with silver, chrome, or brass bases, pedestals, or lids. Shakers sold to DeVilbiss were made into atomizers. Irving W. Rice & Co. purchased Candlewick tray handles and trays, assembled boudoir sets, and sold Candlewick clocks.

References: Gene Florence, *Elegant Glassware of the Depression Era, Sixth Edition*, Collector Books, 1994; National Imperial Glass Collector's Society, *Imperial Glass Encyclopedia, Vol. 1: A-Cane*, The Glass Press, 1995; —, *Imperial Glass Catalog Reprint*, Antique Publications, 1991; Virginia R. Scott, *Collector's Guide to Imperial Candlewick*, 4th ed., available from author (275 Milledge Terrace, Athens, GA 30606); Mary M. Wetzel-Tomalka, *Candlewick: The Jewel of Imperial, Book I*, available from author (P.O. Box 594, Notre Dame, IN 46556), 1980; —, *Candlewick: The Jewel of Imperial, Book II*, available from author, 1995; —, *Candlewick, The Jewel of Imperial, Personal Inventory & Record Book*, available from author, 1998; —, *Candlewick, The Jewel of Imperial, Price Guide '99 and More*, available from author, 1998.

Periodicals: *Glasszette,* National Imperial Glass Collector's Society, P.O. Box 534, Bellaire, OH 43528; *The Candlewick Collector Newsletter,* National Candlewick Collector's Club, 275 Milledge Terrace, Athens, GA 30606.

Videotapes: National Imperial Glass Collectors Society, *Candlewick, at Home, in Any Home*, Vol. I, *Imperial Beauty* (Candlewick display), Vol. II, Seminar by Mary Wetzel and Virginia Scott, 1993 National Imperial Glass Collectors Society Convention (P.O. Box 534, Bellaire, OH 43528).

Collectors' Clubs: California Candlewick Collectors, 1360 Lomay Place, Pasadena, CA 91103; Candlewick Crystals of Arizona, 2430 E. Sheridan, Phoenix, AZ 85008; Maryland Imperial Candlewick Club, 23 Ashcroft Ct., Arnold, MD 21012; Michigan Assoc. of Candlewick Collectors, 17370 Battles Rd., South Bend, IN 46614; National Candlewick Collector's Club, 275 Milledge Terrace, Athens, GA 30606; National Imperial Glass Collector's Society, P.O. Box 534, Bellaire, OH 43528; Ohio Candlewick Collector's Club, 613 S Patterson, Gibsonburg, OH 43431; Texas Regional Imperial Glass Group, P.O. Box 911, Decatur, TX 76234; Fox Valley Northern Illinois Imperial Enthusiasts, 38 W. 406 Gingerwood, Elgin, IL 60123.

Museum: Bellaire Museum, Bellaire, OH 43906.

Reproduction Alert: When Imperial Glass Corp. was liquidated in 1985, all the molds were sold, but no accurate records were kept of all the buyers. It is known that Mirror Images, Lansing, Michigan, purchased more than 200 of the molds, and Boyd Crystal Art Glass, Cambridge, Ohio, purchased 18 small ones. Other molds went to private individuals and groups.

Since the late 1980s, Boyd Crystal Art Glass has used Candlewick molds to make items in various slag and clear colors. Boyd has marked its reproductions with its trademark, a "B" inside a diamond, which is pressed on the bottom of each article.

In 1985, Mirror Images had Viking Glass Co., New Martinsville, W.V., make the six-inch Candlewick basket, 400/40/0, in Alexandrite, and a four-piece child's set (consisting of a demitasse cup and saucer, six-inch plate, and five-inch nappy) in pink. In 1987, Viking produced clear plates, bowls, saucers, flat-based sugars and creamers (400/30 and 400/122), and the 400/29 tray for Mirror Images in crystal. These pieces have ground bottoms, are somewhat heavier than original Candlewick pieces, and are not marked. Shapes of items may differ from original Candlewick.

In late 1990, Dalzell-Viking Corporation, successor to Viking, began making Candlewick in Mirror Image's molds. It made five-piece place settings in crystal, black, cobalt, evergreen, and red. Most of these are marked, either "DALZELL" for the first-quality pieces, or "DX" for seconds. In January 1991, Dalzell added handled plates, bowls, and a five-section 400/112 center-well relish in crystal. A new pastel shade, Cranberry Mist, was added in 1992.

Since late 1995, Dalzell Viking has offered Candlewick Gold, clear with gold beads; Candlewick Pastels, also called Satins, in azure, crystal, green, yellow, and cranberry; 8", 10", and 12" plates, cups, and saucers, and 6" bowls were made, all marked only with a paper label.

In 1996, Dalzell added a punch bowl set with gold beads and also began to make Candlewick with silver beads. The Pastel Satin production has been extended to include the following: 400/231 three-piece square bowl set; 400/161 butter dish; 400/154 deviled-egg tray; 400/68D pastry tray with a heart center handle; 400/87C and /87F vases; a six-inch bowl on an eight-inch oval tray; and a four-ounce sherbet, similar to 400/63B compote. Dalzell also added Candlewick Frosts, dark amber, plum, blue, and sage green with frosted finish. All of the above were marked only with a Dalzell Viking paper label.

Ashtray
   400/18 bridge, crystal 6.00
   400/134/1, crystal 6.00
   400/150, 6" d, round, large beads
      Caramel slag 14.00
      Cobalt blue 30.00
      Crystal 8.00
      Pink 14.00
   400/450, nested set, 4", 5", and 6"
      Crystal 20.00
      Pink 32.00
   400/450, nested set, 4", 5", and 6", patriotic dec
      Pink 72.00
      Red, white, and blue 175.00
Atomizer
   400/96 shaker, atomizer top, made by DeVilbiss 125.00
   400/167 shaker, atomizer top, amethyst 75.00
   400/167 shaker, atomizer top, aqua 75.00
   400/247 shaker, atomizer top, amethyst 75.00
   400/247 shaker, atomizer top, aqua 65.00
Banana Stand, 11" d, 2 turned-up sides, 4-bead stem, crystal 800.00
Basket, crystal
   400/37/0, 11", applied handle 130.00
   400/40/0, 6-1/2", turned-up sides, applied handle........30.00
   400/273, 6", rolled-in edge 350.00
Bell, crystal
   400/108, 5" 85.00
   400/179, 4", 4-bead handle.......................................50.00
Bon Bon, 400/51T, 6", heart shape, curved-over center handle, beaded edge
   Crystal 25.00
   Light Blue 75.00
   Ruby red, crystal handle 200.00
Bowl
   400/1F, 5" d, crystal...12.00
   400/3F, 6", nappy, crystal...10.00
   400/42B, 4-3/4" d, crystal...12.00
   400/52, 6" d, divided, crystal....................................15.00
   400/62B, 7" d, two handles, red 250.00
   400/63B, 10-1/2" d, belled, crystal 55.00
   400/73H, 9" w, heart-shape, handle...........................125.00
   400/74B, 8-1/2" d, 4 ball toes, black 275.00
   400/74B, 8-1/2", 4 ball toes, crystal..........................125.00
   400/74SC, 9" d, 4 ball toes, crimped
      Black 200.00
      Crystal 85.00
      Light blue...100.00
      Red 200.00
   400/75B, 10-1/2" d, crystal 35.00
   400/92B, 11" d, float bowl, cupped edge, crystal.........35.00
   400/104B, 14" d, belled, large beads on sides.............75.00
   400/106B, 12" d, belled, crystal 70.00
   400/131B, 14" l, oval, crystal 350.00
   400/427B, 4-3/4" d, 6" d, 7" d and 8-1/2" d, crystal, price for nested set 65.00
Bridge Set, 400/118, 4 pc, crystal 34.00
Bud Vase, crystal
   400/25, 3-3/4" h, beaded foot, ball shape, crimped top 35.00
   400/28C, 8-1/2", trumpet shaped top, crimped, beaded ball bottom 50.00
   400/107, 5-1/4" h, beaded foot, large beads, crimped top 45.00

Butter Dish, cov, #400/144, $40.

400/227, 8-1/2" h, beaded ball bottom, narrowed top slants, applied handle 100.00
Butter, cov, crystal
   400/144, 5-1/2" d, round, 2-bead finial..........................40.00
   400/161, quarter pound, graduated beads on cov.......30.00
   400/276, 6-3/4" x 4", California
      Beaded top, c1960..95.00
      Plain top, c1951..115.00
Cake Stand, crystal
   400/67D, 10" d, dome ftd, wedge marks on plate, 1-bead stem, c1939..80.00
   400/103D, 11" h, tall, 3-bead stem...............................75.00
   400/160, 14" d, 72 candle holes..................................300.00
Canapé Plate, 400/19, 6" d, off-center indent, crystal 15.00
Candleholders, pr, crystal
   400/CV, 5" h, round bowl, beaded, vase insert, 2 pc 175.00
   400/CV, 5" h, round bowl, fluted, vase insert, 2 pc 175.00
   400/79R, 3-1/2" h, rolled saucer, small beads 30.00
   400/81, 3-1/2" h, dome ftd, small beads, round handle... 100.00
   400/86, mushroom, pr...90.00
   400/115, 9" h, oval, beaded base, 3 candle cups 200.00
   400/115/1-2, 9" h, oval, beaded base, 3 candle cups, 2 eagles...500.00
   400/175, 6-1/2" h, 3-bead stem...................................150.00
   400/190, 5" h, handle 100.00
   400/207, 4-1/2" h, 3 toed..160.00
   400/224, 5-1/2" h, ftd, 3 sections of arched beads on stem..450.00
   400/280, 3-1/2" h, flat 30.00
   400/1752. 6-1/2" h, 3-bead stem, adapter, prisms 250.00
Candy Dish, cov, crystal
   400/59, 5-1/2" d, 2-bead finial......................................35.00
   400/110, 7" d, 3-part, 2-bead finial
      Cut and mirror finish...400.00
      Typical finish..70.00
   400/140, 8" d, 1-bead stem
      Flat, c1944...150.00
      Footed, beaded foot dome, c1943........................225.00
   400/245, 6-1/2" d, round bowl, sq cov, 2-bead finial ..125.00
   400/260 ....85.00
Celery Tray, crystal
   400/46, 11" l, oval, scalloped edge.............................50.00
   400/105, 13" l, oval, 2 curved beaded handles 40.00
Champagne, 3400, saucer, flared belled top, 5 oz, 4 graduated beads in stem, crystal..16.00
Cheese and Cracker Set, 400/88, 5-1/2" ftd 400/88 cheese compote, 10-1/2" d 400/72D handled plate, crystal..........45.00

Cheese, Toast or Butter Dish, 400/123, 7-3/4" d plate with cupped edge, domed cov with bubble knob, crystal............ 200.00
Cigarette Set, crystal
   400/29/6, 6 pc set 60.00
   400/29/64/44, dome ftd 3" 400/44 cigarette holder, small beads, 4 nested 400/64 ashtrays, c1941 ....60.00
Claret, 3400/5, flared belled top, 4 graduated beads in stem, crystal...55.00
Clock, 4", large beads, New Haven works, crystal..........400.00
Coaster, crystal
   400/78, 4" d, ten rays 7.00
   400/226, 3-1/2" d, spoon rest.......................................12.00
Cocktail, 4000/190, bell-shaped bowl, beads around foot, 4 oz, 3 bead stem, crystal 20.00
Compote, crystal
   400/48F, 8" d, beaded edge, 4-bead stem 65.00
   400/48F, 8" d, beaded edge, 5-bead 350.00
   400/67B, 9" d, flat, large bead stem, c1943 ....65.00
   400/67B, 9" d, ribbed bowl, dome ftd, large bead stem ... 75.00
   400/220, 5" d, 3-part, beaded edge, arched...............90.00
Console Set, crystal
   400/100, 12" 400/92F flat bowl, cupped edge, pr 2-lite candleholders, center circle of large beads 95.00
   400/8692L, 13" 400/92L mushroom bowl on 400/127B 7-1/2" d base, pr 400/86 mushroom candleholders 200.00
Condiment Set, crystal
   400/1589, jam set, two cov 400/89 marmalade jars, 3-bead ladles, oval 400/159 tray 95.00
   400/2946, oil and vinegar, pr 400/164 and 400/166 beaded foot cruets, kidney-shaped 400/29 tray....................90.00
Cordial, 3400, flared belled top, 4 graduated beads in stem, crystal 20.00
Cordial Bottle, 15 oz, beaded foot, 3-bead stopper
   400/82, crystal, handle, c1938....................................195.00
   400/82, crystal, handle, red stopper and base, c1938....275.00
   400/82/2, crystal, no handle, c1941 ....175.00
Creamer and Sugar Set
   400/29/30, flat base, beaded question mark handles, 400/30, 7" l 400/29 tray, crystal 30.00
   400/30, flat base, beaded question mark handles, sterling silver floral dec 100.00
   400/31, beaded foot, plain handles, c1937
      Crystal 40.00
      Blue 60.00
   400/31, plain foot, question mark handles, c1941, crystal 30.00
Cup and Saucer, beaded question mark handles
   400/35, tea, round 400/35 cup, 400/35 saucer.............15.00
   400/37, coffee, slender 40/37 cup, 400/35 saucer 15.00
   400/77, after dinner, small, slender 5-1/2 d beaded saucer..20.00
Decanter
   400/18, crystal...365.00
   400/163, beaded foot, round stopper
      Crystal 195.00
      Crystal with red foot and stopper, c1938 ....250.00
Deviled Egg Tray, 400/154, 11-1/2" d, twelve indents for eggs, heart-shaped center handle, crystal 115.00
Epergne Set, 400/196, 9" ftd 400/196FC flower candle holder, 1-bead stem, 7-3/4" h 2-bead peg vase, beaded top, peg to fit into candle cut, crystal 175.00
Fruit Tray, 400/68F, center handle, crystal 350.00
Goblet, water, crystal
   400/190 Line, bell shaped bowl, hollow trumpet shaped stem with beads around foot, 10 oz 17.50
   3400 Line, flared bell bowl, 4 graduated beads in stem, 9 oz...16.00

Marmalade, cov, spoon, #400/1989, $30.

Iced Tea Tumbler, crystal, 12 oz, ftd
    400/18, domed beaded foot, rounded top....................40.00
    400/19, beaded base, straight sides 22.00
Icer, no inserts, 400/533, crystal.......................................75.00
Jelly Server, crystal
    400/52, 6" d, divided dish, beaded edge, handles.......18.00
    400/157, 4-3/4" d, ftd, 1-bead stem, 2-bead cov..........50.00
Juice Tumbler, 400/19, beaded base, straight sides, 5 oz, ftd,
    crystal...12.50
Ladle, 3 bead, crystal
    Large...12.00
    Medium 12.00
    Small...12.00
Lamp, Hurricane
    400/79R, 3-1/2" saucer candleholder, 9" chimney, 2 pc set
        Bohemian, cranberry flashed chimney, gold bird and
        leaves dec 125.00
        Crystal 75.00
    400/152R, candleholder, chimney, and 100/152 adapter,
        crystal, 3 pc..95.00
Lemon Tray, #400/221, 5-1/2" l, handle, crystal................55.00
Manhattan Pitcher, 400/18, 40 oz, crystal.......................245.00
Marmalade, 400/89, 4 pc, crystal....................................45.00
Mayonnaise Set, bowl, plate with indent, and ladle, crystal
    400/23, 5-1/4" d 400/32D bowl, 7-1/2" d 400/23B plate,
        400/135 3-bead ladle..30.00
    400/52/2, 6-1/2" d 400/52/B bowl with 2 handles, 400/52D
        handled pate, 400/135 3-bead ladle......................40.00
Mint Dish, 400/51F, 5" d, round, applied handle 20.00
Mint Tray, 400/149, 9" d, heart-shaped center handle 30.00
Mirror, domed beaded base, crystal, brass holder and frame,
    2-sided mirror flips on hinges, made for I. Rice Co.,
    1940s...85.00
Mustard Jar, 400/156, beaded foot, notched beaded cov with
    2-bead finial, 3-1/2" glass spoon, fleur-de-lis handle, crys-
    tal...40.00
Nappy, 400/3F, 6" d, beaded edge, crystal......................10.00
Pastry Tray
    400/49D, handle, 400/19, crystal 28.00
    400/68D, 11-1/2" d beaded plate, center heart-shaped handle
        Crystal 35.00
        Crystal, floral cutting...80.00
Pitcher, crystal
    400/16, 16 oz, beaded question mark handle, plain
        base...125.00
    400/18, 16 oz, plain handle, beaded base 200.00
    400/18, 80 oz, plain handle, beaded base 300.00

40/24, 80 oz, beaded question mark handle, plain
    base..145.00
Plate, crystal
    400/1D, 6" d, bread and butter 8.00
    400/3D, 7" d, salad..7.00
    400/5D, 8-1/2" d, salad/dessert.................................10.00
    400/7D, 9" d, luncheon...15.00
    400/10D, 10-1/4" d, dinner..30.00
    400/72C, 10" d, w handles, crimped...........................25.00
    400/145D, 12" d, 2 open handles................................30.00
Platter, crystal
    400/124D, 13" l 90.00
    400/131D, 16" l 190.00
Punch Bowl Set, crystal
    400/20, 13" d six quart 400/20 bowl, 10" belled 400/128 base,
        twelve 400/37 punch cups, 400/91 ladle, 15 pc set ... 250.00
    400/20, 13" d six quart 400/20 bowl, 17" d 400/20V plate, twelve
        400/37 punch cups, 400/91 ladle, 15 pc set 225.00
    400/210, 14-1/2" d ten quart 400/210 bowl, 9" belled
        400/210 base, twelve 400/37 punch cups, 400/91 ladle,
        15 pc set 450.00
Relish, beaded edge, crystal
    400/54, 2-part, 6-1/2" l, 2 tab handles........................15.00
    400/55, 4-part..30.00
    400/57, 8-1/2" l, oval..20.00
    400/84, 2-part, 6-1/2" l 25.00
    400/102, 13" l 85.00
    400/208, 3-part, 3 toes, 10" d 175.00
    400/215, 3-part on one side, 1 section on other, 5-1/2" l, 2 tab
        handles...100.00
    400/256, 2-part, 10-1/2" l, oval, 2 tab handles 25.00
    400/262, 3-part, 10-1/2" l, 2 tab handles...................100.00
Relish and Dressing Set, 400/1112, 10-1/2" 5-part 400/112 rel-
    ish, 400/89 jar fits center well, long 3-bead ladle, crystal,
    c1942... 115.00
Rose Bowl, 400/132, crystal.. 425.00
Salad Fork and Spoon, 400/75, 5-bead handles, crystal 32.00
Salad Set, crystal
    400/735, 9" d handled heart-shaped 400/73H bowl, 700/75
        fork and spoon set...110.00
    400/75B, 10-1/2" d beaded 400/75B bowl, 13" d cupped
        400/75V plate, 5-bead handles 400/75 fork and spoon
        set...85.00
Salt and Pepper Shakers, pr, beaded foot, crystal
    400/96, bulbous, 8 beads, chrome tops 25.00
    400/116, one ball stem...225.00
    400/190, trumpet foot, chrome tops............................90.00
Salt Dip, crystal
    400/61, 2"...10.00
    400/19, 2-1/4"...10.00
Salt Spoon, 400/616, crystal, 3" 10.00
Sauce Boat Set, 400/169, oval gravy boat with handle, 9" oval
    plate with indent 135.00
Sauce Bowl, 400/243, 5-1/2" d, crystal 110.00
Sherbet, 400/190, belled bowl, 5 oz, tall, crystal 15.00
Sugar, 400/18, domed foot 115.00
Tidbit Server, 400/2701, two tiers, 7-1/2" d and 10-1/2" d plates
    joined by metal rod, round handle at top
    Crystal 60.00
    Emerald green..350.00
Torte Plate
    400/20D, 17" d, flat, crystal 50.00
    400/20V, 17" d, cupped, crystal.................................50.00
Tray
    400/42E, 5-1/2" l, upturned handles, crystal 20.00
    400/51T, 6" l, handle bent to center of dish, crystal......25.00

400/62E, 8-1/2" l, black, hand painted gold flowers, handle..250.00
Tumbler, water, ftd, crystal
    400/18, domed beaded foot, rounded top, 9 oz...........32.00
    400/19, beaded base, straight sides, 10 oz, 4-3/4" h ...16.00
Vase, crystal
    400/87C, 8" h, crimped beaded top, graduated beads down sides 50.00
    400/87R, 7" h, rolled beaded flange top, solid glass arched handles with small bead edging, flat foot 40.00
    400/143C, 8" h, crimped, flip, cut leaves 195.00
Wine
    400/190 Line, belled bowl, hollow trumpet stem with beads, 5 oz, crystal 28.00
    3400 Line, flared belled bowl, four graduated stems in base, 9 oz
        Crystal 25.00
        Ruby red bowl 100.00
        Yellow, c1977 ....30.00

CARNIVAL GLASS

History: Carnival glass, an American invention, is colored pressed glass with a fired-on iridescent finish. It was first manufactured about 1905 and was immensely popular both in America and abroad. More than 1,000 different patterns have been identified. Production of old carnival glass patterns ended in 1930.

Most of the popular patterns of Carnival Glass were produced by five companies: Dugan, Fenton, Imperial, Millersburg, and Northwood. Northwood patterns frequently are found with the "N" trademark. Dugan used a diamond trademark on several patterns.

In Carnival glass, color is the most important factor in pricing carnival glass. The color of a piece is determined by holding it to the light and looking through it.

References: Gary E. Baker et al., *Wheeling Glass*, Oglebay Institute, 1994 (distributed by Antique Publications); Elaine and Fred Blair, *Carnival Hunter's Companion: A Guide to Pattern Recognition*, published by authors (P.O. Box 116335, Carrolton, TX 75011), 1995; Carl O. Burns, *Collector's Guide to Northwood Carnival Glass*, L-W Book Sales, 1994; —, *Imperial Carnival Glass 1909-1930 Identification and Values,* Collector Books, 1996; Bill Edwards, *Standard Encyclopedia of Carnival Glass*, 6th ed., Collector Books, 1998; Ruth Grizel, *A Notebook of Imperial's Modern Carnival Glass,* WGCN (P.O. Box 143, North Liberty, Iowa, 52317-0143); Marion T. Hartung, *First Book of Carnival Glass to Tenth Book* of Carnival Glass (series of 10 books), published by author, 1968 to 1982; William Heacock, James Measell and Berry Wiggins, *Dugan/Diamond*, Antique Publications, 1993; ——, *Harry Northwood, The Wheeling Years, 1901-1925*, Antique Publications, 1991; Heart of America Carnival Glass Assoc., Educational Series 1 (1990); Educational Series 2, (1992), Educational Series 3 (1996) (3048 Tamarak Dr., Manhattan, KS 66502); James Measell, *Imperial Glass Encyclopedia, Volume II, Cape Cod-L,* National Imperial Glass Collectors' Society, 1997; Marie McGee, *Millersburg Glass*, Antique Publications, 1995; Tom and Sharon Mordini, *Carnival Glass Auction Price Reports, 1989-1996,* published by authors (36 N. Mernitz, Freeport, IL 61032);

Lloyd Reichel, *Carnival Glass Collectors Book I (1971) and II (1971),* published by author, (P.O. Box 236, Jamestown, MO 65046); Jerry Reynolds, *Iridescent Hatpins & Holders of the Carnival Glass Era,* published by author (1305 N. Highland Pkwy, Tacoma, WA 98406); The Australian Carnival Enthusiasts Associated, Inc., *Carnival Glass of Australia,* Australian Carnival Enthusiasts Associated, Inc.; *The Sanctified Cross-Eyed Bear's Price Trend Guide for Carnival Glass and Individual Sales Supplemental Guide for 1996, 3rd Edition,* The Sanctified Cross-Eyed Bear (P.O. Box 1296, Huntsville, AL 35807), 1996; Cecil Whitney, *The World of Enameled Carnival Glass Tumblers,* published by author (1041 Cheshire Lane, Houston, TX 77018), 1985.

Periodical: *Network,* PageWorks, P.O. Box 2385, Mt. Pleasant, SC 29465.

Collectors' Clubs: Air Capital Carnival Glass Club, 15201 E. 47th St., Derby, KS 67037; American Carnival Glass Assoc., 9621 Springwater Lane, Miamisburg, OH 45342; Australian Carnival Enthusiasts Assoc. (SA) Inc., P.O. Box 1028, New Haven, SA, 5018; Australian Carnival Enthusiasts Assoc. (Victoria) Inc., RSD Fryerstown, Victoria, 3451; Canadian Carnival Glass Assoc., 107 Montcalm Dr., Kitchner, Ontario N2B 2R4 Canada; Carnival Club of Western Australia, 179 Edgewater Drive, Edgewater, Western Australia 6027; Carnival Glass Collectors Assoc. of Australia, Inc., 24 Kerstin St., Quakers Hill, NSW 2763; Collectible Carnival Glass Assoc., 2360 N. Old S. R. 9, Columbus, IN 47203-9430; Gateway Carnival Glass Club, 108 Riverwoods Cove, East Alton, IL 62024; Great Lakes Carnival Glass Club, 612 White Pine Blvd., Lansing, MI 48917; Heart of America Carnival Glass Assoc., 43-5 W. 78th St., Prairie Village, KS 66208; Hoosier Carnival Glass Club, 944 W. Pine St., Griffith, IN 46319; International Carnival Glass Assoc., P. O. Box 306, Mentone, IN 46539; Keystone Carnival Glass Club, 719 W Brubaker Valley Rd, Lititz, PA 17543; L'Association du Verra Carnaval du Quebec, 3250 rue Leon Brisbois, Ile Bizard, QC, H9C IT6 Canada; Lincoln-Land Carnival Glass Club, N951, Hwy 27, Conrath, WI 54731; National Duncan Glass Society, P.O. Box 965, Washington, PA 15301; National Imperial Glass Collectors, P.O. Box 534, Bellaire, OH 43906; New England Carnival Glass Club, 10 Seminole Rd., Canton, MA 02021-1212; Northern California Carnival Glass Club, 4325 Raiders Way, Modesto, CA 95355; Pacific Northwest Carnival Glass Club, 5340 Market Rd, Bellingham, WA 98226; San Diego County Carnival Glass Club, 5395 Middleton Rd., San Diego, CA 92019; San Joaquin Carnival Glass Club, 3906 E. Acacia Ave., Fresno, CA 93726; Southern California Carnival Glass Club, 31091 Bedford Dr., Redlands, CA 92373; Tampa Bay Carnival Glass Club, 101st Ave. N, Pinellas Park, FL 34666; Texas Carnival Glass Club, 4736 CR 310, Cleburne, TX 76031; The Carnival Glass Society (UK), 162 Green Lane, Edgeware, Middsix HA8 8EJ, England; WWW.CGA at http://woodland.com/woodland.carnival glass.

Videos: *Hooked on Carnival, Volume I and II,* Glen and Steve Thistlewood, P.O. Box 83, Alton, Hampshire Gu34 4YN England.

Museums: National Duncan Glass Society, Washington, PA; Fenton Art Glass Co., Williamstown, WV.

Acanthus, Imperial, bowl, 7-1/2" d, smoke 50.00
Acorn, Fenton, bowl, 8" d, marigold...............................100.00
Acorn Burrs, Northwood
    Punch Cup, pastel...85.00
    Water Set, pastel...525.00
Advertising and Souvenir
    Elks, Detroit, 1910, Fenton, bowl, purple 975.00
    John Brand, open basket, marigold............................90.00
Amaryllis, Northwood, compote, purple 150.00
Apple Blossom Twigs, Dugan, bowl, low, ruffled, marigold... 70.00
April Showers, Fenton, vase
    6" h, squatty, amethyst.....................................125.00
    13" h, blue 50.00
Asters, ice cream bowl, marigold, 9" d 125.00
Beaded, Dugan, basket, amethyst 80.00
Beaded Bulls Eye, Imperial, vase, 9" h, purple...............170.00
Beaded Cable, Northwood, rose bowl
    Marigold 75.00
    White 425.00
Beaded Shell, Dugan, mug, blue................................115.00
Beauty Twig, Dugan, bud vase, marigold, 9" h 100.00
Blackberry, Fenton
    Basket, open edge, ruffled, blue.............................90.00
    Bowl, 3" h, 6-1/2" d, open edge, basketweave ext., amber/
        horehound...255.00
    Vase, swung, open edge, dark marigold................2,250.00
Blackberry Bramble, Fenton, compote, ruffled, green 35.00
Blackberry Spray, Fenton
    Hat, red 300.00
    Hat, reverse amberina opal, ruffled 1,000.00
    Jack in the Pulpit, crimped edge, red......................800.00
Blackberry Wreath, Millersburg
    Compote, green 75.00
    Ice Cream Bowl, 5/12" d, amethyst............................50.00
    Ice Cream Bowl, 6-3/4" d, marigold 45.00
    Ice Cream Bowl, 10" d, green 200.00
    Sauce, 3 in 1, green 85.00
Blaze, ice cream bowl, 9" d, marigold 60.00
Borderland Plants, Dugan, plate, hand grip, peach opale-
    scent..175.00
Brocaded Acorns, Fostoria, plate, 7-1/2" d, lavender......225.00
Boutonniere, Millersburg, compote, amethyst, satin 110.00
Bull's Eye and Beads, vase, 12" h, amber 260.00
Bushel Basket, Northwood
    Amethyst 250.00
    Marigold, pastel 250.00
    Sapphire Blue...2,000.00
    White 200.00
Butterfly, Fenton, calling card tray, blue 55.00
Butterfly and Berry, Fenton
    Bowl, 9" d, scalloped, 3 claw and ball feet, bronze, green,
        and blue irid, cobalt blue ground.......................450.00
    Vase, 7" h, tightly crimped edge, blue 80.00
Butterfly and Fern, Fenton, tumbler, amethyst.................50.00
Butterfly and Tulip, ice cream bowl, 10" d, ftd, marigold 285.00
Captive Rose, Fenton, plate, 9" d, blue 375.00
Carolina Dogwood, Westmoreland, bowl, 7-3/4" d, six ruffled,
    blue opalescent..425.00
Caroline, Dugan, peach opalescent
    Bowl, 9" d 95.00
    Plate, hand grip...100.00
Cherry, Dugan
    Bowl, 9" d, collar base, pastel opalescent.................135.00
    Bowl, ftd, pastel opalescent................................95.00
Cherry, Millersburg
    Milk Pitcher, marigold......................................750.00

Captive Rose, Fenton, plate, blue, 9" d, $375. Photo courtesy of Mickey Reichel Auction Center.

    Spooner, green 125.00
Coin Spot, Dugan, compote, peach opalescent 80.00
Colonial, Imperial, lemonade mug, marigold, clear handle and
    base... 22.50
Concave Flute, Westmoreland, bowl, flat, marigold, 9" d...... 55.00
Concord, Fenton, ice cream bowl, ruffled
    Amethyst...300.00
    Green, gold, red, and blue irid.............................350.00
    Pumpkin Marigold 250.00
Corinth, Dugan
    Banana boat, 8-1/2" l, 2 sides up, teal 25.00
    Jack in the Pulpit Vase, 8-1/2" h, yellow.....................80.00
Corn Vase, Northwood, vase, flower base, ice green 270.00
Cosmos, Millersburg, ice cream bowl, 6" d, green........... 65.00
Cosmos and Cane, berry bowl, white............................. 40.00
Country Kitchen, Millersburg, butter, cov, amethyst....... 445.00
Courthouse, Millersburg, bowl, 7-1/2" d, low, ruffled,
    amethyst... 725.00
Cut Flowers, Jenkins, vase, 10" h, green 110.00
Dahlia, Dugan, berry bowl, amethyst............................. 65.00
Dandelion, Northwood, tumbler, marigold 55.00
Diamond Point, Northwood, vase, 10" h, ice blue.......... 300.00
Diamond Ring, Imperial, bowl, ruffled, 8" d
    Marigold 50.00
    Smoke 50.00
Diamonds, Millersburg
    Pitcher, marigold, chip base filled 35.00
    Tumbler, marigold 40.00
Dogwood Sprays, Dugan, bowl, tricorn, dome ftd, peach
    opalescent.. 50.00
Dolphins, Millersburg, compote, amethyst, rosalind int.... 1,500.00
Double Stem Rose, Dugan
    Bowl, domed foot, peach opalescent 160.00
    Plate, dome foot, white....................................175.00
Dragon and Lotus, Fenton
    Bowl, ruffled, plain back, amber 120.00
    Bowl, 3 in 1, light amethyst, irid pink and blue
        highlights...225.00
    Ice Cream Bowl, cobalt blue.................................185.00
    Ice Cream Bowl, marigold, chip...............................40.00
Dragon and Strawberry, Fenton, bowl, ftd, large, green....1,600.00
Dragonfly, hatpin, marigold 95.00
Drapery, Northwood
    Candy Dish, ice blue.......................................175.00

Candy Dish, N mark, marigold 135.00
Rose Bowl, aqua opalescent 450.00
Rose Bowl, electric blue...500.00
Rose Bowl, white 425.00
Vase, 8" h, marigold, small chip 35.00
Vase, 8" h, white 175.00
Vase, 8-3/4" h, ice lime green 125.00
Dutch Mill, ashtray, marigold 30.00
Egyptian Scarab, hatpin, pastel....................................60.00
Embroidered Mums, Northwood, bowl, 9" d, ruffled
    Blue 400.00
    Marigold 400.00
Fanciful, Dugan
    Bowl, ruffled, peach opalescent 160.00
    Ice Cream Bowl, peach opalescent......................160.00
Fans, English, pitcher, marigold 90.00
Fashion, Imperial, rose bowl, green...........................300.00
Feather Stitch, Fenton, plate, marigold 600.00
Fine Cut, Jenkins, vase, 10" h, marigold 80.00
Fine Cut and Roses, Northwood
    Candy Dish, ftd, amethyst..................................75.00
    Rose bowl, ice blue 195.00
    Rose bowl, white 225.00
Fine Rib, Dugan, Fenton, or Northwood, vase, 9" h, fiery
    amethyst...375.00
Fish Net, Dugan, epergne, crimped edge, center lily vase, pastel
    opalescent..275.00
Fish Scale and Beads, Dugan
    Bowl, low, candy ribbon crimping, pastel, 7" d...........155.00
    Plate, 7" d, white 125.00
Fleur De Lis, Millersburg, bowl, ruffled, large, amethyst....525.00
Floral and Grape, Fenton, water set, pitcher, two tumblers,
    blue..150.00
Flowers and Frames, Dugan, bowl, dome foot, peach
    opalescent..155.00
Flowering Dill, Fenton, hat, amethyst 40.00
Flowers and Frames, Dugan, bowl, 9" d, peach opale-
    scent..175.00
Fluffy Peacock, tumbler, cobalt blue 95.00
Flute, Millersburg, berry bowl, aqua 20.00
Flute and Cane, Imperial, bowl, 8-1/2" d, deep ruffle,
    marigold..25.00
Frosted Block, Imperial, bowl, 8-1/2" oblong, marigold.....30.00
Fruits and Flowers, Northwood
    Bon Bon, handled, stemmed, green.........................275.00
    Bon Bon, handled, stemmed, electric blue, 4" h,
    8-1/2" d 250.00
    Bon Bon, handled, stemmed, sapphire blue 2,500.00
    Bowl, 7" d, green 110.00
Garden Mums, Northwood, bowl, 5-1/4" d, amethyst 375.00
Garden Path Variant, Dugan, bowl, 10" d, white.............300.00
Good Luck, Northwood
    Bowl, pie crust edge, basketweave ext., green..........225.00
    Bowl, pie crust edge, pastel 250.00
    Bowl, ribbed, dark marigold 175.00
    Bowl, ribbed back, blue 450.00
    Plate, dark ice blue 3,400.00
Grape, Imperial
    Bowl, ruffled, green...90.00
    Cup and Saucer, marigold....................................40.00
    Decanter, stopper, marigold..................................75.00
    Tumbler, marigold...40.00
    Tumbler, pastel...30.00
Grape and Cable, Northwood
    Banana Boat, amethyst..210.00
    Berry Bowl, 6" d, ruffled, basketweave ext., pastel.......40.00

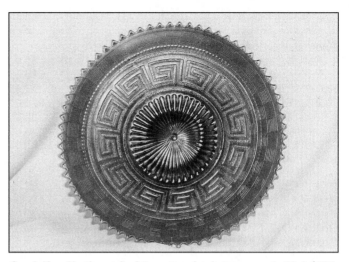

Greek Key, Northwood, plate, green, basketweave ext., 9" d, $825. Photo courtesy of Mickey Reichel Auction Center.

Bowl, 7-1/4" d, basketweave ext., green.....................80.00
Bowl, ruffled, basketweave ext., marigold 35.00
Bowl, stippled, pie crust edge, ice blue 750.00
Breakfast Creamer, pastel 100.00
Candle Lamp, marigold 600.00
Cracker Jar, cov, marigold..350.00
Dresser Tray, ice blue...1,100.00
Dresser Tray, marigold..140.00
Hatpin Holder, green...400.00
Hat Bowl, pastel 45.00
Ice Cream Bowl, 10-1/2" l, white, sgd 175.00
Nappy, pastel 75.00
Orange Bowl, banded, blue......................................800.00
Pin Tray, ice blue..875.00
Plate, 7-3/4" d, hand grip, basketweave ext., green,
    sgd 135.00
Plate, 8" d, 2 sides up, basketweave ext., green........120.00
Plate, 9" d, plain back, marigold 80.00
Powder Jar, cov, amethyst.......................................200.00
Punch Cup, green..35.00
Punch Cup, marigold 22.50
Sherbet, amethyst 40.00
Spooner, marigold, chip..25.00
Sugar Bowl, cov, green..175.00
Sweetmeat, cov, amethyst 95.00
Tumbler, marigold...35.00
Water Set, dark marigold, 7 pc 325.00
Grape and Gothic Arches, Northwood, creamer, pastel, sgd
    "N" 75.00
Grape Delight, Dugan
    Nut Bowl, white...90.00
    Rose Bowl, amethyst...145.00
    Rose Bowl, marigold...125.00
    Rose Bowl, white 100.00
Grape Leaves, Millersburg or Northwood, bowl, dark ice
    blue..2,450.00
Grapevine Lattice, Dugan
    Bowl, low, ruffled, white..85.00
    Plate, 7" d, white..75.00
Greek Key, Northwood, plate, 9" d, basketweave ext.,
    green 825.00
Hanging Cherries, bowl, 8-1/2" d, ftd, peach opalescent ...145.00
Hearts and Flowers, Northwood
    Bowl, ruffled, pie crust edge, marigold.....................500.00
    Bowl, ruffled, ribbed back, ice blue 500.00

Compote, blue...625.00
Compote, Renninger's Blue 1,100.00
Compote, sapphire opalescent.............2,000.00
Compote, white..200.00
Plate, marigold 1,850.00
Heavy Grape, chop plate, marigold 135.00
Heavy Iris, tankard, marigold........................375.00
Holly, Fenton
  Bowl, crimped, ruffled edge, 9" d, marigold 135.00
  Bowl, low, ruffled, blue...............................100.00
  Bowl, ruffled, aqua......................................85.00
  Compote, goblet shape, blue 50.00
  Compote, ribbed, blue 40.00
  Compote, ruffled, green 135.00
  Goblet, red 875.00
  Hat, crimped, ruffled edge, red 450.00
  Hat, 4 sides up, aqua...................................60.00
  Hat, ruffled, blue...55.00
  Hat, ruffled, red, amber, yellow..................150.00
  Ice Cream Bowl, scalloped, 9" d, marigold..................25.00
  Plate, 9-1/4" d, white..................................300.00
  Plate, 9-1/2" d, white..................................210.00
Holly and Berry, Dugan, bowl, ruffled, peach opalescent.... 110.00
Holly Sprig (Whirl), Millersburg
  Bon Bon, 2 handles, green 80.00
  Bowl, 6" d, deep, crimped, ruffled edge, green............70.00
  Bowl, 9-3/4" d, ruffled, amethyst 115.00
  Bowl, 9-3/4" d, ruffled, green......................120.00
  Calling Card Tray, green...............................80.00
Horse Head Medallion
  Bowl, ruffled, blue 150.00
  Nut Bowl, ftd, vaseline................................550.00
Inverted Strawberry, Cambridge, lady's spittoon, marigold, sgd
  "Near Cut," 3" h, 5-1/2" w........................750.00
Kittens, Fenton, cereal bowl, marigold 290.00
Lattice and Grape, Fenton, tumbler, marigold..................30.00
Lattice and Points, Dugan, vase, 9-1/2" h, marigold..........40.00
Leaf Chain, Fenton
  Bowl, blue, 9" d 100.00
  Plate, 7" d, marigold, 7" d...........................100.00
  Plate, white, 7" d, ...300.00
Leaf Column, Northwood, vase, 10" h, white 125.00
Lined Lattice, Dugan
  Vase, 9-1/2" h, white..................................75.00
  Vase, 11" h
    Light lavender/smoke...............................220.00
    Pastel...165.00
Lion, Fenton, bowl, ruffled, 7" d, marigold 110.00
Little Fishes, Fenton, sauce, ftd, dark marigold...............200.00
Little Stars, Millersburg, bowl, 8" d, low, ruffled, pastel
  marigold 105.00
Long Thumbprint, Dugan, vase, 7" h, aqua 35.00
Lotus and Grape, Fenton
  Bowl, low, ruffled, marigold.........................65.00
  Bowl, 7" d, ftd, marigold 25.00
Louisa, Westmoreland
  Plate, ftd, marigold 70.00
  Rose Bowl, amethyst 105.00
Lustre Rose, Imperial
  Ice Cream Bowl, collared base, flared edge, smoke 150.00
  Ice Cream Bowl, ftd, pastel, 10" d, ...220.00
  Plate, 9" d, amber 120.00
Many Stars, Millersburg, ice cream bowl, 5 points,
  marigold 1,400.00
Mayan, Millersburg, bowl, 7-3/4" d, green.........................85.00
Memphis, Northwood, punch cup, marigold 7.50

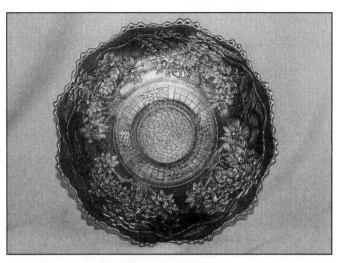

Orange Tree, Fenton, plate, marigold, 9-1/4" d, $425. Photo courtesy of Mickey Reichel Auction Center.

Mikado, Fenton, compote, ruffled, blue 650.00
Milady, Fenton, tumbler, blue 75.00
Morning Glory, Millersburg, vase, 7" h, pastel, radium... 200.00
Nippon, Northwood, bowl, pie crust edge
  Ice Blue 375.00
  White 285.00
Northern Star, Fenton, plate, 6" d, two sides turned up, very light
  marigold 20.00
Octagon, Imperial, wine, marigold.................................25.00
Ohio Star, Millersburg, vase, green 2,800.00
Omnibus, U. S. Glass, tumbler, marigold 225.00
Orange Tree, Fenton
  Bowl, ruffled, 9" d, white.............................110.00
  Hat Pin Holder, cobalt blue, 7" h................150.00
  Ice Cream Bowl, 7-3/4" d, trunk center, electric blue 250.00
  Mug, blue, 3-1/2" h 185.00
  Mug, Persian Blue 60.00
  Orange Bowl, blue 150.00
  Plate, 9" d, white.......................................175.00
  Plate, 9-1/4" d, marigold............................425.00
  Plate, 9-1/4" d, white.................................250.00
  Punch Bowl, matching base, blue 360.00
  Tumbler, marigold.......................................70.00
Pansy, Imperial, dresser tray, stippled amber...............135.00
Panther, Fenton, bowl, ruffled, claw feet, blue, 10" d 900.00
Peacock and Dahlia, Fenton
  Bowl, spatula ftd, amethyst........................100.00
  Plate, 7" d, ruffled, blue 450.00
Peacock and Grape, Fenton
  Bowl, ftd, lime opalescent..........................585.00
  Bowl, ruffled, pumpkin marigold 325.00
  Ice cream bowl, spatula foot, amethyst 120.00
  Ice cream bowl, spatula foot, green 60.00
  Plate, collar base, marigold 1,100.00
Peacock and Urn, Fenton
  Bowl, 8" d, ruffled, marigold.......................150.00
  Compote, blue...45.00
  Ice Cream Bowl, dark marigold 600.00
  Plate, 9" d, blue...550.00
  Plate, 9" d, deep marigold..........................375.00
  Plate, 9" d, white.......................................400.00
  Sauce Bowl, pastel......................................95.00
Peacock at Fountain, Northwood
  Bowl, marigold 235.00
  Compote, ice blue....................................1,100.00

Peacocks, Northwood, plate, stippled, ribbed back, blue, $800. Photo courtesy of Mickey Reichel Auction Center.

Poppy Show, Northwood, ruffled, blue, $1,400. Photo courtesy of Mickey Reichel Auction Center.

Pitcher, light blue 2,000.00
Tumbler, light blue 175.00
Tumbler, dark marigold..25.00
Peacocks, Northwood
   Berry Bowl, 5-1/4" d, amethyst.....................................90.00
   Bowl, ruffled, electric blue...650.00
   Bowl, ruffled, ribbed back, marigold.........................325.00
   Plate, ribbed back, cobalt blue..................................850.00
   Plate, ribbed back, ice blue.....................................2,400.00
   Plate, stippled, ribbed back, blue...............................800.00
Peacocks on the Fence, Northwood
   Bowl, ruffled, 9" d, ice green....................................1,100.00
   Bowl, ruffled, ribbed back, blue..................................600.00
   Bowl, ribbed back, whimsy type, ice blue...............2,000.00
   Plate, 9" d, ice green...300.00
   Plate, 9" d, lavender..550.00
   Plate, 9" d, ribbed back, white..................................475.00
Peacock Tail, Fenton, dish, triangular, sides pulled up to 2"
   peach, 7" d, marigold..85.00
Peacock Tail Variant, Millersburg, compote, green.........125.00
Persian Garden, Dugan
   Bowl, 10-1/2" d, deep, ruffled, peach 450.00
   Plate, 6" d, white...65.00
   Plate, 6-1/2" d, blue..135.00
   Plate, 6-3/4" d, dark marigold.....................................80.00
   Plate, 7-12" d, white...125.00
Persian Medallion, Fenton
   Bon Bon, aqua, four sided 200.00
   Bon Bon, reverse amberina 850.00
   Bowl, 8-1/2" d, 3 in 1 edge, amethyst 140.00
   Compote, amethyst...125.00
   Hair Receiver, sq top, marigold 50.00
   Ice Cream Bowl, crimped edge, amethyst 165.00
   Plate, 6" d, blue..135.00
   Plate, 6" d, marigold..50.00
Petal & Fan, Dugan
   Bowl, 5" d, peach opalescent, ruffled 75.00
   Bowl, 10" d, peach opalescent 200.00
Pine Cone, Fenton
   Ice Cream Bowl, 6-3/4" d, blue 110.00
   Plate, 6" d, amethyst..225.00
   Plate, 6" d, blue, silvery iridescent 95.00
   Plate, 6" d, marigold..70.00
Plum Panels, Fenton
   Compote, green 40.00

Vase, 10-1/2" h, red..650.00
Vase, 12" h, green 100.00
Poinsettia, Northwood, milk pitcher, marigold 185.00
Pony, Dugan, bowl, amethyst 435.00
Poppy Show, Northwood
   Bowl, ruffled, blue, mkd 1,400.00
   Plate, amethyst..1,150.00
   Plate, 9"d, green...3,000.00
Question Marks, Dugan
   Bon Bon, 2 handled, stemmed, amethyst....................75.00
   Compote, crimped ruffled edge, peach opalescent...140.00
Rainbow, Northwood
   Bowl, basketweave back, green 105.00
   Compote, amethyst..95.00
Raspberry, Northwood, milk pitcher, green, gold bronze color,
   7-1/2" h 165.00
Rays and Ribbons, Millersburg, bowl, fluted, amethyst 200.00
Ribbon Tie, Fenton, bowl, 3 in 1, amethyst.................... 130.00
Rings, Jeanette, vase, gold irid, 8" h 45.00
Ripple, Imperial
   Vase, 10-1/2" h, green...50.00
   Vase, 10-1/2" h, pastel 150.00
   Vase, 11-1/2" h, pastel 165.00
Robin, Imperial, water pitcher and 4 tumblers, marigold 750.00

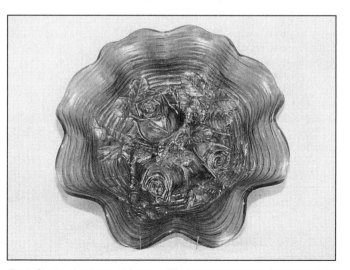

Rose Show, Northwood, bowl, ruffled, sapphire blue, $2,250. Photo courtesy of Mickey Reichel Auction Center.

Rococo, Imperial.
    Bowl, ruffled, marigold 20.00
    Vase, marigold 120.00
    Vase, ruffled, 3-1/2" h, smoke 65.00
Rose Columns, Millersburg, vase, green....................5,500.00
Rose Show, Northwood
    Bowl, dark marigold 1,500.00
    Plate, electric blue...2,100.00
Round-Up, Dugan
    Bowl, 8-1/2" d, low, ruffled, marigold 85.00
    Bowl, 8-1/2" d, low, pastel opalescent 195.00
    Plate, 8-3/4" d, white..175.00
Rustic, Fenton, vase
    6-1/2" h, white...70.00
    19-1/2" h, 5-1/4" d, marigold 700.00
    20" h, 5" d base, green..1,500.00
Sailboats, Fenton, bowl, 6" d, ruffled, marigold 75.00
Scales, Westmoreland, bowl, amethyst.........................40.00
Scroll Embossed, Imperial
    Berry Set, File pattern ext., 6 pc, pastel.....................175.00
    Compote, large, deep amethyst 80.00
    Plate, green 60.00
Shell and Sand, bowl, 8" d, ruffled, teal green................125.00
Singing Birds, Northwood
    Berry Bowl, master, green...2,500.00
    Mug, amethyst 75.00
    Mug, aqua opalescent 1,350.00
    Mug, green, straight sides 165.00
    Mug, light blue 550.00
    Tumbler, green, sgd "N" 135.00
Single Flower, Dugan
    Bowl, 3-1, peach opalescent..35.00
    Plate, 7" d, peach opalescent 40.00
Ski Star, Dugan
    Banana Boat, peach opalescent....................................50.00
    Bowl, 8" d, ruffled, peach opalescent 50.00
    Bowl, 10" d, tri-corner, dome ftd, peach opalescent 125.00
    Bowl, 11" d, ruffled, peach opalescent 400.00
Smooth Ray, Westmoreland
    Bowl, 8" deep, teal 25.00
    Bowl, 9-1/2" d, deep ruffled, vaseline 35.00
Soldiers and Sailors, Fenton, plate, marigold 2,250.00
Spearhead and Rib, Fenton, vase, dark marigold, ruffled top,
    14" h..50.00
Spiralex, English, vase, 11" h, peach opalescent.............45.00
Springtime, Northwood
    Tumbler, green..65.00
    Water Pitcher, green 900.00
    Water Pitcher, marigold...600.00
S-Repeat, Dugan, punch cup, amethyst 12.50
Stag and Holly, Fenton, ice cream bowl, 8" d, spatula foot
    Cobalt blue..350.00
    Marigold 90.00
Starfish, Dugan, compote, peach opalescent 85.00
Star of David and Bows, Northwood, bowl, amethyst........70.00
Stippled Flower, Dugan, bowl, tri-corner, peach opale-
    scent 65.00
Stippled Rays, Fenton
    Bowl, 6" d, amberina 300.00
    Bowl, 6-1/2" d, six ruffles, Scale Band ext., red 300.00
Stippled Rays, Northwood, bowl, amethyst......................60.00
Stippled Strawberries, Jenkins
    Bowl, pie crust edge, blue 300.00
    Plate, 9" d, ribbed back, green 1,250.00
Stork and Rushes, Dugan
    Mug, banded top, amethyst..70.00

Tumbler, blue 40.00
Tumbler, lattice banded, marigold 20.00
Water set, deep blue, 8" h pitcher, four 4" h tumblers 400.00
Strawberry, Millersburg and Northwood
    Bowl, 8" d, crimped ruffled edge, green, radium,
      Millersburg...275.00
    Bowl, 8-1/2" d, pie crust edge, stippled, blue.............450.00
    Bowl, 9" d, plain back, pastel marigold......................200.00
    Bowl, 9"d, stippled, pastel 250.00
    Compote, amethyst 400.00
    Compote, marigold, Millersburg 450.00
    Ice Cream Bowl, amethyst 150.00
    Plate, basketweave ext., marigold 76.00
    Plate, 7-1/2" d, hand grip, green, "N" mark.................300.00
    Plate, 9" d, amethyst, mkd..170.00
    Plate, 9" d, green, "N" mark 265.00
    Plate, 9" d, marigold, "N" mark....................................150.00
Strawberry Scroll, Fenton, tumbler, blue.......................140.00
Sunflower, Millersburg, pin tray
    Green 90.00
    Pastel 75.00
Swan, Dugan, master salt
    Celeste blue 20.00
    Florentine ice green 50.00
Swirl, Northwood, compote, tricorn, 3-1/2" d, marigold .. 100.00
Ten Mums, Fenton, bowl, 9-1/2" d, 3 in1 edge, amethyst ... 300.00
Thin Rib, Dugan, vase
    5" h, squatty, peach opalescent....................................80.00
    15" h, pastel 25.00
Thin Rib, Northwood, vase, 10" h, blue, electric highlights ... 115.00
Thistle, Fenton
    Banana Boat, blue..500.00
    Banana Boat, deep marigold...140.00
    Banana Boat, green..600.00
    Bowl, crimped ruffled edge, , blue................................175.00
    Bowl, 9" d, 3 in 1, green 70.00
Three Fruits, Northwood
    Bowl, ruffled, basketweave ext., marigold, sgd 200.00
    Bowl, ruffled, collar base, stippled, pastel opal sapphire
      blue...950.00
    Bowl, ruffled, meander ext., stippled, ftd, butterscotch aqua
      opal...450.00
    Bowl, stippled, pumpkin marigold 400.00
    Bowl, stippled, ribbed back, collar base, white.........250.00
    Plate, basketweave ext., green 200.00
    Plate, 9" d, stippled, marigold 185.00
    Plate, 9" d, stippled, ribbed back, dark marigold 375.00
    Plate, 9" d, stippled, ribbed back, amethyst 450.00
    Plate, 9-1/2" d, pale amethyst horehound 800.00
Tiger Lily, Imperial, tumbler, pastel.................................125.00
Top of the Morning, variant, hatpin, pastel 75.00
Tree Trunk, Northwood, vase, 12" h, 4-3/4" d base, amethyst,
    sgd 245.00
Trout and Fly, Millersburg, ice cream bowl, low, amethyst ... 750.00
Tulip, Millersburg, plate, 9" d, marigold 90.00
Tulip and Cane, Imperial, goblet, marigold 40.00
Triplets, (Daisy Dear), Dugan, bowl, 7" d, ruffled, vaseline ... 20.00
Twins, Imperial, berry bowl, 6" d, marigold.....................40.00
Two Flowers, Fenton
    Bowl, ruffled, ftd, large, blue.......................................150.00
    Rose bowl, ftd, blue 100.00
Victorian, bowl, 11" d, ruffled
    Amethyst 400.00
    Pastel 475.00
Vineyard, Dugan, water pitcher, marigold 90.00
Vintage, Fenton, Millersburg, Northwood
    Bowl, 8" d, candy ribbon edge, green 175.00

Bowl, 8" d, cherry red 1,600.00
Bowl, 9" d, ruffled, green 60.00
Compote, marigold 65.00
Plate, 7" d, blue 200.00
Plate, 7-1/2" d, amethyst 450.00
Vintage Leaf, Fenton
Ice Cream Bowl, tightly crimped, lavender 150.00
Plate, marigold 1,400.00
Waffle Block, Imperial, punch bowl, teal 100.00
Water Lily and Cattails, Northwood
Butter, cov, marigold 325.00
Tumbler, pastel 850.00
Whirling Leaves, Millersburg, bowl, 8-1/2" d, ruffled
Amethyst 150.00
Green, cut leaves 400.00
Wide Panel, Imperial, vase, 10" h, red 300.00
Wide Rib, Dugan, vase, 11" h, cobalt blue 50.00
Wild Blackberry, Fenton, bowl, crimped ruffled edge,
green 225.00
Wild Strawberry, Northwood
Bowl, 10" d, basketweave back, amethyst 250.00
Bowl, 10" d, basketweave back, marigold 135.00
Bowl, 10" d, pastel 225.00
Plate, 701/4" d, hand grip, green 175.00
Wildflower, Dugan, nappy, handle, marigold 80.00
Wishbone, Northwood
Bowl, 3 ftd, marigold 135.00
Bowl, ruffled, 3 ftd, amethyst 110.00
Bowl, ruffled, 3 ftd, white 300.00
Epergne, single lily, green 550.00
Wishbone and Flowers, bowl, 3 ftd, green 140.00
Zig Zag, Millersburg, bowl, amethyst, 3 in 1, amethyst 450.00
Zippered Heart, Imperial, berry set, 7 pc, pastel 250.00
Zipper Loop, Imperial
Lamp, 8" h, 4-3/4" base, marigold 325.00
Lamp, 9" h, 5-1/8" base, marigold 285.00

CENTRAL GLASS WORKS

History: Central Glass Works, Wheeling, W.V., was established as a cooperative in 1863 by workmen from J. H. Hobbs, Brockunier and Company. It failed shortly thereafter and was reorganized as a stock company in 1867. Production continued until 1939.

Early goods were bottles, lamps, and barware. Around 1900, production began of crystal and decorated tablewares, as well as barware and tumblers for homes and famous hotels. In 1919, Central Glass acquired the molds for Benjamin W. Jacob's very successful Chippendale pattern. The trademark, Krys-Tol (and sometimes the pattern date) is marked in the mold. Chippendale was made in more than 300 forms and was widely distributed. It achieved such great popularity in England that molds were sent to an English firm in 1933.

Central Glass produced a large line of optic glassware, as well as selling blanks to decorating companies. Several etched patterns were also popular.

Reference: Hazel Marie Weatherman, *Colored Glassware of the Depression Era, Book 2,* Glassbooks, Inc., 1982.

Periodical: *The Daze,* Box 57, Otisville, MI 48463.

Bon Bon, Balda, Morgan etch, 2 handles, black 95.00

Vase, Ebony, gold encrusted Morgan etching, 10" h, $255.

Bowl
9-1/2" d, Frances, green 35.00
11" d, Frances, green, crimped, ... 40.00
11" d, Frances, green, rolled, 3 toes 40.00
11-1/2" d, Balda, lavender, rolled edge 50.00
Butter Dish, cov, Chippendale pattern colorless 20.00
Candlesticks, pr, Frances, 3-1/2" h, green 40.00
Champagne, Balda, light amethyst, 5-3/4" h 30.00
Cocktail, Balda, lavender 30.00
Console set, bowl and pr candlesticks, colorless
Memphis 50.00
Zoricor 55.00
Creamer
Balda, lavender 30.00
Chippendale, colorless 25.00
Frances, green 15.00
Cream Soup and liner, Balda, lavender 40.00
Decanter Set, decanter, 6 cordial glasses, Balda,
lavender 660.00
Fruit Bowl, Frances, 10" d, 3 toes, green 35.00
Goblet, water
Acorn, colorless 15.00
Balda, lavender 30.00
Frances, colorless 18.00
Hester, colorless 15.00
Morgan, blue and crystal 95.00
Sheila, colorless 15.00
Veninga, colorless 15.00
Hair Receiver, cov, Chippendale, colorless 15.00
Mayonnaise, Morgan, ftd, 2 handles, matching ladle,
rose 165.00
Pitcher, water
Acorn, colorless 35.00
Balda, lavender 300.00
Ring Holder, Chippendale, colorless 15.00
Server, Morgan, 10" d, center handle, green 135.00
Sherbet, 4-7/8" h, Balda, lavender, 4-7/8" h 18.00
Sugar, cov
Balda, lavender 30.00
Chippendale, colorless 25.00

Frances, green..15.00
Tumbler
    Balda, light amethyst, 3" d, ftd 37.50
    Balda, lavender, 5-1/8" d, ftd,.......................25.00
    Hester, colorless 15.00
    Morgan, cone shape, 4-1/2" h, 6 oz, cone shape.........40.00
Tumble-Up, Thistle etching................................25.00
Wine
    Balda, lavender, 5-1/2" h, 2-1/2 oz.............40.00
    Chippendale, colorless 20.00

CHILDREN'S TOY DISHES

History: Dishes made for children often served a dual purpose–play things and a means of learning social graces. Dish sets came in two sizes. The first was for actual use by the child when entertaining her friends. The second, a smaller size than the first, was for use with dolls.

Children's dish sets often were made as a sideline to a major manufacturing line either as a complement to the family service or as a way to use up the last of the day's batch of materials.

Children's toy dishes were made by many of the major manufacturers, such as Cambridge, Akro Agate, Jeannette Glass Co., and Hazel Atlas. Collectors prefer complete sets and mint pieces; sometimes this is difficult to achieve because the pieces were toys and enjoyed by children of years ago.

Children's toy dishes are commonly sold in combinations such as berry sets, table sets, and water sets. Due to the small size of the items, the display desirability of a grouping of pieces has increased their value.

Unlike toy dishes meant for play, children's feeding dishes are the items actually used in the feeding of a child. Their colorful designs of animals, nursery rhymes, and children's activities are meant to appeal to the child and make mealtimes fun.

References: Maureen Batkin, *Gifts for Good Children, Part II, 1890-1990*, Antique Collectors' Club, 1996; Gene Florence, *The Collectors Encyclopedia of Akro Agate Glassware, Revised Edition,* Collector Books, 1975, 1992 value update; Roger and Claudia Hardy, *The Complete Line of Akro Agate: Marbles, General Line and Children's Dishes With Prices*, published by authors, 1992; Doris Lechler, *Children's Glass Dishes, China and Furniture, Volume I*, Collector Books, 1982, 1991 value update; Doris Lechler, *Volume II*, Collector Books, 1986, 1993 value update; Doris Lechler, *French and German Dolls, Dishes, and Accessories*, Antique Publications, 1991; Doris Lechler, *Toy Glass*, Antique Publications, 1989; Lorraine May Punchard, *Child's Play,* published by author, 1982; —, *Playtime Kitchen Items, and Table Accessories*, published by author, 1993; Margaret & Kenn Whitmyer, *Children's Dishes,* Collector Books, 1984, 1995 value update.

Collectors' Club: Toy Dish Collectors, P.O. Box 351, Camilus, NY 13031.

Additional Listings: Also see Akro Agate.

Reproduction Alert: Reproductions exist in several types of Children's Glass and are indicated with an asterisk.

Mug, Degenhart, stork, cobalt blue carnival, 2-5/8" h, $50.

Child-Sized Dishes

Bowl
    Breakfast of Champions.............................55.00
    Children, red dec 12.00
    Davy Crockett, brown and white 20.00
    Dutch Girl 10.00
    Wheaties, red and white.............................25.00
Cereal Bowl, Circus, red, Pyrex 15.00
Mug
    Batman, Wakefield 16.00
    Bo Peep, red and white.............................10.00
    Circus, red and white................................6.00
    Circus Clowns, red and white 12.00
    Davy Crockett, brown and white 10.00
    Davy Crockett, red and white.....................13.00
    Esso Tiger 5.00
    Indians, red 9.00
    Ranger Joe, blue......................................11.00
    Robin Hood, red and white 15.00
    Smokey the Bear 20.00

Play Dishes

Akro Agate

Dinner Set, Interior Panel, small, amber, orig box,
    21 pcs...200.00
Tea Set, Octagonal, large, green and white, Little American
    Maid, orig box, 17 pcs 225.00

Akro Agate, tumblers, Interior Panel and Stacked Disc, cobalt blue, $50.

Water Set, Play Time, pink and blue, orig box, 7 pcs 125.00
Bohemian, decanter set, ruby flashed, Vintage dec,
  5 pcs..135.00
Contemporary Glass, Mosser Glass
  Jennifer Pattern, pink, green or yellow, made to resemble
    Depression Glass Cameo pattern
    Berry Set, master bowl, four rimmed bowls 20.00
    Console Set 20.00
    Cup and Saucer, 8 pc set 22.00
    Dessert Set, cake plate, four plates 25.00
    Goblet, 4 pc set 20.00
    Grill Plate, 4 pc set 25.00
    Ice Tub 12.00
    Juice Set, juice pitcher, 4 tumblers 25.00
    Plate, dinner, 4 pc set 20.00
    Salad Set, divided relish, 4 sq plates 22.00
    Table Set, cov butter, creamer, sugar......................18.00
    Tumbler, cone shape 10.00
    Vase..10.00
  Lindsey Pattern, modern version of Cambridge Caprice pat-
    tern, cobalt blue or moonlight blue
    Console Set 25.00
    Cup and Saucer 20.00
    Plate, dinner, 4 pc set 20.00
    Punch Set, punch bowl and six cups........................35.00
    Relish Set, elongated 3-part dish, salt dips 25.00
    Water Set, pitcher, 4 tumblers.................................30.00
Depression-Era Glass
  Bowl, Little Deb, ribbed..15.00
  Creamer
    Cherry Blossom
      Delphite 50.00
      Pink 47.50
    Doric and Pansy
      Pink 35.00
      Ultramarine 45.00
    Laurel
      Green..35.00
      Green, Scotty dec..115.00
      Ivory, Scotty dec...85.00
      Plain...20.00
      Moderntone, rust 6.50
  Creamer and Sugar, Moderntone, pink 30.00
  Cup
    Cherry Blossom*
      Delphite 35.00
      Pink 35.00
    Doric and Pansy
      Pink 32.50
      Ultramarine 48.00
    Homespun
      Crystal..22.00
      Pink 32.00
    Laurel
      Green..30.00
      Green, Scotty dec..60.00
      Ivory, Scotty dec...40.00
      Plain...18.00
    Moderntone
      Blue..14.25
      Burgundy..13.50
      Gray 12.00
      Pink 14.25
      Yellow...14.25
  Mixer, Glassbake, 3 ftd 40.00
  Plate
    Cherry Blossom, 6" d

Delphite 13.00
      Pink 12.50
  Doric and Pansy
    Pink 15.00
    Ultramarine 18.00
  Homespun
    Crystal 10.00
    Pink 15.00
  Laurel
    Green...17.50
    Green, Scotty dec...55.00
    Ivory, Scotty dec..35.00
    Plain..10.00
    Red trim 15.00
  Moderntone
    Blue...12.00
    Chartreuse..9.00
    Gold..9.50
    Gray 8.50
    Green...12.00
    Rust...8.50
    Turquoise 12.50
    Yellow..12.00
Saucer
  Cherry Blossom
    Delphite 7.50
    Pink 6.50
  Doric and Pansy
    Pink 7.00
    Ultramarine 8.50
  Homespun
    Crystal 9.00
    Pink 12.00
  Laurel
    Green...10.00
    Green, Scotty dec...55.00
    Ivory, Scotty dec..25.00
    Plain..8.00
  Moderntone
    Blue...9.75
    Green...9.75
    Pink 9.75
Set
  Cherry Blossom, 14 pc set
    Delphite 425.00
    Pink 400.00
  Diana, crystal, gold trim, rack, price for 12-pc set..... 125.00
  Doric and Pansy, 14 pc set
    Pink 320.00
    Ultramarine 375.00
  Homespun, pink, 4 plates, 4 saucers, 3 cups........195.00
  Laurel, McKee, red trim, 14 pc set........................355.00
  Moderntone, turquoise, gold, 14 pc set 210.00
Sugar
  Cherry Blossom
    Delphite 50.00
    Pink 47.50
  Doric and Pansy
    Pink 35.00
    Ultramarine 45.00
  Laurel
    Green...40.00
    Green, Scotty dec...115.00
    Ivory, Scotty dec..85.00
    Plain..20.00
  Moderntone
    Beige 20.00

Gray 15.00
Pastel Pink 15.00
Rust 6.50
Teapot
  Homespun
    Crystal 65.00
    Pink 75.00
  Moderntone
    Gray 115.00
    Green 95.00
    Lemon 75.00
    Pink 75.00
    White 75.00

Goofus Glass, banana stand, folded, two cupids 35.00

Milk Glass
Butter, cov
  Versailles, emb roses, raised scalloped draping, blue trim,
    Ditheridge, c1900 .... 165.00
  Wild rose 65.00
Creamer, Wild Rose 65.00
Cup, Nursery Rhyme 24.00
Ice Cream Platter, Wild Rose 60.00
Mug
  Gooseberry 35.00
  Little Bo Peep 85.00
Punch Bowl, Wild Rose 45.00
Punch Bowl Set, punch bowl and six cups
  Nursery Rhyme
    Blue 460.00
    White 225.00
    Wild Rose, lemon stain dec 225.00
Stein, Monk, rings on top 25.00
Table Set, cov butter, creamer, cov sugar, spooner
  Thumbelina 95.00
  Wild Rose, 4 pc 275.00

Pattern Glass (colorless unless otherwise noted)
Banana Stand, Beautiful Lady, stemmed 45.00
Berry Bowl
  Fine Cut X 20.00
  Flute 8.00
  Lacy Daisy 8.00
  Pattee Cross 10.00
  Wheat Sheaf 9.00
Berry Set, Wheat Sheaf, 7 pcs 85.00
Butter, cov
  Alabama 215.00
  Amazon 75.00
  Austrian, canary 250.00
  Button Arches, ruby stained, enamel flowers, souv-
    enir 175.00
  Doyle's 500, amber 100.00
  Drum 145.00
  Hawaiian Lei 60.00
  Hobnail with Thumbprint base, blue 95.00
  Lion Head 175.00
  Mardi Gras 125.00
  Michigan, rose stain 185.00
  Pennsylvania, dark green 115.00
  Stippled Forget-Me-Not 100.00
  Tulip and Honeycomb 105.00
  Wee Branches, alphabet base 110.00
Cake Stand
  Beautiful Lady, 4" h, 5" d, c1905 .... 25.00
  Fine Cut and Fan 40.00
  Hawaiian Lei 35.00
  Palm Leaf Fan 35.00
  Rexford 35.00

Ribbon Candy, green 48.00
Candlesticks, pr, Star, Cambridge, light blue 35.00
Castor Set, glass bottles, SP metal base
  American Shield, four bottles 125.00
  Gothic Arches 165.00
Condiment Set
  English Hobnail 45.00
  Hickman, open salt, pepper shaper, cruet, and leaf shaped
    tray 75.00
Creamer
  Alabama 60.00
  Amazon, pedestal 30.00
  Austrian, canary 75.00
  Buzz Saw 15.00
  Colonial, blue 22.00
  Dewdrop 30.00
  Drum 70.00
  Fernland 18.00
  Grapevine with Ovals 40.00
  Hawaiian Lei 15.00
  Hobnail with Thumbprint base, amber 40.00
  Hobnail with Thumbprint base, blue 40.00
  Lamb 75.00
  Lacy Medallion, green, gold trim, souvenir 25.00
  Liberty Bell 65.00
  Lion Head 65.00
  Mardi Gras, ruby stain 75.00
  Nursery Rhyme 30.00
  Pennsylvania 35.00
  Pert 30.00
  Sawtooth Band, Heisey 55.00
  Stippled Forget-Me-Not 80.00
  Tappan, amethyst 35.00
  Tulip and Honeycomb 20.00
  Twin Snowshoes 20.00
  Twist, opalescent, blue 80.00
  Wee Branches 80.00
  Whirligig 230.00
Cruet, English Hobnail, green 25.00
Cup and Saucer, Lion 50.00
Goblet, Vine, cobalt blue 60.00
Honey Jug, Mardi Gras, ruby stain, 2-1/2" h 85.00
Horseradish Dish, Menagerie, bear 120.00
Ice Cream Platter, ABC 125.00
Lemonade Pitcher
  Lily of the Valley 125.00
  Oval Star 65.00
Mug, handle
  Austrian 45.00
  Fighting Cats 35.00
  Grape and Festoon with Shield, cobalt blue 90.00
  Grapevines 20.00
  Grapevine with Ovals 21.00
  Heron 15.00
  Liberty Bell 125.00
  Michigan 45.00
  Old Butterfly 30.00
  Ribbed Forget-Me-Not 25.00
  Robin, amber 25.00
  Robin, translucent blue, Atterbury, 2-1/2" h 35.00
  Robin in Tree, amber 45.00
  Stippled Forget-Me-Not 60.00
  Wee Branches 25.00
Nappy, Michigan 50.00
Pepper Shaker, English Hobnail 10.00

Pitcher
Brick Work 45.00
Colonial 20.00
Hobb's Hobnail 45.00
Michigan, rose stain 50.00
Nursery Rhyme 100.00
Oval Star 20.00
Pattee Cross, gold trim 48.00
Waffle and Button 32.00

Plate
Dog's face 140.00
Sitting Dog, numerals border 125.00
Wee Branches 48.00

Punch Bowl
Inverted Strawberry 75.00
Oval Star, gold trim 55.00
Rex 110.00
Thumbelina 30.00
Whirligig 20.00

Punch Bowl Set, punch bowl and six cups
Flattened Diamond and Sunburst 75.00
Star Arches 75.00
Tulip and Honeycomb 90.00
Wheat Sheaf 75.00

Punch Cup
Inverted Strawberry, Cambridge 17.50
Thumbelina 35.00
Wheat Sheaf 8.00

Spooner
Amazon, pedestal, sawtooth rim 30.00
Austrian, canary 90.00
Colonial, green 20.00
Diamond and Panels 20.00
Doyle's 500, amber 35.00
Duncan & Miller #42, some gold trim 30.00
Hawaiian Lei 35.00
Lion Head 90.00
Mardi Gras 45.00
Menagerie Fish, amber 150.00
Michigan, rose stain 120.00
Mitered Sawtooth 26.00
Pennsylvania 20.00
Stippled Forget-Me-Not 80.00
Tulip and Honeycomb 20.00
Twist, opalescent, vaseline 75.00
Whirligig 20.00

Sugar, cov
Alabama 90.00
Amazon, pedestal 35.00
Austrian, canary 150.00
Beaded Swirl 40.00
Colonial, blue 30.00
Drum 65.00
Fernland 20.00
Hawaiian Lei, with bee 40.00
Liberty Bell 135.00
Lion Head 125.00
Mardi Gras 65.00
Michigan 55.00
Nursery Rhyme 48.00
Oval Star 30.00
Stippled Forget-Me-Not 115.00
Tappan, amethyst 45.00
Tulip with Honeycomb 25.00

Table Set, 4 pcs, cov butter dish, creamer, cov sugar, spooner
Arrowhead in Oval 100.00
Beaded Swirl 125.00

Clear and Diamond Panels, blue 185.00
Hobnail Thumbprint Base, 4 pc set on matching
  tray 75.00
Oval Star, 4 pcs 75.00
Sweetheart 90.00
Thumbelina, 3 pcs 85.00
Tray, Doyle's 500, amber 50.00

Tumbler
Michigan 12.00
Nursery Rhyme 20.00
Oval Star 12.00
Pattee Cross 12.00
Sandwich Ten Panel, sapphire blue 145.00
Water Set, Nursery Rhyme, pitcher, 6 tumblers 225.00

COCKTAIL COLLECTIBLES

History: The cocktail shaker traces its origins as far back as 7000 B.C. and the South American jar gourd, a closed container used to mix liquids. The ancient Egyptians of 3500 B.C. added spices to fermented grain–perhaps history's first cocktails. Alcoholic drinks have been a part of recorded history into the modern era.

By the late 1800s, bartenders used a shaker as a standard tool. Passing the liquid back and forth between two containers created a much appreciated show.

The modern cocktail shaker arrived on the scene in the 1920s, when martinis were in vogue. Shapes tended to be stylish, and materials ranged from glass to sterling silver. Perhaps nothing symbolizes the Jazz Age more than the flapper dress and cocktail shaker. When Prohibition ended in 1933, the cocktail shaker enjoyed another surge of popularity.

Movies helped popularize the cocktail shaker. William Powell showed a bartender how to mix a proper martini in "The Thin Man," a tradition continued by James Bond in the 007 movies. Tom Cruise's portrayal of a bartender in "Cocktail" helped solidify the collecting interest in cocktail shakers during the 1980s.

Following World War II, a bar became a common fixture in many homes. Every home bar featured one or more cocktail shakers and/or cocktail shaker sets. Chrome-plated stainless-steel shakers replaced the sterling-silver shakers of the 1920s and 1930s. Major glass companies, such as Cambridge, Heisey, and Imperial, offered cocktail shakers. Life in the fabulous '50s was filled with novelties; cocktail shakers were no exception. Figural and other forms of novelty shakers appeared.

Run your fingers around the edge of glass shakers to check for chipping. A small chip reduces the price by a minimum of 30 percent. Shakers with brilliant sharp colors are more desirable than those made of clear glass. Be on the constant alert for cracks and fractures. Most individuals want shakers that are usable and are at least in fine condition.

Reference: Tom and Neila Bredehoft, *Fifty Years of Collectible Glass, 1920-1970*, Antique Trader Books, 1997; Stephen Visakay, *Vintage Bar Ware*, Collector Books, 1997.

Periodicals: *Collector Glass News*, 108 Poplar Forest Dr., P.O. Box 308, Slippery Rock, PA 16057; *Root Beer Float*, P.O. Box 571, Lake Geneva, WI 53147.

Collectors' Club: The Shot Glass Club of America, 5071 Watson Dr., Flint, MI 48506.

Ad, The latest in Beverage Sets, courtesy of Macbeth Evans, Crockery and Glass Journal, 1933.

Additional Listings: Also see specific manufacturers.

Beverage Set
    Depression Glass, pitcher, decanter, orig stopper, seven 4" h tumblers, eight 3-1/2" h tumblers, Scottie dog dec on each, price for set 135.00
    Weston, cobalt blue, ribbed pitcher with ice lip, applied crystal handle, five matching tumblers 175.00
Brandy Snifter, Cambridge, Nude, Tahoe blue 325.00
Champagne
    Duncan Miller, Terrace, red 95.00
    Fostoria, American, amethyst...22.50
Claret
    Cambridge, Nudes, forest green 150.00
    Fostoria, Navarre, 6" h...60.00
Cocktail
    Cambridge
        Moonlight Blue...10.00
        Nude, amethyst 110.00
    Fostoria
        American 15.00
        Buttercup 24.00
    Heisey, Steeplechase, pale yellow, frosted base 100.00
    Tiffin, June Night 45.00
Cocktail Set
    Art Deco style, glass shaker, six tall glasses, five shorter glasses, stippled frosted surface, gold and colored mid bands, 1950s...65.00
    Dorflinger, 6" h colorless glass mixing beaker, enameled cock rooster, six 4-3/4" h martini glasses with matching fighting hens, 7 pc set...290.00
    Fostoria, #2518 Line, ruby decanter and six matching cordials, 7 pc set 200.00
    Rockwell Silver Overlay, 11" h Czechoslovakian black glass vasiform decanter topped with corked lid, pouring spouts and stopper, Art Deco silver overlay floral design, two 5-1/4" h martini glasses with Flambo red bowls, black stems, matching dec, Rockwell shield mark on bases........690.00
    Steuben, crystal, 6-1/2" h carafe, two pedestal base glasses, orig case, orig cloth bags 400.00
Cocktail Shaker
    Cambridge, Diane pattern, clear, matching glass top ... 150.00
    Hawkes, 11-3/4" h, 5" w, cut glass, all over brilliant period cutting featuring ovals and bands, sterling silver top and shaker both sgd "Hawkes"..................................200.00
    Heisey, #4036, rooster head stopper, 1 quart 225.00
    Macbeth Evans, Crackle pattern, crystal 18.00
    New Martinsville, Moondrops, green, handle, top missing 20.00
    Paden City, Utopia, clear 165.00
    Sportsman Series, cobalt blue, white image
        Ship dec 60.00
        Windmill dec...25.00
Cordial, McKee, Rock Crystal....................................12.00
Cordial Set
    Central Glass Co, Balda Orchid pattern, decanter, six matching cordial glasses..375.00
    Cambridge, amber, 12 oz decanter 3400/119 and four 1 oz 1341 cordials..50.00
    Duncan Miller, Mardi Gras, decanter, six 4-1/2" #5301 cordials, crystal *75.00*
    Rooster, martini pitcher, four matching tumblers, clear, red, and black dec...35.00
Decanter, orig stopper, glass
    Duncan Miller, First Love, 32 oz...................................295.00
    Erickson, two tone, green and crystal, controlled bubble stopper 220.00

Farber Ware, Mandarin gold, 32 oz, 3400/92 ....60.00
Fostoria, American pattern, 24 oz, 9-1/2" h.................100.00
Heisey, #980 Moonglo cutting, 1 pint 210.00
Imperial, Cape Cod, etched "Rye"..................................70.00
Decanter Set, Art Deco
    6-3/4" h decanter, faceted cylindrical form, squared stopper, black and burgundy enameled peacock feathers, etched stripes on four sides, six glasses with conforming dec 400.00
    8-1/2" h decanter, globular form, raised sq stopper, etched and enameled black criss-cross design, sq base, four glasses with conforming dec 700.00
    8-1/2" h decanter, globular form, raised tapered stopper, molded and faceted rectangles, black and red accents, six glasses with conforming dec.........................650.00
    9-1/4" h decanter, lozenge form, attenuated stopper, red, black, and white enamel dec, five glasses with conforming dec 500.00
Hors D'oeuvre Pick
    Fruit, set of twelve 20.00
    Man, top hat 3.50
Ice Bucket
    Cambridge, Apple Blossom, amber 30.00
    Duncan Miller, Canterbury, clear 35.00
    Fostoria
        Baroque, yellow..125.00
        Bouquet, Century, clear 80.00
        Chintz, clear with etching 135.00
    Hazel Atlas, white windmill dec, cobalt blue.................30.00
    Imperial Glass, Cape Cod, clear.................................125.00
Low Ball, 8 oz, #4052 National, Heisey......................... 45.00
Martini Glass, 5-3/4" h, cobalt blue, colorless stem, gold rimmed foot, etched border with Art Deco figures, 4 pc set.... 175.00
Martini Pitcher
    Cambridge
        Apple Blossom, clear 200.00
        Diane, clear, etching 600.00
    Tiffin, Twilight, 11-1/2" h 450.00
Martini Set, 32 oz stainless steel martini shaker, James Bond silhouette logo, two 8 oz martini glasses with satin etched 007 gun logo, United Artist exclusive set, MIB 70.00
Old Fashion Tumbler, Catalonia, Consolidated, yellow, 3-7/8" h 20.00
Pilsner, Old Sandwich, Heisey, 10 oz, Moongleam green 45.00
Pitcher
    Modernistic, orange, red, and black screen print, ice lip, 8" h, Bartlett-Collins, c1954 ....24.00
    Scotties, two red Scotties, two black Scotties, red and black stars, ice lip, 8" h, Bartlett-Collins, c1942.................55.00
    Spanish Dancers, 86 oz, ice lip 47.50
    Weston, ruby, ribbed, ice lip, applied crystal handle 120.00
Punch Bowl Set
    Cambridge, Tally Ho, emerald green, mugs, price for 12 pc set...295.00
    Heisey, Lariat, crystal, seven quart punch bowl, ten cups, price for set 255.00
    Heisey, Plantation, Dr. Johnson, six cups, ladle, price for set...950.00
    Westmoreland, Paneled Grape, milk glass, 15 pcs....795.00
Roly Poly, Macbeth Evans, 5 oz, cobalt blue................... 10.00
Shot Glass, Sure Shot, green, gold trim, Imperial............ 22.00
Swizzle Stick
    Advertising, colored 3.50
    Amber...1.50
    Amethyst 1.00
    Black 2.00

Cobalt Blue..2.50
Christmas, set of six................................30.00
Christmas Tree, gold, set of 4.................15.00
Crystal 1.00
Dark Green...3.00
Man, top hat...3.50
Medium Green...3.00
Nude, Art Deco 18.00
Souvenir, Hotel Lexington, amethyst, 1939 World's Fair 20.00
Spatter knob, clear stirrer........................1.00
Toddy Mixer, crystal, green, 12 oz 24.00
Tom and Jerry Set, Fostoria, American pattern, bowl and eight
    mugs...340.00
Tumbler
    Central Glass Co, Balda, light amethyst, ftd, 3" h.........37.50
    Duncan Miller, Terrace, red 37.50
    Fostoria
      June, yellow, ftd...........................32.50
      Versailles, blue, ftd......................45.00
    Heisey, New Era, ftd, 12 oz.............25.00
    Macbeth Evans, Golfer, green or pink satin.................75.00
    Sportsman Series, cobalt blue, white windmill dec,
      12 oz..27.50
    Weston, cobalt blue 12.00
Whiskey
    Duncan and Miller, amethyst, 1 oz........15.00
    Farber Ware, 3400/92, amethyst, 2 oz, price for 6 pc
      set..55.00
    Fostoria, June, ftd, yellow.................75.00
    New Martinsville, Moondrops, cobalt blue....17.00

CONSOLIDATED GLASS COMPANY

History: The Consolidated Lamp and Glass Company was formed as a result of the 1893 merger of the Wallace and McAfee Company, glass and lamp jobbers of Pittsburgh, and the Fostoria Shade & Lamp Company of Fostoria, Ohio. When the Fostoria, Ohio, plant burned down in 1895, Corapolis, Pennsylvania, donated a seven-acre tract of land near the center of town for a new factory. In 1911, the company was the largest lamp, globe, and shade works in the United States, employing more than 400 workers.

In 1925, Reuben Haley, owner of an independent design firm, convinced John Lewis, president of Consolidated, to enter the giftware field utilizing a series of designs inspired by the 1925 Paris Exposition (l'Exposition Internationale des Arts Décorative et Industriels Modernes) and the work of René Lalique. Initially, the glass was marketed by Howard Selden through his showroom at 225 Fifth Avenue in New York City. The first two lines were Catalonian and Martele.

Additional patterns were added in the late 1920s: Florentine (January 1927), Chintz (January 1927), Ruba Rombic (January 1928), and Line 700 (January 1929). On April 2, 1932, Consolidated closed it doors. Kenneth Harley moved about 40 molds to Phoenix. In March 1936, Consolidated reopened under new management, and the "Harley" molds were returned. During this period, the famous Dancing Nymph line, based on an eight-inch salad plate in the 1926 Martele series, was introduced.

In August 1962, Consolidated was sold to Dietz Brothers. A major fire damaged the plant during a 1963 labor dispute and in 1964 the company permanently closed its doors.

References: Ann Gilbert McDonald, *Evolution of the Night Lamp*, Wallace-Homestead, 1979; Jack D. Wilson, *Phoenix & Consolidated Art Glass, 1926-1980*, Antique Publications, 1989.

Collectors' Club: Phoenix and Consolidated Glass Collectors, P.O. Box 3847, Edmond, OK 73083-3847.

Almond Dish, Ruba Rombic, smoky topaz, 3" l 235.00
Animal
    Dragonfly, brown and green stained milk glass 80.00
    Screech Owl, brown stained milk glass 90.00
Ashtray, Santa Maria, green wash 200.00
Basket, Catalonian, green... 48.00
Berry Bowl, master
    Cone, pink, glossy, silverplated rim 110.00
    Criss-Cross, cranberry opalescent, 8" d 175.00
Boat, Lovebirds, 13" l, frosted and clear......................... 350.00
Bon Bon, Ruba Rombic, 6" d, smoky topaz................... 125.00
Bowl
    5-1/2" d, Coronation, Martelé, flared, blue 75.00
    8" d, Dancing Nymph, dark blue wash 365.00
    8" d, Ruba Rombic, smoky topaz...............................900.00
    9-1/2" d, Catalonian, yellow.......................................45.00
Box, cov, 7" l, 5" w, Martelé line, Fruit and Leaf pattern, scalloped
    edge..85.00
Butter Dish, cov
    Cosmos, pink band 200.00
    Guttate, white, gold trim 150.00
Candlesticks, pr
    Five Fruits, Martelé line, green 60.00
    Hummingbird, Martelé line, oval body, jade green,
      6-3/4" h..245.00
    Ruba Rombic, smoky topaz 215.00
    Tropical Fish, blue wash 500.00
Celery Tray, Florette, pink 35.00
Cigarette Box, cov, Phlox, slate blue 150.00
Cocktail, Dancing Nymph, French Crystal........................ 90.00
Cologne Bottle, orig stopper, 4-1/2" h, Cosmos 120.00
Compote, Fish, green 90.00
Console Bowl, Cockatoo, blue, frosted highlights 250.00
Cookie Jar
    6-1/2" h, Regent Line, #3758, Florette, rose pink over white
      opal casing..370.00
    9" h, Con-Cora, white milk glass, gilt dec 60.00
Creamer and Sugar
    Catalonia, light green 45.00
    Cosmos 300.00
    Ruba Rombic, sunshine yellow 350.00
Cruet, orig stopper
    Cone, yellow satin 300.00
    Florette, pink satin 225.00
Cup and Saucer
    Catalonian, green..30.00
    Dancing Nymph, ruby flashed 265.00
Goblet, Dancing Nymph, French Crystal.......................... 90.00
Humidor, Florette, pink satin.. 225.00
Jar, cov, Con-Cora, #3758-9, pine cone dec, irid 165.00
Jug
    Five Fruits, half gallon, French Crystal 250.00
    Spanish Knobs, 5-1/2" h, handle, pink 125.00
Lamp
    Cockatoo, 13" h, figural, orange and blue, black beak, brown
      stump, black base...450.00
    Dogwood, brown and white 135.00
    Elk, 13" h, chocolate brown, blue clock mounted between
      horns, black bass base, shallow annealing mark... 1,000.00

Flower Basket, 8" h, bouquet of roses and poppies, yellows, pinks, green leaves, brown basketweave, black glass base 300.00
Lovebirds, 10-1/2" h, two green lovebirds, orange crest, brown and yellow stump, black base 350.00
Owl, 8-1/2" h, brown owl, black eyes, black glass base 400.00
Mayonnaise Comport, Martelé Iris, green wash 55.00
Miniature Lamp, Cosmos
    7" h, fish net ground 350.00
    9" h, pink, yellow and blue dec, electrified 90.00
Night Light, Santa Maria, block base 450.00
Old Fashioned Tumbler, 3-7/8" h, Catalonian
    Lavender 24.00
    Yellow 20.00
Pickle Castor, Cosmos 525.00
Pitcher, water
    Catalonian, yellow 135.00
    Florette, pink satin 200.00
Plate
    7" d, Catalonian, green 25.00
    7" d, Catalonian, yellow 15.00
    8-1/4" d, Bird of Paradise, amber wash 40.00
    8-1/4" d, Dancing Nymph, French Crystal 85.00
    8-1/4" d, Dancing Nymph, pink 145.00
    8-1/2" d, Five Fruits, green 40.00
    10-1/4" d, Catalonian, yellow 40.00
    12" d, Five Fruits, white 65.00
    12" d, Martelé, Orchid, pink, birds and flowers 115.00
Platter, Dancing Nymph, Palace
    Dark Blue wash 1,000.00
    French Crystal 500.00
Puff Box, cov
    Hummingbirds, milk glass 75.00
    Lovebirds, blue 95.00
Salt and Pepper Shakers, pr
    Cone, green 75.00
    Cone, pink 75.00
    Cosmos 185.00
    Guttate, green 85.00
    Guttate, pink satin 100.00
Sauce, Criss-Cross, cranberry opalescent 55.00
Scent Bottle, orig stopper, Cosmos, pink and blue floral 140.00
Sherbet, ftd
    Catalonian, green 20.00
    Dancing Nymph, blue 85.00
    Dancing Nymph, French Crystal 80.00
Snack Set, Martelé Fruits, pink 45.00
Spooner
    Cosmos 140.00

Criss-Cross, cranberry opalescent 75.00
Sugar Bowl, cov
    Catalonian, green 30.00
    Catalonian, yellow 40.00
    Guttate, cased pink 120.00
Sugar Shaker, orig top
    Cone, green 95.00
    Guttate, cased pink, pewter top 200.00
    Guttate, cranberry, pewter top 450.00
Sundae, Martelé Russet Yellow Fruits 35.00
Syrup
    Cone, squatty, pink 295.00
    Cosmos, SP top 275.00
Toilet Bottle, Ruba Rombic, cased jade green 650.00
Toothpick Holder
    Florette, cased pink 75.00
    Guttate, cranberry 185.00
Tumbler
    Catalonian, ftd, green, 5-1/4" h 30.00
    Cosmos 85.00
    Dancing Nymph, frosted pink, 6" h 175.00
    Guttate, pink satin 60.00
    Katydid, clambroth 165.00
    Martelé Russet Yellow Fruits, ftd, 5-3/4" h 5.00
    Ruba Rombic, jade, 5-1/2" h 325.00
Umbrella Vase, Blackberry 550.00
Vase
    Catalonian, lavender, fan, 6-5/8" h 45.00
    Catalonian, #1101, triangle, rubena, 10" h 90.00
    Catalonian, #1183, three tiers, honey, 6" h 165.00
    Con-Cora, milk glass, hp flowers, 12" h, 8-1/2" d 95.00
    Con-Cora, #8c, pine cone dec, irid 65.00
    Con-Cora, #6X13, tall, pine cone dec 65.00
    Con-Cora, #4916C, pine cone dec, irid 75.00
    Dancing Nymph, crimped, ruby stain, reverse French Crystal highlights, 5" h 135.00
    Dancing Nymph, crimped, rust stain, reverse highlights, 5" h 140.00
    Florentine, collared, flat, green, 12" h 275.00
    Freesia, white ceramic wash, fan 225.00
    Hummingbird, #2588, turquoise on satin custard, 5-1/2" h 90.00
    Katydid, blue wash, fan shaped top, 8-1/2" h 300.00
    Katydid, white frost, 8-1/4" h 115.00
    Katydid, white frost, fan shaped top, 8-1/2" h 165.00
    Lovebirds, custard yellow ground, pale green birds, coral colored flowers, 11-1/4" h, 10" w 600.00
    Peonies, pink, green and brown, 6-1/4" h 80.00
    Poppy, green cased 550.00
    Purple leaf and berry design, opalescent, 9-3/4" h 225.00
    Regent Line, #3758, cased blue stretch over white opal, pinched, 6" h 175.00
    Ruba Rombic, French Silver, 9-1/2" h 4,000.00
Water Pitcher, Florette, pink satin 195.00

CONTEMPORARY COLLECTOR GLASSES

History: Contemporary collector glasses date back to the premiere of "Snow White and the Seven Dwarfs" in December 1937. Libbey Glass and Walt Disney designed tumblers with a safety edge and sold them through variety stores and through local dairies. The glasses were popular with the public, and today, collector glasses can be found with almost every Disney char-

Salt shaker, Bulging Loops pattern, pigeon blood, 3-1/4" h, $100.

acter and movie theme. In 1953, Welch's began to use decorated tumblers as jelly containers and featured Howdy Doody and his characters. These glasses were eagerly received, and Welch's soon added other cartoon characters, like Mr. Magoo, to the designs. By the late 1960s, fast food restaurants began to use tumblers as advertising premiums. Soft drink manufacturers like the Coca-Cola Co. and the Pepsi-Cola Co. saw the advertising potential and helped develop marketing plans for the characters and soft drink products.

Contemporary Collector Glasses are usually produced in series, and it is important to collectors to assemble all the different color variations and items in a series.

Care should be taken when using these tumblers as several early examples were decorated with a lead-based paint. Collectors should try to purchase examples with brightly colored decorations, and avoid faded examples. Because these bright tumblers were mass produced, collectors may be able to find very good to excellent examples.

References: Myles Bader and John Hervey, *Hervey & Bader Collectors' Guide To Glass Collecting,* published by authors, 1988; Mark E. Chase and Michael Kelly, *Contemporary Fast Food and Drinking Glass Collectibles,* Wallace-Homestead, 1988; —, *Collectible Drinking Glasses,* Collector Books, 1995; —, *Collectible Drinking Glasses,* Collector Books, 1998; John Hervey, *Collector's Guide to Cartoon & Promotional Drinking Glasses,* L-W Sales, 1990; Carol and Gene Markowski, *Tomart's Price Guide to Character & Promotional Glasses,* Wallace-Homestead, 1990.

Periodicals: *Collector Glass News*, 108 Poplar Forest Dr., P.O. Box 308, Slippery Rock, PA 16057; *Root Beer Float*, PO Box 571, Lake Geneva, WI 53147.

Collectors' Club: International Glass Collectors Assoc., 3991 Bethel Rd., New Wilmington, PA 16142.

Al Capp, Pappy Yokum, green, 1949, 4-3/4" h 20.00
Alice in Wonderland, Queen of Hearts and Rabbit............22.00
American Greeting Corp
    Christmas is a Gift of Love 5.00
    Holly Hobbie, Coke, Happiness Is 4.00
Amtrak, mug, red and blue logo, 5-1/4" h set of 4 ....10.00
Aquaman..10.00
Arby's
    Actors, Laurel and Hardy...10.00
    Actors, W. C. Fields, 1979...8.00
    Arkansas Razorbacks, 1977 ....4.00
    BC Ice Age, anteater, 1981...8.00
    BC Ice Age, Thor on wheels, 1981 ....8.00
    Bicentennial Stars and Stripes, 1976................................9.00
    Dudley takes tea at sea, 12 oz, 1976..............................23.00
    Memphis State Univ. Tigers, mug.....................................5.00
    Monopoly, College #200 as you pass Go, 1985...........28.00
    Wizard of Id, Wizard, 1983...14.00
    Zodiac, Libra, 1976...3.00
Archie Comic Publications
    Archie Gets A Helping Hand, © 1971, 4 oz....................6.00
    Jughead Wins The Pie Eating Contest, © 1971, 4 oz 4.00
    Reggie Makes The Scene, Veronica etched in bottom, © 1971, 4 oz...6.00
Archie Bunker, mug, "To the rear, march with Arch," blue and white, 5-1/2" h 3.00

Armour, Transportation Series, The Pony Express, 5" h 4.00
Batman
    Bat Mobile, 1989, Canada, 4-1/4" h 4.00
    With Robin The Boy Wonder, blue and gray 45.00
Betty Boop, King Features Syndicate, 1988 ....9.00
Bicentennial Collection, Red Steer Restaurant, 1976
    Cataldo Mission...5.00
    Oregon Trail 5.00
    Silver City 5.00
Borden's, Elsie and Friends, Bicentennial theme 4.00
Bozo the Clown, 1950s 9.00
Burger Chief, Endangered Species Collection, Bald Eagle, 1978.. 5.00
Burger King
    Burger Thing, 1979 ....5.00
    Coca-Cola, Star Wars, Chewbacca, © Twentieth Century-Fox Film Corp., 1977 ....18.00
    Coca-Cola, Star Wars, Ewok Village and C-3PO, © Lucasfilm Ltd., 1983, 16 oz......................................15.00
    Coca-Cola, Star Wars, Luke Skywalker, © Lucasfilm Ltd., 1980, 16 oz...15.00
    Coca-Cola, Whopper, Canadian, 1997.............................5.00
    Dr. Pepper, D. D. Lewis, Dallas cowboys, 5-1/2" h.......10.00
    Duke of Doubt, 1979...5.00
    King Series, 1978...6.00
Cabbage Patch Kids, juice, 3-1/2" h.................................. 5.00
Chili's, Big Chili's Reunion, 1985, 6" h 5.50
Chuck E. Cheese
    All The Characters & Lots of Activity, 5-1/2" h..............20.00
    Chuck E. Cheese, milk glass mug, pedestal, 1981 ....3.00
Cinderella, 1950, Cinderella attending stepsisters............. 8.00
Coca-Cola
    Atlanta, mug...7.00
    Caltex/Coca-Cola, 1996 Worldwide Olympic Partner, 1928-1996 Coca-Cola logo, back reads "South African Olympic Team Proud Sponsor of the South African Team to the 1996 Olympic Games in Atlanta," red star on white circle Texaco logo...15.00
    Classic Golf, red and green plaid background, white lettering...10.00
    Coca-Cola Around The World, 8 pc set, orig box, 1960s...120.00
    Coke/Eat' N Park, Pittsburgh Steelers Hall of Fame, 1996, set of 4...16.00
    Diet Coke, Romain, stirring pot of Diet Coke over fire, Canada...12.00

Braum's Mug, Frost Before Using, black lettering and cow image, $3.

Enjoy Coca-Cola Logo, bell shaped, 6" h
  Bears, NFL..6.00
  Dallas Cowboys..6.00
  Miami Dolphins...6.00
Heritage Collector Series, Monticello.........................26.00
King Kong, New York Subway 3.50
Magnificent Ladies, flared, #5...................................4.00
Mickey's Christmas Carol: Goofy as Marley's Ghost,
  1982...3.50
Olympics, Enjoy Coca-Cola
  1976, slogan in English, Japanese, Hebrew, Arabic, and
    Chinese, set of 4, MIB 40.00
  1996, Atlanta logo, other side with 1919 Olympic Games
    in Stockholm 15.00
  1996, Atlanta logo, other side with 1948 Olympic Games
    in London..15.00
  St. Vincent and the Grenadines, 5-1/8" h.................24.00
World Cup Soccer, Enjoy Coca-Cola, Italia '90, Delhaize,
  Food Lion Star logo 15.00
Dairy Queen
  Beatles, Canada, 16 oz...11.00
  Boy and girl with cone and sundae, 1976 ....6.00
Davy Crockett
  American Pioneer, grew up in the forests, shooting deer,
    red...32.00
  Fighting bear, on horse, Indian pal, brown, frosted, 5" h....35.00
D. C. Comics
  Batman, Super Series, 1976 ....12.00
  Superman, Super Powers, 1993 ....10.00
Disney
  America on Parade, 5-5/8" h 6.00
  Disneyworld, Minnie with purse, 5-5/8" h.................5.00
  Mickey Mouse Club, Donald building brick wall...........14.00
  Mickey Mouse Club, Mickey waving........................8.00
  Nice Shot, Mickey shooting basketball, 6-1/4" h.............6.00
  101 Dalmatians, French, 3-7/8" 15.00
  Pinocchio, Jiminy Cricket, green, 4-3/4" h..............25.00
  Sleeping Beauty, touching the spindle, 1958 ....18.00
  Snow White and Seven Dwarfs, Happy, 4-5/8" h 12.00
Domino's Pizza, Dick Tracy 175.00
Dr. Pepper
  Happy Days, Ralph, 1977......................................10.00
  Happy Days, The Fonz, 1977................................11.00
Star Trek, Kirk, Spock, McCoy and The Enterprise, 1978, set
  of 4...140.00
Esso Tiger, slogan in eight languages, 5-1/2" h 15.00
Hanna-Barbera
  Barney, Pizza Hut, 1986..10.00
  Flintstone children, gold lettering, 3-1/4" h.................55.00
  Fred, Wilma, and Dino, "Wilma," mug, 1991.................3.00
  Going to the Drive-In, Hardee's, 1991 ....10.00
  Here's Your Lunch Fred, Wilma and Fred, European, gold
    rim, 4-3/4" h 35.00
  You Really Like Football, Don't You Fred, Football is it, mug,
    1994...5.00
Hardee's, The Chipmunks, © Bagdasarian Productions, 1985,
  16 oz
  Alvin...10.00
  Chipettes...10.00
  Simon...10.00
  Theodore...10.00
Hess Gas Station, classic truck series, 1996, set of 4.......20.00
Kentucky Derby
  1953 ....90.00
  1954 ....135.00
  1956, 1 star, 2 tails 150.00

1961 ....66.00
1962 ....58.00
1964 ....25.00
1968 ....35.00
1970, Festival 8.00
1972 ....20.00
1975 ....8.00
1978 ....8.00
Marathon Oil, Apollo, carafe, 1970s 7.50
McDonald's
  Big Mac, slogan in several languages, late 1970s 5.00
  Camp Snoopy
    #1, There's No Excuse For Not Being Properly Pre-
      pared 6.00
    #2, Civilization is overrated! 6.00
    #3, The struggle for security is no picnic! 6.00
    #4, Morning People Are Hard To Love 6.00
    #5, Rats! Why is having fun always so much work?....6.00
  Capt. Cook, 12 oz, thick base...............................11.00
  Classic 50's, 1993 ....5.00
  Great Muppet Caper, 5-1/2" h, © Henson Associations, Inc.,
    1981
    Happiness Hotel Bus...6.00
    Hot Air Balloon..6.00
    Kermit..7.00
    Miss Piggy...7.00
  Monopoly, black and white 15.00
Pepsi
  Beaky Buzzard, white letter, Brockway, 1973.................6.00
  Bianca, Disney Rescuers 8.50
  Brutus and Nero, Disney Rescuers.........................9.00
  Bugs Bunny, Broadway, © Warner Bros., 1973, 16 oz 12.00
  Cool Cat and Beaky Buzzard, © Warner Bros., 1976,
    16 oz...15.00
  Daffy Duck and the Tasmanian Devil, 1976, 16 oz 15.00
  Dudley Do-Right, © P.A.T. Ward, 1970s, 16 oz.............20.00
  Minnie Mouse, © Walt Disney Productions, 16 oz 20.00
  Natasha, slight fading, © P.A.T. Ward, 12 oz 35.00
  Porky Pig, © Warner Bros., 1973, 16 oz...................15.00
  Richie Rich, © Harvey Cartoons, white lettering, some color
    registration off...20.00
  Road Runner and Wili E. Coyote Catapult, © Warner Bros.,
    1976, 16 oz..8.00
  Shazam!, © DC Comics, 1978, 16 oz 10.00
  Snidley Whiplash, green lettering, © P. A. T. Ward,
    16 oz...20.00
  Super Action Baseball, 1981, George Brett................18.00
  Superman, faded, © DC Comics, 1975, 16 oz 8.00
  Tweety, Sylvester, and Spike, © Warner Bros., 1976, 16 oz,
    some color registration off..................................8.00
  Underdog, black lettering, © Leonardo, 16 oz 18.00
  Wile E. Coyote, © Warner Bros., 1973, 16 oz, black lettering,
    faded...5.00
  Wonder Woman, © DC Comics, 1978, 16 oz, faded 15.00
  Woody Woodpecker, white lettering, © Walter Lantz, 1970s,
    16 oz,..20.00
Pepsi/Sea World/Pizza Hut, Monster Marsh Dinosaur, 1994,
  central OH issue, set of 4 ....16.00
Pike's Peak, Streamline Cog Train at Summit House, Auto High-
  way, Pikes Peak Cog Railroad, 5" h 9.00
Pizza Hut, Boris and Bullwinkle, faded, registration off on most
  colors...45.00
Preakness, official
  1979 ....35.00
  1981 ....35.00
  1984 ....25.00

1987 ....20.00
Red Lobster, Tropical Explosion, 7" h................................5.00
7-11 Quickshop, Thor, 16 oz......................................30.00
Taco Bell, Star Trek series, 1984, © Paramount Pictures Corp., 16 oz
    Fal-Tor-Pan...12.00
    Lord Kruge..12.00
    Spock Lives, 5-3/4" h......................................10.00
Ultramar Petroleum, Batman, © DC Comics, 1989, 4-1/4" h.. 15.00
Universal Studios, Battlestar Galactica, Apollo, 1979, 16 oz.. 15.00
Warner Bros.
    Bugs Leads A Merry Chase, Yosemite Sam etched in bottom, 1974, 4 oz...5.00
    Daffy Duck, 1976, 4 oz....................................15.00
Wendy's, 1982 World's Fair, Knoxville, TN 8.00
Welch's Looney Tunes, 10 oz round bottom jelly jar, orig lid, © Warner Bros.
    Bugs Bunny, Daffy Duck, and Elmer Fudd, 1994, #11 of 12...125.00
    Daffy Duck and Porky Pig, 1994, #4 of 12 ....5.00
    Foghorn Leghorn and Henry Hawk, 1995, #4 of 6..........5.00
    Roadrunner and Wile E. Coyote, 1994, #8 of 12.............5.00
    Sylvester and Tweety, 1994, #6 of 12...........................5.00
    Tasmanian Devil, 1995, #5 of 6....................................5.00
Wheeling Downs 10th Anniversary, 1976-1986, red, 3-3/8" h... 3.00

CORALENE

History: Coralene refers to glass or china objects which have the design painted on the surface of the piece, along with tiny colorless glass beads which were applied with a fixative. The piece was placed in a muffle to fix the enamel and set the beads. The design and technique were named "coralene" by Mt. Washington Glass, believed to be the originator of American coralene decoration.

Several American and English companies made glass coralene in the 1880s. Seaweed or coral were the most common design. Other motifs were Wheat Sheaf and Fleur-de-Lis. Most of the base glass was satin finished.

Reproduction Alert: Reproductions are on the market, some using an old glass base. The beaded decoration on new coralene has been glued and can be scraped off.

Bowl
    4-1/2" d, blue ground, flowers and leaves, SP holder..... 165.00
    5-1/2" d, blue MOP satin herringbone pattern, pink seaweed coralene, deeply crimped top, applied rim............625.00
    5-1/2" d, peachblow, ruffled, yellow coralene seaweed dec 190.00
Cruet, pink satin, yellow coralene, orig stopper 410.00
Fairy Lamp, 7" h, six rows of yellow coralene, white opaque shade with yellow tinting, brass colored metal holder 375.00
Pickle Castor, 7" h, rubena inverted thumbprint insert, coralene butterflies, floral wreath, bird finial cov, cucumbers and leaves on vine, ring handle, low silverplated frame, marked "Derby Silver Co. #147" 825.00
Pitcher
    5-1/4" h, cased white ground, bright pink lining, gold seaweed coralene, applied amber reeded handle......225.00
    6-1/4" h, shaded yellow ground, white lining, coralene seaweed dec..350.00
    6-1/2" h, pink and white satin stripes, yellow branch coralene, rose int., bulbous shape, tricorner mouth, amber applied handle, polished pontil............................500.00

Sweetmeat, blue ground, flowers and leaves, SP holder 400.00
Toothpick Holder, 2-1/2" h, glossy peachblow, sq raised rim, bulbous body, opaque lining, yellow seaweed coralene dec 275.00
Tumbler, 3-3/4" h, satin glass, medium to light pink, white int., gold seaweed coralene, gold rim.......................... 225.00
Vase
    4-1/2" h, 3-3/8" d, Diamond Quilted pattern, shaded pink, yellow beaded coralene starts in centers of diamonds, white enameled beading around top edge 500.00
    5" h, 4" d, white ground, rose dec 65.00
    5-3/8" h, golden yellow snowflake MOP satin ground, white lining, yellow wheat coralene dec 520.00
    5-1/2" h, 4-5/8" d, fan shaped top, opaque pink satin ground blends to frosted base, all over dec of yellow three leaf sprays with coralene beads 235.00
    6" h, white cased to yellow, yellow coralene beading, ruffled rim...250.00
    7" h, pink shaded and cased to white, diamond pattern, gold beading within design, price for pr 440.00
    7" h, ruffled pink top shading to white mother of pearl, coralene flowers and butterfly 90.00
    7-1/2" h, blue ground, bulbous, yellow coralene seaweed dec 265.00
    7-1/2" h, peachblow satin, deep rose shading to pale pink, yellow coralene seaweed dec, gold trim top, white casing, polished pontil, c1870, mkd "PATENT"...........850.00
    7-3/4" h, 4-3/4" d, pink and green striped satin ground, off-white lining, heavy yellow beaded coralene 475.00
    8" h, blue ground, large pink, green, and white center coralene rose, Japanese 400.00
    8" h, 5" d, alternating pink, white, and green striped satin ground, shades to white base, yellow coralene beading.........520.00
    8-1/2" h, green shaded ground, green beading, gold tracery 350.00
    8-1/2" h, yellow shaded to pale pink cased to opal white, diamond and cross pattern, yellow beading, gold trim, slight bead loss 175.00
    8-1/2" h, 7" w, sapphire blue, two pastel colored coralene lilies, stems, and foliage, reverse with cream colored foliage, 4 clear scrolled feet, gold enamel trim, Moser, some loss of glass beads 950.00
    10-1/2" h, Diamond Quilted pattern, MOP pink satin shaded ground, yellow wheat coralene 1,200.00

CRACKLE GLASS

History: The history of crackle glass has not definitely been established. It is known that the Venetians made some examples as early as the 16th century. The Bohemians are also credited with early examples. Their method of creating this sparkly finish was to plunge red hot glass into cold water and then to reheat it as the piece was re-blown. Martin Bach claimed his Egyptian and Moorish Art Nouveau-influenced designs were reproductions of these ancient civilizations' glass when he created his form of crackle for the Durand Glass Company in 1928. By the late 1930s to the early 1970s, crackle was quite popular in the West Virginia glass houses, including Pilgrim, Blenko, Kanawha, and Viking, and many others.

One popular theory for the development of this technique was to hide imperfections in the glass. By creating a crackling effect, defects could be disguised. Other companies used this technique to create more reflective surfaces on a plain body, adding sparkle and interest without the costly process of cutting or hand decorating.

There are several ways to create the crackle effect: (1) The glassblower takes a hot glob of glass and while still attached to the blow pipe, he dips it into cold water. The glass blob is then returned to the hot oven and reheated, sealing the cracks. The glass is then shaped, producing a large crackle design; (2) A desired style is created, then submerged in cold water. After the crackle effect is achieved, it is then reheated to seal the large cracks; (3) The hot glass is rolled in moist sawdust or covered with sand in order to give the surface a coarse finish, submerged in water, causing the surface to crack, without destroying the glass, a second layer of glass is then added and reheated until the cracks fuse together slightly, adding stability. Kanawha uses a hot mold process, where the molds are preheated to accept the molten glass. Harmon Glass blew its glass into metal paste molds that had been lined with paste and cork.

Like many other types of glassware, Crackle Glass can be found from colorless to a rainbow of intense colors. Collectors may use colors to date some examples of Blenko and Pilgrim Glass, as their color production has been carefully documented.

References: Judy Alford, *Collecting Crackle Glass with Values*, Schiffer, 1997; Stan and Arlene Weiman, *Crackle Glass Identification and Value Guide*, Book I (1996), Book II (1998), Collector Books.

Collectors' Club: Collectors of Crackle Glass Club, P.O. Box 1186, Massapequa, NY 11758.

Museum: Pilgrim Glass Corp., P.O. Box 395, Ceredo, WV 22507.

Basket, 7-1/2" h, 6" w, white crackle ext., brilliant blue int., crystal V-shaped thorn handle, Victorian 125.00
Beaker, 7" h, 5-1/2" d top, Leaf pattern, crystal, green applied leaves, hand blown, Blenko, c1940-50 ....90.00
Candleholders, amberina, squatty form, pr 30.00
Cigarette Lighter, 7" h, amberina, metal top 35.00
Cocktail Shaker, Macbeth Evans, crystal 18.00
Cruet, 6" h, amber, hand blown, Rainbow Glass Co, c1940-60 ....35.00
Decanter, orig stopper
    7-1/2" d, 5-1/4" d, blue, straight neck, bulbous base, air bubbles in colorless ball stopper 75.00
    8-1/2" d, amber, hand blown, pontil mark.....................70.00
    8-1/2" h, orange, hand blown, Rainbow Glass Co., c1940-60...65.00
    10-1/2" h, amberina, hand blown, pontil mark 85.00
Dish, 8-3/4" w, 6" l, 3-1/2" h, smoke gray, crimped folded up sides, hand blown, pontil mark, Blenko 85.00
Drink Mixer, 8-1/4" h, blue, applied crystal open end handle, hand blown, Pilgrim Glass Co., orig label 75.00
Pitcher
    4" h, blue, applied reeded handle................................20.00
    5-1/4" h, blue, applied clear handle, mold blown, Kanawha..30.00
    5-1/4" h, green, applied green handle, mold blown, Kanawha..25.00
    5-1/2" h, 5" d, amberina, applied glass handle, hand blown, pontil mark...65.00
    10-1/2" h, amberina, red top shades to orange to amber to orange, slender body, wide flaring top, applied orange

Ad, Pilgrim Glass Pitcher Collection, available in 18 shapes and 5 colors! China Glass & Tablewares, February 1962.

        handle, hand blown, pontil scar 115.00
    12-1/2" h, amberina, mold blown, Kanawha 55.00
    13" h, lemon-lime, applied handle, hand blown, pontil mark, Pilgrim Glass Co..115.00
Plate, green, US Glass.. 5.00
Punch Cup, clear, cobalt blue ring handle, Fry.............. 45.00
Rose Bowl, 5-1/4" h, 4-1/4" w, reddish-orange, pinched top, hand blown, pontil mark, Pilgrim Glass Co. 60.00
Tankard
    7" h, bright yellow, applied crystal handle, Pilgrim Glass Co. 65.00
    7-1/2" h, peach crackle body, enamel and gold overlay, applied handle, polished pontil, Moser, c1920 ....125.00
    12" h, clear, applied clear handle 35.00
Tumbler, 5-1/4" h, clear body, Delft green handle, Fry..... 70.00
Vase
    4-3/4" h, deep blue, 2 pulled up sides 15.00
    5" h, flashed cranberry, hand blown 35.00
    5" h, 3" d, two shades of orange, flared at top, hand blown, pontil scar, Blenko..35.00
    7" h, amber, flared crimped top, straight body, bulbous foot, hand blown, pontil mark, Bischoff Glass Co. 45.00
    7-1/4" h, 7-1/2" w, Jonquil, crimped, ftd, Blenko 125.00
    7-3/4" h, dark orange-red, slender, flared top, mold blown, Kanawha..40.00
    10" h, baluster, flared neck, clear, free blown...............35.00
    10-1/2" h, 8-1/2" d, reddish-orange, crimped top, hand blown, pontil mark, Blenko 135.00
    10-3/4" h, crystal, crackled on bottom half only, sgd "R. Strong 7/76," ground pontil 125.00
    Large, petal pink, Fenton 75.00

CRANBERRY GLASS

History: Cranberry glass is transparent and named for its color, achieved by adding powdered gold to a molten batch of amber glass and reheating at a low temperature to develop the cranberry or ruby color. The glass color first appeared in the last half of the 17th century, but was not made in American glass factories until the last half of the 19th century.

Cranberry glass was blown, mold blown, or pressed. Examples often are decorated with gold or enamel. Less-expensive cranberry glass, made by substituting copper for gold, can be identified by its bluish purple tint.

Reference: William Heacock and William Gamble, *Encyclopedia of Victorian Colored Pattern Glass: Book 9, Cranberry Opalescent from A to Z*, Antique Publications, 1987; Kenneth Wilson, *American Glass 1760-1930*, 2 vols., Hudson Hills Press and The Toledo Museum of Art, 1994.

Collectors' Club: Pilgrim Glass Cranberry Collector's Club, P.O. Box 395, Ceredo, WV 25307.

Reproduction Alert: Reproductions abound. These pieces are heavier, off-color, and lack the quality of older examples.

Additional Listings: See specific categories, such as Bride's Baskets; Cruets; Jack-in-the-Pulpit Vases; etc.

Barber Bottle, Inverted Thumbprint pattern 270.00
Basket
    5-1/2" h, 6" w, star shaped top, ruffled edge, colorless thorn loop handle, c1890...195.00
    7" h, 5" w, ruffled edge, petticoat shape, colorless loop handle, c1890...250.00
    7-1/2" h, 6-3/4" w, boat-shaped basket, dark cranberry, all over gold dec, white florals, wide gold band, brass ftd vase with flower form handle..................................200.00
    8" h, 5" w, deep color, ruffled edge, applied colorless handle, Victorian..90.00
    8-1/2" h, 5" w, rose bowl form, Diamond Quilted pattern, ruffled edge, applied wishbone feet, V-shaped loop handle...150.00
    9" h, 5" w, deep cranberry int., amber casing on ext., white and gold aventurine flecks, applied amber feet, amber U-shaped handle 90.00
    9" h, 5" w, very deep cranberry int., slight ribbed int., applied colorless wishbone rigaree around top, twelve applied feet, applied colorless twisted loop handle, Victorian, flake on one foot...100.00
Biscuit Barrel, frosted, bear finial top.............................450.00
Bottle
    7-3/4" h, 4" d, flattened bulbous, frosted, gold church scene, small boats on back, gold around top 135.00
    8" h, 3" d, gold mid-band, white enameled trim, colorless faceted stopper...145.00
    8-1/2" h, 3-1/4" d, Inverted Thumbprint pattern, white enameled dot flowers and bands, gold trim, colorless cut faceted stopper..155.00
    9-3/4" h, 3-1/2" d, dainty white enameled flowers around middle, white enameled dots dec, colorless teardrop stopper...175.00
Bowl
    5-1/2" d, 6-1/2" d underplate, swirl pattern....................65.00
    7-3/4" d, paneled, flower dec, brass standard, mirrored base..120.00
Bride's Bowl, 9" sq, 3-1/2" h, finely executed enameled apple blossom dec, fancy ornate SP orig holder mkd "Middletown Silver Co.," Mt. Washington 950.00
Butter Dish, cov, round, Hobnail pattern 125.00
Candlestick
    10-1/2" h, applied yellow eel dec 120.00

10-5/8" h, heavily encrusted gold and polychrome dec, pr 190.00
Celery Vase, 10" h, Thumbprint pattern, enameled flowers and birds, ornate handles, ftd mount, orig silverplated Jas. Tufts Co. frame 550.00
Claret Jug, 10-3/4" h, n4-5/8" h, French emb pewter hinged top, foot, and handle 320.00
Cologne Bottle
    7" h, dainty blue, white, and yellow enameled flowers, green leaves, gold outlines and trim, orig colorless ball stopper 195.00
    8-5/8" h, 2-3/8" d, gold scrolls, small gold flowers, matching sq cranberry bubble stopper 185.00
Creamer, 5" h, 2-3/4" d, Optic pattern, fluted top, applied colorless handle 95.00
Cruet, orig stopper
    6-1/2" h, 2-3/4" d, applied colorless wafer foot, applied colorless twisted rope handle with flower prunt at base, colorless ribbed bubble stopper 135.00
    10-1/2" h, 3-7/8" d, acid cut herringbone double band around middle, applied colorless foot, applied colorless handle, colorless cut faceted stopper.................................190.00
    13" h, 4" d, heavy gold roses dec, colorless cut faceted stopper..195.00
Cup and Saucer, gold bands, enameled purple and white violets, gold handle 135.00
Decanter
    10" h, cut to colorless, flattened colorless oval, obverse medallion engraved "Mollies Pony 1869" centering scene with horse, cut star on reverse, conforming teardrop stopper, some internal bubbles 990.00
    10-1/2" h, 3-1/4" d, cut to colorless, matching mushroom bubble stopper...250.00
    11-1/2" h, 3-7/8" d, bulbous base, pinched-in sides, lacy gold enamel dec, dark red flowers, gold enameled centers, applied colorless handle, colorless cut faceted stopper..250.00
Epergne, 19" h, 11" d, 5 pc, large ruffled bowl, tall center lily, 3 jack-in-the-pulpit vases 1,150.00
Fairy Lamp, 4-1/2" h, applied colorless hand tooled petals, colorless insert mkd "Clarke" 350.00
Finger Bowl, scalloped, matching underplate 145.00
Mantel Lusters, pr, orig prisms 550.00
Mug, 4" h, 2-3/4" d, Baby Inverted Thumbprint pattern, applied colorless handle and pedestal foot 65.00
Music Box, 12-1/4" h, 5-1/4" d decanter, emb ribs with etched leaves and stars, orig colorless cut bubble stopper, not working 310.00

Finger bowl, Inverted Thumbprint pattern, $85.

Night Light, 6-1/4" h, 3-1/4" d, cranberry shade with white sanded scallops, grapes, and leaves, openwork brass top rim, gold-washed ormolu ftd frame 275.00

Perfume Bottle, 7-1/4" h, 2-3/4" d, gold stars dec, star cut under base, colorless bubble stopper 150.00

Pitcher
    6-1/4" h, 4-3/8" d, Ripple pattern, bulbous, round mouth, applied colorless handle 110.00
    6-1/2" h, 4-1/8" d, Ripple and Thumbprint pattern, bulbous, round moth, applied colorless handle 110.00
    7-1/2" h, 4-1/2" d, Optic pattern, bulbous, round mouth, applied colorless reeded handle 145.00
    10" h, 5" d, bulbous, ice bladder int., applied colorless handle..............................220.00
    11-3/8" h, 9" w, bulbous shape, colorless loop handle, white and blue floral leaf dec, int. vertical ribs, c1895 ....275.00
    Venetian pattern, large..............................120.00

Rose Bowl
    3-3/4" h, 3-3/4" d, worn gold rim, six-crimp top 90.00
    4" h, optic ribs, scalloped turned in rim, colorless ruffled applied pedestal base..............................125.00

Salt, master
    Crystal rigaree around middle 150.00
    Enameled floral dec, ftd 200.00

Sauce, Hobbs Hobnail pattern 45.00

Smoke Bell, 6-1/2" d, swirled, ruffled edge 600.00

Spooner, Paneled Sprig pattern 125.00

Sugar Bowl, cov, 6-1/8" h, 4" d, applied wafer foot, colorless ribbed bubble finial 110.00

Sugar Shaker
    Inverted Thumbprint pattern, nine panels 150.00
    Parian Swirl pattern 120.00
    Optic pattern, orig top 225.00

Tankard, 11" h, 5-1/4" d, hinged SP top, collar, applied colorless handle 275.00

Tumble-Up, Inverted Thumbprint pattern 195.00

Tumbler, Inverted Thumbprint pattern 65.00

Urn, 11-1/2" h, 2 applied colorless handles, enameled flowers and leaves 400.00

Vase
    6-3/8" h, 4-3/8" d, frosted, white daisies, blue forget-me-nots, green leaves, price for pr 210.00
    7-1/2" h, emb ribs, applied colorless feet, 3 swirled applied colorless leaves around base 110.00
    8" h, vertical bands below diamond points, deep cut to colorless..............................315.00
    8" h, vertical bands of ribbed thumbprints cut to colorless, ground pontil 110.00
    8-7/8" h, bulbous, white enameled lilies of the valley dec, cylinder neck..............................115.00

Water Set, Frazier pattern, enameled flowers, pitcher, 6 matching tumblers..............................265.00

Wine Decanter
    8-1/2" h, 4-1/2" d, small gold stars dec, orig gold trim cranberry bubble stopper 165.00
    10-3/4" h, 4-3/4" d, flattened bulbous shape, colorless wafer foot, applied colorless spun rope handle, orig bubble stopper 185.00
    12" h, opaque white cased over cranberry, enameled flowers and gilt scrollwork dec, pr..............................500.00
    13" h, 4" d, gold roses and foliage dec, applied colorless handle, colorless cut faceted stopper....................200.00
    13-1/2"h, blown swirl, colorless applied ruffled top, 3 colorless applied feet, gilt and enamel surface dec of leaves and flowers, some paint wear 350.00

CROWN MILANO

History: Crown Milano is an American art glass produced by the Mt. Washington Glass Works, New Bedford, Massachusetts. The original patent was issued in 1886 to Frederick Shirley and Albert Steffin.

Usually, it is an opaque-white satin glass finished with light-beige or ivory-colored ground embellished with fancy florals, decorations, and elaborate and thick raised gold.

When marked, pieces carry an entwined CM with crown in purple enamel on the base. Sometimes paper labels were used. The silver plated mounts often have "MW" impressed or a Pairpoint mark as both Mount Washington and Pairpoint supplied mountings.

References: John A. Shuman III, *The Collector's Encyclopedia of American Art Glass,* Collector Books, 1988, 1994 value update; Kenneth Wilson, *American Glass 1760-1930,* 2 Vols., Hudson Hills Press and The Toledo Museum of Art, 1994.

Collectors Club: Mount Washington Art Glass Society, P.O. Box 24094, Fort Worth, TX 76124-1094

Museum: New Bedford Glass Museum, New Bedford, MA.

Atomizer, 6-1/2" h, trumpet vine dec, swirled body 600.00

Biscuit Jar, cov
    5-1/2" h, squatty, round, opal ground, all over hand painted rose blossoms, buds, leaves, and thorny stems, gold outlines, SP rim, bail, and cover, imp "MW," purple "CM" and crown mark..............................400.00
    6" h, painted Burmese ground, all over bamboo design, green, gold and brown enamel, ornate silver hardware 1,150.00
    7" h, enameled floral dec, SP collar, lid, and bail handle, base sgd, lid mkd "Pairpoint"..............................750.00
    7" d, 6" h, blown blank, hobnail dec, underwater scene, jeweled starfish and enameled sea creature, sea plants, period fancy SP hardware and cover, mkd "MW".......1,610.00
    7-1/2" d, 9" h, colorful painting of couple in Colonial garb covers entire front, reverse side is a small white reserve, outlined in raised gold, gold line-drawn florals, cream colored body, base is signed "3912/80," lid is signed, "M.W.4419/c"..............................975.00

Bowl
    4" h, cov, delicate multicolored flowers, applied gold scrolling, handles, finial, base mkd "CM" under crown in blue 700.00
    6" h, cov, shiny finish, Colonial opalware, applied reeded prunt handles, multicolored blossoms and elaborate gold enameling, red wreath and crown mark and number "1013," some wear 800.00
    9" d, 3" h, tricorn, rolled edge, roses, asters, cornflowers, pansies and bachelor buttons, shaded yellow ground, gold trim, gold scrolls on ext., sgd "C. M. Monogram 74" 1,740.00
    10" d, 4-1/4" h, heavy walls, square and crimped top rim, coppery and gilt enamel oak leaf and acorn dec, ivory satin ground, mkd "300," work gold rim 175.00

Bride's Basket
    4" h, 8" d, multicolored roses, asters, and pansies, lusterless white ground, tricorn, colored and cut rim bowl, SP mounting, black crown mark, worn 500.00

11-1/2" h, 11" d, six large pansies, purple and orange tracery medallions, pale yellow int., tricorn, tightly ruffled, orig tricorn ftd stand, sgd "Pairpoint" 2,950.00

12" h, 9" w, triangular, gold edged fluted bowl, white ground, pink roses, yellow and purple pansies dec, gold dec, soft beige int. with gold scrolls, ornate SP Pairpoint stand 3,165.00

Candlesticks, pr, 8-1/4" h, 3-3/4" d base, silver-plated base and socket, opal glass cylinder, deep maroon background, gold leaf and bow encircle central portrait of young woman in low-cut pink dress, sgd on metal "Pairpoint Mfg. 6139" 1,750.00

Cracker Jar, 8-1/2" h, 5-1/2" d, yellow and purple mums, pink and yellow roses, gold dec, stationary handle, Aldoph Frederick dec, c1895-1900 ....985.00

Creamer and Sugar, petticoat shape, 4-1/2" h creamer, 4-3/4" h cov sugar with two applied leaf handles, blue cornflowers, purple asters, pink, and yellow roses, red wild roses, soft beige ground, heavy gold embellishments, faint hairline in sugar, sgd "Crown Milano" 1,250.00

Ewer

6-1/2" h, 7-1/2" d, Colonial Ware, two reserves of colorful blossoms, rococo borders of gold scrolls, bordered by fancy scrolls, gold cross-hatching, cream colored shoulder, white body, some loss to color wash around rope handle, sgd "0100"..975.00

8" h, 8" d, bulbous, gold lotus blossoms, green and gold pods outlined in raised gold, light green ground, aqua serpentine handle with gold scales, spout dec with aqua and scrolled leaves, c1894 ....1,650.00

10" h, beige, tan, rust, jeweled shadow flowers outlined in heavy gold, seven green jewels on each flower, rope handle, c1893..1,375.00

10" h, 8" w, pillow, handled, landscape dec, central front cartouche with idyllic English countryside, shepherd, sheep, and thatched roof house, plants and trees in bloom, heavily raised gold floral and scroll design around perimeter of design, soft green ground, numerous gold floral traceries of pansies, roses, and asters, gold scrolling on neck and handle, sgd and numbered................4,315.00

11-1/2" h, yellow shaded body, all over white enameled blossom clusters, connected by delicate raised gold leaves and vines, applied twisted handle, sgd 1,450.00

12" h, opaque white ground, freeform pastel enamel clusters, raised gold swirled stripes 1,350.00

12" h, white neck and body, background shadow dec of sepia colored scrolls and florals, spout with raised gold dec, abstract dec, twisted handle with brushed gold highlights, hundreds of individual dots in dark blue, light bleu, rust, coral, pink, yellow, green, black and gold form stylized florals and geometric designs 1,750.00

Jar, cov

4" h, squatty, star molded, custard colored ground, apricot chrysanthemums and jeweled starfish, SP rim, bail handle, and floral cov, imp "M. W. 4417"......................675.00

5-1/4" h, melon ribbed bowl, enamel dec, applied gold bead dec, SP rim, bail and crab motif cov, one bead missing, worn SP 600.00

5-1/2" h, deeply ribbed melon-form, applied yellow-amber surface, gold enameled roses and thorny branches, silver plated rim, bail handle, crab dec cov, mkd "MN4415," base stamped "CM" under crown in blue 1,400.00

6-3/4" h, melon ribbed bowl, blue body, gold enhanced floral dec, SP rim and raised cov, unsgd.......................350.00

10-1/2" h, molded floral ground, pink, green, and white blossoms and broad leaves, elaborate SP Rogers Bros. han-

Vase, egg shaped body, cylindrical neck, flattened bulbous top, two applied handles, gold floral dec, blue highlights, beige flower bud, star mark, 10" h, $950.

dled frame, some corrosion to stand 1,350.00

Jardiniere, 6" h, 8" d, blue, yellow, and pink chrysanthemum blossoms, shiny pink ground, scrolling gilt borders, blue crown mark, numbered 400.00

Pickle Castor, 9" h, shaded pink to white ground, pink and white enameled flowers, all over raised hobnail pattern, period fancy SP Pairpoint frame.................................. 1,725.00

Pin Tray, 5-3/4" d, glossy, folded rim, pansy dec, red wreath mark with crown 275.00

Pitcher, 12" h, hand painted, portrait of costumed couple in center, attributed to Frank Guba, scrolled gilt borders, applied rope twist handle, red crown and wreath mark.................. 675.00

Rose Bowl

4-1/4" h, swirled gold enamel stylized sq floral, yellow shaded opal ground, unsgd...250.00

4-1/2" h, 5" d, shaded Burmese yellow to soft brown ground, purple, pink, and yellow orchids, green and brown foliage, sgd and numbered in purple 500.00

Rose Jar, 8-1/2" h, raised bulbed rim, molded stylized borders, oval body with eight ribs, hand painted roses, gold dec, unsgd 500.00

Salt Shaker

2-1/2" h, hen, hand painted dec...................................350.00

4" h, ribbed, dainty blue and white daisy blossoms, Burmese-colored background.....................................185.00

Sugar Shaker, Muffineer

3" h, 4" d, melon-ribbed shape, chalk-white body, sprays of violet-colored Johnny-Jump-Up blossoms, silvery-bright metal collar and lid, embossed with butterfly, dragonfly, and blossoms 585.00

3" h, 4" d, melon ribbed, tomato shape, white ground, tendrils with multicolored ivy leaves, two part metal collar and lid emb with butterfly, dragonfly, and blossoms 585.00

Syrup Pitcher, 6" h, 4" w, melon ribbed body, alternating pale pink with gold netting and brilliantly colored Dresden type floral dec, handle, sgd and numbered............... 2,875.00

Sweetmeat Jar, cov, 5" h, ivory ground, deeper colored ribs, worn enameled floral design, SP fittings and lid, sgd "M.W." 550.00

Tumbler, 3-3/4" h, shiny finish, gold bow and swag enameling, red wreath mark, pr 525.00

Vase

4" h, amber and umber organic swirls, beaded pinwheel dec, ribbed and swirled lusterless ground, black crown and CM mark..550.00

4-1/2" h, bulbous, 8 pulled-up ribs, soft beige ground, deep beige traceries, heavily raised gold enameled petit point dec of stylized iris, leaves, and scrolls...................875.00

4-1/2" h, 4-1/4" d, jeweled, gilt enameled apple blossoms, gold beaded dec, two applied handles, orig paper label on base, three beads missing...............................675.00

4-1/2" h, 5" w, squatty bulbous form, painted gingko dec, green and brown leaves, shaded pale pink ground 550.00

5" h, 6" d, bulbous, ribs, pulled edges, gingko dec, green and brown leaves, pink ground, Albertine.............785.00

5" h, onion-shape, narrow neck with four turned-down folds, shadow dec, buff colored fern leaves, gold dec of four large fern leaves in two shades of gold, 24 molded-in swirls, white int. 885.00

5" h, 7" w, bulbous, peach and yellow mottled ground, gold wild rose dec, leaves, buds, and stems, glass jewels, two applied leaf handles...1,200.00

5-1/2" h, squatty, pastel yellow body, gold outlined pink and lavender orchid blossoms, applied ribbed handles, sgd 990.00

6" h, flared eight-lobed rim on ribbed sphere, peach colored ground, polychrome spring blossoms, overlaid with gold medallions, purple crown "CM" mark with "583" below 1,725.00

6" h, onion shape, twenty-four molded swirls, narrow neck, four turned down folds, flower like mouth, four large fern leaves and shadow of buff colored fern leaves, white int., attached SP stand...400.00

6" h, 5-3/4" d, cream-colored body, 24 swirling molded-in ribs, white peony blossoms.................................1,250.00

6" h, 6" d, springtime blossoms, glorious pastel hues, opposite side of flowering white dogwood, 4 raised gold circular embellishment, large circle with cherub riding mystical sea creature, 1 with a sun face surrounded by stylized dolphins, 2 smaller circles with geometric designs, Crown Milano logo and "583" 1,950.00

6-1/4" h, deeply ruffled quatraform rim, swirled opal oval, blue medallions under gold outlined white peony blossom and buds, unsigned 1,035.00

8-1/2" h, ribbed oval, bulbed molded border motif, hand painted pink rose blossoms, unsgd 1,200.00

8-3/4" h, 6-1/2" w, ball shaped, 2-1/2" neck, allover gold fern dec, beige and white ground, gold and beige scrolls around neck 1,200.00

9-1/4" h, opaque white body, cup-shaped top, exquisite floral decoration, 2 applied handles, orig paper label.....1,750.00

9-1/2" d, h, encrusted gold, thorny rose branches laden with single petaled blossoms, buds and leaves, orig paper label 1,450.00

9-3/4" h, extended think neck, bulbous base, pink tinted body, raised gold and blue enameled pansy dec, one sgd, matching pr...1,900.00

10-1/2" h, creamy yellow ground, green, brown, and gilt enamel blossoms, leaves, and blackberries, unsgd 450.00

10-1/2" d, shaded yellow lusterless ground, gilt enameled green and brown scrolling designs, winged dragons 2,550.00

12" h, Colonial Ware, shiny finish, dainty pastel pink roses, festoons of leafy vines, two rows of applied rigaree, brushed gold on rigaree, rim, and base, sgd with Colonial Ware crown in wreath logo and "1041"...............1,750.00

12" h, cone shape, flared, fluted top, Albertine, gold dec, gilded prunts, mkd, c1893 ....770.00

12-1/4" h, creamy lusterless ground, gilt enameled pink, green, and blue thistle dec, unsgd 1,500.00

12-1/2" h, 5-1/2" w, soft beige ground, green and pink thistles, light green/blue leaves, gold trim 1,100.00

13-3/4" h, double bulbed elongated shape, pink seed

thistle blossoms, green, brown, and white leaf dec, unsgd 1,250.00

14-1/2" h, Burmese colored ground, white, yellow, amber, and brown cymbidium orchids, unsgd 2,500.00

Vase, cov, 5" h, 8-1/2" d, Colonial Ware, shiny finish, bowl form, applied reeded prunt handles, conforming cov, multicolored blossoms, elaborate gold enameling, red wreath, crown mark, and "1013" on base, some gold wear 825.00

CRUETS

History: Cruets are small glass bottles used on the table and holding condiments such as oil, vinegar, and wine. The pinnacle of cruet use occurred during the Victorian era when a myriad of glass manufacturers made cruets in a wide assortment of patterns, colors, and sizes. All cruets had stoppers; most had handles. Cruets also have pouring lips or spouts. Perfume bottles are often the same size, but do not have a pouring lip.

Pattern glass manufacturers included cruets as part of their patterns. Later, Depression era manufacturers also included cruets in their lines, often offering different sizes.

References: Elaine Ezell and George Newhouse, *Cruets, Cruets, Cruets*, Vol. I, Antique Publications, 1991; William Heacock, *Encyclopedia of Victorian Colored Pattern Glass: Book 6, Oil Cruets from A to Z*, Antique Publications, 1981; Dean L. Murray, *More Cruets Only,* Killgore Graphics, Inc., 1973.

Additional Listings: Pattern Glass and specific glass categories such as Amberina, Cranberry, and Satin.

Amber
8" h, 3-1/8" d, blue enameled daisies, gold leaves, three petal top, applied amber handle, amber ball stopper 145.00

8" h, 4" d, four dimpled sides, gold trim, applied sapphire blue handle, sapphire blue bubble stopper...........165.00

8-5/8" h, 3-5/8" d, emb bands, dainty white, green, pink, yellow, and blue enameled flowers and foliage, two small insects, applied amber handle, matching amber bubble stopper with enameled leaves 190.00

9-1/4" h, 4-1/2' d, engraved butterfly and ferns, star cut base, applied blue handle, blue cut faceted stopper......250.00

10-1/4" h, 4-1/8" d, Inverted Thumbprint pattern, encased in emb French pewter frame, mask heads on side, lacy openwork, bird's head on handle, orig amber bubble stopper encased in matching pewter 225.00

Amberina
3" h, ball shape, Baby Inverted Thumbprint pattern, polished pontil, orig stopper 250.00

5-3/4" h, Inverted Thumbprint pattern, applied amber handle, orig amber stopper, Mt. Washington...............375.00

7" h, Inverted Thumbprint pattern, three petal top, amber applied handle, cut faceted stopper 185.00

Art Glass, 6" h, ruby cut to colorless, intricate design cut into body, oval panels cut in to neck, notches cut into spout, 16 pointed star cut into base, colorless glass handle, orig faceted stopper 400.00

Bluerina, 6-3/4" h, vivid blue neck and spout, amber body, Optic Thumbprint pattern, ribbed handle, colorless faceted stopper 395.00

Bohemian, 5-1/2" h, ruby flashed, cut back jumping stag design, replaced stopper 110.00

Burmese, 6-1/4" h, ribbed, orig stopper, Mt. Washington ... 720.00

Crackle, 8" h, vaseline, double neck, c1920 .... 125.00

Cranberry

6" h, 4" w, Diamond Quilted pattern, blown molded, colorless applied handle, cut stopper 125.00

10-3/4" h, 4-3/4" d, applied colorless wafer foot, applied spun rope handle with colorless flower prunt at base, orig colorless flattened bulbous ribbed bubble stopper....220.00

12-1/2" h, 4-1/2" d, gold scrolls and basket of flowers, applied colorless patterned foot, applied colorless handle, colorless bubble stopper 225.00

Swirled Ribs pattern, Fenton 65.00

Custard Glass

Louis XV pattern, colorless faceted stopper 150.00

Wild Bouquet pattern, 6-1/2" h, fired-on dec...............525.00

Cut Glass, sgd "Sinclair"..125.00

Lime Green

7" h, 3-1/2" d, bulbous, small white enameled flowers, rust centers, gold leaves, applied green handle, orig green bubble stopper 125.00

9" h, 3-1/2" d, small white enameled flowers, gold-colored centers, green leaves, applied green handle, orig green ball stopper 135.00

9-3/4" h, 3-1/8" d, dainty pink enameled floral sprays, gold bird in flight, applied green handle, orig green bubble stopper 140.00

Mary Gregory, 9-1/2" h, 3" d, amber ground, Optic pattern, white enameled young boy, three-petal top, amber applied handle, orig amber bubble stopper 250.00

Opalescent Glass

Circled Scroll, green 650.00

Daisy Fern, blue, Parian mold, no stopper.................195.00

Everglades, blue 600.00

Parian Swirl, blue...495.00

Stripes, pale blue, orig hollow stopper, solid amber handle, 7-1/4" h, polished pontil mark...............................345.00

Sunburst on Shield, blue..900.00

Swag with Brackets, green 485.00

Wild Bouquet, blue...495.00

Pattern Glass

Argonaut Shell, custard, gold trim 975.00

Beaded Ovals in Sand, blue, dec 400.00

Big Button, ruby stained...250.00

Block and Lattice, no stopper 45.00

Brilliant, amber stained, orig stopper..........................225.00

Bull's Eye with Points...100.00

Column Block, vaseline..295.00

Chrysanthemum Sprig, blue, opaque 1,250.00

Chrysanthemum Sprig, custard 495.00

Croesus, large, green, gold trim 395.00

Double Circle, apple green...225.00

Empress, green, os 295.00

Esther, green, gold trim...465.00

Everglades, vaseline, gold trim..................................595.00

Florette, pink, satin 225.00

Fluted Scrolls, blue, dec 295.00

Inverted Thumbprint, cranberry 265.00

Jackson, vaseline...225.00

Louis XV, green, gold trim...350.00

Medallion Sprig, green...395.00

Millard, amber stain..345.00

Nestor, blue, dec, orig stopper....................................195.00

O'Hara's Diamond, ruby stained 295.00

Palm Beach, colorless...75.00

Riverside's Ranson, vaseline 210.00

Royal Ivy, rubena 465.00

Shosone 65.00

Stars and Stripes, cranberry, heat check 650.00

Tiny Optic, green, dec 140.00

Truncated Cube, ruby stained 285.00

Waffle, no stopper..35.00

X-Ray, green, gold trim 175.00

Peachblow

6-1/2" h, petticoat shape, orig cut amber stopper, Wheeling 1,750.00

7" h, acid finish, enameled fish, water lilies and cattails, gold outlines, applied amber handle, orig faceted amber stopper 1,250.00

8" h, acid finish, applied reeded handle 775.00

Rubena, Royal Ivy pattern, frosted, orig stopper............ 450.00

Rubena Verde

Ball shape, applied colorless handle, colorless ball shaped stopper 485.00

Hobnail pattern, applied colorless handle, colorless hobnail stopper 650.00

Inverted Thumbprint pattern, 6-3/4" h, 4" w, petticoat shape, orig cut vaseline stopper, Wheeling.....................395.00

Tee Pee pattern..485.00

Sapphire Blue

7-1/4" h, 3-3/4" d, bulbous, round mouth, white enameled wreaths, scrolls, and dots, applied blue handle, orig blue ball stopper with matching enamel dec.................200.00

8-1/2" h, 3" d, white enameled flowers and foliage, yellow centers, gold trim, applied amber handle, amber ball stopper 185.00

9" h, 4" d, bulbous, round top, enameled lavender flowers, green leaves, gold trim, applied colorless handle, colorless bubble stopper 190.00

Satin

Diamond Quilted pattern, 7" h, yellow, applied frosted handle, faceted colorless stopper...............................300.00

Diamond Quilted pattern, 8-1/4" h, white shaded to gold, colorless frosted handle, orig frosted colorless knobby stopper 595.00

Florette pattern, pink 225.00

Seaweed pattern, blue, orig stopper 475.00

Slag, 6-3/4" h, Hobstars pattern, matching stopper 65.00

Spangle, Leaf Mold pattern, cranberry ground, white spatter, mica flecks, orig stopper...................................... 375.00

Spatter

4-1/2" h, red and white spatter, white ground, tricorn top, applied colorless handle 175.00

8-3/4" h, 3-1/2" d, blue ground, white spatter, applied colorless handle, colorless heart-shaped stopper.........145.00

Threaded Swirl pattern... 650.00

Opalescent, Daisy and Fern pattern, Apple Blossom mold, blue ground, applied blue handle, colorless faceted stopper, $250.

CUP PLATES

History: Many early cups were handleless and came with deep saucers. The hot liquid was poured into the saucer and sipped from it. This necessitated another plate for the cup, hence the "cup plate."

The first cup plates made of pottery were of the Staffordshire variety. From the mid-1830s to 1840s, glass cup plates were favored. The Boston and Sandwich Glass Company was one of the main manufacturers of the lacy glass type.

It is extremely difficult to find glass cup plates in outstanding (mint) condition. Collectors expect some marks of usage, such as slight rim roughness, minor chipping (best if under the rim), and in rarer patterns, a portion of a scallop missing. Some allowances are made for the techniques used to create this little plates. As such, overfills or underfills of the molds may detract slightly from the value. Condition can detract from the value, but color may drastically increase it. Most cup plates were made of clear glass, but many deeply colored green, blue, and purple cup plates are known, as well as some opaque white and fiery opalescent cup plates.

References: Ruth Webb Lee and James H. Rose, *American Glass Cup Plates*, published by author, 1948, Charles E. Tuttle Co. reprint, 1985; Kenneth Wilson, *American Glass 1760-1930*, 2 Vols., Hudson Hills Press and The Toledo Museum of Art, 1994.

Collectors' Club: Pairpoint Cup Plate Collectors of America, P.O. Box 890052, East Weymouth, MA 02189.

Notes: The numbers used are from the Lee-Rose book in which all plates are illustrated. Prices are based on plates in average condition.

LR 1, clear, flint, polished pontil..35.00

LR 2, 3-5/8" d, amber, blown, 18 ribs, Midwest origin 1,200.00

LR 4-A, 4-1/8" d, clear, swirled red and white latticino, gold flecks in rim, attributed to Nicholas Lutz, Sandwich.............185.00

LR 10, 3-5/8" d, clear, plain rim, New England origin........75.00

LR 11, 2-13/16", clear, New England origin, small shallow rim chips and roughage..85.00

LR 13, 3-3/4" d, deep blue, A-type mold, plain rim, New England origin..75.00

LR 21, 3-7/16" d, clear, 15 scallops with shelves rim, stars between shoulder fans, strawberry diamond center, New England origin 115.00

LR 22-A, 3-7/16" d, clear, 15 scallops with shelves, circles between shoulder fans, six pointed star center, New England or Sandwich origin 100.00

LR 22-B, 3-7/16" d, clear pontil, New England origin, slight roughage...95.00

LR 26, 3-7/17" d, clear, 15 even scallops, 11 lance points center, attributed to New England Glass Co. or Sandwich ... 165.00

LR 28, 3-1/4" d, clear, 17 even scallops, 12 lance points, attributed to New England Glass Co. or Sandwich origin 35.00

LR 36, 3-1/4" d, opal opaque, 17 even scallops, seven stalk sheaves with round points, rosettes in spandrels between eight central leaves, New England origin...............475.00

LR 37, 3-1/4" d, opalescent, 17 even scallops, seven stalk sheaves with round points, rosettes in spandrels between eight central leaves, attributed to New England Glass Co. or Sandwich..475.00

LR 41-A, 3-1/6" d, clear, 17 even scallops, six stalk sheaf, radial lines dividing cross-hatched band, attributed to

New England Glass Co. or Sandwich origin, minor roughness 200.00

LR 45, 3-9/16" d, pale opalescent, 19 even scallops, rope top and bottom, wide cap ring, attributed to New England Glass Co. or Sandwich, mold overfill, slag deposit near center 120.00

LR 46, 3-1/2" d, lavender, 15 even scallops, geometric shoulder design, strawberry diamond pattern, Eastern origin.......125.00

LR 51, 3-3/4" d, clear, pontil, 15 scallops with points between, stippled center background, New England origin, moderate rim roughage, few shallow flakes 185.00

LR 52, 3-3/4" d, opalescent, 15 scallops with points between, stippled, Eastern origin 200.00

LR 58, 3-3/8" d, cloudy, unlisted color, plain rope, band of radial lines on inner and outer edge of underside of shoulder, bull's eyes on plain band, waffle center, Eastern origin......285.00

LR 70, 3-7/16" d, colorless, plain rope, Midwest origin .. 125.00

LR 75-A, 3-13/16" d, clear, rope rim top and bottom, strawberry diamond between border sheaves, attributed to New England Glass Co., one tiny rim flake 90.00

LR 79, 3-3/8" d, pink tint, rope top and bottom, rope table ring with tiny feet, New England origin 60.00

LR 80, 3-3//4" d, opalescent, rope top and bottom, plain table ring, New England origin......................................250.00

LR 81, 3-3/4" d, fiery red opalescent, rope top and bottom, rope table ring with tiny feet, New England origin.........360.00

LR 82, 3-5/8" d, clear, plain rim, five pointed star center, attributed to New England Glass Co. 125.00

LR 82, 3-5/8" d, opalescent, plain rim, five pointed star center, attributed to New England Glass Co., minor rim roughness 375.00

LR 88, 3-11/16" d, deep opalescent opaque, rope top, shoulder baskets, pinwheel with stars center, attributed to New England Glass Co. or Sandwich...............................250.00

LR 95, 3-5/8" d, opalescent opaque, ten sided, rope top and bottom, New England origin.................................180.00

LR 100, 3-1/4" d, clear, plain rim, stippled background, attributed to Philadelphia area, normal mold roughness..........110.00

LR 121, 3-16" d, clear, lacy, portholes shoulder pattern, stippled, Midwest origin, slight rim roughage.............115.00

LR 135, 3-7/16" d, clear, 24 bull's eyes, points between, peacock feather pattern, Midwest origin......................85.00

LR 150,-B, 2-15/16" d, clear, plain rim, rope on bottom, Midwest origin..60.00

LR 163, 3-1/4" d, light green, 24 scallops, radial lines beneath, irregular stippling, Midwest origin 75.00

LR 179, 3-7/16" d, lavender, 10 scallops, rope top and bottom, attributed to Philadelphia, PA, area......................145.00

LR 197-E, 3-1/8" d, clear, Midwest origin......................75.00

LR 200, 96 sawtooth scallops, Midwest origin.................45.00

LR 215-C, 3-5/8" d, clear, Scotch Plaid, 60 even scallops, Curling, Ft. Pitt Glass Works 35.00

LR 242-A, 3-1/2" d, black amethyst, lacy, 60 even scallops, Eastern origin, mold overfill and underfill 675.00

LR 247, 3-7-16" d, emerald green, lacy, twelve-sided, 60 scallops, attributed to New England Glass Co. or Sandwich, small chip on one scallop....................................750.00

LR 257, 3-3/8" d, clear, attributed to New England Glass Co. or Sandwich... 40.00

LR 259, 3-7/16" d, clear, 12 large stippled scallops, points between, Eastern origin...200.00

LR 271, clear, attributed to New England Glass Co. or Sandwich 65.00

LR 272, clear, 43 scallops, Eastern origin 70.00

LR 276, 3-7/16" d, blue, lacy, 55 even scallops, arcs of central quadrants outlined in heavy dots, dots in centers of cen-

tral diamond-shaped figures, coarse rope table ring, Boston and Sandwich Glass Co....................................395.00
LR 279, 2-7/8" d, light green, lacy, 24 scallops, points between, rope band on shoulder, Eastern origin....................295.00
LR 284, 3-3/16" d, clear, 24 large bull's eyes divided by points, attributed to Philadelphia, PA, area, minute rim roughness..260.00
LR 323, 3-1/2" d, opalescent, attributed to New England Glass Co. or Sandwich,...80.00
LR 332-B, 2-1/2" d, clear, attributed to New England Glass Co. or Sandwich,..55.00
LR 343-B, 3-7/16" d, plain, dotted below, fire polished, attributed to Philadelphia, PA, area....................................35.00
LR 391, 3-7/16" d, clear, Eastern origin 20.00
LR 395, 3-3/4" d, clear, 44 points, unknown origin 20.00
LR 396, 3-1/4" d, clear, Sandwich origin...........................15.00
LR 399, 3-5/16" d, clear, Eastern origin, normal mold roughness..110.00
LR 412, 3-3/16" d, clear, 10 sided, star center, Sandwich origin..120.00
LR 416, 3-1/16" d, clear, unknown origin, minor roughness... 25.00
LR 433, 4-1/8" d, clear, two chips, mold roughness..........80.00
LR 456, 3-3/8" d, clear, 41 even scallops, Sandwich origin... 40.00
LR 458-A, 3-1/2" d, clear, unknown origin 20.00
LR 459-M, 3-3/4" d, jade opaque, 43 even scallops, 12 hearts on shoulder, Sandwich origin.................................475.00
LR 500, 3-1/4" d, clear, 48 even scallops, unknown origin 65.00
LR 503, 3-1/4" d, clear, 56 even scallops, Eastern, possibly Sandwich, origin..20.00
LR 522, 3-5/16" d, amber, flint, 66 even scallops, Sandwich origin..375.00
LR 538, 3-1/4" d, clear, 66 even scallops, Sandwich origin... 20.00
LR 561-A, octagonal, colorless, gray striations, Washington, tilted head, Midwest orig....................................4,500.00
LR 565-A, 3-9/16" d, clear, 25 flat scallops, points between, Sandwich origin..35.00
LR 575, 3-1/2" d, clear, 25 large scallops with 2 smaller ones between, Sandwich origin 75.00

Glass, historical

LR 568, 3-7/16" d, clear, Harrison, 67 even scallops, swags and black lozenges on shoulder, attributed to Sandwich, mold roughness..85.00
LR 576, 3-9/16" d, medium blue, Victoria, 25 large scallops, two small scallops between, Sandwich origin 100.00
LR 586-B, 3-7/16" d, clear, Ringgold, Palo Alto, stippled ground, small letters, Philadelphia area, 1847-48 ....650.00
LR 605-A, 3-1/2" d, clear, octagonal, 7 scallops between corners, ship, stippled and plain rope rigging 100.00
LR 615-A, 3-7/8" d, clear, Constitution, 25 scallops, points between, unknown origin...650.00
LR 653, 3" d, clear, plain rim, acorns on shoulder, central eagle in laurel wreath, Midwest origin..............................175.00
LR 658, emerald green, Boston & Sandwich origin, two tiny scallops missing...4,250.00
LR 670, 3-7/16" d, 36 bull's eyes, Midwest or Pittsburgh origin..75.00
LR 676, 3-11/16" d, clear, 60 even scallops, "Fort Pitt" in banner held by central eagle, Curling's Ft Pitt Glass works..... 95.00
LR 677-A, 3-3/16" d, clear, 44 even scallops, Midwest origin..45.00
LR 695, 3" d, clear, Midwestern origin, normal mold roughness...150.00
LR 836, 4-3/4" d, Geo. Peabody, Heart & Crown..............90.00

CUSTARD GLASS

History: Custard glass was developed in England in the early 1880s. Harry Northwood made the first American custard glass at his Indiana, Pennsylvania, factory in 1898.

From 1898 until 1915, many manufacturers produced custard glass patterns, e.g., Dugan Glass, Fenton, A. H. Heisey Glass Co., Jefferson Glass, Northwood, Tarentum Glass, and U.S. Glass. Cambridge and McKee continued the production of custard glass into the Depression era years.

The ivory or creamy yellow custard color is achieved by adding uranium salts to the molten hot glass. The chemical content makes the glass glow when held under a black light. The more uranium, the more luminous the color. Northwood's custard glass has the smallest amount of uranium, creating an ivory color; Heisey used more, creating a deep yellow color.

Custard glass was made in patterned tableware pieces. It also was made as souvenir items and novelty pieces. Souvenir pieces are include a place name or hand-painted decorations, e.g., flowers. Patterns of custard glass often were highlighted in gold, enameled colors, and stains.

References: Gary E. Baker et al., *Wheeling Glass 1829-1939*, Oglebay Institute, 1994, distributed by Antique Publications; William Heacock, *Encyclopedia of Victorian Colored Pattern Glass, Book IV: Custard Glass from A to Z*, Peacock Publications, 1980; William Heacock, James Measell and Berry Wiggins, *Harry Northwood: The Early Years 1881-1900*, Antique Publications, 1990; —, *Harry Northwood, The Wheeling Years, 1901-1925,* Antique Publications, 1991.

Reproduction Alert: L. G. Wright Glass Co. has reproduced pieces in the Argonaut Shell and Grape and Cable patterns. It also introduced new patterns, such as Floral and Grape and Vintage Band. Mosser reproduced toothpicks in Argonaut Shell, Chrysanthemum Sprig, and Inverted Fan & Feather.

Banana Boat
    Geneva, Northwood, 11" l, oval....................................145.00
    Grape and Gothic Arches, Northwood, 6" h, 12" l.......200.00
    Grape and Thumbprint, Northwood 375.00
    Maple Leaf, Northwood...200.00
Berry Bowl, master
    Argonaut Shell, Northwood, 10-1/2" l 150.00
    Beaded Circle, Northwood..185.00
    Cherry and Scale, Fenton 120.00
    Chrysanthemum Sprig, Northwood................................165.00
    Diamond with Peg, Jefferson 225.00
    Everglades, Northwood...200.00
    Grape and Cable, Northwood, 7-1/2" d, ruffled edge.....85.00
    Inverted Fan and Feather, Northwood 225.00
    Louis XV, Northwood, gold trim....................................145.00
    Maple Leaf, Northwood...250.00
    Ring Band, Heisey 125.00
    Victoria, Tarentum 175.00
Berry Set
    Chrysanthemum Sprig, Northwood, master and six individual bowls, sgd "Northwood" in script 590.00
    Everglades, Northwood, gold trim 400.00
    Geneva, Northwood, , master and four sauces 225.00
    Ring Band, Heisey 375.00

Bowl
    Delaware, US Glass 65.00
    Grape and Cable, Northwood, 7-1/2" d, basketweave ext.,
        nutmeg stain, Northwood 60.00
Butter Dish, cov
    Argonaut Shell, Northwood 250.00
    Beaded Circle, Northwood...........................275.00
    Cherry and Scale, Fenton 240.00
    Chrysanthemum Sprig, Northwood, blue..................750.00
    Everglades, Northwood................................375.00
    Fan, Dugan...225.00
    Geneva, Northwood, red and green dec 165.00
    Georgia Gem, Tarentum, enamel dec 150.00
    Intaglio, Northwood 225.00
    Inverted Fan and Feather, Northwood 250.00
    Jefferson Optic, Jefferson 200.00
    Maple Leaf, Northwood................................200.00
    Ribbed Drape, Jefferson...............................275.00
    Ring Band, Heisey 200.00
    Tiny Thumbprint, Tarentum, dec 300.00
    Victoria, Tarentum 300.00
    Wild Bouquet, Northwood 275.00
    Winged Scroll, Heisey, dec............................185.00
Celery
    Chrysanthemum Sprig, Northwood.......................565.00
    Georgia Gem, Tarentum 195.00
    Ivorina Verde, Heisey 250.00
    Ring Band, Heisey 300.00
    Victoria, Tarentum, gold trim 190.00
Cigarette Box, Ivorina Verde, Heisey.....................250.00
Cologne Bottle, orig stopper
    Ivorina Verde, Heisey 250.00
    Northwood Grape, Northwood, nutmeg stain 425.00
Compote
    Argonaut Shell, Northwood 80.00
    Geneva, Northwood 45.00
    Intaglio, Northwood, 9" d............................385.00
    Ring Band, Heisey, roses dec, gold trim 170.00
Condiment Set
    Chrysanthemum Sprig, Northwood, 4 pcs..............2,000.00
    Creased Bale, Dithridge, 4 pcs.........................200.00
    Ring Band, Heisey, 5 pcs 800.00
Condiment Tray
    Chrysanthemum Sprig, Northwood.......................650.00
    Ring Band, Heisey 110.00
Cracker Jar, cov, Grape and Cable, Northwood, two
        handles..700.00
Creamer
    Argonaut Shell, Northwood 150.00
    Beaded Circle, Northwood, 4-1/2" h, slight gold loss 350.00
    Cherry and Scale, Fenton 145.00
    Chrysanthemum Sprig, Northwood, blue, gold dec ...395.00
    Delaware, US Glass, rose dec 85.00
    Diamond with Peg, Jefferson 90.00
    Everglades, Northwood................................125.00
    Fan, Dugan...100.00
    Fluted Scrolls, Heisey................................85.00
    Geneva, Northwood 85.00
    Grape and Cable, Northwood..........................115.00
    Heart with Thumbprint, Tarentum......................80.00
    Intaglio, Northwood 115.00
    Inverted Fan and Feather, Northwood 150.00
    Jackson, Northwood 100.00
    Jefferson Optic, Jefferson 95.00
    Louis XV, Northwood 85.00
    Maple Leaf, Northwood................................125.00

Northwood Grape, Northwood, nutmeg stain 115.00
Ribbed Drape, Jefferson...............................120.00
Ring and Beads, Heisey 50.00
Vermont, US Glass Co. 100.00
Victoria, Tarentum 125.00
Wild Bouquet, Northwood 145.00
Winged Scroll, Heisey, dec............................110.00
Cruet
    Argonaut Shell, Northwood, gold trim 885.00
    Beaded Circle, Northwood, 6-1/2" h, slight gold loss.... 1,250.00
    Chrysanthemum Sprig, Northwood, blue, clear stopper..600.00
    Chrysanthemum Sprig, Northwood, custard, orig
        stopper 500.00
    Chrysanthemum Sprig, Northwood, custard, worn goofus dec,
        clear stopper 125.00
    Georgia Gem, Tarentum, green, orig stopper 300.00
    Louis XV, Northwood, clear faceted stopper 185.00
    Maple Leaf, Northwood................................950.00
    Ribbed Drape, Jefferson...............................400.00
    Ring Band, Heisey 400.00
    Wild Bouquet, Northwood 525.00
Custard Cup
    Empress, Riverside, green, gold trim..........................45.00
    Winged Scroll, Heisey 65.00
Ferner, Grape and Cable, Northwood, 7-1/2" d, ftd........ 185.00
Glove Holder, Victoria, Tarentum, 7" h, fan shaped, enameled,
        gilt wire frame, ... 450.00
Goblet
    Beaded Swag, Heisey..................................75.00
    Grape and Gothic Arches, Northwood, nutmeg stain...75.00
    Grape and Cable, Northwood..........................70.00
Hair Receiver
    Georgia Gem, Tarentum 50.00
    Winged Scroll, Heisey 125.00
Humidor, Winged Scroll, Heisey 225.00
Ice Cream Bowl, individual size
    Fan, Dugan...60.00
    Peacock and Urn, Northwood..........................40.00
Jelly Compote
    Argonaut Shell, Northwood, dec 145.00
    Beaded Circle, Northwood............................365.00
    Chrysanthemum Sprig, Northwood......................200.00
    Geneva, Northwood 100.00
    Intaglio, Northwood, gold trim........................150.00
    Inverted Fan and Feather, Northwood 325.00
    Maple Leaf, Northwood................................375.00
    Ribbed Drape, Jefferson...............................190.00
    Ring Band, Heisey 200.00

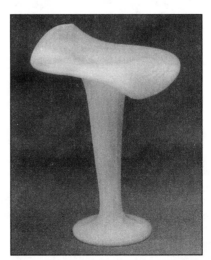

Jack in the pulpit vase, bamboo type dec on flared top, $25.

Lamp, Heart with Thumbprint, Tarentum, kerosene 400.00
Mug
    Diamond with Peg, Jefferson 60.00
    Punty Band, Heisey 70.00
    Ring Band, Heisey 60.00
Napkin Ring, Diamond with Peg, Jefferson 150.00
Nappy
    Northwood Grape, Northwood 60.00
    Prayer Rug, Imperial 65.00
    Winged Scroll, Heisey 65.00
Pickle Dish
    Beaded Swag, Heisey 265.00
    Vermont, U.S. Glass 60.00
    Winged Scroll, Heisey 65.00
Pin Dish, Delaware, U.S. Glass, dec................................80.00
Pin Tray/Dresser Tray
    Chrysanthemum Sprig, Northwood 70.00
    Delaware, U.S. Glass, dec 90.00
    Grape and Thumbprint, Northwood 150.00
    Ivorina Verde, Heisey 200.00
    Northwood Grape, Northwood, nutmeg stain 225.00
    Winged Scroll, Heisey, hand painted dec 200.00
Pitcher
    Argonaut Shell, Northwood 325.00
    Beaded Circle, Northwood 350.00
    Cherry and Scale, Fenton 350.00
    Chrysanthemum Sprig, Northwood 375.00
    Diamond with Peg, Jefferson, tankard 275.00
    Inverted Fan and Feather, Northwood 400.00
    Maple Leaf, Northwood 385.00
    Ring Band, Heisey, floral dec 450.00
    Vermont, U.S. Glass 250.00
    Winged Scroll, Heisey, dec 270.00
Plate
    Grape and Cable, Northwood, nutmeg stain 60.00
    Prayer Rug, Imperial, 7-1/2" d 35.00
    Three Fruits, Northwood, 7-1/2" d 30.00
Punch Bowl, matching base, Grape and Cable, North-
    wood..900.00
Punch Cup
    Diamond with Peg, Jefferson 70.00
    Grape and Cable, Northwood 50.00
    Inverted Fan and Feather, Northwood 200.00
    Northwood Grape, Northwood 50.00
    Ring Band, Heisey 60.00
Rose Bowl, Grape and Gothic Arches, Northwood 90.00
Salt and Pepper Shakers, pr
    Argonaut Shell, Northwood 350.00
    Beaded Circle, Northwood 275.00
    Carnelian, Northwood 450.00
    Chrysanthemum Sprig, Northwood 175.00
    Diamond with Peg, Jefferson 125.00
    Fluted Scrolls with Flower Band, Northwood 150.00
    Geneva, Northwood 185.00
    Georgia Gem, Tarentum, orig top 100.00
    Heart, Northwood 175.00
    Intaglio, Northwood 175.00
    Louis XV, Northwood 350.00
    Maple Leaf, Northwood 475.00
    Punty Band, Heisey 90.00
    Ribbed Band, Heisey 125.00
    Trailing Vine, Couderspot Glass 165.00
    Winged Scroll, Heisey 185.00
Sauce/Berry Bowl, individual size
    Argonaut Shell, Northwood, dec 90.00
    Beaded Circle, Northwood 65.00

    Beaded Swag, Heisey 65.00
    Cane Insert 35.00
    Chrysanthemum Sprig, Northwood 85.00
    Delaware, U.S. Glass, rose stain...................................65.00
    Fan, Dugan 70.00
    Geneva, Northwood, oval 45.00
    Georgia Gem, Tarentum 40.00
    Intaglio, Northwood 35.00
    Inverted Fan and Feather, Northwood 55.00
    Klondyke, Dazell 45.00
    Louis XV, Northwood, gold trim 45.00
    Louis XV, Northwood, green 50.00
    Maple Leaf, Northwood 80.00
    Peacock and Urn, Northwood 45.00
    Ribbed Drape, Jefferson 45.00
    Ring Band, Heisey, gold and rose dec 48.00
    Victoria, Tarentum 50.00
    Wild Bouquet, Northwood 50.00
    Winged Scroll, Heisey 45.00
Spooner
    Argonaut Shell, Northwood, 4-3/4" h, script signature, bright
        gold dec, scalloped rim 275.00
    Beaded Circle, Northwood, 4-1/4" h, slight gold loss 350.00
    Chrysanthemum Sprig, Northwood 125.00
    Everglades, Northwood 145.00
    Fan, Dugan 85.00
    Geneva, Northwood 50.00
    Grape and Gothic Arches, Northwood 95.00
    Intaglio, Northwood 95.00
    Louis XV, Northwood 75.00
    Maple Leaf, Northwood 140.00
    Ribbed Drape, Jefferson 65.00
    Trailing Vine, Couderspot Glass, blue 70.00
    Victoria, Tarentum 65.00
    Wild Bouquet, Northwood 70.00
    Winged Scroll, Heisey 100.00
Sugar, cov
    Argonaut Shell, Northwood 150.00
    Beaded Circle, Northwood, 6-3/4" h, slight gold loss 485.00
    Cherry and Scale, Fenton 145.00
    Chrysanthemum Sprig, Northwood, blue, gold dec ...395.00
    Delaware, U.S. Glass, rose dec 85.00
    Diamond with Peg, Jefferson 110.00
    Everglades, Northwood 125.00
    Fan, Dugan 100.00
    Fluted Scrolls, Heisey 85.00
    Geneva, Northwood 85.00
    Grape and Cable, Northwood 115.00
    Heart with Thumbprint, Tarentum..................................80.00
    Intaglio, Northwood 115.00
    Inverted Fan and Feather, Northwood 150.00
    Jackson, Northwood 100.00
    Jefferson Optic, Jefferson 165.00
    Louis XV, Northwood 85.00
    Maple Leaf, Northwood 125.00
    Northwood Grape, Northwood, nutmeg stain 115.00
    Ribbed Drape, Jefferson 120.00
    Ring and Beads, Heisey 50.00
    Vermont, U.S. Glass Co. 100.00
    Victoria, Tarentum 125.00
    Wild Bouquet, Northwood 145.00
    Winged Scroll, Heisey 175.00
Syrup, orig top
    Geneva, Northwood 250.00
    Ring Band, Heisey 315.00
    Winged Scroll, Heisey 350.00

Table Set, cov butter, creamer, cov sugar, spooner
  Argonaut Shell, Northwood 425.00
  Carnelian 850.00
  Geneva, Northwood 550.00
  Georgia Gem, Tarentum, gold trim 300.00
  Intaglio, Northwood 500.00
  Louis XV, Northwood, gold trim..................................500.00
  Ring Band, Heisey 550.00
Toothpick Holder
  Argonaut Shell, Northwood, dec 465.00
  Chrysanthemum Sprig, Northwood, blue, gold trim....315.00
  Diamond with Peg, Jefferson 85.00
  Georgia Gem, Tarentum, souvenir 45.00
  Inverted Fan and Feather, Northwood 350.00
  Ivorina Verde, Heisey 85.00
  Maple Leaf, Northwood 475.00
  Ribbed Drape, Jefferson..150.00
  Vermont, U.S. Glass, green dec 145.00
  Wild Bouquet, Northwood, blue trim, enameled dec 90.00
Tumbler
  Argonaut Shell, Northwood 90.00
  Beaded Circle, Northwood, 4" h, enameled blue blossoms,
    six tiny flowers with green leaves, slight loss to gold high-
    lights 250.00
  Cherry and Scale, Fenton 50.00
  Delaware, U.S. Glass, green dec.................................65.00
  Fan, Dugan...60.00
  Fluted Scrolls, Heisey..45.00
  Geneva, Northwood, red and green enamel dec 60.00
  Grape and Cable, Northwood, nutmeg stain 50.00
  Grape and Gothic Arches, Northwood, 6" h 65.00
  Intaglio, Northwood, green trim....................................45.00
  Inverted Fan and Feather, Northwood 90.00
  Jackson, Northwood 45.00
  Louis XV, Northwood, gold trim....................................60.00
  Prayer Rug, Imperial 80.00
  Punty Band, Heisey, souvenir 40.00
  Ribbed Drape, Jefferson, floral dec............................100.00
  Vermont, U.S. Glass 110.00
  Wild Bouquet, Northwood 35.00
  Winged Scroll, Heisey..70.00
Vase
  Diamond with Peg, Jefferson, 8" h 120.00
  Grape Arbor, Northwood, nutmeg stain 85.00
  Prayer Rug, Imperial 65.00
  Victorian, baluster, crown-style top, gold dec, intertwining foli-
    age around center, 15" h, 4-1/2" h, matched pr......2,500.00
  Winged Scroll, Heisey..100.00
Water Set, Winged Scroll, Heisey, pitcher, 4 tumblers 500.00
Whiskey, Diamond with Peg, Jefferson souvenir...............45.00
Wine
  Beaded Swag, Heisey..70.00
  Diamond with Peg, Jefferson 50.00
  Punty Band, Heisey..50.00
  Tiny Thumbprint 50.00

CUT GLASS, AMERICAN

History: Glass is cut by grinding decorations into the glass by means of abrasive-carrying metal or stone wheels. A very ancient craft, it was revived in 1600 by Bohemians and spread through Europe to Great Britain and America.

American cut glass came of age at the Centennial Exposition in 1876 and the World Columbian Exposition in 1893. The American public recognized American cut glass to be exceptional in quality and workmanship. America's most significant output of this high-quality glass occurred from 1880 to 1917, a period now known as the American Brilliant Period.

The Early Period was from 1765 to 1829, and glass from this period is rare. Early Period designs reflect the influence of English and Irish cut glass. Motifs include prisms, flutes, single star, diamonds, and a simple form of the strawberry diamond. The Middle Period from 1830 to 1870 produced simple, typically American designs in reaction to European patterns. Flute cuttings, engraved fine lines, etching, engraving historical scenes, and cut colored glass were predominate. Brilliant Period patterns are much more complex and usually cut deeper into the blank. Motifs include prisms, notched prisms, hobstars, curved miter splits, fans, and pinwheels, as well as stars and blocks and many design components of the earlier periods.

All cut glass blanks were hand blown until 1902. The H. C. Fry Glass Company of Rochester, Pennsylvania, produced the first pressed blanks in 1902.

About 1890, some companies began adding an acid-etched "signature" to their glass. This signature may be the actual company name, its logo, or a chosen symbol. Signatures are often rather pale and may be difficult to find. Today, signed pieces command a premium over unsigned pieces since the signature clearly establishes the origin. However, signatures should be carefully verified for authenticity since objects with forged signatures have been in existence for some time. One way to check is to run a finger tip or fingernail lightly over the signature area. As a general rule, a genuine signature cannot be felt; a forged signature has a raised surface.

Many companies never used the acid-etched signature on their glass and may or may not have affixed paper labels to the items originally. Dorflinger Glass and the Meriden Glass Co. made cut glass of the highest quality, yet never used an acid-etched signature. Furthermore, cut glass made before the 1890s was not signed. Many of these wood-polished items, cut on blown blanks, were of excellent quality and often won awards at exhibitions.

Consequently, if collectors restrict themselves only to signed pieces, many beautiful pieces of the highest quality glass and workmanship may be missed.

References: Bill and Louis Boggess, *Collecting American Brilliant Cut Glass 1876-1916*, Schiffer Publishing, 1992; ——, *Identifying American Brilliant Cut Glass*, 3rd ed., Schiffer Publishing, 1996; ——, *Reflections on American Brilliant Cut Glass*, Schiffer Publishing, 1995; City of Corning, New York, Centennial, *Corning, N. Y., 1891, Illustrated*, Corning-Painted Post Historical Society, 1990; Jo Evers, *Evers' Standard Cut Glass Value Guide*, Collector Books, 1975, 1995 value update; E. S. Farrar & J. S. Spillman, *The Complete Cut & Engraved Glass of Corning*, Crown Publishers, Corning Museum of Glass monograph, 1979; John Feller, *Dorflinger America's Finest Glass, 1852-1921*, Antique Publications, 1988; Bob Page and Dale Fredericksen, *A Collection of American Crystal*, Page-Fredericksen Publishing, 1995; ——, *Seneca Glass Company 1891-1983*, Page-Fredericksen Publishing, 1995; J. Michael Pearson, *Encyclopedia of American Cut & Engraved Glass*, Vols. I to III, published by author, 1975; Albert C. Revi, *American Cut & Engraved Glass*, Schiffer Publishing, 1965; Estelle F. Sinclaire & Jane Shadel Spillman, *The Complete Cut & Engraved Glass of Corning, Second Edition*, Syracuse University Press, 1997, Martha Louise Swan, *American Cut and Engraved Glass*, Wallace-Homestead, 1986, 1994 value update; H. Weiner and F. Lipkowitz, *Rarities in American Cut Glass*, Collectors House of Books, 1975; Kenneth Wilson, *American Glass 1760-1930*, 2 Vols., Hudson Hills Press and The Toledo Museum of Art, 1994.

Collectors' Club: American Cut Glass Assoc., P.O. Box 482, Ramona, CA 92065.

Museums: Chrysler Museum, Norfolk, VA; Corning Museum of Glass, Corning, NY; High Museum of Art, Atlanta, GA; Huntington Galleries, Huntington, WV; Lightner Museum, St. Augustine, FL; Toledo Museum of Art, Toledo, OH.

Note: A common abbreviation associated with Cut Glass is ABP–American Brilliant Period.

Ambrosia Bowl, 12" d, 10-1/4" h, panel and cut fruit design...150.00
Atomizer
 4" h, 2-1/2" sq, Harvard pattern, gold washed atomizer, ABP..145.00
 6-1/2" h, all over cutting, mkd "DeVilbiss," ABP..........145.00
 8" h, 2-1/2" h sq, Harvard pattern, gold washed atomizer, ABP..125.00
Banana Bowl, 11" d, 6-1/2" d, Harvard pattern, hobstar bottom, ABP...210.00
Basket
 5-1/2" h, 6" d, brilliant and gravic style cutting, Wild Rose pattern, applied crystal handle, sgd "Tuthill," ABP 1,125.00
 6" h, 6" d, step cut base with large hobstar, band of four hobstars with diamond point, fan and cane cutting, triple notched handle, ABP 950.00
 6" h, 7" d, four cut hobstars, strawberry, diamond, and fan cutting, triple notched square cut handle, brilliant blank, ABP..350.00
 6" h, 8" d, low form, eight-sided, all over brilliant cut design of hobstars and numerous brilliant cuttings, applied twisted rope handle, ABP...225.00
 6-1/2" h, 8" d, low, floral and leaf design, applied crystal twisted rope handle, ABP.......................................150.00
 6-1/2" h, 5" d, pattern of two large pinwheels, star cut base, notched handle, sgd "Frye," ABP 160.00
 7-1/2" h, 8-1/2" d, all over heavy brilliant pattern, and of Harvard with hobstars, viscera cutting, applied crystal twisted rope handle, low form, ABP 325.00
 7-1/2" h, 8-1/2" d, four large hobstars, two fans applied crystal rope twisted handle, ABP................................350.00
 7-1/2" h, 8-1/2" d, hobstars and Harvard pattern cutting, low bowl, twisted crystal handle, ABP........................200.00
 8" h, 7" d, Cactus pattern, Pairpoint 275.00
 8" h, 7" d, hobstars, fans, tiny buttons, cut scalloped rim, 3 applied feet, cut notched applied handle..............300.00

8" h, 8-1/2" d, Angelica pattern, applied loop crystal rope handle, deep cut pattern, sgd "Fyre"....................550.00
8" h, 9" d, six cut flowers and leaves, bands of cane, notch and cut etch, twisted rope handle, ABP.................125.00
8-1/2" h, 6-1/2" w, square-shaped, three large cut hobstars with panels of floral cut leaf design, double notched handle, ABP...500.00
9" h, 10-1/2" d, low flaring basket, bands of twelve hobstars around side with fan cutting and panels of cross hatching, cut with huge hobstar in base, flat arched handle with notched edges and leaf cutting in center, clearly sgd "Hoare" on int. 3,500.00
9-1/2" h, 11-1/2" d, five large hobstars, fancy emb floral silver handle and rim, ABP...225.00
10-1/2" h, 10-3/4" d, brilliant and heavy glass blank, four hobstars with fan and strawberry point cutting, double notched handle, ABP...425.00
12-1/2" h, 8" d, all over scrolls and leaf design, quadruple notched handle resembles snake with tongue coming out, sgd "Hawkes Gravic" 900.00
13" h, 9" d, notched cut step pedestal, open flaring shaped basket, band of hobstars, brilliant cutting, applied crystal rope twisted handle, large hobstar cut base, ABP 1,850.00
14" h, 9" w, engraved thistles and leaves, triple notched handle..200.00
14-1/2" h, 10" d, cut cosmos and Harvard type band, double notched handle, ABP 175.00
14-1/2" h, 10" d, cut plums, leaf, and floral design, double notched handle, ABP 750.00
16" h, 10" d, ruffled shaped form, dahlia-like flower cut with leaves, elaborate swirls, cut and notched applied loop handle, base sgd "Hawkes Gravic Glass" 1,800.00
17" h, 11-1/2" d, numerous cut hobstars, step cutting, heavy serrated edge, large star cut base, triple notched handle, ABP..2,900.00
17-1/2" h, 12" w, floral and leaf design, large double notch handle, ABP...500.00
18" h, 10" d, Harvard design, pattern of four cut carnations and leaves, double notched handle, ABP.............850.00
18" h, 12" d, alternating hobstars and pinwheels, double notched handle, extremely heavy and brilliant blank, ABP..1,200.00
18" h, 12" d, floral and brilliant pattern, poppy-like design, bands of triple diamond cut pattern, ABP...........2,900.00
21" h, 13-3/4" h, heavy blank, hobstars and pinwheels, double notched handle, ABP 1,500.00
21" h, 16" d, floral and leaf design, double notched handle, American Brilliant and Floral Period 600.00
Beaker, 8-1/2" h, 6-1/2" w, crystal blank with gravic cutting, finely engraved all over with wild rose buds, blooms, and leaves 100.00
Bell
 5-3/4" h, hobstars, fans, strawberry diamond, ABP 275.00
 6-3/4" h, sharply cut strawberry diamond and fans, pattern also cut on stem end knob 550.00
Bon Bon, 8" d, 2" h, Broadway pattern, Huntly, minor flakes 135.00
Bone Dish, 7" l, 5" w, Russian pattern, crescent shape, set of 4.. 360.00
Bowl
 7" d, low, Pontiac pattern, sgd "Clark" 60.00
 7-3/4" d, 3-1/2" h, China Aster pattern, highly cut pattern, sgd "Hawkes Gravic"...450.00
 8" d, Checker Board pattern 250.00
 8" d, clusters of hobstars and cross hatched diamonds, ABP..90.00

Bowl, hobstar, strawberry, diamond, and other cuttings, notched scalloped rim, sgd Hawkes, $300.

8" d, feathered buzz saws, nail head filled diamonds, ABP, minor flakes 90.00

8" d, Heart pattern 250.00

8" d, hobstars, arches, and cane, ABP, chips 50.00

8" d, hobstars, fans, and pointed diamonds, sgd "Hawkes," ABP, minor chips..100.00

8" d, large feathered buzz saws and hobstar medallions, ABP...100.00

8" d, low, circle motifs of hobstar and cane 150.00

8" d, low, "Y" in center, 3 large hobstars.......................80.00

8" d, sunbursts and feathered arches, ABP...................90.00

8" sq, 4 large hobstars in corners, double-mitre vesicas with cane and Russian motifs 115.00

8" d, 2" h, eight lobes, hobstars and triangular panels cut on base, cross hatching and small star cutting 90.00

8" d, 3-1/2" h, slanted sides cut in pattern of eight hobstars, hobstar base, vertical panels of notches, ABP 50.00

8" d, 3-3/4" h, large hobstar with band of 8 hobstars, ABP, large chip on rim 110.00

9" d, deep cut, medallions, large pointed ovals, arches, and base, ABP...110.00

9" d, Manitou pattern, clear uncut tusk surrounded by brilliant overall cutting, Hoare 400.00

9" d, six large deep cut hobstars and Gothic arches, ABP, minor flakes 250.00

9" d, 4" h, hobstar, fan...125.00

9" d, 4-1/4" deep, Russian pattern, ABP 275.00

9" d, 5-1/2" h, hobstar, checkerboard, ABP 135.00

9-1/4" d, 5" h, golden amber blank attributed to Union Glass Co., Somerville, MA, upper bowl cut in cane pattern above faceted edge, eight scallop rim, star-cut base, unsigned..3,450.00

10" d, deep cut buttons, stars, and fans, ABP 220.00

10" d, Lotus pattern, Eggingston...................................275.00

11" d, 5" h, engraving of glass basket with large bouquet of flowers within scroll, large pattern of diamonds, Hawkestype...150.00

12" d, Holland pattern, rolled rim, sgd "Hawkes"........700.00

12" d, 4-1/2" h, rolled down edge, cut and engraved flowers, leaves, and center thistle, notched serrated edge 275.00

Box, cov

   5" d, 2-3/4" h, cut paneled base, cover cut with large eight-pointed star with hobstar center surrounded by fans, C. F. Monroe 275.00

6-1/2" d, hinged, hobstars, cross hatching, fan, Hawkes, ABP..400.00

6-1/2" d, 4-1/4" h, Bishop's hat shape, large center hobstar, cross hatching and fans on lid, silver plated fittings ... 850.00

Bread Tray

   11-1/2" x 8", Blazed Star...90.00

   12" x 7-1/2", Wedgemere pattern, Libbey, tooth chip..... 250.00

   13-3/4" x 6-1/4", hobstars and cane, rim flake 250.00

Butter Dish, cov

   Hobstar, ABP...250.00

   Russian and florals, 7" d..385.00

Butter Pat

   Cypress, Laurel..35.00

   Hobstar, elongated thumb hold, ABP, set of 4 ....200.00

Candlesticks, pr

   8" h, hobstars, hobnail, and diamonds, hollow teardrop stems, rayed bases 975.00

   9-1/2" h, hobstars, teardrop stem, hobstar base 250.00

   10" h, faceted cut knobs, large teardrop stems, ray base 425.00

   12" h, Adelaide pattern, amber, Pairpoint 250.00

Candy Basket

   3-3/4" h, engraved florals, sterling rim and handle, Hawkes..175.00

   4" d, 6" h, Beaver pattern, Fry, hobstars, whirling stars, cross hatching, cut notched rim and handle, ABP 225.00

Candy Dish, 7-3/4" l, oval, deeply cut Elfin pattern, Hoare.... 90.00

Canoe

   2" l, Harvard pattern, ABP 75.00

   11-1/4" l, Harvard pattern sides, hobstar base, ABP ..185.00

   13-1/2" l, 4-1/2" w, floral and leaves 85.00

Celery Tray

   10" l, 4-1/2" w, hobstar center, buzzstars, ABP.............85.00

   11" l, nailhead filled diamonds and sunbursts, ABP 90.00

   11" x 6", Pattern #70450, Marshall Field catalog, Boggess, pg 156, #568 ....140.00

   12" l, Bakers Gothic pattern, folded, sgd "Libbey" 85.00

Celery Vase, 7-3/4" h, blown, scalloped rim, bowl cut with panels, strawberry diamonds, and fans, knop stem, star cut foot, Pittsburgh 275.00

Centerpiece, 10-3/4" d, wheel cut and etched, molded, fruiting foliage, chips 490.00

Champagne

   Double teardrop stems, strawberry diamonds and fans, set of six 360.00

   Flared bowls, delicate stems, hobstar chain, set of nine..450.00

   Kalana Lily pattern, Dorflinger.......................................75.00

   Monarch pattern, saucer style, set of 12.................1,200.00

   Rayed Button Russian pattern, Russian bases, tumbler type, set of six, ABP 500.00

   Stone engraved rock crystal, Dorflinger, c1890 ....85.00

Champagne Bucket, 7" h, 7" d, sgd "Hoare," ABP 400.00

Champagne Pitcher

   10" h, hobstars and cane, double thumbprint handle 210.00

   11" h, Prism pattern, triple notch handle, monogram sterling silver top 425.00

   12-1/2" h, Cane pattern, other cuttings, sterling silver rim, ABP..400.00

   13-1/4" h, allover cut hobstars, cane bars, stars, and fan, 24 point hobstar base, triple notch handle, fluted spout 600.00

Cheese Dish, cov

   6" h dome, 9" d, plate, cobalt blue cut to clear, bull's eye and panel, large miter splints on bottom of plate, ABP 250.00

   8" h, 10-1/2" d plate, swirling pattern serving plate, matching high dome cov, faceted knob top, ABP, flat edge chip, minor wear..550.00

Cider Pitcher
  Hobstar, cross-cut diamond, jewels and fan, zipper cut and tear drop handle..325.00
  Hobstars, zippers, fine diamonds, honeycomb cut handle, 7" h, ABP..175.00
  Pinwheel and chain of hobstar cut, triple notch handle... 220.00
  Split vesica motifs, hobstar, star, and tan, triple notch handle..150.00
Cigarette Set, 4-1/4" x 3-1/2" cov box, 2 ashtrays, Millicent pattern, Hawkes, sgd 145.00
Cocktail Shaker
  10-1/2" h, 4-1/2" w, steeple case with rider, horse, and fox, band of heavy cut diamonds, notched thumbprint on base, glass sgd "Hawkes," cover and rim marked "Sterling" 450.00
  12-1/2" h, 5-1/2" w, mallard duck in flight over marsh, fancy sterling silver rim and cover, both glass and sterling rim sgd "Hawkes"..210.00
Cologne Bottle
  5-1/4" h, alternating bull's eye and cross-cut squares, faceted cup stopper, sgd "Libbey"....................325.00
  6" h, Hob and Lace pattern, green cased to clear, pattern cut stopper, Dorflinger 625.00
  6-1/4" h, sq, red cut to clear, Octagon Diamond pattern, horizontal stepped shoulder, matching starred stopper, ABP, chips at inner stopper edge 575.00
  7-1/2" h, Holland pattern, faceted cut stopper............275.00
  7-1/2" h, 2-3/4" d, Parisian pattern, sq shape, Dorflinger, ABP, pr..700.00
Compote
  6" h, flared rim, deep bowl with hobstars and pointed triangles, similar cut base, minor flakes, ABP.................95.00
  6" h, hobstar and arches, flared pedestal, ABP..........150.00
  9" h, Hawkes, blank #1224..............................200.00
  9" h, Pairpoint, intaglio cut fruit.......................445.00
  9" h, deep cut buzz saws and pointed arches below, thumbprint stem, ABP...110.00
  9" h, deep cut sunburst, arches and buttons, zippered stem, starcut petal base, ABP.....................................150.00
  9" h, sunburst and fan cuttings, zipper stem, star cut base, minor flakes, ABP..190.00
  9" d, 6" h, Hobstars, fans, buttons, mitres, octagonal notched standard, ABP 150.00
  9-1/4" d, 7" h, Pittsburgh, blown, cut panels, strawberry diamonds and fans, foliage band at rim, finely scalloped lip, knob stem, star cut foot, minor wear and scratches .. 385.00
  9-1/2" h, deep star and arch cutting, star cut base, ABP...180.00
  Tuthill, wild rose pattern, large teardrop stem, all over cut designs, sgd, 8" h, 6" w 250.00
Condiment Dish, 11" d, 6-1/2" h, notched center handle, tripartite condiment servers 2,100.00
Console Set
  12" d #1074 bowl, pr 3-1/2" h #12928 candleholders, Elfin Green, engraved Como pattern, Sinclaire 350.00
  12" d ftd bowl with wide flat rim, p 9-1/8" h baluster form candlesticks, cross-hatched diamond and flute cutting, ABP 750.00
  15" d bowl, 14" h candlesticks, bright floral and webbed motif on bowl, matching candlesticks with horizontal stepped cutting on upper shafts, trefoil T. G. Hawkes mark on each base, "1925" engraved at center of rayed base.....3,125.00
Cordial, engraved, faceted stem, sgd "Hawkes" 75.00
Cracker Jar, cov, 7" d, floral cut, silver plate and bail handle, Pairpoint 275.00

Creamer and Sugar
  3" h, hobstar, ABP......................................50.00
  6" d, 4" h, large center hobstar with triangular panels of cross hatching, handles with large notches and end in three leaf clover at base, unsigned brilliant heavy blank.......350.00
  6-1/2" h, hobstar and arches, stepped hexagonal pedestal, ABP...415.00
  8-1/2" d, hobstars and sunburst, plantation size, ABP ... 385.00
  Zenda, sgd "Libbey" 90.00
Cruet, orig stopper
  6" h, Chrysanthemum pattern, tri-pour spout, cut handle and stopper, sgd "Hawkes," ABP 350.00
  7" h, buzz saws, ABP 70.00
  9-1/2" h, Alhambra pattern, honeycomb handle, tall pyramidal shape, ABP..675.00
  9-1/2" h, sunburst, arches, and horizontal cut ovals, St. Louis handle, ABP..250.00
Decanter, orig stopper
  6-1/2" h, blown, colorless, cut panels, fans, and diamond point roundels, applied foot and 2 rings, Pittsburgh, small chips..220.00
  7-1/4" h, blown, colorless, cut flutes, diamond point, strawberry diamonds and panels, 3 applied rings, Pittsburgh, small flakes, lip ground 110.00
  7-3/8" h, blown, colorless, cut panels, strawberry diamonds and fans, 3 applied rings, Pittsburgh, pinpoint flakes, mismatched stopper 55.00
  8" h, blown, colorless, cut panels, strawberry diamonds and fans, applied foot, 3 applied rings, Pittsburgh, slight stain in bottom, very small chips...............................250.00
  8-1/2" h, blown, colorless, cut panels and fans, 3 applied rings, Pittsburgh, small flakes 140.00
  11-1/2" h, stars, arches, fans, cut neck, star cut mushroom stopper 95.00
  12-3/4" h, hobstar and fan pattern, large notched handle, sgd "Hoare," firing check at handle 75.00
  13" h, cranberry cut to clear, bulbous body, fan and diamond cutting, notched panel neck, applied cut handle, faceted stopper, star-cut base, ABP 3,450.00
  13" h, paneled neck above sunburst, fine diamond and pineapple cuttings, ABP, minor flake at bottom of stopper.... 100.00
  14" d, eight panels, hollow pointed stopper, sgd "Hawkes" 220.00
Dish
  5" d, heart shape, handle, ABP 45.00
  5" d, hobstar, pineapple, palm leaf, ABP 45.00
  8" d, scalloped edge, all over hobstar medallions and hobs, ABP..175.00
Dresser Box, cov, mirror lid, ABP
  4" h, 8" w, heavy brilliant blank, panel side cuttings, star cut bottom, lid cut with center hobstar surrounded by chain of hobstars with notched fan cuttings, orig hinged beveled mirror, mkd "C. F. M. Co. Sterling" trim, fully sgd at hinge, slight dent at hinge....................................750.00
  7" h, 7" w, Harvard pattern variation, three-ftd, silver plated fittings, orig beveled mirror on swivel hinge under lid, cut by Bergen Glass Co, couple of minute flakes........750.00
Epergne, 11" h, one piece, bowl cut in intaglio thistle, lily cut in honeycomb and cross hatch, rolled rim............... 850.00
Fern Dish
  3-3/4" h, 8" w, round, silver-plate rim, C. F. Monroe, minor roughness to cut pattern, normal wear on base, no liner.... 200.00
  5" h, 9-1/2" d, brass rim, C. F. Monroe 400.00
Finger Bowl, strawberry diamond, sgd, Hawkes 55.00
Flower Center
  4-1/4" h, 5-1/2" d, hobstars with strawberry diamond points

and fans, 16 point rayed base, blue and notch cut
neck 315.00

5" h, 6" d, hobstars, flashed fans, hobstar chain and base,
ABP 325.00

7-1/2" h, paneled zipper and pointed stem above bulbous
bowl, star cut sunburst arches and medallions 200.00

7-1/2" h, zippered neck, bulbous bowl with sunburst, arrows,
and four pointed ovals, ABP..................................110.00

7-3/4" h, 12" d, etched and wheel cut motif, honeycomb
flared neck, some wear 500.00

8" d, large hobstar base, step cut neck, ABP 325.00

10" d, hobstars, fan, and diamond, horizontal step-cut neck,
scalloped rim, large hobstar base, ABP 600.00

Goblet
Buzzstar, pineapple, 7" h, marked "B & B," ABP..........40.00
Clear Button Russian pattern, facet cut teardrop stem,
ABP 140.00
Intaglio vintage cut, 8-1/2" h, sgd "Sinclaire" 80.00
Rayed Button Russian, 6" h, teardrop stems, sgd "Hawkes,"
set of nine 1,200.00
Strawberry diamond and fans, double teardrop stems, wood
polished, set of twelve 800.00
Strawberry diamond, pinwheel, and fan, notched stem, 7 pc
set 350.00

Hair Receiver
4-1/4" d, deep cut arches, diamonds, engraved florals ... 60.00
5-1/2" d, Harvard pattern, 2 pc 140.00

Humidor, cov
6-3/4" h, 6" d, deep cranberry cut to clear, Prism and Punty
pattern, elaborate sterling silver cover, Mt. Washington,
ABP, several chips on base rim, cover dented, two jewels
missing 650.00
7-1/2" d, Middlesex, hollow stopper, sponge holder in lid,
Dorflinger, ABP..490.00
9" h, hobstars, beaded split vesicas, hobstar base, matching
cut glass lid with hollow for sponge, ABP 575.00
9" h, Monarch pattern, hobstar base, matching cut glass lid
with hollow for sponge, Hoare, ABP 625.00

Ice Bucket
6" d, Jewel pattern, hobstar bases, two handles, 8-1/2" d underplate, Clark, ABP..550.00
6-1/2" h, 7" w, Harvard pattern, floral cutting, eight sided
form, ABP, minor edge flaking on handles.............100.00
7" h, hobstars and notched prisms, 8" d underplate, double
handles, ABP..940.00

Ice Cream Server, floral engraved................................175.00

Ice Cream Set, Russian pattern, eight 7" d dishes, 8-1/2" d serving bowl, 11" d cake plate, some chips to edges, ABP,
price for 10 pc set 500.00

Ice Cream Tray
14" x 7-1/2", 24 point hobstar center surrounded by cane,
pinwheel border 100.00
15" x 11", hobstars, arches, and gravic cut florals, ABP, mi-
nor flakes..150.00

Ice Tub, two handles, hobstars, ABP..............................395.00

Jar, 6" h, 6" d, deep cranberry cut to clear, star and leaf design,
star cut bottom, Sinclaire, no lid 875.00

Jug, 7" h, spherical body, offset stoppered spout, applied
notched handle, Sinclaire, ABP..............................520.00

Knife Rest, 4-1/2" l, ABP..145.00

Lamp, ABP
13" h, 6-1/2" d mushroom shade with engraved and clear cut
large flowers and leaves, vining tendrils, notch cup stepped
base with matching pattern cut on bottom................350.00
13-1/2" h, domed shade with strawberry diamond and horizontal ribbed cutting, Hawkes-Sinclaire manner, silvered
metal two-socket electrical fittings 690.00

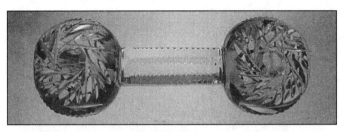

Knife Rest, pinwheel cutting, $90.

14" h, teardrop shade with engraved tulip blossoms, star-cut
closed top, columnar shaft with sq silver plated platform
base, dec with cherubs in vineyard scene, attributed to
Pairpoint 550.00

15" h, 5" h x 10" d mushroom shade done cut with gravic cut
style daisies and leaves, matching base, orig prisms,
Pairpoint style 500.00

18" h, mushroom shade, Pattern #69359, orig pendants, T. B.
Clark 2,450.00

21" h overall, 14" h vasiform cut and engraved standard,
double stepped reticulated silver plated bases, matching
faceted finial, pr..490.00

23" h, large mushroom shade, pedestal base, shade cut with
ten large hobstars with panels of cross-hatching base cut
in Queen pattern with step cutting below fixture, orig ring
and prisms..2,750.00

23-3/4" h, 10" d shade, large expanding cut star in heavy brilliant period pattern of band of daisy-like flowers and
leaves, matching conforming base, inverted trumpet
form, with matching band of flowers, notched prism band,
band of strawberry, diamond, and fan circling base, orig
prisms 2,000.00

26" h, 10-1/2" d Turkish domed shade with pagoda top, Harvard pattern shade and base, 40 step notched prism cut
base, silver plated fittings, orig cut prisms 3,750.00

32" h, 7" d font, 9-1/2" w base, banquet type, solid medium
green, strawberry, diamond, and fan pattern, three-sec-
tion, large flaring hollow blown base, cut knob and large
matching cut font, orig double wick hardware, attributed
to Dorflinger factory 5,250.00

Liquor, stemmed, buzzstar, pineapple, marked, "B & B,"
ABP... 25.00

Loving Cup, 6-1/2" h, sterling rim, prism cut, three triple notched
handles, ABP... 575.00

Luncheon Set, mirror black crystal, opaque white rim wraps, 12-1/2"
d centerpiece bowl, six 8-1/2" d luncheon plates, 6-1/2" dessert plates, twelve 4-3/4" bowls, Sinclaire, 26 pc set ..750.00

Mayonnaise Bowl, 5" d, deep cut, hobstar, medallions, and
arches, ABP... 50.00

Milk Pitcher, pinwheel, strawberry diamond and notched
fan... 90.00

Mustard Pot, cov, 3-1/2" h, panel and notched prism, underplate, sgd "Maple City Glass" 225.00

Napkin Ring, hobstars and bow-tie fans.......................... 90.00

Nappy, two handles
6" d, hobstar center, intaglio floral, strawberry diamond button
border, 6" d..45.00
6" x 7", step-cut pulled handle, checker board bottom, diamond
cut sides 70.00
7" d, four part, hobstar in each section, double thumbprint
handles, 7"..160.00
9" d, deep cut arches, pointed sunbursts and medallions,
ABP..135.00

Orange Bowl
9-3/4" x 6-3/4" x 3-3/4" h, hobstars and strawberry diamond,
ABP..200.00

10" d, pinwheel, notched prism and hobstar in vesicas, ABP 185.00

Parfait, Renaissance, faceted and teardrop stems, Dorflinger, 6 pc set 200.00

Perfume Bottle

3-1/4" l, canary yellow, cut facets, silver mounted cap ... 300.00

3-1/2" l, cranberry overlay, shaped sides, notched cuts, S. Mordan & Co., silver mounted cap 325.00

3-1/2" l, pistol shape, sterling silver fittings 225.00

5-1/2" h, 3" d, six-sided, alternating panels of Harvard pattern and engraved florals, rayed base, matching faceted stopper, ABP 175.00

6-1/2" h, bulbous, all over cutting, orig stopper, ABP 220.00

7" l, oval cut column, hinged sterling silver cov with polychrome portrait center 225.00

Perfume Flask, 5-1/2" l, diamond cut cylindrical bottle, screw mount on one end, hinged spring cap on other, hallmark "EG," well worn orig velvet lined leather case........230.00

Pickle Tray, 7" x 3", checkerboard, hobstar 45.00

Pitcher

6-3/8" h, blown, cut panels, strawberry diamonds, fans, roundels, and rays with foliage rim, fluted lip, Pittsburgh, recut rim with chip 95.00

9" h, cranberry cut to clear with detailed woodland scene, tapered straight sided form, elaborate star and fan-cut base, applied colorless handle, American.............635.00

9-1/2" h, button and daisy cut wide borders, floral center, ABP 125.00

Plate

7" d, Thos. Singleton for Mt. Washington 110.00

10" d, Carolyn pattern, J. Hoare...................................525.00

12" d, alternating hobstar and pinwheel 100.00

Pokal, cov, 16" h, 6-1/2" w, Harvard pattern, tall cut knob, ABP...850.00

Powder Box, cov

3" h, star and zipper cut, emb silvered lid, ABP 75.00

4-1/2" d, flashed hobstar on top, alternating pinwheel and vesica motif 120.00

5-1/2" d, buzz saw base and large buzz saw lid 125.00

Punch Bowl

11" h, 10" w, 2 pc, Elgin pattern, Quaker City 600.00

11" h, 10" w, pc, pinwheel and hobstar pattern, heavy blank with unusual lapidary cut domed base, ABP 500.00

12-1/4" d, 5" h, four star-cut devices spaced by notched vertical ribbing, star-cut base, silver rim mounted with ornate grape clusters and vines, silver mkd "sterling" with mark for Wilcox..1,035.00

14" d, 7" h, five large hobstars, central large hobstar, ABP..550.00

Pitcher, floral cutting, basketweave-type base cutting, applied notched handle, $375.00

17" h, 11-1/2" d, chalice shape, pedestal base, engraved all over with pattern of stars among leaves and hanging blossoms, band of leaf etching around top and base 500.00

Punch Cup

Cranberry cut to clear, cross-cut diamond, clear handle, 2-1/2" h 95.00

Hobstars, pedestal, handle...85.00

Monarch pattern, set of ten 320.00

Punch Ladle

11-1/2" l, silver plated emb shell bowl, cut and notched prism handle...165.00

14" l, 5-1/4" w, Harvard pattern, ornate Pairpoint silver plate stem and double spout bowl.................................325.00

Relish

6" l, pinwheel, hobstars, fans, and prisms, ABP 90.00

8" l, two handles, divided, Jupiter pattern, Meriden....120.00

13" l, leaf shape, Clear Button Russian pattern, ABP 375.00

Rose Bowl

6-1/2" h, ABP 175.00

8" d, 7-1/2" h, ftd, all over strawberry diamond, ray base, Mt. Washington..575.00

10" d, 9-1/2" h, sphere shape, integrated disk foot, overall Russian pattern variant cutting without buttons, top rim polished, base also cut, ABP 575.00

Rum Jug, 7-1/2" h, all over notched prisms 325.00

Salad Bowl and Underplate

10" d, 6" h bow, 11-1/2" d underplate, Spilane (Trefoil & Rosette) pattern, cross-cut vesicas, notched prism, hobstars and fans, sgd "Libbey" 2,200.00

10" d, 7" h, strawberry diamonds, minute nicks 325.00

Salad Serving Fork and Spoon, silver plated, cross-cut diamond glass handles 300.00

Salt

Feather 20.00

Sawtooth, ftd, individual size......................................30.00

Salt Shaker

Garland pattern, green, 4" h, sterling silver lid..............60.00

Notched prism columns 30.00

Sandwich Tray, 10" d, gravic floral cut, center handle, ABP...90.00

Scent Bottle, 6-1/4" l, cane pattern, tapered bottle, hinged cover and rim, imp "Tiffany & Co. Sterling," ABP, cover misaligned, glass stopper missing 175.00

Spooner, 5" h, hobstar and arches, ABP 90.00

Sweet Pea Vase, 3-1/2" h, 6" w, Kalana Pansy, Dorflinger .. 110.00

Tankard Pitcher

10-1/4" h, Harvard cut sides, pinwheel top, mini hobnails, thumbprint notched handle, ABP 200.00

11" h, hobstar, strawberry diamond, notched prism and fan, flared base with bull's eye, double thumbprint handle 275.00

12" h, diamond band and leaf design, large applied notched handle, ABP...200.00

17-1/4" h, 7" w base, three rows of hobstars, diamond point cutting, fancy silver rim, applied loop cut handle, ABP ... 700.00

Tantalus Set, three matching 6" h Dorflinger cut glass bottles in patent #210 with orig matching stoppers, elaborate metal holder sgd "The Tantalus Betjemann's Patented London 6588," some minor flaking to bottles 1,100.00

Tazza, 8" d, shallow bowl, buzz star and arches, paneled zippered stem, starcut base, ABP 125.00

Tobacco Jar, 9" h, 6" d, straight sided canister, panels of fine cut cane pattern alternating with faceted thumbprints, matching cut glass top with star cutting repeated on base, ABP... 1,150.00

Tray

4-1/2" w, 1-3/4" h, cutting of diamond notches, star cut base, floral emb silver plated rim, C. F. Monroe 75.00

10" l, all over hobstars, ABP 495.00

10" l, deep cut hobstar medallions and cross hatched arches, ABP...225.00

12" l, similar to Hawkes Nelson pattern, sgd "Straus".....700.00

12" l, 8" w, cane pattern, ABP.......................................400.00

14" x 7-1/2", Sillsbee pattern, Pairpoint 335.00

Tumble-Up, handled pitcher and matching tumbler, geometric and floral..450.00

Tumbler

Bristol Rose pattern, Mt. Washington...........................75.00

Clear Button Russian pattern 95.00

Cut panels, fans, sheaves, roundels, strawberry diamonds, 3-1/8" h, flint, Pittsburgh 40.00

Harvard, rayed base...45.00

Hobstars...40.00

Hobstars, strawberry diamonds, fans, hobstar cluster and base, set of six 360.00

Panel, sgd "Hawkes," rare 400.00

Russian Button pattern, set of nine 350.00

Star of David pattern, 4" h, set of four 300.00

Vase

5" h, 2" w, Kalana, lily dec, Dorflinger 150.00

8" h, monogrammed and inscribed silver flared neck, body cut with thumb notching and elongated panels, ABP, c1901, minor chips..230.00

8" h, trumpet set, hobstar and diamond arches, ABP.....90.00

9" h, cylindrical, star, strawberry diamond, cross-cut diamond and fan, attributed to Dorflinger 130.00

9" h, deep cut zippered ribs with panels of sunburst and fine cut, ABP, minor flake 150.00

9-1/2 h, deep cut arched stars, windows, and zippered ribs, ABP...100.00

10" h, arches, pointed triangles and buzz stars, ABP.....100.00

10" h, ovoid shape bowl, cut with buzz saw, button and daisy, deep arches, zipper cut paneled stem, faceted paperweight and fine cut foot, ABP.........................275.00

10" h, trumpet, zipper and thumbprint cut, star cut paperweight base...100.00

10-1/4" h, engraved dragon, clear ground, deep amber flashing, applied sterling rim, both glass and silver rim sgd "Hawkes"...250.00

11" h, bulbous top, fluted rim, tapering cylindrical stem, wide base, bulbous top cut with double row of thumbprints and diamond patterns and cross hatching, step cutting underneath, stem cut with hobstars, cross hatching, and flat flutes, heavy brilliant blank, clearly sgd "Hawkes" 550.00

11" h, sunburst and finecut pattern, zippered panel stem, star cut base...175.00

11-1/2" h, 6" w, medium green, floral engraving, gold band, sgd "Hawkes," int. crazed 150.00

12" h, hobstars, florals, and zippered ribs 85.00

12" h, strawberry diamond, buzzstars. ABP...............150.00

12" h, 5-1/2" w, triangular, three large and three small hobstars, double notched pedestal and flaring base, ABP 150.00

12-1/4" h, corset shape, cone and file band, deep cut leaves and flowers 85.00

12-1/2" h, 6-1/2" d, floral and diamond point engraving, sgd "Hawkes"...250.00

14" h, bowling pin shape, Comet pattern, sgd "J. Hoare," professionally repaired...200.00

14" h, bowling pin shape, three 24 point hobstars on sides surrounded by notched prisms, strawberry diamond, hobstars, star, and checkered diamond fields 700.00

14" h, corset shape, Harvard pattern, deep floral engraving 925.00

14" h, trumpet shape, 8" w at top, Venetian pattern, Hawkes, ABP...750.00

15" h, corset shape, Primrose pattern, Dorlinger 1,250.00

16" h, corset shape, well cut hobstar, strawberry diamond, prism, flashed star and fan...................................300.00

16" h, tapered cylinder, bulbed scalloped top, intricately carved in a variety of motifs, ABP, some small int. rim chips...1,840.00

17" h, 7" w at widest point, tulip shape, hobstar, strawberry diamond and fan, 24 point hobstar base...............425.00

19-1/2" h, funeral, hobstars, strawberry diamond, and fan motifs 500.00

Water Carafe

Brunswick pattern, thin neck, sgd "Hawkes" 240.00

Harvard pattern, ABP 185.00

Hobstars and notched prisms, ABP............................125.00

Pinwheel and Fan cutting, notched neck, 8" h, 4" w ...125.00

Russian pattern, 7-1/2" h, 6" w, all over brilliant design, minor flaking to pattern, ABP..225.00

Thumbprint and chain of hobstar, honeycomb neck, sgd "Hawkes"...180.00

Wedgemere pattern, Libbey, 9" h, ABP 1,200.00

Water Pitcher

9-1/2" h, Harvard pattern panels and intaglio cut sprays of flowers and foliage, ABP.......................................300.00

10" h, Keystone Rose pattern 190.00

11" h, Harvard pattern, rayed base, double punty handle, sgd "Hawkes," ABP...400.00

Water Set, pitcher and tumblers, two bands of hobstars, flat pillar cut, 3 panels of intaglio wild florals, sgd "Sinclaire," 6 pcs...575.00

Whiskey Jug, 6-1/4" h, bulbous, thistle and grape cutting, orig stopper, sgd "Sinclaire" 295.00

Wine

4" h, flint, cut panels, strawberry diamonds, and fans, Pittsburgh 60.00

4-1/8" h, flint, Gothic Arch, sheaf like ferns, Pittsburgh..... 75.00

4-1/4" h, flint, strawberry diamonds, fans, leaves, and panels, Pittsburgh...65.00

6" h, buzz saws and cross hatched diamonds, ABP, 1 chipped, set of 4 ....100.00

Vase, sunflower motif, 12" h, $450.

CUT VELVET

History: Several glass manufacturers made cut velvet during the late Victorian era, c1870-1900. An outer layer of pastel color was applied over a white casing. The layers were fused and blown into a mold. Then the piece then was molded or cut in a high-relief ribbed or diamond shape, exposing portions of the casing. The pieces were usually acid finished, which gives the piece a satin velvety feel, hence the name "cut velvet." Some glossy pieces have been found.

This exquisite glassware was made in many forms. Bowls, ewers, pitchers, and vases are the most common. Ruffled edges, rigaree, and applied clear handles are sometimes added to enhance the beauty or usefulness of a piece. Although two-toned bodies have been found, most are single colors, shaded by the shape and technique. Colors include amethyst, apple green, apricot, blue, butterscotch, pin, tan, turquoise, and yellow with white linings.

Basket, 11-1/2" h, 9" w, brilliant yellow ext., Diamond Quilted pattern, bright pink shaded int., tightly crimped and ruffled edge, applied crystal loop handle 300.00
Biscuit Jar, cov, pink, SP mountings and lid....................275.00
Celery Vase, 6-1/2" h, deep blue over white, Diamond Quilted pattern, box-pleated top...725.00
Creamer
    3-1/2" h, Diamond Quilted pattern, cranberry, applied multicolored enamel dec 385.00
    5-1/4" h, raised ribbed pattern, butterscotch body, white lining 200.00
Cruet, 6" h, shiny pink, Diamond Quilted pattern, clear faceted stopper, clear handle 750.00
Finger Bowl, 4-1/2" d, Diamond Quilted pattern, blue 185.00
Rose Bowl, 3-1/4" d, 3-3/4" h, egg shape, raised Diamond Quilted pattern, rose body, white lining, six crimp top 195.00
Vase
    5-1/4" h, blue body, quatrefoil top...............................145.00
    5-1/2" h, 3" w, deep pink over white, vertical ribs, two minor surface chips..85.00
    6-1/4" h, opaque white body, pale pink lining, ribbon candy rim...150.00
    6-1/2" d, stick type, raised Diamond Quilted pattern, rose body, white lining 250.00
    6-3/4" h, bulbous, raised Diamond Quilted pattern, pink body, ruffled rim 220.00
    7-1/2" h, 3-1/2" w, bulbous shape, ruffled top, Herringbone pattern, deep Alice Blue, white lining, c1880.........450.00
    8-3/4" h, bulbous, raised Diamond Quilted pattern, pale blue body 265.00
    9" h, cylindrical, raised Diamond Quilted pattern, blue body, ruffled rim 250.00
    9" h, slight flare to end of elongated neck, robin's egg blue, diamond quilt body, daisy blossom like design at base 385.00
    9" h, 6" tall cylinder over short bulbous base, deeply ruffled 9" w top, deep orange Diamond Quilted pattern ...675.00
    10" h, ruffled and crimped top, purple cased to opal white body, Diamond Quilted pattern, Victorian..............575.00
    11-1/2" h, 6" w, glossy satin, Herringbone pattern, deep blue shading to pale blue, bright opaque white lining, applied crystal edge...250.00
    13-1/2" h, 6" d base, double gourd shape, long pumpkin stem neck, pale gold, Diamond Quilted pattern 650.00

CZECHOSLOVAKIAN ITEMS

History: Objects marked "Made in Czechoslovakia" were produced after 1918, when the country claimed its independence from the Austro-Hungarian Empire. The people became more cosmopolitan and liberated and expanded the scope of their lives. Their porcelains, pottery, and glassware reflect many influences.

A specific manufacturer's mark may be identified as being much earlier than 1918, but this only indicates the factory existed in the Bohemian or Austro-Hungarian Empire period.

Czechoslovakian glassware can range from exquisite gut glass to Art Deco designs executed in bright colors. Vivid color combinations of orange, blue, and black with white are common. Spatter-type wares and bright streaks of color also are readily found. Modern Czech craftsmen are producing some lovely pieces and should be included in any collection of Czechoslovakian glassware. The mass-produced bowls, perfume bottles, vases and other types of items are starting to command high prices as collectors seek these colorful pieces of glassware.

References: Dale and Diane Barta and Helen M. Rose, *Czechoslovakian Glass & Collectibles* (1992, 1995 values), Book II (1996) Collector Books; *Bohemian Glass*, n.d., distributed by Antique Publications; Ruth A. Forsythe, *Made in Czechoslovakia*, Antique Publications, 1993; Jacquelyne Y. Jones-North, *Czechoslovakian Perfume Bottles and Boudoir Accessories*, Antique Publications, 1990; Leslie Piña, *Pottery, Modern Wares 1920-1960*, Schiffer Publishing, 1994.

Periodical: *New Glass Review*, Bardounova 2140 149 00 Praha 4, Prague, Czech Republic.

Collectors' Club: Czechoslovakian Collectors Guild International, P.O. Box 901395, Kansas City, MO 64190; Friends of the Glass Museum of Novy Bor, Kensington, MD 20895.

Atomizer, 7-1/2" h, brilliant period cut glass 115.00
Basket
    Amber, six-prong cobalt blue handle 45.00
    Bright yellow, six-prong cobalt blue handle..................60.00
    Lemon yellow, black trim, clear handle, emb floral design, 7-1/2" h, 6-1/2" w, matched pr 100.00
    Multicolored spatter cased in cobalt blue, cobalt blue handle, 7" h...100.00
    Pink, six-prong cobalt blue handle 50.00
    Powder blue, glossy, floral design, black trim, clear frosted handle, 7-1/2" h, 6-1/2" w...90.00
    Red, colorless handle 95.00
    Yellow and orange spatter, clear twisted thorn handle ..110.00
Bowl
    Cased, yellow int., black ext., polished pontil..............60.00
    Clear and smoke with oxblood and orange drippings, 9" d, 4" h..100.00
    Flared opal-green oval, three black applied ball feet, black rim wrap, design attributed to Michael Powolny, 10-1/2" d, 5" h...290.00
    Low, glossy finish yellow and orange spatter, deep purple base, 7-1/2" w..75.00
    Multicolored spatter cased in cobalt blue, cov.............85.00
Box, cov
    6" d, amber ground, white enameled boy and bird, orig paper label "Bohemian glass, made in Czechoslovakia" 75.00
    7" d, 3-1/2" h, lemon yellow, enamel dec of black tree with brilliant orange fruit, black leaves, sgd "Delafine Ltd".... 150.00
Console Set, 10" x 6" x 2-1/2" bowl, Art Deco design, turquoise raised drapery, knotted corners, bowl and pr candlesticks 85.00
Decanter Set, figural owl decanter, four matching cups, blue ground, painted eyes 200.00

Dresser Set, 6" h colorless bottle, covered powder with enameled florals 50.00
Fairy Lamp, 5" h, 2 pc, ruby flashed, cut back design of jumping stag, orig paper label "Egermann, Czechoslovakia" 90.00
Fernery, 4-1/2" d, amber cased with cream mottling, orig frog 95.00
Flask, 12-1/2" h, Burmese type ground, birds perched on stems, foliage, moon, sgd "Tischler #426" 500.00
Inkwell, 3-1/4" h, colorless, figural, sitting Scottie dog, SP collar, mkd 85.00
Jack in the Pulpit Vase, 12" h, white and yellow irid, deep red interior, green-red criss-cross looping, mkd "Czechoslovakia" 325.00
Jam Jar, cov, 4" h, 3-1/2" d, pear shape, glossy finish, multicolored spatter, applied black trailing 75.00
Jar, cov
    4" h, mottled red and yellow, applied florals 50.00
    4" h, swirled cased orange and yellow, colorless finial..... 35.00
Lamp
    9" h, vanity, cased red mushroom shade, coralene floral dec on matching base..250.00
    9" h, vanity, mushroom shade hand dec with windmill scene, matching base, orig bulb 250.00
    22" h, figural, bronzed metal figure of kneeling woman supporting diamond hobbed art glass mottled art glass shade, minor damage to shade 250.00
    25" h overall, pale pink and deep blue cased to clear honeycomb pattern glass, orig cast iron and metal fittings 95.00
Lamp Shade, beaded 50.00
Luncheon Set, partial, flowing irid magenta, orange, brown and lavender, mother of pearl ground, sgd, 40 pcs 280.00
Perfume Bottle
    3" h, colorless, integrated engraved stopper..............125.00
    4" h, mottled blue and turquoise, art glass stopper under brass hinged cap 90.00
    5" h, colorless, etched and engraved stopper............125.00
    5" h, red, black stopper, ground pontil on dauber, paper label mkd "Made in Czechoslovakia" 100.00
    6" h, amethyst, faceted, integrated engraved stopper ... 145.00
    6-3/4" h, amber, large intaglio floral stopper................175.00
Pitcher, 9-1/2" h, cranberry, white enameled boy with bird, orig paper label "Bohemian glass, made in Czechoslovakia"...110.00
Plate, 9-1/2" d, gilt foliate designs, wide burgundy border, Epiag, early 20th C, light wear, 11 pc set 290.00
Powder Box, cov, round, yellow, black knop.....................60.00
Rose Bowl, 5-1/2" h, enameled florals and orange lattice dec 80.00
Scent Bottle, 6-1/4" h, molded green malachite glass, elaborate cherub and foliate design, conforming stopper with floral bouquet, polished base, pr.....................................260.00
Vase
    4" h, mottled white and brown, large mottled red base with metallic green...50.00
    4-3/4" h, blue, ftd, applied black rim, cased 70.00
    5" h, irid opalescent, red threading, red int., ground pontil, mkd "Czechoslovakia" 165.00
    5" h, 5" w, bright red, applied cobalt blue rim, applied cobalt blue leaf dec around center 75.00
    5-1/8" h, tripod, ovoid, mottled red internally striped in black, red glass legs supporting struts applied and tooled all in one piece, polished at top rim..............................270.00
    6" h, cased red over white, irid finish 110.00
    6-1/2" h, ftd urn form, rose pink irid bowl, blue oil-spot motif, partial acid stamp "CZECHO/SLOVAKIA" 1,000.00
    6-1/2" h, bright yellow, mottled base.............................75.00
    7" h, bright tomato red...65.00

Vase, cased, ringed body, blue , orange spatter, white ground, 6" h, $25.

    7" h, ribbed orange, bright cobalt blue leaf trim, matched pr 100.00
    7" h, 3" w, glossy finish, ivory, bulbous tortoise shell spatter base, pr 145.00
    7-1/4" h, yellow and orange, ftd, applied black rim, cased..65.00
    7-1/2" h, raised rim, bright yellow cased oval body, hand painted blue clown above spiked design elements, painted black rim, sgd "Czech/Slovakia" on base, pr ...290.00
    8" h, green, fine orange threading at fan shaped rim, ground pontil..220.00
    8" h, mottled red over yellow, blown out mold of ribs and snails 100.00
    8" h, yellow and orange spatter, four clear feet 90.00
    8" h, wave design of charcoal and white with bubbles, colorless cased ground, applied black serpent 90.00
    8-1/2" h, red and white mottled ground, black snake dec, ruffled...125.00
    8-1/2" h, yellow, orange, red, blue spatter, cobalt applied trim, clear feet...95.00
    8-1/2" h, 5" w, glossy finish, bulbous, red and gray spatter, applied reeded black handles, pr.........................155.00
    9" h, orange, black center spiral and rim 95.00
    9" h, wrought iron reticulated frame, blown-in glass body with splotched blue, orange and green cased to white, base stamped "Czechoslovakia" 460.00
    9" h, 3" w, red, cobalt blue spiral and trim 95.00
    9" h, 4" w, bright red, bulbous base, flaring rim, applied cobalt blue leaf dec around center 100.00
    10" h, 5" w, acid finish, orange and yellow spatter, clear ground, dark purple base 100.00
    10-1/2" h, applied black rim, three horizontal ribs, wide ftd flange, mkd "Czechoslovakia" 150.00
    10-1/2" h, trumpet form, deep rose bowl with blue oil-spot motif, acid stamped "CZECHO/SLOVAKIA" 1,800.00
    10-1/2" h, 8" w, matte finish, bright orange, yellow, white, and green spatter, pr..150.00
    11" h, 5" w, pale blue ground, white and pink spatter 90.00
    12" h, ribbed bright orange, brown, yellow, and orange spatter base 110.00
    14-3/4" h, raised rim, irid colorless oval body cased to opal glass, internal layer of bright red, green, orange, and olive green splotched dec, base stamped "Czechoslovakia"...520.00
    15" h, 9-1/4" h, acid finish, brilliant yellow and orange swirls, dark lavender spatters, flaring acid finish pedestal base with lavender flames up the side...........................200.00
Wine, 5" h
Orange bowl, black stem, enameled jester design 50.00
Red bowl, black stem..35.00

DAUM NANCY

History: Daum Nancy glassware originates in the Nancy, France, region and most pieces are attributed to members of the Daum family. Also known as Cristalleries de Nancy, the glassworks has been in operation since 1875.

1895–1942

Daum family members include the founder, Jean Daum (1825-1885), Jean-Louis Auguste Daum (1853-1909), Jean-Antonin Daum (1864-1930), Paul Daum (1890-1944), Henri Daum, (1894-1930), Michel Daum (b. 1900), and Jacques Daum (b. 1919). Both Jean-Louis Auguste and Jean-Antonin were greatly influenced by Emile Gallé.

Cameo glasswares were carefully crafted in addition to colored glassware with enameled decoration, etch glass, cased glass, and several other techniques. Crystal glassware and pate-de-verre were reintroduced into the firm's lines during the late 1960s.

All items made are marked with an engraved signature, which varies from artist to artist.

References: Victor Arwas, *Glass Art Nouveau To Art Deco*, Rizzoli International Publications, Inc., 1977; Harold Newman, *An Illustrated Dictionary Of Glass*, Thames and Hudson, 1977; Wolf Ueker, *Art Nouveau and Art Deco Lamps and Candlesticks*, Abbeville Press, 1987.

Reproduction Alert: Examples of period Daum Nancy items have been copied and reproduced. Most lack the details and exquisite cutting of the originals.

Animal, modern, crystal
15" h, catalog #02039, stork, head overlooking back, inscribed "Daum France" 230.00
18-1/2" h, catalog #02038, stork, head extended upward, inscribed "Daum France" 235.00
Beverage Set, 9" h ribbed oviform pitcher, applied handle, carved circular stopper, six matching footed goblets, clear glass, finely carved with thistle blossoms, gilt highlights, enameled "Daum Nancy" 2,250.00
Bottle, 4-1/2" h, cameo, rhomboid shape, short, narrow cylindrical neck, everted rim, mottled and streaked green and white, dark red splashes on base, green and gray overlay, cut pendant leafy branches and stems of deep orange berries, sgd in cameo, c1900 ....2,000.00
Bowl
6" d, 2" h, trefoil rim, colorless and brick-orange body, frosted int., dec as branches of mistletoe with white berries, gold enhancement, base sgd "Daum (cross) Nancy" 920.00
6-3/4" d, 3-1/8" h, mottled yellow-pink dish, metal foil inclusions blown into simple wrought iron framework, base sgd "Daum Nancy/L. Majorelle" 1,100.00
7-3/4" h, circular, pinched quatrefoil rim, burgundy mottled yellow ground, etched berried branches, black enamel highlights, enameled "Daum Nancy/France" 1,800.00
8-1/2" h, 5-1/4" h, flared, ftd, inverted rim, mottled burgundy ground, overlaid in puce, etched wooded lake scene, cameo sgd "Daum Nancy" 1,600.00
Box, cov
2-3/4" h, sq, frosted colorless, white, and amber ground, amethyst-purple blossoms and buds, delicate green leafy stems, conforming cov, sgd in green "Daum Nancy (cross)" 2,100.00
6" w, 5-1/4" h, brilliant blue mottled ground, shades of turquoise blue and cobalt blue, gold foil dec, sgd "Daum Nancy" 275.00
Candlesticks, pr, 6-3/4" h, 9" l, 3-lite, molded colorless form, engraved "Daum (cross) Nancy," c1960 .... 175.00
Centerbowl, 23" l, 8" h, modern, crystal, heavy walled elliptical colorless, inscribed "Daum France"..................... 175.00
Chandelier, 41" l, flared trumpet hanger, wide domed shade, rich yellow glass etched with vertical geometric devices, etched "Daum Nancy"..................................... 25,000.00
Cologne Bottle, 6" h, mold blown Art Deco sq colorless bottle, cased to opaque amethyst, capped with conforming orange stopper, lower edge engraved "Daum (cross) Nancy," pr... 920.00
Coupe, 16" d, flared circular form, etched geometric pattern, faceted base, smoky topaz, incised "Daum Nancy France" 1,100.00
Creamer, 3-1/8" h, 3" d, cameo, squared bulbous, round mouth, mottled gold shading to mottled brown frosted ground, enameled green leaves and brown berries, single acid cutting, cameo sgd 1,750.00
Cruet, 7-1/4" h, green ground, stylized foliate branch with white enamel berries, gold enamel accents, applied brushed gold highlights, sterling silver edged matching flag sided stopper, orig silver holder with cut out edge, gold enamel sgd "Daum Nancy," cross of Lorraine............... 1,850.00
Cup and Saucer, 3-1/4" d cup, 5-1/4" d saucer, etched and enameled black on white to colorless, handled cup with Dutch lowlands scene, woman walking on tree lined roadway, passing sailboats, saucer with scene of windmill, farm, each pc mkd in gold "Daum (cross) Nancy" 1,150.00
Dealer's Sign, crystal, France 60.00
Decanter, 9" h, bulbous Art Deco style, bubbly orange, applied aubergine handle and stopper, sgd "Daum (cross) Nancy/France" at lower edge 690.00
Egg, 5" h, fiery opalescent egg shaped oval, acid etched eggshell texture, shallow cameo, cut ducks in groups of three, sgd on glass base, mounted to gilt metal beaded pedestal foot... 1,600.00
Flower Pot, 5-3/4" h, heavy walled colorless molded body, internally dec by tiny bubbles, lower edge engraved "Daum (cross) Nancy-France" 345.00
Goblet
5-1/2" h, colorless glass, black and gold enameled floral and painted dec, sgd 1,250.00
Dali, sgd, orig presentation box...................................400.00
Hops Pitcher, 3" h, flattened miniature, fiery yellow amber, scrolling stylized etched and enameled black and gold dec, base mkd "Daum (cross) Nancy" 1,850.00
Jar, cov
2-1/4" h, 4" w, light and dark blue textured crystal ground, cameo carved pale gray and black poppies, leaves, and buds, gold accents, sterling lid with "E" monogram and emb poppies, minute wear to edge rim of jar 200.00
3-3/4" h, apple shape, green bowl, matching cove, bright orange finial, side inscribed "Daum (cross) Nancy".....260.00
Jar, open, 1-3/4" h, polished rim, colorless, white and purple bowl, wheat shaft and grasses dec, base sgd "Daum (cross) Nancy" in gold... 850.00
Lamp Base
10-1/2" h, oviform, yellow ground overlaid in burgundy, etched and polished with stylized flowering vines, carved "Daum Nancy France," drilled and mounted in gilt-metal base..1,500.00
15-3/4" h, elliptical mottled amber and brown vase, deeply etched and wheel-cut mushrooms growing wild under branches, pine cones and needles, all over naturalized

enameling, drilled and mounted with gilt metal lamp fittings top and base 4,600.00

Lamp, table

19-1/2" h, trumpet form standard, domed shade with open top, tangerine ground shading to yellow, etched and enameled sailboats, enameled "Daum Nancy".......................8,500.00

20" h, 11-1/4" d domed gray glass shade, etched vertical lines, etched "Daum Nancy France," wrought iron standard dec with pine cone clusters, circular foot with conforming dec, stamped "Katona".........................2,500.00

20-1/4" h, gray-white glass elongated slender dome shade acid etched in furrows, zig-zag border, wrought iron mount, base, and shade inscribed "Daum Nancy France" with cross de Lorraine 135,000.00

21-1/2" h, 12" d orange domed glass shade with scalloped rim, etched stylized chrysanthemums, etched "Daum Nancy France," reticulated scrolled wrought iron base 2,200.00

Miniature Pitcher, 2-1/2" h, 3" w, clear glass, int. ribbing, black enameled landscape, gold trim, applied loop handle, sgd "Daum Nancy"...2,000.00

Miniature Vase

1-1/2" h, shaped cylindrical, mottled tangerine ground, etched and enameled snow scene with trees, enameled "Daum Nancy"...800.00

1-3/4" h, bright yellow ground, enameled brown landscape design...850.00

Paperweight, cactus 125.00

Perfume Flacon, 5-3/4" h, colorless bottle, shaded emerald green at top, etched poppy blossoms and pod, starry background, mounted with silver taster foot, screw rim, and swirled cov, base mkd "Daum (cross) Nancy" 1,380.00

Platter, 17-3/4" d, round, topaz ground, ext. etched with concentric textured Art Deco style rings, base edge inscribed "Daum (cross) Nancy France," minor scratches...................650.00

Salt, 1-1/4" h, 1-1/4" w, bucket shape, two tab handles, snowy landscape scene...900.00

Sculpture, 8-1/4" h, clear and frosted, designed by Folon, #81 of limited edition of 300, etched "Folon Daum France 81/300" 175.00

Toothpick Holder, 2" h, orange and yellow mottled ground, winter trees in snowy landscape dec, base sgd "Daum (cross) Nancy"...1,150.00

Perfume Bottle, cameo, gold irid and foliage, purple ground, replaced stopper, 7-1/2" h, $1,430. Photo courtesy of Jackson's Auctioneers & Appraisers.

Vase

3" h, flattened form, gray and tan ground, enameled floral dec, molded "Daum Nancy/France" 1,300.00

3-1/2" h, oviform, mottled frosted white ground shading to violet base, etched and enameled violets, cameo sgd "Daum Nancy"...2,000.00

3-1/2" h, 7-1/4" d, quatraform rim, mottled burgundy red bowl-form, three encased gold foil elements, lower edge inscribed "Daum (cross) Nancy," some int. scratches 460.00

3-7/8" h, squared rim, goblet form, yellow-orange mottled ground, winter trees above snowy ground, minimal chip on pedestal foot, base inscribed "Daum (cross) Nancy" 2,185.00

4" h, bulbed oval, sunset red and orange, overlaid in dark burgundy-black, cameo etched leafy waterfront trees with boats, lower side sgd "Daum (cross) Nancy" 865.00

4-1/2" h, diamond form, cased yellow and mottled orange body, etched and enameled orange poppy blossoms and buds, delicate green stems, gold enhanced leaves, side sgd "Daum Nancy (cross)"..........................1,785.00

4-1/2" h, ftd trumpet form, rich opalescent ground, etched and enameled thistle branch, engraved "Daum Nancy" ...700.00

4-1/2" h, waisted lozenge form, opalescent ground, delicate enamel and gilt foliate dec, painted "Daum Nancy" 1,500.00

4-1/2" h, 2" w, single layer of pale opalescent yellow, cutting of thistles and leaves, sgd.........................350.00

4-3/4" h, square etched colorless body, cased to yellow and deep purple, overall painted naturalized cornflowers, side sgd in cameo "Daum Nancy (cross)"..........3,550.00

4-7/8" h, barrel, mottled red, orange, and green body, overlaid in olive green, etched riverside landscape, lower side sgd "Daum (cross) Nancy" 1,380.00

4-7/8" h, barrel, mottled orange-amber body, maroon and sienna colored riverside scene, side sgd "Daum Nancy (cross)"...1,265.00

4-7/8" h, square cylinder of colorless and sky-blue glass, etched and painted as leafy birch trees at riverside, "Daum (cross) Nancy" inscribed in base............2,415.00

4-7/8" h, square cylinder of green over colorless, cameo etched iris blossom, border scene above and gold enamel highlights, "Daum (cross) Nancy" in gold on base...........690.00

5" h, oval body, gold highlighted iris blossoms, raised on hallmarked silver pedestal foot, side sgd "Daum (cross) Nancy"...375.00

5-1/4" h, blue-green bowl-form, amber splotches raised on aubergine-black pedestal foot, smooth flougravure finish, inscribed "Daum (cross) Nancy" on lower side 600.00

5-1/2" h, enameled, conical vessel, four pinched sides, enamel painted yellow and amethyst frosted surface, orange blossoms, tall spike leaves, "Daum Nancy (cross)" painted on side...1,610.00

5-1/2" h, etched and Enameled, pinched trumpet form, mottled yellow shading to apricot, etched and enameled white flowering branches, cameo sgd "Daum Nancy".......... 2,200.00

5-1/2" h, etched, Art Deco, monochromatic translucent yellow sphere, alternating glossy and etched panels, base rim inscribed "Daum (cross) Nancy France" 345.00

6" h, bulbous, fluted panels, smoky gray, wheel carved "Daum Nancy France"...500.00

6" h, elongated oval, intercalaire etched, seagreen glass internally dec with burgundy trailings, etched aquatic foliage, gilt highlights, seagreen finely enameled with seaweed, fish, and squid, enameled "Daum Nancy" 6,000.00

6" h, wheel-carved, fire-polished, squatty bulbous form, everted rim, opalescent ground, overlaid with cranberry and spruce, etched and carved wild roses on thorny branches, martele surface, engraved "Daum Nancy"............................ 4,500.00

6-1/4" h, elliptical opalescent body, free-form decorative rim, etched tall leafy trees in foreground, red landscape in distance enhanced by enamel dec, base sgd in black "Daum (cross) Nancy"..4,100.00

6-1/4" h, tooled double pointed rim, yellow amber tapered cylinder, brown and black sailboats in harbor scene, base inscribed "Daum (cross) Nancy"................2,300.00

6-3/4" h, two handled oval, opaque green shaded into orange-amber, delicate cameo etched spring flowers painted in natural palette, enhanced by gold repeating on applied handles, base inscribed in gold "Daum (cross) Nancy"..2,875.00

6-7/8" h, raised rim, urn-form, frosted amber, orange, and mottled green body, etched and realistically colored orchid blossoms, delicate stems, above wild grasses, side sgd "Daum Nancy (cross)" 1,265.00

7" h, broad oval bowl form, pedestal foot, colorless glass, rose red mottled powders below bright royal blue border, internally decorated, base inscribed "Daum (cross) Nancy"..435.00

7-3/4" h, bulbous, polished rim, monochromatic topaz body, repeating etched panels of Art Deco geometric devices, lower edge engraved "Daum (cross) Nancy France" 375.00

7-3/4" h, oviform, everted rim, overlaid in red and blue, etched and wheel-carved iris blossoms and foliage against martele ground, engraved "Daum Nancy" 3,250.00

8-3/4" h, compressed cylindrical, mottled sky-blue ground, etched mountainous landscape with trees and lake in foreground, enameled "Daum Nancy" 4,000.00

8-7/8" h, colorless, blown, applied blue and brown glass medallion, diagonal cut lines, engraved "Daum France," orig paper label 225.00

9-1/4" h, baluster, overlaid in orange and green, etched and carved poppy blossoms and foliage, frosted martele ground, engraved "Daum Nancy" 2,000.00

9-1/4" h, slender bud, creamy amber, blue foot, smooth flougravure finish, inscribed "Daum (cross) Nancy" on lower side...650.00

9-1/2" h, ftd trumpet form, opalescent ground, etched and enameled thistle blossoms, gilt highlights, gilded "Daum Nancy"..2,000.00

10-3/4" h, elongated oval, mottled white, colorless, and deep purple-blue body, etched overall and cameo enamel painted as naturalized stalks of wheat and grasses, gold accents and embellishments, base mkd in gold "Daum (cross) Nancy"..5,750.00

11-3/4" h, waisted cylinder, mottled autumnal colors, etched thorny branches and leaves, cameo sgd "Daum Nancy"... 1,400.00

12-1/4" h, flattened flask form, mottled burgundy and lemon ground, overlaid in puce, etched wooded lace scene, sailboats, cameo sgd "Daum Nancy" 2,500.00

13-1/4" h, modern, crystal, heavy walled colorless trapezoidal body, inscribed "Daum" near base, tiny top chips.... 175.00

14-1/2" h, flared oviform, flattened sq foot, deep smoky topaz, etched vertical skyscraper motif bands, wheel carved "Daum Nancy France" 7,000.00

15-1/2" h, raised rim, oval shaded gray to sky-yellow to gray, vitrified autumn colors on falling leaves above and below landscape scene, medial cameo mark "Daum Nancy (cross)"..6,900.00

19-3/4" h, cylindrical, bulbous base, frosted ground shading to emerald green, etched and enameled storks in flight, lotus blossom lake below en griaisille, gilt highlights, gilt sgd "Daum Nancy"...5,750.00

20" h, trumpet form, bulbous foot, lavender ground, deep violet overlay, etched and wheel-carved flowering clematis blossoms and foliage, fine martele ground, sgd "Daum Nancy"..6,000.00

27" h, elongated extended neck, bulbous body, mottled pastel blue-green, multicolored yellow-red acid finished surface, etched repeating geometric and foliate dec, mkd "Daum Nancy (cross)" in cameo at side 2,100.00

Veilleuse Lamp Shade, 6" h, mottled frosted yellow, amber, and orange, side inscribed "Daum (cross) Nancy" 460.00

Wine, 3-1/2" h, entire surface of glass cut and polished with gold dec, sgd, set of 9 .... 325.00

DEPRESSION GLASS

History: Depression glass was made from 1920 to 1940. It was an inexpensive machine-made glass and was produced by several companies in various patterns and colors. The number of forms made in different patterns also varied.

Depression glass was sold through variety stores, given away as premiums, or packaged with certain products. Movie houses gave it away from 1935 until well into the 1940s.

Like pattern glass, knowing the proper name of a pattern is the key to collecting. Collectors should be prepared to do research.

References: Tom and Neila Bredehoft, *Fifty Years of Collectible Glass, 1920-1970*, Antique Trader Books, 1997; Gene Florence, *Collectible Glassware from the 40's, 50's, 60's*, 4th ed., Collector Books, 1997; ——, *Collector's Encyclopedia of Depression Glass*, 13th ed., Collector Books, 1997; ——, *Elegant Glassware of the Depression Era*, 7th ed., Collector Books, 1997; ——, *Kitchen Glassware of the Depression Era*, 7th Edition, Collector Books, (1995, 1997 value update); ——, *Pocket Guide to Depression Glass & More, 1920-1960s*, 10th ed., Collector Books, 1996; ——, *Stemware Identification Featuring Cordials with Values, 1920s-1960s*, Collector Books, 1997; ——, *Very Rare Glassware of the Depression Era*, 1st Series (1988, 1991 value update), 2nd Series (1991), 3rd Series (1993), 4th Series (1996), 5th Series (1996), Collector Books; Ralph and Terry Kovel, *Kovels' Depression Glass & American Dinnerware Price List*, 5th ed., Crown, 1995; Carl F. Luckey and Mary Burris, *Identification & Value Guide to Depression Era Glassware*, 3rd ed., Books Americana, 1994; Ellen T. Schroy, *Warman's Depression Glass*, Krause Publications, 1997; Kent G. Washburn, *Price Survey*, 4th ed., published by author, 1994; Hazel Marie Weatherman, *Colored Glassware of the Depression Era*, Book 2, published by author 1974, available in reprint; ——, *1984 Supplement & Price Trends for Colored Glassware of the Depression Era, Book 1*, published by author, 1984.

Periodicals: *Fire-King News*, P.O. Box 473, Addison, AL 35540; *Kitchen Antiques & Collectible News*, 4645 Laurel Ridge Dr., Harrisburg, PA 17110; *The Daze, Inc.*, P.O. Box 57, Otisville, MI 48463.

Collectors' Clubs: Big "D" Pression Glass Club, 10 Windling Creek Trail, Garland, TX 75043; Buckeye Dee Geer's, 2501 Campbell St., Sandusky, OH 44870; Canadian Depression Glass Club, P.O. Box 104, Mississaugua, Ontario L53 2K1 Canada; Clearwater Depression

Glass Club, 10038 62nd Terrace North, St. Petersburg, FL 33708; Crescent City Depression Glass Club, 140 Commerce St., Gretna, LA 70056; Depression Era Glass Society of Wisconsin, 1534 S. Wisconsin Ave., Racine, WI 53403; Depression Glass Club of Greater Rochester, P.O. Box 10362, Rochester, NY 14610; Depression Glass Club of North East Florida, 2604 Jolly Rd, Jacksonville, FL 33207; Fostoria Glass Collectors, Inc., P.O. Box 1625, Orange, CA 92668; Greater Tulsa Depression Era Glass Club, P.O. Box 470763, Tulsa, OK 74147-0763; Heart of America Glass Collectors, 14404 E. 36th Ter., Independence, MO, 64055; Illinois Valley Depression Glass Club, RR 1, Box 52, Rushville, IL 62681; Iowa Depression Glass Assoc., 5871 Vista Dr., Apt. 725, West Des Moines, IA 50266; Land of Sunshine Depression Glass Club, P.O. Box 560275, Orlando, FL 32856-0275; Lincoln Land Depression Glass Club, 1625 Dial Court, Springfield, IL 62704; National Depression Glass Assoc., Inc., P.O. Box 8264, Wichita, KS 67209; Northeast Florida Depression Glass Club, P.O. Box 338, Whitehouse, FL 32220; North Jersey Dee Geer's, 82 High Street, Butler, NJ 07405; Peach State Depression Glass Club, 4174 Reef Rd., Marietta, GA 30066; Phoenix and Consolidated Glass Collectors' Club, P.O. Box 182082, Arlington, TX 76096-2082; Southern Illinois Diamond H Seekers, 1203 N. Yale, O'Fallon, IL 62269; 20-30-40 Society, Inc., P.O. Box 856, LaGrange, IL 60525; Western Reserve Depression Glass Club, 8669 Courtland Drive, Strongsville, OH 44136.

Website: *DG Shopper Online,* The WWW Depression Era Glass Magazine, http://www.dgshopper.com; *Mega Show,* http://www.glassshow.com; *Facets Antiques & Collectibles Mall,* http://www.Facets.net

Videotape: *Living Glass: Popular Patterns of the Depression Era*, 2 Vols., Ro Cliff Communications, 1993.

Reproduction Alert: Reproductions of Depression Glass patterns can be a real problem. Some are easy to detect, but others are very good. Now that there are reproductions of the reproductions, the only hope for collectors is to know what they are buying and to buy from reputable dealers and/or other collectors. Most of the current Depression Glass reference books have excellent sections on reproductions. The following items with an asterisk have been reproduced, but beware that they are more reproductions being brought into the marketplace.

Note: The examples listed below are only a small sampling of the patterns and variety of objects found in this large collecting area. Please refer to one of the reference books mentioned above for more detailed listings of a particular pattern or manufacturer.

Ashtray
    Adam, Jeannette Glass Co., 4-1/2" d
        Green..25.00
        Pink..32.00
    Cloverleaf, Hazel Atlas, 5-3/4" d, green.........................20.00
    Diana, Federal Glass Co., pink 4.00
    Early American Prescut (Anchor Hocking), crystal
        4" d 3.00
        7-3/4 d 12.00
    Floragold, Jeannette Glass Co., irid............................10.00

    Forest Green, Anchor Hocking Glass Co., 4-5/8" sq,
        green 5.50
    Harp, Jeannette Glass Co., crystal 4.50
    Homespun (Fine Rib), Jeannette Glass Co., crystal or
        pink 6.00
    Manhattan (Horizontal Ribbed), Anchor Hocking Glass Co.,
        crystal 11.00
    Moroccan Amethyst, Hazel Ware, amethyst, 3-1/2" d.....5.75
    Pineapple & Floral, 4-1/2" d, amber 20.00
    Sunflower, Jeannette Glass Co., green........................14.00
    Windsor (Windsor Diamond), Jeannette Glass Co., 5-3/4" d,
        pink 35.00
Berry Bowl, individual
    Adam, Jeannette Glass Co., pink 16.50
    Anniversary, Jeannette Glass Co., 4-7/8" d, irid 4.50
    Bowknot, green 16.00
    Cherry Blossom, Jeannette Glass Co., delphite*..........15.00
    Colonial Fluted (Rope), Federal Glass Co., green........11.00
    Doric and Pansy, Jeannette Glass Co., ultramarine 20.00
    Fruits, Hazel Atlas, green..28.00
    Heritage, Federal Glass Co., blue................................55.00
    Madrid, Federal Glass Co., amber.................................6.00
    Normandie (Bouquet and Lattice), Federal Glass Co., 5" d,
        irid 5.00
    Old Café, Hocking Glass Co., ruby.................................6.00
    Patrician (Spoke), Federal Glass Co., amber 12.00
    Pyramid (No. 610), Indiana Glass Co., green 25.00
    Rose Cameo, Belmont Tumbler Co., green 12.00
    Sharon (Cabbage Rose), Federal Glass Co., pink 10.00
    Windsor (Windsor Diamond), Jeannette Glass Co., 4-3/4" d,
        crystal 4.00
Berry Bowl, master
    Aunt Polly, U.S. Glass Co., blue..................................45.00
    Cameo (Ballerina, Dancing Girl), Hocking Glass Co.,
        pink 150.00
    Colonial Fluted (Rope), Federal Glass Co., crystal.......16.00
    Doric, Jeannette Glass Co. delphite 135.00
    Floral and Diamond Band, pink 13.00
    Florentine No. 2 (Poppy No. 2), Hazel Atlas, 9" d, yellow... 30.00
    Heritage, Federal Glass Co., pink................................42.00
    Indiana Custard, (Flower and Leaf Band), Indiana Glass Co.,
        French Ivory 32.00
    Lorain, Indiana Glass Co., green 85.00
    Newport (Hairpin), Hazel Atlas, amethyst 35.00
    Raindrops (Optic Design), Federal Glass Co., green...45.00
    Strawberry, US Glass Co., green or pink 20.00
    Windsor (Windsor Diamond), Jeannette Glass Co., 8-1/2" d,
        green 17.50
Bon Bon
    Flower Garden with Butterflies (Butterflies and Roses), U.S.
        Glass Co., black 265.00
    Moonstone, Anchor Hocking Glass Co., opal, heart
        shape...14.00
    Royal Ruby, Anchor Hocking, ruby...............................18.00
Bowl
    Adam, Jeannette Glass Co.
        9" d, open, green..45.00
        10" l, oval, pink...40.00
    American Pioneer, Liberty Works, crystal, 9" d.............24.00
    Bamboo Optic, Liberty, 4-1/4" d, green 6.00
    Carolyn, Lancaster, 11" d, topaz.................................36.00
    Cube (Cubist), Jeannette Glass Co., 4-1/2" d, green 7.00
    Diamond Quilted, (Flat Diamond), Imperial Glass Co., 7" d,
        green or pink 10.00
    Early American Prescut, (Anchor Hocking), crystal
        4-1/4" d, smooth edge...2.50

5-1/4 d, ruffled edge..4.00
5-1/2" d, flat edge..3.00
6-3/4" d, 3 legs...4.50
7-3/4" d, round, cov...6.00
8-3/4" d, ruffled..9.00
Floragold, Jeannette Glass Co., 5-1/4" d, ruffled, irid...16.00
Georgian (Lovebirds), Federal Glass Co., 6-1/2" d,
    green...65.00
Iris (Iris and Herringbone) Jeannette Glass Co., 9-1/2" d,
    irid..10.00
Jody, Lancaster, 12" l, oval, topaz...........................35.00
Jubilee, Lancaster Glass Co., 8" d, pink...................265.00
Manhattan (Horizontal Ribbed), Anchor Hocking Glass Co.,
    crystal
    4" d..10.00
    4-1/2" d, handles..9.00
    7" d, 2 handles..16.00
Moonstone, Anchor Hocking Glass Co., cloverleaf, opal...13.00
Oyster and Pearls, Anchor Hocking Glass Co., 5-1/4" w,
    heart shape, ruby..15.00
Primo (Paneled Aster), U.S. Glass Co., 7-3/4" d, green....25.00
Queen Mark
    6" d, pink...20.00
    9" d, crystal..10.00
Roxana, Hazel Atlas, golden topaz...........................12.00
Sandwich, Anchor Hocking, crystal
    4-3/4" d, scalloped..17.00
    7-1/2" d, scalloped..8.00
    8-1/2" l, oval, scalloped.....................................7.00
Sharon (Cabbage Rose), Federal Glass Co., 8" d,
    amber...5.00
Sphinx, Lancaster, 12" d, green..............................135.00
Tulip, Dell Glass Co., 13-1/4" l, amber, crystal, or green....40.00
Windsor (Windsor Diamond), Jeannette Glass Co.
    7" x 11-3/4", boat shape, green...........................35.00
    8" d, 2 handles, crystal......................................9.00
    10-1/2" l, pointed edge, pink..............................32.00
Butter Dish, cov
    Adam, Jeannette Glass Co., pink*........................95.00
    Anniversary, Jeannette Glass Co., pink.................60.00
    Block Optic (Block), Hocking Glass Co., green.........50.00
    Cameo (Ballerina, Dancing Girl), Hocking Glass Co.,
        yellow...1,400.00
    Colonial, (Knife and Fork), Hocking Glass Co., green......60.00
    Colonial Block, Hazel Atlas, Hazel Atlas, green or pink....45.00
    Doric, Jeannette Glass Co. green..........................90.00
    Floral, (Poinsettia), Jeannette Glass Co., green.........90.00
    Georgian (Lovebirds), Federal Glass Co., green.........80.00
    Hex Optic (Honeycomb), Jeannette Glass Co., green.....75.00
    Holiday (Buttons and Bows), Jeannette Glass Co., pink....45.00
    Miss America, (Diamond Pattern), Hocking Glass Co.,
        crystal*..200.00
    Moderntone, Hazel Atlas, cobalt blue, metal cov.......100.00
    Royal Lace, Hazel Atlas, pink.............................150.00
    Sandwich, Anchor Hocking, low, crystal..................45.00
    Sierra Pinwheel, Jeannette Glass Co., green............75.00
    U.S. Swirl, U.S. Glass Co., green or pink................115.00
    Windsor (Windsor Diamond), Jeannette Glass Co.,
        pink..60.00
Cake Plate
    Adam, Jeannette Glass Co., green........................32.00
    Anniversary, Jeannette Glass Co., crystal, round.......7.50
    Block Optic (Block), Hocking Glass Co., crystal.........18.00
    Cameo (Ballerina, Dancing Girl), Hocking Glass Co., 10" d,
        green..22.00
    Cherry Blossom, Jeannette Glass Co., pink*............25.00

Candlesticks, Adam, pink, 3-3/4" h, pr, $100.

    Doric, Jeannette Glass Co. pink............................30.00
    Harp, Jeannette Glass Co., crystal, 9" d.................20.00
    Holiday (Buttons and Bows), Jeannette Glass Co., 10-1/2" d,
        pink..100.00
    Miss America, (Diamond Pattern), Hocking Glass Co.....25.00
    Primo (Paneled Aster), U.S. Glass Co., green or yellow...23.50
    Sunflower, Jeannette Glass Co., green or pink...........16.00
    Thistle, Macbeth-Evans, green............................150.00
Candlesticks, pr
    Adam, Jeannette Glass Co., 4" h, pink..................100.00
    Bamboo Optic, Liberty, hexagon base, pink.............25.00
    Holiday (Buttons and Bows), Jeannette Glass Co., 3" h,
        pink..110.00
    Laced Edge (Katy Blue), Imperial Glass Co., Imperial, 2-lite,
        green..180.00
    Madrid, Federal Glass Co., 2-1/4" h, pink*...............28.00
    Moonstone, Anchor Hocking Glass Co., opal.............18.00
    Old Colony (Lace Edge, Open Lace), Hocking Glass Co.,
        pink..250.00
    Patrick, Lancaster Glass Co., pink........................150.00
    Tea Room, Indiana Glass Co., green......................48.00
Candy Dish, cov
    Cloverleaf, Hazel Atlas, green.............................45.00
    Floragold, Jeannette Glass Co., irid......................15.00
    Flower Garden with Butterflies (Butterflies and Roses), US
        Glass Co., heart shape, pink.........................195.00
    Fortune, Hocking Glass Co., pink.........................25.00
    Iris (Iris and Herringbone) Jeannette Glass Co.,
        crystal*...150.00
    Moroccan Amethyst, Hazel Ware, amethyst, tall........32.00
    Ovide, Hazel Atlas, Platonite..............................12.00
    Princess, Hocking Glass Co., green*......................65.00
    Queen Mary (Prismatic Line, Vertical Ribbed), Hocking Glass
        Co., crystal...22.00
    Ribbon, Hazel Atlas, black..................................38.00
Candy Jar, cov
    Aunt Polly, U.S. Glass Co., green.........................26.00
    Cube (Cubist), Jeannette Glass Co., pink................28.00
    Diana, Federal Glass Co., amber..........................36.00
    Moonstone, Anchor Hocking Glass Co., opal.............30.00
Casserole, cov
    Adam, Jeannette Glass Co., green........................90.00
    Dewdrop, Jeannette Glass Co., crystal...................24.00
    Floral, (Poinsettia), Jeannette Glass Co., pink..........28.00
    New Century, Hazel Atlas, crystal or green..............60.00
Cereal Bowl
    Adam, Jeannette Glass Co., 5-3/4" d, green.............46.00
    Aurora, Hazel Atlas, pink...................................14.00
    Cherry Blossom, Jeannette Glass Co., green*...........35.00

Candy Jar, cov, Miss America, pink, $175.

Daisy (No. 620), Indiana Glass Co., fired-on red 25.00
Floragold, Jeannette Glass Co., irid 35.00
Hobnail, Hocking Glass Co., crystal, red trim 4.25
Horseshoe (No. 612), Indiana Glass Co., green or
    yellow 25.00
Old Café, Hocking Glass Co., crystal or pink 8.00
Ring (Banded Rings), Hocking Glass Co., decorated 5.00
Thistle, Macbeth-Evans, green 27.50

Cheese and Cracker Set
    Jubilee, Lancaster Glass Co., yellow 255.00
    Patrick, Lancaster Glass Co., pink 150.00

Chop Plate
    Columbia, Federal Glass Co., flashed 12.00
    Windsor (Windsor Diamond), Jeannette Glass Co., 13-5/8" d,
        green 18.00

Coaster
    Adam, Jeannette Glass Co., pink 32.00
    Cherry Blossom, Jeannette Glass Co., green or pink ...15.00
    Floragold, Jeannette Glass Co., irid 10.00
    Harp, Jeannette Glass Co., crystal 4.50
    Miss America, (Diamond Pattern), Hocking Glass Co.,
        crystal 20.00
    Primo (Paneled Aster), U.S. Glass Co., green or yellow 8.75

Cocktail
    American Pioneer, Liberty Works, amber 45.00
    Block Optic (Block), Hocking Glass Co., green 35.00
    Iris (Iris and Herringbone) Jeannette Glass Co. 24.00
    Patrick, Lancaster Glass Co., pink or yellow 85.00
    Ring, (Banded Rings), Hocking Glass Co., decorated or
        green 18.00

Comport
    Anniversary, Jeannette Glass Co., crystal, ruffled 6.50
    Floragold, Jeannette Glass Co., irid, 5-1/4" d, ruffled 695.00
    Floral and Diamond Band, U.S. Glass Co., green 16.50
    Manhattan (Horizontal Ribbed), Anchor Hocking Glass Co.,
        crystal, 5-3/4" h 32.00
    Miss America, (Diamond Pattern), Hocking Glass Co.,
        crystal 14.00
    Pineapple & Floral, (No. 618) Indiana Glass Co., diamond
        shape, crystal 3.00
    Windsor (Windsor Diamond), Jeannette Glass Co.,
        crystal 6.00

Console Set
    Block Optic (Block), Hocking Glass Co.,11-3/4" d bowl,
        pr 1-3/4" h candlesticks, amber 160.00
    Diamond Quilted, (Flat Diamond), Imperial Glass Co.,
        10-1/2" d bowl, pr candlesticks, green 55.00

Cookie Jar, cov
    Manhattan (Horizontal Ribbed), Anchor Hocking Glass Co.,
        crystal 35.00
    Mayfair (Open Rose), Hocking Glass Co., green* 575.00
    Princess, Hocking Glass Co., blue 875.00
    Royal Lace, Hazel Atlas, cobalt blue 500.00
    Sandwich, Anchor Hocking, crystal 40.00

Cordial
    Diamond Quilted, (Flat Diamond), Imperial Glass Co.,
        pink 15.00
    Hobnail, Hocking Glass Co., crystal 6.00
    Jubilee, Lancaster Glass Co., yellow 245.00

Creamer
    Adam, Jeannette Glass Co., green 22.00
    Bamboo Optic, Liberty, ftd, green 10.00
    Block Optic (Block), Hocking Glass Co., yellow 15.00
    Cameo (Ballerina, Dancing Girl), Hocking Glass Co., 4-1/4" h,
        pink 85.00
    Christmas Candy (No. 624), Indiana Glass Co., crystal... 12.00
    Cube (Cubist), Jeannette Glass Co., green 10.00
    Floragold, Jeannette Glass Co., irid 10.00
    Georgian (Lovebirds), Federal Glass Co., green, 3" 15.00
    Holiday (Buttons and Bows), Jeannette Glass Co., pink ... 12.50
    Newport (Hairpin), Hazel Atlas, cobalt blue 20.00
    Ovide, Hazel Atlas, black 7.00
    Raindrops (Optic Design), Federal Glass Co. 8.00
    Strawberry, US Glass Co., small, crystal irid 12.00
    Sunflower, Jeannette Glass Co., green or pink 20.00
    Tulip, Dell Glass Co., amethyst or blue 20.00
    Vernon (No. 616), Indiana Glass Co., green or yellow 25.00

Creamer and Sugar, cov
    Colonial Block, Hazel Atlas, Hazel Atlas, pink 40.00
    Florentine No. 1 (Old Florentine, Poppy No. 1), Hazel Atlas,
        ruffled, green 45.00
    Forest Green, Anchor Hocking Glass Co., green 14.00
    Iris (Iris and Herringbone) Jeannette Glass Co., crystal... 30.00
    Lake Como, Hocking Glass Co., opaque white, blue
        scene 65.00
    Madrid, Federal Glass Co., amber 15.00
    Moderntone, Hazel Atlas, cobalt blue 22.00
    Moonstone, Anchor Hocking Glass Co., opal 18.00
    Normandie (Bouquet and Lattice), Federal Glass Co.,
        irid 14.00
    Patrician (Spoke), Federal Glass Co., amber 20.00
    Pretzel (No. 622), Indiana Glass Co. 9.00
    Sandwich, Anchor Hocking, no lid 30.00
    Tea Room, Indiana Glass Co., with tray, pink 75.00
    Windsor (Windsor Diamond), Jeannette Glass Co.,
        crystal 10.00

Cream Soup
    American Sweetheart, Macbeth-Evans , monax 120.00
    Floral, (Poinsettia), Jeannette Glass Co., green or pink ... 735.00
    Madrid, Federal Glass Co., amber 15.00
    Mayfair, Federal Glass Co., amber 18.00
    Moderntone, Hazel Atlas, 5" d, ruffled, amethyst 30.00
    Patrician (Spoke), Federal Glass Co., amber 16.00
    Petalware, Macbeth-Evans, Cremax 12.50
    Windsor (Windsor Diamond), Jeannette Glass Co.,
        green 30.00

Cup
    Adam, Jeannette Glass Co.
        Green 22.00

Pink...24.00
Anniversary, Jeannette Glass Co.
    Irid..4.00
    Pink..9.00
Aurora, Hazel Atlas
    Cobalt blue..18.00
    Green..9.00
Bamboo Optic, Liberty
    Green..7.00
    Pink..10.00
Bowknot, unknown maker, green.....................15.00
Cherry Blossom, Jeannette Glass Co., crystal or pink* 20.00
Cloverleaf, Hazel Atlas, green...........................8.00
Egg Harbor, Liberty
    Green..6.00
    Pink..8.00
Harp, Jeannette Glass Co., crystal 26.00
Mayfair (Open Rose), Hocking Glass Co., pink 18.00
Miss America, (Diamond Pattern), Hocking Glass Co.,
    crystal..10.00
Moroccan Amethyst, Hazel Ware, amethyst 5.00
Peanut Butter, unknown maker, crystal...............4.00
Pretzel (No. 622), Indiana Glass Co., crystal 6.00
Pineapple & Floral, (No. 618) Indiana Glass Co., amber or
    red..10.00
Queen Mary, pink..7.00
Round Robin, green..7.00
Sunflower, Jeannette Glass Co., pink 16.00
Victory, Diamond Glass-Ware Co., pink.............8.00
Cup and Saucer
    Cameo (Ballerina, Dancing Girl), Hocking Glass Co.,
      crystal..14.00
    Colonial Fluted (Rope), Federal Glass Co., crystal.........7.00
    Diamond Quilted, (Flat Diamond), Imperial Glass Co.,
      blue...24.00
    Dogwood, Macbeth-Evans, green 40.00
    Doric & Pansy, Jeannette Glass Co., ultramarine.........21.00
    Forest Green, Anchor Hocking Glass Co., green 8.00
    Fortune, Hocking Glass Co., crystal 12.50
    Lake Como, Hocking Glass Co., opaque white, blue
      scene..42.00
    Lorain, Indiana Glass Co., crystal or green 15.00
    Madrid, Federal Glass Co., amber................9.00
    Parrot (Sylvan), Federal Glass Co., green ...55.00
    Patrician (Spoke), Federal Glass Co., amber 20.00
    Royal Lace, Hazel Atlas, green....................25.00
    Royal Ruby, Anchor Hocking, ruby, round 12.00
Demitasse Cup and Saucer
    Diana, Federal Glass Co., crystal 12.00
    Iris (Iris and Herringbone) Jeannette Glass Co., irid.......350.00
Dessert Bowl
    Fortune, Hocking Glass Co., crystal or pink 4.50
    Moonstone, Anchor Hocking Glass Co., crystal 8.00
    Royal Ruby, Anchor Hocking, ruby, sq.........5.25
    Star, Federal Glass Co., amber....................4.00
Domino Tray
    Cameo (Ballerina, Dancing Girl), Hocking Glass Co., 7" l,
      pink...250.00
    Round Robin, unknown maker, green...........40.00
Dresser Tray, Floral, (Poinsettia), Jeannette Glass Co.,
    green..700.00
Egg Cup
    Egg Harbor, Liberty
      Green..12.00
      Pink..14.00
    Old English (Threading), Indiana Glass Co., crystal.....10.00

Ovide, Hazel Atlas, green 4.50
Flower Frog, Floral, (Poinsettia), Jeannette Glass Co.,
    green 850.00
Fruit Bowl
    Bubble (Bullseye Provincial), Hocking Glass Co., crystal,
      4-1/2" d..5.00
    Cherry Blossom, Jeannette Glass Co., crystal............32.00
    Dogwood, Macbeth-Evans, green 250.00
    Floragold, Jeannette Glass Co., irid............8.50
    Heritage, Federal Glass Co., crystal 15.00
    Iris (Iris and Herringbone) Jeannette Glass Co., 11-1/2" d,
      ruffled..15.00
    Oyster and Pearls, Anchor Hocking Glass Co., pink 10.00
    Raindrops (Optic Design), Federal Glass Co., green...11.00
    Royal Ruby, Anchor Hocking, ruby 6.00
    Thistle, Macbeth-Evans, pink 200.00
Goblet
    Block Optic (Block), Hocking Glass Co., green............24.00
    Bubble (Bullseye Provincial), Hocking Glass Co., forest
      green..15.00
    Colonial Block, Hazel Atlas, crystal..............9.00
    Diamond Point, ruby stained, 7-1/2" h.........35.00
    Hobnail, Hocking Glass Co., crystal 7.50
    Iris (Iris and Herringbone) Jeannette Glass Co., 5-1/2" h, irid,
      clear foot..25.00
    Jubilee, Lancaster Glass Co., 7-1/2" h, yellow..............75.00
    Moroccan Amethyst, Hazel Ware, amethyst 10.00
    Old English (Threading), Indiana Glass Co., amber, green,
      or pink...30.00
    Ring, (Banded Rings), Hocking Glass Co., crystal.........7.00
Hot Plate
    Georgian (Lovebirds), Federal Glass Co., green..........48.00
    Parrot (Sylvan), Federal Glass Co., 5" d, amber 875.00
Iced Tea Tumbler, ftd, 12 oz
    Adam, Jeannette Glass Co., green..............60.00
    Circle, Hocking Glass Co., green or pink 17.50
    Dewdrop, Jeannette Glass Co., crystal 17.50
    Diamond Quilted, (Flat Diamond), Imperial Glass Co., green
      or pink...10.00
    Florentine No. 1 (Old Florentine, Poppy No. 1), Hazel Atlas,
      yellow..24.00
    Hobnail, Hocking Glass Co., crystal 8.50
    Homespun (Fine Rib), Jeannette Glass Co., crystal or
      pink...32.00
    Miss America, (Diamond Pattern), Hocking Glass Co.,
      pink...85.00
    Princess, Hocking Glass Co., pink...............50.00
    Roulette (Many Windows), Hocking Glass Co., green 25.00
    Ships (Sailboat, Sportsman Series), Hazel Atlas, cobalt
      blue...18.00
Juice Tumbler, ftd
    Fortune, Hocking Glass Co., crystal 8.00
    Holiday (Buttons and Bows), Jeannette Glass Co., pink ...55.00
    Old Café, Hocking Glass Co., crystal or pink 10.00
    Peanut Butter, unknown maker, crystal.........9.00
    Royal Ruby, Anchor Hocking, ruby 5.00
    S-pattern, Macbeth Evans, pink...................14.00
    Thumbprint, Federal Glass Co., green.........6.00
Lemonade Tumbler, Floral, (Poinsettia), Jeannette Glass Co.,
    green 60.00
Mayonnaise Set, Underplate, Orig Ladle
    Christmas Candy (No. 624), Indiana Glass Co., crystal... 24.00
    Diamond Quilted, (Flat Diamond), Imperial Glass Co.,
      blue...65.00
    Flower Garden with Butterflies (Butterflies and Roses), U.S.
      Glass Co., amber 70.00

Jubilee, Lancaster Glass Co., pink 315.00
Landrum, Lancaster, topaz..150.00
Patrick, Lancaster Glass Co., yellow.........................80.00
Mint Tray, Old Café, Hocking Glass Co., ruby...................15.00
Mug
Block Optic (Block), Hocking Glass Co., green............35.00
Cherry Blossom, Jeannette Glass Co., pink 250.00
Moderntone, Hazel Atlas, white 8.50
Nappy
Coronation (Banded Fine Rib, Saxon), Hocking Glass Co.,
    crystal or ruby...15.00
Floragold, Jeannette Glass Co., irid............................8.00
Floral and Diamond Band, (Poinsettia), Jeannette Glass Co.,
    pink..11.00
Pickle
Aunt Polly, U.S. Glass Co., green or irid 17.50
Cherryberry, U.S. Glass Co., crystal 10.00
Pyramid (No. 610), Indiana Glass Co., green or pink 35.00
Pitcher
Adam, Jeannette Glass Co., 32 oz, pink....................125.00
Aunt Polly, U.S. Glass Co., crystal 175.00
Bamboo Optic, Liberty, 8-1/2" h, green 50.00
Coronation (Banded Fine Rib, Saxon), Hocking Glass Co.,
    pink..500.00
Crystal Leaf, Macbeth Evans, pink 45.00
Floragold, Jeannette Glass Co., irid............................40.00
Florentine No. 1 (Old Florentine, Poppy No. 1), Hazel Atlas,
    ice lip, pink..115.00
Forest Green, Anchor Hocking Glass Co., 22 oz, green....22.50
Fruits, Hazel Atlas, green...85.00
Hex Optic (Honeycomb), Jeannette Glass Co., 32 oz, 5" h,
    green or pink 24.00
Horseshoe (No. 612), Indiana Glass Co., 64 oz, green... 250.00
Jubilee, Lancaster Glass Co., pink 950.00
Mac Hob, Macbeth Evans, 72 oz, crystal 40.00
Miss America, (Diamond Pattern), Hocking Glass Co., crystal,
    8" h*...45.00
New Century, Hazel Atlas, ice lip, 80 oz, cobalt blue ...45.00
Ring, (Banded Rings), Hocking Glass Co., 60 oz, decorated
    or green..25.00
Sandwich, Anchor Hocking, crystal, ice lip 85.00
Star, Federal Glass Co., crystal, 60 oz........................14.00
U.S. Swirl, U.S. Glass Co. green 55.00
Windsor (Windsor Diamond), Jeannette Glass Co., 4-1/2" h,
    pink..115.00
Plate
Adam, Jeannette Glass Co.
    6" d, sherbet, green..9.50
    7-3/4" d, salad, green 17.00
    9" d, dinner, pink 32.00
    9" d, grill, green or pink 20.00
American Pioneer, Liberty Works, 6" d, crystal 12.50
American Sweetheart, Macbeth-Evans , 9" d, monax...10.00
Anniversary, Jeannette Glass Co., 9" d...........................5.00
Aunt Polly, U.S. Glass Co.
    6" d, blue 12.00
    8" d, crystal..20.00
Aurora, Hazel Atlas, 6-1/2" d, cobalt blue 12.00
Bamboo Optic, Liberty, octagonal
    5-3/4" d, bread and butter, green.................................4.00
    7" d, salad, green 7.50
    8" d, luncheon, pink..10.00
    10" d, dinner, green...24.00
Block Optic
    6" d, crystal..1.50
    8" d, green..5.50

Plate, Sharon, amber, dinner, 9" d, $12.

9" d, dinner, green...27.50
9" d, grill, yellow..42.00
Bowknot, 7" d, green 12.50
Bubble (Bullseye Provincial), Hocking Glass Co.
    6-3/4" d, crystal..3.50
    9-3/8" d, dinner, forest green....................................20.00
    9-3/8" d, dinner, ruby...22.00
    9-3/8" d, grill, sapphire blue 22.00
Cameo (Ballerina, Dancing Girl), Hocking Glass Co., 8" d
    Crystal..14.00
    Green...12.00
    Pink..36.00
Cherry Blossom, Jeannette Glass Co.
    6" d, green*...6.00
    7" d, pink..17.00
    9" d, crystal* 18.00
    9" d, grill, green or pink..22.00
Christmas Candy (No. 624), Indiana Glass Co.
    6" d, teal..16.00
    9-5/8" d, crystal..12.00
Circle, Hocking Glass Co., 8-1/4" d, green or pink.......11.00
Colonial Fluted (Rope), Federal Glass Co., 8" d, green ... 10.00
Columbia, Federal Glass Co., 9-1/2" d, pink................32.00
Daisy (No. 620), Indiana Glass Co.
    6" d, amber...3.00
    8-3/8" d, crystal...5.00
    9-3/8" d, dark green...7.50
Diana, Federal Glass Co.
    6" d, amber...3.00
    9-1/2" d, crystal...6.00
Dogwood, Macbeth-Evans
    6" d, pink..9.50
    8" d, green..9.00
    10-1/2" d, grill, green or pink 20.00
Doric
    6" d, green or pink 6.50
    7" d, green...20.00
    9" d, pink...18.00
    9" d, grill, pink...25.00

Doric & Pansy, Jeannette Glass Co., ultramarine, dinner ...35.00
Early American Prescut, (Anchor Hocking), crystal
    11" d 10.00
    13-1/2" d 12.00
Egg Harbor, Liberty, luncheon
    Green 9.00
    Pink...9.00
Floragold, Jeannette Glass Co., 8-1/2" d, dinner, irid 35.00
Floral, (Poinsettia), Jeannette Glass Co.
    6" d, sherbet, green.......................................7.50
    8" d, salad, pink...15.00
    9" d, dinner, delphite 145.00
    9" d, grill, green 185.00
Floral and Diamond Band, (Poinsettia), Jeannette Glass Co.,
    8" d, luncheon, green or pink 40.00
Florentine No. 1 (Old Florentine, Poppy No. 1), Hazel Atlas
    6" d, sherbet, crystal......................................6.50
    8-1/2" d, salad, green 9.00
    10" d, dinner, green.......................................16.00
    10" d, grill, yellow..22.00
Florentine No. 2 (Poppy No. 2), Hazel Atlas, 10" d, yellow,
    dinner 15.00
Fortune, Hocking Glass Co., 8" d, luncheon, crystal or
    pink...17.50
Georgian (Lovebirds), Federal Glass Co., green
    6" d, sherbet..6.50
    8" d, luncheon..10.00
    9-1/4" d, dinner 30.00
Hobnail, Hocking Glass Co., 8-1/2" d, luncheon, crystal 5.50
Holiday (Buttons and Bows), Jeannette Glass Co., pink
    6" d, sherbet..6.00
    9" d, dinner 17.50
Homespun (Fine Rib), Jeannette Glass Co., 9-/2" d, dinner,
    crystal or pink 17.00
Horseshoe (No. 612), Indiana Glass Co.
    6" d, sherbet, green or yellow.......................9.00
    8-3/8" d, salad, green or yellow...................10.00
    9-3/8" d, luncheon, green.............................13.00
    10-3/8" d, grill, green or yellow....................85.00
Iris (Iris and Herringbone) Jeannette Glass Co.
    8" d, luncheon, crystal 125.00
    9" d, dinner, irid 45.00
Jubilee, Lancaster Glass Co.
    7" d, salad, pink...25.00
    9-3/4" d, luncheon 16.50
Laced Edge (Katy Blue), Imperial Glass Co., 10" d,
    blue...90.00
Madrid, Federal Glass Co.
    6" d, amber..4.00
    8-7/8" d, amber..8.00
    Grill, amber..9.00
Manhattan (Horizontal Ribbed), Anchor Hocking Glass Co.,
    7" d, crystal..6.00
Mayfair (Open Rose), Hocking Glass Co., 8-1/2" d, pink ...25.00
Miss America, (Diamond Pattern), Hocking Glass Co., dinner,
    crystal 15.00
Moderntone, Hazel Atlas, 7-3/4" d, cobalt blue 12.50
Moroccan Amethyst, Hazel Ware, amethyst
    5-3/4" d, sherbet 4.50
    7-1/4" d, salad 4.75
    9-3/4" d, dinner 7.00
Newport (Hairpin), Hazel Atlas
    6" d, sherbet, amethyst...................................7.50
    8-1/2" d, luncheon, cobalt blue 16.50
    8-1/2" d, dinner, fired on color 15.00
Normandie (Bouquet and Lattice), Federal Glass Co.

    6" d, irid 3.00
    Grill, irid 9.00
Old Café, Hocking Glass Co., crystal or pink
    6" d, sherbet..4.00
    10" d, dinner 10.00
Old Colony (Lace Edge, Open Lace), Hocking Glass Co.,
    crystal
    Dinner..33.00
    Luncheon 23.00
    Salad..25.00
Parrot (Sylvan), Federal Glass Co.
    5-3/4" d, sherbet, amber...............................24.00
    7-1/2" d, green 40.00
    9" d, dinner, green 38.00
    10-1/2" d, grill, amber...................................32.00
Patrician (Spoke), Federal Glass Co.
    7-1/2" d, amber..15.00
    9" d, amber...12.00
    11" d, amber..6.00
Patrick, Lancaster Glass Co.
    7" d, sherbet, pink...20.00
    7-1/2" d. salad, yellow 20.00
    8" d, luncheon, pink......................................45.00
Peanut Butter, unknown maker, crystal, 8" d, luncheon....5.00
Petalware, Macbeth-Evans
    6" d, sherbet, cremax, gold trim 50.00
    8" d, salad, fired-on color 8.00
    9" d, dinner, monax 10.00
Pineapple & Floral, (No. 618) Indiana Glass Co.
    6" d, sherbet, amber.......................................6.00
    8-3/8" d, salad, amber or crystal 8.00
Pretzel (No. 622), Indiana Glass Co., 9-3/4" d, dinner,
    crystal 10.00
Primo (Paneled Aster), U.S. Glass Co., 10" d, dinner,
    green 22.50
Princess, Hocking Glass Co.
    5-1/2" d, sherbet, apricot..............................10.00
    8" d, salad, green...15.00
    9-1/2" d, dinner, pink....................................35.00
    9-1/2" d, grill, green or pink.........................15.00
Queen Mary (Prismatic Line, Vertical Ribbed), Hocking
    Glass Co., 6" d, crystal...................................4.00
Romansque, 8" d, octagonal
    Gold...8.00
    Green...9.00
Rose Cameo, Belmont Tumbler Co., 7" d, salad, green 16.00
Rosemary (Dutch Rose), Federal Glass Co.
    6-3/4" d, salad, green....................................11.00
    9-1/2" d, dinner, green 15.00
    9-1/2" d, grill, amber......................................8.50
Roulette (Many Windows), Hocking Glass Co., 8-1/2" d, lun-
    cheon, crystal 7.00
Round Robin
    6" d, sherbet, irid or green..............................7.00
    8" d, luncheon, green 12.50
Roxana, Hazel Atlas, 6" d, sherbet, crystal 4.00
Royal Lace, Hazel Atlas
    6" d, sherbet, green.......................................15.00
    8-1/2" d, luncheon, cobalt 30.00
    9-7/8" d, dinner, pink....................................20.00
    9-7/8" d, grill, cobalt blue 35.00
Royal Ruby, Anchor Hocking, ruby
    6-1/4" d, sherbet..4.00
    7" d, salad...3.00
    7-3/4" w, salad, sq 2.00
    8-3/8" w, luncheon, sq 11.00

9-1/8" d, dinner 14.00
Sandwich, Anchor Hocking, 9" d, crystal....................20.00
Ships (Sailboat, Sportsman Series), Hazel Atlas, 9" d, dinner,
    cobalt blue..32.00
Sierra Pinwheel, Jeannette Glass Co., 9" d, dinner,
    green 18.00
Starlight, Hazel Atlas, 9-1/2" d, dinner, crystal...............7.00
Tea Room, Indiana Glass Co.
    6-1/2" d, sherbet, pink............................32.00
    8-1/4" d, luncheon, green..........................37.50
Thistle, Macbeth-Evans
    8" d, luncheon, green 22.00
    10-1/2" d, grill, pink..............................28.00
Vernon (No. 616), Indiana Glass Co., 8" d, luncheon, green
    or yellow 10.00
Waterford (Waffle), Hocking Glass Co., dinner, crystal 10.00
Windsor (Windsor Diamond), Jeannette Glass Co.
    6" d, sherbet, crystal.............................3.75
    9" d, dinner, green or pink........................25.00

Platter
Cherry Blossom, Jeannette Glass Co., green..............48.00
Daisy (No. 620), Indiana Glass Co., crystal or dark
    green...11.00
Dogwood, Macbeth-Evans, Macbeth Evans, 12" l, oval,
    pink..650.00
Georgian (Lovebirds), Federal Glass Co., green..........70.00
Indiana Custard, (Flower and Leaf Band), Indiana Glass Co.,
    French Ivory.......................................30.00
Laced Edge (Katy Blue), Imperial Glass Co., 13" l, blue.. 165.00
Madrid, Federal Glass Co., amber...............................14.00
Petalware, Macbeth-Evans, Monax......................20.00
Royal Lace, Hazel Atlas, pink 40.00
Windsor (Windsor Diamond), Jeannette Glass Co., 11-1/2" l,
    oval, green..25.00

Puff Box, cov, Moonstone, Anchor Hocking Glass Co.,
    opal 25.00

Punch Bowl
Forest Green, Anchor Hocking Glass Co., green 25.00
Moroccan Amethyst, Hazel Ware, amethyst.................85.00

Punch Bowl Set
Dewdrop, Jeannette Glass Co., bowl, 12 cups, crystal.... 65.00
Royal Ruby, Anchor Hocking, bowl, 12 cups, ruby 110.00

Relish
Doric, Jeannette Glass Co. green.............................32.00
Early American Prescut, (Anchor Hocking), crystal, 4-part,
    11 d 10.00
Lorain, Indiana Glass Co., 4-part, 8" d, crystal or green... 17.50
Miss America, (Diamond Pattern), Hocking Glass Co., 4-part,
    crystal 11.00
Pretzel (No. 622), Indiana Glass Co., 3-part, crystal 9.00
Princess, Hocking Glass Co., 4-part, apricot.............100.00
Tea Room, Indiana Glass Co., divided, green..............30.00

Salad Bowl
Cherryberry, US Glass Co., green 22.00
Cloverleaf, Hazel Atlas, yellow 48.00
Cube (Cubist), Jeannette Glass Co. 15.00
Early American Prescut, (Anchor Hocking), crystal,
    10-1/2" d 10.00
Forest Green, Anchor Hocking Glass Co., green 6.50
Fortune, Hocking Glass Co., crystal 15.00
Hobnail, Hocking Glass Co., crystal 5.00
Horseshoe (No. 612), Indiana Glass Co., green or
    yellow 24.00
Landrum, Lancaster, pink 110.00
Pineapple & Floral, (No. 618) Indiana Glass Co.,
    amber*...10.00

Tea Room, Indiana Glass Co., pink 135.00
Twisted Optic, Imperial, blue...............................15.00

Salt and Pepper Shakers, pr
Adam, Jeannette Glass Co., green.............................100.00
American Sweetheart, Macbeth-Evans , monax.........325.00
Cameo (Ballerina, Dancing Girl), Hocking Glass Co.,
    green*...70.00
Cube (Cubist), Jeannette Glass Co., green or pink......36.00
Diana, Federal Glass Co., amber...............................100.00
Floral, (Poinsettia), Jeannette Glass Co., green* 45.00
Florentine No. 2 (Poppy No. 2), Hazel Atlas
    Green..40.00
    Yellow...45.00
Hex Optic (Honeycomb), Jeannette Glass Co., green or
    pink..30.00
Manhattan (Horizontal Ribbed), Anchor Hocking Glass Co.,
    crystal 50.00
Moderntone, Hazel Atlas, white 18.00
New Century, Hazel Atlas, crystal.............................25.00
Ovide, Hazel Atlas, black or green 28.00
Patrician (Spoke), Federal Glass Co., amber 50.00
Princess, Hocking Glass Co., green 50.00
Ribbon, Hazel Atlas, green 25.00
Waterford (Waffle), Hocking Glass Co., crystal, tall........7.00

Sandwich Server, center handle
Bamboo Optic, Liberty, octagonal
    Green..20.00
    Pink...25.00
Daisy (No. 620), Indiana Glass Co., amber 14.50
Flower Garden with Butterflies (Butterflies and Roses), U.S.
    Glass Co., green...................................75.00
Landrum, Lancaster, topaz................................55.00
Old English (Threading), Indiana Glass Co., amber.....60.00
Ring, (Banded Rings), Hocking Glass Co., decorated or
    green 15.00
Spiral, Hocking Glass Co., green..........................30.00
Twisted Optic, Imperial, canary 35.00

Saucer
Adam, Jeannette Glass Co., green or pink...................7.00
Aurora, Hazel Atlas
    Cobalt blue 6.00
    Green..2.00
Bamboo Optic, Liberty
    Green..3.00
    Pink...3.00
Block Optic (Block), Hocking Glass Co., crystal 2.00
Bubble (Bullseye Provincial), Hocking Glass Co., crystal.... 1.50
Cloverleaf, Hazel Atlas, green or pink.........................4.00
Harp, Jeannette Glass Co., crystal 10.00
Madrid, Federal Glass Co., amber...............................4.00
Miss America, (Diamond Pattern), Hocking Glass Co.,
    crystal 4.00
Peanut Butter, unknown maker, crystal........................3.00
Round Robin, irid or green
Twitch, No. 92, Bartlett-Collins, green.......................3.00

Sherbet
Adam, Jeannette Glass Co., green...........................40.00
April, Macbeth Evans, 4" h, ftd, pink.........................15.00
Bowknot, unknown maker, green...............................24.00
Cherry Blossom, Jeannette Glass Co., pink 17.00
Cloverleaf, Hazel Atlas, green.................................12.00
Coronation (Banded Fine Rib, Saxon), Hocking Glass Co.,
    green 70.00
Doric, Jeannette Glass Co. delphite 10.00
Florentine No. 1 (Old Florentine, Poppy No. 1), Hazel Atlas,
    yellow...16.00

Sherbet, Patrician, green, $14.

Florentine No. 2 (Poppy No. 2), Hazel Atlas, yellow 8.00
Forest Green, Anchor Hocking Glass Co., Boopie,
    green 7.00
Fruits, Hazel Atlas, pink..7.50
Hex Optic (Honeycomb), Jeannette Glass Co., green or
    pink...5.00
Iris (Iris and Herringbone) Jeannette Glass Co., 2-1/2" h,
    irid..15.50
Lorain, Indiana Glass Co., yellow* 35.00
Madrid, Federal Glass Co., amber.................................7.00
Moderntone, Hazel Atlas, cobalt blue.........................13.00
Moonstone, Anchor Hocking Glass Co., opal.................7.00
Normandie (Bouquet and Lattice), Federal Glass Co.,
    irid...8.00
Old Café, Hocking Glass Co., ruby.............................12.00
Old English (Threading), Indiana Glass Co., green......20.00
Parrot (Sylvan), Federal Glass Co., cone shape, green ... 24.00
Peanut Butter, unknown maker, crystal..........................4.00
Raindrops (Optic Design), Federal Glass Co., crystal......4.50
Rose Cameo, Belmont Tumbler Co., green 16.00
Sandwich, Anchor Hocking, crystal 8.00
Sunflower, Jeannette Glass Co., green........................13.50
Thumbprint, Federal Glass Co., green...........................7.00
Windsor (Windsor Diamond), Jeannette Glass Co., pink...13.00
Snack Set, plate with indent, matching cup
    Columbia, Federal Glass Co., crystal 35.00
    Dewdrop, Jeannette Glass Co., crystal 9.00
    Harp, Jeannette Glass Co., crystal 47.00
    Moroccan Amethyst, Hazel Ware, amethyst.................15.00
    Sandwich, Anchor Hocking, 9" d, crystal.......................7.00
Soup Bowl
    Holiday (Buttons and Bows), Jeannette Glass Co., 7-3/4" d,
        pink...50.00
    Indiana Custard, (Flower and Leaf Band), Indiana Glass Co.,
        French Ivory...32.00
    Laced Edge (Katy Blue), Imperial Glass Co., blue.......18.00
    Royal Ruby, Anchor Hocking, ruby.............................14.00
Sugar, cov
    Bamboo Optic, Liberty, ftd, green 10.00
    Cameo (Ballerina, Dancing Girl), Hocking Glass Co., 3-1/4"
        h, pink...100.00

Cube (Cubist), Jeannette Glass Co., 3" , green or pink ... 25.00
Diana, Federal Glass Co., amber or crystal.................10.00
Egg Harbor, Liberty
    Green..3.00
    Pink...4.00
Floragold, Jeannette Glass Co., irid............................15.00
Georgian (Lovebirds), Federal Glass Co., 3" d, green.....15.00
Heritage, Federal Glass Co., crystal 22.00
Holiday (Buttons and Bows), Jeannette Glass Co., pink...25.00
Madrid, Federal Glass Co., amber.................................7.00
Ring, (Banded Rings), Hocking Glass Co., decorated....10.00
Sierra Pinwheel, Jeannette Glass Co., pink 20.00
Tulip, Dell Glass Co., blue..20.00
Vernon (No. 616), Indiana Glass Co., crystal...............12.00
Syrup Pitcher, Cameo (Ballerina, Dancing Girl), Hocking Glass
    Co., green... 225.00
Tid-Bit Server
    Anniversary, Jeannette Glass Co., crystal 14.00
    Bubble (Bullseye Provincial), Hocking Glass Co., ruby ... 35.00
    Christmas Candy (No. 624), Indiana Glass Co., crystal....12.00
    Dogwood, Macbeth-Evans, pink.................................90.00
    Laced Edge (Katy Blue), Imperial Glass Co., 2 tiers,
        blue...110.00
Tray
    Cube (Cubist), Jeannette Glass Co., pink 5.00
    Floral, (Poinsettia), Jeannette Glass Co., 6" sq, green ... 195.00
    Harp, Jeannette Glass Co., rect, crystal 35.00
    Manhattan (Horizontal Ribbed), Anchor Hocking Glass Co.,
        14" d, crystal inserts 50.00
    Patrick, Lancaster Glass Co., 11" d, pink...................145.00
    Windsor (Windsor Diamond), Jeannette Glass Co., 4" sq,
        green...12.00
Tumbler
    Bamboo Optic, Liberty, 5-1/2" h, 8 oz, ftd, pink...........15.00
    Block Optic (Block), Hocking Glass Co.,3-1/4" h, green....27.50
    Bubble (Bullseye Provincial), Hocking Glass Co., crystal....5.00
    Cherryberry, US Glass Co., 3-5/8" h, irid 20.00
    Columbia, Federal Glass Co., 4 oz, crystal.................30.00
    Crystal Leaf, Macbeth Evans
        3-1/2" h, green...5.00
        4-1/2" h, 9 oz, pink...10.00
        4-3/4" h, 12 oz, pink...12.00
    Dogwood, Macbeth-Evans, 4-3/4" h, pink...................45.00
    Doric, Jeannette Glass Co. 5-1/2" h, pink 60.00
    Forest Green, Anchor Hocking Glass Co., 9 oz, green 7.00

Sugar, open, Cameo, yellow, 3-1/4" d, $12.00

Hex Optic (Honeycomb), Jeannette Glass Co., 7 oz, 4-3/4" h, green or pink 8.00
Horseshoe (No. 612), Indiana Glass Co., 9 oz, ftd, green 22.00
Madrid, Federal Glass Co., 5-1/2" h, amber 18.00
Mayfair (Open Rose), Hocking Glass Co., 6-1/2" h, ftd, pink 40.00
Moderntone, Hazel Atlas, cone, white 4.00
Patrician (Spoke), Federal Glass Co.
    4" h, amber 25.00
    5-1/2" h, amber 40.00
Peanut Butter, unknown maker, crystal, milk glass.........7.00
Princess, Hocking Glass Co., 9 oz, green 28.00
Pyramid (No. 610), Indiana Glass Co., 8 oz, ftd, crystal or pink 50.00
Rose Cameo, Belmont Tumbler Co., green 22.50
Ships (Sailboat, Sportsman Series), Hazel Atlas, 9 oz, cobalt blue 14.00
Vernon (No. 616), Indiana Glass Co., yellow 35.00
Vase
Moonstone, Anchor Hocking Glass Co., 6-1/2" h, ruffled, crystal 8.00
Moroccan Amethyst, Hazel Ware, 8-1/2" h, amethyst.....40.00
Old Café, Hocking Glass Co., 7-1/4" h, ruby 24.00
Old English (Threading), Indiana Glass Co., 12" h, amber, green, or pink 60.00
Pineapple & Floral, (Poinsettia), Jeannette Glass Co., cone, red 45.00
Tea Room, Indiana Glass Co., 11" h, green................200.00
Vegetable, open
Cameo (Ballerina, Dancing Girl), Hocking Glass Co., green 30.00
Christmas Candy (No. 624), Indiana Glass Co., teal 235.00
Colonial, (Knife and Fork), Hocking Glass Co., green 25.00
Daisy (No. 620), Indiana Glass Co., dark green 10.00
Doric, Jeannette Glass Co. pink 30.00
Florentine No. 2 (Poppy No. 2), Hazel Atlas, yellow, cov ...55.00
Horseshoe (No. 612), Indiana Glass Co., 8-1/2" d, green or yellow..30.00
Lake Como, Hocking Glass Co., opaque white, blue scene, 9-3/4" l...60.00
Madrid, Federal Glass Co., 10" l, oval, amber*............18.00
Normandie (Bouquet and Lattice), Federal Glass Co., irid..18.00
Parrot (Sylvan), Federal Glass Co., amber 65.00
Pineapple & Floral (No. 618), Indiana Glass Co., amber or crystal 30.00
Rosemary (Dutch Rose), Federal Glass Co., green......37.00
Sharon (Cabbage Rose), Federal Glass Co., amber, oval 20.00
Star, Federal Glass Co., amber....................................10.00
Tea Room, Indiana Glass Co., green............................75.00
Wall Pocket, Anniversary, Jeannette Glass Co., pink 30.00
Whiskey
Diamond Quilted, (Flat Diamond), Imperial Glass Co., pink..12.00
Hex Optic (Honeycomb), Jeannette Glass Co., green or pink..8.50
Hobnail, Hocking Glass Co., crystal 5.00
Miss America, (Diamond Pattern), Hocking Glass Co., crystal..22.00
Raindrops (Optic Design), Federal Glass Co., green.....9.00
Roulette (Many Windows), Hocking Glass Co., green or pink..15.00
Ships (Sailboat, Sportsman Series), Hazel Atlas, cobalt blue 30.00

Wine, Colonial (Knife & Fork), green, $28.

Thumbprint, Federal Glass Co., green..........................6.50
Tulip, Dell Glass Co., amethyst 20.00
Wine
Anniversary, Jeannette Glass Co., crystal 8.00
Cameo (Ballerina, Dancing Girl), Hocking Glass Co., green 65.00
Circle, Hocking Glass Co., green or pink 15.00
Hobnail, Hocking Glass Co., crystal 6.50
Iris (Iris and Herringbone) Jeannette Glass Co., 4" h, irid..25.00
Mayfair (Open Rose), Hocking Glass Co., pink 75.00
Moroccan Amethyst, Hazel Ware, amethyst.................10.00

DUNCAN AND MILLER

History: George Duncan, Harry B. and James B., his sons, and Augustus Heisey, his son-in-law, formed George Duncan & Sons in Pittsburgh, Pennsylvania, in 1865. The factory was located just two blocks from the Monongahela River, providing easy and inexpensive access by barge for materials needed to produce glass. The men, from Pittsburgh's south side, were descendants of generations of skilled glassmakers.

The plant burned to the ground in 1892. James E. Duncan Sr. selected a site for a new factory in Washington, Pa., where operations began on Feb. 9, 1893. The plant prospered, producing fine glassware and table services for many years.

John E. Miller, one of the stockholders, was responsible for designing many fine patterns, the most famous being Three Face. The firm incorporated and used the name The Duncan and Miller Glass Company until the plant closed in 1955. The company's slogan was "The Loveliest Glassware in America." The U.S. Glass Co. purchased the molds, equipment, and machinery in 1956.

References: Tom and Neila Bredehoft, *Fifty Years of Collectible Glass, 1920-1970*, Antique Trader Books, 1997; Gene Florence, *Elegant Glassware of the Depression Era*, 6th ed., Collector Books, 1995; Gail Krause, *The En-*

cyclopedia Of Duncan Glass, published by author, 1984; —, *A Pictorial History of Duncan & Miller Glass,* published by author, 1976; —, *The Years of Duncan,* published by author, 1980; Naomi L. Over, *Ruby Glass of the 20th Century*, Antique Publications, 1990, 1993-94 value update.

Collectors' Club: National Duncan Glass Society, P.O. Box 965, Washington, PA 15301.

Museum: Duncan Miller Glass Museum, Washington, PA.

Miscellaneous Patterns and Etchings

Animal
   Donkey and pheasant 425.00
   Goose, fat 275.00
   Heron 95.00
   Swan
     5-1/2", crystal, #122 Sylvan 38.00
     6-1/2", opal pink 95.00
     7", medium green, pall mall 55.00
     7-1/2", crystal bowl 12.00
     7-1/2", red bowl 40.00
     10", ruby, partial sticker 285.00
     10-1/2", crystal bowl 24.00
     10-1/2", dark green bowl 55.00
     10-1/2", red bowl 75.00
Bowl
   Chrysanthemum, blue, 13-1/2" d 145.00
   Murano, 10" d, crimped
     Milk Glass 55.00
     Twilight 145.00
Candlesticks, pr
   American Way, crystal 15.00
   Sculptured fish, one with small crack 500.00
Candy Dish, Murano, 7" d, crimped, crystal 38.00
Celery Vase, Homestead, 5" h, milk glass 28.00
Console Bowl, #16, winged shape, cobalt blue 250.00
Console Set, American Way, star plate and pr candlesticks, citron 35.00
Cornucopia Vase
   #121, Swirl, blue opalescent, shape #2, upswept tail 75.00
   #131, 14" h, shape #3, deep ruby 125.00
Creamer, Zipper Slash, amber stain, etched dec 45.00
Cruet, Starred Loop, orig stopper, crystal 36.00
Goblet
   Croecus, crystal 35.00
   Eternally Yours, crystal 15.00
   Festival of Flowers, crystal 28.50
   Plaza, cobalt blue 37.50
Iced Tea Tumbler, ftd, Croecus, crystal 35.00
Jelly Compote, Mardi Gras, #42, crystal, 5" h 32.00
Juice Tumbler, Eternally Yours, crystal 18.00
Plate, Chantilly cutting, #115, 7-1/2" d, 2 handles, crystal 22.00
Punch Bowl and Base, Mardi Gras, #42, crystal, 12-1/2" d 250.00
Punch Cup, Mardi Gras, #42, crystal 15.00
Salad Plate, Chantilly cutting, #115, 7-1/2" d, crystal 18.00
Sugar Shaker, Duncan Block, crystal 40.00
Tumbler, Mardi Gras, #42, crystal , 4" h, 8 oz, gold trim, 6 pc set 120.00
Urn
   3" sq base, ruby, no handles 35.00
   3" sq base, light chartreuse, round applied handles 45.00
   3" sq base, ruby, round applied handles 45.00
   5-1/2" sq base, crystal, round applied handles 25.00
   5-1/2" sq, base, light chartreuse, no handles 36.00
   5-1/2" sq, milk glass, green handles 395.00

Water Carafe, Mardi Gras, #42, crystal, 8-1/2" d 135.00
Water Set, Button Panels, crystal, gold trim, 7 pc set 160.00
Whiskey
   Ducks and Cattails etching, crystal, 2 oz, orig label 28.00
   Seahorse, etch #502, red and crystal, ftd, 2 oz 45.00
Wine, Festival of Flowers, crystal 26.50

Patterns and Etchings

Astaire
   Cordial, ruby 45.00
   Finger Bowl, ruby 35.00
   Plate, ruby, 7-1/2" d 12.50
   Tumbler, ruby, 10 oz 18.00
Canterbury, #115 Extensive dinnerware pattern made in Cape Cod blue (opalescent), chartreuse, cranberry pink, crystal, jasmine yellow, ruby, and sapphire blue. Made 1937.
   Ashtray, rect, crystal 10.00
   Basket
     5-1/2" d, cranberry pink 70.00
     10" l, oval, crystal 85.00
   Bowl
     6-1/2", sapphire blue 30.00
     8" d, 2 part, crystal 16.00
     12" d, flared, crystal 25.00
   Cake Plate, 14" d, chartreuse 30.00
   Candlesticks, pr, 3-1/2" h, crystal 25.00
   Candy Box, cov
     Chartreuse, 3 part 55.00
     Crystal, 3 part, 6" d, 3-1/2" h 65.00
   Celery Tray, 11" l, crystal 25.00
   Champagne, sapphire blue 20.00
   Cheese Comport, crystal 25.00
   Cigarette Box, ruby, small 125.00
   Claret, sapphire blue 25.00
   Cocktail, crystal 10.00
   Comport, 5-1/2" h
     Crystal 28.00
     Ruby, crystal foot, orig label 138.00
   Condiment Tray, 4-part, crystal 20.00
   Cordial, blown, cut, crystal 20.00
   Creamer and Sugar, tray, crystal
     2-3/4" h, 3 oz 35.00
     3-3/4" h, 7 oz 25.00
   Cup and Saucer, crystal 17.50
   Decanter, stopper, crystal 100.00
   Flower Arranger
     Jasmine yellow 65.00
     Dark green, 5-1/2" h 55.00
   Goblet
     Chartreuse 20.00
     Crystal, 9 oz, ftd 12.00
   Ice Cream, crystal 6.00
   Mayonnaise, plate, orig ladle 40.00
   Oyster Cocktail, jasmine yellow 15.00
   Plate
     8" d, chartreuse 15.00
     8-1/2" d, sapphire blue 15.00
     9" d, chartreuse 18.00
     11-1/4" d, crystal 25.00
   Relish, crystal
     3-part, 11" d 25.00
     3-part, 3 handles, silver overlay 27.50
   Salt and Pepper Shakers, pr, crystal 24.00
   Sherbet, crimped, sapphire blue 15.00
   Sugar, large, crystal 10.00
   Tumbler, 6-1/4" h, crystal 15.00

Ad, Introducing "The New Puritan," Pottery, Glass & Brass Salesman, May 1930.

Vase

    4-1/2" h, sapphire blue 20.00
    5-1/2" h, crystal...24.00
    7-1/4" h, inverted candle type, crystal...................115.00
Violet Vase, cranberry pink opalescent 40.00
Wine, crystal..25.00

Caribbean Extensive dinnerware pattern made in amber, blue, crystal, and ruby. Made 1936-55.
Ashtray, 6" d, blue 35.00
Bowl

    5" d, blue 35.00
    8-1/2" d, blue 70.00
Candy, cov, 7" d, flared, blue.......................................95.00
Champagne, blue 45.00
Cheese Dish, cov, blue 35.00
Cocktail, 3-3/4" oz, 4-1/8" h, blue 45.00
Console Bowl, 12" d, flared edge, crystal 40.00
Creamer, blue 25.00
Cruet, orig stopper, crystal 75.00
Cup and Saucer, crystal 22.00
Epergne, 9-1/2" h, blue 95.00
Fruit Plate, 6" d, handle, blue 20.00
Goblet, blue...40.00
Mayonnaise, 5-3/4" d, handle, orig liner, spoon, blue.....85.00
Milk Pitcher, blue...295.00
Plate

    6-1/4" d, bread and butter, crystal 6.00
    7-1/2" d, salad, blue 20.00
    8-1/2" d, luncheon, blue 35.00
    10-1/2" d, dinner, crystal 45.00
Punch Bowl, crystal...90.00
Punch Cup, crystal, red handle 15.00
Relish, 2-part, round, 6" d, blue 30.00
Salt and Pepper Shakers, pr, metal tops, crystal..........35.00
Server, 6-1/2" d, center handle, blue 48.00
Torte Plate, 16" d, crystal 35.00
Tumbler, 5-1/2" h, ftd, crystal 22.00

Vase

    5-3/4" h, ftd, ruffled edge, blue................................60.00
    7-1/2" h, ftd, flared, bulbous, crystal 38.00
    9" h, flared, blue 125.00
Water Pitcher, blue...965.00
Wine, blue, 3 oz, 4-3/4" h 45.00

First Love Extensive dinnerware etched pattern made only on crystal. Made in 1937.
Ashtray, 5" l, rect 35.00
Bowl

    5-1/2" d, handle 40.00
    10" d, flared 50.00
Bud Vase, 9" h 75.00
Butter Dish, 7" sq, Terrace blank 120.00
Cake Plate, 14-1/2" d, small base 60.00
Candelabra, pr, 2-lite, #30 ....75.00
Candlesticks, pr, 4" h 60.00
Candy, open, 3-part 40.00
Celery Tray, 11" l 42.00
Champagne 16.00
Cheese and Cracker 95.00
Cocktail, #65111-1/2 ....20.00
Comport, 5-1/2" 50.00
Cornucopia Vase, #117 ....60.00
Creamer and Sugar, matching tray, individual size......35.00
Cup and Saucer 20.00
Decanter, 32 oz...295.00
Deviled Egg Plate, 12" d 115.00
Goblet

    Low 25.00
    Tall 28.00
Honey Dish, 5" x 3" 30.00
Ice Bucket, orig handle 75.00
Iced Tea Tumbler, ftd, #5111-1/2, 6-1/2" h, 12 oz........15.00
Martini Pitcher 165.00
Mayonnaise, 5-1/4" x 3" , divided, 7-1/2" underplate 40.00
Nappy, 5-1/2" x 2" , handle, heart shape 30.00

New! № 21 Pattern Greeted with instant favor

BUYERS have given this new Duncan & Miller line an enthusiastic welcome because it gives them an opportunity to give their customers style plus quality in glassware at very modest cost. It is easily one of the leaders of 1931.

Available in crystal, green, amber and rose.

Immediate shipment from stock at the factory.

DESIGN PATENT PENDING

Salesrooms

NEW YORK
Paul Joseph
200 Fifth Avenue

BOSTON
Murt Wallace
111 Summer St.

CHICAGO
F. T. Renshaw
58 E. Washington St.

PHILADELPHIA
William C. Byrnes
Burd Bldg.
9th & Chestnut Sts.

CALIFORNIA
Cliff B. Rhodes
San Francisco Office—
412 Kamm Bldg.
Los Angeles Office—
122 East 7th St.

Factory Representatives:
E. B. Hill
A. A. Graeser
WASHINGTON, PA.

The DUNCAN and MILLER GLASS CO

Manufacturers of Fine Table Glassware

WASHINGTON P.A.

Ad, Introducing No. 21, Crockery and Glass Journal, 1931.

Oyster Cocktail, 3-3/4" 22.00
Perfume Bottle, 5" h, #5200......................................65.00
Plate
    6" d, bread and butter, #111 ....15.00
    7-1/2" d, salad, #115 ....20.00
    8-1/2" d, luncheon, #30 ....22.00
    11" d, dinner, #111 ....45.00
Relish
    2-part, 2 handles, Terrace blank........................30.00
    3-part, feather...50.00
    4-part, 9" 45.00
    5-part, 10" d...65.00
Salad Dressing Bottle..200.00
Salt and Pepper Shakers, pr 32.00
Urn, 7" h...50.00
Tumbler, 8 oz, flat..30.00
Vase, 10" h, cylinder..72.00

Hobnail
Bowl, 12" d, crimped rim, blue..................................65.00
Candlesticks, pr
    Amethyst...75.00
    Blue opalescent, 4" h..60.00
Champagne, pink..20.00
Cologne Bottle, 8 oz
    Blue opalescent...115.00
    Pink opalescent...85.00
Cruet, orig stopper, amber.......................................60.00
Cup and Saucer, blue opalescent.............................22.00
Goblet, ftd, 9 oz, blue opalescent............................40.00
Hat, 6", blue opalescent...195.00
Ivy Ball, #118, 5", small opening
    Amber..25.00
    Light Green..36.00
    Milk Glass..38.00
Plate
    8" d, blue opalescent...15.00
    8-1/2" d, pink...30.00
Violet Vase, green, ftd, ruffled.................................30.00

Indian Tree made in crystal.
Candy, cov, #115, 3 compartments...........................75.00
Champagne...25.00
Creamer and Sugar, #115...55.00
Iced Tea Tumbler, ftd...22.00
Juice Tumbler, ftd, 4-3/4" h.....................................22.50
Pickle/olive, 8-1/2"...40.00
Plate, 8-1/2" d..18.00
Sherbet/champagne, tall...12.00

Language of Flowers made in crystal.
Bowl, 12" d, flared...37.50
Candlesticks, pr 45.00
Oyster Cocktail, crystal..15.00
Sherbet, crystal..15.00
Sugar..15.00

Passion Flower
Bowl, 12-1/2" d, crystal..30.00
Creamer and Sugar, #38, crystal..............................40.00
Plate, 14-1/2" d, crystal...30.00
Relish, divided, crystal, 10-1/2" l..............................25.00

Sandwich #41. Extensive dinnerware pattern made in amber, cobalt blue, crystal, green, and pink. Made by Duncan and Miller from 1924 to 1935. The molds have been sold and some forms of this pattern have been made by other companies, such as Lancaster Colony and Tiffin.
Ashtray, individual, sq...8.00
Basket, 10", oval, loop handle.................................150.00
Bon Bon, 5" l, heart shape, ring handle 18.00

Bowl
    11-1/2" d...48.00
    12" d, shallow 50.00
Cake Plate, pedestal, 13" d......................................85.00
Candelabra, pr
    10" h, pr 150.00
    16" h, 3-lite, bobeches and prisms.....................225.00
Candy Basket, ftd, loop handle.................................50.00
Candy, cov, ftd...55.00
Celery Tray, 10" l...22.50
Champagne...20.00
Cheese Comport...15.00
Coaster...15.00
Cocktail..15.00
Comport, 7"...25.00
Creamer, 4"...12.00
Creamer and Sugar, tray, individual size..................37.50
Cruet, stopper 40.00
Cruet Set, 5 pc...70.00
Cup and Saucer...16.00
Deviled Egg Plate...80.00
Float Bowl, 11-1/2" d..50.00
Fruit Bowl
    5-1/2" d...10.00
    12" d, flared, crystal..45.00
Goblet, water, 9 oz, ftd...18.00
Grapefruit Bowl, rimmed, 7"......................................18.00
Ice Cream Bowl, 5 oz...12.00
Jelly Compote...10.00
Juice Tumbler, ftd...13.00
Mayonnaise, 5" d..20.00
Nappy, 5" d...8.00
Pickle, 7" l, oval...15.00
Plate
    6" d, bread and butter 6.00
    7" d, dessert..7.50
    8" d, salad...11.00
    9-1/2" d, dinner...50.00
Relish
    2-part, round, ring handle 15.00
    2-part, 5-1/2" d, handle......................................15.00
    3-part, 6" x 10"..27.50
    3-part, 10-1/2", oblong.......................................20.00
    4-part, 10" d, round, 2 handles..........................45.00
Salad Bowl, 10" d...70.00
Salt and Pepper Shakers, pr, metal tops 20.00
Sandwich Plate, 16" d...115.00
Sherbet...10.00
Sugar, 2-3/4"..10.00
Syrup Jar..65.00
Torte Plate, 12" d...50.00
Tray, 7" l, oval...15.00
Tumbler
    4-3/4" h, 9 oz, ftd..12.00
    5-1/4" h, 13 oz, flat...18.00
Vase
    9-3/4" h, ftd...70.00
    10" h, ftd, #41...90.00
Water Pitcher, ice lip..135.00
Wine..20.00

Sanibel
Bowl
    8" d, blue opalescent...80.00
    14" d, yellow opalescent....................................85.00
Celery Tray, 13" l, 3-part, pink opalescent................45.00
Floating Garden Bowl, 13-1/2" l, pink opalescent.........50.00

Mint Tray, 7" l, blue opalescent 30.00
Plate, 8" d, pink opalescent..30.00
Relish, 2-part, blue opalescent 30.00
Salad Plate, 8-1/2" d
    Blue opalescent...25.00
    Yellow opalescent 25.00

Spiral Flutes. Made in amber, crystal, green, and pink. Introduced
    in 1924.
    Almond Bowl, 2" , amber..15.00
    Bowl, 6-3/4" d, flange, green....................................9.00
    Celery Tray, 10-3/4" x 4-3/4", green 20.00
    Chocolate Box, cov, amber....................................225.00
    Cigarette Holder, green, cutting 70.00
    Cocktail, 2-1/2 oz, ftd 10.00
    Compote, 6" d, amber 20.00
    Console Bowl, 12" d, pink 40.00
    Creamer, green 10.00
    Cup and Saucer, amber..10.00
    Demitasse Cup and Saucer, green.........................20.00
    Finger Bowl, green 11.00
    Grapefruit, ftd, green 20.00
    Juice Tumbler, ftd, 4-1/2" h, pink 20.00
    Mug, 7" h, amber..40.00
    Nut Bowl, individual, green 20.00
    Parfait, 5-1/2" h, green..20.00
    Pickle, 8-1/2" l, green 18.00
    Plate
        6" d, dessert, pink..5.00
        7-1/2" d, salad, green 6.00
        8-1/2" d, luncheon, amber 8.00
        10-1/4" d, dinner, crystal 22.00
    Relish, 10" x 7-1/2" d, oval, two inserts, green 75.00
    Seafood Sauce Cup, green......................................24.00
    Sherbet, 4-3/4" h
        Green...10.00
        Pink...10.00
    Tumbler, 5-1/4" h, ftd, green....................................12.50
    Vase, 8-1/2" h, green...20.00

Tear Drop. Extensive dinnerware pattern made only in crystal.
    Made from 1936 to 1955.
    Ashtray, individual...5.00
    Basket, ruby handle, large size...............................110.00
    Bon Bon, 6"...27.50
    Bowl, 12" sq, handle..42.50
    Butter Dish, cov, quarter pound..............................22.00
    Cake plate, 13" d, ftd..48.00
    Candy Dish, 7-1/2" d, heart shape 15.00
    Celery Tray, 11" l, 2 handles, oval...........................15.00
    Champagne, 5-1/8" h, bead stem.............................10.00
    Cocktail, 3-1/2 oz 12.00
    Condiment Set, 5 pcs..75.00
    Cordial..25.00
    Creamer and Sugar..15.00
    Cruet, orig stopper, 3 oz 18.00
    Cup and Saucer, ftd..8.00
    Iced Tea Tumbler, ftd, 14 oz....................................18.00
    Marmalade, cov, orig spoon 40.00
    Mayonnaise, ftd, spoon...21.00
    Nut, 2-part, handle, 6" d..25.00
    Olive Dish, oval, 2 handles......................................18.00
    Oyster Cocktail, 3-1/2 oz, ftd...................................8.00
    Plate
        6" d, bread and butter 5.00
        7-1/2" d, salad...6.00
        8-1/2" d, luncheon 8.00
        10-1/2" d, dinner..35.00

Relish, 2-part, 2 handles 15.00
Sherbet, low 5.00
Sweetmeat, center handle, 6-1/2" 30.00
Torte Plate, 13" d, rolled edge....................................30.00
Tumbler, 14 oz, 5-1/4" h, flat 9.00
Wine, 4-3/4" h, #5301...14.00

Terrace
    Ashtray, red, sq..35.00
    Bon Bon, rolled up handles, cobalt blue.....................20.00
    Bowl, 5", crystal 12.50
    Candy, cov
        6" h, crystal, floral sterling overlay.........................135.00
        Tall, cobalt blue 400.00
    Champagne, red 95.00
    Comport, 7", amber...45.00
    Creamer, crystal...15.00
    Cup, crystal..15.00
    Cup and Saucer, crystal 20.00
    Demitasse Set, cup, saucer, and plate......................45.00
    Jug, floral sterling overlay 350.00
    Mayonnaise Bowl, divided, Eternally Yours cutting 40.00
    Plate
        7-1/2" d, cobalt blue 37.50
        8-1/2" d, crystal..12.50
    Relish
        4-part, 9" d, round, floral sterling overlay 45.00
        5 part, gold trim 125.00
    Tray, 4" d, round, handle, floral sterling overlay..........135.00
    Tumbler
        Cobalt blue 30.00
        Red 37.50

DURAND

History: Victor Durand (1870-1931), born in Baccarat, France, apprenticed at the Baccarat glassworks where several generations of his family had worked. In 1884, Victor came to America to join his father at Whitall-Tatum & Co. in New Jersey. In 1897, father and son leased the Vineland Glass Manufacturing Company in Vineland, New Jersey. Products included inexpensive bottles, jars, and glass for scientific and medical purposes. By 1920 four separate companies existed.

When Quezal Art Glass and Decorating Company failed, Victor Durand recruited Martin Bach Jr., Emil J. Larsen, William Wiedebine, and other Quezal men and opened an art-glass shop at Vineland in December 1924. Quezal-style iridescent pieces were made. New innovations included cameo and intaglio designs, geometric Art Deco shapes, Venetian Lace, and Oriental-style pieces. In 1928, crackled glass, called Moorish Crackle and Egyptian Crackle, was made.

Durand died in 1931. The Vineland Flint Glass Works was merged with Kimble Glass Company a year later, and the art glass line was discontinued.

Many Durand glass pieces are not marked. Some have a sticker with the words "Durand Art Glass," others have the name "Durand" scratched on the pontil or "Durand" inside a large V. Etched numbers may be part of the marking.

Reference: Kenneth Wilson, *American Glass 1760-1930: The Toledo Museum of Art, Volume I, Volume II*, Hudson Hills Press and The Toledo Museum of Art, 1994.

Ashtray, 5" d, irid blue and green ground, match holder
center 750.00
Bowl
4-1/4" d, 2" h, irid blue body, white heart and vine dec, base
mkd in silver "V Durand #3" 575.00
4-1/2" d, 2" h, irid blue, white heart and vine design, highly
irid surface, sgd 500.00
5" d, luster glass, opal and blue floral, sgd and
numbered 3,350.00
8" d, 6-1/2" h, orange cased to opal, irid green leaf and vine
dec, sgd "Durand" in "V" 1,500.00
9-3/4" d, butterscotch, partial silver sgd 325.00
Box, cov
3-1/2" d, King Tut, green luster ground, gold luster
dec 1,200.00
4-1/2" d, 3-1/4" h, King Tut, Lady Gay Rose, round, gold int.,
applied ambergris disk foot, cover cut-star at center top
pontil mark, unsigned...1,610.00
Candlesticks, pr
2-3/4" h, mushroom, red, opal pulled florals, pale yellow
base...700.00
7" h, irid opal white with random dec, int. gold luster, un-
signed..375.00
9-1/2" h, amber baluster, pulled blue tip feathers, etched
wheat and leaves on flanged rim 325.00
10" h, No. 315, transparent ambergris baluster form, simple
foliate cutting on top bobeche rim, unsigned 520.00
Charger
14" d, transparent green ground, five center colorless, green,
and gray feathers, few small seed bubble.................900.00
14-1/4" d, transparent blue ground, five center colorless,
lighter blue, and gray feathers, numerous bubbles within
glass surround..750.00
Compote, cov, 10-1/2" h, Spanish yellow cased glass, etched
and wheel-cut Bridgeton Rose floral dec cut to clear, conforming matching cover, base marked with "Durand" in
"V," possibly added latter..375.00
Compote, open
5-1/2" d, 4-1/2" h, irid gold and opal, King Tut, sgd....325.00
8" d, white feather center design, blue ground, pale green
stem and foot...750.00
Decanter, 12" h, blue cut to clear, mushroom shaped stopper,
unsgd..600.00
Dessert Set, ten white rimmed ruby ftd bowls, seven plates, 15"
d center bowl, pr ruby with topaz candlesticks 950.00
Dish and Undertray, 4-1/2" d dish, 7" d undertray, transparent
Spanish Yellow, green rim wraps, unsgd...............225.00
Ginger Jar, cov, 10-1/2" h, gold and green King Tut
dec 1,950.00
Goblet, 5-1/2" h, irid ruby ground, pale yellow stem and base,
sgd 500.00
Jack in the Pulpit Vase, 10-3/4" h, gold irid, strong orange and
fuchsia highlights 700.00
Jar, 8-1/2" h, gold ground, blue swirl vine dec 1,200.00
Lamp Base
8" h, turquoise green over opal, silver and blue leaves, random irid threading, gilt-metal Egyptian Revival platform
base, replaced socket...800.00
8-1/2" h, ruffled rim, oval vasiform lamp shaft, transparent
amber, blue pulled feathers, cut Bridgeton Rose design,
mounted to gilt-metal lamp fittings, metal work, sockets
replaced 230.00
11" h glass shaft, 40" h with finial and riser, King Tut, green
irid vasiform shaft, elaborate gilt-metal and giltwood
Egyptian Revival lamp fittings 1,200.00
12" h vase, blue, green, orange King Tut dec, opal ground,
drilled..400.00

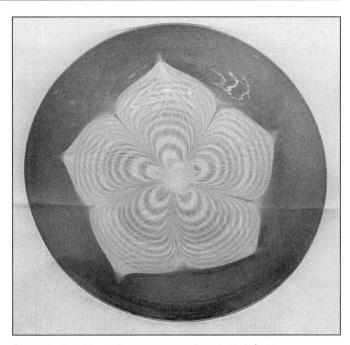

Plate green, white pulled center, unsigned, 8" d, $200.

23-1/2" h, brilliant blue, all over spider web dec, purple, gold,
and blue highlights..1,000.00
Mantel Lamp, 6-1/2" h, opal glass oval, applied gold threading
and irid, mounted to elaborate gilt-metal single socket
lamp base, some thread loss, pr...........................550.00
Mint Bowl, 6" d, shallow, gold scalloped rim, sgd "V.
Durand" 195.00
Plate
7-3/4" d, cobalt blue ground, opal pulled feather, cross
hatched pontil, sgd 500.00
8-1/2" d, ruby, paneled, ten-sided, hand blown, sgd 215.00
8-5/8" d, feather pattern, blue, opal, and clear, cross hatched
cut center 225.00
Rose Bowl, 4" h, colorless, air traps, sgd and numbered ... 350.00
Sherbet, 3-3/8" h, ruby and opal, feather pattern 175.00
Stemware, cobalt blue cut to clear 175.00
Vase
4" h, colorless sphere, controlled bubble, int. dec, base inscribed "V. Durand 1995-4" 290.00
4-1/4" h, oviform, irid blue, white cobweb dec, sgd
"Durand"..800.00
6" h, ambergris oval, flared rim, overall lustrous gold surface,
inscribed "V. Durand 1710-6" 375.00
6" h, oval, fine blue irid, inscribed "Durand 1722 1/2-6"...435.00
6-1/4" h, King Tut, classic baluster form, irid green swirls and
coils, warm orange glass cased to white, lustered orange
int., Larson foot...690.00
6-3/4" h, flared oval, opal ground, green gold leaves, silvery
gold threading, gold irid int., sgd "V. Durand 1812-6" on
base, some thread loss 635.00
7" h, flared trumpet, integrated pulled King Tut dec, inscribed
"Durand" in script straight across polished pontil 690.00
7" h, irid amber, intaglio florals, unsgd.........................195.00
7-1/8" h, baluster, ftd, King Tut, pale green ground, gold
swirling dec, sgd "Durand" 750.00
8" h, collared oval, ambergris, extended folded rim, blue irid,
inscribed "V. Durand 20161-8" 1,265.00
8" h, tooled beehive, brilliant blue irid ambergris, silver signature 1,000.00
8-1/2" h, flared rim, oval ground, red and white crackled surface, bright irid gold luster, rough base..............1,610.00

8-1/2" h, folded over white rim, light green, shiny, sgd and numbered 600.00

8-3/4" h, 8" w, deep orange-gold, purple and blue irid surface, sgd, numbered 1710, minor int. wear 600.00

9" h, flared, bulbous, irid blue, sgd and numbered 1,600.00

9" h, gold irid oval cased to white, inscribed "Durand" across pontil, water stained int. 625.00

9-1/4" h, irid cobalt blue, vertical gold heart and vine motif, purple shading, incised signature........................1,250.00

9-3/4" h, Lady Gay Rose, flared orange lined oval body, cased to white, red-rose surface, King Tut irid swirling gold and silver design...1,495.00

10-1/2" h, ten prominent vertical ribs, oval amber body, rough deeply crackled surface with over all irid, base inscribed "Durand"...1,840.00

12" h, flared cylinder, bright transparent green shaded to clear, five pulled green and white striped pulled peacock feathers..750.00

12" h, flared ten-ribbed yellow amber body, emerald green crackled surface, base inscribed "V. Durand"....1,610.00

12" h, 4-3/4" w, oyster white exterior, random threading, heart leaf dec, brilliant yellow irid interior, gold irid foot, very minor loss to threading...800.00

12-1/4" h, flared trumpet, shaded purple-blue luster, applied gold pedestal foot, heart and vine dec, mkd "Durand 20120-12" 1,725.00

15" h, "Genie" form, elongated tapered neck, bulbous amber body, fine gold irid, flattened indentation on bulbed side, base inscribed "V Durand 1974-15" 1,150.00

EARLY AMERICAN GLASS

History: The term "Early American glass" covers glass made in America from the colonial period through the mid-19th century. As such, it includes the early pressed glass and lacy glass made between 1827 and 1840.

Major glass-producing centers prior to 1850 were Massachusetts (New England Glass Company and the Boston and Sandwich Glass Company), South Jersey, Pennsylvania (Stiegel's Manheim factory and many Pittsburgh-area firms), and Ohio (several different companies in Kent, Mantua, and Zanesville).

The Lacy Period of American glass began with the advent of pressing machines in the 1820s and continued until about 1850. The earliest pressing machines led to a revolution in the was glassware was made, as well as the detailed patterns now referred to as lacy. Lacy patterns tried to convey the delicate and intricate cut glass patterns in the new pressing techniques without using the more time-consuming copper wheel grinding and engraving methods.

Intricate lacy patterns often contain florals, scrolls, as well as historical and commemorative elements. Many lacy patterns have such an elaborate pattern that they resemble embroidery or lacy backgrounds, hence their name. Lacy patterns were adapted to create almost every type of glass household item, from decanters and drawer pulls to goblets, plates, salts, and vegetable dishes.

Researchers today often contend that many of other lacy patterns were also designed to hide small blemishes in the batches of glass used by early manufacturers. Many lacy patterns do indeed hide some imperfections such as pieces of sand and even small pebbles. Lacy patterns remain a vivid reminder of the pride and craftsmanship of early moldmakers and glasscrafters.

Early American glass was collected heavily during the years between 1920 and 1950. It has now regained some of its earlier popularity. Leading sources for the sale of Early American glass are the auctions of Early Auction Co., Garth's Auction, Inc., Norman C. Heckler & Co., and Robert W. Skinner Auctions.

References: Raymond E. Barlow and Joan E. Kaiser, *The Glass Industry in Sandwich, Vol. 2, Vol. 3, and Vol. 4*, distributed by Schiffer Publishing; William E. Covill, *Ink Bottles and Inkwells*, William S. Sullwold Publishing, 1971; Lowell Inness, *Pittsburgh Glass, 1797-1891*, Houghton Mifflin, 1976; Ruth Webb Lee, *Early American Pressed Glass, 36th Edition*, Lee Publications, 1966; Ruth Webb Lee, *Sandwich Glass Handbook*, Charles E. Tuttle, 1977; George and Helen McKearin, *American Glass*, Crown, 1975; ——, *Two Hundred Years of American Blown Glass*, Doubleday and Company, 1950; Helen McKearin and Kenneth Wilson, *American Bottles and Flasks*, Crown, 1978; L.W. and D. B. Neal, *Pressed Glass Dishes of the Lacy Period, 1825-1850*, published by author, 1972; Adeline Pepper, *Glass Gaffers of New Jersey*, Schribners, 1971; Dick Roller (comp.), *Indiana Glass Factories Notes*, Acorn Press, 1994; Jane S. Spillman, *American and European Pressed Glass*, Corning Museum of Glass, 1981; Kenneth Wilson, *American Glass 1760-1930*, 2 vols., Hudson Hills Press and The Toledo Museum of Art, 1994; ——, *New England Glass and Glassmaking*, Crowell, 1972.

Periodicals: *Antique Bottle & Glass Collector*, P.O. Box 187, East Greenville, PA 18041; *Glass Collector's Digest*, Antique Publications, P.O. Box 553, Marietta, OH 45750-0553.

Collectors' Clubs: Early American Glass Traders, RD 5, Box 638, Milford, DE 19963; Early American Pattern Glass Society, P.O. Box 266, Colesburg, IA 52035; Glass Research Society of New Jersey, Wheaton Village, Glasstown Rd., Millville, NJ 08332; The National American Glass Club, Ltd., P.O. Box 8489, Silver Spring, MD 20907.

Museums: Bennington Museum, Bennington, VT; Chrysler Museum, Norfolk, VA; Corning Museum of Glass, Corning, NY; Glass Museum, Dunkirk, IN; Historical Glass Museum Foundation, Redlands, CA; New Bedford Glass Museum, New Bedford, MA; Sandwich Glass Museum, Sandwich, MA; Toledo Museum of Art, Toledo, OH; Wheaton Historical Village Assoc. Museum of Glass, Millville, NJ.

Additional Listings: Blown Three Mold; Cup Plates; Flasks; Sandwich Glass; Stiegel-Type Glass.

Back Bar Bottle, 10-1/4" h, fancy pattern mold, cylindrical, pale opalescent yellow green, opalescent stripes swirled to the right, rolled mouth, ground pontil scar, 1870-1900 ... 200.00

Bank, 6-1/2" h, freeblown and pattern molded, sea green with mulberry colored spiral striation patterned molded bowl with coin slot, applied rigaree trailing and three applied birds, freeblown pedestal base, applied flat circular foot, knob contains US dime1841, tooled rim, pontil scar, 1841-60 .... 17,000.00

Bottle
  5" h, opaque white, polychrome enameled floral dec, some opalescent, pewter fittings and cap 360.00
  6-3/8" h, colorless, blown, cased, finely engraved floral swags with bows, medallion with "B. R.," mismatched stopper 125.00
  7-5/8" h, blown, amber, globular, 24 swirled ribs, applied lip, appears to have terminal ring, minor wear and scratches, tiny broken blister, small stones, trace of stain, Zanesville, OH 330.00
  7-7/8" h, blown, deep amber, globular, 24 swirled ribs, Zanesville, OH, minor int. stain 470.00
  8-1/2" h, pattern molded, globular, 24 ribs swirled to the left, medium reddish amber, outward rolled mouth, pontil scar, Midwest America, 1820-40 .... 650.00

Bowl
  4-1/2" d, 3-3/8" h, pattern molded, 16 ribs swirled to the right, medium sapphire blue, sheared rim, plain applied foot with pontil scar, attributed to Mantua, OH, 1822-29 .... 700.00
  4-3/4" d, 3-1/8" h, blown, cobalt blue, expanded diamond, applied foot 250.00
  4-7/8" d, 2-7/8" h, blown, puce, sixteen vertical ribs, broken swirl to right, inward folded rim, ftd, pontil 265.00
  5" d, 3-5/8" h, blown, cobalt blue, 15 swirled ribs, flared lip, applied foot 440.00
  5-1/2" h, free blown, aquamarine, tooled rim, pontil scar, attributed to New York state glasshouse, 1840-70 .... 475.00
  5-7/8" d, 3" h, blown, amber, folded rim, early 19th C, minor burst bubble 690.00
  6-1/2" d, 1-7/8" h, blown, light green, lily pad dec, rolled rim, attributed to NJ 1,495.00
  6-1/2" d, 4-5/8" h, blown, amber, folded rim, Mid-western 715.00

Candlesticks, pr
  6-7/8" h, clambroth, hexagonal 500.00

9-1/8" h, flint, dolphin base, hexagonal socket, small edge
flakes, one glued socket, pr 110.00

Canister, blown, colorless
9-5/8" h, 2 applied rings and finial, Pittsburgh 110.00
9-7/8" h, colorless, dolphin, minor roughage to base,
single 200.00
11" h, 2 applied rings, pressed lid with chips 140.00
11-1/8" h, 3 applied blue rings, colorless applied finial,
Pittsburgh 770.00

Celery Vase
8-1/4" h, cut, waisted with band of alternating cross hatched
diamonds and ovals, foliate band at rim, Bakewell, Pittsburgh, c1825 ....375.00
8-3/8" h, flint, colorless, cut sheaf of wheat pattern, Pittsburgh, rim chips 385.00
8-1/2" h, 5-1/8" d, colorless, engraved elaborate pattern of
festoons, small flowers, and leaf band, twenty ga-
drooned ribs, applied foot and knob stem, early 19th C,
slight crazing 250.00
9-1/2" h, colorless, pillar molded, copper wheel engraved
panels, Pittsburgh, c1820 ....145.00
10" h, flint, colorless, round foot, hexagonal foot and bowl
with oval and round thumbprint and Gothic Arches, chips
on foot..145.00

Chamberstick, 1-7/8" h, miniature or toy, pressed pattern, deep
amethyst, American, 1840-70 ....140.00

Cologne Bottle
5-1/2" h, hexagonal, canary yellow, Star and Punty, cut stopper with ground edges......................................330.00
5-1/2" h, pattern molded, sixteen vertical ribs, bright sapphire blue, inward rolled mouth, faint pontil scar, Midwest
America, 1820-60...240.00
8-1/8" h, free blown, slender conical for, brilliant medium amethyst, inward rolled mouth, pontil scar 325.00

Compote
5-3/4" d, 5-7/8" h, fiery opalescent, Colonial, rim chip 535.00
4-1/4" h, 6-1/2" d, 4-1/4" h, Lacy period, Heart and Shield pattern,
colorless, New England Glass Co., small rim chip..... 750.00
7-1/4" h, freeblown, colorless, copper wheel engraving of vintage pattern, leaves and fruit, ground rim, pontil scar, attributed to Pittsburgh district, Pittsburgh, PA, 1840-70.... 210.00
10" d, 7-3/4" h, flint, colorless, blown. bowl with cut sheaf of
wheat pattern, knop stem, star foot, Pittsburgh, wear and
small flakes..385.00

Creamer
3" h, pattern molded, amethyst, 18 ribs swirled to the right,
modified pear form, applied handle, inward rolled rim with
pour spout, pontil scar, c1820-50 ....600.00
3-1/4" h, pattern molded, sapphire blue, faint darker blue striations, 14 ribs, tooled rim with pour spout, applied handle, attributed to Pittsburgh, 1820-60, small pc of rigaree
at tail end of handle missing 150.00
3-1/2" h, cobalt blue, expanded diamond, applied handle,
check at handle...165.00
3-1/2" h, cobalt blue, 20 diamond pattern, ovoid, applied
handle, sheared rim with pour spout, pontil scar, 1770-
1830..450.00
3-1/2" h, freeblown, cobalt blue, ovoid, applied base and
handle, sheared rim with pour spout, pontil scar, 1830-
60..400.00
3-1/2" h, freeblown, sapphire blue, ovoid, applied base and
handle, sheared rim with pour spout, pontil scar,
1830-60 ....150.00
4-5/8" h, pattern molded, deep sapphire blue, 11 diamond
pattern, elongated ovoid, applied solid handle, tooled
rim, pour spout, applied ribbed base with inward rolled
rim, pontil scar, c1820-40 ....650.00

Flask, pattern molded, swirled to the right, Emil Larson, NJ, c1930, amethyst, sheared mouth, pontil scar, 7-3/8" h, some ext. high-point wear, $250. Photo courtesy of Norman C. Heckler and Co.

Decanter, colorless, blown
9-3/8" h, cut fluting and panels, engraved swags and tassels,
lip flakes 165.00
9-1/2" h, copper wheel engraved floral design, stopper re-
ground 110.00
9-3/4" h, blown, colorless, applied chain dec, attributed to
Thomas Cains, Boston, first half 19th C, very minor chips,
scratches to int. 230.00
10-5/8" h, pillar molded, 8 pillar mold, colorless with amethyst
highlights on each rib, heavy collar molded mouth, ground
pontil scar, attributed to Pittsburgh, 1835-70 .... 1,000.00

Dish, 5-1/8" d, fiery opalescent, Plume, minor chips 165.00

Ewer, 11-3/4" h, flint, colorless, pillar mold, applied foot and handle, pewter top, hinged lid with finial, Pittsburgh 495.00

Flask
4-1/4" h, pattern molded, plump chestnut form, 20 ribs
swirled to the right, deep purple tooled flared mouth, pontil scar, attributed to early Pittsburgh district, Pittsburgh,
PA, 1800-30...650.00
5-1/8" h, freeblown, deep olive amber, sheared mouth, pontil
scar, 1800-30, some minor ext. wear 160.00
5-1/4" h, pattern molded, plump form, twenty diamond pattern over faint twenty flute pattern, brilliant amethyst,
sheared mouth, pontil scar, attributed to American Flint
Glass Manufactory, Manheim, PA, 1763-74 ....2,200.00

Flat Iron, miniature, light green, one shallow chip, several small
flakes at base, handle check 450.00

Gaffing Tool Holder, 4-3/4" h, blown, peacock blue, applied
base, segmented stem... 580.00

Goblet
6-1/2" h, blown, deep amethyst, applied pedestal foot, polished pontil, Ohio, c1830 ....165.00
7" h, colorless, applied foot, hollow hourglass stem and bowl,
copper wheel engraved ivy and "B.D.C.," attributed to
New England Glass Co. 125.00

Hat, blown, colorless, polished pontil, applied cockade....... 40.00

Jar, free blown
4-1/2" x 6-3/8", golden amber, cylindrical, wide flat folded
rim, tubular pontil...325.00
8" h, colorless, two horizontal ribs, domed cov, air trap
finial 200.00

Jigger, 2-1/8" h, fiery opalescent, paneled 75.00

Lamp, flint
8-1/8" h, canary, pressed, loop design, hexagonal base, mi-
nor cracks...375.00

Pitcher, free blown, attributed to South Jersey glasshouse, 1840-60, bulbous body, type 1 lily pad dec, applied solid handle, applied circular foot, golden amber, sheared rim with pour spout, pontil scar, McKearin plate 17, $7,000. Photo courtesy of Norman C. Heckler and Co.

10-1/4" h, colorless, hexagonal base, comet font, soldered repair on brass collar, chips on foot........................165.00

10-1/4" h, free blown, lace maker's, colorless, globular font, hollow stem, applied circular foot, applied handle with thumb rest, tooled rim, smooth base, American, 1800-30....250.00

12-1/4" h, colorless, sq base, hexagonal stem, four printee font, pewter collar..180.00

Mug, handle, colorless

3-3/4" h, twenty-four wide ribs, applied strap handle with curl, copper wheel engraved tendrils, and letter "P" 150.00

5-1/2" h, applied foot and handle, Stiegel type copper wheel engraved tulip 175.00

Pan, 7" d, blown, colorless, applied cobalt blue rim, ground pontil...165.00

Pitkin

7" h, blown, aqua, half post neck, 30 ribs with broken swirl, flake at pontil and bottom edge 330.00

7-1/4" h, blown, olive green, half post neck, 36 ribs with broken swirl...275.00

Pitcher

4-3/8" h, blown, deep olive green, applied foot and handle, Mt. Vernon Glass Works....................................1,760.00

4-5/8" h, lily-pad, blown, amber, applied handle, broken blister in second gather near one pulled up peak, Ellenville, NY...2,255.00

5" h, blown, colorless, applied chain dec, attributed to Thomas Cains, Boston, first half 19th C, minor crack to handle...690.00

5-1/2" h, blown, amber, incised rim, applied ribbed handle, petal foot, Midwestern, minute chips 4,315.00

5-1/2" h, freeblown, lily pad, bulbous body, type I lily pad dec, applied solid handle, applied circular foot, golden amber, sheared rim, pour spout, pontil scar, attributed to South Jersey glass house, 1840-60, McKearin plate 17........7,000.00

5-3/4" h, pillar mold, flint, colorless, applied handle and tooled lip, Pittsburgh 315.00

6" h, freeblown, lily pad, bulbous body, type II lily pad dec, applied handle, applied flat circular foot, bluish aquamarine, tooled rim, pour spout, pontil scar, attributed to Ellenville Glassworks, Ellenville, NY, 1830-60 ....6,000.00

7" h, blown, colorless with slight blue-gray tint, threaded neck, applied handle, check at base of handle, Midwestern 220.00

9" h, mold blown, flint, Cleat pattern, applied handle, minor edge roughness 300.00

Preserving Jar, 7-1/4" h, blown, colorless, tin lid, recessed gallery lip for wax 220.00

Rose Bowl, pillar molded, colorless, Pittsburgh 30.00

Salt, master, 2-1/4" h, 2-1/8" d, pattern molded, light amethyst, 17 ribs swirled to the right, double ogee bowl with short stem drawn from same gather, applied plain foot, tooled rim, pontil scar, Midwest, 1820-50 ....800.00

2-1/2" h, blown molded, light green, diamond pattern on petal foot, late 18th C/early 19th C, minute chips 815.00

2-1/2" h, 2-3/4" d, cobalt blue, pattern molded, checkered diamond, applied solid foot, Amelung 850.00

2-7/8" h, pattern molded, cobalt blue, 16 ribs swirled slightly to the right, double ogee bowl, short stem of same gather, applied circular foot, sheared mouth, pontil scar, Midwest, 1820-60 ....90.00

2-7/8" h, 2-1/4" d, pattern molded, cobalt blue, checkered diamond pattern, double ogee bowl with short stem from same gather, plain applied circular foot, sheared rim, pontil scar, attributed to Amelung Glass Works, Frederick, MD, 1785-1797 ....1,200.00

3" h, pattern molded, colorless, double ogee bowl, short stem, applied petal foot, sheared rim, pontil scar, 1770-1830...175.00

3-5/8" h, pattern molded, colorless with pale gray cast, 15 ribs, outward folded rim, pontil scar, freeblown foot, flat rim chip...170.00

Sand Shaker, free blown, opaque blue 275.00

Scent Bottle, 3" h, teardrop form, colorless, pattern molded, ribbed and swirled to the right, 15 ribs, sheared mouth, pontil scar...300.00

Spooner

4-1/8" h, cobalt blue, Bigler variant 415.00

4-3/8" h, fiery opalescent, Excelsior, chips on base ...330.00

Sugar Bowl, cov

5-1/8" h, blown, colorless, applied chain dec, attributed to Thomas Cains, Boston, first half 19th C 920.00

5-1/4" h, Lacy period, Acanthus Leaf pattern, canary yellow, octagonal, Boston and Sandwich Glass Co., slight roughage...2,900.00

5-3/8" h, flint, vaseline, Gothic Arch, octagonal, acanthus leaf lid, small flakes on base, lid with rim chips 550.00

5-3/4" h, Lacy period, Gothic Arch pattern, canary yellow, Boston and Sandwich Glass Co., c1840.............2,500.00

7-3/8" h, freeblown, light green, applied sq base, applied double solid handles, flanged cover with elaborate applied swan finial, sheared rim, pontil scar, attributed to South Jersey...5,500.00

Sugar Bowl, open

5-5/8" h, deep blue, paneled, small flakes on foot......200.00

8-3/4" h, cobalt blue, paneled, small flakes 660.00

Syrup, 8-1/4" h, colorless, hexagonal, Star and Punty, applied hollow handle, tin top with hinged lid, pewter finial 220.00

Tumbler

3-1/8" h, blown, cobalt blue, paneled, pinpoint flakes on foot...125.00

3-1/8" h, blown, cobalt blue, Ashburton, pinpoint flakes on foot...150.00

3-1/4" h, Lacy period, Eye and Scale pattern, colorless, pillar flute motif, Boston and Sandwich Glass Co., 1827 ... 900.00

4" h, blown, olive green, , old paper label, broken blisters, Midwestern 715.00

6-3/4" h, copper wheel engraved floral design 100.00

Vase, blown

8" h, emerald green, flared baluster, circular foot, attributed to Pittsburgh, 19th C..2,185.00

9-3/4" h, colorless, trumpet, applied foot, folded edge, tear drop stem 200.00

9-7/8" h, colorless, applied flared foot, folded rim 300.00

12-5/8" h, amethyst, trumpet, applied foot, hollow stem, folded rim 250.00
Whiskey Bottle, 7-1/4" h, blown molded, amber, pear-shape, applied handle, "Griffith Hyatt & Co. Baltimore" around semicircular panel enclosing paper label, circular panel on reverse enclosing paper label of *U.S.S. Constitution*, wear, losses to labels 750.00

Wine
5-1/8" h, colorless, blown, Pittsburgh-type engraved foliage, tapered stem and bowl, applied foot 85.00
6-3/8" h, colorless, blown, folded rim, hollow stem, applied dome foot attributed to Amelung............................600.00
7-1/2" h, free blown, panel cut flared bowl, baluster stem, applied foot, pr 225.00
7-3/4" h, air twist stem, wear and scratches 50.00
Wine Funnel, 3-3/8" x 5-3/4", colorless, engraved border of leaves and flowers, eight cut flutes continue down stem........95.00

ENGLISH GLASS

History: The English have been manufacturing fine glassware for centuries. This category is a catchall for some examples of the many fine glasswares produced by the English. English glassmakers, just like their contemporaries around the world, often did not mark their wares. Research and a familiarity with techniques and colors often allow collectors and dealers to correctly attribute a lovely piece of glass as English.

References: Victor Arwas, *Glass Art Nouveau to Art Deco*, Rizzoli International Publications, Inc., 1977; Ray and Lee Grover, *English Cameo Glass*, Crown Publishers, Inc., 1980; Charles A. Hajdamach, British Glass, 1800-1914, Antique Collectors' Club, 1991; Albert C. Revi, *Nineteenth Century Glass*, reprint, Schiffer Publishing, 1981.

Barber's Bowl, 7-1/2" h, 5-1/2" d, cylindrical, spring green ground, white enameled dec of stylized leaves, gold band of diamonds and half diamonds 750.00
Basket
6" h, 6-1/2" w, deep cranberry, rolled over rim, applied crystal ruffled edge, shell ftd base, applied crystal looped handle, Victorian...175.00
7" h, 8" w, vaseline opalescent shading to pink, diamond quilted design, petal shaped edge, pale pink handle 100.00
12" h, 10" w, heavy threaded body, applied rigaree shell base with double row of rigaree, three large rows of applied rigaree including two done in shell pattern, double crossed crystal handle with matching applied rigaree 450.00
Beverage Set, 8-3/4" h x 5-3/4" w pitcher, two 4" tumblers, deep emerald green shading to purple, allover enameled floral dec of Queen Anne's lace, leaves, and wild roses, applied transparent green handle..............................850.00
Bowl
5" d, 3" h, opalescent yellow shading to vaseline, applied blue edge, yellow rigaree, Victorian.........................50.00
8" w, 3-3/4" h, triangular shape, Tartan, blue, white, and pale pink, clockwise swirl on ext., reversed on int., applied feet, sgd "Tartan Rd. No. 46498," registered by Henry Gething Richardson, Wordsley Flint Glass Works, near Stourbridge, Feb 24, 1886 ....1,250.00
Candlesticks, 10" h, cut glass, Anglo/Irish, 19th C, set of 4...850.00
Celery vase, 7-1/4" h, 4-7/8" d, emb ribs, blue opalescent, mkd "RD. #217752" 95.00

Centerpiece, 20-1/2" h, 15-1/2" d, three part, center vase, compote dish, and base, cut glass, Anglo/Irish, 19th C 1,500.00
Compote
6" h, 8" w, deep rose shading to pink satin int., white ext., silver plated stand, Victorian 150.00
11-3/4" h, baluster form pedestal, fan and diagonal cut bowl, Irish...400.00
Creamer, 4-1/2" h, 3-3/4" d, daisies and panel type pattern, vaseline opalescent, mkd "Rd. #176566" 75.00
Dish, cov, 9-1/2" d, cut glass, crosshatching and fans, Anglo/Irish, 19th C, chips, pr 400.00
Hanging Basket
8-1/2" h, 3" w basket, pink overlay over white, crystal stand with thorn handle and holder.................................200.00
9" h, 5-1/2" h x 3-1/4" w basket, pink and white cut overlay basket, clear applied thorn handle cut with flower and leaf design, clear crystal ribbed thorn base 600.00
Humidor, 6-1/4" h, 4-1/4" w, white milk glass, shades from yellow to brown, large pink and burgundy enameled roses, green leaves, brass finish, emb flower finial, Victorian, small chip on rim 50.00
Jar, cov, 5-1/2" h, spatter, minor roughness 65.00
Pokal, cov, 17-3/4" h, 8" d, cut glass, wide paneled cut design, tulip like edge, Anglo-Irish, matching pr 700.00
Rose Bowl, spatter, cased 75.00
Spirits Bottle, 5" h, 6-1/8" d, free blown, cylindrical squatty shape, dense olive green, sheared mouth, string rim, pontil scar, 1/2" chip on string rim, small chips, some ext. wear, 1680-1730... 325.00
Syrup Pitcher, 7" h, 3-1/2" w, pear shape, body shades from blue to white, beige flowers, green leaves and ferns, silver plated top and handle, Victorian 100.00
Sweetmeat
6" h, 6" w, vaseline, applied vaseline rigaree in middle, fancy Sheffield holder 100.00
8" h, 10" l, two bowls, vaseline, applied ruby red edge, fancy metal holder with center handle 125.00
Urn, cov, 12" h, colorless cut crystal, Anglo Irish, pr 800.00
Vase
5" h, marbleized, striated red, yellow, orange, blue, and green, cased, opal white lining, enamel dec at flared neck and rim 215.00
8" h, floriform, opalescent yellow, internally dec by four stylized flowers, attributed to Powell or Whitefriars 350.00
10" h, 5-3/4" d, colorless crystal over blue overlay, crystal rigaree around top and near base, blue overlay pedestal foot, multicolored enameled birds and flowers 425.00

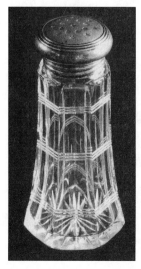

Sugar shaker, cut-glass base, star cut base, star shaped holes in hallmarked sterling silver top, $85.

10-1/4" h, Moss Agate, cobalt blue ground, multi-chromatic swirls of color overlaid with colorless glass, engraved mark "W. & C. England," (Webb Corbett), minor tooling blemish at shoulder 700.00

EPERGNES

History: Epergnes were made by early glass craftsmen. Beautiful glassware used for serving food was often an important decorating element in early society, and epergnes of glass and silver adorned many dining rooms. Epergnes usually consist of one or multiple lily-type vases supported on elaborate frames and are often found with large round bases which could be filled with additional fruit or floral displays. Epergnes can be found in almost every glass color and historical period, right up to the present. Their peak popularity was during the Victorian period when they were considered necessary to every well-appointed dining room.

Reference: John Mebane, *Collecting Bride's Baskets and Other Glass Fancies*, Wallace-Homestead, 1976.

4-3/4" h, 4-3/8" d base, single bulbous Burmese ruffled vase, red berries, green and brown leaves dec, enameled highlights, notched mirrored plateau, base cov in red velvet, Webb 350.00

8" h, 7" w, three Burmese fairy lamps with satin glass shades, prunus blossom dec, colorless pressed glass candle cups, gilt metal ftd stand fitted with four undecorated Burmese satin glass flower holders, ruffled rims 3,200.00

Custard glass ground, applied pink flowers, green leaves, amber rigaree, two piece, attributed to Stevens and Williams, $195.

8-1/2" h, clear glass base with two tree trunk apertures, each has hanging pink cased basket, English 350.00

8-1/2" h, trumpet form, blue edge, highly dec figural glass dragon encircling stem, enameled florals and gold highlights, no holder 75.00

12" h, 7-1/2" d, cranberry, center ruffled top single lily, fancy crystal applied spiral trim, ruffled cranberry bowl, brass connection... 250.00

13-1/2" h, 10" w, colorless ground, eight miniature baskets with handles and berry prunts, all hanging from center vase, Stevens and Williams 475.00

14-1/2" h, 10-1/2" d, ruffled lift out opalescent vase, nickel plated foot and vase holder 275.00

15" h, Baccarat, three trumpet shaped vases with scalloped edges, Rose Tiente coloration............................. 475.00

16" d, 10-1/2" d, shaded blue int., white ext., green and maroon flowers and lacy foliage on int., lift out center lily 450.00

19" h, 11" d, 3 lily, pink and white cased, ruffled bowl, heavy wire holder with figural strawberries and leaves winding around 10" l lilies 350.00

20" h, 3 lilies, cranberry, two clear twisted basket arms, Victorian... 600.00

20" h, 3 lilies, turquoise and white cased, scalloped bowl, fancy rigaree around lilies.. 450.00

21" h, 16" d, cranberry, enter flower vase, two candleholders supported with colorless glass branches, cut and etched leaf and berry design, cranberry prism drops, Victorian ...575.00

23" h, green opalescent, four lily shaped vases stemming from flower bowl, Victorian 660.00

24" h, emerald green, central lily shaped vase, five diamond cut bowls with fluted edges, silver plated frame mkd "WMF EP IX," c1880.. 2,650.00

Cut Glass, three 9" h trumpets, one 13-1/2" trumpet, three handled hanging baskets, 10-1/2" bowl, strawberry, diamond, and fan design, attributed to Dorflinger, American Brilliant Period 5,500.00

Single lily, rubena overshot, fishnet dec 300.00

EUROPEAN GLASS

History: European glassmakers have been creating utilitarian and decorative glassware items for centuries. The necessity of food and beverage storage vessels created a demand for early pieces. Other items, such as wine goblets, and other types of stemware, exist today as fine examples of the many craftsmen who worked throughout Europe.

Because of the variation in raw materials from one region to another, differences in techniques and colors exist. These differences provide clues to scholars and collectors when determining the origin of a piece. The existing examples also reflect the political and religious views of the periods. It was not unusual for a reigning monarch to shelter and encourage a glassblower. Unfortunately, wars and changes in monarchs caused shortages of money and materials for glassmakers. During some periods, production halted and often years passed before techniques were reinstated or developed by later craftsmen.

Brilliant colors, exquisite detailed cuttings, and engravings are frequently found on European glassware. The addition of enamel and gilt decorations further enhanced the glassware. Utilitarian pieces, such as bowls and bottles, were frequently left plain. Most pieces are unmarked. Glass composition, design, and texture are the most important keys to identifying regions and periods.

Today, European craftsmen are beginning to capture international markets with innovative and colorful glassware. Leading auction houses, such as Skinner's and William Doyle Galleries, Inc., include these examples and are finding that they do quite well with today's collectors.

References: Sheldon Barr, *Venetian Glass, Confections in Glass, 1855-1914*, Harry N. Abrams, Inc., 1998; Brigitte Klesse and Hans Mayr, *European Glass from 1500-1800, The Ernesto Wolf Collection*, Kremayr & Sheriau, 1987; Leslie Pina, *Fifties Glass*, Schiffer Publishing, 1993.

Museum: Corning Museum of Glass, Corning, NY.

Basket
    6" h, 5-1/2" w, ruby cut glass, red and white candy stripe spiral twist handle 175.00
    7" h, 12" w, amber, wide banner of enameled floral dec in Persian manner, gold, blue, red, and green, two large applied open handles, applied matching ruffled glass base, Austria 125.00
    8-1/2" h, 8" w, irid green, applied crystal handle with prunts 50.00
    10-1/2" h, 6" w, olive green, mottled white, maroon, blue, and gold, applied fancy loop handle with gold dec, crackle finish, base inscribed "Eleveille Harris," French 150.00
    12-1/2" h, 9-1/2" d, cranberry shaded to clear, engraved and cut bouquets of wild roses, triple notched handle..... 150.00
    14" h, 8" w, deep red border shading to pale green and clear, highly irid surface, applied clear shaped handle.....100.00
Beaker, 4-1/2" h, German, engraved, seven irate women fighting over pair of trousers, verse..............................825.00
Bowl
    3-3/4" h, heavily walled, conical, translucent amber ground, etched graduated depths with descending, overlapping squares, etched artist's monogram of Jean Luca, c1925, French 800.00
    4-3/4" d, 3" h, colorless glass, pinched quatreform rim, green and aubergine leaves and berries against mustard colored background, sgd "Leg." (Legras) at side, "Made in France" stamped on base......................................175.00
    7-3/4" d, 3" h, splotched and mottled amber, blue, and turquoise powders within colorless glass round, internal silver foil spangles, foot inscribed "Muller Fres Luneville" 345.00
Box, cov, 5" d, 2-3/4" h, transparent green, orange-amber int., etched naturalistic crab on cov, seaweed springs around base, black etched mark "Nancea" 435.00
Centerbowl, 10-1/4" h, 9-3/4" d, half round, colorless, frosted pedestal base of figural Atlas, arms extended supporting bowl, labeled and stamped "Sevres Cristal France" 520.00
Centerpiece Set, 14" d x 5-1/2" h heavy walled bowl with folded-in edge, maroon, colorless, white, and olive green dec, matching pr of 4-1/2" h candleholders, WMF Wurttenberg...230.00
Compote, 3-3/4" h, conical lime green body, circular black glass foot, everted circular rim, black enameled lattice dec, attributed to Wiener Werkstaette, early 20th C..................225.00
Cordial Service, two 9" h decanter, nine matching 2-1/2" tumblers, stylized Art Deco foliate and orange, amber, green blue, and black enamel motif, bottles sgd "Serves" at side...700.00
Flower Holder, 6" h, 7-1/2" w, irid, diamond quilted, oyster design..60.00
Goblet, 7" h, 3" d top of bowl, hand painted magenta, yellow, and green flowers and foliage on ext., flower painted in center of int., long delicate green stem, gilt edge around green base, each numbered "350" and artist initialed "W.R." on bottom, Austrian, c1890, set of 8 ....3,600.00

Jack in the Pulpit Vase, 8-1/4" h, green, deep brown random threading, slight irid finish 125.00
Jar, 6-7/8" h, 4-3/4" d base, formed from squatty bottle, globular, elongated neck, expanded sheared mouth with string rim, pontil scar, olive amber, painted red, tan, gold, blue, white, and flesh tone dec of George Washington, sixteen star flag painted on reverse, Netherlands, c1730-60, some scaling to paint dec 1,700.00
Jar, cov, 13" h, ftd, colorless, molded and etched, crown, motto, dated "1847" 250.00
Lamp Shade
    5-1/4" h, 2-1/4" fitter rim, bell form, red striped ruffled edge, four green heart leaves, random green threading, irid amber spotted surface, Austrian, minor chips at top edge....260.00
    13-3/4" d, shallow frosted colorless body, molded fanciful floral design, sgd "Degue" at side, "France" on rim, not drilled, small unseen chip inside rim......................230.00
Lamp, table, 16" h, 11-1/2" d molded mushroom cap colorless shade, irid raised honeycomb design, adjustable turned brass lamp shaft, weighted base, Austrian........... 575.00
Marble, 1-5/8" d, end of day, blue, red, white, and yellow streaks, mica flecks, German, 1880-1915............. 425.00
Perfume, 41/4" l, tapered body, ball form knob, black glass, silver foil dec... 150.00
Pitcher, 9" h, colorless bottle body, etched all over, enameled violet blossoms, gold enhanced, mounted with elaborate silvered metal handle, spouted rim, and hinged cov imp "V (ship) S," (Verre de Serves) mark repeated on glass base.. 935.00
Pokal, cov, 11-3/4" h, colorless lead glass, hollow Sileasian stem on goblet and cov finial, goblet finely engraved with falconers and coat of arms, German inscription translates as "Let your allegiance soar as the falcons fly," small chip on cov finial base, blown and engraved in Germany, late 19th C 2,400.00
Rose Bowl
    4-1/2" h, tricorn, spotted red rose body, amber-gold irid pulled wavy banded dec, polished pontil, Austrian 575.00
    4-3/4" h, ruffled rim, purple ground, irid coin spot circles, matching vertical lines, polished pontil, Austrian.....420.00
Tea Canister, canary, crudely sheared mouth, smooth base, Russian, c1860
    4" h, sq, chamfered corners, emb sunburst motif, applied brass collar and cap, smooth base,.......................100.00
    4-3/4" h, sq, chamfered corners, emb waffle pattern on four panels, tin soldered cap, smooth base, 5/8" l chip on mouth...50.00
Vase
    3-3/4" h, oyster white, deep pink and green threading, one side of ruffled rim turned up 100.00
    4-1/8" h, 5-1/4" d, flared bowl-form, colorless body layered in black and amber, etched and engraved stylized leaf motif, dec abstractions in Josef Hoffman manner, labeled "Made in Germany" 175.00
    6-1/4" h, 9-1/2" w, deep red shading to clear, pale green mottled finish, highly irid, ruffled 850.00
    8" h, clear, Art Deco cut dec of trees, woodsman, Karhula 135.00
    8" h, opalescent, spherical form, concentric molded dot pattern, molded "VERVIL FRANCE" 400.00
    8" h, 11-1/2" d, frosted and selectively polished white bulbous ground, molded medial band of alternating male and female lions in high relief, amethyst patine in recesses, base imp "D'Avesen Made In France" 1,840.00
    9" h, oviform, orange ground, red cameo flowers shading to burgundy base, etched "Le Verre Francais France"..... 1,300.00

Vase, De Vez, cameo cut, black poppy dec, three layers, black, green, and red, 9-3/4" h, $925.

9-1/8" h, raised rim, oval ambergris body, irid and lightly etched, spotted background, elaborate overall floral dec, polished pontil, Austrian, attributed to Loetz..........460.00

9-1/4" h, colorless flattened body, enameled red and blue stylized basket of flowers painted in Marcel Goupy style, cartouche on base mkd "France" 815.00

9-1/2" h, round colorless flattened form, applied handles, polychrome enameled medallions front and back with parrots and blossoms, in Marcel Goupy manner, cartouche on base mkd "France"....................................815.00

9-3/4" h, 4" w, elongated egg-shaped, frosted green ground, enameled winter scene of houses, trees, and woman stacking wood, Legras, base numbered "#4114" 350.00

10" h, broad bulbous oval, transparent olive green, etched and selectively frosted in repeating curvilinear Art Deco elements, "Legras" etched in motif, internal blemish at mid section...800.00

10-1/2" h, transparent topaz colored goblet-form, green and yellow repeating Art Deco devices, base inscribed "M. Goupy" 1,380.00

11" h, shouldered vase, bun foot, mottled tangerine ground, etched stylized flowers and stems, acid stamped "Le Verre Francais France".......................................1,100.00

11" h, 3-1/2" d w, cylinder, finely enameled border of pink, magenta, and white poppies, stylized design at top and base, colorless center with stylized yellow, white, and light green buds and foliage, Art Nouveau style, French, c1910..675.00

11" h, 4-1/2" h, clear ground, painted and frosted in the matter of Daum, blue sailing ships against bright yellow/orange ground...100.00

12" h, raised ruffled rim, transparent royal purple body, acid textured and etched stylized Art Deco lily blossom and scrolling leaves, blue irid on raise dec, polished pontil, Austrian 920.00

12-1/4" h, 5-1/2" w, deep cobalt blue over crystal, cut band of floral and leaf design, large square star cut base, slight roughage on base...100.00

12-3/8" h, cylinder, gold irid surface, combed dec, blue-green luster, polished pontil, Austrian....................815.00

12-1/2" h, emerald green bulbed body, all over irid, mounted in bronzed metal frame with swirling foliate design, Austrian..635.00

13" h, elongated oviform, bun foot, yellow ground, orange cameo flowers shading to blue, etched "Le Verre Francais" 1,200.00

13" h, 6-1/2" w, mottled pink and yellow, white ground, five leaf-like pulled decorations near base, highly irid surface...225.00

13" h, 7" w, deep red mottled ground, swirled pattern, highly irid..200.00

14" h, tapered bulbous body, cylindrical neck, mottled yellow ground, overlaid with green shading to red, etched geometric bands, engraved "Le Verre Francais" 1,200.00

14-1/2" h, 5" w, cobalt blue, flaring rim, pedestal base, cut all over with raised panels mixed with recessed diamond and heart-shaped panels, heavy gold dec, intricate tiny leaves, slight wear to gold....................................400.00

15" h, gooseneck, cased rose glass overlaid with threading network, polished pontil, Pallme-Konig 290.00

15-1/2" h, yellow ground, stylized cameo orange scarabs, applied handle 950.00

16" h, 4" d, enameled and painted, yellow and orange sunset, green and brown landscape, sgd "Legras" 500.00

22-1/2" h, 7" w, deep emerald green shading to clear, realistic cut pattern of large oriental poppy, leaves, and buds, Austrian, attributed to Moser or Harrach................575.00

Veilleuse, (night light), 5-1/2" h, bulbous mottled green and blue shade, patinated wrought iron mount surrounded by three curling tendrils, inscribed "Robj, Paris," c1920 .... 650.00

Wine, 5-3/4" h, freeblown, engraved, colorless, large bowl with engraved bird and floral motif, lettered "Fn Die Huhe," long stem with wide knop, domed circular foot with inward rolled edge, tooled rim, pontil scar, early 19th C 325.00

FAIRY LAMPS

History: Fairy lamps, which originated in England in the 1840s, are candle-burning night lamps. They were used in nurseries, hallways, and dim corners of the home.

Two leading candle manufacturers, the Price Candle Company and the Samuel Clarke Company, promoted fairy lamps as a means to sell candles. Both contracted with glass, porcelain, and metal manufacturers to produce the needed shades and cups. For example, Clarke used Worcester Royal Porcelain Company, Stuart & Sons, and Red House Glass Works in England, plus firms in France and Germany. Clarke's trademark was a small fairy with a wand surrounded by the words "Clarke Fairy Pyramid, Trade Mark."

Fittings were produced in a wide variety of styles. Shades ranged from pressed to cut glass, from Burmese to Nailsea. Cups are found in glass, porcelain, brass, nickel, and silver plate.

American firms selling fairy lamps included Diamond Candle Company of Brooklyn, Blue Cross Safety Candle Co., and Hobbs-Brockunier of Wheeling, West Virginia.

Fairy lamps are found as two-pieces (cup and shade) and three-pieces (cup with matching shade and saucer). Married pieces are common.

References: Bob and Pat Ruf Pullin, *Fairy Lamps*, Schiffer Publishing, 1996; John F. Solverson (comp.), *Those Fascinating Little Lamps: Miniature Lamps Value Guide*, Antique Publications, 1988; Kenneth Wilson, *Americana Glass 1760-1930: The Toledo Museum of Art, Volume I, Volume II*, Hudson Hills Press and the Toledo Museum of Art, 1994.

Periodical: *Light Revival*, 35 West Elm Ave., Quincy, MA 02170; *Night Light Newsletter,* 38619 Wakefield Ct., Northville, MI 48167.

Collectors' Club: Night Light Club, 38619 Wakefield Ct., Northville, MI 48167.

Reproduction Alert: Reproductions abound.

Amber, 3-5/8" h, 3" d, pyramid, white opal swirl glass shade, clear mkd Clarke candle cup 125.00
Burmese
    4" h, acid finished pyramid dome shade, clear mkd Clarke base, two slight bruises on base............................175.00
    5-1/2" h, 7-1/2" d, Cricklite, frilly pleated skirted base, clear candle holder mkd "Clarke's Cricklite Trade Mark" 1,085.00
    5-3/4" h, undecorated dome shade, Burmese quadrafold base, clear mkd Clarke candle cup, bottom edge of shade lightly ground...325.00
    7" h, salmon pink shaded to yellow, acid finish, matching ruffled base mkd "Clarke's Patent Fairy Lamp," clear mkd Clarke candle cup, brass frame with 2 scrolling arms 825.00
Cased, 6-1/4" h, glossy aqua blue, ribbed dome shade, non-matching complimentary blue satin base, lined white set in Clarke sgd cup 225.00
Cranberry
    4-1/4" h, pyramid shade with 3 rows of down turned petals, matching cranberry petaled base, clear mkd Clarke candle cup, some of the petals have been ground and polished...150.00
    4-1/2" h, crown shape, overshot shade, clear base, clear mkd Clarke candle cup, c1887 ....220.00

Figural, 4-1/4" h, dog's head, satinized white glass, matching pyramid-sized base, blue eyes, faint caramel-colored streak runs throughout head 450.00
Nailsea
    4-3/4" h, citron ground, clear mkd Clarke Cricklite candle cup and base 190.00
    5" h, pink and white, clear mkd Clarke candle cup and base...200.00
Opalescent
    4-1/8" h, blue pyramid done shade, rose and foliage dec creamware base sgd "Clarke & Tunnicliffe" 450.00
    5-3/8" h, Cleveland Swirl, pink, white, and opaque, upward fluted base, clear mkd Clarke candle cup, several small chips on top post of base......................................600.00
    5-3/4" h, Cleveland Swirl, blue, white, and opaque, dome shade with emb ribs, 6-sided ruffled matching under bowl, clear mkd Clarke candle cup, slight roughness to base of shade, base lighter than shade.................350.00
Overshot
    3" h, 3-3/4" d, green pyramid shade, clear mkd Clarke candle cup 125.00
    3-1/2" h, yellow swirl cased pyramid shade, clear mkd Clarke candle cup 175.00
Peachblow, matching shade and base
    3-7/8" h, cream lining, acid finished rose shaded pink, black lacy flower and leaf dec, clear mkd Clarke candle cup, gold washed metal stand, attributed to Thomas Webb..... 350.00
    3-3/4" h, green leaves dec, clear mkd Clarke candle cup, attributed to Thomas Webb................................400.00
    4-1/2" h, 2-7/8" d, colorless, opalescent overshot, crown shaped pyramid shade, clear mkd Clarke candle cup, made for Queen Victoria's 1887 Jubilee 190.00
    5-1/4" h, clear mkd Clarke candle cup, Mt. Washington ..250.00
    6-3/8" h, blue, white, brown, and green enamel dec, white int., clear mkd Clarke Cricklite candle cup 425.00
Sapphire Blue, 4-5/8" h, DQ, melon ribbed, clear mkd Clarke candle cup 175.00
Satin
    3-1/2" h, 2-7/8" d, rose DQ, MOP shade, white lining, clear mkd Clarke candle cup 185.00
    3-5/8" h, apple green opaque shade, emb Swirl pattern, clear mkd Clarke candle cup 150.00
    3-3/4" h, blue Diamond Quilted, mother of pearl pyramid shade, Clarke sgd base 150.00
    3-3/4" h, pink Diamond Quilted, mother of pearl pyramid shade, Clarke sgd base 150.00
    3-3/4" h, pink cased pyramid shade with white lining, Clarke sgd base 125.00
    4" h, pale pink smocked pattern pyramid shade, Clark sgd base..100.00
    4-1/4" h, 5-3/4" w base, blue, lined cream, matching ruffled base, unsigned white satin cup 200.00
    5" h, dark pink shading to light pink dome with imp stars, ruffled inverted saucer-shaped base, clear cup 550.00
    6" d, lavender ruffled dome top, 3 gold inset jeweled medallions, ruffled base 350.00
    7-1/2" h, orange pyramid shade, 12 rows of frosted tooled loopings, make-do frosted finger shade cup 225.00
Spatter, 5-1/2" h, white spatter, chartreuse cased in crystal ground, swirled rib mold, heavy applied crystal feet and base trim, clear mkd Clarke candle cup 550.00
Vaseline, 3-1/2" h, 2-7/8" d, ribbed dome, green c mkd Clarke candle base... 175.00
Verre Moiré (Nailsea)
    4" h, red frosted ground, white loopings, clear Clarke candle cup mkd "S. Clarke's Patent Pyramid Trade Mark" and "C.W.S. Night Light" 495.00

4-3/4" h, blue dome shade, clear mkd Clarke candle cup 325.00

4-3/4" h, citron dome shade, Clarke sgd base, clear mkd Clarke candle cup 225.00

4-7/8" h, rose dome shade, Clarke sgd base, clear mkd Clarke candle cup...............................4,300.00

5-1/4" h, cranberry frosted ground, white loopings, clear base, clear mkd Clarke candle cup 250.00

6-1/4" h, citron, matching 3 cornered ftd base, clear mkd Clarke candle cup, very minor roughness to bottom edge of shade...725.00

6-1/2" h, 8" w, sweeping white loopings blend into delicate blue background, done shaped shade, triangular shaped base with pinch-in folds, clear glass cup holder with ruffled edge, sgd "S. Clarke Patent Trade Mark Fairy"....................945.00

FENTON GLASS

History: The Fenton Art Glass Company began as a cutting shop in Martins Ferry, Ohio, in 1905. In 1906, Frank L. Fenton started to build a plant in Williamstown, W.V., and produced the first piece of glass there in 1907. Early production included carnival, chocolate, custard, and pressed glass, plus mold-blown opalescent glass. In the 1920s, stretch glass, Fenton dolphins, jade green, ruby, and art glass were added.

In the 1930s, boudoir lamps, Dancing Ladies, and slag glass in various colors were produced. The 1940s saw crests of different colors being added to each piece by hand. Hobnail, opalescent, and two-color overlay pieces were popular items. Handles were added to different shapes, making the baskets they created as popular today as then.

Through the years, Fenton has beautified its glass by decorating it with hand painting, acid etching, color staining, and copper-wheel cutting. Several different paper labels have been used. In 1970, an oval raised trademark also was adopted.

References: Tom and Neila Bredehoft, *Fifty Years of Collectible Glass, 1920-1970*, Antique Trader Books, 1997; Robert E. Eaton, Jr. (comp.), *Comprehensive Price Guide to Fenton Glass: The First Twenty-Five Years, 1995*, Antique Publications, 1995, 1997 value update —, *Comprehensive Price Guide to Fenton Glass: The Second Twenty-Five Years 1995*, Antique Publications, 1995, 1997 value update; —, *Comprehensive Price Guide to Fenton Glass: The 80s' Decade*, Antique Publications, 1996, 1997 value update; Fenton Art Glass Collectors of America (comp.), *Fenton Glass: The Third Twenty-Five Years Comprehensive Price Guide, 1995*, Antique Publications, 1995; Shirley Griffith, *A Pictorial Review of Fenton White Hobnail Milk Glass*, published by author, 1984; William Heacock, *Fenton Glass: The First Twenty-Five Years* (1978), *The Second Twenty-Five Years* (1980), *The Third Twenty-Five Years* (1989), available from Antique Publications; Alan Linn, *Fenton Story of Glass Making*, Antique Publications, 1996; James Measell (ed.), *Fenton Glass: The 1980s Decade*, Antique Publications, 1996; Naomi L. Over, *Ruby Glass of the 20th Century*, Antique Publications, 1990, 1993-94 value update; Ferill J. Rice (ed.), *Caught in the Butterfly Net*, Fenton Art Glass Collectors of America, Inc., 1991; Margaret and Kenn Whitmyer, *Fenton Art Glass 1907-1939*, Collector Books, 1996.

Periodical: *Butterfly Net*, 302 Pheasant Run, Kaukauna, WI 54130.

Collectors' Clubs: Fenton Art Glass Collectors of America, Inc., P.O. Box 384, Williamstown, WV 26187; National Fenton Glass Society, P.O. Box 4008, Marietta, OH 45750; Pacific Northwest Fenton Assoc., 8225 Kilchis River Rd., Tillamook, OR 97141.

Videotape: Michael Dickensen, *Glass Artistry in the Making Fenton*, Fenton Art Glass, 1992.

Museum and Factory Tour: Fenton Art Glass Co., 420 Caroline Ave., Williamstown, WV 26187

Ashtray

#848 Mandarin Red..75.00

#3773 Dogwood Flowered Hobnail, pipe 65.00

#3810 Hobnail, milk glass, 2 pc.................................18.00

Lincoln Inn, Aqua or Ruby...25.00

Banana Bowl, #3720 Hobnail, milk glass........................ 40.00

Basket

#192 Mulberry, 10-1/2" h, c1942 ....475.00

#203 Black Rose, 7" h 250.00

#389 Cranberry Hobnail, 10-1/2" h...........................285.00

#389 Topaz Hobnail, 10-1/2" h..................................450.00

#680 Aqua Crest, 5" h, handle 120.00

#1353 Coin Dot, French Opalescent, 12" h...............200.00

#1522 Cranberry Coin Dot, 10-1/2" h........................385.00

#1523 Aqua Crest, 13" h...250.00

#1924 Coin Dot, French Opalescent, 5" h....................35.00

#3830 10" Cranberry Opal, Hobnail 95.00

#3834 Hobnail, French Opalescent, 4-1/2" 60.00

#3835 Hobnail, Cranberry Opalescent, 5-1/2" h.........125.00

#6437 Aventurine, green with blue, 11" h 125.00

#7237 Rose Crest, 7" h..45.00

#6137 Beatty Waffle, Green Opal 47.50

#6458 Vasa Murrhina, blue mist, 11" 95.00

#7437 Burmese, Maple Leaf decal 75.00

#7437 DV Violets in the Snow, milk glass 75.00

#9137 Olde Virginia Thumbprint, 7" h 30.00

#9235 Embossed Rose, 9" h..40.00

Beverage Set

#230 Celeste Blue, pitcher and six tumblers, cut 350.00

#222 Rib Optic, Blue Opalescent, six tumblers, royal blue coasters..550.00

#3967 Hobnail, Cranberry Opalescent, 80 oz pitcher, four #3947 barrel tumblers 275.00

Christmas Snowflake, Cobalt Blue water pitcher, six tumblers (L.G. Wright) 210.00

Bell

#7466 CV hp Christmas Morn 45.00

#8466 OI Faberge, Teal Marigold 55.00

#8466 RE Faberge, Rosalene 45.00

#9064 Velva Rose, Whitton 25.00

Bon Bon

#1533 Dolphin, tangerine stretch, crimped, sq 85.00

#1621 Dolphin Handled, Green 32.50

#3935 Hobnail, blue opalescent, 5", handle 30.00

#7225 Silver Turquoise, 5-1/2" h 20.00

#8230 Rosalene Butterfly, two handled 35.00

Bowl

#249 Ming, Fenton Rose, 3 ftd 110.00

#846 Pekin Blue, cupped...37.50

#848 Chinese Yellow, 8 Petal.................................45.00
#950 Mandarin Red, 11" oval..............................125.00
#1562 Satin Etched Silvertone, oblong bowl 55.00
#1601 Ebony, oval, dolphin handles, ftd..................145.00
#1605 Stag and Holly, green, ftd.........................130.00
#1800 Sheffield, halo etching, 11-1/2" d 50.00
#7221 Silver Crest, 10" d, yellow jonquil dec, gold trim......46.00
#7224 Aqua Crest, 13" d.................................130.00
#7224 Silver Crest, 10" d.................................50.00
#7423 Milk Glass bowl, hp Yellow roses.....................65.00
#8222 Rosalene, Basketweave..............................30.00
#9020 Peach Crest, 10" d.................................90.00
#9020 Peach Crest, Charleton dec........................105.00
Cake Plate, #7213 Ebony Crest, 13" d.........................135.00
Candlestick
#950 Ming, pink, pr....................................130.00
#951 Silver Crest Cornucopia, single.....................37.50
#3974 Hobnail Topaz Opalescent 60.00
#7272 Silver Crest, single 17.50
Candy Box, cov
#7258 Thumbprint, pink, oval.............................30.00
#7380 Custard hp Pink Daffodils Louise Piper dated March
1975...160.00
#9282 Rose, orange.....................................35.00
#9394 UE 3 pc. Ogee, Blue Burmese......................110.00
#9394 RE 3 pc. Ogee, Rosalene.........................100.00
Ruby Iridized, Butterfly, for FAGCA 100.00
Candy Dish, cov
#835 Aquamarine......................................70.00
#835 Cameo Opalescent 45.00
Hobnail Topaz Opalescent, ftd 130.00
Comport
#3728 PO Plum Opal Hobnail 5-1/2" 75.00
#7228 Emerald Crest, ftd................................30.00
#8422 Flowered, ftd. Rosalene 30.00
#8422 Waterlily ftd, Rosalene............................30.00
#9222, Blue Marble Roses...............................25.00
Cocktail Shaker, #6120 Plymouth, Crystal.....................55.00
Condiment Set, #3809 Hobnail, 7 pc.........................40.00
Console Bowl, Ming, oval
Green 85.00
Pink...85.00
Console Set, #1900 Daisy and Button, mermaid blue, pr 2-lite
candlesticks, cloverleaf bowl 190.00
Cracker Jar, #1681 Big Cookies
Jade 125.00
Lilac, no lid, handle...................................250.00
Creamer
#1502 Diamond Optic, Black.............................35.00
#1502 Diamond Optic, Ruby.............................30.00
#1924 Coin Dot, cranberry opalescent, 4" h................75.00
#6464 RG Aventurine Green w/Pink, Vasa Murrhina 45.00
Creamer and Sugar, cov
#489 Hobnail, Topaz Opalescent, miniature................25.00
#1903 Daisy and Button, Blue Opalescent.................35.00
#9103 Fine Cut & Block (OVG) 20.00
Creatures (Animals and Birds)
Alley Cat
Burmese 75.00
Pink Carnival......................................75.00
Stiegel Green Carnival 75.00
#5174 Springtime Green Iridized Blown Rabbit...........45.00
#5178 Springtime Green Iridized Blown Owl...............45.00
#5193 RE Rosalene Fish, paperweight....................25.00
#5197 Happiness Bird, Cardinals in Winter................32.50
#5197 Happiness Bird, Rosalene 40.00

Cruet
#208 Coin Dot, 7" h
Cranberry 150.00
French Opalescent.................................100.00
#7701 QJ 7" Burmese, Petite Floral....................175.00
Cup and Saucer, #7208
Aqua Crest...35.00
Emerald Crest 45.00
Decanter Set
#389 Blue Opalescent, decanter and four wines........250.00
#3761 Hobnail, Cranberry Opalescent 375.00
Epergne
#3701 Hobnail, milk glass, 4 pc..........................60.00
#3801 Hobnail, milk glass, 4 pc..........................50.00
#3902 Petite Blue, Opal 4" h............................125.00
#3902 Petite French Opal, 4" h...........................40.00
#7308 SC Silver Crest, 3 Horn..........................125.00
Fairy Light
#1167 RV Rose Magnolia Hobnail 3 pc. Persian Pearl Crest,
Signed Shelly Fenton.................................80.00
#3380 CR Hobnail, 3 pc. Cranberry Opal.................75.00
#3608 Hobnail amber, 2 pc.............................30.00
#3804 CA Hobnail 3 pc. Colonial Amber 25.00
#3804 CG Hobnail 3 pc. Colonial Green 20.00
#8406 WT Heart, Wisteria...............................65.00
#8406 PE Heart, Shell Pink.............................25.50
#8408 BA Persian Medallion 3 pc. Blue Satin.............35.00
#8408 VR Persian Medallion, 3 pc. Velva Rose–75th
Anniv..75.00
Flower Pot, #401 Snow Crest ,green........................... 35.00
Fruit Bowl, #846 Mandarin Red, 9-3/4" d, black glass stand ..85.00
Ginger Jar
#893 Persian Pearl w/base and top 150.00
#893 Crystal, wisteria satin etching, 3 pc 125.00
Goblet
#203 Silver Crest.......................................60.00
#1620 Plymouth, ruby 22.00
#1700 Lincoln Inn, royal blue............................30.00
#1942 Flower Windows Blue 55.00
Guest Set, 2 pc
#200, Florentine Green..................................375.00
Opal Curtain Optic, topaz, blue handle 1,350.00
Hat
#1922 Peach Crest, 10" h..............................125.00
#1922 Swirl Optic, French Opalescent 110.00
Hurricane Lamp, Topaz Opal Daisy and Fern 300.00
Hurricane Shade, Snow Crest, emerald green 95.00
Jug
#192 Diamond Optic, 8", handle, mulberry................230.00
#6068 Cased Lilac, Handled, 6-1/2" 50.00
#7264 Aqua Crest, 9" h, handle, roses dec................70.00
Hobnail, blue opalescent, 4-1/2" 70.00
Lamp
#670 boudoir
Black embossed, satin shade.......................200.00
Coin Spot, French Opalescent.......................225.00
Jade 250.00
Pink, floral cut....................................250.00
#1790 Colonial, orange, courting, oil 65.00
#2606 Candy Stripe French Colonial, 20" 650.00
#2700 Ruby Overlay Mariners..........................150.00
#3782 CA Courting, Amber Hobnail, Kerosene...........65.00
#7312 BD Hurricane Candle Lamp, 5 Petal Blue Dog-
wood..75.00
#7398 Black Rose, Hurricane, White Base, 9" h 100.00
Lavabo, #3867 Hobnail, milk glass.............................. 130.00

Of course Shelley is too young to court . . .

. . . but it really doesn't matter, for her Fenton Courting Lamps are actually lamps of many uses.

In the bedroom, in the living room, or wherever these richly colored lamps are used, they add a gentle light.

Adapted to oil or electricity, the attractive price and versatility of these handmade "early American" lamps will lead many of your customers to buy them in pairs.

May we send you our catalog?

Suggest Fenton Courting Lamps for the patio — They will make every party an occasion.

THE FENTON ART GLASS COMPANY • WILLIAMSTOWN, WEST VIRGINIA

Ad, lovely young lady with several examples of Fenton Art Glass wares. China Glass & Tablewares, February 1962.

Liquor Set, #1934 Flower Stopper, floral silver overlay, 8 pc
  set...250.00
Liquor Tray, #1934, light blue satin, 12".........................140.00
Mayonnaise Set, #3903 Hobnail, Cranberry Opalescent,
  3 pcs..150.00
Mother's Day Plate, 1979, amethyst carnival, Madonna of the
  Rose Hedge, orig box, stand, and literature.............25.00
Mustard, cov, spoon, #3889 MI, hobnail 35.00
Nut Bowl
  #3428 Cactus, Topaz Opalescent, Levay....................25.00
  Sailboats, Marigold Carnival 50.00
Paperweight, eagle, chocolate, orig literature 25.00
Pitcher
  #100 Honeycomb & Clover, Crystal/Gold 45.00
  #821 Cannonball, cobalt dec.....................................150.00
  #1653 Ming Green, black handle................................165.00
  #9166 Jacqueline, honey amber.................................75.00
  Burmese, hp log cabin scene 275.00
  Christmas Snowflake, Cranberry Opal, water (L.G.
    Wright)...350.00
  Coin Dot, Cranberry Opalescent, #1353....................250.00
  Daisy & Fern, Topaz Opal, water (L.G. Wright)...........170.00
  Dot Optic, Cranberry Opalescent 250.00
  Plum Opal, Hobnail, water, 80 oz..............................190.00
Plate
  #107 Ming Rose 8" 30.00
  #175 Leaf, Blue Opalescent, 7" d 25.00
  #1614 9-1/2" Green Opal with Label New World 65.00
  #1621 Dolphin Handled, Fenton Rose, 6" 25.00
  #1720 Emerald Crest, 10" d 50.00
  #5118 Leaf, 11" Rosalene (Sample)............................120.00
  Lafayette & Washington, Light Blue Iridized, Sample.....80.00
Powder Box
  #6080 Blue Overlay, Wave Crest 90.00
  #6080 Coral, Wave Crest 226.00
Rose Bowl
  Black Rose, 6-1/2" 40.00
  Crystal, Wisteria satin etching, crimped, #894 ....35.00
  Silver Crest, 6" d, ftd...55.00
Salt and Pepper Shakers, pr
  #1605 Rib Optic, Cranberry Opalescent 95.00
  #1605 Rib Optic, Lime Opalescent..............................85.00
  #3806 Hobnail, Cranberry Opalescent, flat 50.00
Sandwich Tray, #1502 Emerald Crest, 10" d, handle 160.00
Sherbet
  #1620 Plymouth, Amber..15.00
  #1700 Lincoln Inn, ruby..25.00
  #1942 Flower Windows, Crystal 35.00
  #4441 Small, Thumbprint, Colonial Blue......................35.00
  #4443 Thumbprint, Colonial Blue................................20.00
Slipper, Hobnail
  Blue Opalescent..25.00
  Crystal 20.00
  Milk Glass, white 15.00
Temple Jar
  #7488 Chocolate Roses on Cameo Satin.....................25.00
  Cranberry Swirl, 3 pc, c1939 ....250.00
Tid-Bit Tray, #7294 Aqua Crest, 2 tiers............................70.00
Toothpick Holder
  Daisy and Button, chocolate, hat shape......................45.00
  Hobnail, Topaz Opalescent 35.00
  Strawberry, Carnival, orange 12.00
Tumbler
  #1634 Diamond Optic, Aqua 6.00
  #3700, Grecian Gold, grape cut 15.00
  #9242 Roses 12.00

Vase
  #186 Aqua Crest, 8" sq 60.00
  #194 Coin Dot, 11" h, double crimped, blue opalescent . 160.00
  #194 Coin Dot, 11" h, 2 handle, blue opalescent........160.00
  #389 Hobnail, 8" h, ftd, blue opalescent 60.00
  #711 Ivy Green, 5" h 70.00
  #847 Mandarin Red, fan, 5-1/2" h 60.00
  #847 Periwinkle Blue, fan..62.50
  #894 Spiral Optic, blue opalescent, 10" h
    Flared 130.00
    Tulip 140.00
  #1452 Peach Crest, 13-1/2" 150.00
  #3756 Plum Opal, bud, 8" h 35.00
  #3759 Plum Opal, Hobnail, Swung 150.00
  #5155 Peach Crest, 10-1/2" h, hand 360.00
  #7258 Silver Crest, 8" h 50.00
  #7357 Crystal Crest, fan, 6-1/4" h 85.00
  #7460 Amberina Overlay crimped, 6-1/2" 80.00
  #7547 Burmese, hp Pink Dogwood, 5-1/2" h 75.00
  #8254 Mermaid Planter/Vase, Dark Carnival 100.00
  #8802 12" French Blue, Oval, Sandcarved 160.00
  Aristocrat Bud Vase, #98 Cutting, Fenton Rose...........45.00
  Art Glass, vaseline with white opalescence, two applied co-
    balt blue handles and rim, 10" h, 6" w 1,100.00
  Fan Vase, Rose Crest, 6-1/2" h 70.00
  Hand Vase, Aqua Crest 290.00
  Hanging Heart, opaque jade green ground, cobalt blue rim,
    irid surface, 11-1/2" h, 6" w.................................1,700.00
  Ivory Crest, 10" 65.00
Wine Bottle, #1667 Rib Optic, cranberry 190.00

FINDLAY ONYX GLASS

History: Findlay onyx glass, produced by Dalzell, Gilmore & Leighton Company, Findlay, Ohio, was patented for the firm in 1889 by George W. Leighton. Due to high production costs resulting from a complex manufacturing process, the glass was made only for a short time.

Layers of glass were plated to a bulb of opalescent glass through repeated dippings into a glass pot. Each layer was cooled and reheated to develop opalescent qualities. A pattern mold then was used to produce raised decorations of flowers and leaves. A second mold gave the glass bulb its full shape and form.

A platinum luster paint, producing pieces identified as silver or platinum onyx, was applied to the raised decorations. The color was fixed in a muffle kiln. Other colors such as cinnamon, cranberry, cream, raspberry, and rose were achieved by using an outer glass plating which reacted strongly to reheating. For example, a purple or orchid color came from the addition of manganese and cobalt to the glass mixture.

References: Neila and Tom Bredenhoft, *Findlay Toothpick Holders*, Cherry Hill Publications, 1995; James Measell and Don E. Smith, *Findlay Glass: The Glass Tableware Manufacturers, 1886-1902*, Antique Publications, 1986; Kenneth Wilson, *American Glass 1760-1930: The Toledo Museum of Art, Volume I, Volume II,* Hudson Hills Press and The Toledo Museum of Art, 1994.

Collectors' Club: Collectors of Findlay Glass, P.O. Box 256, Findlay, OH 45839.

Spooner, cinnamon ground, tulip, daisy, and thistle motif, 4-1/4" h, $650.

Bowl
  7" d, 2-3/4" h, silver onyx 320.00
  7-1/2" d, cream onyx 390.00
  7-1/2" d, raspberry onyx...425.00
Butter Dish, cov, 5-1/2" d, silver onyx 850.00
Celery, 6-1/4" h, cream 450.00
Creamer, 4-1/2" h, platinum colored dec, opalescent glass handle
  Cream onyx..525.00
  Raspberry onyx..550.00
Dresser Box, cov, 5" d, cream, round............................675.00
Mustard, cov, 3" h, hinged metal cov, orig spoon mkd "sterling"
  Cream onyx..400.00
  Raspberry onyx..600.00
Pitcher
  7-1/2" h, cream, applied opalescent handle, polished rim
    chip...800.00
  8" h, cream onyx, amber florals and handle, minor bubbles
    in inner liner...700.00
Salt and Pepper Shakers, pr, 3" h, platinum onyx 550.00
Spooner, 4-1/2" h
  Cream onyx, bright silver dec, few small rim flakes....485.00
  Platinum blossoms, rough edge 265.00
  Raspberry onyx..650.00
Sugar Bowl, cov, 5-1/2" h
  Cream onyx..475.00
  Raspberry onyx..650.00
Sugar Shaker, 6" h
  Raspberry onyx..495.00
  Silver onyx...400.00
Syrup, 7" h, 4" w, silver dec, applied opalescent handle....1,150.00
Toothpick Holder, 2-1/2" h
  Cinnamon onyx 425.00
  Cream onyx, metallic silver dec, minimal flaking at rim... 475.00
Tumbler, raspberry onyx, Floradine pattern 785.00
Water Set, water pitcher, four barrel-shaped tumblers,
  cream 2,500.00

FIRE-KING

History: Fire-King dinnerware and kitchenware were products of the Anchor Hocking Glass Corporation. In 1905, Isaac J. Collins founded the Hocking Glass Company along the banks of the Hocking River near Lancaster, Ohio. On March 6, 1924, fire completely destroyed the plant, but it was rebuilt in six months.

Hocking produced pressed glass dinnerware, many patterns of which are considered Depression glass. In 1937, Hocking Glass Company merged with the Anchor Cap Company and became Anchor Hocking Glass Corporation. Shortly thereafter, the new company began to manufacture glass ovenware that could withstand high temperatures in a kitchen oven.

Production of oven-proof glass marked "FIRE-KING" began in 1942 and lasted until 1976. Dinnerware patterns include Alice, Charm, Fleurette, Game Bird, Honeysuckle, Jane Ray, Laurel, Primrose, Turquoise Blue, Swirl, and Wheat. Utilitarian kitchen items and ovenware patterns also were produced.

Housewives eagerly purchased Fire-King sets and could also assemble sets of matching dinnerware and ovenware patterns. Advertising encouraged consumers to purchase prepackaged starter, luncheon, baking, and snack sets, as well as casseroles. Oven glassware items included almost everything needed to completely stock the kitchen.

Fire-King patterns are found in azurite, forest green, gray, ivory, jadeite, peach luster, pink, plain white, ruby red, sapphire blue, opaque turquoise, and white with an assortment of rim colors. To increase sales, decals were applied. Collectors tend to focus on the older patterns and colors, as well as ovenware items.

Fire-King was sold in sets. Add an additional 25-35% to the price of the individual pieces for an intact set in its original box.

Anchor Hocking used a molded mark for Fire-King, as well as oval foil paper labels.

References: Gene Florence, *Anchor Hocking's Fire King & More,* Collector Books, 1998; ——, *Collectible Glassware from the 40's, 50's, 60's,* 4th ed., Collector Books, 1998; ——, *Kitchen Glassware of the Depression Years*, 5th ed., Collector Books, 1995, 1997 value update; Shirley Glyndon, *The Miracle in Grandmother's Kitchen,* published by author, 1983; Gary and Dale Kilgo and Jerry and Gail Wilkins, *Collectors Guide to Anchor Hocking's Fire-King Glassware*, K & W Collectibles Publisher, 1991; ——, *Collectors Guide to Anchor Hocking's Fire-King Glassware, Volume II,*, K & W Collectibles Publisher, 1998; April M. Tvorak, *Fire-King*, 5th ed., published by author (P.O. Box 126, Canon City, CO 81215), 1997; ——, *Fire-King '95*, published by author, 1995; ——, *Fire-King II*, published by author, 1993; ——, *History And Price Guide to Fire-King*, VAL Enterprises, 1992

Periodicals: *Fire-King Monthly*, P.O. Box 70594, Tuscaloosa, AL 35407; *Fire-King News*, K & W Collectibles, Inc., P.O. Box 374, Addison, AL 35540.

Collectors' Club: Fire-King Collectors Club, 1406 E. 14th St., Des Moines, IA 50316.

Alice pattern, cup and saucer, Jade-ite, $12

Dinnerware

Alice Jade-ite, white with blue trim, and white with red trim, Introduced as Quaker Oats premium, 1945.
Cup and Saucer
    Jade-ite...12.00
    White, blue trim...15.00
    White, red trim 20.00
Plate, 9-1/2" d
    Jade-ite...22.00
    White, blue trim...24.00
    White, red trim 27.50

Anniversary Rose. Translucent white, rose design, 22K gold trim, heat resistant, 1964-65.
Berry Bowl 4.00
Creamer 5.00
Cup and Saucer 5.00
Plate
    7-3/8" d, salad 4.00
    10" d, dinner 4.50
Platter, 9" x 12" 7.00
Soup Bowl 6.00
Sugar, cov 5.00
Vegetable Bowl 6.00

Blue Mosaic. Solid white, blue mosaic pattern, 1966-68.
Berry Bowl 4.00
Creamer 5.00
Cup and Saucer 4.50
Plate
    7-1/4 to 7-3/8" d, salad 6.00
    10" d, dinner 8.00
Salad Bowl 5.00
Soup Bowl 6.00
Sugar, cov 5.00
Vegetable Bowl 6.50

Bubble. Heat resistant, often found with blue and silver paper labels, 1930s-60s.
Berry Bowl, blue 17.50
Bowl, 8-3/8" d, Peach Lustre 8.00
Cereal Bowl, blue 15.00
Creamer and Sugar, white 7.50
Cup and Saucer, blue 6.00
Mug, Peach Lustre 3.00
Plate, blue
    7" d, salad...4.00
    9-1/4" d, dinner 8.00

    9-1/4" d, grill 14.00
Soup Bowl 16.00
Vegetable Bowl 6.00
Candleglow
Cake Plate, 9" d, round 9.00
Casserole, 1-1/2" sq, knob cover 9.00
Custard Cup 2.00
Charm. Azur-ite and Jade-ite, square shapes, 1950s.
Bowl, 4-3/4" d, Azur-ite..5.00
Cereal Bowl, 6" d, Azur-ite 18.00
Creamer
    Azur-ite 6.50
    Jade-ite..17.00
Cup and Saucer
    Azur-ite 11.00
    Jade-ite..12.00
Plate
    6-5/8" d, salad, Jade-ite...5.00
    7-1/4", dessert, Azur-ite...15.00
    8-3/8" d, luncheon, Azur-ite 7.00
    9-1/2" d, dinner, Azur-ite.......................................20.00
    9-1/2" d, dinner, Jade-ite.......................................25.00
Platter, 11" x 8"
    Azur-ite 15.00
    Jade-ite..30.00
Salad Bowl, 7-3/8" d
    Azur-ite 15.00
    Jade-ite..30.00
Sugar
    Azur-ite 6.00
    Jade-ite..17.00
Children's Ware, alphabet mug 12.00
Colonial Lady, snack set, ruby and crystal 10.00
Country Kitchens, cake plate, 9" d, ...5.00
Diamond, mug, Peach Lustre 3.00
Fishscale, demitasse cup and saucer, Lustre.................35.00
Game Bird. White background, four different decals, heat resistant.
Ashtray 5.00
Chili Bowl, 5" d 5.00
Creamer, Pheasant dec 10.00
Dessert Bowl
    Canada Goose dec 5.00
    Mallard Duck dec 5.00
    Pheasant dec 5.00

Bubble pattern, platter, sapphire blue, orig label, 12" l, $18.

Mug
  Canada Goose dec 10.00
  Mallard Duck dec 10.00
  Ruffled Grouse dec 12.00
Plate, 10" d, dinner
  Canada Goose dec 9.00
  Mallard Duck dec 9.00
  Pheasant dec 9.00
  Ruffled Grouse dec 9.00
Sugar, Pheasant dec 10.00
Tumbler
  Canada Goose dec 22.00
  Mallard Duck dec 12.00
  Pheasant dec 12.00
  Ruffled Grouse dec 12.00
Golden Shell Swirl. Milk white swirl, 22K gold scalloped edg-
  es, ovenproof, 1963-76.
  Berry Bowl, 4-7/8" d 4.00
  Cereal Bowl 6.00
  Creamer and Sugar, ftd 7.00
  Cup and Saucer 5.00
  Demitasse Cup and Saucer 12.00
  Dessert Bowl, 4-3/4" d 2.00
  Plate
    7-1/2" d, salad 3.00
    9" d, dinner 5.00
  Soup Plate, flat, 7-5/8" d 6.00
  Souvenir Plate, 10" d, World's Fair, 1964 ....45.00
  Vegetable Bowl 8.00
Honeysuckle, cup and saucer 6.00
Ivory, snack set, gold trim 5.00
Jade-ite. Restaurant Ware, heat resistant. 1950-56.
  Berry Bowl, small 6.00
  Bowl, 10" d 15.00
  Butter Dish, cov 75.00
  Cereal Bowl, flared 18.00
  Chili Bowl 12.00
  Coffee Mug, 7 oz 10.00
  Cup and Saucer 10.00
  Demitasse Cup and Saucer 70.00
  Egg Cup, double 20.00
  Hot Chocolate Mug 20.00
  Milk Pitcher 32.00
  Plate
    5-1/2" d, bread and butter 4.00
    6-3/4" d, pie or salad 6.00
    8" d, luncheon 10.00
    8-7/8" d, oval, partitioned 20.00
    9" d, dinner 15.00
    9-5/8" d, grill, 3 sections 15.00
    9-5/8" d, grill, 5 sections 18.00
    9-3/4" l, oval, sandwich 15.00
  Platter, 11-1/2" l, oval 20.00
  Refrigerator Dish, 4" x 4", clear top 18.00
  Relish, 5-part 18.00
Jane Ray. Made in Ivory, Jade-ite, Peach Lustre, white, and
  white with gold trim. First jade colored heat resistant din-
  nerware, 1945-63.
  Cereal Bowl
    Ivory 8.00
    Jade-ite 15.00
    White 8.00
  Chili Bowl
    Ivory 8.00
    Jade-ite 6.00
    White 8.00

Creamer and Sugar
  Ivory 19.00
  Jade-ite 10.00
  Peach Lustre 20.00
  White 19.00
Cup and Saucer
  Ivory 7.00
  Jade-ite 8.00
  Peach Lustre 10.00
  White 9.00
Oatmeal Bowl, 8" d
  Ivory 8.00
  Jade-ite 10.00
  White 8.00
Plate
  7-3/4" d, salad, ivory or white 9.00
  9-1/8" d, dinner, Jade-ite 10.00
Soup Bowl
  Ivory 8.00
  Jade-ite 16.00
Starter Set, Jade-ite, 12 pcs, orig box, orig labels 75.00
Vegetable Bowl, 8-1/4" d
  Ivory 14.00
  Jade-ite 18.00
  White 14.00
Leaf and Blossom
  Bowl 9.00
  Plate, 10" d, dinner, green and pink 8.00
Meadow Green
  Bowl, 4-1/2" d 4.00
  Plate
    7-1/4" d, salad 4.00
    10" d, dinner 5.00
  Soup Bowl 6.00
Milano, pitcher, aqua, ice lip 35.00
Peach Lustre. Copper tinted lustre, scratches easily, heat resis-
  tant, 1951-65.
  Creamer
    Gray Laurel 5.00
    Peach Lustre 2.50
  Cup and Saucer
    Gray Laurel 5.50
    Peach Lustre 6.00
  Custard Cup, ruffled, Peach Lustre 1.00
  Dessert Bowl, 4-7/8"
    Gray Laurel 4.50
    Peach Lustre 4.00
  Plate
    7-1/2" d, salad, Peach Lustre 3.00
    9" d, Gray Laurel 8.00
    9" d, dinner, Peach Lustre 6.50
  Serving Plate, 11" d
    Gray Laurel 15.00
    Peach Lustre 14.00
  Soup Bowl, 7-5/8" d
    Gray Laurel 6.00
    Peach Lustre 6.50
  Sugar, ftd
    Gray Laurel 6.00
    Peach Lustre 2.50
  Vegetable Bowl, 8-1/4" d
    Gray Laurel 12.00
    Peach Lustre 9.00
Philbe. Made in blue, crystal, green and pink, from 1937-38.
  Candy Jar, cov, 4" d, low, blue 800.00
  Cereal Bowl, 5-1/2" d
    Blue 65.00

Crystal 20.00
Green...42.00
Pink 42.00
Cookie Jar, cov, crystal.......................................625.00
Creamer, 3-1/4" h, ftd
    Blue 135.00
    Crystal 40.00
    Green...115.00
    Pink 115.00
Cup and Saucer
    Blue 225.00
    Crystal 95.00
    Green...175.00
    Pink 175.00
Iced Tea Tumbler, ftd
    Blue 165.00
    Crystal 90.00
Plate
    6" d, sherbet, crystal.......................................35.00
    8" d, luncheon, blue..50.00
    8" d, luncheon, green or pink 40.00
    10-1/2" d, grill, blue 75.00
Sandwich Plate, 10" d
    Blue 110.00
    Crystal 30.00
    Green...65.00
    Pink 65.00
Sherbet, 4-3/4" h, blue....................................1,500.00
Sugar, 3-1/4" h, ftd
    Blue 135.00
    Crystal 40.00
    Green...115.00
    Pink 115.00
Tumbler, ftd, blue 175.00
Primrose, sugar, open 4.00
Red Rose, mug 3.00
Royal Ruby #R4000
Bowl
    4-1/2" d 6.00
    6-1/2" d 15.00
Creamer 6.00
Cup and Saucer 8.00
Dessert Bowl 6.00
Plate
    Dinner 10.00
    Salad 10.00
Saucer 2.00
Sugar..6.00
Sapphire Blue Light blue, also made in Ovenware.
Cereal Bowl, 6" d..22.00
Custard Cup, 5 oz 3.00
Mug 25.00
Hot Plate, tab handle..16.00
Utility Bowl
    6-7/8" d 16.00
    10-7/8" d 22.00
Shell. Molded swirl design, scalloped edge, 1963.
Berry Bowl, Jade-ite 6.00
Creamer, Jade-ite 7.50
Cup and Saucer, Jade-ite......................................6.00
Demitasse Cup and Saucer, Lustre 6.00
Fruit Bowl, Jade-ite 7.00
Plate
    7" d, salad, Jade-ite...6.50
    10" d, lustre 10.00
Sugar, Peach Lustre, cov.......................................8.00

Vegetable Bowl, Lustre 6.00
Swirl. Made in Azure-ite, ivory, ivory with gold trim, ivory with red trim, Jade-ite, pink, sunrise, white, and white with gold trim.
Bowl
    Lustre, 8-1/2" d...11.00
    Sunrise..8.00
Creamer, flat
    Azure-ite 6.00
    Ivory 4.00
    Pink 9.00
    White 4.50
Creamer, ftd
    Ivory 5.00
    Jade-ite 6.00
    White 5.00
    White with trim 6.00
Cup and Saucer
    Azur-ite 8.50
    Ivory 4.00
    Jade-ite 6.00
    Pink 4.00
    White 7.00
    White with trim 10.00
Plate
    7-1/8" d, salad, azur-ite 6.50
    7-1/8" d, salad, jade-ite 8.50
    7-1/8" d, salad, sunrise 8.00
    9-1/8" d, dinner, azur-ite 9.50
    9-1/8" d, dinner, ivory 4.50
    9-1/8" d, dinner, jade-ite 11.00
Platter, 12" x 9"
    Azur-ite 18.00
    Ivory 7.00
    Sunrise..20.00
    White 7.00
    White with trim 20.00
Soup Bowl, 7-5/8" d
    Azur-ite 9.00
    Ivory 8.00
    Jade-ite 8.50
    Pink 12.00
    White 4.00
    White with trim 5.00
Sugar, flat, tab handles
    Azure-ite 6.00
    Ivory 4.00
    Pink 9.00
    White 4.50
Sugar, ftd, open handles
    Ivory 5.00
    Jade-ite 6.00
    White 5.00
    White with trim 6.00
Three Band, cup, Peach Lustre 2.00
Turquoise Blue. Some pieces with 22K gold trim, heat resistant, 1957-58.
Bowl, 8" d 15.00
Cereal Bowl, 5" d 12.00
Creamer 6.00
Cup...3.00
Deviled Egg Plate, gold edge 15.00
Mug 10.00
Plate
    7" d 11.00
    9" d 7.00
Relish, 3-part, gold trim 12.00

Saucer
    Round 75
    Square 1.00
Snack Set, plate with ring and cup, gold trim 9.00
Soup Bowl, 6-5/8" d 16.00
Sugar 7.00
Vegetable Bowl, 8" d 9.75

Vienna Lace
Creamer 2.50
Dessert Bowl 2.00
Plate, 10" d, dinner 3.00
Platter, oval 8.00
Sugar, cov 5.00
Vegetable Bowl, 8-1/4" 8.00

Wheat
Bowl, 4-5/8" d 3.00
Platter 10.00

Kitchenware

Batter Bowl, 7-1/2" d, 1 handle
    Jade-ite..24.00
    White, hand painted floral 20.00
Butter Dish, clear lid, 2-3/4" x 6-3/4"
    Clear 5.00
    Ivory 9.00
    Jade-ite..17.50
Casserole, 10 oz, individual size, tab handle, Sapphire
    Blue 13.00
Coffee Maker, Silex, 2 cup, 2 pc 20.00
Hot Plate, Sapphire Blue, handle 22.00
Loaf Pan, Sapphire Blue, 9" x 5" 20.00
Measuring Cup, Sapphire Blue, 1 spout 18.00
Mixing Bowl
    Beaded Rim, 4-7/8" d, white 6.00
    Sapphire Blue, turned rim 23.00
    Swirl
        6" d, jadeite...12.00
        9" d, white 10.00
    Turquoise Blue
        Quart, round 13.00
        Quart, tear shape...15.00
Mixing Bowl Set, 6", 7", 8", ivory swirl 30.00
Mug
    Jade-ite..8.00
    Sapphire Blue, thick 30.00
Nurser, Sapphire Blue, 4 oz 8.50
Pie Plate, Sapphire Blue, 8" d 7.00
Refrigerator Dish
    4-1/2 x 5-1/2", open, jadeite 16.00
    5 x 9", cov, emb lid, jadeite 40.00
Table Server, Sapphire Blue 20.00
Utility Bowl, Sapphire Blue
    6-7/8" d 15.00
    8-1/4" d 18.00

Ovenware

Baker, Sapphire Blue, 6 oz, individual 3.25
Cake Pan, 8" sq, Primrose, white, decal 9.00
Casserole, cov
    Ivory, knob, 1-1/2 qt, knob lid.....................................15.00
    Peach Lustre, copper tint, French-style, tab lids, orig
        label 5.00
    Sapphire Blue, 1 pint...14.00
Custard Cup, 6 oz
    Crystal, orig label 2.00

Ovenware, cov individual casserole, light blue, $8.50.

    Sapphire Blue...3.00
Loaf Pan, Sapphire Blue 16.00
Mixing Bowl Set, nested, 3 bowls 60.00
Mug 27.50
Nurser, 4 oz 15.00
Percolator Top, Sapphire Blue 5.00
Pie Plate
    Crystal, 10 oz, deep, orig label 3.00
    Ivory, 15 oz 16.00
    Sapphire Blue, 9-1/2" d 7.00
Pie Plate Cover, Sapphire Blue, 9" d 15.00
Popcorn Popper, Sapphire Blue 35.00
Roaster, 2 pcs
    8-3/4" l...50.00
    10-3/8" l...75.00
Set, Peach Lustre, copper tint, 1-1/2 qt casserole, 5 x 9"
    deep loaf, 9" d pie plate, 6 x 10" utility pan, 8" round cake
    plan, 6 oz custard cup, orig box and labels 45.00
Table Server, Sapphire Blue 19.00
Utility Bowl, Sapphire Blue, 7" d 12.00

FLASKS

History: A flask, which usually has a narrow neck, is a container for liquids. Early American glass companies frequently formed them in molds which left a relief design on the front and/or back. Historical flasks with a portrait, building, scene, or name are the most desirable.

A chestnut is hand-blown, small, and has a flattened bulbous body. The pitkin has a blown globular body with a spiral rib overlay on vertical ribs. Teardrop flasks are generally fiddle-shaped and have a scroll or geometric design. Pocket flasks are generally small enough to fit conveniently in a pocket and can have a variety of designs.

Dimensions may differ for the same flask because of the variations in the molding process. Color is an important pricing factor, with scarcer colors demanding higher prices. Aqua and amber are the most common colors. Flasks found with a "sickness" or opalescent scaling which obscures the clarity, are worth much less.

Decorators have long favored the shapes and colors of flasks and often included them in decorating schemes. Of course, reproduction flasks were soon made to meet this need.

References: Gary Baker et al., *Wheeling Glass 1829-1939*, Oglebay Institute, 1994, distributed by Antique Publications; Ralph and Terry Kovel, *Kovels' Bottles Price List*, 10th ed., Crown Publishers, 1996; George L. and Helen McKearin, *American Glass*, Crown Publishers, 1941 and 1948; John Odell, *Digger Odell's Official Antique Bottle and Glass Collector Magazine Price Guide Series*, Vol. 3, published by author (1910 Shawhan Rd., Morrow, OH 45152), 1995; Michael Polak, *Bottles Identification and Price Guide, 2nd Edition,* Avon Books, 1997; Kenneth Wilson, *American Glass 1760-1930*, 2 vols., Hudson Hills Press and The Toledo Museum of Art, 1994.

Periodical: *Antique Bottle & Glass Collector*, P.O. Box 187, East Greenville, PA 18041.

Collectors' Clubs: Federation of Historical Bottle Clubs, 88 Sweetbriar Branch, Longwood, FL 32750; The National American Glass Club, Ltd., P.O. Box 8489, Silver Spring, MD 20907.

Chestnut
   4-3/4" h, Zanesville, OH, blown, 24 vertical ribs, amber, half pint, minor wear...250.00
   10" h, Germany, 1650-1700, freeblown, olive yellow, sheared mouth, applied decorated string rim, smooth base ... 325.00
Historical
   Baltimore Monument-Sloop, Baltimore Glass Works, Baltimore, MD, 1840-60, light yellow with olive tone, sheared mouth, pontil scar, half pint, some ext. high point wear and scratches..2,100.00
   Clasped Hands-Cannon, Pittsburgh district, Pittsburgh, PA 1860-80
      Aquamarine, applied collared mouth with ring, smooth base, pint, McKearin GXII-41, some minor int. haze..........70.00
      Golden yellow, applied collared mouth with ring, smooth base, pint, McKearin GXII-41, some minor ex. Scratches below cannon, 1/8" chip on top of mouth 300.00
   Double Eagle, Coventry Glass Works, Coventry, CT, 1830-48, yellow olive, sheared mouth, pontil scar, pint, McKearin GII-70...200.00
   Double Eagle, Granite Glass Works, Stoddard, NH, 1846-50, yellow olive, sheared mouth, pontil scar, pint, McKearin GII-81, slight misshapen shoulder 250.00
   Double Eagle, Kentucky Glass Works, Louisville, KY 1850-55, attributed to, brilliant copper, sheared mouth, pontil scar, pint, McKearin GII-24, 2" vertical crack.........325.00
   Double Eagle, Louisville Glass Works, Louisville, KY, 1855-60, vertically ribbed, pale blue green, sheared mouth, pontil scar, pint, McKearin GII-32A, manufacturer's mouth roughness, some int. haze 575.00
   Double Eagle, Stoddard glasshouse, Stoddard, NH, 1846-60
      Light yellow amber with olive tone, sheared mouth, pontil scar, half pint, McKearin GII-86a......................180.00
      Olive amber, sheared mouth, pontil scar, quart, McKearin GII-79...160.00
      Yellow amber with olive tone, sheared mouth, pontil scar, pint, McKearin GII-82 ....110.00
   Double Eagle, Pittsburgh district, Pittsburgh, PA, 1860-80, yellow olive, applied collared mouth with ring, smooth base, pint, McKearin GII-105, pinhead flake at base 150.00
   Eagle-Cornucopia, attributed to Keene Marlboro Street Glassworks, Keene, NH, 1830-50

Bright aquamarine with bluish bone, sheared mouth, pontil scar, pint, McKearin GII-74 ....140.00
Brilliant aquamarine, sheared mouth, pontil scar, pint, McKearin GII-74, small int. open bubble on shoulder..... 90.00
Brilliant yellowish green with olive tone, sheared mouth, pontil scar, pint, McKearin GII-63......................180.00
Emerald green, sheared mouth, pontil scar, pint, McKearin GII-74, pinhead sized flake on top of mouth, two 3/8" potstone cracks 210.00
Pale aquamarine, sheared mouth, pontil scar, pint, McKearin GII-72, some minor int. stain near base ...130.00
Yellow amber with olive tone, sheared mouth, pontil scar, pint, McKearin GII-72 ....120.00
Yellowish olive amber, sheared mouth, pontil scar, pint, McKearin GII-72...150.00
Eagle-Cornucopia, attributed to early Pittsburgh district, 1820-40, sheared mouth, pontil scar
   Colorless, half pint, McKearin GII-11 ....600.00
   Light greenish-aquamarine, pint, McKearin GII-6 ..... 475.00
Eagle-Stag, Coffin and Hay Manufacturers, Hammonton, NJ, 1836-47, aquamarine with pale yellowish green tint. Sheared mouth, pontil scar, half pint, McKearin GII-50.............325.00
Eagle-Westford Glass Co., Westford Glass Co., Westford, CT, 1860-73, bright medium reddish amber, malformed applied double collared mouth, smooth base, half pint, McKearin GII-65 ....120.00
Eagle-Willington/Glass Co., Willington Glass Works, West Willington, CT, 1860-72
   Bright medium yellowish-olive, applied double collared mouth, smooth base, half pint, McKearin GII-63....210.00
   Golden red amber, applied double collared mouth, smooth base, quart, McKearin GII-61, some ext. highpoint wear 200.00
   Medium yellow olive, double collared mouth, smooth base, pint, McKearin GII-64................................150.00
   Yellow-olive, sloping collared mouth, smooth base, quart, McKearin GII-61 ....200.00
For Pike's Peak Prospector-Hunter Shooting Deer, attributed to Ravenna Glass Works, Ravenna, OH, 1860-80, aquamarine, applied mouth with ring, smooth base, quart, McKearin GXI-47, 1/4" shallow flake 325.00
Horse and Cart-Eagle, Coventry Glass Works, Coventry, CT, 1830-48, bright light yellow amber with olive tone, sheared mouth, pontil scar, pint, McKearin GV-9 ....170.00
Lowell/Railroad-Eagle, Coventry Glass Works, Coventry, CT, 1830-48, yellow amber with olive tone, sheared mouth, pontil scar, half pint, McKearin GV-10, some minor ext. highlight wear, lettered emb weak 170.00
Masonic-Eagle, Keene Marlboro Street Glassworks, Keene, NH, 1815-30
   Deep bluish aquamarine, shared mouth, pontil scar, pint, McKearin GIV-27 ....275.00
   Deep greenish aquamarine, wide tooled collared mouth, pontil scar, pink, McKearin GIV-5......................850.00
   Light blue green, inward rolled mouth, pontil scar, half pint, McKearin GIV-28 ....300.00
   Light yellow amber with olive tone, sheared mouth, pontil scar, half pint, McKearin GIV-24 ....160.00
   Olive amber, sheared mouth, pontil scar, pint, McKearin GIV-71...150.00
   Pale bluish-green, tooled collared mouth, pontil scar, pint, McKearin GIV-7a 950.00
Masonic-Eagle, New England, possibly CT glasshouse, 1815-30, brilliant aquamarine, inward rolled mouth, pontil scar, pint, McKearin GIV-16 ....3,000.00
Masonic-Eagle, White Glass Works, Zanesville, OH, 1820-30

Light blue green, sheared mouth, pontil scar, pint, McKearin GIV-32..325.00

Light yellow amber, sheared mouth, pontil scar, pint, McKearin GIV-32, shallow bubble burst on left column of Masonic emblem 500.00

Masonic-NEG Eagle, attributed to New England Glass Bottle Co., Cambridge, MA, 1820-30, deep greenish aquamarine, sheared mouth, ground pontil, half pint, McKearin GIV-26 ....1,200.00

Seeing Eye Masonic, attributed to Stoddard glasshouse, Stoddard, NH, 1846-60, olive amber, sheared mouth, pontil scar, pint, McKearin GIV-43, moderate ext. high-point wear..150.00

Success to the Railroad, Coventry Glass Works, Coventry, CT, 1830-48

Brilliant light yellowish olive, sheared mouth, pontil scar, pint, McKearin GV-8, pinhead sized flake on side of mouth...325.00

Yellow amber with olive tone, sheared mouth, pontil scar, pint, McKearin GV-8, narrow 1/2" area on top of mouth ground 160.00

Success to the Railroad, Keene Marlboro Street Glassworks, Keene, NH, 1830-50

Brilliant yellow amber with olive tone, sheared mouth, pontil scar, pint, McKearin GV-3, sandgrain on medial rib...160.00

Light yellow amber with olive tone, sheared mouth, pontil scar, pint, McKearin GV-3 ....250.00

Success to the Railroad, Lancaster Glass Works, Lancaster, NY, 1849-60, aquamarine, sheared mouth, tubular pontil scar, pint, McKearin GV-1a, 3/8" brush on inside of mouth, other minor mouth roughness 200.00

Success to the Railroad, Mount Vernon Glass Works, Vernon, NY, 1830-44

Deep yellow olive, sheared mouth, pontil scar, pint, McKearin GV-5...160.00

Forest green, sheared mouth, pontil scar, pint, McKearin GV-5, pinhead sized flake on medial rib 375.00

Pattern Molded

4-5/8" l, Midwest, 1800-30, 24 ribs swirled to the right, golden amber, sheared mouth, pontil scar 190.00

7-3/8" l, Emil Larson, NJ, c1930, swirled to the right, amethyst, sheared mouth, pontil scar, some exterior highpoint wear..250.00

Pictorial

Baltimore/Glass Works and anchor-Resurgam Eagle, Baltimore Glass Works, Baltimore, MD, 1860-70, variegated yellow amber, applied collared mouth, smooth base, pint, McKearin GXIII-54, two 1/4" shallow flakes at side of base..475.00

Cornucopia-Large Medallion, Midwest America, 1820-40, very pale blue green, sheared mouth, pontil scar, half pint, McKearin GIII-1 ....3,000.00

Cornucopia-Urn, attributed to Coventry Glass Works, Coventry, CT, 1830-48, bright green, sheared mouth, pontil scar, pint, McKearin GIII-4, small flake appears to have been ground...230.00

Cornucopia-Urn, attributed to New England, 1830-50, yellow olive, sheared mouth, pontil scar, half pint, McKearin GIII-2, small chip 130.00

Cornucopia-Urn, Lancaster Glass Works, NY, 1849-60, blue green, applied sloping collared mouth, pontil scar, pint, McKearin GIII-17, some minor stain......................350.00

Flora Temple/Horse, Whitney Glass Works, Glassboro, NJ, 1860-80, cherry puce, applied collared mouth with ring, smooth base, pint, handle, McKearin GXIII-21 ......170.00

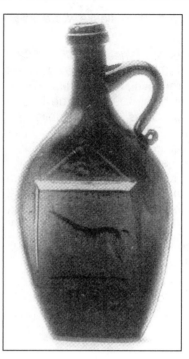

Pictorial, Sailor-Banjo Player, Maryland Glass Works, Baltimore, MD, 1840-60, aquamarine, inward rolled mouth, pontil scar, half pint, McKearin GXIII-8, $180. Photo courtesy of Norman C. Heckler and Co.

Isabella/Glass Works and anchor-Factory, Isabella Glass Works, Brooklyn, NJ, 1850-60, aquamarine, sheared mouth, pontil scar, qt, McKearin GXIII-55, 3/4" open bubble burst to right of factory 210.00

Monument-Sloop, Baltimore Glass Works, Baltimore, MD, 1840-60, medium variated yellow green, sheared mouth, pontil scar, half pint, McKearin GVI-2, some exterior highpoint wear, overall dullness................................1,100.00

Sailor-Banjo Player, Maryland Glass Works, Baltimore, MD, 1840-60, aquamarine, inward rolled mouth, pontil scar, half pint, McKearin GXIII-8 ....180.00

Sheaf of Wheat-Star, attributed to Bulltown Glass Works, Bulltown, NJ, 1858-60, bright medium green, applied double collared mouth, pontil scar, pint, McKearin GIII-39.....750.00

Sheaf of Wheat-Westford Glass Co., Westford Glass Works, Westford, CT, 1860-73

Golden amber, reddish tone, applied double collared mouth, smooth base, pint, McKearin GXIII-35 ....120.00

Reddish amber, applied double collared mouth, smooth base, pint, McKearin GXIII-35 ....140.00

Yellow olive, applied double collared mouth, smooth base, pint, McKearin GXIII-36 ....120.00

Yellow olive, applied double collared mouth, smooth base, pint, McKearin GXIII-37 ....120.00

Summer-Winter, attributed to Baltimore Glass Works, Baltimore, MD, 1860-70, citron with olive tone, applied double collared mouth, smooth base, pint, McKearin GX-15..............900.00

Pitkin Type

Midwest, 1800-30

4" h, ribbed and swirled to the right, 26 ribs, brilliant golden amber, outward rolled mouth, pontil scar, some ext. high point war, some minor int. stain, 1/4" shallow chip near base..1,200.00

6-1/4" l, ribbed and swirled to the right, 16 ribs, olive green with yellow tone, sheared mouth, pontil scar, some int. stain...300.00

New England, 1783-1830, sheared mouth, pontil scar

5" h, 36 ribs swirled to the right, yellow olive..........400.00

5-1/4" h, 36 swirled ribs, olive green, half post neck...255.00

5-1/4" l, ribbed and swirled to the left, 36 ribs, light olive yellow, ...375.00

Pitkin, ribbed and swirled to the right, sixteen ribs, Midwest, 1800-1830, olive green with a yellow tone, sheared mouth, pontil scar, 6-1/4" h, some int. stain, $350. Photo courtesy of Norman C. Heckler and Co.

6" l, ribbed and swirled to the right, distinct popcorn pattern, 36 ribs, yellow-olive, 1/4" fissure 220.00

6-1/2" h, 31 ribs, broken swirl, olive green, half post neck 315.00

6-7/8" h, 36 ribs, ribbed and swirled to left, light yellow amber 500.00

Portrait

Adams-Jefferson, New England, 1830-50, yellow amber, sheared mouth, pontil scar, half pint, McKearin GI-114...325.00

General Jackson, Pittsburgh district, 1820-40, bluish-aquamarine, sheared mouth, pontil scar, pint, McKearin GI-68...1,500.00

Lafayette-DeWitt Clinton, Coventry Glass Works, Coventry, CT, 1824-25, yellowish-olive, sheared mouth, pontil scar, half pint, 1/2" vertical crack, weakened impression, McKearin GI-82..2,100.00

Lafayette-Masonic, Coventry Glass Works, Coventry, CT, 1824-45, yellowish-olive, sheared mouth, pontil scar, half pint, McKearin GI-84, some minor exterior highpoint wear...1,700.00

Rough and Ready Taylor-Eagle, Midwest, 1830-40, aquamarine, sheared mouth, pontil scar, pint, McKearin GI-77..1,200.00

Washington-Albany Glass Works/NY, Albany Glass Works, Albany, NY, 1847-50, greenish-aquamarine, sheared mouth, pontil scar, half pint, McKearin GI-30......2,200.00

Washington-Eagle, Kensington Glass Works, Philadelphia, PA, 1820-38, bright aquamarine, sheared mouth, pontil scar, pint, McKearin GI-14 ....375.00

Washington-Monument, Baltimore Glass Works, Baltimore, MD, 1830-50, jade green, sheared mouth, pontil scar, pint, McKearin GI-20, ext. high point wear..........2,400.00

Washington-Sheaf of Wheat, Dyottville Glass Works, Philadelphia, PA 1840-60, medium yellow-olive, inward rolled mouth, pontil scar, half pint, McKearin GI-59......9,000.00

Washington-Taylor, Dyottville Glass Works, Philadelphia, PA 1840-60

Bright bluish-green, applied double collared mouth, pontil scar, quart, McKearin GI-42 ....400.00

Brilliant olive yellow, sheared mouth, pontil scar, pint, McKearin GI-38 ....900.00

Scroll

America, 1845-60

Brilliant golden amber, applied collared mouth, iron pontil mark, pint, McKearin GIX-10 ....425.00

Brilliant golden amber, sheared mouth, pontil scar, pint, McKearin GIX-14, 3/8" potstone crack near medial rib...140.00

Cornflower blue, sheared mouth, pontil scar, pint, McKearin GIX-10 1-4" flake on int. of mouth 190.00

Medium lime green, sheared mouth, iron pontil mark, McKearin GIX-11, 1/4" flat flake on top of mouth......... 325.00

Miniature, America, 1845-60, cobalt blue, inward rolled mouth, pontil scar, 2-5/8" h, approx. 1 oz, McKearin GIX-40, extremely rare, deep color.. 5,000.00

Portrait, Lafayette-Masonic, Coventry Glass Works, Coventry, CT, 1824-25, yellowish olive, sheared mouth, pontil scar, half pint, McKearin GI-84, $1,700. Photo courtesy of Norman C. Heckler and Co.

Scroll, America, 1845-60, medium lime green, sheared mouth, iron pontil mark, McKearin GIX-11, 1/4" flake on top of mouth, $325. Photo courtesy of Norman C. Heckler and Co.

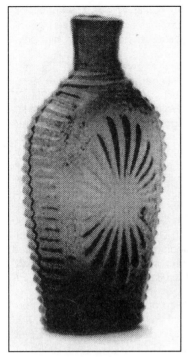

Sunburst, Coventry Glass Works, Coventry, CT, 1814-30, variated brilliant yellowish green with olive tone, sheared mouth, pontil scar, half pint, McKearin GVIII-18, $850. Photo courtesy of Norman C. Heckler and Co.

Sunburst
>   Baltimore Glass Works, Baltimore, MD, 1820-30, attributed to, sheared and tooled mouth, pontil scar
>>   Colorless, light gray hue, pint, McKearin GVIII-26, some light overall int. haze...375.00
>>   Copper amber, pint, McKearin GVIII-20 ....1,900.00
>>   Deep yellow olive, pint, McKearin GVIII-26.........2,750.00
>>   Olive green, half pint, McKearin GVIII-27............3,000.00
>   Coventry Glass Works, Coventry, CT, 1814-30
>>   Brilliant light olive yellow, sheared mouth, pontil scar, pint, McKearin GVIII-3 ....450.00
>>   Brilliant light yellowish olive, sheared mouth, pontil scar, half pint, McKearin GVIII-16 ....500.00
>>   Brilliant medium yellowish olive, sheared mouth, pontil scar, McKearin GVIII-3, some highpoint wear 325.00
>>   Variegated brilliant yellowish amber with olive tone, sheared mouth, pontil scar, half pint, McKearin GVIII-18 ... 850.00
>   Keene Marlboro Street Glassworks, Keene, NY, 1815-30
>>   Brilliant yellow amber with olive tone, sheared mouth, pontil scar, half pint, McKearin GVIII-8, 3/4" faint fissure in one of rays 200.00
>>   Pale yellowish amber, sheared mouth, pontil scar, pint, McKearin GVIII-2, some ext. highpoint wear.....350.00
>>   Yellow olive, "P & W," sheared mouth, pontil scar, half pint, McKearin GVIII-10 ....350.00
>>   Yellow olive, sheared mouth, pontil scar, pint, McKearin GVIII-8, some ext. highpoint wear 325.00
>   New England, 1820-30, attributed to, blue green, inward rolled mouth, pontil scar, half pint, McKearin GVIII-29 .... 190.00

FOSTORIA GLASS

History: Fostoria Glass Co. began operations at Fostoria, Ohio, in 1887, and moved to Moundsville, W.V., its present location, in 1891. By 1925, Fostoria had five furnaces and a variety of special shops. In 1924, a line of colored tableware was introduced. Fostoria was purchased by Lancaster Colony in 1983 and continues to operate under the Fostoria name.

Fostoria is known for tableware and stemware of high quality. These fine wares included clear, colored, etched, gilded, lustered, and pressed items. Fostoria reacted to the market and the times by actively competing with its contemporaries, such as Cambridge, Heisey, and Westmoreland. Some of the Fostoria patterns and colors were designed to directly compete with these companies. Careful study of its patterns will show the similarities in design and color. Fostoria's Azure blue compare to Cambridge's blue. Etched patterns such as June or Navarre compare to Cambridge's Rose Point and Heisey's Orchid pattern.

Fostoria produced patterns in a wide range of items, allowing a bride to set her table from ashtrays to vases. Plates of every size and use complemented the stemware. She could use a different piece of stemware to serve grapefruit, oysters, parfait, sherbets, as well as water and wine.

One of the most popular patterns every produced by Fostoria is American. Its production began in 1915 and continued until the merge with Lancaster Glass. Most production was in clear glass, although some color pieces were made. This pattern was very popular with World War II brides and was made in many forms. More than 50 different sizes of bowls were made for use as serving pieces.

Reference: Tom and Neila Bredehoft, *Fifty Years of Collectible Glass, 1920-1970*, Antique Trader Books, 1997; Gene Florence, *Elegant Glassware of the Depression Era*, 7th Edition, Collector Books, 1997; Ann Kerr, *Fostoria: An Identification and Value Guide of Pressed, Blown, & Hand Molded Shapes* (1994, 1997 values), *Etched, Carved & Cut Designs* (1996, 1997 values) Collector Books; Milbra Long and Emily Seate, *Fostoria Stemware*, Collector Books, 1995; Leslie Piña, *Fostoria Designer George Sakier*, Schiffer Publishing, 1996; ——, *Fostoria*, Schiffer Publishing, 1995; JoAnn Schleismann, *Price Guide to Fostoria*, 3rd ed., Park Avenue Publications, n.d.

Periodical: *The Daze*, P.O. Box 57, Otisville, MI 48463.

Collectors' Clubs: Fostoria Glass Assoc., 109 N. Main St., Fostoria, OH 44830; Fostoria Glass Collectors, P.O. Box 1625, Orange, CA 92668; Fostoria Glass Society of America, P.O. Box 826, Moundsville, WV 26041.

Museums: Fostoria Glass Museum, Moundsville, WV; Huntington Galleries, Huntington, WV.

Note: Prices listed are for crystal (colorless) unless otherwise noted.

Animal
>   Colt, standing, 3-7/8" h..50.00
>   Duckling, frosted amber, head back 35.00
>   Duck, Mama, frosted amber 35.00
>   Flying Fish, ruby 55.00
>   Pelican..65.00
>   Polar Bear..75.00
>   Seal 85.00
Bookend
>   Eagle..125.00
>   Lyre, pr 100.00
>   Owl...250.00
>   Seahorse...200.00
Candlestick, Rebecca at the Well
>   Crystal Satin 125.00

Marsh Green 225.00
Figure, Madonna, #2635
    Crystal 55.00
    Silver Mist 55.00
Window Box, #2373, with frog
    Ebony, small 85.00
    Green, large 75.00
    Rose, small 90.00

Miscellaneous Patterns and Etchings

After Dinner Cup, Fern, pink 50.00
Bowl
    #2315, Paradise, ftd, rolled edge, orchid.......85.00
    #2324, 10" d, green 60.00
    #2545, Flame, 12-1/2" l, oval, crystal.........45.00
Brandy, #6012, 2 oz, crystal 22.00
Candleholders, pr
    #2297, 7" h, turquoise 42.50
    #2395-1/2, black, ...50.00
    #2447, topaz...75.00
    #2447, wisteria 200.00
    #2470-1/2, wisteria 300.00
    #2472, Fuchsia, etch #310, duo 100.00
    #2545, crystal 75.00
    #2630, Milkweed, crystal 36.00
    #2666, Flora, crystal, wheat cutting 30.00
Centerpiece Bowl, Grape, #2371, oval, 2 pc flower holder,
    orchid 255.00
Chalice, cov, Crown, Windsor, gold, 9-1/2" h 85.00
Champagne
    Chapel Bell, #6080 ....10.00
    Christiana, #6030, 5-1/2" h 10.00
    Distinction, red 14.00
    Heraldry, #6012 ....10.00
    Precedence, #6108, onyx bowl 38.00
    Shooting Stars, crystal 30.00
Champagne Set, Spiral Optic, crystal body, green stem...85.00
Claret
    Sampler, 4" h, crystal 25.00
    Splendor, #6131, 7 oz, 5-1/2" h, blue 15.00
    Wilma, blue, blank #6016 ....38.00
Coaster, #2272, crystal 6.00
Cocktail
    Heraldry, #6012 ....9.00
    Laurel, crystal...15.00
    Spiral Optic, crystal body, green stem.........18.00
    #6008, crystal 8.00
Comport
    #2327, 7-1/2", turquoise 40.00
    #2470, rose, 6" low 28.00
Console Bowl, #2297, 10-1/2" d, "C" rolled edge,
    turquoise 55.00
Cordial
    Heraldry, #6012, crystal 28.00
    Westchester, #6012, ruby 60.00
Creamer and Sugar
    Coronet 25.00
    Skyflower, crystal.....................................45.00
Cruet, orig stopper, Glacier, crystal.................45.00
Cup and Saucer
    Coronet 9.75
    Florentine, crystal 15.00
    Shirley, crystal 24.00
Decanter, #4020, ftd, orig stopper, crystal, green foot....125.00
Goblet
    Announcement, #6103/666, 7-1/4", crystal 12.00

Comet, #4020, 11 oz, crystal.........................22.00
Diadem, #6202, crystal, green stem...............35.00
Grand Majesty, etched blue bowl, 9 oz 30.00
Grand Majesty, etched blue bowl, 13 oz 35.00
Heraldry, #6012, crystal 18.00
Lotus, 11 oz, crystal, mist base......................21.00
Lovelight, #6107/671, 8-1/4", crystal.............20.00
Needlepoint, #64, 12 oz, amber.....................22.00
Pine, 5-7/8" h, crystal 20.00
Rhapsody, #6055, 6-1/8" h, crystal 12.00
Sampler, 10 oz, 5-1/2" h, crystal...................25.00
Spiral Optic, 7-1/2" h, #5093, crystal body, green stem,
    set of 6 ....150.00
Triumph, #6112, 10 oz, gold 15.00
#6008, crystal 12.00
Iced Tea Tumbler, Tradition, red.....................22.00
Jug
    Daisy, #5000, crystal 350.00
    Oriental, #303, crystal 125.00
Juice Tumbler, ftd
    Christiana, #6030 ....11.00
    Laurel, 4-3/4" h, crystal 15.00
    Stardust, 4-5/8" h, crystal 15.50
    Wistar/Betsy Ross, 3-3/4", #2620, crystal.....12.00
    #6008, crystal 10.00
Mint Tray, Seascape, opalescent pink, 7-1/2" l.....30.00
Nut Cup, Grape Leaf, milk white, individual size 10.00
Oyster Cocktail, Florentine, 3-1/2", crystal 15.00
Parfait, Spinet 10.00
Pitcher, #2666/807, 10" h, lilac.......................20.00
Place Card Holders, #2538/543, Azure Blue, set of 8....165.00
Plate, Wistar/Betsy Ross, 7" d, #2620, crystal.....10.00
Relish
    #2470, 5-part, 12" l, topaz 45.00
    Shirley, #2496, 3-part, 10" l, crystal 50.00
    Silver Spruce, 3-part, 10" l 35.00
Salad Set, Thistle, 12" bowl, 13-1/2" d plate, crystal.....95.00
Saucer
    Florentine, crystal 3.00
    Minuet, green 5.00
Server, center handle, Morning Glory cutting, crystal 45.00
Sherbet
    Lovelight, #6107/671, 9 oz, crystal...........10.00
    Pine, 4-3/8", crystal 15.00
    Spinet, #6033/821, 4", low, crystal 15.00
    Spray, #6055/841, 4-1/2", crystal 10.00
    Westchester, #6012, low, ruby 25.00
    Wistar/Betsy Ross, 4-1/8", #2620, crystal.....12.00
    Woodland, #2921, brown 15.00
    Woodland, #2921, crystal..........................12.00
Sugar
    Flemish, crystal..15.00
    Fuchsia, etch #310 ....24.00
    Glacier, crystal 15.00
Toothpick Holder
    Brazilian 55.00
    Frisco 45.00
Tray, #2470, 8-3/4" l, pink..............................30.00
Tumbler
    Congo, 5" h, pink 45.00
    Florentine, 5-1/2", ftd, crystal...................20.00
    Laurel, 6" h, ftd, crystal 18.50
    Oriental, #4911, 8 oz, crystal....................20.00
    Queen Anne Etch, #4020, 5" h, ftd 22.00
    Queen Anne Etch, #4020, 5-5/8" h, ftd 25.00
Vase
    #101, Images, 4" h, white cased 200.00

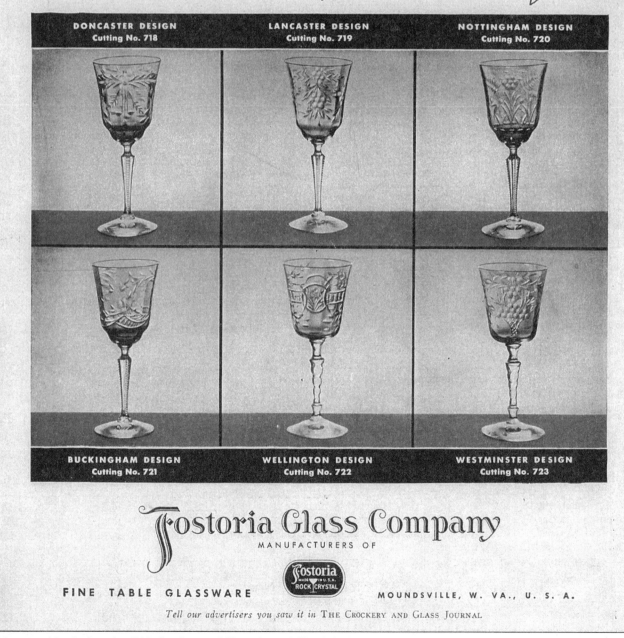

Ad, new goblet designs for 1933, Crockery and Glass Journal, March 1933.

#2292, Royal Blue, 8" h, flared 175.00
#2292, Spiral Optic, 8" h, flared, amber 65.00
#2385, fan, azure blue 95.00
#4105, 9-3/4" h, Draped Optic 160.00
7" h, Images, rolled edge, lilac, orig pamphlet 200.00
Wine
Laurel, 5-1/2" h, crystal..........................28.00
Woodland, #2921, brown 15.00
Woodland, #2921, crystal.........................12.00
#6008, crystal 12.00

Patterns

Acanthus. Plate Etching #282. Dinnerware pattern. Made 1930-1933. Made in amber, green, or amber with crystal base and green with crystal base.
After Dinner Cup and Saucer, amber 50.00
Candlestick, amber 55.00
Cocktail, amber with crystal base 25.00
Goblet, green with crystal base 28.00
Jelly, amber...20.00
Lemon dish, amber 24.00
Plate, 8" d, green.....................................20.00
Server, center handle, amber 25.00
Sugar, cov, handle, green..........................185.00
Tumbler, ftd, 5-1/4" h.................................22.50

Alexis, Pattern #1630. Made 1909-1925. Made in crystal.
Celery Vase, tall 35.00
Creamer and Sugar, hotel, cutting..............95.00
Decanter, Kentucky Tavern, no stopper 75.00
Jug, half gallon..195.00
Vase, 8" h 65.00

American, Line #2056. Made 1915-1986. Made in some amber, blue, crystal, green, some pink shading to purple (late 1902s), red (1980s), white, and yellow. Dalzell Viking continues to make some forms. Prices for colors fluctuate greatly. Some pieces made under Whitehall label. Prices listed below are crystal unless otherwise noted.
Appetizer, individual size.............................35.00
Ashtray
Large 100.00
Oval 25.00
Oval, with match stand............................30.00
Square 6.00
Baby Bowl, flared 25.00
Basket, reed handle, 4" x 9" 95.00
Beer Mug...75.00
Bell 650.00
Biscuit Jar..800.00
Bitters Bottle 50.00
Bon Bon, 6" d, ftd 16.00
Bowl
4-1/2" d 14.50
8-1/2" d, 2 handles 60.00
10" d, ground base..................................55.00
11" d, rolled edge 42.50
11" d, three corners 42.50
11-3/4" d, oval, deep 45.00
Brick Ice Cream 75.00
Bud Vase, 8-1/4" h, white 65.00
Butter Dish, cov..95.00
Butter Dish, cov, metal holder, label 140.00
Cake Plate
10" d, 2 handles......................................32.00
12" d, 3 toes..45.00
Cake Stand
Round 70.00

Square 80.00
Candleholders, pr
2-lite, bell 125.00
2-lite, flat 110.00
3"..25.00
7" h, columnar, sq..................................95.00
Candle Lamp, chimney and cup 175.00
Candy Dish, cov, 3-part 90.00
Celery Dish, 10"...20.00
Centerpiece Bowl, 9-1/2" d 42.50
Cheese Comport 25.00
Chip and Dip 190.00
Cigarette Box, cov......................................40.00
Claret 75.00
Coaster 10.00
Cocktail, ftd, cone, 2-7/8" h 12.00
Commemorative Bowl, ftd 490.00
Comport, cov, 9" d, high standard 35.00
Condiment Bottle, stopper.........................125.00
Console Bowl..35.00
Cookie Jar...325.00
Cordial Decanter, stopper...........................95.00
Cosmetic Box, cov
1-1/2" 700.00
2-1/2" 700.00
Creamer and Sugar, hexagonal.................1,800.00
Creamer and Sugar, matching tray, tea size 50.00
Creamer and Sugar, matching tray, green 165.00
Cruet, no stopper 25.00
Cup and Saucer 12.00
Decanter, stopper
Gin 180.00
In metal holder.....................................190.00
Large 125.00
Rye 180.00
Scotch 180.00
Wine..85.00
Finger Bowl 90.00
Floating Garden
10" d 60.00
11" d 60.00
Fruit Bowl, 16" h 120.00
Goblet, water, hex, 7" h 15.00
Hat
3" d, medium 25.00
4", large 45.00
Honey Jar, cov, orig spoon 400.00
Hurricane Lamp and Chimney 325.00
Ice Bucket, metal handle 70.00
Ice Cream Platter 300.00
Iced Tea Tumbler, ftd, 20 oz.......................20.00
Ice Tub, 6-1/2" 65.00
Jam jar, cov..70.00
Jelly, cov 35.00
Jewel Box, cov 600.00
Jug, 3 pint, ice lip......................................60.00
Juice Tumbler
Flat..12.00
Footed 13.00
Lemon dish, cov..40.00
Luncheon Tumbler, ftd 12.00
Marmalade, cov, orig spoon 110.00
Mayonnaise, 2 pc, ground base 55.00
Mustard, cov 80.00
Napkin Ring...35.00
Nappy, handle
5" d, tricorn 12.00

Why this is America's best-loved crystal...

AMERICAN giftware by Fostoria has the fiery beauty found only in handcrafted crystal. In typically American fashion, it is as practical and durable as it is lovely to look at. Fostoria craftsmen hand-mold each piece.

Then they fire-temper AMERICAN so you can use it day after day with confidence. **Send for our folder** — it shows you all 118 of the beautiful pieces. Items shown here from $1.50. (Slightly higher West.)

See Fostoria AMERICAN for yourself. You'll find it — in all its lovely facets — on display at your favorite store. Fostoria Glass Company, Dept. AH, Moundsville, W. Virginia.

Fine Crystal with Fashion Flair . . . made by hand in America

Fostoria

Ad, American pattern, American Home Magazine, 1961.

8" x 4-3/4", deep 125.00
9-1/2" x 3", flared 125.00
Old Fashioned Tumbler..10.00
Olive Dish, 6" l 14.00
Oyster Cocktail 3-1/4", ftd 18.00
Pastry Stand...500.00
Perfume Bottle, round, replaced stopper.................675.00
Pickle Dish, 8"...15.00
Picture Frame, oval 22.00
Pin Tray
    5" l, rect...125.00
    Jenny Lind, milk glass..30.00
Pitcher, pink 40.00
Platter
    10-1/2" l, oval..40.00
    12" l..50.00
Pomade Set..875.00
Puff Box, cov, amber...460.00
Punch Cup, flared 10.00
Relish
    2-part, 12" l, boat shape......................................22.00
    3-part, 6" x 9"...35.00
    3-part, 9-1/2" l..34.00
    4-part, 6-1/2" x 9"...55.00
Relish Boat
    8-1/2" l...12.00
    12" l..18.00
Ring Tree...750.00
Rose Bowl, 3-1/2" d..25.00
Salad Plate, crescent 110.00
Salt Dip, orig spoon...20.00
Salt and Pepper Shakers, glass tops........................50.00
Sandwich Tray, center handle 48.00
Sauce Boat..40.00
Serving Plate, center handle...................................35.00
Sherbet, 5 oz, 3-1/2" h, low, round base 8.00
Shrimp and Dip...375.00
Soap Dish...3,100.00
Straw Jar, cov...185.00
Sugar Bowl, cov, tea size 8.50
Sugar Bowl, cov, handle, table size..........................24.00
Sugar Cube Holder 335.00
Sundae, 6 oz, 3-1/8" h..9.50
Sweet Pea Vase...85.00
Syrup, 3 pc, ground base 225.00
Syrup, glass lid, 10 oz..145.00
Tom and Jerry Mug..42.00
Tom and Jerry Punch Bowl.....................................250.00
Tomato Juice Tumbler, ftd 10.00
Toothpick Holder..22.50
Torte Plate
    13-1/2" l, oval..70.00
    20" d..150.00
Tray
    Rect, 6-3/4" l..35.00
    Oval, 10-1/2" l, handles 55.00
    Rect, 10-1/2" l...125.00
    Rect, 14-1/8" l, cobalt blue, 5-part......................200.00
Trifle Bowl, 8" d..250.00
Trophy Bowl, handles..140.00
Tumbler
    5 oz, 3-5/8" h, flat..12.00
Vase
    6" h, straight sides...30.00
    9" h, sq, ftd..37.50

9-1/2" h, flared, swung...395.00
10" h, flared, ftd...90.00
10" h, sq, ftd..90.00
10" h, straight sides..90.00
11" h, swung...175.00
12" h, straight sided..135.00
16" h, swung...345.00
19" h, swung...375.00
Wash Bowl, 19" d, flared..500.00
Wedding Bowl, cov
    Crystal 130.00
    Milk glass..125.00
Whiskey, 2-1/2"...15.00
Wine..16.50

American Lady. Line #5056. Made 1933-73. Made in crystal, and crystal with amber, burgundy, emerald green or regal blue bowl.
Bowl, #495, crystal..10.00
Claret, #27, emerald green and crystal 35.00
Cocktail, #21, crystal...12.00
Goblet, 6-1/8" h
    Burgundy..40.00
    Crystal..20.00
Iced Tea Tumbler, #63, burgundy and crystal............35.00
Oyster Cocktail, #33, crystal.....................................12.00
Sherbet, 4-1/8", crystal..12.50
Tumbler, 5-3/9" h, amber and crystal.........................15.00

Argus. Pattern #2770. Giftware line. Made for Henry Ford Museum. Made 1960s-85 in cobalt blue, crystal, gray (1972), olive green, and ruby.
Bowl, 4-1/2" d, ruby...18.50
Cocktail, 2-7/8" h, crystal...10.00
Compote, cov, 8", cobalt blue...................................40.00
Dessert Plate, 8" d, olive green...................................9.00
Goblet, ruby..25.00
Juice Tumbler, 2-7/8" h, cobalt blue..........................15.00
Sherbet, ruby..16.00
Wine, ruby..25.00

Baroque. Line #2496. Made 1936-66 in azure blue, black amethyst, cobalt blue, crystal, green, pink, red, and topaz yellow.
Bon Bon, 3 toes, azure blue.....................................40.00
Bowl
    7" d, topaz yellow, ruffled, 3 feet 20.00
    10-1/2", handle, crystal 95.00
    12" d, flared
        Crystal..30.00
        Topaz yellow..60.00
Candlestick
    2-lite, crystal, pr...45.00
    2-lite, topaz yellow, pr..130.00
    2-lite, 8-1/4" h, 16 prisms, azure blue...................90.00
    5-1/2" h, topaz yellow, pr....................................130.00
Candy, cov, 3-part, crystal..80.00
Celery, azure blue...85.00
Comport, 5-1/2" w, topaz yellow................................40.00
Comport, short
    Azure blue...38.00
    Topaz yellow...40.00
Creamer and Sugar
    Individual size, topaz yellow.................................55.00
    Table size, topaz yellow 40.00
Cup and Saucer
    Azure blue...30.00
    Crystal 12.00
    Topaz yellow...30.00
Dessert, handle, azure blue......................................90.00

Goblet, water, azure blue...25.00
Ice Bucket, topaz yellow..130.00
Iced Tea Tumbler, 6" h, ftd
    Azure blue..90.00
    Crystal...70.00
    Topaz yellow...70.00
Mayonnaise, underplate
    Azure blue..65.00
    Topaz yellow...25.00
    Mint, tab handle, azure blue...................................28.00
Nappy, handle
    4" d, round, crystal 12.00
    4" d, square, azure blue 45.00
    4" w, square, crystal 12.00
    5" d, ftd, crystal..55.00
Nut, 3 toes
    Azure blue..40.00
    Topaz yellow...35.00
Oil and Vinegar, azure blue 595.00
Oil, orig stopper, crystal...90.00
Oyster Cocktail, azure blue..22.00
Pickle Dish, azure blue..55.00
Pitcher, ice lip, azure blue, light use 1,400.00
Plate
    6" d, azure blue 12.00
    6" d, topaz yellow 10.00
    7" d, azure blue 15.00
    8" d, azure blue 20.00
Preserve, cov, topaz yellow 270.00
Punch Cup, crystal..12.00
Relish
    2-part, 6-1/2" l, azure blue 55.00
    3-part, azure blue 75.00
    3-part, topaz yellow 45.00
Rose Bowl, topaz yellow 95.00
Salt and Pepper Shakers, pr
    Individual size, azure blue...................................340.00
    Table size, azure blue 170.00
    Table size, topaz yellow 120.00
Sauce Bowl, divided, azure blue 72.00
Saucer, crystal 3.50
Server, center flame shaped handle, crystal 60.00
Sherbet, 5 oz, 3-3/4"
    Azure blue..25.00
    Crystal...10.00
    Topaz yellow...20.00
Sweetmeat
    6", sq, handle, azure blue.....................................48.00
    9-1/2", cov, topaz yellow.....................................300.00
Tidbit, 3 toes, azure blue..45.00
Torte Plate, 14" d
    Crystal...40.00
    Topaz yellow...45.00
Tumbler, ftd, 5" h, azure blue......................................45.00
Vase
    6-3/4" h, crystal..95.00
    7" h, azure blue...170.00

Beacon. Cutting #767. Made 1937-55 in rock crystal.
Champagne 15.00
Cocktail 9.00
Goblet, water..24.00
Plate, 7-1/2" d...9.00
Sherbet...8.00
Sweetmeat...25.00
Tumbler, ftd, 9 oz..12.00

Beverly. Plate Etching #276. Made 1927-34 in azure blue

(1928-31); amber, crystal, green (1927-34); orchid (1927-28); amber and green with crystal bowl (1927-34).
Ashtray, crystal..12.00
Bouillon and Liner
    Amber..20.00
    Green...24.00
Candy Box, cov, 3", crystal 90.00
Celery, crystal..25.00
Cereal Bowl, green...30.00
Comport, 8", ftd, #2350, amber..................................85.00
Demitasse Cup and Saucer
    Amber..45.00
    Green...30.00
Finger Bowl and Liner, green......................................25.00
Pitcher, amber..125.00
Pitcher, water, ftd, green 225.00
Plate
    6" d, crystal...4.00
    7-1/2" d, crystal 5.00
    7-1/2" d, green 8.00
    8-1/2" d, crystal 7.50
    10-1/4" d, dinner, amber.......................................35.00
    10-1/4" d, dinner, green..35.00
Platter, 15" l, amber...120.00
Salt and Pepper Shakers, pr, #5000.........................135.00
Sherbet, amber..20.00
Tumbler, ftd, 12 oz, green and crystal 22.00
Underplate, 6-1/4" d, amber...6.00

Bouquet. Plate Etching #342. Made 1949-1960 in rock crystal only.
Bud Vase, 6" h...45.00
Candlesticks, pr, #2630, duo......................................75.00
Champagne, 4-3/4" h..24.00
Cocktail...18.00
Goblet, 6-1/4" h..30.00
Juice Tumbler, ftd, 4-1/2" h 20.00
Oyster Cocktail..24.00
Sherbet..24.00
Tumbler, ftd. 5-7/8" h...26.00

Buttercup. Etching #340. Made only in crystal.
Ashtray, #2364, 2-3/8", individual size 20.00
Candlestick
    #2324, 4" h...30.00
    #6023, 2-lite, pr 95.00
Champagne 20.00
Cocktail 24.00
Fruit Bowl, 13" d...75.00
Goblet, #6030, 7 oz, luncheon 35.00
Plate
    7-1/2" d...16.50
    9-1/2" d, dinner 50.00
Relish, 3-part, 10"...50.00
Salt and Pepper Shakers, pr, #2364 ....48.00
Server, center handle...50.00
Sherbet, #6030, 6 oz..22.00
Vase, #6021, 6" h, ftd...65.00
Wine, #6030...35.00

Camelia. Plate Etching #344. Made 1952-65 in rock crystal only.
Butter, cov, quarter pound 55.00
Candlestick, #2630, 7" l, single..................................65.00
Champagne 22.50
Cocktail 24.00
Juice Tumbler, ftd 20.00
Parfait 25.00
Pitcher, #2630, 6-1/8" h, pint....................................115.00
Wine...30.00

Capri. Pattern #6045. Made 1952-65. Blown lead glass stemware made in solid crystal and crystal bowls on bitter green or cinnamon base.

Claret-wine, cinnamon 22.00
Finger Bowl, crystal 8.00
Goblet, cinnamon 20.00
Iced Tea Tumbler, ftd, crystal with cinnamon base 17.00
Juice Tumbler, crystal with bitter green base 10.00
Plate, 7" d, crystal 8.00
Sherbet, 4" h
    Cinnamon 18.00
    Crystal 15.00

Century. Made 1949-85 in crystal only.
Bowl
    4-1/2" d, thin 20.00
    5" d 15.00
    8" d, two handles, deep, oval 50.00
    11" d, ftd, rolled 45.00
Butter Dish 28.75
Cake Salver, ftd, cutting 50.00
Candlesticks, triple, pr 125.00
Cereal Bowl 22.50
Comport, 4-3/8" 20.00
Creamer and Sugar, large, floral silver overlay 50.00
Creamer and Sugar, matching tray, individual size 40.00
Cruet, orig stopper 50.00
Cup and Saucer 18.00
Dessert Bowl, two handles 45.00
Goblet, water 20.00
Ice Bucket 50.00
Iced Tea Tumbler, 5-7/8" h, ftd 20.00
Mayonnaise, divided, two ladles 42.50
Pitcher
    Ice Lip, 7" h 85.00
    Pint 70.00
Plate
    7" d 12.00
    9-1/2" d 25.00
    10" d, handle 18.00
Preserve, cov, ftd 40.00
Relish
    2-part, 7-1/2" l 18.50
    3-part, handle 35.00
Salad Plate, crescent 35.00
Salt and Pepper Shakers, pr 40.00
Salt and Pepper Shakers, pr, matching tray, individual
    size 40.00
Server, center handle 45.00
Serving Bowl, center handle, 9-1/2" oval 20.00
Sherbet 20.00
Tumbler, 12 oz, ftd 27.50
Vase, 8-1/2" h, oval 65.00
Vegetable, oval 45.00
Wine 28.00

Chintz. Plate Etching #338. Made c1950s in crystal only.
Bon Bon, 7-5/8" 28.00
Bowl
    10" d, handle 75.00
    10-1/2" d, handle 65.00
    10-1/2" d, 4 toes 70.00
Cake Plate, #2496, handle 28.00
Candlestick, #2496
    4" h, 1-lite, pr 60.00
    5-1/2" h, 1-lite, pr 130.00
    2-lite, pr 130.00
Champagne, 6 oz, tall 24.00
Cheese and cracker 145.00

Cheese Compote, 3-1/2" h 50.00
Cocktail, 5", 4 oz 25.00
Comport, 5-1/2" d, 4-3/4" h 40.00
Console Set, bowl and pr double candlesticks 125.00
Creamer and Sugar, ftd 40.00
Creamer and Sugar, matching tray, individual size 110.00
Cup and Saucer 26.00
Dessert Bowl, 2 handles 70.00
Goblet, water
    6-1/8" h 25.00
    7-3/4" h 32.00
Iced Tea Tumbler, ftd 35.00
Jelly, cov 65.00
Juice Tumbler, ftd, 5 oz 25.00
Mayonnaise and Underplate, #2496 ....65.00
Nappy, triangular, handle 40.00
Pickle 35.00
Plate
    7" d 16.50
    7-1/2" d 8.00
Relish
    2-part, 6" sq 35.00
    3-part 45.00
Sauce Dish, handle 80.00
Server, center handle 75.00
Sherbet, 4-3/8", 6 oz, low 20.00
Sugar, 3-1/2", ftd 15.00
Torte Plate, 14" d, minor scratches 70.00
Tumbler, ftd, 6" h 22.50
Wine, 4-1/2 oz 45.00

Coin. Line #1372. Made 1958-82 in amber, blue, crystal, empire green, olive green, and ruby red.
Ashtray
    3" x 9", oblong, empire green 20.00
    7-1/2" d, center raised coin, ruby red 30.00
    7-1/2" d, plain center, ruby red 26.00
Bowl
    8" d, amber 35.00
    8-1/2" d, ftd, amber 60.00
Bud Vase, amber 22.50
Candlesticks, pr, 4-1/2" h
    Amber 40.00
    Crystal 40.00
    Olive green 20.00
Candy Dish, cov
    Amber 35.00
    Blue 75.00
    Ruby red, frosted 55.00
Candy Jar, cov #347, amber 40.00
Cigarette Box, cov, amber 40.00
Comport, ftd
    Empire green 40.00
    Olive green 45.00
    Ruby red, 8-1/2" 75.00
Creamer
    Amber 10.00
    Olive green 15.00
Creamer and Sugar, crystal 22.00
Cruet, olive green, 7 oz 50.00
Iced Tea Tumbler, ftd, 14 oz, 5-3/16" h, crystal 45.00
Nappy, handle, ruby red 24.00
Old Fashioned Tumbler, crystal 35.00
Pitcher
    Amber 95.00
    Olive green 65.00
Plate, 8" d, ruby red 40.00

Punch Set, bowl , base, 12 cups, crystal....................650.00
Salt Shaker
    Olive green...17.50
    Ruby red..32.50
Sugar, cov, olive green...30.00
Urn, cov, ftd, 12-3/4" h, amber...............................45.00
Vase, 8" h, ftd, red..45.00
Wedding Bowl, 8-1/2" d
    Amber...50.00
    Crystal 60.00
    Ruby red..60.00

Colonial Dame. Pattern #5412. Made 1948-82 in solid crystal and Empire Green with crystal base. Designed to compliment Colony pattern dinnerware.

Claret/Wine, Empire Green 30.00
Cocktail, 3-1/2 oz, 4", Empire Green.......................12.00
Cordial, 3-1/4", crystal..20.00
Goblet, 11 oz, 6-3/8", Empire Green........................30.00
Juice Tumbler, ftd, Empire Green with crystal base.....12.00
Oyster Cocktail, crystal...8.00
Plate, 7" d, crystal..8.00
Sherbet/champagne, 6-1/2 oz, 4-5/8", Empire Green.....24.00

Colony. Line #2412. Made 1938-72 in crystal only.

Almond, ftd..20.00
Bowl
    7" w, triangular, ftd..20.00
    8-1/4" d, flared...65.00
    8-1/2" d, handle..35.00
    10-1/2" l, low, ftd...75.00
    11" d, flared..30.00
    11" l, oval, ftd..55.00
    14" l, oval, ftd..70.00
Butter Dish, cov, 1/4 lb..60.00
Candlesticks, pr, 2-lite..120.00
Candy Dish, cov, milk glass......................................70.00
Celery Dish...30.00
Centerpiece, 13"..90.00
Cheese and Cracker Set...50.00
Comport, low, cov..55.00
Console Set, 9" h ftd bowl, pr 14-1/2" h candlesticks,
    amber..600.00
Creamer and Sugar...35.00
Creamer and Sugar, matching tray...........................45.00
Cruet, stopper..55.00
Cup, 3 toes..22.00
Goblet, 5-1/4" h...16.00
Ice Bowl, ftd...200.00
Ice Cream, 5-1/2" w, sq...40.00
Iced Tea Tumbler..20.00
Ice Jug, ftd, 3 pint...200.00
Inkwell, cascade, brass hinged lid 150.00
Mayonnaise, underplate...25.00
Muffin Tray..40.00
Nappy, 4-1/2"..22.00
Nut Bowl, 5-1/2" d, 3 ftd...18.00
Oil Bottle, stopper 55.00
Oyster Cocktail..22.00
Pitcher, ftd, 48 oz..225.00
Plate
    9" d, dinner..35.00
    10" d, handle..35.00
Platter, 12-1/2" l...95.00
Punch Cup...20.00
Relish, 3-part, 10-1/2" l, handle..............................35.00
Rose Bowl, 6" d..130.00
Salver, 12" d, ftd..100.00

Sandwich Server, center handle...............................35.00
Sherbet..9.00
Sponge Cup, 3" d, round..30.00
Sugar
    2-7/8" h..12.50
    Large..15.00
Torte Plate, 15" d...50.00
Tumbler, 12 oz, flat...32.50
Urn, cov
    Patterned..85.00
    Plain..125.00
Vase
    7" h, ftd, cupped..95.00
    7-1/2" h, flared..45.00
    12" h, flared...325.00
Wine, 4-1/4" h...27.00

Contour. Pattern #2638, #6060, #2666. Made 1955-77 in amber, crystal, and crystal with pink.

Ashtray, amber, 2 lip..25.00
Champagne, crystal and pink....................................20.00
Goblet, water, crystal...30.00
Iced Tea Tumbler, crystal and pink 25.00
Relish, 3-part, crystal...25.00
Sherbet, 4-1/2", crystal..15.00

Corsage. Plate Etching #325. Made 1935-60 in crystal only.

Bowl
    9" d, handle, #2536...90.00
    11-1/2" d..50.00
Candlesticks, pr, 2-lite, #2496...............................130.00
Cocktail, 5" h...20.00
Cordial, 1 oz...55.00
Cup and Saucer..24.00
Iced Tea Tumbler, ftd...30.00
Nappy, tricorner, handle...50.00
Oyster Cocktail..22.00
Plate, 8-1/2" d..15.00
Relish
    2-part, Lafayette blank, #2440..........................50.00
    5-part, chipped...75.00
Sauce Dish, 6-1/2" l, oval...70.00
Sherbet, tall...20.00
Tumbler, ftd, 6"...25.00
Wine, 3 oz, 5-1/4" h, crystal.....................................30.00

Dolly Madison. Cutting #876. Made 1939-74 in rock crystal with hand-cut flutes. Designed and sold as a companion to Raleigh pattern tableware.

Champagne...22.00
Cocktail..20.00
Goblet..25.00
Sherbet..20.00

Fairfax. Pattern #2375, dinnerware line. Made 1927-60 in amber and green (1927-41); orchid (1928-28); azure and rose (1928-41); topaz (1929-36); selected items in ebony (1930-42); selected items in ruby (1935-39).

After Dinner Creamer, rose.......................................35.00
After Dinner Cup, azure blue 35.00
After Dinner Cup and Saucer
    Green..30.00
    Rose 30.00
Berry Bowl, 5" d
    Amber...10.00
    Rose 15.00
    Topaz..12.00
Bon Bon, cov, 2 handles
    Rose 20.00
    Topaz..22.50

Bouillon
  Amber, with liner 15.00
  Green, with liner 17.50
  Rose 18.50
  Topaz 23.00
Bowl
  5" d, green 6.00
  8" d, rose 27.50
  9-1/2" d, rose 10.00
Butter Dish, cov
  Green 125.00
  Rose 125.00
Cake Plate, #2375, 10" d, handle
  Amber 35.00
  Azure blue 50.00
Candlesticks, pr
  #2375, 3", azure blue 60.00
  #2394, 3-toed
    Azure blue 45.00
    Rose 40.00
    Topaz 35.00
Candy, cov, 3-part, green 68.00
Champagne, #5298
  Azure blue 30.00
  Rose 30.00
Cheese and Cracker Set, #2375
  Azure blue 75.00
  Rose 75.00
  Topaz 80.00
Claret, #5299, topaz 35.00
Combination Bowl and Candlesticks, #2415, azure
  blue 160.00
Comport
  4-1/2", crystal 30.00
  5-1/2" d, #5297, tall, green 60.00
  5-3/4" d, rose 75.00
  6", #2400
    Azure blue 45.00
    Topaz 24.00
  7", orchid 70.00
  #5298, blown, low, rose 125.00
Confection, cov
  Orchid 130.00
  Rose 90.00
Cordial, amber, #5298 ....45.00
Cracker Plate, #2375, handle, topaz 30.00
Creamer, azure blue, individual size 30.00
Creamer and Sugar, individual size
  Amber 70.00
  Rose 70.00
  Ruby 60.00
  Topaz 70.00
Creamer and Sugar, table size
  Azure blue 25.00
  Green, ftd 20.00
  Rose 23.00
  Topaz, ftd 20.00
Cream Soup
  Rose 40.00
  Liner, topaz 15.00
Cruet, open, topaz 70.00
Cup and Saucer
  Amber 10.00
  Azure blue, ftd 17.00
  Green 12.00
  Rose 16.00

Topaz 12.00
Dessert Bowl, large, handle, rose 48.00
Finger Bowl, blown
  Green 15.00
  Rose 15.00
Goblet, water, #5299, topaz 24.00
Grape Fruit, liner, amber, #945-1/2 ....25.00
Gravy Boat, liner
  Green 75.00
  Topaz 90.00
Ice Bucket, azure blue 45.00
Icer
  Black 15.00
  Green 10.00
Mayonnaise and liner, topaz 35.00
Mayonnaise, ftd, green 35.00
Mayonnaise Underplate, orchid 14.00
Nut, individual, 3 toes
  Azure blue 30.00
  Green 18.50
Oil Bottle and Stopper, ftd, rose 135.00
Parfait, #5299, topaz 35.00
Pickle Dish
  8" l, green 20.00
  8-1/2" l, divided, rose 20.00
Pitcher, ftd, #5000, orchid 350.00
Plate, 6" d, bread and butter
  Amber 2.50
  Azure blue 6.00
  Green 3.00
  Rose 4.00
  Topaz 5.00
Plate, 7" d, green 5.50
Plate, 7-1/2" d
  Azure blue 7.50
  Rose 8.00
  Topaz 6.00
Plate, 8-3/4" d, salad
  Amber 6.00
  Blue 12.00
  Green 5.00
  Rose 10.00
  Topaz 7.00
Plate, 9-1/2" d, luncheon
  Green 20.00
  Orchid 60.00
  Rose 15.00
Plate, 10-1/4" d, dinner, rose 40.00
Plate, 10-1/4" d grill
  Amber 18.50
  Rose 40.00
Platter
  10-1/2" l, oval, topaz 25.00
  12-1/4" l, green 45.00
  14-1/8" l, green 45.00
Relish, 2-part, topaz 17.00
Salad Bowl, green, 9-1/4" d 25.00
Salt and Pepper Shakers, pr, green 60.00
Sandwich Server, topaz 38.00
Sauce Boat
  Azure blue 50.00
  Crystal, flower cutting 15.00
Saucer
  Amber 2.00
  Green 3.00
  Rose 2.50

Topaz...3.00
Server, center handle, rose...30.00
Service Tray, amber...95.00
Shaker, ftd, azure blue...40.00
Sherbet
    Azure blue, #5298, low.......................................22.50
    Topaz, 6 oz...11.00
Sugar Bowl
    Individual size, amber......................................10.00
    Individual size, azure blue..................................15.00
    Individual size, green......................................10.00
    Table size, ftd, green......................................10.00
    Table size, ftd, flat top, rose...............................15.00
    Table size, topaz...12.50
Sugar Pail, rose..75.00
Sweetmeat, handle
    Rose..24.00
    Topaz...18.50
Tomato, icer, rose..52.50
Tumbler, 9 oz, ftd, #5296
    Azure blue...20.00
    Topaz...13.00
Tumbler, ftd, #5298, azure blue......................................24.00
Vase
    7" h, ftd, #2369, crystal....................................150.00
    8" h, flip, loop optic, #4100, amber.........................90.00
    8" h, ftd, #22902, green....................................80.00
    10" h, flip, #4100, crystal, cutting..........................130.00
    10" h, loop optic, #4105, green..............................130.00
Vegetable Bowl
    Azure blue, cov, oval......................................70.00
    Green, 10" l, oval...45.00
Whipped Cream Pail, handle
    Azure blue...75.00
    Rose..60.00
    Topaz...35.00
Whiskey, #5298, ftd, topaz..25.00
Wine, topaz..18.00

Glacier. Acid-Etched Design #2510. Made 1935-44 in crystal only.
Candy, cov, ftd...95.00
Creamer, ftd..9.00
Cruet, orig stopper..45.00
Ice Bucket..60.00
Jelly, cov..25.00
Nappy, sq...10.00
Old Fashioned Tumbler...12.00
Onion Soup, cov...25.00
Pickle Dish, handle..9.00
Plate, 8" d...9.00
Rose Bowl, 5" d...25.00
Salad Bowl...25.00
Sugar, large..15.00
Torte Plate, 15" d...35.00
Tumbler, 9 oz...18.00

Heather. Etching #343. Made only in crystal.
Bon Bon, 3 toed...30.00
Bowl
    5" d..30.00
    8" d, flared...50.00
    8-1/4" d, handle...45.00
    10-3/4" d, flared, ftd.....................................70.00
Bud Vase, 8-1/2" h, #5902...120.00
Butter Dish, cov, 1/4 lb...95.00
Cake Plate, handle..40.00
Candy, cov...75.00
Cereal Bowl..40.00

Champagne...22.00
Cheese and Cracker...120.00
Cocktail...20.00
Compote...30.00
Comport, 4-3/8" h...35.00
Creamer and Sugar
    Individual size, matching tray...............................75.00
    Table size...35.00
Cup and Saucer...24.00
Juice Tumbler..20.00
Mayonnaise, 2 pc...70.00
Muffin Tray, handle...75.00
Nappy, 3 toed, tricorner...32.50
Party Plate Set, 2 pc..70.00
Pickle, 8"...30.00
Plate
    6" d..10.00
    7-1/2" d..14.00
    8" d..16.50
    9-1/2" d..60.00
Platter, 12" l..90.00
Relish, 2-part, 7-3/8" l, #2360, handle...............................25.00
Salt and Pepper Shakers, pr, open....................................25.00
Sherbet..18.00
Sugar
    Individual size...17.50
    Large...25.00
Tumbler, 12 oz, 6-1/8" h, ftd..25.00
Vase, 5" h, #6021...130.00
Vegetable, oval...70.00
Wine..40.00

Hermitage. Pattern #2449. Made 1931-45 in amber, crystal and green (1931-42); topaz (1932-38); gold tint (1938-44); wisteria (1932-38); selected items in ebony (1932-38).
Ashtray Set, set of 4 stacking ashtrays, crystal........25.00
Beer Mug, ftd, 12 oz, crystal..35.00
Celery, 11", green..70.00
Coaster, green...15.00
Cocktail, cone, topaz...10.00
Coupe Salad, 6-1/2", crystal...8.50
Cup and Saucer, crystal...18.50
Icer, 4-3/4"
    Crystal..12.50
    Green...15.00
Jug, 3 pint
    Crystal..125.00
    Topaz...130.00
Plate
    8" d, amber...20.00
    9" d, crystal...24.00
Sandwich Plate, 12" d, green...20.00
Sherbet, 3", low, wisteria...15.00
Tumbler, 2-7/8" h, ftd
    Crystal..8.00
    Green...10.00
    Topaz...10.00
Tumbler, 4-1/4" h, ftd, topaz...15.00
Vase, 6" h, green...70.00

Holly. Cutting #815. Made 1942-80 in rock crystal only.
Champagne...18.00
Claret, 6"...35.00
Cocktail
    3-1/2 oz, 5-1/4" h..20.00
    5-1/4"..22.50
Cordial, 1 oz, 3-7/8"...35.00
Goblet, #6030
    10 oz, 6-1/2" h..25.00

10 oz, 7-7/8" h..30.00
Iced Tea Tumbler, #6030, 12 oz, 6" h................20.00
Juice Tumbler, ftd, 4-5/8" h.............................20.00
Pickle, 8"...24.00
Plate, 7-1/2" d..20.00
Salt and Pepper Shakers, pr, #2364, 2-5/8"......45.00
Sherbet, 6 oz...20.00
Sherbet, low..14.00
Wine...25.00

Jamestown. Pattern #2719. Made 1958-85 in amber, azure blue, azure tint, crystal, green, pink, ruby, and smoke.

Bowl, 4-1/2" d, amber......................................12.00
Butter Dish, cov, pink......................................50.00
Creamer and Sugar, amber..............................30.00
Goblet, luncheon, amber..................................12.00
Goblet, water, 5-7/8" h
    Amber...10.00
    Azure blue..20.00
    Crystal..15.00
    Green..19.50
    Smoke..8.00
Iced Tea Tumbler, ftd, 12 oz, 6" h
    Amber...10.00
    Azure blue, 6" h..20.00
    Ruby...20.00
Juice Tumbler, ftd, 4-3/4" h
    Amber...10.00
    Azure blue..18.00
    Green..20.00
    Ruby...20.00
Pitcher
    Amber...75.00
    Green...110.00
    Smoke...45.00
Sherbet, 7 oz, 4-1/2" d
    Amber...10.00
    Azure tint, 7 oz..18.00
    Crystal..10.00
    Green..12.50
    Ruby...16.00
    Smoke..6.50
Tumbler, 5-1/4" h, flat, ruby.............................22.00
Tumbler, 6" h, ftd
    Amber...10.00
    Azure blue..24.00
    Green..24.00
Tumbler, 9 oz, flat, smoke................................10.00
Tumbler, 12 oz, flat, azure blue.........................20.00
Wine, ftd, azure blue.......................................20.00

June. Made 1928-44 in azure blue, crystal, rose pink, and topaz yellow.

After Dinner Creamer and Sugar
    Rose pink..300.00
    Topaz yellow...150.00
After Dinner Cup and Saucer
    Azure blue...200.00
    Rose pink..200.00
    Topaz yellow...60.00
Ashtray
    Azure blue..80.00
    Rose pink...55.00
Baker, oval, rose pink.....................................180.00
Bar Tumbler, topaz yellow, 2 oz.........................75.00
Berry Bowl, 5" d
    Azure blue..65.00

Crystal..45.00
Rose pink...60.00
Topaz yellow...40.00
Bon Bon, azure blue...25.00
Bouillon
    Azure blue..60.00
    Topaz yellow..40.00
Bouillon and Liner
    Crystal..40.00
    Rose pink...85.00
Bowl
    9" d, 2 handles, topaz yellow.........................85.00
    11-1/2" d, 3-toed, rose pink...........................85.00
    12" d, #2394, crystal...................................65.00
Canapé Plate, crystal......................................35.00
Candlesticks, pr
    3" h, #2375, topaz yellow..............................75.00
    4" h, crystal...70.00
    5" h, scroll, #2395-1/2, topaz yellow..............150.00
Celery
    Azure blue...130.00
    Crystal..80.00
    Rose pink..130.00
Centerpiece Bowl, 12" d, topaz yellow.................80.00
Cereal Bowl, yellow...85.00
Champagne
    Azure blue..55.00
    Crystal..30.00
    Rose pink...48.00
    Topaz yellow..30.00
Chop Plate, 13" d
    Rose pink..230.00
    Topaz yellow...160.00
Claret, yellow...60.00
Club Plate, blue...300.00
Cocktail
    Rose pink...65.00
    Topaz yellow..40.00
Comport
    4", crystal..45.00
    6", #2400, topaz yellow.................................45.00
    6-1/2" h, azure blue....................................110.00
Console Set, 12" d ftd bowl, pr 3" h candlesticks, topaz
    yellow..105.00
Creamer and Sugar, individual size, crystal.........125.00
Creamer, ftd, topaz yellow................................30.00
Cream Soup
    Azure blue..95.00
    Topaz yellow, orig liner.................................80.00
Cup and Saucer
    Crystal..30.00
    Rose pink...44.00
    Topaz yellow..40.00
Finger Bowl
    Azure blue...100.00
    Crystal..45.00
    Rose pink..100.00
    Topaz yellow..42.50
Goblet, water
    Azure blue..75.00
    Crystal, #5298..45.00
    Rose pink...75.00
Grapefruit and Liner
    Crystal...130.00
    Topaz yellow...250.00
Ice Bucket, crystal..95.00

Iced Tea Tumbler, ftd
 Azure blue 75.00
 Rose pink 75.00
 Topaz yellow 45.00
Icer Bowl
 Crystal 60.00
 Topaz yellow 55.00
Icer and Tomato Insert, crystal 80.00
Juice Tumbler, ftd, blue 65.00
Lemon Dish
 Azure blue 45.00
 Rose pink 45.00
Mayonnaise and Liner
 Azure blue 190.00
 Topaz yellow 120.00
Mayonnaise Ladle
 Crystal 19.50
 Topaz yellow 35.00
Mint, 4-1/2" d, 3 toed, #2394 ....45.00
Oil and Vinegar Bottle, crystal 300.00
Oyster Cocktail, 5-1/2 oz
 Azure blue 55.00
 Topaz yellow 35.00
Parfait
 Crystal 70.00
 Topaz yellow 60.00
Pickle, 8" l, green 20.00
Pitcher
 Crystal 500.00
 Rose pink 600.00
 Topaz yellow 425.00
Plate
 6" d, rose pink 13.00
 6" d, topaz yellow 10.00
 7" d, rose pink 18.50
 7-1/2" d, rose pink 20.00
 7-1/2" d, topaz yellow 15.00
 8-1/4" d, azure blue 25.00
 8-1/4" d, rose pink 22.00
 8-1/2" d, topaz yellow 18.50
 9-1/2" d, topaz yellow 50.00
 10-1/4" d, dinner, rose pink 175.00
 10-1/4" d, dinner, topaz yellow 85.00
Platter
 Azure blue, 11" l 175.00
 Crystal, 12" l 90.00
 Rose pink, 12" l 230.00
Relish, 2-part, rose pink 70.00
Salt and Pepper Shakers, pr
 Azure blue 250.00
 Crystal 60.00
 Topaz yellow 170.00
Sauce Boat, topaz yellow 110.00
Server, center handle
 Azure blue 120.00
 Topaz yellow 75.00
Sherbet
 Azure blue, 6" 35.00
 Topaz yellow 24.00
Sugar, cov, topaz yellow 230.00
Sweetmeat, rose pink 55.00
Tomato Juice Insert, topaz yellow 20.00
Tumbler, water, 9 oz, ftd
 Azure blue 44.00
 Rose pink 44.00
Tumbler, water, 12 oz, ftd, topaz yellow 40.00

Vase, 8" h, bulbous base, topaz yellow 400.00
Vegetable, oval, azure blue 165.00
Whipped Cream Bowl
 Rose pink 35.00
 Topaz yellow 45.00
Whiskey, ftd
 Azure blue 225.00
 Topaz yellow 85.00
Wine
 Azure blue 115.00
 Topaz yellow 75.00

Kashmir. Plate Etching #281. Made 1930-34 in crystal, azure blue, topaz, green, and crystal with azure, topaz, or green base.
After Dinner Cup and Saucer, topaz 55.00
Berry Bowl, azure blue 38.00
Celery, azure blue 85.00
Cereal Bowl, 6", topaz 35.00
Champagne
 Azure blue 42.50
 Topaz 28.50
Cheese Comport, #2375, azure 45.00
Cocktail, crystal bowl, green base 28.00
Cruet, azure blue 995.00
Jug, ftd, #4020, crystal, green base 300.00
Mayonnaise, ftd, azure blue 40.00
Pickle, azure blue 28.00
Soup, flat, azure blue 195.00
Tumbler, ftd, #4020, 10 oz, crystal, green base 24.00

Lafayette. Pattern #2440. Made 1931-60 in amber, green, and rose (1933-38); burgundy, empire green and regal blue (1935-42); crystal (1931-60); gold tint (1938-44); ruby red (1935-39); topaz (1932-38); and wisteria (1931-38).
Almond, individual, crystal 8.00
Bon Bon, 5" d, handle
 Amber 9.50
 Burgundy 40.00
Cake Plate, crystal 20.00
Candlesticks, pr, 2-lite, #2447, wisteria 200.00
Champagne, wisteria 60.00
Creamer and Sugar, wisteria 125.00
Cup and Saucer, wisteria 35.00
Finger Bowl, #869, wisteria 65.00
Goblet, wisteria 25.00
Iced Tea Tumbler, ftd, #5299, wisteria 60.00
Pickle, 9" l, wisteria 75.00
Plate
 6" d, wisteria 12.00
 7" d, wisteria 20.00
 8" d, handle, burgundy 75.00
 8-1/2" d, wisteria 25.00
 9" d, crystal 14.00
Relish, 2-part, handle
 Burgundy 50.00
 Regal blue 85.00
Sauce Boat and Liner, burgundy 130.00
Sauce Bowl, rose 70.00
Sugar, 3-5/8", crystal 15.00
Torte Plate, 13" d, empire green 70.00
Wine, #5298, wisteria 165.00

Lido. Plate Etching #329. Made 1937-55 in azure blue, crystal and azure blue with crystal base (197-43).
Bowl, 10-1/2" d, handle, 4 toed, azure blue ...140.00
Candle, duo flame, single, crystal 40.00
Candlesticks, pr, 5-1/2" h, crystal 90.00
Candy, cov, 3-part, crystal 65.00
Champagne, saucer, #6017
 Azure blue 48.00

Crystal 18.00
Cheese and Cracker, azure blue 170.00
Compote, 5-1/2", crystal 18.50
Creamer and Sugar, #2496, crystal 40.00
Dessert, 2 handles, crystal 70.00
Goblet, #6017, azure blue with crystal base 28.00
Nappy, tricorner, handle, crystal 30.00
Pitcher, 53 oz, ftd, crystal 145.00
Plate, 7-1/2" d, crystal 12.00
Relish, 3-part
  Azure blue, handle 100.00
  Crystal 40.00
Tumbler, 12 oz, ftd, crystal 22.00

Manor. Plate Etching #286. Made 1931-44 in crystal (1931-44); green (1931-35); topaz (1931-38); green bowl with crystal base (1931-35); topaz bowl with crystal base (1931-37); crystal bowl with wisteria base (1931-35).
Ashtray, #2412, crystal 15.00
Bowl, 12" d, green 45.00
Candlesticks, pr, #2433, 3" h, topaz 75.00
Champagne, #6007, crystal 22.00
Claret, 4-1/2 oz, crystal bowl, green base 30.00
Cocktail, 3-1/2 oz, crystal bowl, wisteria base 30.00
Comport, 6", green 35.00
Finger Bowl, crystal bowl, green base 12.00
Goblet, crystal
  #6003, 6-1/4" h 22.50
  #6007, 6-1/2" h 25.00
Icer, orig insert, topaz 50.00
Sherbet, #6007, crystal 22.00
Tumbler, #6003, 9 oz, crystal bowl, topaz base 20.00
Whiskey, ftd, #6003, crystal 25.00

Mayfair. Pattern #2419. Made 1930-44 in crystal (1930-44); azure blue and green (1930-31); topaz (1930-38); gold tint (1938-44); amber and rose (19300-1942); selected items in ebony, wisteria, and ruby red (1930-42).
After Dinner Cup and Saucer, ebony 12.00
Ashtray, Rosette intaglio etch, crystal 20.00
Baker, rose 45.00
Celery, 11", topaz 16.00
Creamer and Sugar, tea size, #2419
  Ebony 45.00
  Rose 38.00
  Topaz 38.00
Cup and Saucer
  Amber 10.00
  Ebony 12.00
Fruit, 5" d, crystal 7.50
Gravy, attached underplate, topaz 65.00
Plate, 10" d, crystal 20.00
Relish, 4-part, 8-3/4" l, handle, topaz 45.00
Saucer, amber 1.75

Mayflower. Plate Etching #332. Made 1939-55 in crystal.
Bon Bon 28.00
Bowl, 8-1/2" d, handle 35.00
Cake Plate, handle 25.00
Candlesticks, pr, 1-lite 70.00
Champagne 18.50
Cocktail 22.00
Compote, 6" d 40.00
Creamer 16.50
Cup and Saucer 24.00
Goblet, water 20.00
Iced Tea Tumbler, 12 oz 30.00
Mayonnaise and Ladle 45.00

Muffin Tray, handle 55.00
Oyster Cocktail 12.00
Pitcher, #4140 ....350.00
Relish, 3-part 35.00
Salt and Pepper Shakers, pr 75.00
Server, center handle, flame 80.00
Sugar 18.00
Vase, 7" h, 2 handle 140.00
Wine 35.00

Meadow Rose. Plate Etching #328. Made 1936-75 in crystal and azure blue with crystal base 1936-44).
Bowl, 10-1/2" d, flared, crystal 22.00
Cake Plate, handle, crystal 22.00
Candlesticks, pr, #2926
  1-lite, azure blue 150.00
  2-lite, crystal 70.00
  3-lite, crystal 95.00
Champagne, saucer, #6016
  Azure blue 45.00
  Crystal 28.00
Cocktail, 3-1/2 oz, crystal 25.00
Cordial, #6016, crystal 60.00
Creamer and Sugar, individual size, crystal 60.00
Cup and Saucer, crystal 24.00
Goblet, water, crystal 38.00
Iced Tea Tumbler, ftd
  Azure blue 55.00
  Crystal 35.00
Juice Tumbler, 5 oz, crystal 22.50
Mayonnaise, 3 pc, crystal 80.00
Oyster Cocktail, crystal 25.00
Pitcher, bulbous, 7" h, crystal 195.00
Plate, 7-1/2" d
  Azure blue 30.00
  Crystal 15.00
Plate, 10" d, handle, crystal 55.00
Plate, 13-1/2" d, crystal 45.00
Relish, 3-part
  Azure blue 90.00
  Crystal 45.00
Salt and Pepper Shakers, pr, azure blue 260.00
Sherbet, 4-1/2", crystal 16.00
Sugar, crystal 17.50
Tray, 11" l, handle, crystal 50.00
Tumbler, 13 oz, ftd, crystal 32.00
Underplate, 7" d, center ring, crystal 15.00
Wine, crystal 45.00

Midnight Rose. Plate Etching #316. Made 1933-57 in crystal only.
Bowl, 10-3/4" d, ftd 65.00
Celery, 11" 60.00
Champagne 24.00
Cocktail 22.00
Creamer and Sugar, matching tray 60.00
Cup and Saucer 25.00
Mayonnaise, 2 part, oval 68.00
Pickle, 9" 45.00
Plate
  7" d 10.00
  7-1/2" d 14.00
Relish, 5-part, round, #2462, 11" d 80.00
Sherbet, #6009 ....18.50
Torte Plate, 14" d, slight use 60.00

Navarre. Plate Etching #327. Made 1936-82 in crystal (1936-82); azure bowl with crystal base (1973-82); pink bowl with crystal base (1973-78).
Bell, azure blue base, crystal handle 80.00

Navarre, iced tea tumbler, crystal, $45.

Bowl, crystal
    12" d, flared 62.50
    12" d, handle, 4 toes................................65.00
Brandy Snifter, crystal 165.00
Candlesticks, pr, crystal
    #2495, 2-lite, flame 90.00
    #2496, 2-lite 90.00
    #2496, 3-lite 190.00
Candy, cov, 3-part, crystal........................130.00
Celery/Relish, 12" l, 5 part, crystal 100.00
Champagne Flute
    Azure blue bowl, crystal base 175.00
    Crystal 175.00
Champagne/saucer, 6 oz, 5-5/8"
    Azure blue 45.00
    Crystal 25.00
    Pink..40.00
Cheese and Cracker, crystal 150.00
Claret, 4-1/2 oz
    Azure blue bowl, crystal base 75.00
    Crystal 50.00
    Pink bowl, crystal base...........................75.00
Cocktail, crystal..25.00
Compote, crystal
    #2400, 4-1/2" 45.00
    #2400, 6-1/2" 70.00
    #2496...45.00
Cordial, 3-7/8" h, crystal............................50.00
Cracker Plate, crystal.................................55.00
Creamer and Sugar, crystal
    Individual size...45.00
    Table size 60.00
Cup and Saucer, crystal 32.00
Goblet, water, 7-5/8" h, crystal 30.00
High Ball, flat, crystal 65.00
Ice Bucket, Baroque style, crystal 160.00
Ice Tea Tumbler, ftd
    Azure blue 52.00
    Crystal 45.00
    Pink..55.00
Jug, contour, crystal.................................450.00

Juice Tumbler, ftd, 5 oz, crystal 25.00
Magnum, 7-1/4", 16 oz, crystal 175.00
Nappy, round, handle, crystal.....................45.00
Old Fashioned Tumbler, crystal 75.00
Pickle, #2496, crystal 75.00
Pitcher, crystal...500.00
Plate, crystal
    7" d 15.00
    7-1/2" d 18.00
    8" d 15.50
Relish, crystal
    2-part, 6", sq 40.00
    3-part, 10" l, #2496 ....50.00
    5-part 130.00
Salt and Pepper Shakers, pr, #2364, 2-1/4", crystal.....98.00
Sauce Dish, #2496, crystal 125.00
Sherbet, 6 oz, 4-3/8", crystal 24.00
Sugar, crystal 18.00
Tumbler, ftd, crystal
    5 oz 25.00
    10 oz 28.00
    13 oz 35.00
Vase, 10" h, ftd, #2470, crystal.................150.00
Wine, 5-1/4", crystal 40.00

Nectar. Plate Etching #332. Made 1936-43 only in crystal.
    Cocktail, #6011 ....9.00
    Cordial, #6011 ....14.00
    Creme De Menthe, #6011, 2 oz 30.00

Neo Classic. Made 1934-late 1950s in crystal and regal blue, burgundy, ruby with crystal base, and crystal bowl with amber base.
    Champagne, saucer, #6011
    Burgundy..20.00
    Crystal 18.50
    Empire Green 20.00
    Cocktail, crystal 18.50
    Goblet, #6011, 10 oz
        Burgundy...35.00
        Ruby..48.00
    Iced Tea Tumbler, ftd, 12 oz, burgundy 25.00
    Sherry, burgundy 26.00
    Tumbler, #6011, 10 oz, Regal Blue...........25.00
    Whiskey, #6011, 2 oz
        Regal Blue..35.00
        Ruby..35.00
    Wine, #6011, 5" h, 3 oz, burgundy 18.00

New Garland. Plate Etching #284. Made in 1929-35 in amber, rose, and topaz. Also made in rose with crystal base (1931-34); crystal bowl with amber base (1930-31).
    After Dinner Cup, green 25.00
    After Dinner Cup and Saucer, topaz..........50.00
    Baker, 10", topaz 60.00
    Claret, rose bowl, crystal optic base..........20.00
    Fruit, 5-1/2" d, topaz 18.00
    Goblet, #4020, 11 oz, topaz.....................30.00
    Plate
        6" d, topaz 8.00
        8" d, topaz 10.00
        9" d, amber 15.00
    Platter, 12" l, amber 30.00
    Salad Dressing Bottle, topaz...................260.00
    Sherbet, #4020, high, 7 oz, topaz 24.00
    Vase, #2430, 8" d, topaz.........................190.00
    Whiskey, #4020, 10 oz, ftd, topaz 16.00

Oak Leaf. Brocade Plate Etching #290. Made in 1928-31 in crystal, green, and rose (1928-31); selected items in ebony (1929-31).

Bon Bon, #2375
    Crystal 24.00
    Green..40.00
Bowl, 12" d, crystal....................................100.00
Centerpiece, oval, green.............................85.00
Cigarette Box, cov, ebony..........................48.00
Ice Bucket, iridized blue 200.00
Lemon Tray, handle, orchid etching, gold trim 60.00
Lunch Tray, octagon, fleur-de-lis handle, green..........75.00
Plate, 7" d, crystal.....................................25.00
Salver, 12" d, rose.....................................60.00
Soup Plate, deep liner, 8-1/2" d, green 20.00
Sweetmeat, amber....................................24.00
Tumbler, 5 oz, crystal................................18.00

Pioneer. Pattern #2350. Made 1926-60. Made in crystal, amber, and green (1926-41); blue (1926-27); selected items in rose, azure blue (1929-36); also selected items in ebony (1929-41); also selected items in burgundy, empire green, regal blue, and ruby (1934-41).
Ashtray, amber...8.00
Bouillon with liner, blue 20.00
Bowl
    5-1/2" d, amber................................5.00
    9-1/4" l, oval, amber........................15.00
Cream Soup, flat, amber.............................9.00
Cup and Saucer, burgundy 20.00
Cup
    flat, green.......................................7.50
    ftd, green..7.50
Demitasse Cup and Saucer, amber..............17.50
Mahjong Set, 8-3/4" d snack plate with sherbet, amber 30.00
Plate
    6" d, green......................................4.00
    7-1/2" d, amber................................4.00
    7-1/2" d, green.................................4.50
    9" d, green......................................7.00
    9-1/2" d, amber..............................10.00
    9-1/2" d, blue.................................25.00
    10-1/2" d, green..............................25.00
Platter, 10-3/4" l, oval, amber 15.00
Sauce Boat, amber 22.50
Saucer, green..3.00
Sugar, cov, green......................................40.00

Plymouth. Plate Etching #336. Made 1939-45 and only in crystal.
Goblet..26.00
Juice Tumbler..12.00
Sherbet..14.00

Priscilla. Pattern #2321. Made 1925-30. Made in amber, blue, crystal, and green (1925-30); azure blue and rose (1929-30).
Bouillon, crystal.......................................10.00
Creamer, rose 10.00
Custard Cup, handle, green 12.50
Goblet, 9 oz, crystal..................................15.00
Mayonnaise, crystal 25.00
Mug, ftd, green...60.00
Pitcher, blue...90.00
Plate, 8" d, blue..20.00

Raleigh. Pattern #2574. Made 1939-55 in crystal only.
Bon Bon...15.00
Bowl, 13" d 30.00
Cake Plate, 10" d......................................15.00
Creamer and Sugar, #681, ftd 20.00
Cruet, orig stopper, crystal 50.00
Cup and Saucer, crystal 12.50
Mayonnaise, underplate, and ladle..............35.00
Plate
    7-1/2" d, crystal................................6.00

    8-1/2" d, crystal................................8.50
Relish, 3-part, 10" l 25.00
Torte Plate, 13" d......................................30.00
Tray, crystal...15.00
Whipped Cream Bowl 30.00

Rambler. Pattern #1827. Made 1911-15 in crystal only. Some items reproduced in 1969.
Berry Bowl, 4-1/2" d..................................10.00
Champagne, hollow stem 30.00
Creamer and Sugar....................................30.00
Goblet..28.00
Iced Tea Tumbler, ftd.................................25.00
Nappy, 10" d 20.00
Oyster Cocktail..20.00
Plate, 8" d 10.00
Relish, 5-part, crystal, plain or gold trim 70.00
Sherbet..14.00
Tumbler, water..15.00

Randolph. Pattern #2675. Made 1961-65 in handmade milk glass only.
Bowl, 5-3/4" sq 10.00
Candlesticks, pr, 6" h.................................45.00
Creamer...17.50
Cup and Saucer 17.50
Egg Cup...15.00
Nappy, sq...14.00
Plate, 9" d, luncheon 14.50
Preserve, cov, ftd......................................27.50
Salt and Pepper Shakers, pr, chrome top.................15.00
Sugar, open..10.00

Rogene. Plate Etching #269. Made 1924-1929 only in crystal.
Champagne 15.00
Goblet, #5082...20.00
Jug, ftd, No. 7...360.00
Mayonnaise 60.00
Pitcher, crystal, ftd..................................225.00
Plate, #2283
    6" d...8.00
    7" d..10.00
    8" d..15.00
Tumbler, 13 oz..45.00

Romance. Plate Etching #341. Made 1942-72 only in crystal.
Bowl
    10" l, oval, handle, orig paper label.................65.00
    11" l, oblong, shallow........................70.00
Candlesticks, pr
    #25984, 5-1/2" h, orig paper label.................65.00
    #6023, 2-lite....................................95.00
Champagne 22.50
Cocktail..25.00
Console Bowl 45.00
Creamer and Sugar....................................40.00
Cup and Saucer 27.50
Fruit Bowl, 12" d..65.00
Oyster Cocktail, 4 oz..................................25.00
Pickle...40.00
Plate
    6" d...10.00
    7-1/2" d..14.00
Relish, 3-part..50.00
Salt and Pepper Shakers, pr, crystal, individual 65.00
Sandwich Server 45.00
Sherbet, low 22.00
Torte Plate, 14" d.......................................65.00
Tumbler, 6"...25.00
Wine 40.00

Royal. Plate Etching #273. Made 1925-32 in amber, black, blue and green.

Bouillon Cup, 3-1/2" d, green 18.50
Candlestick, 3", green, pr 50.00
Centerpiece Bowl, 12" d, rolled edge, amber 45.00
Champagne, amber 20.00
Console Bowl, amber 32.00
Cup and Saucer, amber 15.00
Finger Bowl, amber 25.00
Goblet, amber 25.00
Grapefruit, blown, ftd
    Amber 45.00
    Crystal 35.00
Jelly Comport, 5", amber 35.00
Parfait, amber 35.00
Pickle, 6-3/8" l, 8-sided oval, worn gold edge 15.00
Plate
    6" d, amber 5.00
    7-1/2" d, amber 5.00
    8" d, amber 10.00
    10" d, green 30.00
Platter, 12" l, amber, slight scratches 40.00
Relish, 8-sided oval, worn gold edge, amber
    8-3/8" l 18.50
    10-1/4" l 22.00
Soup, flat, amber 35.00
Tumbler, water, ftd, 9 oz, amber 18.00
Underplate, 6-1/8" d, amber 6.50
Urn, 10" h, ftd, #2324, amber 125.00
Vase
    7" h, #2292, amber, flared 95.00
    8" h, #2292, amber, gold edge 95.00

Seville. Plate Etching #274. Made 1926-34 in amber, blue, crystal, and green.

Bowl, amber 10.00
Butter, cov, crystal 85.00
Candy Box, cov, #2331, crystal 80.00
Centerpiece, 11" d, blue 95.00
Cheese and Cracker, crystal 40.00
Cream Soup, amber 30.00
Dinner Plate, amber 12.00
Plate, 7-1/2" d, green 6.50
Saucer, amber 3.00
Salad plate, amber 6.00
Sherbet, 4", amber 18.50
Tumbler, ftd, 5", amber 20.00
Underplate, 6-1/2" d, green 5.00

Sprite. Cutting #823. Made 1950-68 in combination gray and polished cutting on crystal only.

Champagne 20.00
Goblet, 6-1/8" h 25.00
Iced Tea Tumbler, ftd, 6" h 25.00
Juice Tumbler, ftd, 41/2" h 21.50
Mayonnaise, #2630/477, 3 pc set 36.00
Sherbet 18.50
Torte Plate, 14" d 42.00

Sun-Ray. Pattern #2510. Made 1935-44. Made in amber, azure blue, crystal, green and topaz (1935-38); gold tint (1938-40); selected items in ruby red (1935-40).

Bon Bon, 7-1/2" d, 3 toed, crystal 22.50
Bowl, 12" d, handle, crystal 45.00
Celery, 10" l, crystal 27.50
Compote, low, crystal 25.00
Creamer and Sugar, individual size, crystal 30.00
Decanter, #25010-1/2, orig stopper, oblong, crystal
    Rye 85.00

Scotch 85.00
Ice Bucket, crystal 45.00
Nappy, 2 handle, tricorn, crystal 12.50
Nut Cup, amber 20.00
Relish
    2-part, handle, crystal 20.00
    2-part, 10" l, crystal 27.50
Salt, individual, crystal 20.00
Sherbet, crystal 9.50
Sugar, 2-3/4", crystal 10.00
Torte Plate, 16-1/2" d
    Crystal 70.00
    Ruby red 75.00
Tumbler, green 18.00
Vase, 9" h, sq, ftd, crystal 75.00

Trojan. Made 1929-44 in rose pink, some green, and topaz yellow.

Ashtray, topaz yellow 55.00
Baker, oval, topaz yellow 100.00
Berry Bowl, topaz yellow 35.00
Candlesticks, pr, #2394, topaz yellow 65.00
Cereal Bowl, topaz yellow 75.00
Champagne
    Rose pink 40.00
    Topaz yellow 30.00
Cocktail, topaz yellow 28.00
Combination Bowl, #2415, topaz yellow 250.00
Comport, 4-1/2", topaz yellow 40.00
Cordial, topaz yellow 75.00
Cream Soup and Liner, topaz yellow 70.00
Cruet, topaz yellow 600.00
Cup and Saucer, topaz yellow 22.00
Demitasse Cup and Saucer, topaz yellow 75.00
Dessert Bowl, large, handle, topaz yellow 95.00
Goblet, topaz yellow 42.00
Grapefruit and Icer, topaz yellow 145.00
Iced Tea Tumbler, ftd, topaz yellow 50.00
Lemon Plate, handle, topaz yellow 24.00
Mint, 6" d, ftd, master, topaz yellow 75.00
Plate, topaz yellow
    6" d 9.50
    7-1/2" d 8.00
    8-1/2" d 16.00
Relish, topaz yellow 40.00
Service Tray, insert, topaz yellow 300.00
Soup, 7" d, flat
    Rose pink 195.00
    Topaz yellow 195.00
Sugar Pail, topaz yellow 250.00
Tomato Juice Insert, topaz yellow 20.00
Vase, 8" h, bulbous bottom, topaz yellow 400.00

Vernon. Plate Etching #277. Made 1927-34 in amber, crystal, and green (1927-34); azure (1928-34); orchid, (1927-28).

Candlesticks, pr, mushroom, green 90.00
Candy, cov, 3-part
    Green 100.00
    Orchid 130.00
Centerpiece Bowl, 13" l, oval, orchid 195.00
Cereal Bowl, orchid 55.00
Cheese and Cracker Plate, round, orchid 90.00
Chop Plate, orchid 140.00
Cup and Saucer, orchid 24.00
Finger Bowl
    Green 20.00
    Orchid 35.00
Grapefruit, green 35.00
Parfait, orchid 55.00

Pitcher, orchid 500.00
Plate, 9-1/2" d, orchid 35.00
Server, center handle, orchid 90.00
Sherbet, orchid 28.00
Tumbler, etched, ftd, crystal 15.00

Versailles. Plate Etching #278. Made 1928-44 in azure blue, green, rose, topaz, and gold tint.

After Dinner Creamer and Sugar, green 65.00
Ashtray
    Azure blue 75.00
    Rose 70.00
    Topaz 65.00
Baker, oval, azure blue 165.00
Bar Tumbler, 2 oz, azure blue 95.00
Berry Bowl, azure blue 55.00
Bon Bon, topaz 35.00
Bowl
    5" d, green 35.00
    5" d, topaz 40.00
    9-1/2" d, scroll handles, topaz 45.00
Candlesticks, pr
    3" h, #2395, azure blue 90.00
    5" h, scroll, topaz 60.00
Celery, green 90.00
Centerpiece, 11" d, round, azure blue 140.00
Cereal Bowl, 6-1/2" d
    Rose 95.00
    Topaz 70.00
Champagne, #5099, 6 oz, 6-1/8" h
    Green 35.00
    Rose 50.00
    Topaz 45.00
Claret, 6" h, 4 oz, rose 195.00
Cocktail
    Green 45.00
    Topaz 60.00
Compote, 7"
    Azure blue 110.00
    Green 75.00
Cracker, handle, azure blue 95.00
Cream Soup, liner
    Azure blue 55.00
    Topaz 20.00
Cruet, topaz 350.00
Cup and Saucer
    Azure blue 45.00
    Green 45.00
    Topaz 25.00
Decanter, stopper missing, topaz 750.00
Demitasse Cup and Saucer
    Rose 42.00
    Topaz 35.00
Dessert Bowl, large, handle, azure blue 145.00
Fruit Bowl
    Rose 65.00
    Topaz, 5" 18.00
Fruit Cocktail Insert, rose 42.50
Goblet
    Azure blue 65.00
    Rose 65.00
    Topaz 65.00
Grapefruit and Liner, green 150.00
Iced Tea Tumbler, #5099, 12 oz, 6" h, ftd
    Azure blue 60.00
    Topaz 45.00
Icer, topaz 50.00

Jug, #5000, ftd
    Green 600.00
    Rose 660.00
Juice Tumbler, ftd, topaz 15.00
Mayonnaise, underplate
    Rose 125.00
    Topaz 40.00
Mayonnaise Ladle, green 35.00
Mint, #2394, 4-1/2", green 50.00
Nut Dish, individual size, azure blue 65.00
Oyster Cocktail, 5-1/2" oz
    Azure blue 55.00
    Green 45.00
    Topaz 25.00
Parfait
    Azure blue 95.00
    Green 65.00
Plate
    4" d, topaz 10.00
    6" d, azure blue 14.50
    6" d, topaz 4.00
    7" d, azure blue 26.00
    7-1/2" d, topaz 18.00
    8-1/2" d, topaz 12.00
    9-1/2" d, topaz 30.00
    10-1/4" d, azure blue 65.00
    10-1/4" d, green 90.00
    10-1/4" d rose 95.00
Platter
    12" l, green 100.00
    15" l, rose 300.00
    15" l, topaz 95.00
Relish, 2-part, 8-1/2" l
    Azure blue 70.00
    Rose 48.00
    Topaz 28.00
Salt and Pepper Shakers, pr
    Azure blue 260.00
    Rose 190.00
Sauce Boat and Liner, topaz 250.00
Seafood Insert, green 22.50
Server, center handle, rose 80.00
Service Tray, insert, green 375.00
Sherbet
    Green 30.00
    Topaz 14.75
Soup Bowl, green 90.00
    Sugar
    Azure blue 40.00
    Green 20.00
Sugar Pail, azure blue 300.00
Sweetmeat, green 45.00
Tomato Juice Insert
    Green 22.50
    Rose 25.00
Tumbler, ftd
    5-1/4" h, orig paper label, azure blue 45.00
    6" h, #5298, azure blue 70.00
Whipped Cream Pail
    Azure blue 185.00
    Rose 275.00

Vesper. Plate Etching #275. Made 1926-34. Made in amber and green (1926-34); selected items made in blue (1926-28).

After Dinner Cup and Saucer, green 50.00
Bouillon, green 14.00
Bowl
    5" d, amber 22.00

10" d, ftd, #2524, amber..85.00
Candlesticks, pr, 3" h, green...............................70.00
Candy Dish, cov, 1/2 lb, green 120.00
Cereal Bowl, amber...30.00
Champagne, amber..24.00
Comport, twist stem, 7-1/2", amber 45.00
Console Bowl
    11" d, rolled edge, amber...............................45.00
    13" d, ftd, green..65.00
Creamer and Sugar, green, ftd............................65.00
Cream Soup, green..30.00
Cup and Saucer, amber...25.00
Goblet, blue..30.00
Grapefruit, ftd, blown, green.................................70.00
Ice Bucket, amber...65.00
Plate
    6" d, green...7.00
    7-1/2" d, amber...8.00
    8" d, amber...10.00
    9-1/2" d, amber...30.00
    9-1/2" d, green...50.00
    10" d, blue 65.00
Vase, 8" h, trumpet, #2292, green.......................95.00
Wine, green..50.00

Victoria. Pattern #4024. Made 1934-43 in crystal, regal blue bowl and crystal base, burgundy bowl and crystal base, empire green, selected pieces made in ruby.
Cocktail, 1-3/4" h, 1 oz, empire green.................20.00
Cordial, 3-1/8" h, regal blue 50.00
Goblet, 5-3/4" h, empire green..............................25.00
Oyster Cocktail, crystal 10.00
Relish, canoe shape, satin highlights 85.00
Sherbet, crystal 8.00

Wakefield. Cutting #820. Made 1942-72 in rock crystal only.
Candlesticks, #6023...75.00
Claret, #6023..20.00
Finger Bowl 10.00
Goblet, luncheon, #6023/63..................................18.00
Jug, ftd..90.00
Juice Tumbler, 4-1/2" h, ftd 22.00
Plate
    6" d 8.00
    7" d 9.00
    8" d 12.00
Sherbet, 4-7/8" h..22.00
Tumbler, 5-3/4" h, ftd..24.00

Willow. Etching #335. Made 1939-45 only in crystal.
Champagne..25.00
Cocktail..18.00
Creamer and Sugar..40.00
Fruit Bowl..10.00
Goblet, 9 oz..25.00
Jug, ftd..360.00
Juice Tumbler...16.00
Sugar, 3", crystal...20.00
Wine 30.00

Willowmere. Plate Etching #333. Made only in crystal.
Bowl
    11" d, handle 65.00
    11-1/2" d, crimped 65.00
    12" d, flared 55.00
Cake Tray, 10-1/2" d, handle................................45.00
Candlesticks, pr, 4", #2560-1/2...........................60.00
Celery, 11"..70.00
Champagne 14.00
Creamer and Sugar
    Individual size...36.00

Table size, ftd..45.00
Cup and Saucer..22.00
Demitasse Cup and Saucer....................................36.00
Mayonnaise and Liner..48.00
Oyster Cocktail...20.00
Pitcher, 8-7/8", qt, flat...300.00
Plate
    7" d 14.00
    7-3/8" d 8.50
Relish, 4-part...70.00
Server, center handle, #2560................................50.00
Sherbet, tall...20.00
Torte Plate, 14" d...65.00
Tumbler, 12 oz, ftd, #6024....................................30.00
Wine, 3-1/2 oz..16.00

FRUIT JARS

History: Fruit jars are canning jars used to preserve food. Thomas W. Dyott, one of Philadelphia's earliest and most innovative glassmakers, was promoting his glass canning jars in 1829. John Landis Mason patented his screw-type canning jar on Nov. 30, 1858. This date refers to the patent date, not the age of the jar. There are thousands of different jars and a variety of colors, types of closures, sizes, and embossings.

References: Douglas M. Leybourne Jr., *Red Book No. 7*, published by author (P.O. Box 5417, N. Muskegon, MI 49445), 1993; Jerry McCann, *Fruit Jar Annual*, published by author (5003 W. Berwyn Ave., Chicago, IL 60630), 1995; Michael Polak, *Bottles Identification and Price Guide, 2nd Edition,* Avon Books, 1997; Dick Roller (comp.), *Indiana Glass Factories Notes*, Acorn Press, 1994; Bill Schroeder, *1000 Fruit Jars: Priced and Illustrated*, 5th ed., Collector Books, 1987, 1996 value update.

Periodical: *Fruit Jar Newsletter*, 364 Gregory Ave., West Orange, NJ 07052.

Collectors' Clubs: Ball Collectors Club, 22203 Doncaster, Riverview, MI 48192; Federation of Historical Bottle Collectors, Inc., 88 Sweetbriar Branch, Longwood, FL 32750; Midwest Antique Fruit Jar & Bottle Club, PO Box 38, Flat Rock, IN 47234.

Adams & Co., Manufacturers, Pittsburgh, PA, aqua, applied mouth, orig stopper, quart....................540.00
A. Dufour & C Bordeaux, greenish aquamarine, barrel form, tooled mouth, pewter screw collar, mkd pewter cap, pontil scar, half gallon, L# 860 ....350.00
Advance, Pat. Appl'd For, aqua, ground lip, quart..........95.00
A. Stone & Co./Philada
    Aquamarine, applied collared mouth, glass lid, smooth base, half gallon, 2 mouth chips, L #2747.............175.00
    Aquamarine, grooved ring ax sealer, tin lid, iron pontil mark, pint, L #2743...950.00
    Aquamarine, internal threaded neck, threaded glass stopple, smooth base, quart plus, 1/4" flat chip on mouth, L #2749-1 ....425.00
Atlas, quart, L #109
    Apple Green...15.00
    Cornflower..35.00
Atlas Mason's Patent, medium yellow green, ABM lip, quart 50.00
Automatic, aqua, quart, L #177 ....225.00

Ball
- Letter "B" reversed, green, quart, L #221 ....15.00
- Mason, yellow green, amber striations, quart 75.00

Beaver, circular, aqua, quart, L #424-1 ....30.00

BBGM Co., aqua, quart, L #197 ....35.00

B. B. Wilcox, aquamarine, ground mouth, glass lid, wire bale, smooth base, half gallon, L #3000 ....100.00

Belle, Pat. Dec 14th 1869, aqua, 3 raised feet, ground lip, metal neck band, wire bail, quart.................................75.00

Best, brown amber, ground mouth, glass lid, wide zinc screw band, smooth base, Canada, 1890-1900, quart, L #453...... 200.00

Brighton, circular, aqua, quart #512 ....85.00

Canton, circular, quart, L #565 ....100.00

Clarke Fruit Jar Co., Cleveland, OH, aqua, ground lip, lid, metal cam lever closure, 1-1/2 pint.................................165.00

Columbia, quart, pale green, L #641 ....30.00

Crown, quart, apple green, L#697 ....20.00

Crystal Jar, Patd Dec. 17, 1878, clear, ground lip.............70.00

Dandy, L #751
- Half Gallon, aqua 70.00
- Quart, amber 225.00

Dodge Sweeney & Co.'s California, aqua, ground lip, glass insert, zinc band, 1-1-2 quart..................................425.00

Dur For, light green, wire clamp, French, 6-1/2" h 40.00

Eagle, deep aquamarine, applied collared mouth, glass lid, iron yoke, smooth base, half gallon, #872....................160.00

E. C. Flaccus Co., milk glass, ground mouth, milk glass lid, stag head, metal band, smooth base, pint, L #1016 .....375.00

Eclipse, aqua, no lid, quart, L#885 ....500.00

Ellwood, aqua, label and gauze, quart, L #1469 ....50.00

Everlasting, L #952
- Pint, aqua 45.00
- Quart, aqua 35.00

Excelsior, aqua, ground lip, insert, zinc band, quart.......575.00

Fahnestock Albree & Co., aqua, applied mouth, quart 35.00

Franklin Fruit Jar, aqua, ground lip, zinc lid, quart 225.00

Friedley & Cornman's Patent Oct. 25th 1958, Ladies Choice, aquamarine, ground mouth, iron rim, gutta percha or leather insert, smooth base, half gallon, iron rim lid rusty, L #1039...1,200.00

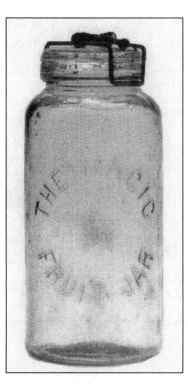

The Magic/star/Fruit Jar, America, 1880-1900, cylindrical, greenish aqua, ground mouth, glass lid, metal and iron metal cam clamp, smooth base, half gallon, chips to mouth, L#1606, $180. Photo courtesy of Norman C. Heckler and Co.

Fruit Keeper, aqua, quart, L #1042....................................65.00

Gem, whittled, half gallon, pale green, no insert, L #1068 .... 15.00

Gilberds Improved Jar, aqua, ground lip, wire band, quart 160.00

Globe, L #1123
- Half Gallon, aqua 40.00
- Quart
  - Amber 100.00
  - Aqua...25.00

Griffen's, aqua, quart, L #1154 ....225.00

Haines Combination, aquamarine, applied sq collared mouth, glass lid, wire clamp, smooth base, quart, c1860, some minor flakes on lid, L #1168 ....85.00

Helmen's Railroad Mills, amber, ground lip, insert, zinc band, pint...70.00

Helmes, amber, quart, L #1235 ....35.00

High Grade, aqua, ground lip, zinc lid, quart 150.00

Imp, aqua, half gallon 150.00

Independent, light purple, quart, L #1308 ....50.00

Johnson & Johnson, New York, cobalt blue, ground lip, orig insert, screw band, quart 325.00

Kerr, aqua, quart, L #1371 ....65.00

Lafayette, aqua, tooled lip, orig 3 pc glass and metal stopper, quart 200.00

L & W—Manufactured for Rice & Burnett, Cleveland, O, aquamarine, applied sq collared mouth, Kline glass stopple, smooth base, quart, shallow 1/4" flake on stopple, L #1529..100.00

Manufactured for N. O. Fansler, Cleveland, OH, aquamarine, applied collared mouth with glass stopple, smooth base, quart, 1/4" shallow chip on top of mouth, L #977 .....160.00

Mason Crystal Jar, clear, ground lip, zinc lid 65.00

Mason's Patent Nov. 30th, 1858
- Light green, profuse amber striations, machined mouth, zinc lid, smooth base, half gallon, some int. stain, L#1787......325.00
- Large snowflake, brilliant variegated golden yellow, ground mouth, zinc fruit depressor lid, smooth base, half gallon, L #1875..2,300.00

Moore's Patent Dec. 3rd 1861, aquamarine, applied collared mouth, glass lid, iron yoke clamp, smooth base, quart, L #2204.. 120.00

Peerless, aqua, applied mouth, iron yoke, half gallon......85.00

Pet, aqua, applied mouth, quart 55.00

Petal, deep bluish aquamarine, petaled shoulders, tooled collared mouth, new cork stopple, iron pontil, quart plus, L #3067.. 500.00

Phoenix, amber, quart, #2364...450.00

Potter & Bodine's Airtight Fruit Jar, aquamarine, grooved ring wax sealer mouth, tin lid, wire closure, smooth base, pint, severe damage to groove rim and discoloration, L #2383.... 400.00

Protector, aquamarine, ground mouth, unmarked tin lid, smooth base, quart, L #2420 .... 70.00

Safety, amber, quart, L #2534 ....175.00

Solidor, light green, wire clamp, name emb on front, French, 7-1/2" h 38.00

Star, aqua, emb star, ground lip, zinc insert and screw band, quart 300.00

Star and Crescent, aquamarine, ground mouth, zinc press down lid, porcelain liner, smooth base, quart, L#2727 .... 425.00

Stark, aqua, quart, L #2730 .... 200.00

Sun, aquamarine, ground mouth, glass lid, iron clamp, smooth base, quart 130.00

The Magic (star) Fruit Jar, greenish-aqua, ground mouth, glass lid, iron clamp, smooth base, half gallon, chips to mouth, L #1606.. 180.00

The Masons' Improved, colorless, swirled flutes at shoulder and base, ground mouth, glass lid, zinc screw band, smooth

base, quart, numerous chips and bruise hidden under lid
and band, unlisted 300.00
The Pearl, aqua, ground lip, screw band, quart...............40.00
The Van Vilet Jar of 1881, aqua, ground lip, orig wire and iron
yoke, quart...365.00
Trademark Lightning, ground mouth, matching glass lid, wire
bale, smooth base
Brilliant yellow with olive tone, mkd "H. W. P.," one half gallon,
1880-90, L #1148......................................170.00
Citron, pint, c1880, L #1499.......................................450.00
T. W. Beach Fruit Grower, aqua, cork closure, emb around
shoulder, 6" h..30.00
Union N1, Beaver Falls Glass Co., Beaver Falls, PA, aqua, ap-
plied wax seal ring, half gallon 45.00
Vacuum Seal, aqua, quart, L #2870 ....200.00
Whitmore's Patent, Rochester, NY, aqua, ground lip, wire closure,
quart..425.00
Wilcox, aqua, quart, L #3000 ....100.00

FRY GLASS

History: The H. C. Fry Glass Co. of Rochester, Pennsylvania, began operating in 1901 and continued in business until 1933. Its first products were brilliant-period cut glass. It
later produced Depression glass tablewares. In 1922, the
company patented heat-resisting ovenware in an opalescent color. This "Pearl Oven Glass," which was produced in
a variety of pieces for oven and table, included casseroles,
meat trays, and pie and cake pans. Most pieces of the oven
glass are marked "Fry," with model numbers and sizes.

Fry's beautiful art line, Foval, was produced only in
1926 and 1927. It is pearly opalescent, with jade green or
delft blue trim. It is always evenly opalescent, never
striped like Fenton's opalescent line. Foval examples are
rarely signed, except for occasional silver-overlay pieces
marked "Rockwell."

Reference: Fry Glass Society, *Collector's Encyclopedia
of Fry Glass*, Collector Books, 1989, 1998 value update.

Collectors' Club: H. C. Fry Glass Society, P.O. Box 41,
Beaver, PA 15009.

Reproduction Alert: In the 1970s, reproductions of Foval were made in abundance in Murano, Italy. These pieces, including items such as candlesticks and toothpicks,
have teal blue transparent trim.

Art glass

Candleholder, Azure blue 25.00
Creamer, 4" h, pinched top, yellow body, three blue-green
loops, applied deep blue handle 175.00
Goblet, Royal Blue, 6-1/4" h 35.00
Ivy Ball, crystal swirl connector
Emerald Green 60.00
Rose 65.00
Pitcher, 9-1/4" h, Diamond Optic pattern, chrome green, ground
pontil..85.00
Plate, 7-1/2" d, jade, sterling silver floral overlay 185.00
Relish, 2-part, irid, holder..60.00
Tumbler, conical, colorless, sterling silver floral overlay, 10
oz, sgd "Rockland" 110.00
Vase, 12" h, opalescent body, pink loopings...............215.00
Wine, Royal Blue, 3-3/4" h..35.00

Bowl, opalescent swirls, cobalt blue rim, 8-1/2" d, $85.

Cut and etched glass

Bowl, 8" d, pineapple design, wheel cutting, sgd.......120.00
Goblet
Rose etch, #7816, 10 oz...24.00
Wild Rose etch, #51 ....30.00
Ice Cream Tray, 14" l, 7" w, Nelson pattern variation, all over
cutting, sgd "Fry" 290.00
Iced Tea Set, Japanese Maid, deeply etched, ftd pitcher, six
handled, ftd tumblers 525.00
Jug, Wild Rose etch, 64 oz, cut fluted neck................165.00
Juice Tumbler, Wild Rose etch, 3-5/8" h, 5 oz, cut fluted
base...20.00
Nappy, 6" d, pinwheel and fan with hobstar center, sgd...60.00
Sherbet, 4" h, Chicago pattern.....................................75.00
Soda Tumbler, Wild Rose etch, 5" h, 12 oz, handle, 16 point
cut star base..28.00
Tumbler
Pinwheel, zipper, and fan motifs, sgd, 6 pc set.....180.00
Wild Rose etch, #51, 3-1/2" h, 8 oz, cut fluted base.... 24.00
Wine, Wild Rose etch, 5-1/4" h, 3 oz, cut fluted stem ...28.00

Foval

Bouillon Cup and Saucer, pearl white, two cobalt blue
handles...85.00
Bud Vase
9-1/2" h, pearl white, Delft blue wafer attachment 125.00
10" h, pearl white, cobalt blue foot 140.00
Canapé Plate, 6-1/4" d, 4" h, cobalt blue center handle .. 175.00
Candlesticks, pr, 12" h, pearl white candlesticks, jade green
threading and trim 1,380.00
Centerbowl, 10-1/2" d, pearl white, Delft blue rim.......125.00
Compote
6-3/4" d, alabaster white bowl and foot, jade green
stem..120.00
8-3/4" d, 6-3/4" h, opalescent pearl white bowl, pale blue
loopings and blue foot.....................................175.00
Creamer and Sugar, Set 200, delft blue handles........175.00
Cream Soup, opalescent 55.00
Cruet, pearl white body, cobalt blue handle, orig
stopper...125.00
Cup and Saucer, pearl white, Delft blue handles 65.00
Decanter, 9" h, ftd, applied Delft blue handle.............195.00
Eggcup, jade base...145.00
Fruit Bowl, 9-7/8" d, 5-1/4" h, pearl white, ridged, delft blue
foot..520.00
Goblet, fiery opalescent pearl white body, pink
loopings..90.00

Lemonade Pitcher
    6" h, Pearl Ware, Delft blue handle..........................145.00
    6-1/4" h, Icicle pattern, green handle 95.00
    10-1/2" h, 5" w, tankard, applied Delft Blue large loop handle
       and foot, strong pearlescence...............................675.00
Parfait, 6-1/2" h, pearl white body, Delft blue stain 175.00
Pitcher, alabaster body, jade green base and handle 295.00
Plate, 9-1/2" d, pearl white, Delft blue rim 75.00
Teacup and Saucer, Delft blue handles 95.00
Teapot, pearl white, cobalt blue spout, handle and
    knob 250.00
Toothpick Holder, pearl white, Delft blue handle..........85.00
Tumbler, 3-7/8" h, waisted..40.00
Vase
    7-1/2" h, jade green, rolled rim and foot.................225.00

9" h, trumpet, pearl white, jade green foot 395.00
Wine, pearl white, Delft blue stem...............................165.00

Ovenware

Bean Pot, 1 quart 35.00
Butter Dish, cov, Pearl Oven Ware................................75.00
Casserole, Pearl Oven Ware, etched gold dec lid, metal
    holder, 1938 ....75.00
Child's Pie Plate, Pearl Oven Ware 50.00
Custard, flared, opaque 12.00
Grill Plate, 10-1/2" d, mkd "Pearl Oven Ware"..............35.00
Pie Plate 35.00
Platter, 17" l, Oven Ware 65.00
Trivet, 8", Oven Ware..20.00

GALLÉ

History: Emile Gallé was one of the most famous glassmakers and designers from Nancy, France. Born in 1846, he learned the art of glassmaking from his father. He furthered his studies in art at Weimar and traveled frequently to Paris and London to study glass and glass techniques.

1867–1904

Gallé opened his own glasshouse in 1867, and began production of art glass in 1874 with his father. This Nancy factory did very well and soon expanded into cameo and cased glass wares. Gallé was a leading exponent of the Art Nouveau movement in glassmaking, furniture, and other decorative arts.

Complicated cameo-cutting techniques allowed intricate glasswares to be crafted to Gallé's exacting standards. One of the more common techniques of the factory was the production of cameo ware with detailed floral patterns on an opaque white background. Opaque colored backgrounds of many other colors were also used. Much like his contemporary, Louis Tiffany, Gallé was a designer and left much of the actual crafting to others. The lovely glass creations he designed were influenced by the Art Nouveau movement, as well as the increasing interest in Japanese and other Oriental-style decoration.

Examples of Gallé's wares were exhibited at the Paris Expositions of 1878 and 1884. They were also exhibited there in 1889 and 1900 and received wide acclaim for their beauty. Gallé's influence on other glasshouses, such as De Verre, in the Nancy region was felt as the "School of Nancy" grew around his factory.

After Gallé's death in 1904, the factory continued production until 1931. Most pieces of Gallé glass were signed. Cameo glasswares have the bold signature cameo carved into the piece. Pieces made after Gallé's death are signed with the classic signature and a star.

References: Victor Arwas, *Glass Art Nouveau to Art Deco*, Rizzoli International Publications, Inc., 1977; Tim Newark, *Emile Gallé,* The Apple Press, 1989; Harold Newman, *An Illustrated Dictionary of Glass*, Thames and Hudson, 1977; Albert C. Revi, *Nineteenth Century Glass*, reprint, Schiffer Publishing, 1981.

Museums: Bergstrom-Mahler Museum, Neenah, WI; The Chrysler Museum, Norfolk, VA; The Corning Museum of Glass, Corning, NY; The Toledo Museum of Art, Toledo, OH.

Cameo

Bonbonniere, cov, 4" h, Verre Parlant, egg shaped, frosted ground overlaid in violet, etched rooster and phrase "Le cou de Village," cameo sgd "Galle" 1,750.00
Bowl
5" d, 4-1/2" h, round, small pedestal base, lime green flowers and leaves over frosted gray and pink ground, top rim pulled to make five points, sgd, two spots re-polished, inclusion on int. base 400.00
11" l, 3-1/4" h, frosted ground, overlaid in blue and violet, etched water lilies floating on water, cameo sgd "Galle" 1,300.00

Box, cov
3-1/2" h, frosted fiery amber-yellow base and cover, orange sienna layer etched all over as blossoming leafy plants, sgd "Galle" on cover and base, some color variation 1,265.00
4-3/8" d, compressed spherical shape, flat lid, amber ground, purple overlay, carved stalk of starflowers, lid and base sgd in cameo.................................800.00
Brush Pot, 5-1/2" h, sq, dark yellow ground, overlay small trumpet flowers and leaves, enameled white, green, and maroon, gilt highlights, sgd in cameo, c1900 .....3,300.00
Cabinet Vase
2-1/2" h, 2-1/4" w, squatty, gray acid ground, lavender at throat, cut with green leaves and purple and green floral spray, sgd 350.00
2-1/2" h, 3-1/2" d, frosted green, yellow, and clear ground, cameo overlay of green and yellow maple leaves and seedlings, sgd, two chips in design..................450.00
Coupe, 4-3/8" d, 2-1/4" h, frosted turquoise body, overlaid in magenta-red, crisply etched as leafy blossoming plants, side sgd "Galle" 750.00
Creamer, 3-1/4" h, 2-1/4" d, frosted peach ground, red berries and leaves, two acid cuttings, applied frosted handle, cameo sgd 1,600.00
Ewer, 9-1/4" h, compressed spherical body and spout, applied handle and vines, colorless body, wheel carved lines simulating opening calla lily, sgd "E Gallé" on base, c1900...3,500.00
Floor Vase, 30-1/2" h, 6-1/4" d top, 12" d base, highly carved ferns in shades of brown and burgundy, crystal and pink ground with clear carved shaded green ferns in background, sgd..8,500.00
Lamp, table
14-1/2" h, 12" d, wrought iron base cast with stylized foliage issuing 3 down turned arms, each with flared frosted yellow glass shade, overlaid in red, etched trumpet flowers and foliage, each cameo sgd "Galle" 6,500.00
25" h, 18" d domed shade, frosted yellow ground, overlaid in red and crimson, etched peony blossoms and foliage, baluster vase base, both shade and base cameo sgd "Galle" 170,000.00
30" h, 18" d domed shade, deep yellow ground, overlaid in periwinkle and indigo, etched berried branches, cameo sgd on shade and ftd base "Galle" 30,000.00
Lamp, wall, 9-1/4" h, 9" " w, half-round frosted amber glass wall pocket, layered in cinnamon colored glass, etched various blossoms, mounted to gilt bronze floral frame and metal back housing light socket, sgd "Galle" on side in cameo...5,500.00
Miniature Vase
2-3/8" h, conical oval, pink within frosted glass, overlaid in green and amethyst, etched as blossoming cluster, sgd "Galle" at lower edge 490.00
3-1/2" h, flattened sphere, green, orange, and frosted, cameo etched acorns and oak leaf branches, sgd "Galle" on reverse...600.00
5" h, slender oval, yellow, frosted, and aubergine, cameo etched wild geraniums, sgd "Galle" near base.... 750.00
Perfume, 4" h, 4-1/4" w, raised rim, wide flattened quatraform bottle, mottled pink ground, layered in moss green and brown, double etched in riverscape scene with man in boat, conforming stopper, sgd "Galle" at reverse 2,650.00
Plaffonier, domed circular shade, cameo sgd "Galle"
20" d, frosted yellow ground, overlaid in crimson red, mold blown and etched oranges among foliage, ...17,000.00
20" d, frosted yellow ground, overlaid in red, etched poppies 6,750.00

Vase, 14" h, three color, blue poppies, green foliage, fading peach to opaque ground, sgd in cameo, $2,800. Photo courtesy of Freeman\Fine Arts of Philadelphia, Inc.

Toothpick Holder, 2-1/2" h, tapered cylinder, orange-amber over frosted colorless body, cameo etched broad blossom and bud on leafy stem, sgd "Galle" in cameo 690.00

Tumbler, 2-3/4" h, frosted colorless and pink opal ground, white, blue, and green overlay cut in four petaled blossoms and leaves, sgd in cameo 800.00

Vase

3-3/4" h, frosted brick-red oval, overlaid in maroon, polished and etched floral motif, side sgd "Galle"...............635.00

4-1/2" h, flared trefoil rim, oval body, layered in red amber, etched leafy vines and grape clusters, surface fire polished, "Galle" sgd in motif...............................1,300.00

5-3/4" h, raised rim, flattened fiery amber oval body, layered in olive green, etched long-leafed branches with figs pendent..1,150.00

6" h, bulbed, orange and colorless body, overlaid in red, cameo carved and etched trailing blossoms, buds, and leafy stems, side sgd "Galle," some int. debris flecks 575.00

6" h, flared green-gray ftd oval, overlaid in purple, leafy branches laden with berries, reverse side sgd "Galle," some minor int. stain...750.00

6" h, oval pink, white, and frosted colorless glass, layered in lavender-purple under green, cameo etched as pendant wisteria blossom clusters, sgd "Galle" at lower side..1,265.00

6-3/4" h, frosted yellow-amber banjo body, overlaid pastel blue-green under mauve, cameo etched mountain landscape..1,955.00

7" h, oviform, everted rim, rich yellow ground overlaid in sky blue and hunter green, etched cornflowers and foliage, cameo sgd "Galle"................................2,750.00

7" h, 3-1/2" w, banjo shape, deep purple fuchsia floral dec, frosted clear and yellow ground, sgd 800.00

7" h, 5" w, bulbous, flaring rim, marbleized shades of orange, small bubbles and dark brown swirls throughout, inscribed "Cristallerie de Galle," small bruise at base...900.00

7-3/4" h, colorless body cased and layered with brilliant pink and amethyst, olive green around raised calyx-rim, deeply etched overall in detailed blossoms, seed pods, berries, and leaves, "Galle" Asian influence mark at side...5,175.00

8" h, flattened oviform, frosted yellow ground, overlaid in white and violet, etched mountainous lake scene, cameo sgd "Galle" 2,000.00

8-1/4" h, pinched quatraform rim, shaded blue to frost to pink tapered body, layered in bright pink and olive green, etched blossoming leafy plants, sgd "(star) Galle" 1,265.00

9" h, elongated ovoid pastel yellow and frosted colorless body, overlaid in burgundy and rose, cameo etched bleeding hearts blossoms, sgd "Galle" in lower design 1,610.00

8-3/8" h, 6" d, marquetry wheel carved and cameo etched, trumpet, ridge raised rim, colorless heavy walled body, cased to opal-pink, overlaid in amethyst-mauve over creamy pink-beige, etched and martelé carved as highly detailed trumpet blossoms and undulating leaf forms, "Galle" Asian influence mark at lower edge, some internal specks and blemishes within glass............. 5,750.00

10" h, elongated trumpet form, everted rim, frosted ground shading to peach, overlaid in lime green and brown, etched ferns, cameo sgd "Galle" 1,500.00

10-1/2" h, 5-1/2" w, blue mountains, frosted pale pink and clear ground, deep brown landscape scene, sgd 3,900.00

11-1/2" h, flared blue-gray oval body, overlaid in blue, green, lavender, and purple, cameo etched riverside landscape, mountains, tall fir trees, side sgd "Galle".............2,645.00

12" h, flattened oval, frosted yellow ground, overlaid in blue and green, etched trees against mountainous landscape, cameo sgd "Galle" 3,000.00

12-1/2" h, bulbous, pink and colorless frosted body, elongated slender neck, overlaid white, green, and lavender cameo etched blossoming leafy branches, sgd "Galle" in cameo on reverse...........................1,380.00

12-1/2" h, 5-1/2" w, 3-1/4" d mouth, elongated oval body, short straight neck, shaded gray frosted ground, cut pine cones and tassels dec, shading from dark brown to light coffee color, sgd....................................800.00

13-3/4" h, ribbed transparent, frosted, and fire-polished aquamarine oval, tricorn rim, applied aubergine cupped pedestal foot, overlaid in glossy sapphire blue, cameo etched two bumblebees among blossoms, leafy morning glory vines, center star blossom, sgd "Verre Parlant Lupine et Caitate," and "Galle" at side.................. 5,750.00

14-3/4" h, 6-1/4" w, round, flat base, tapered stem opens to wide ovoid shoulder, rolled-in top rim with four indentations, large orange nasturtiums and leaves circle around shaded gray, pink, and pale orange ground..... 1,550.00

15-1/4" h, flared elongated trumpet, green and pink frosted body, overlaid in dark olive green and lavender, cameo etched tall spiked blossoms, leafy stems, medial cameo mark "(star) Galle" 1,495.00

15-1/2" h, 5-1/2" w, 3-1/2" w mouth, lavender columbine flowers over clear frosted to shaded yellow ground, sgd..2,000.00

17" h, pilgrim flask form, rich yellow frosted ground, overlaid in periwinkle and indigo, etched mountainous landscape and chalets, cameo sgd "GALLE," orig paper label...19,500.00

23" h, elongated flared ovoid body, frosted colorless, pink, and lavender, overlaid in purple-amethyst, cameo etched wisteria blossom cluster, long leafy stems at side, "(star) Galle" in cameo...........................2,875.00

Enameled

Cup, 2" h, 2-3/4" w, pale amber body, seven enamel fleur-de-lis dec, applied rope handle, sgd "E. Galle Nancy," set of 4 ....600.00

Cup and Saucer

2-1/4" h cup, 5" d saucer, pale topaz transparent crystal, matching pastel stylized floral designs, cups inscribed "E. Galle Nancy" on base, price for 8 pc set....1,495.00

2-5/8" d cup, 4-1/4" d saucer, handleless cup, scalloped edge, blue, green, rose, white, and gold repeating border dec, plate inscribed "Galle" and retailer "Gilman Collamore & Co. New York".....................345.00

Flacon, 5-1/4" h, 5-1/2" l, Verre Parland, figural bird, transparent topaz bird-form vessel, applied disk foot, notched handle, body enameled with multicolored scrolling devices, golden stylized bird with phrase "Je Suis ill Roi," base engraved "E. Galle - Nancy," topaz stopper above beak rim.......3,105.00

Miniature Vase
2-5/8" h, wide blue-green oval cased to opal, overlaid olive green, etched with seed pods on leafy branch, rim wrapped with conforming leaf and pod silver collar, sgd "Galle" at side, lightly dented......................825.00
3-1/4" h, frosted pink oval, layered in lime green, etched broad leaf blossoming plant, sgd "Galle" in cameo..435.00

Perfume Bottle, 6" h, 3-1/2" w, clear crystal body, blue enameled floral and ribbon design, sgd "E. Galle Nancy".......1,650.00

Tray, 10-1/4" d, scalloped and folded pale topaz, praying mantis above stylized leaf and blossom branches, enameled black, brown, blue, and red, disk foot, mkd "E. Galle a Nancy"...1,265.00

Tumbler, 4-1/2" h, faceted, slightly tapering cylinder, enameled French peasant woman holding umbrella in the rain, two acanthus leaves, inscription on reverse, blue, yellow, red, and white, enameled "Emile Gallé Depose," c1870..1,650.00

Vase
3-3/4" h, 5" d, aquamarine transparent bowl form, six-sided angular rim, raised star above gold centered pink cameo etched blossoms, gold enameled leaves, base inscribed "Galle/Depose/GesGesch" in flower outline 1,840.00
4-3/4" h, transparent colorless sphere, applied rope twist collar, Japonesque fish over blue waves, floral elements, gold painted ocean waves, ripples, base inscribed "E. Galle a Nancy," two sliver chips under collar at rim..1,380.00
5" h, bulbous emerald green transparent oval body, surface etched all over and cameo cut chrysanthemums, enhanced by enamel polychrome coloring, sgd "Galle" at lower side..1,035.00
6-1/4" h, three footed ribbed body, pastel Japonesque floral dec, base mkd "E. Galle/a Nancy," rim polished..320.00
12" h, double bulbed transparent colorless glass, ribbed, blue enameled fleur-de-lis with gold accents, base inscribed "Emile Galle Nancy"..............................980.00

Whimsey, 4-1/4" h, three blue and amethyst butterflies on frosted cap with "Galle" mark, mounted on wrought iron tripod holder..1,265.00

Wine, 4-3/8" h, colorless rib-molded bowl, amber knop, topaz cupped stem foot, 3 applied red, amber, green jewels as etched blossom centers, gold enameled outlines, "E. Galle" etched on leaf on foot, some wear to gold..............1,380.00

Marquetrie Sur Verre

Vase, 7-1/2" h, Les Roses De France, applied, internally dec, and wheel-carved, opalescent glass flecked with pink, purple and turquoise, dec with 3 rose colored applied high relief roses, applied high relief lime green scrolling stems and leaves, surrounded by low relief pale pink with thistle-like flowers, ftd base, surfaces finely wheel carved, inscribed "Galle," series introduced in 1903.........82,000.00

GOOFUS GLASS

History: Goofus glass, also known as Mexican ware, Hooligan glass, and pickle glass, is a pressed glass with relief designs that were painted either on the back or front. The designs are usually in red and green with a metallic gold ground. It was popular from 1890 to 1920 and was used as a premium at carnivals.

The cold painted, unfired, decoration did not wear well and easily chipped off. This may be why the name goofus was derived: the manufacturers "goofed" with this technique. The goofus decoration was applied to colorless, transparent green, blue, or amber grounds, as well as opalescent and milk glass grounds. Surfaces were sometimes acid etched (giving a satin ground), crackled, or pressed in a basketweave pattern.

Goofus Glass was produced by several companies: Crescent Glass Company, Wellsburg, W.V.; Imperial Glass Corporation, Bellaire, Ohio; LaBelle Glass Works, Bridgeport, Ohio; and Northwood Glass Co., Indiana, Pennsylvania, Wheeling, W.V., and Bridgeport, Ohio. Goofus glass made by Northwood includes one of the following marks: "N," "N" in one circle, "N" in two circles, or one or two circles without the "N."

Goofus glass lost its popularity when people found that the paint tarnished or scaled off after repeated washings and wear. No record of its manufacture has been found after 1920.

Reference: Carolyn McKinley, *Goofus Glass,* Collector Books, 1984.

Periodical: *Goofus Glass Gazette,* Steve and Judy Gillespie, #9, NW 61st St., Gladstone, MO 64118-4002.

Website: http://sundial.sundial.net~gballens, Goofus Glass Information Center, David and Maureen Ballentine.

Ashtray, red rose dec, emb adv 12.00
Basket, 5" h, strawberry dec.. 50.00
Bon Bon, 4" d, Strawberry pattern, gold, red, and green dec 40.00
Bowl
4-1/2" d, red roses dec, gold trim 20.00
5-1/2" d, La Belle Rose pattern, sq 35.00
6-1/2" d, Grape and Lattice pattern, red grapes, gold ground, ruffled rim..45.00
7" d, Iris pattern, gold and red dec 35.00
7" d, thistle and scrolling leaves, red dec, gold ground, ruffled rim...35.00
8-3/4" d, fluted, beaded rim, relief molded, teardrops and red hearts..45.00
9" d, Carnation pattern, red flowers, relief molded 30.00
9" d, Cherries pattern, red dec, gold ground...............30.00
9" d, Roses pattern, red roses, ruffled, relief molded ...30.00
10" d, Dahlias pattern, scalloped 50.00
10" d, pears and apples dec...35.00
10-1/2" d, red roses, molded, gold ground...................45.00
10-1/2" d, water lilies dec...50.00
11" d, red cherries, relief molded, ruffled....................35.00
Bread Plate, 7" w, 11" l, Last Supper pattern, red and gold, grapes and foliage border...65.00
Cake Plate
11" d, Dahlia and Fan, red dec, gold ground 40.00
12" d, red roses dec, gold ground 20.00
Candle Holder, red and gold 20.00
Candy Dish, 8-1/2" d, figure eight design, serrated rim, dome foot..60.00
Coaster, 3" d, red floral dec, gold ground 12.00

Compote
 4" d, Grape and Cable pattern 35.00
 6" d, Strawberry pattern, red and green strawberries and foliage, ruffled 40.00
 6-1/2" d, Poppy pattern, red flowers, gold foliage, green ground, sgd "Northwood" 40.00
 9-1/2" d, red and green floral and foliage dec, green ground, crimped and fluted rim, pedestal foot, sgd "Northwood" 40.00
 9-1/2" d, Strawberry pattern, red and green strawberries and foliage, gold ground, ruffled 50.00
 10-1/4" d, red fruit, relief molded 65.00
Decanter, orig stopper
 La Belle Rose 50.00
 Single Rose pattern, basketweave ground, emb rose stopper 65.00
Dish, 11" d, chrysanthemum sprays, red and gold, scalloped rim 75.00
Dresser Tray, 6" l, Cabbage Rose pattern, red roses dec, gold foliage, clear ground 35.00
Fairy Lamp, red roses dec, green trim, clear candle cup 45.00
Flask, zig-zag pattern, milk glass ground, gold paint, metal screw top 50.00
Jar, cov, butterflies, red and gold 35.00
Jewel Box, 4" d, 2" h, basketweave, rose dec 50.00
Miniature Lamp, 12" h, Cabbage Rose pattern 45.00
Mug, Cabbage Rose pattern, gold ground 35.00
Nappy, 6-1/2" d
 Cherries pattern, red cherries, gold foliage, clear ground 35.00
 Strawberry pattern, red strawberries, green leaves, molded applied ring handle 20.00
Perfume Bottle, 3-1/2" h, pink tulips dec 20.00
Pickle Jar, aqua, molded, gold, blue, and red painted floral design 50.00
Pin Dish, 6-1/2" l, oval, red and black florals 20.00
Pitcher, red rose bud dec, gold leaves 60.00
Plate
 6" d, Rose and Lattice pattern, relief molded 20.00
 6" d, Sunflower pattern, red dec center, relief molded 20.00
 7-1/2" d, apples, red dec, gold ground 24.00
 7-3/4" d, Carnations pattern, red carnations, gold ground 20.00
 8" d, red applies, relief molded 20.00
 8-1/2" d, Gibson Girl cameo, red and gold 45.00
 8-1/2" d, red apples, gold ground, relief molded 35.00
 10-1/2" d, grapes dec, gold ground, irid pink edge 35.00
 11" d, Dahlia pattern, red and gold 40.00
 11" d, roses, red and gold, scalloped rim 45.00
 12" d, Bird and Strawberry, gold, blue and red dec ... 100.00
Platter, 18" l, red rose dec, gold ground 65.00
Powder Jar, cov
 3" d, puffy, rose dec, red and gold 40.00
 4-1/2" d, Cabbage Rose pattern, white cabbage rose, relief molded 35.00
Salt and Pepper Shakers, pr
 Grape and Leaf pattern 45.00
 Poppy pattern 40.00
Syrup, relief molded
 Red roses dec, lattice work ground, orig top 85.00
 Strawberry pattern, red strawberries, green foliage, gold ground 75.00
Toothpick Holder, red rose and foliage dec, gold ground 40.00
Tray, 8-1/4" d, 11" d, red chrysanthemum dec, gold ground .. 45.00
Tumbler, 6" h, red rose dec, gold ground 35.00
Vase
 6" h, Cabbage Rose pattern, red dec, gold ground 45.00

 6-1/2" h, Grape and Rose pattern, red and gold dec, crackle glass ground 35.00
 7-1/4" h, Grapes pattern, purple dec 35.00
 7-1/2" h, brown, red bird 30.00
 8" h, Grapes pattern, purple dec 35.00
 9" h, bird sitting on grapevine, red and gold, satin glass ground 45.00
 9" h, Poppies pattern, blue and red dec, gold ground 45.00
 10-1/2" h, Peacock pattern 75.00
 2" h, Parrot pattern, red and blue bird, molded foliage 85.00
 12" h, red roses, molded, gold ground 60.00

GREENTOWN GLASS

History: The Indiana Tumbler and Goblet Co., Greentown, Indiana, produced its first clear, pressed glass table and bar wares in late 1894. Initial success led to a doubling of the plant size in 1895 and other subsequent expansions, one in 1897 to allow for the manufacture of colored glass. In 1899, the firm joined the combine known as the National Glass Company.

In 1900, just before arriving in Greentown, Jacob Rosenthal developed an opaque brown glass, called "chocolate," which ranged in color from a dark, rich chocolate to a lighter coffee-with-cream hue. Production of chocolate glass saved the financially pressed Indiana Tumbler and Goblet Works. The Cactus and Leaf Bracket patterns were made almost exclusively in chocolate glass. Other popular chocolate patterns include Austrian, Dewey, Shuttle, and Teardrop and Tassel. In 1902, National Glass Company bought Rosenthal's chocolate glass formula so other plants in the combine could use the color.

In 1902, Rosenthal developed the Golden Agate and Rose Agate colors. Golden Agate was the color used for the Holly Amber pattern, designed by Frank Jackson, in January 1903. More than 30 forms were developed for this pattern, which featured a gold colored body with a marbleized onyx color on raised design elements. All work ceased on June 13, 1903, when a fire of suspicious origin destroyed the Indiana Tumbler and Goblet Company Works.

After the fire, other companies, e.g., McKee and Brothers, produced chocolate glass in the same pattern designs used by Greentown. Later reproductions also have been made, with Cactus among the most-heavily copied patterns.

Reference: James Measell, *Greentown Glass*, Grand Rapids Public Museum, 1979, 1992-93 value update, distributed by Antique Publications; Brenda Measell and James Measell, *A Guide To Reproductions of Greentown Glass*, 2nd ed., The Printing Press, 1974; James Measell, *Greentown Glass, The Indiana Tumbler & Goblet Co.*, Grand Rapids Public Museum, 1979, 1992-93 value update, distributed by Antique Publications; Kenneth Wilson, *American Glass 1760-1930: The Toledo Museum of Art, Volume I, Volume II*, Hudson Hills Press and The Toledo Museum of Art, 1994.

Collectors' Clubs: Collectors of Findlay Glass, P.O. Box 256, Findlay, OH 45839; National Greentown Glass Assoc., 19596 Glendale Ave., South Bend, IN 46637.

Videotapes: *Centennial Exhibit of Greentown Glass* and *Reproductions of Greentown Glass*, National Greentown Glass Assoc., PO Box 107, Greentown, IN 46936.

Museums: Grand Rapids Public Museum, Ruth Herrick Greentown Glass Collection, Grand Rapids, MI; Greentown Glass Museum, Greentown, IN.

Reproduction Alert.

Animal, covered dish
    Bird with Berry, blue 475.00
    Bird with Berry, chocolate, minor repair 650.00
    Cat, hamper base, amber 465.00
    Cat, hamper base, blue 465.00
    Cat, hamper base, chocolate 425.00
    Dolphin, chocolate, chip off tail 195.00
    Hen on Nest, blue 265.00
    Hen on Nest, chocolate 725.00
    Rabbit, dome top, amber 250.00
    Robin, nest base, opaque white 225.00
Berry Set, Leaf Bracket, chocolate, 7 pcs 275.00
Bowl
    6-1/4" d, No. 11, blue 200.00
    6-1/2" d, Cactus, chocolate 100.00
    7-1/4" d, Herringbone Buttress, green 135.00
    7-1/2" d, Cactus, chocolate 120.00
    7-1/2" d, Holly Amber, oval 375.00
    8-1/2" d, Holly Amber 395.00
    10-1/4" d, Geneva, chocolate 450.00
Butter, cov
    Cactus, chocolate 300.00
    Cupid, chocolate 575.00
    Daisy, opaque white 100.00
    Herringbone Buttress, green 250.00
    Holly Amber 1,875.00
    Leaf Bracket, chocolate 250.00
    Oval Lattice, colorless 75.00
    Shuttle, chocolate 1,100.00
Cake Stand, Holly Amber 2,500.00
Celery Vase, Beaded Panel, colorless 100.00
Compote
    Cactus, chocolate 225.00
    Geneva, 4-1/2" d, 3-1/2" h, chocolate 150.00
    Holly Amber, 8-1/2" h, 12" d, cov 2,500.00
Cookie Jar, Cactus, chocolate 300.00
Cordial
    Austrian, canary 125.00
    Overall Lattice, colorless 45.00
    Shuttle, colorless 45.00
Creamer
    Austrian, colorless 40.00
    Cactus, chocolate 125.00
    Cord Drapery, colorless 65.00
    Cupid, Nile green 400.00
    Holly Amber, 4" h, 3-1/2" w, golden agate, professionally pol-
        ished rim, small burst bubble 75.00
    Holly Amber, 4-1/2" h 650.00
    Indian Head, opaque white 450.00
    Indoor Drinking Scene, chocolate, 5-1/2" h 500.00
    Shuttle, colorless, tankard style 65.00
Cruet, orig stopper
    Cactus, chocolate 325.00
    Chrysanthemum Leaf, chocolate 1,275.00
    Dewey, vaseline 300.00
    Geneva, chocolate 1,000.00
    Holly Amber 1,850.00
    Leaf Bracket, chocolate 275.00
    Wild Rose and Bowknot, chocolate 350.00
Dish, Dolphin, chocolate, sawtooth 200.00
Dresser Tray, Wild Rose and Bowknot, chocolate 350.00

Lamp, Wild Rose and Bowknot, clear font with chocolate base, 8" h, $450. Photo courtesy of Green Valley Auctions, Inc.

Goblet
    Beehive, colorless 65.00
    Diamond Prisms, colorless 70.00
    Overall Lattice, colorless 40.00
    Shuttle, chocolate 500.00
Honey, cov, Holly Amber 850.00
Jelly Compote
    Cactus, chocolate 200.00
    Pleat Band, chocolate 130.00
Lemonade Tumbler, Cactus, chocolate 100.00
Mug
    Elf, green 115.00
    Herringbone Buttress, chocolate 80.00
    Holly Amber, 4-1/2" h, ring handle 550.00
    Outdoor drinking scene, Nile green 200.00
    Overall Lattice, colorless 45.00
    Serenade, colorless 75.00
    Troubadour, 6-1/2" h, opaque white, cov 70.00
Mustard, cov, Daisy, opaque white 75.00
Nappy
    Holly Amber 385.00
    Leaf Bracket, chocolate, triangular 85.00
    Masonic, chocolate 85.00
Paperweight, Buffalo, Nile green 600.00
Parfait, Holly Amber 600.00
Pitcher, water
    Cord Drapery, colorless 95.00
    Fleur De Lis, colorless 265.00
    Racing Deer and Doe, colorless 200.00
    Ruffled Eye, chocolate 550.00
    Shuttle, chocolate 3,500.00
    Squirrel, colorless 200.00
    Teardrop and Tassel, cobalt blue 200.00
Plate, Serenade, 8-1/2" d, chocolate 125.00
Punch Cup
    Cord Drapery, colorless 20.00
    Shuttle, colorless 15.00
Relish
    Cord Drapery, amber 110.00
    Holly Amber, oval 300.00
    Leaf Bracket, 8" l, oval, chocolate 75.00
Rose Bowl, Austrian, colorless 45.00
Salt and Pepper Shakers, pr
    Cactus, chocolate 150.00
    Holly Amber 500.00
Salt, wheelbarrow shape, Nile green 350.00
Sauce
    Cactus, chocolate, ftd 65.00
    Geneva, chocolate 90.00
    Holly amber 250.00
    Leaf Bracket, chocolate 50.00
    Six Fluted, chocolate 225.00
    Water Lily and Cattails, chocolate 100.00

Wild Rose and Bowknot, chocolate 95.00
Spooner
Austrian, colorless..65.00
Cactus, chocolate 80.00
Cupid, colorless...145.00
Holly Amber...475.00
Wild Rose and Bowknot, chocolate 150.00
Stein, Serenade, colorless 50.00
Sugar, cov
Cupid, opaque white...115.00
Dewey, cobalt blue 145.00
Syrup
Cord Drapery, chocolate.......................................350.00
Holly Amber, 5-3/4" h, SP hinged lid 2,000.00
Indian Feather, green...175.00
Toothpick Holder
Cactus, chocolate 75.00
Holly Amber, 2-1/4" h 585.00

No. 11, green 85.00
Tumbler
Cactus, chocolate, 4" h 85.00
Cord Drapery, chocolate.......................................245.00
Dewey, canary 65.00
Fleur de Lis, chocolate...75.00
Geneva, chocolate 115.00
Holly Amber...400.00
Icicle, chocolate 150.00
Leaf Bracket, chocolate 125.00
Sawtooth, chocolate..70.00
Shuttle, chocolate..70.00
Teardrop and Tassel, blue 65.00
Wildflower, amber 45.00
Vase, Holly Amber, 6" h 500.00
Wine
Cord Drapery, colorless 85.00
Shuttle, colorless...20.00

HANDEL & CO.

History: Handel & Co., was established in 1893 by Philip Handel. This Meriden, Connecticut, firm is known mainly for lamps, although it also did some decorating on glasswares. Vases and other items were etched, enameled, or painted.

Handel & Co. patented a method of "chipping" glass in 1904. This method required that a piece be sandblasted, covered with glue, and refired, creating a "chipped ice" or frosted finish. This textured finish was applied to many items, including lamp shades.

Well known for its beautiful lamps, the company also produced its own metalwork, including spelter bases with a patinated bronze finish. Styles ranged from plain to sculptured nudes and stylized tree trunks. A patent was issued to Handel for a pond lily lamp in 1902. Several variations of this lamp were made.

The period before World War I saw a rapid expansion in the production of lamps; many new patents were taken out by Philip Handel. The company also made great strides in adapting kerosene lamps to electric. The company's production slowed during the war years and was affected by the death of Philip Handel in 1914. However, the company successfully reorganized and began a second prosperous period directly after World War I. A national sales force helped to market the beautiful lamps to the middle class. The high-quality lamps were loved, but prices soon rose out of the range of the average buyer, resulting in declining sales and hard economic times of the company. It continued to produce some glassware and lamps, and even tried china decorating before closing in 1936.

Most of the decorators signed their works, along with a vertical mark. Decorators included Henry Bedigie, F. Gubisch, Albert Parlow, George Palme, William Runge, and Walter Wilson.

References: Victor Arwas, *Glass Art Nouveau to Art Deco*, Rizzoli, 1977; Robert De Falco, Carole Goldman Hibel, John Hibel, *Handel Lamps, Painted Shades & Glassware*, H & D Press, 1986; John A. Shuman III, *The Collector's Encyclopedia of American Art Glass, Collector Books, 1988, 1994 value update*; Kenneth Wilson, *American Glass 1760-1930: The Toledo Museum of Art, Volume I, Volume II*, Hudson Hills Press and The Toledo Museum of Art, 1994.

Museums: New Bedford Museum, Bedford, NH; The Corning Museum of Glass, Corning, NY; The Toledo Museum of Art, Toledo, OH.

Ashtray, 3" d, 1" h, glossy brown exterior, Boston Terrier painted on interior, sgd "Handelware" and artist mkd, wear to dog's face...100.00
Fernery, 4" h, 9" d, opalware, ftd, white glass, painted yellow and pink spider mums, green leaves, stems, buds, sgd in gold on base 1,800.00
Hanging Globe, 10" h, 10" d, chipped ice finish, Birds in Flight dec, red trees, green leaves, Baltimore Oriole-type birds flying among branches, one perched, brass finish hanging attachments..3,250.00
Humidor
    6" h, 4-1/2" w, dark brown and green ground, male and female golfers in appropriate attire, base sgd "Handelware PJ Handel, Meriden, CT #2379/136"...................1,500.00

Lamp, boudoir, dome shade, hand painted ext. surface, white birch trees on foreground shore, river and island beyond, artist sgd "AL Handel 5892," bronze Handel baluster base, fine patina, 14-1/2" h, 7" d, shade, $2,200. Photo courtesy of Skinner, Inc.

    6-1/2" h, 6" w, melon ribbed, opal ground with dark green and brown, metal cover with pipe finial, wear to paint, sgd "Handelware" 550.00
    7-1/2" h, 5-1/2" w, dark green and brown glossy ground, three running dog heads, sgd "Handelware" 1,100.00
    7-1/2" h, 6" w, dark brown and green ground, scene of doe and buck, metal cover with full pipe finial, sgd with shield mark and #4060/3 ....1,000.00
Jewelry Box, cov, 4-1/2" w, 3-1/2" h, soft beige opal ground, pink carnation dec, sgd "Handelware #71/941" ... 675.00
Lamp, boudoir
    8" h, amber dec shades, red and yellow florals, sgd and numbered on bronze base, pr 1,250.00
    13-1/2" h, 7" d tucked under dome shade, pond lilies and cat-o-nine tails on blue ground, mkd "Handel 6554," two rim chips, Handel metal single socket base, corroded finish, finial missing 1,840.00
    14" h, 7' d bell shaped reverse painted shade, natural palette meadow landscape, rim sgd "Handel 6231," bronzed metal ribbed single socket base imp "Handel"..........2,645.00
    14" h, 7-1/2" d, six-sided conical moonlit scenic shade, blue, green, sunset pink on int., landscape hand painted on ext. surface, sgd "Handel 6232," six-sided metal base with gray-green patina, imp "Handel," cap indented 2,185.00
    14" h, 7" x 5" scenic dome shade, chipped ice finish, windmill and landscape, orange, green, and brown, bronze finish base...1,750.00
    14" h, 7 x 5" scenic dome shade, sunset landscape and trees in shades of brown, No. 6112 ....1,600.00
    14" h, 8-1/4" w squared domed shade with scalloped border, chipped sand-finish, int. painted with red flowers and foliage, each sgd "Handel 6698," one with "C. M.," metal bases painted white, tag stamped "HANDEL," pr............. 2,750.00
    14-1/2" h, 7" d domed glass shade, four sets of four vertical ribs, int. painted with tall sailing ships in port with windmills on background shore, painted pastel sea and sky, lower edge sgd "Handel 6356," mounted in single socket ribbed Handel base 2,415.00
Lamp, ceiling, 25" d bent slag glass paneled shade, octagonal forest scene bronzed frame, green pine cone needle apron, Handel three-socket cluster fixture with hanging hood, two panels cracked.................................. 3,750.00
Lamp, desk
    8" w shade, Design No. 6975, cylindrical lipped shade, chipped finish, painted on int. with fully rigged sailing ship in tropical bay, palm trees, fool moon, green, brown, blue, and gray, pivoted bronzed metal base, adjustable arm, orig Handel cloth tag, one tiny chip on inner shade rim..............2,350.00
    14" h, 8" l, bright yellow ground, band of pink roses against black, orig sgd base 1,100.00

19" h, 7-1/2" d six-sided paneled amber slag glass shade, six green dec elements at rim, harp type bronzed metal base, adjustable swivel socked 1,500.00

Lamp, floor

24" d leaded glass shade, border of pink tulips, green leaves, bronze base...6,500.00

67" h torchiere, oval glass shade acid-etched and enamel painted with shield coat of arms, mounted on orig metal weighed lamp base, 3 significant chips at top rim of shade...425.00

Lamp, hanging, 9-1/2" d, obverse painted model 6885 sphere, irid orange-amber, hand painted and sgd by artist Henry Bedigie, three birds among leafy background trees, orig metal fittings, inside socket, decorative tassel, minor rim chips, needs rewiring 2,550.00

Lamp, table

15" d, 21" h, Hawaiian, pale yellow background shading to orange, palm trees, ferns, shade sgd "6310," pr.......5,500.00

16" d, Shade No. 6958, black ground, pink roses, twelve blue and yellow parrots 13,500.00

18" d, Bird of Paradise, blue green ground, purple, fuchsia, blue, yellow, and orange birds, orig lamp base supported with 3 columns, sgd "B. D. #7036"....................10,500.00

18" d, 26" h, Rain Forest, deep colors, yellow goldenrod flowers, sgd bronze lamp base 10,500.00

19" h, 12" d Tam o'Shanter shade, converted fluid type, obverse painted shade with green stylized leaf motif, shaded int., rim sgd "Handel Co. 2642," mounted on three-arm spider with swastika border above cast metal six-band base, corrosion, socket repair................................550.00

20" d, 22" h, caramel slag panel with green painted and metal overlay Art Nouveau shade, orig sgd bronze base, some damage to metal overlay 1,450.00

20" h, 14" domed reverse painted shade, butterscotch yellow ground, stylized Arts and Crafts multicolored border design, two-socket ribbed organic design base, imp "Handel," repaired copper finish, sockets replaced, int. glass bubble on shade 1,380.00

21" h, 14" d hipped Arts and Crafts-style shade, tan-brown textured shade, light reflective opal white int., molded basketweave border design, four drop-ring buckles, mounted on baluster-form copper colored Handel base, finish worn 2,300.00

21" h, 14" d textured Teroma-style obverse and reverse painted dome shade, colorless ground, six red roses, thorny leafy green stems, mkd in rd "Handel 1521," and "A.C." in the design, bronzed sq two-socket base, imp "Handel," rewired, replaced fitter cap.................2,300.00

22" h, 15" d domed glass shade basketweave molded with vertical ribs and horizontal ridges, painted with profusion of pastel rose blossoms in shades of pink, rose, and yellow, interspersed green leaves, imp "Handel" top rim, mounted on ridged quatraform single socket base with "Handel" threaded label, small int. chip on rim 2,185.00

22" h, 18" d textured domed shade, clear cased to opal white reflective int., outside hand painted with repeating foliate Arts and Crafts style motif below yellow amber color, inner rim inscribed "Handel 6778 HG," three-socket Handel tripartite base, bronzed finish................................4,600.00

22" h, 18" d textured domed shade, hand painted colorful riverscape, tall green trees under sunset orange skies, sgd on edge "Handel 7124(?)," three-socket bronzed turned baluster base...4,025.00

22-1/2" h, 15" d reverse painted domed shade, hand painted summer scene, sgd "Handel 7452," two-socket bronzed metal base, twist shaft, reticulated platform........4,600.00

22-1/2" h, 16" d molded octagonal Teroma shade with dropped apron, hand painted yellow-pink roses on latticework ground, sgd "Handel," at edge, mounted on three-socket bulbed and sectioned bronzed base stamped "Handel," base refinished.....................................2,645.00

22-1/2" h, 18" d textured dome reverse painted Meadowlands scenic shade, maroon red and green grass, blue gray and orange clouds, blue sky overhead, rim inscribed "Handel 6937," three-socket ribbed quatraform bronzed platform base 5,500.00

23" h, 18" d domed reverse painted shade, riverfront landscape with split rail fence, moon through autumn trees, inscribed "Handel 8025," heavy bronzed base with four scrolled legs around central shaft, sq platform, base unsigned, restored 5,175.00

23-1/2" h, 18" conical obverse painted Daffodil shade, hand painted green and yellow naturalized blossoms, mkd "Handel 5648," mounted on three-socket gilt metal tripartite base with Handel label, old repaint on metal base..........5,750.00

23-1/2" h, 18" d textured dome shade, hand painted realistic pastel rose blossoms, three crystal yellow butterflies in flight, sgd "Handel 7032," mounted on dark gold metal three-socket base with split tripartite columns 10,350.00

23-1/2" h, 18" d textured domed shade, three brilliantly colored macaws among exotic jungle foliage and wisteria blossoms, sgd "Handel 6974," mounted on three-socket bronzed metal base with Japonesque motif, tiny rim chip, one socket replaced...16,100.00

24-1/2" h, 16" d textured domed reverse painted shade, hand painted delicate wild roses and varicolored leaves on thorny branches, edge sgd "Handel," mounted on three-socket ribbed shaft in orig white paint, Japonesque fretwork stepped platform base, some wear to paint 5,475.00

24-1/2" h, 17" diagonal paneled glass shade, ten sunset orange slag glass bent panels above shaped green slag border, framed in bronzed leafy tree overlay motif, raised on bronzed simulated tree trunk base with dark patination, needs rewiring 4,025.00

24-1/2" h, 18" d eight-ribbed domed reverse painted shade, enameled naturalized landscape scene, sgd "Handel 6640(?)," mounted on large three-socket bronze base, repeating cast leaf Arts and Crafts motif................8,100.00

24-1/2" h, 18" d textured glass dome shade, two pairs of long-tailed brightly colored birds perched in brilliant yellow-green blossoming foliage, black background, edge sgd "Handel 7026 Palme," mounted on three-socket Handel gilt metal and gesso base, urn-form tripartite shaft with amber glass beads 11,500.00

28" h, 18" d shade composed of four tapered curved panels, two etched and enameled with brilliant orange parrots, two with brown-amber jungle leafage, lower edge sgd "Handel 7686 Palne," mounted on Handel lamp base, replacement socket, rewired 4,025.00

Lamp Shade

6" h, 3-1/8" d outside rim, ball shaped, irid orange int., scenic hand painted landscape with two birds in flight, rim sgd "Handel 7004," base hole drilled, some under edge rim chips..1,495.00

10" h, 27-1/2" w, 4-3/4" d opening, octagonal conical shade, leaded amber slag and tan panels in geometric arrangement, green-amber rippled ladderwork, drop apron dec by bronzed metal scenic tree framework hand painted to enhance forest motif, imp "Handel" tag at side, replaced electrical mounts 1,840.00

Sketch Book, 13" x 10-1/2", orig cover inscribed "P. J. Handel August 22nd, 1904," labeled "Pearl E. Lambert, Richmond,

Oil Craft Painting," approx. ten pages showing Handel wares, including lamps, leaded shades, hanging domes, lilies, numerous orig artist sketches, black and white line drawings of designs used on Handel porcelain and opal humidors, orig design numbers and prices for shades, watercolor of two elves advertising Pabst Blue Ribbon done by unknown Handel artist, pages loose, some wrinkling and minor edge tears 700.00

Tazza, 5-1/2" w, 9" h, shaded cream, and green opal ground, strawberries, leaves, and blossoms dec, beaded white top, sgd "Handelware" 1,000.00

Vase

6-1/2" h, 4-3/4" d, Teroma Art, landscape scene, naturalistic fall colors, artist sgd "John Bailey" 1,500.00

8" h, Teroma, etched ext. surface hand painted wood landscape scene, in muted colors, unsigned, tiny chip near base..690.00

9-3/4" h, 4-1/2" w, Teroma Art, landscape and mountain design, purple and blue mountains, green and yellow trees and leaves, Shape #4218.................................2,500.00

11" h, flared and ftd oval, colorless glass overlaid in golden amber double etched repeating stylized floral motif, etched "Palme" in design, and "Handel 4258" on base, some rim skips, int. etching................................1,150.00

HEISEY GLASS

History: The A. H. Heisey Glass Co. began producing glasswares in April 1896, in Newark, Ohio. Heisey, the firm's founder, was not a newcomer to the field, having been associated with the craft since his youth.

1900–58

Many blown and molded patterns were produced in crystal, colored, milk (opalescent), and Ivorina Verde (custard) glass. Decorative techniques of cutting, etching, and silver deposit were employed. Glass figurines were introduced in 1933 and continued in production until 1957 when the factory closed. Imperial Glass Corporation purchased several of the molds after they closed.

Heisey sold blanks to Tiffin Glass and the T. G. Hawkes Company. No glassware was marked until November 1901, when paper labels became popular. The "H" in diamond mark was introduced later. This mark was never used on the foot or bowl, only on the stem; however, not every piece was marked.

All Heisey glass is notable for its clarity. Popular patterns were widely sold through stores, and today's collectors delight in finding Heisey glass advertisements in women's magazines of the era.

Heisey colors include rainbow hues of Alexandrite, amber, black, blue, cobalt blue, dawn, emerald green, flamingo (pink), heliotrope, marigold (deep amber-yellow), Moongleam (green), red, Sahara (yellow), tangerine, vaseline, and zircon.

References: Neila Bredehoft, *Collector's Encyclopedia of Heisey Glass, 1925-1938*, Collector Books, 1986, 1997 value update; Lyle Conder, *Collector's Guide to Heisey's Glassware for Your Table*, L-W Books, 1984, 1993-94 value update; Gene Florence, *Elegant Glassware of the Depression Era*, 7th edition, Collector Books, 1997.

Periodicals: Heisey Herald, P.O. Box 23, Clinton, MD 20735; The Heisey News, 169 W. Church St., Newark, OH, 43055; The Newscaster, P.O. Box 102, Plymouth, OH 44865.

Collectors' Clubs: Bay State Heisey Collectors Club, 354 Washington St., East Walpole, MA 02032; Heisey Collectors of America, 169 W Church St., Newark, OH, 43055; National Capital Heisey Collectors, P.O. Box 23, Clinton, MD 20735; Southern Illinois Diamond H Seekers, 1203 N. Yale, O'Fallon, IL 62269.

Videotape: Heisey Glass Collectors of America, Inc., *Legacy of American Craftsmanship: The National Heisey Glass Museum*, Heisey Collectors of America, Inc., 1994.

Museum: National Heisey Glass Museum, Newark, OH.

Reproduction Alert: Some Heisey molds were sold to Imperial Glass of Bellaire, Ohio, and certain items were reissued. These pieces may be mistaken for the original Heisey. Some of the reproductions were produced in colors which were never made by Heisey and have become collectible in their own right. Examples include: the Colt family in Crystal, Caramel Slag, Ultra Blue, and Horizon Blue; the mallard with wings up in Caramel Slag; Whirlpool (Provincial) in crystal and colors; and Waverly, a 7-inch, oval, footed compote in Caramel Slag.

Note: Glassware is colorless (clear, crystal, or etched) unless other color indicated.

Miscellaneous Accessories, Etchings, and Patterns

Animal

Asian Pheasant..280.00

Clydesdale 325.00

Donkey, #1 ....225.00

Gazelle 1,450.00

Goose, wings half up 80.00

Mallard, wings down 260.00

Mallard, wings up 150.00

Plug Horse, Oscar 115.00

Pony, kicking 175.00

Pony, standing...95.00

Rabbit...225.00

Ringneck Pheasant 175.00

Sealyham Terrier 125.00

Scottie..120.00145.00

Sparrow 145.00

Ashtray

Lodestar, dawn...110.00

Military Cap, #1536 ....35.00

Basket

Daisy...140.00

No. 417, colorless, sgd, minor base nick.................80.00

No. 417, medium green, floral and band engraving, sgd, 8-1/4" h, 6-1/2" h 175.00

No. 417, pale amethyst, sgd, 8-1/2" h, 6" w 300.00

No. 417, pink, sgd, 8-1/2" h, 6" w 125.00

No. 459, butterfly and floral engraving, sgd, 13-1/2" h, 7" w 175.00

No. 459, daisy and leaf engraving, sgd, 14" h, 7" w ...175.00

No. 460, heavy press, cut glass imitation, patent date 2-22-16, sgd, 12" h, 7-1/2" w................................225.00

No. 461, Pickett, moongleam, 7" 450.00

No. 463, Bonnet, 7"...160.00

September, 1931   *Page 5*

Expressing Fine Traditions in Early American Glass

Simple lines and delightful sturdiness are carried out with true craftsmanship in recent Early American glass by Heisey. In this glass is expressed the many fine traditions of the period.

An example is the new 1404 line — the Thumb Print pattern. The charm of its design was inspired by the famous Sandwich glass, of which the Heiseys own the original models.

A variety of stemware and other pieces is offered in the 1404 pattern, in clear crystal, Sahara gold, Moon Gleam green, and Flamingo rose.

It is a design with a great deal of appeal—right in the fashion to go with the vogue for Early American dining-rooms.

Other glass in this period offered by Heisey is the Scroll Design—No. 1405—and fine lead-brown stemware with quaint Chintz etchings. You will want to stock one or another of these patterns for the fall.

A. H. HEISEY & COMPANY
Newark, Ohio

Shown here is the goblet of the new 1404 line, the Thumb Print pattern. Available in stemware and other pieces in the following colors: Clear Crystal, Moon Gleam, Flamingo and Sahara.

SALES OFFICES

E. G. Nock, 358 Fifth Avenue Building, New York.

W. S. Redfield, 1560 Merchandise Mart, Chicago.

H. S. Bokee, 122 W. Baltimore Street, Baltimore.

H. M. Bortz, 218 E. Sedgwick Street, Philadelphia.

G. A. Granville, 111 Summer Street, Boston.

R. C. Irwin, 1560 Merchandise Mart, Chicago.

R. E. Phillips, 129 Putnam Avenue, Zanesville, Ohio.

C. S. Whipple, 622 S. Westlake Avenue, Los Angeles.

Davis & Braisted Co., 120 N. 4th Street, Minneapolis.

Hal M. Copeland, 3608 Springdale Avenue, Baltimore.

The Edminster Co., 612 Howard Street, San Francisco.

E. F. Redfield, 6432 Oak Street, Kansas City, Mo.

Heisey's
GLASSWARE Ⓗ *for your table*

Tell our advertisers you saw it in THE CROCKERY AND GLASS JOURNAL

Ad, Line #1404, Thumb Print pattern, introduced in Crockery and Glass Journal, September 1931.

No. 465, paneled, sgd, 12-3/4" h, 9-1/4" l 100.00
No. 477, leaf and floral engraving, sgd, 10-1/2" h,
10-1/2" l..100.00
No. 480, floral cutting, round shape, sgd, 9-1/2" h,
8" w...175.00
No. 480, floral leaf and basketweave engraving, sgd, 10-1/2"
h, 8" w..225.00
Picket, engraved...225.00
Bell, Victorian Belle...35.00
Berry Bowl, Beaded Swag, opalescent, metal foot.......25.00
Beverage Set, Gallagher, pitcher and six handled lemon-
ades...450.00
Bitters Bottle, #5003, tube......................................165.00
Bookends, pr, horse head.......................................225.00
Bowl
9-1/2" d, 3" h, cut basket of flowers design, 3 applied
glass feet 70.00
10" d, Priscilla, ftd, mkd...295.00
Brandy, #3416 Barbara Fritchie, 3/4 oz
Crystal..45.00
Moongleam bowl, crystal stem, rare 900.00
Butter Dish, cov, #341-1/2, Puritan 60.00
Candelabrum, pr
#17 Classic 16" h..300.00
#300 Hemisphere, 5-light, 3-1/2" d........................150.00
#1445 Grape Cluster, 1-lite, 4" prisms 325.00
Candle Block, #1469, 3" pr...85.00
Candleholder, #1428, Warwick, 2-lite, trial blue 1,500.00
Candlesticks, pr
#22 Windsor, 7-1/2" h..140.00
#33 Jack Be Nimble 35.00
#99 Little Squatter 35.00
#112, Mercury, Sahara yellow 70.00
#114 Pluto, Hawthorne orchid 155.00
#118 Miss Muffet, diamond optic base, Moongleam....55.00
#121 Pinwheel 90.00
#126 Trophy, flamingo pink.....................................275.00
#1433 Thumbprint and Panel 140.00
#1504 Regency, 2-lite...98.00
Tea Rose, 2-lite, fern blank......................................120.00
Candy Dish, cov, #3350 Wabash, 6", ftd, Flamingo....100.00
Candy Jar, cov, #1590 Zodiac, 10" h, ftd......................55.00
Card Box, cov, Windsor, Royal Sensation cutting 125.00
Center Piece, Buttress, low...35.00
Champagne, Rampo, Moongleam green saucer-shaped
bowls, applied flamingo pink base, 6 pc set 360.00
Champagne Flute, #422 Cumberland, #3336 Lady Leg, 7" h,
4-1/2 oz...38.00
Cigarette Box, cov
#1280 Winged Scroll, emerald green, 2-7/8" 170.00
#1489 Puritan, 6", horse head 100.00
#1533 Wampum 75.00
Cocktail
#3333 Old Glory, 3 oz, monogrammed "EMS".........80.00
#3481 Glenford, Hawthorne, 3 oz, checker optic 60.00
#5038 Rooster stem 80.00
#5063 Bantam Rooster...375.00
Cocktail Shaker
#4225 Cobel, one quart, horse head stopper 110.00
#4225 Cobel, one quart, silver trim, unknown cutting ...70.00
#4225 Cobel, pint, rooster stopper, etched "US"...150.00
#4225 Cobel, two quart..55.00
#4255 Sportsman etching, #4255, 2 qt, #455
etching 290.00
Cologne, #1489, cut stopper, 4 oz.............................155.00
Commemorative Plaque, 5-1/2" h, cobalt blue, diamond

shape, emb "H," manufactured by Heisey Collectors of
America 100.00
Cordial, 5th Avenue-Mitchell, #829 ....45.00
Cornucopia, Warwick, #1426, 9" h.............................190.00
Creamer and Sugar, cov
#325 Pillows, crystal, gold trim...............................165.00
#335 Quator, cutting..30.00
#354 Wide Flat Panel, oval, hotel size, Sahara
yellow..175.00
#479 Petal, Moongleam..75.00
#1483 Stanhope, black knobs....................................90.00
#1506 Whirlpool, individual size................................65.00
Cup
#502 Crinoline etching, #1509 Queen Ann blank 38.00
#1483 Stanhole, crystal, black knob 12.00
Custard Cup, Pinwheel & Fan, Moongleam green........20.00
Decanter
#305 Punty and Diamond Point, orig stopper 185.00
#367 Prism Band, flamingo pink, crystal #48 cut
stopper...200.00
#3397 Gascony, 1 pint, ftd, crystal stopper and foot, cobalt
bowl 160.00
#4036 Sherry, half pint, paler label, #4004 Maryland cutting,
silver dec stopper 140.00
Floral Block, #15, Hawthorne, 5", duck insert 200.00
Floral Bowl
10 Gibson Girl, 10" d, Hawthorne, star base............50.00
#134 Trident, Monterey cutting 235.00
#1632 Lodestar, dawn, 12" d 110.00
Fruit Basket, #480, 8", cutting 245.00
Goblet
#419 Sussex, Moongleam Green, 8 oz 100.00
#458 Olympiad, #3411 Monte Cristo, 8-3/8" h, 9 oz....60.00
#4091 Kimberly, #1015 Dolly Madison, rose cutting,
10 oz...85.00
#3324 Delaware, flamingo, diamond optic 20.00
#3333 Old Glory, monogrammed, 8 oz....................25.00
#3333 Old Glory, Renaissance cutting 30.00
#3368 Albemarle, 8-1/2" h, 8 oz, diamond optic 35.00
#5025 Tyrolean, 10 oz, orchid etch.........................75.00
#5077 Legionaire, 10 oz, ftd, amber stem 65.00
#8005 Galaxy 25.00
Hair Receiver, Pin Wheel and Fan, #350, metal lid.......60.00
Horseradish Jar, #352..55.00
Iced Tea Tumbler, ftd
Fred Harvey, amber 45.00
Kimberly, #4091, Dolly Madison, #1015, rose cutting ..70.00
Ivy Vase, #4224 Tangerine...105.00
Jar, 11-1/2" h, 5" w, floral cutting, gold banding, sgd 70.00
Jug
#3362 Charter Oak, flamingo, diamond optic, half
gallon...200.00
#4165 Shaw, cobalt blue, 8" h.................................300.00
Juice Tumbler, Patio, amber, 5 oz, ftd 125.00
Lamp, Dolphin, candlestick type 180.00
Lavender Jar, cov, #352 Flat Panel, 1-1/2 oz..............140.00
Madonna, 9" h
Frosted 110.00
Limelight..1,600.00
Martini Pitcher, #4054 Coronation, 30 oz 25.00
Mayonnaise Ladle, #6, Alexandrite.............................245.00
Mug, Whaley, #4163, 16 oz
Etched club drinking scene 150.00
Etched fisherman scene...260.00
Mustard, cov, #352 Flat Panel....................................48.50
Nappy, #357 Prison Stripe, 4-1/2" d............................22.00

Oyster Cocktail, #4085 Kohinoor, zircon bowl, 4 oz ...125.00
Parfait, #3362 Charter Oak, #3362, marigold, 4-1/2" h 50.00
Perfume, 6-1/4" h, amber and crystal, floral and leaf cutting,
   long crystal stopper, pr 150.00
Pickle, #1191 Lobe, flamingo..28.00
Powder Jar, Pin Wheel and Fan, #350, silver lid.........165.00
Punch Cup
   Fancy Loop, #1205, 4-1/2" h, 5 oz.............................48.00
   Locket on Chain 35.00
   Pillows 35.00
Punch Ladle, #11 ....95.00
Relish
   Crenoline, 3-part..65.00
   Normandie, #1466 Relish, star etch 95.00
Rose Bowl
   Mermaid, 6" d 500.00
   Plateau, #3369, flamingo...65.00
Steele, #4157, 5-1/2" d, moongleam 85.00
Salad Plate
   #4004 Impromptu, 7" d...12.00
   #4901 Kimberly, #1015 Dolly Madison, rose cutting,
     8" d...40.00
Sherbet
   Gascony Line, #3397, Ambassador, #452 etching, 2-3/8"
     h, 6 oz...35.00
   Priscilla, 4 oz, high 15.00
Sherry, #5058 goose stem, 2 oz 130.00
Soda Tumbler
   #170 Cleopatra, diamond optic, 5 oz........................20.00
   #235 Newton, Fronetnac etch, 8 oz 20.00
   #1486 Coleport, 13 oz..60.00
   #3389 Duquesne, tangerine, ftd, 12 oz...................210.00
   #3397 Gascony, #452 Ambassador, etching, 5-1/2" h,
     12 oz...35.00
   #3416 Barbara Fritchie, #457 Springtime etching, restored
     rim, 5-5/8" h, 12 oz..15.00
   #3481 Glenford, moongleam green and flamingo,
     8 oz 165.00
   #4054 Coronation, 10 oz 9.50
   #4083 Stanhope, ftd, zircon bowl and foot, 8 oz....155.00
   #4091 Kimberly, #1015 Dolly Madison rose cutting,
     5 oz...55.00
Sugar, cov, #1225 Pineapple and Fan, gold trim 48.00
Syrup
   McGrady, 5 oz, Flamingo, #372...............................65.00
   Punty Band 200.00
   Urn...130.00
Tankard, #335 Pillows, flamingo, 2 quart.................1,750.00
Toothpick Holder
   Fancy Loop, emerald, small base flake, wear to gold
     trim..120.00
   Puritan, ftd 90.00
   Sunburst 80.00
   Waldorf Astoria, #333..110.00
Tumbler, #1417 Arch, orig red and white factory identification
   label, 9 oz..55.00
Vase
   Cathedral, #1413, flared, Sahara yellow 250.00
   Pineapple and Fan, 6" h, green, worn gold trim.......40.00
   Prison Stripe, #357, cupped, 5".................................55.00
Water Bottle, Waldorf Astoria 60.00
Wine
   #1125 Plain Band 20.00
   #3397 Gascony, 2 oz, Sahara 55.00
   #3397 Gascony, 2 oz, Sportsman etch 60.00
   #4091 Kimberly, 2 oz, Dolly Madison rose etch, paper
     label..75.00

Patterns

Acorn
   Plate, dinner..60.00
   Sherbet, Flamingo pink 20.00
   Syrup..80.00

Arcadia, #1025
   Champagne, saucer 18.00
   Goblet, water..20.00

Banded Flute, #150
   Beer Mug, handle...240.00
   Celery Tray, 11-1/2" l, oval..30.00
   Chamberstick..45.00
   Champagne, 4-1/2 oz..110.00
   Claret..25.00
   Compote, 10" d, ftd..145.00
   Cordial..100.00
   Cup 100.00
   Flower Center 60.00
   Goblet
     7 oz 120.00
     9 oz 100.00
   Horseradish Jar, cov..95.00
   Iced Tea Tumbler, 12 oz...190.00
   Match Box, cov 100.00
   Nappy, flared
     9-1/2" d...30.00
     10-1/2" d...65.00
   Pitcher, half gallon...150.00
   Plate, 6" d..50.00
   Punch Bowl and Base 140.00
   Punch Cup 65.00
   Punch Set, 14" d punch bowl, high base, five cups ...295.00
   Salt Shaker...50.00
   Schoeppen, 14 oz, ftd...325.00
   Sherbet, 3 oz, saucer, ftd..20.00
   Soda Tumbler, tapered, 12 oz 70.00
   Tray, round, 13" d
     Flamingo pink..265.00
     Moongleam green 300.00
   Water Carafe 125.00
   Wine..50.00

Beaded Panel & Sunburst, #1235
   Punch Bowl and Stand, 7-3/4" h, 14-1/2" w, 5-3/4" h x 9-1/2"
     w stand, chip under bottom bowl rim, c1896-1905,
     sgd 625.00
   Water bottle..115.00

Carcassone, #3390
   Cordial, Sahara yellow 115.00
   Jug, 3 pint 120.00
   Sherbet, crystal 20.00

Chintz #1401 (Empress Blank) and #3389 (Duquesne Blank).
Made in Alexandrite orchid, crystal, flamingo pink,
Moongleam green, and Sahara yellow, 1931-38.
   Celery Tray, 10" l, crystal..20.00
   Champagne, crystal..22.00
   Claret, crystal 20.00
   Cocktail, Sahara yellow 42.00
   Cordial, #3389, Duquesne, crystal...........................115.00
   Creamer, Sahara yellow 40.00
   Cup and Saucer, crystal...30.00
   Finger Bowl, Sahara yellow 15.00
   Goblet, crystal 25.00
   Grapefruit, crystal..22.00
   Ice Bucket, ftd, crystal...90.00
   Iced Tea Tumbler, #3389, 12 oz, ftd, Sahara yellow.....25.00
   Juice Tumbler, #3389, 5 oz, ftd, crystal 15.00

Mint Dish, Sahara yellow 32.00
Nasturtium Bowl, 7-1/2" d, crystal 20.00
Oyster Cocktail, #3389, Sahara yellow 25.00
Pickle and Olive Bowl, 2-part, 13" d, crystal 20.00
Pitcher, three pint, dolphin foot, Sahara yellow...........185.00
Plate, square
  6" w, bread and butter, crystal 8.00
  7" w, salad, Sahara yellow 20.00
  8" w, luncheon, crystal 12.00
  8" w, luncheon, Sahara yellow 25.00
  10-1/2" d, dinner, crystal 45.00
  10-1/2" d, Sahara yellow 90.00
Platter, 14" l, oval, crystal 28.00
Preserve Bowl, handle, crystal 18.00
Sandwich Tray, center handle, 12" sq, crystal.............40.00
Sugar, Sahara yellow 42.00
Tumbler, ftd, 10 oz
  Crystal 25.00
  Sahara yellow 30.00

Colonial, #359
Bowl, 9" d, cupped, scalloped, shows wear..............40.00
Candy Dish, cov..60.00
Celery, 12" 35.00
Champagne 18.00
Claret 18.00
Toaster 10.00
Cocktail, 3 oz...15.00
Cordial 15.00
Cruet, Flamingo pink, octagonal stopper...................620.00
Crushed Fruit Jar
  Large 190.00
  Small 180.00
Custard Cup, flared, handle...................................10.00
Goblet 20.00
Horseradish and Mustard, cov, pr 75.00
Jug, pint 165.00
Plate
  4-3/4" d 4.75
  6" d, scalloped 10.00
Punch Bowl, matching base, 13" d 175.00
Sherry, 2 oz 15.00
Tumbler, 6 oz, ftd 50.00

Creole, #3381
Soda Tumbler, 12 oz, ftd, diamond optic Alexandrite bowl,
  crystal foot 167.50
Wine, 2-1/2 oz, Alexandrite 165.00

Crystolite, Blank #1503. Made in amber, crystal, Sahara yellow, and Zircon/Limelight.
  Ashtray, zircon..65.00
  Basket, 6" h...175.00
  Cake Plate...325.00
  Candle Block, sq 20.00
  Candlesticks, pr
    Round 40.00
    3-lite 75.00
  Celery Tray, 12" l, rect...35.00
  Cheese Comport, ftd..25.00
  Cheese Plate, 8" d, 2 handles 45.00
  Cigarette Holder..25.00
  Coaster
    Sahara yellow 35.00
    Zircon 45.00
  Cordial...110.00
  Creamer and Sugar
    Individual size..20.00
    Table size, round 50.00

Floater Bowl, 12" l, oval 48.00
Floater Candles, 4-1/2" sq, pr 38.00
Floral Bowl, 10" d 25.00
Gardenia Bowl, 12" d 175.00
Jelly Compote, 4-1/2" h, 5" d 28.00
Mayonnaise Set, 3 pc
  Oval 62.00
  Round 48.00
Nut, master, swan, 7" 45.00
Oil Bottle, no stopper 30.00
Pitcher, swan...260.00
Plate, 7" d 10.00
Puff Box, cov, 4-3/4" 80.00
Punch Cup 10.00
Relish, 5-part, 10" d, aluminum Lazy Susan...............90.00
Sherbet, 6 oz 35.00
Spring Salad Bowl 70.00
Sugar, cov 30.00
Torte Plate, 18-1/2" d 80.00
Tumbler, 10 oz 20.00
Urn, 7" h...20.00

Empress Blank #1401. Made in Alexandrite, cobalt blue, flamingo pink, Moongleam green, Sahara yellow, and some tangerine. This pattern was also made later in crystal and the name changed to Queen Ann.
  Ashtray
    Alexandrite 150.00
    Sahara yellow 90.00
  Bowl
    6" d, dolphin foot, Moongleam green 45.00
    7-1/2" d, dolphin foot, Sahara yellow 50.00
    11" d, ftd, flower frog, Sahara yellow.......................75.00
  Candelabra, 3-lite, Sahara yellow, crystal bobeches,
    pr 950.00
  Candlesticks, pr
    Alexandite, #135...500.00
    Pink, 6" h, dolphin foot 185.00
  Candy Dish, cov, silver overlay, ftd...........................75.00
  Celery Tray, 13" l, Sahara yellow 45.00
  Compote, 6" l, oval, fuschia cutting...........................60.00
  Console Bowl, 11" d, #497 Rosalie etch 55.00
  Creamer and Sugar
    Crystal, Old Colony etching 80.00
    Moongleam, individual size..................................95.00
    Sahara yellow 60.00
  Cream Soup, Sahara yellow 25.00
  Cruet, orig stopper
    Flamingo...140.00
    Moongleam green foot and stopper.......................250.00
  Cup and Saucer
    Alexandrite, sq 115.00
    Moongleam green, sq 50.00
    Sahara yellow, round...45.00
  Goblet, pink, etched..50.00
  Grapefruit, 6" sq, Sahara yellow 20.00
  Iced Tea Tumbler, ftd, pink, etched...........................50.00
  Ice Tub, #1401, arctic etch 170.00
  Jelly Compote, 6" h, Sahara yellow 35.00
  Lemon Server, cov, oval...50.00
  Marmalade, cov, ladle...60.00
  Mayonnaise
    Alexandrite 190.00
    Crystal..40.00
    Flamingo pink 45.00
    Sahara yellow, dolphin feet 50.00
  Nut Dish, individual
    Alexandrite 175.00

Flamingo pink...35.00
Sahara yellow...20.00
Plate
6" d, sherbet, Sahara yellow, round 13.00
6" sq, sherbet, Sahara yellow, square.....................13.00
7" d, Alexandrite...50.00
7" sq, Alexandrite..100.00
7" sq, cobalt blue..230.00
7-1/2" d, Alexandrite..45.00
7-1/2" d, Sahara yellow.......................................22.00
8" d, salad, Alexandrite, round..............................80.00
8" d, salad, Sahara yellow, round...........................20.00
8" d, salad, Sahara yellow, square..........................22.00
10-1/2" d, dinner, Alexandrite, round......................520.00
10-1/2" d, dinner, crystal, square...........................90.00
Relish, 3-part
Minuet etch...90.00
Moongleam, 7"...30.00
Sahara yellow...35.00
Salt and Pepper Shakers, pr, Sahara yellow................75.00
Tray, center handle, 12" sq, Sahara yellow.................65.00
Vase, 8" h, three handles, Arctic etch.....................85.00
Vegetable, 10" l, Sahara yellow.............................45.00

Greek Key. #433. Made in crystal.
Almond Dish, individual 35.00
Banana Split Dish, 9" l, ftd.................................25.00
Butter Dish, cov...170.00
Candy Dish, cov, ftd...65.00
Celery Tray, 12" l...45.00
Champagne..40.00
Creamer and Sugar, medium size.............................100.00
Cruet, no stopper..35.00
Egg Cup..45.00
Flower Center..75.00
Horseradish, cov...60.00
Ice Tub, cov..140.00
Jelly Compote, handle..25.00
Nappy..10.00
Orange Bowl, 14" d, flared rim...............................65.00
Pitcher, 3 pint...200.00
Plate
4-1/2" d...12.00
6" d...15.00
7" d...18.00
8" d...20.00
9" d...24.00
Punch Bowl Base..40.00
Relish, 9" l, oval...55.00
Sherbet, low, flared...60.00
Spooner..90.00
Straw Jar, top missing......................................250.00
Tankard, 3 quart..250.00
Tray, 13" l, oblong..60.00
Tumbler, 12 oz, flared rim...................................30.00
Water Bottle..185.00

Heisey Minuet, #503, etching
Champagne, #5010 Symphone, 61/8" h, 6 oz...................55.00
Goblet, #5010 Symphone, 8-1/8" h, 9 oz.....................65.00
Iced Tea Tumbler, ftd, #5010 Symphone, 6-15/16" h,
    12 oz...60.00
Mayonnaise, ftd, #1511 Toujours............................85.00
Oyster Cocktail, #5010 Symphone, 3-3/8" h, 4-1/2 oz....48.00
Plate
7" d, #1511 Toujours...24.00
8" d, #1511 Toujours...24.00
Sundae, #5010 Symphone, 3-1/2" h, 6 oz....................45.00

Wine...65.00
Ipswich. Blank #1405. Made in Alexandrite, cobalt blue, crystal, flamingo pink, Moongleam green, and Sahara yellow.
Candlestick Centerpiece, ftd, vase, prisms, pr...........300.00
Champagne/Sherbet, tall, #150 ....12.00
Cocktail Shaker..285.00
Creamer..20.00
Finger Bowl, underplate, Moongleam Green..................45.00
Floral Bowl, 11" d, ftd......................................70.00
Jug, 1/2 gallon...350.00
Juice Tumbler, ftd, Sahara yellow...........................42.00
Mantel Lusters, pr, cobalt blue, orig inserts and
    prisms...900.00
Plate
7" sq, flamingo pink...25.00
8" sq, Sahara yellow...30.00
Sherbet, Sahara yellow.......................................35.00
Sugar, flamingo pink...30.00
Tumbler, Sahara yellow.......................................52.00
Lariat. Blank #1540. Made in crystal, limited production in amber and black.
Ashtray, 4" d..15.00
Bon Bon, 7-1/2" d, hand painted dec........................100.00
Bowl, 12" d..40.00
Bud Vase, 15" h, swung......................................185.00
Buffet Plate, 21"..70.00
Camellia Bowl, 9-1/2" d......................................40.00
Candlesticks, pr
Low..40.00
2-lite, #1150..95.00
3-lite..125.00
Candy Basket, Moonglo cutting...............................45.00
Candy Dish, cov, dec...80.00
Caramel, cov, 7"...75.00
Celery Tray, 10" l...30.00
Champagne, 6 oz, saucer, Moonglo cutting...................40.00
Cheese Dish, cov, ftd..40.00
Coaster...8.00
Cocktail, Moonglo cut..12.00
Creamer and Sugar, individual size, floral cutting.......30.00
Deviled Egg Plate, 13" d....................................125.00
Floral Bowl, small, 9" d.....................................27.00
Gardenia Bowl, 12" d...32.00
Goblet
Moonglo cutting..55.00
Plain..12.00
Hurricane Lamps, dec, pr....................................100.00
Iced Tea Tumbler, 12 oz......................................20.00
Juice Tumbler, ftd, 5 oz.....................................10.00
Plate
7" d, dessert...8.00
8" d, salad..12.00
10-1/2" d, service...24.00
14" d, floral cutting..48.00
Punch Bowl, Set, 14" d punch bowl, 21" d underplate, 8 punch
    cups, orig hooks, and ladle 225.00
Punch Cup..12.50
Punch Bowl Underplate 95.00
Relish
2-part, 11", 2 handles, oval.................................40.00
3-part, 10-1/2"..24.00
3-part, 12" l, Moonglo cutting 45.00
Salad Bowl, 10-1/2" d..40.00
Sandwich Plate, 13" d..28.00
Wine, 3-1/2 oz
Moonglo cutting..35.00

Plain...15.00

Narrow Flute, #393

Champagne, 4-1/2 oz 80.00
Creamer and Sugar, individual size............................40.00
Cube Sugar Holder, 7", rim, patent date....................25.00
Goblet..28.50
Jug, three pint 75.00
Mustard, cov..60.00
Nut Dish, Moongleam...15.00
Pitcher
    3 pint...55.00
    1 quart, wear on base, roughness on handle 20.00
Soda Tumbler, 10 oz, ftd, gold trim, enameled flowers 85.00
Strawberry Dip Plate, with rim 195.00

New Era. #4044. Made in crystal, frosted crystal, and some cobalt blue with crystal stem and foot. Original pattern made 1934-41. Stemware, candlesticks, and celery added 1944-57. Made pieces of this Art Deco style tableware were monogrammed. Deduct 20 percent for monogrammed pieces.

Ashtray 30.00
Candlesticks, pr 90.00
Celery 40.00
Cocktail 18.00
Console Bowl..85.00
Cordial...40.00
Cup and Saucer..50.00
Floral Bowl, 11" d, frosted 40.00
Nut Cup..50.00
Pilsner...50.00
Plate
    6" d 25.00
    Luncheon..40.00
Relish, 3-part..45.00
Rye Bottle, orig stopper, monogram.........................115.00

Octagon, Blank #500, #1229, and #1231 (ribbed). Made in crystal, Dawn, flamingo pink, Hawthorne orchid, Marigold, Moongleam green, and Sahara yellow.

After Dinner Cup and Saucer, flamingo pink 25.00
Basket, 5" h, Hawthorne orchid etching....................120.00
Bon Bon, sides up..10.00
Celery Dish, Moongleam green...................................35.00
Creamer and Sugar, Moongleam green 75.00
Hors D'oeuvre Plate, 13" d, flamingo pink..................30.00
Ice Tub, Hawthorne orchid etching.............................65.00
Mayonnaise, ladle, Moongleam green.........................70.00
Muffin Plate, 12" d, Moongleam green.........................47.50
Nut Dish, individual
    Flamingo pink 15.00
    Moongleam green 35.00
Plate, 8" d, luncheon, Moongleam green.....................20.00
Salad Bowl, 12-1/2" d, Sahara yellow........................25.00
Soup Plate, 9" d, Sahara yellow 20.00
Tray, 12" d, 4 compartments, Clermont cutting 70.00
Vegetable Bowl, 9" d, flamingo pink..........................20.00

Old Dominion, Blank #3380, 1930-39.

Bar Tumbler, Moongleam green 30.00
Bouillon Cup, two handles, ftd, flamingo pink..............20.00
Champagne/saucer, marigold, Empress etch bowl, crystal
    stem..30.00
Cigarette Holder...20.00
Cocktail, marigold, Empress etch bowl, crystal stem 30.00
Cordial, diamond optic, Sahara yellow 145.00
Creamer and Sugar, cov, etched, Sahara yellow 70.00
Cup and Saucer, flamingo pink 40.00
Goblet, marigold, 8-3/4"..55.00
Grapefruit, 6" d, Moongleam green.............................40.00

Nappy, 8" d, Sahara yellow 40.00
Plate
    6" d, Sahara yellow, round....................................9.00
    7" w, flamingo pink, square 18.00
    9" d, colorless, round..20.00
    10-1/2" w, Moongleam green, square 65.00
Oyster Cocktail..65.00
Sandwich Plate, 12" d, center handle, flamingo pink....60.00
Sherbet, low, marigold, Empress etch bowl, crystal
    stem..25.00
Soda Tumbler, 12 oz, ftd, diamond optic Alexandrite 90.00
Wine, Sahara yellow 20.00

Old Colony Etching made on #1401 Empress blank, #3390 Caracassone blank, and #3380 Old Dominion blank. Made on cobalt blue, crystal, flamingo pink, marigold, Moongleam green, and Sahara yellow; c1930-39.

Beverage Set, 11 oz pitcher, six goblets, Sahara yellow, Carcassone blank, sq base 525.00
Bouillon Cup, Moongleam green 30.00
Cocktail, 3 oz, Sahara yellow, Old Dominion blank, round
    base..28.00
Finger Bowl, #4075
    Crystal 8.00
    Flamingo pink 12.00
    Marigold 28.00
    Moongleam green 18.00
    Sahara yellow 15.00
Creamer, dolphin foot, flamingo................................35.00
Mayonnaise, 5-1/2" d, dolphin foot, flamingo pink........75.00
Plate
    6" d, crystal, round 8.00
    7" w, flamingo pink, square 15.00
    8" d, Sahara yellow, round..................................30.00
    9" d, Moongleam green, round.............................72.00
    10-1/2" d, crystal, round....................................32.00
    10-1/2" d, crystal, square...................................30.00
Soda Tumbler, 9 oz, ftd,, Sahara yellow 28.00
Sugar, dolphin foot, Moongleam green 35.00
Vase, 9" h
    Crystal 80.00
    Flamingo pink 135.00
    Moongleam green 175.00
    Sahara yellow 160.00
Wine, 2-1/2 oz
    Crystal 50.00
    Flamingo pink 145.00
    Moongleam green 175.00
    Sahara yellow 135.00

Old Sandwich. Blank #1404. Made in amber, cobalt blue, crystal, flamingo pink, Moongleam green, and Sahara yellow.

Ashtray, Moongleam, individual size 67.50
Beer Mug
    Amber..450.00
    Stiegel blue...400.00
Bowl, 11" d, oval, ftd, Moongleam green 120.00
Catsup Bottle...35.00
Creamer and Sugar, oval, Flamingo pink 50.00
Decanter, Moongleam green 185.00
Goblet, 12 oz...20.00
Iced Tea Tumbler, ftd, 12 oz 15.00
Jug, Sahara yellow, half gallon 225.00
Parfait 15.00
Pitcher, half gallon, ice lip, pressed handle.................120.00
Plate, 7" w, flamingo pink, square 20.00
Popcorn Bowl, cupped, Moongleam green 70.00
Salt Shaker 30.00

Soda Tumbler
    8 oz, Moongleam green 48.50
    10 oz, flat, tangerine..495.00
Sundae, 6 oz 55.00
Old Williamsburg, crystal.
Candelabra, 3-lite, #301, short base.........................310.00
Cocktail 10.00
Epergne, 5-1/2" d, orig paper label..............................62.50
Wine 14.00
Orchid Etching #1507 on #1519 Waverly blank, and #1509 Queen Ann blank. Made only in crystal; 1940-57.
Ashtray, 3" sq 30.00
Bowl
    10" d, Queen Anne blank 68.00
    11" d, 3 dolphin feet 165.00
    13" d 100.00
Butter Dish, cov 245.00
Cake Plate, 13-1/2" d, ftd 245.00
Candlesticks, pr
    2-lite, Trident blank, #134.....................................120.00
    2-lite, Waverly blank 120.00
Celery, Waverly blank 65.00
Champagne 30.00
Cheese and Cracker Set, 12" d...................................135.00
Cigarette Holder, ftd 165.00
Cocktail, 4 oz..40.00
Cocktail Shaker, sterling foot 200.00
Compote, 6", Waverly blank 50.00
Condiment Bottle, orig stopper 250.00
Cordial...115.00
Creamer and Sugar, individual size...............................50.00
Cruet, Waverly 160.00
Cup and Saucer, ftd 40.00
Gardenia Bowl, #1519 Waverly, 9-1/4" d 85.00
Goblet...40.00
Iced Tea Tumbler, 12 oz 60.00
Jelly, #1519 Waverly, 7" h, ftd 65.00
Jug, 1/2 gallon, ice lip 525.00
Juice Tumbler, ftd 50.00
Mayonnaise, liner, orig spoon, ftd................................165.00
Pitcher, tankard 625.00
Plate, 7-1/4" d..18.00
Relish, 3-part, 11" l, Waverly blank................................65.00
Serving Tray, center handle
    12" d, Queen Ann blank 200.00
    13" d 150.00
Sherbet, low 20.00
Torte Plate, 14" d 90.00
Wine, 3 oz..75.00
Pied Piper, crystal.
Beverage Set, pitcher and six goblets.........................500.00
Champagne, saucer 30.00
Oyster Cocktail..15.00
Plantation, Blank #1567. Made in crystal and some amber.
Butter, cov, round...120.00
Cake Plate 200.00
Candlesticks, pr, 2-lite 150.00
Candy, cov, 3-part 250.00
Coaster, 4" d 60.00
Compote 30.00
Coupe Plate, 7"..500.00
Creamer and Sugar..35.00
Cruet, orig stopper 155.00
Gardenia Bowl, 13" d 45.00
Honey, ivy etch, 6-1/2" 80.00
Hurricane Lamps, globes, electrified, pr 1,150.00

Iced Tea Tumbler, ftd 75.00
Marmalade Jar, pineapple shape, cov, sgd spoon 115.00
Mayonnaise, liner, matching underplate, etched........115.00
Pitcher, 1/2 gallon, ice lip 415.00
Plate, 8-1/2" d 25.00
Punch Bowl, some wear 450.00
Relish
    4-part, 8" d, round 110.00
    5-part, 13" l, oval 75.00
Salt and Pepper Shakers, pr, salt cloudy......................75.00
Sandwich Plate, 14" d 65.00
Sherbet...25.00
Sugar Shaker 115.00
Syrup 150.00
Torte Plate, 14" d, ivy etch...95.00
Tumbler, ftd, 12 oz, pressed 80.00
Vase, 5" h, ftd 35.00
Wine 35.00
Pleat and Panel. Blank #1170. Made in crystal, flamingo pink, and Moongleam green.
Bowl, flamingo pink 25.00
Bread Plate, 7" d 20.00
Candle Dish, cov
    Flamingo pink 55.00
    Moongleam green 95.00
Champagne, 5 oz, flamingo pink 25.00
Cheese and Cracker Set, flamingo pink 45.00
Compote, cov, 7" h, flamingo pink, gold trim 75.00
Creamer and Sugar, hotel size 25.00
Goblet, 5-1/4" h, 7-1/2 oz, luncheon, flamingo pink 30.00
Iced Tea Tumbler, flamingo pink 25.00
Jelly Compote
    Flamingo pink 30.00
    Moongleam green 25.00
Lemon Dish, cov, 5" l, flamingo pink 55.00
Marmalade Jar, ftd 25.00
Nappy, 8" d, flamingo pink 58.00
Plate
    6" d, flamingo pink 12.00
    7" d, crystal 10.00
    7" d, flamingo pink 15.00
Sandwich Plate, 14" d, Moongleam green 35.00
Spice Tray, 10" d, flamingo pink 35.00
Provincial. Blank #1506. Made in crystal, Moongleam green, and Zircon/Limelight.
Butter Dish, cov 85.00
Candy Dish, zircon 500.00
Creamer and Sugar, ftd 30.00
Cruet, orig stopper, 4 oz 35.00
Goblet...15.00
Mustard, cov 50.00
Nut Bowl, 5" d 15.00
Oil Bottle, 4 oz..15.00
Plate, 18" d 40.00
Relish, 12"...35.00
Snack Plate, 7" d, two handles 20.00
Torte Plate, 17" d, #1506 ....45.00
Violet Vase, 3-1/2" h, Moongleam green 65.00
Ridgeleigh. Blank #1469. Made in crystal, Sahara yellow and zircon; 1935-44.
Ashtray
    Club shape 10.00
    Square, 6" 35.00
Candlesticks, pr
    2" sq...80.00
    7" h, bobeches and prisms 150.00

Celery and Relish Tray, oblong, 2-part 40.00
Centerpiece Bowl, 11" d.....................................225.00
Champagne, 5 oz, #872 Mariemont cutting...............155.00
Cigarette Holder...20.00
Claret, 4 oz...35.00
Coaster, stacking set of 6 ....36.00
Cocktail, 3-1/2 oz, #872 Mariemont cutting 100.00
Cologne, 4 oz, #105 stopper....................................75.00
Creamer 20.00
Cruet, orig stopper 50.00
Floral Bowl, 11-1/2" w..55.00
Goblet
    Luncheon...18.50
    8 oz, etching..65.00
Jelly, handle, 6" 20.00
Marmalade, violet vase base, slotted chrome cover 50.00
Mustard, cov 20.00
Nappy, pink...8.00
Old Fashioned Tumbler, 8 oz....................................20.00
Pitcher, half gallon, ice lip 80.00
Plate, 8" d 10.00
Platter, small..40.00
Punch Bowl 170.00
Salt and Pepper Shakers, pr, double cone shape..........4.00
Salt Dip 15.00
Sherbet..20.00
Tid-Bit Tray, 11" and 13" plates................................75.00
Torte Plate, 13" d 60.00
Tumbler, 8 oz 45.00
Vase
    6" h, Zircon, candle 235.00
    8" h, Sahara yellow, cylinder 245.00
Wine, flared bowl..85.00

Rose. Etching #1515 on #1519 Waverly blank. Made only on crystal; 1949-57.
Ashtray 35.00
Butter Dish, cov, horsehead finial 160.00
Cake Plate, 15" d, pedestal.....................................325.00
Candlesticks, pr, low, flat......................................65.00
Candy Dish, cov, seahorse 250.00
Celery, 12" 48.00
Champagne, saucer 35.00
Claret, #5072, 4 oz..125.00
Cocktail..32.50
Compote, low, ftd, 6-1/2" h.....................................65.00
Cordial..100.00
Cracker Plate, 12" d 130.00
Cup and Saucer 75.00
Goblet, crystal, 9 oz...42.00
Honey, ftd, 6-1/4" d..80.00
Iced Tea Tumbler, 12 oz, ftd....................................65.00
Juice Tumbler, ftd, 5-1/2" h, 5 oz 58.00
Mayonnaise, underplate, ftd 85.00
Relish
    3-part...65.00
    4-part, 9" d, round 70.00
Salad Plate, 7" d 20.00
Salt and Pepper Shakers, pr.....................................85.00
Server, center handle...175.00
Sherbet, 6 oz, low...30.00
Sugar, ftd..35.00
Tumbler, ftd, 12 oz 50.00
Wine, 3 oz..115.00

Saturn, #1485.
Baked Apple 20.00
Creamer and Sugar...55.00

Cruet, orig stopper, dawn, crystal stopper 290.00
Cup and Saucer, ball handle, zircon 200.00
Sherbet, 5 oz, zircon 40.00
Soda Tumbler, limelight, 5 oz...................................70.00
Tidbit Tray, zircon..95.00
Tumbler, 9 oz 20.00

Spanish, #3404.
Champagne, 5-1/2 oz, crystal
    Barcelona, #941, cutting...............................40.00
    Strawberry diamond cutting, 5-7/8" h 50.00
Cocktail, 3-1/2 oz, crystal, Barcelona, #941, cutting 38.00
Goblet
    Cobalt blue...155.00
    Crystal, Barcelona, #941, cutting 58.00
    Crystal, strawberry diamond cutting, 7-1/2" h, 10 oz.... 65.00
Soda Tumbler
    4-1/4" h, 5 oz, cobalt blue, strawberry diamond
    cutting..95.00
    6-1/4" h, 12 oz, #457 Springtime etching, restored
    rim...15.00

Tudor, #411.
Bar Tumbler, 2 1-2 oz..15.00
Champagne 12.00
Floral Bowl, 12-1/2" d, ftd, moongleam 80.00
Goblet, 6 oz...12.00
Jug, 1/2 gallon, floral cutting 100.00
Mayonnaise, Hawthorne orchid 95.00
Nappy, rolled edge
    8-1/2" d..30.00
    10" d...35.00
Sherbet, 5-1/2 oz 10.00

Twist, Blank #1252. Made in some Alexandrite, crystal, flamingo pink, marigold amber/yellow, Moongleam green, and Sahara yellow.
Baker, Moongleam green...30.00
Bowl
    8" sq, ftd, marigold 80.00
    9" d, flamingo pink....................................35.00
Celery Tray, 13" l
    Flamingo..35.00
    Marigold..45.00
Cheese Plate, Kraft, Moongleam green 62.50
Console Bowl, 12-1/2" d, Moongleam green, gold bird
    border..85.00

Twist, oil bottle, 2-1/2 oz, #78 stopper, flamingo, orig label, $75.

Creamer and Sugar, oval, Sahara yellow.....................165.00
Cruet, orig stopper, Moongleam green.........................80.00
Cup and Saucer, flamingo 55.00
Floral Bowl, 9" d, Moongleam green...........................70.00
Goblet, 9 oz, flamingo pink 40.00
Ice Bucket, Moongleam green.....................................95.00
Juice Tumbler
    5 oz, 4-3/8" h, ftd, flamingo pink.......................48.00
    6 oz, flamingo pink......................................30.00
Lemon Plate, 2 handles, Moongleam green 20.00
Nasturtium Bowl, 8" oval
    Flamingo pink...110.00
    Moongleam green 110.00
Pickle Tray, 7" l, flamingo pink 20.00
Plate
    6" d, flamingo pink..18.00
    7" d, flamingo pink..22.00
    8" d, marigold 15.00
Relish, flamingo pink, 13" l..40.00
Salt and Pepper Shakers, pr, flat, Sahara yellow..........85.00

Victorian, #1425. Made in cobalt blue, crystal, Sahara yellow, and some zircon; 1933-53.
Celery Tray, 12" l...45.00
Champagne/saucer, 2 ball stem.................................17.50
Claret, two ball stem, 4 oz..20.00
Cologne Bottle, orig stopper......................................50.00
Creamer and Sugar...35.00
Goblet, one ball stem..24.00
Juice Tumbler, 5 oz...10.00
Punch Bowl Set, 15" d bowl, twelve cups 325.00
Salt and Pepper Shakers, pr, sanitary tops 55.00
Wine, 2-1/2 oz..20.00

Waverly. Blank #1519. Made in crystal, some amber. Often found with Orchid or Rose etchings.
Bowl
    10" d, crimped, rose etch...............................95.00
    12" d, rose etch, seahorse foot, floral.............235.00
Box, cov, 5" l...35.00
Butter Dish, cov, rose etching...................................175.00
Candle Epergnette, 2 part..25.00
Candlesticks, pr, 2-lite, #942 Harvester cutting..........125.00
Candy Box, cov, 6" l, bow tie knob 40.00
Compote, 6" dl low foot...20.00
Creamer and Sugar
    Orchid etch..75.00
    Plain..55.00
Cup and Saucer 12.00
Epergne, 5" d, orig blue label 24.00
Floral Bowl, cutting...45.00
Honey Dish, 6-1/2" d, ftd...15.00
Mayonnaise, 5-1/2" d, 3 ftd, rose etch 55.00
Plate
    7" d...8.00
    8" d, Narcissus etching 20.00
    11" d...20.00
Relish, 6-1/2", divided, 3 ft.......................................25.00
Salt and Pepper Shakers, pr, plume shape, sterling top....50.00
Sherbet..18.00
Torte Plate, 14" d, rose etch......................................50.00
Vegetable Bowl, 9" d...35.00

Yeoman. Blank #1184. Made in some cobalt blue, crystal, flamingo pink, Hawthorne orchid, marigold, Moongleam green, and Sahara yellow.
Ashtray, Hawthorne orchid...35.00
Banana Split Dish, Moongleam green, ftd 35.00
Bon Bon, Sahara yellow, 6-1/2" d, handle....................45.00

Bouillon Cup, ftd...20.00
Candle Vase, short prisms, inserts, crystal..................95.00
Celery Tray
    Moongleam green, 13" l.................................40.00
    Sahara, 9" l..35.00
Coaster, 4-1/2" d
    Crystal 4.00
    Flamingo pink...7.00
    Moongleam green 15.00
    Sahara yellow 12.00
Compote, Moongleam green, 5" w, 3-3/4" h 45.00
Cream Soup, Moongleam green....................................20.00
Creamer and Sugar, Hawthorne orchid 60.00
Cruet, orig stopper
    Flamingo pink...80.00
    Moongleam green, 4 oz..................................85.00
    Sahara yellow, 2 oz.......................................75.00
Cup and Saucer, flamingo pink 25.00
Egg Cup, Flamingo pink...25.00
Grapefruit, ftd, marigold..48.00
Gravy, underplate, Moongleam green 35.00
Hors D'oeuvre Tray, 13" d, center handle, Sahara
    yellow..65.00
Lemon Dish, Sahara yellow..85.00
Marmalade Jar, cov, Sahara yellow 50.00
Oyster Cocktail, crystal...12.00
Parfait, crystal..15.00
Plate
    6" d, crystal...4.00
    6" d, flamingo pink..18.00
    6" d, Hawthorne orchid..................................20.00
    6" d, marigold...18.00
    6" d, Moongleam green..................................15.00
    8" d, crystal...15.00
    8" d, crystal, #847 streamline cutting 55.00
    10-1/2" d, crystal..18.00
Relish, 3-part, Moongleam green, handle....................60.00
Salt, open, flamingo pink...10.00
Sherbet, flamingo pink 12.00
Soda Tumbler, flamingo pink, 4-1/2 oz.........................10.00
Sugar Shaker, Moongleam green.................................70.00
Tray, 11" l, 3-part, crystal..20.00
Tumbler
    8 oz, Sahara yellow, ftd.................................20.00
    10 oz, flamingo pink, straight sides.................20.00
Whiskey, 2-1/2 oz
    Crystal 5.00
    Flamingo pink...10.00
    Moongleam green 18.00
    Sahara yellow 15.00

HOBBS, BROCKUNIER & CO.

History: The Hobbs Glass Company was located in Wheeling, W.V. from 1845 until 1891. Its principal production was brilliant cut glass. John L. Hobbs and James B. Barnes founded the firm after leaving the New England Glass Company. Their sons, John H. Hobbs and James F. Barnes, soon joined the business. In 1863, the name was changed to Hobbs, Brockunier & Co. to reflect changes in management by John L. Hobbs, John H. Hobbs, and Charles Brockunier. Brockunier was formerly a superintendent at the New England Glass Company. William Lehighton Sr., was in charge of production.

William Lehighton devised a formula for soda lime glass in 1864. Lehighton's formula was responsible for production of a cheaper, but also clear type of glassware, which revolutionized the glass industry.

By the 1880s, the firm was producing fine art glass, including amberina, spangled, and several opalescent patterns. It is generally these colored wares that are considered when the name Hobbs, Brockunier is mentioned.

Reference: Neil and Tom Bredehoft, *Hobbs, Brockunier & Co. Glass*, Collector Books, 1997; Kenneth Wilson, *American Glass 1760-1930: The Toledo Museum of Art, Volume I, Volume II*, Hudson Hills Press and The Toledo Museum of Art, 1994.

Barber Bottle, Francesware Hobnail pattern, frosted ground, amber stain..125.00
Basket, Leaf and Flower pattern, ruby stain, scalloped, pressed rope handle..65.00
Berry Bowl, master
    Francesware Swirl pattern..85.00
    Hexagon Block pattern, pointed scalloped rim, 7" d 25.00
Bowl
    5-1/4" d, Hobnail pattern, cranberry opalescent, ruffled.....75.00
    7" l, Francesware Hobnail pattern, oval 45.00
    8" d, 4" h, satin, soft pink ground, applied yellow edge, thirty crimps...450.00
Bride's Basket, 10-3/4" h, 9" d x 3" h bowl, Daisy and Button, amberina with deep fuchsia, red to bright amber, orig fancy Meriden silver plated holder, numerous edge flakes and chips...100.00
Cake Plate, Hand, frosted base..250.00
Castor Set, Francesware Swirl pattern, salt and pepper shakers, oil and vinegar cruets, orig SP holder 650.00
Celery Vase, 6-1/2" h, 5" w, cranberry opalescent, opaque white swirls, satin finish, flared ruffled rim, polished pontil... 100.00
Compote, 7" d, Hexagon Block pattern, amber stain, high standard, pointed scalloped rim 65.00
Creamer, applied handle
    Francesware Hobnail pattern, clear and frosted 45.00
    Hexagon Block pattern, ftd...35.00
    Hobbs Block pattern, clear 35.00
    Leaf and Flower pattern, amber stain 45.00
Cruet, 7" h, Rubena Verde, tee pee shape, flashed ruby-red color at trefoil spout and two-thirds way down, intense vaseline lower third, handle, and faceted stopper 550.00
Custard Cup, Hexagon Block pattern, applied handle, ftd ... 50.00

Goblet
    Hexagon Block pattern, amber stain 50.00
    Hobbs' Block pattern, amber stain 95.00
Lamp Shade, Francesware Swirl pattern, bulbous........... 90.00
Lemonade Set, Francesware Hobnail pattern, frosted ground, amber stain, pitcher and six lemonade mugs....... 425.00
Miniature Lamp, Francesware Swirl pattern 425.00
Mustard, cov, Francesware Swirl pattern 90.00
Pitcher
    5" h, 5" w, spangle, light gold ground, diamond quilted body, gold mica flecks, white lining, applied amber shell reeded handle...285.00
    7-1/4" h, Hobnail pattern, frosted rubena, applied handle...350.00
    7-3/4" h, sq mouth, shaded pink satin ground, yellow coralene seaweed dec, applied frosted handle..........750.00
    8-1/2" h, Francesware Hobnail pattern, frosted ground, amber stain...250.00
Salt Shaker, Stripe, blue opalescent, ring neck.............. 110.00
Sauce
    Francesware Hobnail pattern, frosted, amber stain, ruffled rim...35.00
    Francesware Swirl pattern, oval 35.00
    Hexagon Block pattern, amber stain, pointed scalloped rim...25.00
    Hobbs' Block pattern, scalloped rim..............................15.00
Spooner
    Francesware Hobnail pattern, frosted, amber stain, ruffled rim...55.00
    Francesware Swirl pattern...65.00
    Hexagon Block pattern, amber stain, pointed scalloped rim...30.00
    Hobbs' Block pattern, scalloped rim..............................35.00
    Leaf and Flower pattern, scalloped 35.00
Sugar Bowl, cov
    Francesware Hobnail pattern, frosted, amber stain......95.00
    Francesware Swirl pattern, faceted knop finial 95.00
    Hexagon Block pattern, amber stain, ftd 125.00
    Hobbs' Block pattern, frosted, amber stain 115.00
    Leaf and Flower pattern, ruby stain 145.00
Sugar Shaker
    Inverted Thumbprint pattern, frosted, amber top........120.00
    Venetian Diamond pattern, cranberry..........................125.00
Syrup, cranberry ground, opalescent hobnails, orig pewter top mkd " Pat. Mar 20 83" 400.00
Toothpick Holder
    Daisy and Button pattern, amberina 300.00
    Francesware Hobnail pattern, frosted, amber stain, 2-1/2" h 65.00
Tumbler
    Francesware Hobnail pattern, frosted, amber stain......45.00
    Francesware Swirl pattern...45.00
    Hexagon Block pattern, amber stain 35.00
    Hobbs' Block pattern 20.00
Waste Bowl, Francesware Hobnail pattern, frosted ground, amber stain, 4" d 55.00
Water Pitcher, cranberry, melon ribbed, ivy mold, ruffled edge 185.00
Water Tray, Francesware Hobnail pattern, frosted, amber stain, leaf shape, 12" l 145.00
Witch Ball, 6-1/2" d, Hobnail pattern, vaseline............... 300.00

Lamps, left: Hobbs Snowflake, blue opalescent, 9-5/8" h, glass sleeve over connector, tiny flake on edge of base, $700; right: Hobbs Snowflake, cranberry opalescent, 9-1/2" h, missing glass sleeve, $450. Photo courtesy of Green Valley Auctions, Inc.

IMPERIAL GLASS

History: Imperial Glass Co., Bellaire, Ohio, was organized in 1901. Its primary product was pattern (pressed) glass. Soon other lines were added, including carni-

val glass, Nuart, Nucut, and Near Cut. In 1916, the company introduced Free-Hand, a lustered art glass line, and Imperial Jewels, an iridescent stretch glass that carried the Imperial cross trademark. In the 1930s, the company was reorganized into the Imperial Glass Corporation, and the firm is still producing a great variety of wares.

Probably the most well-known Imperial glass pattern is Candlewick. Because of the high collectibility of this pattern, it is listed in a separate category. It is one of those patterns known by pattern name first, and the manufacturer second. Imperial produced many other patterns, including Cape Cod and Crystolite, but these never achieved the success of the Candlewick line.

Imperial recently acquired the molds and equipment of several other glass companies: Central, Cambridge, and Heisey. Many of the retired molds of these companies are once again in use.

Marks: The Imperial reissues are marked to distinguish them from the originals.

References: Margaret and Douglas Archer, *Imperial Glass*, Collector Books, 1978, 1993 value update; Tom and Neila Bredehoft, *Fifty Years of Collectible Glass, 1920-1970*, Antique Trader Books, 1997; Carl O. Burns, *Imperial Carnival Glass 1909-1930 Identification & Values*, Collector Books, 1996; Gene Florence, *Elegant Glassware of the Depression Era*, 6th ed., Collector Books, 1994; Myrna and Bob Garrison, *Imperial Cape Cod Tradition to Treasure*, printed by author, 1982; Myrna and Bob Garrison, *Imperial's Vintage Milk Glass*, published by authors, 1992; Frank L. Hahn and Paul Kikeli, *Collector's Guide to Heisey and Heisey by Imperial Glass Animals*, Golden Era Publications, 1991; James Measell, *Imperial Glass Encyclopedia, Volume II, Cape Cod-L*, National Imperial Glass Collectors Society, 1997; National Imperial Glass Collectors Society, *Imperial Glass Encyclopedia: Volume I, A-Cane*, Antique Publications, 1995; ——, *Imperial Glass 1966 Catalog*, reprint, 1991 price guide, Antique Publications; Mary M. Wetzel-Tomalka, *Candlewick: The Jewel of Imperial, Book I*, available from author (P.O. Box 594, Notre Dame, IN 46556), 1980; ——, *Candlewick: The Jewel of Imperial, Book II*, available from author, 1995; ——, *Candlewick: The Jewel of Imperial, Personal Inventory & Record Book*, available from author, 1998; ——, *Candlewick: The Jewel of Imperial, Price Guide '99 and More*, available from author, 1998.

Periodical: *Glasszette*, P.O. Box 534, Bellaire, OH 43906.

Collectors' Clubs: National Candlewick Collector's Club, 275 Milledge Terrace, Athens, GA 30606; National Imperial Glass Collectors Society, P.O. Box 534, Bellaire, OH 43906.

Videotapes: National Imperial Glass Collectors Society, Candlewick: At Home, In Any Home, Vol. I: Imperial Beauty, Vol. II: Virginia and Mary, RoCliff Communications, 1993; ——, Glass of Yesteryears: The Renaissance of Slag Glass, RoCliff Communications, 1994.

Carnival

Bell
    Hobnails, marigold 25.00
    Santa, white 45.00
    Star Medallion, ice green 27.50
    Suzanne, cobalt blue...55.00
Bowl, Fashion, red..40.00
Candleholders, pr, Rose, ice blue and amber..............20.00
Compote
    Acanthus, red 35.00
    Zodiac, smoke, cov 35.00
Creamer and Sugar, Acanthus, red 35.00
Dish, Pansy, oblong, marigold 27.50
Mug, #474, smoke..15.00
Perfume, pink..40.00
Pickle Dish, Grape, amber 25.00
Plate
    Nu-Homestead, ribbed back, marigold 700.00
    Nu-Homestead, vaseline 75.00
    Mums, amethyst 75.00
Powder Box, cov
    Amber...35.00
    Smoke..25.00
Relish, 2-part, Arrow, red 45.00
Sugar Shaker, ice blue 35.00
Vase
    Daisy, ice blue...25.00
    Floral with Button, 7" h, 3" d, red 45.00
    Loganberry, 10" h, green....................................300.00
    Swirl, ice pink, tall...35.00
    Swirled Interior, fan shape, two handles, smoke and multicolor irid 80.00
    Three Swans, 9" h, necks curve to form handle, irid blue, emb "IG" 75.00
Water Carafe, Grape, ice green 35.00
Water Set
    Grape, amber, 7 pc 150.00
    Robin, cobalt blue, 7 pc 175.00

Engraved or hand cut

Bowl
    6-1/2" d, flower and leaf, molded star base 25.00
    9-1/2" d, three sprays with flowers, molded star base .. 45.00
Candlesticks, pr, 7" h, Amelia 35.00
Celery Vase, 3 side stars, cut star base 25.00
Nut Dish, Design No. 112, 5-1/2" d 30.00
Pitcher, 6" h, daisies, molded star base......................65.00
Plate, 5-1/2" d, Design No. 12.....................................15.00
Sherbet, Design No. 300, engraved stars, ftd 15.00
Syrup, Design No. 112, SP top 45.00
Table Set, cov butter, reamer, cov sugar, and spooner, Design No. 4, cut star pattern....................................215.00
Tankard, Design No. 110, flowers, foliage, and butterfly cutting..60.00
Tumbler, buzz star dec 20.00

Jewels

Bowl
    6-1/2" d, purple Pearl Green luster, mkd.................75.00

Humidor, Checkerboard pattern, faceted knob finial, $90.

8-1/2" d, 3-1/2" h, round base ending in cornered top, blue and purple jewel finish, stretch type irid, sgd 300.00
Candlesticks, pr
   7-3/4" h, dark purple stretch form...........................500.00
   9" h, 3-3/4" d, bright orange, small pulled pontil on one...500.00
Compote, 7-1/2" d, irid teal blue 65.00
Plate
   8" d, irid pale green...50.00
   9" d, white luster 70.00
Rose Bowl, amethyst, green irid 75.00
Vase
   5-1/2" h, bulbed gold irid, lightly stretched luster, base molded cross trade mark 325.00
   5-1/2" h, 6-1/2" w, round body ending in square dimpled top, dark blue, silver blue irid, sgd "Imperial" on base..250.00
   6" h, 4-1/2" d, classic baluster, brilliant blue glossy ext., orange irid lining..550.00
   7-3/4" h, classic baluster, white body, mirror bright tray-blue surface, deep orange irid interior rim 320.00

Lustered (Freehand)

Bud Vase, 7" h, 3-1/4" d, bulbous base, tall cylindrical neck, orange and heart vine dec, irid purple ground 600.00
Candlesticks, pr
   10-3/4" h, cobalt blue, white vine and leaf dec 325.00
   10-3/4" h, 4-1/8" d, crystal, selenium red knobs, threaded dec around stem, polished pontil...................1,550.00
Hat, 9" w, ruffled rim, cobalt blue, embedded irid white vines and leaves...120.00
Lamp Shade, 5" l, art Nouveau, irid ivory, gold, and green feather pattern, colored threading, sgd 190.00
Pitcher, 10" h, pale yellow luster, white pulled loops, applied clear handle...240.00
Rose Bowl, 6" h, irid orange, white floral cutting...........85.00
Vase
   6-1/4" h, 4-1/2" d, classic shape, bulbous base, flaring neck, glossy yellow ext., orange lining..............400.00
   6-1/2" h, flared orange lined rim, opal oval body, chartreuse imreen heart and vine dec 750.00
   6-1/2" h, 6" d, bulbous, flaring top, blue pulled loop over bright orange exterior, orange and white lining 650.00

7" h, irid metallic finish, green, purple, and blue, white veining..350.00
7" h, opal white irid body, bright blue heart and vine dec, applied cobalt blue wrap, subtle orange lustered interior..800.00
7-1/4" h, brilliant orange irid flared oval body cased to white, lustered green pulled dec, unsigned polished white pontil...345.00
7-1/2" h, 4-1/4" d, bulbous, slender neck, flaring top, blue glossy finish, orange interior...............................450.00
8-1/2" h, irid green, blue, and purple concentric lines over red ground, polished pontil 330.00
8-1/2" h, 2-1/2" w, slender, white drag loops over yellow, bright orange interior 400.00
8-1/2" h, 3" d, yellow ground, white drag loop dec, orange irid interior, small black spot on interior rim from firing...400.00
8-3/4" h, 2-1/2" w, white opal ground, orange interior casing, green hanging hearts and vines, minor wear to interior lining..350.00
8-3/4" h, 3" d, cylindrical, flaring and rim, brilliant orange, applied blue threading, minute wear to threading in two spots 400.00
10" h, red irid ext., int. with irid alligatored caramel surface over white irid 450.00
10" h, 5-1/2" d, bulbous, flaring neck and top rim, blue pulled drag loops over orange, brilliant orange interior.... 900.00
11" h, tricorn rim, extended tooled handles on oval body, brilliant golden bronze, heart and vine dec, orig label on base...2,300.00
11-1/4" h, irid purple, amber, and white pulled ext., purple int. 300.00
11-1/4" h, 4-1/2" w, dark blue matte finish, pale blue drag loops, blue and purple irid interior 800.00
11-1/4" h, 5" w, oyster white exterior, deep orange neck, hanging heart and vine dec 850.00
11-1/2" h, 5" w, bright orange ground, deep blue loops over bright white, irid surface...........................875.00

Nuart

Ashtray, mkd "Nuart"...20.00
Lamp Shade
   Crystal, cluster electric type, frosted int., flower etching, mkd "Nuart" 35.00
   Marigold 50.00
   Pearl Ruby, fan and star etching, mkd "Nuart" 45.00
Vase, 7" h, bulbous, irid green 125.00

Nucut

Berry Bowl
   4-1/2" d, handles 15.00
   7-1/2" d, mkd "Nucut" 22.00
Bowl, 8-1/2" d, Rose Marie, pink, ftd, mkd "Nucut".......45.00
Celery Tray, 11" l, mkd "Nucut"....................................18.00
Creamer, mkd "Nucut" 20.00
Fern Dish, 8" l, brass lining, ftd 30.00
Nappy, 6" w, heart shape, mkd "Nucut" 22.00
Orange Bowl, 12" d, Rose Marie 48.00
Punch Bowl Set, 13" d punch bowl, six cups, Rose Marie, mkd "Nucut" 185.00
Salad Bowl, 10-3/4" d, mkd "Nucut"..............................35.00
Sauce, 4-1/2" d, handles, mkd "Nucut".........................18.00
Tumbler, flared rim, molded star, mkd "Nucut" 15.00

Pressed

Animal Dish, cov
   Chicken on Nest, amethyst slag.............................100.00

Ad, introducing new Jefferson pattern, China, Glass & Tablewares, 1962.

Rabbit, white milk glass, 4-1/2" h 85.00
Rooster, lacy basket base, amethyst slag 125.00
Ashtray, Cathay, jade..65.00
Baked Apple
　Cape Cod, crystal 10.00
　Tradition, crystal, 6" d.......................................5.00
Berry Bowl, Katy, blue opalescent, flat rim 30.00
Birthday Cake Plate
　Cape Cod, crystal 325.00
　Tradition, crystal 95.00
Bookends, pr, Cathay, jade 110.00
Bowl
　5" d, Empress, blue 25.00
　9" d, Roses, milk glass 20.00
　10" d, Pillar Flutes, light blue 35.00
　13" d, Cape Cod...40.00
Butter, cov
　Cape Cod, 2 handles 42.00
　Fancy Colonial, rose 55.00
Cake Stand, Cape Cod
　10-1/2" d, ftd 40.00
　11" d, ftd 100.00
Champagne
　Cape Cod, azalea 22.00
　Cape Cod, green 18.00
Cheese Dish, cov, Monticello....................................40.00
Claret, 5 oz
　Cape Cod, azalea 35.00
　Cape Cod, crystal 8.00
Coaster/Spoon Rest, Cape Cod, crystal 9.00
Cocktail
　Cape Cod, crystal 9.00
　Mt. Vernon 8.00
Cologne Bottle, Hobnail, blue milk glass, ruffled, orig stopper,
　pr 45.00
Compote
　Brocaded Orchid, 6" , d, green 94.00
　Cape Cod, crystal, 7" , ftd 40.00
　Pillar Flutes, light blue 25.00
Cordial
　Cape Cod..18.00
　Park Lane, amber 10.00
　Riviera, blue...10.00
　Wakefield, amber 12.00
Creamer and Sugar
　Cape Cod, crystal, sq foot 40.00
　Pillar Flutes, light blue 48.00
Cruet, stopper
　Cape Cod, crystal 35.00
　Cape Cod, green, #119......................................30.00
Cup and Saucer, Cape Cod, crystal............................15.00
Decanter, stopper
　Blown out grapes, orchid, IG mark 70.00
　Cape Cod, crystal, 30 oz....................................65.00
　Grape pattern, milk glass 25.00
Epergne, Crocheted, crystal 140.00
Fruit Bowl, 4-1/4" d, Cape Cod....................................10.00
Goblet
　Cape Cod, amber, #1602.....................................12.00
　Cape Cod, crystal 7.00
　Monticello, crystal..12.00
　Park Lane, amber 10l00
　Provincial, green..15.00
　Tradition, crystal, 5-3/8" h 8.00
Hot Sauce Bottle, Cape Cod, ceramic tube.................50.00
Ivy Ball, 4" h, Spun, red, crystal foot 60.00

Juice Tumbler
　Cape Cod, 6 oz, flat, crystal.................................9.00
　Cape Cod, 6 oz, ftd, amber................................12.00
　Cape Cod, 6 oz, ftd, 5-1/8" h, crystal 10.00
　Georgian, red 14.00
Junk Boat, Cathay, crystal, sgd "Virginia B Evans" 125.00
Lemon Dish, cov, Grape, milk glass, tab handles, notched
　lid..40.00
Marmalade, Cape Cod, crystal 30.00
Mayonnaise, underplate, orig spoon, Monaco, amber 35.00
Mint Dish, Cathay, peach blossom 40.00
Mint Tray, Molly, 8-1/2" l, heart-shaped center handle,
　ruby..40.00
Mug, Cape Cod, 12 oz, handle, crystal......................42.50
Mustard, cov, Cape Cod...22.50
Nappy, 5" d, handle, Floral pattern, caramel slag, IG
　mark..30.00
Parfait, Cape Cod, crystal, ball stem 10.00
Pepper Mill, Cape Cod, 236, large 85.00
Pitcher
　Spun, 80 oz, teal..95.00
　Traditions, 40 oz, ice lip 35.00
Plate
　Cape Cod, 6-1/4" d, bread and butter 6.00
　Cape Cod, 7-1/2" d, depressed center 25.00
　Cape Cod, 8-1/2" d..9.00
　Fancy Colonial, 7-1/2" d, pink..............................10.00
　Monticello, sq 18.00
　Tradition, 8" d 6.00
　Windmill, glossy, green slag, IG mark......................45.00
Powder Box, cov, 6" d, pocket watch form, green, emb
　"IG"..40.00
Punch Bowl Set
　Cape Cod, 15 pcs 175.00
　Crocheted, crystal, bowl, liner, 12 cups.................290.00
　Mt. Vernon 150.00
Relish
　4-part, 9-1/2", Cape Cod, crystal...........................35.00
　5-part, 11" d, Cape Cod, crystal............................65.00
Salt and Pepper Shakers, pr
　Cape Cod, ftd...25.00
　Huckabee, aluminum tops 30.00
Sherbet
　Cape Cod, amberina...20.00
　Cape Cod, crystal, ball stem, tall............................8.50
　Cape Cod, green, tall 15.00
　Mt. Vernon, low..7.00
　Park Lane, amber 10.00
　Tradition, crystal 5.00
Sundae, #1602 ....8.00
Sweet Pea Vase, 4" h..15.00
Tea Cup and Saucer, Cape Cod, crystal......................12.00
Tumbler
　Cape Cod, 12 oz, flat 12.50
　Calente, cobalt blue, 4" h....................................8.00
　Georgian, red 18.00
Vegetable Bowl, Cape Cod, oval, 11" l 70.00
Whiskey
　Cape Cod, 2-1/2 oz..12.50
　#1602, crystal...15.00
Whiskey Decanter, Cape Cod, chrome holder 175.00
Wine
　Cape Cod, #1602, 3 oz 9.00
　Mt. Vernon 8.00
　Old Williamsburg, pink or yellow 18.00
　Park Lane, amber 10.00
　Provincial, green..15.00
　Wild Rose etch 16.50

INKWELLS

History: Most of the commonly found inkwells were produced in the United States or Europe between the early 1800s and the 1930s. The most popular materials were glass and pottery because these substances resisted the corrosive effects of ink.

Inkwells were a sign of the office or wealth of an individual. The common man tended to dip his ink directly from the bottle. The years between 1870 and 1920 represent the golden age of inkwells when elaborate designs were produced. Glass inkwells are well represented in this interesting collecting area.

Inkwells are frequently sold by their Covill number (C#), referring to the excellent reference book by William E. Covill Jr.

References: Veldon Badders, *Collector's Guide to Inkwells: Identification and Values,* Book I (1995), Book II, (1997), Collector Books; William E. Covill Jr., *Inkbottles and Inkwells,* William S. Sullwold Publishing, out of print.

Amber, 4-1/2" h, 2-1/2" sq, fine stippling on base, deep plain dimple on each side, polished brass hinged mountings 240.00
Austrian, 3-1/2" h, art glass green irid ground, irid threading, bronze floral base, hinged cap, mkd "D.R.G.M." 360.00
Blown Three Mold, glass
　1-5/8" h, Keene Marlboro Street Glassworks, Keene, NH, 1820-40, cylindrical, deep olive amber, tooled disc mouth, pontil scar, McKearin GIII-28 .... 180.00
　1-5/8" h, Mount Vernon Glass Works, Vernon, NY, 1820-40, dense olive amber, tooled disc mouth, pontil scar, McKearin GII-15.. 150.00
　1-3/4" h, Boston and Sandwich Glass Works, Sandwich, MA, 1860-90, cylindrical, vertical flues, fiery opalescent milk glass, crudely sheared mouth, smooth base, small areas of roughness and flaking, C #1173 ....200.00
Figural
　1-7/8" h, snail, America, 1830-70, colorless glass, ground mouth, smooth base, flat chip on int. 140.00
　2-3/4" h, Benjamin Franklin head shape, France, 1830-60, colorless glass with pale gray cast, sheared mouth, smooth base, C#1289 .... 230.00
Freeblown Glass, 1-3/4" h, attributed to America, 1840-60, sq, opaque electric blue, flared mouth, pontil scar 120.00
Paperweight, 6-1/4" h, 4-1/2" d, multicolored concentric millefiore, base with 1848 date canes, Whitefriars 175.00

Blown Three Mold, Mount Vernon Glass Works, Vernon, NY, 1820-40, dense olive amber, tooled disc mouth, pontil scar, 1-5/8" h, McKearin GII-15, $150. Photo courtesy of Norman C. Heckler and Co.

Pattern Molded Glass, 2" h, America, 1840-60, cylindrical, vertical ribs, cobalt blue, sheared rim, pontil scar, C #1066 ... 140.00
Pitkin Type, 1-7/8" h, New England, 1780-1830, 36 ribs swirled to left, cylindrical, deep yellow-olive, tooled mouth, pontil scar, C #1160 .... 400.00
Teakettle, attributed to America, 1830-60, cut and polished octagonal form
　1-5/8" h, orange amber, ground mouth, applied brass collar, smooth base, brass cap missing, C #1268............325.00
　2" h, opalescent electric blue, ground mouth, smooth base, C #1255 ....400.00
　2-1/8" h, canary, ground moth, smooth base, missing closure, C #1268 ....250.00
　2-5/8" h, brick red and burgundy slag glass, ground mouth with brass cap, smooth base, two small chips, C#1261 .. 110.00
　3-1/4" h, additional applied ink reservoir on top, opaque blue, gilt highlighted dec, ground mouth, smooth base, no collar and cap, wear to gilt...............................350.00
Teakettle, attributed to America, 1830-60, 2" h, five loped body form, raised floral and leaf dec, fiery opalescent milk glass ground, orange painted and gilt dec highlights, ground mouth with brass collar and cap, smooth base, similar to C#1223... 275.00
Tiffany, 4-1/2" h, double bulbed transparent green-amber Favrile glass, dark red pulled feather motif dec, base inscribed "X 1353," hinged silver rim and cap both imp "Tiffany & Co. Maker Sterling S3099" 2,990.00

JACK-IN-THE-PULPIT VASES

History: Trumpet-shaped jack-in-the-pulpit glass vases were in vogue during the late 19th and early 20th centuries. The vases were made in a wide variety of patterns, colors, and sizes by many manufacturers.

The form imitates the wildflower known as Jack-in-the-Pulpit. These vases are generally found with a bulbous base, slender stem, and a flaring throat that develops into a lovely diamond-shaped back. Art glass examples provide collectors with lovely shaded and colorful additions to their glassware collections.

3-1/2" h, 6-1/2" w, red carnival glass, Leaf and Berry
    pattern 300.00
4" h, squatty, blossom form, white satin ground, emerald green
    lining, seven applied and frosted feet.....................75.00
4-1/4" h, satin glass, peachblow colored ground, applied cam-
    phor glass ruffled pedestal foot 400.00
4-1/2" h, opaque jade green, ruffled emb ribbed base, enam-
    eled small white flowers, gold trim 95.00
5" h, opaline, ruffled purple top..90.00
5-1/2" h, 3-1/2" w, spangled blue, yellow, and brown, white
    ground, all over silver flecks, applied crystal edge,
    swirled, Mt. Washington 250.00
5-3/4" h
    Spangle, white ground, pink lining, mica flecks, ruffled rim,
      clear edging 125.00
    6-1/4" d, Leaf Chalice pattern, opalescent blue............85.00
6" h
    Steuben, bright gold Aurene, strong irid, sgd "Aurene
      2699" 1,450.00
    Vaseline, clear bulging opalescent body, cranberry flared
      rim, ftd 165.00
    5" w, frosted pink and white stripes, large bulbous base,
      broad flange, Webb 375.00
6-1/2" h
    Loetz type, gold luster, pinched body 200.00
    3" w top, Burmese, matte finish, ruffled top, Mt. Washington,
      c1880..425.00
6-3/4" h
    Burmese, crimped edge, delicate coloration.............230.00
    Stevens and Williams, rainbow swirl, trefoil crimped
      top 500.00
7" h, cased pink over white, enameled bell flowers,
    Victorian..100.00
7-1/4" h
    Creamy opaque ext., white and yellow flowers, green leaves
      gold trim, deep rose pink int., amber edge, ormolu leaf
      feet..165.00
    Spatter, green, peach, yellow, and white spatter at top,
      green diamond quilted pattern body 75.00
7-1/2" h
    Nailsea, frosted chartreuse green ground, white loopings,
      applied frosted feet 165.00
    Opalescent, chartreuse, ruffled 90.00
8" h, 7" w, Burmese, scalloped rim, applied base, Pair-
    point 725.00
8-1/2" h
    Spatter, white, green, and cranberry 115.00
    Squirrel and Acorn pattern
      opalescent, blue..150.00
      opalescent, green 145.00
      opalescent, vaseline..175.00
      opalescent, white 115.00

Opalescent swirled stripe, cobalt blue rim, 9" h, $95.

9" h
    Emerald green crooked neck, tree bark surface, snipped rim
      manipulated to blossom form, gold irid surface, polished
      pontil, Loetz 690.00
    5" w, cranberry, white opal edge, applied crystal base,
      Hobbs..325.00
9-1/2" h, 5" w, lusterless white, Mt. Washington, randomly scat-
    tered floral dec, flared pie crimped top 300.00
9-3/4" h, 4-3/4" d top, Crown Milano, painted opalware, Bur-
    mese yellow base, Peachblow pink top, white mid sec-
    tion, small flower and leaves floral dec, 36 crimps at top,
    Mt. Washington..785.00
10" h
    Cranberry, applied crystal rigaree and feet................225.00
    4" w, Burmese, Mt. Washington, tightly pleated ruffled top,
      delicate pink with re-fired yellow edge, yellow steam and
      base..450.00
11-3/4" h, cased floriform, gold irid flower, green and gold pulled
    feather dec opaque opal body, unsigned, attributed to Mar-
    tin Bach, Quezal, two int. skips in blossom.............1,400.00
12" h, Loetz, green, silver-blue irid spots, c1920............450.00
12-1/2" h, trumpet, satin, white, lavender and white flowers,
    green leaves, ruffled rim, Mt. Washington.............375.00
13-1/4" h, amberina, Inverted Thumbprint pattern, New England
    Glass Works 325.00
13-1/2" h
    Blue opalescent, eight petal top, yellow enameled inside of
      top and down front 275.00
    Czechoslovakian, brilliant yellow baluster form, colorless
      glass overlay, black rim wrap..............................225.00
14" h, purple stretch, butterscotch pulled feather design on
    base..270.00
15-3/4" h, cased, blue, white lining, ruffled, applied crystal spiral
    trim, clear foot with scalloped shell trim 250.00

JEWELRY

History: Jewelry has been a part of every culture. It is a way of displaying wealth, power, or love of beauty. In the current antiques marketplace, it is easiest to find jewelry dating after 1830.

Glass elements have been an important part of the jewelry design and manufacturing process for a long time.

Designers discovered that glass could be blown, molded, and cut to imitate expensive gemstones. Some designers saw the beauty of the glass beads and cabochons as they eagerly incorporated the bright colors and shapes into bracelets, brooches, earrings, and pins. While much of the jewelry found today with glass elements is classified as costume jewelry, it often exhibits fine craftsmanship, prong settings, and a variety of metal settings.

Many examples of jewelry are found with glass elements. Rene Lalique started as a jewelry designer and experimented with molded glass brooches and pendants, some of which were adorned with semi-precious stones. Bohemian manufacturers were known for their exquisite glasswork and beads. After World War I, production of glass beads and molded and faceted glass stones became a primary industry, and consequently, primarily export items from the new country named Czechoslovakia. Czechoslovakian examples are now widely sought and highly prized by collectors. Black glass was used as a design element for many Victorian mourning pieces. Jewelry with glass elements offer every color of the gemstone world, from sapphire blue to ruby red and many other combined colors, resulting in millefiori beads and goldstone.

Authentic copies of period jewelry pieces were made for the movie industry and often contained glass and other materials. The fashion industry responded to the demand of movie inspired consumers by offering styles of clothing and jewelry. Costume jewelry designers continued to use glass elements for the mass-produced styles influenced by this ever growing group of consumers.

Today's collectors of jewelry with glass elements can find many good values as many jewelry collectors overlook these treasures.

References: Lillian Baker, *100 Years of Collectible Jewelry, 1850-1950*, Collector Books, 1978, 1997 value update; Jeanne Bell, *Answers to Questions about Old Jewelry*, 4th ed., Books Americana, 1996; Maryanne Dolan, *Collecting Rhinestone & Colored Jewelry, Third Edition,* Books Americana, 1993; Ginny Redington Dawes and Corinne Davidov, *Victorian Jewelry*, Abbeville Press, 1991; Ulysses Grant Dietz, Janet Zapata et. al., *The Glitter & the Gold, Fashioning America's Jewelry,* The Newark Museum, 1997; Martin Eidelberg, (ed.), *Messengers of Modernism, American Studio Jewelry 1940-1960,* Flammarion, 1996; Lodovica Rizzoli Eleuteri, *Twentieth-Century Jewelry*, Electa, Abbeville, 1994; Stephen Giles, *Jewelry, Miller's Antiques Checklist,* Reed International Books Ltd., 1997; S. Sylvia Henzel, *Collectible Costume Jewelry, Third Edition,* Krause Publications, 1997; Sibylle Jargstorf, *Baubles, Buttons, and Beads: The Heritage of Bohemia,* Schiffer, 1991; Penny Proddow, Debra Healy, and Marion Fasel, *Hollywood Jewels,* Harry L. Abrams, 1992; Jerry Reynolds, *Iridescent Hatpins & Holders of the Carnival Glass Era,* published by author (1305 N. Highland Pkwy, Tacoma, WA 98406); Christie Romero, *Warman's Jewelry*, 2nd ed., Krause Publications, 1998; Sheryl Gross Shatz, *What's It Made Of? A Jewelry Materials Identification Guide*, 3rd ed., published by author (10931 Hunting Horn Dr., Santa Ana, CA 92705), 1991; Doris J. Snell, *Antique Jewelry with Prices, Second Edition,* Krause Publications, 1997; Janet Zapata, *Jewelry and Enamels of Louis Comfort Tiffany*, Harry N. Abrams, 1993.

Periodicals: *Auction Market Resource for Gems & Jewelry*, P.O. Box 7683, Rego Park, NY 11374; *Gems & Gemology*, Gemological Institute of America, 5355 Armada Drive, Carlsbad, CA 92008; *Jewelers' Circular Keystone/Heritage*, P.O. Box 2085, Radnor, PA 19080.

Collectors' Clubs: American Society of Jewelry Historians, Box 103, 1B Quaker Ridge Rd., New Rochelle, NY 10804; Leaping Frog Antique Jewelry and Collectable Club, 4841 Martin Luther Blvd., Sacramento, CA 95820; National Cuff Link Society, P.O. Box 346, Prospect Heights, IL 60070; Society of Antique & Estate Jewelry, Ltd., 570 7th Ave., Suite 1900, New York, NY 10018.

Museums: Glass and Costume Jewelry Museum, Jablonec-Nisou, Czech Republic; Jewelers Museum, Providence, RI.

Bar Pin, large oval red glass cabochon bezel set within rope twist frame, mounted on scrolled and pierced shaped rectangular stamped gold plated brass plaque, flanked by small oval and round red glass cabochons and green enameled C-scrolls, reverse mkd "Czechoslovakia," safety pin catch, c1925, 2" w 50.00

Beads

3/4" l, colorless irid bead molded in spiraled five-rib design, set of 53 beads..575.00

1-1/4" l, Fleurettes, Lalique, gray glass, lavender-mauve patine over floral motif, set of 11 beads 1,380.00

1-1/4" l, Renaissance, Lalique, bright green beads pierced above and below medial panel, set of 11 beads ...490.00

23 beads, 14" l, solid oval beads composed of fused millefiori murrine canes, bright multicolored palette, strung on black silk, Murano 275.00

70" l, bronze multicolored irid carnival glass beads 50.00

108 beads, frosted colorless bead molded with four raised medallions, strung and knotted, attributed to Rene Lalique..815.00

Bracelet

Flexible, hinged white metal plaque bezel set with three rounded rect red glass cabochons in rope twist frames within black enamel scroll and floral design, silvered imitation marcasite rhinestones, set in bosses and bezels, terminating in snake chain at each end, spring ring clasp, reverse mkd "Czechoslovakia," c1920, 7-1/2" l 90.00

Link, sterling silver, five light blue glass convex rect plaques prong set in engraved sterling silver frames alternating with prong set square cut open backed colorless lead crystal stones, spring ring clasp mkd "sterling," c1920, 7" l.....90.00

Rondelles Plates, green glass discs strung on extensible cord, Rene Lalique 1,840.00

Brooch/Pin

Gilt metal frame, clear and frosted glass roundel, four flying moths, bright blue foil backing, frame stamped "Lalique," sq "RL" trademark, 1-3/4" d................................1,200.00

Gold, ornate setting with applied twisted border, center goldstone plaque with multicolored floral dec 65.00

Sterling Silver, S-scroll and flowered suspending two large faceted aquamarine colored glass drops on chains, set with rhinestones, DeRosa......................................475.00

White Metal, openwork butterfly motif, foliate and floral design within rope twist rect white metal frame, round, square, rect, and lozenge shaped blue glass prong set in upper left corners, set throughout with imitation marcasites, trombone catch, Czechoslovakia, c1920 ....70.00

Kosta Boda, Monica Backström, 1998, Sweden. Photo courtesy of Kosta Boda.

Hatpin, carnival glass
    Bubble Bee, amethyst..225.00
    Butterfly, amethyst..70.00
    Butterfly, blue 70.00
    Dragon Fly, blue..25.00
    Moire Taffeta, blue 75.00

Rooster, amber..175.00
Rooster, blue 100.00
Six Plums, blue..85.00
Necklace, Lalique
    18" l, Feuilles de Lievre, twenty green leaf form beads restrung as choker, green silk cord.......................2,100.00
    18" l, Fleurs et Reinceauc, twelve molded blue beads on blue cord 2,300.00
Pendant
    Fioret, molded figures, frosted glass, woven silk cord, silk tassel, Rene Lalique, 2-1/4" h, ...125.00
    Rectangular pillow shape, colorless glass, orange, gray, green, and black enamel painted bird on reverse, tree on obverse, engraved mark "M Goupy" at side.......1,150.00
    Sainte-Odile, pierced molded blue disc, woman's profile portrait, sgd "R. Lalique" at lower edge, 1-3/4" d 635.00
Stickpin, oval goldstone, gold filled setting and stickpin, orig box... 35.00
Suite
    Aurora Borealis, bib necklace of faceted beads, graduated fringe of glass beads and rhinestones suspended from rhinestone chain, matching flexible bracelet with glass bead clusters, matching clip earrings, c1960.......225.00
    Lalique, Dahlias, necklace and matching extensible bracelet, molded colorless frost glass with petal motif 1,725.00

KITCHEN GLASSWARE

History: The Depression era brought inexpensive kitchen and table products to center stage. Anchor Hocking, Hazel Atlas, McKee, U. S. Glass, and Westmoreland were companies which lead in the production of these items.

Kitchen glassware complimented Depression glass. Many items were produced in the same color and style. Because the glass was molded, added decorative elements included ribs, fluting, arches, and thumbprint patterns. Kitchen glassware was thick to achieve durability. The resulting forms were difficult to handle at times and often awkward aesthetically. After World War II, aluminum products began to replace Kitchen glassware. Today's microwaves are seeing a resurgence in kitchen glassware forms.

Kitchen glassware was made in large numbers. Although collectors do tolerate signs of use, they will not accept pieces with heavy damage. Many of these products contain applied decals; these should be in good condition. A collection can be built inexpensively by concentrating on one form, such as canister sets, measuring cups, etc.

References: Ronald S. Barlow, *Victorian Houseware*, Windmill Publishing, 1992; Tom and Neila Bredehoft, *Fifty Years of Collectible Glass, 1920-1970*, Antique Trader Books, 1997; Gene Florence, *Anchor Hocking's Fire King & More,* Collector Books, 1998; ——, *Collectible Glassware from the 40's, 50's, 60's*, 4th ed., Collector Books, 1998; ——, *Kitchen Glassware of the Depression Years*, 5th ed., Collector Books, 1995, 1997 value update; Linda Campbell Franklin, *300 Years of Housekeeping Collectibles*, Books Americana, 1992; ——, *300 Hundred Years of Kitchen Collectibles*, Krause Publications, 1997; Shirley Glyndon, *The Miracle In Grandmother's Kitchen,* printed by author, 1983; Gary and Dale Kilgo and Jerry and Gail Wilkins, *Collectors Guide to Anchor Hocking's Fire-King Glassware*, K & W Collectibles Publisher, 1991; —, *Collectors Guide to Anchor Hocking's Fire-King Glassware, Volume II*, K & W Collectibles Publisher, 1998; Jan Lindenberger, *The 50s & 60s Kitchen*, Schiffer Publishing, 1994; ——, *Fun Kitchen Collectibles*, Schiffer Publishing, 1996; Kathryn McNerney, *Kitchen Antiques 1790-1940*, Collector Books, 1991, 1997 value update; Gary Miller and K. M. Mitchell, *Price Guide to Collectible Kitchen Appliances*, Wallace-Homestead, 1991; Susan Tobler Rosgove and Marcia Buan Steinhauer, *Pyrex by Corning*, Antique Publications, 1993; Susan Tobler Rosgove, *Pyrex by Corning A Supplement and 1997-98 Price Guide,* 1997; Diane Stoneback, *Kitchen Collectibles*, Wallace-Homestead, 1994; April M. Tvorak, *Fire-King*, 5th ed., published by author (P.O. Box 126, Canon City, CO 81215), 1997; ——, *Fire-King '95*, published by author, 1995; ——, *Fire-King II*, published by author, 1993; ——, *History And Price Guide to Fire-King*, VAL Enterprises, 1992; ——, *Pyrex Price Guide*, published by author, 1992.

Periodicals: *DG Shopper Online,* The WWW Depression Era Glass Magazine, http://www.dgshopper.com/~dgshoppr, *Fire-King News,* P.O. Box 473, Addison, AL 35540; *Kitchen Antiques & Collectible News*, 4645 Laurel Ridge Dr., Harrisburg, PA 17110; *The Daze, Inc.,* P.O. Box 57, Otisville, MI 48463.

Collectors' Clubs: Glass Knife Collectors Club, 711 Kelly Dr., Lebanon, TN 37087; National Reamer Collectors Assoc., 47 Midline Court, Gaithersburg, MD 20878.

Museums: Corning Glass Museum, Corning, NY; Kern County Museum, Bakersfield, CA; Landis Valley Farm Museum, Lancaster, PA.

Anchor Hocking, Post–1930

Federal Glass Co.

Hazel Atlas

Hocking Pre–1938

Jeannette Glass Co.

Owens Illinois

MACBETH
No
PEARL GLASS

Apothecary Set, Chalaine	195.00
Ashtray	
Butterfly, crystal, Jeannette	7.00
Cowboy Hat, Delphite, Jeannette	22.75
Green, fluted, Federal	12.00
Jadeite	60.00
Banana Split Dish, Jeannette, oval, crystal	5.00
Batter Bowl	
Anchor Hocking, set of 7", 8", 9", and 10" d, rimmed, transparent green	95.00
Hocking, crystal, spout	15.00
Tufglass, two handles, two spouts	45.00
Batter Pitcher, 2 cup	
Milk Glass, Federal	15.00
Pink, US Glass	55.00
Beer Mug, yellow	40.00
Berry Bowl, Hazel Atlas, crimped	
Large, green	21.00
Large, pink	25.00

Wonderful, wonderful PYREX WARE
is extra smart in COLOR!

IMAGINE THESE beautiful dishes on *your* table . . . they're strikingly designed, vibrant with color, real "show-off" pieces when you're entertaining.

And think of what a joy they are to own . . . for they're honest-to-goodness *Pyrex Ware!*

All of these sturdy beauties go in the oven, then right to the table! Any leftovers? Put your Pyrex Ware dish in the refrigerator, ready to heat up again.

Illustrated above: the new Pyrex Color Ware Casserole Set . . . a 48-ounce casserole complete with cover and four individual dishes (7-ounce size). In gay red or sunny yellow.

Pyrex Color Ware Casserole Set, complete **$3.95**

Extra 7-ounce individual dishes   39¢ each

80 ounce bowl with four 12-ounce dishes. Red or yellow.
Oven-and-Table Set
$3.95

4 gay-colored dishes with clear glass covers. For baking, serving, storing.
Oven-and-Refrigerator Set
$4.15

Wonderful mixing bowls to use a dozen ways. A size for every use.
Color Bowl Set
$4.15

80-ounce size for buffet suppers. Bake in it, serve in it. Red or yellow.
Covered Casserole
Medium Size **$2.75**
Large Size **$3.15**

PYREX BRAND WARE

If it's Pyrex Ware the trade-mark is on it

Ad, Pyrex Ware, Chatelaine Magazine, December 1951.

Small, cobalt blue..15.00
Small, green...7.00
Small, pink...7.00
Bowl
    5-1/2" d, red, platonite, Criss-Cross.............................12.50
    6" d, Delphite, Pyrex...13.00
    6" d, jadeite, Jeannette..16.00
    6" d, Jennyware, Jeannette, crystal................................8.00
    6-1/2" d, cobalt blue...23.00
    7-1/2" d, cobalt blue, Hazel Atlas................................45.00
    7-3/4" d, cobalt blue..55.00
    8" d, Delphite, vertical rib...85.00
    8" d, green, Hocking...15.00
    8-1/2" l, oval, Pyrex, beige, two handles, blue dec, 1-1/2
        quart...15.00
    9" d, Delphite, Pyrex...17.00
    10" d, emerald glo..50.00
Butter Box, cov, Federal, green, 2 pound size................145.00
Butter Dish, cov, 1 pound size
    Criss Cross
        Cobalt Blue..120.00
        Crystal...20.00
    Hazel Atlas
        Cobalt blue..195.00
        Green...60.00
        Iridescent, round...25.00
    Hocking, crystal...25.00
    Jadeite..95.00
Cake Plate, Snowflake, pink......................................35.00
Canister
    3" h, jadeite, Jeannette
        Allspice...65.00
        Ginger...65.00
        Nutmeg...65.00
        Pepper..65.00
    5-1/2" h, coffee, jadeite, sq, Jeannette........................55.00
    6" h, green, screw-on lid, smooth...............................38.00
    20 oz, tea, Delphite, round.......................................275.00
    20 oz, tea, screw-on lid, Vitrock................................27.00
    29 oz, cereal, Delphite, sq.......................................375.00
    29 oz, sugar, Delphite, sq..425.00
    40 oz, coffee, Delphite, round...................................400.00
    40 oz, sugar, Delphite, round....................................450.00
    Rice, Ruff N' Ready, green..24.00
Casserole, cov, white, Pyrex......................................25.00
Cereal Bowl, green, Federal..8.00
Coffeepot, 4 cup, Pyrex...15.00
Creamer, Criss Cross, crystal.....................................15.00
Creamer and Sugar
    Hocking, crystal, dec...12.00
    Hocking, green...24.00
    Jeannette, green..15.00
Cruet, stopper
    Crystolite, amber..30.00
    Hocking, transparent green.......................................25.00
Cup, handle
    Federal, green...5.00
    Hazel Atlas, diamond quilted, pink..............................10.00
Curtain Tiebacks, pr
    2-1/2" d, knob-type, pink..35.00
    3-1/2" d, flat, floral, green and pink.............................20.00
    4-1/2" d, flat, floral, amber.......................................25.00
Custard Cup
    Hazel Atlas, ftd, green..5.00
    Tufglas, green...6.00
Drawer Pull, crystal

Double type...10.00
Knob..3.00
Drippings Jar, cov, jadeite, Jeannette...........................32.00
Egg Cup, double
    Black...12.00
    Green, Hazel Atlas...7.00
    Yellow, Hocking..7.50
Egg Nog Set, bowl, six cups, white, Hazel Atlas..............30.00
Epsom Salt Container, ribbed, jade.............................150.00
Fish Bowl, 6" d, transparent green...............................22.00
Fork and Spoon, amber handle....................................45.00
Funnel, green
    Medium..35.00
    Large..110.00
Furniture Caster
    Hazel Atlas, 3" d, transparent green...........................40.00
    Hocking, green, set of 4..14.00
Ginger Jar, Chalaine blue..55.00
Grease Jar, Tulips, cov, Hocking..................................15.00
Hand Beater, 32 oz measuring cup base
    Green..45.00
    Green, stippled texture...45.00
Ice Bucket, Hocking, crystal, handle.............................25.00
Iced Tea Spoons, colored handles, set of 12..................60.00
Icing Tray, 10-1/2" d, Chalaine blue............................175.00
Juicer, lemon/lime, green, Federal...............................20.00
Juice Tumbler, Hocking, pink, ribbed, 3-3/8" h................6.50
Knife
    Block, 8-1/4" l
    Crystal, orig box..28.00
    Green..45.00
    Pinwheel, crystal..15.00
    Plain, 9-1/8" l, green..40.00
    Stonex
        Dark amber, MIB...375.00
        Light amber, MIB..300.00
        Opalescent...40.00
    Three Leaf
        Crystal...15.00
        Green...35.00
    Three Star
        Blue...38.00
        Crystal, orig box..38.00
        Pink...25.00
Loaf Pan, cov, 5 x 8", Glassbake, clear, knob finial..........35.00
Match Holder, Jeannette, Delphite, round
    Black lettering "Matches"..95.00
    No lettering...50.00
Mayonnaise Ladle
    Amber, flat..9.75
    Pink, transparent..20.00
Measuring Cup
    2 oz, 1/4 cup, jadeite, Jeannette...............................40.00
    8 oz
        Crystal, 1 spout, Fire-King..................................18.50
        Crystal, 1 spout, Hocking...................................16.00
        Green, Hazel Atlas...32.00
        Green, transparent...18.00
        Milk white, Hazel Altas.......................................25.00
    16 oz
        Cobalt Blue, Hazel-Atlas....................................225.00
        Crystal, US Glass..20.00
        Fired-on Green..20.00
        Green, Hocking..32.00
        Green, stick handle, US Glass.............................50.00
        Milk glass, white..22.00

Mixing Bowl
    5-3/4" d, yellow banded dot, Pyrex 8.00
    6" d, crystal, Hazel Atlas 12.00
    6" d, crystal, Jeannette 16.00
    6-1/2" d
        Amber, Federal...10.00
        Cobalt Blue, Hazel-Atlas 35.00
        Green, Restwell..10.00
    6-5/8" d, cobalt blue, Hazel Atlas...........................25.00
    7-1/4" d, yellow banded dot, Pyrex 10.00
    7-1/2" d, cobalt blue, Hazel-Atlas...........................42.00
    7-3/4" d, amber, Federal 15.00
    8-1/2" d, cobalt blue, Hazel-Atlas...........................50.00
    9-1/2" d, amber, Federal 18.00
    11" d, Vitrock, white 15.00
    #90, Pyrex, set of 3, crystal, measure, mix, and pour.....25.00
    #120, Pyrex, 3 quart, crystal 12.00
    Nested Set, white, ivy dec, Hazel Atlas 50.00
Mug
    Ranger Joe, Hazel-Atlas
        Blue 9.50
        Red 9.50
    Red Transparent, New Martinsville, polka dot pattern....15.00
Napkin Holder, Nar-O-Fold, white, mkd "Napkin Company, Chi-
    cago, reg. U.S.A." 50.00
Percolator Lid, green, Hocking 12.00
Pie Lifter, Pine Cone..15.00
Pitcher
    Criss-Cross, green, Hocking 12.00
    Crystal, painted, Hocking..18.00
    Fired-On, orange, ball shape, tilt 20.00
    Green, tall, Hocking 36.00
    Jadeite, sunflower in base 40.00
    Pheasants dec, green, Hocking.................................25.00
Plate, 8" d, green, Federal 6.00
Platter
    Glassbake, crystal, large 20.00
    Pyrex, 14" l, oval 12.00
Range Shaker
    Black, arch
        Flour...35.00
        Salt and pepper, pr 45.00
        Sugar 40.00
    Chalaine, salt, pepper, sugar, and flour, set..............450.00
    Custard
        Arch, flour 25.00
        Arch, sugar 28.00
        Three Small Lines, spice 25.00
    Delphite
        Arch, sugar 250.00
        Rib, salt and pepper, pr 85.00
    Green, emb
        Flour...75.00
        Salt...40.00
        Sugar 90.00
    Jadeite, Jeannette, flour, sq....................................30.00
    Pink
        Emb, salt and pepper, pr 110.00
        Jenny...28.00
    Seville
        Arch, sugar 35.00
        Three Large Lines, flower....................................25.00
        Three Large Lines, ginger 35.00
        Three Large Lines, spice.....................................65.00
    Ultramarine, Jenny 35.00
Reamer, lemon

    Criss Cross, pink 325.00
    Hazel Atlas, pink 35.00
    Jeannette
        Delphite 100.00
        Jadeite...35.00
Reamer, orange
    Criss Cross
        Blue 375.00
        Crystal 10.00
        Pink..250.00
    Federal
        Large, loop handle, crystal................................14.00
        Small pointed cone, green 25.00
    Hazel Atlas, cobalt blue, tab handle 325.00
    Jeanette, pink..175.00
    Lindsay
        Green..475.00
        Pink..425.00
    Sunkist
        Black...800.00
        Caramel...375.00
        Chaline 275.00
        Crown Tuscan 375.00
        Opalescent...200.00
    US Glass, Handy Andy, green 50.00
Refrigerator Dish, cov
    4" x 4"
        Criss Cross, cobalt blue 35.00
        Delphite blue, Jeannette 40.00
    4" x 5", jadeite...65.00
    4" x 8"
        Criss Cross, green..60.00
        Delphite 65.00
        Floral carved, transparent green, US Glass.............30.00
    4-1/2" x 4-1/2" sq
        Jadeite, Jeannette 15.00
        Pink, Jennyware 35.00
    4-1/2" x 4", crystal, vertical ribs, Hocking...................14.00
    6 x 3", transparent green, Tufglass 45.00
    6-1/2" sq, Poppy Cocklebur, transparent green, US
        Glass 55.00
    8" x 8", sq
        Amber, Federal..25.00
        Criss Cross, crystal 25.00
        Pink, Federal...45.00

Refrigerator Dish, Hazel Atlas, cobalt blue, 4" x 4", $25.

8-1/2 x 4-1/2" , jadeite, Jeannette..................32.00
32 oz, round, jadeite, Jeannette..................35.00
Relish, 8-1/2 x 13" oval, Delphite, divided, Pyrex 20.00
Rolling Pin
   Clambroth, metal handles..................125.00
   Cobalt blue, wood handles 650.00
   Custard, screw cap..................275.00
   Peacock blue, wood handles..................250.00
Root Beer Dispenser, amber 350.00
Salad Fork and Spoon, blue 55.00
Salt and Pepper Shakers, pr
   Cobalt Blue, red lids, Hazel-Atlas 30.00
   Delphite, round..................125.00
   Ribbed, jadeite, Jeannette..................22.00
   Roman Arches, black, minor damage to lids..................45.00
   White, Hazel Atlas, red dec, 3-1/2" h 24.00
Salt Box
   4 x 5-1/2" d, round, yellow, no writing on lid 100.00
   Green, wood lid..................900.00
   Pink, glass lid..................150.00
   Ultramarine..................175.00
Sherbet
   Federal, pink 5.00
   Hocking, plain yellow 7.50
Soup Bowl, Glassbake..................2.00
Spice Jar, Hazel Atlas, cobalt blue..................75.00
Spice Shaker
   Delphite
      Paprika, black lettering..................185.00
      Pepper, round, black lettering..................60.00
      Pepper, sq, black lettering..................150.00
   White
      Cinnamon, red and blue dec, Hocking..................12.00
      Ginger, red and blue dec, Hocking..................12.00
      Nutmeg, red and blue dec, Hocking..................12.00
      Paprika, red and blue dec, Hocking..................12.00
Spoon, clear, Higbee..................25.00
Straw Holder, crystal, lid missing..................100.00
Sugar Bowl, cov
   Criss-Cross design, transparent green, Hazel-Atlas ... 35.00
   Federal, ftd, green..................12.50
Sugar Cube Dispenser, crystal..................225.00

Sugar Shaker
   Amber, paneled 225.00
   Delphite, round..................185.00
   Green
      Hex optic..................250.00
      Pinch..................250.00
      Plain..................145.00
      Spiral 250.00
      Jadeite..................175.00
Sundae, ftd, pink, Federal..................12.00
Syrup Pitcher
   Crystal, gold catalin handle 12.00
   Crystal, flower etch..................35.00
   Green, Hazel-Atlas..................45.00
Thermos, Cambridge, cobalt blue 450.00
Tom and Jerry Set, Hazel Atlas
   7 pc, Auld Lang Syne..................15.00
   7 pc, eggnog..................15.00
   7 pc, red and green dec 15.00
   9 pc, red and green dec 25.00
   9 pc, red and green dots 25.00
Towel Bar, 24" l, crystal, orig hardware 15.00
Tray, sq, Jeannette, handle, pink..................18.00
Trivet, 9" d, round, Pyrex, crystal 12.00
Tumbler
   Federal, Lido, 15 oz, ftd, pink 15.00
   Hazel Atlas
      Crystal, flat..................4.50
      Pink, diamond quilted..................12.00
      White, 3-1/2" h, 9 oz..................5.00
      White, 4-1/2" h, 16 oz..................7.00
   Hocking, cobalt blue, flat..................1.50
   Jeannette, Cosmos pattern, irid 4.50
Vase
   Hazel Atlas, 6-3/4" h, milk glass, c1930..................12.00
   Hocking, bud, dark amethyst..................18.00
   Jeannette, bud, jadeite 14.00
Water Bottle, clear, glass lid, Hocking..................24.00
Water Cooler, Smith, cobalt blue 400.00
Water Dispenser, 17" h, black base, crystal bowl, silver
   trim..................95.00
Water Set, Jeannette, pitcher, seven tumblers, irid 32.00

LALIQUE

History: René Lalique (1860-1945) first gained prominence as a jewelry designer. Around 1900, he be-

gan experimenting with molded-glass brooches and pendants, often embellishing them with semi-precious stones. By 1905, he was devoting himself exclusively to the manufacture of glass articles.

In 1908, Lalique began designing packaging for the French cosmetic houses. He also produced many objects, especially vases, bowls, and figurines, in the Art Nouveau and Art Deco styles. The full scope of Lalique's genius was seen at the 1925 Paris l'Exposition Internationale des Arts Décorative et Industriels Modernes. He later moved toward his well-known Art Deco forms.

The mark "R. LALIQUE FRANCE" in block letters is found on pressed articles, tableware, vases, paperweights, and automobile mascots. The script signature, with or without "France," is found on hand-blown objects. Occasionally, a design number is included. The word "France" in any form indicates a piece made after 1926.

The post-1945 mark is generally "Lalique France" without the "R," but there are exceptions.

References: Patricia Bayer, *The Art of Rene Lalique*, Book Sales, 1996; Nicholas Dawes, *Lalique Glass*, Crown, 1986; Hugh D. Guinn (ed.), *Glass of René Lalique at Auction*, Guindex Publications, 1992; *Lalique Glass From The Collection of Charles and Mary Maguil*, Clark Art Institute; *Lalique Glass The Complete Illustrated Catalogue for 1932*, Dover Publications, 1981; Robert Prescott-Walker, *Collecting Lalique Glass*, Wallace-Homestead, 1996; 1986; Mary Lou Utt, et. al., *Lalique Perfume Bottles*, Crown, 1990;

Periodicals: Lalique Magazine, 400 Veterans Blvd., Carlstadt, NJ 07072; T & B, P.O. Box 15555, Plantation, FL 33318.

Collectors' Club: Lalique Collectors Society, 400 Veterans Blvd., Carlstadt, NJ 07072.

Videotape: Nicholas M. Dawes, World of Lalique Glass, Award Video and Film Distributors, 1993.

Reproduction Alert: The Lalique signature has often been forged, the most common fake includes an " R" with the post-1945 mark.

Animal
    Fish, 7" l, sgd "Lalique, France," orig paper label 550.00
    Fox, 2-3/4" h, frosted, circular, engraved script sgd "R. Lalique France"..550.00
    Rooster, 9" h, numbered, sgd "R. Lalique, France," orig paper label 2,000.00
Ashtray
    3-1/2" h, Soucis, opal figure of vase with flowers at center, base stamped "R. Lalique France" 460.00
    5-3/4" d, lion, molded gargoyle form rim, extended mane ridges, engraved script sgd...................................180.00
    8" d, frosted cherubs, orig paper label 185.00
Atomizer, cylindrical
    2-1/2" h, Epines, clear, molded thorny bramble design, lav-

ender patine, raised molded signature, gilt metal atomizer fittings, damage to orig bulb and net.................300.00
    3-3/4" h, relief molded frieze of six nude maidens, holding floral garland, waisted gilt metal mount, Le Provencal fragrance, molded "R Lalique, Made in France"........265.00
    4-3/4" h, relief molded frieze of six nude maidens, holding floral garland, waisted gilt metal mount chased with ribbon tied floral festoons, stamped "LE Parisiene Bte S.G.D. G. Made in France/O/F," base low relief molded "R. Lalique Made in France" 900.00
Auto Mascot
    5-1/4" h, 6-1/4" l, Chrysis, nude woman, frosted, clear, chromed radiator cap, mkd "R. Lalique, France".................. 3,850.00
    6-3/4" h, Falcon, molded, polished and frosted, circular platform base, raised molded mark, numbered on base..........950.00
    8-1/4" h, rooster, molded, polished and frosted, ruffled tail feathers, low disk base, etched block mark, numbered on base..750.00
Beverage Set, Selestat, 10-1/2" h carafe with orig stopper, six 6" fluted glasses, six 5-1/4" h fluted glasses, each with molded foliage dec, black glass knop, molded "R. Lalique," minor rim nicks, 30 pc set 1,035.00
Bon Bon Box, cov
    8-1/4" d, Boites Ronde Grande Libellulis, irid dragonfly, sgd "R. Lalique No. 51" 1,295.00
    10-1/4" d, Lily of the Valley, mkd "Claire d'Lune," block sgd 695.00
Bookends, pr
    6-1/4" h, florals, birds, sgd 500.00
    7-1/8" h, three molded putti bearing garlands, frosted, stenciled "Lalique France" 600.00
Bottle, 13" h, double dove, swirl, stopper, never opened, signed, numbered 900.00
Bowl
    5-1/4" d, Coquilles, opalescent, scallop shell molded ext. design, etched reverse signature "R. Lalique, France No. 3204" 185.00
    8" d, 3-1/2" h, Gui, molded, clear, imp mistletoe leaves and stems, gray patine, berry clusters in relief form feet, raised block letter mark...350.00
    8-1/2" d, 2-1/8" h, Vernon, opalescent, press molded sunflower design, "R. Lalique France" molded below rim 690.00
    9" h, Actina, clear and frosted, blue opalescence 400.00
    9-1/4" d, nesting sparrow rim design, etched signature and paper label 250.00
    9-1/4" d, 3-5/8" h, Dahlia No. 1, press molded design, blos-

Automobile Mascot, Cinq Cheveaux, clear and frosted, c1925, orig Breves Galleries chromium plated brass mount, modern glass base, molded "R. Lalique," wheel-cut "France," $8,850.

som feet, raised motif, recessed leaf elements, circular center mark "R. Lalique France" 1,100.00

9-1/2" d, Chicoree, clear and frosted, molded Verrerie d'Alsace mark..385.00

9-3/4" d, Perruches, twenty repeating birds executed in high relief, blue patine enhancing blossom recessed panels, base acid stamped in center "R. Lalique/France" 2,990.00

12-1/4" d, opalescent, lily of the valley dec, sgd "R. Lalique" 600.00

13-1/4" d, 3" h, band of 29 daisies, frosted, clear bottom with stems, sgd "R. Lalique France"...............................550.00

Bowl and Platter, Poissons, 9-1/8" bowl, 11-3/4" platter, repeating fish curved to bubbled center, each sgd "R. Lalique" raised lettering molded on int..............................1,150.00

Box, cov
3-1/8" d, " h, Quatre Pappillons, four butterflies spaced at top, delicate floral motif on sides, faint molded "Lalique Depose" on base..920.00

3-1/2" d, Emiliane, frosted, molded flowerheads, engraved "R. Lalique France" 250.00

3-3/4" d, molded with dancing nude nymphs, molded "D'ORSAY" 275.00

Candlestick, 3-1/" h, sgd "R. Lalique"...............................600.00

Carafe, 7-1/4" h, clear, indented and molded large blossoms, brown patine in recesses, inscribed "R. Lalique" 450.00

Center Bowl
Bamako 1,050.00

Daisy, 14" d, broad molded rim, clear, brown patine on floral border...465.00

Champagne Glass, 4-1/2" h, Strasbourg, frosted androgynous nude couple on stem, Art Deco pattern exhibited at Paris Exhibition, 1925, Rene Lalique, set of 6.................920.00

Chandelier, 13-1/2" d domed shade, Charmes, frosted all over leaf pattern, rect components with similar pattern, orig metal fixtures, molded "R. Lalique".....................4,000.00

Charger
12" d, Peacock Feather...550.00

14-1/2" d, Martigues, opalescent, deeply molded swimming fish, molded mark "R. Lalique"...........................2,700.00

Cigarette Lighter, 5" h, highly emb frosted lion's heads, pedestal, sgd in script...90.00

Clock, 8-1/2" l, 6" h, demilune, circular mate finished silvered metal face, stylized dahlia encircled by polished Arabic numerals, arching frosted "R. Lalique France," dial inscribed "ATO" and impressed "Made in France," c1930 ....2,750.00

Cordial Set, Wingen, 8" h bulbous bottle, conforming stopper, two 3" h wine glasses, each with fine vertical striping, molded "R. Lalique" 575.00

Coupe, 9-3/8" d, 3-1/4" h, shallow bowl, Vases No. 1, colorless, repeating polished urn-forms alternating frosted stylized bouquets, center molded "R. Lalique," Marcilhac 3216, p 750...230.00

Dresser Jar, 3-1/2" h, Epines, domical stopper bottles, molded thornbushes, colorless ground
Sepia patine, raised "R. Lalique" and "France" on base...460.00

Strong blue patine, molded mark "R. Lalique," one stopper frozen, chip under edge, price for pr 230.00

Dressing Table Mirror, 12" l, 6-1/2" d, Narcisse Couche, frosted glass frame and handle, molded foliate motif centering male nude above handle, orig gray patine in recesses, inscribed "R. Lalique, France" top rim, mirror slightly stained, Marcilhac 675, p 359................................980.00

Illuminare, Crucification, #12001, 20" , sgd "Marc Lalique" 2,750.00

Jardiniere, 18-1/4" l, 5-1/8" h, Saint Hubert, frosted elliptical

Limited Edition Plate, 1967, Fish Ballet, $70.

bowl, ends spreading to form reticulated ear shaped handle, molded relief of leaping antelope among clear leafy branches, wheel cut block letters "R. Lalique/France," incised script "No. 3461," c1932 ....3,500.00

Lamp, 14" h Grande Ovalen Joueuse de Flute, oval glass blossom framed plaque with center fiery opal raised figure of draped woman playing double flute, platform base incised "R. Lalique/France" in block letters, mounted to giltmetal base and framework of two-socket table lamp, statuette not drilled... 17,250.00

Limited Edition Plate, orig box
1965, 8-1/2" d 100.00
1967 ....95.00
1968 ....95.00
1969 ....70.00
1970 ....55.00
1971 ....55.00
1972 ....55.00
1973 ....55.00
1974 ....55.00

Madonna, 14-1/2", black base, Marc Lalique, 1945 .... 875.00

Mascot/Paperweight, 8" h, rooster, frosted molded cock, tall feathered tail, stamped "Lalique France" on base, also mkd "R. Lalique" in the mold 490.00

Medallion, 1-3/8" d, Dana les Fleurs, 1924 model, frosted low relief of nude female under blossoms, made for Fioret perfume box, mkd "R. Lalique/Fioret/Paris"................ 520.00

Paperweight, Tete D'Aigle, eagle head, clear and frosted, sgd in mold at side "R. Lalique" 1,200.00

Perfume Bottle
2-1/2" h, Imprudence, ridged bottle, silver trim, mkd "R. Lalique France," orig Worth box 275.00

3-1/4" h, Le Jade, flattened snuff bottle form, molded jungle bird dec, bright green crystal, matching stopper, mkd "Le Jade/Roger et Gallet Paris/R. Lalique" in mold 2,185.00

3-1/2" h, Courer Joie, frosted heart-shaped floral bottle mkd "Bottle Made by Lalique," orig Nina Ricci box 295.00

3-1/2" h, Serpent, frosted, molded as striking snake, patine within recessed areas, stamped "Lalique"..........2,750.00

3-3/4" h, Elgance, for D'Orsay, sq molded bottle, two nude

women standing among flowering ranches, molded "D'ORSAY" 2,000.00

4-3/4" h, Bouchon Cassis, vertically ribbed colorless barrel form, integrated tiara stopper molded as currant berries, selectively polished and frosted, base molded, also engraved "R. Lalique" 7,200.00

19" h, Richard Hudnut Master Violet Sec, sq colorless bottle, orig contents, labels intact, some wear, corrosion at rim .. 145.00

Perfume Flacon

3-1/2" h, Marquila, frosted navy blue, molded artichoke lappet design, matching stopper, sgd and numbered...... 1,955.00

3-3/4" h, Salamandres, colorless flattened oval, polished roundels surrounded by curving lizards, gray-green patine in recesses, motif repeated on stopper, base inscribed "L. Lalique, France"................................1,495.00

5-1/4" h, Ambre, polished sq bottle, molded draped women recessed at each corner, black sq stopper with floral motif, base mold mark "Lalique/Ambre D'Orsay," small chips inside top...1,380.00

5-1/2" h, Bouchon Fleurs de Pommier, colorless barrel-shaped bottle, green patine in scalloped ridges, molded flawless tiara stopper with matching patine on blossom motif, base inscribed "R. Lalique France N 493" 10,065.00

5-1/2" h, Bouchon Mures, colorless barrel-shaped bottle, black ribbing, molded flawless matte black tiara stopper with berry clusters, molded "R. Lalique" on base 9,200.00

5-3/4" h, Quatre Cigales, colorless rect bottle, molded cicadas at each corner, recessed frosted white wings extending to base, integrated blossom stopper, base inscribed "R. Lalique France No. 475"...............................1,150.00

Place Card Holder, 1-5/8" h, demilune form, clear and frosted, molded baskets of flowers and fruit, engraved "R. Lalique," set of 8 ....850.00

Plaque, 4" h, 3-1/2" w, frosted and clear, floral design, mkd "Lalique," orig velvet lined box 100.00

Plate

9-1/4" d, Coquilles, four stylized shells, molded cameo mark, set of six 750.00

10-1/2" d, Volutes, opalescent, molded spiral design, stamped "R. Lalique France" at center..................575.00

11-1/4" d, Assiette Plate Ondine, opalescent, mermaids among bubbles, inscribed "R. Lalique France" 1,500.00

13-1/2" d, Felix, clear and frosted, stylized petals, stenciled "R. Lalique France" 300.00

Powder Box, cov, sepia wash, 2 ladies, arms entwined, fancy scrolls and flowers on cov, sepia washed garlands of flowers on base, sgd "Coty" and "Lalique Depose," c1915..600.00

Shot Glass, two cherubs, sgd...60.00

Statuette

6-3/4" h, dove, frosted molded birds, engraved "Lalique France," pr..490.00

9-3/4" l, Pigeon Burges and Pigeon Grand, press molded colorless frosted solid crystal, each engraved "Lalique France"..435.00

14-1/2" h, Madonna and Child, frosted colorless form, integrated black glass sq plinth, acid stamped in block letters "Lalique France," design attributed to Mark Lalique........ 700.00

Table Ornament, Groupe Luxembourg, 7-3/4" h, molded as three cherubs, frosted, colorless

Long hair version 700.00
Short hair version 700.00

Tray, 10-1/2" d, blue opalescence, all over shell pattern, sgd "R. Lalique" 300.00

Vase

3-1/2" h, Oleron, opalescent, molded fish dec............375.00

4-1/2" h, Eglantines, frosted oval, polished thorny branches and rose blossoms in relief, center base inscribed "R. Lalique" 400.00

5-3/4" h, Avallon, amber, molded birds among berry branches..1,100.00

6" h, Boulouris, flared cylinder, opalescent band of sparrows on shoulders, vertical ribbing, stamped "R. Lalique".... 1,775.00

6-1/4" h, Meander, frosted and clear, engraved "R. Lalique, France," c1935...1,200.00

6-1/2" h, Courlis, broad shouldered oval, stylized sea terms in flight above ocean waves, Art Deco style, red-amber, inscribed "R. Lalique France" 3,690.00

6-5/8" h, Gerriers, flared rim, stepped conical emerald green body, five repeating rows of flowers, base inscribed in script "R. Lalique France No. 1019" 3,740.00

6-5/8" h, Gui, broad oval body, molded mistletoe motif, base rim inscribed in script "R. Lalique France No. 948"......... 980.00

6-3/4" h, Druide, frosted opalescent ground, medium relief molded berries and branches, engraved "R. Lalique, France No. 937" 750.00

6-3/4" h, Formose, frosted and clear, molded "R. Lalique" 1,350.00

7" h, Espalion, raised rim, bulbous body, molded fern motif, base inscribed in script "R Lalique France No. 996" 1,150.00

7" h, Satyrs, cylindrical, frosted and clear, traces of blue patine, center bands of satyrs among ivy leaves, acid etched "R. Lalique, France" 1,2900.00

7" h, St. Tropez, frosted, molded berried stems, engraved "R. Lalique France" 550.00

7-1/4" h, Dandaides, opalescent, molded in low relief, standing water maidens, orig pale blue patine, molded "R. Lalique," etched "France" 2,500.00

7-1/2" h, Ornis, chalice form, two bird handles, smoky topaz, wheel carved "R. Lalique France" 1,000.00

8-1/4" h, snail motif, blue staining, relief signature 4,900.00

9" h, Ceylan, extended rim, four pairs of lovebirds in high relief, perched among stylized leafy branches, frosted and clear, blue patine, several small necks on rim edges.....4,025.00

9" h, Malasherbes, frosted, low relief, rows of overlapping flowers, acid stamped "R. Lalique," inscribed "France"..2,000.00

9-1/2" h, Ceylon, molded in medium relief, four pairs of parakeets perched in leafy branches, inscribed "R. Lalique" 3,800.00

9-1/2" h, Figurines et Masques, oval, molded full length nude women above grotesque mask faces alternating blown-out panels, base inscribed "Lalique/France" 2,415.00

10" h, Perruches, molded with fourteen pairs of love birds perched on flowering branches, frosted and polished to enhance design, electric blue, base inscribed "R. Lalique/France" at center with "H. H. Battles/Philada" label 9.775.00

10-1/4" h, Archers, frosted and clear, engraved "R. Lalique, France No. 893" 3,000.00

10-1/2" h, frosted and clear oval, molded repeating montage of male archers shooting at birds in flight, gray patine in recessed areas, base inscribed "R. Lalique France N 893" 2,760.00

3-1/2" h, 6" w, scantily clad female figure, holding torch, modern 550.00

LAMP SHADES

History: Lamp shades were made to diffuse the harsh light produced by early gas lighting fixtures. These early shades were made by popular Art Nouveau manufacturers including Durand, Quezal, Steuben, and Tiffany. Many shades are not marked.

Lamp shades offer a glass collector exciting shapes and colors. Many of the art glass and decorated shades make lovely cabinet pieces. Preservationists also seek period lamp shades as replacements for antique lighting fixtures.

References: Dr. Larry Freeman, *New Lights on Old Lamps,* American Life Foundation, 1984; Denys Peter Myers, *Gaslighting in America: A Pictorial Survey, 1815-1910,* Dover Publications, Inc., 1978; Jo Ann Thomas, *Early Twentieth Century Lighting Fixtures,* Collector Books, 1980.

Reproduction Alert: Lamp shades have been widely reproduced.

Aladdin
   Cased, green 870.00
   Satin, white, dogwood dec............................65.00
Artichoke, 10" d
   Green 1,000.00
   White 800.00
Ball, 7-1/2" d, pink opalescent, white hobnails, 4" fitter, two small chips, 1-1/4" crack in fitter ring................................25.00
Bigelow Kennard
   22" d, 9-1/2" h, conical leaded dome, white opalescent brickwork segments above and below border of repeating red amber ripple glass pine cones, shaded green needle leaves, yellow border glass, rim tag "Bigelow Kennard Boston Studios," four border glass segments broken out........ 2,760.00
   24-1/2" d, 5-1/4" h, broad parasol shape, 32 tapered panels in Prairie School manner, rim tag "Bigelow Kennard Boston," small split in metal rim.................................1,610.00
Bohemian, 6" h, 2" outside rim, attributed to Loetz, bell form, gold papillon surface, green and red raised spots and vertical stripes 435.00
Cameo, 3" x 6" fitter, bright yellow and fuchsia, clear frosted ground, floral cutting 250.00
Cased art glass, 5-1/2" h, 2-1/4" d fitter rim, cased gold, opal glass ruffled bell shade, green pulled feather motif, gold irid luster, price for 4 pc set 435.00
Ceiling Shade, 22" d, 9-1/2" deep, 5" opening, hipped O' Brien dome, leaded green glass segments arranged in brickwork geometric progression, three orig int. bronze reinforcements, rim imp "Tiffany Studios, New York 1501".............. 10,350.00
Durand
   5" h, 5" l, gold and black heart dec, ivory ground, random gold trailings, highly irid gold int., set of 4 ....900.00
   9-1/2" l, gold Egyptian crackle, blue and white overlay, bulbous, ruffed rim, sgd..225.00
Fenton, 4" d, white opal hobnails, blue ground 90.00
Fostoria
   5-1/2" d, Zipper pattern, green pulled dec, opal ground, gold lining 225.00
   8" h, long tapered ruffled bell form, intricate gold and green zipper pattern, gold irid int. 290.00
Frosted, 10-1/4" h, 14" w, dome shade, floral cut dec, set of flat 6" prisms..95.00
Gas, 5-1/2" h, 8-1/2" w, 4" d fitter ring, frosted glass, ruffled six panel top, emb pattern of 15 vertical rows of banding separated by 15 vertical plain ribs, cranberry top edge, price for 3 pc set 250.00
Handel
   6" d, 15" h, tulip shape, caramel and green, soldered repair to base...600.00

9" d, 4" fitter rim, round crackle glass gall, transfer printed Art Deco parrots, gilt metal and tassel mountings.......635.00
10" d, tam o'shanter, hand-painted green silhouette village scene with windmill and harbor, sgd "Handel 2862"...325.00
27-1/2" d, 10" h, octagonal conical shade, leaded green slag panels geometrically arranged, green-amber rippled ladderwork, drop apron dec by bronzed metal scenic tree framework handpainted to enhance forest motif, Handel tag imp on side..2,875.00
Imperial, NuArt, marigold 65.00
Leaded Glass, hanging dome
   16" d, 3-1/2" opening, rose pink slag glass segments, green acorn shaped leaf on vine dec belt, attributed to Bigelow & Kennard, areas of restoration, ...1,150.00
   20" d, leaded and paneled, band of grapes, apples, pears, and cherries, one piece missing, leading poor, numerous rust spots and pitting...100.00
   20" d, leaded and paneled, 8 panes on top in caramel glass, band of bluebirds and fruit, caramel and green slag panels, crack to one panel 300.00
   20" d, 15" h, sections of green and brown, border of apples, pears, and cherries, Wilkinson 550.00
   21" d, 14" h, green, amber, and red, border of mottled brown, orange and red, some small fractures in panel 350.00
   22" d, caramel colored glass, red and green floral border, 5 cracked panels at top 250.00
   24" d, caramel colored glass, border of red and green grapes and leaves...350.00
   26" d, 14" h, conical, raised amber slag grown and brickwork shoulder above wide colorful border of grape clusters, puffed bend glass apples, pears, peaches, and figures of birds 690.00
   27" d, amber caramel and white squares in geometric design, replacement ceiling and electrical fittings.............1,200.00
Leaded Glass, table, 17-1/2" d, 3" d opening, narrow topped umbrella-shape, dropped apron, four bright red starburst blossoms with yellow disks on green stems, green slag background segments, conforming motif on apron, some restoration to inside leading 635.00
Lithophane, 12" d, color courting scene 10,500.00
Loetz, 8-1/2" d, irid green oil spotting, ribbon work, white glass int., c1900.. 250.00
Luster Art, 5-1/4" h, 2-1/8" d outer rim, bell shape, sixteen ribs, opal, gold int., rim mkd "Luster Art," 3 pc set 230.00
Lutz Type, 8" sq, 6-1/4" h, opaque white loopings, applied cranberry threading, ribbon edge 195.00
Macbeth Evans, 10" d drilled bowl, dogwood pattern, pink, frosted int... 150.00
Miniature Lamp, 5-3/4" h, #288-I, orange satin, one flake and chip on fitter.. 50.00
Muller Freres, 6" h, frosted satin, white top, cobalt blue base, yellow highlights, 3 pc set 400.00
Opalescent
   Coin Spot pattern, amber ground, c1880 ....70.00
   Swirl pattern, cranberry ground, 8-1/2" d...................110.00
Pairpoint
   7" h, puffy, flower basket, reverse painted pink and yellow poppies and roses 425.00
   14" d, Saville design reverse painted shade, monochrome green, three sets of bird pairs amid scrolling foliate elements 1,840.00
Quezal
   5-1/2" d, dark green, platinum feathers, gold lining....650.00
   5-1/2" l, 6-1/4" w, 2-1/2" d fitter, green pulled feather, butterscotch loopings, white ruffled edge, gold int., unsigned, set of 4 ....600.00

Rubena, 7-1/4" d, 3-7/8" d fitter ring, cranberry shading to clear, frosted and clear etched flowers and leaves, ruffled 460.00
Satin Glass, 6" h, brown enameled dec of sail boat in lake scene..45.00
Smoke Bell
   3" h, 4" w, white milk glass, aqua blue edge, metal loop .. 75.00
   4" h, 4-1/4" w, white milk glass, medium blue edge, metal loop...85.00
   6-3/4" h, 5-3/4" w, white milk glass, forest green edge, applied milk glass loop, some smoke staining.............50.00
   7-1/4" h, 6-1/2" w, white milk glass, blue edge, applied milk glass loop 95.00
Steuben
   Aurene, irid brown, platinum applied border 425.00
   Aurene, irid gold, twenty-four vertical ribs on slightly tapered form, 6-1/2" h, 2-1/8" fitter rim, set of 4 ....635.00
   Pulled green feather, oyster white exterior, brilliant green interior, 2-1/4" fitter, 5-1/2" h, sgd, set of 3 ....550.00
   Threaded and heart dec, brilliant gold irid, 2-1/4" fitter, 4-1/2" h, sgd, set of 4..1,200.00
Tartan, 6" h, 3-1/4" fitter ring, gaslight, bands of white, yellow, and pink, sgd "Tartan Rd. No. 46498," registered by Henry Gething Richardson, Wordsley Flint Glass Works, near Stourbridge, Feb. 24, 1886 ....285.00
Tiffany
   1" d, fitter, 4-3/4" l, lily, gold irid, unmarked, pr 1,990.00
   2-3/4" h, flared bell-form, similar swirled combed dec, one gold, other amber, lustrous irid surface, inscribed "A2253," and "A2261," pr 1,035.00
   4-1/2" x 3", gas type, green pulled feather over yellow and gold spattered ground, slightly dimpled edge, sgd "LCT" 650.00
   4-3/4" l, 4" w, tulip shape, slightly ruffled edge, white opal stripes, green and lavender full feather dec at top, sgd 1,000.00
   5" h, 2-7/8" fitted rim, rib-molded opal shade, glossy int., pink Damascene-type dec, rims inscribed "LCT Favrile," one cracked, pr...1,380.00
   5-1/4" d, bell shape, irid gold ground, 4 pc set 1,200.00
Verlys, 3-5/8" d, 5-3/4" h, raised birds and fish dec.........285.00

LAMPS AND LIGHTING

History: Lighting devices have evolved from simple stone-age oil lamps to the popular electrified models of today. Aimé Argand patented the first oil lamp in 1784. Around 1850, kerosene became a popular lamp-burning fluid, replacing whale oil and other fluids. In 1879, Thomas A. Edison invented the electric light, causing fluid lamps to lose favor and creating a new field for lamp manufacturers. Companies like Tiffany and Handel became skillful at manufacturing electric lamps, and their decorators produced beautiful bases and shades.

References: James Edward Black (ed.), *Electric Lighting of the 20s-30s* (1988, 1993 value update), *Volume 2 with Price Guide* (1990, 1993 value update), L-W Book Sales; J. W. Courter, *Aladdin Collectors Manual & Price Guide #17*, published by author (3935 Kelley Rd., Kevil, KY 42053), 1997; —, *Aladdin, Electric Lamps,* published by author, 1989; —, *Aladdin, Electric Lamps, Price Guide #1,* published by author, 1989; —, *Aladdin, The Magic Name In Lamps, Revised Edition,* published by author, 1997; J. W. and Treva Courter, *Aladdin, Electric Lamps, Price Guide #3,* published by author, 1997; —, *Angle*

Lamps: Collectors Manual & Price Guide, published by author, 1992; —, *The Light That Never Fails,* published by author, 1996; Robert De Falco, Carole Goldman Hibel, John Hibel, *Handel Lamps,* H & D Press, Inc., 1986; Larry Freeman, *New Light On Old Lamps,* American Life Foundation, 1984; Arthur H. Hayward, *Colonial and Early American Lighting,* 3rd ed., Dover Publications, 1962; L-W Book Sales (ed.), *Quality Electric Lamps,* L-W Book Sales, 1997; Marjorie Hulsebus, *Miniature Victorian Lamps,* Schiffer Publishing, 1996; Edward and Sheila Malakoff, *Pairpoint Lamps,* Schiffer, 1990; Nadja Maril, *American Lighting,* Schiffer Publishing, 1995; Richard Miller and John Solverson, *Student Lamps of the Victorian Era*, Antique Publications, 1992, 1992-93 value guide; Bill and Linda Montgomery, *Animated Motion Lamps 1920s to Present*, L-W Book Sales, 1991; Denys Peter Myers, *Gaslighting in America*, Dover Publications, 1990; Leland and Crystal Payton, *Turned-On: Decorative Lamps of the Fifties,* Abbeville Press, 1989; Henry A. Pohs, *Miner's Flame Light Book*, Hiram Press, 1995; *Quality Electric Lamps*, L-W Book Sales, 1992; Jo Ann Thomas, *Early Twentieth Century Lighting Fixtures,* Collector Books, 1980; Catherine M. V. Thuro, *Oil Lamps*, Wallace-Homestead, 1976, 1992 value update; ——, *Oil Lamps II*, Collector Books, 1983, 1994 value update; Wolf Ueker, *Art Nouveau and Art Deco Lamps and Candlesticks,* Abbeville Press, 1987; Kenneth Wilson, *American Glass 1760-1930*, 2 vols., Hudson Hills Press and The Toledo Museum of Art, 1994.

Periodical: *Light Revival*, 35 West Elm Ave., Quincy, MA 02170.

Collectors' Clubs: Aladdin Knights of the Mystic Light, 3935 Kelley Rd., Kevil, KY 42053; Coleman Collector Network, 1822 E. Fernwood, Wichita, KS 67216; Historical Lighting Society of Canada, P.O. Box 561, Postal Station R, Toronto, Ontario M4G 4EI, Canada; Incandescent Lamp Collectors Assoc., Museum of Lighting, 717 Washington Place, Baltimore, MD 21201; Night Light, 38619 Wakefield Ct., Northville, MI 48167; Rushlight Club, Inc., Suite 196, 1657 The Fairway, Jenkintown, PA 19046.

Museums: Kerosene Lamp Museum, Winchester Center, CT; Pairpoint Lamp Museum, River Edge, NJ.

Reproduction Alert: The following is a partial list of reproduction kerosene lamps. Colors in italics indicate a period color:

   Button & Swirl, 8" high: *clear, cobalt blue,* ruby
   Coolidge Drake (a.k.a. Waterfall), 10" high: *clear, cobalt blue, milk glass,* ruby
   Lincoln Drape, short, 8-3/4" high: *amber, clear, green, and other colors*
   Lincoln Drape, tall, 9-3/4" high: *amber, clear, cobalt blue, moonstone, ruby*
   Shield & Star, 7" high: *clear,* cobalt blue
   Sweetheart (a.k.a. Beaded Heart), 10" h: *clear, milk glass, pink,* pink cased font with clear base

General clues that help identify a new lamp include parts that are glued together and hardware that is lacquered solid brass.

Astral

Astral

American, 19th C

23" h, acid etched shade, foliate standard ending in stepped marble base, electrified, minor imperfections 460.00

26-1/2" h, acid etched globe, gilt brass lotus font hung with prisms above overlay shaft cut ruby to clear, stepped marble base, electrified 865.00

Cornelius & Co., Philadelphia, 24" h, patent date April 18, 1845, marble base, later blue rimmed wheel cut and acid finish shade, electrified, gilt wear, minor base chips 635.00

Boudoir

Aladdin

14-1/2" h, 8" d, reverse painted bell shade, pine border, floral molded polychromed metal base.............225.00

G-16, Alacite..500.00

Cambridge, #3500/45, urn shape, gold dec...............330.00

Cut Glass, 9" h, mushroom shade, flared base, sunburst design..400.00

French, 11" d, 6" d, weighted brass base, crystal glass paneled insert, brass emb leaves and berries, rod curving upward holding night light, brass chains, and mounts, glass night light, holds candle 215.00

Handel, 14-1/2" h, 8" d ribbed glass domed shade with squared scalloped rim, obverse painted with snowy winter scene, pastel yellow orange sky, sgd "Handel 5637" on rim, raised on bronzed metal tree trunk base, threaded Handel label 3,335.00

Obverse Painted Scenic, 13-1/2" h, closed top mushroom-cap glass shade with textured surface mounted on gilt metal handled lamp base, weighted foot, handpainted silhouetted forested landscape scenes, rim mkd "Patented April 29th, 1913"...1,150.00

Pairpoint, 15" h, 9" d Stratford puffy shade, pansies, wild roses, and red roses, shade and base both sgd..............3,100.00

Phoenix, 14" h, 8" reverse painted shade, brilliant yellow and orange, green trees, blue and orange mountains, pr.... 850.00

Chandelier

Art Glass, 21" drop, 6-1/2" h shade, three scrolling gold metal light arms, flared and bulbed gold irid glass shades, green pulled feather dec.....................................1,150.00

Bradley & Hubbard, 25" d, hand beaten curled heavy brass frame, six caramel colored bent slag glass panels, 19" of heavy brass chain and mounting 980.00

Muller Fres, 23" d, 42" h, one center and three side bell-form shades of mottled orange, yellow, and blue, each marked "Muller Fres Luneville," black wrought iron ceiling mount with elaborate foliage dec framework, minor chip on side rims..1,500.00

Venetian Glass, 48" d, 58" h, threaded and blown cranberry glass shaft, clear glass scrolled rods suspend faceted swags, 14 scrolled candle arms with molded drip pans..825.00

Desk

Austrian, 17" h, closed top teardrop opal green irid shade with Loetz-type papillon surface and spiraled gold threading, single socket base with ribbed foliate cast motif, base mkd "Rose Bros. & Co., Lancaster, PA".........................1,500.00

Bradley & Hubbard, 13" h, 8-1/2" d adjustable tilt shade, narrow ribbed panels, reverse painted green, blue, and brown Arts and crafts border motif, single socket metal base..460.00

Emeralite, 17" h, adjustable roll etched glass shade, polychrome Arts and Crafts style border, silvered metal lamp base, conforming enameled curvilinear devices, orig "Emeralite" tag...920.00

Handel

14" h, 10" w, orig chipped ice dec opal shade, floral etched pattern, sgd "Handel, No. 6573" 1,300.00

15" h, 8" flared glass cylindrical shade, green textured surface cased to reflective opal white, mkd "Mosserine Handel 6010," adjustable bronzed metal weighted base, threaded Handel label on felt liner 1,380.00

Student

22" h, double, brass frame, electrified, cased green shades 605.00

23-1/2" h, brass frame and adjustable arm, white glass shade, early 20th C 260.00

Tiffany

13-1/2" h, 7" d swirl dec irid green ribbed dome Damascene shade cased to white, mkd "L.C.T" on rim, swivel-socket bronze harp frame, rubbed cushion platform, five ball feet, imp "Tiffany Studios New York 419"...........3,740.00

17-1/2" h, 7" d swirl dec irid green cased dome Damascene shade, mkd "L.C.T. Favrile," swivel-socket dark patina bronze harp frame with baluster shaft, ribbed cushion platform, five ball feet, imp "Tiffany Studios New York 7907" 4,025.00

18" h, 10-1/2" d gold irid Steuben bell shade, swivel socket dark etched bronze wide harp frame, adjustable shaft above leaf and petal base, imp "Tiffany Studios New York 569" 1,100.00

Early American

Banquet

20-1/2" h, blue cut to clear overlay punty font, matching standard, double stop marble base, collar missing, font has been drilled.....................................3,550.00

28-1/2" h, 10" d floral etched ruby ball shade, brass, sgd "The Rochester Company," electrified 500.00

28-3/4" h, 10" d reverse frosted gold dec ball shade sgd "Baccarat" on fitter, artist sgd "Beaucaire," brass font shell sgd "Miller," spelter stem and foot, electrified 700.00

Blown, colorless, 10" h, drop burners, pressed stepped base, chips on base, pr 385.00

Fluid

9" h, free blown teardrop font, heavy pressed octagonal sided base, small chips to base........................115.00

10" h, sapphire blue, eight paneled, floral engraved font, brass stem, marble font, twin-tube burner, one chip to panel, normal wear to marble base....................125.00

10-1/2" h, vertical rib and diamond point, flint, some roughness to foot edges....................................80.00

11" h, pressed four-printie block, cobalt blue pressed hexagonal base, twin-tube whale oil burners mounted on pewter collars, significant chipping and roughness on underside of one font, foot chip, pr 1,700.00

11-1/4" h, white cut to cranberry, brass stem, double step marble foot, normal wear to edges of marble base..500.00

12" h, Adams & Co., flower display under glass center, clear and frosted font, clear and stippled four column base, orig label...950.00

12-3/8" h, white cut to cranberry with gold trim, font mounted on brass stem, double step marble foot............ 1,200.00

13" h, pink cut to white cut to clear font, large white clam-broth base, 3 discolored bubble bursts 900.00

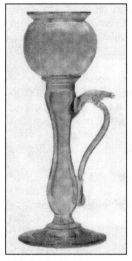

Lace Maker's, 10-1/4" h, free blown, globular font, hollow stem, applied circular foot, applied handle with thumb rest, colorless, tooled rim, smooth base, America, 1800-1830, $250. Photo courtesy of Norman C. Heckler and Co.

Hand, 2-7/8" h, Hobbs Glass Co., Snowflake pattern, cranberry ground, white opalescent pattern, applied clear handle...550.00

Hour Glass, 7" h, clear blown glass, pine and oak frame, whittled baluster posts, old brown finish, glued break in bottom plate 275.00

Lace Maker's
10" h, free blown, clear, cut circles ring font..........325.00
17-1/2" h, cranberry thumbprint shade, electrified brass base, multiple small dents on base...................170.00

Oil (kerosene)
Acanthus Leaf, 12" h, jade green font, double stepped clambroth colored semi-opaque base, minor roughness, several small base chips 1,900.00

Acorn and Drapery, 9-1/2" h, cut and frosted free blown font, three ring knob, pewter collar, stepped pressed base, New England Glass Works....................................250.00

Blackberry, 8" h, Boston and Sandwich......................225.00

Chapman, 8-1/4" h, clear, Atterbury & Co....................75.00

Columbian Coin, 9-1/4" h, milk glass, Central Glass Co. 125.00

Duncan Ribbed Band, 2 handles..................................90.00

Gem, 7-1/2" h, clear font, amber pressed textured match striker panels on stem, Atterbury & Co. 150.00

Hobb's Optic, flat, finger......................................575.00

King Melon Optic Dot, opal white, finger grip handle, Crimp & Galfurid chimney...155.00

Little Beauty, orig label...60.00

Loop, 9-1/4" h, flint, clear, slight roughness to base.....85.00

Optic, 8-7/8" h, silver stained band, frosted leaves and flowers, Beaumont Glass Works, Bellaire, OH.............285.00

Queen of Hearts, 8" h, clear font, medium green base, Dalzell, Gilmore & Leighton, Findlay, OH, ...275.00

Ripley, two handles..70.00

Shieldon Swirl, 8-3/4" h, blue opalescent font, clear base, two small chips and roughness under base, $350. Photo courtesy of Green Valley Auctions, Inc.

Snowflake, cranberry opalescent, large 745.00

Waffle and Thumbprint, 10-5/8" h, flint, clear, several small nicks 100.00

Wave, 9-1/4" h, clear, panel base, mkd "October 7, 1873," Atterbury & Co. 75.00

Floor

Bradley and Hubbard, 56" h, 7" d, small domed leaded glass shade, green slag glass, gold key border, open framework adjustable standard, domed circular foot 400.00

Handel, harp base, bronze finish, 2 parrots on yellow ground shade, sgd "Handel #7073 G A" 8,000.00

Tiffany, 55" h, 9-1/2" d linenfold shade, twelve-sided etched bronze shade #1936 with panels of gold-amber favrile fabrique glass, swing socket harp base, tripod legs, spade feet, shade and base imp "Tiffany Studios New York," bronze base hammered "423".................1,380.00

Tiffany/Aladdin, 50" h, 10" d spun bronze shade, reflective white int., mkd "Tiffany Studios New York," adjustable bridge lamp base with Arabian Nights motif, orig dark bronze patina, elaborate platform base, stamped "Tiffany Studios New York 576" 2,990.00

Wilkinson, 64" h, 24" d leaded domed shade, opal white segments banded by wide border of multicolored and shaded blossoms with buds rising through brickwork and around top rim, elaborate five-socket ribbed floor base with medial leaves, stepped lappet bordered platform...........7,200.00

Hanging

American, 19th C
18" h, patinated metal and cut glass, hall type, candle socket, Gothic arches, diamonds and flowerheads dec..1,380.00
23" h, clear blown glass, hall type, elaborate wheel cut dec of birds and deer in landscape, foliate devices, pressed brass mounts....................................2,415.00

Arts and Crafts, brass washed metal, 4 lanterns, hammered amber glass...1,000.00

Candle, 12" w, 6-1/2" h heavy blue opaline shade, fancy gold trim, pearl like jewel highlights, fancy stamped brass chains and canopy, outside of body satinized, glossy bottom protruding disk, some wear to gold trim 400.00

Cranberry, glossy cranberry shade, white enameled Arabesque dec, mounted in yellow brass frame with satinized vertically ribbed cranberry and white spatter font shell and drop in font, white milk glass smoke bell with cranberry edge...2,250.00

Handel, 10" d, hall type, spherical form, acid cut, translucent white, brown, vase and foliate dec, ornate orig hardware 4,200.00

Satin Glass, blue Diamond Quilted mother of pearl shade mounted in jeweled brass frame, cobalt blue edged white milk glass smoke bell 3,500.00

Steuben, 13" w, 6-1/2" d, gold calcite dome, large star cut center, orig rim and chains, unsgd 1,100.00

Tiffany, 18" l, 15" d, attributed to Tiffany Glass and Decorating Co., late 19th C, square green and opalescent diamond-shaped glass jewels arranged as central pendant chandelier drop, twisted wire frame....................2,990.00

Piano

Handel, 9" h, 22" l, 7" d conical leaded glass shade with straight apron of green slag and granite glass segments arranged in geometric design, mounted to adjustable socket, curved "dog's leg" shaft above weighed lappet dec base imp "Handel" 1,265.00

Tiffany, 6-3/4" h, 19" l tripartite gold amber glass turtleback shade, framed in bronze, three center gold irid turtleback tiles, single-socket swiveling "dog leg" shaft, shade and weighted base imp "Tiffany Studios New York"......4,025.00

Table

Bigelow Kennard, Boston

19" h, 13-1/4" d domed leaded shade, fiery opal white brickwork above amber, slate blue, and white lappet border motif, converted fluid lamp font with three-arm spider inserted within Japonesque art pottery base with shaded pink, blue, green glaze, imp "600"......1,840.00

22" h, 18" d domed leaded shade, red cluster gladiola blossoms, green leaf stalks, opal white glass segments, blue and mottled segments, rim tagged "Bigelow Studios Boston," and "Bigelow Kennard," three-socket stem shaft above ftd bronze platform base 3,740.00

26" h, 18" d domed leaded shade, opalescent white segments in geometric progression border, brilliant green leaf forms repeating motif, edge imp "Bigelow Kennard Boston/Bigelow Studios," three socket over Oriental-style bronze base cast with foo dog handles, Japonesque devices 2,875.00

Bradley & Hubbard

12" h, six sided bent panel slag glass shade, brickwork frame, metal base with three owl shaft, "B & H" imp on base, shade labeled, damage to some panels and glass eyes...690.00

21-1/2" h, 15" sq octagon shade, Prairie School, shade with geometric overlay on green and white slag glass panels with red squares, sgd on base and shade 1,150.00

22" h, 20" d dome shaped leaded shade, caramel colored pieces in honeycomb pattern, rimmed at base, border of pink and ivory panels, framed with continuous double narrow green strip, base sgd "Bradley & Hubbard Mft. Co. Patent Applied For," brass finished pedestal with design of draped swags and medallions above raised leaves, wide paneled foot, raised rim, two or three panels with cracks................................1,600.00

23-1/2" h, 18" d bent glass shade, eight emerald green slag panels, octagonal flame motif in green-black metal frame, two-socket black painted metal base with "B&H" triangular patent mark 575.00

Classique, 22-1/2" h, 18" d, brilliantly colored sunset scene with trees, bell shaped shade, bronze six-sided base ... 1,350.00

Duffner and Kimberly, New York

21-1/2" h, 16-1/2" d leaded mosaic Colonial No. 501 shade, pink, lavender, amber, yellow, and green glass segments arranged in four repeating arches centering candleform element, three-socket Duffner bronze base with ribbed shat, crossed ribbon platform, c1906 .... 4,025.00

23" h, 17-1/2" d leaded glass conical shade, sixteen amber caramel slag panels, Prairie school-type ground sq belt border, three-socket gilt bronze ribbed shaft, weighted platform base...................................2,530.00

24" h, 21" d conical leaded glass shade, amber slag background panels, three repeating intricate heraldic elements of lavender-amethyst glass superimposed on crimson red medial band, lower border glass in chevron motif, amber granite and mauve ripple accent colors, three-socket bronzed shaft with cast foliate devices 4,600.00

26" h, 24-1/2" d dome leaded glass shade with tuck-under irregular rim, multicolored blossoms with yellow centers, green leaves, long stemmed flowers extending to top on segmented white background, three socket bronze lobed shaft with quatraform shaped base 7,435.00

28" h, 21-1/2" d shaped domical leaded glass shade, repeating sections of stylized floral motif separated by raised curved panels, green, amber, glass, and elaborate dore overlay, imp tag "The Duffner & Kimberly Co. New York," matching four-socket gilt bronze base with swirling scrolls and shell-form devices...........26,450.00

Durand, 29-1/2" h, brass, blue glass standard, opaque white and clear feather pattern.......................................300.00

Handel

15" h, 10" l, 5-1/2" d elongated oval glass shade, glossy irid int., ext. handpainted with colorful woodland scene with center bird in flight on front and back, sgd on rim "Handel 6427," mounted on integrated oval base with "Handel" threaded label 5,462.00

20" h, 12" d brilliant yellow shade with sunrise, green trees, reddish-orange accents, sgd "Handel, #4216," chip out of shade rim 1,350.00

21" h, 16" d framed bent panel shade, six curved amber slag glass panels overlaid with oak leaf metal framework, conforming applied color, two socket baluster base, orig bronzed finish, work, finial missing, rim repair...... 920.00

22" h, 16" d domed shade, shaded green and amber int., obverse painted riverside landscape, muted naturalistic earthen tones, metal rim stamped "Handel," two socket bronzed ribbed base 4,140.00

22" h, 17" d nine-sided leaded shade, caramel and white panels, green border, heavy brass overlay, six-sided brass column base, raised edge design, minor separation on shade...1,800.00

23" h, 17-7/8" d reverse painted dome shade, brilliant blue and red parrots among trees and wisteria blossoms, base cast with blossoming prunus branches, brown patina, shade painted "Handel 6874R" 22,000.00

23" h, 18" d reverse painted shade, chipped ice finish, orange-yellow ground, panels of red, blue, and green foliate dec and leaves, 1" rim orange and red band, textured bronze finish base, shade sgd "Handel #7918" 2,000.00

23" h, 18" d textured glass dome shade, reverse painted garden bouquet of wild rose blossoms, Schribner pink, red, and yellow, three crystal yellow butterflies in flight, rim sgd "Handel 6688" and by artist, mounted on orig finish bronze metal simulated tree trunk base, threaded Handel label on front liner.............14,950.00

23-1/2" h, 18" d domed glass shade with eight subtle ribs, reverse painted scene of beach front trees and leafy colorful bushes, sailboats and see gulls on blue background ocean, sgd on rim "Handel 6749," mounted on bronzed base with four handles, four splayed feet, mkd "Handel," some metal surface corrosion..........5,750.00

Jefferson

22" h, 16" d shade, landscape of trees, houses, and water, earth tone of yellow, brown, and green, orig copper-colored base 1,100.00

22" h, 16" d reverse painted domical shade, painted border of violet and pink butterflies in green ferns, orange brown ground, molded bronze metal vasiform base, stepped round foot 1,750.00

23-1/2" h, 17-3/4" d reverse painted domical shade, brown and russet palm trees, orange and yellow sky and beach scene, mountains in background, brass finish urn shaped base with molded handles, round circular base...1,500.00

Leaded, 21" h, 18 d shade, hydrangea flowers, orig finish on metal base...3,000.00

Moe Bridges, 23" h, 18" d shaped domed reverse painted shade, expansive riverside landscape, sgd on lower rim "Moe Bridges Co. 186," orig gilt metal base, replaced sockets, worn finish 1,650.00

Pairpoint

12" h, puffy shade, red and orange poppies, variegated green ground, orig base, some restoration to shade..4,250.00

19" h, 14" d conical textured reverse painted shade, orange and fuchsia inside, green and black Arts and Crafts geometric motif on ext., married two-socket thistle patterned cast metal base.............................865.00

20-1/2" h, 11-1/2" d domed closed top mushroom-cap glass shade, Vienna, coralene yellow int., painted stylized olive green leaves and red berries, gold outline on ext., ball-decorated ring supported by four arms, quatraform base molded with foliate devices, imp "Pairpoint Mfg Co., 3052".......................................2,070.00

21" h, 12" d puffy rose bouquet shade, pink and white roses, yellow accents, green leaves, unsgd shade, base sgd "Pairpoint Mfg Co. 3054"................2,300.00

21" h, 16" d Berkley reverse painted flared shade, broad moonlit scene of man in rowboat approaching buildings, leafy summer trees, artist sgd "C. Durand," dark gold three-dolphin base, imp "Pairpoint D3076" 4,025.00

22" h, 16" d Berkley reverse painted shade, Hawaiian seascape, birds and distant ships, tropical foliage, artist sgd "H. Fisher," stamped "The Pairpoint Corp'n," bronzed metal two socket base with bulbed paneled shaft, imp trademark and "Pairpoint"...................................4,600.00

23" h, 16" d mold-blown reverse painted shade, fruiting orange branches among green leaves, white blossom, and butterflies, base cast as tree trunk, brown-green patina, shade stamped "The Pairpoint Corp" 32,000.00

24" h, 20" d Copley design flared shade reverse painted with two ships and six sea gulls, swirling ocean waves, artist sgd "H. Fisher" on rim, raised matching glass lighted lamp base, stamped "Pairpoint D3000," rewired, new sockets 8,625.00

Pittsburgh

18" h, 14" d labeled conical reverse painted shade, orange, amber, and pink int., black Arts and Crafts geometric motif painted on textured ext. surface, two-socket base with matching motif, base paint worn..................1,265.00

18" h, 14" d reverse painted shade, pale yellow, green, brown, and white landscape, orig metal base, mkd "41384"..925.00

19" h, 16" d reverse dec shade, Lakes of Killarny, purple mountains, green, and brown landscape, slight roughness to top rim..850.00

22" h, 14" d textured glue-fired domed reverse painted shade, water wheel mill scene on int., obverse painted in leafy trees with dark coloration, mounted on orig two-socket metal base, floral medial hand.....2,100.00

26" h, 18" d textured and glue-fired glass dome shade, front and back scenes of Taj Mahal, mounted on bulbous three-socket Arts and Crafts bronzed metal telescoping metal base, new sockets, mismatched finial 2,415.00

Steuben, Carder, 23" h, 11" h moss agate angular shouldered oval glass shaft, purple and lavender with mica flecks, green aventurine, amber, red, and blue swirls, gilt metal two socket lamp fittings, catalog #8026....1,610.00

Tiffany

22" h, 16" d dome leaded shade, Bellflower, favrile glass segments leaded as clusters of vivid red and red-orange bellflowers, yellow and fiery-amber scrolling foliate devices against green shaded background, stamped "Tiffany Studios New York" on rim, dark bronze urn-form lamp base set into three-arm shaft above sq platform, early TS circular imp mark 12,075.00

22-1/2" h, 12" d dome shade, irid swirl dec green Damascene shade cased to reflective white and amber, dark bronze three-arm spider and fluid unit, four-legged base, imp "S1089" on frame and font, also stamped "Tiffany Studios New York" with TG&D Co. logo...5,175.00

Wilkinson Co.

24-/12" h, 18" d leaded dome, pink and white waterlily blossoms interspersed with green and red ripple glass leaves and buds, amber granite glass ground, three-socket cast bronze base with beaded lappet motif................3,450.00

27-1/2" h, 20" d scalloped conical leaded glass shade, yellow centered pink and peach colored blossoms, green leaves bordering amber and green slag glass segments arranged in ladderwork progression, locking mechanism with three baluster shaft, bulbed turnings, stepped platform base, imp "Wilkinson Co/Brooklyn, NY" 3,220.00

30" h, 22" d mosaic conical shade, multicolored glass segments arranged as blossoming red, orange, and yellow hollyhock spikes, white ground, curved drop apron of lavender and granite textured golden amber border glass, three-socket cast foliage dec base with locking mechanism...6,325.00

30" h, 23" d broad tucked under domed mosaic shade, pink and white pond lilies, rippled dark amber cat-o-nine tails, background water shaded with blue, lavender, and green, three-socket simulated tree trunk base with Wilkinson locking mechanism 7,475.00

Williamson, Richard, & Co., Chicago, 25" h, 20" d peaked leaded glass dome, amber slag bordered by red tulips, pink and lavender-blue spring blossoms, green leaf stems, carved glass, mounted on four-socket integrated shaft with stylized tulip blossoms above leafy platform, imp "R. Williamson & Co./Washington & Jefferson Sts./Chicago, Ill," restored cap at top rim 3,220.00

Wall, Bradley and Hubbard, wall mount bracket, sapphire blue expanded bull's eye shade 400.00

LIBBEY GLASS

History: Edward Libbey established the Libbey Glass Company in Toledo, Ohio, in 1888 after the New England Glass Works of W. L. Libbey and Son closed in East Cambridge, Massachusetts. The new Libbey company produced quality cut glass which today is considered to belong to the brilliant period.

1896–1906

In 1930, Libbey's interest in art-glass production was renewed, and A. Douglas Nash was employed as a designer in 1931.

The factory continues production today as Libbey Glass Co.

References: Carl U. Fauster, *Libbey Glass Since 1818-Pictorial History & Collector's Guide,* Len Beach Press, 1979; Bob Page and Dale Frederickson, *Collection of American Crystal*, Page-Frederickson Publishing, 1995; Kenneth Wilson, *American Glass 1760-1930*, 2 vols., Hudson Hills Press and The Toledo Museum of Art, 1994.

Manufacturer: Libbey Glass, One Sea Gate, Toledo, OH 43666.

Additional Listings: Amberina Glass; Cut Glass.

Art glass

Bell, 5-3/4" h, colorless, acid etched dec "1893 World's Fair," circular logo surrounded by acid-etched florals and banners, shoulder int. molded "1893 World's Columbian Xposition" (sic), twisted frosted handle with star at top, metal clapper 285.00

Bon Bon, 7" d, 1-1/2" h, amberina, shape #3029, six pointed 1-1/2" w fuchsia rim, shallow pale amber bowl, sgd .. 600.00

Bowl
   7" d, amberina, ruffled, flared rim, sgd...................350.00
   8-1/4" d, Wave pattern, scalloped rim, turned over ruby border, amberina body, three applied amber feet, acid stamped "Libbey" in circle, c1900 ....450.00
   10" d, 4" h, amberina, fold down rim, sgd 850.00
   12-1/2" d, black cut to colorless, sgd..................1,250.00

Bud Vase, 9" h, elongated, ribbed, colorless..............615.00

Cologne Bottle, 8-1/2" h, honey amber on nine optic panels, deep fuchsia neck, quatraform opening, color blushed on orig stopper, Libbey, #3041 ....1,750.00

Compote, 10-1/2" w, 4" h, colorless, pink Nailsea-type loops, flaring top, sgd "Libbey" 595.00

Console Set, green and white pulled feather, sgd......825.00

Hair Receiver, cov, 4-1/2" w, 2" h, two pc, amberina, deep fuchsia shading to amber, partial label..............1,750.00

Pickle Castor, amberina, Swirled Rib pattern, ftd Meriden frame 475.00

Pitcher, 5-1/2" h, ribbed opal body, combed peppermint pink striping, applied cased glass handle, colorless foot stamped "Libbey" in circular mark.........................350.00

Rose Bowl, 3-1/2" w, 2-1/2" h, melon ribbed bowl, beige ground, two pansies and leaves, white beads, sgd "Libbey Cut Glass" 550.00

Tazza, 7" d, 5-3/4" h, colorless, opalescent feet, white and pink pulled feather bowl, pr.....................................300.00

Vase
   8" h, oviform, ribbed, wasted neck, wafer and ball stem 720.00
   8-1/4" h, tapered optic fern and pink threaded design, colorless foot, sgd 325.00
   9" h, cylindrical, slightly flaring, light vertical ribbing, blue threaded dec, opal ground, c1933 ....275.00
   10" h, turquoise zipper pattern, colorless ground, sgd..425.00
   11-1/4" h, 4" d, deep red ball shaped bowl, 7-1/2" l hollow amber stem, 4" d circular base, sgd 1,000.00
   11-1/2" h, 2-1/2" w, amberina, deep fuchsia shading to amber, slight ribbing, flaring edge, orig label 850.00
   15" h, floriform, amberina, c1917 ....990.00

Cut glass

Banana Boat, American Brilliant Period
   12-1/2" l, 6-3/4" w, 6-3/4" h, hobstars, cane, and trellis cutting, double sabre signature, flake and chip out of edge 900.00
   13" x 7" x 7", scalloped pedestal base, 24 point hobstar, hobstar, cane, vesica, and fan motifs, sgd 1,500.00

Basket, American Brilliant Period
   14-1/2" h, 9-3/4" w, cut carnation, graphic style cutting, unusual cut handle, sgd 275.00
   18-1/2" h, 9" w, pedestal base, berry and leaf design, notched edge, fancy cut handle, sgd 1,000.00

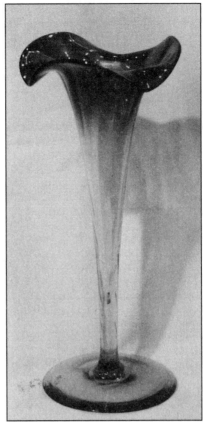

Vase, amberina, lily shape, tricorn, $390.

   19-1/2" h, 8-3/4" w, pedestal base, floral pattern of roses, band of diamond point and leaves, double notched handle, sgd...800.00

Bowl
   8" d, hobstar, bands of strawberry diamond and fans, sgd...110.00
   9" d, Somerset pattern, sgd...................................150.00

Candy Dish, cov, 7", divided, clover shape, hobstar and prism, sgd 90.00

Champagne, Rock Sharpe, #1014, Frontenac Cut.......35.00

Charger, 14" d, hobstar, cane, and wreath motifs, sgd ... 300.00

Cocktail
   Rock Sharpe, #1014, Frontenac Cut 28.00
   Vanity Cut, #300, 4-5/8" h, 4 oz, crystal...................25.00

Cordial
   American Prestige pattern, c1930...........................50.00
   Cut glass, 2" h, American brilliant period, mkd "Libbey," pr..90.00
   Rock Sharpe, #1013 variant 25.00

Cordial Set, 11-1/4" h decanter, six 3-1/2" h goblets, Knickerbocker pattern, Walter Dorwin Teague/Edwin W. Fuerst manner, each stamped "Libbey," c1939 ....400.00

Goblet, Rock Sharpe, #1014, Frontenac Cut 42.00

Ice Cream Tray, 10 x 14", Gloria pattern.....................275.00

Nut Cup, 1-1/2" h,, faceted pedestal, sgd, six pc set..... 220.00

Pitcher, 10" h, copper wheel cut leaves and butterfly dec, sgd 195.00

Plate
   Gloria pattern, 7" d 165.00
   Strawberry diamond and fans border, sunburst center, sgd..75.00
   Tumble-Up, star burst, hobstar, fern, and fan motifs, minor handle check...725.00

Vase
   8-3/4" h, eight faceted panels, deeply cut iris, frosted foliate motif, stamped "Libbey" in circle 635.00

12" h, floral pattern, flutes and horizontal ladder, precise cutting, colorless blank, 1906-19 trademark 450.00

13-1/2" h, baluster, emerald green cut flower panels, ftd, sgd base...............700.00

Wine, Harvard pattern, faceted cut knob stems, sgd, 12 pc set...............350.00

Pressed Patterns

Butter Dish, cov, 7-1/4" d, 6" h, Maize, pale green kernels, gold trimmed husks...............500.00

Candlesticks, pr, Silhouette pattern, colorless candle cup, opalescent figure of camel in stem 385.00

Celery Vase, 6-1/2" h, 5" w, Maize, Pomona dec, amber kernels, blue leaves...............395.00

Champagne, Silhouette pattern, colorless bowl, figural squirrel stem...............200.00

Cocktail, Silhouette pattern, colorless bowl, black figure of kangaroo in stem...............300.00

Goblet

Liberty Bell pattern, 12 oz, 7" h, crystal...............25.00

Silhouette pattern, colorless bowl, black figure of cat in stem, sgd...............300.00

Pitcher, 8-3/4" h, 5-12" d, Maize, barrel shaped, creamy opaque kernels, green husks, applied strap handle...............575.00

Plate, Optic Swirl pattern, green 45.00

Salt and Pepper Shakers, pr, Maize 75.00

Sherbet

#3006-2, 5-1/2" h, 6 oz, crystal...............20.00

Silhouette pattern, black rabbit, sgd...............145.00

Sherry, 5" h, Silhouette pattern, colorless bowl, black monkey silhouette in stem...............125.00

Spooner, Maize, creamy opaque kernels of corn, blue husks, gold trim...............190.00

Sugar Bowl, cov, 2-3/4" h, Optic Rib pattern, pale blue opalescent, satin finish, gold enameled "World's Fair 1893"...............175.00

Sugar Shaker, Maize, creamy opaque kernels of corn, yellow husks, gold trim, orig top...............245.00

Toothpick Holder, Maize, creamy opaque kernels of corn, blue husks, gold trim...............300.00

Tumbler, Maize, creamy opaque kernels of corn, yellow husks 125.00

Water Carafe, Maize, creamy opaque kernels of corn, yellow husks, gold trim...............325.00

Wine, 7" h, Silhouette pattern, colorless bowl, black cat silhouette in stem, sgd...............200.00

LOETZ

History: Loetz is a type of iridescent art glass that was made in Austria by J. Loetz Witwe in the late 1890s. Loetz was a contemporary of L. C. Tiffany's, and he had worked in the Tiffany factory before establishing his own operation; therefore, much of the wares are similar in appearance to Tiffany products. The Loetz factory also produced items with fine cameos on cased glass. Some pieces are signed "Loetz," "Loetz, Austria," or "Austria."

Reference: Robert and Deborah Truitt, *Collectible Bohemian Glass: 1880-1940*, R & D Glass, 1995.

Basket

6-1/2" h, 5" w, brilliant green mottled on clear ground, highly irid blue and purple finish...............100.00

10-1/2" h overall, 4-1/2" h x 7" w glass, oyster white glass,

mottled medium yellow raindrop patter, four bands of pulled deep ruby brown horizontal stripes, pinched and dimpled, four pulled down edges, fancy ormolu and silver bronzed Art Nouveau holder with Japanese chrysanthemum dec 600.00

16" h, 10" w, mottled oyster white int., deep gold mottled ground, applied tall crystal loop handle with floral prunts 250.00

17-1/2" h, 10" w, deep red to clear, green hooked and pulled design, highly irid surface, applied crystal handle....250.00

18-1/4" h, 11-1/2" w, medium green, purple and blue irid...............200.00

Bottle, 11-3/4" h, bulbous, extended neck, everted rim, four up-turned handles, rose gold irid ground, rainbow irid oil spot dec 19,800.00

Bowl

5" d, 3" h, white, applied punties and rim...............130.00

5-3/4" d, cylindrical, ruffled rim, orange int., green shading to silver ext...............600.00

7" d, 4" h, rolled rim, applied green tadpoles, highly irid, white ground...............110.00

9" d, 6" h, irid gold, textured crackle finish, polished pontil...............250.00

10" d, Onyx, dec...............395.00

10" d, 3" h, oyster white ground, diamond quilted design, applied deep black-green edge, highly irid surface 120.00

13" l, 7-1/2" h, large shell form, resting on seaweed base, green ground, blue irid...............1,700.00

Bride's Bowl, 12" h, 9-1/2" d glass basket, clear to green glass, mottled with deep purple spatter, brilliant green and purple irid finish, silver plated Victorian holder 300.00

Candlesticks, pr

9-1/2" h, slender baluster form, raised circular foot, gold irid...............300.00

15-3/8" h, cobalt blue ground, annulated round tapering stem, stepped cushion foot, bell form nozzle, conical drip pan, rainbow irid oil spot dec...............2,400.00

Centerpiece Bowl

10" h, 15" l, deep gold bronze with deep purple dec glass bowl, highly irid surface, fancy bronze Art Nouveau holder with pine cone and leaf dec...............1,500.00

13" d, speckled green irid finish, blown-out scrolls, ormolu ftd frame mkd "L. Henry," bowl unmarked...............550.00

Chalice, 5-1/2" h, blue-green irid round, tear drop motif, engraved "Loetz, Austria," c1900...............2,550.00

Chandelier, five hanging irid shades with purple and blue highlights, Art Nouveau-style fixture...............3,500.00

Compote

10" d, 9-1/2" h, brilliant irid green, diamond quilted raised pattern, highly irid surface, fancy Art Nouveau reticulated floral design metal holder...............300.00

10-5/8" d, 5-1/4" h, bright orange int., deep black ext., white flaring circular rim, 3 ball feet, c1920...............310.00

Dish, 8-1/2" d, 2-3/4" h, three applied pulled out handles, brilliant gold base, outstanding color, sgd in pontil with monogram "M" and "L"...............200.00

Garniture Set, blood red, multicolored variegated oil-spot motif, matched pr of sq 9-3/4" h vases in metal frames, rect matching 4-1/2" h x 9" l x 4" d planter in ornate brass mounted frame, emb pond lily dec...............1,950.00

Inkwell

3-1/4" h, 4" w, highly textured and irid surface, four blown-out corners, deep cobalt blue glass, brass fittings......300.00

3-1/2" h, amethyst, sq, irid, web design, bronze mouth...125.00

Jack in the Pulpit Vase

10" h, Persian flask shape, dimpled bulbous body, spotted irid papillon surface dec, polished pontil...............635.00

11-1/2" h, gold irid flower and stem, applied raised large leaf on dome foot, blue irid...............1,300.00

14" h, silver blue gold irid surface, floriform blossom, green body, knotty tree bark texture, polished pontil.......425.00

Lamp Shade
  3-3/4" h, 3-3/4" d, mottled yellow shaded to blue sphere, layered in brick red, etched as leafy branches with berry clusters, sgd "Richard" at side...............................230.00
  5" h, 2-1/4" fitter, deep butterscotch bronze, band of deep blue irid gold spots, slight roughness on fitter rim 300.00

Lamp
  7-1/4" h shade, 29" drop, 21" wingspan, ceiling, bronze figural full bodied flying bat suspended from bronze chains and ceiling mount, Loetz art glass teardrop form shade with irid red over gold spotted and threaded dec..............5,750.00
  19-1/2" h, 9-1/2" d, table, globular shade, bulbous base, all over irid oil-spot motif, orig brass oil fittings........3,000.00

Pitcher, 8-5/8" h, pinched bulbous body, purple and green irid, applied handle, gilt metal mount with cast foliate motif...650.00

Rose Bowl, 6-1/2" d, ruffled purple irid raindrop dec 265.00

Salt, 2-3/4" d, 1" h, irid blue ground, blue and gold oil-spot motif..600.00

Sweetmeat Jar, cov, 5" h, irid silver spider web dec, green ground, sgd..450.00

Town Pump and Trough, 10" h, 9" w, all over random threading, slight irid colors, applied base with pale pink-peach open flower, green leaves 400.00

Urn, 9-1/4" h, ovoid, irid, blue oil-spot motif, inscribed "Loetz, Austria" 1,600.00

Vase
  4" h, 3" w, deep green, blue irid, raised pattern..........150.00
  4" h, 4" w, pale irid green, gold scale-like dec............300.00
  4-1/4" h, 4" w, pinched form, irid blue/gold 300.00
  4-1/2" h, lozenge form, deep blue irid ground, silver irid lines and spots, engraved "Loetz Austria" 4,800.00
  4-1/2" h, 4" w, transparent pink, irid surface with blue and gold highlights, ground pontil 450.00
  5" h, bulbous, green irid body, pinched shoulder, ruffled rim, silver Art Nouveau floral overlay.........................1,600.00
  5" h, colorless oval, tricorn ruffled rim and dimpled sides, overall small gold circles and large red roundels, polished pontil, attributed to Koloman Moser for Loetz..............1,725.00
  5" h, ftd urn form, chartreuse body, blue oil-spot motif...900.00
  5" h, 3-1/4" w, four pinched-in sides, pale gold ground, blue wave design, irid surface 550.00
  5" h, 6" d, raised bowl form, lemon yellow, irid int., horizontal lustered striping, amber pulled vertical fingers, dark aubergine-purple foot and border, silver irid accents, inscribed "Loetz Austria" on polished pontil..........7,200.00
  5" h, 10-1/2" w, pillow shape, short squatty form, brilliant red, multicolored irid, oval base continues to rect top, six crimps on rim...225.00
  5-3/4" h, bulbous irid green body, pulled, dripping dec around rim, engraved "Loetz Austria" 1,600.00
  5-3/4" h, flared cylinder, everted rim, cobalt blue ground, silver-blue oil-spot motif, three molded glass butterflies 700.00
  6" h, chalice form, chartreuse bowl, blue oil-spot motif ..900.00
  6" h, 5" w, irid gold, deep blue and gold highlights, large bronze Raindrop spots, dimpled body, large ground pontil ..750.00
  6" h, 9" w, ftd nautilus shell, frosted oyster clear color, pink base, irid finish in verde de soiree style.................400.00
  6-1/2" h, ruffled trefoil rim, ambergris body, symmetrical dec with three gold and silvery irid pulled feathers, base inscribed "Loetz Austria"...865.00
  6-1/2" h, tadpole neck, white irid ground, green rig-aree..200.00
  6-1/2" h, 4-1/2" d, cameo, deep amethyst over frosted white ground, four Art Deco style roses, numerous round circles..1,000.00

Vase, purple irid, 7-5/8" h, unmarked, $175.

6-1/2" h, 7" d, pale green vaseline ground, all over white swirl pattern, aventurine flecks, highly irid surface, pinched-in shape, attributed to Loetz 100.00

7" h, Federzeichnung, oval body, opal mother of pearl, internal octopus motif, brown-gold surface, some wear to gold 1,380.00

7" h, irid blue body, silver plated holder 330.00

7" h, melon shape, Carneol 295.00

7" h, textured body, three pinch bottom, ground pontil, unmarked 275.00

7" h, 4-1/2" w, bulbous, three applied loop handles, silver overlay on handles and 2" top band, irid body 975.00

7" h, 7" w, blue green irid, all over spider web dec, orig Art Nouveau pewter metal frame 250.00

7-1/4" h, pinched bulbous body, flared bifurcated green rim, low relief dec, blue wavy string-like dec 800.00

7-1/2" h, enameled Marmorierte Agate, quatraform rim, striated amber-red-gray stone body cased to pink int., white enamel dec on upper body, polished pontil 300.00

7-1/2" h, ftd cylindrical form, everted rim, cobalt blue, blue oil-spot motif, three applied molded glass butterflies...1,000.00

7-1/2" h, pinched baluster, three applied handles, irid body with striated pattern in low relief, burgundy and gold speckles 400.00

7-1/2" h, 4-1/2" w, ovoid, purple and brown irid ground, large blue and purple pulled raindrops......................1,150.00

7-3/4" h, 3" d, ruffled rim, light green irid ground, deep orange oil-spot motif, irid emerald green, cobalt blue, and blue aurene elongated ovals..............................1,350.00

8" h, tapered rect, violet swirls, bronze mount on rim cast as bats with wings spread 3,200.00

8-1/4" h, flared form, inverted rim, teal green shading to burgundy base, cased, irid 2,000.00

8-1/2" h, irid green, pimpled texture, polished pontil, mkd "Loetz Austria" 450.00

8-3/4" h, Marmorierte, oval body, marbleized green, aubergine, and turquoise blue striations, cased to opal, lined in blue, dec with gilt enamel sunbursts, red glass "jewel" centers..460.00

9-1/2" h, floriform, flattened circular base, slender stem supporting conical bowl, amber ground, silver oil-spot motif..800.00

9-1/2" h, floriform, flattened circular base, slender stem supporting conical bowl, green ground, irid oil-spot motif..... 800.00

9-3/4" h, pinched cylindrical form, triangular rim, gold irid ground, orange spots...700.00

10" h, flattened gold foot rising to flared double gourd blue irid body, applied spiraling gold irid snake around standard 1,500.00

10" h, pinched conical body, flared triangular rim, deep cobalt blue, silver striated dec 650.00

10-1/4" h, flared, applied green dec around base with blue oil-spot motif, engraved "Loetz Austria"................900.00

10-1/4" h, oviform, twisted peaked rim, cobalt blue ground, silver-blue oil-spot motif 1,500.00

10-1/4" h, slender oviform, cracked green dec shading to burgundy at top, cased, irid............................1,400.00

10-1/4" h, 5" w, irid dimpled and swirled, bright red ground, irid finish with streaks of pink, purple, green, and blue...400.00

10-1/2" h, flared oval, irid ambergris int., pulled rose-red ribbon ext., gold irid spots, polished pontil.............5,175.00

10-1/2" h, 6" w, bulbous swirl, applied shell handles, Rainbow, white lining, gold trim, cased in crystal, pink, yellow, and blue irid surface, pr 675.00

11" h, pinched ewer form, irid, blue oil-spot motif, mounted in Art Nouveau gilt metal stand 1,500.00

11" h, trumpet form, applied ribbed crimped handles, irid body 2,800.00

12-5/8" h, colorless ribbed body, blue, green, and gold combed irid horizontal striping, base inscribed with circular crossed arrow mark above "Austria"................980.00

13-1/2" h, ftd cylinder, ruffled rim, lemon yellow ground, stylized green and burgundy leaf motif.......................500.00

14-1/2" h, oviform, pinched sides and everted quatrefoil rim, irid salmon pink, silver waves.............................1,500.00

15-1/4" h, 8-1/2" d, Papillion, lustered gold, purple, and green 750.00

16" h, slender extended neck, bulbous orange body, pulled and coiled gold irid dec, fine colorful luster, polished pontil and base...6,900.00

16-3/4" h, conical ambergris-green body, three overlapping rows of integrated hot-applied dec, irid silver, gold, blue luster, polished pontil 2,760.00

Wishing Well, 11" h, 7" w, figural, green irid bowl, spider web design, bronzed grape leaves and vines...............200.00

LOTUS GLASS COMPANY

History: The Lotus Glass Company was located in Barnesville, Ohio. It was incorporated in 1912 and concentrated on decorating glassware. In the 1920s and 1930s, fine handmade blanks were purchased from manufacturers such as Bryce, Cambridge, Central, Duncan and Miller, Fostoria, Heisey, Paden City, and other American companies. The blanks were purchased in crystal and a rainbow of colors.

The Lotus Glass Company decorators used several different kinds of techniques. They were experts at light and

Ad, Gold Brocade, Silver Brocade, China, Glass & Tablewares, October 1967.

heavy cuttings. They perfected a deep plate etching process. Some wares were hand painted, while others were iridized. The most distinguishing characteristic of Lotus Glass is the 24K gold or sterling silver bands they used frequently.

Early advertisements for Lotus Glassware claimed it "Glassware for every purpose. A wide range of shapes, colors, and decorations. Complete matched patterns. Rose, Green, Amber, Crystal, and Black...Decorated in Gold and Silver." Modern collectors are starting to recognize and document many of the beautiful patterns.

Reference: Hazel Marie Weatherman, *Colored Glassware of the Depression Era, Book 2,* Glassbooks, Inc., 1982.

Periodical: *The Daze,* Box 57, Otisville, MI 48463.

Bowl, La Furiste, crystal, gold trim, 8-1/2" d, two handles 45.00
Candlesticks, pr, La Furiste, 5-3/4" h, pink 85.00
Cheese Plate, La Furiste, green, gold encrusted 50.00
Compote
    Brocade, 6" h, crystal, gold trim.................................35.00
    Butterfly etch, black 80.00
Cordial, Vesta etch, crystal..28.00
Cracker Plate, La Furiste, 10" d, green, gold encrusted......75.00
Goblet, La Furiste, pink..30.00
Ice Bucket, La Furiste, pink, green trim.............................75.00
Iced Tea Tumbler, ftd, Bird of Paradise etch, green cube stem,
    crystal bowl and foot 35.00
Jug, Bridal Bouquet, ball shape, crystal, gold encrusted...... 75.00
Pitcher, La Furiste, pink 450.00
Plate
    Brocade, 12" sq, crystal, gold trim...............................65.00
    McGuire etch, 8" sq, black..20.00
Rose Bowl, La Furiste, 7-3/4" h, ftd, crystal, gold trim 85.00
Sandwich Plate, La Furiste, green, gold trim, 2 handles 60.00
Server, La Furiste, center handle, green 55.00
Vase, La Furiste, Heisey #4029 oval, diamond optic,
    moongleam..185.00

LUTZ-TYPE GLASS

History: Lutz-type glass is an art glass attributed to Nicholas Lutz, who made it while at the Boston and Sandwich Glass Co. from 1869 until 1888. Lutz is believed to have made two distinct types of glass, striped and threaded. The striped glass was made by using threaded glass rods in the Venetian manner, and this style is often confused with authentic Venetian glass. Threaded glass was blown and decorated with winding threads of glass.

Since Lutz-type glass was popular, copied by many capable glassmakers, and unsigned, it is nearly impossible to distinguish genuine Lutz products.

References: Raymond E. Barlow and Joan E. Kaiser, *Glass Industry in Sandwich*, Vol. 1 (1993), Vol. 2 (1989), Vol. 3 (1987), and Vol. 4 (1983), distributed by Schiffer Publishing; ——, *Price Guide for the Glass Industry in Sandwich Vols. 1-4*, Schiffer Publishing, 1993; Ruth Webb Lee, *Sandwich Glass Handbook*, Charles E. Tuttle, 1966; ——, *Sandwich Glass*, Charles E. Tuttle, 1966; George S. and Helen McKearin, *American Glass*, Random House, 1979; Catherine M. V. Thuro, *Oil Lamps II*, Collector Books, 1994 value update; Kenneth Wilson, *American Glass 1760-1930*, 2 Vols., Hudson Hills Press and The Toledo Museum of Art, 1994.

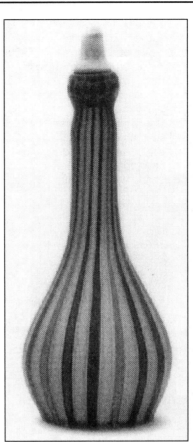

Barber bottle, 8-1/4" h, cylindrical, bulbous form, long neck, latticino stripes, colorless frosted ground, white, red, and pale green vertical stripes, tooled mouth, pontil scar, $190. Photo courtesy of Norman C. Heckler and Co.

Museum: Sandwich Glass Museum, Sandwich, MA.

Barber Bottle, 8" h, colorless ground, multicolored threaded latticino and opaque stripes..................................... 250.00
Beverage Set, 70-1/2" h tankard pitcher, four lemonade tumblers, four large tumblers, colorless ground, cranberry threading, engraved pattern of water plants and Grape Blue Heron on pitcher 650.00
Bowl
    3-1/4" d, 3" h, colorless, white, amethyst, and yellow latticino, goldstone border..75.00
    5" d, 2-7/8" h, colorless, white latticino, red rim, colorless applied baby face handles..275.00
Cake Stand, threaded, colorless, white threads............. 125.00
Compote
    7" h, colorless ground, lavender, pink, and opalescent swirls, entwined serpent stem..275.00
    8-7/8" h, 6-1/2" d, DQ, threaded, amberina, colorless hollow stem..500.00
Dish, 12" w, leaf shape, colorless, white latticino, goldstone and white waves.. 175.00
Epergne, 3 pcs, pink threads 275.00
Finger Bowl and Underplate, 7" d, ruffled edge, amber swirls, amethyst latticino, gold metallic borders 165.00
Lamp, 11" h, cranberry and white latticinio font, brass stem, double step marble foot, normal wear to edges of foot, font appears to be glued onto metal socket, Barlow 2129 .... 1,400.00
Lamp Shade, 8" sq, 20-1/2" fitter ring, opaque white loopings, applied cranberry threading, ribbon edge........... 180.00
Lemonade Tumbler, 5-1/2" d, colorless ground, cranberry threading, engraved dec, applied colorless handle............ 145.00
Marble
    1-3/4" d, colorless ground, green, red, white, and blue threaded twists, minor bruises, some roughness.................35.00

2-1/8" d, colorless ground, cranberry and white swirl....... 95.00
2-3/8" d, multicolored, minor roughness and bruises 110.00
Pitcher, 10" h, colorless ground, pink threading..............200.00
Plate, 6-1/4" d, threaded, rose shading to amber body, goldstone dec, ruffled 125.00
Punch Cup, 3" x 2-5/8", cranberry threading, colorless ground, circular foot, applied colorless handle.....................85.00
Scent Bottle, 2-1/8" l, blown, colorless, figural sea horse, opaque white spiral ribs, applied blue rigaree 115.00
Syrup Pitcher, blue ground, white stripes, frosted handle...175.00
Tea Service, creamer, cov sugar, two cups and saucers, colorless ground, light pink, blue, and white latticino 250.00

Tumbler, colorless ground
3" h, gold and white latticino, threaded, six applied strawberries, ftd...115.00
3-1/2" h, white, green, and orange latticino 120.00
3-3/4" d, white and amethyst latticino goldstone highlights 75.00
Vase, colorless ground
7" h, cylindrical, cranberry threading 125.00
8" h, bulbous, white latticino, applied colorless handle ... 150.00
Whimsy, 6-3/8" h, tiny Frozen Charlotte doll in colorless glass tube, latticino rings dec, bulbous finial, knob stem, colorless foot 375.00

MARY GREGORY TYPE GLASS

History: The use of enameled decoration on glass, an inexpensive way to imitate cameo glass, developed in Bohemia in the late 19th century. The Boston and Sandwich Glass Co. copied this process in the late 1880s.

Mary Gregory (1856-1908) was employed for two years at the Boston and Sandwich Glass factory when the enameled decorated glass was being manufactured. Some collectors argue that Gregory was inspired to paint her white enamel figures on glass by the work of Kate Greenaway and a desire to imitate pate-sur-pate. However, evidence for these assertions is very weak. Further, it is questionable whether Mary Gregory even decorated glass as part of her job at Sandwich. The result is that "Mary Gregory type" is a better term to describe this glass. Collectors should recognize that most examples are either European or modern reproductions.

Reference: R. and D. Truitt, *Mary Gregory Glassware*, published by authors, 1992; Kenneth Wilson, *American Glass 1760-1930: The Toledo Museum of Art, Volume I, Volume II,* Hudson Hills Press and The Toledo Museum of Art, 1994.

Museum: Sandwich Glass Museum, Sandwich, MA.

Reproduction Alert: Mary Gregory Type Glassware has been reproduced for years. Careful inspection of the details of the enameling is critical to determining age. Check for facial features of an American nature rather than European or Oriental features.

Atomizer, cranberry ground, white enameled little girl, gold washed atomizer mounting 345.00
Barber Bottle
    7-1/8" h, deep sapphire blue, white enameled youngster playing tennis, cylindrical bulbous form, long neck, tooled mouth, pontil scar..150.00
    7-1/2" h, cobalt blue ground, white enameled boy and girl playing badminton..135.00
    7-5/8" h, deep amethyst ground, white enameled young girl, landscape setting pr 300.00
Beverage Set, pitcher and six tumblers, colorless ground, white enameled girl, garden setting 295.00

Barber bottle, 8" h, cylindrical, bulbous form, long neck, deep sapphire blue, white enamel dec of girl playing tennis, tooled mouth, pontil scar, $150. Photo courtesy of Norman C. Heckler and Co.

Bowl, 8-1/2" w, 9-1/2" h, amber molded glass bowl, white enameled young woman with fishing pole catching fish in landscape scene, elaborate fancy holder with four griffins for feet, rococo open work handle...............................125.00
Box, cov
    3-3/4" l, 2-1/4" deep, 3" h, oval, white enameled boy with bunch of flowers in hand, deep amethyst ground, metal fittings, orig key missing..375.00
    5-3/4" d, 4-3/4" h, sapphire blue ground, white enameled young girl holding basket of flowers on lid, multicolored enamel dec on base, fancy wire legs 645.00
    6-1/2" d, 6-1/2" h, round, ebony color, white enameled young boy offering nosegay to young girl sitting on bench beneath overhanging tree, white enamel garland around perimeter, gold colored metal fittings and scrolled legs..........1,085.00
Bud Vase, 7" h, 2-1/2" w, amber ground, white spatter background, young boy and girl among foliage, facing pr............550.00
Cologne Bottle, sapphire blue, white enameled child 155.00
Cruet, orig stopper
    7-1/2" h, green, white enameled girl and trees 145.00
    8-1/2" h, sapphire blue, sq dimpled sides, white enameled two girls facing each other, blue handle 495.00
    9-1/2" h, amber ground, white enameled boy, applied colorless handle, colorless bubble stopper 295.00
Decanter, stopper, 12" h, colorless, white enameled woman with basket 175.00
Dresser Set, pr 10-1/2" h perfume bottles, 7" cov dresser jar, deep cobalt blue, enameled young children and angels, sprays of flowers, crown tops............................... 895.00
Dresser Tray, 10-1/2" l, 8" w, oval, emerald green ground, white enameled boy and girl dancing white another girl plays the mandolin.. 295.00
Ewer, 10" h, 3-1/8" d, cranberry ground, white enameled girl in garden setting, applied colorless handle.............. 225.00
Jewel Box
    3" x 3-1/2", cranberry ground, hinged lid 420.00
    10" l, 4" w, blue ground, white enameled boy and girl pulling cart, girl astride huge bottle, boy carrying goblet, floral garlands, SP edges, base and feet, sgd "Middletown Plate Co."...850.00
Milk Pitcher, 6" h, cranberry ground, white enameled girl, colorless applied handle.. 50.00
Miniature, pitcher, 1-3/4" h, cranberry ground, white enameled little girl blowing bubbles, colorless glass handle with gold highlights.. 200.00
Mug
    3" h, 2-1/8" d, cranberry ground, white enameled boy, applied colorless handle 85.00
    3" h, 2-1/4" d, cranberry ground, white enameled girl, applied colorless handle 85.00
    3-7/8" h, 2-1/4" d, amber ground, applied amber handles, white enameled boy on one, girl on other, pr.........150.00
    4-1/2" h, amber ground, ribbed, white enameled girl praying 65.00
    5" h, blue ground, white enameled boy with butterfly..... 125.00
Paperweight, 2-1/2" w, 4" l, deep black ground, white enameled young boy and girl in garden setting 295.00
Patch Box
    Emerald green..295.00
    Topaz, 2" d, hinged 230.00
Perfume Bottle
    4" h, sq, blue ground, white enameled boy on one, girl on other, cut glass stoppers, pr 250.00
    4-5/8" h, 2" d, cranberry ground, white enameled little girl dec, colorless bubble stopper 165.00
    5-3/4" h, 3" d, sapphire blue ground, white enameled boy

chasing butterfly, tinted facial features, blue ball
stopper 225.00
Pitcher
6-1/2" h, blue ground, white enameled boy with boat..... 150.00
6-5/8" h, 4-1/4' d, lime green ground, bulbous, optic effect,
round mouth, white enameled boy, applied green
handle..145.00
7-1/2" x 9-1/2", medium green ground, white enameled boy with
bird and trees, girl with bowl and brush dec, pr 275.00
9" h, colorless ground, colored enamel of three
women..325.00
11-1/2" h, colorless ground, white enameled woman, bird,
and trees 275.00
12" h, 6-1/2" w, sapphire blue ground, bulbous, applied amber handle, white enameled young woman holding her
hat and staff, standing in scenic spot, minor paint loss on
front 150.00
Plate, 6-1/4" d, cobalt blue ground, white enameled girl with butterfly net 125.00
Rose Bowl, cranberry ground, crimped top, white enameled girl
holding flower 325.00
Salt Shaker, 5" h, blue ground, paneled, white enameled girl in
garden, brass top..190.00
Tumble-Up, cranberry ground, white enameled girl on carafe,
boy on tumbler 415.00
Tumbler
2-1/2" h, 1-3/4" d, cranberry ground, white enameled boy on
one, girl on other, facing pr 100.00
4-1/4" h, cranberry ground, white enameled girl holding basket of flowers 115.00
4-1/2" h, sapphire blue ground, white enameled boy, ribbed
body 85.00
5" h, 2-1/2" d, sapphire blue ground, white enameled girl carrying basket of flowers 90.00
5-1/2" h, cobalt blue ground, white enameled girl picking
flowers, narrow gold band at top 115.00
5-3/4" h, transparent light blue ground, white enameled boy,
gold band at top, pedestal foot...............................140.00
Urn, 12" h, green ground, white enameled young woman with
swan, gold handles 450.00
Vase
2-1/2" h, 1-1/2" w, cobalt blue ground, white enameled figure
of young man standing among foliage, gold trim 325.00
4" h, cranberry ground, white enameled boy and
wagon...95.00
4-1/2" h, cranberry ground, 3 ftd, white enameled girl and
boy 110.00
5-1/2" h, cranberry, white enameled girl 100.00
6-1/4" h, 2-1/4" d, blue ground, white enameled child,
matched pr 275.00
6-1/2" h, green ground, white enameled young man....90.00
6-3/4" h, 3" d, pale amber ground, young girl in forest scene,
reverse with spray of flowers and leaves, neck and shoulder with dec band 225.00
7" h, cobalt blue ground, gilded rim, white enameled flowers
and cupids 175.00
7-1/2" h, green satin ground, white enameled lady 200.00
7-3/4" h, mottled blue ground, cut scalloped top, white
enameled boy and girl, matched pr.......................450.00
8" h, double ring shape, sapphire blue ground, young boy
dec 195.00
8-1/4" h, 3-1/2" d, amber ground, ruffled top, white enameled
young girl..185.00
8-7/8" h, 4" d, cranberry ground, white enameled young girls
carrying watering cans, facing pr 425.00
9" h, 4" d, frosted emerald green ground, white enameled girl
holds flowers in her apron and hand.....................165.00

9-7/8" h, cranberry ground, white enameled boy running with
butterfly net, girl with bouquet of flowers, holding apron,
colorless pedestal foot, facing pr..........................475.00
10-1/2" h, 5" w, cranberry ground, white enamel of young girl
holding a flower, paneled int. 295.00
10-5/8" h, 4" d, cylinder shape, lime green ground, white
enameled young girl carrying butterfly net 185.00
12" h, emerald green ground, finely white enameled scene of
boy picking flowers 190.00
13" h, 6-7/8" d, cranberry ground, white enameled girl with
flowers in her apron, scalloped top, applied colorless
reeded snail handles...420.00
Wine Bottle, 9" h, 3-1/8" d, cranberry ground, white enameled girl
holding floral spray, orig colorless bubble stopper... 195.00

McKEE GLASS

History: The McKee Glass Co. was established in 1843 in
Pittsburgh, Pennsylvania. In 1852, it opened a factory to produce pattern glass. In 1888, the factory was relocated to
Jeannette, Pennsylvania, and began to produce many types
of glass kitchenwares, including several patterns of Depression glass. The factory continued until 1951 when it was sold
to the Thatcher Manufacturing Co.

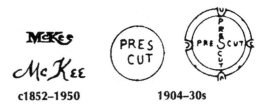

c1852–1950   1904–30s

The McKee Glass Co. produced many types of glass,
including window panes, tumblers, tablewares, Depression glass, milk glass, and bar and utility objects.

McKee named its colors Chalaine Blue, Custard, Seville
Yellow, and Skokie Green. McKee glass may also be found
with painted patterns, e.g., dots and ships. A few items were
decaled. Many of the canisters and shakers were lettered in
black to show the purpose for which they were intended.

There are many so-called "McKee" animal-covered
dishes. Caution must be exercised in evaluating pieces
because some authentic covers were not signed. Furthermore, many factories have made, and many still are making, split-rib bases with McKee-like animal covers or with
different animal covers. The prices below are for authentic
McKee pieces with either the cover or base signed.

References: Tom and Neila Bredehoft, *Fifty Years of Col-
lectible Glass, 1920-1970*, Antique Trader Books, 1997;
Gene Florence, *Kitchen Glassware of the Depression
Years*, 5th ed., Collector Books, 1997; ——, *Very Rare
Glassware of the Depression Years*, 5th Series, 1996,
Collector Books; Lowell Innes and Jane Shadel Spillman,
M'Kee Victorian Glass, Dover Publications, 1981; M'Kee
and Brothers, *M'Kee Victorian Glass*, Dover Publications,
1971, 1981 reprint.

Animal Dish, cov
Canary, nest base, milk glass 145.00
Cat, milk glass..190.00
Dove, round base, beaded rim, vaseline, sgd............365.00

Hen, milk glass, orig eyes 140.00
Horse, milk glass..195.00
Rabbit, milk glass...170.00
Squirrel, split rib base, milk glass 150.00
Basket, 15-1/2" h, 11" w, cut and pressed, floral and bird with
butterfly...50.00
Berry Set, Hobnail with Fan pattern, blue, master berry and 8
sauce dishes..170.00
Bird House, gray body, red roof 165.00
Bowl
5" d, 4-1/2" h, Skokie Green 8.75
6-1/2" d, Skokie Green 16.00
8" d, Star Rosetted pattern................................18.00
9" d, Laurel pattern, Skokie Green 15.00
9" d, Seville Yellow, green dots.........................35.00
9-1/2" d, Skokie Green, flower band pattern.....35.00
10" l, oval, Skokie Green, Autumn pattern........50.00
10-1/2" d, Chalaine Blue...................................145.00
Bread Plate
Queen pattern, canary yellow 40.00
Star Rosetted pattern, "A Good Mother Makes A Happy
Home"...65.00
Butter Dish, cov
Eureka pattern, heavy brilliant flint....................75.00
Gothic pattern, colorless, pyramid shaped finial 50.00
Queen pattern, canary yellow, domed lid..........85.00
Red ships, white ground......................................27.50
Star Rosetted pattern, colorless........................45.00
Strigil pattern, colorless....................................45.00
Wiltec pattern, Pre-Cut Ware, frosted 70.00
Cake Stand
Queen pattern, amber...65.00
Rock Crystal, green, low.....................................55.00
Candlesticks, pr
9" h, Rock Crystal, amber..................................130.00
9" h, Rock Crystal, colorless..............................165.00
10" h, crucifix form, Christ figure and "INRI" plaque, hexagonal
base, colorless...125.00
Candy Dish, cov, 7-3/4" h, orange body, gold trim, gold finial,
colorless pedestal base 35.00
Canister, cov
Drippings, 2-3/4" h, 4-1/4" d, Skokie Green 30.00
Flour, 24 oz, Skokie Green...............................55.00
Sugar, 40 oz, Seville Yellow 75.00
Sugar, 40 oz, Skokie Green 65.00
Castor Set, 3 bottle, toothpick handle...........................270.00
Celery Vase
Eugenia pattern, heavy brilliant flint..................95.00
Gothic pattern, colorless, ruby stain, scalloped 90.00
Strigil pattern, colorless....................................25.00
Cereal Canister, cov, Skokie Green, 48 oz, round..............35.00
Champagne, colorless, heavy brilliant flint
Eugenia 90.00
Eureka 90.00
Cheese and Cracker Set, Rock Crystal, red...................170.00
Clock, Daisy and Button pattern, tambour shape,
vaseline..450.00
Coffee Canister, cov, Skokie Green, 24 oz, faded............30.00
Compote
Brittanic pattern, green 60.00
Eugenia pattern, heavy brilliant flint, 8" d.......150.00
Queen pattern, apple green................................85.00
Star Rosetted pattern, colorless, 8-1/2" d 70.00
Console Bowl, 8-1/2" d, Autumn pattern, Skokie Green.......40.00
Cookie Jar, cov, 6" h, Skokie Green, diagonal Art Deco design,
ftd 95.00

Cordial, colorless
Eugenia pattern, heavy brilliant flint 90.00
Eureka pattern, heavy brilliant flint 85.00
Gothic pattern 45.00
Rock Crystal 35.00
Creamer
Comet pattern, colorless 55.00
Eugenia pattern, heavy brilliant flint 190.00
Eureka pattern, heavy brilliant flint 155.00
Gothic pattern, ruby stain.................................65.00
Masonic pattern, colorless................................45.00
Queen pattern, canary yellow 45.00
Rock Crystal, colorless.....................................35.00
Star Rosetted pattern, colorless.......................40.00
Strigil pattern, colorless...................................35.00
Decanter Set, decanter, six whiskey glasses, pink ground, ring
dec 125.00
Dinnerware, Oxford pattern, 26 pc set, c1940 .... 42.00
Dish
4 x 5", red ships, white ground..........................20.00
6" sq, Sunbeam pattern, turned up corners, green 30.00
Dripping Dish, 4 x 5", cov, Skokie green 30.00
Egg Beater Bowl, spout
Ivory..30.00
Skokie Green...32.00
Egg Cup, Custard 8.00
Fish Dish, 7" l, oval, Skokie green 14.00
Flour Shaker
Chalaine Blue...125.00
Red Dots, Seville Yellow ground 115.00
Red Ship, white ground, red ship 30.00
Roman arch, custard..30.00
Fruit Bowl, 12" d, Colonial pattern
Caramel..140.00
Seville Yellow...80.00
Skokie Green..95.00
Goblet
Eugenia pattern, heavy brilliant flint 90.00
Eureka pattern, heavy brilliant flint 75.00
French Ivory 40.00
Gothic pattern, ruby stain.................................65.00
Puritan pattern, pink stem 35.00
Queen pattern, amber..45.00
Rock Crystal, colorless.....................................25.00
Star Rosetted pattern, colorless.......................40.00
Strigil pattern, colorless...................................35.00
Grapefruit Bowl, Rock Crystal, red 45.00
Iced Tea Tumbler, Rock Crystal, red 35.00
Jelly Compote, Gothic pattern, colorless, scalloped rim 20.00
Lamp
Dance de Lumierre, green 750.00
Eugenia pattern, heavy brilliant flint, whale oil burner 165.00
Nude, green 175.00
Ribbed Tulip pattern, 9-1/2" h, colorless font, milk glass
base..125.00
Measuring Cup
Glassbake, 4 cup, crystal, red lettering 25.00
Red ships, white ground 28.00
Seville Yellow, ftd, 4 cup 150.00
Seville Yellow, red dots, 2 cup 55.00
Skokie Green, nested set, 4 pc 125.00
Measuring Pitcher, white.. 25.00
Mixing Bowl, Red Ship, white ground, red or black dec
6" d 15.00
7" d 20.00
8" d 20.00
9" d 24.00

Plate, Rock Crystal, amber, 9" d, $24.

Mug, Bottoms Down, Seville Yellow 150.00
Mustard Bottle, Eugenia pattern, heavy brilliant flint 35.00
Pepper Bottle, Eugenia pattern, heavy brilliant flint 30.00
Pickle Dish, oval
    Queen pattern, blue 25.00
    Star Rosetted, colorless 20.00
Pin Tray, hand shape, milk glass 20.00
Pitcher
    Aztec pattern, 5" h, colorless 20.00
    Dark Skokie Green, 16 oz 75.00
    Eugenia pattern, heavy brilliant flint 125.00
    Gothic pattern, colorless 75.00
    Queen pattern, blue 85.00
    Skokie Green, 16 oz 37.00
    Star Rosetted pattern, colorless 70.00
    Sunburst, marked "Prescut" 65.00
    Yutec, Eclipse, marked "Prescut" 45.00
    Wild Rose and Bowknot, frosted, gilt dec, 8" h 65.00
Plate
    Holly pattern, 8" d, Skokie Green 12.00
    Laurel pattern, 9" d, Skokie Green 10.00
    Rock Crystal pattern, 12" d, colorless 18.00
    Serenade pattern, 6-3/8" d, opaque white 60.00
Platter, Glassbake, 17-1/2" l, fish shape, crystal 25.00
Punch Bowl Set, bowl, 12 mugs, Tom and Jerry, red scroll
    dec 65.00
Razor Hone, stropper, milk glass 20.00
Reamer, pointed top, Skokie Green 45.00
Refrigerator Dish, cov
    Custard, 4" x 5" 22.00
    Red Ship, 5" x 8", white ground, red dec 25.00
    Seville Yellow, 6-1/2" sq 55.00
    Skokie Green, 4" x 5" 12.00
    White, 5" x 8" 18.00
Relish
    Gothic pattern, colorless 20.00
    Hickman, 8" l, green, gold trim 30.00
    Prescut, milk glass 25.00
    Ring Box, cov, Seville Yellow 20.00

Salt and Pepper Shakers, pr
    Red Dots, Seville Yellow ground 75.00
    Red Ships, white ground, red dec, black tops 35.00
    Roman Arches, black 60.00
    Roman Arches, Seville Yellow ground, black lettering .48.00
    Skokie Green, 2-1/4", sq 14.00
Sauce
    Eugenia pattern, heavy brilliant flint 12.00
    Gothic pattern, ruby stain 20.00
    Queen pattern, colorless, ftd 12.00
    Strigil pattern, colorless 8.00
Sandwich Server, center handle
    Brocade, pink, 10-1/2" d 50.00
    Rock Crystal, red 140.00
Sherbet
    Laurel pattern, Skokie Green 10.00
    Rock Crystal pattern, colorless 12.00
Skillet, Range-Tee, crystal 5.00
Spooner
    Eugenia pattern, heavy brilliant flint 45.00
    Queen pattern, amber 35.00
    Stars and Stripes pattern, colorless, minor roughness 22.00
    Strigil pattern, colorless 20.00
Sugar Bowl, cov
    Comet pattern, colorless 55.00
    Eugenia pattern, heavy brilliant flint 190.00
    Eureka pattern, heavy brilliant flint 155.00
    Gothic pattern, ruby stain 65.00
    Laurel pattern, Skokie Green 15.00
    Masonic pattern, colorless 45.00
    Queen pattern, canary yellow 45.00
    Rock Crystal, colorless 35.00
    Star Rosetted pattern, colorless 40.00
    Strigil pattern, colorless 35.00
Sugar Shaker
    Chalaine Blue 125.00
    Red Dots, Seville Yellow ground 115.00
Toothbrush Holder, Skokie Green 20.00
Toothpick Holder
    Aztec pattern, colorless 25.00

Wren house, gray body, red roof, $150.

Figural, hat shape, vaseline 35.00
Gothic pattern, ruby stain, scalloped rim......................85.00
Rock Crystal, colorless..40.00
Tumbler
   Bottoms Up, orig coaster, Seville Yellow 180.00
   Bottoms Up, orig coaster, Skokie Green....................170.00
   Eugenia pattern, heavy brilliant flint...........................45.00
   Flower Band, 3-1/2" h, Skokie Green 1.00
   Gladiator pattern, cobalt blue, gold trim 50.00
   Gothic pattern, colorless...35.00
   Ivory, 4" h, flat..12.00
   Ivory, 4-1/2" h, ftd 12.00
   Queen pattern, blue 45.00
   Ribbed Palm pattern, colorless.................................70.00
   Rock Crystal pattern, colorless 25.00
   Sextec, colorless, 4" h, flat......................................20.00
   Seville Yellow, 4-1/2" h, ftd 14.00
Vase
   Auto, 6-1/4" h, crystal 45.00
   Auto, 6-1/2" h, Colonial, Cut No. 1, crystal 45.00
   Brocade, 7-1/2" h, crystal, two handles, gold trim 50.00
   Clothed Woman, 3 sided, Skokie Green.....................175.00
   Hickman, 10" h, green, gold trim................................65.00
   Nude, 8-1/2" h, Chalaine Blue..................................175.00
   Rock Crystal, 11" h, amber.......................................85.00
   Sarah, Chalaine Blue...85.00
   Sarah, Skokie Green, 8" h 48.00
Water Bottle, 21" h, Radium Emanator Filter, vaseline, orig
   box...325.00
Window Box, 5" x 9", lion, Skokie Green 85.00

MERCURY GLASS

History: Mercury glass is a light-bodied, double-walled glass that was "silvered" by applying a solution of silver nitrate to the inside of the object through a hole in its base.

F. Hale Thomas of London patented the method in 1849. In 1855, the New England Glass Co. filed a patent for the same type of process. Other American glassmakers soon followed. The glass reached the height of its popularity in the early 20th century.

Atomizer, colored floral bud shaped glass stopper 50.00
Bottle, 7-1/2" h, 4-1/4" d, bulbous, flashed amber panel cut
   neck, etched grapes and leaves dec, corked metal stopper, c1840 ....175.00
Bowl
   4-3/4" d, enameled floral dec, gold luster int. 50.00
   6" d, enameled white floral dec..................................45.00
Cake Stand, 8" d, pedestal base, emb floral dec 80.00
Candlesticks, pr
   4" d, plain 40.00
   5-1/2" d, enameled white floral dec, domed base 70.00
   8" h, baluster 150.00
   10-1/2" h 225.00
   11" h, enameled floral dec 150.00
   12-3/4" h, baluster, domed circular foot, amber, enameled floral springs...300.00
Candy Dish, cov, 8-1/4" h, 4-1/4" d, pedestal base, colorless
   glass domed cov 45.00
Carafe, 12" h, 5-1/2" d, mushroom stopper, dated 1909 .....65.00
Christmas Ornament, 7" d, ball, brass collar and hanger,
   c1900..50.00
Cologne Bottle, 4-1/4" x 7-1/2", bulbous, flashed amber panel,
   cut neck, etched grapes and leaves, corked metal stopper, c1840 ....160.00

Lightning rod ball, quilt raised diamond pattern, silver mercury, sheared collared mouths with metal collars marked "Kretzer Brand/Trademark," America, 1870-1920, 5" d, $300. Photo courtesy of Norman C. Heckler and Co.

Compote, 7" h, 6-1/2" d, enameled white floral dec, gold luster
   int. 65.00
Creamer
   6" h, etched grapevine dec, applied colorless handle... 115.00
   6-1/2" h, etched ferns, applied colorless handle, attributed to
   Sandwich...140.00
Cup and Saucer, etched floral dec..................................65.00
Curtain Tieback, 2-5/8" d, pewter fitting, starflower dec 65.00
Garniture, 14" h, baluster, raised circular molded foot, everted
   rim, enameled foliate motif 215.00
Goblet
   5" d, gold, white lily of the valley dec 40.00
   6-7/8" h, silver, etched Vintage pattern, gold luster int. 65.00
   7-1/2" h, Ivy pattern, engraved grape leaves and
   grapes 145.00
Mug, 2-7/8" h, silver, applied colorless handle 35.00
Perfume Bottle, emerald green ground, cut and enameled dec,
   orig stopper 225.00
Pitcher
   9-3/4" h, 5-1/2" d, bulbous, panel cut neck, engraved lacy florals
   and leaves, applied colorless handle, c1840 ....225.00
   12-1/2" h, bulbous, applied colorless handle..............185.00
Salt, 3 x 3", price for pr..100.00
Scent Bottle, 4" l, cobalt blue over mercury glass ground, cut with
   shaped oval panels, silver mounted, early 20th C 320.00
Spooner, Vintage pattern 75.00
Sugar Bowl, cov, 4-1/4" d, 6-1/4" h, low foot, enameled white
   foliage dec, knob finial 65.00
Sweetmeat Dish, cov, 4" d, 7-1/2" h, pedestal base, colorless
   cov 50.00
Tazza, 5-3/4" d, 2-3/4" h, etched birds and leaves dec.... 75.00
Toothpick Holder
   3-1/2" h, gold, pedestal base 40.00
   5" h, gold, pedestal base, etched ferns 45.00
Urn, 13" h, baluster, mkd "Harnish & Co. London" 250.00
Vase
   4-3/4" h, silver, sanded foliage dec............................45.00
   8" h, cut to show emerald glass ground, mkd "Harnish & Co.
   London Pat." 115.00
   8-3/4" h, emerald green, hand painted floral dec, c1890,
   pr 185.00
   9-3/4 h, cylindrical, raised circular foot, everted rim, bright
   enameled yellow, orange, and blue floral sprays and insects, pr...225.00
   10-1/4" h, paneled sides, frosted palm trees, flowers, gold
   luster int., pr...225.00
   10-1/2" h, cylindrical, hand painted floral and leaf band
   around center 125.00
   12" h, ribbed, emerald green, enameled floral and bird
   dec 145.00

13" h, trumpet shape, enameled panel of orange, yellow, green, and blue floral clusters and butterflies........220.00
Wig Stand, 10-1/4" h 150.00
Wine, engraved Vintage dec, amber int. 100.00
Witch Ball, emerald green, attached base 185.00

MILK GLASS

History: Opaque white glass attained its greatest popularity at the end of the 19th century. American glass manufacturers made opaque white tablewares as a substitute for costly European china and glass. Other opaque colors, e.g., blue and green, also were made. Production of milk glass novelties came in with the Edwardian era.

The surge of popularity in milk glass subsided after World War I. However, milk glass continues to be made in the 20th century. Some modern products are reissues and reproductions of earlier forms. This presents a significant problem for collectors, although it is partially obviated by patent dates or company markings on the originals and by the telltale signs of age.

Collectors favor milk glass from the pre-World War I era, especially animal-covered dishes. The most prolific manufacturers of these animal covers were Atterbury, Challinor-Taylor, Flaccus, and McKee.

References: E. McCamley Belknap, *Milk Glass*, Crown Publishers, 1949, out of print; Regis F. and Mary F. Ferson, *Today's Prices for Yesterday's Milk Glass*, published by authors, 1985; ——, *Yesterday's Milk Glass Today*, published by authors, 1981; Myrna and Bob Garrison, *Imperial's Vintage Milk Glass,* published by authors, 1992; Everett Grist, *Covered Animal Dishes*, Collector Books, 1988, 1993 value update; Lorraine Kovar, *Westmoreland Glass*, 2 vols., Antique Publications, 1991; S. T. Millard, *Opaque Glass*, 4th ed., Wallace Homestead, 1975; Betty and Bill Newbound, *Collector's Encyclopedia of Milk Glass*, Collector Books, 1995; Kenneth Wilson, *American Glass, 1760-1930: The Toledo Museum of Art, Volume I, Volume II*, Hudson Hills Press and The Toledo Museum of Art, 1994.

Collectors' Club: National Milk Glass Collectors Society, 46 Almond Dr., Hershey, PA 17033.

Museum: Houston Antique Museum, Chattanooga, TN.

Notes: Numbers in listings prefixed with a letter refer to books listed in the references, wherein the letter identifies the first letter of the author's name.

Animal Dish, cov
    Baboon, fleur de list base, seated baboon, facing to one side, attributed to Flaccus (F114) 600.00
    Chick emerging from egg, basketweave base 80.00
    Deer, fallen tree base, sgd "E. C. Flaccus Co., Wheeling, WV" (F34) 185.00
    Dog, setter, white base, sgd "Flaccus," repair to lid.....150.00
    Elephant with Rider (F1)...700.00
    Fish, 8-3/4" l, walking, divided horizontally, 5 central fins support body, detailed scales, red glass eyes (B167b) 195.00
    Hen, large, almond..90.00
    Hen, large, blue head, white body...............................45.00
    Hen, large, gray, Kemple 300.00
    Hen, marbleized, head turned to left, lacy base, white and deep blue, Atterbury (F8) 165.00

Bowl, Daisy, Challinor, Taylor, enameled pink, blue, and green dec, 8-1/4" d, $40.

Hen on sleigh 90.00
Lamp, octagonal picket base, blue body, white head, Westmoreland (F87) 115.00
Pintail Duck, basketweave base, traces of old paint, numbered 65.00
Rabbit, patent date on base, Atterbury (F48) 175.00
Robin with Berry (F217)..75.00
Squirrel, acorn base (F15) 145.00
Swan, closed neck, basketweave base (M278) 95.00
Turkey, small, blue, Kemple...200.00
Bon Bon, scoop shape, Eagle Glass Co., 1899 (F597) 45.00
Bottle, figural
    Bear, 10-1/4" h, facing forward, sitting, forelegs folded across chest (F132)..125.00
    Duck, 11-1/2" h, vertical bill, head, and neck form flanged opening, rimmed oval for label, no closure, Atterbury (F433) 350.00
Bowl
    Arch Border pattern, 8" d, alternating wade curved arches and interlocking narrow pointed arches, Challinor, Taylor (B100a)..50.00
    Ball and Chain pattern, 8" d, openwork rim (B100b) 50.00
    Cut Star pattern, 7-1/4" d, blue, scalloped edge, twelve rated stars (F289) 75.00
    Daisy, 8-1/4" d, allover leaves and flower design, open scalloped edge (F165)..85.00
    King's Crown, 8" d, basketweave pattern, slanted sides, vertical bar pattern on base, eight triangular points forming crown (B1078b)..75.00
Bread Tray, basketweave border, motto "Give Us Our Daily Bread" inscribed on rim, Atterbury (F345) 75.00
Butter Dish, cov
    Crossed Fern pattern, 6" d, animal claw grasping ball feet and finial, scalloped edge, Atterbury (F232)...........75.00
    Gooseberry pattern, narrow beaded edges, band of fruit on cov and base, berry finial, Sandwich (F248)..........120.00
    Roman Cross pattern, 4-7/8" w, sq, ftd base curves outward toward top, cube shape finial (F240) 75.00
Calling Card Receiver, bird, wings extended over fanned tail, head resting on leaf, detailed feather pattern (F669) 150.00
Candlestick
    3-3/8" h, clown, bust rises from wide curved neck ruffle (F129) 75.00
    7-3/4" h, swirl, ribbing twists counter-clockwise from base, column, cup, and was guard (F522) 50.00
Candy Container, figural, top hat, tin threaded lid (W12A)....45.00

Celery Vase
    Blackberry Pattern, 6-5/8" h, scalloped rim, plain band above vertical surface, Hobbs
        Brockunier (F317)...110.00
        Burred Hobnail pattern.......................................45.00
Child's Mug, Little Bo Peep (M-92)....................................85.00
Compote
    Atlas, lacy edge, blue 185.00
    Blackberry pattern, 9" h, large figural blackberry finial on cov, Hobbs Brockunier (B121)..............................160.00
    Chick and Eggs, 11" h, pedestal, chick emerging from heaped eggs, finial cov, mounted on curved tripod, central support, rounded lacy edge base, emb Atterbury patent date, Aug. 6, 1889 inside cov (F362)..........185.00
    Lattice Edge pattern, 8-1/2" d, floral dec, Daisy and Button type pattern pedestal base, Challinor, Taylor (M116a)...... 100.00
    Prism pattern, 8" d, 5-1/2" h, wafer connection between Prism bowl and foot...155.00
Creamer
    Beaded Circle pattern, applied handle (F322) 65.00
    Blackberry pattern...45.00
    Burred Hobnail pattern.......................................45.00
    Forget Me Not pattern..40.00
    Melon with Leaf and Net pattern, Atterbury 45.00
    Paneled Wheat pattern, Hobbs Brockunier (F255).......65.00
    Roman Cross pattern (F239)...............................50.00
    Trumpet Vine pattern, fire painted dec, sgd "SV".........70.00
Cruet, Tree of Life pattern, blue.......................................80.00
Dresser Box, cov, horseshoe, horse, floral dec.................40.00
Egg Cup, cov, 4-1/4" h, bird, round, fluted, Atterbury
    (F130) 135.00
Fish Set, figural fish platter, four serving dishes, Atterbury, emb patent date 250.00
Hurricane Lamp, 10-1/2" h, Rainbow Art Co., #183, ruby and gold hand painted dec, 2 pc, c1947 ....125.00
Inkwell, horseshoe, circular inkwell in center, pen rests
    (F449) 45.00
Jar, cov, figural
    Eagle, "Old Abe," leafy base, "E. Pluribus Unum" on encircled banner, gray (F568).......................................115.00
    Owl, glass eyes..85.00
Lamp, 11" h, Goddess of Liberty, bust, 3 stepped hexagonal bases, clear and frosted font, brass screw connector, patent date, Atterbury (F329) 300.00
Match Holder
    Indian Head (B219)...125.00
    Jolly Jester, patent date on rear (F201) 135.00
    Minstrel Boy..195.00
    Trilby, patent date with reversed " 9" 150.00
Match Safe, 4-1/2" h, baby in black hat, corrugated match striker (F534) 350.00
Mug
    Ivy in Snow pattern, 3" h.....................................40.00
    Liberty Bell, Centennial dates emb between two bells (F674) 185.00
Mustard, cov, bull's head (F14) 150.00
Pitcher
    Birds on Branch pattern, trio of small birds on leafy branch, cold painted dec (F519)......................................110.00
    Dart and Bar pattern, 8" h, blue, rect handle, ftd (B85a) . 100.00
    Fish pattern, 71/4" h, finely detailed, Atterbury (F328) 185.00
Plate
    Ancient Castle, 7" d...50.00
    Cats, 6" d, 2 cats form upper edge, bracketed dog head, open work, swirling leaves, emb "He's all right" (B20d) 125.00
    Colonial Hearth, center black decal, lacy edge, Kemple Glass 15.00

Plate, Trumpet Vine dec, lattice border, Challinor, Taylor, 10-5/8" d, $35.

    Columbus, 9-3/4" d, center bust with dates 1492-1892 across chest, shell and club border........................45.00
    Cupid and Psyche, 7" d 45.00
    Dog and Cats (B20d) 50.00
    Donkey, 7" d 45.00
    Easter Horseshoe (W150Ac)................................85.00
    National, flag, eagles, patent date on back, 7" d..........50.00
    Roger Williams Memorial, 7-1/4" d, Williams monument emb in center, flags, eagles, and fleur de lis, patent date, Westmoreland (F639) 150.00
    Roses, 12" d, Imperial, c1950 ....35.00
    Small Mouth Bass, multicolored center dec, lacy heart border, Kemple Glass, 6-1/2" h 15.00
    Star, 5-3/8" d, six pointed center star, lacy filigree fills in spaces between points 15.00
    Woof Woof 45.00
Platter
    Blaine Logan Campaign, 13-1/8" l, emb bust of Blaine faces Logan, notched border (F564) 365.00
    Retriever, 13-1/4" l, swimming dog pursuing duck through cattails, lily pad border (B53) 120.00
Salt Shaker
    Atterbury Dredge, 3-3/8" h, combination octagonal paneled and pepper shapers shaped as small cov stein (F415) 95.00
    Brownie, 2-3/8" h, Palmer Cox Brownies in different poses on each of four vertical sides (F448)..........................120.00
    Diamond Point and Leaf pattern, 2-3/4" h, blue (F489) 50.00
Spooner
    Beaded Circle pattern, 5-5/8" h, scalloped, ftd, flint, attributed to Sandwich (F321) 70.00
    Melon with Leaf and Net, Atterbury.............................40.00
    Monkey, scalloped top, 5-1/8" h (F275) 125.00
    Paneled Flower, 4-5/8" h, ribbing separates six diamond point panels, stylized floral dec, scalloped edges, Challinor, Taylor (F284) 60.00
Sugar Bowl, cov
    Almond Thumbprint, 7-1/2" h, large scalloped edges (F367) 120.00
    Beaded Circle pattern, applied handle (F322) 65.00
    Blackberry pattern...45.00

Burred Hobnail pattern...45.00
Ceres pattern, 7-1/4" h, cameo profiles in beaded circles, leafy sprays, bust finial (B127) 115.00
Forget Me Not pattern 40.00
Melon with Leaf and Net pattern, Atterbury 45.00
Nine Panel patter, Ihmsen Glass Co., flared bowl, cov fits inside base edge (F670) 450.00
Paneled Wheat pattern, Hobbs Brockunier (F255) 65.00
Roman Cross pattern (F239) 50.00
Sunflower pattern (B82b) 65.00
Trumpet Vine pattern, fire painted dec, sgd "SV" 70.00
Sugar Shaker
    Netted Oak pattern, 4-1/4" h, oak leaf centered on netted panels, green top band, Northwood (F495)..............85.00
    Royal Oak pattern 90.00
Syrup Pitcher, orig top
    Alba pattern, 6-1/2" h, enameled floral sprays, Ditheridge (F139) 150.00
    Beehive, 5-5/8" h, emb beehive center, ribbed top and base, strap handle (F372) 185.00
    Bellflower pattern, single vine, dated, Collins & Wright (F155C0) 245.00
Toothpick Holder, Tramp Shoe (F194) 65.00
Tumbler, Royal Oak, orig fired paint, green band 50.00
Whimsy, rowboat, Atterbury, patent date 45.00
Wine, Feather pattern 40.00

MILLEFIORI

History: Millefiori (thousand flowers) is an ornamental glass composed of bundles of colored glass rods fused together into canes. The canes were pulled to the desired length while still ductile, sliced, arranged in a pattern, and fused together again. The Egyptians developed this technique in the first century B.C. It was revived in the 1880s.

Reference: Kenneth Wilson, *American Glass, 1760-1930: The Toledo Museum of Art, Volume I, Volume II*, Hudson Hills Press and The Toledo Museum of Art, 1994.

Reproduction Alert: Millefiori items, such as paperweights, cruets, and toothpicks, are being made by many modern companies.

Basket
    3-1/4" h, blue and amber canes, matte finish, orig millefiori handle, Italian 100.00
    3-1/2" h, yellow and blue canes, matte finish, orig millefiori handle, Italian 100.00
    10-1/2" h, 6-1/2" w, random pattern of millefiori canes, white opal ground cased in colorless, butterscotch irid surface, applied pale pink loop handle..............................200.00
Bowl
    2" d, pink, green, and white canes, applied colorless handles..48.00
    4" d, blue and white canes, applied colorless handles 80.00
    8" d, tricorn, scalloped, folded sides, amethyst and silver deposit...125.00
Box, cov, 3" d, multicolored 125.00
Creamer
    4" h, white ground, scattered millefiori, applied handle... 250.00
    4-1/2" h, 3" d, white and cobalt blue canes, yellow centers, satin finish...110.00
Cruet
    6" h, bulbous, multicolored canes, applied frosted rope handle, c1920 ....400.00

7" h, slender, multicolored canes, matte finish, Italian, c1950..75.00
Cup and Saucer, white and cobalt blue canes, yellow center, satin finish... 90.00
Decanter, 12" h, deep black ground, all over multicolored flux and canes, including peachblow, and opal, enamel dec, Gundersen... 1,450.00
Dish
    4-3/8" d, 1-1/2" h, close concentric millefiori, blue, white, and amethyst canes, signature Whitefriars monk cane, dated "1977"...80.00
    5" d, octagonal, blue and white canes 125.00
Door Knob, 2-1/2" d, paperweight, center cane dated 1852, New England Glass Co. 395.00
Flask, 4-1/2" x 3" x 1", millefiori separated by blue and white filigrana threads 275.00
Goblet, 7-1/2" h, multicolored canes, colorless stem and base.. 150.00
Jack in the Pulpit Vase, multicolored canes, matte finish, Italian, c1950 .... 65.00
Inkwell, 4-1/2" h, sgd "Paul Ysart" 200.00
Jut, 2-1/4" h, multicolored canes, applied colorless handle.. 95.00
Lamp, 14-1/2" h, 8-1/2" d dome shade, glass base, electric.. 795.00
Miniature Lamp
    8-1/2" h, mushroom cap shade, bulbous base, multicolored canes...375.00
    11" h, mushroom cap shade, matching glass lamp shaft, red, blue, and white, gilt metal "Bryant" electrical fittings... 1,200.00
Perfume Bottle, round body, seven portrait canes, orig metal mountings, Venetian, c1930-40............................ 450.00
Pitcher, 6-1/2" h, multicolored canes, applied candy cane handle... 195.00
Rose Bowl, 6" h, crimped top, multicolored, cased, white lining... 145.00
Slipper, 5" l, camphor ruffle and heal............................. 140.00
Sugar, cov, 4" h, 3-1/2" d, white canes, yellow centers, satin finish... 125.00
Toothpick Holder, ruffled top, multicolored canes, c1890 .. 200.00
Tumble-Up, 8-3/4" h, multicolored canes, matte finish, Italian, c1950... 85.00
Vase
    3-1/2" h, waisted, ruffled top, light blue, cobalt blue, medium blue, and white canes, four applied knob handles ..65.00
    4" d, handkerchief, red ground, gold dust ext. 180.00
    4" d, multicolored canes, applied double handles 100.00
    5-1/2" h, purple bands, white oval lines and bands, red flowers, yellow centers...175.00
    8" h, ruffled rim, multicolored canes, applied colorless handles...190.00
    11" h, bulbous, yellow and green canes, red dots......125.00

MINIATURE LAMPS

History: Miniature oil and kerosene lamps, often called "night lamps," are diminutive replicas of larger lamps. Simple and utilitarian in design, miniature lamps found a place in the parlor (as "courting" lamps), hallway, children's rooms, and sickrooms.

Miniature lamps are found in many glass types, from amberina to satin glass. Miniature lamps measure 2-1/2 to 12 inches in height, with the principle parts being the base, collar, burner, chimney, and shade. In 1877, both L. J. Atwood and L. H. Olmsted patented burners for miniature lamps. Their burners made the lamps into a popular household accessory.

References: Marjorie Hulsebus, *Miniature Victorian Lamps*, Schiffer Publishing, 1996; Ann Gilbert McDonald, *Evolution of the Night Lamp*, Wallace-Homestead, 1979; Frank R. and Ruth E. Smith, *Miniature Lamps* (1981), Book II (1982) Schiffer Publishing; John F. Solverson, *Those Fascinating Little Lamps: Miniature Lamps and Their Values*, Antique Publications, 1988, includes prices for Smith numbers.

Collectors' Club: Night Light, 38619 Wakefield Ct., Northville, MI 48167.

Reproduction Alert: Study a lamp carefully to make certain all parts are original; married pieces are common. Reproductions abound.

Note: The numbers given below refer to the figure numbers found in the Smith books.

Figure III-I, Artichoke, pink 225.00
Figure VII-I, Santa Claus 2,700.00
Figure VII-II, satin, rainbow, Kosmos Brenner burner, 10-1/2" h 2,750.00
Figure VIII-I, cameo, white maidenhair fern and butterflies, citron ground 5,500.00
Figure XVIII-II, overshot, frosted, house scene, 5-1/2" h 850.00
Figure XXIX-II, satin, swirled emb ribbed rose shade, emb scene, SS pedestal base, 13-1/2" h 800.00
#9-I, opaque white, Fire Fly, orig dated burner 250.00
#11-1, milk glass pedestal base and shade, clear pressed font, Sandwich, 6-3/4" h 275.00
#20-II, blue glass shade, Aladdin type 275.00
#25-II, cranberry, Berger lamp 275.00
#28-II, milk glass, Glow Lamp, melon ribbed 165.00
#29-I, nutmeg, white milk glass, brass band and handle 80.00
#30-I, green glass shade, tin holder, acorn border 120.00
#36-I, Little Buttercup, blue 75.00
#40-I, opalescent, cranberry, Spanish Lace pattern, applied handle, hornet border 325.00
#49-I, cobalt blue, Little Butter Cup, 2" h, pr 275.00
#49-II, Little Banner 90.00
#50-I, log cabin, blue, handle 1,100.00
#59-II, clear, emb "Vienna" 125.00
#68-I, finger lamp, blue with stars, emb "Wide Awake," 115.00
#82-II, Block pattern, milk glass, matching globe, 6-1/2" h .. 100.00
#95-II, clear, applied handle 70.00
#106-I, clear, block font and base, nutmeg burner 90.00
#109-I, Beaded Heart, clear, emb 115.00
#110-I, Bull's Eye, clear, stem 45.00
#111-I, Bull's Eye, teal blue, stem, 4-7/8" h 190.00
#112-I, Bull's Eye, green, burst bubble on one of the points on foot 45.00
#116-I, Fishscale pattern, amber, nutmeg burner, clear glass chimney 150.00
#121-I, mercury glass, acorn shape, emb acorn cap base, acorn burner 125.00
#125-I, Christmas Tree, white milk glass, gold trim 125.00
#143-I, Lincoln Drape, frosted amber, acorn burner 140.00
#144-I, Westmoreland pattern 325.00
#153-I, milk glass, pink and gold, emb 115.00
#156-I, milk glass, emb flower and scrolls, 8" h 125.00
#165-II, clear, fine ribbing, acorn burner, patent collar ... 115.00
#166-I, Greek Key, clear, acorn burner 90.00
#171-I, Pond Lily, emb, inside painting 140.00

Satin, MOP, diamond quilt pattern body, pink, 8-1/2" h, $1,350.

#177-I, custard glass, rough shade 55.00
#184-II, Swirl, orig reflector 85.00
#190-I, Block and Dot pattern, milk glass, 7-3/4" h 140.00
#192-I, Block pattern, clear, hand painted blue and green flowers, acorn burner, 6-1/2" h 85.00
#203-I, Plume pattern, opaque white, gilt dec, nutmeg burner, 8-1/4" h 115.00
#211-I, Medallion, milk glass, emb 45.00
#212-I, pink milk glass with shells, base of shade damaged 145.00
#213-I, milk glass, emb, yellow, pink, and white 135.00
#214-I, Maltese Cross, milk glass, emb rough top shade 50.00
#230-I, Acanthus, milk glass, emb, yellow and white 125.00
#231-I, Drape pattern, pink and white milk glass 75.00
#240-I, Defender, green milk glass, 8-1/2" h 250.00
#241-I, Paneled Cosmos, white milk glass, multicolored floral dec, 8-1/4" h, small chip on top rim of shade 370.00
#286-I, Cosmos, white milk glass, multicolored floral dec, pink trim bands, 7-1/2" h 275.00
#311-I, white milk glass, orange, green and brown ground, 8" h, no harm fish scale flake on shade fitter edge 350.00
#317-I, milk glass, pink and yellow flowers, shaded green ground 300.00
#325-I, pink milk glass, angel dec 165.00
#327-II, swan, milk glass, shade with crack 300.00
#330-II, elephant, wrong shade 225.00
#368-I, Beaded Rib, spatter glass, hornet burner 400.00
#368-II, milk glass, blue bands, pink flowers, green leaves, Dietz Night Light burner 475.00
#369-I, Beaded Swirl, end of day 300.00
#370-I, cranberry, Beaded Swirl 200.00
#389-I, satin, blue, melon ribbed base, pansy ball shade, chip on shade 155.00
#390-I, melon ribbed, cased, yellow 525.00
#394-I, satin, blue, puffy diamond quilted pattern base and umbrella shade, nutmeg burner, clear glass chimney, 9" h ... 475.00
#400-I, green beaded 125.00
#403-I, Beaded Drape, cranberry opalescent, nutmeg burner, 9-1/2" h 350.00
#409-II, cranberry, threaded base 125.00
#421-II, milk glass, banquet style shape, three tiers, brass pedestal base 550.00

#432-I, Twinkle, cobalt blue, 7" h, slight flake on shade fitter edge 175.00

#439-I, cranberry, Hornet burner, 8" h, some roughness at top of shade...200.00

#459-II, satin, red shading to pink, emb scrolled leaves and swirl, 10" h 1,650.00

#460-I, cranberry, white enamel floral dec, 11-5/8" h 450.00

#474-I, Spanish Lace filigree 750.00

#482-I, Daisy and Cube, vaseline, nutmeg burner, 8" h 365.00

#483-II, satin, light blue, enameled tulips and leaves, gold trim...450.00

#488-II, amber, applied handle 75.00

#490-I, Skeleton, 5-1/2" h...8,000.00

#497-I, owl, black, gray, orange eyes..........................1,100.00

#499-I, swan, glossy pink slag, 7-3/4" h, 3 very small flakes on top of shade 2,250.00

#502-I, opalescent, amber, pink feet...........................3,000.00

#508-I, Spanish Lace, opalescent, nutmeg burner 350.00

#509-I, Reverse Swirl, opalescent, 7-3/8" h, roughness and chips to top edge of shade 125.00

#536-I, cranberry shading to clear on both shade and base, applied colorless feet, 7-1/2" h 450.00

#538-I, amberina, paneled, amber fee, 9-1/4" h............1,500.00

#546-I, Swirl, blue, 8-1/2" h..600.00

#555-I, glossy satin glass, pink and butterscotch 1,550.00

#595-I, satin, MOP, DQ, shading from pink to apricot, burner ring damaged...1,050.00

#600-I, satin, MOP, Raindrop, four petal feet, 8-3/4" h 600.00

#610-I, Burmese, Webb, brown and green foliage, red berries 4,000.00

#625-I, Glow Lamp, amber, replaced glass burner, 4-1/2" h 40.00

#625-I, Glow Lamp, ruby, orig glass burner, 4-1/2" h......100.00

#625-I, Glow Lamp, white milk glass, floral dec, burner....30.00

MONART GLASS

History: Monart glass is a heavy, simply shaped art glass in which colored enamels are suspended in the glass during the glassmaking process. This technique was originally developed by the Ysart family in Spain in 1923. John Moncrief, a Scottish glassmaker, discovered the glass while vacationing in Spain, recognized the beauty and potential market, and began production in his Perth glassworks in 1924.

The name "Monart" is derived from the surnames Moncrief and Ysart. Two types of Monart were manufactured: a commercial line which incorporated colored enamels and a touch of aventurine in crystal, and the art line in which the suspended enamels formed designs such as feathers or scrolls. Monart glass, in most instances, is not marked. The factory used paper labels.

Collectors' Club: Monart & Vasart Collectors Club, 869 Cleveland St., Oakland, CA 94606.

Basket, brown to light tan opal vertical striations, Cluthra type..600.00

Bowl

7-1/4" d, 1-3/4" h, Cluthra, internally swirled and hooked green, amber, and aubergine, yellow ground, gold dust, orig label "Monart Glass/Moncreiff Scotland/YXI"..225.00

9" d, Aventurine, blue, mottled brown, and goldstone, pebbled texture 150.00

10-1/2" d, white, gray crackle, yellow and green flecks, oxblood red base and rim.......................................190.00

11-1/2" d, mottled orange and green 195.00

Candlestick, two shades of green, goldstone mica, paper label...120.00

Lamp Shade, 6-1/2" d, white opal....................................95.00

Vase

5-7/8" h, 5-5/8" d, mottled shades of blue, goldstone flecks, orig paper label...200.00

6-1/2" h, mottled shades of red and blue, white lining... 225.00

7" h, colorless, interior sapphire blue pulled elements enhanced by golden amber threading, blue rim border 250.00

7" h, 7" w, gray, blue, and white swirls on dark red ground, orig paper label..215.00

8" h, bulbous angular bright orange body, gray powder overlay cracked on surface, prominent pontil button smooth, Moncrieff, attributed to Monart/Ysart studios 435.00

8-1/2" h, goldstone shading to clear, cylindrical, flaring rim, Scottish Cluthra 225.00

8-1/2" h, 8" d, blue, silver, mica, and orange streaks, small bubbles 250.00

11" h, mottled orange shade to deep orange at flared rim...260.00

14" h, bulbous, tapered, extended neck, flared rim, blue shaded to pink, gold highlights, Cluthra 650.00

14-1/2" h, blue irid ground, tree-bark texture 250.00

16" h, green, flecked neck, orange body, dark inclusions, gold Cluthra centers..465.00

MONT JOYE GLASS

History: Mont Joye is a type of glass produced by Saint-Hilaire, Touvier, de Varreaux & Company at their glassworks in Pantin, France. Most pieces were lightly acid etched to give them a frosted appearance and were also decorated with enameled florals.

Bowl, 3-3/4" d, frosted ground, enameled floral dec, sgd ... 275.00

Ewer, cov, cameo cutting, crystal, green, and gold, brass spout and handle, removable cover, artist sgd "Cristalle Rie Depantin"..550.00

Jar, cov, 8" h, cylindrical, crystal ground, etched, enameled iris, gilt leaves, crystal knob, gilt factory mark, c1900............275.00

Pitcher, 10" h, amethyst, enameled flowers, aqua, blue, pink, and gold, sgd 350.00

Rose Bowl, 3-3/4" h, 4-1/4" d, pinched sides, acid etched, enameled purple violets, gold stems and dec......295.00

Vase

4" h, pink enameled poppy and gold leaves, frosted textured ground, mkd 275.00

5-1/8" h, spherical, cylindrical neck and foot, frosted ground, etched and gilt oak leaves and acorns, gilt signature..215.00

5-1/2" h, swirled shape, green, enameled flowers, c1890, sgd "Mont Joye" 445.00

5-3/4" h, green glitter body, gold leaf painted dec, applied opal glass spheres 375.00

6-1/2" h, green frosted ground, cut poppies, crimson enamel and gilt trim...265.00

7-1/2" h, dark green satin ground, enameled pink iris dec 400.00

8" h, light turquoise ground, etched iris dec, gold highlights, acid etched frosting, gold band around crimped edge 395.00

8-1/2" h, cameo, icy frosted ground, enameled leaves, deep red poppies, sgd 450.00

9" h, frosted ground, enameled purple orchids, green leaves 200.00

9-1/2" h, 6" w, ovoid, acid etched, lilies outlined in gold, body slightly ribbed, indented fluted top with gold accents, sgd, c1900 ....600.00

10" h, bulbous, narrow neck, clear to opalescent green, naturalistic thistle dec, gold highlights........................375.00

11" h, tomato red ground, lacy gold dec, enameled iris and foliage dec...250.00

13-3/4" h, flattened ovoid shape, cameo, crystal ground, etched, molded and enameled iris, gilt leaves, c1900 .... 350.00

18" h, green, enameled purple flowers, gold leaves, sgd 325.00

25-3/4" h, flaring waisted bottle form, green metallic flaked ground, overlaid foliate dec, MOP beads, base stamped "Mont Joye," c1910 ....1,200.00

Violet Vase, 6" h, frosted etched surface, colorless glass, naturalistic enameled purple violet blossoms, gold highlights, base mkd "Dimier Geneve" 260.00

MORGANTOWN GLASS WORKS

History: The Morgantown Glass Works, Morgantown, W.V., was founded in 1899 and began production in 1901. Reorganized in 1903, it operated as the Economy Tumbler Company for 20 years until, in 1923, the word "Tumbler" was dropped from the corporate title. The firm was then known as The Economy Glass Company until reversion to its original name, Morgantown Glass Works, Inc., in 1929, the name it kept until its first closing in 1937. In 1939, the factory was reopened under the aegis of a guild of glassworkers and operated as the Morgantown Glassware Guild from that time until its final closing. Purchased by Fostoria in 1965, the factory operated as a subsidiary of the Moundsville-based parent company until 1971, when Fostoria opted to terminate production of glass at the Morgantown facility. Today, collectors use the generic term, "Morgantown Glass," to include all periods of production from 1901 to 1971.

Morgantown was a 1920s leader in the manufacture of colorful wares for table and ornamental use in American homes. The company pioneered the processes of iridization on glass, as well as gold and platinum encrustation of patterns. They enhanced Crystal offerings with contrasting handle and foot of India Black, Spanish Red (ruby), and Ritz Blue (cobalt blue), and other intense and pastel colors for which they are famous. They conceived the use of contrasting shades of fired enamel to add color to their etchings. They were the only American company to use a chromatic silk-screen printing process on glass, their two most famous and collectible designs being Queen Louise and Manchester Pheasant.

The company is also known for ornamental "open stems" produced during the late 1920s. Open stems separate to form an open design midway between the bowl and foot, e.g., an open square, a "Y," or two diamond-shaped designs. Many of these open stems were purchased and decorated by Dorothy C. Thorpe in her California studio, and her signed open stems command high prices from today's collectors. Morgantown also produced figural stems for commercial clients such as Koscherak Brothers and Marks & Rosenfeld. Chanticleer (rooster) and Mai Tai (Polynesian bis) cocktails are two of the most popular figurals collected today.

Morgantown is best known for the diversity of design in its stemware patterns, as well as for its four patented optics: Festoon, Palm, Peacock, and Pineapple. These optics were used to embellish stems, jugs, bowls, liquor sets, guest sets, salvers, ivy, and witch balls, vases, and smoking items.

Two well-known lines of Morgantown Glass are recognized by most glass collectors today: #758 Sunrise Medallion and #7643 Golf Ball Stem Line. When Economy introduced #758 in 1928, it was originally identified as "Nymph." By 1931, the Morgantown front office had renamed it Sunrise Medallion. Recent publications erred in labeling it "dancing girl." Upon careful study of the medallion, you can see the figure is poised on one tiptoe, musically saluting the dawn with her horn. The second well-known line, #7643 Golf Ball, was patented in 1928; production commenced immediately and continued until the company closed in 1971. More Golf Ball than any other Morgantown product is found on the market today.

References: Jerry Gallagher, *Handbook of Old Morgantown Glass*, Vol. I, published by author (420 First Ave. NW, Plainview, MN 55964), 1995; ——, *Old Morgantown, Catalogue of Glassware*, 1931, Morgantown Collectors of America Research Society, n.d.; Ellen Schroy, *Warman's Depression Glass,* Krause Publications, 1997; Hazel Marie Weatherman, *Colored Glassware of the Depression Era*, Book 2 published by author, 1974, available in reprint; ——, *1984 Supplement & Price Trends for Colored Glassware of the Depression Era*, Book 1, published by author, 1984.

Periodical: *Morgantown Newscaster,* Morgantown Collectors of America, 420 First Ave., NW, Plainview, MN 55964.

Collectors' Clubs: Old Morgantown Glass Collectors' Guild, P.O. Box 894, Morgantown, WV 26507.

Bowl

#1 Berkshire, Crystal w/#90 Starlet cutting, 8" d 58.00

#12 Stella, Nanking Blue, #2 Cover, 8" d 315.00

#12-1/2 Woodsfield, Genova Line, 12-1/2" d 545.00

#12-1/2 Woodsfield, Pomona Line, 12-1/2" d..............550.00

#14 Fairlee, Glacier decor, 8" d 525.00

#17 Calypso, Spanish Red, 7-3/4" d 235.00

#19 Kelsha, Danube Line, 12" d................................425.00

#19 Kelsha, Genova Line, 12" d................................425.00

#22 Linwood, Topreen Line, Spiral Optic, 10" d 355.00

#26 Greer, Neubian Line, 10" d.................................750.00

#26 Greer, Topreen Line, 10" d.................................465.00

#35-1/2 Elena, Old Amethyst, applied Crystal rim, 8" d ... 425.00

#35-1/2 Elena, Old Bristol Line, 9-1/2" d 745.00

#67 Fantasia, Bristol Blue, 5-1/2" d 75.00

#71 Vienna, Steigel Green w/Crystal Italian Base, 12" d 1,400.00

#101 Heritage, Gypsy Fire, matte finish, 8" d...............70.00

#101 Heritage, Peacock Blue, 8" d 48.00

#103 Elyse, Steel Blue, 7" d 48.00

#111 Dodd, Bristol Blue, 5" d 65.00

#1102 Crown, Moss Green, 9" d 45.00

#1102 Crown, Steel Blue, 9" d.....................................50.00

#1933 El Mexicana, Console, Seaweed, 10" d 385.00

#1933 El Mexicano Console, Ice, 10" d 285.00

#1933 El Mexicano Console, Seaweed, 10" d 285.00

#1933 El Mexicano Ice Tub, Ice, 6" d 210.00

#1933 El Mexicano Ice Tub, Seaweed, 6" d 210.00

#4355 Janice, Crystal, #787 Maytime etch, 13" d.......195.00

Ad, showing Golf Ball, #7643, ruby bowls. The Crockery and Glass Journal, September 1931.

#4355 Janice, Crystal, Glacier Decor w/Snow Flowers, 13" d 565.00
#4355 Janice, 14K Topaz, Carlton/Madrid, 13" d 185.00
#4355 Janice, Ritz Blue, 13" d 445.00
#4355 Janice, Spanish Red, 13" d 445.00
#7643 Celeste, Spanish Red, Crystal trim, covered, 6" d 1,200.00
#7643 Truman, Spanish Red, Crystal trim, rare, 10" d 4,500.00
#9937 Revere, Ruby, 6" d 75.00

Candleholders, pair
#37 Emperor, Genova Line, 8" h 625.00
#37 Emperor, Stiegel Green, 8" h................................625.00
#37 Emperor, 14K Topaz, 8" h......................................625.00
#60 Rhoda Hurricane Lite, plain rim, Lime, 8" h..........110.00
#80 Modern, Moss Green, 7-1/2" h.................................70.00
#81 Bravo, Gypsy Fire, 4-1/2" h.....................................70.00
#81 Bravo, Peacock Blue, 4-1/2" h...............................528.00
#81 Bravo, Thistle, 4-1/2" h...135.00
#82 Cosmopolitan, Moss Green, slant, 7" h...................75.00
#82 Cosmopolitan, Gypsy Fire, slant, 7" h......................75.00
#87 Hamilton, Evergreen, 5" h.......................................75.00
#87 Hamilton, Steel Blue, 4" h.......................................50.00
#88 Classic, Nutmeg, 4-3/4" h..55.00
#105 Coronet, Cobalt Blue, slant, 8-3/4" h...................120.00
#105 Coronet, Ebony, slant, 8-3/4" h............................120.00
#7620 Fontanne, Ebony filament, #781 Fontinelle etch..1,000.00
#7643 Dupont, Crystal, rare, 4-5/8" h...........................385.00
#7643 Golf Ball, Torch Candle, single, Ritz Blue, 6" h 280.00
#7643 Jacobi, Anna Rose, rare, 4" h............................525.00
#7643 Jacobi, Venetian Green, rare, 4" h 525.00
#7662 Majesty, Randall Blue, 4" h................................750.00
#7662 Majesty, Spanish Red, 4" h 395.00
#7690 Monroe, Ritz Blue, 7" h, rare 1,200.00
#7949 Bertonna, DanubeLine, 8-3/4" h.........................835.00
#7951 Stafford, Crystal w/#25 gold band, 3-1/8" h 685.00
#9923 Colonial, Burgundy, 2-pc hurricane, 8-1/2" h.....130.00
#9923 Colonial, Pineapple, 2-pc hurricane, 8-1/2" h 140.00

Candy Jar
#14 Edmond, Danube Line, #4 cover, rare, 8-1/2" h.......625.00
#14 Guilford, Genova Line, #3 cover, 10-3/4" h..........500.00
#15 Lisbon, Crystal w/#734 American Beauty etch, #2 cover, 8-1/2" h 525.00
#16 Rachel, Crystal, Pandora cutting, 6" h 385.00
#71 Jupiter, Steel Blue, 6" h...95.00
#108 Bethann, Topreen Line, 5" h.................................595.00
#127 Yorktown Steel Blue, 7-1/2" h.................................75.00
#200, Mansfield, Burgundy matte, 12" h.......................195.00
#1114 Jerome, Bristol Blue, 11-1/2" h...........................135.00
#1212 Michael, Spanish Red, Crystal finial, 5-1/2" h.... 1,000.00
#2938 Helga, Anna Rose, Meadow Green finial, 5" h... 1,500.00
#7643-1 Alexandra, Randall Blue/Crystal Duo-Tone, 5" h...825.00
#9949 Christmas Tree, Crystal, 4 part stack jar, 11" h.... 140.00
#9952 Palace, Ruby, 6-12" h...60.00

Champagne
#7565 Astrid, American Beauty etch, 6 oz....................45.00
#7577 Venus, Ritz Blue, Pillar Optic, 5-1/2 oz...............55.00
#7606-1/2 Athena, Ebony filament, #777 Baden etch, 7 oz..75.00
#7621 Ringer, Anna Rose, 7 oz 65.00
#7621 Ringer, Aquamarine, 6 oz 55.00
#7623 Pygon, D.C. Thorpe satin open stem, 6-1/2 oz.... 165.00
#7630 Ballerina, #757 Elizabeth etch, 6 oz..................55.00
#7640 Art Moderne, Ebony open stem, 5 oz 85.00

#7643 Golf Ball, 5-1/2 oz, Ritz Blue..............................55.00
#7643 Golf Ball, 5-1/2 oz, Spanish Red 50.00
#7643 Golf Ball, 5-1/2 oz, Stiegel Green......................50.00
#7660 Empress, Spanish Red, 6 oz..............................48.00
#7664 Queen Anne, Azure, #758 Sunrise Medallion etch, 6-1/2 oz..95.00
#7678 Old English, 6-1/2 oz, Ritz Blue..........................52.00
#7678 Old English, 6-1/2 oz, Spanish Red 45.00
#7678 Old English, 6-1/2 oz, Stiegel Green...................40.00
#7705 Hopkins, Toulon gold decor, 5 oz 145.00
#7860 Lawton, Azure, Festoon Optic, 5 oz 50.00

Cocktail
Chanticleer, Pink Champagne bowl, 4 oz.....................45.00
Mai Tai, Topaz stem, 4 oz...50.00
Old Crown, 6-1/4" h, 5-1/2 oz..85.00
#7577 Venus, Anna Rose, Palm Optic, 3 oz 38.00
#7577 Venus, Azure, Palm Optic, 3 oz 38.00
#7577 Venus, Venetian Green, Palm Optic, 3 oz.........35.00
#7586 Napa, Azure, Festoon Optic, 3-1/2 oz...............48.00
#7620 Fontanne, Ebony filament, #781 Fontinelle etch, 3-1/2 oz...135.00
#7630 Ballerina, #765 Springtime etch, 3 oz 45.00
#7643 Golf Ball, 3-1/2 oz, Ritz Blue...............................42.00
#7643 Golf Ball, 3-1/2 oz, Spanish Red 42.00
#7643 Golf Ball, 3-1/2 oz, Stiegel Green.......................42.00
#7654-1/2 Legacy, Spanish Red, 3 oz...........................45.00
#7654-1/2 Legacy, Manchester Pheasant Silk Screen, 3-1/2 oz...185.00

Compote
#201 Inverness, Meadow Green, Peacock Optic, 4-1/2" d, 7-1/2" h...155.00
#203 Marietta, Ruby, 9-1/2" h...5.00
#206 Colette, Burgundy, 7-1/2" h....................................65.00
#7556 Helena, low with cover, Crystal, Snowberry cutting, 4-1/2" d...265.00
#7556 Toledo, high with cover, Crystal, Forever cutting, 4-1/2" d...315.00
#7620 Rarey, Spanish Red bowl, 6" d, 6-1/2" h 255.00
#7654 Reverse Twist, Aquamarine, 6-1/2" d, 6-3/4" h 195.00

Cordial
788-1/2 Roanoke, Spanish Red, 1-1/2 oz 50.00
7565 Astrid, Anna Rose, #734 American Beauty etch, 3/4 oz...155.00
7570 Horizon, #735 Richmond etch, 1 oz.....................55.00
7577 Venus, Anna Rose, #743 Bramble Rose etch, 1-1/2 oz...165.00
7587 Hanover, #733 Virginia etch w/#25 Minton Gold band, 1 oz..55.00
7643 Golf Ball, 1-1/2 oz, Pastels 55.00
7643 Golf Ball, 1-1/2 oz, Ritz Blue................................58.00
7643 Golf Ball, 1-1/2 oz, Spanish Red 55.00
7643 Golf Ball, 1-1/2 oz, Stiegel Green.........................52.00
7617 Brilliant, Ritz Blue, 1-1/2 oz 135.00
7617 Brilliant, Spanish Red, 1-1/2 oz 135.00
7640 Art Moderne, Ebony stem, 1-1/2 oz 135.00
7654 Lorna, Nantucket etch, 1-1/2 oz..........................105.00
7660-1/2 Empress, Spanish Red, 1-1/2 oz 87.50
7668 Galaxy, Mayfair etch, 1-1/2 oz 87.50
7668 Galaxy, #810 Sears' Lace Bouquet etch, 1-1/2 oz.... 50.00
7673 Lexington, Ritz Blue filament, #790 Fairwin etch, 1-1/2 oz...165.00
7909 Blake, Spanish Red filament, 1 oz 65.00

Goblet
300 Festival, Gloria Blue, 8 oz......................................35.00
7565 Astrid, #734 American Beauty etch, punty cut stem, 10 oz..65.00

March, 1933

5

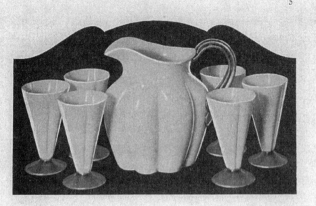

An Interpretation of Old Morgantown Quality in
MILK GLASS

There's a triple sales appeal in the new Beverage Set, No. 20069, pictured above. While the set is blown, of course, in the finest of opal milk glass —so very popular now—the ingenuity of the designers is apparent in two additional qualities. A dash of Ritz Blue in the tumbler feet and pitcher handle increases the charm of the white. And the simple, distinctive "melon" shape makes the tumblers easy to grasp.

The "melon" set is available also in solid Stiegel Green, Ruby, or Ritz Blue. You'll like the prices.

MORGANTOWN GLASS WORKS
Morgantown, W. Va.

The simple lines of this opal milk glass bowl and quaint candlestick reveal unusual decorative character. Both articles are trimmed with edges of Ritz Blue.

BOWL, WHITE AND BLUE   CANDLESTICK, WHITE AND BLUE

Old Morgantown
GLASSWARE

HOLLYHOCK

MARTHA WASHINGTON SWAN DRESDEN MARINE

BETTER BATHROOM SETS
3 bottles and 1 tumbler per set, same decoration, in white box. Bottles round, with flat shoulders marked *Astringent, Lotion, Toilet Water.* Priced to sell.

Tell our advertisers you saw it in THE CROCKERY AND GLASS JOURNAL

Ad, No. 20069, milk glass. The Crockery and Glass Journal, March 1933.

7568 Horizon, #735 Richmond etch, 10 oz.................48.00
7577 Venus, Anna Rose, Azure foot, Tulip Optic, 9 oz... 145.00
7577 Venus, Anna Rose, Palm Optic, 9 oz 55.00
7577 Venus, Anna Rose, #743 Bramble Rose etch,
      9 oz...125.00
7577 Venus, Crystal, #743 Bramble Rose etch, 9 oz....80.00
7589 Laurette, #735 Richmond etch, 9 oz 42.00
7604-1/2 Heirloom, 14-K Topaz, #751 Adonis etch,
      9 oz...125.00
7614 Hampton, Anna Rose stem, Queen Louise Silk Screen,
      9 oz...225.00
7614 Hampton, Golden iris, Virginia etch, 9 oz 65.00
7617 Brilliant, Ritz Blue, 10 o z.................................125.00
7617 Brilliant, Spanish Red, 10 oz 95.00
7623 Pygon, D. C. Thorpe satin open stem, 9 oz 185.00
7624 Paragon, Ebony open stem, 10 oz....................200.00
7625 Paramount, Meadow Green open stem, #765 Spring-
      time etch, 10 oz 165.00
7630 Ballerina, Aquamarine/Azure, Yukon cutting,
      10 oz...120.00
7636 Square, open stem, 9 oz 245.00
7637 Courtney, D.C. Thorpe satin open stem, 9 oz....195.00
7638 Avalon, Venetian Green, Peacock Optic, 9 oz.....45.00
7640 Art Moderne, Ritz Blue, Crystal open stem, 9 oz... 155.00
7643 Golf Ball, 9 oz, Alabaster................................150.00
7643 Golf Ball, 9 oz, Pastels 55.00
7643 Golf Ball, 9 oz, Ritz Blue..................................58.00
7643 Golf Ball, 9 oz, Spanish Red 55.00
7643 Golf Ball, 9 oz, Stiegel Green 52.00
7644-1/2 Vernon, Venetian Green, Pineapple Optic,
      9 oz...55.00
7646 Sophisticate, Picardy etch, 9 oz.........................65.00
7659 Cynthia, #746 Sonoma etch, 10 oz 68.00
7664 Queen Anne, #758 Sunrise Medallion etch, 10 oz....95.00
7664 Queen Anne, Manchester Pheasant Silk Screen,
      10 oz...275.00
7678 Old English, 10 oz, Ritz Blue.............................55.00
7678 Old English, 10 oz, Spanish Red 55.00
7678 Old English, 10 oz, Stiegel Green 45.00
7690 Monroe, Golden Iris, Amber, 9 oz 80.00

Guest Set
  23 Trudy, 6-3/8" h
      Alabaster 175.00
      Anna Rose, Palm Optic 90.00
      Baby Blue 85.00
      Baby Blue carafe, India Black tumbler...................140.00
      Bristol Blue 125.00
      Jade Green..90.00
      Opaque Yellow carafe, India Black tumbler...........195.00
      Venetian Green, Palm Optic..................................95.00
  24 Margaret, 5-7/8" h
      Anna Rose, enamel decor...................................170.00
      Azure/Aquamarine, enamel decor 575.00
      Jade Green..185.00
      Golden Iris, pulled spout, handled........................425.00

Jug
  6 Kaufmann, Old Bristol line, 54 oz..........................1,500.00
  6 Kaufmann, #510 Doric Star Sand Blast, 54 oz.........275.00
  8 Orleans, #90 Starlet cutting, 54 oz........................315.00
  8 Orleans, #131 Brittany cutting, 54 oz.....................385.00
  14 Eiffel, #282 needle etch, 65 oz............................325.00
  33 Martina, #518 Lily of the Valley Sand Blast dec, 46 oz,
      7-piece set..585.00
  33 Rawsthorne, Anna Rose, Peacock Optic, 48 oz....465.00
  36 Bolero, Pomona Two-Tone Line, 54 oz 985.00
  37 Barry, Anna Rose handle and foot, Palm Optic,
      48 oz...390.00
  37 Barry, Zurich Two Tone Line, covered, 48 oz 860.00

303 Cyrano, #203 needle etch, 54 oz 385.00
545 Pickford Spiral, Amber, 54 oz 135.00
1933 LMX Del Rey, Randall Blue non-opaque, rare,
      54 oz...675.00
1933 LMX Ockner, Ice, 64 oz...................................210.00
1933 LMX Ockner, Seaweed, 64 oz...........................210.00
1962 Ockner, Crinkle Line, 64 oz, Amethyst..............145.00
1962 Ockner, Crinkle Line, 64 oz, Pink Champagne 115.00
1962 Ockner, Crinkle Line, 64 oz, Pink Champagne,
      frosted 165.00
1962 Ockner, Crinkle Line, 64 oz, Topaz Mist 95.00
1962 San Juan, Crinkle Line, Amethyst, Tankard,
      64 oz...125.00
1962 Tijuana, Crinkle Line, Peacock Blue, Juice/Martini,
      34 oz...80.00
7622-1/2 Ringling, 54 oz, Golden Iris.........................650.00
7622-1/2 Ringling, 54 oz, Randall Blue 535.00
7622-1/2 Ringling, 54 oz, Spanish Red 695.00
9844 Swirl, Burgundy, 54 oz.....................................195.00
20069 Melon, Alabaster, Ritz Blue trim 1,250.00

Plate, #1500
  Alexandrite, #776 Nasreen etch, dessert, 7" d 135.00
  Anna Rose, #734 American Beauty etch, dessert, 7" d ... 55.00
  Anna Rose, #743 Bramble Rose etch, salad/luncheon,
      8-1/2" d 55.00
  Crystal, Hollywood Platinum/Red band decor, torte,
      14" d 395.00
  Crystal, #734 American Beauty etch, dessert, 7" d 45.00
  Crystal, #810 Sear's Lace Bouquet etch, dessert, 7" d.... 25.00
  Meadow Green, #737 Victoria Regina decor, dessert,
      7" d 22.00
  Ritz Blue, Vernay decor, dessert, 7-1/2" d 135.00
  Old Bristol, dessert, 7-1/4" d 185.00
  Stiegel Green, salad/luncheon, 8-1/2" d 55.00
  14-K Topaz, #751 Adonis etch, dessert, 7" d 58.00
  14-K Topaz, Carlton Madrid, liner, 6" d.......................35.00
  14-K Topaz, Carlton Madrid, dessert, 7-1/4" d 50.00
  14-K Topaz, #776 Nasreen etch, salad, 7-3/4" d 55.00

Sherbet
  #1962 Crinkle, 6 oz, Pineapple 32.50
  #1962 Crinkle, 6 oz, Pink...24.00
  #1962 Crinkle, 6 oz, Ruby...27.50
  #3011 Montego, Gypsy Fired, 6-1/2 oz.......................38.00
  #3011 Montego, Peacock Blue, 6-1/2 oz.....................24.00
  #7620 Fontanne, #781 Fontinelle etch, 6 oz 165.00
  #7640 Art Moderne, Ritz Blue, 5-1/2 oz.....................65.00
  #7643 Golf Ball, 5-1/2 oz, Pastels 35.00
  #7643 Golf Ball, 5-1/2 oz, Ritz Blue...........................45.00
  #7643 Golf Ball, 5-1/2 oz, Spanish Red 38.00
  #7643 Golf Ball, 5-1/2 oz, Stiegel Green 35.00
  #7646 Sophisticate, Picardy etch, 5-1/2 oz 48.00
  #7654 Lorna, Meadow Green stem, #766 Nantucket etch,
      5-1/2 oz..55.00
  #7654-1/2 Legacy, Manchester Pheasant Silk Screen,
      6-1/2 oz...135.00
  #7668 Galaxy, #787-1/2 Mayfair etch, 5-1/2 oz 30.00
  #7690 Monroe, Old Amethyst, 6 oz.............................85.00
  #7690 Monroe, Spanish red, 6 oz 70.00
  #7780 The President's House, 6 oz 20.00

Tumbler
  #1928 Ivy, Stiegel Green, ice tea, 15 oz 75.00
  #1962 Crinkle, Amberina, flat water, 10 oz 120.00
  #1962 Crinkle, India Black, flat juice, 6 oz 85.00
  #7621 Ringer, Spanish Red, ice tea, 14 oz 65.00
  #7622 Bracelet, Ritz Blue, ice tea, 14 oz 85.00
  #7664 Queen Anne, Aquamarine/Azure, #758 Elizabeth
      etch, 11 oz...115.00
  #7668 Galaxy, Pink Champagne, ftd, 9 oz 22.00

#7668 Galaxy, #778 Carlton etch, 9 oz...........................22.00
#7703 Sextette, Old Bristol, ftd tea, 11 oz...................185.00
#9051 Zenith, Venetian Green, Peacock Optic, bar,
    2 oz..45.00
#9074 Belton, Golden Iris, #733 Virginia etch, 12 oz......48.00
#9074 Belton, Primrose, Vaseline, Pillar Optic, 9 oz...125.00
Vase
#12 Viola, Rainbow Line, Spiral Optic, 8" d.................120.00
#24 Roseanne, Baby Blue, Allegheny Bird Screen Print,
    10" h..350.00
#25 Olympic, #734 American Beauty etch, 12" h 650.00
#26 Catherine 10" bud, Anna Rose, #758 Sunrise Medallion
    etch..745.00
#26 Catherine 10" bud, Azure, #758 Sunrise Medallion
    etch..270.00
#26 Catherine 10" bud, Jade Green, Enamel Floral Decor,
    crimped 250.00
#35-1/2 Electra, Continental Line, Old Amethyst, 10"... 1,000.00
#43 Encino, Peacock Blue, 10-1/4" h......................1,255.00
#53 Serenade 10" bud, Opaque Yellow......................430.00
#53 Serenade 10" bud, Spanish Red..........................425.00
#53 Serenade 10" bud, Venetian Green, #756 Tinker Bell
    etch..595.00
#54 Media, Golden Iris, Pillar Optic, 10" 225.00
#67 Grecian, Ebony, Saracenic Art Line, 6" h..........1,200.00
#73 Radio, Ritz Blue, 6"..895.00
#90 Daisy, Crystal, Green and White Wash, 9-1/2" w 450.00
#91 Lalique, Crystal Satin, 8-1/4" h 650.00
#1933 Gaydos, LMX Seaweed, 6-1/2" 785.00
#7261 Ringer, 8" flip vase, Aquamarine/Azure 295.00
#7621 Ringer, 10" bud, Opaque Yellow......................475.00
#7643 Kennon, Ivy Ball Vase, Ritz Blue, 4" 195.00
Wine
#7565 Astrid, Anna Rose, #734 American Beauty etch,
    3 oz..125.00
#7560 Horizon, #735 Richmond etch, 3 oz...................55.00
#7577 Venus, Anna Rose, #743 Bramble Rose etch, 3-1/2
    oz...145.00
#7587 Hanover, #733 Virginia etch w/#25 Minton Gold band,
    3 oz..45.00
#7643 Golf Ball, 3 oz, Alabaster.................................145.00
#7643 Golf Ball, 3 oz, Pastels 60.00
#7643 Golf Ball, 3 oz, Ritz Blue 65.00
#7643 Golf Ball, 3 oz, Spanish Red 60.00
#7643 Golf Ball, 3 oz, Stiegel Green.............................55.00
#7617 Brilliant, Ritz Blue, 2-1/2 oz 120.00
#7640 Art Moderne, ebony stem, 3 oz........................145.00
#7654 Lorna, Nantucket etch, 3 oz...............................85.00
#7660-1/2 Empress, Spanish Red, 3 oz.......................85.00
#7662 Majesty, Spanish Red, 3-1/2 oz 85.00
#7668 Galaxy, #810 Sears' Lace Bouquet etch,
    2-1/2 oz..48.00
#7673 Lexington, Ritz Blue filament lament, #790 Fairwin
    etch, 3 oz..135.00
#7693 Warwick, Stiegel Green, 2-1/2 oz......................55.00
#7720 Palazzo, Violet, 3-1/2 oz 120.00
#7721 Panama, Sharon decor, 3 oz............................225.00
#8445 Plantation, Lotus Green, 3 oz 125.00
#8446 Summer Cornucopia, Copen Blue bowl, 3 oz....325.00

MOSER GLASS

History: Ludwig Moser (1833-1916) founded his polishing and engraving workshop in 1857 in Karlsbad (Kar-

lovy Vary), Czechoslovakia. He employed many famous glass designers, e.g., Johann Hoffmann, Josef Urban, and Rudolf Miller. In 1900, Moser and his sons, Rudolf and Gustav, incorporated Ludwig Moser & Söhne.

Moser art glass included clear pieces with inserted blobs of colored glass, cut colored glass with classical scenes, cameo glass, and intaglio cut items. Many inexpensive enameled pieces also were made.

In 1922 Leo and Richard Moser bought Meyr's Neffe, their biggest Bohemian art glass rival. Moser executed many pieces for the Wiener Werkstätte in the 1920s. The Moser glass factory continues to produce new items.

References: Gary Baldwin and Lee Carno, *Moser—Artistry in Glass*, Antique Publications, 1988; Gary Baldwin, *Moser—Artistry in Glass, Second Edition*, Antique Publications, 1997; Mural K. Charon and John Mareska, *Ludvik Moser, King of Glass*, published by author, 1984; Jan Mergl and Lenka Pankova, *Moser 1857-1997,* Austrian Publisher, English version distributed to Eaton's Glass Books, (http://glassbooks.com), 1997.

Basket, 5-1/2" h, green malachite ground, molded cherubs dec,
    pr 800.00
Bell, 5-1/2" h, cranberry cut to colorless, gold scrolling, orig
    clapper 110.00
Beverage Set, 10-1/4" h, frosted and polished smoky topaz decanter, 4 cordials, molded nude women, 5 pc set.... 265.00
Bowl
7-1/4" d, 5-5/8" h, opalescent pink shaded ground, multicolored enameled oak leaves and foliage, applied lustered
    acorns, sgd in gold on base 1,200.00
8" d, sapphire blue ground, colorless applied feet, enameled
    and gilt floral dec, script sgd "Moser"....................200.00
Box, cov
3-3/8" h, circular, deep purple ground, gold enameled fauns
    and maidens, fitted cov, four ball feet, etched "Made in
    Czechoslovakia Moser Karlsbad" 1,200.00
4-1/2" l, red ground, enameled blue and white floral motif, gilt
    highlights 550.00
6" d, 3-3/4" h, cranberry ground, white enameled woman carrying cornucopia and grapes, gold enameled vine and
    berries 650.00
Cabinet Vase, 2" h, 2-1/2" w, bulbous, citron green ground, applied brass rim, three black glass acorns, gold and yellow
    florals and leaves, three flying insects, sgd "Moser Carlsbad" under base 200.00
Calling Card Holder
Cranberry ground, turquoise jewels, gold prunts, four scrolled
    feet 375.00
Crystal ground, two multicolored enameled birds of paradise
    in center, bird on ruffled rim 225.00
Centerpiece
5" x 9", green ground, intaglio cut flowers...................425.00
11" d oval bowl, intaglio, emerald green shading to clear
    ground, sgd...215.00
Chalice, cov, 9-1/2" h, amber and colorless ground, faceted,
    central landscape frieze, gold leaves outlined in white,
    gold and black dots, white dotted blossoms, neck, base,
    and orange stopper heavily gold encrusted 425.00
Cologne Bottle
7-1/2" h, 3-1/2" d, amethyst shaded to clear ground, deep intaglio cut flowers and leaves, orig stopper, sgd ...695.00
9-1/2" h, deep cobalt blue ground, enameled floral scene,
    matching stopper, script engraved "Moser" 225.00

Compote

4" h, 8-1/4" d, hollow base, pale amber ground, electric blue rigaree and four applied dec, int. deck of twelve painted leaves, brown branches, gold leaves, white cherries, matching branch on base 650.00

9-1/2" h, quatraform, crystal ground, gilt enameled heavy scrollwork reserves, matching dec on pedestal foot, crystal stem, pr..400.00

Cordial, 1-3/8" h, cranberry bowl, colorless stem, multicolored enameled flowers, bee, and insect dec on base.....100.00

Cruet, 13" h, pigeon blood ground, eleven raised acorns, raised enameled tracery branches and dragonfly, trefoil spout, applied handle, orig paper label.........................1,850.00

Cup and Saucer, amber ground, gold scrolls, multicolored enameled flowers 295.00

Decanter

10-1/2" h, ovoid, flattened sides, colorless ground.....125.00

11-1/2" h, 4-1/4" d base, cranberry and white opaque overlay, six opaque petal shapes with gold tree and branch design, gilt dec around each petal, top formed by six cut petals edged in gold, gold vertical lines, tulip-shaped stopper with six opaque white petal shapes with conforming dec, c1880 ....1,375.00

Decanter, Underplate, 10" h, white overlaid in pink, cut to crystal, thumbprints and leafage, script engraved "Moser" ... 275.00

Demitasse Cup and Saucer, amber shading to white, enameled gilt flowers 100.00

Ewer

5-3/4" h, 2-3/4" d, crystal shaded to gold ground, multicolored enameled flowers and green leaves, pedestal base, unsgd 285.00

9" h, cov, horn shape, aquamarine ground, all over gold leaves, vines and flowers, pedestal base 925.00

10-3/4" h, cranberry ground, gilt surface, applied acorns and clear jewels...2,000.00

Fernery, 7" d, deep amethyst ground, inverted thumbprint, enameled florals, script sgd "Moser".....................450.00

Finger Bowl, matching underplate

6" d bowl, 7" d underplate, scalloped, shaded pink to lavender ground, gold, silver, and blue enameled Arabesque dec, white petit-point dec.....................................975.00

6-1/2" d bowl, Alexandrite ground, sgd 250.00

Flask, 7-1/2" l, powder horn shape, deep cranberry ground, multicolored enameled fern dec, brass spigot, fittings and orig chain 775.00

Goblet

4-1/2" h, cranberry ground, enameled, gold overlay, wheel cut design, ftd stem with gold overlay on base, 6 pc set..500.00

5-1/4" h, 3-1/2" d, colorless ground, gold overlay, relief amethyst sq blocks 225.00

8" h, cranberry ground, Rhine-style, enameled oak leaves, applied acorns, 4 pc set 1,800.00

Ice Cream Set, master bowl and four serving bowls, clear shading to gold ground, mermaid relief, gilt highlights...........395.00

Jar, cov, 10-3/4" h, goblet form, amber ground, polished faceted panels, conforming inset cov...............................315.00

Juice Tumbler, colorless ground, enameled florals, lace-type trim, 83 applied glass jewels..................................235.00

Lamp, 18" h, 7-1/4" w globe, cranberry opaque ground, multicolored enamel floral dec, gilt scroll dec, finely cut pattern on globe and base, acid etched signature on base, c1920..4,800.00

Mug, 4-1/4" h, topaz colored crackle ground, heavy gold handle and base edging, four applied insects with polychrome dec 345.00

Nappy, 5" w, 1-3/4" h, pastel green, yellow, blue, and pink, four enameled foxes, applied loop handle, polished disc base...500.00

Pansy Vase, 14" h, colorless ground, multicolored dec ... 1,000.00

Perfume Bottle

4-3/4" h, pink-lavender Alexandrite ground, faceted panels, matching stopper, sgd in oval...............................275.00

5" h, emerald green ground, all over floral dec, orig stopper 275.00

6-1/2" h, 4-1/4" d, Malachite ground, molded bottle and stopper, slab polished sides and top 295.00

Pitcher

6-3/4" h, amberina ground, inverted thumbprint pattern, four yellow, red, blue, and green applied glass beaded bunches of grapes, pinched in sides, 3-dimensional bird beneath spout, allover enamel and gold leaves, vines, and tendrils...3,200.00

8-1/2" h, amber ground, multicolored enameled florals ...275.00

11-3/4" h, bright transparent blue ground, heavy gilding, enameled fern fronds, birds, and insects, applied salamander handle 2,400.00

Plate, 7-3/8" d, amber ground, gold dec 150.00

Pokal, cov, 8" h, cut, faceted, and enameled, amethyst body with cut panels, gold and high relief floral dec, wafer foot with cut stem 700.00

Portrait Vase, 8-1/2" h, colorless ground, multicolored portrait of woman, gold leaves, light wear........................... 450.00

Rose Bowl, 6" h, 6-1/2" d, colorless ground, outward flared ruffled top, all over gold enamel dec, vines, flowers, and lattice, c1858... 475.00

Scent Bottle

5" h, emerald green ground,, multicolored leaves and berries, ball stopper..195.00

11" h, cranberry ground, leaves, white and gold dec 400.00

Sherry, 4-1/4" h, crystal ground, gold and white beading, knobbed stem, wafer base.................................. 225.00

Sweetmeat Dish, round, cranberry ground, engraved, gold band 225.00

Toothpick, cranberry ground, colorless pedestal, cut, sgd ..145.00

Tumbler

3-1/2" h, octagonal, ruby cut to clear ground, gold dec... 85.00

4" h, green, red, and blue, elaborately dec with floral, scrolled, beading, and gild, some beads missing, 9 pc set...460.00

Urn, 15-3/4" h, cranberry ground, 2 gilt handles, studded with green, blue, clear, and red stones, highly enameled surface, multicolored and gilt Moorish dec............. 3,500.00

Vase

5-1/4" h, 2-5/8" w, light green ground, coralene beaded dec around top, gilt coralene leaf design, white enameled branches, blue dot enameled highlights, center 5-petal flower with 2 sprays of leaves, white enameled opaque scene of tree and mountains, between spray of leaves on front, c1890 ....500.00

6" h, flared vaseline goblet form, faceted, gold medial band of etched Amazon women, sq base inscribed "Moser Czecko/Slovakia Karlsbad" 420.00

6-1/2" h, cranberry ground, heavy applied dec of scrolls, abstract flowers, and butterflies, four ftd, #2208........950.00

7" h, paneled amber baluster body, wide gold medial band of women warriors, base inscribed "Made in Czechoslovakia-Moser Karlsbad" 550.00

7-3/4" h, long neck shading from emerald green shading to clear ground, bulbous base, gold and platinum floral dec, diamond point signature 375.00

8-1/4" h, 6-1/2" w, bulbous base, narrow neck, three applied rolled handles, blue ground, enameled dec of green and pink grasshopper, delicate pastel flowers, and leaves, round pink enameled circle with brown and turquoise beetle and spray of pink and blue flowers with green leaves, gilt dec, vertical stripe, enameled pink and white flowers, gilt and turquoise green leaves 1,200.00

9" h, cranberry ground, two gilt handles, medallion with hp roses, sgd...1,050.00

10" h, flared purple cylinder, broad medial band of etched griffins, urns, and swags, enameled in gold, polished pontil..375.00

10" h, heavy walled dark amethyst faceted body, etched and gilded medial scene of bear hunt, spear-armed men and dogs pursuing large bear..345.00

10" h, trumpet, red Venetian ground, heavy gold filigree surrounding central Greek Goddess Diana wearing clinging dress, one bare breast, standing next to buck, other side with Diana holding bird, standing next to doe 450.00

11" h, emerald green ground, intricately enameled fish, four applied pickerel, handles..900.00

11" h, stick, cranberry ground, enameled gold florals and scrolls, script engraved "Moser" 150.00

11-1/2" h, alternating blue and yellow bands, ivory enameled florals, script engraved "Moser".............................385.00

12" h, triangular baluster, ruby ground, gold enameled children dec..265.00

12-1/8" h, 3-7/8" w, flaring neck, stepped pedestal base, delicate gold all over fern and floral design on neck and body, 2-3/8" border with gold design, acid cutback dots above and below border, pink, white, purple, orange and magenta floral dec of pansies, bell flowers, mums, daisies and clematis, shaded green foliage all around base, orig paper label with design number, c1880 ......2,800.00

12-1/4" h, cobalt blue ground, large enameled florals and gold dec, script engraved "Moser" 220.00

12-1/2" h, cranberry ground, stylized gilt florals, script engraved "Moser" 275.00

12-1/2" h, green ground, six gold cartouche with jewels surrounded by seed pearls, gold filigree around neck and base, minor wear..300.00

12-1/2" h, 5-1/2" w, aventurine glass, deep emerald green, all over gold flecking, Art Nouveau style gold and painted enamel dec, sgd "Bares Moser Karlsbad".............275.00

14-1/2" h, cranberry shading to colorless, swirled body, enameled florals, script engraved "Moser".............175.00

15-1/2" h, clear and frosted ground, deeply etched thistles, inscribed "Moser/Karlsbad" 420.00

23-1/2" h, cranberry ground, enameled leaf surface, applied acorns, three dimensional eagle and bird, sgd "Moser," stand...8,250.00

Wine

Rainbow glass, funnel shaped cup, Inverted Baby Thumbprint pattern, enameled grapes and leaves dec, applied row of gold knobs around top 365.00

Turquoise shading to clear ground, all over gold leaf dec, heavy applied prunts...425.00

MOUNT WASHINGTON GLASS COMPANY

History: In 1837, Deming Jarves, founder of the Boston and Sandwich Glass Company, established the Mount Washington Glass Company in Boston, Massachusetts for George D. Jarves, his son. In the following years, the leadership and the name of the company changed several times, as George Jarves formed different associations.

In the 1860s, the company was owned and operated by Timothy Howe and William L. Libbey. In 1869, Libbey bought a new factory in New Bedford, Massachusetts. The Mount Washington Glass Company began operating again there under its original name. Henry Libbey became associated with the company early in 1871. He resigned in 1874 during the general depression, and the glassworks was closed. William Libbey had resigned in 1872 when he went to work for the New England Glass Company.

The Mount Washington Glass Company opened again in the fall of 1874 under the presidency of A. H. Seabury and the management of Frederick S. Shirley. In 1894, the glassworks became a part of the Pairpoint Manufacturing Company.

Throughout its history, the Mount Washington Glass Company made different types of glass including pressed, blown, art, lava, Napoli, cameo, cut, Albertine, and Verona.

References: George C. Avila, *The Pairpoint Glass Story,* Reynolds-DeWalt Printing, Inc., 1968; Edward and Sheila Malakoff, *Pairpoint Lamps*, Schiffer Publishing, 1990; Leonard E. Padgett, *Pairpoint Glass,* Wallace-Homestead, 1979; John A. Shuman III, *Collector's Encyclopedia of American Art Glass*, Collector Books, 1988, 1994 value update; *Pairpoint Manufacturing Company 1894 Catalogue Reprint,* Antique Publications, 1997; Kenneth Wilson, *American Glass 1760-1930: The Toledo Museum of Art, Volume I, Volume II,* Hudson Hills Press and The Toledo Museum of Art, 1994.

Collectors Club: Mount Washington Art Glass Society, P.O. Box 24094, Fort Worth, TX 76124-1094.

Museum: The New Bedford Glass Museum, New Bedford, MA.

Additional Listings: Burmese; Crown Milano; Peachblow; Royal Flemish.

Basket, mother of pearl satin

6-3/4" h, 6-1/2" w, deep pink shading to pale pink, Diamond Quilted pattern, applied frosted loop handle 200.00

9" h, 7" w, deep blue shading to pale white, Herringbone pattern, applied camphor edge, large twisted and frosted thorn handle 300.00

9-1/2" h, 5" w, shaded apricot pink to off white, Herringbone pattern, applied frosted loop handle......................150.00

9-1/2" h, 7-1/2" w, bright spring daffodil yellow shading to pale yellow, Herringbone pattern, ruffled edge, applied frosted loop handle with thorns 250.00

11" h, 11" w, deep yellow shaded ext. bright pink shading to deep red int., Diamond Quilted patterned, applied ruffled camphor edge, applied camphor thorn handle 500.00

Beverage Set, mother of pearl satin

Coralene, yellow sea weed dec, glossy finish, 9" h, bulbous water pitcher, three spout top, applied reeded shell handle, three matching 4" h tumblers, 2 blisters on pitcher, 3 pc set..750.00

Herringbone, 9" h bulbous water pitcher, 7" w, applied frosted handle, deep rose to deep pink to pink, to off white, enameled and painted white wild roses, green, brown, and gold leaves, stems, branches, and thorns, 4 3/4" h tumblers, damage to tumbler, 5 pc set...............1,750.00

Biscuit Jar, cov, 7" h, 5" w, raised swirl patter, white shading to beige, white enamel beading, pink and white enameled rose, orig silver plated fittings 200.00

Bowl
  4-1/2" d, satin, pink floral dec......................................95.00
  4-1/2" d, 2-3/4" h, Rose amber, fuchsia, blue swirl bands, bell tone flint..295.00
  10-1/2" d, blue satin int., chrysanthemums and leaves dec on ext., ruffled...280.00

Box, cov
  4" h, 7" d, colorless frosted ground, molded swirls, Royal Flemish type dec, yellow blossoms on leafy blossoms, central enamel outlined cartouche with single red bead, gilt-metal hinged rim, wear, no lining 2,645.00
  4" h, 7" d, colorless frosted ground, molded swirls, Royal Flemish type dec, Wavecrest style dancing flamingoes, gilt-metal hinged rim, wear, lining soiled.............3,450.00
  4-1/2" h, 6-1/2" d, opalware, mint green ground, deep pink roses, small red cornflowers, gold trim, blown-out floral and ribbon design, #3212/20............................1,750.00
  4-3/4" h, 6-1/2" d, opalware, soft beige ground, portrait of reclining colonial lady, base numbered "3212/90," repairs needed to hinge..1,100.00

Bride's Basket, opal pink and white ribbed bowl, SP Pairpoint frame, c1894..1,250.00

Calling Card Tray, 6-1/4" d, white lusterless, ruffled, flowers and two butterflies dec..65.00

Candlestick, 12" h, pink and white, hand painted florals, ftd SP Pairpoint holder..215.00

Caster Set, satin, multicolored enameled floral dec, SP Pairpoint holder..250.00

Collars and Cuffs Box, opalware, shaped as 2 collars with big bow in front, cov dec with orange and pink Oriental poppies, silver poppy-shaped finial with gold trim, base with poppies, white ground, gold trim, bright blue bow, white polka dots, buckle on back, sgd "Patent applied for April 10, 1894," #2390/128............................950.00

Compote
  5-1/2" h, 7-3/8" d, Napoli, colorless dish, reverse painted maroon with blue and yellow blossoms and leaves, gold highlights on int., silvered ribbed metal base mkd "Pairpoint B4702"..500.00
  11" h, 4-1/2" h, Ambero, thick bowl with reverse painted enameled grapes and leaves, thin layer of lemon flashing on base and wafer foot, rolled over rim, sgd "Ambero C".......950.00
  11" h, 10-1/4" d, Napoli, deep cranberry colored ground, painted and gilded dec of peaches, green leaves, naturalistic colors, Art Nouveau style silver plated Pairpoint base with elaborate poppy design, some orig gold wash on base, sgd "Pairpoint Manufacturing Company, New Bedford, Mass Quadruple Plate #B4704"............650.00

Cracker Jar, 9-1/2" h, 7-1/2" w, opalware, bright yellow ground, pink Oriental poppies, green leaves dec, blown-out floral and leaf design on base, orig metal hardware, base mkd "3930/230," cov mkd "Pairpoint"............................525.00

Creamer, 3" h, melon ribbed, enameled leaf and floral dec, SP handle and spout..200.00

Cruet
  Acid Cut, enameled blue and white flowers, soft yellow shaded throat, handle, and stopper............................1,950.00
  Acid Cut, white body, leaves and blue berries, yellow throat, handle, and stopper......................................1,950.00

Dresser Box, cov, 6-1/4" h, 8" w, painted satin finish ground shading from tan to gold and brown, large enameled poppies, buds, and leaves, shades of yellow, tan, brown, red, and white, top with large blown out central flower with gold highlights, hinged, orig emb silver plated trim, worn orig green satin lining, base numbered "4655/820"..................1,750.00

Ewer
  7-3/4" h, conical lusterless white ground, hand painted and

Jar, cov, apricot, white daisies dec, silver plated fittings sgd "Pairpoint," 3" h, $190.

enameled thistle blossoms and leaves, elongated pouring lip, applied reeded handle...............................195.00
  13" h, satin, shaded blue mother of pearl, white lining, applied frosted and twisted rope handle, white pedestal base..775.00

Flower Holder, 5-1/4" d, 3-1/2" h, mushroom shape, white ground, blue dot and oak leaf dec,.......................425.00

Flower Frog, 3" h, 5-1/2" d, mushroom shape, pedestal base, painted Burmese coloration, top dec with white, yellow, and tan daisies and leaves...................................250.00

Fruit Bowl, 10" d, 7-1/2" h, Napoli, solid dark green ground painted on clear glass, outside dec with pale pink and white pond lilies, green and pink leaves and blossoms, int. dec with gold highlight traceries, silver-plated base with pond lily design, 2 applied loop handles, 4 buds form feet, base sgd "Pairpoint Mfg. Co. B4704"........2,200.00

Humidor, 5-1/2" h, 4-1/2" d top, hinged silver-plated metalwork rim and edge, blown-out rococo scroll pattern, brilliant blue Delft windmills, ships, and landscape, Pairpoint.......950.00

Jewel Box, 4-1/2" d top, 5-1/4" d base, 3-1/4" h, opalware, Monk drinking glass of red wine on lid, solid shaded green background on cover and base, fancy gold-washed, silver-plated rim and hinge, orig satin lining, artist sgd "Schindler"..550.00

Jug
  6" h, 4" w, satin, Polka Dot, deep peachblow pink, white air traps, Diamond Quilted pattern, unlined, applied frosted loop handle..475.00
  6" h, 5-1/2" w, Verona, yellow, gold, and purple spider mums and buds, green leaves dec...............................450.00

Lamp, parlor, four dec glass oval insert panels, orig dec white opalware ball shade with deep red carnations, sgd "Pairpoint" base, c1890..1,750.00

Lamp Shade, 4-1/4" h, 5" d across top, 2" d fitter, rose amber, ruffled, fuchsia shading to deep blue, Diamond Quilted pattern..575.00

Miniature Lamp, 17" h, 4-1/2" d shade, banquet style, milk glass, bright blue Delft dec of houses and trees, orig metal fittings, attributed to Frank Guba............................795.00

Mustard Pot
  3-1/4" h, 1-3/4" w, melon ribbed, satin finish, yellow shaded to white ground, enameled pink apple blossom dec, green leaves, orig silver plated notched cover, brass bail handle..175.00

4-1/2" h, ribbed, bright yellow and pink background, painted white and magenta wild roses, orig silver-plated hardware..185.00

Perfume Bottle
5-1/4" h, 3" d, opalware, dark green and brown glossy ground, red and yellow nasturtiums, green leaves, sprinkler top..375.00
6" h, 2-1/4" w, sq, satin, woman in 1890s dress, script on back "Hout's Milk White March 19, 1894-50th Performance Boston Theatre Boston," orig threaded atomizer............. 175.00

Pickle Castor, deep cranberry satin ground, Optic Diamond and Inverted Thumbprint pattern insert, gold spider mums dec, ftd Simpson Hall frame, ornate engraved cov, orig silvering...700.00

Pitcher
5" h, 5" w, Verona, gold fish swimming among coral, rust, purple, and green sea plants, blue ground, green plants on handle, gold trim, spout and rim....................1,000.00
5-1/2" h, 3-1/4" d, Hobnail pattern, Burmese, deep salmon shading to bright yellow ground, acid finish, applied bright yellow handle...1,600.00
6" h, 3" w, satin, Diamond Quilted pattern, mother of pearl, large frosted camphor shell loop handle..............325.00
8" h, Verona, bulbous, maiden hair fern dec, gold highlights, applied colorless reeded handle..........................265.00

Plate
7" d, country scene of stone bridge, cottage, and lake, factory dec, orig paper label.......................................125.00
12" d, twin cupids, leaf and floral border....................125.00

Rose Bowl, 4" h, 5" d, satin, bright yellow, enameled red berries, pale orange leaves and branches, 8 large ribbed swirls...145.00

Salt and Pepper Shakers, pr, egg shape
Chicks, 2-1/4" h, 2-1/2" l, opal, hand painted floral dec, figural metal chicken head covers..............................450.00
Egg in Blossom...135.00
Holly dec, holder...385.00
Melon ribbed, shades from pink to white, yellow and white daisy dec, screw on pewter lid, 2" h, 2" w.............150.00
Tomato shape, opal glass, pink and yellow pansy dec, 2-1/4" h, 2-1/2" w...95.00

Salt Shaker, fig shape, 2-1/2" h
Mauve, forget-me-not dec, orig top.............................225.00
Pastel yellow ground, pine cone motif, orig top..........200.00
White ground, floral dec, orig top...............................225.00

Scent Bottle, lusterless white ground, reserve with couple, basket of flowers on reverse...200.00

Sugar Shaker
4" h, 3-1/4" d, egg shape, pastel pansies, pronged top..590.00
5-1/2" h, Inverted Thumbprint pattern, lighthouse shape, Bluerina, orig metal top...350.00

Syrup Pitcher, 7-1/2" h, opaque white, violets and leaves dec, silver plated lid, collar, and handle have oxidized, pitcher inscribed "351"...1,250.00

Toothpick Holder, satin glass, Brownie Policeman, billy club in hand, holding another Brownie by scruff of neck, sitting Brownie on back...575.00

Tumbler, 4" h, satin, c1880
Diamond Quilted, heavenly blue................................165.00
Diamond Quilted, shaded yellow to white...................165.00
Herringbone, shaded blue...165.00

Vase
5" h, 4" w, melon ribbed, ruffled tricorn top, mother of pearl satin, Alice Blue, white lining, applied frosted edge, 1880s..275.00
5-1/4" h, 4-1/2" w, bulbous, flaring neck, Lava, glossy black

Salt shaker, Egg and Blossom, 2-1/2" h, $135.

ground, numerous green, blue, white, and gray flux, one large burst bubble near surface...........................1,200.00
5-3/4" h, Lava, dense black vasiform, surface dec with irregular squares of blue, green, pink, and gray, applied reeded handles at shoulders, some bubbles at surface........... 2,100.00
5-3/4" h, Lava, flared black glass oval, surface dec with irregular patches of red, blue, pink, green, gray, and small opal white speckles, applied reeded handles at shoulders, some bubbles, minor surface scratches...............1,840.00
5-3/4" h, 4-1/4" w, satin, heavenly blue shading to white, white lining, hobnails, 4 fold, folded in-top.............675.00
6" h, 3-1/4" w, bulbous stick, satin, flaring rim, apricot shading to white, Diamond Quilted pattern....................375.00
6-1/4" h, 5-1/2" w, satin, melon ribbed, mother of pearl, Bridal White, muslin pattern, applied frosted edge, c1880... 425.00
6-1/2" h, satin, Alice Blue, pr..275.00
6-1/2" h, 3" w, satin, Raindrop, Bridal White, mother of pearl, applied frosted edge, pr.....................................550.00
6-1/2" h, 6" w, satin, bulbous, Diamond Quilted pattern, deep rose shading to pink, two applied frosted "M" handles with thorns, cut edge, c1880.................................750.00
8" h, Ring, black ground, gold storks in flight, gold floral dec, spoke bottom, pr...550.00
8" h, mother of pearl satin, Raindrop, butterscotch, applied camphor edge...375.00
8" h, trumpet, Napoli, pedestal, chrysanthemums and daisies dec inside ribbed vase and underside, gilt edges, trim, sgd, numbered...500.00
8" h, 7" w, bulbous, mother of pearl satin, Alice Blue, Muslin pattern, applied frosted edge, 3 petal top.............675.00
8-1/4" h, 5" w, satin, amberina coloration, mother of pearl Diamond Quilted pattern, deep gold diamonds, white lining, slightly ruffled top...1,250.00
8-1/2" h, 5" d at base, Napoli, int. dec in turquoise, blue, green, and rust, ext. outlined in gold, frog sitting in bulrushes dec, 8 vertical ribs, some paint loss on int........................975.00
9" h, 3-1/2" w at shoulder, mother of pearl satin glass, deep gold, Raindrop pattern sheet lining, applied tightly crimped camphor edge, c1880...........................285.00
9" h, 5-1/2" w, pink opalware, Delft windmill with person in front, gold trim top and base, Pairpoint..................725.00
9-1/4" h, 4-1/4" w, mother of pearl satin, shaded rose, Diamond Quilted pattern, ruffled edges, white lining, c1880, pr..875.00
9-1/2" h, 6" w, mother of pearl satin, shaded yellow to white, Diamond Quilted pattern, painted and enameled landscape design, white and blue floral dec.................150.00

10" h, Neapolitan Ware, yellow, purple, rust, and gold spider mums, green leaves, gold spider webbing on ext., sgd "Napoli," #880 ....1,450.00

11-1/4" h, gourd shape, 6" l flaring neck, satin, deep brown shading to gold, white lining, enameled seaweed design all over...550.00

11-1/2" h, Napoli, 1-1/4" mouth, int. painted bouquet of spring flowers, eight exterior swirling ribs delineated on int. with black dots, brilliant gold ext., each petal and leaf outlined, fine gold network, brushed gold highlights to crown-like top, sgd "Napoli 821".........................2,950.00

11-7/8" h, bulbous stick, Colonial ware, glossy white, gold dec, all over vine and berry dec, two wreath and bow dec at top, sgd, #1010 ....550.00

12-3/4" h, 5-1/2" w, Colonial ware, shaped like Persian water jug, loop handle on top, small spout, bulbous body, pedestal base, glossy white ground, pale pink and purple lilies, green leaves and stems, overlaid gold dec of leaves, stems, and daisies, sgd and #1022.....................2,200.00

17-1/2" h, hp floral dec, white satin glass, swirl ribbed tall cylinder body 400.00

18" h, Napoli, snipped and flared tricorn rim, elongated ribbed colorless oval body, hand painted chrysanthemum blossoms on int., gold tracery on ext., inscribed "Napoli 841" on base, some wear to gold, rim possibly retouched 635.00

MURANO GLASS

History: Murano, Italy, is the home of several interesting Italian glassmakers. The Barovier and Toso Studio and the Ermanno Nason Murano Studio are modern makers who produced glassware in the 1950s. The Venini Glassworks was established in 1925 by Paolo Venini and is currently operated by his descendants.

Venini Glassworks revived several old Venetian glass techniques, such as millefiori, and has also developed several new distinctive styles.

Principal designers of Venini Glassworks include Ludovico Diaz De Santillana, and the Finnish designer, Tapio Wirkkala, who served as art director of the firm for many years.

Modern Italian glassware is currently selling quite well in some of the major auction houses. Works by artists such as Ermanno Nason are realizing high prices.

Items made by the Barovier and Toso Studio are often identified by a signature which reads "Murano/Antica Vetreia/F 11: TOSO," and may even include a design or style number. Items made by Venini Glassworks may be engraved or acid stamped. Some are marked "Venini Murano, Made in Italy," or "Venini Murano, Italia."

Bowl
6" d, Cordonato Oro, ribbed colorless, gold and yellow inclusions, Barovier & Toso, c1953.................................225.00
9" d, 4" h, folded rim, round bowl with panels of stepped window squares of brilliant yellow and red outlined in white, sutured at each corner with black-aubergine dots, side label "Archimeded Seguso/Made in Italy/Murano".....690.00
9-1/4" l, leaf-shape, white on colorless filligrana internal design, figurative medial pattern, base stamped "Venini Murano Italia," Trya Lundgren design........................345.00
13-1/2" d, ruffled edges, swirling red and white striated pattern, orig label "Goodfriend, Italy. Handmade," attributed to Aurelliano Toso..120.00

Brandy Snifter, 12" h, fused transparent red, green, blue, and colorless stripes in diagonal design, cobalt blue pedestal stem and foot, design attributed to Fulvio Bianconi for Venini..1,725.00
Candlesticks, pr, 9-1/2" h, Soffiato, clear glass baluster form, domed circular foot, applied cobalt blue dec, Venini..800.00
Centerbowl, 18" d, broad shallow colorless irid bowl, bright blue rim wrap, molded dished pattern at center, Venetian Revival style 300.00
Charger, 22" d, shallow bowl, applied rows of stringing, wide rim, attributed to Zecchin Martinuzzi....................550.00
Figure
Bird, 6-3/4" h, 8" l, colorless swallow, latticino core and gold, bipartite pedestal foot, attributed to Barovier & Toso... 175.00
Clown, dark red body, orig sticker.................................75.00
Fish, 11-1/2" h, aventurine, black glass oval body, applied fish-face lips, eyes, and fins, round platform base inscribed "Salviani Murano" 260.00
Fish, 12-1/2" l, flat sided, opaque white cased with clear glass, internally dec with beige and turquoise stripes, aubergine glass eyes, acid stamped "VENINI MURANO ITALIA," orig paper label, designed by Ken Scott, c1962 ....650.00
Rooster, 8-1/2" h, multicolored striated dec, applied gilt glass dec, orig paper label, Fratelli Toso..............350.00
Fountain, attributed to Barovier and Toso, c1940
38" h, 26" d, pink ftd bowl with gold inclusions central pink and gold fixture supporting five intricately blown nude female figures with florets, bowl cracked and restored.......... 3,000.00
60" h, 28" h, sectional pedestal base with gold inclusions, supporting broad blue plastic basin with light fittings, central blue and gold fixture supporting five intricately blown nude opalescent female figures holding gold garlands alternating with striated rose flowerheads 9,500.00
Fruit, Cordonato Oro, two gourds and two squashes, internally dec, scalloped gold bands, applied stems, Barovier & Toso... 220.00
Hat, 13" l, 5" h, mottled dark navy blue body, white hat band, symmetrical red threading on curved brim........... 345.00
Lamp, table
11-3/4" h, red, white, and blue canes arranged in baluster form, fitted with electrical fixtures, circular paper label "Made in Italy," attributed to Fratelli Toso 260.00
24" h, figural glass lamp post, inebriated clown chased by fantasy dog, base inscribed "Cenedese Murano 1973," small fracture at dog's foot...................................345.00
Lamp Shade, hanging, Venini
14" h, cigar shape, orange ground, blue, green and red horizontal striped border 700.00
14" h, cigar shape, yellow ground, blue, green, and red horizontal striped border 700.00
14" h, waisted cylindrical form, thin stripes, cobalt blue, green, and red horizontal striped border 400.00
20" h, cigar shaped, white ground, blue, red, and green horizontal striped border 1,200.00
20" h, onion form, white ground, thin caramel stripes..... 700.00
Paperweight, 7-1/2" l, Neopolitico, stylized fish form, white stone dec, yellow eyes, designed by Ercole Barovier for Barovier and Toso, c1954, pr 400.00
Pitcher, 8" h, 5-1/4" w, blue, ribbed, applied flowers and handle... 1,200.00
Plate, 11" d, black aubergine with oro antico aventurine, six matching pcs of glass fruit, design by Ercole Barovier for 1934 Biennale... 320.00
Sculpture
6-1/4" d, face, Fucina Degli Angeli, freeblown fiery amber, corroso green-black surface, engraved signature and

"Alfo3" on reverse, designed by Max Ernest, from 1966 series 575.00

6-1/2" h, 14" d foot, Desert Bandits, whimsical cactus with etched and colored faces, arms raising holding wide removable sky bowl, among tumbleweeds and rabbit, base inscribed "Bandits in the Desert US of America 1952/Dis. Bruno Saeeti/Seguso Murano" 920.00

12" h, Apparenza, colorless head, applied turban ornament, burgundy colored masquerade mask with eye slits, button mouth, ruffled collard base, lower edge inscribed "Max Ernst" and below Ferro e Lazzarini - Murano," designed by Max Ernst, executed by Ferro-Lazzarini 1,035.00

13-1/2" h, portrait in red glass, applied blue eye and ear, raised on colorless columnar candlestick body base, etched and painted polka dot skirt, stockings, and black pumps, base engraved "Miro/Messega IVR Murano," design by Jean Miro, execution attributed to Ermanno Nason, chip on back corner of base 2,300.00

13-3/4" h, form of woman, hands on hips, anger in stance, black on white glass, mkd "Picasso" at lower edge, base engraved "Picasso IVR Mazzega Murano," design by Pablo Picasso, rigaree chip 2,530.00

29" h, 36" w, six black cylinder designs in style of Pablo Picasso, Joan Miro, Jean Hans Arp, Mark Chagall, Georges Braque, Jean Cocteau, raised upon Plexiglas mount with center green glass apparanza of Max Ernst inscribed at lower edge "Gailliano Ferro Murano 1955," attributed to Gailliano Ferro 5,175.00

Vase

6" h, Neopolitici, baluster, pulled dec in shades of gray, white, and black, Barovier and Toso, pr 300.00

7" h, intricate stepped window square of brilliant yellow and red outlined in white, sutured with black-aubergine at each corner, design attribute to Archimede Seguso 575.00

7-1/2" h, colorless oval body, twelve gold enhanced leaves suspended within, attributed to Ercole Barovier, Rilieve Aurati 980.00

7-1/2" h, 7-1/2" w, round, shades of dark and medium green interspersed with blue spiral swirls, narrow top opening 50.00

8" h, Pezzato Istanbul, flared body, purple, gray, colorless, and pale yellow patchwork squares, stamped "Venini Murano Italia," design by Fulvio Bianconi, c1952 ....6,900.00

8-1/2" h, Pezzato, flattened oval, fused red, blue, green, and colorless squares, some with vertical stripes, enhanced on ext. with gold foil surface dec, base inscribed "Vittorio Ferro '85," Bianconi design adapted by Vittorio Ferro 635.00

8-3/4" h, Pezzato, triangular form, undulating rim, red, blue, green, and clear patchwork, circular acid stamped "Venini Murano ITALY" 6,250.00

9" h, Fazzoletto Handkerchief, cased white ground, seafoam green int., orig paper label, designed by Fulvio Bianconi 500.00

9" h, Occhi, bulbed barrel shape, colorless and dark purple-aubergine patchwork in window gridwork, base stamped "Venini Murano Italia," designed by Tobia Scarpa, c1960 ....3,750.00

9-1/4" h, white opal sphere, two colorless spirals, inscribed "Barbini Murano 33" 175.00

9-1/2" h, Double Incalmo, medial band of black and red on white murrine, brilliant transparent green above, blue below, base stamped "Venini Murano Italia," designed by Riccardo Licata 1953-56 ....7,475.00

9-1/2" h, Spichi, flared oviform, irregular rim, alternating wide vertical bands of black, teal, yellow, and clear, designed by Fulvio Bianconi 7,000.00

9-7/8" h, six rows of fused black/red on white alternating murrine with transparent green glass above, blue below, designed by Riccardo Licata, c1953-56, Double Incalmo, base stamped "Veini Murano Italia," Venini sq paper label numbered 3835 ....7,200.00

10-1/4" h, Soffiato, flattened circular body, long tapered neck, circular foot, neck applied with ruffled collar, pale green, gold flecks 300.00

10-1/2" h, Apparenzia, multicolored and aventurine swirling canes between colorless and opaque white layers, folded asymmetrical rim, Fratelli Toso 425.00

10-1/2" h, Fazzoletto Handkerchief, cased yellow ground, white int., acid stamped "Venini Murano ITALIA," designed by Fulvio Bianconi 500.00

11" h, Archimede Seguso, oval glass body, netted white and amethyst square windows, arranged in progressive diagonal pattern 550.00

11" h, Spirali Vaso a Canna, fused transparent green and red alternating colorless diagonally striped filligrana, labeled and incised "venini italia," designed by Bianconi, c1983 ....220.00

11" h, 14" h, paperweight, cased green/yellow glass cone, colorless glass surround, solid ball foot, inscribed "Venini Italia Launa," one inscribed '83, the other '85, labeled, pr 690.00

11" h, 14" w, handkerchief, deep purple over white....100.00

11-1/2" h, deep red, crackled, applied clear ribbons along sides, heavy disc foot, Barovier & Toso, c1940 .....450.00

11-1/2" h, Incalmo, cylindrical, red base, clear body, irregular gunmetal waves, acid stamped "Venini Murano ITALY," partial orig paper label, designed by Thomas Sterns, 1962 ....4,000.00

11-1/2" h, Saturneo, freeblown bottle form, colorless glass internally dec by five double rows of teal green aqua bull's eye murrine separated by latticino white filigrana vertical rods highlighted by aventurine accents, Erocle Barovier, 1951 ....9,200.00

11-3/4" h, Incalmo, oval body, transparent cobalt blue banded with red, fused to black-speckled white cased to colorless, base inscribed "Tagliapeitra/Angelin by Effett International/Murano 1985/8/100," c1985 ....865.00

12-1/2" h, red cased and silver speckled bulbous body, multicolored latticino and millefiori canes, colorless rim wrap, medial rigaree, A.V.E.M. Studio 260.00

13" h, Veronese Soffiato, bulbous ftd body, blown light amber, attributed to Venini 1,300.00

13-1/2" h, Veronese Soffiato, bulbous ftd body, blown deep turquoise, attributed to Venini 800.00

14" h, Mosaic Tessuto, flared cylindrical form, slanted rim, gray ground dec with white zafirico patches, acid stamped "Venini Murano Italy" 6,000.00

14-1/2" h, heavy walled sommerso cylinder, cobalt blue within blush pink ext., polished base, attributed to Angel Seguso 275.00

15" h, 16" d, broad shouldered oval vessel of colorless glass, broad incalmo blue band, engraved and etched with Cocteau portraits colored and embellished, "Jean Cocteau" at side, inscribed "AVEM Murano" on base, in the style of Jean Cocteau, execution attributed to AVEM 1,725.00

16-1/2" h, Messa Filagrana, alternating spiral bands of latticino white and aubergine black, applied black angular handles, dark platform base, Murano Studio 290.00

17" h, Fasce Orizzontali, flared oval transparent body with brilliant red, blue, green, aubergine, and colorless stripes, base stamped "Venini Murano Italia," designed by Fulvio Bianconi 1953, minor water stain at base only 12,650.00

NAILSEA-TYPE GLASS

History: Nailsea-type glass is characterized by swirls and loopings, usually white, on a clear or colored ground. One of the first areas where this glass was made was Nailsea, England, 1788-1873, hence the name. Several glass houses, including American factories, made this type of glass.

Reference: Kenneth Wilson, *American Glass 1760-1930: The Toledo Museum of Art, Volume I, Volume II,* Hudson Hills Press and The Toledo Museum of Art, 1994.

Basket, 5-1/2" h, 5" w, pink loopings, white satin ground, applied frosted feet, applied frosted handle 385.00
Bell, 11-3/4" h, white, rose loopings...................................95.00
Bottle
    6-1/2" h, medium gray-blue ground, white loopings, pewter threading, pontil scar, cap missing, attributed to Germany, mid 18th C 1,750.00
    7-5/8" h, rect, beveled edges, medium sapphire blue ground, white loopings, pewter threads, pontil scar, attributed to Germany or Northern Europe, c1750 ....1,250.00
    8" h, gemel, flattened ovoid body, 2 necks, white casing, red, white, and blue loopings 400.00
    8-1/2" h, gemel, colorless ground, white loopings, sheared lip, pontil scar, 1860-80...200.00
    8-3/4" h, gemel, cranberry ground, white loopings, applied rigaree 275.00
Bowl, 4-1/4" d, 2-1/4" h, citron ground, narrow white looping, applied rigaree loop dec, rim, ground pontil..............200.00
Candlestick, 10" h, colorless, white loopings, folded socket rim, hollow blown socket drawn out to a double knop, bulb shaped stem, 2 additional knops, inverted cone shaped base, early 19th C 375.00
Cologne Bottle, 5-3/8" h, opaque white body, blue and cranberry loopings, colorless stopper with white, pink, and blue loopings, pontil scar, New England, 1840-60 ....485.00
Fairy Lamp
    5-1/4" h, 6-1/4" d, frosted blue, opaque white loopings, colorless Clarke insert...695.00
    6" h, blue shade, matching ruffled trifold rim base, colorless glass candle cup insert...750.00
    6-1/2" h, red, sweeping white loops, dome shaped shade, ruffled triangular base, colorless glass candle cup with ruffled edge, orig "Price's Royal Castle Night Light" candle..985.00
Finger Bowl, 4-1/4" d, ftd, colorless ground, swirled streaks of deep blue ad white, foot drawn from body, applied colorless handles imp with cherub's face.........................85.00
Flask
    6-1/2" h, 5" w, cranberry ground, white and deep pink feathering 150.00
    6-3/4" h, colorless ground, white loopings, flattened round body, short sheared lip, small rough pontil, attributed to South Jersey...185.00
    7-1/4" h, broad oval form, ruby red ground, white herringbone type loopings, applied double collared mouth, pontil scar 400.00
    7-1/4" h, opaque white ground, pink loopings, sheared lip, pontil scar, attributed to England, 1960-80............200.00
    7-1/2" h, 4-1/2" w, opal white ground, deep cobalt blue loops...250.00
    7-3/4" h, pocket, elongated teardrop form, milk glass ground, blue and rose loopings, sheared mouth, pontil scar...300.00
    8" l, colorless ground, white loopings, sheared lip, pontil scar, 1860-80 ....150.00

    8-3/4" h, pocket, teardrop form, teal green, profuse white loopings, sheared mouth, pontil scar.....................240.00
Lamp, 11-1/2" h, colorless ground, pink and white loopings on font and ruffled shade, applied colorless feet, berry prunt 2,500.00
Mug, 5-1/4" h, 3-5/8" d, colorless ground, white and blue loopings, cylindrical, tapering slightly to rim, applied colorless solid handle, rough pontil...................................... 375.00
Pipe, 18" l, white ground, red loopings, bulbous bowl, knopped stem.. 275.00
Pitcher
    6-1/2" h, 4" d, colorless ground, white loopings, ftd, solid applied base, triple ribbed solid handle with curled end, flaring formed mouth, attributed to South Jersey, c1840-60 ....1,200.00
    9-1/2" h, cranberry ground, thick white loopings, applied clear handle with five crimps, applied colorless handle with five crimps, applied colorless foot, pontil scar, attributed to South Jersey, c1840-50 ....4,100.00
Powder Horn
    11" h, colorless ground, blue and white loopings, tooled lip, pontil scar, ground lip, mid 19th C 125.00
    13" l, colorless ground, white loopings and red stripes, stand...250.00
Rolling Pin
    13-3/4" l, free blown, rose and white loopings, colorless ground, ground mouth, smooth base, 1850-80 .....220.00
    16-1/2" l, colorless ground, deep ruby loopings, 1883 English coin trapped inside, attributed to Nailsea district, England, 1880s 400.00
    18" l, colorless ground, pink and white loopings 265.00
Salt, open, 3-1/4" d, 1-1/4" h, colorless ground, white loopings, wide gauffered rolled rim, applied cobalt blue rim band, applied solid foot, polished pontil 450.00
Tankard, 7" h, aqua ground, white loopings, applied solid aqua handle, pontil scar, crack at upper handle attachment, attributed to South Jersey, mid-19th C..................... 425.00
Tumbler, white ground, blue loopings 120.00
Vase
    8" h, 5" d, cylindrical, flared mouth and base, colorless, white loopings, plain sheared rim, pontil, attributed to South Jersey..200.00
    9-3/4" h, medium blue ground, white loopings, hollow knop stem containing 1842 dime, applied foot, pontil scar, stem previously broken off and re-glued, attributed to Pittsburgh or South Jersey, 1840-50......................................625.00
    9-7/8" h, bulbous, flaring neck, ftd, colorless ground, spiraling white bands, applied colorless swagging, applied colorless baluster stem, thick round base, attributed to New England, 19th C 3,200.00
Witch Ball
    4-3/8" d, white ground, pink and blue loopings 450.00
    5-1/4" d, colorless ground, opaque white casing, red loopings, attributed to Pittsburgh 275.00
    16" h, matching ball and vase stand, colorless ground, white loopings, pontil scar, attributed to Pittsburgh or New Jersey, 1840-50..1,250.00

NASH GLASS

History: Nash glass is a type of art glass attributed to Arthur John Nash and his sons, Leslie H. and A. Douglas. Arthur John Nash, originally employed by Webb in Stourbridge, England, came to America and was employed in 1889 by Tiffany Furnaces at its Corona, Long Island, plant.

While managing the plant for Tiffany, Nash designed and produced iridescent glass. In 1928, A. Douglas Nash purchased the facilities of Tiffany Furnaces. The A. Douglas Nash Corporation remained in operation until 1931.

Reference: Kenneth Wilson, *American Glass 1760-1930: The Toledo Museum of Art, Volume I, Volume II,* Hudson Hills Press and The Toledo Museum of Art, 1994.

Bottle, 4-1/2" h, squatty, pinched sides, amber irid, green and amber irid striated feather dec, inscribed "LCT B1," c1890..1,250.00
Bowl
    5-1/4" d, inverted rim, leaf design, sgd 200.00
    7-3/4" d, 2-1/2" h, Jewel pattern, gold phantom luster 285.00
    13" d, Diamond Optic pattern, colorless ground, cranberry threads, wide rim..295.00
    15-1/2" d, Chintz amber, blue, and green opalescent, turned down rim...325.00
Candlestick
    4" h, Chintz ruby and gray, sgd 450.00
    4-1/2" h, irid blue, sgd and numbered 500.00
    5" h, Chintz blood red and silver dec...........................550.00
Champagne, 5" h, pale irid amber, shallow cup splitting to three stems continuing to domed circular base..............750.00
Cologne Bottle
    5" h, flaring bulbed base, Chintz wide pale green stripes separated by wide pale green stripes with thing blue centers, clear stopper with controlled bubble, sgd "Nash/1008?jj"..600.00
    6" h, cylindrical, Chintz paperweight stopper 275.00
Compote
    6" d, 2" h, fold over rim, Chintz, green-blue bowl, colorless pedestal foot, sgd 225.00
    7-1/2" d, 4-1/2" h, Chintz transparent aquamarine, wide flat rim of red and gray-green controlled stripe dec, base inscribed "Nash RD89" 865.00
Cordial, 5-1/2" h, Chintz, green and blue...........................95.00
Creamer, 4-1/4" h, pale orchid and green design, applied colorless handle 325.00
Dish, cov, 5" d, 2-1/2" h, internally molded leaf design, amber ground, lustrous gold irid, conforming cover, rim chips..260.00
Finger Bowl, 4-3/4" d, matching underplate, opalescent rays, cranberry rim, sgd..225.00
Goblet
    6-1/2" h, Chintz 185.00
    6-3/4" h, feathered leaf motif, gilt dec, sgd.................295.00
Perfume Bottle
    7-1/2" h, bulbous bottle shape over blown-in-mold apron, irid gold, conforming stopper with 7" l wand, sgd "Nash 523"...975.00
    7-7/8" h, blue and lilac rays, pale blue foot, silver-blue irid, orig pointed amber stopper...850.00
Plate
    4-1/2" d, irid amber, scalloped edge, sgd and numbered..325.00
    6-1/2" d, Spiral pattern, orchid and clear spirals, sgd 200.00
    8" d, Chintz, green and blue 195.00
Salt, open, 4" d, 1-1/4" h, irid gold, ruffled rim, sgd and numbered..350.00
Sherbet, bluish-gold texture, ftd, sgd, #417 ....275.00
Vase
    4-3/4" h, blue-gold irid, pedestal base, inscribed "Nash 644"...350.00
    5-1/2" h, Chintz, brilliant red oval, controlled black, brown, gray striped dec, base inscribed "Nash"...............865.00

Vase, ftd, irid gold, mkd "544 Nash," 4-1/8" h, $375.

    5-1/2" h, Chintz, brilliant red oval, controlled black, brown, gray striped herringbone dec, base inscribed "Nash," internal split in red glass layer, as made 175.00
    5-1/2" h, Chintz, deep rose red-red oval, alternating wide and narrow vertical silver luster stripes, base inscribed "Nash RD 66" 990.00
    5-1/2" h, Chintz, pastel, transparent oval, internally striped with pastel orange alternating with yellow chintz dec....... 175.00
    6-1/4" h, 3-1/2" d, trumpet shade, Chintz, sgd and numbered 375.00
    7-1/2" h, beaker, Chintz, blood red, sgd "Nash RD 1025" 475.00
    7-3/4" h, baluster, brilliant irid pumpkin, lemon-yellow int...3,500.00
    8-1/2" h, Chintz, green, brown, and gold flecks..........325.00
    9" h, Chintz, blood red and ray, ball shaped clear stem 475.00
    9" h, Polka Dot, deep opaque red oval, molded with prominent sixteen ribs, dec by spaced white opal dots, base inscribed "Nash GD154".......................................1,100.00
    9-1/2" h, green and gold irid body, colorless irid circular base..325.00
    12" h, trumpet shape, orange and yellow vertical stripes, inscribed "Nash 62AA" 450.00
    13-1/4" h, 4-1/4" w, hourglass shape, bright orange, cobalt blue vertical stripes, polished pontil......................350.00
Wine, 6" h, Chintz, pink and green................................. 175.00

NEW MARTINSVILLE VIKING

History: The New Martinsville Glass Manufacturing Company, founded in 1901, took its name from its West Virginia location. Early products were opal glass decorative ware and utilitarian items. Later productions were pressed crystal tableware with flashed-on ruby or gold decorations. In the 1920s, innovative color and designs made vanity, liquor, and smoker sets popular. Dinner sets in patterns such as Radiance, Moondrops, and Dancing Girl, as well as new colors, cuttings, and etchings were produced. The 1940s brought black glass formed into perfume bottles, bowls with swan handles and flower bowls. In 1944, the company was sold and reorganized as the Viking Glass Company.

The Rainbow Art Glass Company, Huntington, West Virginia, was established in 1942 by Henry Manus, A Dutch immigrant. This company produced small, hand-fashioned animals and decorative ware of opal, spatter, cased, and crackle glass. Rainbow Art Glass also decorated for other companies. In the early 1970s, Viking acquired Rainbow Art Glass Company and continued the production of the small animals.

New Martinsville glass predating 1935 appears in a wide variety of colors. Later, glass was made only in crystal, blue, ruby, and pink.

Look for cocktail, beverage, liquor, vanity, smoking, and console sets. Amusing figures of barnyard and sea animals, dogs, and bears were produced. Both Rainbow Art Glass and Viking glass are handmade and have a paper label. Rainbow Art Glass pieces are beautifully colored, and the animal figures are more abstract in design than those of New Martinsville. Viking makes plain, colored, cut and etched tableware, novelties, and gift items. Viking began making black glass in 1979.

References: Tom and Neila Bredehoft, *Fifty Years of Collectible Glass, 1920-1970*, Antique Trader Books, 1997; James Measell, *New Martinsville Glass, 1900-44*, Antique Publications, 1995; Hazel Marie Weatherman, *Colored Glassware of the Depression Era, Book 2*, Glassworks, Inc., 1982.

Manufacturer: Dalzell-Viking Glass, P.O. Box 459, New Martinsville, WV 26155.

Animal, crystal
  Bear, baby, sun colored 35.00
  Bear, mama 225.00
  Chick, baby 45.00
  Hen, 5" h, head down 45.00
  Horse, head up 90.00
  Horse, rearing 100.00
  Piglet, standing 145.00
  Polar Bear 50.00
  Rooster, large 80.00
  Seal, baby 70.00
  Squirrel on base 45.00
  Swan, Janice, 12" 55.00
  Tiger, head up 190.00
Ashtray
  4" d, fish 12.00
  5" d, skillet 15.00
Basket
  8-3/4" d, 5" d, Radiance, amber, ftd, 1937-38 .... 35.00
  14" h, sq, crystal 30.00
Bon Bon
  Janice, crystal 20.00
  Radiance, amber 15.00
Bookends, pr, crystal
  Cornucopia, 5-3/4" h 80.00
  Daddy Bear, 4-1/4" h 150.00
  Elephants, 5-1/2" h, #237 .... 200.00
  Lady's Heads 250.00
  Nautilus Shell 65.00
  Police Dog 85.00
  Ship 65.00
  Squirrels 120.00

Starfish 170.00
Wolfhound 90.00
Bowl
  5" h, Peach Blow, yellow-caramel shading to peach to beige, scalloped rim 60.00
  5" h, swan, sweetheart shape, emerald green, crystal handle 30.00
  5-1/4" d, 2-1/4" h, Muranese, peachblow, ruffled 165.00
  5-1/2" d, Meadow Wreath 10.00
  8-1/2" d, 3 toed, Moondrops, amber 25.00
  10" d, Janice, light blue, 3 ftd, cupped 75.00
  12" d, Janice, crystal 55.00
  12" d, Prelude etching, ftd 25.00
  12" d, Radiance, amber 40.00
  13" d, Radiance, ruby 70.00
Butter Dish
  Moondrops, cobalt blue 325.00
  Radiance, crystal, sterling silver overlay 110.00
Cake Plate
  Basket etching 20.00
  Hostmaster, amber 25.00
  Prelude etching 57.00
Candlesticks, pr
  #414 .... 40.00
  #4531, 6" h 40.00
  Hostmaster, 8-1/2" h, cobalt blue, sterling silver trim 40.00
  Janice, #4554, 5" h, red 60.00
  Prelude etching, 5" h, 1-lite, #4554 .... 130.00
  Moondrops, 4" h, unlisted brocade dec, #37/2, crystal ... 130.00
  Radiance, 2-lite
    #42, light blue, pr 230.00
    #4536, blue, pr 125.00
Candy Box, cov, Moondrops, 3-part, amber, etch #26 .... 160.00
Celery Tray
  Janice, #4521, 11" l, crystal 40.00
  Meadow Wreath, 10" l 15.00
Cheese and Cracker Set, Prelude etching 85.00
Cigarette Holder, cart shape 20.00
Cocktail Shaker, Hostmaster, c1935, red 80.00
Compote, 11" d, Radiance, crystal, sterling base 55.00
Console Bowl, Moondrops, ruby, winged 125.00
Console Set, 10-1/2" s swan-shaped center bowl, 4-1/2" h pr swan shaped candlesticks, amber bodies, crystal necks, c1940-60 .... 75.00
Cordial, 1 oz, Moondrops
  Amber, silver dec 25.00
  Cobalt blue, metal stem and foot 40.00
  Ruby 15.00
Creamer and Sugar
  Eagle, crystal 25.00
  Florentine, crystal 27.50
  Janice, light blue 65.00
Cup
  Hostmaster, 5-1/2" d, cobalt blue, c1935 .... 15.00
  Moondrops, ftd, red 14.00
Decanter
  Moondrops, amethyst, 10" h 65.00
  Roberto, evergreen, fan shaped crystal stopper 55.00
Goblet
  Hostmaster, cobalt blue 24.00
  Mt. Vernon, cobalt blue 20.00
  Prelude etching, crystal 28.00
Honey Jar, cov, Radiance, ruby 45.00
Iced Tea Tumbler, ftd, Prelude etching, crystal 15.00
Ice Tub, 5-1/2" h, Hostmaster, c1935
  Amber 40.00

Ad, Viking Cabbage Salad Set. China Glass Tablewares, December 1970.

Ruby 55.00
Juice tumbler, Moondrops, cobalt blue 18.00
Lamp Base, police dog, pink........................125.00
Luncheon Set, Janice, blue, twelve luncheon plates, cups, and saucers, two serving plates..................275.00
Marmalade, cov, Janice, crystal 25.00
Mayonnaise, cov, underplate, Radiance, amber..............25.00
Mug, Georgian, ruby......................................18.00
Nut Dish, Radiance, amber, two handles 10.00
Paperweight, pear, red, green stem 45.00
Perfume, heavy, tall stopper, applied swan handles.........50.00
Pitcher, Oscar, pink 125.00
Plate
  Florentine, 9" d, crystal...................................15.00
  Janice, 13" d, ruby, two handles 65.00
  Meadow Wreath, 11" d, crystal 20.00
  Moondrops, 9-1/2" d, green 25.00
  Prelude etching, 16" d......................................85.00
Powder Jar
  Cinderella Coach, crystal...........................35.00
  Diamond, three toes, frosted, lavender, celluloid lid 25.00
Punch Bowl, Radiance, black........................245.00
Relish
  Prelude etching, 4-part,   crystal, 8" d, sterling base 45.00
  Moondrops, 8-1/2" l, 3 toed, amber 12.00
  Radiance, blue, 3-part, #26 etch 65.00
Salad Bowl, 11" d, Wild Rose etching.............................25.00
Salt and Pepper Shakers, pr, Radiance, pink.................275.00
Server, center handle, Prelude etching 55.00
Sherbet, #34, jade green 12.00
Sugar, cov
  Florentine..15.00
  Meadow Wreath 12.00
  Moondrops, amber....................................10.00
Torte Plate, 15" d, Prelude etching 60.00
Tumble-Up, Volstead Pup, carafe and tumbler
  Crystal 65.00
  Pink..80.00
Tumbler
  Georgian, ruby, 9 oz 25.00
  Hostmaster, cobalt blue 10.00
  Moondrops, cobalt blue, 5 oz 24.00
  Moondrops, ruby...15.00
  Oscar, amber, 9 oz 12.00
Vanity Set
  Jade green cologne with black stopper, jade green power box with black lid, black tray......................215.00
  Judy, 3 pcs, green and crystal, cologne bottle, stopper, tray..95.00
  Thousand Eye, puff box and pr colognes.....................90.00
  #18/2, pink, puff box and two colognes, slight chips ...100.00
Vase
  Janice, 8" h, 3 ftd, flared, black...................................125.00
  Modern, pink satin..125.00
  Radiance, #4232, 10" h, crimped, etch #268, crystal 135.00
Whiskey
  Moondrops, 2 oz, amethyst............................20.00
  Moondrops, 2 oz, cobalt blue 16.00
  Mount Vernon, ruby......................................15.00

NORTHWOOD GLASS

History: The Northwood Glass Company was incorporated in 1887 in Martins, Ferry, Belmont County, West Virginia by Henry Helling, Henry Floto, William Mann, Thomas Mears, and Harry Northwood. Production started in early January 1888, with blown ware, consisting of lamp shades, tablewares, water sets, and berry sets. Harry Northwood was the designed and general manager and surely used the years of experience he had working with the former Hobbs, Brockunier, and La Belle Glass Works to develop new glass techniques and patterns. The Northwood Company soon became known for its numerous patterns and items, as well as the vivid colors and types of art glass it produced.

Harry Northwood was also responsible for obtaining several patents for glass manufacturing devices. In November of 1888, he obtained a patent for a speckled type of glassware. This technique was often used with colored grounds, such as cranberry and produced an innovative type of glassware known as spatter. Production reports of many types of colorful wares can be found. By April 1889, however, the directors dissolved the company and attempted to settle affairs. It appears from most written accounts that, although the products were wonderful, the sales force could not carry through. The Northwood Company reorganized as an Ohio corporation. Accomplished glassmakers continued to produce quality products and added fine examples of cased, satin, and agate type wares. Patterns requiring skilled workmanship such as Royal Ivy were developed and widely advertised.

By 1898, the Northwood Glass Company was beginning to feel pressure from the giant United States Glass conglomerate. Natural supplies were becoming more expensive; Harry Northwood even invested in a natural gas company in an effort to keep prices low. Plans to relocate developed and in 1892, incorporation papers were filed in Pennsylvania. Lawsuits related to the business began to shake its foundation as the company moved to Ellwood City, Pa. By 1898, the company was failing and closed late in the year.

Harry Northwood went on to the Indiana Glass Company, Indiana, Pa. His presence became quickly known as new products were developed, including some intricate pressed patterns to rival cut glass.

Northwood & Co. was founded in 1902 by Harry Northwood and Thomas Dugan in Wheeling, West Virginia. The first items produced by the new company were ornate tableware patterns as well as lemonade sets. Ironically, the company was located in the former Hobbs, Brockunier plant, where the young Englishman, Harry Northwood, held his first glassmaking job.

By 1907, H. Northwood & Co. was established as one of America's finest glassware manufacturers. Novelties and pressed patterns were produced in opalescent colors, as well as solid green, amethyst, and blue–some of which featured gold decorations. Carnival glass production began in 1908, but continued only until 1915. Despite its popularity, it was discontinued due to hard financial times. H. Northwood & Co. continued to pioneer glass formulas and produced a fine line of custard patterns as well as an imitation marble-type glass.

Harry Northwood died in 1919, and the company reorganized. Several new patterns and colors were added. Competition from companies such as Westmoreland, Fenton, and Imperial was becoming fierce and the company began to falter. By 1925, Northwood & Co. ceased production and the plant was closed.

References: Marion T. Hartung, Northwood *Pattern Glass In Color, Clear, Colored, Custard, and Carnival*, privately printed, 1969; William Heacock, James Measell, Berry Wiggins, *Harry Northwood: The Early Years, 1881-1900*, Antique Publications, 1990; —*Harry Northwood: The Wheeling Years, 1901-1925*, Antique Publications, 1992; Kenneth Wilson, *American Glass 1760-1930: The Toledo Museum of Art, Volume I, Volume II,* Hudson Hills Press and The Toledo Museum of Art, 1994.

Museums: The Chrysler Museum, Norfolk, VA; The Corning Museum of Glass, Corning, NY; The Toledo Museum of Art, Toledo, OH.

Additional Listings: See Carnival Glass, Custard Glass, Opalescent Glass, and Pattern Glass.

Basket
    4" h, white carnival, basketweave, eight sided, open handles, ftd, sgd 125.00
    4-1/2" h, 4-1/2" d, bushel basket shape, blue opalescent...140.00
    11-1/2" h, 12" w, deep red with pale orange cream color, bright shocking pink int. lining, applied crystal edges, four applied rosette prunts, four large thorn ribbed feet, double applied crystal rope handle, Victorian 1,250.00
Berry Set, master and six individual sauces
    Leaf Medallion pattern, cobalt blue, gold trim 315.00
    Memphis pattern, green...200.00
Biscuit Jar, cov, Cherry Thumbprint pattern, colorless, ruby and gold trim 150.00
Bon Bon, Stippled Rays pattern, carnival, blue.................60.00
Bowl
    Cobalt Blue, 6-1/2" d, gold highlighted florals and beaded pattern, gold on rim, sgd "Northwood" 50.00
    Satin, 4-1/2" h, 9" d, gold and pink stripes on white ground, white int., applied frosted crimped edge 500.00
    Vintage pattern, blue..50.00
Bud Vase, six-sided, pulled top, green, mkd 35.00
Butter, cov
    Cherry Thumbprint pattern, colorless 110.00
    Leaf Umbrella pattern, cranberry................................600.00
    Peach pattern, colorless, gold and red trim..................95.00
    Spanish Lace pattern, vaseline opal..........................445.00
    Springtime pattern, carnival, purple...........................215.00
    Venetian pattern, cobalt blue, gold trim, enamel dec.....135.00
Calling Card Tray, ftd, Opal, blue opalescent 40.00
Candlesticks, pr
    4-1/2" h, #636, blue irid stretch 55.00
    10" h, Chinese Red pattern 115.00
Candy Dish, cov
    #636, blue irid stretch, one pound size.......................70.00
    #659, russet stretch, half pound size..........................60.00
Celery Vase
    Block pattern, blue opalescent 55.00
    Leaf Mold pattern, cranberry 135.00
    Ribbed Pillar pattern, pink and white spatter................95.00
Cologne Bottle, Leaf Umbrella pattern, mauve, cased, orig stopper 275.00
Compote, Pearl and Scale pattern, green 80.00
Condiment Tray, Chrysanthemum Sprig pattern, custard, gold and color dec, script mark 450.00
Console Set, Chinese Red pattern, 9-1/2" d ftd compote, pr matching candlesticks 185.00
Creamer
    Cherry and Plum pattern, colorless, ruby and gold trim.....85.00

Leaf Umbrella pattern, cranberry, breakfast size 225.00
Lustre Flute pattern, carnival, green 50.00
Paneled Sprig pattern, blue opalescent, white spatter, 6" h...95.00
Peach pattern, colorless, gold and red trim..................60.00
Pods and Posies pattern, green, gold trim 70.00
Creamer and Sugar, No. 12 pattern, colorless, gilt trim, mkd... 75.00
Cruet, orig stopper
    Daisy and Fern pattern, blue opalescent, Parian Swirl mold..175.00
    Intaglio pattern, white opalescent 165.00
    Wild Bouquet pattern, custard, enamel dec 550.00
Finger Bowl, Leaf Umbrella pattern, blue, cased 100.00
Goblet
    Grape and Gothic Arches pattern, custard, nutmeg stain...75.00
    Nearcut, colorless 35.00
    Strawberry and Cable pattern, colorless 40.00
Jelly Compote
    Intaglio pattern, white opalescent, c1903 ....45.00
    Poppy pattern, green 35.00
Lady's Spittoon, Inverted Fan and Feather, blue opalescent, c1903 .... 275.00
Marmalade Jar, cov, Paneled Sprig pattern, cranberry, SP rim, cov, and bail handle... 195.00
Nappy
    Lustre Flute pattern, carnival, marigold 35.00
    Memphis pattern, "Compliments L. H. Cahn & Co/Furniture/236-240 W. Federal St" in center, "N" in circle mark, c1900...65.00
Nut Bowl, Leaf and Beads pattern, carnival, purple......... 65.00
Pitcher
    Cherry and Plum pattern, colorless, gold trim 165.00
    Chrysanthemum Sprig, 9" h, lime green, white spatter, satinized handle 475.00
    Coin Dot pattern, carnival, marigold 170.00
    Daisy and Fern pattern, cranberry, ball shape 175.00
    Leaf Mold pattern, cranberry, white spatter...............300.00
    Leaf Umbrella pattern, blue opaque, 72 oz 650.00
    Paneled Holly pattern, green, gold trim 250.00
    Royal Oak pattern, colorless 75.00
Plate
    Paneled Cherry pattern, colorless, red cherries, gold leaves, 10-1/2" d 45.00
    Thistle pattern, colorless, 10" d 30.00
    Three Fruits pattern, custard, 7-1/2" d 25.00
Rose Bowl
    Pearl and Scale pattern, stem, blue...........................90.00
    Pull Up, 8" h, 6" w, deep green and red, brilliant pink lining, three applied crystal thorn feet 1,200.00
Salt and Pepper Shakers, pr, orig tops
    Bow and Tassel pattern, milk glass 65.00
    Carnelian pattern, custard 450.00
    Leaf Umbrella pattern, mauve, cased........................165.00
Sauce
    Cherry Thumbprint pattern, colorless, ruby and gold trim...15.00
    Regent pattern, amethyst, gold trim............................40.00
    Wild Bouquet pattern, white opal, no dec....................20.00
Server, 11" d, center handle, #698, blue irid stretch 48.00
Spooner
    Aurora pattern, pink satin ground, white patter 85.00
    Cherry and Plum pattern, colorless, ruby and gold trim... 75.00
    Chrysanthemum Sprig pattern, opaque blue, gold trim ..245.00
    Gothic Arches pattern, colorless..................................35.00

Sugar Castor, Leaf Umbrella, cased blue, $225.

Memphis pattern, green...75.00
Singing Birds pattern, colorless....................................70.00
Sugar, cov
    Cherry and Plum pattern, colorless, ruby and gold trim.....85.00

Cherry Thumbprint pattern, colorless, ruby and gold
    trim...100.00
Paneled Sprig pattern, milk glass, green and gold dec ..125.00
Peach pattern, colorless, ruby and gold trim...............85.00
Utopia Optic pattern, cranberry..................................120.00
Syrup, Leaf Umbrella pattern, cranberry, white spatter....... 250.00
Table Set, cov butter, creamer, spooner, and cov sugar
    Belladonna pattern, green, gold trim........................325.00
    Nearcut, colorless, gold trim....................................250.00
    Paneled Holly pattern, green, gold trim....................475.00
    Peach pattern, green, gold trim, mkd "N".................350.00
Toothpick Holder
    Maple Leaf pattern, custard.....................................550.00
    Memphis pattern, green..50.00
    Ribbed Optic pattern, rubena...................................165.00
    Threaded Swirl pattern, rubena 250.00
Tumbler
    Atlas pattern, opaque pink...35.00
    Flower and Bud pattern, colorless.............................50.00
    Oriental Poppy pattern, colorless, gold trim 25.00
    Paneled Holly pattern, colorless 45.00
    Peach pattern, colorless 45.00
    Regent pattern, amethyst, gold trim...........................75.00
    Strawberry and Cable pattern, colorless 40.00
Vase
    7-1/2" h, 6" w, Jewel, medium blue over white satin body, ver-
        tical pattern of 30 ribs, orig white lining 450.00
    Daisy and Drape pattern...300.00
    Diamond Point pattern, 7" h 150.00
Whiskey Tumbler, Threaded Swirl pattern, Rubena 65.00
Wine Set, Cornflower pattern, green, gold trim, decanter, orig
    stopper, 4 matching wines 165.00

OPALESCENT GLASS

History: Opalescent glass, a clear or colored glass with milky white decorations, looks fiery or opalescent when held to light. This effect was achieved by applying bone ash chemicals to designated areas while a piece was still hot and then refiring it at extremely high temperatures.

There are three basic categories of opalescent glass: (1) blown (or mold blown) patterns, e.g., Daisy & Fern and Spanish Lace; (2) novelties, pressed glass patterns made in limited quantity and often in unusual shapes such as corn or a trough; and (3) traditional pattern (pressed) glass forms.

Opalescent glass was produced in England in the 1870s. Northwood began the American production in 1897 at its Indiana, Pennsylvania, plant. Jefferson, National Glass, Hobbs, and Fenton soon followed.

References: Gary Baker et al., *Wheeling Glass 1829-1939*, Oglebay Institute, 1994, distributed by Antique Publications; Bill Banks, *Complete Price Guide for Opalescent Glass*, 2nd ed., published by author, 1996; Bill Edwards, *Standard Encyclopedia of Opalescent Glass*, Collector Books, 1997; William Heacock, *Encyclopedia of Victorian Colored Pattern Glass*, Book II, 2nd ed., Antique Publications, 1977; William Heacock and William Gamble, *Encyclopedia of Victorian Colored Pattern Glass*, *Book 9, Cranberry Opalescent from A to Z*, Antique Publications, 1987; William Heacock, James Measell, and Berry Wiggins, *Dugan/Diamond*, Antique Publications, 1993; ——, *Harry Northwood* (1990), Book 2 (1991) Antique Publications; ——, *Harry Northwood: The Early Years 1881-1900*, Antique Publications, 1990; ——, *Harry Northwood: The Wheeling Years 1901-1925*, Antique Publications, 1991.

Blown

Barber Bottle
    Raised Swirl, cranberry 295.00
    Spanish Lace, cranberry 700.00
    Swirl, blue 225.00
Basket, Daisy and Fern, vaseline, looped handle.......190.00

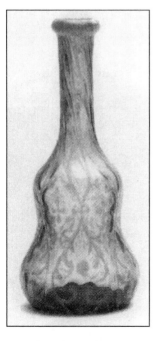

Barber bottle, cylindrical, flattened bulbous body, long neck, cranberry, Coin Spot, tooled mouth, smooth base, 7-1/2" h, $180. Photo courtesy of Norman C. Heckler and Co.

Berry Bowl, master, Chrysanthemum Base Swirl, blue, satin 95.00
Biscuit Jar, cov, Spanish Lace, vaseline....................275.00
Bowl
    Ruffles and Rings, green 40.00
    Seaweed, white, 9" d 80.00
    Swirling Maze, cranberry, ruffled 145.00
Bride's Basket, cranberry, SP holder
    Bubble Lattice 200.00
    Poinsettia, ruffled top..275.00
Butter Dish, cov
    Hobbs Hobnail, vaseline 250.00
    Spanish Lace, blue..265.00
Celery Vase
    Consolidated Criss-Cross, rubena, satin finish 250.00
    Daffodils, blue 115.00
    Reverse Swirl, cranberry 175.00
    Ribbed Lattice, cranberry 245.00
    Seaweed, cranberry 250.00
    Windows, cranberry, ruffled rim 115.00
Cheese Dish, Hobb's Swirl, cranberry 350.00
Compote, Ribbed Spiral, blue.......................................70.00
Creamer
    Buckeye Lattice, cranberry 450.00
    Coin Dot, cranberry 190.00
    Windows Swirl, cranberry 500.00
Cruet, orig stopper
    Chrysanthemum Base Swirl, white, satin 175.00
    Fern, blue 345.00
    Hobb's Hobnail, blue..225.00
    Ribbed Opal Lattice, white 135.00
    Spanish Lace, canary yellow..................................185.00
    Stripe, blue, applied blue handle 185.00
    Windows, Plain, cranberry......................................375.00
    Windows, Swirled, cranberry..................................350.00
Custard Cup, Panel Hobnail, white 15.00
Finger Bowl
    Hobb's Hobnail, cranberry 65.00
    Hobb's Optic Diamond, cranberry 70.00
    Spanish Lace, blue..50.00
Lamp, oil
    Inverted Thumbprint, white, amber fan base 145.00
    Snowflake, cranberry...800.00
Miniature Lamp, Reverse Swirl, vaseline 95.00
Mustard, cov, Reverse Swirl, vaseline 65.00
Pickle Castor, Daisy and Fern, blue, emb floral jar, DQ, resilvered frame 650.00
Pitcher
    Arabian Nights, white 450.00
    Buttons and Braids, blue..220.00
    Christmas Snowflake, cranberry 2,100.00
    Coin Spot, cranberry, clover leaf crimp 325.00
    Coin Spot, cranberry, triangular crimp, windows mold, #261 ....400.00
    Daisy and Fern, cranberry.....................................500.00
    Fern, blue 450.00
    Fern, cranberry, applied crystal handle, 9" h, 6" d 600.00
    Hobb's Hobnail, cranberry 315.00
    Reverse Swirl, blue, satin, speckled 495.00
    Seaweed, blue...525.00
    Stars and Stripes, cranberry 2,100.00
    Windows, cranberry 695.00
Rose Bowl
    Opal Swirl, white...40.00
    Piasa Bird, blue 100.00
Salt Shaker, orig top

Coin Spot, cranberry 200.00
Consolidated Criss-Cross, cranberry.....................85.00
Reverse Swirl, blue..65.00
Ribbed Opal Lattice, cranberry...............................95.00
Spooner
   Bubble Lattice, cranberry......................................145.00
   Reverse Swirl, cranberry 165.00
   Ribbed Spiral, blue..110.00
Sugar, cov
   Bubble Lattice, cranberry......................................195.00
   Reverse Swirl, cranberry 350.00
   Spanish Lace, blue...175.00
Sugar Shaker
   Bubble Lattice, rubena...250.00
   Coin Spot, blue, ring neck.....................................160.00
   Coin Spot, cranberry 275.00
   Fern, white...115.00
   Paneled Sprig, cranberry......................................195.00
   Ribbed Opal Lattice, cranberry..............................325.00
   Spanish Lace, cranberry.......................................535.00
   Windows, Swirled, blue...245.00
Syrup
   Coin Dot, blue...145.00
   Coin Spot, cranberry 175.00
   Coin Spot and Swirl, blue, applied loop handle, orig tin
      cover...150.00
   Daisy and Criss-Cross, white 545.00
   Daisy and Fern, blue, bulbous 285.00
   Reverse Swirl, cranberry 1,145.00
Tankard
   Chrysanthemum Swirl Variant, cranberry...........2,500.00
   Poinsettia, cranberry 2,500.00
Toothpick Holder
   Consolidated Criss-Cross, cranberry.....................500.00
   Overall Hobnail, blue...65.00
   Ribbed Lattice, blue...165.00
Tumbler
   Acanthus, blue 90.00
   Beatty Honeycomb, blue.......................................275.00
   Bubble Lattice, cranberry......................................135.00
   Christmas Snowflake, blue, ribbed 125.00
   Maze, swirling, green..95.00
   Reverse Swirl, cranberry 65.00
   Seaweed, cranberry..150.00
   Spanish Lace, green...65.00
   Swirl, blue...95.00
   Windows, cranberry 125.00
Vase, Dahlia, blue..60.00
Waste Bowl, Hobbs Hobnail, vaseline 75.00
Water Set, Christmas Snowflake, cobalt blue, 6 pc 400.00
Whimsy, bowl, Piasa Bird, blue....................................85.00

Novelties

Back Bar Bottle, 12-1/4" h, robin's egg blue ground, opalescent stripes swirled to the right 100.00
Barber Bottle, 8" h, sq, diamond pattern molded form, light
   cranberry, white vertical stripes 275.00
Basket
   4" h, 5" w, cranberry, white opalescent stripes and clear
      ribbing interspersed with silver mica, ruffled edge, ap-
      plied clear twisted center loop handle 150.00
   7-1/2" h, 5" w, rose bowl form, cranberry, deep white opal-
      escent extends half way down, applied clear rigaree
      top, applied crystal five-footed base, small loop ap-
      plied crystal handle 200.00

Lamp, Cobweb, cranberry ground, clear Eason base, ground under foot, $550. Photo courtesy of Green Valley Auctions.

Bowl
   Cashews, blue, crimped 60.00
   Grape and Cherry, blue 85.00
   Greek Key and Ribs, green......................................75.00
   Jolly Bear, white..85.00
   Leaf and Beads, green, twig feet 60.00
   Many Loops, blue, crimped, fluted 65.00
   Ruffles and Rings, white...35.00
   Winter Cabbage, white...45.00
Bushel Basket, blue 75.00
Chalice, Maple Leaf, vaseline 45.00
Compote
   Dolphin, vaseline...95.00
   Squirrel and Acorn, green, ruffled 175.00
Cruet, Stars and Stripes, cranberry 575.00
Hanging Vase, 8-1/2" h, green opalescent vase with thorns,
   clear crystal vine as holder for vase, pressed green daisy-
   like flower on holder, Victorian 115.00
Hat, Opal Swirl, white...35.00
Mug, Singing Birds, blue..145.00
Plate, Wishbone and Drape, green 35.00
Rose Bowl
   Leaf Chalice, green, pedestal 65.00
   Palm and Scroll, green, three ftd............................75.00
Vase, corn, white..125.00

Pressed

Banana Boat, Jewel and Fan, green............................115.00
Berry Bowl, master
   Alaska, blue...195.00
   Everglades, vaseline, gold trim 200.00
   Tokyo, green...75.00
Berry Set
   Beatty Swirl, blue, 7 pcs.......................................325.00
   Inverted Fan and Feather, white.............................260.00
   Iris and Meander, blue, 6 pcs 380.00
   Swag with Brackets, green, 7 pcs...........................275.00
Bowl
   Argonaut Shell, vaseline, shell ftd 100.00
   Beaded Stars, low base, green................................45.00
   Beatty Rib, blue, rect...65.00
   Diamond Spearhead, 9" d, blue 45.00
   Iris with Meander, 8" d, vaseline...........................135.00
   Jewel and Fan, blue 35.00
   Jeweled Heart, green, crimped................................40.00
   Many Loops, crimped, green 25.00
   Peacock, Northwood, white...................................145.00
   Peacock and Fence, blue 300.00
   Waterlily and Cattail, blue......................................65.00
Butter Dish, cov
   Argonaut Shell, white..245.00

Beatty Rib, white...95.00
Drapery, blue, gold trim.................................215.00
Everglades, vaseline......................................345.00
Fluted Scrolls, blue.......................................200.00
Idyll, green...350.00
Jackson, blue...155.00
Sunburst and Shield, blue..............................345.00
Swag with Brackets, green.............................100.00
Tokyo, blue..300.00
Water Lily and Cattails, blue..........................300.00
Water Lily and Cattails, white........................230.00

Calling Card Receiver
Fluted Scrolls, white..40.00
Inverted Feather, vaseline..............................225.00

Celery Vase
Alaska, blue, dec...150.00
Diamond Spearhead, green............................275.00
Wreath and Shell, vaseline, dec.....................140.00

Compote
Diamond Spearhead, vaseline.........................150.00
Intaglio, vaseline...70.00
Tokyo, blue..60.00

Cracker Jar, cov
Beaded Drape, pale blue ground, mate finish, silver plated
    hardware, 11" h, 6-1/2" w, wear to silver plate...... 100.00
Wreath and Shell, vaseline.............................750.00

Creamer
Alaska, blue...85.00
Beaded Shell, green.......................................165.00
Fluted Scrolls, blue..70.00
Fluted Scrolls, vaseline....................................85.00
Gonterman Swirl, blue, frosted.......................625.00
Inverted Fan and Feather, blue.......................125.00
Intaglio, white..85.00
Paneled Holly, white...70.00
Scroll with Acanthus, green..............................65.00
Swag with Brackets, green................................90.00
Tokyo, blue..125.00
Wild Bouquet, green......................................140.00
Wreath and Shell, vaseline, dec.....................135.00

Cruet
Alaska, vaseline, enameled dec......................275.00
Christmas Pearls, white..................................260.00
Everglades, vaseline......................................275.00
Fancy Fantails, blue.......................................375.00
Fluted Scrolls, blue, clear stopper..................295.00
Jackson, blue...185.00
Scroll with Acanthus, blue..............................200.00

Epergne, Jackson, blue......................................155.00
Goblet, Diamond Spearhead, cranberry................85.00

Jelly Compote
Diamond Spearhead, vaseline...........................85.00
Everglades, blue, gold trim...............................85.00
Intaglio, blue...55.00
Iris with Meander, vaseline...............................95.00
Wild Bouquet, blue..160.00

Match Holder, Beatty Rib, white...........................35.00

Mug
Diamond Spearhead, cobalt blue.......................85.00
Stork and Rushes, blue.....................................90.00

Pitcher
Beatty Swirl, canary yellow.............................195.00
Fluted Scrolls, vaseline..................................300.00
Gonterman Swirl, amber top...........................375.00
Intaglio, blue...215.00
Jeweled Heart, blue.......................................250.00

Swag with Brackets, vaseline.........................225.00
Wild Bouquet, blue..300.00

Plate
Palm Beach, blue, 10" d, set of 6...................895.00
Tokyo, ftd, green..70.00
Water Lily and Cattail, amethyst.......................85.00

Rose Bowl
Beaded Drape, blue..60.00
Fancy Fantails, cranberry, four clear applied feet..... 650.00
Fluted Scrolls, blue..125.00
Fluted Scrolls, vaseline..................................115.00

Salt and Pepper Shakers, pr
Everglades, vaseline......................................400.00
Jewel and Flower, canary yellow, orig tops...........250.00

Salt, open, individual
Beatty Rib, white...42.00
Wreath and Shell, blue.....................................65.00

Sauce
Alaska, blue...65.00
Alaska, white..20.00
Argonaut Shell, blue...40.00
Circled Scrolls, blue...50.00
Drapery, Northwood, dec, blue..........................35.00
Iris with Meander, yellow...................................25.00
Jewel and Flower, white....................................25.00
Regal, green...65.00
Water Lily and Cattails, white............................35.00
Wild Bouquet, blue...40.00

Spooner
Argonaut Shell, French Opal...........................170.00
Beatty Rib, white..45.00
Flora, blue..110.00
Fluted Scrolls, blue, dec...................................70.00
Intaglio, white..45.00
Iris with Meander, canary yellow.......................95.00
Palm Beach, vaseline..95.00
Tokyo, blue..85.00
Swag with Brackets, blue..................................50.00
Wreath and Shell, vaseline..............................120.00
Wreath and Shell, white..................................285.00

Sugar, cov
Alaska, vaseline...155.00
Circled Scroll, green...85.00
Diamond Spearhead, vaseline.........................235.00

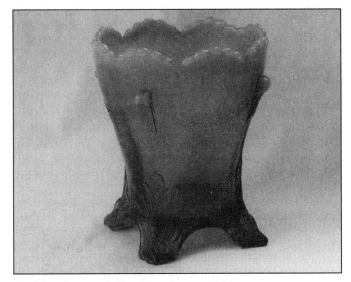

Spooner, Swag with Brackets, green, $60.00

Fluted Scrolls, blue..130.00
Gonterman Swirl, amber...........................235.00
Intaglio, blue..75.00
Jewel and Flower, vaseline 90.00
Swag with Brackets, blue...........................95.00
Tokyo, blue, gold trim...............................115.00

Syrup
Diamond Spearhead, green..................350.00
Flora, white, gold trim............................275.00

Toothpick Holder
Beatty Rib, white......................................30.00
Diamond Spearhead, green........................75.00
Diamond Spearhead, vaseline.....................80.00
Flora, white, gold trim.............................150.00
Gonterman Swirl, amber top 150.00
Iris with Meander, blue...........................115.00
Ribbed Spiral, blue...................................90.00
Wreath and Shell, blue............................275.00

Tumbler
Alaska, blue..110.00
Alaska, vaseline..85.00
Beatty Rib, white.......................................35.00
Beatty Swirl, white 45.00
Drapery, blue...90.00
Everglades, vaseline....................................50.00
Fluted Scrolls, vaseline..............................75.00
Intaglio, white..45.00
Jackson, green...50.00
Jeweled Heart, blue 85.00
Paneled Holly, blue 100.00
S-Repeat, blue..45.00
Wild Bouquet, white..................................25.00
Wreath and Shell, collared, blue 90.00
Wreath and Shell, ftd, blue.......................375.00

Vase
Fluted Scrolls and Vine, blue....................70.00
Inverted Fan and Feather, blue 85.00
Northwood Diamond Point, blue 75.00
Water Lily and Cattail, amethyst...............75.00

Water Set
Diamond Spearhead, tankard pitcher, six tumblers,
green 445.00
Everglades, pitcher, six tumblers.........700.00
Fluted Scrolls, blue, pitcher and six tumblers 645.00
Jeweled Heart, blue 650.00
Swag with Brackets, vaseline...............695.00
Tokyo, green...675.00

OPALINE GLASS

History: Opaline glass was a popular mid- to late 19th-century European glass. The glass has a certain amount of translucency and often is found decorated with enamel designs and trimmed in gold.

Basket
5" h, ruffled, applied colorless handle............................60.00
6-1/2" h, 6" d, clambroth color, applied pink snake loop around handle, gold rim...100.00
Biscuit Jar, cov, white ground, hp, florals and birds dec, brass lid and bail handle..165.00
Bouquet Holder, 7" h, blue opaline cornucopia shaped gilt dec flower holders issuing from bronze stag heads, Belgian black marble base, English, Victorian, early 19th C, pr...725.00
Bowl, 8" d, 2 h, rose opaque body...................................50.00

Box, cov, gilt metal, blue, Continental, early 20th C
5-3/8" l, rect, domed................................250.00
7-1/2" l, egg-shaped.................................295.00
Candelabra, Louis XV style, late 19th C
18-1/2" h, gilt bronze and blue opaline, scrolled candle arms and base, two-light.............................175.00
26-1/2" h, gilt metal and blue opaline, five-light.........400.00
Candlestick, 7-1/4" h, white opaque clambroth body, rib molded 150.00
Chalice, white ground, Diamond Point pattern 35.00
Cheese dish, cov, white opaque body, gold enamel dec... 185.00
Child's Mug, 2-1/4" h, paneled scenes of Dutch children, pr 65.00
Clock, 6" d, white opaque body, hanging type, circular frame, hand painted, Welch Company, Forestville, CT, clockworks, orig brass chain 275.00
Cologne Bottle
6" h, jade green opaque body, orig stopper.................95.00
8-3/4" h, jade green opaque body, gold ring dec, orig stopper 90.00
Creamer, shaded yellow to white opaque body, pink roses and blue forget me nots, SP rim and handle................ 125.00
Cup Plate, Lee-Rose 258, white opaque body, minute rim roughage 75.00
Dresser Jar, 5-1/2" d, egg shape, blue ground, heavy gold dec 200.00
Ewer, 13-1/4" h, white ground, Diamond Point pattern ... 135.00
Fairy Lamp, 17" h, French blue, four large faceted purple and dark blue jewels, filigree brass mountings............ 285.00
Jack in the Pulpit Vase, 5-1/2" h, robin's egg blue opaque body, applied amber feet................................ 95.00
Jardinieres, 5-1/4" h, gilt bronze and blue opaline, sq, Empire style, tasseled chains, paw feet, early 20th C, pr............. 1,610.00
Mantel Lusters, 12-3/4" h, blue, gilt dec, slender faceted prisms, Victorian, c1880, damage, pr.................................. 250.00
Match Holder, 1-3/8" h, blue opaque body, gold flowers and leaves 40.00
Oil Lamp, 24" h, dolphin-form stepped base, clear glass oil well, frosted glass shade, late 19th C, converted to electric, chips.. 460.00
Oil Lamp Base, 22" h, blue, baluster turned standard on circular foot, 20th C, converted to electric, pr.................... 635.00
Perfume Bottle
2-3/4" h, blue opaque body, gold flowers and leaves, matching stopper 60.00
3-1/8" d, 7-3/4" h, tapering cylinder, flat flared base white, ring of white opaline around neck and matching teardrop stopper, gold trim 115.00
4" h, blue opaque body, gold, white, and yellow dec, matching stopper 75.00
Pitcher
4-1/4" h, pink opaque body, applied white handle 75.00
12" h, pink, applied ruby paste stones, beaded enamel swag, applied handle, French, 19th C 110.00
Posy Holder, 8" h, blue opaque body, figural hand holding small vase, ruffled rim....................................... 85.00
Salt and Pepper Shakers, pr, 4" h, pansy dec, damage to both covers, worn dec, pr 45.00
Salt, open, boat shaped, blue dec, white enamel garland and scrolling 75.00
Sugar, cov, shaded yellow to white opaque body, pink roses and blue forget me nots, SP cover, rim, and handle 150.00
Toothpick Holder, lavender opaque body, small ball feet..... 85.00
Tumbler, white opaque body, enameled pink rose 25.00
Tumble-Up, carafe, tumbler, and underplate, pale green opaque body, gold beading, black and white jeweled dec, three pcs 325.00

Urn, 13" h, blue opaque body, enameled blue flowers, gilt trim,
    flared rim, pr 350.00
Vase
    5" h, blue, platinum stars dec, Czechoslovakian 55.00
    5-1/2" h, cased light blue opaline, blue applied ribbon han-
        dles, mkd "Czecho-slovakia" 50.00
    8" h, swirled and mottled colors over opaline, applied clear
        pinched handles, Czechoslovakian 35.00
    16-1/4" h, oviform, circular cushioned foot, parcel gilt, enam-
        eled, turquoise blue opaque body, gilt rimmed molded
        border and handles, oval panels with artists' portraits,
        one with Raphel, other Van Dyke, brown, claret, white,
        and flesh tones, gilt borders with scrolling foliate edges,
        French, 19th C, pr 2,500.00
Violet Bowl, 3-1/2" d, 3" h, peachblow pink ground, blue and
    white enameled flowers, gray leaves and vines, base
    sgd, Mt. Washington 275.00
Water Pitcher, 12-1/4" h, blue, high looped handle, bulbous,
    early 20th C 230.00
Whiskey Taster, white opaque clambroth colored body
    Lacy, Sandwich, Lee, plate 150-5, minute rim nicks 45.00
    Ten Panel, handle, small chip on bottom......................85.00

ORREFORS, KOSTA BODA

History: Orrefors Glasbruck, Sweden, was established in
1898. First production items were glass windows and ink
bottles. New ownership in 1913 introduced more items.
The firm now produces fine art glass, table wares, and
limited edition plates.

One of the most sought after types of Orrefors glass is
Graal. Simon Gate, F. Hald, and Knut Bergqvist were all
instrumental in the development of this line around 1916.
Cased glasswares were developed by Simon Gate and
Advard Hald around 1920. The Ariel line was developed
in 1939 by Edvin Ohrstrom. Internally decorated wares
were introduced by Jan Johansson, c1970.

Designers employed by Orrefors include: Knut
Bergqvist (c1919), Gunnar Cyren (c1959), Simon Gate
(c1915), Advard Hald (c1917), F. Hald and Jan Johansson (c 1970), Nils Landberg (c1925), Vicke Lindstrand
(c1928-41), Ingegorg Lundin (c1947), Edvin Ohrstrom
(c1936), Sven Palmqvist (c1936), John Selbin (c1927),
and Heinrich Wollman (c1919).

Today Orrefors is part of Orrefors Kosta Boda which
was established by a merger in 1990. The present group
consists of five glassworks, Orrefors, Sendvik, Kosta, Boda, and Åfors. The glass sold under the Orrefors or Kosta
Boda names is produced at these glass centers.

Kosta Boda was founded in 1742 by Anders Koskull
and George Bogislaus Staël von Holstein. The village they
established used the first syllables of their names "Ko-Sta."
Boda was founded in 1864 by three glass masters from
Kosta, long a center for manufacturing glassware. In 1920,
Fritz Kallenberg designed a series of glassware which was
produced until the 1960s. Erik Höglund came to Boda in
1953 with blown soda glass and changed the glassmaking industry. Åfors was founded in 1876 by four master
glassblowers and was owned by the Åfors family until
1975. It was then acquired by Kosta Boda.

The marks used by Orrefors include the name engraved
on the base, often including a design number, and the de-

Bowl, Skal Ravenna, S. Palmquist, 1961. Photo courtesy of Orrefors.

signer's name. A "U" in the mark indicates that the piece
was machine fire polished. Finding an "A" after the mark indicates the piece is a handworked piece of cut glass.

Website: Orrefors Kosta Boda has a visually delightful Internet site at http://www.orrefors.

Bottle, blue, fishnet dec, deep blue neck, sgd "Sven Palmquist
    Kraka" 775.00
Bowl
    4-1/2" d, 2-3/4" h, aubergine, bright blue, and colorless, ver-
        tical trapped air stripes, applied foot engraved "Orre-
        fors/Ariel 246 F/Edvin Ohstrom" 400.00
    6-1/2" d, 4-1/4" h, heavy walled, teal blue surface, cut to
        clear, polished oval and circular facets, inscribed "Kosta
        56693 Lindstrand" 875.00
    8-1/2" h, Graal, internally tinted purple body, clear lattice
        work dec, inscribed "Orrefors Sweden/Graal nr S05/Ed-
        vard Hald" 600.00
    9-5/8" l, hexagonal, flaring sides, colorless, engraved seminude
        women with wide flaring long hair, geometric borders, star-
        burst base, designed by Simon Gate, c1925 .... 2,2500.00
    11" d, shallow, colorless, molded balloons encircling
        center 150.00
Bucket, 6-3/4" d, 7" h, heavy walled cylinder, transparent teal
    blue, notable clarity, base inscribed "Orrefors Esp. PA.
    245-62 Sven Palmqvist" 200.00

Carousel, Ewald Dahlskog, 1926. Photo courtesy of Kosta Boda.

Compote, Heliopora, Kjell Engman, Kosta Boda, Sweden. Photo courtesy of Kosta Boda.

Candleholders, pr, colorless, ball shaped.........................90.00
Center Bowl, 12" d, 6-3/4" h, half-round, raised on heavy solid glass pedestal, open at center base with teardrop aperture, labeled "Orrefors Sweden" 345.00
Charger, 14-1/4" d, colorless crystal platter, folded rim, internally dec by concentric rings of aubergine windows, and gold-yellow swirls, all around central dark core, base inscribed "Aqua Graal No. 481P/Edward Hald/Orrefors '58" 815.00
Cordial Set, 12" h decanter, five 2-1/2" glasses, colorless squared decanter engraved with nude male diver underwater, glasses dec with different mermaid on each, decanter inscribed "Orrefors/Lindstrand 2983 B. L. O," glasses numbered 175.00
Decanter
    8-1/4" h, 8" l, figural pheasant, head stopper, engraved feathers, base mkd "Kosta 8218/V. Lindstrand" 420.00
    10-1/4" h, 6" l, domed rect form, sailor playing accordion at reverse, vignette of sailors on shore leave on obverse, base inscribed "Orrefors Landberg 138 C IAD," slight nick to stopper...1,150.00
    11-3/4" h, squared crystal bottle with Romeo on one side, Juliet on reverse, labeled and inscribed "Orrefors/Lundberg 1880-111-F5" 175.00
Finger Bowl, 5" h, 8-3/4" l underplate, colorless, oval tapering bowl, finely engraved frieze of cavorting nude females, holding lengths of drapery and fringed festooned fabric, scalloped borders, designed by Simon Gate, c1926, sgd "OF F 109.26 C" 2,750.00
Goblet, 8" h, heavy, crystal, etched frosted design on bowl and part of stem, sgd "Orrefors Palmquest 3397 61.5" 550.00

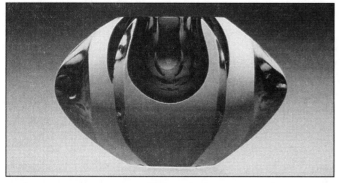

Scultpure, Ventana, Mona Morales-Schildt, 1963, Kosta Boda. Photo courtesy of Kosta Boda.

Paperweight
    2-1/4" h, squared colorless block, sky blue and yellow vitrified surface sheared to reveal engraved petroglyphs at reverse, base inscribed "Kosta 96736".................365.00
    5-1/2" h, mushroom shaped crystal, bubbled core, blue green looping inclusions within base, inscribed "Kosta 97070 Warff," by Ann or Goran Warff....................260.00
Perfume Bottle, 3-3/4" h, 2" w, bulbous, flat front and back, colorless, engraved swan, ball stopper 100.00
Rose Bowl
    5-1/2" h, globular, layered, sgd "Orrefors H 7 48," c1948...200.00
    7" h, cut and polished surface, raised stylized Art Deco floral panels, incised "Kosta 1936 Came 4"....................430.00
Sculpture
    2-3/4" h, 3-3/4" h, 4-1/2" h, colorless figural owl, engraved eye and feather embellishments, each inscribed "Kosta V. Lindstrand" and numbered, 3 pc set.................150.00
    4-3/4" h, solid wedge, two vitrified surfaces engraved with petroglyphs revealed through polished front surface, base inscribed "Kosta 95689 Warff" 690.00
    5-3/4" h, 9-1/2" l, colorless glass oval block, flat polished surface, back of vitrified yellow-sky blue engraved at edge with row of ten antlered elk reflected in base, inscribed "Kosta 967—Warff," designed by Ann Warff..........460.00
    6" l, 8-3/4" l, 10-1/2" l, and 11" l, colorless figural fish, internal teardrop body bubble and eye, each inscribed "Kosta" and numbered, 4 pc set..260.00
    9-3/4" h, solid colorless bird, looped tail, curved branch, inscribed "Orrefors 4288.111 Olle Alberius".............275.00
    15-1/4" h, shore birds, solid elongated figural sculptures, internally colored gray-green within colorless surround, capped with bright red crests lower edge engraved "Kosta '84," wooden block plinth, pr...........................345.00
Vase
    4" h, bird on branch, Orrefors, modern 50.00
    4" h, heavy walled colorless abstract cone-form, internal blue spiral motif, base stamped "Lind/Strand/Kosta," designed by Vicke Lindstrand...................................260.00
    4-1/2" h, conical, tinted deep blue, etched running figures, animals, and horse-drawn cart, landscape with rain clouds etched at rim, designed by Edvard Hald, inscribed "Orrefors Hald"..900.00
    5" h, heavy walled pale green crystal oval, internally dec and colored in underwater scene with fish and aquatic plants, base inscribed "Orrefors Sweden/Graal N. 231D/Edward Hald"...980.00
    5-1/2" h, 3-3/4" sq mouth, colorless, Art Deco style, four bulbous sides, thick engraved panel of woman holding baby above her head, polished pontil, artist sgd............200.00
    5-3/4" h, 4" w, pale green ground, internal paperweight dec of purple and green sea plants, sgd "Kosta" and "V. Lindstrand" 100.00
    6" h, colorless, black foot, Orrefors, modern.................85.00
    6-1/4" h, Ariel pattern, colorless, straight sides with trapped air bubbles in various geometric shapes against olive-green ground, designed by Ingeborg Lundin, sgd, c1960..900.00
    6-1/4" h, heavy walled colorless oval, lined in bright emerald green, wheel cut to clear on interior in circles, base inscribed "Kosta B 2779" 290.00
    6-1/2" h, oblong, colorless, engraved, two nude children carrying basket of flowers, designed by Sven Palmquist....400.00
    6-3/4" h, expanded oval fire dec with colorful shards and multi lines, base inscribed "Kosta Boda/Artist Coll. B. Vallien 48280"...320.00

Vase, Gunnar Wennerberg, 1909, Kosta Boda, Sweden. Photo courtesy of Kosta Boda.

6-3/4" h, 4-1/2" w, paperweight form, dark green and black fish swimming among sea plants, sgd "Orrefors Graal" 750.00

6-3/4" h, 8" d, opaque white, blue, red, and yellow lines running down left side, designed by Bartil Vallien, Kosta Boda 175.00

6-7/8" h, Venta, veiled, colorless, central cavities cased blue, olive green, orange, ext. concave panels to maximize optic illusory effect, base inscribed "Kosta SS 122" 690.00

7" h, heavy walled oval, colorless, internally dec by stylized black-brown trees, yellow, red, and orange falling leaves, base inscribed "Kosta LU 2011," designed by Vicke Lindstrand, shallow scratch at side............................2,645.00

7" h, blue, amber, and colorless, internally dec with tiny controlled bubbles and netting, one engraved "Orrefors/Karka Nr 349/Sven Palmqvist" 400.00

7-1/8" h, colorless crystal cylinder, internally dec by teal blue amorphous element, enhanced by cut and polished surface ovals, base engraved "Kosta 46693 V Lindstrand," designed by Vicke Lindstrand 520.00

7-1/4" h, Graal, colorless pyriform, thick walls, internally dec with fish swimming among sea grasses, sgd "Edvard Hald," c1960..550.00

7-1/2" h, heavy walled colorless internally dec oval, vertical trapped air panels alternating subtle gray feather panels, base inscribed "Orrefors Aerial No. 111F/Edvin Ohrstrom" 2,530.00

7-3/4" h, heavy walled colorless internally dec oval, aubergine spiral decorative core, inscribed "Kosta" and numbered..325.00

7-3/4" h, heavy walled colorless internally dec oval, baluster form, half white, half aubergine vertical stripes, inscribed "Kosta" and numbered..335.00

7-3/4" h, heavy walled colorless internally dec oval, central royal blue vertically lined network horizontally banded by pale peach colored divisions in symmetrical alignment, base inscribed "Orrefors S. Graal No. 194 N. Edward Hald"..2,100.00

8" h, bud, smoke, clear casing....................................120.00

8" h, titled "The Girl and the Dove," heavy walled amber tinted colorless and sapphire blue oval, internally air dec with framed bird and woman in profile among blossom elements, base engraved "Orrefors/Ariel R. 235N/Edwin Ohrstrom" 5,175.00

8-1/2" h, heavy walled colorless crystal oval, blue shadowed int., inscribed "Kosta" and numbered 335.00

8-1/2" h, light blue, engraved scene of three seagulls in flight..220.00

8-3/4" h, Graal, colorless, internally dec, amorphic figures playing games, designed by Edwin Ohostrom, inscribed "Orrefors 1938 Graal" 6,500.00

9" h, bullet shape, crystal casing, amber to blue, bubble in base, Kosta, pr 200.00

9-1/2" h, carved nude Medusa-like woman beside fawn, sgd "Orrefors/Lindstrand" and numbered.....................225.00

10" h, octagonal faceted crystal, engraved nude woman with scarf, base engraved "Orrefors/Lindstrand, 1702.A4.9," designed by Vicke Lindstrand, 1938 ....230.00

10-1/4" d, frosted slender nude female archer holding bow aloft, sgd "Orrefors/Lindstrand/1484/B1/SR," minor surface scratches..125.00

11" h, blue, amber, and colorless, internally dec with tiny controlled bubbles and netting, one engraved "Orrefors/Karka Nr 322/Sven Palmqvist" 425.00

11-3/4" h, internally dec with vertically striped motif, opal white with aubergine, base acid stamped "Kosta/Lind/Strand"..420.00

12-1/4" h, elliptical vessel, engraved with stylized trees, occasional small birds among polished leaves, base engraved "Kosta LG2268," designed by Vicke Lindstrand.... 1,100.00

12-1/4" h, elongated bulbous body internally dec with vertical stripes in shaded blue and maroon, applied disk foot stamped "Lind/Strand/Kosta," designed by Vicke Lindstrand 750.00

12-1/2" h, internally dec with vertically striped motif, green with white, base acid stamped "Kosta/Lind/Strand" 400.00

17" h, elongated goose neck flattened oval bottle form, colorless, engraved with tall stylized grasses which form intricate spider webs, labeled and inscribed "Kosta L G 2384," attributed to Vicke Lindstrand....................450.00

OVERSHOT GLASS

History: Overshot glass was developed in the mid-1800s. To produce overshot glass, a gather of molten glass was rolled over the marver upon which had been placed crushed glass. The piece then was blown into the desired shape. The finished product appeared to be frosted or iced.

Early pieces were made mainly in clear glass. As the demand for colored glass increased, color was added to the base piece and occasionally to the crushed glass.

Pieces of overshot generally are attributed to the Boston and Sandwich Glass Co. although many other companies also made it as it grew in popularity.

Museum: Sandwich Glass Museum, Sandwich, MA.

Basket

7" h, 9" w, pink opalescent ruffled body, 3 rows of hobnails, twisted vaseline handle 190.00

7-1/4" h, 5" d, transparent green shading to colorless, ruffled swirled edge, sq thorn handle, melon-ribbed base with pineapple-like design, entire surface with overshot finish 285.00

10" h, 7-1/2" d, rect, shaded cranberry to crystal, applied crystal ruffled edge, applied thorn overshot handle..............225.00

Biscuit Jar, cov, 7" h, 5" d, colorless melon ribbed body, applied cranberry overshot, coiled snake handle...............250.00

Bowl, 6" d, 3-7/8" h, pale blue opaque, applied amber rigaree around top, applied green leaves, white, pink, and blue applied flowers......................................235.00

Bride's Bowl, 8-5/8" d, 6-5/8" h, shaded clear to blue ground, lobed, crimped edge, dec brass holder 215.00

Celery Vase, 6" h, 3-1/2" d, scalloped top, cranberry ground...90.00

Cheese Dish, dome cov, 8" d, 7" h, cranberry ground, enameled crane and cattails, applied colorless faceted finial.... 425.00

Compote

6-3/4" h, 8-3/8" d, cranberry shaded to clear bowl, applied clear scalloped and ruffled edge, fancy brass dome ftd pedestal base..125.00

9" h, 8-7/8" d, colorless ground, applied gold dec, cranberry serpent around stem 125.00

10-1/4" h, 10" d, cranberry ground, wide rounded bowl, scalloped crown gilt trimmed rim, compressed knop on cylindrical pedestal, wide flaring foot, late 19th C.........300.00

12-3/4" h, 8-1/2" d, rubena overshot bowl, white metal bronze finished figural standard...135.00

14" h, 9" d, rubena overshot bowl, white meal bronze finished figural standard 165.00

Custard Cup, pink ground, applied clear ground, Sandwich 60.00

Decanter, colorless ground, ice bladder, orig stopper ...750.00

Ewer, 13-1/2" h, trefoil top, colorless ground, twisted rope handle, Sandwich.......................................275.00

Fairy Lamp, 4-1/4" h, 3" d, opalescent, figural, crown shape, colorless pressed "Clarke" base................................195.00

Finger Bowl, pink ground, fluted and swirled 115.00

Goblet, flint, cut cotton twist stem, American 300.00

Ice Cream Tray, 13" l, colorless, gold trim, Portland..........40.00

Lamp Shade, 7-7/8" d, 2-7/8" d fitter ring, sapphire blue shaded to clear ground, ruffled...125.00

Marmalade Jar, cov, matching underplate, green ground, gold snake entwined on cov, attributed to Boston and Sandwich Glass Co. 315.00

Mug, 3" h, colorless ground, applied colorless handle 35.00

Pitcher

6" d, cranberry ground, bulbous, applied colorless reeded handle...125.00

8" d, bulbous, colorless ground, heavy enamel dec of white roses, blue forget me nots and green leaves, applied colorless handle...150.00

8" d, ovoid, cranberry ground, swirled melon ribbed body, cylindrical neck, pinched spout, applied colorless reeded handle...250.00

8-1/4" h, green ground, amber shell handle, Sandwich, c1875, brown age line near lip...............................225.00

9" h, tankard, cranberry ground, applied colorless reeded handle, hinged metal lid.......................................195.00

10-1/2" h, colorless, rope twist handle, ice bladder......90.00

Punch Cup, pink ground, applied colorless handle, attributed to Boston and Sandwich Glass Co. set of 8.............. 300.00

Rose Bowl, 3-3/4" d, rubena ground, applied flowers and pale green leaves.. 165.00

Tazza, 5-3/4" h, 7-3/4" d, colorless ground, flint glass.... 195.00

Vase

5-1/2" h, pink ground, applied random amber threading 225.00

7-1/2" h, bulbous base, slender neck, colorless ground, gold overshot, silver floral dec 125.00

8-1/2" h, opalescent pink ground, fluted, applied colorless handle...135.00

11" h, cranberry ground, two applied pink flowers, green branch and leaves, clear ruffled edge, applied amber feet...300.00

PADEN CITY GLASS

History: Paden City Glass Manufacturing Co. was founded in 1916 in Paden City, W.V. David Fisher, formerly of the New Martinsville Glass Manufacturing Co., operated the company until his death in 1933, at which time his son, Samuel, became president. A management decision in 1949 to expand Paden City's production by acquiring American Glass Company, an automated manufacturer of bottles, ashtrays, and novelties, strained the company's finances, forcing them to close permanently in 1951.

Although Paden City glass is often lumped with mass-produced, machine-made wares into the Depression Glass category, Paden City's wares were, until 1948, all handmade. Their products are better classified as "Elegant Glass" of the era as it ranks in quality with the wares produced by contemporaries such as Fostoria, New Martinsville, and Morgantown.

Paden City kept a low profile, never advertising in consumer magazines of the day. They never marked their glass in any way because a large portion of their business consisted of sales to decorating companies, mounters, and fitters. The firm also supplied bars, restaurants, and soda fountains with glassware, as evidenced by the wide range of tumblers, ice cream dishes, and institutional products available in several Paden City patterns.

Paden City's decorating shop also etched, cut, hand painted, and applied silver overlay and gold encrustation. However, not every decoration found on Paden City shapes will necessarily have come from the factory. Cupid, Peacock and Rose, and several other etchings depicting birds are among the most sought after decorations. Pieces with these etchings are commanding higher and higher prices even though they were apparently made in greater quantities than some of the etchings that are less-known (but just as beautiful).

Paden City is noted for its colors: opal (opaque white), ebony, mulberry (amethyst), Cheriglo (delicate pink), yellow, dark green (forest), crystal, amber, primrose (reddish-amber), blue, rose, and great quantities of ruby (red). The firm also produced transparent green in numerous shades ranging from yellowish to a distinctive electric green that always alerts knowledgeable collectors to its Paden City origin.

Contrary to popular belief and previously incorrect printed references, The Paden City Glass Manufacturing Company had absolutely no connection with the Paden City Pottery Company, other than their identical locale.

References: Jerry Barnett, *Paden City, The Color Company,* published by author, 1978; Tom and Neila Bredehoft, *Fifty Years of Collectible Glass, 1920-1970,* Antique Trader Books, 1997; Lee Garmon and Dick Spencer, *Glass Animals of the Depression Era,* Collector Books, 1993; Naomi L. Over, *Ruby Glass of the 20th Century,* The Glass Press, 1990, 1993–94 value update; Hazel Marie Weatherman, *Colored Glassware of the Depression Era 2,* Glassbooks, 1974.

Animals
    Bunny, ears down, cotton dispenser, satin finish 95.00
    Dragon Swan, crystal..175.00
    Dragon Swan, light blue...650.00

    Goose, crystal 60.00
    Goose, light blue...125.00
    Horse, rearing (Barth Art)..175.00
    Pheasant, light blue...170.00
    Pony, tall...90.00
    Pony, 12" h, light blue...150.00
    Banana Split Dish, #191 Party Line, green 20.00
Bookends, pr
    Eagle, crystal..300.00
    Pouter Pigeons, crystal 170.00
Bowl
    #191 Party Line, pink, 4-5/8" d 9.00
    #300 Archaic, Peacock and Rose etching, pink, 11" d.... 130.00
    #412 Crow's Foot, round, 3 ftd, flared, ruby 65.00
    #881 Gadroon, cobalt blue, 8" d................................85.00
    Cupid etch, rolled edge, pink, 10-1/2" d 350.00
    Emerald Glo, Coppertone metal base, 10" d 40.00
    Gazebo etching, crystal, 13" d..................................55.00
Cake Salver
    Cupid etch, green 245.00
    Crow's Foot Square, Orchid etching, low, ftd, crystal 40.00
    Crow's Foot Square, Orchid etching, low, ftd, ruby 120.00
    Gazebo etch, crystal 65.00
Candleholders, pr
    #191 Party Line, dome foot, Gypsy cutting, medium
        blue...25.00
    #300 Archaic, Nora Bird etching, amber 100.00
    #412 Crow's Foot Square, mushroom, black 90.00
    #412 Crow's Foot Square, red, 5-1/4" h 125.00
    #412 Crow's Foot Square, white, silver Venus and Cupid
        design...85.00
    #890 Crow's Foot Round, triple, red 165.00
    Nora Bird, pink 125.00
Candy Box, cov, flat
    #412 Crow's Foot Square, cobalt blue, 3-part 170.00
    #412 Crow's Foot Square, crystal, 3 ftd, chip edge of lid,
        flower cut 18.00
    Black Forest etch, crystal 65.00
    Gazebo etch...60.00
Candy Jar, cov, ftd, #191 Party Line, pink....................... 45.00
Candy Tray, #300 Gothic Garden, 11" d, center handle, light
    green 150.00

Orchid Etch, compote, yellow, 6-5/8" h, 7" w, $42.

Cheese and Cracker, plate with compote style, Black Forest, pink..250.00
Cheese and Cracker, plate with dome lid style, Nerva, crystal...65.00
Cocktail Shaker
    #191 Party Line Green, with spout...............................95.00
    Speakeasy, green 45.00
Compote
    #191 Party Line, pink, ftd, 11" 35.00
    #191 Party Line, with cutting, green............................28.00
    #300 Archaic, Lela Bird etch, green, tall......................65.00
    #411 Mrs. B, 7-1/2" d, yellow, tall................................35.00
    #411 Mrs. B, Gothic Garden etching, yellow, tall..........45.00
    #412 Crow's Foot Square, amethyst 65.00
Condiment Set, Emerald Glo, cut stars, orig lids and spoons...45.00
Console Bowl, 7", three-footed base, #503, amber, cutting ... 25.00
Console Bowl, 11" sq, Orchid, yellow 115.00
Creamer
    #411 Mrs. B, amber..12.50
    #412 Crow's Foot Square, Orchid etching, ruby...........40.00
    #700, Cupid etch, 5" h, ftd, pink................................135.00
Creamer and Sugar, #411 Gothic Garden etch, topaz......85.00
Cream Soup Bowl, #412 Crow's Foot Square, amber, ftd... 9.00 .... 10.00
Cruet, orig stopper, Emerald Glo, cut stars.......................45.00
Cup and Saucer
    #215 Glades, ruby, set of 8..110.00
    #220 Largo, light blue 25.00
    #411 Mrs. B, amber..7.50
    #411 Mrs. B, cobalt blue, set of 8 ....120.00
    #411 Mrs. B., ruby..10.00
    #412 Crow's Foot Square, amber 10.00
    #412 Crow's Foot Square, red 18.50
    #991, Penny Line, red 22.00
Finger Bowl, #991, Penny Line, ruby 35.00
Goblet
    #991 Penny Line, amethyst, low foot............................18.50
    #991 Penny Line, ruby 32.50
    #994 Popeye & Olive, 6-1/8" h, cobalt blue 35.00
Ice Bucket, #902, metal bail, cobalt blue 75.00
Ice Tub
    #300 Archaic, Cupid etch, green, 4-3/4".....................300.00
    #991 Penny Line, green 25.00
Ice Cream Soda, ftd, Party Line, 7" h
    Amber..18.50
    Pink..25.00
Iced Tea Tumbler, ftd, Penny Line, 12 oz
    Amethyst 22.50
    Ruby...35.00
Lemonade Pitcher, cov, #210 Regina, Black Forest etch, 10-1/4" h, pink...870.00
Marmalade, #191 Party Line, crystal, chrome cov 20.00
Mayo Bowl, black, Ardith, ftd..58.00
Mayonnaise Set, 3 pc, Cupid, green 275.00
Old Fashioned Tumbler, Georgian, 3-1/4" h, ruby.............15.00
Plate
    #191 Party Line, 6" d, amber..3.00
    #215 Glades, 6" d, ruby, set of 8.................................50.00
    #411 Mrs. B, 8-1/2" d, amber 6.00
    #412 Crow's Foot Square, 6" w sq, ruby.......................5.00
    #890 Crow's Foot Round, 6-1/2" d, blue 6.00
    #890 Crow's Foot Round, 8-1/2" d, amber.....................7.00
Punch Bowl Set, #555, crystal, bowl, 7 cups....................75.00
Relish, #890 Crow's Foot Round, 3-part, 11" l oblong, crystal, star cut..30.00

Saucer
    #411 Mrs. B, amber..2.00
    #411 Mrs. B, pink 2.00
    #411 Mrs. B, yellow 2.00
    #412 Crow's Foot Square, ruby......................................5.00
    #890 Crow's Foot Round, ruby.....................................7..00
Serving Plate, center handle
    #220 Largo, ruby..95.00
    #300 Archaic, Cupid etching, pink 200.00
    #300 Archaic, Peacock & Rose etch, green, 10-3/4" d.... 145.00
    #411, Mrs. B., amber..18.00
    #411 Mrs. B., pink..20.00
    #411 Mrs. B., Gothic Garden etch, yellow 55.00
    #1504, Chaucer, crystal 35.00
Sherbet
    #69 Georgian, ruby 12.50
    #191 Party Line, pink..8.50
    #991 Penny Line, amethyst, low foot............................12.50
    #991 Penny Line, ruby, tall...13.00
Soup Bowl, #412 Crow's Foot, green, 7" d, tiny base nick......20.00
Sugar Bowl
    #411 Mrs. B, amber..12.50
    #411 Mrs. B, Gothic Garden etching, green.................35.00
    #412 Crow's Foot Square, amber 10.00
    #412 Crow's Foot Square, ruby.....................................15.00
Sugar Pourer, #94 bullet-shape, screw-on nickel base, green 175.00
Tumbler
    #69 Georgian, 3-1/2" h, ftd, "V" shape, ruby.................10.00
    #191 Party Line, 3-1/2" h, ftd, amber..............................9.50
    #191 Party Line, 5" h, cone shape, green.......................7.75
    #191 Party Line, 5-3/4" h, cone shape, green................8.75
    #191 Party Line, 5-3/4" h, cone shape, pink 9.75
    #210 Regina, Coca-Cola type, 5 oz, crystal 3.00
    #890 Crow's Foot Round, amber 35.00
    #991 Penny Line, red, 3 1/4" h, red...............................8.00
    #991 Penny Line, red, 4 1/8" h, red.............................10.00
    #991 Penny Line, red, 5 1/4" h, red.............................12.00
Vase
    #182 Lela Bird etch, black, elliptical 250.00
    #184 Gothic Garden etch, ebony................................125.00
    #191 Party Line, fan, green..38.00
    #210 Regina, Black Forest etch, 6-1/2" h, black, squatty..175.00
    #210 Regina, Black Forest etch, 6-1/2" h, green 150.00
    #210 Regina, Black Forest etch, 10" h, black..............250.00
    #210 Regina, Black Forest etch, 10" h, crystal 195.00
    #210 Regina, Delilah Bird etch, 6-3/4" h, green..........125.00
    #184 Utopia etch, 10" h, black....................................195.00
    #184 Utopia etch, 10" h, yellow....................................85.00
    #412 Crow's Foot Square, amber, 11-1/2" h, flared 150.00

PAIRPOINT

History: The Pairpoint Manufacturing Co. was organized in 1880 as a silver-plating firm in New Bedford, Massachusetts. The company merged with Mount Washington Glass Co. in 1894 and became the Pairpoint Corporation. The new company produced specialty glass items often accented with metal frames.

Pairpoint Corp. was sold in 1938 and Robert Gunderson became manager. He operated it as the Gunderson Glass Works until his death in 1952. From 1952 until the plant closed in 1956, operations were maintained under the name Gunderson-Pairpoint. Robert Bryden reopened the glass manufacturing business in 1970, moving it back to the New Bedford area.

References: George C. Avila, *The Pairpoint Glass Story,* Reynolds-DeWalt Printing, Inc., 1968; Edward and Sheila Malakoff, *Pairpoint Lamps,* Schiffer, 1990; Leonard E. Padgett, *Pairpoint Glass,* Wallace-Homestead, 1979; John A. Shuman III, *Collector's Encyclopedia of American Art Glass,* Collector Books, 1988, 1994 value update; *Pairpoint Manufacturing Company 1894 Catalogue Reprint,* Antique Publications, 1997; Kenneth Wilson, *American Glass 1760-1930: The Toledo Museum of Art, Volume I, Volume II,* Hudson Hills Press and The Toledo Museum of Art, 1994.

Collectors' Clubs: Mount Washington Art Glass Society, P.O. Box 24094, Fort Worth, TX 76124-1094; Pairpoint Cup Plate Collectors, P.O. Box 890052, East Weymouth, MA 02189.

Museum: New Bedford Glass Museum, New Bedford, MA; Pairpoint Museum, Sagamore, MA.

Bell, 9-3/4" h, ruby base, crystal swirled handle..............200.00
Bowl
   7-3/4" d, 3-1/4" h, Peppermint Stick, star-cut frosted round form, rosaria rim cut in vertical stripes, medial band of cut diamond motif, fitted into silvered metal Aesthetic design holder 185.00
   8" d, 6-1/2" h, cov, raised gold chrysanthemum blossoms and foliage, eggshell white ground, gold striped handles, fish floral, sgd and numbered 600.00
   8-1/2" d, 3-1/2" h, Ambero, heavy walls, textured ext., int. painted with trailing vines, three pink lotus blossoms, lush green leaves floating on pool of lime green water, sgd "Ambero L"...................775.00
Box, cov, 7-1/4" l, 2-3/4" h, molded quatraform oval, opal ground, gold enameled floral dec, hinged metal rim fittings, sgd on base "PMC 9524"...................475.00
Candle Lamp
   8" h, blown-out pansy dec reverse painted shade, multicolored, mahogany pedestal with glass candleholder 920.00
   8" h, 4-1/2"d puffy blown-out poppy shade, orange, purple, and yellow flowers, orig wooden base, shade glued onto base...................1,100.00
Calling Cad Receiver, 5" d, engraved floral dec, clear controlled bubble ball connector, saucer base 145.00

Box, cov, molded quatraform oval shape, gold enameled floral dec, hinged metal rim fittings, base sgd "PMC 9524," 2-3/4" h, 6-1/4" l, $475. Photo courtesy of Skinner, Inc.

Candlesticks, pr, 9-1/2" h, Mt. Washington opalware glass, silver-plated overlay, deep pink painted ground, white peony dec, fancy Art Nouveau styled silver overlay base and socket, sgd "Pairpoint Mfg. Co."...................1,250.00
Centerpiece, 12" h, 13" l, swan, ruby glass brown body, applied clear swan's neck and head 450.00
Champagne, 5-1/8" h, Flambo pattern, crystal 60.00
Cologne Bottle, 8" h, applied vertical cranberry ribbing, elaborate flower form cranberry and clear stopper 115.00
Compote
   Cov, 8-1/2" d, ruby, bubbled finial and ball stem........145.00
   Open, 10" h, 5-1/2" d, Fine Arts Line, Aurora, brilliant cut deep amber glass bowl, brass and onyx base with full figured cherub holding up bowl, mkd "C1413 Pairpoint" 475.00
Console Set, 3 pc set
   12" d bowl, matching 3" h candlesticks, Tavern glass, bouquet of red, white, and green flowers...................575.00
   12" d, bowl, matching mushroom candlesticks, Flambo Ware, tomato red, applied black glass foot, c1915 ....1,950.00
Cracker Jar, cov
   5" h, squatty, shaded pink to yellow ground, floral and leaf dec, enameled flowers, ormolu molded base, sgd "P" in diamond on lid...................275.00
   6-1/2" h, 6" d, 16 panels, gold/beige ground, white and deep pink roses, green leaves, cov sgd "Pairpoint-3932," base sgd "3932/222," fancy metal work 595.00
   6-3/4" h, 7-1/2" w, Mt. Washington opalware, pistachios green top and bottom, 3-1/2" w band of deep pink and red roses, green leaves, gold trim, fancy silver-plated cov, handle, and bail, cov sgd "Pairpoint -3912," base sgd "3912-268" 725.00
   7" h, 6" d, molded bulbous base, hand painted, daisy dec, apricot ground, SP rim, cov, and bail handle, sgd and numbered 300.00
Decanter, 10" h, Old English pattern, quart, matching stopper 1,250.00
Hat, 4-1/4" h, deep red ground, white spatter, controlled bubbles, orig paper label 90.00
Inkwell, 4" h, colorless, all over controlled bubbles, sterling silver cap 200.00
Jewel Box, cov, robin's egg blue opal glass, six scalloped pink, yellow, and coral rose medallions with green leaves, brown traceries, painted gold trim, four ball feet, gold washed silver plated base, sgd and numbered...................350.00
Lamp, boudoir
   11-3/4" h, 5-1/2" d puffy pansy shade with open top, yellow, orange, red, and purple pansies, green ground, sgd "Pat. Applied for" in gold on outside bottom edge, urn-shaped base with antique brass finish sgd "Pairpoint"....3,300.00
   14-3/4" h, 9" closed top Papillon shade, pink and red roses, yellow and green butterflies, brass Pairpoint base with green paint 4,750.00
Lamp, floor, 16" d Springfield shade, 57" h, painted soft yellow and peach ground, purple azalea flowers, sgd "Pairpoint Corp." 2,000.00
Lamp, table
   20" h, 12" d, blown-out, deep green ground, brilliant colored deep rose azaleas, orig brass collared base with fancy floral design, sgd "Pairpoint Mfg Co. 3099," slight flake on int. rim, covered by ring 11,000.00
   22" h, 17" d Berkeley shade, wisteria design, trees with pale pink and yellow leaves, rare glass dec base with green finish, flat chip on base 2,700.00
   22-1/2" h, 16" d, Directorie, clipper ship dec, triple dolphin base, orig vertie finish on base, shade and base sgd "C. Durand," small rim chip...................4,000.00

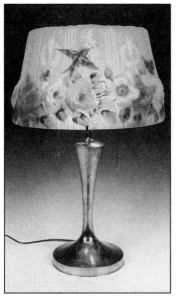

Lamp, Hummingbird and Rose puffy blown-out shade, white, yellow, and orange flowers and buds, green and tan foliage, $10,450. Photo courtesy of Jackson's Auctioneers & Appraisers.

23" h, Pisa shade, Egyptian scenes including Sphinx and two pyramids, camels, oasis, and merchants, dec attributed to Adolph Frederick, shade sgd "Pairpoint Corp. patented July 1907," Pairpoint sgd metal base with brass finish... 8,000.00
23" h, 16" d shade, landscape scene with man and deer by pond 1,800.00
23" h, 17" d Exeter shade, pink, yellow, and purple chrysanthemums on brown and black border, orig paper label, fancy silver plated sgd Pairpoint base................4,700.00
23" h, 17" d flared and domed Four Seasons shade, etched glass sections reversed painted depict Spring, Summer, Autumn, and Winter, three-socket baluster metal base with bronzed finish, sgd and numbered "D3051" 3,750.00
23-1/2" h, 17-1/2" d Carlisle conical reverse painted shade, exotic tropical trees and plants, four brightly colored cockatoos, silvered tripartite urn form metal base, imp "Pairpoint D3070" 6,625.00
27-1/2" h, 17" d Directorie scenic hexagonal heavy walled shade, reverse painted as six continuing panels, colorful landscaped ground with columned waterfront building, irid background coloring, paneled borders above and below, "The Pairpoint Corp.n" on border, gilt metal, onyx, and cut glass candle lamp form base, imp "Pairpoint Mfg. Co. E30001" 2,645.00
Mushroom shape, cut glass, dome shade with orig prisms, cut Viscaria pattern, c1915 ....1,850.00
Pitcher, 8-1/2" h, amberina, applied ruby handle 190.00
Plate, 5-1/8" d, enameled floral dec, artist sgd "P. Kiluk," diamond mark with "P" 125.00
Salt, master, colorless, controlled bubbles........................85.00
Scent Bottle, 5" h, 3-1/4" d, patterned millefiori stopper with two rose canes, other pastel canes, yellow translucent ground, clear controlled bubbles in body................................70.00
Smoking Stand, three opal bowls, 3-3/4" x 3-1/2" h, 3" x 2" h, and 2-1/4" x 2-1/4" h, Delft dec, windmills, houses, people, trees, and sailing ships, brass rims, maple shield shape, fancy brass trim and feet, brass cigar holder 565.00
Urn, ruby, swirl connector, applied cactus handles 350.00
Vase
    5-1/2" h, 4-1/2" w, Tavern glass, bulbous, enameled floral dec of vase of flowers, base numbered.................225.00
    6" h, Tavern glass, bulbous, enameled sailing galleon on wavy sea, sgd "D. 1507," c1900-38....................300.00
    9" h, Ambero, int. painted with scene of couple strolling down country lane, textured finish 750.00

10" h, purple, hexagonal sides, sgd 120.00
14-1/2" h, flared colorless crystal trumpet form, bright-cut floral dec, gilt metal foliate molded weighted pedestal base, imp "Pairpoint C1509" 490.00
15" h, winged cherub I flowing pink drape with tray of peonies, reverse with spray of multicolored poppies, gold borders, powder blue rim shading to cobalt blue ground, applied cobalt blue openwork handles...............1,400.00

PAPERWEIGHTS

History: Although paperweights had their origin in ancient Egypt, it was in the mid-19th century that this art form reached its zenith. The finest paperweights were produced between 1834 and 1855 in France by the Clichy, Baccarat, and Saint Louis factories. Other weights made in England, Italy, and Bohemia during this period rarely match the quality of the French weights.

In the early 1850s, the New England Glass Co. in Cambridge, Mass., and the Boston and Sandwich Glass Co. in Sandwich, Mass., became the first American factories to make paperweights.

Popularity peaked during the classic period (1845-1855) and faded toward the end of the 19th century. Paperweight production was rediscovered nearly a century later in the mid-1900s. Contemporary weights still are made by Baccarat, Saint Louis, Perthshire, and many studio craftsmen in the U.S. and Europe.

References: *Annual Bulletin of the Paperweight Collectors Association, Inc.*, available from association (P.O. Box 1263, Beltsville, MD 20704), 1996; Monika Flemming and Peter Pommerencke, *Paperweights of the World*, Schiffer, 1994; John D. Hawley, *Glass Menagerie*, Paperweight Press, 1995; Sibylle Jargstorf, *Paperweights*, Schiffer, 1991; Paul Jokelson and Dena Tarshis, *Baccarat Paperweights and Related Glass*, Paperweight Press, 1990; George N. Kulles, *Identifying Antique Paperweights-Lampwork,* Paperwork Press, 1987; Edith Mannoni, *Classic French Paperweights*, Paperweight Press, 1984; Bonnie Pruitt, *St. Clair Glass Collectors Guide*, published by author, 1992; Pat Reilly, *Paperweights*, Running Press, Courage Books, 1994; Lawrence H. Selman, *All About Paperweights*, Paperweight Press, 1992; ——, *Art of the Paperweight*, Paperweight Press, 1988; ——, *Art of the Paperweight, Perthshire*, Paperweight Press, 1983; ——, *Art of the Paperweight, Saint Louis*, Paperweight Press, 1981 (all of the Paperweight Press books are distributed by Charles E. Tuttle Co., 1996); Kenneth Wilson, *American Glass 1760-1930*, 2 vols., Hudson Hills Press and The Toledo Museum of Art, 1994.

Periodicals: *Paperweight Collectors Bulletin,* Paperweight Collectors Assoc., Inc., P.O. Box 1263, Beltsville, MD 20704; *Paperweight Gaffer,* 35 Williamstown Circle, York, PA 17404; *Paperweight News,* 761 Chestnut Street, Santa Cruz, CA, 95060; *The Gatherer,* Museum of American Glass at Wheaton Village, Glasstown Rd., Millville, NJ 08332.

Collectors' Clubs: Arizona Paperweight Collectors, 21405 N. 142nd Drive, Sun City West, AZ 85375; Caithness Collectors Club, 141 Lanza Ave., Building 12, Garfield, NJ 07026; Cambridge Paperweight Circle, 34 Huxley Rd.,

Welling, Kent DA16 2EW, U.K.; Delaware Valley Chapter, Paperweight Collectors International, 49 East Lancaster Ave., East Frazer, PA 19355-2120; Evangline Bergstrom Paperweight Collectors, 1008 North 14th St., Manitowoc, WI 54220; Indiana Paperweight Collectors, 123 North 9th St., Zionsville, IN 46077-1217; International Paperweight Society, 761 Chestnut St., Santa Cruz, CA 95060, http://www.paperweight.com; MD-DC-VA Paperweight Collectors, P.O. Box 20083, Baltimore, MD 21284-0083; Mid-Atlantic Paperweight Collectors, P.O. Box 6259, High Point, NC 27262; Montreal Paperweight Collectors, 3275 Sherbrooke St., East, #2, Montreal, Quebec H1W IC3 Canada; New England Paperweight Collectors, 168 Oxbow Rd., Wayland, MA 01778; Northern California Paperweight Collectors, 10110 Longview, Atwater, CA 95301; Ohio Paperweight Collectors, 2303 Glendon Rd., University Heights, OH 44118; Ontario Paperweight Collectors, 16 Tanburn Place, Don Mills, Ontario M3A 1X5 Canada; Paperweight Club of Deutchland, Postfach 1733, D-82145 Planegg, Germany; Paperweight Collectors Assoc. Inc., P.O. Box 1264, Beltsville, MD 20704, http://www.collectoronline.com/paperweights/PCA.html; Paperweight Collectors Assoc. of Chicago, 535 Delkir Ct., Naperville, IL 60565; Paperweight Collectors Assoc. of Texas, 19302 Marlstone Ct., Houston, TX 77094-3082; San Diego Paperweight Collectors, P.O. Box 881463, San Diego, CA 92168.

Museums: Bergstrom-Mahler Museum, Neenah, WI; Corning Museum of Glass, Corning, NY; Degenhart Paperweight & Glass Museum, Inc., Cambridge, OH; Museum of American Glass at Wheaton Village, Millville, NJ; Toledo Museum of Art, Toledo, OH.

Antique

Baccarat
  Anemone, three-dimensional ridged white petals trimmed in blue, central star honeycomb millefiori cane, star cut base, 2-1/4" d, 1-3/4" h, minor wear on base 750.00
  Butterfly meadow scene...18,700.00
  Clematis, six red buds, green stems and leaves, star cut base, 3" d, 2-1/8" h 2,050.00
  Close Concentric Millefiori, several arrowhead, whorls, and six-pointed star canes, green, red, blue, and white, 2-3/8" d, 1-3/4" h 475.00
  Close Pack Millefiori
    Miniature, Gridel silhouettes of dog, deer, horse, other complex canes with arrowheads, stars, signature, dated "B 1848," 2" d, 1-3/8" h...............................1,300.00
    Mushroom, various millefiori canes, including arrowheads, six-pointed stars, quatrefoil lobes, blue and white torsade, star cut base, 2-5/8" d, 1-7/8" h 2,200.00
    Various complex canes, 3" d, 2" h........................1,100.00
  Dog, central star honeycomb millefiori cane surrounded by five blue and white petals, five green leaves and stem, star cut base, 2" d, 1-3/8" h, minor surface spalls and surface scratches..800.00
  Dog Rose, central millefiori cluster of pink whorl and white star canes, five red and white petals, well centered with six and one facing, star cut base, 2-1/4" d, 1-5/8" h, several surface scratches, one spall, minor nicks and dings............800.00
  Primrose, center cluster of pink whorl and white stars, six red and white petals, star cut base, 2" d, 1-1/2" h........900.00
  Scattered Gridel Silhouette, thirteen millefiore and animal

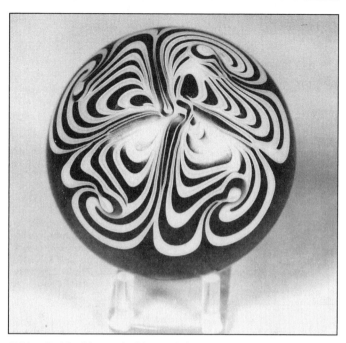

Crider, Swirls, blue and white, sgd, $90.

canes, upset muslin background, date cane "B1848," 2-1/4" d 1,380.00
  Scattered Millefiori, densely packed canes, Gridel animals including dancing devil, goose, deer, goat, kangaroo, dated "B1848," seriously cut down, 2" d................865.00
  Silhouette canes, lace background 2,900.00
  Trefoil, double interlaced, arrowhead, six-pointed stars and whorl canes, pedestal base with pink and white torsade, 3" d, 2-6/8" h 2,500.00
Clichy
  Close Packed Millefiori, various complex canes including signature "C" cane, stave basket, 2-3/8" d, 1-5/8" h, annealing crack in stave 700.00
  Concentric Millefiori
    Central pink rose cane, surrounded by row of pink, white, and green canes, outer concentric row of pink/white and amethyst/white and green canes, multi-faceted surface, 2" d, 1-3/16" h, ring of carbon and bubbles surrounds design..200.00
    Miniature, one row of nine Clichy roses, one row of green moss canes, blue and white stave basket, 1-3/4" d, 1" h..2,500.00
  Faceted Pattern Millefiori, miniature, central cluster of white star canes, blue whorl cane with two rows of complex canes, five side facets, one top facet, 1-3/4" d, 1-1/4" h, minor chip on top facet 250.00
  Garland Trefoil, pink and white whorl canes clustered in green cane, central Clichy rose and five other complex canes, 2" d, 1-1/4" h, minor surface scratches, wear to base...900.00
  Millefiori, multi-colored complex canes, central pink and green Clichy rose, upset muslin background, ten side facets, one bruise at side, 2-1/8" d........................490.00
  Millefiori, white center, red surround, green and purple outer rim...200.00
  Mushroom, close concentric design, large central pink and green rose surrounded by pin, white, cobalt blue, and cadmium green complex millefiori, middle row of canes with ten green and white roses alternating with pink pastry mold canes, pin and white stems, 2-3/4" d 6,600.00

Nosegay, three floral canes, including a Clichy rose on 5 green leaves and stem, 2" d, 1-1/4" h 600.00

Open concentric, Florette and millefiori canes, pink, blue, white, and green, on clear background, well centered, 2-1/4" d, 1-1/2" h..425.00

Miniature, eight Clichy roses and other complex canes, turquoise background, 1-5/8" d, 1-1/4" h...........800.00

Patterned Millefiori

Central floret surrounded by pink and green cog canes, garland of six-pointed star canes and bundled rods, 2" d, 1-1/2" h, minor roughage on base, minor surface imperfections...250.00

Central millefiori cane surrounded by ring of nine white and green Clichy roses, outside ring of ten pink and green Clichy roses, purple millefiori canes, 1-3/4" d, 1-1/4" h, minor wear on base 800.00

Central pink and green Clichy rose surrounded by clusters of white six-pointed stars and a garland of pink and green canes, 1-3/4" d, 1-1/4" h, minor surface wear 600.00

Two concentric millefiori white and green rings, central green and white complex cane, outer garland of white, green, blue, and red canes, red background, 2-3/8" d, 1-3/4" h, two surface spalls, one surface pit......800.00

Quatrefoil Patterned Millefiori, pink and white quatrefoil canes, spaced complex millefiori blue and green canes, sodden snow background, 3" d, 2" h 2,150.00

Scattered millefiori

Clear background, six Clichy roses, florets, and other complex canes, 2-3/4" d, 1-1/2" h......................850.00

Cobalt blue background, one Clichy rose cane, other complex canes, 3" d, 2-1/4" h.........................2,650.00

Scramble, whole and partial canes, one whole and one partial rose cane, 2-3/4" d, 2-1/8" h, minor surface scratches, wear on bottom...700.00

Star, purple and green canes around pink circlet, central cane centered white star, base scratches, 2" d.....215.00

Swirl

Alternating purple and white pinwheels emanating from white, green, and pink pastry mold cane, minor bubbles, 2-5/8" d...2,200.00

Central cane cluster of white florets, pink cog canes,

Degenhart, portrait of Elizabeth Degenhart, designed by Jack Choko of Millville, NJ, made by Imperial Glass for Crystal Art Co., introduced 1977, $175.

2-1/4" d, 1-1/4" h, minor surface wear, minor wear on base...800.00

Green and white, central cane cluster of pink whorls and white florets, 2" d, 1-1/2" h, minor surface wear, wear on base..900.00

Trefoil, interlaced, blue and pink canes, upset muslin background, large central millefiori cane, 2-5/8" d, 1-7/8" h 850.00

Degenhart, John, window, red crystal cube with yellow and orange upright center lily, one to window, 4 side windows, bubble in center of flower's stamens, 3-3/16" x 2-1/4" x 2-1/4" 1,225.00

Gillinder

Buddha, amber, opalescent, sgd 325.00

Turtle, orange, moving appendages in hollow center, pale orange background, molded dome, 3-1/16" d.......500.00

Millville, umbrella pedestal, red, white, green, blue, and yellow int., bubble in sphere center, 3-1/8" d, 3-3/8" h..... 800.00

New England Glass Co.

Concentric Millefiori, canes on muslin background, faceted, many internal fractures, 2-3/4" d 115.00

Crown, red, white, blue, and green twists interspersed with white latticino emanating from a central pink, white, and green complex floret/cog cane, minor bubbles in glass, 2-3/4" d 2,400.00

Double Overlay, red rose, yellow over white cut to clear, six side facets, one top facet, 2-3/4" d 230.00

Fruit Bouquet

Five apples, four cherries, eight green leaves, white spiral latticino background, design off-center, piece of cullet hovers above design 110.00

Five pears, four cherries, four green leaves, latticino background, well centered, polished pontil, 2-1/2" d, 1-3/4" h 550.00

Leaf Spray, three clusters of pink, blue, green, and amethyst leaves, latticino background, 2-1/2" d, one leaf spray has two separated leaves 200.00

Open Concentric Millefiori, complex canes including three rabbit canes, upset muslin background, ten side facets, one top facet, 2" d, 1-3/4" h 1,000.00

Poinsettia, central yellow millefiori cluster, cobalt blue petals, green stem, three green leaves, red jasper background, 2-3/4" d, 1-5/8" h, flower off-center, two of the petals have splits, polished pontil, wear on base......................100.00

Scramble, pieces of millefiori canes, rods, and muslin, 201/2" d, 1-5/8" h, minor surface nicks, scratches, and spalls, wear on base 75.00

Pinchbeck

Equestrian Scene, two men and one woman sit on horses with dogs at their feet, scene mounted in hollow clear dome, 2-5/8" d, 1-3/4" h...450.00

Pastoral dancing scene, couple dancing before grouped of onlookers, 3-3/16" d...650.00

Saint Louis

Clematis, twelve pastel blue ribbed petals, green leafy stem, white latticino bed, six outer facets, center "SL 1972" cane, 3" d 260.00

Faceted Posey, central floral arrangement of four millefiori canes, green leaves, surrounded by ring of blue and green millefiori canes, six-sided facets, one top facet, 2-1/4" d, 3" h 600.00

Fruit Bouquet, apple, two pears, three cherries, six green leaves, latticino background, polished base, 2-1/2" h, 1-3/4" h 800.00

Millefiori, close concentric millefiori, central silhouette of couple dancing, chartreuse, cadmium green, white, opaque pink, mauve, salmon, peach, powder blue, and ruby florets, cross canes, cogs, and bull's eyes canes, 3-3/16" d 5,750.00

Nosegay, four millefiori flower canes nestled on five green leaves and stems, blue, white, and yellow cane garland, strawberry cut base, 2-1/2" d, 1-3/4" h 600.00

Pattern Spaced Millefiori

Canes of six-pointed stars and cogs in six clusters, red jasper background, 2-1/4" d, 1-1/2" h 125.00

Miniature, complex millefiori cane clusters, millefiori garland on clear background, 1-1/2" d, 1-1/2" h 100.00

Red, white, blue, and yellow canes, upset muslin background, 3" d, 2" h, polished pontil, wear on base... 300.00

Pear, yellow and russet, sq cookie base, 2-3/4" h, 3" sq, broken stem 300.00

Pompon, pink petals, bundle of yellow rod canes in center of flower, one pink blossom, five green leaves with stem, star cut base, 2-3/4" d, 2" h, one bubble floats about flowers, minor surface scratches, wear on base 850.00

Scramble, various pieces of complex canes, polished pontil, 2-3/4" d, 1-3/4" h, wear on base 200.00

Upright Bouquet, four upright flowers and green leaves, white spiral torsade, star cut base, 3" d, 2-1/2" h, very minor surface scratches and wear on base............ 2,600.00

Sandwich Glass Co.

Cruciform, blue and red cross, red petals, two green leaves, 2-1/8" d, 1-1/2" h, polished pontil, wear on base.... 400.00

Cruciform and Heart, pink and green cruciform, red and green heart sits among four branches, two with pink leaves, two with blue leaves, green stems, 2-3/4" d, 1-3/4" h, one pink step separated from stem, surface scratches on top 350.00

Poinsettia

Double poinsettia, red flower with double tier of petals, green and white Lutz rose, green stem and leaves, bubbles between petals, 3" d 1,200.00

Central white and yellow rose cane, two tiers of red petals, green stem, two green leaves, polished pontil and polished base, 2-3/4" d, 1-1/2" h 450.00

Central yellow and blue millefiori cane, two tiers of light blue petals, six well-laced bubbles, green stem, two green leaves, well centered, polished pontil and base, 2-7/8" d, 1-1/2" h 500.00

Sulphide

Queen Victoria, French, 3-3/16" d, 2-1/5" h, scratches to surface and base, 2 pieces of cullet within glass 150.00

Shakespeare, William, cameo type, clear background, French, 2" d, 3/4" h, minor surface scratches, very low profile 125.00

Woman, unidentified, diamond-cut background, attributed to Saint Louis, 3" d, 2-1/8" h, minor surface spalls and roughage to base 100.00

Union Glass Co. (Somerville)

Bird, pair of egrets and egg-filled nest, 3-3/4" d 300.00

Central red flower, words "E. E. Rines, Somerville," garland of twelve flowers surrounds design, 4" d, 2-7/8" h, surface scratches, central flower has in-the-making imperfection 175.00

Fantasy Flower, blue petals with yellow dots, green leaves, sitting on red, white, and blue background, 3-1/4" d, 3" h, one surface spall 500.00

Poinsettia, red, split petals, 3-1/8" d, scratched 50.00

U.S. Glass Co., Colombian Exposition, frosted center, woman with long tresses................. 145.00

Val St. Lambert, patterned millefiori, four red, white, blue, pistachio, and turquoise complex canes circlets spaced around central pink, turquoise and cadmium green canes circlet,

canes set on stripes of lace encircled by spiraling red and blue torsade, minor blocking crease, 3-1/2" d 950.00

Whitefriars, close concentric millefiori, pink, blue, purple, green, white, and yellow cog canes, 1948 date cane, minor bubble in dome, 3-5/8" d 900.00

Modern

Ayotte, Rick

Bird, miniature

Cardinal, red cardinal sits on branch of three pink roses, green leaves and stems, script sgd "Ayotte M-14 '85," 2" d, 1" h................. 250.00

Finch, yellow bird perched on branch, faceted, sgd and dated, limited ed. of 25, 1979, 2-3-16? D 750.00

House Wren, brown house wren sits on branch with green leaves, powder blue background, script sgd "Ayotte 8/50 1980," 2-1/2" d, 1-3/4" h 500.00

Mocking Bird, gray and white mocking bird sits on branch with three orange blossoms and leaves, script sgd "Ayotte M-45 '93," 2" d, 1-1/4" h 325.00

Titmouse, gray and white bird sits on holly leaves and berries, snowy white background, script sgd and dated "Ayotte M-27/87," 2" d, 1-1/4" h 350.00

Hawaiian Floral Bouquet, two Lady Slipper orchids, six Hawaiian flowers, green and brown leaves, sgd in script "Rick Ayotte ED/50 '95," 3-1/2" d, 2" h................... 600.00

Baccarat

Animal Series, centers surrounded with millefiori and animal canes, 3-1/4" d

Dancing Devil, 1975 .... 310.00

Deer, dated 1976 .... 275.00

Elephant, 1973 .... 315.00

Grouse, 1975 .... 310.00

Horse, 1973 .... 315.00

Hunter, 1974 .... 325.00

Monkey, 1976 .... 300.00

Pair of Partridges, 1976 .... 275.00

Pelican, 1974 .... 300.00

Rooster, dated 1971 .... 310.00

Squirrel, 1972 .... 310.00

Swan, 1974 .... 315.00

Church, closed pack millefiori, zodiac silhouette canes, date cane "1968," acid etch mark underneath, 2-3/4" h, 1-3/4" h 400.00

Concentric Millefiori, concentric rings of reds, whites, and greens, acid-sgd on reverse, 2-3/8" d, 1-3/4" h, some distortion to canes during making................................. 50.00

Gridel pelican cane surrounded by five concentric rings of yellow, pink, green, and white complex canes, pink canes contain eighteen Gridel silhouette canes, lace background, 1973 date cane, signature cane, sgd and dated, limited ed. of 350, 3-1/16" d 850.00

Peace on Earth, sgd "Baccarat, France" 130.00

Sulphide, double overlay

Bonaparte, yellow on white, 3" d 125.00

Mount Rushmore, oval, red, white and blue, 4" l.... 100.00

Mozart, green on white, 3" d 125.00

Baccarat-Dupont

Looped garland, six loops, three yellow and three green surround white and pink ring of millefiori canes, center cane with four arrow heads, six side facets and one top facet, c1932. 2-3/4" d, 2" h 225.00

Open Concentric Millefiori, red, white, and green complex millefiori canes, c1932, 2" d, 1-5/8" h 50.00

Banford, Bob

Daffodil, two yellow blossoms, two buds, green leaves, cobalt blue background, multifaceted base, sgd with signature red "B" cane, 2-7/8" d, 2-1/2" h 376.00

Wheat Flower, yellow twelve-petaled flower with brown dots, yellow stamens, one partially opened bud, green leaves, stems, sgd with red "B" signature cane and star on base, 2-7/8" d, 2" h 225.00

Banford, Ray

Iris, purple iris blossom, two buds, green leaves, star cut white background, sgd with signature "B" cane, 3" d, 2" h 275.00

Rose Bouquet, three white roses, green leaves, powder blue pebble background, sgd in underside with black "B," 2-3/8" d, 2-1/8" h 275.00

Barker, Joe, amethyst six-petaled flower, blossom with one bud, six leaves, transparent amber background, script sgd on bottom "Joe Barker," 2-1/4" d, 1-1/2" h 80.00

Buzzini, Chris

Bindwind and Wild Flax, two pink morning glories entwined with wild flax blossoms, buds, and leaves, numbered "33/40," sgd and dated with signature cane, script sgd "Buzzini '94," 3" d, 2-1/4" h 700.00

Floral Bouquet

Four wild rose bouquet, three pink wild roses, one yellow wild rose, five buds, green leaves, brown stems, numbered "37/40," sgd and dated in script "Buzzini '90," sgd and dated with "Buzzini 90" signature cane, 3" d, 2-3/8" h..450.00

Three red azaleas surrounded by purple bellflowers, three yellow wild flowers, sgd and dated with signature cane, script sgd "Buzzini '87," 3" d, 2" h 500.00

Two purple asters with bud, one yellow wild rose with two buds, green leaves, brown stems, sgd and dated with signature cane, script sgd "Buzzini '91," numbered "25/40," 3" d, 2-1/4" h..500.00

Lupine, three pink and amethyst blossoms, three white blossoms, yellow stamens, green leaves, brown stems, numbered "69/75," sgd and dated "Buzzini '90" with signature cane and script, 3" d, 2-5/8" h................................450.00

Orchid, pink, white, and orange orchid, bud, leaves, and roots, sgd and dated "Buzzini '87" with signature cane and script, 2-7/8" d, 2-1/4" h..........................475.00

Vetch, amethyst and white blossoms, green leaves and stems, brown roots, sgd and dated with signature cane, script sgd "Buzzini '91," numbered "16/40," 3" d, 2-1/4" h.......... 400.00

Violet, two purple flowers, yellow and orange centers, green stems, two buds, four heart-shaped green leaves, bulbous root system, signature and date cane "Buzzini '89," also sgd in script "Buzzini LSV 8912," 3" d, 2-1/4" h 550.00

Correia, orchid, orange flower, green stem and leaves, black background, frosted ext. front window facet, limited edition of 200, numbered "106," sgd "Correia," dated "1983," 2-58" d, 2-1/4" h 180.00

D'Albret, sulphide series, 2-3/4" d

Columbus, blue background 50.00

Kennedy, Jack and Jackie, green background............65.00

Roosevelt, Franklin, amethyst background...................50.00

DePalma, Tony, rose, pink to white crimped petals, four green leaves, clear pedestal foot, sgd and dated on bottom "A DePalma 1986," 3-1/4" d, 4-1/2" h..........................150.00

Grubb, Randall, floral bouquet, eleven flowers, pastel pink, blue, and amethyst, green leaves and stems, sgd in script "Randall Grubb '92," 3" d, 2-3/8" h..........................375.00

Hamon, Bob, crimped blue flower, green leaves, clear pedestal, six side facets, one top facet, sgd on bottom with emb "H," 2" d, 2-1/8" h..75.00

Hansen, Robert, lily of the valley, three white blossoms, eight

buds on green stem with leaves, pink background, six side facets, one top facet, base sgd "Robert Hansen," 2-1/8" d, 1-1/2" h 125.00

Hansen, Ronald E., single flower, blue five-petaled flower, central millefiori cane, six green leaves, cobalt blue background, six side facets, one top facet, base sgd "Ronald E. Hansen," 1-3/4" d, 1-1/4" h 50.00

Kaziun, Charles

Concentric Millefiori

Central cane cluster with red heart surrounded by eight millefiori red, white, and green canes, upset muslin background, underside sgd with blue on white "K" signature cane, 1-1/2" d, 1-1/8" h, several minute bubbles exist within muslin 375.00

Heart, turtle silhouette, shamrocks, six pointed stars, and floret canes encircled by purple and white torsade, turquoise background flecked with goldstone, K signature cane, 2-1/16" d 1,200.00

Open Concentric Millefiori, central fish silhouette cane surrounded by six silhouette canes of turtles and shamrocks, robin's egg blue with gold aventurine background, pink torsade surrounds design, sgd with black and white signature cane, reverse side sgd with gold "K"..........500.00

Pedestal, millefiori spider lily, gold "K," 1-1/4" h, 2" h

Blue cushion background 350.00

Gold aventurine on amethyst 375.00

Gold flecked white background 375.00

Green background 365.00

Pink background 365.00

Yellow background..350.00

Silhouette, black and white portrait silhouette surrounded by green, white, and pink canes, opaque pink background, six side facets, one top facet, miniature, sgd on underneath side with gold "K," 1-3/8" d, 7/8" h...............425.00

Lewis, Pete, rose, pink crimped petals, four green leaves, pedestal base, sgd on underside with signature "PL" cane, 2-3/8" d, 2-3/4" h... 185.00

Lotton, Charles

Surface Decorated

All over irid swirled blue and white dec, reverse sgd "Lotton 1974," 2-3/4" d, 1-7/8" h...............................65.00

Iridescent floral yellow, white, and blue dec, reverse side sgd in script "Charles Lotton 1975 Multi Flora," 2-3/4" d, 1-3/4" h 75.00

Lundberg Studios

Jonquil

Five orange and white jonquil blossoms, green leaves, script signature "Steven Lundberg, Lundberg Studios 1986 101623," 3" d, 2-1/2" h 250.00

Three blossoms, red and white stripped petals, yellow stamens, green leaves, sgd in script "Steven Lundberg, Lundberg Studios 1989 0600532," 2-7/8" d, 2-1/4" h..200.00

Rose, pink rose, nine leaves, sgd in script "Daniel Salazar, Lundberg Studios 1989 05Z672," 2-7/8" d, 2-1/2" h..150.00

Orient & Flume, complex central millefiori cluster, marbrie green, maroon, and white background, script sgd "Orient & Flume C152 May 1978," 2-3/4" d, 2-1/4" h 100.00

Parabelle

Patterned millefiori, central Clichy rose surrounded by seven green and white millefiori canes in ring of twelve Clichy type roses, garland of eight circlets, green moss carpet background, sgd and dated on reverse side with cane "PB1992," 2-3/4" d, 2" h......................................650.00

Spaced millefiori, various complex canes, red opaque background, signature and date cane "PB1990," orig paper label, 2-3/4" d, 1-5/8" h 145.00

Perthshire

Christmas

1983, Christmas holly wreath, green and red bow, upset muslin background, sgd and dated on bottom with signature cane, 2-5/8" d, 2" h 150.00

1984, poinsettia and white Christmas flower bouquet, sgd with "P" signature cane, strawberry cut base, 2-3/4" d, 2-1/4" h............................125.00

1987, word "Noel," white Christmas flower, two boughs of holly and five white stars, six side facets, one top facet, sgd "P 1987," 3" d, 2" h 150.00

Crown, central complex cane with projecting red and blue twisted ribbons alternating with latticino ribbons, 1985 date cane, signature cane, limited edition of 268, 3" d 850.00

Double Overlay

Single pink flower resting on latticino background, cut red and white double overlay, sgd with "P" signature cane, orig label, 2-7/8" d, 2-1/4" h 225.00

Single upright flower, pink petals, green leaves, central "P" signature cane, blue and white double overlay, eight side facets, one top facet, strawberry cut bottom, 2-1/4" d, 1-1/2" h 200.00

Three flower bouquet, three white lily-of-the-valley flowers, swirl cut green and white double overlay, "P" signature cane, 2-3/8" d, 1-3/4" h 175.00

Miniature, six-petaled pink flower, central "P" signature cane, two green leaves, stem hovering over pink and white basket, 1-3/4" d, 1-1/2" h............................175.00

Silk Worm, green, black, and red silk worm rests on two green leaves, top and side faceting, sgd underneath leaf with "P" signature cane, 2-3/8" d, 2-1/4" h..............150.00

Single Flower, five-petaled amethyst and white flower, central "P" signature cane, green leaves and stems, eight side facets, one top facet, strawberry cut base, 2-1/4" d, 1-1/2" h 100.00

Randolph, Grant, Oriental tree with millefiori blossoms, irid and bubbled background, applied lamp-worked humming bird on surface, egg-shaped, bottom sgd "Grant Randolph 1993 A2012," orig paper label, 2-1/4" d, 2-1/2" h..................50.00

Rosenfield, Ken

Floral bouquet, two pink and yellow flowers, three pink buds, green leaves and stem, egg-shaped, sgd in script on bottom "Ken Rosenfield '93," 2-3/4" d, 3-5/8" h 175.00

Scenic Aquatic, colorful sea creates and grasses arranged on sanded blue background, side inscribed "Ken Rosenfield '91" and "R" cane, 3-1/4" d............................400.00

Spring Bouquet, blue, pink, and white spring flowers suspended above bright transparent claret background, side inscribed "Ken Rosenfield '87" near "R" cane, 3-1/4" ... 345.00

Saint Louis

Abundance Fruit Basket, latticino fruit basket filled with lamp worked bananas, applies, pears, cherries, plums, and leaves, limited edition of 150, sgd in script "St. Louis 1993," numbered "114/150," 4-1/4" l, 3-1/4" w 750.00

Butterfly, blue, red, white, black, and amethyst millefiori, white star dust carpet background, sgd and dated with signature cane on underside, 2-7/8" d, 1-7/8" d.....300.00

Clematis, six-petaled red flower, central signature and date cane "SL 1982" on cobalt blue background, orig paper label, 2-1/2" d, 2" h 175.00

Egg Shape, hand cooler type, oval, white latticino alternating with pink to blue twists, "SL1976" cane, 2-7/8" h ...230.00

Five Flower Bouquet, three blue clematis, one white double clematis, red and white primrose, green leaves and

stems, underside with date and signature cane "SL 1986," 2-3/4" d, 2" h................................350.00

Mushroom, double overlay, close concentric millefiori, central signature cane "SL 1970," encased in pistachio over white double overlay, five side facets, one top facet, 2-7/8" d, 2" h 425.00

Pie Douche, close concentric millefiori, complex canes, latticino pedestal basket, signature and date "1972" cane, 3" d, 3" h............................950.00

Red and white honeycomb carpet background, rings of C-shaped red and white complex canes, central signature and date "1974" cane, sgd "SL 1974," 2-3/4" d, 2-1/4" h....350.00

Rose, single pink rose and bud, green leaves and stems, pale amethyst background, six side facets, one top facet, sgd and dated on reverse with "SL1978" signature cane, 3-1/8" d, 2" h 275.00

Rose Spray, red bud and blossoms, thorny branch, six side facets, sgd "SL1976" cane under white cushion, 3" d 175.00

Sulphide

Amour, garland of five blue flowers, red background, six side facets, one top facet, sgd and dated "1979" with signature cane on bottom, 2-7/8" d, 1-5/8" h 125.00

Double eagle, blue background, encased in red over white double overlay, five side facets, one top facet, acid etched signature on base, 3" d, 2" h 125.00

Upright Bouquet, three flowered upright bouquet, red, white, and blue, green leaves, latticino cushion, white flower has a date and signature cane "SL 1978," six side facets, one top facet, 2-7/8" d, 2" h 275.00

Smith, Gordon

Lady Slipper, sgd on side "GES 1983," 2-5/8" d, 1-3/4" h 195.00

Strawberry, one red strawberry, one green strawberry, one blossom, three leaves, script sgd on side "GES 1985 EXP," 2-3/4" d, 1-3/4" h............................255.00

Smith, Hugh, cattail, three cattails among green leaves, green and white jasper background, five side facets, one top facet, sgd with "HS" signature cane, sgd and dated "1973 Hugh Edmond Smith" on base, 2-1/4" d, 1-1/2" h 100.00

Stankard, Paul

Blackberry Bouquet, three blackberries, three orange and white stylized flowers, two white blossoms and buds, green stems and leaves, acid signature "Paul J. Stankard A027 1988," 3-3/8" d, 2-1/4" h 1,600.00

Blueberry and Spirit, clusters of pink blossoms, blueberries, and yellow flowers, complete under system with roots labeled "seeds, ripe, moist, nature's continuum," male nude spirit below, PS96 cane at side, edge inscribed " Paul J. Stankard M5 '96," 3-1/4" d 2,415.00

Dogwood, delicate four petal white blossoms, cobalt blue background, sgd "PS" within cane and inscribed '73................................990.00

Epiphytic Orchid, green stems, brown root system, black "S" on yellow signature cane, engraved "B590, 1982," 3" d, 1-3/4" h 800.00

Floral Bouquet

Two pink roses, three pink buds, one yellow rose, three white wild roses, green leaves, brown stems, sgd with black "S" on yellow signature cane, engraved "B621 1982," 3" d, 2" h 1,500.00

Yellow meadow wreath, blue forget-me-nots, red St. Anthony's fire, white bellflowers, and white chokeberry blossom and buds, 1977, 3" d........................2,400.00

Indian Pipes and Spirit, three white blossoms, brown bud over tangled root system, nude woman "spirit" and "seeds, pollen, fertile" canes below, sgd "PS94" at side, inscribed "Paul J. Stankard S1594" lower edge, 3-1/4" d 2,300.00

Lady's Slipper, two blossoms, bud, green leaves on stem, root system, seed pod, deep green background side "S" cane, inscribed '81, 3-1/4" d 1,495.00

Spring Beauty

Six petal white blossom, curved green stem with roots "S" cane at side, inscribed "PJS '72," 2" d 1,035.00

Three striped pink on white blossoms, six buds on stems with roots, tiny red "S" cane at side, inscribed '79, 3" d 1,840.00

Stylized Flowers

Fourteen striped petal blossom, leafy stem, black background, base inscribed "PJS '71," 2-1/8" d 990.00

Five petal red centered purple blossom and bud, twisted stem and roots, white background, base fully inscribed "Paul J. Stankard '71," 2-1/8" d 1,035.00

Six pink flowers, green leaves, buds, and stems, powder blue background, sgd with black "S" signature cane on side, dated with black "71" cane, 2-1/8" d, 1-3/8" h, three bubbles appear within design 450.00

Trillium, three red and white petals, three large green leaves, three smaller leaves, clear background, sgd with "PS" signature cane, dated "1973" in script, 2-3/8" d, 2" h 500.00

Wildflower, yellow blossom and buds, seed pod, green stem, root system, edge fully inscribed "Paul J. Standard," 3" d 1,265.00

Wild Rose, pink five-petaled wild rose flower, yellow stamens, green leaves and stems, clear background, fifteen side window facets, top facet, criss-cross pattern side cut, sgd with "PS" signature cane, 2-5/8" d, 1-7/8" h 550.00

Tarsitano, Debbie

Bouquet, yellow and blue centered pink blossom, bright blue flowers on green leafy vines, "DT" cane on reverse, 3" d 415.00

Dahlia, purple flower, yellow stamens, green leaves, centered on star cut base, DT signature cane, 3" d, 2" h 650.00

Orange and purple bird of paradise flower on stalk, striped green leaves, star cut background, DT signature cane, 2-15/16" d 550.00

Three flower bouquet, three pink five-petaled blossoms, two buds, four smaller pale blue flowers, green leaves, brown stems, star cut base, signature cane present, but unreadable, 3-1/8" d, 2-1/4" h 650.00

Yellow centered purple-blue, yellow, and pink zinnia blossoms with red and blue buds, leafy stems, "DT" cane on reverse, 3-1/4" d 850.00

Tarsitano, Delmo

Coiled green snake, realistic earth and translucent green background, sgd with "DT" signature, 3-3/8" d, 2-1/4" h 750.00

Earth Life Series, open mouth snake entwined in pink, lavender, and blue flowers, rocky ledge background, "DT" cane in design, 4-1/4" d 1,750.00

Tarsitano, Victor, red trumpet flower, yellow centers, one single bug on branch, four green leaves, rock background, sgd underneath with "T" signature cane, 3" d, 2-1/4" h 400.00

Trabucco, David and John

Floral Bouquet, two yellow flowers, two blue flowers with yellow centers, six blue buds, seven small yellow flowers, green leaves and stems, sgd in script "Trabucco 1990 DJ," 3" d, 2-1/2" h 150.00

Raspberry Bouquet, three red raspberries, two pink flowers, yellow center stamens, four pink buds on branch, seven green leaves, signature "T" cane underneath one leaf, sgd in script "Trabucco 1991 DJ," 3" d, 2-3/4" h 225.00

Wild Rose, fourteen petal pink and white flower, white stamens, one bud and five small white flowers, nine green leaves, sgd underneath one leaf with black on green "T," script sgd

"Trabucco 1992 DJ," 1-7/8" d, 1-5/8" h 125.00

Trabucco, Victor

Lavender Rose, three flowers on green and brown leafy stems, "VT" leaf cane, inscribed "Trabucco 1994," 3-3/4" d 815.00

Raspberry and Roses Magnum, red berries, white blossoms, "VT" leaf cane, side inscribed "Trabucco 1996," 3-3/4" d 690.00

Rose Bouquet, single large pink rose, two pink buds, eight white bellflowers, eight green leaves and stems, translucent cobalt blue background, sgd underneath one leaf with a "VT" signature cane, script sgd "Trabucco 1987," 3" d, 2-5/8" h 250.00

Violet, three violet blossoms, two buds, five heart-shaped leaves, green stems, sgd underneath one leaf with "VT" signature cane, 1983, 3" d, 2-3/8" h 175.00

Ward, Mayauel, floral bouquet, four blue trumpet flowers, two orange blossoms, one pink and yellow flower, one orchid, three yellow and orange berries, black background, large top facet, sgd on bottom "Mayauel Ward 1995," 3-3/4" d, 2" h 375.00

Whitefriars

Close Pack Millefiori, multi side facets, one top facet, sgd and dated "1978" with Whitefriars monk cane, 3" d, 2" h ... 250.00

Rectangular Block, millefiori canes arranged in block form, sgd and dated with signature monk cane and "1973" date cane, 2-5/8" x 2-1/8" x 1-1/2" 300.00

Whittemore, Francis

Acorns, two green and brown acorns on branch with three brown and yellow oak leaves, translucent cobalt blue background, circular top facet five oval punties on sides, 2-3/8" d 300.00

Nosegay, titled four flower nosegay, one contains a "W" signature cane and five green leaves, opaque white background, clear pedestal base, also sgd on reverse with blue and white "W" signature cane, 1-3/8" d, 2-3/4" h 250.00

Pompon Bouquet, seven pink pompons, green leaves and stems, snow white background, sgd with signature black on yellow "W" signature cane, 2-3/8" d, 1-3/4" h 325.00

Rose

Pink rose and bud, green leaves and stems, cobalt blue background, sgd with black on yellow "W" signature cane on underneath side of one petal, 201/2" d, 1-7/8" h 225.00

Yellow crimped rose, three green leaves, clear pedestal foot, signed with signature black on white "W" cane, 1-3/4" d, 2-1/2" h 225.00

Three flower bouquet, single five-petaled clematis blossom, white and yellow calla lily, yellow and green stylized blossom, green leaves and stems, red translucent background, sgd with signature black on yellow "W" cane, 2-3/8" d, 2" h 200.00

Violet, two partially opened violets, one bud, green stems and leaves, opaque white background, sgd with signature black on white "W" cane, seven side facets, one top facet, 1-7/8" d, 1-5/8" h 150.00

Ysart, Paul, green fish, yellow eye, yellow and white jasper background encircled by pink, green, and white complex cane garland, PY signature cane 550.00

Zimmerman, Joe, doorstop, five pink, blue, white, orange, and yellow ice-pick flowers, white background, green leaves, script sgd on base "Joe Zimmerman," emb "S," minor surface scratches 50.00

PATE-DE-VERRE

History: The term "pate-de-verre" can be translated simply as "glass paste." It is manufactured by grinding lead

glass into a powder or crystal form, making it into a paste by adding a 2 percent or 3 percent solution of sodium silicate, molding, firing, and carving. The Egyptians discovered the process as early as 1500 B.C.

In the late 19th century, the process was rediscovered by a group of French glassmakers. Almaric Walter, Henri Cros, Georges Despret, and the Daum brothers were leading manufacturers.

Contemporary sculptors are creating a second renaissance, led by the technical research of Jacques Daum.

Ashtray
 3-1/2" sq, mottled turquoise and midnight blue, two rect compartments, molded bumblebee with black and orange body, green wings, deep brown head, molded signature "A Walter/Nancy" and "Berge/SC," c1925 .... 900.00
 6-1/4" l, 3-1/2" w, center medallion with Egyptian head, molded in reds and purples, small flower buds around edge, raised lattice work on bottom 1,650.00
Atomizer, 5-3/4" h, red berries, green leaves, molded signature "H. Berge" 1,200.00
Bookends, pr, 6-1/2" h, Buddha, yellow amber pressed molded design, seated in lotus position, inscribed "A Walter Nancy"...2,450.00
Bowl
 4" d, 8-3/4" h, Almeric Walter, designed by Jules Cayette, molded blue green glass, yellow center, green around border, three brown scarab beetles with long black antennae, inscribed "A. Walter Nancy," and also "J. Cayette," "Made in France" on base 4,600.00
 4-3/4" h, oviform, turquoise blue ground, molded green band of stylized flowers, molded "A. Walter Nancy" 1,600.00
 6-1/2" d, 4" h, mottled violet bowl, molded with animated hunting scene of wild boar, deer, and fowl being speared by arrows, molded "G. Argy-Rousseau" 8,250.00
 9-3/4" d, 4" h, octagonal coupe, solid foot, dec by swags of stylized leafy purple and black branches, mottled colorless near transparent background, ext. molded "G. Argy Rousseau" 6,500.00
Center Bowl, 10-3/8" d, 3-3/4" h, blue, purple, and green press molded design, 7 exotic long legged birds, central multi-

pearl blossom, repeating design on ext., raised pedestal foot, sgd "G. Argy-Rousseau" 6,750.00
Clock, 4-1/2" sq, stars within pentagon and tapered sheaves motif, orange and black, molded sgd "G. Argy-Rousseau," clock by J. E. Caldwell 2,750.00
Dagger, 12" l, frosted blade, relief design, green horse head handle, script sgd "Nancy France" 1,200.00
Dish
 6" l, 5" w, brilliant yellow, orange, and blue ground, large blue moth, detailed, sgd "A. Walter" 2,500.00
 Large, butterfly, script sgd "Daum Nancy, France"....200.00
Display Plaque, 4-4/5" l, 2-5/8" h, rect, golden amber, brown, and colorless, raised molded brown lettering "Les Pates de Verre d'Argy-Rousseau" 2,530.00
Inkwell, double, 6-1/2" l, 3" h, black and brown beetle, brilliant orange and yellow glass, central beetle motif, orig conforming covers, sgd "Walter" 4,500.00
Jewelry
 Earrings, pr, 2-3/4" l, teardrop for, molded violet and rose shaded tulip blossom, suspended from rose colored swirl molded circle 2,200.00
 Pendant, 1-1/4" d, molded amethyst portrait of Art Nouveau woman, flowing hair, gilt metal mount 400.00
 Pendant, 2-1/8" x 2-1/4", pierced glass, butterfly, blue, green, red-orange wings, colorless and gray ground, inscribed "GAR" in design (G. Argy-Rousseau) 2,415.00
 Pendant, 2-1/2" x 1-3/4", deep amethyst, red and brown spatter, detailed moth, orig silk tassel, necklace, and red bead, G. Argy Rousseau 1,750.00
Paperweight
 2-1/2" h, 3-1/2" w, brown snail, realistic detailing, brilliant green, blue base, sgd "A. Walter".......................2,500.00
 2-5/8" h, Papillion de Nuit, cube, internally streaked gray, deep forest green highlights, molded full relief moths, molded "G. Argy-Rousseau," c1923 ....2,400.00
 3-1/2" h, mouse, gray body, eating from green walnut shell perched on green grassy knoll, mkd by designer and "A. Walter Nancy" in mold.......................................7,500.00
 3-3/4" h, 3-1/2" w, lizard, naturalistic dark brown and black, brilliant blue and green sculptured base, sgd "A. Walter"..5,250.00
Plaque
 5" d, blue, black, and brown moth, Art Deco inspired patterned base, sgd "Walter" 2,400.00
 6-1/2" d, 7-1/4" h, amber ground, two stalking black striped orange tigers emerging from stylized panels ribbed as tall grasses, molded "G. Argy-Rousseau," No. 28.11, designed as lighting plate on electrolier stand...................... 5,750.00
 8-1/2" l, 4" w, figural, white ground, salmon pink mythical creature with blue eyes 1,500.00
Sculpture
 8" h, Faune, man/goat, gray-green glass, inscribed "66/250" on base, mkd "Daum/J.P. Demarchi" on neck and plinth, 1980s 690.00
 9-5/8" l, crab in sea grasses, lemon yellow, chocolate brown, pale mauve, and sea green, sgd "A. Walter/Nancy" and "Berge/SC" 8,500.00
 10-3/4" h, seated cat, gray-green glass, inscribed "53/250" on base, mkd in mold, c1980 ....690.00
Tray
 6" x 8", apple green, figural green and yellow duck with orange beak at one end, sgd "Walter, Nancy"..........950.00
 7" l, 5" w, angular mottled orange-yellow oval, full bodied black and brown center scarab, imp "A. Walter/Nancy" ...2,750.00
Vase
 4" h, smoky gray mottled with violet, rose, and green, relief

Bowl, yellow leaves and purple vines, mkd "Argy-Rousseau," 3-3/4" d, 2" h, $900.

molded with clusters of white berried branches, violet leaves, molded "G. Argy-Rousseau France" 7,250.00

4-3/4" h, spherical, black spiders spinning intricate webs from yellow, orange, amber, and black bramble bushes, side molded "A. Argy-Rousseau," base molded "France" internal 1/2" fracture at mid center 2,990.00

5-1/8" h, striated aubergine purple and colorless cone shaped body, integrated disk foot molded with four repeating spiked devices, imp "Decorchemont" in horseshoe stamp, numbered C199 on base................3,600.00

5-1/4" h, 4-7/8" l, golden amber and brown ground, central conical bud vase in oval plinth base, molded and stylized birds of prey at each side, mkd "G. Argy-Rousseau" 4,025.00

5-1/2" h, press molded and carved, mottled amethyst and frost ground, 3 black and green crabs, red eyes, naturalistic seaweed at rim, center imp "G. Argy-Rousseau," base imp "France"..5,500.00

9" h, molded goblet form, yellow amber ground, shaded green to orange at base, highly detailed and realistic green-black lizard wrapped around stem, imp "A. Walter" and "H. Berge SC," orig thin rim area 6,325.00

Veilleuse, night light

6-1/2" h, domed form, deep aqua blue glass, molded trailing vines, yellow flower, mounted on circular wrought-iron stand, removable domed cap molded "A. Walter Nancy"..6,000.00

7-1/4" h, gray body, molded with amethyst accents on medial band of black and brown leafy branches, wrought iron cap and base with lamp socket, molded "G. Argy-Rousseau" at side..4,900.00

8-1/4" h, oval molded shade, mottled gray-lavender, three repeating red-centered purple blossoms within black V-shaped devices, molded "G. Argy-Rousseau," four ball feet on wrought iron base, fitted with night light, conforming cap 5,300.00

8-1/2" h, press molded oval lamp shade, frosted mottled gray glass, elaborate purple arches with three teardrop-shaped windows of yellow, center teal-green stylized blossoms on black swirling stems, imp "G. Arty-Rousseau" at lower edge, wrought iron frame, three ball feet centering internal lamp socket, conforming iron cover 6,900.00

Vide Pouche, irregular shaped dish

6-1/4" l, welled crescent shape, mottled tangerine shading to pale lemon, molded along with side with two spotted langoustines, one teal, the other burgundy, molded "A. Walter Nancy" and "Berge S.C."..........................4,000.00

6-3/4" l, 3-3/4" h, shallow oval, mottled orange and black, surmounted by green spotted black lizard molded in full relief, molded "A. Walter Nancy Berge" 4,500.00

7-1/4" l, 2-3/4" h, petal shape, seafoam green, molded in low relief with amber seaweed, full relief molded orange and brown seashell, molded "A. Walter Nancy Berge S.C." 4,000.00

11" l, elongated rectangular, mottled sky blue, molded at each end with burgundy and black moth, stylized star burst, molded "A. Walter Nancy Berge S.C."......4,000.00

PATTERN GLASS

History: Pattern glass is clear or colored glass pressed into one of hundreds of patterns. Deming Jarves of the Boston and Sandwich Glass Co. invented one of the first successful pressing machines in 1828. By the 1860s, glass-pressing machinery had been improved, and mass production of good-quality matched tableware sets began. The idea of a matched glassware table service (including goblets, tumblers, creamers, sugars, compotes, cruets, etc.) quickly caught on in America. Many pattern glass table services had numerous accessory pieces such as banana stands, molasses cans, and water bottles.

Early pattern glass (flint) was made with a lead formula, giving many items a ringing sound when tapped. Lead became too valuable to be used in glass manufacturing during the Civil War; and in 1864, Hobbs, Brockunier & Co., West Virginia, developed a soda lime (non-flint) formula. Pattern glass also was produced in transparent colors, milk glass, opalescent glass, slag glass, and custard glass.

The hundreds of companies that produced pattern glass experienced periods of development, expansions, personnel problems, material and supply demands, fires, and mergers. In 1899, the National Glass Co. was formed as a combination of 19 glass companies in Pennsylvania, Ohio, Indiana, West Virginia, and Maryland. U.S. Glass, another consortium, was founded in 1891. These combines resulted from attempts to save small companies by pooling talents, resources, and patterns. Because of this pooling, the same pattern often can be attributed to several companies. Sometimes various companies produced the same patterns at different times and used different names to reflect current fashion trends. U.S. Glass created the States series by using state names for various patterns, several of which were new issues while others were former patterns renamed.

References: Gary Baker et al., *Wheeling Glass 1829-1939,* Oglebay Institute, 1994, distributed by Antique Publications; E. M. Belknap, *Milk Glass,* Crown, 1949; George and Linda Breeze, *Mysteries of the Moon & Star,* published by authors, 1995; Bill Edwards, *The Standard Encyclopedia of Opalescent Glass,* Collector Books, 1992; Elaine Ezell and George Newhouse, *Cruets, Cruets, Cruets,* Antique Publications, 1992; Regis F. and Mary F. Ferson, *Yesterday's Milk Glass Today,* published by author, 1981; William Heacock, *Encyclopedia of Victorian Colored Pattern Glass (all published by Antique Publications): Book 1: Toothpick Holders from A to Z,* 2nd ed. (1976, 1992 value update); —, *Book 2, Opalescent Glass from A to Z, (1981);* ——, *Book 3, Syrups, Sugar Shakers, and Cruets,* (1981); ——, *Book 4, Custard Glass from A to Z,* (1980); ——, *Book 5: U. S. Glass from A to Z* (1980), ——, *Oil Cruets from A to Z, (1981);* ——, *Book 7: Ruby Stained Glass from A To Z* (1986), *Book 8: More Ruby Stained Glass* (1987), Antique Publications; ——, *Old Pattern Glass,* Antique Publications, 1981; ——, *1000 Toothpick Holders,* Antique Publications, 1977; ——, *Rare and Unlisted Toothpick Holders,* Antique Publications, 1984; William Heacock, James Measell, and Berry Wiggins, *Dugan/Diamond: The Story of Indiana, Pennsylvania, Glass,* Antique Publications, 1993; ——, *Harry Northwood: The Early Years, 1881-1900,* Antique Publications; 1990; ——, *Harry Northwood: The Wheeling Years,* Antique Publications; 1991; Ann Hicks, *Just Jenkins,* published by author, 1988; Kyle Husfloen, *Collector's Guide to American Pressed Glass,* Wallace-Homestead, 1992; Bill Jenks and Jerry Luna, *Early American Pattern Glass—1850 to 1910,* Wallace-Homestead, 1990; Bill Jenks, Jerry Luna, and Darryl Reilly, *Identifying Pattern Glass Reproductions,* Wallace-Homestead, 1993; William J. Jenks and Darryl

Reilly, *American Price Guide to Unitt's Canadian & American Goblets Volumes I & II*, Author! Author! Books (P.O. Box 1964, Kingston, PA 18704), 1996; —, *U. S. Glass: The States Patterns*, Author! Author! Books, Inc., 1998.

Minnie Watson Kamm, *Pattern Glass Pitchers*, Books 1 through 8, published by author, 1970, 4th printing; Lorraine Kovar, *Westmoreland Glass: 1950-54, Volume I (1991); Volume II (1991)*, Antique Publications; Thelma Ladd and Laurence Ladd, *Portland Glass: Legacy of a Glass House Down East*, Collector Books, 1992; Ruth Webb Lee, *Early American Pressed Glass*, 36th ed., Lee Publications, 1966; —, *Victorian Glass*, 13th ed., Lee Publications, 1944; Bessie M. Lindsey, *American Historical Glass*, Charles E. Tuttle, 1967; Robert Irwin Lucas, *Tarentum Pattern Glass*, privately printed, 1981; Mollie H. McCain, *Collector's Encyclopedia of Pattern Glass*, Collector Books, 1982, 1994 value update; George P. and Helen McKearin, *American Glass*, Crown Publishers, 1941; James Measell, *Greentown Glass*, Grand Rapids Public Museum Association, 1979, 1992-93 value update, distributed by Antique Publications; James Measell and Don E. Smith, *Findlay Glass: The Glass Tableware Manufacturers, 1886-1902*, Antique Publications, 1986; Alice Hulett Metz, *Early American Pattern Glass*, published by author, 1958; —, *Much More Early American Pattern Glass*, published by author, 1965; S. T. Millard, *Goblets I* (1938), *Goblets II* (1940), privately printed, reprinted Wallace-Homestead, 1975; John B. Mordock and Walter L. Adams, *Pattern Glass* Mugs, Antique Publications, 1995.; Kirk J. Nelson, *50 Favorites: Early American Pressed Glass Goblets: Sections from the Dorothy and Jacque D. Vallier Collection*, University of Wisconsin, 1993;

Arthur G. Peterson, *Glass Salt Shakers*, Wallace-Homestead, 1970; Ellen T. Schroy, (ed.), *Warman's Pattern Glass*, Wallace-Homestead, 1993; Jane Shadel Spillman, *American and European Pressed Glass in the Corning Museum of Glass*, Corning Museum of Glass, 1981; —, *Knopf Collectors Guides to American Antiques, Glass*, Vol. 1 (1982), Vol. 2 (1983), Alfred A. Knopf; Ron Teal, R., *Albany Glass, Model Flint Glass Company of Albany, Indiana*, Antique Publications, 1997; Doris and Peter Unitt, *American and Canadian Goblets*, Clock House, 1970, reprinted by The Love of Glass Publishing (Box 629, Arthur, Ontario, Canada NOG 1AO), 1996; —, *Treasury of Canadian Glass*, 2nd ed., Clock House, 1969; Peter Unitt and Anne Worrall, *Canadian Handbook, Pressed Glass Tableware*, Clock House Productions, 1983; John and Elizabeth Welker, *Pressed Glass in America: Encyclopedia of the First Hundred Years, 1825-1925*, Antique Acres Press, 1985; Kenneth Wilson, *American Glass 1760-1930*, 2 Vols., Hudson Hills Press and The Toledo Museum of Art, 1994.

Periodicals: *Glass Collector's Digest*, The Glass Press, P.O. Box 553, Marietta, OH 45750; *Glass Shards,* The National American Glass Club, Ltd., P.O. Box 8489, Silver Spring, MD 20907; *News Journal,* Early American Pattern Glass Society, P.O. Box 266, Colesburg, IA 52035.

Collectors' Clubs: Early American Pattern Glass Society, P.O. Box 266, Colesburg, IA 52035; Moon and Star Collectors Club, 4207 Fox Creek, Mount Vernon, IL 62864; The National American Glass Club, Ltd., P.O. Box 8489, Silver Spring, MD 20907.

Museums: Bennington Museum, Bennington, CT; Corning Museum of Glass, Corning, NY; Historical Glass Museum, Redlands, CA: Jones Museum of Glass and Ceramics, Sebago, ME; National Museum of Man, Ottawa, Ontario, Canada; Sandwich Glass Museum, Sandwich, MA; Schminck Memorial Museum, Lakeview, OR; The Chrysler Museum, Norfolk, VA; The Toledo Museum of Art, Toledo, OH; University of Wisconsin-Stevens Point, Stevens Point, WI; Wheaton Historical Village Assoc. Museum of Glass, Millville, NJ.

Reproduction Alert: Pattern glass has been widely reproduced.

Additional Listings: Bread Plates; Children's Toy Dishes; Cruets; Custard Glass; Milk Glass; Sugar Shakers; Toothpicks; and specific companies.

Notes: Research in pattern glass is continuing. As always, we try to use correct pattern names, histories, and forms. Reflecting the most current thinking, the listing by pattern places colored, opalescent, and clear items together, avoiding duplication.

Abbreviations:

ah	....	applied handle
GUTDODB	....	Give Us This Day Our Daily Bread
hs	....	high standard
ind	....	individual
ls	....	low standard
os	....	original stopper

Prices listed below are for colorless (clear) pieces, unless otherwise noted.

Ale
    Ashburton, flint, 5" h 90.00
    Dancing Goat, frosted goat...55.00
    Mephistopheles...95.00
Banana Stand
    Amazon (Sawtooth Band), etched 95.00
    Art (Jacob's Tears, Job's Tears, Teardrop and Diamond Block) 70.00
    Broken Column (Irish Column, Notched Rib) 185.00
    Delaware (American Beauty, Four Petal Flower)
    Green, gold trim 75.00
    Rose, gold trim 150.00
    Eyewinker (Cannon Ball, Crystal ball, Winking Eye), flat....85.00
Bar Bottle
    Nine Panel Flute, flint, pint..65.00
    Waffle, flint, quart 155.00
Basket
    Broken Column (Irish Column, Notched Rib), applied handle, 15" l...135.00
    Dakota (Baby Thumbprint, Thumbprint Band), etched ...250.00
    Paneled Thistle (Delta) 85.00
    Portland, gold trim..85.00
    Snail (Compact, Idaho, Double Snail).........................85.00
    Vermont (Honeycomb with Flower Rim, Inverted Thumbprint with Daisy Band), gold trim 45.00
Berry Bowl, master
    Adonis (Pleat and Tuck, Washboard) canary-yellow....20.00
    Croesus (Riverside's #484), green.............................165.00

Daisy and Button, oval, amber..................................45.00
Jacob's Ladder (Maltese), ornate SP holder, ftd........125.00
O'Hara Diamond (Sawtooth (Diamond Point, Mitre Diamond)
    and Star) 25.00
Shell and Tassel (Duncan No. 555, Shell and Spike) 35.00
Three Panel, amber...45.00
Wreath and Shell, 8-1/2" d..45.00
Berry Set
Bull's Eye and Daisy, green stain, 5 pcs....................115.00
Cord Drapery...75.00
Croesus (Riverside's #484), amethyst, 7 pcs 625.00
Delaware (American Beauty, Four Petal Flower), green, gold
    trim, 7 pcs...175.00
Feather (Doric) Duster, gold rim, 7 pcs 55.00
Jacob's Coat, master berry, 11 flat sauces, emerald
    green 60.00
Manhattan, 7 pc...50.00
Biscuit Jar, cov
All-Over Diamond (Diamond Block, Diamond Splendor)...65.00
Broken Column (Irish Column, Notched Rib)................85.00
Minnesota, ruby stained...165.00
Pennsylvania (Balder), emerald green........................100.00
Reverse Torpedo (Bull's Eye and Diamond Point)......145.00
Three Face 300.00
Bon Bon, Georgia (Peacock Feather)..............................35.00
Bowl, open
All-Over Diamond (Diamond Block, Diamond Splendor)...25.00
Buckle (Early Buckle), flint, 10" d 65.00
Daisy and Button, blue, triangular................................45.00
Delaware (American Beauty, Four Petal Flower), boat shaped
    bowl, orig SP frame, rose..400.00
Fleur-de-lis, 9" d..28.00
Honeycomb, flint, 8" d, ftd..20.00
King's #500, Dewey Blue, gold trim, 7" d.....................35.00
New Hampshire (Bent Buckle, Modiste) , gold trim, flared,
    8-1/2" d...20.00
Royal Lady, Belmont's, 11-1/4" l, flat, oval, cov 145.00
Thousand Eye, blue 85.00
Utah (Frost Flower, Twinkle Star) 20.00
Westmoreland, 4-1/4" x 7" sq, orig SP frame 125.00
Brandy Tray, Willow Oak (Acorn, Acorn and Oak Leaf, Bryce's
    Wreath, Stippled Daisy, Thistle and Sunflower),
    amber 125.00
Bread Plate
Actress (Theatrical), Miss Neilson................................80.00

Bowl, Heart with Thumbprint, gold trim, scalloped, 10" d, $45.

Basketweave, canary-yellow..35.00
Cape Cod...45.00
Cupid's Hunt 90.00
Deer and Pine Tree, amber...110.00
Lion, motto, blue...135.00
Roman Rosette, 9" x 11"...55.00
Train 75.00
Butter, covered
Alaska, vaseline opal 350.00
Beaded Loop (Oregon #1)...75.00
Bird and Strawberry (Bluebird, Flying Bird and Strawberry,
    Strawberry and Bird), color....................................100.00
Bull's Eye and Daisy, cranberry eyes, gold trim 65.00
Croesus (Riverside's #484), amethyst 275.00
Deer, Dog, Hunter..225.00
Empress 125.00
Garfield Drape..95.00
Galloway (Mirror Plate, U.S. Mirror, Virginia, Woodrow)
    Colorless...50.00
    Maiden's blush 85.00
Holly 150.00
Horn of Plenty, flint, Washington head finial................995.00
Illinois 55.00
Jockey Cap 400.00
Jumbo 550.00
Liberty Bell, 1876...85.00
Loop and Jewel..95.00
Maryland (Inverted Loop and Fan, Loop and Diamond),
    goldtrim...75.00
Nestor, amethyst, dec..125.00
Pennsylvania (Balder) 50.00
Reverse 44, cranberry, gold trim 125.00
Rose in Snow (Rose), sq..50.00
Thousand Eye, vaseline..90.00
Wreath and Shell, vaseline...250.00
Zipper (Cobb, Late Sawtooth (Diamond Point, Mitre
    Diamond))..75.00
Butter Pat
Horn of Plenty (flint)...20.00
Shell and Tassel (Duncan No. 555, Shell and Spike) ...15.00
Cake Stand
Bird and Strawberry (Bluebird, Flying Bird and Strawberry,
    Strawberry and Bird) 75.00
Crystal Wedding...95.00
Festoon..48.00
Finecut and Panel (Russian, Button and Oval Medallion,
    Nailhead and Panel), blue.....................................75.00
Good Luck, 10" d..75.00
Hand (Pennsylvania #2)..60.00
Holly, 10-1/2" d..110.00
Missouri (Palm and Scroll) 35.00
Pogo Stick..45.00
Rose in Snow..95.00
Shosone, 10-1/2" d..45.00
Texas (Loop with Stippled Panels)..............................125.00
Willow Oak (Acorn, Acorn and Oak Leaf, Bryce's Wreath,
    Stippled Daisy, Thistle and Sunflower), amber 55.00
Calling Card Receiver
Colorado (Lacy Medallion), blue..................................45.00
Heart with Thumbprint (Bull's Eye in Heart, Columbia, Co-
    lumbian, Heart and Thumbprint) 20.00
Carafe
Block 30.00
Bull's Eye...45.00
Excelsior..150.00
Galloway, rose stained..85.00

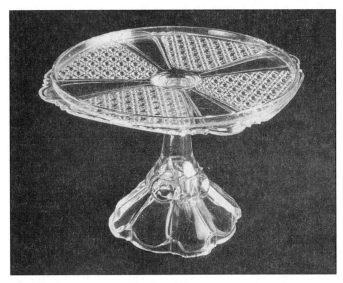

Cake Plate, Two Panel, vaseline, $85.

Honeycomb 100.00
Castor Set
　Alabama (Beaded Bull's Eye and Drape) four bottles, glass
　　frame 125.00
　Bellflower, five bottles, pewter stand 250.00
　Daisy and Button, vaseline, four bottles, glass stand 85.00
　King's Crown 185.00
Celery Tray
　Broken Column (Irish Column, Notched Rib) 45.00
　Nail, etched 45.00
Celery Vase
　Chandelier (Crown Jewel) 25.00
　Diamond Thumbprint, flint 150.00
　Francesware Swirl 75.00
　Good Luck 35.00
　Heart with Thumbprint (Bull's Eye in Heart, Columbia, Colum-
　　bian, Heart and Thumbprint) 145.00
　Jacob's Ladder (Maltese), 9" 30.00
　Honeycomb, flint 45.00
　Moon and Star (Palace) 35.00
　Plume 35.00
　U.S. Coin, quarters 210.00
　Waffle and Thumbprint, flint 95.00
　Wreath and Shell
　　Blue 140.00
　　Vaseline 225.00
Champagne
　Flamingo Habitat 50.00
　Mardi Gras 26.00
　New York, flint 65.00
　Sawtooth (Diamond Point, Mitre Diamond), flint 65.00
Cheese Dish, cov
　Actress (Theatrical) 225.00
　Flamingo Habitat 150.00
　Horseshoe (Good Luck, Prayer Rug) 215.00
　Lion (Frosted Lion), rampant lion finial 400.00
　Snail (Compact, Idaho, Double Snail) 95.00
　Thumbprint, etched 145.00
　Zipper (Cobb, Late Sawtooth) 65.00
Claret
　Broken Column (Irish Column, Notched Rib) 85.00
　Diamond Point, flint 90.00
　Three Face 115.00
Cologne Bottle

Bull's Eye, flint, orig stopper 50.00
Massachusetts (Arched Diamond Points, Cane Variant, Gene-
　va #2, MD-131, Star and Diamonds) 45.00
Thousand Eye, apple green 100.00
Compote, covered
　Barley, 7" d, hs 65.00
　Beaded Band, 8" d 85.00
　Crystal Wedding 75.00
　Dakota (Baby Thumbprint, Thumbprint Band), 5" d, hs, etched
　　leaf 30.00
　Dakota (Baby Thumbprint, Thumbprint Band), 6" d, hs 40.00
　Frosted Chicken, 7" d, hs 200.00
　Frosted Circle, 7" h 125.00
　Frosted Eagle, 8" d, ls 275.00
　Frosted Lion, 7" d, oval 85.00
　Frosted Lion, 8-1/4" d, oval 95.00
　Good Luck, 8" d 175.00
　Heart Stem, 6" 85.00
　Honeycomb, 8" d, hs, melon finial 90.00
　Jumbo 275.00
　Lion and Cable, hs, etched leaf and berry, frosted lion finial,
　　9" d 150.00
　Paneled Forget Me Not, 7" d, hs 50.00
　Peacock Feather, 8" d 125.00
　Pleat and Panel, 8" d, hs 145.00
　Ribbon, 10-7/8" h, 7-3/4" d 55.00
　Ribbon Candy, 7" d 85.00
　Sequoia 55.00
　Snail, (Compact, Idaho, Double Snail) 7" d, 12" h 145.00
　Texas (Loop with Stippled Panels), 6" d, scalloped lid... 195.00
Compote, open
　Almond Thumbprint 45.00
　Amazon (Sawtooth Band) 45.00
　Bird and Strawberry (Bluebird, Flying Bird and Strawberry,
　　Strawberry and Bird), 8" d, ruffled edge 110.00
　Brilliant, Royal's, 6" d 20.00
　Broken Column (Irish Column, Notched Rib), 5-1/2" 75.00
　Cable, 8" d, flint 75.00
　Frosted Foot 45.00
　Good Luck, 9" d 235.00
　Grape Band 35.00
　Horn of Plenty, 7" d, flint 75.00
　Interlocking Crescents 35.00

Compote, Stippled Forget Me Not, open, high standard, $50.

Jacob's Ladder (Maltese), 6" x 8-1/2", flared 30.00
Locket on Chain, hs, 8-1/2" d 145.00
New England Pineapple, 8" d 70.00
Paneled Forget Me Not 35.00
Rope and Thumbprint, amber 40.00
Sawtooth (Diamond Point, Mitre Diamond) 55.00
Teardrop and Tassel 55.00
Two Panel, blue, hs..140.00

Cordial
Almond Thumbprint (Almond, Finger Print), flint...........50.00
Basketweave, apple green 45.00
Bellflower, single vine, vine ribbed, knob stem, rayed base,
 barrel shape 115.00
Feather (Doric) 95.00
King's Crown 45.00
Star and File 20.00
Thousand Eye 30.00

Creamer
Actress (Theatrical)...90.00
Adonis (Pleat and Tuck, Washboard) 20.00
Alaska, vaseline opal 85.00
Barberry (Berry, Olive, Pepper Berry)...........................55.00
Beaded Band 30.00
Bird and Strawberry (Bluebird, Flying Bird and Strawberry,
 Strawberry and Bird) 65.00
Bird in Ring 25.00
Bleeding Heart 55.00
Block and Fan 25.00
Block and Honeycomb 65.00
Broken Column (Irish Column, Notched Rib)...............40.00
Cabbage Rose 55.00
Cardinal Bird 25.00
Chain and Shield...20.00
Chandelier, leaf and berry etch 25.00
Classic Medallion..40.00
Cord and Tassel..30.00
Cottage...30.00
Croesus (Riverside's #484), amethyst, individual size....170.00
Croesus (Riverside's #484), green...............................140.00
Dart...30.00
Dewey, cov, amber 75.00
Diamond Point Band 60.00
Drapery 45.00
Early Thistle, applied handle...75.00
Egyptian 50.00
Frosted Stork 35.00
Garland of Roses, triple stem..35.00
Garfield Drape...45.00
Georgia Gem, gold trim 35.00
Good Luck...40.00
Grace 65.00
Grape 20.00
Grape and Festoon 55.00
Grasshopper, no insect..30.00
Heart with Thumbprint (Bull's Eye in Heart, Columbia, Colum-
 bian, Heart and Thumbprint), individual size 25.00
Hobnail, ball foot 20.00
Horseshoe (Good Luck, Prayer Rug)............................25.00
Intaglio..35.00
Jumbo 150.00
Louis XV, green...45.00
Mascotte, etched 45.00
Memphis, green 75.00
Minerva..50.00
Nailhead 30.00
Oasis 30.00

One-O-One..21.00
One Hundred One...40.00
Paneled Chain...36.00
Pennsylvania (Balder), gold trim 35.00
Popcorn...32.00
Pressed Leaf 45.00
Prize, ruby..110.00
Psyche and Cupid...50.00
Reverse 44, ftd, platinum trim 40.00
Roman Rosette..60.00
Seedpod, green, gold trim, c1899 ....65.00
Stashed Swirl..20.00
Stippled Chain...25.00
Stippled Grape and Festoon..25.00
Sunbeam 45.00
Teardrop and Tassel, opaque white 85.00
Threading 15.00
Three Face 85.00
Torpedo, 6"..36.00
Tremont 20.00
Truncated Cube, individual size, ruby stain..................40.00
Two Band 36.00
Wheat and Barley..15.00
Wreath and Shell
 Blue, decorated...235.00
 Vaseline...145.00

Cruet, orig stopper
Croesus (Riverside's #484)
 Amethyst, small 375.00
 Clear, no stopper...85.00
 Green, small 325.00
Cut Log 40.00
Duchess, maiden's blush, no stopper 125.00
Empress, gold trim 195.00
Illinois, sq 50.00
King's Crown 45.00
Oneida 20.00
Paneled Thistle...30.00
Sterling, amber stained 225.00
Sunflower...40.00
Tacoma 20.00
Zipper and Panel, faceted stopper 30.00

Cruet Tray
Croesus (Riverside's #484)
 Amethyst...110.00
 Green..100.00
Nestor, blue, gold trim...65.00

Cup and Saucer
Basketweave, blue 35.00
Cornell, green, gold grim 30.00
Currier and Ives...30.00
Fleur de Lys with Drape 30.00
King's Crown 55.00
Star and Ivy 35.00
Torpedo...50.00
Wisconsin (Beaded Dewdrop) 50.00

Custard Cup
Bull's Eye and Fan..12.00
New Hampshire (Bent Buckle, Modiste), rose stain 15.00
Snail (Compact, Idaho, Double Snail)...........................32.00
Wisconsin (Beaded Dewdrop).......................................25.00

Decanter
Bigler, bar type, flint..60.00
Fine Rib with Cut Ovals, flint, quart, tiny nick..............200.00
Honeycomb, flint, quart, no stopper 40.00
Peerless, flint...45.00

Sandwich Star, quart, no stopper 25.00

Sawtooth (Diamond Point, Mitre Diamond), flint, quart, orig
stopper 135.00

Tulip and Sawtooth, flint, pink, bar lip, orig stopper ...150.00

Waffle and Thumbprint, orig stopper 135.00

Dish

Heart with Thumbprint (Bull's Eye in Heart, Columbia, Columbian, Heart and Thumbprint), heart shaped, handle 32.50

Shell and Tassel (Duncan No. 555, Shell and Spike), 8" w,
octagonal, amber 50.00

Shoshone, 5" l, handle, Dewey Blue 65.00

Doughnut Stand

Paneled Thistle (Delta) 45.00

Prayer Rug 75.00

Egg Cup, flint

Ashburton 25.00

Bellflower 45.00

Cable 55.00

Colonial 35.00

Frosted Lion 50.00

Hamilton 45.00

Hercules Pillar, double 65.00

Horn of Plenty 45.00

Huber 25.00

New England Pineapple...60

Ribbed Palm...45.00

Fruit Bowl, Shell and Tassel (Duncan No. 555, Shell and Spike),
10" d, Meriden SP holder.......................................100.00

Goblet

Almond Thumbprint..10.00

Apollo (Canadian Horseshoe) Good Luck, Prayer Rug), Shield
Band), etched 35.00

Arched Grape 35.00

Arched Grape Variant 35.00

Argus, barrel, flint...40.00

Ashburton, flint

Knobbed stem..42.50

Plain stem..25.00

Ashman 30.00

Atlas (Bullet, Cannon Ball, Crystal Ball), etched............45.00

Austrian (Finecut Medallion) 35.00

Banded Portland (Virginia #1, Maiden's Blush) 30.00

Bar and Swirl 25.00

Barberry (Berry, Olive, Pepper Berry)..........................35.00

Barred Forget Me Not 20.00

Basketweave, amber...16.00

Beaded Acorn 25.00

Beaded Bands, 20.00

Beaded Panels 20.00

Bessiner Flute, flint...25.00

Bigler, flint 35.00

Blackberry 35.00

Bradford Grape, flint 135.00

Broken Column (Irish Column, Notched Rib)................60.00

Buckle, flint 35.00

Bull and Swirl Band with Etched Leaf and Fern............20.00

Bull's Eye with Daisy

Colorless..25.00

Green stain...40.00

Bull's Eye and Spearhead...50.00

Cabbage Rose 25.00

Canadian 55.00

Cape Cod 45.00

Chain with Star 25.00

Cord and Tassel 85.00

Cottage..20.00

Curled Leaf..27.00

Currant 25.00

Curtain Tieback 35.00

Currier and Ives...30.00

Dakota (Baby Thumbprint, Thumbprint Band), etched 55.00

Deer and Dog, etched 50.00

Deer and Pine Tree 50.00

Dewdrop 20.00

Diamond Point, flint 45.00

Diamond Ridge 30.00

Drapery 35.00

Duquesne, flint 25.00

Egg in Sand 25.00

Egyptian 50.00

Excelsior, barrel, flint...30.00

Falcon Strawberry 20.00

Fairfax Strawberry 45.00

Fan with Diamonds...20.00

Feather (Doric) 35.00

Finecut and Block 30.00

Finecut and Panel

Colorless..20.00

Vaseline...20.00

Fine Diamond Point, flint 30.00

Fishscale 20.00

Flamingo..195.00

Flower Band, frosted 95.00

Flying Stork 65.00

Frosted Lion 70.00

Frosted Magnolia 100.00

Frosted Stork 50.00

Fruit Panels...20.00

Garfield Drape...20.00

Giant Baby Thumbprint, flint 85.00

Girl with Fan 100.00

Good Luck, knob stem..35.00

Gooseberry 35.00

Grand 20.00

Grape Band..20.00

Grape Vine Under 35.00

Grape with Thumbprint 32.00

Hairpin with Thumbprint, flint 35.00

Harvard Yard, rose...45.00

Harvest Blackberry...35.00

Heart with Thumbprint (Bull's Eye in Heart, Columbia, Columbian, Heart and Thumbprint) 65.00

Hidalgo, etched..20.00

Honeycomb..20.00

Honeycomb, Elongated, flint...30.00

Horsemint 20.00

Huber 20.00

Hummingbird

Blue 140.00

Colorless..65.00

Inverted Fern, flint 30.00

Jacob's Ladder 55.00

Knobby Bull's Eye, gold trim, amethyst stain................20.00

Kokomo 35.00

Loganberry and Grape, round rim 20.00

Loop and Dart, Diamond Ornament...............................20.00

Loop and Pyramid 16.00

Maryland 30.00

Melrose, etched 42.50

Michigan (Loop and Pillar) 40.00

Minnesota 36.00

Nail, etched...45.00

Nailhead 32.00
Netted Swan, amber 95.00
New England Centennial............................245.00
New Hampshire (Bent Buckle, Modiste), gold trim.......20.00
New Jersey (Loops and Drops), gold trim....................25.00
Nickel Plate's Richmond 25.00
Nova Scotia Grape and Vine........................60.00
Odd Fellow 48.00
Open Rose 25.00
Oval Mitre, flint 25.00
Oval Panels, vaseline 35.00
Owl and Possum 85.00
Paneled Forget Me Not 45.00
Paneled Ovals, flint 40.00
Paneled Potted Flower 55.00
Paneled Diamonds....................................20.00
Pavonia..30.00
Persian Spear, flint 85.00
Plain Sunburst 20.00
Pleat and Panel 35.00
Plume, engraved 20.00
Polar Bear..125.00
Polar Bear, frosted 100.00
Prism U Flute, flint 32.00
Queen, amber 15.00
Queen, colorless 38.00
Reverse 44, burgundy, gold trim 65.00
Reverse 44, platinum trim 25.00
Ribbed Droplet Band, frosted, amber stained, etched 55.00
Rose in Snow...20.00
Rose Leaves..20.00
Rosette Palm...20.00
Sawtooth (Diamond Point, Mitre Diamond), flint 40.00
Scarab, flint 175.00
Seneca Loop 30.00
Shell and Tassel (Duncan No. 555, Shell and Spike) ...55.00
Shrine 85.00
Star in Box 65.00
Star in Bull's Eye..32.00
Stippled Peppers 35.00
Stocky Mirror, flint......................................45.00
Stork 85.00
Straight Huber, flint, etched 35.00
Strawberry..55.00
Strawberry and Currant..............................35.00
Tape Measure, (Shields), flint 20.00
Teardrop and Tassel...................................175.00
Teardrop and Thumbprint............................20.00
Texas (Loop with Stippled Panels)..............95.00
Texas Bull's Eye...20.00
Texas Centennial.......................................95.00
Thousand Eye, blue 60.00
Three Panel, vaseline 30.00
Thumbprint, hotel style...............................21.00
Tulip with Sawtooth, flint............................45.00
US Coin, frosted dimes 575.00
Vermont (Honeycomb with Flower Rim, Inverted Thumbprint
     with Daisy Band), green, gold trim..........68.00
Waffle with Fan Top.....................................20.00
Ways Current..35.00
Wildflower...20.00
Willow Oak (Acorn, Acorn and Oak Leaf, Bryce's Wreath,
     Stippled Daisy, Thistle and Sunflower)
     Amber..32.00
     Blue 65.00
     Colorless..25.00

Yoked Lump, flint 25.00
Yuma Loop, flint 25.00
Zenith 20.00
Zig Zag 36.00
Hat
     Daisy and Button, blue, large..................45.00
     Thousand Eye, vaseline 48.00
Honey Dish
     Alabama (Beaded Bull's Eye and Drape) cov 60.00
     Beaded Grape Medallion, open...................12.00
     Diamond Thumbprint, flint........................25.00
     Lily of the Valley 12.00
     Oregon #1 (Beaded Loop)........................12.00
Horseradish Dish, Duncan Block #331, ground stopper.....40.00
Ice Cream Tray, Block and Fan 75.00
Jelly Compote
     Croesus (Riverside's #484)
          Green, gold trim 225.00
          Purple, gold trim 245.00
     Diamond Spearhead, cobalt blue 200.00
     Florida (Emerald Green Herringbone, Paneled Herringbone),
          green 25.00
     Reverse Torpedo (Bull's Eye and Diamond Point)........35.00
Juice Tumbler
     Cut Log (Ethol, Cat's Eye and Block).........35.00
     Daisy and Button, amber 15.00
     Massachusetts (Arched Diamond Points, Cane Variant, Gene-
          va #2, MD-131, Star and Diamonds) 15.00
     Pennsylvania (Balder) 8.00
Lamp, oil
     Beaded Bull's Eye and Fleur-de-Lis, green, tall
          standard 115.00
     Crystal Wedding...................................245.00
     Excelsior, flint, 4-3/4" h, finger type.........195.00
     Fishscale, finger type 85.00
     Harp, flint
          4" h, finger type 365.00
          9" h..290.00
     One-O-One, finger type 95.00

Lamp, oil, Torpedo, plain font, pattern on base, $90.

Pleat and Panel 250.00
Star and Punty, flint, 9" h 245.00
Ringed Framed Ovals, flint, 9" h 140.00
Lamp Shade
    Button Arches, gas type 55.00
    Mardi Gras, electric type 45.00
    Teepee, electric type 70.00
Lemonade Pitcher
    Bull's Eye and Fan 85.00
    Pavonia (Pineapple Stem) 125.00
Lemonade Tumbler
    Bull's Eye and Fan 20.00
    Honeycomb, flint 40.00
    Plume 30.00
Marmalade Jar, cov
    Actress (Theatrical) 95.00
    Atlanta (Square Lion, Clear Lion Head) 95.00
    Bow Tie, pewter lid 75.00
    Butterfly with Spray 80.00
    Deer and Pine Tree (Deer and Doe) 90.00
    Log Cabin 275.00
    Snail (Compact, Idaho, Double Snail) 95.00
    Three Face 200.00
    Viking (Bearded Head), ground stopper 175.00
    Wisconsin (Beaded Dewdrop) 125.00
Milk Pitcher
    Cane Horseshoe 40.00
    Cape Cod 65.00
    Colorado (Lacy Medallion), green, gold trim 325.00
    Cupid and Venus 95.00
    Daisy and Button with Crossbars, vaseline 130.00
    Eyewinker (Cannon Ball, Crystal Ball, Winking Eye) 75.00
    Francesware Swirl 125.00
    Good Luck ....90.00 ....225.00
    Paneled Thistle (Delta) 65.00
    Pleat and Panel 155.00
    Rosette 50.00
    Tiny Lion 70.00
    Willow Oak (Acorn, Acorn and Oak Leaf, Bryce's Wreath, Stippled Daisy, Thistle and Sunflower) 40.00
Mug
    Arched Fleur-De-Lis, ruby stained 30.00
    Beaded Swirl (Swirled Column) 15.00
    Bird and Owl 80.00
    Cupid and Venus 30.00
    Kansas (Jewel with Dewdrop) 45.00
    Lyre with Bird on Nest, 3" h 30.00
    Minnesota 15.00
    Thousand Eye, apple green 30.00
    U.S. Coin 185.00
Mustard, cov
    King's Crown 75.00
    Wisconsin (Beaded Dewdrop) 70.00
Nappy
    Amazon (Sawtooth Band), 4" 12.00
    Bird and Strawberry (Bluebird, Flying Bird and Strawberry, Strawberry and Bird) 70.00
    Colorado (Lacy Medallion), emerald green 35.00
    Galloway, rose stain 50.00
    Heart with Thumbprint (Bull's Eye in Heart, Columbia, Columbian, Heart and Thumbprint), green, handle 85.00
    Lily of the Valley 25.00
Olive
    Arched Fleur-De-Lis 17.50
    Beaded Grape (California) 20.00
    Illinois 20.00

Plate, Paneled Thistle, bee mark, 10" d, $35.

    Kentucky 25.00
    Maryland (Inverted Loop and Fan, Loop and Diamond), gold trim 15.00
    Thousand Eye, amber 40.00
Pickle Castor
    Broken Column (Irish Column, Notched Rib) 175.00
    Cupid and Venus, silver plated frame 295.00
    Daisy and Button with V Ornament (Van Dyke), vaseline 120.00
    Feather (Doric) 150.00
Pickle Dish
    Aegis (Bead and Bar Medallion, Swiss) 20.00
    Barberry (Berry) 25.00
    Lily of the Valley, scoop shape 20.00
    Jacob's Ladder (Maltese), handle 10.00
    Maryland (Inverted Loop and Fan, Loop and Diamond) ... 18.00
    Missouri (Palm and Scroll) 20.00
    U.S. Coin, frosted, chips 40.00
    Utah (Frost Flower, Twinkle Star) 20.00
Plate
    Arched Fleur-De-Lis, 7" sq 18.00
    Beautiful Lady, 8" d 20.00
    Beaded Grape (California), 8-1/4" sq 30.00
    Croesus (Riverside's #484), 8" d 145.00
    Egyptian, 10" d, tab handle 95.00
    Elaine, swan border 110.00
    Illinois, 7" d 55.00
    Jacob's Ladder (Maltese), 6" d 27.00
    King's Crown, 7" w, sq 65.00
    Maryland (Inverted Loop and Fan, Loop and Diamond), gold trim, 7" d 25.00
    O'Hara Diamond (Sawtooth and Star), 8" d 30.00
    Ribbed Grape, flint, 5-3/4" 45.00
    Stippled Cherry, 6" d 12.00
    Stippled Forget Me Not, 9" d, kitten center 55.00
    The States (Cane and Star Medallion), 6" d 12.00
    Willow Oak (Acorn, Acorn and Oak Leaf, Bryce's Wreath, Stippled Daisy, Thistle and Sunflower), 9" d, blue 45.00
    Wisconsin (Beaded Dewdrop), 7" d 45.00
Platter
    Actress (Theatrical), Miss Neilson 60.00
    Cape Cod 45.00
    Frosted Stork, One Hundred One border 85.00

Maple Leaf, blue, oval..55.00
Pleat Panel 25.00

Punch Bowl Set
Aztec, bowl, stand, 20 cups.............................100.00
Manhattan, bowl, 12 cups..................................80.00
The States (Cane and Star Medallion), bowl, 8 cups...... 125.00

Punch Cup
Bird and Strawberry (Bluebird, Flying Bird and Strawberry,
Strawberry and Bird)..22.00
Button Panels 10.00
Galloway..8.50
Hickman 10.00
Iowa, gold trim...15.00
Kentucky 8.00
King Arthur 8.00
Louise..8.00
Pennsylvania (Balder) 10.00
Roman Rosette..15.00
U.S. Rib, green, gold band 15.00

Relish
Amazon (Sawtooth Band), etched 30.00
Broken Column (Irish Column, Notched Rib), rect........25.00
Bull's Eye and Fan, pink stain 20.00
Currier and Ives...20.00
Dewey, flower flange, serpentine, amber 45.00
Horn of Plenty, flint, 5" x 7"......................................42.50
Jacob's Ladder (Maltese), 9-1/2" x 5-1/2" 12.00
King's #500, Dewey Blue, gold trim...........................30.00
Magnet and Grape (Magnet and Grape with Stippled Leaf),
stippled leaf...18.00
New Hampshire (Bent Buckle, Modiste), rose stain, diamond
shape...24.00
Oregon #1 (Beaded Loop)...18.00
Texas (Loop with Stippled Panels), blushed................55.00
Wisconsin (Beaded Dewdrop)...................................25.00
Zipper (Cobb, Late Sawtooth)...................................18.00

Rose Bowl
Galloway..30.00
Kokomo, small...20.00
Paneled Thistle (Delta)...50.00
Snail (Compact, Idaho, Double Snail), 5" h.................45.00
Wreath and Shell
Blue 140.00
Vaseline 140.00
Zippered Swirl with Diamond, emerald green 35.00

Salt and Pepper Shakers, pr
Actress (Theatrical)...120.00
Atlas (Bullet, Cannon Ball, Crystal Ball) 25.00
Columbia, Belmont's 85.00
Croesus (Riverside's #484), green...........................250.00
Cut Log, orig tops 130.00
Delaware (American Beauty, Four Petal Flower), green, gold
trim..500.00
Diamond Ridge 45.00
Flower Band 100.00
Westmoreland 60.00
X-Ray, green, gold trim 225.00

Salt, Individual
Atlanta (Square Lion, Clear Lion Head), frosted 42.00
Button Arches...15.00
Illinois 15.00
Lacy Daisy...5.00
Moon and Star 18.50
Snail (Compact, Idaho, Double Snail).........................20.00
Zipper (Cobb, Late Sawtooth)...................................8.00

Salt, Master
Amazon (Sawtooth Band) 20.00

Argus..30.00
Cabbage Rose, ftd 25.00
Electric..12.00
Excelsior, flint 30.00
Jacob's Ladder (Maltese) 22.00
Lily of the Valley, cov...125.00
Royal Lady 30.00
Sawtooth (Diamond Point, Mitre Diamond)..................50.00
Torpedo...25.00

Sauce/individual berry bowl
Acorn, 5" d..18.00
Actress (Theatrical), ftd 27.00
Adonis (Pleat and Tuck, Washboard), 4" d 12.00
Alaska, vaseline opal 45.00
Amazon (Sawtooth Band) 10.00
Bleeding Heart, flat 15.00
Colorado (Lacy Medallion), ruffled.............................18.00
Cupid and Venus, ftd 18.00
Dakota (Baby Thumbprint, Thumbprint Band), ftd, 4" d......6.00
Derby, Riverside, vaseline 35.00
Diagonal Band with Fan, set of 6...............................95.00
Duncan's 2000, amber stained, 4-3/4" d.....................40.00
Florida (Emerald Green Herringbone, Paneled Herringbone),
sq, emerald green...10.00
Frosted Lion, ftd, 4" 20.00
Good Luck, 4" d, ftd 15.00
Grace, Duncan, 4-1/2" d...17.50
Jacob's Ladder, flat, 4-1/2" d 8.00
Japanese, ftd...15.00
Leaf Medallion, amethyst 30.00
Minerva..10.00
Reverse Torpedo (Bull's Eye and Diamond Point)........12.00
Shell and Tassel (Duncan No. 555, Shell and Spike), ftd,
4" d 8.00
Squirrel in Bower..10.00
Thumbprint, flint 12.00
Wreath and Shell, vaseline 40.00
Zipper (Cobb, Late Sawtooth), ftd 15.00

Shoe, Daisy and Button, colorless, sole dated "Pat'd 1888"...95.00

Spill Vase
Buckle with Star...60.00
Diamond Point, flint 50.00
Honeycomb, flint 30.00
Sandwich Star 30.00

Spittoon, Wreath and Shell, vaseline 150.00

Spooner
Alaska, vaseline opal 55.00
Berry Cluster 28.00
Cable, flint 55.00
Cathedral...25.00
Columbian Coin, frosted coins...................................100.00
Croesus (Riverside's #484)
Amethyst..115.00
Clear 100.00
Green 100.00
Fine Rib, flint...45.00
Garfield Drape..38.00
Grace, Duncan...55.00
Grape and Festoon 35.00
Hexagon Block 25.00
Japanese..35.00
Klondike 75.00
Lorraine, frosted 45.00
Louis XV, green..45.00
Magnet and Grape, Frosted Leaf, flint 95.00
Mascotte
Etched 25.00

Sugar, cov, Swan, $175.

Plain	20.00
Pleat and Panel	28.00
Prize, ruby	95.00
Snail (Compact, Idaho, Double Snail)	25.00
Victor, green	75.00

Wreath and Shell
Blue, decorated	224.00
Blue, plain	135.00
Vaseline, decorated	175.00
Vaseline, plain	125.00
X-Ray, amethyst, gold trim	110.00

Sugar, covered
Alaska, vaseline opal	300.00
Bellflower, single vine	110.00
Bradford Grape	55.00
Cathedral, amber	45.00
Cranesbill	40.00

Croesus (Riverside's #484)
Clear	155.00
Green	170.00
Diamond Cut with Leaf	50.00
Frosted Eagle	200.00
Heart with Thumbprint (Bull's Eye in Heart, Columbia, Columbian, Heart and Thumbprint), individual size	25.00
Hinto, flint	75.00
Horseshoe (Good Luck, Prayer Rug) (Good Luck)	85.00
Log Cabin	455.00
Louis XV, green	90.00
Mascotte, etched	450.00
Nail, etched	48.00
New England Pineapple	65.00
New Jersey (Loops and Drops)	50.00
Plain Band, Heisey #1225, gold band	35.00
Rose Point Band	65.00
Snail (Compact, Idaho, Double Snail), breakfast size	85.00
Way's Beaded Swirl (Model)	35.00

Sugar, open
Actress (Theatrical)	50.00

New England Pineapple	45.00
Ray, flint	65.00
Roman Rosette	18.00

Sweetmeat, cov
Almond Thumbprint (Almond, Finger Print), flint	70.00
Bellflower, single vine, 6" h, high standard	300.00
New Jersey (Loop and Drops, Red Loop and Finecut), gold trim	50.00
Ohio, etched	30.00

Syrup
Adonis (Pleat and Tuck, Washboard), canary-yellow	175.00
Alba, white, colored florals	65.00
Cord Drapery, chocolate	350.00
Currier and Ives	95.00
Dahlia, amber	85.00
Jeweled Moon and Star, dec, lid missing	185.00
Knobby Bull's Eye	85.00
Louise	75.00
Patee Cross	65.00
Robin with Nest	175.00
Star and Punty, blown, flint	385.00
Thousand Eye, blue	225.00
York Herringbone	125.00

Table Set
Atlanta, 4 pc	450.00
Empress, green, gold trim, 4 pc	325.00
Tazza, Paneled Daisy and Button, etching	95.00

Toothpick Holder
Atlas (Bullet, Cannon Ball, Crystal Ball), etched leaf and berry	20.00
Banded Portland (Virginia #1, Maiden's Blush)	40.00
Beaded Grape (Beaded Grape and Vine, California, Grape and Vine), green, gold trim	70.00
Box in Box	30.00
Box in Box, green, gold trim	70.00
Bull's Eye and Fan	40.00
Colonial, blue, 2 handles	35.00
Croesus (Riverside's #484), green	125.00
Daisy and Button with "V" Ornament	35.00

Delaware (American Beauty, Four Petal Flower)
Green, gold trim	100.00
Rose stained	120.00
Diamond Spearhead, green	50.00
Empress, gold trim	85.00
King's Crown	45.00
Lower Manhattan, amethyst stain	35.00
Medallion Sunburst	35.00

Michigan (Loop and Pillar)
Colorless	45.00
Yellow stained, floral dec	85.00
Minnesota, green	165.00
Paneled Cherry	25.00
Portland	20.00
Queen's Necklace	35.00
Scalloped Skirt, green, enamel dec	55.00
Reverse 44, platinum trim	95.00
Rising Sun, pink suns	25.00
The States (Cane and Star Medallion)	50.00
Thousand Eye, amber	35.00
Tree of Life, amber, 2 small nicks	75.00
Washington (States Series), Knights Templar enameling	60.00
X-Ray, green, gold trim	25.00

Tray
Bulky Mule, 10" d	40.00

Columbian Shield
Blue	475.00

Vaseline...295.00
Feather Duster, 11", green 32.00
Nellie Bly, oval, minor chips.......................200.00
Scroll Cane (Cane Insert, Hobnailed Diamond and Star)
  Band, amber stain 60.00

Tumbler
  Amazon (Sawtooth Band), etched 42.50
  Beaded Swirl, green, gold trim 40.00
  Bellflower, flint 90.00
  Bird and Strawberry (Bluebird, Flying Bird and Strawberry,
    Strawberry and Bird) 45.00
  Bleeding Heart, ftd.....................................95.00
  Broken Column (Irish Column, Notched Rib), ruby trim ... 65.00
  Bull's Eye and Diamond Panels 50.00
  Cherry and Cable, color trim.......................20.00
  Cranes and Herons, etched.........................30.00
  Croesus (Riverside's #484)
    Amethyst...85.00
    Green...70.00
  Dakota (Baby Thumbprint, Thumbprint Band)
    Etched Fern and Berry 33.00
    Ruby stained 40.00
  Delaware (American Beauty, Four Petal Flower), cranberry,
    gold trim 40.00
  Empress, green, gold trim...........................55.00
  Esther, green, gold trim..............................45.00
  Excelsior, bar 75.00
  Festoon...20.00
  Flower with Cane (Cane Insert, Hobnailed Diamond and Star),
    colorless, green stain, gold trim 20.00
  Gibson Girl 75.00
  Hand..75.00
  Heavy Drape 20.00
  Herons, etched fish in mouth 25.00
  Hobnail...40.00
  Horn of Plenty...50.00
  Hummingbird 50.00
  Illinois 55.00
  King's #500, cobalt blue, gold trim 50.00
  Memphis, emerald green, faded gold trim 25.00
  Michigan (Loop and Pillar), narrow gold stripe near rim 35.00
  Peacock Feather 30.00
  Pillow Encircled, ruby 40.00
  Shell and Jewel 15.00
  Stag, etched, yellow and mauve tints 40.00
  Stippled Leaf 45.00
  Wildflower
    Amber...30.00
    Apple green..45.00
  Wreath and Shell
    Blue 80.00
    Vaseline 85.00
  X-Ray, amethyst, gold trim 65.00

Vase
  Colorado (Lacy Medallion), blue, 12" h.........90.00
  Illinois, 6" h, sq 25.00
  Massachusetts (Arched Diamond Points, Cane Variant, Gene-
    va #2, MD-131, Star and Diamonds), green, 10" h 65.00
  Michigan, bud 18.00
  New Hampshire (Bent Buckle, Modiste)
    Amethyst stain 25.00
    Green stain, twist stem, gold trim................40.00
  Paneled Thistle (Delta) 9-1/4" h....................25.00

Vegetable Bowl
  Beaded Grape Medallion, cov, ftd.................75.00

Eyewinker (Cannon Ball, Crystal Ball, Winking Eye),
  6-1/2" l..35.00
Horseshoe (Good Luck, Prayer Rug).................35.00
Lily of the Valley 35.00

Violet Bowl
  Chandelier (Crown Jewel)............................40.00
  Colorado (Lacy Medallion), blue....................35.00
  Snail (Compact, Idaho, Double Snail)..............50.00

Waste Bowl
  Block and Fan 30.00
  Festoon..38.00
  King's #500, frosted 45.00
  Pavonia (Pineapple Stem) 65.00
  Polar Bear 95.00
  Two Panel, amber 35.00

Water Pitcher
  Aquarium 165.00
  Classic, log feet.......................................315.00
  Cleat, flint 325.00
  Cut and Block, amber trim 125.00
  Dewey, Gridley...95.00
  Diamond Thumbprint, flint.........................1,350.00
  Feather (Doric), green................................200.00
  Florida (Emerald Green Herringbone, Paneled Herringbone),
    emerald green...45.00
  Honeycomb, flint, "pat'd 1865" 90.00
  Horn of Plenty, flint, heat check on handle 875.00
  Huckle, green 65.00
  Hummingbird 125.00
  Klondike, amber stained, sq 900.00
  Nestor, blue, dec.......................................150.00
  Peapods..40.00
  Reverse 44, burgundy, gold trim, jug 65.00
  Squirrel..350.00
  Swan..295.00
  Valentine...325.00
  Wildflower 35.00
  Wreath and Shell, vaseline...........................525.00
  X-Ray, green 140.00

Water Set
  Basketweave, pitcher, 6 goblets, 12" d scenic tray,
    amber 425.00
  Delaware (American Beauty, Four Petal Flower), tankard, 6
    tumblers, green, gold trim...........................375.00
  Hexagon Block, tankard, 2 tumblers, etched, amber
    stain 225.00
  Inverted Thistle, green, gold trim, 7 pc 280.00
  Shell and Jewel, pitcher, 8 tumblers 295.00
  Two Panel, blue..345.00

Water Tray
  Currier and Ives, bulky mule center 35.00
  Daisy and Button with Thumbprint, yellow stain 95.00
  Hummingbird, amber 95.00
  Polar Bear, frosted 300.00

Whiskey
  Argus, applied handle.................................75.00
  Bellflower, single vine, fine ribbed, 3-1/2" h 160.00
  Bull's Eye..85.00
  Diamond Point, flint, applied handle 85.00
  Excelsior..95.00

Wine
  Ashburton, flint 40.00
  Banded Portland (Virginia #1, Maiden's Blush), gold
    trim..42.00
  Barberry (Berry, Olive, Pepper Berry)................40.00
  Beaded Band 32.00

Beaded Tulip...25.00
Bleeding Heart..225.00
Canadian..42.00
Candlewick...12.00
Cathedral
    Amber...40.00
    Blue...45.00
Co-op, Royal...15.00
Cupid and Venus...70.00
Currier and Ives, blue..55.00
Cut Log..20.00
Daisy and Button with Crossbar
    Amber...25.00
    Blue...25.00
    Vaseline..25.00
Dakota (Baby Thumbprint, Thumbprint Band)
    Fern and berry etch..15.00
    Leaf and berry etch..12.00
Diamond Quilted, blue...25.00
Diamond Ridge...25.00
Galloway (Mirror Plate, U.S. Mirror, Virginia, Woodrow) ... 45.00
Halley's Comet..15.00
Hartley...22.00
Heart with Thumbprint (Bull's Eye in Heart, Columbia, Colum-
    bian, Heart and Thumbprint) 42.50
Hourglass...15.00
Jacob's Ladder (Maltese)..24.00
King's Crown, yellow stain 15.00
Lady Hamilton...25.00
Lattice with Oval Panels, flint 35.00
Magnet and Grape, Frosted Leaf, flint.......................115.00
Mascotte...25.00
Massachusetts (Arched Diamond Points, Cane Variant, Gene-
    va #2, MD-131, Star and Diamonds).......................35.00
Melrose...15.00
Minnesota..15.00
Mirror and Fan..24.00
Nailhead..15.00
Paisley..20.00
Paneled Nightshade..35.00
Popcorn...35.00
Portland, gold trim...30.00
Primrose, green..40.00
Prize, ruby..225.00
Rose Point Band...20.00
Spirea Band, blue 20.00
S-Repeat, blue 50.00
Teardrop and Thumbprint, etched.................................25.00
The States 18.00
Three Face...150.00
Two Panel, green..35.00
U.S. Coin (American Coin)..225.00
Wisconsin (Beaded Dewdrop)......................................75.00
Wyoming (Engima)...85.00
Wine Decanter, S-Repeat, blue 120.00
Wine Set, Daisy and Button with Narcissus, decanter, tray,
    6 wines 345.00

PEACHBLOW

History: Peachblow, an art glass which derives its name from a fine Chinese glazed porcelain, resembles a peach or crushed strawberries in color. Three American glass manufacturers and two English firms produced peach-blow glass in the late 1880s. A fourth American company resumed the process in the 1950s. The glass from each firm has its own identifying characteristics.

Hobbs, Brockunier & Co., Wheeling peachblow: Opalescent glass, plated or cased with a transparent amber glass; shading from yellow at the base to a deep red at top; glossy or satin finish.

Mt. Washington "Peach Blow": A homogeneous glass, shading from a pale gray-blue to a soft rose color; some pieces enhanced with glass appliqués, enameling, and gilding.

New England Glass Works, New England peachblow (advertised as Wild Rose, but called Peach Blow at the plant): Translucent, shading from rose to white; acid or glossy finish; some pieces enameled and gilded.

Thomas Webb & Sons and Stevens and Williams (English firms): Peachblow-style cased art glass, shading from yellow to red; some pieces with cameo-type relief designs. Occasionally found with cameo-type designs in relief.

Gunderson Glass Co.: Produced peachblow-type art glass to order during the 1950s; shades from an opaque faint tint of pink, which is almost white, to a deep rose.

Marks: Pieces made in England are marked "Peach Blow" or "Peach Bloom."

References: Gary E. Baker et al., *Wheeling Glass 1829-1939*, Oglebay Institute, 1994, distributed by Antique Publications; Neila and Tom Bredehoft, *Hobbs, Brockunier & Co. Glass*, Collector Books, 1997; James Measell, *New Martinsville Glass*, Antique Publications, 1994; John A. Shuman III, *Collector's Encyclopedia of American Glass*, Collector Books, 1988, 1994 value update; Kenneth Wilson, *American Glass 1760-1930*, 2 Vols., Hudson Hills Press and The Toledo Museum of Art, 1994.

Museums: Huntington Museum of Art, Huntington, WV; New Bedford Glass Museum, New Bedford, MA; Oglebay Institute Glass Museum; The Corning Museum of Glass, Corning, NY; The Toledo Museum of Art, Toledo, OH.

Gundersen-Pairpoint

Butter Dish, cov, 9" d, 5" h, satin finish, scalloped edge, applied finial, c1960 ....415.00
Candlesticks, pr 275.00
Compote, 5" h, Pairpoint 250.00
Creamer and Sugar, 3-1/2" h, 5-3/4" d, acid finish, deep pink,
    vertical stripes, applied reeded handles................475.00
Cruet, 8" h, 3-1/2" w, matte finish, ribbed shell handle, match-
    ing stopper with good color 875.00
Cup and Saucer..275.00
Decanter, 10" h, 5" w, Pilgrim Canteen form, acid finish, deep
    raspberry to white, applied peachblow ribbed handle,
    deep raspberry stopper 950.00
Goblet, 7-1/4" h, 4" d top, glossy finish, deep color, applied
    Burmese glass base...285.00
Hat, 3-1/4" h, satin finish, Diamond Quilted pattern 150.00
Jug, 4-1/2" h, 4" w, bulbous, applied loop handle, acid
    finish 450.00
Mug, satin finish, dec, orig paper label, c1970 ....125.00
Pitcher
    5-1/2" h, Hobnail, matte finish, white with hint of pink on
      int., orig label 550.00
    6-1/4" h, 3-1/2" w, Camellia, peachblow body, pedestal, ap-
      plied clear handle, waffle pontil, orig silver label.. 950.00
Plate, 8" d, luncheon, deep raspberry to pale pink, matte
    finish 375.00

Punch Cup, acid finish 275.00
Tumbler, 3-3/4" h, matte finish...................................275.00
Urn, 8-1/2" h, 4-1/2" w, two applied "M" handles, sq cut base,
    matte finish 550.00
Vase
    4-1/4" h, 3" d, acid finish.......................................225.00
    5" h, 6" w, ruffled top, pinched-in base 525.00
    9" h, 3-1/4" w, Tappan, acid finish.........................425.00
Wine Glass, 5" h, glossy finish 175.00

Mount Washington

Biscuit Jar, cov, 7-1/4" h, satin finish, enameled and jeweled
    dec, sgd 700.00
Bowl, 3" x 4", shading from deep rose to bluish-white, MOP
    satin int. 150.00
Bride's Basket, 11" d, pink ext., peachblow int., gold stylized
    flowers dec, ornate SP holder with aquatic motif, mkd
    "Pairpoint Mfg Co." 875.00
Condiment Set, 3" h salt and pepper shakers, mustard pot,
    acid finish, ribbed barrel form, enameled flub and white
    forget-met-nots, delicate green leaves and tracery, orig
    SP tops, replated SP stand mkd "Pairpoint Mfg Co. New
    Bedford Mass 705"..3,850.00
Cream Pitcher, 3-1/4" h, paper-thin walls, apple blossom
    pink to blue/gray base, tiny pointed spout, applied
    blue/gray handle 3,250.00
Perfume Bottle, 5" h, satin finish, enameled sprays of dainty
    white flowers, orig matching faceted cut stopper...... 650.00
Pitcher, 6-7/8" h, bulbous, sq handle 3,750.00
Tumbler, satin finish, band of apple blossom pink shades to
    soft blue-gray 1,500.00
Vase, satin finish
    7" h, trumpet, fold-over rim.....................................800.00
    8" h, slender neck, bulbous body.........................1,400.00
    8-1/4" h, lily form 1,850.00

New England

Bowl
    5-1/2" d, 3" h, ten ruffled top, deep raspberry shading to
      creamy white 750.00
    6" d, 3" h, acid finish, soft pink shading to off-white base,
      ruffled rim, polished pontil.................................325.00
Celery Vase, 7" h, 4" w
    Hobnail, satin finish, pale creamy white to rose
      pink 475.00
    Square top, deep raspberry with purple highlights shad-
      ing to white 785.00
Creamer and Sugar, 2-3/4" h creamer, 3-1/4" h open sugar,
    satin finish, ribbed, applied white handles.............500.00
Cruet, 6-3/4" h, 4" d at base, petticoat form, applied white
    handle and stopper, 3 lip top, acid finish...........1,950.00
Darner 175.00
Finger Bowl, 5-1/4" d, 2-1/2" h, ruffled rim...................385.00

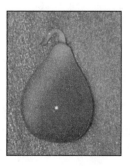

Pear, hollow, free blown, crooked stem, pink shading to white coloring, 4-1/4" h, $300.

Pear, 4-1/4" h, hollow, free blown, crooked stem, pink to
    white coloring 300.00
Pitcher
    6-1/4" h, satin finish, ten crimp top, applied white
      handle 1,200.00
    6-3/4" h, 7-1/2" w, 3-1/4" w at top, bulbous, sq top, applied
      frosted handle, ten rows of hobs 550.00
Punch Cup, satin finish, deep rose shading to white, applied
    white acid finished handle..450.00
Rose Bowl, 4" d, 4" h, glossy finish, deep color..........495.00
Salt Shaker, 3-3/4" h, acid finish, deep color, orig SP
    top 550.00
Spooner, sq top, acid finish 825.00
Toothpick Holder, 5" h, 2-3/8" h peachblow holder, shiny fin-
    ish, silver plated Kale Greenaway holder, little girl holding
    peachblow toothpick holder in outstretched arms, holder
    sgd "James W. Tufts Warranted Quadruple Plate 3405,"
    incised "XM 89," and "Mother 7 10" 1,075.00
Tumbler
    3-3/4" h, shiny finish, deep color upper third, middle fad-
      ing to creamy white bottom, thin walls 445.00
    3-3/4" h, velvety satin finish, deep raspberry red extends
      2/3 down, faces to 1/2" pure white band...........400.00
Vase
    3-1/4" h, 2-1/2" d, bulbous bottom, ring around neck, flar-
      ing top, matte finish 550.00
    5-1/2" h, satin finish, bulbous 485.00
    6-1/2" h, 3" w at top, lily, glossy finish, deep pink shading
      to white 650.00
    7" h, lily, satin finish, wafer base..............................945.00
    8-3/4" h, 4" w, bulbous stick, deep raspberry to white,
      matte finish 950.00
    9-1/2" h, trumpet, deep rose tricorn rim 375.00
    10-1/2" h, 5" w at base, bulbous, tapering neck, cup top,
      deep color, orig glossy finish 1,250.00
    10-1/2" h, 5" w at base, bulbous gourd shape, deep rasp-
      berry with fuchsia highlights to white, coloring extends
      two-thirds way down, 4 dimpled sides 1,450.00
    15-1/2" h, 6" w at top, lily, deep raspberry pink to
      white 1,450.00

New Martinsville

Bowl, 5" d, scalloped rim, yellow-caramel shading to peach
    to beige 65.00
Bride's Bowl, 11" d, wavy ruffled rim, cased int. 125.00
Dish, 5" d, 2-1/2" h, wavy ruffled rim 100.00

Webb

Biscuit Jar, cov, 6" h, 4-1/2" d, acid finish, heavy gold prunus
    blossoms, pine needles and butterfly dec, rich creamy
    white lining, SP rim, lid, and handle 950.00
Celery Vase, 6-1/2" h, acid finish 220.00
Cologne, 5" h, bulbous
    Raised gold floral branches, silver hallmarked dome
      top..900.00
    Shaded rose to amber, cased to opal white, gold enamel
      prunus blossoms and flying butterfly, hallmarked silver
      screw cap 750.00
Creamer, satin finish, coralene dec, rolled rim, flat
    base..650.00
Finger Bowl, 4-1/2" d, cased 195.00
Mustard Jar, 2-1/2" h, satin finish, hand painted prunus dec,
    gold trim 425.00
Plate, 8-1/4" d, glossy finish, crimped edge, gold enameled
    butterfly and blossoming prunus branches 450.00

Punch Cup, glossy finish, creamy white lining............150.00
Scent Bottle, 3-7/8" h, 2-3/4" d, satin finish, dainty blue, white, and yellow enameled flowers, green leaves, monarch butterfly, creamy white lining, hallmarked sterling silver top 725.00
Vase
  6" h, satin finish..375.00
  8-1/4" h, oval body, shaded pink, cased to creamy opal ground, repeating foliate and geometric devices dec...230.00
  10" h, shaded pink, white opal casing, enameled gold pendant blossoming branches............................300.00
  11-1/4" h, 6-1/2" d, pine needles, boughs, and trailing prunus blossoms, buds, and branches, two butterflies in flight, deep cherry red shading to pink-peach, creamy white lining, gold trim at top and base, dec by Jules Barbe 750.00
  12-1/4" h, 4-1/4" d base, coral shades to rose then to light pink, white opaque lining, pink, mauve, and gilt flowers and leaves, gilt around base, polished pontil ...785.00

Wheeling

Bowl, 3-3/4" d, satin finish, ground rim.........................190.00
Carafe, glossy finish...725.00
Cream Pitcher, 4" h, glossy finish, sq top, name etched on shoulder..700.00
Cruet, 6-1/4" h, ball shaped, mahogany neck and spout, fuchsia shoulders, cream base, Hobbs, Brockunier......1,950.00
Decanter, 9-1/8" h, satin finish, applied amber twisted handle, orig stopper...1,250.00
Ewer, 6-3/4" h, 4" w, glossy finish, duck bill top, applied amber loop handle 3,500.00
Jardiniere, 6-1/8" h, bulbous form, Hobbs, Brochure, top rim ground evenly...600.00
Lamp, 11" h, base of glossy Morgan vase affixed to P & A Hornet fluid lamp fittings, glass chimney 500.00
Mustard, SP cov and handle...475.00
Pear, hollow blown
  4-3/4" w, 3" w base, matte finish, bright red and yellow, white lining, very tip of stem gone.....................900.00
  5-1/2" h, 3" w base, glossy finish, tip of stem gone....800.00
Punch Cup, 2-1/2" h, Hobbs, Brockunier.....................535.00
Salt and Pepper Shakers, pr, 2-3/4" h, squatty round form, extra deep fuchsia color shading to amber, orig pewter caps..690.00
Sugar Shaker, 5-1/2" h, satin finish, orig metal top 700.00
Toothpick Holder, 2-3/4" h, 2-1/2" d, bulbous, deep color, glossy finish, two external cracks on outer layer of glass 70.00
Tumbler
  3-1/2" h, shiny finish, deep colored upper third shades to creamy base..385.00
  3-7/8" h, top rim ground..290.00
Vase
  8" h, Morgan stick-form, blue-fuchsia shading to amber, cased to opal white 575.00
  9-1/4" h, ball shaped body, 5" slender neck, shape #11..735.00
  9-1/2" h, flared and ruffled rim, applied amber edge above oval body, molded drapery design, Hobbs Brockunier 1,200.00
  13" h, acid finish 975.00

PEKING GLASS

History: Peking glass is a type of cameo glass of Chinese origin. Its production began in the 1700s and continued well into the 19th century. The background color of Peking glass may be a delicate shade of yellow, green, or white. One style of white background is so transparent that it often is referred to as the "snowflake" ground. The overlay colors include a rich garnet red, deep blue, and emerald green.

Reference: Gloria and Robert Mascarelli, *Oriental Antiques*, Wallace-Homestead, 1992.

Bottle, 10" h, opaque yellow ground, carved birds in flight and orchid plants... 425.00
Bowl
  5-3/4" d, rounded form, ext. with cranes and lotus plants, green overlay, whit ground......................................90.00
  6-1/8" d, floral shaped rim, ext. with birds among lotus, lotus leaf form foot, red overly, white ground...............1,150.00
  7" d, raised lotus petals on ext., opaque blue with white int., 19th C 375.00
  7" d, rounded form, shaped rim, ext. with flowering lotus continuing to a lotus leaf-form foot rim, green overlay, white ground 575.00
Candlestick, cock's foot... 230.00
Cup, 2-1/2" h, deep form, gently flaring rim, ring foot, continual band of overlapping dragons, cloud collar border, lappet border, red overlay, Snowflake 2,185.00
Dish, 11-3/4" l, flattened round form, bright yellow, 19th C....850.00
Rose Jar, cov, 7-1/2" h, 8" d, emerald green over flint white ground, carved bird on hawthorn tree, matching carved cover... 325.00
Snuff Bottle, green, jade stopper, Chinese...................... 45.00
Vase
  7" h, high shouldered form, ducks swimming among tall lotus plants, green overlay, white ground, pr 500.00
  7-1/2" h, ovoid, elongated neck, red overlay, Snowflake pattern, body with 2 dragons and 2 phoenix, neck with dragon and phoenix, Qianlong period, pr 4,600.00
  8" h, high shoulder form, red overlay, white ground, female figures in garden, 18th C, pr 1,840.00
  9" h, opaque white ground, Chinese red cameo, deep cut leaves and berries, baluster, c1900.........................575.00
  9-1/4" h, ovoid, opaque raised yellow flowers, translucent yellow ground, 19th C 525.00
  10" h, baluster, opaque white ground, carved red overlay, goldfish and water lily dec, pr 700.00
  11-1/2" h, hand carved cobalt blue florals and butterflies, white satin ground, Chinese, 19th C 1,100.00
  12" h, baluster, opaque white ground, yellow overlay cut with exotic fish, pond, lilies, pads, and aquatic grasses, pr...700.00

PELOTON

History: Wilhelm Kralik of Bohemia patented Peloton art glass in 1880. Later, it was also patented in America and England.

Peloton glass is found with both transparent and opaque grounds, although opaque is more common. Opaque colored glass filaments (strings) are applied by dipping or rolling the hot glass. Generally, the filaments (threads) are pink, blue, yellow, and white (rainbow colors) or a single color. Items also may have a satin finish and enamel decorations.

Basket, shaded purple to white ground, pink, yellow, blue, and white filaments, applied crystal rigaree edge, wishbone feet, solid crystal rope thorn handle with pr of prunts........ 500.00
Biscuit Jar
  6-3/4" h, pale blue ground, multicolored filaments, white lining, melon ribbed body, SP rim, cover, and bail handle ...550.00

7" h, 6-1/2" d, powder blue body, white, yellow, blue, and vivid pink filaments, 48 molded-in vertical ribs, silverplated fittings, barn swallow emb on lid 785.00

Bowl

3-1/2" d, 2-1/2" h, pinched top, ribbed sides, clear ground, white, pink, blue, and olive green filaments, fiery opal pastel orchid lining 185.00

6-1/2" d, 6" h, white ground, brown and yellow filaments, all-over ribbed surface, 3 applied crystal thorn feet, 8 point star top 325.00

Fairy Lamp, white ground, pastel filaments, undulating ruffled saucer base, colorless Clarke insert 365.00

Finger Bowl, colorless, multicolored filaments...................75.00

Pitcher

6-1/2" h, sq blown colorless body, applied colorless, pink, yellow, blue and white striped yellow filaments, applied colorless handle 250.00

7" h, cranberry ground, multicolored filaments, swirled body, applied colorless reeded handle 385.00

9-3/4" h, colorless ground, red, yellow, and white filaments, swirled body, applied colorless reeded handle.....300.00

11" h, amber ground, multicolored filaments, applied colorless reeded handle..600.00

Plate, 7-3/4" d, colorless ground, blue strings, enamel floral dec 125.00

Punch Cup, turquoise ground, multicolored filaments, enameled florals, set of six...325.00

Rose Bowl

4" h, 4" w, ftd, 4 pulled edges, sq shape, applied crystal edge, 6 shell feet, glossy finish shaded blue ground, yellow, pink, white, blue, and red filaments................395.00

6" h, 5-1/2" w, ftd, 8 point star shaped top, white lining, ribbed and swirled, brown shaded filaments.........325.00

Sweetmeat, cov, 2-1/2" h, 5-1/2" w, white ribbed satin body, random blue, white, yellow, and pink filaments, sgd "Pairpoint" silver plated lid..200.00

Toothpick Holder, 3" h, colorless, white filaments 145.00

Tumbler, 3-3/4" h, colorless ground, yellow, pink, red, light blue, and white filaments...125.00

Vase

3-1/2" h, 3 x 3-7/8" d, orchid pink cased body, emb ribs, pink, blue, and yellow filaments, pinched together in center 195.00

4" h, 4-3/4" d, bulbous base, folded over tricorn shape top, white ribbed cased body, pink, yellow, blue, and white applied filaments..290.00

4-1/4" h, 4-3/4" d, tricorn folded down rim, clear ground rose, yellow, blue, and white filaments, white lining, squatty, melon ribbed body...325.00

5" h, 4-3/4" w, crystal body, heavily applied blue all over threading, pink, yellow, and white enameled floral dec, green leaves, yellow and brown spotted butterfly, minor wear to threading..75.00

6" h, 4-1/2" d, shaded lavender to off-white opaque ground, cased in crystal, all over pink, white, yellow, blue, and red filaments, corset type shape, vertical ribs, tightly crimped top 450.00

6" h, 5" w, ribbed, bright pink ground, yellow, blue, white, red, pink, and purple filaments, white lining, two applied ribbed handles 450.00

7" h, bulbous, colorless ground, cranberry red strings.... 275.00

PERFUME, COLOGNE, and SCENT BOTTLES

History: The second half of the 19th century was the golden age for decorative bottles made to hold scents. These bottles were made in a variety of shapes and sizes.

An atomizer is a perfume bottle with a spray mechanism. Cologne bottles usually are larger and have stoppers which also may be used as applicators. A perfume bottle has a stopper that often is elongated and designed to be an applicator.

Scent bottles are small bottles used to hold a scent or smelling salts. A vinaigrette is an ornamental box or bottle that has a perforated top and is used to hold aromatic vinegar or smelling salts. Fashionable women of the late 18th and 19th centuries carried them in purses or slipped them into gloves in case of a sudden fainting spell.

References: Joanne Dubbs Ball and Dorothy Hehl Torem, *Commercial Fragrance Bottles*, Schiffer, 1993; —, *Fragrance Bottle Masterpieces*, Schiffer, 1996; Carla Bordignon, *Perfume Bottles*, Chronicle Books, 1995; Glinda Bowman, *Miniature Perfume Bottles*, Schiffer, 1994; ——, *More Miniature Perfume Bottles*, Schiffer, 1996; Jacquelyne Jones-North, *Commercial Perfume Bottles*, revised and updated ed., Schiffer, 1996; Christie Mayer Lefkowith, *Art of Perfume*, Thames and Hudson, 1994; Monsen and Baer, *Beauty of Perfume*, published by authors (Box 529, Vienna, VA 22183), 1996; ——, *Legacies of Perfume*, published by authors (Box 529, Vienna, VA 22183), 1997; John Odell, *Digger Odell's Official Antique Bottle and Glass Collector Magazine Price Guide Series*, Vol. 6, published by author (1910 Shawhan Rd., Morrow, OH 45152), 1995; Jeri Lyn Ringblum, *Collector's Handbook of Miniature Perfume Bottles*, Schiffer, 1996.

Periodical: *Perfume & Scent Bottle Quarterly*, P.O. Box 187, Galena, OH 43021.

Collectors' Clubs: International Perfume Bottle Assoc., P.O. Box 529, Vienna, VA 22180; Mini-Scents, 7 Saint John's Rd., West Hollywood, CA 90069; Parfum Plus Collections, 1590 Louis-Carrier Ste. 502, Montreal Quebec H4N 2Z1 Canada; Perfume and Scent Bottle Collectors, 2022 East Charleston Rd., Las Vegas, NV 89104.

Atomizers

3" h, opaque black ground, gold Art Deco dec 75.00

4-1/2" h, Moser, sapphire blue, gold florals, leaves, and swirls, melon ribbed body, orig gold top and bulb.............. 275.00

6-1/4" h, Cambridge, stippled gold, opaque jade, orig silk lined box..140.00

7" h, Carder Steuben, gold aurene tapered body, gilt metal DeVilbiss fittings, orig rubber bulb intact, but hardened ...865.00

8" h

Czechoslovakian, cobalt blue, large enameled and faceted crystal stopper, c1930...................................80.00

Gallé, cameo, lavender flowers and foliage, shaded yellow and frosted ground 1,250.00

9-1/2" h, 3" w, green cut to clear overlay, floral and panel cutting, fancy metal holder, emerald and pearl jewel accents, attributed to Czechoslovakia 400.00

10" h

DeVilbiss, dark amethyst, goldstone spiderweb dec, bulb missing 90.00

Faceted citron green transparent bottle suspended from conforming angular chromed metal holder, Art Deco style, some int. stains, minor metal scratches 700.00

Cologne

3-1/8" h, apple green, pressed base, cut stopper 150.00

3-5/8" h, C & B, irregular six-sided form, bulbous neck, sapphire blue, tooled mouth, pontil scar, attributed to America, 1840-60 ....140.00

4" h, satin, heat reactive rose-red shaded to green, cased to opal glass int., threaded silver rim and hammered screw-on cap, imp "Gorham Sterling" 345.00

4-1/2" h, vaseline, attributed to New England Glass Co., flint, orig stopper 225.00

4-3/4" h, figural, elephant with rich trappings, colorless, tooled flared mouth, pontil scar, America, 1840-60 ....500.00

5" h, diamond form, full figured Indians on two sides, oval label panels on other two sides, aquamarine, inward rolled mouth, pontil scar, America, 1840-60 ....90.00

5-1/2" h, flat corseted form, palmette, scrolled acanthus, and cross hatching, brilliant sapphire blue, inward rolled mouth, pontil scar, America, 1840-60 ....1,800.00

5-7/8" h, Baccarat, colorless, panel cut, matching stopper 75.00

6-1/4" h, front panel with bunch of grapes with leaves, back panel with fancy leaf designs, two sides panels are fluted, aquamarine, tooled flared mouth, pontil scar, America, 1840-60, old label on side panel with medication adv..............375.00

6-3/4" h, Biedermeier style, vaseline, elaborate faceted cutting, conforming stopper, small chip on medial border.....230.00

7" h

   Cut glass, cranberry cut to colorless, cane cut, matching stopper 250.00

   5" d, paperweight, double overlay, crimson red over white over colorless squatty bottle, five oval facet windows reveal concentric millefiore cane int., matching stopper 460.00

7-1/4" h, Tiffany Favrile, irid gold, double bulbed amber body, eight applied prunts trailing threads to base, matching gold irid stopper, inscribed "L. C. T. Q4736," some int. stain 2,415.00

11" h, art glass, transparent green bottle, delicate floral design, colorless pedestal foot, faceted teardrop stopper.....175.00

Cologne Bottle, two-pc mold, twelve body panels, deep sapphire blue, flared mouth, period stopper, smooth base, attributed to Boston and Sandwich Glass Works, Sandwich, MA, 1860-80, $250. Photo courtesy of Norman C. Heckler and Co.

Perfume Bottle, silver deposit, bulbous, floral and flowing leaf motif, 3-3/8" h, $175.

Perfume

2" h, 1-1/2" d, German, green glass, colored enamel coat of arms, fine enamel trim on body and matching green stopper 60.00

2-3/8" h, Venetian, globular body, Lion of Venice portrait cane on surface of opaque yellow and silver glass, crowned with ornate cap dec with flowers, no stopper 335.00

2-1/2" l, dark cobalt blue, sheared top, cork closure, c1890..75.00

3" h, cobalt blue, sheared top, c1890 ....65.00

3-3/4" h, 2-3/8" d, cranberry, bulbous, enameled blue and gray flowers, blue, orange, and white leaves, clear flattened ball stopper 110.00

3-9/16" h, cherub sulphide surrounded by ornate faceting on all sides, gilded copper cap, glass stopper 365.00

3-11/16" h, Clichy, ext. dec with alternating blue and white swirled bands, stopper and base dec with 16K gold chased with delicate patterns, base mkd "D. J.," fitted leather carrying case..990.00

4-3/8" h, Mary Gregory, cranberry, white enameled girl dec, colorless ball stopper 175.00

4-1/2" h, 2-3/4" d, melon ribbed body, emb, lacy gold enameled fern leaves, colorless cut faceted stopper 165.00

4-3/4" h, Steuben, Verre- de Soie, jade green 310.00

5" h

   Paperweight type, spherical bottle, teardrop stopper, each with multi-petaled yellow rose blossom, Francis Whittemore "W" canes..450.00

   Quezal, flattened teardrop form, irid multicolored ground, foliate mounts, bulbous stopper, c1915 ....625.00

5-1/4" h, amethyst overlay, Thousand Eye Honeycomb cutting to clear ground, hinged silver rim and cap 690.00

5-1/2" h, Rene Lalique, Sirenes, frosted mermaids with traces of gray patina, molded signature on base, no cover..... 250.00

6-3/8" h, Baccarat, molded and frosted, acid stamped "Baccarat/France," mid-20th C 650.00

6" l, satin, Diamond Quilted MOP, shading yellow to white, lay down horn type 415.00

6-1/2" h, American Brilliant Period Cut Glass, Button and Star pattern, rayed base, faceted stopper 125.00

Scent

2-1/4" h, teardrop form, ruby, enameled, gilt metal mounting, Victorian, late 19th C, stopper missing 80.00

2-1/2" h

   Early American glass, amethyst, teardrop shape, emb sunburst design..225.00

Scent, cylindrical, flared base, frosted and cut glass, light to dark blue, gold plated cap and chain, orig dauber, 2-3/4" l, $150.

1-1/4" d, Frances Whittemore, paperweight type, white rose with four green leaves, sgd underneath with black on yellow "W" signature cane, white swirl stopper..........115.00

2-3/4" h, teardrop form, blue, enameled, gilt metal mounting, Victorian, late 19th C, stopper missing....................80.00

2-7/8" h, Early American glass, teardrop form, nineteen vertical ribs, citron, sheared mouth, pontil scar, attributed to America, 1840-60, light overall int. haze................230.00

3" h, Early American glass, teardrop form, twenty-vie swirled ribs, emerald green, sheared mouth, pontil scar, c1840-60, some light int. residue..100.00

3-1/4" h, double overlay, pink over white, early 20th C, cap and stopper missing..100.00

3-1/2" h, double overlay, cobalt blue over white, early 20th C, cap and stopper missing 100.00

3-3/4" h, satin, Peacock Eye, MOP, bridal white, orig glass stopper, push-on silverplated lid with monogram "C" 435.00

4" d, satin, bridal white, 24 white vertical stripes, 12 silk ribbons alternating with 12 muted satin ribbons, sterling silver flip top cap, collar stamped "CS, FS, STd, SILr," engraved name 400.00

4-1/8" h, Early American, blown, colorless, cranberry and white stripes, white and gold metallic twist..............95.00

4-1/4" h, ruby, faceted sides, double silver mounts with repoussé molded top, early 20th C 175.00

4-1/2" h, white overlay, ruby glass body, silver mount, early 20th C 185.00

4-5/8" h, 2-1/2" w at base, Perthshire, paperweight type, white and blue canes, amethyst ground, amethyst striped stopper 80.00

4-3/4" h, cobalt blue, faceted sides, double silver mounts with repoussé molded top, early 20th C 175.00

5" l, cobalt blue cut to clear, orig metal mounting.........75.00

5-1/2 h
  Double, cobalt blue, faceted cylindrical sides, silver mounted repoussé tops.....................................225.00
  Four triangular scenes encased in trelliswork banding, dec gilt metal foliate mounts, cut glass stoppers, French, early 20th C 115.00

Vinaigrettes

2-1/4" x 1", cranberry, rect, allover cutting, enameled tiny pink roses, green leaves, gold dec, hinged lid, stopper, finger chain...185.00

3-7/8" l, cut glass, cobalt blue, yellow flashing, SS overlay, emb SS cap...125.00

PHOENIX GLASS

History: Phoenix Glass Company, Beaver, Pennsylvania, was established in 1880. Known primarily for commercial glassware, the firm also produced a molded, sculptured, cameo-type line in 1932 when 45 to 50 molds from the Consolidated Glass Company were moved to Phoenix and used until early 1936.

The earliest art glass production at Phoenix was called the "Reuben Line." These items were made with a oval paper label. One key to identifying Phoenix's Reuben Line is to watch for solid color finishes in light blue, dark blue, green, white, and yellow. Another popular Phoenix line was their Sculptured Art Ware. Most of the designs are credited to Kenneth Haley. This early items in this line were marked with silver paper labels. Later items featured a gold paper label. This line was produced on and off again into the 1960s. The company is still in business, but do not have facilities to make hand molded glass or the Sculptured Art Ware.

References: Jack D. Wilson, *Phoenix & Consolidated Art Glass*, Antique Publications, 1989; Kenneth Wilson, *American Glass 1760-1930: The Toledo Museum of Art, Volume I, Volume II,* Hudson Hills Press and The Toledo Museum of Art, 1994.

Collectors' Club: Phoenix & Consolidated Glass Collectors, P.O. Box 3847, Edmond, OK 73083-3847.

Ashtray
  Phlox, large, white, frosted...86.00
  Praying Mantis, white ground, relief molded insect, triangular 65.00
Basket, 4-1/2" h, pink ground, relief molded dogwood dec....65.00
Bowl
  Bittersweet, relief molded, white ground, 9-1/2" d, 5-1/2" h 165.00
  Swallows, purple wash..150.00
Bowl, cov, Lace Dew Drop, #811, 8-1/2" d, blue and white 275.00
Candlesticks, pr
  3-1/4" h, blue ground, bubbles and swirls 65.00
  4" h, blue ground, frosted..50.00
Canoe
  8" l, white ground, sculptured green lemons and foliage..95.00
  13-1/2" l, opal ground, sculptured blue lovebirds.......325.00
Centerpiece Bowl, 14" d, opaque white ground, sculptured diving nudes, three colors 250.00
Charger, blue ground
  14" d, relief molded white daffodils 100.00
  18" d, relief molded white dancing nudes...................525.00
Cigarette Box, Phlox, white milk glass
  Cocoa Brown...140.00
  Wedgwood Blue...125.00
Compote, 8-1/2" d, butterscotch ground, relief molded dragonflies and water lilies dec 85.00
Floor Vase, 18" h, Bushberry, light green 450.00
Dish, cov, 8-1/2" l, oval, amber ground, sculptured lotus blossoms and dragonflies..100.00
Ginger Jar, cov, frosted ground, bird finial.......................80.00
Lamp
  Boudoir, Wild Rose, brown highlights, milk glass ground 150.00

Ceiling, 15" sq, Flying Birds, heavy custard glass, metal mounts..1,500.00
Table, 22-1/2" h, 18" reverse painted dome shade, blue shading to yellow to blue, water landscape of Indian paddling canoe, rib molded round ftd base.............2,500.00
Table, 23" h, 16" d reverse painted shade, landscape with windmill, cottage, and barn, pale pink, yellow, and blue ground, green and brown landscape, minor edge flake.........650.00
Table, 28" h, Lovebirds, green opalescent glass, brass fixtures..225.00
Table, 26" h, 16" d, reverse painted shade, brilliant yellow and pink ground, large trees and rocks by stream, orig fancy metal Art Nouveau style base, emb floral design ... 1,250.00
Thistle, umbrella shape, blue and irid white, 25" h 400.00
Lamp Base, Cockatoos, blue, brown, custard 200.00
Planter, 8-1/2" l, 3-1/4" h, white ground, relief molded green lion...95.00
Plate, 8-1/2" d, frosted and clear ground, relief molded cherries...60.00
Powder Box, cov, 7-1/4" d, pale lavender ground, sculptured white violets...115.00
Rose Bowl, rose pink ground, relief molded starflowers and white bands...150.00
Tumbler, Lace Dew Drop, blue and white, set of 4 ....75.00
Umbrella Stand, 18" h, 9" w, Thistle
    Green wash..600.00
    Pearlized blue ground..................................450.00
Vase
  Bellflower
    Burgundy pearlized......................................75.00
    Cocoa brown, white milk glass..........................100.00
  Bittersweet
    Gold over milk glass, gold worn, 9-1/2" h..............125.00
    Whited stained crystal, Reuben line....................150.00
  Bluebell, brown, 7" h.....................................125.00
  Cameo, #345, sculptured, blue highlights, 6" h...........130.00
  Cockatoos, aqua, bulbous, cream ground, beige branches, lavender berries, 9" h, 9" w.........................325.00
  Cosmos
    Cocoa brown, white milk glass..........................125.00
    Wedgwood Blue, white milk glass........................150.00
  Daisies, white milk glass, pale blue/gray painted ground, all over daisies, 9-1/2" h, 9" w.....................500.00
  Fern, #261
    Blue, pearlized white fern, silver label...............225.00
    Sculptured crystal, very light blue frosted design, 7" h..130.00
  Figures, satin, milk glass, orig label....................90.00
  Flying Geese
    Cocoa brown, white milk glass..........................220.00
    Pillow form, white on brown............................260.00
  Foxglove, rose, green, white, 10-1/2" h..................125.00
  Freesia, fan, cocoa brown, white milk glass 125.00
  Gold Fish, pale green, peach colored fish, 9-1/4" h, 8" w..425.00
  Grasshoppers and reeds dec, clear and frosted, 8-3/4" h..125.00
  Jewel, powder blue, pearlized.............................80.00
  Line 700, blue crystal, 6-1/2" h.........................350.00
  Madonna, cocoa brown, white milk glass...................220.00
  Peony, yellow, green, custard, 9-1/2" h..................160.00
  Philodendron
    Blue, ormolu mounts, 14" h.............................400.00
    Cocoa brown, white milk glass..........................160.00
    Wedgwood Blue, white milk glass........................160.00
  Starflower
    Cocoa brown, white milk glass..........................140.00

Wedgwood Blue, white milk glass.............................140.00
Thistle, powder blue pearlized..............................520.00
Wild Geese, #357
    Oval, tan shadow, milk glass ground, 9-1/4" h.........230.00
    Pearlized white birds, light green ground, 10" h 195.00
Wild Rose
    Amber...175.00
    Blown out, pearlized dec, dark rose ground, orig label, 11" h...275.00
    Cocoa brown, white milk glass.........................125.00
    Medium green, milk glass ground, partial label, 10-1/2" h..150.00
Zodiac, raised white figures, peach colored ground, 10-1/2" h...700.00

PICKLE CASTORS

History: A pickle castor is a table accessory used to serve pickles. It generally consists of a silver-plated frame fitted with a glass insert, matching silver-plated lid, and matching tongs. Pickle castors were very popular during the Victorian era. Inserts are found in pattern glass and colored art glass.

Amber
    Daisy and Button pattern insert, silver plated frame 370.00
    Inverted Thumbprint pattern, silver plated frame........275.00
Amberina, melon ribbed Inverted Thumbprint pattern insert, silver plated lid, ftd frame, lid, tongs, c1875-95 .... 720.00
Blue
    Currier and Ives pattern insert, orig silver plated frame... 195.00
    Daisy and Button pattern insert, silver plated Wilcox frame, lid, and tongs..................................250.00
    Sprig pattern insert, ornate Reed and Barton frame, orig fork and fancy lid..200.00
Colorless
    Acid etched insert, floral dec with bird medallion, octagonal 11-3/4" h silver plated frame, mkd "Meriden Co. 182"...200.00
    Cupid and Venus patterned insert, silver plated frame ...295.00
    Engraved insert, dark Brittania frame, leafy gingerbread-type dec, orig tongs, matching finial on lid, c1865............ 115.00
Cranberry
    Barrel shaped insert, multicolored enamel flowers, figural frame with acorns and dog's paw feet 425.00
    Bulbous cranberry insert, Inverted Thumbprint pattern, fancy Tuffs frame with emb floral design, 12-3/4" h, internal crack near rim, frame appears to have been dropped, minor repair 475.00
    Inverted Thumbprint pattern insert, enameled blue and white florals, green leaves, shelf on frame dec with peacocks and other birds 325.00
    Paneled Spring insert, silver plated frame, c1875-95..... 450.00
Double
    Colorless inserts, emb fans and flowers, matching cov, fancy tulip finials, Viking head ftd oval handled frame, sgd "Meriden"..275.00
    Vaseline, pickle leaves and pieces, resilvered frame..... 800.00
Emerald Green, paneled insert with enameled florals, ornate silver plated frame 245.00
Mt. Washington, 11" h, 6" d, decorated satin glass insert, blue enamel and painted yellow roses, green leaves, orange and yellow blossoms, silver-plated Rogers stand and tongs.. 875.00
Opal Insert, 11" h, shaded pale green to white ground, pink flowers, fancy silver plated frame with tongs 500.00

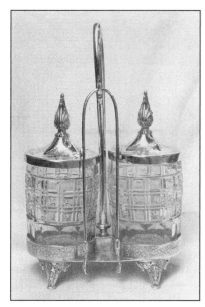

Double, pressed Block and Star patterned insert, Viking feet, Meriden, c1884, 10-1/2" h, 6-3/4" w, $325.

Opalescent
    Coin Spot, cranberry ground, polychrome enameled flowers, opalescent spots, silver plated frame with lion and shield finial 225.00
    Daisy & Fern, blue, emb DQ floral jar, resilvered frame ...650.00
    Vertical white stripes, colorless ground, resilvered angel frame, elephant's head and trunk feet 725.00
Pigeon Blood, Torquay pattern, silver plated frame and tongs........................400.00
Pink, shiny pink Florette pattern insert, white int., bowed out frame 325.00
Satin
    Cranberry, Optic Diamond and Inverted Thumbprint pattern insert, gold spider chrysanthemum dec, ftd Simpson Hall frame, ornate engraved cov, orig silvering 625.00
    Yellow barrel shaped insert, flowers and butterfly dec, cherubs on front and back corners of frame, mkd "Rogers".... 750.00
Sapphire Blue, Beaded Dart pattern insert, fancy silver plated Simpson, Hall & Miller stand 350.00
Vaseline, blown insert, fancy silver plated Meriden frame, orig tongs, 12" h.....................375.00

PIGEON BLOOD GLASS

History: Pigeon blood refers to the deep orange-red-colored glassware produced around the turn of the century. Do not confuse it with the many other red glasswares of that period. Pigeon blood has a very definite orange glow.

Berry Bowl, 9" d, master, Torquay, silver plated rim........110.00
Biscuit Jar
    Florette 275.00
    Torquay pattern, silver plated rim, cov, and handles 295.00
Bowl
    4-1/2" d, Inverted Thumbprint pattern 50.00
    8-1/2" d, Venecia pattern, enameled floral dec...........125.00
    12-1/2" d, three applied colorless lion head prunts on front, applied colorless feet and handles 260.00
Bride's Bowl, 12" h, 10" d, Drapery and Dot pattern, fancy Victorian silver plated holder......................400.00
Butter Dish, cov
    Coreopsis pattern.......................275.00
    Venecia pattern, enameled dec..................350.00
Celery Vase, 6" h, Torquay pattern, silver plated rim.......225.00

Tumbler, alternating panels and ribs, 3-1/2" h, $80.

Cracker Jar, cov, Quilted Phlox pattern, Consolidated Glass Co., resilvered hardware 325.00
Creamer
    Coreopsis pattern.......................125.00
    Florette pattern, satin 75.00
    Venecia pattern, enameled dec.......................125.00
Decanter, 9-1/2" h, orig stopper.......................145.00
Goblet, bucket shaped bowl, cushioned stem, enameled medallion with landscape and country scenes, heavy gold swirls, beads, and feathers, mkd "face de Venise," German, early 19th C 225.00
Hand Cooler, 5" l, cut panels, 2 compartments, SS fittings... 145.00
Pickle Castor
    Beaded Drape pattern, Consolidated Glass Co., orig silver plated frame, cov, and tongs 425.00
    Cone pattern 600.00
    Torquay pattern, silver plated frame and tongs..........400.00
Pitcher
    Bulging Loops pattern, 9-1/2" h, applied clear handle, ground pontil 425.00
    Coreopsis pattern.......................400.00
    Torquay pattern, silver plated rim 450.00
Salt and Pepper Shakers, pr
    Bulging Loops pattern, orig top 150.00
    Flower Band pattern, glossy 150.00
    Globule.......................160.00
Spooner, Torquay pattern
    All glass.......................150.00
    Silverplated rim 225.00
Syrup, Beaded Drape pattern, Consolidated Glass Co., orig hinged lid.......................250.00
Tumbler, 3-1/4" h, alternating panel and rib 85.00
Vase
    6" h, gourd shape, cased, gold leaf dec, applied elephant head handles, Webb, pr.......................400.00
    7-1/4" h, enameled floral and jeweled dec..................175.00
Water Carafe, Coreopsis pattern 250.00
Water Set, Bulging Loop pattern, pitcher, five tumblers. 500.00

PINK SLAG

History: True pink slag is found only in the molded Inverted Fan and Feather pattern. Quality pieces shade from pink at the top to white at the bottom.

Reproduction Alert: Recently, pieces of pink slag made from molds of the now-defunct Cambridge Glass Company have been found in the Inverted Strawberry and Inverted Thistle patterns. This is not considered true pink slag and brings only a fraction of the price of the Inverted Fan and Feather pieces.

Videotape: National Imperial Glass Collectors Society, *Glass of Yesteryears, The Renaissance of Slag Glass by Imperial*, RoCliff Communications, 1994.

Bowl
    9" d, ftd 600.00
    10" d 750.00
Butter Dish, cov, 7-5/8" d, 7" h cov, 2-1/4" h base with 4 molded
    feet, fiery opalescent coloring 1,485.00
Creamer 465.00
Cruet, 6-1/2" h, orig stopper......................................1,300.00
Jelly Compote, 5" h, 4-1/2" d, scalloped top...................375.00
Marmalade Jar, cov 875.00
Pitcher, water 775.00
Punch Cup, 2-1/2" h, ftd...275.00
Salt Shaker 300.00
Sauce Dish, 4-1/4" d, 2-1/2" h, ball feet 225.00
Spooner..350.00
Sugar Bowl, cov 550.00
Toothpick Holder...825.00
Tumbler, 4-1/2" h 475.00

POMONA GLASS

History: Pomona glass, produced only by the New England Glass Works and named for the Roman goddess of fruit and trees, was patented in 1885 by Joseph Locke. It is a delicate lead, blown art glass which has a pale, soft beige ground and a top one-inch band of honey amber.

There are two distinct types of backgrounds. First ground, made only from late 1884 to June 1886, was produced by making fine cuttings through a wax coating followed by an acid bath. Second ground was made by rolling the piece in acid-resisting particles and acid etching. Second ground was made in Cambridge until 1888 and until the early 1900s in Toledo, where Libbey moved the firm after purchasing New England Glass works. Both methods produced a soft frosted appearance, but fine curlicue lines are more visible on first-ground pieces. Some pieces have designs which were etched and then stained with a color. The most familiar design is blue cornflowers.

Do not confuse Pomona with Midwestern Pomona, a pressed glass with a frosted body and amber band.

References: Joseph and Jane Locke, *Locke Art Glass*, Dover Publications, 1987; Kenneth Wilson, *American Glass 1760-1930*, 2 Vols., Hudson Hills Press and The Toledo Museum of Art, 1994.

Bowl
    4-1/2" d, 3" h, first ground, rich deep amber staining 275.00
    5" d, Rivulet pattern, second ground, fluted, blue stain... 125.00
    5-1/4" d, Cornflower pattern, second ground, fluted.....85.00
    10" d, Cornflower pattern, second ground...................450.00
Butter Dish, cov, 4-1/2" h, 8" d underplate, first ground, gold stained
    acacia leaf dec, reeded curlicue handle 1,275.00
Celery Vase, 6-1/8" h, 4-1/2" d, first ground, acacia leaf
    dec 550.00
Champagne, 5" h, stemmed, second ground, amber
    staining...245.00

Creamer
    Cornflower pattern, second ground, blue flower, ruffled top,
      applied crystal crimped base, 3" h, 6" w 225.00
    Daisy and Butterfly pattern, second ground, applied color-
      less handle, three applied colorless feet 275.00
Cruet, orig ball stopper
    5-1/2" h, Blueberry pattern, first ground, gold leaves, applied
      colorless handle 300.00
    7-1/4" h, Cornflower pattern, first ground 365.00
    7-1/4" h, Pansy and Butterfly pattern, second ground, un-
      stained dec and handle, irid amber stopper..........500.00
Finger Bowl, Cornflower pattern, first ground 75.00
Goblet, 6" h, first ground, little amber stain remains....... 115.00
Lemonade Mug, 5-3/4" h
    Cornflower pattern, first ground, blue flowers.............295.00
    Optic Diamond Quilted patterned, first ground, irid, colorless
      handle and upper border 200.00
Mustard, 3-1/8" h, Flower and Pleat pattern, light stain, SP
    top 95.00
Nappy, 5-1/4" d, Cornflower pattern, first ground, blue flowers,
    applied handle 150.00
Pitcher
    3" h, 6-1/2" d, ruffled rim, bowl form, tooled spout rim, etched
      first ground, blue floral dec band, gold leaves and border,
      applied handle 900.00
    5-1/2" h, first ground, applied unstained handle, sq
      mouth..235.00
    6-1/4" h, Cornflower pattern, first ground 400.00
    8-3/4" h, 4-1/2" w, acanthus leaf dec, first ground, deep am-
      ber stain...465.00
    12" h, Diamond Quilted pattern, second ground, slightly ta-
      pering cylindrical body, amber stain at top and applied
      handle, polished pontil 200.00
Punch Cup
    Cornflower pattern, first ground, blue staining............145.00
    Cornflower pattern, second ground 110.00
    Inverted Thumbprint pattern, first ground, amber
      staining 85.00
    Rivulet pattern, second ground, amber stained rim......185.00
Tankard Pitcher, 6-3/4" h, first ground, optic diamond quilted body,
    gold stain on clear glass handle and upper border ...385.00
Tumbler
    Cornflower pattern, second ground, diamond quilted body,
      excellent staining, 4" h..95.00

Mustard, Flower and Pleat, washed color, silver plated top, 3-1/8" h, $45.

Cornflower pattern, second ground, diamond quilted body, honey amber stain top and bottom, rich blue stained flowers, 3-3/4" h, 2-5/8" d 145.00

Oak Leaf Band pattern, second ground 100.00

Pansy and Butterfly pattern, first ground 145.00

Vase

3" h, 6" w, fan, Cornflower pattern, first ground, blue stained flower dec and violet spray 250.00

6" h, first ground, rigaree around ruffled top and neck ring, etched waisted body, first ground, faded amber stain 215.00

Water Set, 7-1/4" h Blueberry pattern, pitcher, six 3-3/4" h expanded diamond tumblers, etched second ground surface, iridized gold stain above and below, some wear to dec 550.00

PURPLE SLAG

History: Challinor, Taylor & Co., Tarantum, Pennsylvania, c1870s-1880s, was the largest producer of purple slag in the United States. Since the quality of pieces varies considerably, there is no doubt other American firms made it as well.

Purple slag also was made in England. English pieces are marked with British Registry marks.

Other slag colors, such as blue, green, and orange, were used, but examples are rare. Another common name for Purple Slag is "Marble Glass" and generally the other color combinations are identified by "Slag" or "Marble Glass."

Videotape: National Imperial Glass Collectors Society, *Glass of Yesteryears*, The Renaissance of Slag Glass by Imperial, RoCliff Communications, 1994.

Additional Listings: Greentown Glass (chocolate slag); Pink Slag.

Reproduction Alert: Purple slag has been heavily reproduced over the years and still is reproduced at present.

Note: Prices listed for purple slag pieces unless otherwise noted.

Animal, Covered Dish

Rabbit 285.00

Rooster, small, caramel slag, Kemple 300.00

Ashtray, 6" sq, chocolate slag, Imperial IG mark..............25.00

Bowl

6" d, Beaded Rib pattern, cov 85.00

8" d, Dart and Bar pattern 60.00

8" d, Heart and Vine pattern 50.00

9" d, Open Rose pattern, caramel slag, Imperial IG mark 50.00

Bread Tray, Notched Daisy pattern, c1890 ....120.00

Butter Dish, cov

Paneled Grape pattern...75.00

Plain paneled sides, cow shaped finial.......................50.00

Cake Stand

Flute pattern 75.00

Plain, pedestal base..60.00

Candlesticks, pr, figural dolphin stems 250.00

Celery Vase

Blackberry pattern, 6-5/8" h, scalloped rim, Hobbs Brockunier..115.00

Jeweled Star pattern, 10" h, c1890 ....125.00

Compote

4-1/2" d, crimped top, plain bowl 70.00

5" d, Beaded Hearts pattern 85.00

8" d, 8" h, Openwork Lattice pattern 95.00

Creamer

Crossbar and Flute pattern 85.00

Figural, fish shape...95.00

Flower and Panel pattern 85.00

Flute pattern 90.00

Oak Leaf pattern 75.00

Scroll with Acanthus patter 90.00

Goblet, Flute pattern 40.00

Jack in the Pulpit Vase, 6" h...45.00

Jar, cov, figural

Bull's head, Westmoreland 50.00

Owl, glossy, green slag, Imperial IG mark...................60.00

Match Holder, Daisy and Button pattern, green 30.00

Monument, obelisk top, English, c1880, 2 flat base chips....125.00

Mug

Bird in Nest, smiling cat, purple, Challinor Taylor, c1890...75.00

Rabbit...65.00

Pitcher

Fan and Basketweave pattern 250.00

Windmill pattern, glossy, Imperial IG mark 45.00

Plate, 10-1/2" d, closed lattice edge 75.00

Platter, oval, notched rim, wildflowers dec, nick..............20.00

Shoe

3-1/4" h, cowboy boot, stirrup and spur.......................65.00

6" h, lady's, high button style, beaded diamond shaped base..75.00

Spooner

Crossbar and Flute pattern 85.00

Flower Panel pattern 80.00

Scroll with Acanthus pattern 65.00

Sugar Bowl, cov

Crossbar and Flute pattern 85.00

Flower Panel pattern 80.00

Flute pattern 190.00

Scroll with Acanthus pattern 125.00

Toothpick Holder

Kettle, three short legs, wire bail handle......................45.00

Scroll with Acanthus pattern 125.00

Tumbler

Flute pattern, 3-1/4" h 50.00

Ribbed pattern, 4-1/2" h...45.00

Scroll with Acanthus pattern 65.00

Vase

5" h, fan shaped, rich variegated purple, emb floral base, Victorian..50.00

10" h, wispy purple swirls against frosted and clear body 125.00

Spooner, Flying Swan, marble glass, aqua and molasses, $95.

QUEZAL

Quezal

1901–25

History: The Quezal Art Glass Decorating Company, named for the quetzal–a bird with brilliantly colored feathers–was organized in 1901 in Brooklyn, New York, by Martin Bach and Thomas Johnson, two disgruntled Tiffany workers. They soon hired Percy Britton and William Wiedebine, two more Tiffany employees.

The first products, which are unmarked, were exact Tiffany imitations. Quezal pieces differ from Tiffany pieces in that they are more defined and the decorations are more visible and brighter. No new techniques were developed by Quezal.

Johnson left in 1905. T. Conrad Vahlsing, Bach's son-in-law, joined the firm in 1918 but left with Paul Frank in 1920 to form Lustre Art Glass Company, which copied Quezal pieces. Martin Bach died in 1924 and by 1925 Quezal had ceased operations.

The "Quezal" trademark was first used in 1902 and was placed on the base of vases and bowls and on the rims of shades. The acid-etched or engraved letters vary in size and may be found in amber, black, or gold. A printed label which includes an illustration of a quetzal was used briefly in 1907.

Reference: Kenneth Wilson, *American Glass 1760-1930: The Toledo Museum of Art, Volume I, Volume II*, Hudson Hills Press and The Toledo Museum of Art, 1994.

Automobile Vase, 10-1/2" h, irid gold amber ground, folded rim, elongated conical form, mkd "Quezal" 165.00
Bowl
   5-1/2" d, irid gold ground, flared rim 275.00
   6-3/4" d, 1-1/2" h, shallow, ambergris, lustrous blue irid, silver base mark...230.00
   7-1/2" d, irid butterscotch ground, ftd, sgd.................350.00
   9-1/2" d, gold calcite ground, stretch rim, pedestal foot, sgd "Quezal" 800.00
   12" d, peacock blue ground, hammered silver base, mid "Oscar B Bach, NY"...475.00
Candlesticks, pr
   6-1/2" h, white opal ground, orange-green King Tut irid dec, flared bobeches rim, ringed hollow baluster, sgd 950.00
   7-3/4" h, irid blue, sgd.......................................575.00
Chandelier, gilt metal
   14" h, 4 elaborated scroll arms, closed teardrop gold, green, and opal shades, inscribed "Quezal" at collet rim, very minor roughness at rim edge 2,000.00
   16" h, 3 shouldered flared opal shades, rib molded design, gold irid int., collet rim inscribed "Quezal," classic shaped socket, wheel with chain drop..................450.00
Cologne Bottle, 7-1/2" h, irid gold ground, Art Deco design, sgd "Q" and "Melba"..250.00
Compote, 4-5/8" h, pale pastel blue ground, pedestal foot, sgd and numbered..525.00
Creamer, 2-1/2" h, irid gold ground, applied lip and handle..550.00
Cruet, white opal ground, green pulled feather design, yellow stopper and applied handle.............................2,500.00
Cup and Saucer, irid gold int., opal hooked feather pattern, sgd and numbered...1,200.00
Finger Bowl and Underplate, 4-1/2" d x 2-5/8" h, 5-3/4" d ribbed, scalloped edge underplate, contoured Flower Pod de-

sign on gold ext. with pink and blue highlights, blue irid int., sgd "Quezal" on base 750.00
Flask, 8-1/2" h, brilliant irid rainbow ground, finely chased silver overlay carnations, inscribed "Quezal," Alvin Corp. mark stamped on silver 1,200.00
Jack in the Pulpit Vase
   8-3/4" h, gold, stretched irid on rounded blossom, sgd "Quezal 176" on base with scrolls..........................1,150.00
   14-3/4" h, irid deep amber ground, green and pink highlights, silvery blue and amber loopings and trailings, wide flaring turned up rim, cylindrical standard, circular domed foot, c1905-20 ....2,500.00
Knife Rest, 3-1/2" l, irid gold ground, two sq ends, twisted bar, polished pontil with signature...............................150.00
Lamp Base, 15-1/2" h, 8" w, deep green hooked feather, bright orange gold ground 1,000.00
Lamp, desk, 14-1/2" h, gold irid shade with green and white pulled feather dec, inscribed "Quezal" at rim, gilt metal adjustable crook-neck lamp.................................575.00
Lamp, mantel
   Gold irid ten rib bell shade, rim mkd "Quezal," gilt metal weighted single socket base, 9" h, pr 575.00
   Opal glass shade with gold outlined green feather dec, inscribed "Quezal" at rim, gilt metal tripod base with twisted shaft, pr 750.00
Lamp Shade
   4-1/2" h, 2-1/4" d outside rim, bell form, ten ribbed, flared rim, irid gold, sgd "Quezal" at top edge 520.00
   5" h, 2-1/8" d outside rim, bell form, five green pulled feathers on opal ground, gold int., rim inscribed "Quezal," 3 pc set...460.00
   5-1/4" h, 2-1/8" d outside rim, bell form, gold irid, ribbed, green and white pulled feather design, inscribed "Quezal" on rim, price for pr...345.00
   5-1/4" h, 2-1/4" d outside rim, hipped opal flared form, green and gold leaves, white ground, gold threading, gold irid int., sgd "Quezal" on inner rim, minimal thread damage, price for 5 pc 750.00
   5-3/4" h, 12-1/2" d, mushroom cap, cased opal to amber, four large pulled and hooked lime green feathers, irid luster, sgd "Quezal" inside curved rim which flares to 9-3/4" d 1,380.00
   6" h, 2-1/8" d, opal bell form, green and gold leaves, white and gold spiderweb threading, gold irid int., sgd "Quezal" on inner rim, price for 3 pc 420.00
Newell Post Lamp, 29-1/2" h, three ball shade, zipper dec, brilliant yellow on oyster white, white meal and brass Victorian newell post 500.00
Nut Dish, irid gold ground, triangular rim, gently rounded body, inscribed "Quezal" 150.00
Perfume Bottle, 5" h, irid gold ground, flattened teardrop shape, bulbous stopper, Gorham sterling silver monogrammed foliate mounts 600.00
Plate
   5-7/8" d, irid gold ground, scalloped rim, sgd on pontil ...200.00
   8" d, irid gold ground, scalloped..............................250.00
   10-3/4" h, fiery irid stretched orange-gold ground, ambergris dec, sgd "Quezal" across polished pontil, set of six 1,500.00
Salt, 2-1/2" d and 3" d, sixteen ribbed body, gold irid, inscribed "Quezal" on base, pr...550.00
Toasting Goblet, 4" h, white opal ground, fiery irid gold int., gold and green pulled feather dec, gold chain border, sgd "Quezal" inside applied hollow stem pedestal, pr 1,750.00
Toothpick Holder, 2-1/4" h, melon ribbed, pinched sides, irid blue, green, purple and gold, sgd 200.00

Vase, blue irid, 11" h, $1,100. Photo courtesy of Jackson's Auctioneers and Appraisers.

Vase

4-1/4" h, irid gold ground, green and gold threads, slender body, circular foot, folded back surface, sgd "Quezal 167" 1,200.00

4-1/2" h, flared rim, bowl form body, translucent amber, delicate green and gold feathers on thin opal surface, folded gold irid rim, base inscribed "Quezal," surface bubbles in feather area 920.00

4-5/8" h, double dec opal body, hooked and pulled gold feathers below green hooked elements, medial gold band, gold irid surface above and within flared rim, base inscribed "Quezal 490" 2,070.00

4-3/4" h, candlestick form, opal cylinders, applied disk foot, green and gold pulled feather dec, gold irid int., inscribed "Quezal" on base, accompanied by gold metal candle cup bobeches, pr..690.00

4-3/4" h, cased cylinder, five pointed gold irid feathers on opal white body, flared golden foot inscribed "Quezal" on base..575.00

4-3/4" h, 3" h, watermelon green body, hooked feather, ricrack, and pulled feather dec on oyster white, irid finish, purple and blue highlights, sgd 2,750.00

4-3/4" h, 5-1/2" w, oyster white ground, green pulled feather, gold trim, sgd 900.00

5" h, lily, pinched quatraform rim, slender transparent golden bud vase, five subtle green spiked feathers, large partial label covers pontil, "Art Quezal - Brooklyn" 1,035.00

5-1/2" h, agate, opaque stone type, obsidian tan, yellow, brown, and green striations, base inscribed "Quezal" 1,380.00

5-1/2" h, cased ivory over amber ground, lavender and yellow swirl dec, bulbous amphora shape, inscribed name and number 750.00

6" h, flared folded rim, cased oval body, gold and green vertical lined leaf dec, base inscribed "Quezal T 918" 1,610.00

6-1/2" h, flared raised rim, oval amber body with gold irid, silver overlaid at rim t shoulder in Art Nouveau floral design, base inscribed "Quezal" with scrolls, "D1193" below, glass stressed at rim silver attachments 1,035.00

7" h, white opal ground, five detailed green pulled feather leaf forms, gold outlines, bright irid gold int., flared trumpet floriform, inscribed "Quezal S 206" 1,200.00

7-1/4" h, 5" d, white opal ground, gold and green feathered leaves, flower form top, sgd 1,750.00

7-3-4" h, 9-1/2" d, large flared bulbous ambergris body cased to opal, dec with green pulled and coiled feathers obscured by lavish overall gold irid, inscribed "Quezal C357" on base..5,175.00

8-1/4" h, baluster, ambergris with blue irid, purple luster above shoulder, inscribed "Quezal" on base 700.00

8-1/2" h, flared oval amber body, gold irid, pulled and hooked white all over tracery, base inscribed "Quezal"...... 1,500.00

8-1/2" h, flared oval amber body, gold irid, white pulled and hooked all over tracery, base inscribed "Quezal," int. manufacturing defect 690.00

9" h, irid ribbon dec, sgd..880.00

9" h, white opal and irid gold ground, gold pulled feather design, gold chain of hearts under rim, bright irid orange-gold int., Martin Bach design, sgd "Quezal 6"....1,200.00

9-1/2" h, white, opal ground, reverse pulled irid gold feathers above symmetrical spider web criss-cross designs, elongated bottle form, sgd "Quezal C 369" 1,500.00

11" h, irid peacock blue, pontil sgd "Quezal" in silver 1,100.00

11-1/2" h, white spatter on black ground, base etched in silver "20120-12 K -QUE-O" 400.00

12-1/4" h, ambergris oval body, cased to white, pulled gold feathers over bright green pulled feather motif, folded gold irid rim, Martin Bach manner, unsigned......3,200.00

14" h, bulbous cased trumpet, green and gold pulled feathers on opaque white ground, gold irid int., base inscribed "Quezal," crack across pontil............................1,150.00

Wall Sconce, 14" h, irid floriform shade, white opal ground, gold pulled feather design, gold int., molded brass sconce, foliage and mirror dec, sgd at base of shade.......... 300.00

Whiskey Taster, 2-3/4" h, oval, gold irid, 4 pinched dimples, sgd "Quezal" on base 200.00

RAINBOW GLASS

History: Rainbow Glass refers to lovely glassware found with rainbow-like stripes of ink, blue, yellow, and often white. Many satin glass objects are found with rainbow coloration and often command a higher price than a similar item in blue or yellow. Edging, feet, and applied handles are common and can be found in both shiny and satinized finishes. Rainbow Glass may also be found in other than satin bodies. Most of the American examples are found unsigned. Many English examples are found signed "Patent."

Reference: John A. Shuman III, *The Collector's Encyclopedia of American Art Glass*, Collector Books, 1988, 1994 value update.

Basket
  9-1/2" h, 5-1/2" w, Diamond Quilted pattern, colorless body with white, pink, blue, and yellow stripes, crystal wishbone handle, Stevens and Williams 350.00
  10" h, 9" w, satin, Herringbone pattern, deep shades of pink, yellow, and blue vertical stripes, white int., applied frosted edge, camphor thorn handle, Mt. Washington 3,400.00
  10-1/2" h, 7" w, brilliant amber cased glass, brilliant white lining, peach and orange stripes, spangle dec, melon rib shape, crystal V-shaped handle 120.00
Bowl, 6" d, 5-1/2" h, MOP satin, strong pink, yellow, and blue shading to white, white lining, triangular, three applied crystal feet, opalescent glass berry prunt, mkd "Patented" 775.00
Celery Vase, 6-3/4" h, 4-3/4" d, blue, pink, and yellow pastel stripes, white opalescent honeycomb ext..............325.00
Creamer, 2-1/2" h, MOP satin, rainbow striped body, elongated spot patterned body, applied frosted handle 350.00
Ewer, 9-1/4" h, MOP satin, deep rose, yellow, blue, apricot, green and lavender stripes, applied frosted handle, ruffled top, Mt. Washington 1,850.00
Fairy Lamp, MOP satin, vertical rainbow stripes, matching base and shade 700.00
Pitcher, 8-1/4" h, MOP satin, rainbow stripes, IVT pattern, reed handle, Mt. Washington..675.00
Rose Bowl, 3-1/4" h, MOP satin, alternating pink, yellow, and narrow blue stripes, white lining, white enamel blossoms 350.00
Sweetmeat Jar, cov, 5-1/2" h, 4-3/4" w, ribbed patterned body, pale blue MOP satin, rainbow stripes, SP bail handle and cov with beehive finial 500.00
Tazza, 7" h, 10-1/2" w, ruffled edge, acid finished bowl, shades from clear frosted into blue, yellow, and pink, enameled bird in flight above branches of flowers in green, pink, white, and yellow, gold highlights, fancy ftd reticulated sterling base..195.00
Vase
  6-1/2" h, red, blue, green, and yellow swirled ground, English, ground pontil..115.00
  6-3/4" h, lily, swirled ribs, vibrant swirls of blue, pink, and yellow on white ground, trefoil crimped top, crystal base 500.00

ROSE BOWLS

History: A rose bowl is a decorative open bowl with a crimped, scalloped or petal top which turns in at the top, but does not then turn up or back out again. Rose bowls held fragrant rose petals or potpourri which served as an air freshener in the late Victorian period. Practically every glass manufacturer made rose bowls in virtually every glass type, pattern, and style.

Rose Bowls usually have a small opening which may be crimped, pinched, scalloped, or even petaled like a flowers. Most rose bowls are round in shape, although a few examples can be found in an egg shape.

Reference: John Mebane, Collecting Bride's Baskets and Other Glass Fancies, Wallace-Homestead, 1976.

Collectors' Club: Rose Bowl Collectors, PO Box 244, Danielsville, PA 18038-0244.

Reproduction Alert: Rose bowls have been widely reproduced. Be especially careful of Italian copies of Victorian art glass, particularly Burmese and Mother-of-Pearl, imported in the 1960s and early 1970s.

Amber, 3" h, white spatter tortoiseshell type dec, applied gold dec 150.00
Amberina, 6" h, 5" d, ribbed, cranberry shaded to olive-amber, enameled white and pink blossoms, tan branches 275.00
Amethyst, squatty, enameled dec, fluted top 115.00
Bohemian, 5" h, deep amber, pinched rim, applied feet, enameled florals 75.00
Crackle, 3-1/4" h, 4-1/4" d, cranberry ground, Arboresque pattern, opaque white design, tightly crimped top 150.00
Cranberry
  4-1/4" h, 4-3/8" d, six crimp top 95.00
  4-1/2" h, 5" d, Coin Spot pattern, eight loops top........195.00
  5-5/8" h, 5-1/4" d 110.00
Cut Glass, small, Hobstars/Panels, American Brilliant Period 45.00
Daum Nancy, 3" h, 3-1/4" d, mottled gold ground, acid cut river's edge landscape, enameled highlights, three petal top 650.00
Fenton, 5-1/2" h, Hobnail pattern, opalescent cranberry..... 165.00
Legras
  9" h, enameled grapes and vines, acid finish background, ground pontil, mkd "LEG" 175.00
  9-1/2" d, 9" h, enamel grape and leaves dec, bright orange-red and black, sgd "Legras" 950.00
Northwood, 301/8" h, 4-1/2" d, satin, light tan ground, mauve pulled feather dec, robin's egg blue lining, tightly crimped top 1,000.00
Opalescent
  Beaded Drape pattern, green.....................................50.00

Opalescent Swirl, blue ground, $70.

Pattern Glass, Champion, emerald green, very worn gold trim, small, $45.

Fancy Fantails pattern, cranberry 65.00
Opalescent Stripe pattern, blue....................................90.00
Opalescent Stripe pattern, cranberry, enameled forget-me-nots dec..95.00
Pattern Glass
    Champion pattern, McKee & Brothers, dec by Beaumont Glass Works, colorless, amber stain.........................60.00
    Eureka pattern, National Glass Co., colorless, ruby stained...85.00
    Heart with Thumbprint pattern, Tarentum Glass Co., colorless, ruby stained 115.00
    Scalloped Six Points pattern, George Duncan Sons & Co., colorless 50.00
    Torpedo pattern, Thompson Glass Co., colorless 90.00
Peachblow, 2-3/8" h, 2-1/2" d, Diamond Quilted pattern, MOP, deep red shaded to amber pink, eight crimp top, Webb 375.00
Peloton, 3-7/8" h, 3-1/2" d, white opaque cased ribbed ground, multicolored filaments, pulled to four points on top 360.00
Rossler, enameled, large
    Cranberry 145.00
    Green 120.00
Rubena, 3-5/8" h, 4-1/4" d, overshot type dec, eight crimps..125.00
Satin
    4-1/2" d, 31/2" h, blue shaded to pale blue ground, mezzotint of cherub wearing bright blue cape, vines and leaves dec, Mt. Washington 200.00
    5-1/2" d, pale blue ground, life-like pansy de, numbered "617" on bottom, Mt. Washington...........................575.00
    5-1/2" h, 5" h, lusterless white ground, eight crimp top, orig matte finish, Mt. Washington, c1870 ....100.00
    5-1/2" h, 5-1/2" w, ovoid, opaque white shading to light blue, three orange flowers and foliage, crimped rim, hand blown 175.00
Stevens and Williams
    4-1/2" h, swirled blue, and yellow, white opalescent edges, ribbed mold, ground pontil.....................................150.00
    4-3/4" h, 5-3/8" d, sapphire blue, 12 crimp top, ribbed effect, enameled pink and white flowers...........................220.00
    6-1/4" h, 4-5/8" d, sapphire blue, applied crystal feet, applied crystal drippings from scalloped top edge 155.00
Webb, 3" h, 3-1/8" d, deep red shading to warm pink-amber, acid finish, cream lining, eight crimp top 250.00

ROYAL FLEMISH

History: Royal Flemish was produced by the Mount Washington Glass Co., New Bedford, Massachusetts. The process was patented by Albert Steffin in 1894. Royal Flemish was only produced for a limited time as the technique involved was labor intensive and therefore costly.

1892

Royal Flemish is a frosted transparent glass with heavy raised gold enamel lines. These lines form sections–often colored in russet tones–giving the appearance of stained glass windows with elaborate floral or coin medallions.

Royal Flemish wares were not all singed, although a round paper label is found on some pieces. A red enameled mark was also used.

References: John A. Shuman III, The Collector's Encyclopedia of American Art Glass, Collector Books, 1988, 1994 value update; Kenneth Wilson, American Glass 1760-1930: The Toledo Museum of Art, Volume I, Volume II, Hudson Hills Press and The Toledo Museum of Art, 1994.

Collectors' Club: Mount Washington Art Glass Society, P.O. Box 24094, Fort Worth, TX 76124.-1094.

Museums: New Bedford Museum, New Bedford, MA; Sandwich Glass Museum, Sandwich, MA; The Corning Museum of Glass, Corning, NY; The Toledo Museum of Art, Toledo, OH.

Biscuit Jar, cov
    8" h, ovoid, large Roman coins on stained panels, divided by heavy gold lines, ornate SP cov, rim, and bail handle, orig paper label "Mt. W. G. Co. Royal Flemish" 1,750.00
    8-1/2" h, 6" d, Roman coin dec, four large medallions, three with coins, one with griffin, deep maroon, beige, and brown ground, orig fancy metal hardware, minor loss to paint..1,100.00
    9" h, 6" w, maroon and rust ground, four Roman coins, replaced SP top..1,150.00
Bowl, 10-1/2" d, 4" h, enameled chrysanthemum dec, gold outlined panels 1,750.00
Box, cov, 5-1/2" d, 3-3/4" h, swirled border, gold outlined swirls, gold tracery blossoms, enameled blossom with jeweled center on lid.. 1,500.00
Cologne Bottle, 5-1/2" h, frosted body, enameled butterfly and daisy dec, heavy gold tracery, dark maroon enameled neck and stopper 4,000.00

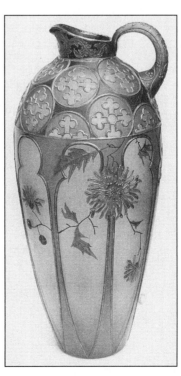

Ewer, alternating pale blue and tan lower panels surmounted by circlets of dark blue with centered light blue crosses, circlets on field of cerise, raised gold separation lines, chrysanthemum blossoms, and foliage, 11-1/2" h, $4,000.

Ewer

9" h, 7" w, Heraldic, brown, rust, and tan dec, gold floral design, 2" band of various coats of armor at neck, rope handle..1,380.00

9-1/2" h, Cupid slaying dragon, raised gold, mythological fish in medallions, pastel blue and violet blossoms within side panels, gold tracery on extended neck, applied twisted rope handle..4,500.00

10-1/2" h, 9" w, 5" d, circular semi-transparent panel on front with youth thrusting spear into chest of winged creature, reverse panel shows mythical fish created with tail changed into stylized florals, raised gold dec, outlines, and scrolls, rust, purple, and gold curlicues, twisted rope handle with brushed gold encircles neck, hp minute gold florals on neck, burnished gold stripes on rim spout and panels........... 4,950.00

12-1/4" h, flag staff dec on segmented stained glass type ground, fierce rampant lion above company masthead double eagle emblem shield, applied rope handle 3,000.00

Jar, 8" h, classical Roman coin medallion dec, simulated stained glass panels, SP rim, bail, and cov, paper label "Mt. W. G. Co. Royal Flemish"..............................1,650.00

Mug, 7" h, tankard form, band of leaves and berries, deep blue band, eighteen circles separated by gold line, gold rope handle...3,510.00

Rose Bowl, eight scalloped top, pale brown shading to frosted, white and blue asters, brown and green stems and leaves, pontil with purple number 1,400.00

Rose Jar, cov, 9" h, bright panels, Roman coins on obverse, raised gold florals on reverse, finial with old repair............2,100.00

Sugar Bowl, cov, 6-1/4" d, 2-1/2" h, pink and yellow apple blossoms, gilt enameled dec, applied reeded handles.... 450.00

Temple Jar, cov, 16" h, 8" d, St. George and the dragon motif, brown, beige, and green shaded background, maroon trim on neck and cover, pinhead flake on top of finial 11,500.00

Vase

6" h, double bulbed, frosted, colorful pansies, all over gold enameling..1,210.00

6" h, 6" w, frosted colorless ground, all over purple violet dec, sgd and numbered "533"....................................1,210.00

7-1/2" h, 7-1/2" d, squatty, smaller squatty form as collar, 14 pastel pansies, clear frosted ground, 4 rayed suns, painted foliage-like gold tracery..................................1,400.00

8" h, 6-3/4" d, tan and brown, raised gold winged gargoyle, stylized florals..2,750.00

8" h, 8" w, central cartouche of two owls sitting on bough, sun in background, reverse with single own sitting on bough, gold scrolling, two snail handles, sgd and numbered "599"...17,250.00

10" h, 4" d, jeweled, colorless frosted ground, gold and red raspberries with leaves, loss to several glass jewels 2,130.00

10" h, 8" d, bulbous, winged serpent and dragon, large pinwheel type stars, deep maroon and green ground........... 4,025.00

14" h, Snow Geese, five geese in flight over bright sun, gold stars, blue, green, and beige stained ground, deep maroon collar..10,350.00

14" h, 4" d, winged creature in flight, gold dec, maroon, tan, brown, beige, and green panels, heavy gold raised dec, 1" gold floral dec band on neck and base..........5,750.00

14" h, 7" d, bulbous, large winged creature, brightly colored lavender, blue, and green ground, heavy gold dec, deep blue sections 6,325.00

Vase, cov

6-1/4" h, squatty bulbous, colorless ground heavily dec with butterflies and colorful stylized blossoms between two maroon tapestry-like reserves, gold enameled embellishments, conforming cov, unsigned.......................3,750.00

15" h, frosted colorless body, elaborately dec with red and opal beaded gold enameled peacock perched o blossom laden branches, scrolling designs, conforming ornamental stopper, base mkd in rd "RF 594," some int. stain, stopper finial flat on one side 4,325.00

RUBENA GLASS

History: Rubena crystal is a transparent blown glass which shades from clear to red. It also is found as the background for frosted and overshot glass. It was made in the late 1800s by several glass companies, including Northwood and Hobbs, Brockunier & Co. of Wheeling, West Virginia.

Rubena was used for several patterns of pattern glass including Royal Ivy and Royal Oak.

Bowl

4-1/2" d, Daisy and Scroll pattern 65.00

9" d, Royal Ivy pattern, frosted 135.00

Butter Dish, cov, Royal Oak pattern, fluted.................... 250.00

Castor set, Venecia pattern, salt and pepper shakers with orig tops, cov mustard jar, cruet with orig stopper, glass handled frame.. 275.00

Cologne Bottle, 6-3/4" h, 2-3/4" d, gold bands, overall stippling, orig cut faceted stopper with gold trim, St Louis .. 150.00

Compote, 14" h, 9" d, rubena overshot bowl, white metal bronze finished figural standard.. 170.00

Cracker Jar, cov

Aurora, inverted rib, Northwood.................................325.00

Cut fan and strawberry design, fancy sterling silver cov, 7" h, 6" w 1,150.00

Diamond Quilted pattern, 7-1/4" h, 6-1/4" d, squatty bulbous body, ornate SP rim, domed cov, and scrolling bail handle, resilvered...375.00

Creamer and Sugar Bowl, cov

Medallion Spring pattern...315.00

Royal Ivy pattern 250.00

Decanter, 9" h, bulbous body, narrow neck, applied colorless handle.. 170.00

Finger Bowl, Royal Ivy pattern 65.00

Marmalade Jar, cov, enameled dec, sgd "Moser" 325.00

Perfume Bottle, 3-1/4" h, SP top rim, cranberry cut stopper 125.00

Pickle Castor, enameled daisy dec, ornate sgd frame with 2 handles, pickle fork in front 245.00

Salt Shaker

Coquette pattern, orig top...150.00

Royal Ivy pattern, frosted, no top 75.00

Sauce Dish, Royal Ivy pattern 35.00

Sugar, cov, Royal Ivy pattern, #79................................. 235.00

Sugar, open, Royal Ivy pattern, #78 .... 135.00

Sugar Shaker

Royal Ivy pattern 275.00

Royal Ivy pattern, frosted 245.00

Royal Oak pattern, frosted 300.00

Syrup, Royal Oak pattern.. 265.00

Tankard

Enameled floral dec, applied reeded handle, 9-1/4" h... 200.00

Reverse rubena, collar etching 175.00

Toothpick Holder

Optic pattern 150.00

Royal Ivy pattern 85.00

Tumbler

Medallion Sprig pattern...100.00

Royal Oak pattern 90.00

Pitcher, enameled apple blossom motif, 7-1/2" h, $475.

Tumble-Up, tumbler and carafe, Baccarat Swirl 175.00
Vase
  6" h, 4-1/2" w, acid etched flowers and leaves, frosted, vertical ribbed int., bell shaped top, Mt. Washington 295.00
  10" h, ruffled rim, hp enameled flowers, gold trim, Hobbs, Brockunier & Co. 175.00
  10" h, trumpet, enameled gold dec.............................150.00
Water Pitcher
  Opal Swirl pattern, Northwood 275.00
  Royal Ivy pattern, frosted 295.00
Water Set, Royal Oak pattern, pitcher and four tumblers 565.00

RUBENA VERDE GLASS

History: Rubena Verde, a transparent glass that shades from red in the upper section to yellow-green in the lower, was made by Hobbs, Brockunier & Co., Wheeling, West Virginia, in the late 1880s. It often is found in the Inverted Thumbprint (IVT) pattern, called "Polka Dot" by Hobbs.

Modern glassblowers have tried to duplicate this technique and some new pieces do exist. But the amount of labor involved to reheat the gather (molten or semi-molten state of glass) to create the color variations prohibits mass production.

Basket, 10" h, 5" d, egg-shaped form, pink and white morning glories, cut-away top, applied green base with gold dec, pale green U-shaped handle 250.00
Bowl, 9-1/2" d, Inverted Thumbprint pattern, ruffled........175.00
Butter Dish, cov, Daisy and Button pattern......................250.00
Celery Vase, 6-1/4" h, Inverted Thumbprint pattern.........225.00
Compote, 8" h, 8" d, Honeycomb pattern 145.00
Creamer and Sugar Bowl, cov, Hobnail pattern, bulbous, applied handle 550.00
Cruet, 7" h, Inverted Thumbprint pattern, teepee shape, trefoil spout, vaseline handle and faceted stopper, Hobbs, Brockunier 550.00
Finger Bowl, Inverted Thumbprint pattern 95.00
Jack in the Pulpit Vase, 8" h...250.00
Pickle Castor, Hobb's Hobnail pattern, SP frame, cov, and tongs...500.00
Salt and Pepper Shakers, pr, Inverted Thumbprint pattern 210.00
Sugar Shaker, Hobb's Coloratura pattern, enameled floral dec, metal lid...320.00

Toothpick Holder, 4" h, Hobnail pattern, opalescent hobs ... 125.00
Tumbler, Inverted Thumbprint pattern 125.00
Vase
  7" h, bulbous, scalloped rim, enameled floral dec......225.00
  9-1/4" h, paneled body, enameled daises dec 85.00
  10-1/4" h, applied colorless edge, sq mouth, colorless rigaree band spiraling from top to base, applied colorless foot...200.00
  12-1/8" h, 5-1/4" d, cranberry shading to green, enameled flowers, green leaves, lacy gold foliage, blue bow ribbon accents...225.00
Water Pitcher
  7-1/2" h, Hobb's Hobnail pattern 395.00
  8" h, Reverse Thumbprint pattern, sq top, applied vaseline handle...295.00
  8-1/2" h, Inverted Thumbprint pattern, applied vaseline handle...350.00

RUBY-STAINED GLASS, SOUVENIR TYPE

History: Ruby-stained glass was produced in the late 1880s and 1890s by several glass manufacturers, primarily in the area of Pittsburgh, Pennsylvania.

Ruby-stained items were made from pressed clear glass which was stained with a ruby red material. Pieces often were etched with a person's name, a place, a date, or an event and sold as souvenirs at fairs and expositions.

Often one company produced the pressed glass blanks and a second company stained and etched them. Many patterns were used, but the three most popular were Button Arches, Heart Band, and Thumbprint.

References: William Heacock, *Encyclopedia of Victorian Colored Pattern Glass*, Book 7, Antique Publications, 1986; Naomi L. Over, *Ruby Glass of the 20th Century*, Antique Publications 1990, 1993-94 value update; Kenneth Wilson, *American Glass 1760-1930: The Toledo Museum of Art, Volume I, Volume II*, Hudson Hills Press and The Toledo Museum of Art, 1994.

Reproduction Alert: Ruby staining is being added to many pieces through the use of modern stained-glass coloring kits. A rash of fake souvenir ruby-stained pieces was made in the 1960s, the best-known example is the "bad" Button Arches toothpick.

Banana Stand
  Art pattern, US Glass Co., 10" d, hs...........................150.00
  Britannic pattern, McKee 100.00
Berry Set
  Sunflower Patch pattern, Duncan Miller, 7 pcs...........275.00
  Thumbnail pattern, 5 pcs 165.00
Biscuit Jar, cov
  Art pattern, US Glass Co..150.00
  Big Button pattern 135.00
  Broken Column pattern, US Glass Co. pattern, US Glass Co. 160.00
Bowl
  Art pattern, US Glass Co...60.00
  Barred Ovals pattern, US Glass Co. pattern, US Glass Co. 7" sq...45.00
  Beveled Diamond and Star pattern, Tarentum Glass Co., 8" d 45.00

Block and Fan pattern, Richards & Hartley Glass Co.,
6" d 40.00
Broken Column pattern, US Glass Co., 8" d 145.00
Button Arches pattern, George Duncan & Sons Co.,
8" d 65.00
Crystal Wedding pattern, US Glass Co., 6" d, scalloped
rim...75.00
Dakota pattern, US Glass Co. 85.00
Heart with Thumbprint pattern, Tarentum Glass Co.,
6" h..75.00
Locket on Chain pattern, Heisey, 8" d....................145.00
Red Block pattern, Bryce Brothers and US Glass Co.,
9" d 85.00
Ruby Thumbprint pattern, US Glass Co., 7" d 50.00
Torpedo pattern, Thompson Glass Co......................75.00
Triple Triangle pattern, Doyle & Co., 10" l, rect............65.00
Truncated Cube pattern, Thompson Glass Co., 8" d....50.00

Bread Plate
Beveled Diamond and Star pattern, Tarentum Glass Co.,
7" d 85.00
Broken Column pattern, US Glass Co.......................140.00
Triple Triangle pattern, Doyle & Co........................125.00

Butter, cov
Art pattern, US Glass Co. 115.00
Atlas pattern, US Glass Co., copper wheel engraving ... 145.00
Beveled Diamond and Star pattern, Tarentum Glass
Co..100.00
Britannic pattern, McKee 125.00
Crystal Wedding pattern, US Glass Co......................145.00
Dakota pattern, US Glass Co., copper wheel engraved
dec 175.00
Duncan's Thumbprint pattern, Duncan Miller 225.00
Eureka pattern, National Glass Co...........................125.00
Locket on Chain pattern, Heisey.............................260.00
Prize pattern 185.00
Ruby Thumbprint pattern, US Glass Co......................150.00
Torpedo pattern, Thompson Glass Co......................150.00
Truncated Cube pattern, Thompson Glass Co. 100.00
Zippered Block pattern, George Duncan & Sons 125.00

Cake Stand, high standard
Atlas pattern, US Glass Co., 9" d 120.00
Beveled Diamond and Star pattern, Tarentum Glass Co.,
9" d 115.00
Button Arches pattern, George Duncan & Sons Co. ..185.00
Red Block pattern, Bruce Brothers, US Glass Co.........95.00
Ruby Thumbprint pattern, US Glass Co., 10" d 175.00

Calling Card Tray, Heart with Thumbprint pattern, Tarentum
Glass Co...85.00

Carafe
Barred Ovals pattern, US Glass Co. 95.00
Champion pattern, McKee, dec by Beaumont Glass
Works...125.00
Heart with Thumbprint pattern, Tarentum Glass Co. ..165.00

Castor Set, Ruby Thumbprint pattern, US Glass Co., four bottles,
orig stoppers and frame..350.00

Celery Tray
Barred Ovals pattern, US Glass Co. 85.00
Britannic pattern, McKee 80.00
Red Block pattern, Bruce Brothers, US Glass Co.........65.00
Triple Triangle pattern, Doyle & Co...........................85.00

Celery Vase
Art pattern, US Glass Co.......................................60.00
Atlas pattern, US Glass Co. 75.00
Beveled Diamond and Star pattern, Tarentum Glass
Co..95.0
Champion pattern, McKee, dec by Beaumont Glass
Works...95.00

Eureka pattern, National Glass Co............................80.00
Ivy In Snow pattern, Co-Operative Flint Glass 145.00
Locket on Chain pattern, Heisey.............................175.00
Hexagon Block pattern, US Glass Co. 130.00
Prize pattern 160.00
Ruby Thumbprint pattern, US Glass Co.
Etched 85.00
Plain..80.00
Torpedo pattern, Thompson Glass Co......................125.00
Truncated Cube pattern, Thompson Glass Co. 115.00
Shoshone pattern, US Glass Co. 120.00

Champagne
Broken Column pattern, US Glass Co.......................175.00
Ivy in snow...85.00
Ruby Thumbprint pattern, US Glass Co......................50.00

Cheese Dish, cov
Esther pattern, Riverside Glass Works, dec by Beaumont
Glass Works..150.00
Red Block pattern, Bryce Brothers and US Glass Co. ... 145.00

Cologne Bottle
Britannic pattern, McKee 145.00
Eureka pattern, National Glass Co...........................95.00
Victoria pattern, Pioneer, orig stopper 95.00

Compote, cov, high standard
Art pattern, US Glass Co., 7" d................................195.00
Broken Column pattern, US Glass Co., 5" d 115.00
Ivy In Snow pattern, Co-Operative Flint Glass, 6" d 185.00
Loop and Block pattern, 8" d 300.00

Compote, open, high standard
Barred Ovals pattern, US Glass Co., 9" d 115.00
Beveled Diamond and Star pattern, Tarentum Glass Co., 7" d,
serrated rim 175.00
Crystal Wedding pattern, US Glass Co., 7" sq, scalloped
rim...95.00

Cordial
Atlas pattern, US Glass Co. 45.00
Red Block pattern, Bryce Brothers and US Glass Co. 50.00

Creamer
Art pattern, US Glass Co., tankard............................55.00
Atlas pattern, US Glass Co. 65.00
Barred Ovals pattern, US Glass Co. 85.00
Beveled Diamond and Star pattern, Tarentum Glass
Co..90.00
Broken Column pattern, US Glass Co.......................135.00
Button Arches pattern, George Duncan & Sons Co., individ-
ual size 65.00
Dakota pattern, US Glass Co. 75.00
Diamonds and Bull's Eye pattern, Dalzell, Gilmore & Leight-
on Glass Co...80.00
Double Fans pattern...80.00
Heart with Thumbprint pattern, Tarentum Glass Co. 95.00
Late Butterfly pattern...115.00
Locket on Chain pattern, Heisey.............................165.00
Red Block pattern, Bryce Brothers and US Glass Co. 75.00
Ruby Thumbprint pattern, US Glass Co......................75.00
Torpedo pattern, Thompson Glass Co......................85.00
Triple Triangle pattern, Doyle & Co...........................65.00
Truncated Cube pattern, Thompson Glass Co. 80.00

Cruet, applied handle, orig stopper
Art pattern, US Glass Co.......................................250.00
Broken Column pattern, US Glass Co., no stopper 525.00
Button Arches pattern, George Duncan & Sons Co. 185.00

Cup and Saucer, Ruby Thumbprint pattern, US Glass
Co. 80.00

Custard Cup
Broken Column pattern, US Glass Co.........................45.00

Champion pattern, McKee, dec by Beaumont Glass
Works..30.00
Ruby Thumbprint pattern, US Glass Co.......................35.00
Triple Triangle pattern, Doyle & Co..............................35.00
Decanter, orig stopper
Aurora pattern, Brilliant Glass Works, 11-3/4" h...........95.00
Corona pattern 110.00
Red Block pattern, Bryce Brothers and US Glass Co.,
12" h...175.00
Torpedo pattern, Thompson Glass Co. pattern, 8" h......150.00
Truncated Cube pattern, Thompson Glass Co., 12" h.....150.00
Finger Bowl
Heart with Thumbprint pattern, Tarentum Glass Co. 65.00
Torpedo pattern, Thompson Glass Co..........................75.00
Goblet
Art pattern, US Glass Co..60.00
Beaded Dart Band 60.00
Beveled Diamond and Star pattern, Tarentum Glass
Co...75.00
Block pattern 90.00
Britannic pattern, McKee 80.00
Broken Column pattern, US Glass Co........................115.00
Button Arches pattern, George Duncan & Sons Co. 45.00
Dakota pattern, US Glass Co.......................................85.00
Esther pattern, Riverside Glass works, dec by Beaumont
Glass Works 85.00
Heart with Thumbprint pattern, Tarentum Glass Co. 110.00
Hickman pattern...55.00
Loop pattern...90.00
Red Block pattern, Bruce Brothers, US Glass Co........ 40.00
Ruby Thumbprint pattern, US Glass Co., vintage
etching...65.00
Truncated Cube pattern, Thompson Glass Co.............50.00
Honey Dish
Britannic pattern, McKee, cov, sq..............................185.00
Broken Column pattern, US Glass Co., open, flat.........45.00
Ruby Thumbprint pattern, US Glass Co., cov, 8" sq, tab
handles...245.00
Marmalade Jar, cov
Atlas pattern, US Glass Co. 115.00
Esther pattern, Riverside Glass works, dec by Beaumont
Glass Works 100.00
Ruby Thumbprint pattern, US Glass Co......................185.00
Milk Pitcher, applied handle
Art pattern, US Glass Co...160.00
Beveled Diamond and Star pattern, Tarentum Glass
Co...145.00
Button Arches pattern, George Duncan & Sons Co. ..130.00
Ruby Thumbprint pattern, US Glass Co......................150.00
Truncated Cube pattern, Thompson Glass Co.........1,100.00
Mug
Brittanic pattern, McKee 35.00
Button Arches pattern, George Duncan & Sons Co. 40.00
Dakota pattern, US Glass Co. 45.00
Shuttle pattern, Greentown 50.00
Mustard, cov, underplate
Button Arches pattern, George Duncan & Sons Co. 115.00
Ruby Thumbprint pattern, US Glass Co......................125.00
Pickle Castor, patterned insert, SP frame
Broken Column pattern, US Glass Co.........................350.00
Ruby Thumbprint pattern, US Glass Co......................250.00
Torpedo pattern, Thompson Glass Co........................275.00
Pickle Dish, rect
Art pattern, US Glass Co..50.00
Barred Ovals pattern, US Glass Co. 45.00
Beveled Diamond and Star pattern, Tarentum Glass
Co...40.00

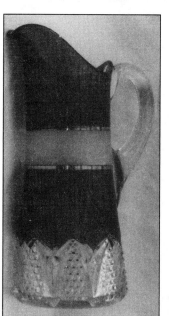

Pitcher, Button Arches, frosted center band with gold trim, applied colorless handle, $125.

Eureka pattern, National Glass Co...............................50.00
Locket on Chain pattern, Heisey.................................90.00
Plate
Broken Column pattern, US Glass Co., 5" d 60.00
Button Arches pattern, George Duncan & Sons Co.,
7" d 35.00
Heart with Thumbprint pattern, Tarentum Glass Co.,
6" d 40.00
Punch Bowl, Ruby Thumbprint pattern, US Glass Co., 12" d, ser-
rated rim 350.00
Punch Cup
Heart with Thumbprint pattern, Tarentum Glass Co. 45.00
Sterling pattern...40.00
Relish
Art pattern, US Glass Co..60.00
Block and Fan pattern, Richards & Glass Co. oval.......45.00
Broken Column pattern, US Glass Co., 11" l, oval 145.00
Crystal Wedding pattern, US Glass Co........................45.00
New Jersey pattern, US Glass Co., 8" l......................110.00
Red Block pattern, Bryce Brothers and US Glass Co. 50.00
Salt and Pepper Shakers, pr
Block and Fan pattern, Richards & Hartley Glass Co. 65.00
Box pattern..115.00
Button Arches pattern, George Duncan & Sons Co. 95.00
Dakota pattern, US Glass Co. 90.00
Flat Diamonds Box pattern...165.00
King's Crown, US Glass Co. 140.00
Nail pattern, Ripley & Co. Glass Co., etched.............135.00
Red Block pattern, Bryce Brothers and US Glass Co. 80.00
Red Block and Lattice pattern 150.00
Torpedo pattern, Thompson Glass Co..........................90.00
Sauce
Atlas pattern, US Glass Co., 4" d, ftd 25.00
Barred Ovals pattern, US Glass Co., 4-1/2" d, flat........25.00
Beveled Diamond and Star pattern, Tarentum Glass Co.,
ftd 25.00
Button Arches pattern, George Duncan & Sons Co., 4" d,
flat 20.00
Crystal Wedding pattern, US Glass Co........................25.00
Eureka pattern, National Glass Co. , 4" sq..................25.00
Locket on Chain pattern, Heisey.................................50.00
Red Block pattern, Bryce Brothers and US Glass Co., 5" d,
ftd 35.00

Ruby Thumbprint pattern, US Glass Co., 4-1/2" d 30.00
Torpedo pattern, Thompson Glass Co., 5-1/2" d 35.00
Triple Triangle pattern, Doyle & Co., 5" d.....................30.00
Truncated Cube pattern, Thompson Glass Co., 4" d......35.00

Spooner
Art pattern, US Glass Co., scalloped rim......................65.00
Beveled Diamond and Star pattern, Tarentum Glass
    Co..75.00
Block and Fan pattern, Richards & Hartley Glass Co.......50.00
Broken Column pattern, US Glass Co...........................85.00
Crystal Wedding pattern, US Glass Co.........................75.00
Eureka pattern, National Glass Co..............................75.00
Heart with Thumbprint pattern, Tarentum Glass Co. 80.00
Locket on Chain pattern, Heisey................................150.00
Red Block pattern, Bruce Brothers, US Glass Co.........50.00
Ruby Thumbprint pattern, US Glass Co.......................65.00
Torpedo pattern, Thompson Glass Co..........................60.00
Triple Triangle pattern, Doyle & Co.............................70.00
Truncated Cube pattern, Thompson Glass Co. 60.00

Sugar Bowl, cov
Art pattern, US Glass Co., tankard..............................55.00
Atlas pattern, US Glass Co..65.00
Barred Ovals pattern, US Glass Co. 85.00
Beveled Diamond and Star pattern, Tarentum Glass
    Co..90.00
Broken Column pattern, US Glass Co........................135.00
Button Arches pattern, George Duncan & Sons Co., individ-
    ual size...65.00
Dakota pattern, US Glass Co......................................75.00
Diamonds and Bull's Eye pattern, Dalzell, Gilmore & Leighton
    Glass Co..80.00
Double Fans pattern...80.00
Heart with Thumbprint pattern, Tarentum Glass Co. 95.00
Late Butterfly pattern...115.00
Locket on Chain pattern, Heisey................................165.00
Red Block pattern, Bryce Brothers and US Glass Co. 75.00
Royal Crystal pattern...90.00
Ruby Thumbprint pattern, US Glass Co.......................75.00
Torpedo pattern, Thompson Glass Co..........................85.00
Triple Triangle pattern, Doyle & Co.............................65.00
Truncated Cube pattern, Thompson Glass Co. 80.00
Zippered Block pattern, George Duncan & Sons 115.00

Sugar Shaker, orig top
Beveled Diamond and Star pattern, Tarentum Glass
    Co..155.00
Block and Fan pattern, Richards & Hartley Glass Co.....125.00

Syrup
Beveled Diamond and Star pattern, Tarentum Glass Co.,
    7" h, orig metal top...195.00
Button Arches pattern, George Duncan & Sons Co. 200.00
Esther pattern, Riverside Glass Works, dec by Beaumont
    Glass Works...250.00

Tankard Pitcher, applied handle
Britannic pattern, McKee 175.00
Button Arches pattern, George Duncan & Sons Co. 145.00

Toothpick Holder
Blocked Thumbprint Band pattern...............................30.00
Douglas pattern...165.00

Eureka pattern, National Glass Co. 70.00
Rib and Bead pattern..55.00
Ruby Thumbprint pattern, US Glass Co.......................50.00
Scalloped Swirl pattern, souvenir................................40.00
Sunk Honeycomb, pattern...75.00
Zipper Stash pattern...30.00

Tray
Atlas pattern, US Glass Co..80.00
Box in Box pattern..50.00
Truncated Cube pattern, Thompson Glass Co. 60.00

Tumbler
Beaded Swirl pattern...55.00
Beveled Diamond and Star pattern, Tarentum Glass
    Co..40.00
Block pattern..80.00
Broken Column pattern, US Glass Co...........................65.00
Button Arches pattern, George Duncan & Sons Co.,
    souvenir..20.00
Dakota pattern, US Glass Co......................................50.00
Ivy In Snow pattern, Co-Operative Flint Glass 65.00
Loop pattern, Central Glass Co...................................80.00
Red Block pattern, Bruce Brothers, US Glass Co., one
    row..30.00
Starred Loop pattern 36.00
Tacoma pattern, Greensburg Glass Co. 40.00
Triple Triangle pattern, Doyle & Co. 35.00

Water Pitcher
Art pattern, US Glass Co., bulbous, half gallon 195.00
Barred Ovals pattern, US Glass Co. 185.00
Beveled Diamond and Star pattern, Tarentum Glass
    Co..180.00
Crystal Wedding pattern, US Glass Co.......................215.00
Ruby Thumbprint pattern, US Glass Co., applied handle,
    serrated rim 245.00
Triple Triangle pattern, Doyle & Co., pressed handle 185.00

Water Set
Blocked Thumbprint, Duncan Miller, 7 pcs.................400.00
Sunflower Patch, Duncan Miller, 6 pcs 435.00

Whiskey
Atlas pattern, US Glass Co. 45.00
Button Arches pattern, George Duncan & Sons Co. 50.00
Sunbeam pattern..55.00

Wine
Beveled Diamond and Star pattern, Tarentum Glass
    Co..50.00
Britannic pattern, McKee 60.00
Button Arches pattern, George Duncan & Sons Co. 40.00
Co-op, Royal...25.00
Crystal Wedding pattern, US Glass Co.........................40.00
Dakota pattern, US Glass Co., dated...........................20.00
Ivy In Snow pattern, Co-Operative Flint Glass 90.00
Red Block pattern, Bryce Brothers and US Glass Co. 45.00
Ruby Thumbprint pattern, US Glass Co.......................40.00
Sunk Honeycomb pattern 60.00
Sterling pattern..80.00
Torpedo pattern, Thompson Glass Co........................115.00
Triple Triangle pattern, Doyle & Co. 65.00
Truncated Cube pattern, Thompson Glass Co. 70.00

SABINO GLASS

History: Sabino glass, named for its creator Ernest Marius Sabino, originated in France in the 1920s and is an art glass which was produced in a wide range of decorative styles: frosted, clear, opalescent, and colored. Both blown and pressed moldings were used. Hand-sculpted wooden molds that were cast in iron were used and are still in use at the present time.

In 1960, the company introduced fiery opalescent Art-Deco style pieces, including a line of one- to eight-inch high figurines. Gold was added to a batch of glass to obtain the fiery glow. These are the Sabino pieces most commonly found today. Sabino is marked with the name in the mold, as an etched signature, or both.

Animal Figure
  Bird, babies, 3" h, two chubby babies perched close on twig with berries leaves, oval molded base, relief molded "Sabino" 35.00
  Bird, feeding, 1-1/2" x 2"......................................90.00
  Bird, five birds perched on branch, 7 x 8" 1,250.00
  Bird, hopping, 1-1/2" x 2".....................................85.00
  Bird, jumping, 3-1/4" x 3-1/2"................................85.00
  Bird, mocking, 6" x 4-1/2" h................................115.00
  Bird, nesting, 1-1/2" x 2".....................................90.00
  Bird, pair, 3-1/2" x 4-1/2" 250.00
  Bird, resting...60.00
  Bird, shivering...75.00
  Bird, teasing, 2-1/2" x 3", wings up 85.00
  Bird, trio, 5" x 5"...265.00
  Butterfly, opalescent, relief molded "Sabino" 25.00
  Cat, napping, 2" h...45.00
  Cat, sitting, 2-1/4" h..50.00
  Chick, drinking, wings down....................................50.00
  Chick, standing, 3-3/4" h, wings up 60.00
  Collie, 2" h..50.00
  Dragonfly, 6" h, 5-3/4" l.....................................125.00
  Elephant..45.00
  Fish, large..110.00
  Fox...35.00
  Gazelle..100.00
  German Shepherd, 2" h...45.00
  Hen...35.00
  Heron, 7-1/2" h...125.00
  Mouse, 3" h...60.00
  Owl, 4-1/2" h...70.00

  Panthers, 5-3/4" x 7-1/4", grouping 225.00
  Pekinese, 1-1/4" h, begged, opalescent, relief molded "Sabino" 35.00
  Pigeon, 6-1/4" h..150.00
  Poodle, 1-3/4" h...35.00
  Rabbit, 1" x 2"...75.00
  Rooster, 7" h...400.00
  Scottie, 1-1/2" x 3" x 4".....................................115.00
  Snail, 1" x 3", relief molded "Sabino" 45.00
  Squirrel, 3-1/2" h, eating acorn, oval molded base, relief molded "Sabino" 45.00
  Stork, 7-1/4" h...145.00
  Turkey, 2-1/4" h, 2-1/2" l, molded signature "Sabino, France" 45.00
  Turtle, small...35.00
  Zebra, 5-1/2" l, 5-1/2" h.....................................165.00
Ashtray
  Shell, 5-1/2" l, 3-1/2" w......................................35.00
  Violet, 4-1/2" d..40.00
Blotter, 6" l, rocker type, crossed American and French flags... 275.00
Bowl
  Beehive..150.00
  Berry, 5-3/4" d, relief molded 70.00
  Fish, 5" d..85.00
  Shell...50.00
Box, cov, Petalia 145.00
Candlestick, 2-lite, relief molded grapes 140.00
Centerbowl, 10-1/4" d, 4-1/4" h, heavy walled, frosted, three high relief oyster shells, tripod feet, star, and pearls between, center mkd "Sabino France," int. wear 500.00
Charger, 11-3/4" d, opalescent, Art Deco molded spiral design, 3 nude women swimming, central molded mark "Sabino Paris" 550.00
Clock, 6-1/8" h, opalescent, arched case, overlapping geometric devices, molded festoons centered by circular chapter ring, molded "SABINO," c1925.................... 1,725.00
Hand, left.. 200.00
Knife Rest
  Butterfly, 4" l...50.00
  Duck...25.00
Luminiere, 9" h, 12" l, deeply opalescent, molded as fish, conforming illuminating gilt-metal base, glass molded "SABINO FRANCE"... 1,300.00
Napkin Ring, birds, opalescent 45.00
Perfume Bottle, opalescent, semi-nudes, 1920s 250.00
Plate, 8-1/2" d, sailing ships................................. 250.00
Powder Box, small 40.00
Scent Bottle
  Nudes, 6" h, inscribed "Sabino France".....................125.00
  Petalia...150.00
  Pineapple, 5" h..175.00
Statue
  Cherub, 2" h...45.00
  Draped Nude, 7-1/4" h.......................................425.00
  Kneeling Nude, 6" h...250.00
  Madonna, 5" h...120.00
  Maiden, 7-3/4" h, opalescent, draped in contrapposto with raised right arm, etched "Sabino Paris" 885.00
  Venus de Milo, large 75.00
Tray
  Butterfly, round..90.00
  Shell, figural...50.00
  Thistle, figural...60.00
Vase
  7" h, press molded sphere, raised bumblebees clustered on

Figure, dragonfly, 6" h, $125.

angular honeycomb and floral latticework, engraved mark on base "Sabino Paris"..................................460.00

7-1/2" h, 9-1/2" d, colorless elliptical body, full-bodied nude women at each side, frosted blossoming flower bends, molded script mark on base "Sabino Paris" 1,495.00

8-1/2" h, blown-out blossoms, eight panels 350.00

9-7/8" h, opalescent, rounded rect form, Art Deco female nude each side, joining hands around vessel, etched "Sabino Paris"..1,870.00

15-1/2" h, tall oval body, molded three swallows in flight, fiery amber, base inscribed "Sabino France" in script.... 1,035.00

SALT AND PEPPER SHAKERS

History: Collecting salt and pepper shakers, whether late 19th-century glass forms or the contemporary figural and souvenir types, is becoming more and more popular. The supply and variety is practically unlimited; the price for most sets is within the budget of cost-conscious collectors. In addition, their size offers an opportunity to display a large collection in a relatively small space.

Specialty collections can be by type, form, or maker. Great glass artisans, such as Joseph Locke and Nicholas Kopp, designed salt and pepper shakers in the normal course of their work.

The colored transparent and colored opaque sets command the highest prices; clear and white sets the lowest. Although some shakers, e.g., the tomato or fig, have a special patented top and need it to hold value, it does not lower the price to replace the top of a shaker.

Sentiment and whimsy are prime collecting motivations, especially in the areas of figural and souvenir shakers. The large variety of shakers and their current low prices indicate a potential for long-term price growth.

Generally, older shakers are priced by the piece, and prices below are noted how they are priced. All shakers are assumed to have original tops unless noted. Arthur Goodwin Peterson's *Glass Salt Shakers: 1,000 Patterns* provides the reference numbers given below. Peterson made a beginning, there are still hundreds, perhaps thousands of patterns to be catalogued.

References: Art Anderson, *Casinos and Their Ashtrays,* privately printed, (P.O. Box 4103, Flint, MI 48504,) 1994; Gideon Bosker, *Great Shakes: Salt and Pepper For All Tastes,* Abbeville Press, 1986; Gideon Bosker and Lena Lencer, *Salt and Pepper Shakers,* Avon Books, 1994; Larry Carey and Sylvia Tompkins, *1002 Salt and Pepper Shakers,* Schiffer, 1995; ——, *Salt and Pepper,* Schiffer, 1994; Melva Davern, *Collector's Encyclopedia of Salt & Pepper Shakers,* 1st Series (1985, 1991 value update), 2nd Series (1990, 1995 value update), Collector Books; Helene Guarnaccia, *Salt & Pepper Shakers,* Vol. I (1985, 1996 value update), Vol. II (1989, 1993 value update), Vol. III (1991, 1995 value update), Vol. IV (1993, 1997 value update), Collector Books; Mildred and Ralph Lechner, *World of Salt Shakers,* 2nd ed., Collector Books, 1992, 1996 value update; Arthur G. Peterson, *Glass Salt Shakers,* Wallace-Homestead, 1970; Mike Schneider, *Complete Salt and Pepper Shaker Book,* Schiffer, 1993.

Periodicals: *Novelty Salt and Pepper Shakers Club Newsletter,* Novelty Salt & Pepper Shakers Club, P.O. Box 3617, Lantana, FL 33465; *The Newsletter Pioneer,* Antique and Art Glass Salt Shaker Collectors Society, 2832 Rapidan Trail, Maitland, FL 32751.

Collectors' Clubs: Antique and Art Glass Salt Shaker Collectors Society, 2832 Rapidan Trail, Maitland, FL 32751; Novelty Salt & Pepper Shakers Club, P.O. Box 3617, Lantana, FL 33465.

Museum: Judith Basin Museum, Stanford, MT.

Art glass (priced individually)

Blue, Inverted Thumbprint, sphere 125.00

Burmese, satin finish, barrel, ribbed, floral motif, two piece pewter top with finial, Mt. Washington....................225.00

Cobalt Blue, 4" h, deep color, sterling push-on lid with English hallmarks "E.E.," "HH" and a lion facing left, sterling collar mkd "E.E.," anchor, and lion facing left........185.00

Cranberry, Inverted Thumbprint, sphere 175.00

Fig, enameled pansy dec, satin, orig prong top, Mt. Washington..120.00

Libbey, satin, egg shape, flat side, pewter top, made for Columbian Exposition, 1893 (28-B) 75.00

Peachblow, Wheeling, bulbous..................................460.00

Scrollware, blue scrolling 170.00

Wave Crest
  2-1/2" h, Erie Twist body, hp flowers 185.00
  5-1/2" h, pink shaded to white ground, hp forget-me-nots 325.00
  Paneled tapered body, floral dec...........................50.00

Depression glass (priced by pair)

Aunt Polly, blue 220.00

Cloverleaf, black 75.00

Colonial, green 140.00

Madrid, amber 125.00

Raindrops, green 315.00

Royal Lace, cobalt blue 250.00

Sandwich (Indiana), crystal..18.00

Sharon, pink 55.00

Swirl, ultramarine 45.00

Tea Room, green 30.00

Figurals (priced by set)

Chick, pedestal, C. F. Monroe, white opal, not dec, 3" h...285.00

Christmas, barrel shape
  Amber...80.00
  Amethyst...145.00

Ducks, 2-1/2" h, sitting, glass, clear bodies, blue heads, sgd "Czechoslovakia" 45.00

Depression Glass, Moderntone pattern, amethyst, $37.50.

Opaque, Butterfly, orig pewter top, made by Eagle Glass Co, c1890, P-23B, $35.

Egg shape
  Opaque white body, holly dec, 23 red raised enameled berries, Mt. Washington..............................185.00
  Pastel tint, pink enameled blossoms, lid loose 65.00

Opalescent glass (priced individually)

Argonaut Shell, blue.......................................65.00
Beatty Honeycomb, blue (22-Q) 45.00
Circle Scroll, blue, tin top (156-S) 85.00
Fluted Scrolls, vaseline 65.00
Jewel and Flower, blue, (164-J), replaced top 45.00
Ribbon Vertical, white 40.00
Seaweed, Hobbs, cranberry...........................60.00
Windows, Hobbs, blue, pewter top..............................50.00

Opaque glass (priced individually)

Acorn, Hobbs, shaded pink to white, tin top (21-A)......50.00
Apple Blossom, milk white, Consolidated Lamp and Glass Co. 35.00
Brownie, 2-3/8" h, rounded cube, 4 vertical sides, Palmer Cox Brownies in different poses on each (F-488)....90.00
Carnelian, custard, Northwood 225.00
Chocolate, Cactus, Greentown.....................................50.00
Creased Waist, yellow, Couderspot Glass Co. 35.00
Chrysanthemum Sprig, custard 150.00
Cone, pink, Consolidated Lamp and Glass Co. 45.00
Daisy Sprig.....................................50.00
Egg in Blossom 100.00
Everglades, purple slag, white and gold highlights, pewter (160-K)...85.00
Guttate, green, Consolidated Lamp and Glass Co.......48.00
Inverted Fan and Feather, pink slag (31-O)...............250.00
Knobby, heavy opaque white, hp pastel flowers, shading to pale yellow, orig pewter top 45.00
Punty Band, custard..45.00
Sunset, white, 3" h, Dithridge (40-U) 35.00
Winged Scroll, custard.......................................80.00

Pattern glass (priced individually)

Actress, pewter top 45.00
Banded Portland, maiden's blush................................40.00
Barred Ovals, ruby stained, orig top............................40.00
Beautiful Lady, colorless, 1905..................................25.00
Block and Fan, colorless, 1891..................................20.00
Cane, apple green 30.00
Croesus, amethyst, gold trim...................................75.00
Crown Jewel, c1880, etched...................................35.00
Dakota, ruby stained, orig top.................................85.00
Diamond Horseshoe, ruby stained 45.00
Diamond Point and Leaf, blue milk glass (F-489).........40.00

Double Deck, opaque green.....................................40.00
Feather (28-N)...25.00
Flower and Rain, red...425.00
Four Square, Billows 100.00
Francesware, Hobbs, Brockunier Co., c1880, hobnail, frosted, amber stained 45.00
Haines 45.00
Leaf, four feet, berry...115.00
Little Apple, ftd 110.00
Lobe, squatty 120.00
Locket on Chain, Heisey, ruby stained, orig top.........125.00
Maine (22-M)...25.00
Medallion Sprig, 3-1/4" h, shaded cobalt blue to white, orig base (33-S)...75.00
Mikado, vaseline 30.00
O'Hara Diamond, ruby stained 35.00
Paneled Sprig, milk glass, green dec 37.50
Scrolled Panel, opaque green 35.00
Stars and Stripes (173-S)...................................25.00
Thousand Eye, vaseline 30.00
Tulip...100.00
Twelve Panel, scrolled pink...................................130.00
Wheat and Barley, blue..40.00
Whirligig, colorless, tin top, (177-A).............................20.00

SALTS, OPEN

History: When salt was first mined, the supply was limited and expensive. The necessity for a receptacle in which to serve the salt resulted in the first open salt, a crude, hand-carved, wooden trencher.

As time passed, salt receptacles were refined in style and materials. In the 1500s, both master and individual salts existed. By the 1700s, firms such as Meissen, Waterford, and Wedgwood were making glass, china, and porcelain salts. Leading glass manufacturers in the 1800s included Libbey, Mount Washington, New England, Smith Bros., Vallerysthal, Wave Crest, and Webb.

Open salts were the only means of serving salt until the appearance of the shaker in the late 1800s. The ease of procuring salt from a shaker greatly reduced the use of and need for the open salts.

References: William Heacock and Patricia Johnson, *5,000 Open Salts*, Richardson Printing Corporation, 1982, 1986 value update; L. W. and D. B. Neal, *Pressed Glass Dishes of the Lacy Period 1925-1950*, published by author, 1962; Allan B. and Helen B. Smith have authored and published ten books on open salts beginning with *One Thousand Individual Open Salts Illustrated* (1972) and ending with *1,334 Open Salts Illustrated: The Tenth Book* (1984). Daniel Snyder did the master salt sections in volumes 8 and 9. In 1987, Mimi Rudnick compiled a revised price list for the ten Smith Books; Kenneth Wilson, *American Glass 1760-1930*, 2 Vols., Hudson Hills Press and The Toledo Museum of Art, 1994.

Periodical: *OSCAR,* Open Salt Collectors of the Atlantic Region, 820 Sunlight Dr., York, PA 17402; *Salty Comments*, 401 Nottingham Rd., Newark, DE 19711; *Salt Talk,* New England Society of Open Salt Collectors, P.O. Box 177, Sudbury, MA 01776.

Collectors' Clubs: New England Society of Open Salt Collectors, P.O. Box 177, Sudbury, MA 01776; Open Salt

Early American, pattern molded, attributed to Amelung Glass Works, Frederick, MD, 1785-1797, checkered diamond pattern, double ogee bowl with short stem from same gather, plain applied circular foot, cobalt blue, sheared rim, pontil scar, 2-7/8" h, 2-1/2" d, $1,200. Photo courtesy of Norman C. Heckler and Co.

Collectors of the Atlantic Region, 820 Sunlight Dr., York, PA 17402.

Note: The numbers in parenthesis refer to plate numbers in the Smiths' books.

Early American glass

2-3/8" h, 2-3/4" d, pressed vaseline, emb rib, SP ftd holder 55.00
2-5/8" l, colorless, variant, Neal MN3, chips 305.00
3" h
  Cobalt blue, paneled with diamond foot 125.00
  Colorless, blown, expanded diamond bowl, applied petal foot...145.00
3" l, colorless, lacy, eagle, Neal EE1, chips.................200.00
3-1/8" l
  Cobalt blue, Neal CN 1a, 2 feet replaced, small chips 200.00
  Fiery opalescent, 3-1/8" l, Neal BS2, chips.............275.00
3-1/4" l, fiery opalescent, eagles, Neal EE3b, chips ...500.00
3-3/8" h, cobalt blue, facet cut, fan rim, sq foot, edges ground 125.00
3-5/8" l, sapphire blue, Neal BT 2, very minor flakes ... 1,075.00

Figurals

Basket, 3" h, 2-3/4" d, coral colored glass, SP basket frame, salt with cut polished facets 55.00
Boat, lacy, colorless, New England, Neal BT-9, slight rim roughness..160.00
Bucket, 2-1/2" d, 1-5/8" h, Bristol glass, turquoise, white, green, and brown enameled bird, butterfly and trees, SP rim and handle 75.00

Individual

Baccarat, double salts, clear, pedestal, paneled sides, one salt frosted panels, sgd (395) 125.00
Cameo Glass
  Galle, green pedestal, enamel dec, sgd, early (205) 295.00
  Webb, red ground, white lacy dec around bowl, matching spoon (137) 600.00
Colored Glass
  Cambridge, Decagon pattern, amber (468) 40.00
  Cobalt blue, Steuben, pedestal (485) 250.00

Cranberry, ruffled salt held by rigaree in wire holder, unmarked (373) 190.00
Milk glass, turquoise, double, sgd "Vallerystahl, Made in France" 45.00
Moser, cobalt blue, pedestal, gold bands, applied flowers sgd (380)...70.00
Opaque blue, double, 3-1/2" h, molded rim form...185.00
Purple Slag, 3" d, 1-1/4" h, emb shell pattern..........50.00
Sapphire blue, white enameled stylized leaves, blossoms, and scrolls, touches of pink, green, and yellow, gold rim and wafer foot, 3-1/8" d, 1-1/2" h 290.00
Cut Glass, 2" d, 1-1/2" h, cut ruby ovals, allover dainty white enameled scrolls, clear ground, gold trim, scalloped top 60.00
Pattern Glass (Colorless unless otherwise noted)
  Crystal Wedding..25.00
  Fine Rib, flint...35.00
  Hawaiian Lei, (477)...35.00
  Liberty Bell, oval..25.00
  Pineapple and Fan...25.00
  Three Face..40.00
  Thumbprint pattern, double salts, octagonal (394) 90.00

Masters

Colored Glass
  Aventurine, narrow base (316) 75.00
  Clambroth, Sawtooth, Sandwich, c1850 ....65.00
  Cobalt blue, master, wafer base, 2-1/6" h, 2-1/16" d... 150.00
  Cranberry, 3" d, 1-3/4" h, emb ribs, applied crystal ruffed rim, SP holder with emb lions heads 160.00
  Green, light, dark green ruffled top, open pontil (449) 90.00
  Opalescent, blue, silver rim, English, registry number (384) 115.00
  Purple Slag, Leaf and Flower (313)........................65.00
  Raspberry, heavy, sq, Pairpoint (444)....................75.00
  Vaseline, 3" d, 2-1/4" h, applied crystal trim around middle, SP stand 125.00
Cut Glass, 2" d, 2" h, green cut to clear, SP holder 115.00
Pattern Glass (Colorless unless otherwise noted)
  Bakewell Pears 30.00
  Barberry, pedestal...40.00
  Basketweave, sleigh (397) 100.00
  Diamond Point, cov 75.00
  Eureka pattern, ruby stained 40.00
  Excelsior 30.00
  Eyewinker, pedestal (346)......................................90.00
  Gothic Arches variant, pedestal, 2-1/2" h, c1865 (3606) 35.00
  Grasshopper 35.00
  Hamilton, pedestal (344) 40.00
  Hobnail, round (407) 40.00
  Horizontal Framed Ovals...30.00
  Horn of Plenty (329)...85.00
  Palmette (471)..65.00
  Paneled Diamond, pedestal (331) 50.00
  Red Block, ruby stained 65.00
  Ruby Thumbprint, ruby stained, sq.........................65.00
  Sawtooth Circle 35.00
  Scrolled Heart, green 275.00
  Snail, ruby stained...75.00
  Square Pillared (341)...35.00
  Sunflower, pedestal (346) 40.00
  Toboggan, (397)..185,99
  Torpedo, ruby stained 65.00
  Viking 30.00
  Vintage (340) 40.00

SANDWICH GLASS

History: In 1818, Deming Jarves was listed in the Boston Directory as a glass factor. That same year he was appointed general manager of the newly formed New England Glass Company. In 1824, Jarves toured the glassmaking factories in Pittsburgh, left New England Glass Company, and founded a glass factory in Sandwich.

Originally called the Sandwich Manufacturing Company, it was incorporated in April 1826 as the Boston & Sandwich Glass Company. From 1826 to 1858, Jarves served as general manager. The Boston & Sandwich Glass Company produced a wide variety of wares in differing levels of quality. The factory used the free-blown, blown three mold, and pressed glass manufacturing techniques. Both clear and colored glass were used.

Competition in the American glass industry in the mid-1850s resulted in lower-quality products. Jarves left the Boston & Sandwich company in 1858, founded the Cape Cod Glass Company, and tried to duplicate the high quality of the earlier glass. Meanwhile, at the Boston & Sandwich Glass Company, emphasis was placed on mass production. The development of a lime glass (non-flint) led to lower costs for pressed glass. Some free-blown and blown-and-molded pieces, mostly in color, were made. Most of this Victorian-era glass was enameled, painted, or acid etched.

By the 1880s, the Boston & Sandwich Glass Company was operating at a loss. Labor difficulties finally resulted in the closing of the factory on Jan. 1, 1888.

References: Raymond E. Barlow and Joan E. Kaiser, *Glass Industry in Sandwich*, Vol. 1 (1993), Vol. 2 (1989), Vol. 3 (1987), and Vol. 4 (1983), distributed by Schiffer; —, *Price Guide for the Glass Industry in Sandwich Vols. 1-4*, Schiffer, 1993; Ruth Webb Lee, *Sandwich Glass Handbook*, Charles E. Tuttle, 1966; —, *Sandwich Glass*, Charles E. Tuttle, 1966; George S. and Helen McKearin, *American Glass*, Random House, 1979; L. W. and D. B. Neal, *Pressed Glass Dishes Of The Lacy Period 1925-1950*, published by author, 1962; Catherine M. V. Thuro, *Oil Lamps II*, Collector Books, 1994 value update; Kenneth Wilson, *American Glass 1760-1930*, 2 Vols., Hudson Hills Press and The Toledo Museum of Art, 1994.

Museum: Sandwich Glass Museum, Sandwich, MA.

Bank, 12" h, colorless, applied peacock blue rigaree, rooster finial, two silver U.S. dimes dated 1835 within knob stem 8,000.00
Barber Bottle, clambroth 70.00
Basket, 5-1/2" h, 5-1/2" w, ruffled box pleated top, White Burmese, candy pink to yellow peachblow-type, applied frosted thorn handle 795.00
Bowl
   6-1/2" d, pressed, Peacock Eye pattern, grape border, lacy, colorless, ftd, shallow flake on foot 500.00
   7-1/2" d, pressed, lacy, Tulip and Acanthus pattern, slight roughness 45.00
   9-1/2" d, pressed, Gothic Arches pattern, lacy, colorless, Lee 129 ....185.00
Butter Dish, cov
   Bluerina, 4-7/8" h, enameled dec 675.00
   Gothic pattern, colorless, flint 200.00

Horn of Plenty pattern, colorless, flint, bust of George Washington finial, small scallop chips 1,700.00
Candlesticks, pr
   6-5/8" h, clambroth, hexagonal petal socket, loop base, ground base with chips, small flakes, roughness 200.00
   7" h
      Canary, pressed, loop base, Barlow #3047, gauffering marks, very minor chips 375.00
      Clambroth, hexagonal petal socket, loop base, small flakes, roughness 230.00
      Colorless, petal and loop design, slight chip on one petal..425.00
   7-1/2" h, hexagonal base, purple-blue petal socket, translucent white 575.00
   7-1/2" h, 3-1/2" w base, Petal and Loop variant, opaque white 100.00
   9-3/4" h, opaque blue and white, stepped base 50.00
   10-1/4" h, clambroth, dolphin, single step base, minor roughage to base 525.00
Celery Vase
   7-3/4" h, Execelsior pattern, colorless, flint 90.00
   8-1/2" h, Diamond Thumbprint pattern, colorless, flint.... 150.00
   9" h, Loop pattern, dark blue, ground base, flakes around base..420.00
   11-1/4" h, Arch pattern, cobalt blue, cascade base ...500.00
Christmas Salt, orig 5" x 5-1/2" box, amethyst, teal blue, canary, yellow, and sapphire blue salts, marked caps and agitators, ground mouth, smooth base, box mkd "Dana K. Alden's World Renowned Table Salt Bottles" 500.00
Claret, 4-1/2" h, Horn of Plenty pattern, flint, set of 8 ...... 500.00
Cologne Bottle
   5-1/2" h, paneled, twelve sided form, teal blue, fiery blue opalescent neck, tooled flared mouth, smooth base, 1860-80 ....350.00
   5-5/8" h, sq tapered form, thumbprint pattern on side panel, herringbone corners, fiery blue opalescent, opaque blue neck and mouth, tooled mouth, smooth base, c1860-80 ....800.00
   6" h, blown three mold, medium amethyst, flared mouth, pontil scar, c1820, McKearin GI-7, type 4....................300.00
   6" h, paneled, corseted form, amethyst, tooled mouth, pontil scar, c1840-60 ....700.00
   6-3/8" h, tapered monument building form, cobalt blue, tooled flared mouth, smooth base, c1860-80, mouth roughness and numerous chips............................120.00
   6-3/4" h, cobalt blue, ribbed, tam o'shanter stopper ..195.00
   7" h, two pc mold, twelve body panels, deep sapphire blue, flared mouth, smooth base, period stopper, c1860....250.00
   7-1/8" h, paneled, twelve sided form, colorless, inward rolled mouth, smooth base, nearly perfect label reads "Daisy/Cologne/Fragrant And Lasting/L. M. Wardner/Druggist/St. Regis Falls, N.Y.," c1860-80........................160.00
   7-1/4" h, paneled, twelve-sided form, sapphire blue with purple tone, outward rolled mouth, pontil scar, 1840-60 ...... 250.00
Compote
   6" d, 5-7/8" h, Horn of Plenty pattern bowl, Waffle pattern base, flint, minor chips and roughness 145.00
   7-1/2" d, 5" h, Waffle pattern, colorless, flint, minute under rim roughness..75.00
   9" d, 12" h, Sandwich Star pattern, electric blue......5,500.00
   10-1/2" d, 4-3/4" h, cranberry overlay, oval cuts, enameled birds and flowers on inner surface, c1890.............495.00
Creamer
   Fish Scale pattern, lacy, colorless 85.00
   Gothic Arches pattern, lacy, deep purple-blue 850.00
   Lily of the Valley, colorless, ftd, applied handle............65.00
Creamer and Sugar, Gothic pattern, colorless, flint 125.00

Cup and Saucer, lacy, colorless.....................................200.00
Cup Plate
    Blue, lacy, ship...125.00
    Violet Blue, lacy, heart..............................325.00
Curtain Tieback, 3" d, flower, white opalescent, orig
    hardware..65.00
Decanter, blown three mold
    McKearin GI-29, sapphire blue, flared mouth, smooth base,
    half pint, 1860-80, top surface of mouth ground, no stop-
    per..70.00
    McKearin GII-18, colorless, flared mouth, pontil scar, pint,
    period stopper, 1820-40.............................110.00
    McKearin GII-18, colorless, flared mouth, pontil scar, quart,
    period stopper, 1820-40.............................130.00
    McKearin GIII-5, colorless, flared mouth, pontil scar, quart, pe-
    riod stopper, 1820-40, some int. haze near base......120.00
    McKearin GIII-6, colorless, flared mouth, pontil scar, pint, no
    stopper, 1820-40.....................................80.00
Dish, colorless
    5-3/4" l, Rayed Peacock Eye pattern, flint...................185.00
    6-1/4" l, Tulip and Arches Leaf pattern, lacy...............145.00
    8" d, Scotch Plaid pattern, lacy, pontil mark...............150.00
    12" l, 9" w, 1-3/4" h, Peacock Eye pattern, flint............800.00
Egg Cup, 3-3/4" h, Horn of Plenty pattern, flint...................90.00
Ewer, 10-7/8" h, clambroth body, green applied handle and
    band, pewter fittings..................................65.00
Flat Iron, amethyst, three minor flakes on edges, handle
    check..650.00
Flip, 5-5/8" h, blown three mold, colorless, sheared rim, pontil
    scar, 1820-40, McKearin GII-18...............................130.00
Goblet, colorless, flint
    Gothic pattern, 12 pc set.............................650.00
    Horn of Plenty pattern, 6" h, pr.......................100.00
Honey Dish, lacy, medium red-amber, two scallops
    missing..120.00
Inkwell
    2-3/8" h, sq, honey amber, applied brass collar, hinged cap,
    smooth base...40.00
    2-9/16", cylindrical domed form, colorless, pink and white
    stripes, sheared mouth, applied pewter collar and cap,
    smooth base...2,300.00
Jewel Casket, cov, 6-1/2" l, oblong, lacy, colorless, Lee
    162..1,200.00
Ladle, 9-1/2" l, clambroth.......................................45.00
Lamp
    8-3/4" h, Blackberry pattern, blue clambroth, brass stem,
    marble foot...750.00
    8-5/8" h, Blackberry pattern, pale blue clambroth, brass
    stem, white clambroth base.............................1,100.00
    10" h, Horn of Plenty pattern, flint, colorless, whale oil
    burner..400.00
    10-5/8" h, free blown tear drop shape font, triangular scrolled
    base, paw feet, whale oil burner.......................850.00
    11-1/4" h, Acanthus Leaf pattern, light peacock blue, sand
    finish, brass standard, brass collar, marble base, 1850-
    60..400.00

11-3/4" h, colorless blown font, sq scrolled pressed base, lion
    head dec, paw feet, very minor chips and cracks....290.00
12-1/2" h, pressed blue glass fonts, clambroth column and
    stepped base, minor base chips and cracks, pr...1,840.00
Marble
    1-3/4" d, spangled, green, red, white, and blue.........150.00
    2-1/8" d, cranberry and white swirl, Lutz-type.............150.00
    2-1/8" d, spangled, multicolored, roughness and some
    nicks...145.00
    2-5/8" d, spangled, red, white, and blue...................525.00
Milk Pan, 7-1/4" d, 3" h, free blown, folded rim, pinched lip,
    green..375.00
Mustard Pot, cov, Peacock Eye pattern, lacy, colorless......395.00
Paperweight, 3-1/2" w, 1-1/4" h, colorless and frosted, portraits
    of Queen Victoria and Prince Consort, 1851........220.00
Pitcher, 10" h
    Amberina Verde, fluted top.............................325.00
    Electric Blue, enameled floral dec, fluted top, threaded
    handle..425.00
    Reverse Amberina, fluted top..........................400.00
Plate, colorless
    6" d, Plaid pattern, few scratches.......................65.00
    6" d, Shell pattern, lacy................................165.00
    7" d, Rayed Peacock Eye pattern.........................125.00
    8" d, Plaid pattern, few chips...........................85.00
    9-1/2" d, Quatrefoil, lacy...............................1,765.00
Pomade, cov, figural, bear, imp retailer's name
    3-3/4" h, clambroth, imp "F. B. Strouse, N.Y.," chips......525.00
    4-1/2" h, blue, base imp "X. Bazin, Philada," chips....300.00
Relish, 8-1/8" l, Pipes of Pan pattern, colorless.............250.00
Salt
    1-3/4" h, blown three mold, cobalt blue, sheared rim, pontil
    scar, c1820-40, McKearin GIII-3........................600.00
    2" h, 3-1/8" d, blue, pressed, floral, Barlow 1460, minor chips,
    mold imperfections.....................................690.00
Sauce Bottle, 5-7/8" h, Horn of Plenty, colorless, flint, arched
    panel engraved "Heswan," two small annealing lines at
    top..120.00
Sauce Dish, colorless
    Beaded Scale and Eye pattern, daisy center...............75.00
    Horn of Plenty pattern, flint, 4-1/2" d...................40.00
    Peacock Eye pattern, flint...............................50.00
    Roman Rosette pattern, fiery opalescent...................100.00
    Shell Medallion pattern, octagonal.......................70.00
    Waffle pattern, flint....................................50.00
Scent Bottle
    Deep emerald green, violin shape, orig pewter screw top,
    McKearin 241-31..225.00
    Medium purple-blue, McKearin 241-55......................150.00
Spillholder, 5" h, Sandwich Star pattern, electric blue, several
    small chips on base corners............................800.00
Spooner, colorless, flint, Gothic pattern.......................85.00
String Holder, 4" h, 3-7/8" d, colorless, cobalt blue rim and ring
    around string hole.....................................375.00
Sugar, cov, colorless, flint
    Acanthus Leaf pattern..................................350.00
    Horn of Plenty pattern, 7-1/2" h.........................250.00
Sweetmeat, cov, Waffle pattern, colorless, flit, one scallop rim
    chipped...95.00
Talcum Shaker, clambroth..35.00
Toddy Plate, 5-7/8" d, star and fan border, eight pointed center
    star, raised sq hobs....................................120.00
Toilet Water Bottle, 5-1/2" h, blown three mold, brilliant light vio-
    let blue, tooled flared mouth, pontil scar, incorrect stop-
    per, McKearin GI-3, type 1.............................240.00
Toy, lemonade cup, 1-5/8" h, canary, pressed, handle, tooled
    rim, pontil scar.......................................140.00

**Inkwell, cylindrical domed form, col-
orless with pink and white stripes,
sheared mouth with applied pewter
collar and cap, smooth base, 2-9/16"
h, $2,300. Photo courtesy of Norman
C. Heckler and Co.**

Toilet-water bottle, blown three mold, brilliant deep sapphire blue, tooled flared mouth, period tam o'shanter stopper, pontil scar, 6-3/4" h, McKearin GI-7, type 4, some light int. residue near base, $180. Photo courtesy of Norman C. Heckler and Co.

Vase
    9-1/4" h, amethyst, Three Printie Block pattern, trumpet shape, gauffered rim, triple ring turned connector, pressed colorless base, hairlines to base 2,900.00
    9-1/2" h, tulip shape, amethyst, McKearin 201-40, tiny flake under point of one foot, pr...................................2,400.00
    10" h, dark amethyst, pressed, tulip, octagonal base, few chips to underside of base, pr 2,500.00
Vegetable Dish
    10-1/2" l, lacy, colorless, grape border, cov, Lee 151-1 ....5,500.00
    10-3/4" l, medium amethyst, thinly blown bell, Three Printie Block pattern, expanded rim, heavy octagonal standard, sq base, c1845-60 ....1,250.00
Vinegar Bottle, 6-3/4" h, blown three mold, deep amethyst, cobalt blue stopper 395.00
Whiskey Taster
    Clambroth, lacy, Lee pate 150-5................................120.00
    Cobalt blue, nine panels 185.00

SATIN GLASS

History: Satin glass, produced in the late 19th century, is an opaque art glass with a velvety matte (satin) finish achieved through treatment with hydrofluoric acid. A large majority of the pieces were cased or had a white lining.

While working at the Phoenix Glass Company, Beaver, Pennsylvania, Joseph Webb perfected mother-of-pearl (MOP) satin glass in 1885. Similar to plain satin glass in respect to casing, MOP satin glass has a distinctive surface finish and an integral or indented design, the most well known being diamond quilted (DQ).

The most common colors are yellow, rose, or blue. Rainbow coloring is considered choice.

Additional Listings: Cruets; Fairy Lamps; Miniature Lamps; Rose Bowls.

Reproduction Alert: Satin glass, in both the plain and mother-of-pearl varieties, has been widely reproduced.

Basket
    4-1/2" h, 4" w, pastel pink, herringbone patterned body, cased in white, very tightly ruffled rim, applied clear frosted handle 150.00
    4-3/4" h, 4" w, pink shaded to white, applied twisted and frosted rope handle 95.00
    5" h, 10" w, deep pink shading to white, leaf form shaped bowl, orange enamel dec, applied frosted leaf basket, large applied frosted thorn handle, Victorian.........150.00
    5-1/2" h, 4" w, blue, herringbone patterned body, MOP, applied frosted camphor feet, ...95.00
    6" h, 4-1/2" w, shaded rose to pink, herringbone patterned body, MOP, applied frosted squared-off handle ...150.00
    7" h, 5-1/2" w, pink and blue stripes, opaque white ext., ruffled edge, ornate twisted frosted handle 100.00
    8" h, 7" w, brilliant robin's egg blue over white, melon rib shape, heavily crimped and ruffled edge, frosted loop handle...100.00
    8-1/2" h, 8-1/2" w, candy stripe, deep pink, red, and white stripes, white int. lining, frosted thorn handle, slight roughage to handle 175.00
    8-3/4" h, 5-1/2" w, glossy, herringbone patterned body, deep pink shading to pale pink, applied amber V-shaped handle 110.00
    9" h, 5-1/2" w, herringbone patterned body, MOP, rose bowl shape, shaded deep rose to pale pink to off white, applied U-shaped handle...225.00
    9-1/2" h, 10" l, deep peach int., pale green ext., fancy ruffled edge, twisted frosted thorn handle, applied leaf feet, Victorian...200.00
    10-1/2" h, 6" w, moiré patterned body, MOP, chartreuse yellow shading to deep cranberry in amberina type coloration, box pleated top on deep basket, four frosted thorn feet, frosted loop handle, minor roughage to one foot.................. 400.00
    11-3/4" h, 8-1/2" w, moiré patterned body, MOP, deep red shading to pink, matching lining shading to white, applied frosted "V" shaped handle, four fancy thorn feet.....600.00
Biscuit Jar, cov, 9" h, 5" d, DQ patterned body, MOP, shiny finish, rainbow stripes, flared cylindrical base, SP bail handle and cov, mkd "Patent".....................................995.00
Bowl
    4-1/2" d, 2-3/4" h, ribbed body, MOP, shaded pink ground, very tightly crimped ribbon edge 350.00
    5-7/8" d, 4-1/2" h, blue DQ patterned body, MOP, three applied frosted thorny glass vases forming feet, white lining, ruffled edge 365.00
    6-1/2" w, 4-1/2" h, bright pink and blue, white lining, Coin Spot pattern, scalloped rose bowl like top, 3 thorn feet, berry prunt...750.00
    10-1/2" d, 4-1/2" h, squatty, MOP, gold, amber, and red moiré, lusterless white lining, deeply crimped rim................ 375.00
Bride's Bowl, 12" d, 14-3/4" h, cream ext., MOP lining, enamel floral dec, ruffled clear edge with gold trim 450.00
Celery Vase, herringbone patterned body, MOP, white base shades to raspberry to deep cranberry rim, applied clear frosted ruffled edge, SP holder mkd "Aurora SPMFG" quadruple plate, attributed to Mt. Washington, c1885.. 1,200.00
Cologne Bottle, long dauber, green, oval foot, green, Lancaster Glass 95.00
Cream Pitcher, 4-1/2" h, 3-1/8" d, blue, raindrop patterned body, MOP, frosted blue reeded handle, white lining, bulbous, round mouth 195.00
Cup and Saucer, 3" h cup, 5" d saucer, pink to white raindrop patterned body, MOP, frosted handle................... 395.00
Dish, 5-1/4" d, raspberry ground, ivory ruffled rim........... 65.00

Ewer
    8-1/2" h, pink, MOP, frilly spout, thorn handle.............385.00
    9-1/2" d, DQ patterned body, MOP, deep apricot shading to light ground, applied colorless thorn handle 350.00
    19-1/2" h, ovoid creamy beige ground, light blue floral sprays, outlined in gold, floral emb metal mount with satyr head on handle, Victorian 900.00
Finger Bowl and Underplate, blue DQ patterned body, MOP, sgd "Patent" 585.00
Hatpin Holder, 3-1/4" h, DQ patterned body, MOP, pink ground, enameled floral dec..175.00
Jar, cov, 6-1/4" h, DQ patterned body, MOP, salmon ground, applied colorless floral final.................................325.00
Marmalade, 4-1/2" h, 3-1/2" d, DQ patterned body, MOP, shaded pink ground, black etched dec of bird among berries and leaves, frosted applied shell ruffled top, SP holder 250.00
Mug
    2-3/4" h, 2-1/4" d, barrel shape, deep rose to amber, DQ patterned body, creamy white lining, frosted loop handle, English...175.00
    3-1/2" h, pink and gold looping, white ground, applied frosted reeded handle..175.00
Nappy, 6" l, 2-1/2" h, handle, white, DQ patterned body, MOP, triangular shaped top, applied frosted handle, allover gold dec, deeply crimped edge 425.00
Perfume Bottle, 4-1/2" h, 4" d, swirl patterned body, MOP, shaded pink ground, white and orange flowers dec, atomizer missing 150.00
Pitcher, bulbous
    6" h, 4-1/2" d, DQ patterned body, MOP, shaded blue ground, enameled pink and yellow floral dec, green leaves, oval top, applied handle..350.00
    7-3/4" h, 6" d, melon ribbed body, MOP, shaded pale pink to white ground, enameled white and gold coral dec, applied frosted handle 750.00
Rose Bowl
    3-3/8" d, 4" h, shaded heavenly blue, herringbone patterned body, MOP, 6 crimp top 195.00
    3-1/2" d, 2-3/4" h, blue, ground pontil mark 385.00
    3-3/4" d, 2-3/8" h, heavenly blue, ribbon pattern, MOP, nine crimp top, white lining 235.00
    4" h, shaded blue to white, Mezzotint cherub dec, Victorian..175.00
    4-1/2" d, bright yellow to white, enameled berries, leaves, and stems, Victorian..145.00
    5" d, 4-3/8" h, shaded blue, white lining, 6 crimp top, lavender enameled leaves dec 115.00
    5-1/2" d, 5" h, bright green shading to pale green, enamel blue, pale yellow, and gold floral dec 295.00
Scent Bottle, 4-3/8" l, tapered conical form, blue, silver repousse top, American, early 20th C, stopper missing...........300.00
Toothpick Holder, 2-1/2" h, DQ patterned body, MOP, yellow ground 160.00
Tumbler
    3-1/2" h, rainbow, DQ patterned body, MOP, enamel floral dec, 3 white and pink single-petaled blossoms, 4 buds, 4 leaves and grass, gold rim.....................................750.00
    3-3/4" h, 2-3/4" d, DQ patterned body, apricot 80.00
    3-3/4" h, 2-3/4" d, DQ patterned body, blue..................70.00
    3-3/4" h, 2-3/4" d, DQ patterned body, pink..................60.00
    3-3/4" h, 2-3/4" d, DQ patterned body, yellow..............60.00
    3-3/4" h, 2-3/4" d, herringbone pattern body, blue........65.00
    3-3/4" h, 2-3/4" d, raindrop pattern body, pink and white 65.00
    4" h, apricot to pink to white, DQ patterned body, MOP, c1880, small blister 60.00

Vase, vertical, ribbed, pinched tricorn top, pink, Stevens and Williams, 3" h, $375.

Vase
    4-1/2" h, 5-5/8" d, ribbon patterned body, MOP, light blue, three way top, pinched in side 375.00
    4-3/4" h, 4" d, DQ patterned body, MOP, shaded heavenly blue, heavy gold floral dec, red enameled spider with mark on base "Whitehouse Glass Works, Stourbridge" 260.00
    5-1/2" h, 2-3/4" d, raindrop patterned body, MOP, blue, frosted amber edge ruffled fan top, white lining 145.00
    5-3/4" h, hobnail, MOP, pink shades to pale pink base, 4 folded-in sides..500.00
    7" h, 3-5/8" d, DQ patterned body, MOP, shaded pink ground, blue flowers and morning glory dec, bee in flight..125.00
    7" h, 4-1/2" d, MOP, Federzeichnung, bold air-traps randomly sweep down around perimeter, chocolate-colored ground, squiggly lines of burnished gold tracery, quadric-form top with gold embellishments in individual folds, gold enamel signature in pontil "Pat 9159" 2,500.00
    9" h, 3-1/2" w, swirl patterned body, MOP, gold to pale pink-white, Mt. Washington 325.00
    10-1/2" h, 5-1/2" w, DQ patterned body, MOP, bulbous, heavenly blue shading to pale blue, creamy white lining, English...265.00
    10-3/4" h, DQ patterned body, MOP, spray of carnations, long green stems, rose pink fading to pale pink at base.... 175.00
    11-1/2" h, 4" w, DQ patterned body, MOP, bulbous, deep blue shading to white, four petal top, white flowers and orange branches dec, Victorian 185.00

SCHNEIDER GLASS

History: Brothers Ernest and Charles Schneider founded a glassworks at Epiney-sur-Seine, France, in 1913. Charles, the artistic designer, previously had worked for Daum and Gallé. Robert, son of Charles, assumed art direction in 1948. Schneider moved to Loris in 1962.

Although Schneider made tablewares, stained glass, and lighting fixtures, its best-known product is art glass which exhibits simplicity of design and often has bubbles and streaking in larger pieces. Other styles include cameo-cut and hydrofluoric-acid-etched designs.

Schneider glass was signed with a variety of script and block signatures, "Le Verre Francais," or " Charder."

Bowl
    4-7/8" d, 2-1/2" h, pink and lavender powders within colorless body, inscribed "Schneider," stamped "France" ...200.00
    4-7/8" d, 3-1/4" h, glossy orange dish, fitted into wrought iron frame, stamped "Schneider/France".....................290.00
    6" d, amethyst, shallow, sgd 175.00
    9" d, 2-3/4" h, flatted flared form, pink and lavender swirls, three aubergine purple bead feet, inscribed "Schneider" ...420.00
Candlesticks, 7" h, 8-1/2" h, 9-1/2" h, colorless crystal, hexagonal shape, ground base, 3 pc set 125.00
Centerbowl, 12" d, 3-1/4" h, mottled orange border, yellow and white body, edge inscribed "Schneider," base inscribed "France-Ovington New York," inside wear.............345.00
Charger, 15-1/2" d, brilliant orange plate, brown-green amorphous centr4al dec, reverse inscribed "Schneider France/Ovington New York" 525.00
Cigarette Lighter Base, 7-1/2" h, 3" h mottled yellow pear shaped glass, etched purple and rose-pink Art Deco elements, inscribed "Le Verre Francais" on gilt metal atomizer top 375.00
Compote
    10" d, 8-1/2" h, Tango red, mottled blue-black rim, shaped bowl, wrought metal pedestal foot, three glass beads, glass stem inscribed "Schneider France"..............690.00
    15" d, 6-1/4" h, folded rim on broad centerbowl, Tango Red streaked with aubergine, applied purple and black stem, foot inscribed "Schneider".....................................525.00
Dish, 13-1/2" x 5-1/2", mottled orange and dark blue, amethyst with white ribbing, pedestal base 275.00
Ewer, 15-1/2" h, ovoid, pointed spout, thick cushion foot, mottled white frosted ground, mottled orange and green overlay, etched floral bands, applied purple angled handle at shoulder, engraved "Charder Le Verre Francais" 1,250.00
Lamp, 15-1/2" d, hanging, creamy glass half-round light bowl, speckled yellow and red, edge inscribed "Schneider," suspended by twisted and knotted cord and wire chain, three matching glass beads................................1,380.00
Night Light, 5" h, 3-3/4" w, round glass globe, acid finish shading from yellow to blue spatter, pewter-style figural ftd base, three butterflies hold the shade, some bends to silver plated base 650.00
Pitcher
    6-1/2" h, bulbous Tango red body, elongated mottled blue-brown neck and spout, applied purple glass handle, inscribed "Schneider" 635.00
    6-1/2" h, motled Art Deco orange bulbous body, aubergine base, applied angular handle, mkd "Schneider" at lower edge 345.00
    13-3/4" h, oval mottled brown and yellow ground, silver foil inclusions, amethyst-purple angular applied handle, point nicked at end 460.00
Serving Plate, 14" d, 3" h, transparent green-yellow dish, mottled orange pedestaled foot, inscribed "Schneider France"...345.00
Tazza, 15-1/2" d, 3-1/2" h, slightly triangular top with three pulled points, shades of yellow, orange, and dark purple spattering, purple striped short pedestal 850.00

Vase
    4" h, flared rim, pink oval body, amethyst shaded to purple layer, etched stylized sunflower motif, lower edge inscribed "Le Verre Francais France" 520.00
    5-3/8" h, creamy yellow body, orange-brown mottled lower oval, purple disk foot, medial border of aubergine-black olives on leafy branches, ftd sgd "Schneider France" in script...3,450.00
    6-3/4" h, 4" w, gourd shape, glossy finish, light and dark orange spattering, dark purple at base....................700.00
    7" h, oviform, wide everted rim, applied black applications on two sides, carved as overlapping flowerheads, carved "Schneider" 1,700.00
    7-1/4" h, squat waisted form, everted rim, internally dec with air bubbles, three applied handles, engraved "Schneider/France" 1,000.00
    9" d, clear shading to bright orange, applied black base, ground pontil 385.00
    9-3/4" h, 5-1/2" w, pale pink and yellow mottled ground, deep amethyst like leaves, four applied glass dec, sgd 700.00
    10" h, flared rim, half cobalt blue, half yellow oval ground, sgd at lower side "Schneider" 550.00
    10-1/4" h, ftd oval pink mottled glass body, amethyst shaded to purple overlay, repeating etched stylized sunflower motif, sgd "Le Verre Francais" on foot, "France/Ovington" on base..1,035.00
    11" h, oval body, mottled red and yellow glass overlaid, etched stylized leaves and berries, foot inscribed "Le Verre Francais," base mkd "France/Ovington" 1,265.00
    11-3/4" h, 6-1/2" w, elongated urn shape, shading from clear top to translucent yellow base, large irregular air trap designs, sgd "Schneider France" 725.00
    12" h, bulbous flared body, mottled red and yellow glass, overlaid and etched stylized leaves and berries, two applied purple handles, lower edge inscribed "Le Verre Francais," base mkd "France-Ovington"............1,380.00
    12" h, bulbous ftd body, internally dec with medium air bubbles, three bright red applied bands around neck, globular spots on body, etched "SCHNEIDER" 5,000.00
    12" h, quatraform, fiery yellow amber int., bright blue and maroon splotches, dark purple platform foot, inscribed "Schneider" above, "France" on base 1,250.00
    12-1/2" h, flattened oval, mottled pastel blue body, bright royal blue overlay, two stripes of etched foliated elements, sgd "Charder" on cameo at side, foot inscribed "Le Verre Francais France" 1,150.00
    12-1/2" h, mottled yellow ground, orange, tan, and brown repeating organic elements, platform foot inscribed "Le Verre Francais" and retailer "Ovington, New York" 865.00
    12-1/2" h, 5-1/2" d, colorless, applied amethyst base, two carved handles in form of Art Deco bouquets, sgd "Schneider France" 4,000.00
    14" h, mottled and veiled oval body, rose pink, yellow, and orange above pink-red and brick glass, two applied amethyst handles at top, foot inscribed "Schneider" 1,265.00
    15-1/2" h, 12" d, oval colorless and mottled white body, internally decorated with broad orange and purple aubergine strokes and splotches, inscribed "Schneider" mark at side...1,725.00
    16-3/4" h, bulbous, elongated neck, translucent orange body with red striations, side inscribed "(vase) Schneider France," some top chips 520.00
    18" h, ftd slender body, bulbous neck, internally dec with yellow and rose swirls shading to purple below, 3 crimped applications, engraved "Schneider" and firm's mark 2,500.00
    20" h, elongated neck, colorless crystal oval with sixteen ribs, accented by orange-amber color, candy cane mark on base, some int. stain 230.00

SENECA GLASS COMPANY

History: Seneca Glass Company, Morgantown, West Virginia, was founded in 1891 by a group of immigrants from the Black Forest countryside of Germany. Although the first site was the former Fostoria Glass Company plant, in Fostoria, Ohio, the company was chartered in West Virginia. In 1896, Seneca moved to Morgantown, and began production of fine blown and cut crystal.

During the Depression era, Seneca Glass Company introduced a variety of colors, but was widely known for its rock crystal production. Seneca also produced plain and cut goblets, sherbets, wine glasses, and other table wares. Colorless casual glassware, specialty Christmas items, and an extensive series of bells, rounds out later production.

Reference: Hazel Marie Weatherman, *Colored Glassware of the Depression Era, Book 2,* Glassbooks, Inc., 1982.

Periodical: *The Daze,* Box 57, Otisville, MI 48463.

Brandy Snifter, Lavalier, #903, crystal 12.00
Champagne, saucer, crystal
    Cut #488, 6" h, 8 oz......................25.00
    Ester 10.00
    Festus 10.00
    Lavalier, #903......................12.00
    Naomi......................10.00
Cocktail
    Driftwood, ruby......................15.00
    Naomi, crystal......................12.00
    #476-4, 6" h, 4 oz, crystal......................25.00
Finger Bowl, Festus, crystal......................12.00
Goblet
    Anais, crystal......................10.00
    Asteric, cut, crystal......................12.00
    Brittany, cut, crystal......................25.00
    Candlewick, crystal......................10.00
    Cut #488, 8" h, 10 oz, crystal......................35.00
    Driftwood, amber......................5.00
    Driftwood, avocado green......................5.00
    Driftwood, emerald green......................7.50
    Driftwood, ruby......................8.50
    Estes, crystal......................10.00
    Fashionables, avocado green......................7.50
    Germania, crystal......................12.00
    Images, crystal......................6.00
High Ball
    Chalice, cut, crystal......................8.00
    Driftwood, avocado green......................5.00
    Driftwood, ruby......................8.00
Iced Tea Tumbler
    Driftwood, avocado green......................5.00
    Driftwood, emerald green......................8.00
    Fashionables, avocado green......................9.00
Juice Pitcher, Driftwood, emerald green......................35.00
Juice Tumbler, Driftwood
    Amber......................4.00
    Brown......................4.00
    Emerald Green......................5.00
    Ruby......................5.00
Old Fashioned, Chalice, cut, crystal......................25.00
Parfait, crystal
    Festus......................12.00
    Naomi......................15.00
Pilsner
    Cut Star, crystal......................18.00

    Slim, #903, amber......................22.50
Sherbet, crystal
    Allegheny......................7.50
    Asteric......................10.00
    Candlewick......................10.00
    Ester......................9.00
Tumbler
    Allegheny, crystal, black scalloped foot, 3-1/2" h, 10 oz....18.00
    Driftwood, amber, dec foot......................5.00
    Driftwood, avocado green, dec foot......................5.00
    Driftwood, emerald green, dec foot......................5.00
    Images, dec foot......................8.00
    Lavalier, #903, crystal......................12.00
    Sherwood, 10 oz, crystal......................9.00
    Sherwood, 12 oz, crystal......................9.00
    Slim, 16 oz, sq foot, burgundy......................28.00
Water Set, pitcher and 6 ftd tumblers, red......................175.00
Wine
    Brittany, cut, crystal......................25.00
    Dorchester, cut, crystal......................32.00
    Driftwood, ftd, ruby......................18.00
    Lavalier, #903, crystal, 3-1/2 oz......................10.00
    Naomi, crystal......................15.00

SILVER DEPOSIT and SILVER OVERLAY GLASS

History: Silver deposit glass was popular at the turn of the century. A simple electrical process was used to deposit a thin coating of silver on glass products. After the glass and a piece of silver were placed in a solution, an electric current was introduced which caused the silver to decompose, pass through the solution, and remain on those parts of the glass on which a pattern had been outlined.

Silver overlay is silver applied directly to a finished glass or porcelain object. The overlay is cut and decorated, usually by engraving, prior to being molded around the object.

Glass usually is of high quality and is either crystal or colored. Lenox used silver overlay on some porcelain pieces. Most designs are from the Art Nouveau and Art Deco periods.

Reference: Lillian F. Potter, *Re-Introduction to Silver Overlay on Glass and Ceramics*, published by author, 1992; Kenneth Wilson, *American Glass 1760-1930: The Toledo Museum of Art,* Volume I, Volume II, Hudson Hills Press and The Toledo Museum of Art, 1994.

Basket, 5" h, 7-1/2" w, deep emerald green ground, applied loop handles with berry prunts, six rows of applied glass openwork forming reticulated base, silver overlay 500.00
Box, cov, 7" d, 4-1/2" h, dark amethyst, int. divided into 3 compartments, repeating silver foliate dec.................230.00
Candlesticks, pr, 7-1/4" h, opal, amber streaked ground, irid threading on base, SS rim, attributed to Loetz......750.00
Compote, 6" h, 6-1/2" d, black ground, overlaid in Art Deco gazelles and stylized foliate motifs, Rockwell type dec, minor silver loss, pr..................225.00
Decanter, 7-1/2" h, squatty colorless base, star cut base, heavily overlaid in silver scrolling devices, monogrammed "FGS" in reverse, stamped "9/1000 fine" and numbered, conforming stopper................550.00
Perfume Bottle
    3" l, colorless......................135.00
    3" l, green......................175.00

Vase, green ground, overlay marked "Sterling Silver Deposit 196," 6" h, 2-3/8" d, $225.

4" h, squatty, colorless ground, silver cut iris blossoms, stems, and scrolls, orig stopper, mkd "999/1000 fine - 3105" 500.00

5-1/2" h, spherical, teal green, layered at shoulder with silver floral dec, stopper missing, stamped "sterling" 345.00

Tankard Pitcher, 10-3/4" h, 6" w, cranberry, heavy silver overlay, grape and vine dec, large shield, applied clear handle..2,800.00

Vase

3-1/4" h, gourd form, orange spotted silver irid vase, overlaid with Secessionist-style silver overlay, enameled "586 M655" 1,600.00

3-1/2" h, bulbous, trefoil rim, blue irid, silver Art Nouveau floral silver, attributed to Loetz...................................800.00

3-5/8" h, flat rim, mold blown green glass irid oval, scroll and floral dec, imp "L Sterling," design worn.................635.00

3-3/4" h, irid green oval body, four applied protrusions, silver floral motif stamped "patented 3419-999/1000 fine," hall-marked 635.00

4-1/2" h, oviform, pinched around neck, silver-blue oil-spot motif, geometric silver overlay, attributed to Loetz.......2,300.00

4-1/2" h, ruffled quatraform rim, dimpled oval body, gold irid surface overlaid in scrolling silver foliage dec, polished pontil, Austrian...550.00

7-1/2" h, green/yellow irid ground, silver plated swan and lily dec, attributed to Loetz 500.00

8-3/4" h, raised flared rim, broad amber oval irid body overlaid on front with pendant berry and leaf silver dec, leaf imp "L. Sterling," Austrian 1,380.00

9" h, oval dark amethyst body, three buttress-form feet, foliage border with animal medallions, "sterling" engraved in design, minor silver loss...175.00

10" h, cased turquoise blue cylinder, layered in sterling dec, full length floral designs, two butterflies.................175.00

10" h, pinched oval ambergris body internally dec with metallic pulled feathers, external silver overlay intricate rose blossoms with stylized Art Nouveau motif, polished pontil, attributed to Loetz 4,600.00

10-1/2" h, 6-1/2" w, deep red shading to green with Loetz

type iridescence, elaborate silver overlay of flowers and vines, minor loss to silver 325.00

12" h, bright rose -red tapered body, opal white int., overlaid in elaborate silver floral motif with scrolls and swirling stems, centering medallion crest 1,380.00

12" h, 5" d, cylindrical, white glass ground, silver floral overlay 175.00

14" h, cobalt blue gooseneck body, silver irid papillon dec, elaborate silver overlay in scrolling foliate designs, recessed polished pontil, Austrian, minor damage 2,415.00

14-1/4" h, colorless oval, internally flashed in amber, amethyst, pink, and frosted landscape scene, overlaid with tall tree, antlered deer center, base stamped "Rockwell" in shield, some paint loss, wear, stain....................690.00

22" h, baluster, peach ground, elaborate stylized silver floral overlay, attributed to Loetz.................................4,500.00

34-1/2" h, emerald green flared body, silvered leaf and vine dec, some silver loss..635.00

SMITH BROS. GLASS

History: After establishing a decorating department at the Mount Washington Glass Works in 1871, Alfred and Harry Smith struck out on their own in 1875. Their New Bedford, Massachusetts, firm soon became known worldwide for its fine opalescent decorated wares, similar in style to those of Mount Washington.

Smith Bros. glass often is marked on the base with a red shield enclosing a rampant lion and the word "Trademark."

References: Kenneth Wilson, *American Glass 1760-1930*, 2 Vols., Hudson Hills Press and The Toledo Museum of Art, 1994.

Reproduction Alert: Beware of examples marked "Smith Bros."

Atomizer, melon ribbed, creamy white satin ground, hand painted carnations outlined in gold, red rampant lion mark ... 625.00

Biscuit Jar

7" h, 5" d, barrel shape, beige ground, 7 deep brown, rust, maroon, green, and gold pansies, metal cov mkd "S. B. 4412," base also sgd 750.00

8-1/2" h, 7-1/2" d, pale pink draped over shoulder with hp lacy border, 4 cream colored textured enameled tassels, six-sectioned body, satin finish, metal fittings, lid sgd "S B 4402" 675.00

8-1/2" h, 7-1/2" d, tan, floral dec, melon shaped, matching lid, lion trade mark...275.00

Bowl

6" d, 2-3/4" h, melon ribbed, two shades of gold prunus dec, beaded white rim...375.00

8-3/4" d, narrow ribbed body, creamy white satin ground, oak leaves and acorns outlined in gold, metal rim, mkd....550.00

9" d, 4" h, melon ribbed, beige ground, pink Moss Rose dec, blue flowers, green leaves, white beaded rim 675.00

Box, cov, 4" d, melon ribbed, beige satin ground, blue florals, sgd 375.00

Bride's Bowl, 9-1/2" d, 3" h bowl, 16" h overall, opal glass bowl, painted ground, 2" band dec with cranes, fans, vases, and flowers, white and gray dec, fancy silver-plated holder sgd and numbered 2117 .... 1,450.00

Creamer and Sugar

4" d, 3-3/4" h, shaded blue and beige ground, multicolored violet and leaves dec, fancy silverplated metalware...... 750.00

4" h, ribbed melon-form, white asters, yellow centers, silver plated scrolled rims, cov with woman's profile cartouche 450.00

Fernery
   10" d, orig insert, melon ribbed, creamy white shiny finished satin ground, hand painted violets and leaves, rampant lion mark, sgd "Smith Bros." 450.00
   10" d, 4" h, squatty, ten ribbed bulbous oval body, wild rose dec, outlined in gold, raised edge, SP rim, red rampant lion mark 600.00

Humidor, 6-1/2" h, 4" d, cream ground, 8 blue pansies, melon-ribbed cov 850.00

Jar, cov, 4-1/2" h, squatty, melon ribbed, creamy white satin ground, hand painted pansy dec, openwork silver top 275.00

Juice Tumbler, blue, stork dec 50.00

Mayonnaise Dish, creamy white satin ground, floral dec, fancy SP top and handle, sgd 275.00

Mustard Jar, cov, 2" h, ribbed, gold prunus dec, white ground 300.00

Perfume, 5" h, creamy white satin ground, enameled floral dec, floral emb cap, rampant lion mark 450.00

Plate, 7-3/4" d, Santa Maria, beige, brown, and pale orange ship, commissioned by Libbey for Columbian Exposition of 1902-03 ....595.00

Potpourri, 5-3/4" d, 3-3/4" h, open white lotus blossom, trailing stem, partially opened bud, framed by two naturalistic tinted leaves, shadowy blue ripples of cream-colored pond, another floating stem with leaf and bud on other side, silver plated lid with lotus blossom finial, lion-in-shield signature 585.00

Rose Bowl
   2-1/4" h, 3" d, cream ground, jeweled gold prunus dec, gold beaded top, sgd 285.00
   4-1/2" d, fat bulbous shape, beige ground, two sprays of daisy-type flowers, beaded top 325.00

Salt, open, 2" w, 1-1/4" h, white satin melon ribbed body, blue, orange, and green small flowers and leaves, orange beaded top 90.00

Sugar Shaker
   5-3/4" h, pillar ribbed, white ground, pink wild rose and pale blue leaves, blue beaded top, orig cov fair 495.00
   6" h, 2-1/2" d, cylindrical, vertical ribs, opaque white body, stylized dec of pink, blue, and gray summer blossoms, wispy stalks, pewter top 575.00

Sweetmeat, Jar, cov, 5-1/4" d, 5-1/4" h, melon ribbed body, creamy white satin ground, enameled daisy spray, emb SP collar and bail, sgd 575.00

Toothpick Holder
   2" h, ribbed blank, purple and blue violets, beaded top 285.00
   2-1/4" h, barrel shape, opaque white body, swag of single petaled blossoms 265.00
   2-1/4" h, pillar ribbed, white ground, pink wild rose and pale blue leaves, blue beaded top 250.00
   2-1/2" h Little Lobe, pale blue body, single petaled rose blossoms, raised blue dots on rim 245.00

Vase
   3-1/2" w, 2-1/4" h, melon ribbed, ivory satin ground, gold prunus blossoms, gold trim, sgd, top rim may be repainted.....40.00
   5-1/4" h, 3-1/2" d, pinched-in, apricot ground, white wisteria dec, gold highlights, sgd 375.00
   5-1/4" h, 4" d, triangular shape, pale yellow ground, white daisy-like flowers, sgd 425.00
   5-1/2" h, petticoat shape, flared base, pink ground, multicolored foliage and herons, stamped mark on base, "Smith brothers-New Bedford, MA," pr.............................850.00

Vase, melon body, white body, Royal dec, gold enamel floral dec, gold beaded rim, rampant lion in shield mark, 3-1/4" d, 2-1/4" h, $195.

7" h, soft pink ground, inverted dec of white pond lily, blue-green and black leaves, brown stems, maroon trim, c1870, pr 375.00

7-1/4" h, 8" d, double canteen, pink rose sprays centered in 3 decorative reserves, lime-yellow ground, two restored enameled dots, small int. chip 325.00

7-1/4" h, 8-1/4" w, 2-1/4" d, double canteen, one side with naturalistic executed enamel dec of wisteria blossoms clinging to vine which sweeps across face and over shoulder, each blossom is outlined in raised gold, olive-green leaves overhang floral cluster, raise gold borders, other canteen visible from that side depicts Roman columns draped with stylized ivory, other side large canteen with Venetian harbor scene, gondolier in foreground, two sail boats, several abstract sails in distance, smaller canteen shows solitary wisteria cluster clinging to vine from other side, background color simulates Mount Washington's Burmese, Smith Bros. lion-in-shield mark 1,950.00

8" h, conical shape, pink, white blossoms and hummingbird dec, script sgd, pr...225.00

8-1/2" h, 3-3/4" w, Verona, colorless ground, painted and enameled pink and yellow orchids, leaves, stems, and buds, int. vertical ribs 495.00

8-1/2" h, 6-1/2" w, 1-1/2" neck, canteen shape, pale pink shading to cream ground, purple wisteria dec, raised heavy gold leaves and branches, beaded top, sgd.................1,250.00

10" h, 6" d, pillow, soft ground, purple wisteria, green, and gold leaves, slight roughage on base....................925.00

10" h, 8" w, shaded rust, brown, yellow and gold ground, white apple blossoms, green leaves, and branches, painted beige int. 595.00

12-1/2" h, Verona, colorless ground, deep purple and white irises, gold trim, green leaves and stems, int. vertical ribs...550.00

L. E. SMITH GLASS COMPANY

History: L. E. Smith Glass Company was founded in Mount Pleasant, Pennsylvania, by Lewis E. Smith in 1907. Although Smith left the company shortly after, it still bears his name. Early products were cooking articles and utilitarian objects such as glass percolator tops, fruit jars, sanitary sugar bowls, and reamers.

In the 1920s, green, amber, canary, amethyst, and blue colors were introduced along with an extensive line of soda fountain wares. The company also made milk glass, console, dresser sets, and the always-popular fish-shaped aquariums. During the 1930s, Smith became the largest producer of black glass. Popular dinner set lines were Homestead, Melba, Do-Si-Do, By Cracky, Romanesque, and Mount Pleasant.

L. E. Smith glass is handmade and usually unmarked. Some older pieces bear a "C" in a circle and a tiny "S." Currently, a paper label is used. If you collect older items, carefully study the black and Depression glass pieces. The Moon and Star pattern has been reproduced for many years. Smith glass of recent manufacture is found in house sales, flea markets, and gift and antiques shops.

References: Lee Garmon and Dick Spencer, *Glass Animals of the Depression Era*, Collector Books, 1993; Hazel Marie Weatherman, *Colored Glassware of the Depression Era 2*, Glassbooks, 1982.

Animal
    Cat, black, reclining, c1930, mkd 35.00
    Goose, black, reclining, c1930, mkd 25.00
    Rooster, black, reclining, c1930, mkd 25.00
    Swan, opaque white..30.00
Aquarium, kingfish
    Crystal 195.00
    Green 250.00
Ashtray, elephant, black 35.00
Bon Bon, ftd, handle
    Cobalt blue...15.00
    Green..10.00
Bookends, pr, rearing horse
    Amber, 8" h, c1940..45.00
    Cobalt blue, c1930..65.00
    Crystal, c1930 ....45.00
Bowl
    10" d, Wig Wam pattern, ftd, oval, cobalt blue............150.00
    10" d, Wig Wam pattern, ftd, round, cobalt blue.........150.00
    10" d, Wig Wam pattern, ftd, round, crystal 95.00
    10-1/2" d, Melba pattern. green, ruffled 35.00
    10-1/2" d, Romanesque pattern, green......................45.00
Cake Plate, Do-Si-Do pattern, handles 17.50
Candlesticks, pr
    By Cracky pattern, green..20.00
    Mt. Pleasant pattern, black 25.00
    Romanesque pattern, pink...20.00
    Veined Onyx pattern, black...40.00

Candlestick, Moon 'n' Star, Heritage Collection, yellow shading to red, 4-3/4" h, $8.00

Wig Wam pattern, black..100.00
Wig Wam pattern, cobalt blue..80.00
Wig Wam pattern, crystal..50.00
Casserole, cov, Melba pattern, 9-1/2" l, oval 15.00
Compote, cov, Moon 'n' Star pattern, amberina..............35.00
Creamer
    Do-Si-Do pattern 6.00
    Homestead pattern, pink...8.00
    Moon 'n' Star pattern, amberina................................12.00
Cruet, Moon 'n' Star pattern, ruby....................................35.00
Cup and Saucer, Melba pattern
    Amethyst 10.00
    Pink..9.00
Fern Bowl, flower frog, Greek Key pattern, 4-1/4" h
    Cobalt blue..75.00
    Dark amethyst 35.00
    Vaseline...85.00
Flower Block, By Cracky pattern, 3" h...............................5.00
Flower Pot, 4" h, black, silver floral dec 15.00
Goblet
    Do-Si-Do pattern 5.00
    Homestead pattern, pink...7.00
    Moon 'n' Star pattern, amberina................................17.50
Jardiniere, Greek Key pattern, 3 ftd, dark amethyst, silver
    overlay 25.00
Mayonnaise, Kent pattern 10.00
Parfait
    Do-Si-Do pattern 7.00
    Homestead pattern, pink...9.00
    Soda Shop pattern 10.00
Plate
    6" d, Melba pattern, amethyst 7.50
    7" d, Romanesque pattern, octagonal, green 10.00
    7-1/8" d, round, aqua...6.00
    8" d, Homestead pattern, pink....................................8.00
    8" sq, Do-Si-Do pattern, amethyst.............................12.00
    8" d, Maple Leaf pattern, cobalt blue.........................15.00
    8" d, Melba pattern, octagonal, pink...........................8.00
    8" d, Mt. Pleasant pattern, pink, scalloped edge...........8.00
    8" w, Romanesque pattern, octagonal, green.............10.00
    9" d, Homestead pattern, pink, grill............................15.00
    9-1/4" d, Lincoln, backward "C" border, milk glass,
    c1960...50.00
    11" w, Romanesque pattern, octagonal, amber...........30.00
Platter, 11-1/2" w, Melba pattern, octagonal, pink 15.00
Salt and Pepper Shakers, pr
    Dresden pattern, white...20.00
    Mt. Pleasant pattern, cobalt blue 30.00
Sherbet
    Do-Si-Do pattern 9.00
    Romanesque pattern, vaseline 15.00
Slipper, Daisy and Button pattern, amber, 2-1/2" h 10.00
Soda Tumbler, crystal
    Jumbo pattern, ribbed, pedestal foot 9.00
    Soda Shop pattern 10.00
Sugar, cov
    Do-Si-Do pattern 9.00
    Homestead pattern, pink..12.00
    Kent pattern...10.00
    Melba pattern 12.00
    Moon 'n' Star pattern, amberina................................15.00
Tray, 15" l, 6" w, oval
    Black 15.00
    Crystal 12.00
Urn, two handles, 7" h, dancing girls, cobalt blue 40.00
Vase
    Moon 'n' Star pattern, blue, 7" h 20.00

Romanesque pattern, green, fan, ftd 45.00
Violet Bowl, Hobnail pattern, white opaque.......................10.00
Window Box, F. W. Woolworth 30.00
Wine
 Moon 'n' Star pattern, amberina.................................15.00
 Ruby body, crystal stem and foot 7.00

SOUVENIR, COMMEMORATIVE and HISTORICAL GLASS

History: Souvenir, commemorative, and historical glass includes those items produced to celebrate special events, places, and people.

Many localities issued plates, mugs, glasses, etc., for anniversary celebrations or to honor a local historical event. These items seem to have greater value when sold in the region in which they originated.

World's fairs and expositions are another source of souvenir glassware. Beautiful examples have survived from the Chicago Columbian Exposition as well as others.

Commemorative and historical glass includes several patterns of pressed glass which celebrate persons or events as well as campaign and memorial items.

Souvenir, commemorative, and historical glass can be found mainly in colorless, custard, and ruby stained glassware.

References: Arene Burgess, *Collector's Guide to Souvenir Plates*, Schiffer, 1996; Bessie M. Lindsey, *American Historical Glass*, Charles E. Tuttle Company, 1967; George S. and Helen McKearin, *American Glass*, Random House, 1979; L. W. and D. B. Neal, *Pressed Glass Dishes of the Lacy Period 1925-1950,* published by author, 1962; Catherine M. V. Thuro, *Oil Lamps II*, Collector Books, 1994 value update; Kenneth Wilson, *American Glass 1760-1930*, 2 vols., Hudson Hills Press and The Toledo Museum of Art, 1994.

Ale Glass, Philadelphia Centennial....................................65.00
Basket, Clitherall, MN, opaque clambroth.......................365.00
Beer Mug
 Chicago, Columbian World's Fair, 1893, eight pressed panels
  at bottom, mkd "M. Gordon, World's Fair, 1893" 45.00
 Philadelphia Centennial 65.00
Bell
 Chicago, Columbian World's Fair, 1893, etched, frosted
  handle...75.00
 Elkhorn Fair, 1913, Button Arches pattern, ruby staining, color-
  less paneled handle, 6-1/2" h 75.00
 Louisiana Purchase, 1904, St. Louis, Liberty Bell replica,
  some gold...50.00
Bottle
 Columbus, oval, lay down, metal screw top 350.00
 Deadwood, SC 115.00
 Dodge city..45.00
Bowl, Centenary, M. E. Church, South Bonne, Terre, MO, scalloped
 edge, blue tint, 6" d.. 20.00
Bread Plate
 Cleveland Reform, hobnail border, 10" d....................45.00
 President Taylor, Curtain Tieback pattern, 10-1/2" x
  7-1/2" 65.00
Bust, Gillinder
 George Washington, round, frosted center 295.00
 Lincoln, frosted...325.00

Bowl, Carnival Glass, Millersburg (Courthouse) Souvenir, low, ruffled, amethyst, very irid, 7-1/2" d, $725. Photo courtesy of Mickey Reichel Auction Center.

 Napoleon, frosted and colorless 300.00
 Shakespeare, frosted 150.00
Candlestick, saucer base, Wellington Hotel, Albany, NY...... 22.50
Canoe, opalescent, Greetings from Texas decal 45.00
Creamer
 3" h, transfer New Central Building, Iowa State College, Ames,
  IA, custard..60.00
 4" h, Chicago Masonic Temple, custard, worn gold trim... 65.00
Cup, Phlox, WI, custard, Heisey 42.00
Dish, cov, Remember the *Maine,* green opaque glass .. 135.00
Ewer, 5" h, The Alamo, Built 1718, Souvenir San Antonio, TX,
 transfer design on custard 75.00
Goblet
 Cassville, WI, Beaded Swag pattern, custard, c1899 ....85.00
 G.A.R., 1887, 21st Encampment..................................100.00
 Mother, Ruby Thumbprint pattern 35.00
Hatchet
 Hazelton, PA, white milk glass, red letters, 6" l.............35.00
 Washington, PA, Centennial, 1810-1910, white milk
  glass..45.00
Jelly Compote, Artesian, SD, ruby stained 45.00
Loving Cup, Oneonta, NY, ruby shading to colorless, gold trim,
 two handles, 3-1/2" h 50.00
Mug
 Bryan, William Jennings, milk glass 40.00
 Cedar City, MI, Button Arches pattern, clambroth........20.00
 Centennial, Philadelphia, waisted 125.00
 Hardwick, VT, custard glass, gold trim 35.00
 Independence Hall, glass 70.00
 Juneau, WI, Homecoming, 1914, clambroth.................40.00
 Lacy Medallion, clambroth..35.00
 New Rockford, ND, custard glass................................35.00
 Saratoga Springs, NY, frosted, weighted bottom, horses
  crossing finish line, spring illus 30.00
 Washington and Lafayette, milk glass 60.00
 White Rock, SD, custard glass....................................55.00
Mustache Cup, Viking, milk glass................................... 375.00
Paperweight
 Brainard, MN, lake scene, 3" d, round 40.00
 Columbian Expo, US Glass, frosted center, woman with up-
  swept hairdo...145.00

Memorial Hall, frosted 150.00
Moses in Bulrushes, frosted center............................145.00
New Salem State Park, 2-3/4" d, round 35.00
Plymouth Rock, colorless..95.00
Ruth the Gleaner, frosted 125.00
Washington, George, round, frosted center 300.00

Pitcher
Bar Harbor, ME, custard glass, gold trim, beaded base ...95.00
Pittsburgh, Button Arches pattern, ruby stained,
    tankard 140.00

Plate
Atlantic City Lighthouse 22.00
Fitzhugh Lee, 5-1/4" d, egg and dart border 35.00
Frieda Hepel, 5-1/4" d, egg and dart border 40.00
Grant, peace, round, maple leaf border, colorless.......40.00
Grant, peace, amber...65.00
Grant, Ulysses, amber glass, emb "Patriot & Soldier,"
    9-1/2" sq...60.00
Mary Had A Little Lamb, 5-1/4" d, egg and dart border ... 25.00
Old Glory, 5-1/2" d, colorless glass................................30.00
Yankee Doodle, 5-1/4" d, egg and dart border, color-
    less...35.00
Yankee Doodle, 5-1/4" d, egg and dart border, green 40.00

Platter
Constitution 65.00
Continental, Memorial Hall 55.00
Garfield Memorial..40.00
Mormon Tabernacle, stippled border 425.00
Remember, three presidents, colorless and frosted
    glass...65.00
Rock of Ages..75.00
Three Presidents 35.00
Washington Centennial, Washington center 125.00

Shovel, Kearney, NE, gold scoop and letters, colorless handle,
    6-1/2" l...30.00
Stein, Centennial...65.00
Tile, 4" d, Detroit Women's League, multicolored irid
    glass...135.00

Toothpick Holder
Glen Ullen, ND, ruby stained glass, gold.....................35.00
Lakewood, NJ, Diamond with Peg pattern, Jefferson, ruby
    stain...45.00
Lewistown, ME, Georgia Gem pattern, custard glass, gold
    trim...45.00
Ottawa, IL, green custard, plain sides 40.00
Providence, Shamrock pattern, ruby stained glass 40.00
Rochester, MN, Punty Band, custard..........................75.00

1000 Islands, 1909, Anna, Delaware pattern, rose stained,
    gold trim...110.00
Tray, flag shape, 38 stars 50.00

Tumbler
Greenburg, FL, yellow, ruby stain trim 55.00
Lord's Prayer, etched...15.00
Louisiana Purchase, milk glass.....................................50.00
Niagara Falls, Prospect Point, gold rim........................20.00
Ten Commandments, etched..13.00
Whittier birthplace, waisted, tall 60.00

Vase
Bristol Exhibition, "A Present From the Bristol Exhibition,
    1893," purple slag..75.00
Cora, San Antonio, 1899, Pineapple & Fan pattern, matched
    pair, one with just name Cora, Heisey.....................95.00
Parkers Prairie, MN, custard glass...............................85.00
Red Wing, MN, custard glass, multicolored scene,
    c1920...95.00

Wine
Ashbury Park, NJ, ruby stained 35.00
Buffalo, 1899, Shriner's Convention, colorless, gold
    trim...115.00
Christmas, Triple Triangle pattern, ruby stained...........40.00

SPANGLED GLASS

History: Spangled glass is a blown or blown-molded variegated art glass, similar to spatter glass, with the addition of flakes of mica or metallic aventurine. Many pieces
are cased with a white or clear layer of glass. Spangled
glass was developed in the late 19th century and still is
being manufactured.

Originally, spangled glass was attributed only to the Vasa
Murrhina Art Glass Company of Hartford, Connecticut,
which distributed the glass for Dr. Flower of the Cape Cod
Glassworks, Sandwich, Massachusetts. However, research
has shown that many companies in Europe, England, and
the United States made spangled glass, and attributing a
piece to a specific source is very difficult.

Apothecary Jar, 6-1/2" h, bulbous, pink and white, silver mica
    flecks, matching stopper...................................... 175.00
Basket
6-1/2" h, 5-1/2" w, bean pot shape, sq top, deep pink int.,
    shaded deep apricot with spangled gold, applied crystal
    loop handle..325.00
7" h, 6" l, ruffled edge, white int., deep apricot with spangled
    gold, applied crystal loop handle, slight flake 225.00
7-1/2" h, 5" w, brown-pink shading to amber, vertical stripes
    with gold spangles, bright pink int., bulbous bean pot type
    form, applied crystal loop edge and handle 150.00
7-1/2" h, 7" w, deep rose shading to pink to white, melon
    ribbed form, twisted crystal handle.......................100.00
8-1/2" h, 10" d, deep heavenly blue shading to white, lighter
    blue edge, large silver mica flecks, three rows of hob-
    nails, ruffled, applied crystal edge, applied crystal rope
    handle, slight amount of edge roughness..............100.00
9" h, 10" l, deep blue shading to pale blue to white int., silver
    spangles, brilliant white ext., deeply crimped and blown-
    out edge, applied crystal rope handle, Victorian 175.00
9-1/2" h, 9" d, opaque white ext., int. of pink, green, amber,
    brown, and silver mica flecks, applied crystal edge, ap-
    plied crystal twisted rope handle 100.00
9-1/2" h, 10" l, 8-1/2" w, pink, yellow, and brown-green spat-

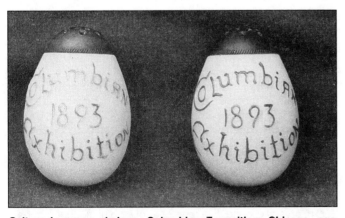

**Salt and pepper shakers, Columbian Exposition, Chicago, egg
shape, orig pewter tops, Mt. Washington, left: matte finish, blue letters, $75; right: glossy finish, blue letters, $65.**

ter, silver flecks, white ext., applied crystal twisted rope handle, c1890..325.00

10" h, 9-1/2" w, cased amber ext., shocking pink int., gold mica flecks, tightly ribbed, applied amber leaf ftd base, applied amber twisted handle, slight edge roughness...........125.00

10-1/2" h, 11-3/4" w, bright pink cased with white, heavy silver mica flecks, tightly ruffled and pleated rim, applied colorless braided V-shaped handle.......................300.00

11" h, 9-1/2" d, large ruffled pulled down rect basket, deep amethyst shading to white, silver mica over opaque white, applied crystal rope handle 150.00

13" h, 9" w, amber glass, green, pink, maroon, and yellow spangles, white lining, very ruffled edge with crystal applied rim, applied shell reeded feet, strap-type handle 150.00

Beverage Set, bulbous pitcher, 6 matching tumblers, rubena, opalescent mottling, silver flecks, attributed to Sandwich, c1850-60 ....250.00

Bowl, 4-3/8" d, 2-1/4" h, rainbow, silver mica flecks, white lining...150.00

Bride's Bowl, 10-3/8" d, multicolored, ruby, cranberry, and green, ivory-yellow ground, silver flecks.................120.00

Candlesticks, pr, 8-1/8" h, pink and whit spatter, green Aventurine flecks, cased white int.....................................115.00

Condiment Set, cranberry, green flecks, SP holder, 3 pcs...215.00

Creamer and Sugar, cov, blue, gold mica flecks............250.00

Cruet, Leaf Mold pattern, cranberry, mica flecks, white casing, Northwood...450.00

Decanter, 12" h, 3-1/2" w, dark lavender, silver flecks through, large matching ball stopper, Italian..........................40.00

Ewer, 11" h, colorless, cased pink, mica flecks, twisted applied handle...125.00

Fairy Lamp, 6-3/8" h, multicolored, gold mica flecks, orig Clarke insert...225.00

Juice Tumbler, 3-3/8" h, white ground, pink spatter, silver mica flecks, white casing...95.00

Pitcher

6-3/4" h, cobalt blue, gold mica flecks, applied amber handle with flecks...250.00

7-1/2" h, bulbous, 4 sided top, apricot, gold mica flecks form diamond pattern, white casing, pontil....................175.00

8-3/4" h, bulbous, crimped rim with applied colorless edge, deep rose, burgundy spatter, silver mica flecks, applied colorless reeded handle...325.00

10" h, peach ground, ruby spatter, gold mica flecks, white casing, applied amber thorn handle......................250.00

Rose Bowl, 3-3/8" d, 3-1/2" h, 8 crimp top, cased deep rose, heavy mica coral like dec, white int. 115.00

Sugar Shaker, cranberry, mica flecks, white casing, North wood 115.00

Tumbler

3-1/2" h, pale blue and white spatter, silver mica flecks form vertical paneled pattern, white casing 85.00

4" h, pink, white, orange, red, yellow, and silver spangles...75.00

Vase

4-3/4" h, 4" d, amethyst ground, collared scalloped top, goldstone flecks around body.......................................145.00

8" h, modified baluster, tulip shaped lip, deep cranberry casing, colorless casing with gold foil flecks in wide vertical swath, brown, green, yellow, and red spatter........250.00

8" h, 4-1/8" d, tan, beige, oxblood red and pink spatter, silver mica flecks, white casing 165.00

8-1/8" h, 3-5/8" d, cranberry ground, emb swirls, goldstone 140.00

9-1/4" h, pink ground, silver mica flecks, white casing, applied vaseline rigaree shell trim, applied vaseline loop handles...165.00

12" h, oviform, squatty circular base, amber, silver mica flecks, pinched neck 100.00

14-1/2" h, melon ribbed, ruffled, pink, white, and green mica flecks 265.00

Witch Ball, 8" h, tortoiseshell glass ball, attached to amber glass stem and foot... 200.00

SPATTER GLASS

History: Spatter glass is a variegated blown or blown-molded art glass. It originally was called "End-of-Day" glass, based on the assumption that it was made from batches of glass leftover at the end of the day. However, spatter glass was found to be a standard production item for many glass factories.

Spatter glass was developed at the end of the 19th century and is still being produced in the United States and Europe. It is still being produced today. Companies like Northwood and Hobbs, Brockunier produced splendid examples of spatter glass. The Czechoslovakians used vivid color combinations creating some striking pieces of glassware.

References: William Heacock, James Measell and Berry Wiggins, *Harry Northwood: The Early Years 1881-1900*, Antique Publications, 1990; —, *Harry Northwood: The Wheeling Years 1902-1925*, Antique Publications, 1991.

Reproduction Alert: Many modern examples come from the area previously called Czechoslovakia. Reproductions of Northwood pieces have also flooded the marketplace.

Basket

6" h, 6" w, yellow, maroon, green, and brown spatter, white int., 3 rows of hobnails, rect form, loop thorn handle 125.00

6" h, 6-1/2" l, 6" w, pink and bright yellow spatter, white int. lining, colorless thorn handle, 8 point star shaped body 250.00

6" h, 8" w, pink and white, air traps, star shaped basket, thorn handle with sag in center 250.00

6-1/2" h, 6-1/4" l, 5" w, rect, maroon, brown, yellow, blue, red, green spatter, white int. lining, colorless thorn loop handle, tightly crimped edge with two rows of hobnails.........250.00

7" h, crystal ground, five rows of applied blue flattened hobs, white and blue spatter, applied crystal twisted thorn handle, Victorian...300.00

Tumbler, Inverted Thumbprint pattern, colorless shading to orange ground, white and silver spangles, 3-3/4" h, $35.

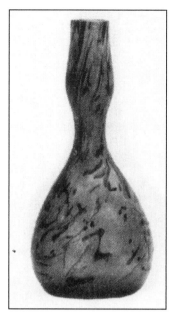

Barber bottle, 7-1/4" h, cylindrical, bulbous body, long bulbous neck, amethyst and light yellow amber mottled design, overall pink irid, ground mouth, smooth base, $325. Photo courtesy of Norman C. Heckler and Co.

7-1/2" h, 5" w, triangular form, bright pink and yellow spatter, white ground, colorless twisted thorn handle, ruffled edge, c1890 ....225.00

7-1/2" h, 6" l, brown and jade green spatter, white ground, thorn handle, ruffled star shaped edge, c1890......275.00

8" h, 13" l, 8" d, tortoiseshell, pale ground with white, red, and brown spatter, heavy gold enameled floral dec, applied gold dec loop handle, minor wear to gold handle..... 150.00

Bottle, 11" h, rubena, opalescent spatter.........................150.00

Bowl

8-1/2" d, 4-1/4" h, Le Gras, Tigre, cranberry int., spattered cream opaque with goldstone, amber glass applied wishbone feet 220.00

9" h, 8" w, triangular shape, white satin ground ext. and int., pink and yellow spatter, large applied twisted thorn handle...100.00

9-1/2" h, 10" w, pink and white spatter, brilliant opaque yellow ground, three rows of hobnails, ruffled and crimped edge, applied crystal shell feet, twisted thorn handle, flake off one foot..200.00

13-1/2" h, 6" h, blown swirl pattern, yellow cased ground, white spatter, two applied amber loop handles, three amber thorn ball feet 100.00

Box, 7-1/2" l, 4-1/2" h, egg shaped, hinged, white casing, yellow and blue flowers, gold and white leaves, three applied colorless feet 275.00

Candlestick, 7-1/2" h, yellow, red, and white streaks, colorless overlay, vertical swirled molding, smooth base, flanged socket..60.00

Cane, 30-1/2" l, aqua, spiral twist at straight end of handle..150.00

Cologne Bottle

8-1/2" h, etched adv "Rich Secker Sweet Cologne, New York," applied colorless handles.............................65.00

Leaf Mold, vaseline spatter, shiny finish 400.00

Creamer, 4-3/4" h, pink and white, applied colorless handle, Northwood...50.00

Cruet, orig stopper, applied colorless handle

Amber and white spatter, polished pontil 95.00

Red and white spatter 125.00

Darner, brightly colored 250.00

Darning Egg, multicolored, attributed to Sandwich Glass.... 125.00

Ewer, cranberry spatter, applied colorless handle............65.00

Fairy Lamp, 3-1/4" h, 2-7/8" d, pyramid shape, pink, yellow, and white, white casing, mkd "Clarke" base............... 100.00

Finger Lamp, 6-1/4" h, 4-1/4" d, peach ground, white and brown spatter, applied colorless handle.........................145.00

Jack in the Pulpit Vase, 9-3/8" h, 5-1/2" d, green, white, and peach spatter body, white and peach spatter top, green base..125.00

Perfume Bottle, 4-3/4" h, yellow shaded to white ground, gold, blue, yellow, and white spatter...............................85.00

Rose Bowl, 3-1/2" h, octagonal, crimped top, rose spatter, white casing..115.00

Salt, 3" l, maroon and pink, white spatter, applied colorless feet and handle 125.00

Sugar Shaker, 4-7/8" h, pink and white, SP top 75.00

Toothpick Holder, Leaf Mold, cranberry and vaseline spatter 225.00

Tumbler

3-1/2" h, Inverted Thumbprint pattern, colorless ground, vaseline and white spatter, c1890 ....45.00

3-3/4" h, emb Swirl pattern, white, maroon, pink, yellow, and green, white int. 65.00

Tumble-Up, bottle and matching tumbler, elongated thumbprint patterned body, green, red, pink, and yellow spatter, white casing, applied colorless feet.....................300.00

Vase

7" h, blue opalescent, white spatter, crimped, Dugan....75.00

7" h, 4-1/2" d, golden yellow and white, enameled bird and flowers, applied colorless handles, colored enamel dec..180.00

7-1/2" h, bulbous, ruffled rim, ruby, white spatter, gold butterflies, flowers, and foliage, pr 475.00

10" h, pink, yellow, and tan swirls, white casing, cupped goblet type neck, pr..300.00

Water Pitcher, cranberry and yellow, cinched, ground and polished pontil 105.00

STEUBEN GLASS

History: Frederick Carder, an Englishman, and Thomas G. Hawkes of Corning, New York, established the Steuben Glass Works in 1904. In 1918, the Corning Glass Company purchased the Steuben company. Carder remained with the firm and designed many of the pieces bearing the Steuben mark.

1903–32

The most widely recognized wares are Aurene, Verre De Soie, and Rosaline, but many other types were produced. Aurene is the name given to glassware that has an iridized golden sheet and may be found on amber, blue, colorless, or topaz colored glass. Examples of Aurene with a red, green, or brown base are rare. Aurene was produced from 1904 through 1933. Verre de Soie is also an iridized type of glass. The silk-like texture is lightly frosted and should have a blue tint. Rosaline is a pink jade type glass with a cloudy appearance. Rosaline pieces are commonly with found alabaster trim, feet, handles, and finials.

Steuben glassware can also be identified by the classic shapes and styles. Catalog reprints and other types of research materials have led to identification of these distinctive shapes.

The firm is still operating, producing glass of exceptional quality.

References: Paul Gardner, *Glass of Frederick Carder*, Crown Publishers, 1971; Paul Perrot, Paul Gardner, and James S. Plaut, *Steuben: Seventy Years Of American Glassmaking,* Praeger Publishers, 1974; Kenneth Wilson, *American Glass 1760-1930*, 2 Vols., Hudson Hills Press and The Toledo Museum of Art, 1994.

Museums: Corning Museum of Glass, Corning, NY; Rockwell Museum, Corning, NY; The Chrysler Museum, Norfolk VA; The Rockwell Museum, Corning, NY; The Toledo Museum of Art, Toledo, OH.

Reproduction Alert: Steuben pieces have been reproduced. The coloration can be duplicated, but the silky and iridized finishes originally produced by Steuben are not usually perfected on reproductions.

Acid Cut Back

Bowl, 8" d, 7-1/4" h, green jade, cut chrysanthemums and leaves dec 650.00
Candlesticks, pr, 14" h, black cut to colorless, Poussin pattern, flowers and leaves 2,400.00
Centerpiece Bowl, 17-1/2" w, 2-3/4" h, black, four baskets filled with flowers, other floral and ribbon designs, applied flint white rim, sgd 800.00
Jar, cov, 5-1/2", white ground, apple green leaves and flowers 800.00
Lamp Base
    10" h, catalog #8492, possibly Marlene pattern, flattened round flask, gold aurene on green jade, cameo etched stylized blossom forms, gold aurene grip glaze shoulder, gilt-metal crest platform base and lamp fittings 3,450.00
    25" h, 5-1/2" d shaft, jade green over alabaster, cut floral and leaves design, fancy orig silver plated mountings and orig finial 550.00
    26" h, 14" h glass shaft, catalog #8006, elongated flared neck over bulbous base, acid etch grape motif, spiraled leaves and vines around neck, mounted to unsigned gilt-metal base and two-socket shaft.....920.00
Vase
    9-1/2" h, baluster, green jade cut back to alabaster, Bird pattern, exotic bids, leafy flowering tree branches... 1,200.00
    10-1/4" h, 3-3/4" d, heavy walled, cobalt blue Aurene ground, silver-blue irid, cut to dark cobalt, broad vintage frieze of grapes, leaves, and vines below shoulder dec of stylized leaves and berries, sgd "Steuben Aurene 2683" on base....................................4,200.00
    12" h, baluster, raised flared rim, triple layers, peach Cintra cased to alabaster, dark amethyst overlay, acid cut back Pagoda pattern, three repeats in shaped medallion windows with Canton landscapes, floral and fretwork borders..2,400.00

Animal, colorless crystal

Angel Fish, 10-1/2" h, 10" w, sgd 750.00
Bear, small 120.00
Beaver, amethyst eyes, sgd
    4" l..300.00
    6-1/4" l...325.00
    10-1/4" l...400.00
Cat, 8-1/4" h, designed by Donald Desky, engraved "Steuben" 300.00

Chick, 4" h, design by George Thompson, inscribed "Steuben" 225.00
Dinosaur, 12-3/4" l, modeled by James Houston........650.00
Eagle, on ball, 12" d, hand etched "Steuben"............225.00
Elephant, 8-1/2" h 375.00
Fish, 7" l, design by George Thompson, engraved "Steuben" 275.00
Frog, 4-3/4" h, design by Lloyd Atkins, 1960s 320.00
Gazelle, 7" h, leaping, inscribed "Steuben," numbered and artist sgd, pr 1,200.00
Kitten, 4" l, design by Lloyd Atkins, inscribed "Steuben" 275.00
Koala Bear, design by Lloyd Atkins, solid glass, applied appendages, mkd "Steuben" on base
    4-1/2" h 550.00
    5-1/4" h 920.00
Mouse, 3-3/4" l, design by Lloyd Atkins, inscribed "Steuben" 225.00
Owl
    5-1/2" h, facing right, frosted eyes, design by Donald Pollard, inscribed "Steuben" 230.00
    7-3/4" h, design by James Houston, 18kt figural owl on curvilinear glass perch 1,840.00
Partridge in a Pear Tree, design by Lloyd Atkins, 18K gold on central bird and fruit laden tree, mkd "Steuben" on base..1,840.00
Penguin, 6-1/2" h, numbered 190.00
Porpoise, 12" l, bottle nose dolphin posed to dive, design by Lloyd Atkins 865.00
Pouter Pigeon, 7-1/2" h, upright position, swelling chest, inscribed "Steuben," pr..900.00
Rooster, 10" h, modeled by Donald Pollard, inscribed "Steuben" 650.00
Squirrel, 4-1/4" h, curving tail, inscribed "Steuben 8120, L.A."..450.00
Songbird, 3" h, design by George Thompson, inscribed "Steuben" 200.00
Swan, 4-3/4" h, graceful necks, one upright, other downturned, pr..600.00
Rabbit, 4" l, design by John Dreves............................500.00
Tropical Fish, 10-1/2" h, molded upright fins, inscribed "Steuben," pr 900.00
Trout, 8-1/2" h, 3" w, bubble interior, script sgd..........650.00

Aurene

Atomizer, 7-1/4" h, catalog #6136, gold, tapered bottle fitted with gilt metal cap and tube for atomizer bulb.......520.00
Basket
    6-3/4" h, 6-1/4" w, irid gold, brilliant gold, purple, and blue highlights, applied loop handle, applied berry prunts, sgd "Aurene 453" 1,750.00
    8" h,2-3/4" h, rolled in rim, three applied glass feet, highly irid blue surface with purple highlights, sgd "Aurene, #2586," minor interior scratches........................600.00
    8-3/4" h, 9-1/2" w, flaring, deep gold, purple and blue irid highlights, sgd "Aurene, #723," minor surface scratching..800.00
    9-1/2" h, 8" w, brilliant gold, applied blue-gold handle, raspberry prunt, inscribed "Aurene, #453" 1,800.00
    9-1/2" h, 8" w, brilliant gold int., calcite ext., blue-green applied handle..1,300.00
    10" d, 2" h, deep irid blue aurene with purple highlights, sgd "Aurene #2586" 500.00
    10-1/4" w, 2-1/2" h, gold aurene on calcite, purple highlights, flaring, minor interior scratches 300.00

13" h, 8" w, gold irid, orig metal mounted floral design handle, sgd "F. Carder".................................2,000.00

15-3/4" h, 10" w, brilliant blue, green, and purple int., oyster white calcite ext., applied loop handle......3,500.00

Bon Bon, 4-1/2" d, 1-1/4" h, catalog #138, blue, scalloped design, silvery blue luster, base inscribed "Aurene 138"..550.00

Bowl
5-1/4" d, design #565, gold, ten prominent ribs, scalloped rim, inscribed "Aurene 565"............................375.00

6" d, 3" h, catalog #2687, gold, oval, irid smooth surface, inscribed..460.00

Bulb Bowl, 9-3/4" d, 1-3/4" h, catalog #2586, shallow, gold, silvery transparent luster, base scratches.............260.00

Candlestick
8-1/4" h, catalog #686, blue, rope twist shaft, shiny foot..635.00

10" h, catalog #686, blue, rope twist shaft, inscribed "Aurene 686," one with partial label, pr................1,840.00

12" h, catalog #6405, blue, rope twist shafts, price for mated pr...575.00

Centerpiece Bowl
8" d, 4" h, gold, deeply pinched scalloped rim manipulated into eight apertures......................................550.00

10" d, 3" h, catalog #158, blue, eight pointed scalloped rim, amber glass, blue irid, strong luster, inscribed on base "Aurene 158"..1,035.00

12" d, 4-3/4" h, catalog #7423, blue, flared form, eight spaced crimps, irid shades from deep purple to golden and silvery cobalt blue.............................2,300.00

14" d, irid gold aurene on calcite, minor interior scratching...825.00

14" d, 2" h, angular, shallow round bowl, gold aurene on calcite, orange irid luster.....................................420.00

14-1/2" d, 2" h, catalog #3579, shallow, gold aurene on calcite, broad decumbent flowers cut on rim, etched white calcite blossoms, one bubble near edge.............690.00

Champagne, 5-3/4" h, catalog #2642, gold, lustrous irid, base inscribed..460.00

Cigarette Holder, 4-1/4" l, blue, ribbed.......................350.00

Cologne Bottle
5" h, catalog #1455, gold, eight-lobed body, conforming stopper, base inscribed "Aurene 1455"...........815.00

6-1/2" h, catalog #1455, gold, eight-lobed body, tapered conforming stopper, very minor chips at stopper rim, inscribed "Aurene 1455"..................................815.00

Compote
6" w, 5" h, deep irid blue, purple highlights, sgd, numbered "2760"..1,100.00

7-1/2" d, 10" d, design #367, deep color, crimped edge, rope twist shaft, base inscribed "Steuben Aurene 367"..1,265.00

8-1/2" d, 7" h, flared deep gold bowl, spiral ribbed calcite shat and round foot..920.00

10" d, 2-3/4" h, gold aurene on calcite, flared bowl, low cupped pedestal foot..460.00

Finger Bowl and Underplate, catalog #171, 5" d bowl, 6-1/4" d plate, gold, pointed scalloped rim, both mkd "Aurene"..690.00

Goblet, 6" h, catalog #2361, gold, flared bell form, applied twist, disk foot, inscribed "Aurene 2361," set of 8............1,840.00

Jardiniere, 6-1/2" h, gold, pedestal base, three applied handles, base engraved "Steuben Aurene 627".......1,210.00

Lamp, 12" h, vase catalog #429, opaque white alabaster glass oval, gold Aurene heart and vine dec, elaborate gilt metal base, electrified cap, three Art Nouveau women as fittings, not drilled..3,737.00

Lamp Shade, 6-1/2" h, 2-1/4" fitter ring, gold, flared ten-rib bell form, fleur-de-lis mark at rim, set of 4.............750.00

Miniature Vase, 1-1/2" h, 2-3/4" d, catalog #649, old aurene on alabaster, irid white body, six coiled feather elements, base inscribed "Aurene 649"..................................920.00

Perfume Bottle
7" h, catalog #3425, blue irid, urn form bottle, orig black mirror stopper, peach to alabaster blossom finial, full length dauber, base inscribed "Steuben Aurene 3425"...1,840.00

7-1/2" h, catalog #6136, strong irid blue, tapered form, unsigned gold DeVilbiss-type fittings, mesh covered bulb..1,100.00

7-1/2" h, catalog #6407, gold, atomizer base, gilt metal DeVilbiss attachment, bulb missing, wear........345.00

Plate, 8-1/2" d, catalog #3059, gold, shallow bowl-form, fine irid lustrous surface, inscribed "Aurene 3059," price for pr...345.00

Salt, 1-1/2" h, 2-1/2" w, gold aurene on calcite, pedestal foot..375.00

Sherbet and Underplate
4" d, 6-1/4" d, catalog #2680, blue, twelve-rib molded dish and underplate, strong blue-purple luster, each inscribed "Aurene 2680"......................................520.00

6" d, 3-3/4" h, catalog #2960, gold stemmed bowl with calcite stem, sgd "F. Carder Aurene" on base......290.00

6" d, 4-1/4" d, gold aurene on calcite, irid..............225.00

Vase
4-1/4" h, catalog #131, gold, early quatraform, ruffled rim, dimpled body, platinum gold irid, base inscribed "Aurene 131"...550.00

4-1/4" h, catalog #550, early ribbed green aurene cased to white, gold aurene leaf and vine motif, sic gold centered white millefiori blossoms, base inscribed "Aurene 550"...500.00

4-1/2" h, pointed quatraform rim, dimpled body, platinum gold irid surface dec by subtle green swirls on ext., base inscribed "Aurene 131B".......................1,265.00

5" h, catalog #2631, flared bulbous form, ten prominent ribs, even blue irid, base inscribed "Steuben"..........1,100.00

6" h, 4" w, platinum, green heart and fine dec, white millefiori flowers, sgd "Aurene #599"..............2,200.00

7" h, 6-3/4" d, catalog #1952, gold, six ruffled rim, white calcite body, fine gold veining on ext. gold irid int., shades from dark to light...................................375.00

7-1/4" h, design #136, platinum gold irid, raised quatraform rim on dimpled bulb above elongated stem, integral foot, mkd "Aurene 136"...........................920.00

8-1/4" h, catalog #2683, irid gold body, inscribed "Steuben"...1,300.00

9" h, catalog #260, gourd-shaped green oval body cased to irid opal, gold Aurene blossoms, vertical stems, inscribed "Aurene 260" on base.........................865.00

9-1/2" h, catalog #2526, elongated cylinder raised on disk platform foot, fine irid blue luster, polished top rim, base inscribed "Aurene/2556"..........................375.00

10" h, catalog #506, style D, gold aurene on irid green body cased to white int., blossom, heart, and vine dec, base inscribed "Aurene 506".........................5,175.00

10-1/2" h, 5" w, brilliant green ground, irid gold flowers, sgd "Aurene, 244"...4,000.00

12" h, catalog #6034, trumpet, molded cone, irid gold, cupped pedestal foot inscribed "Steuben Aurene," numbered and labeled...................................1,265.00

12" h, elongated slender baluster, organic green leaf-forms pulled into alabaster white dec by gold aurene peacock feathers centering four gold hearts with green peacock eyes, inscribed on base "Aurene/535," 1/2" shallow scratch at side 3,950.00

12-1/4" h, catalog #6034, gold, swirled trumpet, cupped pedestal foot, inscribed "Steuben Aurene 6034" 1,380.00

12-1/2" h, catalog #273, six ruffle rim, smooth oval opaque white body, four green eye peacock feathers, gold Aurene dec, inscribed "Aurene 273" on base 4,600.00

18-1/4" h, catalog #6239, stick, elongated narrow cylinder, gold luster, disc foot inscribed "Aurene" ...520.00

Bristol Yellow

Cake Set, 10-1/2" d plate, eight 7" d serving plates, two with "Steuben" in block letters, some edge chips, blemishes, 9 pc set..350.00

Centerbowl, 16" d, 4-1/2" d, low ruffled rim, mirror black threads on ext., Steuben fleur-de-lis mark on base.................420.00

Decanter, 9" h, quatraform buttressed form, swirled rib-mold, solid matching stopper..575.00

Dresser Jar, 5-1/4" h, square, swirl molded, matching stopper 225.00

Vase

10" h, catalog #6030, flared oval optic ribbed design, strong twist to the right, fleur-de-lis mark on bulbed foot, small sand grain bubble at side................200.00

12" h, catalog #6034, trumpet form, ribbed flared body, applied cupped pedestal foot, fleur-de-lis mark on base..490.00

Celeste Blue

Box, cov, 5-1/2" d, 4-1/2" h, catalog #7540, round swirled blown box, conforming cov, threaded Celeste finial, flat rim chip inside cover 175.00

Centerbowl, 12" d, 5-1/4" h, ribbed Celeste blue bulbed bowl, cupped transparent topaz amber pedestal foot........300.00

Creamer and Sugar, applied amethyst handles 400.00

Dresser Jar, 5-1/4" h, square, swirl molded, matching stopper 225.00

Finger Bowl and Underplate, 5" d bowl, 6-1/4" d underplate, catalog #204..200.00

Goblet, 6" h, ribbed design, crystal stem, fleur-de-lis mark, set of six 300.00

Urn, cov, 19" h, catalog #3114 variant, sixteen rib oval vasiform brilliant transparent blue body, conforming raised cover with figural red and yellow glass pear finial with applied green stem, ribbed leaf, some glass bubbles 1,650.00

Vase

6" h, catalog #6287, fan, optic ribbed version, triple wafer stem, pedestal base stamped with fleur-de-lis mark..320.00

8-3/4" h, broad oval, round applied disk foot, fleur-de-lis mark..290.00

Cintra

Bowl, 8" d, 7" h, catalog #6856, scalloped rim, mottled and crackled pink, blue, and frosted colorless ground, applied blossoms, three applied twig feet, int. water stain, annealing cracks where 2 twigs attach to body......................1,500.00

Cologne Bottle, 5-1/2" h, oval #3048 bottle, opalescent ground with applied pink-blue-purple Cintra handles, and rim wrap, amethyst turret stopper and dauber........................1,500.00

Lamp, 32" h, 14" h glass shaft, heavy walled green Cintra oval body overlaid in translucent alabaster, acid etched naturalized wheat stalks and angular grasses, matching

wheel molded gilt metal platform base, Art Deco gazelle finial above three-socket fittings.........................1,725.00

Plate, 8-1/2" d, opalescent body, blue and red Cintra edge 185.00

Vase, 12" h, catalog #3279, speckled pastel green in colorless and white surround, overlaid with Rosa glass, acid-etched twice to shade stylized blossoms and vertical geometric devices, four chips on blossom petals 3,450.00

Cluthra

Bowl, 15" d, 7-1/2" h, heavy conical walls, shaded black-gray to clear and white crystal, irregular swirling bubbles throughout 850.00

Vase

8-1/4" h, catalog #6882, angular Art Deco form, two color, rose at rim shading to white base, elongated bubbles throughout 575.00

10-1/2" h, catalog #2683, classic flared oval, creamy white and colorless, swirled and bubbled.........920.00

10-1/2" h, catalog #7273, triangular Art Deco body, swirled cluthra, applied colorless polished rim wrap and foot, fleur-de-lis mark.................................750.00

12-1/4" h, catalog #8494, colored oval cluthra body, yellow at top shading to bright rose-pink base, overlaid in Rosa, etched in Carder's Cliftwood pattern, quintessential Art Deco elements................................3,737.00

12-1/2" h, 10-1/2" d, bulbous, paneled, two applied crystal handles, various sized all over random bubbles, brilliant green ground, lighter striations, in making tool mark near one handle, sgd 2,450.00

Crystal

Audobon Plate, 10" d

Set, great blue heron, white pelican, flamingo, barred owl, horned grebe, swallow-tail kit, four engraved "Steuben," other two "S," unused condition, set of 6 ....2,990.00

Wild Turkey, base engraved "Steuben" 345.00

Bowl

7-3/4" d, 3-1/2" h, engraved, orig box, pr 175.00

9" d, 7" h, catalog #8084, square prunts on pedestal base, design by Donald Pollard, 1957 ....345.00

Candleholders, pr, catalog #8017, two-arm candelabra, scroll motif, engraved "Steuben" on base, design by Lloyd Atkins 490.00

Centerpiece Bowl

10-3/4" d, 7" h, broad conical form, deep well applied in four swirled leaf forms, "Steuben" engraved on base..320.00

16" d, catalog #3579, rib-molded colorless body, pale Rosa pink folded rim, engraved floral, webbed, and scrolled dec, fleur-de-lis mark on base, some wear scratches 345.00

Cocktail Set, 6-1/2" h, carafe, two pedestal base glasses, orig case, orig cloth bags 400.00

Exhibition Bowl

9-1/2" h, X1924A designed by George Thompson, engraving by Donald Wier, wood sprite playing stringed instrument among blossoms and bees, below "Sounds and Sweet Airs That Give Delight," inscribed "Steuben" on base..1,495.00

11-3/4" h, American Ballard Series, "The Arts," design by George Thompson, engraving designed by Sidney Waugh, from patriotic wartime series, conforming cover with finial, matching pedestal knob, inscribed "Steuben" on base...1,840.00

Figure, Guardian Angel, catalog #1027, solid crystal angel, wings outspread, head wreathed in 18K gold vermeil halo, base inscribed "Steuben" 1,955.00
Goblet
7" h, catalog #7737, elegant fluted bowl, broad bubbled stem, engraved "Steuben," designed by Sidney Waugh, 6 pc set 550.00
7-1/2" h, catalog #8212, first in Seven Sins series, engraved woman watching man from behind tree, inscribed "Steuben" on base, designed by Sidney Waugh 1,380.00
17-1/2" h, catalog #8202, bowl held aloft by spiral twisted stem, base inscribed "Steuben," 1958 design by Golda Fishbein, light int. stain................................260.00
Luminiere, 13" h, molded glass gazelle set into illuminating rect black plastic base issuing six curved arms each suspending a glass drop, glass inscribed "Steuben," pr 2,000.00
Martini Glass, 4-3/4" h, hourglass shape, teardrop bubble in solid base, inscribed "Steuben," 8 pc set..............425.00
Paperweight
3-1/4" h, faceted hand-polished solid crystal rock base embedded with removable 8-1/2" l sterling silver sword, 18 carat gold scabbard, red velvet and leather case, inscribed "Steuben"............................1,300.00
3-1/2" h, spiraled, central teardrop, inscribed "Steuben"...345.00
4-1/4" h, tree in snow, inscribed "Steuben"............300.00
Plate, 8" d, central monogram "J" above "EF," 8 pc set...300.00
Prismatic Ornament
3-1/2" h, catalog #4107, Empire Ellipse, engraved Shakespeare Twelfth Night inscription, inscribed "Steuben," design by George Thompson...............................200.00
5-3/4" d, catalog #8609, Plant Saturn, designed by James Noll...650.00
Sculpture, 7" h, cut and polished glass rock supporting golden thistle, design by James Houston, inscribed "Steuben" on base, velvet lined red leather case 2,185.00
Urn, 12-3/4" h, 7" h, catalog #7548, Strawberry Mansion, flared bulbed form, sq plinth base, two applied "M" handles, designed by Frederick Carder 750.00
Vase
6" h, catalog #2683, Mansard, frosted colorless crystal cut in repeating stylized Art Deco blossoms, etched fleur-de-lis "Steuben" mark at lower edge......1,500.00
6" h, Sidney Waugh design, wheel-cut parallel lines compacted as squares in quintessential curvilinear expression, mkd "Steuben" on base......................230.00
7-1/4" h, Sidney Waugh design, Angus Dei, winged sacred figure, mkd "Steuben" on base.................345.00
7-1/4" h, Sidney Waugh design, stylized Art Deco gazelle figure, mkd "Steuben" on base 400.00
7-1/4" h, 7-5/8" h, 8" h, Trials of Hercules, set of three vases engraved to depict Nemean Lion struggle, the Trial of the Lernaean Hydr, and Ceryneian Hind Trial, designed by Bernard X. Wolff, limited edition, nos. 3050, 0351, 0352, 1984...4,600.00
10" h, catalog #6761, Mansard, flared bowl-form top, frosted colorless body, acid etched repeating stylized Art Deco blossoms, etched "Steuben" fleur-de-lis mark at lower edge...690.00
15" h, six-prong, catalog #1=7129, triangular flower holders attached to central disk base, lightly crizzled.......920.00
Wine, 5-1/4" h, trumpet shape, wide angular teardrop stems, designed by Sidney Waugh, 12 pc set.................750.00

Flemish Blue

Bowl, 8" l, 4-1/2" l, catalog #6380, rect body, optic ridges swirled to right, four applied feet, fleur-de-lis mark on base..490.00
Perfume Jar, 3-3/4" h, catalog #6887 variant, swirled optic ribbing and threading, conforming stoppers, fleur-de-lis mark on back, price for pr.....................................460.00
Vase, #5441 ....225.00

Grotesque

Bowl
5" d, red pillar molded 375.00
11" d, 6" h, open flower form, Grotesque, deep green shading to colorless, sgd 550.00
12" l, 7-1/4" h, catalog #7535, Grotesque, topaz, four-pillar ruffled oval body, light topaz color, "Steuben" inscribed on base foot...400.00
12-1/2" l, 4-1/4" h, catalog #7535, pillar molded, colorless, green upper body, script sgd "Steuben" on base, small chip on foot edge....................................175.00
Compote, Catalog #7171, 7-1/4" d, 6-1/4" h, green, two line pillar molded design, grotesque suggestion in scalloped rim, hollow flared colorless base, fleur-de-lis mark, price for pr 490.00
Vase
5-1/2" h, 10" d, pillar ribbed abstract form, ivory, minor surface stain 345.00
6-1/4" h, catalog #7311, jade green, modified four-pillar grotesque design, vertical shading...................400.00
9-1/4" h, flared quatraform, amethyst, pillar molded ...575.00
11" h, catalog #7090, flared quatraform, celeste blue edges, some water stains.......................................200.00
19-1/2" h, 7-1/2" w at top, shaded amethyst to clear, sgd, minor interior scratches 1,000.00

Ivrene/Ivorine

Bowl, 6" x 4", catalog #7233, unsigned.........................95.00

Vase, Ivorine, flared flattened oval body, ten rib design, irid white Aurene, partial paper label on base, 9-1/2" h, 10-1/2" w, $550. Photo courtesy of Skinner, Inc.

Candleholder

    3" h, catalog #7564, irid opaque white glass, ruffled and folded bobeche about integrated disk foot.......435.00

    10-1/2" h, catalog #7317, floriform, ribbed stems support two candle cups, applied leaf form accents, cupped disk foot.......................550.00

Centerbowl, 10" d, 4-1/4" h, catalog #7023, classic flared bowl, integrated disk foot, applied rim wrap of lustrous blue Aurene, satin irid, some minor int. wear.........900.00

Lamp, 15" h, 11" d shade, catalog #2384, matching twelve-rib base and shade, irid opaque calcite white, engraved floral motif interspersed through wheel-cut geometric medial design, minimal chipping at top under shade cap.....2,070.00

Urn, 12" h, catalog #7468, translucent irid white, flared, stepped sq pedestal foot, applied "M" handles, pr..............2,100.00

Vase

    5" h, 5" d, catalog #2533, flared body, ten prominent optic ridges.....................460.00

    8-1/4" h, #2683 design, oval, raised floral rim........520.00

Jade

Bowl

    7-1/2" d, 2" h, catalog #5062, light blue, wide flattened rim, cased glass body.......................375.00

    12" d, 3-1/4" h, catalog #6774, bulbed and flared jade centerbowl, int. and ext. iridescence, wide Aurene threading.........................865.00

Centerbowl, 16" d, 5-1/2" h, catalog #3200 variant, broad, flared, opaque yellow, bulbed integrated foot, two small sand grain spots on int.........................230.00

Compote, 7" d, 3" h, catalog #3234, translucent light blue jade above applied opal white alabaster stem and disk foot..........................575.00

Cornucopia, 8-1/4" h, 4-1/2" w at top, green, doomed alabaster foot, sgd, pr.......................1,150.00

Lamp Base

    6" h, catalog #6199, etched yellow jade, sculptured floral pattern, rectangular glass body, silvered metal platform base and harp lamp fittings.......................520.00

    7" h, green jade glass stick vase shaft mounted with etched silvered metal base, rim, and electrical socket fittings, Roycroft orb mark on base...............1,840.00

    9-1/2" h, catalog #8002, flared vasiform green jade glass shaft, applied mirror black looped rigaree handles, gilt metal lamp fittings attributed to Crest Lamp Co.....460.00

Perfume Bottle, 5-3/4" h, green, internally ribbed and tooled, white glass stopper, sgd "F. Carder-Steuben"......675.00

Puff Box, green, catalog #2910..................375.00

Ring Tree, 5-1/2" h, light blue, stemmed pedestal foot, base inscribed "F. Carder/Steuben"..............345.00

Sherbet Set, 3-3/4" h, 4" d sherbet, 6" d plate, light blue sherbet with flint white stem and foot, light blue jade underplate, Carder.......................575.00

Vase

    6" h, catalog #2987, slender light blue cased bud vase, two applied Venetian handles, twisted flint white rings, flint pedestal base, tiny annealing crack in each handle...........................425.00

    6" h, catalog #6199, rect, yellow jade, foliate sculptured pattern....................900.00

    6-1/4" h, catalog #2683, classic oval, green..........815.00

    6-1/2" h, catalog #1565, Oriental Jade, flared parfait form, swirled opal stripes in green body, opal disk foot........................520.00

    7" h, 7-1/2" d, catalog #6078, spherical body, green, acid-

etched cone dec, lower edge etched fleur-de-lis "Steuben".......................1,035.00

    7" h, 8" d, catalog #6078, spherical body, green, acid-etched chrysanthemums and leaves in high relief.........1,265.00

    9-1/2" h, 5-3/4" l, 3-1/4" w, catalog #6199, rect, green, polished at top rim, rib molded, some int. stain.....290.00

    10-1/4" h, catalog #2939, deep green jade, applied "M" handles on each shoulder, stamped in script "Steuben" at center of base.......................750.00

    10-1/2" h, catalog #6199, rect, green, sculptured acid-etched chrysanthemums.......................1,100.00

    10-1/2" h, catalog #7128, triangular, three green cones applied to round alabaster foot, stamped "Steuben".......................865.00

Matsu Noke

Candlestick, 10-1/2" h, colorless crystal, applied rim wraps, handles, and Matsu Noke dec in light Pomona Green glass.......................520.00

Glass, catalog #2239, green handle.......................290.00

Vase, catalog #3359, rose dec.......................340.00

Mirror Black

Bowl

    8" d, 3-1/4" h, catalog #5023, opaque flared form, fleur-de-lis mark on foot, minor scratches.......................435.00

    8" d, 4-3/4" h, glossy, wide ribbed pattern ending as four scallops at top.......................450.00

Jar, cov, sq

    4-3/4" h, gold aurene threaded stopper.......................200.00

    5" h, Celeste blue ground, mirror black reeding, angular black stopper.......................250.00

Vase

    6-1/4" h, 8" l, catalog #7564, modified four pillar grotesque form, ivory bowl raised on capped black foot.....460.00

    6-1/2" h, catalog #7307, modified grotesque manner, waffle pontil.......................175.00

    10-1/2" h, catalog #6873, prong-type, three triangular holders applied to conforming oval pad foot, one with fleur-de-lis stamp mark, price for pr.................920.00

    12" h, catalog #6391, polished raised rim, broad glossy oval, five repeated foliate panels and scrolling devices.......................1,500.00

    12" h, catalog #6391, polished raised rim, broad glossy oval, Matzu, three full length stylized Ming trees over cloud formations, fleur-de-lis mark on base.....1,265.00

    12" h, 11-1/2" d, catalog #2683, classic form, deeply cameo etched Shelton foliate Art Deco pattern against alabaster ground, Carder.......................6,900.00

    12-1/4" h, catalog #6989/7008, classic oval, curved rim flare, base gold foil triangular label "Steuben Made in Corning, NY".......................635.00

Miscellaneous

Bon Bon, 4-1/2" d, 6-3/4" h, catalog #5128, pear-shaped Citron Yellow body, Celeste Blue twisted stem, full bodied, ribbed leaf finial, partial triangular Steuben paper label on base.......................920.00

Bookends, pr. 6-1/2" h, catalog #7399, leaping gazelles, colorless with frosted finish, Art Deco base, stamped "Steuben" script mark.......................1,725.00

Bowl, Catalog #2896, topaz and cobalt blue, weave effect.......................325.00

Candleholders, pr, 3-3/4" h, catalog #6384, Rosa, swirled

rib-molded cup and foot joined by colorless knob with applied rosettes, one stamped "Steuben" 290.00
Candy Dish, ram's head, colorless 300.00
Centerbowl with Flower Frog, clear bowl with controlled bubbles, green threads, green flower frog, chips to frog 200.00
Cologne
   Catalog #6605, 5-3/4" h, bright Antique Green squared bottles, matching random threading and faceted stoppers, minor chips at base edges, price for pr 345.00
   Catalog #6887, light amethyst................................325.00
   Catalog #6887, Rosa..240.00
Compote
   7" d, 3-1/2" h, dense citron yellow cone-shaped bowl, colorless disk foot base, inscribed "F. Carder/ Steuben" 230.00
   Catalog #6043, Cerise Ruby crystal, twisted 360.00
Flower Frog, 9" h, catalog #7133, Kuan Yin, Buddhist goddess, two-tier flower holder, amethyst....................425.00
Jewelry, pendant, crystal and gold, strawberry, design #1055 by Donald Pollard, naturalistic 18K gold hull leafage, bubbled crystal berry suspended from 14kt mesh braided 24" chains, red leather velvet lined presentation case 690.00
Lamp
   25" h overall, catalog #8431, Rose Quartz, 10" h covered urn-forms, heavy walled cased rose quartz glass, etched in dragon motif front and back, conforming etched removable cover, lighted within, intricately mounted in gilt bronze lamp fittings, offset dragon shaft, adjustable finial, price for pr 1,725.00
   29" h overall, catalog #6467, Rose Quartz, 15" h oval baluster body, lightly crackled variegated rose etched all over with classical scene of three draped women in various poses under full length trees in garden setting, drilled and mounted to gilt metal Crest lamp fittings 2,530.00
Luncheon Set, ruby, four rib-molded and scalloped goblets, four ftd dishes, four 9" plates, some color variation, 12 pc set 460.00
Perfume Bottle, 10-1/2" h, 1-1/2" d, Cerise Ruby, swirl rocket shape, orig long colorless dauber, clear base 550.00
Plate, rouge flambe, sixteen rib semi-transparent body, hand polished base, attributed to Frederick Carder 690.00
Sherbet, 3-3/4" h, amethyst, rib-molded, colorless stem, amethyst disk foot, fleur-de-lis mark 250.00
Tray, 5-1/2" d, catalog #7244, ivory, autographed round dish, applied back stem handle, base sgd "F. Carder, Steuben," leaf missing, stem damage 115.00
Urn, cov, catalog #3134, cobalt blue..........................495.00
Vase
   8-1/2" h, catalog #2744, tripartite knobby vases, Special Green (transparent teal green), applied to rustic disk foot, pr 490.00
   10" h, 8" d, medium green, Swirl pattern, flaring 75.00
   10-1/2" h, catalog #7208, faintly ribbed, double bulbed, pedestal, transparent wisteria, pale blue shading to pink-lavender, three applied rippled handles at mid section, Steuben fleur-de-lis mark.....................815.00
   10-3/4" h, catalog #2683, oval, creamy ivory, etched Stanford design, Art Deco motif of leaping stag and doe gazelles, mat finish, integrated "Steuben" fleur-de-lis mark at lower edge.......................................2,300.00
Wine, 4-1/2" h, Special Green, vertical rib-molded, stamped fleur-de-lis mark, set of 12......................................700.00

Moss Agate

Lamp, 30" h overall, catalog #8026, 11" h angular shouldered oval glass shaft of purple and lavender with mica flecks, swirls of green aventurine, amber, red, and blue, mounted to gilt metal single-socket lamp fittings..........1,610.00
Torchere, 15" h, flared glass shade, eight scalloped rim, mottled amber, green, yellow, rust, red swirled with cluthra bubbles and crackling, black painted cast iron lamp base..1,200.00
Vase, 6" h, flared rim, oval body, mottled green, internally dec with multicolored red, blue, white, brown, black, and metallic clusters swirling powders, recessed polished pontil, attributed to Frederick Carder 635.00

Oriental Poppy

Box, cov, 5-1/2" d, 3-1/4" h, catalog #7540, mold blown round dish, opal striped poppy pink transparent crystal, matching five petal blossom on conforming cov.............1,035.00
Champagne, green stem 375.00
Cordial, green stem and foot, sgd 325.00
Goblet, 8-1/4" h, flared rib-molded, pink opal, applied Pomona green straight stem 490.00
Lamp, catalog #6501 ....1,500.00
Lamp Base, 10-3/4" h, catalog #8490, rib-molded satin pink opal, elaborate gilt-metal fittings 575.00
Perfume Bottle, 10-1/2" h, opal, rose, c1925............1,200.00
Sherbet, 4-1/2" h, green stem 275.00
Vase
   6" h, catalog #650, satin smooth flared oval body, pink ground, sixteen integrated opal stripes, two potstone blemishes at side...1,380.00
   10-1/4" h, catalog #8422, flared oval body, vertical opal rib-stripes, rosy-pink surround, applied Pomona Green pedestal foot.......................................1,495.00

Pomona Green

Bowl, 10-1/2" d, 6" h, catalog #6241, angular rib-molded green bowl, topaz pedestal foot............................230.00
Candlesticks, 4" h, catalog #6384.................................90.00
Centerbowl, 10" d, 5-1/4" h, catalog #3080, air trap bubbled variation, four hollow stems around central opening.........345.00
Compote, 8-1/2" d, 8-1/4" h, catalog #6044, rib-molded amber topaz bowl, solid green stem, double cupped base..435.00
Finger Bowl and Underplate, 5" d bowl, 6-1/4" d underplate, catalog #204..200.00
Pitcher, 8-1/2" h, catalog #6232, ribbed oval green body, applied amber handle 230.00
Vase
   6-3/4" h, catalog #6031 variant, ribbed sphere......200.00
   8" h, catalog #6441, trefoil pinched rim, rib-molded cone form..240.00
   11" h, catalog #6287, green round, ridged topaz engraved in floral swag dec, fleur-de-lis mark on base, annealing flaw at pontil.....................................175.00
   11" h, 9" d, broad flared ftd oval, five repeating foliate elements centering wheel-cut vertical designs....345.00
   11" h, 10" d, catalog #6914 variant, wide flared oval, Silverina decoration of mica flecks in diamond pattern, stamped "Steuben" 490.00
   12" h, ribbed conical body, wide grapevine dec border, applied topaz flared foot, fleur-de-lis mark on base..460.00

Rosaline

Bowl, 12-1/2" l, catalog #6081 variant, oval, Roseline cut to alabaster, grapes pattern, raised applied handles at each end, heat crack on one at rim 2,30.00

Compote, 12" d, 2-3/4" h, catalog #506, elegant pink bowl, applied alabaster glass foot, int. bubble................375.00

Powder Box, cov, 4" x 3", catalog #2910, unsigned 210.00

Vase

4-3/4" h, catalog #1500 variant, diminutive oval ginger jar form, double etched Chinese pattern surface, alabaster ground 1,265.00

6-1/2" h, 7-1/2" d, catalog #6078, bowl-form sphere, sea holly pattern, acid etched Art Deco style, broad spiked leaves in pink, rough textured alabaster ground, fleur-de-lis "Steuben" etched at lower side 1,610.00

8" h, catalog #1979, flared oval, pink jade, applied alabaster cupped foot, added engraved "Steuben" mark.... 600.00

Catalog #346, alabaster 335.00

Selenium Red

Bowl, 4-1/2" d, 2-3/4" h, oval, fleur-de-lis mark on base, 6 pc set..325.00

Centerbowl, 14" d, 6" h, catalog #3196, sgd "F. Carder/Steuben"...425.00

Goblet, engraved grape vine motif, base mkd "Steuben" and fleur-de-lis mark...250.00

Vase

6" h, 4" w at top, red dome foot, rolled edge, deep color..300.00

12" h, catalog #6034, ridged trumpet form, brilliant red, grape and vine dec, fleur-de-lis mark on base, four int. bubbles at top rim 920.00

Silverina

Candlesticks, pr

5" h, catalog #6637, amethyst, mica flecked body, controlled bubble pattern 865.00

12" h, catalog #3328 variant, colorless crystal internally dec by diamond patterned air-trap mica flecks, mirror black cupped bases stamped "Steuben" 900.00

Vase, 12" h, topaz bulbous bud vase, decorative mica flecks throughout, applied Pomona Green disk foot 400.00

Spanish Green

Candlestick, 12" h, catalog #2596, optic ribbed baluster form, double ball below candle cup, fleur-de-lis mark on base..250.00

Centerpiece Bowl, 14" d, bubbles and reeded dec 200.00

Champagne Goblet, 6-1/4" h, floriform, five applied ribbed leaves under bubbled bowl, raised on nubby stem, folded rim pedestal foot, stamped mark on base, price for 10 pc set..1,380.00

Compote, 7" h, bubbled and reeded design, pr.........325.00

Shot Glass, threading, bubbles, sgd 60.00

Table Service, twelve 8" d plates, twelve bouillon cups, fourteen serving bowls, 36 pc set 575.00

Vase, 8" h, trumpet form, bubbled and reeded design, pr..400.00

Threaded

Cocktail Pitcher, catalog #7056, crystal body, applied strap handle

9-1/4" h, rose reeding, conforming cov, some loss to threading 225.00

10-1/2" h, green threading, conical cover, minor damage, some loss to threading 200.00

Compote, catalog #2018, crystal, green machine threading, engraved 285.00

Dresser Jar, catalog #1169, colorless puff jars, one with ruby random threads, one with black threads, price for pr 325.00

Goblet, 5-3/4" h, colorless, diamond molded, Pomona blue reeding, applied Bristol yellow disk foot, stamped "Steuben," 3 pc set..225.00

Plate, 10-7/8" d, colorless, bright blue concentric threads on back rim, inscribed "F. Carder/Steuben" 220.00

Salt, 2" h, 2-1/4" d, colorless, Rosa threading applied under flared rim, pedestal 175.00

Verre de Soie

Basket

10-3/4" h, catalog #5069, irid silky body, berry prunt at applied handles 920.00

13" h, 8" w, ruffled rim...600.00

14" h, 10" l, irid, engraving of flowers, leaves, and swags, applied loop handle, sgd "Hawkes Steuben" ...900.00

Bowl

4" d, catalog #2687, pr 300.00

12" d, 2-3/4" h, catalog #2586, three applied prunt feet, shallow planter form 230.00

Centerbowl, catalog #2775, eight pinched apertures around rim...290.00

Chandelier, 16" w, four verre de soie ruffled glass #892 shades, mounted to gilt metal ceiling lamp with acorn and oak cluster motif, adjustable drop 1,840.00

Compote, 6-1/2" h, flared bow, "C" monogram on baluster stem, disk foot 175.00

Console Set, 12" d flared #2764 bowl, pr 3" h mushroom candleholders, ruby reeding on outer rims, stamped fleur-de-lis mark, some threads damage 520.00

Jar, 5-1/4" h, square, gold aurene solid stopper.........200.00

Sherbet Set, 4" h, 3-3/4" d sherbet, 6" d undertray, tinted aquamarine/green 220.00

Tableware, four plates, two goblets, three sherbets, six wines, stamped "Hawkes" at center pontil.............750.00

Tumbler, 4" h, 3-1/4" w at top, flaring rim, sgd "F. Carder Steuben"...450.00

Vase

12-3/4" h, catalog #334, baluster candlestick form, irid colorless frosted glass, triangular gold foil label on base...435.00

14" h, aquamarine, green cast to Verre de soie vessel, two applied ring handles, small annealing crack at one side...375.00

STEVENS AND WILLIAMS

History: In 1824, Joseph Silvers and Joseph Stevens leased the Moor Lane Glass House at Briar Lea Hill (Brierley Hill), England, from the Honey-Borne family. In 1847, William Stevens and Samuel Cox Williams took over, giving the firm its present name. In 1870, the company moved to its Stourbridge plant. In the 1880s, the firm employed such renowned glass artisans as Frederick C. Carder, John Northwood, other Northwood family members, James Hill, and Joshua Hodgetts.

Stevens and Williams made cameo glass. Hodgetts developed a more commercial version using thinner-walled blanks,

19th C

acid etching, and the engraving wheel. Hodgetts, an amateur botanist, was noted for his brilliant floral designs.

Other glass products and designs manufactured by Stevens and Williams include intaglio ware, Peach Bloom (a form of peachblow), moss agate, threaded ware, "jewell" ware, tapestry ware, and Silveria. Stevens and Williams made glass pieces covering the full range of late Victorian fashion.

After World War I, the firm concentrated on refining the production of lead crystal and achieving new glass colors. In 1932, Keith Murray came to Stevens and Williams as a designer. His work stressed the pure nature of the glass form. Murray stayed with Stevens and Williams until World War II and later followed a career in architecture.

References: R.S. Williams-Thomas, The Crystal Years, Stevens and Williams Limited, England, Boerum Hill Books, 1983.

Basket
  7-1/2" h, 6" sq, transparent amber glass, applied green leaves, large amber apples, amber feet, amber thorn loop handle...550.00
  10" h, 6-1/2" d, deep pink int., creamy white ext., three applied amber loop feet which extend up to form three green with cranberry highlights leaf designs which attach and swirl around body, applied amber rope handle with applied cranberry rigaree, top knot finial on center of handle 400.00
  10" h, 9" w, brilliant green over pale yellow, blue lining int., applied blue flowers, four applied vaseline feet, green thorn loop handle, button pontil 400.00
  11" h, 6" w, pale yellow custard body, large applied amber glass flower, applied emerald green leaves, feet and twisted thorn handle 425.00
  13" h, 10-1/2" d, white ribbed ext., blown-out hobnails cased in bright pink shading to pale pink, ornate amber trim, twisted amber handle, applied amber thorn feet, two feet may have been polished in the making 175.00
  13-3/4" h, 8-3/4" d, arabesque, colorless body, white arabesque designs, seven applied bands of cranberry and yellow dec, applied ribbed foot, large crystal loop handle...165.00
  14" h, 7" w, cranberry egg-shaped body, pale cream outer casing, three green applied leaf-like feet which form loops on base, thorn cut edge, large applied amber thorn crossed handle..200.00
Biscuit Jar, 5-1/2" d, 7-3/4" h, creamy opaque ground, applied amber and green leaves, deep pink lining, SP rim, cov, and handle 295.00
Bowl
  5" d, 2-3/4" h, Jewell Glass, pale dusty-rose, zipper-like air-trap ribs, incised in pontil "Rd 55693"....................215.00
  6" d, 3" h, Matsu No Ke, creamy yellow satin bowl, branch of twisted, knurled, and thorny frosted crystal glass winds around perimeter, 36 florets, 3 feet, one slight chip on 1 flower...1,250.00
  8" d, Peachblow, double tier of applied shell rigaree at rim, polished pontil...250.00
Bride's Basket, 10-1/2" h, 10" l, 5" w, off-white ext., Rose Du Barry pink int., two clear red cherries on one side, two amber Anjou pears on other, rambling leafed amber branches, golden-amber pie crust ribbon edge and four knurled feet, golden-amber looping handle....................1,750.00
Calling Card Tray, 10" l, applied amber handle, rolled edge, translucent opalescent ground, three applied berries, blossoms,

and green leaves, three applied amber feet 750.00
Cologne Bottle, 8-1/2" h, cut and engraved crystal, square panel-ribbed crystal with bright-cut floral dec, repeated on conforming cover, stopper chipped at base......... 375.00
Compote, 5" w, 4" h, blue bowl, alabaster foot, sgd 100.00
Creamer and Sugar, open, blue opalescent, snail feet, applied raspberry prunts.. 175.00
Ewer, 5-1/4" h, Silveria, silver foil sandwiched between layers of glass, crimson, ruby-red, and gold on upper half, large areas of vivid purple accented by splotches of gold on lower portion, clear green glass entwining vertical trailing overlaid, applied handle, sgd "S&W" in pontil mark.............. 3,450.00
Lemonade Pitcher, 9" h, amber, thumbprint molding, applied blue handle.. 325.00
Mug, blue, applied plums 300.00
Perfume Bottle, 6-1/2" h, 3-3/4" w, Pompeiian Swirl, deep gold, brown to red, turquoise blue lining, orig cut frosted stopper 895.00
Pitcher
  6" h, 5" d, yellow opalescent, vertical stripes, shell reeded handle..225.00
  7" h, 4-1/2" d, overlay, mint green ext., robin's egg blue int., three white and pink tinted blossoms, amber leaves attached to twisting, curling amber tendril continues to form handle, end of tendril ground smooth 385.00
Rose Bowl, 5-1/4" d, 5" h, Pompeiian Swirl, shaded brown to gold, robin's egg blue lining, box pleated top, 6 ruffles 850.00
Salt, irid gold ground, sterling silver basket, hanging spoon, English hallmarks... 165.00
Toothpick Holder, green ground cut to clear, hallmarked sterling silver rim 275.00
Toupee Stand, mushroom shape, rose alabaster........... 295.00
Tumbler, 5" h, cut and engraved crystal, oval, foliate dec including foxglove blossoms and birds in flight.............. 125.00
Vase
  5-3/4" h, egg shape, opal and cranberry vertical stripes, gold an black floral dec, applied colorless rigaree extends to three feet, pr 250.00
  6" h, 6" w, 4-3/4" w at top, applied dec, Matso Nuke style, ftd, pink-peach peachblow ground, bright cream-yellow lining, colorless applied band of shell-like rigaree at top, 3 rosettes, 3 large 5-1/4" l leaf feet, applied raspberry prunt over pontil 750.00
  6-1/2" h, 4" w, Sylvaria, silvery white shading to raspberry, random green threading 1,200.00
  6-1/2" h, 5-1/2" d, amber ruffled top edge, amber loop feet, rose lined cream opaque body, three appliqué amber,

Vase, blue body, applied amber rim, rigaree, and feet, sgd, 7-1/2" w, 7-1/2" h, $325.

green, and cranberry ruffled leaves.......................260.00

7" h, swirled satin, amber shaded to blue cased to opal and yellow, spiraled air trap swirls 575.00

7-1/4" h, Pompeiian Swirl, MOP, powder blue body, pink air-traps, shiny pink ribbons swirl down neck to body, two small ext. flakes..545.00

7-1/4" h, satin, Swirl, shading blue to pink, spiral trapped bubble pattern...750.00

7-1/2" h, swirled satin, tooled crimped rim, green shaded to rose body, cased to opal and yellow with spiraled air trap swirls..815.00

7-1/2" h, 5" w, striped Swirl, frosted deep pink, rose, and yellow stripes, frosted ground, 36 vertical ribs...........425.00

7-3/4" h, 3-3/4" w, double gourd, Pompeiian Swirl, light brown shading to gold 475.00

8" h, 4-1/2" w, bulbous, Pompeiian Swirl, deep rose, white int..575.00

10" h, intaglio cut, pale rose pink cased to transparent green, wheel cut foliate panels below horizontal stepped flared rim...1,265.00

10" h, slender refined shape, six medallions of applied colorless glass, trailing stems swirling to base, engraved ornate stylized petals and foliage, sgd in pontil "Frederick Carder," Stevens and Williams logo.......................900.00

10-1/2" h, flared trumpet form, colorless, four panels of intaglio blossoms and swirling prunts separated by horizontal notched ribs 300.00

10-3/4" h, 5-3/4" w, bulbous, pedestal base, Pompeiian Swirl, MOP, pale lime green, white lining.........................850.00

11" h, 6-1/2" base, stick with bulbous base, Pompeiian Swirl, deep amber to bright red 950.00

11-1/2" h, 4" w, rose shading to pink, white and colorless applied flowers and leaves, ruffled top, flaring ribbed neck.... 225.00

12" h, 6-1/2" w, gourd, Pompeiian Swirl, brilliant blue, brown swirls, bright yellow lining...................................1,750.00

STIEGEL-TYPE GLASS

History: Baron Henry Stiegel founded America's first flint-glass factory at Manheim, Pennsylvania, in the 1760s. Although clear glass was the most common color made, amethyst, blue (cobalt), and fiery opalescent pieces also are found. Products included bottles, creamers, flasks, flips, perfumes, salts, tumblers, and whiskeys. Prosperity was short-lived; Stiegel's extravagant lifestyle forced the factory to close.

It is very difficult to identify a Stiegel-made item. As a result, the term "Stiegel-type" is used to identify glass made during the time period of Stiegel's firm and in the same shapes and colors as used by that company.

Enamel-decorated ware also is attributed to Stiegel. True Stiegel pieces are rare; an overwhelming majority is of European origin.

References: Frederick W. Hunter, *Stiegel Glass*, 1950, available in Dover reprint; Kenneth Wilson, *American Glass 1760-1930*, 2 vols., Hudson Hills Press and The Toledo Museum of Art, 1994.

Reproduction Alert: Beware of modern reproductions, especially in enamel wares.

Beaker, 5" h, blown peacock blue glass, six panels, enameled birds, dog, tiger, stag, fruit, and florals, loop design around base, polished pontil, c1840, slight lower crizzling ... 425.00

Creamer, pattern molded, fifteen diamond pattern, ovoid form, applied handle, emerald green, tooled rim with pour spout, pontil scar, 3-1/8" h, $2,000. Photo courtesy of Norman C. Heckler and Co.

Bottle, flattened globular, colorless, polychrome enameled lovebirds with heart, German inscription and "America" 1,595.00

Bottle, half post, colorless, pewter lip, minor enamel flaking
5-1/8" h, polychrome enameled flowers and birds, stain 110.00

5-3/8" h, polychrome enameled flowers and birds 360.00

5-3/8" h, polychrome enameled flowers, man with wine glass 165.00

5-1/2" h, polychrome enameled flowers, bird in medallion, some residue, threads incomplete.........................250.00

5-3/4" h, polychrome enameled flowers, man with bell, threads on lip incomplete, broken blister on man's arm.......... 55.00

5-7/8" h, polychrome enameled flowers, inscription, fox with birds in basket...300.00

6-3/4" h, polychrome enameled flowers, man with yoke, and buckets..175.00

Christmas Light, 4" h, yellow-green, expanded diamond pattern, metal fixture...150.00

Creamer
3-1/8" h, pattern molded, 15 diamond pattern, emerald green, ovoid, applied handle, tooled rim, pour spout, pontil scar...2,000.00

3-7/8" h, deep cobalt blue, 20 diamond mold, applied foot and handle, flake on bottom of handle, pinpoint rim flake 500.00

4-1/8" h, cobalt blue, 20 expanded diamonds............350.00

Firing Glass, blown, colorless, European, late 19th C
4" h, Masonic engraving, traces of gilding, pontil scar... 200.00

4-1/4" h, copper wheel engraving around rim, hollow stem, pontil scar...175.00

Flask
4-3/4" h, amethyst diamond and daisy.........................495.00

5" h, amethyst, globular, 20 molded ribs, minute rim chip...1,380.00

5" h, blown, flattened oval, enameled Masonic dec, florals and inscription, sheared lip, pontil, scar, German, mid 18th C 295.00

6" h, blown, colorless, chestnut, checkered diamond pattern, wear, sickness, pinpoint rim flake 725.00

Flip Glass, colorless, sheared rim, pontil scar
3-1/2" h, handle, engraved repeating swag motif around rim, lower body emb with graduated panels, form similar to McKearin plate 22, #2 ....210.00

5-1/4" h, engraved top border frieze of ovals, leaves, and berries beneath loop ribbon design.......................150.00

6-1/4" h, engraved floral motif and sunflower, form similar to

McKearin plate 22, #2 ....300.00
7" h, engraved basket and floral motif, form similar to McKearin plate 22, #2..350.00
7" h, engraved bird in heart dec within sunburst motif, form similar to McKearin plate 22, #2............................400.00
7-3/4" h, 6" d, engraved Phoenix bird between two tulips 175.00
7-7/8" h, engraved pair of birds perched on heart within sunburst motif, form similar to McKearin plate 22, #2...... 475.00
8" h, engraved large flower and floral motif, form similar to McKearin plate 22, #2 ....325.00
8-1/4" h, engraved tulip and floral design, pontil scar, European, late 18th C 245.00
Humpen, 9-1/4" h, blown colorless glass, enameled men smoking pipe, florals, and inscriptions, pontil scar, etched "FH 304/1" on base, European, late 19th C 275.00
Jar, cov, 10-1/2" h, colorless, engraved sunflower and floral motifs, repeating dot and vine dec on cov, applied finial, sheared rim, pontil scar, form similar to McKearin plate 35, #2 and 3 ....750.00
Miniature, flip glass, 3" h, colorless, engraved bird within sunburst motif, seared mouth, pontil scar....................325.00
Mug, blown, colorless
3-3/8" h, enameled polychrome dec of birds, hearts, and flowers, applied strap handle, European, 18th C 395.00
5-1/4" h, engraved floral design, pontil scar, applied strap handle with medial crease, Bohemia, mid 18th C ...275.00
6" h, cov, engraved floral motif, strap handle 425.00
6-1/8" h, elaborate frosted engraving, large applied strap handle...265.00
Perfume Bottle, Daisy in Hexagon pattern, flake on neck...4,000.00
Pitcher, 9-3/4" h, blown, aqua, twelve bands of threading around neck, enameled polychrome floral design, c1820-40..2,000.00
Salt, blown
2-5/8" h, blue, checkered diamond pattern 750.00
2-3/4" h, colorless, ogee bowl, 18 vertical ribs, applied petaled foot...225.00
3" h, deep violet-blue, 11 diamond mold, applied foot, minor pinpoint rim flakes 365.00
Sugar, cov, deep sapphire blue, 11 expanded diamond pattern 2,650.00
Tankard, handle, cylindrical, applied solid reeded handle, flared foot, sheared rim, pontil scar, form similar to McK-

earin plate 22, #4
5-1/2" h, milk glass, red, yellow, blue, and green enameled dec of house on mountain with floral motif, old meandering fissure around body of vessel 150.00
5-3/4" h, colorless, engraved with bird in elaborate sunburst motif...500.00
6-1/4" h, colorless, engraved elaborate bird and tulip dec 475.00
Tumbler, blown, colorless
2-7/8" h, paneled, polychrome enameled flowers.......220.00
3-1/8" h, enameled polychrome dec of bird, heart, and foliage, minor enamel wear.......................................265.00
3-5/8" h, enameled polychrome floral dec and phrase "We two will be true," minor enamel wear......................650.00
4-3/8" h, 3-1/2" d, 22 vertical flutes, engraved dec, crosshatched ovals 50.00
Whiskey Tumbler, blown
Cobalt blue, pattern mold, 12 ogival diamonds over 12 flutes design...500.00
Colorless, enameled man on prancing horse 275.00

STRETCH GLASS

History: Stretch glass was produced by many glass manufacturers in the United States between 1915 through 1935. The most prominent makers were Cambridge, Fenton (which probably manufactured more stretch glass than any of the others), Imperial, Northwood, and Steuben. Stretch Glass is pressed or blown-molded glass, with little or no pattern, that is sprayed with a metallic salt mix while hot, creating a iridescent, onionskin-like effect, that may be velvety or shiny in luster. Look for mold marks. Imported pieces are blown and show a pontil mark.

References: Kitty and Russel Umbraco, *Iridescent Stretch Glass,* published by authors (6019 Arlington Blvd., Richmond, CA 94805) 1972; Berry Wiggins, *Stretch Glass*, Antique Publications, 1972, 1987 value update.

Collectors' Club: Stretch Glass Society, P.O. Box 573, Hampshire, IL 60140.

Ashtray, sapphire blue... 18.00
Basket
6" h, blue, applied colorless reeded handle 65.00
10-1/2" d, white ground, applied colorless handle 140.00
Bobeches, pr, vaseline, scalloped 45.00
Bowl
7-1/2" d, 3" h, green, ftd 35.00
7-1/2" w, sq, orange, Imperial 65.00
9" d, low, blue irid...45.00
9" d, 4" h, orange, flared, Imperial cross mark.............65.00
10" d, green, rolled rim...25.00
10" d, irid green, straight sided, flared, Dugan.............28.00
10" d, 4-1/2" h, yellow irid, Imperial 85.00
12" d, white, Fenton...45.00
13" d, blue, wide rim, collared base............................115.00
Cake Server, green, center handle.................................. 35.00
Candlesticks, pr
8-1/2" h, Colonial Panels, olive-green 85.00
9-1/2" h, light green...60.00
10" h, emerald green..70.00
10-1/2" h, vaseline...60.00
Candy Dish, cov, topaz, Fenton...................................... 60.00
Cheese Dish, 4-1/2" d, 2-1/2" h, yellow ground, black edge,

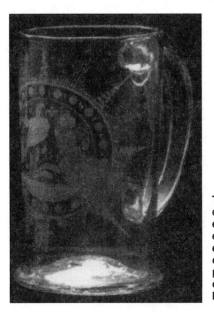

Tankard, 5-3/4" h, cylindrical, applied solid reeded handle and flared foot, engraved with bird within elaborate sunburst motif, colorless, sheared rim, pontil scar, $500. Photo courtesy of Norman C. Heckler and Co.

pedestal base, Northwood 50.00
Compote
    6-1/2" d, 5-1/2" h, bright green, zipper notched pedestal
      base..50.00
    7-5/8" d, 4-1/2" h, irid green, clear stem, amber base 75.00
    9-1/2" d, 5-1/2" h, vaseline, tree bark patterned stem, sgd
      "Northwood" 175.00
Console Bowl
    11-1/2" d, orange, rolled rim..............................40.00
    14" d, red..175.00
Creamer and Sugar, tangerine, Rings pattern..................75.00
Hat, 4" h, purple, Imperial 55.00
Lemonade Pitcher, celeste blue, applied cobalt blue
    handle..215.00
Mayonnaise, ftd, orig liner, Twisted Optic, Iris Ice,
    Imperial...68.00
Mayonnaise Ladle, Celeste...25.00
Nappy, 7" w, vaseline, Fenton..40.00
Nut Cup, yellow, Northwood 50.00
Plate
    6" d, red, paneled, Imperial...............................50.00
    9" d, green, laurel leaf dec 25.00
    8-1/4" d, Aurene, gold 75.00
    8-1/2" d, blue...35.00
    9" d, amethyst ice, paneled, Imperial..................48.00
    10" d, brown and orange.....................................35.00
    11-1/2" d, Panels, russet 65.00
Powder Jar, cov, ice blue 50.00
Ring Tree, 5" d, yellow, enameled floral dec 45.00
Salad Set, 14" d bowl, six 8-1/2" plates, mayonnaise bowl with
    underplate, vaseline, c1920 ....125.00
Sandwich Server, sq, green, center handle 30.00
Sherbet
    4" h, red, melon ribbed..60.00
    5-1/2" h, green, fluted...40.00
Tumbler, Colonial Panels pattern, red 95.00
Vase
    5-1/2" h, baluster, pink, Imperial 75.00
    5-1/2" h, 6" w at top, 3-1/2" d base, Smooth Panels,
      white 60.00
    5-1/2" h, 7-1/2" w at top, 3-1/2" d base, Smooth Panels,
      white 60.00
    6" h, cylindrical, rolled rim, clear ribbed int., hand painted flo-
      rals and leaves 45.00
    6" h, fan, green, ribbed 45.00
    7" h, vaseline, fan shape 40.00
    10" h, blue, vertical cut 60.00
    11-3/4" h, bud, pink 50.00

STUDIO ART

History: Studio art of the 1990s may be the collectibles of the 21st century. Collectors are becoming aware of some of the distinctive examples of studio glassware being currently produced. Many of the fine art glass examples we treasure today began as studio art in the preceding decades.

Collectors may decide to center their collections on specific types of glassware or a particular craftsman. Collectors should buy studio glass to be enjoyed, as well as treasured. Careful documentation of additions to collections will be valuable as the collector's interests grow Well-made, tastefully decorated glassware will surely increase in collectibility. Collectors of studio art often include paperweights in this collecting category as they are individual works of art. This is one of the most inter-

esting and unexplored glass collecting categories in the antiques and collectibles field.

Reference: Sheldon Barr, Venetian Glass, Confections in Glass, 1855-1914, Harry N. Abrams, Inc., 1998; Leslie Piña, Fifties Glass, Schiffer, 1994.

Periodicals: *Glass Art Society Journal*, 1305 4th Ave. #711, Seattle, WA 98101-2401; *Glass Magazine*, New York Experimental Glass Workshop, Inc., 142 Mulberry St., New York, NY 10013; *Neu Glaz* (New Glass), Rudolf - Diesel - Str. 5-7, Frechen 50226 Germany; *Vetri, Italian Glass News*, P.O. Box 191, Fort Lee, NJ 07024-0191.

Museums: The Chrysler Museum, Norfolk, VA; The Corning Museum of Glass, Corning, NY.

Additional Listings: Murano Glass, Orrefors and Paperweights.

Basket, 14" h, 9" w, large free flowing basket, shelf attached
    overhead handle, bright red, control bubbles, mica
    flecks, cased in clear, Barbini type 70.00
Bottle, 4-1/4" h, irid ovoid vessel, swirling elements below moon
    and earth representations, base inscribed "Lewis '74,
    John Conrad Lewis Studio" 345.00
Bowl
    3-1/2" h, deep blue int., white ext., blue and purple flowers,
      Robert Levin 350.00
    6-1/4" d, 3" h, Geod, low, layers of lavender, ruby, cased in
      clear, unsigned Rommerso 95.00
    8" d, 6-3/4" h, sea-form, seedy colorless body shaded to
      smoky topaz, dark red doted repeating rim border, base
      inscribed "For Tommy/Chihuly 1980," Dale Chihuly, minor
      int. water stain 1,035.00
    8-1/4" d, 2-1/2" h, Michael Higgins, speckled, green and
      aqua, three white and yellow circular designs, gold high-
      lights 100.00
Charger, 17" d, Michael Higgins, amethyst, chartreuse and blue
    geometric inclusions, sgd in gold 125.00
Decanter
    8-1/2" h, colorless oval bottle cased to opal white internally
      dec with lavender-pink pulled striations, conforming ball
      stopper, base fully signed "Joel Phillip Myers," dated
      1973...230.00
    18" h, figural, colorless, applied colored glass hair, eyes,
      nose-mouth, nipples and navel, stamped and labeled
      "Rosenthal," designed by Jean Hans Arp..............990.00
Disk, 21" d, broad freeblown form, bluish-tined transparent
    glass, dec by hot manipulated squares and bits of color,
    attributed to Rhode Island School of Design 175.00
Fantasia Cup, 5" h, purple, black, and red, Robert Levin.... 650.00
Goblet
    7-3/8" h, whimsical, glass banana supporting curved striped
      stem, cased yellow and green goblet glass, frosted base,
      inscribed "Levin 1977," titled "Cup with A-Peel," Robert
      Levin Studio...1,150.00
    9-1/4" h, colorless goblet with minute filligrana webbing, blue
      and white latticino figural teapot as stem, applied black
      base, white checked murrine on foot, base inscribed "Mar-
      quis © 1991," design by Richard Marquis.............. 1,500.00
Sculpture
    3" h, 3-1/2" w, solid colorless body, central oval bubble and
      three int. spiraled green, blue, and red veils, polished fac-
      ets, stepped ridges on ext. surface, base inscribed "K.
      Karbler 787120 Michael David" 175.00
    7-3/4" h, 14" l, abstract vessel, nippled protrusions, colorless
      body cased with striated opal, beige, yellow, and turquoise
      inclusions, base sgd "Marvin Lipovsky" dated '74 .....345.00

Eye To Eye, Göran Wärff, 1996, Kosta Boda, Sweden. Photo courtesy of Kosta Boda.

9" h, 13" l, transparent teal glass abstraction, flowing protuberances rising from single ringed base opening, inscribed at lower edge "Samuel J. Herman," England, c1970..635.00

10" h, 9" l, freeform vessel with nippled inclusions of colorless glass, internally dec with amber circles on opal white core, sgd "Marvin Lipovsky," dated '74.................420.00

17" h, figurative glass blossom titled "Midnight Iris," purple, blue, green, and brown coloration crest to roots, sgd "Yaffa Sikorsky-Todd," dated 1988..............................460.00

28" w, Persian Series, each component comprised of brilliant red-orange and golden amber stripes, bright cobalt blue rim wraps, includes slumped centerpiece with colorless ribbed superstructure, folded bowl, wide rim vasiform, two conical vessels, elongated Persian water sprinkler, inscribed "Chihuly 1988" (Dale Chihuly)...........16,100.00

Scent Bottle, Charles Lotton, Lansing, IL, multi-floral, gold and ruby 700.00

Stemware Set, crystal, colorless Art Deco style, square gray-to-paz base, five water goblets, four wines, six cordials, eight sherbets, each stamped "Rosenthal" with trademark, 29 pcs..435.00

Tray, 17" d, orange, red, and amber ornamentals, curvilinear geometric devices, edge marked in gold "higgins," (Michael Higgins) 100.00

Vase

4-3/4" h, contorted ovoid transparent body, shaded red and maroon swirls, base inscribed "Labino 1966" (Dominick Labino) 345.00

5" h, bottle shape, opal, green and gold hooked pattern, Mark Pelser...425.00

5" h, stick, deep rose, interior pulls, Paul Manners, sgd 250.00

5" h, 5-1/4" h, irid, Cypriot type finish 125.00

5-1/2" h, 5" w, irid, green waves 125.00

5-1/2" h, 10-1/2" l, Merletto, pinched circular form, fine network of white threads interspersed with aubergine spots, Seguso 3,000.00

7" h, hummingbird, four-color oval, topaz layered in blue-white, and maroon, deeply etched morning glories with bird hovering at side, fully inscribed "Kelsy/Pilgrim 9/20," 320.00

7-1/4" h, bulbed transparent amberina cylindrical body, hobnail type dec shading from red rim to topaz-amber to red, pontil inscribed "Labino 1965" 350.00

7-1/2" h, brilliant transparent emerald green, occasional opalescent inclusions pulled and tooled into dec protuberances, base inscribed "Labino 5-1083" 425.00

7-1/2" h, 4" w, irid, loop dec 50.00

7-3/4" h, 5-1/2" w, brown glass, blue feather dec, c1979..145.00

8-1/2" h, frosted gray glass bucket form, applied stripes of color etched and polished in linear design, base inscribed "T. Noe 1983 ©," Rhode Island School of Design...175.00

8-1/2" h, mold blown raised rim, bulbous oval of amber cased to colorless, central opal white core stabilizing honey-amber swirls, bubbles, and convolutions, inscribed "Kent F. Ipsen/Richmond VA 1975" 230.00

9-1/2" h 5-3/4" d, cylinder, pastel yellow shaded rose-pink base, internal and surface dec to represent architectonic creation and weaving of Native American blankets, medially signed in cane by artist "Chihuly," Dave Chihuly, c1976..8,100.00

10" h, opaque red striated oval, engraved with fire-breathing dragon motif, gold filled incising, sgd "Chris Heilman," dated April 10, 1979, series #4 of 5 ....230.00

10-1/2" h, heavy walled colorless body, trapped tiny bubbles in symmetrical design, base engraved "G. Nyman/Nuttajarvi—57," designed by Gunnel Nyman, Finnish ...425.00

Blue Snails, Green Seahorses, Ann Wahlström, 1994, Kosta Boda, Sweden. Photo courtesy of Kosta Boda.

10-7/8" h, 11-1/4" d, Soffiato, bulbous, cobalt blue, two handles, acid etched "MADE IN ITALY," Seguso 1,000.00

11-3/4" h, 5-1/8" w, upper portion of smoky topaz, triangular crystal control bubble base, sgd "Erickson" 50.00

13" h, 8" w at base, brilliant yellow, white snail like dec, highly irid, Palmer Konig 500.00

Globular, turquoise and gold, flattened mouth, Medina, sgd..195.00

14-3/4" h, Yokohama, double neck, blue ground, internally dec with gold flecks, green/blue/white murrhines, engraved "Nason Aldo," c1960..............................4,750.00

19-1/2" h, pink bulbous base, long cylindrical blue neck, hand-etched "J. P. Holmes BG89 Organic Vase Series," American, c1989 ....250.00

SUGAR SHAKERS

History: Sugar shakers, sugar castors, or muffineers all served the same purpose: to "sugar" muffins, scones, or toast. They are larger than salt and pepper shakers, were produced in a variety of materials, and were in vogue in the late Victorian era.

Reference: William Heacock, *Encyclopedia of Victorian Colored Pattern Glass*, Book III, Antique Publications, 1976, 1991-92 value update.

Bristol, 6-1/4" h, tall tapering cylinder, pink, blue flowers and green leaves dec...75.00

Crown Milano, melon shape, ribbed, dec, Mt. Washington two pc top 395.00

Custard, Paneled Teardrop 110.00

Cut Glass, Russian pattern alternating with clear panels, orig SS top 375.00

Mt. Washington, Albertine, egg shape, orig top..............295.00

Opalescent

    Beatty Rib, blue...250.00

    Bubble Lattice, blue, bulbous ring neck, orig top.......225.00

    Coin Spot, blue, ring neck...135.00

    Daisy and Fern, Parian Swirl mold, cranberry.............385.00

    Leaf Umbrella, orig top, Northwood...........................295.00

    Spanish Lace, cranberry, orig top 150.00

Opaque

    Acorn, pink, heavy floral enamel.................................225.00

Diamond Side, orig top, $70.

Parian Swirl, green, dec 110.00

Ruby Stained, Duncan Late Block, orig top...................294.00

Satin, Leaf Mold, cased blue, orig top, Northwood 375.00

Smith Bros., Ribbed Pillar, dec 375.00

Wave Crest, 3" h, 3-1/4" d, Helmschmeid Swirls, pale lime-yellow ground, pastel pink rococo swags, raised gold borders, tendrils of gray blossoms rising from base of each of eight swirls, metal lid with emb florals and rococo swags 585.00

SWANKYSWIGS

History: Swankyswigs are decorated glass containers that were filled with Kraft Cheese Spreads. The first Swankyswigs date from the early 1930s. Production was discontinued during the last days of World War II because the paint was needed for the war effort. After the war, production resumed and several new patterns were introduced, including Posy or Cornflower No. 2 (1947), Forget-Me-Not (1948), and Tulip No. 3 (1950). The last colored pattern was Bicentennial Tulip (1975).

In the mid-1970s, several copycat patterns emerged. These include Wildlife Series (1975) and Sportsman Series (1976)–most likely Canadian varieties–Rooster's Head, Cherry, Diamond over Triangle, and Circus. Kraft Cheese Spread is still available but is sold in crystal-type glass.

Swankyswigs were very popular with economy-minded ladies of the Depression era. After the original contents had been consumed, the containers, which could be used as tumblers or to store juice, served as perfect companions to Depression glass table services. Their cheerful designs helped to chase away the Depression blues.

The first designs were hand applied. When the popularity of Swankyswigs increased, more intricate machine-made patterns were introduced. Designs were test marketed and those that did not achieve the desired results are hard to identify and find.

The lack of adequate records about Swankyswigs makes it very difficult to completely identify all patterns. Since 1979, quite a few look-alikes have appeared. Although these glasses were similar to the originals, only Kraft glasses are considered Swankyswigs.

Ideally, select glasses with clear patterns and bright colors. Rarer patterns include Carnival, Checkerboard, and Texas Centennial. Look-alike patterns from other manufacturers include the Rooster's Head, Cherry, Diamond over Triangle, and Circus. The look-alike patterns date from the 1930s to the 1960s.

References: Gene Florence, *Collectible Glassware from the 40's, 50's, 60's*, 2nd ed., Collector Books, 1994; Ian Warner, *Swankyswigs*, Revised, The Daze, 1988, 1992 value update.

Periodical: *The Daze*, P.O. Box 57, Otisville, MI 48463.

Notes: Lids are valued at $5 each when found in good condition. Certain advertisements can bring a higher price. Glasses with original labels will bring approximately 50 percent more.

Antelope and Star, black and red, 3-1/2" h........................ 4.00

Antiques, 3-3/4" h

    Churn and cradle, orange..5.00

Coffee Grinder and Plate, green 5.00
Spinning Wheel and Bellows, red 5.00
Teapot and lamp, blue...5.00
Band #2, red and black 2.50
Band #3, 3-3/8" h 3.00
Bear and Pig, light blue, 3-3/4" h 5.00
Bird and elephant, red, 3-3/4" h.....................................5.00
Bustlin' Betsy, 3-3/4" h
    Brown 6.00
    Orange 2.75
    Red 2.75
    Set, red, blue, brown, yellow, and green 25.00
Carnival, 3-1/2" h
    Blue 4.25
    Green 4.50
    Red 3.00
Cars and Wagon, black and white, 3-3/4" h 4.00
Checkerboard, 3-1/2" d, red and white............................16.00
Circle and Dot
    Black 4.25
    Blue 4.25
    Red 4.25
Cornflower
    #1, light blue
        3-1/2" h 9.00
        3-3/4" h 15.00
        4-1/2" h 18.00
    #2
        3-1/4" h
            Dark Blue 12.75
            Light Blue 12.50
            Yellow 12.00
        3-1/2" h
            Dark Blue 2.75
            Light Blue 2.50
            Red 2.50
            Yellow 2.00
Daisy
    3-1/4" h
        Red and white 35.00
        Red, white, and green 15.00
    3-1/2" h, red and white 25.00
    3-3/4" h, red, white, and green..................................2.00
    4-1/2" h, red, white, and green..................................17.50
Davy Crockett, 3-1/2" h 8.50
Dog and rooster, orange, 3-3/4" h 5.00
Dots, red, 3-1/2" h 3.00
Duck and horse, black, 3-3/4" h......................................5.00
Flying Geese, red, yellow, and blue, 3-1/2" h 4.00
Forget Me Not
    3-1/4" h
        Dark Blue...15.00
        Light Blue 12.75
        Red 14.00
        Yellow 13.00
    3-1/2" h
        Dark Blue...2.75
        Light Blue 2.75
        Red 4.00
        Yellow 3.00
Horizontal Lines, black and red, 3-1/4" h.........................3.00
Kiddie Cup
    3-1/4" h
        Black...13.50
        Brown 12.75
        Green..12.75

Kiddie Cup, Squirrel and Deer, brown, 4-1/2" h, $18.

        Orange 12.75
    3-3/4" h
        Black...3.50
        Brown 2.75
        Green..2.75
        Orange 2.75
    4-1/2" h
        Black...20.00
        Brown 18.00
        Green..18.00
        Orange 18.00
Posy
    Jonquil, yellow
        3-1/4" h 18.00
        3-1/2" h 6.00
        4-1/2" h 20.00
    Tulip, red
        3-1/4" h 15.00
        3-1/2" h 4.00
        4-1/2" h 12.00
    Violet, purple
        3-1/4" h 18.00
        3-1/2" h 5.00
        4-1/2" h 20.00
Scotty, red dog, blue fence, 3-1/2" h 6.00
Squirrel and Deer, brown, 3-3/4" h...................................5.00
Spaceships, blue, 3-1/2" d..6.00
Stars, 3-1/2" h
    Black 2.00
    Green 3.00
    Red..4.00
Tulip
    #1
        3-1/4" h, green 14.00
        3-1/2" h
            Black...3.00
            Dark Blue 2.75
            Green..2.75
            Red...3.50
        4-1/2" h
            Blue...15.00

Green..14.00
Red...15.00
#2
3-1/4" h, dark blue...15.00
3-3/4" h, dark blue...4.00
4-1/2" h, dark blue...18.00
#3
3-1/4" h
Light Blue..14.00
Yellow...14.00
3-3/4" h
Dark Blue...2.75
Light Blue..2.75
Red...2.75
Yellow...3.00
4-1/2" h, red..15.00

SWAROVSKI CRYSTAL

History: The Swarovski family has been perfecting the glassmaker's art in Wattens, Austria, since 1895, and is responsible for many technical advances in the glass industry. For decades, this company has been a leading producer of colored and faceted stones for the costume jewelry and fashion industry, and also is widely respected for its industrial abrasives and quality optics.

Silver Crystal collectible figurines and desk accessories were introduced in 1977, with the creation of a sparkling crystal mouse, followed soon after with a spiny crystal hedgehog. Formed of crystal with lead content of at least 30 percent, these crystal critters have unmistakable sparkle, and were immediately popular.

Sophisticated design and custom fabricated components of the clearest crystal are some of the criteria that distinguish Swarovski crystal from other collectible crystal figurines. The most popular array of Swarovski items falls within the Silver Crystal line, which has included animals, candlesticks, paperweights, and decorative accessories since 1977. Most items are marked, and this is helpful to collectors. The first mark for Silver Crystal items was a block style "SC," sometimes accompanied by the word "Swarovski." Since 1989, an impressionistic swan has been used as the Swarovski symbol. The logo accompanied by a small copyright symbol indicates that the piece was manufactured for the American market.

Other items produced by the Swarovski company are also of interest to collectors, and these include Trimlite, Savvy, Swarovski Selections, Daniel Swarovski Collection, Ebeling & Reuss, and Giftware Suite assortments.

Swarovski crystal collecting has attracted a worldwide following, with a vigorous secondary market. New collectors will find the Swarovski company's Product Listing leaflet very helpful as a beginning checklist of retired and current items. Condition is critical when contemplating an item for resale, and presence of original packaging with enclosures, where applicable, is important. Also desirable is an artist's autograph, occasionally found on the underside of a figurine. Some figurines were produced in more than one version, and the pursuit of various configurations of a design is one type of collection pursued by some Swarovski enthusiasts.

Some crystal figurines have metal trim, usually in one of two colors: shiny silvertone is called "Rhodium" and usually predates the goldtone version of the same item. Examples include the In Flight series of Bee, Butterfly, and Hummingbird, which were produced with both types of trim.

In addition to stunningly clear crystal, color appears in some Swarovski items. For a number of years, paperweights were produced in assorted colors, few of which were sold at retail in the United States. These paperweights, which were colored by applying a vaporized chemical coating to the bottom, have sparked interest among collectors. Recently, the company has introduced several figurines with integrally colored glass.

Few Swarovski pieces are serially numbered, and the items that are numbered have attracted considerable interest. In 1995, the Eagle was produced in an edition of 10,000 pieces. In 1995 and 1996, the company collaborated with perfume makers to create serially numbered perfume flacons in limited quantities.

The Swarovski Collectors Society, which was formed in 1987, extends exclusive offers to members to purchase annual limited editions. The first SCS series, called Caring and Sharing, features three different pairs of birds. The second series, titled Mother and Child, focuses on three sets of sea mammals with their young. The third SCS series, with the Inspiration Africa theme, offers three different African wildlife figurines. A new series, called Fabulous Creatures, was launched in 1997, and the first offering is a Unicorn. All SCS figurines are limited to one per member during the year it is offered, and each piece comes with special packaging and a certificate of authenticity.

References: Swarovski, *Swarovski, The Magic of Crystal*, Harry N. Abrams, 1995; Jane and Tom Warner, *Warner's Blue Ribbon Book on Swarovski Silver Crystal*, 3rd ed. (separate pocket guide included), published by authors (7163 W. Frederick-Garland Rd., Union, OH 45322), 1996.

Periodical: *Swarovski Collector*, General Wille Strasse 88, SH-8706, Feldmeilien, Switzerland.

Collectors' Clubs: Swan Seekers, 9740 Campo Rd., #134, Spring Valley, CA; Swarovski Collectors Society, 2 Slater Rd., Cranston, RI 02920.

Reproduction Alert: Nefarious reproductions haven't been a problem, but copycats are widespread. Collectors who are alert to correct proportions and quality material rarely are mistaken about a piece of Swarovski crystal, and the presence of the maker's mark and correct packaging make acquisition almost foolproof. Replica mouse, replica hedgehog, and replica cat were issued by the company in 1995. Although similar to early figurines, these reissues are clearly marked with the swan logo and also have design distinctions that will keep collectors from becoming confused.

Notes: All prices shown are approximate retail replacement cost for items in perfect condition with correct original packaging and enclosures. Deduct 15 percent for missing boxes or certificates

Accessories

Apple, photo, apple hinged at side, when top is tilted back, it reveals a photograph
#7504nr030R, 30 mm d, rhodium, SC logo............225.00

#7504n050, 50 mm d, gold, SC or swan logo........200.00
#7504nr060, 60mm d, SC logo, gold 400.00
Ashtray, #7641nr100, sculpted crystal, 3-3/8" d, SC or swan logo..225.00
Bell, #7467nr071000, 5-3/4" h, SC or swan logo.........125.00
Candleholder
  #7600nr116, for 5 candles, found with sockets or pickets, SC logo..1,250.00
  #7600nr131, pickets, set of six, 15/16" h, SC logo..... 350.00
  #7600nr136001, gold metal foliage, pineapple, SC logo...500.00
Christmas Ornament
  1981, not dated, crystal snowflake, hexagonal metal trim ring and neck chain, hexagonal ring is stamped "SC" at top on back side, orig blue velour pouch, silver logo box, called the "First Annual Edition," only ornament produced in the Silver Crystal Line 365.00
  1987, dated, Giftware Suite, etched baroque teardrop shape, first in "Holiday Etching" series, no mark .. 150.00
  1991, dated, Giftware Suite, star/snowflake series 150.00
Cigarette Holder, #7463nr062, sculpted crystal, 2-3/8" h, SC or swan logo...130.00
Cigarette Lighter, #7462nr062, 3-1/2" h, chrome lighter in crystal base, SC or swan logo...............................275.00
Grapes, #7550nr30015, cluster of thirty 1-1/8" d clear grapes, clear stem, SC logo, USA only...............1,000.00
Paperweights
  #7451nr60095, Carousel, 2-3/4" h, flared sides, vertical facets, clear, SC logo, often found without logo, sometimes paper label on felted bottom....................800.00
  #7452nr600, Cone, 3-1/8" h, facets that spiral around cone, Bermuda Blue, shades from dark to light blue, SC or swan logo 275.00
  #7452nr600, Cone, 3-1/8" h, facets that spiral around cone, Volcano color, SC or swan logo 450.00
  #7452nr600878, Cone, 3-1/8" h, facets that spiral around cone, clear, SC or swan logo 185.00
  #7453nr60088, Barrel, 2-5/8" h, rect facets that line up vertically, Bermuda Blue, shades from dark to light blue, SC logo, often found without logo, sometimes paper label on felted bottom 400.00
  #7453nr60095, Barrel, 2-5/8" h, rect facets that line up vertically, clear, SC logo, often found without logo, sometimes paper label on felted bottom...........250.00
  #7454nr600, Atomic, 2-3/4" h, hexagonal facets, Bermuda Blue, shades from dark to light blue, SC logo, often found without logo, sometimes paper label on felted bottom...975.00
  #7454nr600, Atomic, 2-3/4" h, hexagonal facets, clear, SC logo, often found without logo, sometimes paper label on felted bottom...................................1,000.00
  #7454nr600, Atomic, 2-3/4" h, hexagonal facets, Vitrail, medium color, SC logo, often found without logo, sometimes paper label on felted bottom........1,700.00
Perfume Bottle, Lancome Trescor, 1994 edition of 5,000 serially numbered, full, with box................................425.00
Picture Frame
  #7505nr75G, oval, 3" h, gold trim, SC or swan logo... 400.00
  #7506nr60, square, gold or rhodium trim, SC or swan logo...250.00
Pineapple, rhodium metal foliage
  #7507nr060002, 2-1/2" h 150.00
  #7507nr105002, 4-1/8" h, SC logo 410.00
Salt and Pepper Shakers, pr, #7508nr068034, 2-3/8" h, rhodium screw on tops, SC logo..............................300.00
Schnapps Glass, #7468nr039000, approx. 2" h, SC or swan logo

Figure, frogs, clear crown, left: clear eyes, $180; right black eyes, $300.

  Europe, set of 3 ....200.00
  USA, set of 6...250.00
Treasure Box, removable lid
  #7464nr50, round shape, flowers on lid, SC or swan logo...200.00
  #7464nr50/100, round shape, butterfly on lid, SC logo...250.00
  #7465nr52, heart shape, flowers on lid, SC logo ...275.00
  #7465nr52/100, heart shape, butterfly on lid, SC or swan logo...250.00
  #7466nr063000, oval shape, flowers on lid, SC or swan logo...275.00
  #7466nr063100, oval shape, butterfly on lid, SC logo...300.00
Vase, #7511nr70, 2-7/8" h, sculpted crystal, three frosted crystal flowers, SC or swan logo 150.00

Figurine

Angel, #7475nr000600...210.00
Baby Lovebirds, #7621nr005...115.00
Bear
  #7636nr112, 4-1/2" h, SC mark only, USA only, SC logo..2,200.00
  #7637nr92, 3-3/4" h, USA only, SC logo..............1,250.00
  #7670nr32, 1-1/8" h, SC logo 200.00
Bee, crystal and metal bee feeding on crystal lotus flower, 4" w, SC logo
  #7553nr100, gold metal bee 1,500.00
  #7553nr200, silver metal bee 2,100.00
Butterfly
  #7551nr100, 4" w, crystal and metal butterfly feeding on crystal lotus flower, gold metal butterfly, SC logo 1,000.00
  #7551nr200, 4" w, crystal and metal butterfly feeding on crystal lotus flower, silver metal butterfly, SC logo 2,200.00
  #7671nr30, 1" h, crystal, metal antennae, no base, USA only SC logo 100.00
Cat
  #7634nr52, 2" h, flexible metal tale, SC logo..........500.00
  #7634nr70, 2-7/8" h, SC or swan logo....................115.00
  #7659nr31, 1-1/4" h, flexible metal tail, SC or swan logo...75.00
Cheetah, #7610nr000001...275.00
Dachshund, metal tail
  #7641nr75, 3" l, rigid, limp, or gently arched, SC or swan logo...120.00
  #7642nr42, 1-1/4" l, SC logo................................150.00
Dog (Pluto on European list), SC or swan logo...........130.00
Dolphin, #7644nr000001..210.00
Duck
  #7653nr45, 1-7/8" l, silver beak, SC logo 90.00
  #7653nr55, 2-1/8" l, silver beak, USA only, SC logo ... 135.00
  #7653nr75, 3" l, crystal beak, USA only, SC logo 275.00
Eagle, #7607nr000001, 1995, edition of 10,000 serially numbered, gray train case type box, wood display pedestal..8,000.00

Elephant

#7640nr40, 2" h, frosted tail, swan logo 100.00

#7640nr55, 2-1/2" h, flexible metal tail, SC logo.....185.00

#7640nr100, Dumbo, 1990, black eyes, clear hat, only 3,000 made, most have swan logo, few unmarked 1,100.00

#7640nr1000001, Dumbo, 1993, blue eyes, frosted hat, swan logo and Disney copyright symbol 375.00

Falcon Head, SC or swan logo

#7645nr45, 1-3/4" h 150.00

#7645nr100, 4" h 1,300.00

Frog

#7642nr48, black eyes, clear crown, SC or swan logo...180.00

#7642nr48, clear eyes, clear crown, usually found with SC logo...300.00

Grand Piano, with stool, #7477nr000006 ....260.00

Hedgehog, silver whiskers

#7360nr30, 1-1/4" h including spines, 30mm body, SC logo, USA only 475.00

#7360nr40, 1-3/4" h including spines, 40mm body, found only with SC mark, worldwide distribution.........180.00

#7360nr50, 2" h including spines, 50mm body, SC logo, worldwide distribution..200.00

#7630nr60, 2-3/8" h including spines, 60mm body, SC logo, USA only 600.00

Hummingbird, crystal and metal hummingbird feeding in crystal lotus flower, 4" w, SC logo

#7552nr100, gold metal hummingbird, green stones on wings 1,500.00

#7552nr200, silver metal hummingbird, red stones on wings 2,500.00

Mallard, #7647nr80, 3-1/2" l, frosted beak, SC or swan logo...160.00

Mouse, silver whiskers, metal coil tail

#763nr23, 13/16" h, SC logo 100.00

#763nr30, 1-3/4" h to top of ears, 30mm body, octagonal base, SC or swan logo............................125.00

#763nr50, 2-7/8" h to top of ears, 50mm body, sq base, USA only, SC mark 300.00

#763nr60, 3-3/4" h to top of ears, 60mm body, sq base, USA only, SC logo 750.00

Pig, #7638n65, 1-3/4" l, crystal "J" shaped tail, SC logo...225.00

Rabbit, ears lay flat on top of head, SC logo

#7652nr20, 1" h 100.00

#7652nr45, 1-1/2" h 250.00

Rose, #7478nr000001 ....155.00

Santa Maria, #7473nr000003 ....375.00

Shell with Pearl, #7624nr055000............................175.00

Sparrow, silver metal open beak

#7650nr20, 3-/4" h, SC or swan logo......................75.00

#7650nr32, 1-1/4" h, SC logo 150.00

Swan, #7658nr27, 1" h, delicate crystal neck connected to body, two wings, tail, SC logo 150.00

Turtle, #7632nr75, 3" l, green eyes, SC logo..............250.00

THREADED GLASS

History: Threaded glass is glass decorated with applied threads of glass. Before the English invention of a glass-threading machine in 1876, threads were applied by hand. After this invention, threaded glass was produced in quantity by practically every major glass factory.

Threaded glass was revived by the art glass manufacturers such as Durand and Steuben, and it is still made today.

Basket
  8" h, 7" w, cranberry shading to amber, white opalescent stripes, threaded surface, pale pink twisted thorn handle, Victorian...125.00
  11" h, 12" d, pink opalescent and amber basket, threaded and raised hobnail design, twisted thorn handle, Victorian...125.00
Bowl
  7" d, 3" h, light pink, green threaded swirl design 45.00
  9-1/2" d, 4-1/2" h, deep amethyst ground, silver-blue threading, highly irid surface, shades of green and purple, inscribed "Loetz, Austria"...100.00
Candlestick, 9-7/8" h, colorless, cut, flared base, bell nozzle with frosted floral and beaded dec, amethyst rim and threading on stem 175.00
Cheese Dish, cov, 7-1/2" h, colorless, light blue opalescent threading on upper half of bell shaped dome, faceted knob...140.00
Claret Jug, 11-1/2" h, 3-1/2" d, chartreuse green, emb scrolled French pewter hinged top, handle, and pedestal foot...245.00
Creamer, 4-3/4" h, colorless with slight blue tint, threaded neck and lip, applied ribbed handle, Pittsburgh 170.00
Epergne, four purple lilies, white threading 375.00
Finger Bowl and Underplate, 2-3/4" h, 7" d, cranberry optic diamond quilted design, fine closely spaced cranberry threads 295.00
Goblet, 5-3/4" h, colorless, diamond molded bowl, Pomona blue reeding, applied Bristol yellow disk foot, stamped "Steuben," set of 3...225.00
Honey Pot, cov, 5-3/4" h, 6-1/2" w, satin finished crystal ground, pulled and twisted pattern of blue and white threads, twig finial on cov, twig-like metal frame 450.00
Lemonade Mug, 5-3/8" h, colorless ground, cranberry threading, Sandwich...125.00

Luncheon Plate, 8-1/2" d, colorless crystal ground, Pomona Green concentric threads applied to ext. rim, Steuben, set of 6...230.00
Mantel Lamp, 13" h, threaded art glass shade with gold, green, and white pulled feather dec, elaborate sculptured metal sphinx base mkd "759E W. B. Mfg. Co. Copyright".............1,150.00
Mayonnaise, underplate, cranberry ground, ground pontil scar...90.00
Mug, 4-3/4" h, colorless, second gather of glass with swirled ribs, applied handle, copper wheel engraved initials and wreath, threaded neck, attributed to New England Glass Co. 1,550.00
Perfume Bottle, 5-1/2" h, colorless ground, pink threading 175.00
Pitcher
  3-7/8" h, colorless, applied threading at neck, applied handle...145.00
  7" h, Lily Pad, aqua, threaded neck and lip, applied hollow handle...550.00
Rose Bowl, 6" h, 5" d, colorless ground, pink threading ... 60.00
Salt, 2-3/4" d, cranberry ground, opaque white threads, applied colorless petal feet 75.00
Tumbler, 3-1/8" h, opalescent ribbed ground, blue threads, Lutz type...30.00
Vase
  6-1/2" h, cone shaped, amber ground, colorless threading, three applied looped feet with strawberry pontils, English...125.00
  7-1/2" h, colorless, Reeded Diamond pattern, Pomona green applied threads, Steuben fleur-de-lis mark............225.00
  8" h, petal top, cranberry ground, white threading, sgd "Stevens and Williams"...150.00
  9-1/2" h, 4" w, deep amethyst body, random web threading, very dark irid purple, green, and gold highlights, Loetz type...175.00
  11-1/2" h, 5-3/4" w, 6" h stick neck, herringbone patterned satin, bridal white, bright pink int., allover clear threading, Victorian...750.00
  12" h, 4" w, red ground, green random threadings at top, flat flared rim, Loetz type...250.00

TIFFANY

History: Louis Comfort Tiffany (1849-1934) established a glass house in 1878 primarily to make stained glass windows.

L.C. Tiffany-Favrile

In 1890, in order to utilize surplus materials at the plant, Tiffany began to design and produce "small glass" such as iridescent glass lamp shades, vases, stemware, and tableware in the Art Nouveau manner. Commercial production began in 1896.

Tiffany developed a unique type of colored iridescent glass called Favrile, which differs from other art glass in that it was a composition of colored glass worked together while hot. The essential characteristic is that the ornamentation is found within the glass; Favrile was never further decorated. Different effects were achieved by varying the amount and position of colors.

Most Tiffany wares are signed with the name "L. C. Tiffany" or the initials "L.C.T." Some pieces also are marked " Favrile" along with a number. A variety of other marks can be found, e.g., "Tiffany Studios" and "Louis C. Tiffany Furnaces."

Pitcher, pink and yellow swirl, 6" h, $175.

Louis Tiffany and the artists in his studio also are well known for their fine work in other areas–bronzes, pottery, jewelry, silver, and enamels.

References: Victor Arwas, *Glass, Art Nouveau and Art Deco*, Rizzoli International Publications, 1977; Alastair Duncan, *Louis Comfort Tiffany*, Harry N. Abrams, 1992; Alastair Duncan and William J. Fieldstein, *Lamps of Tiffany Studios,* Harry N. Abrams, 1983, reprint 1992; Robert Koch, *Louis C. Tiffany, Rebel in Glass*, Crown Publishers, 1966; John A. Shuman III, *Collector's Encyclopedia of American Art Glass*, Collector Books, 1988, 1994 value update; Moise S. Steeg, *Tiffany Favrile Art Glass,* Schiffer, 1997; Kenneth Wilson, *American Glass 1760-1930: The Toledo Museum of Art,* Volume I, Volume II, Hudson Hills Press and The Toledo Museum of Art, 1994.

Museums: Bergstrom-Mahler Museum, Neenah, WI; Corning Glass Museum, Corning, NY; Historical Glass Museum, Redlands, CA; Chrysler Museum, Norfolk, VA; The Toledo Museum of Art, Toledo, OH; University of Connecticut, The William Benton Museum of Art, Storrs, CT.

Basket, 7" h, 8" w, Favrile, pastel green, deep opalescent white, Diamond Quilted pattern, applied vaseline-yellow colored base, bronze edge handle, enameled dec, bronze mountings inscribed "Louis C. Tiffany Furnaces," numbered 1,000.00
Bottle, 6-1/2" h, sq, orange translucent Favrile, metallic blue, purple and green swirled and pulled opaque bottom, sgd "L. C. T. T5224," small bubble burst hole on base........700.00
Bowl, Favrile
  4" d, 2-1/4" h, flared ten-scalloped rim dish, gold irid, base inscribed "L. C. Tiffany Favrile 1104 6619L" 490.00
  4" d, 2-1/2" h, irid gold, pulled rat tail design, purple and green highlights, sgd, pr 750.00
  5" d, 2-3/4" h, colorless fourteen-rib oval, ruffled top rim, body dec with amethyst-purple pulled feather motif, base inscribed "L. C. T. 1979" 575.00
  5" d, 3-1/2" h, flared rim, diamond quilted cobalt blue body, low conforming foot, folded edge, base inscribed "L. C. Tiffany Favrile" 1,150.00
  5-1/4" d, irid gold, ten swirling ribs, numbered "06902," pr 850.00
  6" d, 3-1/2" h, upright ruffled rim, rib mold blown gold irid body, four pulled feet, inscribed "L. C. T. 4115B," some chips to feet..460.00
  6" d, 4" h, double bulbed bowl-form, scalloped rim, four integrated peg feet, irid gold, base inscribed "L. C. Tiffany Favrile 8979B," tiny chip on one foot.....................690.00
  6-1/4" h, curved sapphire blue and opal, crackled irid, gold disk foot, base inscribed "L. C. Tiffany Favrile" 980.00
  6-1/2" d, 1-1/4" h, ribbed, irid peacock blue, sgd "L. C. T. Favrile, #X308" 450.00
  6-1/2" d, 2-1/8" h, colorless planter form, internally dec by bright green lily pad leaf and vine motif, base inscribed "L. C. Tiffany Favrile 811J" 575.00
  6-1/2" d, 3" h, flared half-round, folded rim, lustrous blue surface, base mkd " L. C. Tiffany Favrile 1690" 550.00
  6-3/4" d, 2-1/4" h, shallow, wide flared rim, gold and blue irid, clear with overall dimpled effect 400.00
  7-1/4" d, 4" h, flared rim, jardiniere form crystal body, internally dec by eight pulled green feather devices, button pontil inscribed "L. C. T. Favrile 387V" and labeled 520.00
  8" d, gold spotted opal dish, emerald green border rim, three

applied reeded shell feet, button pontil inscribed "L. C. Tiffany Favrile" 1,610.00
  8" d, 3" h, gold, multicolored highlights, twisted rim, sgd "Favrile," minor surface scratching 400.00
  10" d, 3-1/2" h, gold irid, multicolored irid, twisted wide rim, base sgd "LCT Favrile" 650.00
Calling Card Holder
  6" l, polished onyx oval fish fitted each end by ribbed gold Favrile handles, inscribed "Schlumberger/Made in France/Tiffany" 865.00
  7-3/4" d, fourteen rib circular form, ambergris with pastel opal coloration, stretched luster, polished pontil, early label "TG&D Co." on reverse 260.00
Candelabrum, 19" h, two ten-rib gold irid bell glass shades fitted to bronze holder with blown out green candlecups above lappet cushion base, sixteen matching glass jewels, base imp TG & D Co. logo, and "Tiffany Studios New York 22323" 2,875.00
Candleholders, pr
  4" h, flared stretched and flatted bobeche rims, pedestaled candlecups, base inscribed "L. F. Tiffany-Favrile 1927," one restored foot 575.00
  4" h, mushroom cap shape, bright irid pink-rose, opal disk stem, conforming foot, each inscribed "L. C. T. Favrile 1826" 1,035.00
Candlesticks, pr, 6" h, 303/4" w, green opalescent top, white opalescent stripped base, sgd "L.C.T. Favrile," 2,250.00
Centerpiece Bowl
  9" d, 5-1/4" h, double bulbed rim, jardiniere form honey amber bowl, ten emerald green lily pads at shoulder, orange-gold smooth irid surface, button pontil inscribed "L. C. Tiffany Inc., Favrile 1521-9735 M," 1" shallow scratch at side...1,610.00
  12-1/4" d, irid gold, green leaf dec, matching frog, each sgd "2039L L.C. Tiffany-Favrile" 1,300.00
  14" d, 9" h, broad shallow brilliant blue irid bowl, strong stretched silver-gold luster, inserted into gold artichoke pattern stem and platform base, imp "Tiffany Studios New York, 1043," bowl inscribed "LC Tiffany-Favrile" 1,380.00
Champagne, Favrile
  3-1/2" h, 4" w, gold, grape and leaf cutting, highly irid surface, blue highlights, sgd......................................350.00
  5" h, 4" d top, pale yellow with deep green yellow opalescent finish, highly irid, sgd "L. C. T. Favrile #1806" 350.00
Cologne Bottle, 7-1/2" h, gold King Tut pattern, ivory ground, purple and blue irid highlights, gold stopper, sgd.......... 950.00
Compote, Favrile
  4-3/4" d, 2" h, flared pattern, transparent bright pastel blue, opal white ext., pedestal foot 550.00
  5" d, ruffled, floriform, gold Favrile 725.00
  5" d, 2-1/4" h, flared opal striped green bowl, conforming pastel white striped foot, inscribed "L. C. Tiffany Favrile" 575.00
  5" d, 4-3/4" h, floriform, oval lustrous gold dish with wide five-ruffled rim, solid stem and blue luster disk foot, inscribed "L. C. Tiffany-Favrile 4780C" 1,035.00
  5-1/4" d, 3-1/4" h, deep pink highly irid ground, opalescent leaf design, sgd "LCT Favrile, #1700," retains part of orig label...750.00
  5-1/4" d, 4-1/4" h, ruffled floriform amber bowl, gold irid, cupped pedestal foot, inscribed "L. C. Tiffany Favrile 3472D"...575.00
  6" d, 2" h, irid gold, blue and purple highlights, mirror base, sgd "L. C. T. Favrile" 550.00
  6" d, 4-1/2" h, floriform, deep ruffled broad blossom rim, stretched bright blue irid, mirror bright blue disk foot inscribed "LC Tiffany Favrile 1529/1484K" 2,100.00

6" h, rib-molded and vertical leaf dec, amber dish, pastel green and opal coloration, stretched irid, transparent amber stem, disk foot, inscribed "LCT Favrile 1702" 1,035.00

8-1/4" d, 4-1/4" h, rolled rim, gold irid shallow bowl, engraved int. of leaf and vine dec, baluster stem, cupped ten-rib disk foot, base inscribed "L. C. T. Favrile," irid worn on edge 290.00

8-1/2 d, 4" h, gold irid, ribbed base, inscribed "L. C. Tiffany #1847" 950.00

10" d, 4-1/2" h, ten rib scalloped cobalt blue dish, conforming blue baluster stem and disk foot, int. with engraved leaf and vine dec, base inscribed "L. C. T. Favrile 1279" 2,760.00

10" d, 5-3/4" h, floriform, wide flat flared blossom rim, conical dish fitted into petals rising from broad disk foot, stretched blue irid, inscribed "L. C. Tiffany Favrile 1976" 2,530.00

10-1/4" d, 5" h, deep emerald green shading to white, diamond quilted pattern, orig metal base mkd "Tiffany Furnaces Favrile 499" 800.00

10-1/4" d, 5-3/4" h, flared flattened rim, amber bowl, bright gold stretched irid , baluster stem, cupped pedestal foot, inscribed "L C Tiffany Inc., Favrile," some inside wear scratches 690.00

14" d, 7" h, opaque white and green stripes radiating to outer lip, shaded pink opal int., sea green foot, sgd 2,350.00

Condiment Dish, 2-1/4" d, flared gypsy pot, four integrated feet, one blue, one green, inscribed "L.C.T" and numbered, pr 650.00

Cordial, 3-1/2" h, Favrile, waisted flared form, inscribed "L.C.T.," 6 pc set 1,400.00

Cordial Set, 9-1/2" h double bulb gourd shaped gold irid decanter with twelve applied trailing prunts, orig knobbed stopper, inscribed "LCT 29," six matching 2-1/4" h glasses mkd "LCT" 2,185.00

Finger Bowl and Underplate, Favrile, circular

4-1/4" d bowl, 6" d underplate, transparent ambergris bowl, matching plate with gold irid, each inscribed "L. C. T." on base 345.00

4-3/4" d bowl, 5-3/4" d underplate, everted rim, matching underplate, gold irid, inscribed "L.C.T.," 8 pc set 4,500.00

5-3/4" d bowl, 6-3/4" d underplate, eight ruffled rim, stretched irid gold surface, inscribed "LCT" 650.00

6" d, 2-3/4" h, irid gold, grape and vine cutting, irid coloration with blue highlights, sgd "Louis Tiffany Favrile" 550.00

6" d, 2-3/4" h, ruffled scalloped rim, deep bronze irid gold, sgd "L. C. T." 600.00

6-1/2" d, 3" h, irid gold, highlights, sgd "Louis C. Tiffany" 575.00

Fire Screen, 33" h, 41-1/2" w, sinuously carved bronze frame, four legs, fitted with six panels of mottled blue Favrile glass, stamped "Tiffany Studios New York 77254" 7,000.00

Flower Bowl

10" d, cobalt blue ground, golden green lily pads, lustrous stretched irid, integrated two-tier blue glass frog flower arranger, engraved "Louis C. Tiffany Inc. Favrile 1730N," small hidden inside rim chip 1,610.00

10-1/2" d, stretched gold irid luster on folded rim, five green lily pads centering integrated two-tier glass frog flower arranger, both inscribed "LC Tiffany Favrile" and numbered 1,850.00

Goblet

8" h, floriform, pastel aqua green, opal ribbed accents, conforming cupped pedestal foot, inscribed "L. C. T. Favrile," one with label, 10 pc set 3,335.00

8-1/2" h, trumpet bowl, slender stem, domed circular foot, pale irid lavender, opaque white stripes, sgd "L. C. Tiffany Favrile" 850.00

Ice Cream Bowl, 5" d, 3-1/4" h, irid gold, blue and green highlights, sgd "L. C. Tiffany Favrile," one base may have been ground, pr 500.00

Jar, cov, 4" h, gold amber Favrile cylinder, five pulled green feathers, silver rim, hinged cov and lift handle, monogrammed, mkd "Tiffany & Co. Sterling Silver 925-1000," glass base inscribed "L. C. Tiffany Favrile" 865.00

Lamp Shade

4-1/2" h, lily shape, eight-rib scalloped rim, irid gold... 1,150.00

5-1/4" h, 3-3/4" d collet rim, angular, six-sided amber body, orange-gold irid, inscribed "L. C. T." on top rim, pr...... 750.00

8" h, 2-1/4" d outside rim, opal gold and Favrile, faint diamond optic pattern, teardrop form, numbered "M925" 520.00

Letter Seal, 1-1/2" h, 1/2" w, gold, blue and purple highlights, scarab type, handle engraved with "W" on base..... 150.00

Loving Cup, 8" d, ambergris vasiform, three applied reeded handles, three green leaf forms among trailing vines, gold irid luster, inscribed "L. C. Tiffany Favrile 2024D," top rim out of round, light blemish inside rim 2,530.00

Miniature (Cabinet) Vase, Favrile

1-3/4" h, bulbous, green and gold irid, peaked dec, celadon shoulder, inscribed "L. C. Tiffany Favrile 718AH"...... 550.00

2-1/4" h, eight ribbed spherical amber body, four pulled dec, gold luster, lower side inscribed "LCT W8607"...... 815.00

2-1/2" h, double bulbed pot shape, bright golden orange, eight ribs, inscribed "L.C.T. K539"......................... 815.00

2-1/2" h, 1-3/4" h, highly irid gold surface, full signature... 300.00

2-1/2" h, 3" d, floriform, gold irid ruffled flower pot, four pulled feet, inscribed "L.C.T. W8686" 575.00

2-7/8" h, double gourd form, opal Favrile body, two pulled handles, base inscribed "LCT" 575.00

3" h, irid gold, two pulled handles, sgd "LCT #7072B" 500.00

3-1/8" h, oval body, pulled aperture handles at each side, brilliant irid blue, inscribed "L. C. Tiffany Favrile 1003-2398 M" on base 750.00

3-1/4" h, 2-1/2" w, highly irid black ground, purple highlights, sgd "L. C. Tiffany," numbered 450.00

3-1/4" h, 3-1/2" w, oyster white opalescent ground, irid finish, two pulled handles, sgd "LCT #8094A," orig Tiffany label 700.00

5" h, elongated eight-rib bottle form, golden orange irid, pulled side openings, base inscribed "L. C. T. Favrile 9E" 750.00

Perfume Bottle, 4-1/4" h, globular, short cylindrical neck, everted lip, ball shaped stopper, irid green trailing vine and ivy leaves dec, irid amber ground, shaded with pink, numbered, inscribed "L. C. Tiffany, Favrile," c1916 ...... 1,000.00

Pitcher, 8-1/2" h, waisted cylindrical amber body, tooled spout, applied handle, gold irid, inscribed "LC Tiffany Favrile," tiny annealing fracture at top handle, inside wear............... 550.00

Plate

8-3/4" d, bright pink rim, opal at reverse, ten dec wedge-shaped sections, inscribed "L. C. T. Favrile" 550.00

10-1/2" d, Favrile, pastel irid green, stretched edge, sgd "L. C. Tiffany" 600.00

Posy Vase, 3-1/8" h, Favrile, flared oval, opal, green, and gold, pulled leaf-feather dec, gold irid int., base inscribed "L. C. T. 7973" 865.00

Rose Bowl, 3-1/2" d, bright cobalt blue body, green centered black heart-shaped leaves and trailing vines, irid luster, base inscribed "LCT Tiffany Favrile 9806E" 2,876.00

Rose Water Sprinkler, 15-1/2" h, bulbous base, slender gooseneck, peaked rim, lemon yellow, inscribed "3016," paper label marked "L3016" 1,500.00

Salt

1-1/4" h, circular, rainbow irid, 12 pc set, 8 inscribed "L.C.T.," 4 inscribed "L.C.T. Favrile" 2,400.00

1-1/4" h, 2" d, ftd, gold Favrile, purple and blue highlights, sgd "L. C. T."..225.00

1-1/2" h, 2" d, ftd, wave dec, gold ground, purple highlights, sgd "L. C. T."..150.00

1-3/4" h, 2-1/4" d, ribbed and scalloped, gold, sgd "L. C. T. Favrile," some variation in color, 8 pc set 1,150.00

2" d, gold irid, eight swirled pulls, mkd "L. C. T."........240.00

2-1/4" d, gold irid, two pulled handles, mkd "L. C. T." 245.00

Smoke Bell, 4-1/2" h, 2-3/4" w, gold irid body, slightly ribbed, clear applied hanger 250.00

Tazza, Favrile

5-1/2" h, 10" w, peacock blue, stretched edge, dome foot with purple highlights, sgd "L. C. Tiffany Favrile" 2,250.00

6-1/2" h, 5-1/4" d, flower form, early opalescent glass, pulled feather design, sgd "L. C. Tiffany Favrile #364"......1,000.00

Tile, 6" x 6-1/4", mosaic, tasserae in foliate geometric design, shades of green, gold, orange, and white, gilt metal frame, four ball feet, partial Tiffany paper label 1,840.00

Tray, 6-1/2" d, raised scalloped rim, colorless plate dec with Nash-style green panels and amethyst rib-stripes, inscribed "L. C. T. 361"..290.00

Tumbler, 3" h, oval, gold irid, eight pulled swirl dec, inscribed "LCT" and numbered, 3 pc set 1,150.00

Vase

3" h, 3-1/2" w, irid gold, ten green heart-shaped leaves, sgd "L. C. Tiffany Favrile #4112" 900.00

3-1/2" h, paperweight-type, transparent emerald green globular body, internally dec with abstract metallic, black, green, and blue biomorphic inclusions, base inscribed around button pontil "Tiffany Favrile 88662" 2,875.00

3-1/2" h, 4-1/2" d, bulbous, ruffled rim, stretched edge, gold Favrile, four pulled feet, sgd "L. C. T. #7633A," chemical stained int. 350.00

3-3/4" h, double flared oval, gold diamond patterned medial border, base inscribed "L. C. Tiffany Favrile 3694E," int. water stain 750.00

4-1/4" h, 6" d, squat oval dark cobalt blue body, dark irid surface dec at shoulder with double pulled swirling green and gold luster irid design, base inscribed "L. C. T. H1814"...2,990.00

Vase, conical white opaque body, white streaks, flat circular pedestal, white opaque base with blue rim, flat top with yellow stretched effect, mkd "1546 L. C. Tiffany, Favrile," orig paper label, 5-1/2" h, 6" top d, $1,125.

4-3/8" h, 5" d, broad amber oval body, embedded with 40 white cane blossoms, green heart-shaped leaves on swirling vines, gold irid, base inscribed around button pontil "LCT 4386A" 4,025.00

4-1/2" h, gently ribbed spherical form, everted rim, opalescent gold and rose stripes, engraved "LCT I354," orig paper label 1,200.00

4-1/2" h, ten rib cobalt blue-purple bulbous oval body, ten dimples around shoulder area, ruffled raised rim, base inscribed "LC Tiffany Favrile 7540" 1,035.00

4-1/2" h, 4" w, gourd shape, Favrile, brilliant butterfly blue, irid, inscribed "L. C. Tiffany Favrile #6333G," int. chemical stain 800.00

4-3/4" h, raised rim, broad oval, emerald green body dec by five amber hooked and coiled organic swirls, lustrous gold irid, inscribed around prominent button pontil "LCT-W6639" 1,955.00

4-3/4" h, raised rim, oval green irid body, five silvery pulled feathers, strong purple luster at lower edge, mkd "LCT Tiffany Favrile 3195C" 1,610.00

4-3/4" h, 3-1/2" w, bulbous, brilliant gold Favrile finish, sgd, int. chemical deposits 400.00

5" h, flared amber Favrile glass oval body, 25 tiny white cane blossoms among emerald green leaf-forms, amber stems, fine golden irid luster, base inscribed around button pontil "LCT Tiffany Favrile 2889C"................1,955.00

5" h, quatraform blown-out transparent ambergris bottle form, hot applied metallic green irid chain network dec, inscribed "L. C. Tiffany Favrile 4852" 3,105.00

5-1/4" h, swirled candlestick type, ten ribbed flared amber body, flattened and flared integral bobeche rim, inscribed "LCT," some int. stain...............................550.00

5-1/2" h, flared ten rib mold oval form, indented dec ridges, base inscribed "L. C. Tiffany Favrile 7901B"..........990.00

5-1/2" h, ten ribbed oval body, corresponding dimples, subtle irid gold surface, base inscribed "LCT U993" 1,150.00

5-1/2" h, 6-1/2" d, floriform, broad flat blossom rim, stretch luster ribbed oval amber body, shaped disk platform foot, folded edge, base inscribed "LC Tiffany Favrile 8999 N 1546" 1,380.00

5-3/4" h, gently waisted oviform, rainbow irid, gold pulled feather dec, inscribed "L. C. T. H1737" 1,000.00

5-3/4" h, hipped oval, deep cobalt blue, fine irid luster, base inscribed "L. C. Tiffany Favrile 1024-8994L"..........990.00

6" h, rib molded oval amber body, pulled handles at each side, applied disk foot, inscribed "LCT," rough foot edge 460.00

6" h, 4-1/2" w, bottle green ground, red hooked and pulled feathering, slight irid surface, inscribed "X1284," int. chemical staining 1,000.00

6-1/4" h, elongated neck, golden sphere, extensive green heart-leaf dec, some with amethyst color spots, base inscribed "L. C. Tiffany Favrile 3531E"..................1,500.00

6-1/4" h, heavy conical oval, bulbous eighteen rib swirled design, cobalt blue cased to opalescent amber, shaded irid surface, button pontil inscribed "U 7071," edge inscribed "LCT" 1,380.00

6-3/4" h, gold and aubergine dec, dark amber irid oval ridged body, elaborate pulled and coiled feather and border motif dec, base inscribed "LCT D288" 2,185.00

7" h, flared raised rim, oval opal body, six pastel gold pulled leaves with delicate veining, base inscribed "L.C. Tiffany Favrile 9193B" 690.00

7" h, gray-green oval body, pulled and coiled border above vertical zigzag band below, base inscribed "LCT D1003"...2,530.00

7" h, 5-1/2" w, peacock eye dec, brilliant purple-green and blue irid ground, sgd "LCT," numbered L645.....2,400.00

7-1/4" h, 3-1/2" d, ribbed bottle form, Favrile, highly irid gold ground, purple and blue highlights, sgd "L. C. T. #W7609"...725.00

7-1/4" h, 4" d, Favrile, paperweight technique, glossy surface, deep brown pulled and hooked dec, irid int. 1,250.00

7-1/4" h, 4" d, gold bowl, cartouche on front of gold lily, set in three-ftd wooden base, mkd "Tiffany Studios New York," base may not be orig 1,100.00

8" h, handled, slender, flattened oval, eight ribbed body, integrated tooled handles, gold luster, inscribed "L. C. T. Favrile"...920.00

8" h, paperweight, bulbed oval amber body, int. gold luster, internally dec by vertical stripes, gold-amber dots in zipper pattern, inscribed "L. C. T. Favrile"...............1,495.00

8" h, raised folded rim, dark blue bulbous body, pulled and hooked irid swirls, inscribed "L. C. T. K1073" around prominent pontil button 4,900.00

8" h, slender reverse trumpet form, cobalt blue ground, five pulled leaf-feather elements, silver-gold irid luster, base inscribed "L. C. Tiffany Favrile 4640K".................1,850.00

8" d, tapered oval transparent green-amber early favrile body, dec at shoulder with double horizontal borders of brick red pulled ribbon design, base inscribed "7380" and "Tiffany Glass & Decorating Co." label 1,150.00

9" h, angular tapered rib-molded amber body, golden luster, base inscribed "L. C. Tiffany Inc., Favrile 1108-80 15M" 980.00

9" h, baluster, gold irid, green leaves and vines, carved trailing leaf and vine dec, inscribed "7661M Louis C. Tiffany Furnaces, Inc., Favrile," pr 7,750.00

9" h, floriform, ruffled opal rim on blossom, copper colored outline on mahogany brown stem and design, cupped pedestal with folded edge, inscribed "LCT M1940," 3/8" burst bubble on ext. blossom.............................1,840.00

9" h, ten ribbed oval body, bulbed stem, conforming ribbed pedestal foot with folded edge, irid gold, inscribed "L. C. Tiffany Favrile 3769K," some int. water stain.......1,100.00

9-1/4" h, 5-1/2" w, Favrile, reddish-brown ground, green pulled shoulder, sgd "L. C. Tiffany E1887 Favrile," orig Tiffany label 1,200.00

9-1/2" h, Morning Glory, elongated flared trumpet blossom, deep sapphire blue throat, opal ext., colorless disk foot inscribed "L. C. T. Favrile 1886"...........................1,265.00

10" h, elongated neck, double bulbed body, eight pulled brown-amber leaf-forms rising from base trailing to top rim, cased, golden irid accents, base inscribed "L. C. Tiffany Favrile 9590K" 1,840.00

10" h, folded raised rim, bulbous oval body, opal Favrile ground cased to green, five repeating pulled and hooked dec devices, base inscribed "L. C. Tiffany Favrile 4932E" 3,220.00

10" h, slender flared cylinder, five pointed leaf dec rising from green base shading to lustrous gold top, base inscribed "LC Tiffany Favrile 436"..........................1,380.00

10" h, 5" d, ovoid, interior ribs, mustard yellow opalescent body, slight irid finish, sgd "L. C. Tiffany" 800.00

10-1/8" h, gold irid zipper, ambergris oval body, shoulder chain borders, vertical zipper motif, pulled band at lower edge, integrated foot inscribed "LCT F819" 2,100.00

10-1/4" h, Cypriote, oviform, moss green textured surface, gold irid swirls above shoulder, inscribed "L. C. T. 1564" 10,500.00

10-1/4" h, floriform, ribbed amber glass blossom, stretched golden luster, bulbed stem, disk foot inscribed "L. C. T. Favrile 1268A" 2,530.00

10-1/4" h, twisted and peaked, translucent yellow, inscribed "L.C.T. B2058" 950.00

10-1/4" h, 2-1/4" w, Favrile, pale hooked feathers, oyster white ground, sgd "Louis C. Tiffany Favrile" 1,450.00

10-1/2" h, floriform, gold irid, stretched edge, orig Tiffany label, sgd "LCT #4008B".....................................2,650.00

10-1/2" h, trumpet, flared ten-rib floriform, knopped stem, conforming cupped pedestal foot, irid blue, inscribed "L. C. Tiffany Favrile X154," base aggressively ground to stand straight..1,955.00

10-1/2" h, 5" d, candlestick form, pale green, hollow blown int...450.00

11" h, tall baluster, splint spiral design, two-tone irid, bright gold above shading to deep purple-blue, base inscribed "L. C. Tiffany Favrile 269K"....................................1,500.00

11-1/2" d, floriform, domed circular foot with green pulled feather motif, knopped slender standard, double gourd cream bowl with green pulled feather motif, engraved "L. C. Tiffany Favrile V352" 3,200.00

12" h, Cyrpiote, broad bulbous oval, irid ambergris dec by alternating wide and narrow vertical stripes of metallic Cypriote texture with gold netted bands, Douglas A. Nash manner, applied pedestal disk foot inscribed "L. C. Tiffany-Favrile N4193" 4,600.00

12" h, floriform, opal glass triangular rim, figurative bulbed blossom body, organic leaf and stem dec, irid copper-orange cupped pedestal foot with green pulled leaf dec, inscribed "L. C. Tiffany Favrile 5504D," int. water stain, impurities in foot 1,100.00

12" h, slender reverse trumpet, amber ground, five emerald green leaf elements around base, irid gold surface, inscribed "L. C. Tiffany Favrile 7056J," int. stain......1,150.00

12-1/2" d, flared trumpet, opal white, five green and gold pulled feathers, lustrous gold irid int., base inscribed "LCT Favrile," inserted into artichoke-form etched bronze pedestal base, stamped "Tiffany Studios New York 1043," worn bronze patina 2,530.00

12-1/2" d, floriform, rib-molded spherical blossom, opal white and rosy irid gold, five green petal forms rising from transparent striated gold stem, conforming ribbed and cupped god an opal pedestal foot, base inscribed "LCT 1622B" 8,625.00

15" h, onion form, opaque white ground, green pulled striations, gold int., inscribed "L. C. T. Favrile" 1,300.00

15" h, paperweight, elongated amber-aquamarine baluster body, internally dec with three repeating clusters of ethereal blossoms centering long slender leaves, warm sienna orange-red irid int., base inscribed "LC Tiffany Favrile 8972D" 6,900.00

15" h, pinched cylinder, circular bun foot, erected rim, irid gold, inscribed "L.C.T. 509A".............................2,250.00

15-1/2" h, outwardly tapering form, slightly scalloped rim, ribbed gold opalescent glass, flattened circular base, hand etched "546 L. C. TIFFANY FAVRILE" 2,000.00

16" h, flared elongated ovoid, colorless glass internally dec with ten paperwhite narcissus blossoms, red and yellow millefiori cane centers, perched on naturalized brown stems, green spike leaves extending from swelled base, inscribed "L. C. Tiffany Favrile 2731G" 17,250.00

16" h, irid floriform trumpet, rolled rim, inserted into doré bronze holder, green enamel highlights, base imp "Louis C. Tiffany Furnaces, Inc. 153," glass insert chipped off at end 690.00

16-1/2" h, trumpet form, deep peacock blue, twelve vertical ribs, knob stem base, mirror finish under foot, inscribed "L. C. Tiffany Inc., Favrile #1528 972N" 2,500.00

18-1/4" h, floriform, opal glass triangular rim, figurative bulbed blossom body, green striated leaf and stem dec, copper-orange irid cupped pedestal foot with repeating leaf dec, inscribed "L.C.T. O 2018," some int. water stain 2,530.00

18-1/2" h, elongated cobalt blue cylinder, angular six-sided tooled rim, purple luster irid, inscribed on base "LCT Favrile," inserted into gold doré artichoke pattern stem, monogrammed platform base imp "Tiffany Studios New York, 1043" 1,380.00

18-1/2" h, floriform, bulbous cream irid section, gold pulled feather motif, conforming dec foot, inscribed "L. C. T. F11," circular paper label.....................................7,000.00

Whiskey Taster, 1-3/4" h, 1-1/2" w, brilliant irid gold, purple highlights, sgd...200.00

Wine

3-3/4" h, 3-3/4" w, Favrile, highly irid gold surface, cut and notched base, stem, and bowl, sgd, 4 pc set.....1,150.00

4" h, ambergris, opalescent green rim, int. enhancements, transparent amber stem, disk foot, inscribed "LCT Favrile," set of 4...980.00

5-1/2" h, clear ext., irid blue int..................................200.00

6" h, 2-3/4" w, sapphire blue, opalescent and irid surface...375.00

Lamps

Candle

11-1/2" h, butterfly blue, 3 part, sgd "L. C. Tiffany," chip on outer rim of shade......................................1,850.00

13-1/2" h, gold irid ruffled shade engraved "L. C. T.," splint bamboo bronze base with rich brown patina, base stamped "Tiffany Studios" 1,800.00

14-1/2" h, Favrile, gold irid base, green and white dec glass column, highly irid gold honeycomb design shade...1,600.00

16-1/2" h, three part Electrolier, swirled rib gold irid holder fitted with gilt metal and favrile glass candle supporting gold irid ruffled shade with green pulled and coiled dec, inscribed "L. C. T" twice, base mkd.......1,610.00

Ceiling

7-1/4" h, 14-1/2" d, domed shaded leaded with brilliant green glass segments, foliate motif centering around turtleback at apex, hinged to elaborate double beaded bronze ceiling mouth, wide border of 18 matching green rect turtleback tiles, orig dark patina ...9.775.00

16" h, 14" d, scalloped beaded rim, fiery golden green translucent leaded Favrile glass shade, curving segments in intricate arrangement ending in hinged trap door framing opalescent glass turtleback, orig hooks on rim attached to bronze beaded chain, single socket ceiling mouth 6,100.00

Chandelier, 54" l, 30" d conical shade, striated amber glass segments in brickwork design, 5" drop apron with center Arts and Crafts decorative circle and bar medial border motif, rim imp "Tiffany Studios New York," supported by six bronze chains suspended from conforming ceiling mount, six-light socket wheel at center 14,950.00

Desk

12-1/2" h, 14" w, 4-1/2" h x 7-1/8" w shade, Damascene shade, green, gold and lavender with spiral swirl pattern, matte white casing, counter balance base in dark patina..6,500.00

13-1/2" h, 7" d Damescene shade, swirled dec cased irid gold ribbed dome shade, mkd "LCT" on rim, swivel socket, etched gold harp desk-type frame, ribbed

cushion platform, ball feet, imp "Tiffany Studios New York 419," one ball missing 4,025.00

14-1/2" h, gold, green, and opal conical 6" d shade, rim inscribed "LCT," four-arm spider support, dark bronze platform base fitted with 16 green glass jewels, base imp "Tiffany Studios New York 255" 3,750.00

17" h, 12" d leaded shade, green and white segments, green-amber acorn shaped lead and vine border, "Tiffany Studios New York" tag at edge, base stamped "Tiffany Studios New York 608," replaced socket, some cracks to glass segments.....................4,600.00

18" h, domed irid shade, three arm bamboo base, brown/green patina, orig finial, shade inscribed "L. C. T. Favrile," base stamped "Tiffany Studios New York" 3,750.00

Floor

54-1/2" h, 9-3/4" d shade, tripod base cast with Aladdin's lamp, suspending adjustable Damascene shade, engraved "L.C.T.," base stamped "Tiffany Studios New York 576" 8,000.00

77" h, 25" d bronze and leaded glass curtain border domed shade, amber white diachronic and mottled favrile glass segments geometrically arranged above arched apron border of rippled gold-amber vertical columnar rectangles, rim impressed "Tiffany Studios, New York," six-socket senior gilt bronze base, coiled dec on fluted cushion platform base, imp "Tiffany Studios New York 376," gold patina worn, one socket out 44,850.00

Hanging

14-1/2" l, creased tapered form milk opalescent ground shade, red pulled feather motif, inscribed "04414," suspended on three chains with bronze mount 3,000.00

20-1/2" d, leaded yellow and opal white rippled glass domed shade, band of green acorn-shaped leaf and vine motif, beaded rim, four integrated hanging hooks, unsigned, central medallion replaced by pierced heart cap...,325.00

Lantern, 10" h, 7" w, hanging globe flares to 8-sided base rim, marigold irid stretch glass shade with random irregular blue and purple threading at top, remaining marigold irid with white calcite lining, sgd "LCT Favrile," hanger and wire replaced 2,000.00

Piano, 11-1/2" h, 9-1/2" d irid gold Damascene shade, ten prominent ribs in amber Favrile glass shade, offset fixed curving shaft, lappet cushion base imp "Tiffany Studios New York 25165" and imp "TG & D Co." mark 4,600.00

Student

21" h, 7" d opal cased green Damascene irid Favrile glass shade, inscribed "LCTif-," telescoping single burner lamp, spiral beading and smoked diamond design on urn-form font, fine patina, imp "22327," orig vented chimney 9,200.00

23" h, 30" l, double student, mottled green geometric leaded glass shades flanking reticulated Moorish globe resting within arch supported by chain of openwork design, circular base with gallery, shade stamped "Tiffany Studios New York 1658" 20,000.00

29" h, 10" d, double, dark patina on wire twist dec central font between double post bronze frame, adjustable arm mechanism, beaded spiral on twin burners mounted with translucent green leaded dome Favrile shades 10,925.00

Table

10-1/2" h, 6" w shade, shade and base irid gold Favrile, applied double band of white and green dec on both base and shade, sgd "L. C. Tiffany" 2,550.00

Lamp, table, domed Peony shade, large mauve, fuchsia, purple, and white flowers, green leaves, emerald green ground, imp "Tiffany Studios, New York 1475" on rim, molded bronze base imp "Tiffany Studios, New York 9514," 26" h, 18" d shade, $34,100. Photo courtesy of James D. Julia, Inc.

17" h, 10" d domed leaded dogwood shade, mottled rose and pink blossoms, variegated green leafage, blue sky interspersed with traces of confetti and rippled glass, stamped "Tiffany Studios New York," octagonal bronze base cast with reticulated ivy leaves, twisted vine standard, stamped "Tiffany Studios New York 697" 15,000.00

18-1/2" h, 14" d acorn shade, shades of green, orig patina, both shade and base mkd, numerous cracked pcs in shade 4,950.00

20" h

14" d hemispherical leaded shade, mottled amber glass, amber "jewels," six dragonflies in mottled blue, red, blue, and green confetti glass and delicate bronze overlay, stamped "Tiffany Studios New York, NY 1585," gilt bronze base case with three dragonflies against golden orange favrile glass mosaic background, stamped "Tiffany Studios New York 356" 75,000.00

16" d domed leaded Spreading Daffodil shade, yellow, green, amber, and opal white glass segments, blossoms on spiked stems, rippled glass double border, rim inscribed "Tiffany Studio New York 1488," mounted on oval urn form slender bronze base, imp with "T. G. & D. Co." logo and number......21,850.00

21" h, 14" d conical leaded Arrowroot shade, twelve repeating green leaf root elements interspersed with yellow centered white blossoms, blue striated and ripple glass ground, tag imp "Tiffany Studios New York," elaborate three-arm fluid lamp urn bronze base, four paw feet, platform base, font and foot imp and numbered ... 18,400.00

22" h, 16" d domed leaded shade

Clusters of pendent bellflowers, striated red flowers, mottled green ground, stamped "Tiffany Studios New York," canister base with red and green patina, four slender legs, flattened circular base, stamped "Tiffany Studios New York 185" 10,000.00

Repeating clusters of multicolored purple, blue, opalescent, and striated pastel pansy blossoms, three supporting arms, dark bronze three-socket ribbed cushion base on five ball feet, imp "Tiffany Studios New York 3602," several segments of shade damaged in one area....................................23,000.00

22-1/2" h, 16" d leaded shade, green and gold Favrile geometric segments above wide belt of red, pink, and

green striated wild rose blossoms and leaves, imp "Tiffany studios New York 1997," three-socket base with flared shaft and pedestal foot imp "Tiffany Studios New York" 33,350.00

23" h

16" d domed leaded shade, multicolored upright tulip blossoms and buds, rare Favrile fractured transparent glass ground, rim imp "Tiffany Studios N.Y. 1456-11," urn form bronze base with twelve green favrile turtleback tiles below pierced rim for heat dispersal of int. lighting device, base also imp and numbered "9535".....................................34,500.00

18" d domed leaded dogwood shade, white blossoms against blue ground, pink dogwoods against aqua ground, confetti, bright granite, striated and fractured glass segments, four-socket doré bronze library base with swirled wire dec shaft, five curved feet 44,850.00

20" d conical leaded daffodil shade, mottle yellow daffodil blossoms, green stems and leaves, blue ground, stamped "Tiffany Studios New York 1497," gilt bronze stick base with alligator finish, stamped "Tiffany Studios New York 1497" 20,000.00

24-1/2" h, 20" d broad conical leaded shade, five clusters of yellow daffodil blossoms, sky-blue ground between green spiked leaves, three-socket base with dec wire wrapped bronze lamp shaft on four ftd foliage cushion base, shade rim and base imp "Tiffany Studios New York," shade 1497, base 360 ....26,450.00

25" h

19" d domed shade, mottled green tiles, stamped "Tiffany Studios New York 0546," base stamped "Tiffany Studios New York 994" 14,000.00

18" d waisted dome shade, striated and mottled rose, violet, and red peonies with yellow centers, striated green and red leafage with confetti glass, rippled teal glass border, rich green/red patina, stamped "Tiffany Studios New York 1475-54," organic bronze base with rich brown/red patina, stamped "Tiffany Studios New York 394," orig finial..............45,000.00

26" h, 20" d conical leaded poppies shade, mottled tangerine, yellow, and red blossoms, centers overlaid with bronze openwork, emerald green leaves with interior overlaid bronze openwork, mottled green ground, tag stamped "Tiffany Studios New York 1531-12," trumpet form base cast with stylized pods, stamped "Tiffany Studios/New York 868"....................33,000.00

27" h, 20" d linen fold shade, sixteen sided Favrile fabrique golden amber glass #1952 model shade, dark gold doré finish on leading and cap arrangement, matching gold doré four socket paneled lamp base, shade and base imp "Tiffany Studios New York" and numbered 10,925.00

27-3/4" h, 21" d broad domed Laburnum shade, Favrile glass segments leaded as yellow cluster pendant blossoms, brown branches, green leaves, sky-blue background, two tags "Tiffany Studios," and "New York 1539," reticulated bronze doré six-socket adjustable base imp "Tiffany Studios/New York 397," lead work conserved 129,000.00

31" h, 22" d domed leaded nasturtium shade, mottled and striated red, yellow, pink, and orange nasturtium blossoms, mottled yellow and enameled green leaves, rim and border with striated sky blue glass, stamped "Tiffany Studios New York 1506," bronze base cast as spreading roots, red/brown patina, stamped "Tiffany Studios 393" 49,000.00

33" h, 24" d shade, shade comprised of five separate domed shades, each emerald green with gold wave pattern, each inscribed "L.C.T.," orig finials, each hung with clear and frosted turtleback type tiled prisms, brown bronze base cast with pods, raised on five curved feet, stamped "Tiffany Studios New York" 49,000.00

Wall/Desk, 11-1/2" h, 7" d irid deep green cased to white opal shade engraved with four clusters of broad cannabis leaves, inscribed "LC Tiffany 8063G" at top rim, mounted on swing swivel bell harp with dark patina bronze base, imp "Tiffany Studios New York 418"....................5,750.00

Wall Sconce, 14" h, 10" w, white opalescent Favrile glass tiles set in sq bronze links forming chain-mail curtain, suspended by demilune bronze frame with wire scrollwork, two-arm wall mounted fixture, pr 17,000.00

TIFFIN GLASS

c1960

History: A. J. Beatty & Sons built a glass manufacturing plant in Tiffin, Ohio, in 1888. On Jan. 1, 1892, the firm joined the U. S. Glass Co. and was known as factory "R." Quality and production at this factory were very high and resulted in fine Depression era glass.

Beginning in 1916, wares were marked with a paper label. From 1923 to 1936, Tiffin produced a line of black glassware called Black Satin. The company discontinued operation in 1980.

References: Fred Bickenheuser, *Tiffin Glassmasters*, Book I (1979); *Tiffin Glassmasters, Book II*, Glassmasters Publications, 1981; Fred W. Bickenheuser, *Tiffin Glassmasters, Book III*, Glassmasters Publications, 1985; Jerry Gallagher and Leslie Piña, *Tiffin Glass*, Schiffer, 1996; Kelly O'Kane, *Tiffin Glassmasters, The Modern Years*, published by author, 1998 (P.O. Box 16303, St. Paul, MN 55116-0303, tiffin@pobox.com); Bob Page and Dale Fredericksen, *Tiffin is Forever: A Stemware Identification Guide*, Page-Fredericksen, 1994.

Collectors' Club: Tiffin Glass Collectors Club, P.O. Box 554, Tiffin, OH 44883.

Note: Prices are for crystal (colorless) unless otherwise noted.

Almond, Flanders, pink, ftd..150.00
Animal Dish, cov, duck, brown 65.00
Ashtray
    Canterbury, #115, 3-1/2 x 4-1/2", desert red.................22.00
    Dog, pink...75.00
    Cloverleaf, 3", #9123-96, twilight..............................25.00
    Cloverleaf, 5", #9123-97, twilight..............................45.00
Basket
    Copen, #6533, blue and crystal, 13".........................165.00
    Emerald Green, #15151, satin, 7" 55.00
    Satin, #9574, sky blue, 6" 45.00
    Twilite, 9" h, 5-1/2" w..295.00
Bell
    Cerise...75.00
    Cherokee Rose...65.00
    June Night, #9743, bead handle...............................48.00
    June Night, #9743, cut dec......................................45.00

Bon Bon, Fuchsia, 6-1/2" d, 3 ftd 60.00
Bowl
    Cadena, 6" d, handle, yellow 22.00
    Canterbury, twilite, 9" d, crimped..............................95.00
    Flanders, pink...50.00
    Fuchsia, #5902, 3-part, 6-3/4" d..............................28.00
    Killarney, 9-1/4" d, ftd, #17430, green......................75.00
    Swedish Optic, #510, Copen blue, large sand carved flower...145.00
    Swedish Optic, #525, 4-1/2" d, 3 ftd 45.00
    Swedish Optic, #17430, 3-1/4" h, 6-1/2" d, Da Vinci foot, wisteria..75.00
    Swedish Optic, #17430, 5" h, 8" l, Da Vinci foot, twilite... 165.00
Bud Vase
    Cherokee Rose, 6" h..30.00
    Cherokee Rose, 8" h..45.00
    Cherokee Rose, 10-1/2" h.......................................65.00
    Fuchsia, 10" h..45.00
    Isabella, 10" h..195.00
    June Night, 8" h..40.00
    June Night, 10-1/2" h...60.00
    Swedish Modern, #85, 5" h, twilite.........................145.00
Café Parfait, Classic, #185..70.00
Cake Plate
    Jack Frost, canary yellow, handle, 9-1/2" d 65.00
    Fuchsia, 10-1/2" d...50.00
Candelabrum, #5831, crystal, pr 38.00
Candlesticks, pr
    Black Satin, #81..65.00
    Black Satin, #15328, 8" h...50.00
    Blue Satin, #10...28.00
    Cerise, 2-lite..75.00
    Cherokee Rose, #5902, 2-lite.................................165.00
    Fuchsia, #5902, 2-lite..125.00
    Green Satin, #66, enameled and painted dec............75.00
    June Night...125.00
    Juno, #348, green...35.00
    Killarney, #17394, 4-1/8" h, green............................65.00
    Medford, squatty..30.00
    Williamsburg, #5902, 2-lite......................................75.00
Candy Dish, cov
    Flanders, pink...590.00
    Oneida..50.00
Candy Jar, cov
    Emerald Green, satin, 10" h 65.00
    Jack Frost, cone shape, green...................................55.00
Celery Tray
    Cherokee Rose, 10-1/2" l...35.00
    Fuchsia, 10" l...135.00
    June Night, #5902, 10-1/2" l.....................................58.00
Centerpiece
    Flanders, #5813, 13" d, rolled edge, mandarin yellow200.00
    Fontaine, #15033, green, slight use..........................85.00
    Rambling Rose, #5902, etched, 12" d.........................55.00
    Swedish Optic, #17430, twilite, 11" d........................225.00
Champagne
    Athens Diana...25.00
    Barber, #14196, blue...28.00
    Byzantine..18.00
    Cadena, yellow...30.00
    Cerise, #17392..18.00
    Cherokee Rose, #17403...20.00
    Classic...25.00
    Consul, #17679...18.00
    Flanders, crystal...14.75
    Flanders, pink, 6-1/4" h..40.00

Ad. Tiffinware, showing Flanders and Priscilla patterns. Good Housekeeping, December 1927.

Fontaine, #15033, pink	35.00
Fontaine, #15033, twilite, clear stem	45.00
Fuchsia, #15803	14.00
June Beau	14.00
June Night, #17403	32.50
King's Crown, blue	10.00
Kingsley cutting, #17392	25.00
Lovelace, #17358	18.00
Optic, twilight	48.00
Persian Pheasant, #17358	25.00
Princess, #13643, etched	10.00
Tea Rose, #17453	22.50
Thistle, #14197, 4-7/8" h	22.00
Touraine, #17328, 6" h	24.00
Wisteria, #17477, 4-1/2" h, 5 oz	30.00

Cheese and Cracker, Flanders, yellow 75.00

Claret
Cherokee Rose, #17399, 6" h, 4 oz	40.00
Fuchsia, #15083	20.00
June Night, #17403	35.00
Panel Optic, 2-1/2 oz, twilight	2.00

Persian Pheasant, #17358, 4-1/2 oz	40.00
Roses, c1931	20.00
Wisteria, #17477	25.00

Cocktail
Athens Diana	18.00
Byzantine	14.00
Cerice, #15071	18.50
Cherokee Rose, #17399	16.00
Cherokee Rose, #17403	20.00
Classic, #14185, 4-7/8" h, 3 oz	32.00
Flanders	22.00
Fuchsia, #15083, 4-1/4" h	22.00
June Night, #17403, 3-1/2 oz	28.00
La Fleure, 4-3/4" h, 3-1/2 oz, mandarin and crystal	24.00
Persian Pheasant, #15083	22.50
Touraine, #17328, 5-3/8" h	15.00

Compote
Black Satin, 10" d, 5-3/4" h, twisted stem, two colorful hand painted cockatoos, sprays of green leaves, white enamel dots	165.00
Blue Satin, #15319, 10" h	50.00
Canterbury, twilite, low ftd	135.00
Cherokee Rose, ball stem	115.00
Crystal Satin, #319, 7-1/2" h, 7-1/2" w, reverse painted enameled parrot dec	135.00
Emerald Green, satin, 4-3/4"	35.00
Flanders, #5831, 4-3/4" d, mandarin yellow	65.00
King's Crown, ruby stained	25.00
Persian Pheasant, blown, 6"	85.00
Swedish Optic, #17350, 4-1/2" h, 7" d, carved roses dec	60.00

Console Bowl
Cadena, 12" d, yellow	25.00
Cerise	65.00
Flanders, pink	110.00

Console Set
8" d green opalescent sculpted form bowl, two matching candle bowls	115.00
#15319, amberina, shading from orange to yellow, 9-1/4" h x 10-1/4" d compote, 10-1/4" h pr candleholders	295.00

Cordial
Byzantine	32.50
Cadena, topaz	80.00
Cherokee Rose, #17399, 1 oz, prism stem	55.00
Cerise	70.00
Etch #601, #2000, 3-5/8" h	35.00
Flanders, crystal	150.00
Flanders, pink	150.00
Fontaine, #15033, green, crystal	35.00
Fuchsia, #15083	45.00
June Night, #17357	45.00
June Night, #17392	45.00
June Night, #17403	45.00
Persian Pheasant, #17358, ribbed stem	42.00
Queen Astrid, crystal	35.00
Rubicon, #17621, 4-1/4" h, 1-1/2 oz, platinum rim	22.00
Tiffin Rose, #17680, 5" h	25.00
Westchester Gold, #17679	95.00

Cornucopia
#6041 Swirl, Copen blue, long tail	165.00
#6041 Swirl, Copen blue, short tail	165.00
#6041 Swirl, twilite, short tail	300.00
#6607 Straight, twilite	145.00

Cream Soup
Cadena, pink	30.00

Flanders, pink..45.00
La Fleure, yellow 40.00

Creamer
Cadena, yellow..35.00
Cerise 20.00
June Night 20.00
Juno, yellow..35.00

Creamer and Sugar
Cherokee Rose, beaded..................................60.00
English Hobnail, white milk glass....................15.00
Flanders, crystal, 3" h, individual size, ftd..................145.00
Flanders, pink..350.00
Flanders, yellow 225.00
King's Crown, ruby stained 65.00

Cruet, orig stopper, English Hobnail, white milk glass,
3-1/2" h..16.00

Cup and Saucer
Athens Diana..22.00
English Hobnail, white milk glass......................7.00
Flanders, yellow 100.00
Fontaine, twilite, blown..................................125.00
King's Crown, ruby stained 17.50
La Fleure, yellow 50.00

Dahlia Vase, Black Satin, 8" h, gold dec..............125.00

Decanter, orig stopper
Flanders, pink..750.00
Flanders, yellow 225.00

Dessert/Champagne, Chalet 40.00

Favor Basket, #310, light blue, 3-1/2" h, plain handle.......20.00

Finger Bowl
Flanders 40.00
Fontaine, 4-7/8" d, ftd, twilite 65.00

King's Crown, cranberry stained 17.50

Finger Bowl and Underplate, Minton, crystal, gold border, 4-3/4" d
bowl, 6-3/4" d underplate 175.00

Flower Arranger
7-1/2" d, Empress, #6552, plum....................185.00
8-1/2" d, Canterbury, desert red 45.00

Flower Basket, Copen, #6553, blue and crystal, 13" 165.00

Fruit Bowl, Open Work, line #310, sky blue, 12" d............75.00

Garden Set, Candlelight, #9153-110, crystal and black, late
green shield crest label................................110.00

Goblet
Byzantine, black..45.00
Byzantine, yellow..28.00
Cadena, pink..35.00
Cadena, yellow..35.00
Cerise 22.00
Chalet 50.00
Cherokee Rose, #17399..................................35.00
Cherokee Rose, #17403..................................35.00
Draped Nude, satin stem................................150.00
English Hobnail, white milk glass, 6" 10.00
Festival, #17640..24.00
Flanders, 8-1/4" h, pink 55.00
Fontaine, #033, twilite..................................65.00
Fontaine, #15033, pink..................................40.00
Fuchsia, #15083, 6-1/4" h..............................25.00
Fuchsia, #15083, 7-1/2" h..............................27.00
June Night, #17403, 9 oz................................32.00
Killarney, #17394..25.00
Kingsley cutting, #17392................................35.00
King's Crown, cranberry stained......................8.00
King's Crown, ruby stained 15.00
Line #011, crystal, green stem, wheel cut 38.00
Palais Versailles, #17594, 6-7/8" h, 11oz..........115.00

Panel Optic, #15066, mandarin yellow, 7" h................20.00
Persian Pheasant, #17358, ribbed stem..............30.00
Princess, #13643, etched................................16.00
Psyche, #15106, crystal, green stem..................45.00
Shamrock, dark green....................................22.00
Tea Rose, #17453, 7-3/8" h............................28.50
Thistle, #14197, 6-1/4" h................................20.00
Touraine, #17328, 8" h..................................25.00
Twilite, #17492..35.00
Wisteria, #17477..40.00

Hat, Black Satin, 4" 245.00

Iced Tea Tumbler, 12 oz, ftd
Cadena, yellow..40.00
Cherokee Rose, #17403..................................35.00
Classic..40.00
Flanders, pink..75.00
Flying Nun, , green, crystal............................60.00
Fontaine, #15033, green, crystal......................33.00
Killarney, #17394, green................................32.00
June Night 32.00
King's Crown, cranberry stained......................16.00
King's Crown, ruby stained, 5-3/8" h................22.00
Spiral Optic, crystal bowl, green foot, 4 pc set........95.00
Tea Rose, #17453..28.50
Wisteria, #17477..35.00

Jug
Athens Diana, #128..260.00
Classic, cov..425.00
Swedish Optic, #5935......................................75.00

Juice Tumbler, ftd
Byzantine..16.00
Cerise, #071, crystal 20.00
Cherokee Rose, 5 oz, ftd................................20.00
Classic, 3-1/2" h..35.00
Flanders, mandarin and crystal, 3-3/4" h, 5 oz 25.00
June Night 25.00
King's Crown, ruby stained, 4 oz......................10.00
Wisteria, #17477, 5-1/2" h, 5 oz......................45.00

Lamp
Killarney, gold criss-cross dec, marble base 150.00
Owl 500.00

Lemonade Set, Swedish Optic, #5959 jug, eight hi-balls....200.00

Lily Plate, Cherokee Rose, 13-1/4" d......................70.00

Martini Jug, Twilite, 11-1/2" 450.00

Mayonnaise Set, 3 pc
Cadena, yellow..30.00
Cerise 35.00
Cherokee Rose..45.00
Flanders, yellow 60.00
Old Gold Bright, #310....................................45.00

Night Light, candle holder with finger hold, green satin,
#319..55.00

Nut Bowl, June Night, 6" d..................................45.00

Oyster Cocktail
Athens Diana..18.00
Cerise 18.00
Flanders 15.00
Persian Pheasant, etched................................20.00

Paperweight, figural
Apple, controlled bubbles................................135.00
Elephant, 6" h, 4" w, controlled bubbles, standing, trumpet-
ing trunk, twilite......................................425.00
Pumpkin, yellow, controlled bubbles 125.00
Strawberry, small, desert rose, controlled bubbles......95.00

Parfait
Byzantine, yellow..32.00

Flanders, yellow 60.00
Fuchsia, #15083 ....60.00
Pickle Dish, Fuchsia, 7-3/8" l 45.00
Pitcher
    Cherokee Rose, ftd 700.00
    Flanders, crystal, cov 500.00
    Flanders, pink 475.00
    Flying Nun, cov, crystal, green base 450.00
    Threaded Optic, cornflower blue, 4-3/4" h, 32 oz pitcher
        crystal handle, four 2-5/8" 4 oz tumblers 95.00
Plate
    Byzantine, 8-1/2" d 7.50
    Cadena, yellow, dinner 45.00
    Cerise, 8" d 15.00
    Classic, 10-1/2" d, crystal 125.00
    Flanders, 6" d, pink 22.50
    Flanders, 7" d, crystal 9.00
    Flanders, 8" d, mandarin yellow 24.00
    Flanders, 8" d, pink 45.00
    Flanders, 9-1/2" d, crystal 195.00
    Flanders, 9-1/2" d, mandarin yellow 60.00
    Fontaine, #8833, 8" d, twilight 30.00
    Fuchsia, #8833, 8-1/8" d 22.00
    June Night, 6" d 16.50
    June Night, 8" d 18.00
    Juno, yellow, 9-1/2" d 40.00
    La Fleure, yellow, 7-1/2" d 15.00
    Mefford, #8836, 10" d, satin finish, gold trim 55.00
    Minton, 8-1/4" d, crystal, gold border 12.50
    Persian Pheasant, 8" d, green 14.00
    Persian Pheasant, 8" d, pink 22.00
    Psyche, 8" d, green 20.00
    Rain, Rain, pink 45.00
    Twilite, luncheon 25.00
    Wisteria, #17477, 8" d 25.00
Puff Bowl, English Hobnail, white milk glass 16.00
Puff Box, cov
    Chipperfield, green 50.00
    Dancing Girl, sky blue satin, 6" d 285.00
Punch Bowl Set, Cascade, punch bowl and 8 cups 200.00
Relish
    Cherokee Rose, 6-1/2" d, round, 3 part 47.50
    Cherokee Rose, 12" d 80.00
    June Night, 12", 3 part 80.00
    Rambler Rose, 3-part, 11" l 45.00
Rose Bowl, Swedish Optic, #17430, 5" h, 8" d, gold crest

Ad. Showing Rosiland etching. Crockery and Glass Journal, September 1931.

label 235.00
Salad Bowl
    Fuchsia, 10-1/2" d 120.00
    King's Crown, ruby stained 65.00
Salt and Pepper Shakers, pr
    Fuchsia 95.00
    June Night 165.00
    Seltzer Tumbler, La Fleure, yellow, ftd 20.00
Server, center handle
    Flanders, pink 245.00
    Green Satin 25.00
    Juno, pink 85.00
Sherbet
    Cadena, low, topaz 15.00
    Cerise 10.00
    Cherokee Rose, #17399, tall 20.00
    Diamond Optic, #028, vaseline, amber foot, set of 8 ..... 225.00
    Flanders, crystal, high 28.00
    Fontaine, #15033, rose pink 33.00
    Forever Yours, #17507 ....8.00
    Fuchsia, #15083, 4-1/8" h 12.00
    Fuchsia, #15083, 5-3/8" h 30.00
    June Night, #17403, tall, reed stem 20.00
    Killarney, #17394, green 9.50
    King's Crown, cranberry stained 10.00
    King's Crown, ruby stained 12.00
    La Fleure, yellow, low 20.00
    Maderia, twilite 10.00
    Wire Optic, #15018, pink, high 36.00
    Wisteria, #17477 ....18.00
Sherry
    June Night, 2 oz 45.00
    Palais Versailles, #17594, 6-3/8" h, 5-1/2 oz 115.00
Snack Set, King's Crown, 10-1/2" d plate and cup
    Cranberry stained 35.00
    Ruby Stained 40.00
Sugar, cov
    Cadena, yellow 37.50
    Cerise 25.00
    Flanders, crystal, 3-1/2" h, ftd 35.00
    June Night 20.00
    Juno, yellow 37.50
Sundae
    Cerise 20.00
    Fontaine, #15033, green 25.00
    La Fleure, 4-1/2" h, mandarin and crystal 18.00
    Minton, crystal, gold border, 4 pc set 55.00
    Sweet Pea Vase, Swedish Modern, Copen Blue and crystal,
        7" h 58.00
Tumbler
    Aster, 8 oz, bell, etched 12.00
    Cerise, 4-7/8" h, ftd 25.00
    Cherokee Rose, #17399, 10-1/2 oz 36.00
    Classic, flat, 8 oz 45.00
    Classic, ftd, 7" h, 7 oz 35.00
    Flanders, 3-3/4" h, 5 oz, pink 60.00
    Flanders, 4-3/4" h, 9 oz, pink 50.00
    Flanders, 5-5/8" h, 9 oz, mandarin and crystal 20.00
    Flanders, 5-7/8" h, 12 oz, ftd, pink 60.00
    Fuchsia, 6-5/16" h, 12 oz, ftd 32.00
    June Night, #17358, 10 oz 20.00
    Killarney, #17394, 6-1/2" h, ftd, green 15.00
    La Fleure, 5-5/8" h, mandarin and crystal, ftd 24.00
    Paulina, #14196, 4-3/4" h, ftd, yellow 15.00
    Wide Optic, #017, rose pink, 4-3/4", 9-1/2 oz, ftd 18.00

Vase

    Black Satin, 7-3/4" h, gold dec 75.00
    Black Satin, 9-1/2" h, #16265, nude torchiere 250.00
    Black Satin, 10" h, U. S. Glass sticker 45.00
    Cerise, #14185, 10" h, gold encrusted 55.00
    Cherokee Rose, crystal, bud, 8" h 40.00
    Emerald Satin, dahlia, Kobi basket, silver dec 350.00
    Flanders, 8" h, ftd, flared top, pink 900.00
    Killarney, #17430, green, crystal base 35.00
    Modern, yellow, ball shaped, Saturn optic 50.00
    Poppy, 5" h, blue satin 40.00
    Swedish Optic
        #5858, Copen blue, 10" h, flip, sand carved bell-
           flowers 185.00
        #13750, Copen blue, 9-1/4", tub type 70.00
Water Lamp, #111, Rose, faint water mark 145.00
Whiskey, Classic, #185, ftd, 2 oz 75.00
Wine
    Byzantine 22.50
    Cadena, topaz 35.00
    Cerise 30.00
    Chalet 55.00
    Flanders, crystal 90.00
    Flanders, mandarin and crystal, 6" h, 3-1/2" oz 40.00
    Flanders, pink 95.00
    Fontaine, #15033, 1-1/2 oz, green, crystal 38.00
    Fontaine, #15033, 1-1/2 oz, rose pink 38.00
    Fuchsia, #1503, 5-1/16" h 35.00
    June Night, #17403, 3-1/2 oz 35.00
    Kingsley cutting, #17392 ....35.00
    La Fleure, 6" h, 3-1/2 oz, mandarin and crystal 30.00
    Maderia, twilite 12.00
    Persian Pheasant, #17358, etched 24.00
    Thistle 17.00
    Tiffin Rose, #17680, 6-3/8" h 25.00
    Twilite, #17507 ....38.00

TOOTHPICK HOLDERS

History: Toothpick holders, indispensable table accessories of the Victorian era, are small containers made specifically to hold toothpicks.

They were made in a wide range of materials: china (bisque and porcelain), glass (art, blown, cut, opalescent, pattern, etc.), and metals, especially silver plate. Makers include both American and European firms.

By applying a decal or transfer, a toothpick holder became a souvenir item; by changing the decal or transfer, the same blank could become a memento for any number of locations.

References: William Heacock, *Encyclopedia of Victorian Colored Pattern Glass*, Book I, 2nd ed., Antique Publications, 1976, 1992 value update; ——, *1,000 Toothpick Holders*, Antique Publications, 1977; ——, *Rare & Unlisted Toothpick Holders*, Antique Publications, 1984; National Toothpick Holders Collectors Society, *Toothpick Holders*, Antique Publications, 1992.

Collectors' Club: National Toothpick Holders Collectors Society, 1224 Spring Valley Lane, West Chester, PA 19380.

Reproduction Alert: Reproduction Toothpick Holders abound. Carefully examining details on these small glass objects can be a challenge, but it is often the best way to spot a reproduction.

Art and Colored Glass

    Alexandrite, Honeycomb pattern, shot glass shape, straight
        rim, 2-1/8" h 500.00
    Amberina
        Daisy and Button pattern, intense fuchsia color-
           ation 385.00
        Diamond Quilted pattern, sq top 350.00
        Inverted Thumbprint pattern, pedestal base, 1000 TPs
           #15 ....195.00
        Venetian Diamond pattern, square top, round
           base 275.00
    Burmese, Gundersen 135.00
    Cameo, Daum Nancy, winter scene, sgd 750.00
    Carnival, Kitten pattern, Fenton, amethyst 160.00
    Cranberry
        Bulbous Base 100.00
        Coin Spot pattern, pedestal base 175.00
        Coralene beaded flowers 285.00
        Optic Thumbprint pattern 100.00
    Cut
        Chain of hobstars, pedestal 145.00
        Diamonds, fans, and cross-hatching, rayed base .125.00
    Latticino, green, gold, and white 60.00
    Pairpoint, Buffalo, 1000 TPs #21 ....200.00
    Pigeon Blood, Bulging Loops pattern 175.00
    Pomona, dec, 1000 TP's #140 ....125.00
    Smith Bros., Columned Ribs pattern, 1000 TPs #31 ...... 125.00
    Spatter, Royal Ivy pattern, cranberry, crackle 250.00
    Steuben, Grecian Urn, pedestal, applied "M" shape handles,
        2-1/2" h 195.00
    Wave Crest
        #32, kitten dec, 1,000 TP's 95.00
        #408, cat dec, 1000 TPs 165.00

Figural

    Baby's Booties, amber, c1890-95 ....50.00
    Bird, yellow ground, opaque body 35.00
    Book 25.00
    Coal Bucket 35.00
    Dog and Stump, blue 60.00
    Domino 50.00
    Elephant, amber, c1890 ....75.00
    Kitten on pillow 95.00
    Petticoat Hat, vaseline, gold trim 135.00
    Pig, pink 75.00
    Pot Belly Stove, amber 45.00
    Purse shape, Fine Cut, blue 60.00
    Saddle, blue 45.00
    Squirrel on Stump 50.00
    Top Hat, fine cut 50.00
    Tramp Shoe, milk glass 60.00
    Two Roosters, frosted 60.00
    Utility Boot 40.00

Opaque glass

    Clambroth, Zipper, fiery opalescent highlights 30.00
    Custard
        Fan, Dugan, 2-1/2" h 875.00
        Harvard 45.00
        Ribbed Drape, Jefferson 350.00
        Washington 120.00
    Milk Glass
        Alligator, c1885 ....70.00
        Florette, turquoise 110.00
        Parrot and Top Hat, c1895 ....45.00

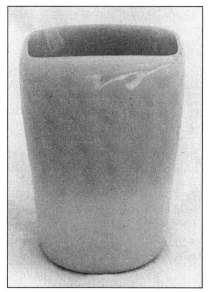

Burmese, glossy finish, 2-5/8" h, $150.

Scroll, claw ftd, light pink and blue dec, c1900 ..... 555.00
Mount Washington, Ribbed pattern, satin finish, white ground, hand painted blue flowers 175.00
Satin, Florette, blue opaque 110.00

Opalescent glass

Beatty Honeycomb pattern, blue ground 165.00
Chrysanthemum pattern, cranberry ground 170.00
Criss-Cross pattern, cranberry ground 600.00
Daisy pattern, vaseline ground, brass rim 110.00
Diamond Spearhead pattern
    Green ground 75.00
    White ground 110.00
Gonterman Swirl pattern, blue ground 300.00
Inverted Strawberry pattern, aqua ground, marked "Near Cut" 45.00
Iris Meander pattern, vaseline ground 110.00
Reverse Swirl pattern, blue ground 85.00
Ribbed Swirl pattern, blue ground 125.00

Ringneck Stripe pattern, white ground 125.00
Shell Wreath pattern, white ground 30.00
Six Panels pattern, blue ground 45.00
Windows Swirl pattern, blue ground 125.00

Pattern glass (colorless, unless otherwise noted)

Arched Ovals pattern 12.00
Banded Portland pattern, cranberry 42.00
Box in Box pattern, green, gold trim 42.00
Continental pattern, Heisey 125.00
Croecus pattern, green, gold highlights, 2-3/4" h 60.00
Dahlia pattern, double, dec 85.00
Daisy and Button pattern
    Amber, barrel shape, brass bands 15.00
    Blue 75.00
Delaware pattern
    Colorless 100.00
    Rose stain, gold dec 175.00
Double Ring Panel pattern 30.00
Florida pattern, ruby-amber 265.00
Francesware pattern, frosted hobnail 65.00
Hobnail pattern, Apple Green, 1000 TPs #205 .... 55.00
Holly pattern, Greentown 65.00
Intaglio Sunflower pattern 20.00
Kansas pattern 45.00
Michigan pattern, clear, yellow stain 175.00
New Jersey pattern, gold trim 55.00
Peerless pattern, Heisey 40.00
Pineapple and Fan pattern, green, Heisey 185.00
Spearpoint Band pattern, ruby stained 195.00
Stars and Stripes pattern 15.00
Sunbeam pattern, emerald 60.00
Swag with Brackets, amethyst 50.00
Texas pattern, gold trim 50.00
Three Face pattern 40.00
Truncated Cube pattern, ruby stained 75.00
Twisted Hobnail pattern 50.00
Vermont pattern 40.00
Vigilant pattern, Fostoria 25.00
Wisconsin pattern 45.00

UNION GLASS

History: Amory and Francis Houghton established the Union Glass Company, Somerville, Massachusetts, in 1851. The company went bankrupt in 1860, but was reorganized. Between 1870 and 1885 the Union Glass Company made pressed glass and blanks for cut glass.

Art-glass production began in 1893 under the direction of William S. Blake and Julian de Cordova. Two styles were introduced: a Venetian style, which consisted of graceful shapes in colored glass, often flecked with gold; and an iridescent glass, called Kew Blas, made in plain and decorated forms. The pieces are similar in design and form to Quezal products but lack the subtlety of Tiffany items.

The company ceased production in 1924.

Museum: Sandwich Glass Museum, Sandwich, MA.

References: John A. Shuman III, The Collector's Encyclopedia of American Art Glass, Collector Books, 1988, 1994 value update; Kenneth Wilson, *American Glass 1760-1930: The Toledo Museum of Art, Volume I, Volume II,* Hudson Hills Press and The Toledo Museum of Art, 1994.

Bowl
    5" d, irid gold ground, flared, ribbed...........................225.00
    5-1/2" d, irid gold ground, shaped rim, shallow round bowl, sgd "Kew Blas" on base.......................................250.00
    14" d, pulled feather, red ground, sgd.....................1,400.00
Candlesticks, pr, 8-1/2" h, irid gold, twisted stems..........750.00
Compote
    4-1/2" h, 3-1/2" d, gold irid, flared rim, applied pedestal foot with folded edge, inscribed "Kew Blas" on base 460.00
    7" h, irid gold ground, pink highlights, ribbed bowl, twisted stem...550.00
Console Set
    10" d compote, 5-1/4" h pr candlesticks, transparent green bowl, control bubbled ball stems...........................590.00
    10" d compote, 6-3/4" h pr candlesticks, Alexandrite, heat reactive red shaded to blue, chocolate shading, central air trap bubble stem...1,265.00
Cuspidor, 5-3/4" d, 2-1/2" h, amber ground, irid gold dec, squatty, flattened flared rim, sgd "Kew Blas"..................285.00
Decanter
    14" h, green-gold irid ground, spherical long stemmed stopper, sgd..375.00
    14-1/2" h, 4-3/4" d base, gold irid, ribbed and painted stopper, purple-pink highlights, sgd on base............1,450.00
Finger Bowl and Underplate
    5" d bowl, 6" d plate, ribbed, scalloped border, metallic luster, gold and platinum highlights............................475.00
    5" d, 7" d plate, twelve ribbed body, scalloped edge, gold irid, inscribed and numbered.................................425.00
Goblet
    4-3/4" h, irid gold ground, curved stem.....................250.00
    6" h, irid gold ground, knob stem...............................350.00
Pitcher
    4-1/2" h, green pulled feather pattern, deep gold irid int., applied swirl handle, sgd "Kew-Blas".......................900.00
    5" h, King Tut, white ground, green and gold irid dec, irid blue lining, blue handle, sgd.............................2,000.00
Rose Bowl, 4" d, scalloped rim, cased glass sphere, green ver-

tical zipper stripes, orange irid int., inscribed "Kew Blas" on base 690.00
Salt, irid gold 220.00
Tumbler
    3-1/2" h, 3" d, brilliant irid gold exterior, purple irid interior, sgd 275.00
    4" h, pinched sides, irid gold, sgd 225.00
Vase
    4-1/4" h, 5-1/4" d, deep emerald green, honeycomb pattern, highly irid purple int., sgd......................................800.00
    4-1/4" h, 5-1/4" d, flared amber ribbed trumpet form, pulled emerald green int. dec, base engraved "Kew-Blas" 815.00
    6-1/4" h, cylinder, rolled rim, gold and green swags, pale orange ground, early 20th C, sgd, orig paper label..... 950.00
    6-1/2" h, 7" w, bulbous, oyster white ground, deep green hooked and pulled feathering, gold irid feathers, gold irid rim on neck, sgd...1,450.00
    7" h, cased ambergris oval body, gold irid feathers on opal body, folded irid rim, base inscribed "Kew-Blas" 980.00
    12-1/2" h, irid gold ground, blue and pink irid highlights, baluster, waisted 950.00
Wine Glass, 4-3/4" h, curving stem, irid gold................. 250.00

VALLERYSTHAL GLASS

History: Vallerysthal (Lorraine), France, has been a glass-producing center for centuries. In 1872 two major factories, Vallerysthal glassworks and Portieux glassworks, merged and produced art glass until 1898. Later, pressed glass animal-covered dishes were introduced. The factory continues to operate today.

Animal Dish, cov
    Cow, 7" h, clear, pasture scene on cov 115.00
    Dog on Rug, amber...135.00
    Fish, white milk glass 95.00
    Hen on nest, opaque aqua, sgd 75.00
    Rabbit, white, frosted..65.00
    Snail, figural strawberry base, white milk glass, sgd...... 115.00
    Squirrel, opaque blue..85.00
    Swan, blue opaque glass..100.00
Box, cov
    4" h, 3-1/2" d, blue milk glass 90.00
    5" x 3", cameo, dark green, applied and cut dec, sgd 950.00
Breakfast Set, hen cov dish, six egg cups, basket form master salt, tray, white milk glass, 9 pc set........................ 500.00
Butter Dish, cov, figural
    Lemon, opaque white, sgd 70.00
    Radish, white milk glass..115.00
    Turtle, opaque white, snail finial.................................100.00
Candlesticks, pr
    Baroque pattern, amber..75.00
    Grecian Girl, frosted...95.00
Candy Dish, 4-1/8" d, white milk glass, basketweave base, rope handles and finial 95.00
Compote, 6-1/4" sq, blue opaque glass 75.00
Goblet, blue milk glass, ftd 75.00
Mustard, cov, swirled ribs, scalloped blue opaque, matching cover with slot for spoon 45.00
Pitcher, Grape and Leaf pattern, vaseline, frosted...........50.00
Plate
    6" d, Thistle pattern, green.......................................65.00

Mustard, cov, swirls, blue opaque, $45.

7-1/2" d, floral dec, blue milk glass 50.00
8" d, Thistle pattern, green 75.00
Salt, cov, hen on nest, white opal 65.00
Sugar, cov, 5" h, Strawberry pattern, opaque white, gold trim,
    salamander finial 85.00
Tumbler, 4" h, blue 40.00
Vase, 8" h, flared folded burgundy red rim, oval pale green
    body, matching red enamel berry bush on front, inscribed
    "Vallerysthal" on base 490.00

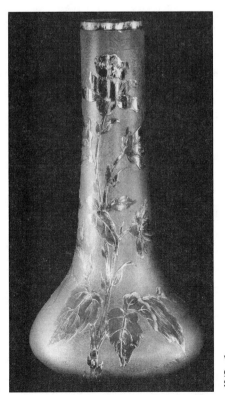

Vase, amberina ground, gold daffodils, 12" h, $3,500.

VAL ST.-LAMBERT

History: Val St.-Lambert, a 12th-century Cistercian abbey, was located during different historical periods in France, Netherlands, and Belgium (1930 to present). In 1822, Francois Kemlin and Auguste Lelievre, along with a group of financiers, bought the abbey and opened a glassworks. In 1846, Val St.-Lambert merged

with the Socété Anonyme des Manufactures de Glaces, Verres à Vitre, Cristaux et Gobeletaries. The company bought many other glassworks.

Val St.-Lambert developed a reputation for technological progress in the glass industry. In 1879, Val St.-Lambert became an independent company employing 4,000 workers. The firm concentrated on the export market, making table glass, cut, engraved, etched, and molded pieces, and chandeliers. Some pieces were finished in other countries, e.g., silver mounts were added in the United States.

Val St.-Lambert executed many special commissions for the artists of the Art Nouveau and Art Deco periods. The tradition continues. The company also made cameo-etched vases, covered boxes, and bowls. The firm celebrated its 150th anniversary in 1975.

Ashtray, shell, gold label... 10.00
Bottle, 6-7/8" h, green vines and flowers dec, acid finished
    ground, green cut to clear overlay edge, sgd "Val/St Lambert" 120.00
Bowl
    6-1/2" d, cov, cameo, deep cut purple florals, frosted
      ground, sgd "Val St Lambert" 750.00
    8" d, floral swag dec, sgd 90.00
    10" d, 4" h, red flashed overlay, sgd 350.00
Cologne Bottle, 61/2" h, textured colorless ground, cranberry
    florals, cut fern, partial paper label, replaced cut
    stopper 220.00
Compote, 3-1/2" d, amberina, ruby rim, mottled glass bow, ap-
    plied amber foot and handles 175.00
Dresser Box, colored 100.00
Finger Bowl, 4-1/2" d, crystal, half pentagon, cut edge,
    sgd 45.00
Goblet, 5-3/8" h, colorless, blown mold, applied foot and
    stem 50.00
Pitcher, colorless, paneled, cut diamond design, sgd 95.00
Sculpture, Madonna, solid 125.00
Tumbler, 3" h, cameo cut blue florals, rim ground........... 40.00
Tumble-Up, decanter and matching tumbler, amber-crystal,
    mkd.. 95.00
Vase
    5-1/4" h, 6-3/4" l, lime green transparent elliptical body, acid
      stamped on base "Val St. Lambert" 345.00
    7-1/2" h, colorless frosted ground, emerald green floral cutting,
      base mkd "Made in Belgium, Val St. Lambert"..........660.00
    8-1/2" h, colorless frosted ground, emerald green bows and
      swags cutting 385.00
    8-1/2" h, heavy colorless oval, engraved rose in center, base
      inscribed "VSG C. Graffart/Piece Unique 1949," attribut-
      ed to Charles Graffart..375.00
    10" h, cameo, cranberry cut to clear, wide band dec with Greek
      figures and nymphs above vertical cut ribs.............. 440.00

Ad, showing the latest in Val. St. Lambert, China and Glass Tablewares, October 1967.

10" h, cameo, cranberry cut to clear, 3" acid cut band of Renaissance style chariots and people, Gothic arch panels, notched rim 300.00

VASART

History: Vasart is a contemporary art glass made in Scotland by the Streathearn Glass Co. The colors are mottled, and sometimes shade from one hue to another. Vasart can be identified by the engraved signature on the base.

Collector's Club: Monart & Vasart Collectors Club, 869 Cleveland St., Oakland, CA 94606.

Basket
    7-1/2" h, flip shape, green and pink, applied handle....85.00
    12" h, mottled green and turquoise, applied handle...120.00
Bowl
    2" d, scalloped rim, mottled green 40.00
    5" d, light green 40.00
    6-1/2" d, pierced handle, pink and gray 70.00
    8" d, gray-green, gold mica flecks 75.00
Hat, mottled blue, sgd 45.00
Mug
    Mottled blue and green...50.00
    Mottled white and lavender..45.00
Plate, 8" d, gray-green, gold mica flecks 80.00
Rose Bowl
    Mottled white and green 50.00
    Mottled white and lavender..60.00
Tray, 12" l, mottled blue shading to green 75.00
Vase
    7-1/2" h, swelled cylinder, internal Cluthra pink and green dec, pulled and hooked swirls dec 125.00
    7-3/4" h, waisted cylinder, internal Cluthra pink and green dec, pulled and hooked swirls de, sgd "Vasart" 125.00
    8" h, oyster white, blue, and pale salmon pink swirl, Cluthra type design, sgd 150.00

VENETIAN GLASS

History: Venetian glass has been made on the island of Murano, near Venice, since the 13th century. Most of the wares are thin walled. Many types of decoration have been used: embedded gold dust, lace work, and applied fruits or flowers.

Reference: Sheldon Barr, *Venetian Glass, Confections in Glass, 1855-1914*, Harry N. Abrams, Inc., 1998.

Videotape: Rosa Barovier-Mentasti, *The Collector Series: Venetian Glass*, Award Video & Film Distributors, Inc., 1992.

Reproduction Alert: Venetian glass continues to be made today.

Beverage Set, 10-1/2" h, pitcher, applied striped handle, 8 flared tumblers, 6 spherical glasses, each striped with opaque orange, transparent yellow-amber, and clear crystal, design attributed to Fulvio Bianconi, 15 pc set 1,950.00
Bowl, 7-1/2" w, 6-1/8" w, deep quatraform bowl, applied quatraform rim, blue, clear internal dec, trapped air bubble square, circles, and gold inclusions, c1950 ....360.00
Candlesticks, pr, 8" h, applied strawberry prunts on amber ruffled bowl, amber base, honeycomb molding, colorless figural swan stem with profuse gold dust dec, applied eyes, attributed to Salviati dott Antonio, late 19th C 380.00
Centerpiece Set, two 8-1/2" baluster ftd ewers, 8-1/2" ftd compote, red and white latticino stripes with gold flecks, applied clear handles and feet, 3 pc set...................150.00
Cordial, 4-1/2" h, colorless bowl, figural swan stem with profuse gold dec, applied eyes, attributed to Salviati dott Antonio, late 19th C 125.00
Decanter, 13" h, figural clown, bright red, yellow, black, and white, aventurine swirls, orig stopper...................250.00
Decanter Set, decanter, six matching goblets with mermaid stems, mermaid dec on decanter 400.00
Dessert Plate, 12" w, cobalt blue, gold and enameled all over dec, rays on back..200.00
Epergne, three lilies, scalloped bowl, pearl satin, DQ, sky blue finish, Victorian 600.00
Goblet
    5-1/4" h, 4-1/4" w, Reticello, gold dust rim band, geometric latticino criss-crossing bands, air bubble trap in junctions, hollow twisted blown stem, three applied gold prunts, designed by Verti de'Arte, late 1940s........400.00
    7" h, etched, enameled biblical scenes 200.00
Jack in the Pulpit, 8" h, white swirled diamond body, profuse gold dust on ext., applied blue flowers and leaves applied clear ruffled rim, rolled edge on hollow raised foot 175.00
Paperweight, 2-3/4" l, 2" w, rect, small micro-mosaic flowers,

black, blue, and gold stone rect base, flowers on brick type background, corners may have been polished, minute roughness to some petals and leaves........175.00
Plate, 7" d, pink and white alternating latticino stripes 65.00
Sherbet, 4" d, 4-1/2" h, ruby bowl, clear stem, gold knob.... 195.00
Sherry, amber swirled bowls, blue beaded stems, 8 pc set................495.00
Tableware, green, applied blue ruffle and prunts, 12 champagnes, compote, 11 dessert plates, 13 sherbets with 12 underplates, 11 tumblers, 10 wines, 70 pc set 2,500.00
Vase
    7" h, handkerchief, striped white and gold threaded latticino, pink, and colorless alternating panels, folded bowl form 150.00
    7-1/4" h, handkerchief, transparent green, cased creamy opaque lining, flat polished pontil 275.00
    11" h, ovoid, colorless, repeating pattern of eight white and one blue spiraling threads, applied opaque white lip and foot with gold speckles.........................275.00
Wine
    4" h, conical bowl with twisted white bands of white latticino farmed in aventurine and light green transparent bands, hollow bubble stem, folded domed foot, one manufacturer's bubble, repair at stem 65.00
    7-3/4" h, colorless, gold flecks in bowl and stem, set of 12.................................225.00

VERLYS GLASS

History: Originally made by Verlys France (1931-1960), this Lalique-influenced art glass was produced in America by The Holophane Co. from 1935 to 1951, and select pieces by the A. H. Heisey Co. from 1955 to 1957. Holophane acquired molds and glass formulas from Verlys France and began making the art glass in 1935 at its Newark, Ohio, facility. It later leased molds to the Heisey Co., and in 1966 finally sold all molds and rights to the Fenton Art Glass Co.

The art glass was made in crystal, topaz, amber, rose, opalescent, and Directorie Blue. Heisey added turquoise. Most pieces have etched (frosted) relief designs.

The French produced glass can be distinguished from the American products by the signature. Verlys France marked the glass with mold impressed "Verlys France" and "A Verlys France." Holophane (also known as Verlys of America) marked pieces with the mold-impressed "Verlys" and a scratched-script "Verlys" signature. The A. H. Heisey Co. used only a paper label which reads "Verlys by Heisey."

Reference: Carole and Wayne McPeek, *Verlys of America Decorative Glass*, revised ed., published by authors, 1992.

Ashtray, frosted
    3-1/2" d, floral dec, script sgd.......................45.00
    4-1/2" d, doves, floral border, script mark....................55.00
    6" d, oval, duck perched on side, wave molded base 60.00
Bowl
    6" d, Cupids and Hearts pattern, colorless....................50.00
    6" d, Pine Cone pattern, French blue.........................110.00
    8-1/2" d, Thistle pattern, three small feet.................150.00
    10" d, Chrysanthemum pattern, frosted 130.00
    13-1/2" d, Poppies, scratched signature....................250.00

Salad Bowl, Poppy pattern, Heisey, Newark, script sgd, 13-1/2" d, $135.

Box, cov, frosted
    6-1/2" d, butterflies, script mark 115.00
    6-3/4" d, relief molded bouquet of coreopsis, molded "Verlys/France" on lid and base.............................200.00
Candy Dish, cov, frosted
    6" h, Pine Cone pattern 50.00
    6-1/2" h, Lovebirds, sgd...............................60.00
    7" h, sculptured florals, opalescent.....................375.00
Candlesticks, pr, 5-1/2" d, leaftip molded nozzle, spreading circular foot with molded nasturtiums, etched signature on base................................ 120.00
Charger
    Flying Geese 75.00
    Tassels, 13" d, script signature 75.00
Plate
    4-7/8" d, Shells pattern, opal 150.00
    5" d, fish, frosted 65.00
    6-1/4" h, Pine Cone pattern, mold sgd 75.00
Powder Box, cov, frosted, lovebirds 85.00
Vase
    4" h, Gems pattern, opal, ground base.........................90.00
    6-1/2" h, 6-3/4" w, frosted and clear, script signature 65.00
    8" d, Thistles pattern, dusty rose...............................275.00
    9" h, ovoid, flared flattened rim, topaz, frosted large blossom and leaves, script sgd "Verlys" on base 600.00
    9-1/4" h, Mandarin, frosted and clear, script signature .. 250.00

VON EIFF, WILHELM

History: Wilhelm Von Eiff was one of the most important glass artists in Germany in the period between World War I and World War II. His first training was as a glass engraver. He later studied in Prague, Vienna, Paris, and northern Bohemia. During these studies, he learned stone-cutting and intaglio techniques, which he later translated to glass.

When he returned to Germany in 1921, he built up the department for glass cutting and glyptic art at the School of

Applied Arts in Stuttgart. His innovative techniques and new creative approach to working with glass attracted world wide attention. Soon his pupils and Von Eiff were working with colorless glass, which had a matte finish, giving the visual impression of tone and weight. The style is easily recognizable. Delicate layering, achieved through polishing the glass in stages, created a decorative element as well as a color gradation of two or three layers of frosted white shades. Rhythmic and sculpture like patterns were created by cutting deep ridges or designs in relief.

Wilhelm Von Eiff was not only a talented glass craftsman, but also a skilled teacher. Several of his pupils mastered his innovative techniques. Irngard Bohn was known as a fine cutter who used her skills as a figural engraver. Arnold Hamann became a master wheel-cutter. Max Hagl, also a master wheel cutter, often was the one chosen to execute Von Eiff's designs. Hans Modell developed a sculptural style of cutting. All of these students later developed their own styles.

It was common during the late 1920s and early 1930s to design glass elements and accessories to compliment the new modernistic architecture. Wilhelm Von Eiff and his students often executed special pieces as well as utilitarian and serving pieces for these exciting homes, leading to patronage and support.

Bowl
   4" d, 2-1/4" h, bulbous, frosted, carved in medium relief, rounded whiplash motif, engraved "K.G.S. STUTTG. ABT PROF. W.V. EIFF," Wilhelm Von Eiff, c1930 ....400.00
   4-3/8" d, tapered circular bowls, fine martele surface, medium relief futuristic abstract patterns, engraved "MH," Hans Modell, c1933, set of 6.................................600.00
   6" d, 4-1/4" d, cov, low circular bowl, sides finely carved with wave pattern, fitted covers with stylized flower head, engraved "K.G.S. STUTTG. ABT W. V. EIFF," c1930, pr 850.00
   6-1/4" d, low circular form, carved martele surface and bottom, deeply carved irregular wave pattern, engraved "MH," Hans Modell, c1933 ....700.00
   6-1/2" d, low circular form, carved prancing deer among stylized foliage, engraved "K.G.S. STUTTG. ABT W. V. EIFF," c1930..600.00
   6-1/2" d, low circular form, medium relief carved wave pattern, engraved "K.G.S. STUTTG. ABT W. V. EIFF,"

c1930..525.00
   8-1/4" d with fitted cov, 4-1/4" d with knobbed cov, carved concentric rings in medium relief, frosted finish contrasts with polished bands, engraved "K.G.S. STUTTG. ABT W. V. EIFF," c1928, pr 1,300.00
   9-1/4" d, ftd flaring form, frosted, carved martele surface dec, low relief large dots, engraved "K.G.S. STUTTG. M. HAGL," designed by Max Hagl, for Wilhelm Von Eiff, c1930..700.00
Bud Vase, 5-3/4" h, ftd tapering vase, fine carved martele surface, low relief carved swag motif, engraved "K.G.S. STUTTG. M. HAGL," pr 500.00
Punch Bowl Set, carved glass punchbowl, cover, eighteen carved glasses, silver and rosewood tray, silver and glass handled cover set with circular medallion of young Hercules strangling serpents, circular lined tray, carved signature "W. V. Eiff," lot as sold by Phillips, NY, includes orig publication of *Moderne Bauformen Monatschefetenfur Architecktur und Raumhunst,* verlag Julius Hoffman Stuttgart, December 1929, illustrating the Oppenheimer house and contents, including this punch bowl set 46,000.00
Punch Bowl Ladle and Underdish, ensuite with punch bowl, silver ladle with medallion of Hercules matching punch bowl cover, carved "Wilhelm Von Eiff," glass underdish matches punch bowl 15,000.00
Sculpture, used as part of a group of twelve that formed a circular light structure in a reception room of the Oppenheimer Villa, designed by Block &Guggenheimer, Stuffgart, Germany, c1927, 13-1/4" h, cylindrical, frosted and carved
   Stylized cowboy, seated nude woman with parasol, engraved "W.V.E.," Wilhelm Von Eiff, c1930 ....2,200.00
   Stylized kneeling woman, diaphanous drapery under moon and stars, reverse with perched owl and flower blossom, engraved "W.V.E.," Wilhelm Von Eiff, c1928 ....2,800.00
Vase
   3-5/8" h, ftd, frosted and carved, flared rim, carved martele surface, medium relief with wave pattern, engraved "K.G.S. SUTT.ABT. PROF. W.V." 500.00
   6-5/8" h, spherical, everted rim, carved martele surface, carved dots in medium relief, engraved "K.G.S., Stuff ABT PROF W.F. Eiff"..1,200.00
   9" h, frosted and carved, medium relief, wave pattern, c1930..500.00
   11" h, ftd trumpet form, carved martele surface, body dec with elongated wave motif, engraved "K.G.S. STUTTG. ABT PROF. W. V. EIFF MAX HAGL," executed by Max Hagl, c1932..800.00

WATERFORD

History: Waterford crystal is high-quality flint glass commonly decorated with cuttings. The original factory was established at Waterford, Ireland, in 1729. Glass made before 1830 is darker than the brilliantly clear glass of later production. The factory closed in 1852. One hundred years later it reopened and continues in production today.

Manufacturer/Distributor: Waterford Wedgwood USA Inc., P.O. Box 1454, Wall, NJ 07719.

Reproduction Alert: Several importers have been exposed as having falsely claimed that their products were genuine Waterford.

Animal
    Bird...65.00
    Fish...65.00
    Seahorse 200.00
Ashtray, 5" d...95.00
Biscuit Barrel..110.00
Bowl
    6" d, allover diamond cutting 70.00
    8" d, DQ, thumbprint stem............................125.00
    8-1/2" d 155.00
    9" d, leaf cut border over trellis work sides 100.00
    10" d, ftd, Benjamin Franklin Liberty Bowl, American Heritage collection 275.00
Bud Vase..60.00
Cake Plate, 10" d, 5-1/4" h, sunburst center, geometric design...85.00
Cake Server, cut glass handle, orig box..........................80.00
Candlesticks, pr, 7" h, pear shape, hollow center, horizontal oval cuts on wafers between fluted to and rayed base, looped cross cuttings in two sizes, downward spray of star cut...175.00

Pitcher, ribbed, applied handle, 10-1/2" h, $215.

Champagne Flute, 6" h, Coleen pattern, 12 pc set.........450.00
Compote, 5-1/2" h, allover diamond cutting above double wafer stem, pr 400.00
Creamer and Sugar, 4" h creamer, 3-3/4" d sugar, Tralee pattern 85.00
Cruet, 5" h, waisted body, short fluted neck, fluted rim, strawberry leaves and fan cutting, faceted stopper 120.00
Decanter, orig stopper, colorless
    10" h, ship's, diamond cutting....................................200.00
    12-3/4" h, allover diamond cutting, monogram, pr......300.00
    13-1/4" h, diamond cutting 100.00
Goblet
    Cameragh pattern 40.00
    Glengarett pattern 45.00
Honey Jar, cov 70.00
Jar, cov, 6" h, diamond cut body, triple spring chain bordering thumb cut rim and star cut lid, faceted knob finial 100.00
Lamp
    14" h, Victorian style 350.00
    23" h, 13" d umbrella shade, blunt diamond cutting, Pattern L-1122 ....450.00
Letter Opener...45.00
Napkin Ring, 8 pc set 165.00
Old Fashioned Tumbler, 3-1/2" h, Comeragh pattern, pr 70.00
Pitcher
    6-3/4" h, Lismore pattern, shaped spout, applied strap handle..125.00
    10" h, diamond cuttings, applied handle 200.00
Plate, 8" d, diamond cut center...............................100.00
Ring Dish, 5" d, colorless, cut glass, price for 3 pc set ..110.00
Rose Bowl, 5-1/2" d, laurel border, spike diamond band......50.00
Salt, 3-7/8" d, oval, diamond cut................................75.00
Scent Bottle, 4-1/2" l, diamond cut..............................75.00
Sweetmeat, cov, pr, double dome cov, Fan pattern, scalloped rim, sq pedestal base, pr 700.00
Tumbler, all over cutting 80.00
Vase
    7" h, bulbous, top to bottom vertical cuts separated by horizontal slash cuts, sgd..............................140.00
    8" h, alternating diamond cut panels and horizontal notches
Wine
    5-1/2" h, Patrick, 8 pc set 220.00
    7-3/8" h, Coleen, 12 pc set.................................725.00
Wine Cooler, 6-1/2" x 6-1/2" 195.00

WAVE CREST

WAVE CREST WARE

c1892

History: The C. F. Monroe Company of Meriden, Connecticut, produced the opal glassware known as Wave Crest from 1898 until World War I. The company bought the opaque, blown-molded glass blanks from the Pairpoint Manufacturing Co. of New Bedford, Massachusetts, and other glassmakers, including European factories. The Monroe company then decorated the blanks, usually with floral patterns. Trade names used were "Wave Crest Ware," "Kelva," and "Nakara."

References: Wilfred R. Cohen, *Wave Crest*, Collector Books, out-of-print; Elsa H. Grimmer, *Wave Crest Ware*, Wallace-Homestead; Kenneth Wilson, *American Glass 1760-1930: The Toledo Museum of Art, Volume I, Volume II*, Hudson Hills Press and The Toledo Museum of Art, 1994.

Collectors' Club: Wave Crest Collectors Club, P.O. Box 2722, Meriden, CT 06450.

Ashtray and Match Holder, 6" w, 3" h, white ground, pink enamel flowers, white centers, green leaves, mkd "Wavecrest," small flat flake on inner rim of match holder, Cohen, page 79, top left...600.00

Biscuit Jar, cov

5" w, 6" h, rococo, square, fancy blown-out mold, white shaded to pale blue ground, all around pink rose dec, green leaves, fancy silver plated emb metal trim, mkd "Wavecrest" 300.00

5-1/2" d, 5-1/2" h, pink and white background, melon ribbed, hp flowers, unmarked..............................250.00

5-1/2" d, 5-3/4" h, tan and white shaded ground, white and magenta transfer lily flowers, no lid, unmarked........45.00

7-1/2" d, 5-1/2" h, squatty, white shaded to ivory ground, raised rococo leaf design, blue, green, yellow, and brown transfer floral dec, small repair to bail handle, unmarked....... 235.00

8" h, blue and white ground, swirled, cherry blossoms dec, lid with handle, unmarked 150.00

8" h, white ground, fern dec, unmarked......................200.00

9" h, 6-1/4" w, white shading to yellow ground, raised rococo swirls on front and back, transfer dec of apple blossoms and leaves, pink, tan, green, and orange, silver plated bail and lid, hardware may be a replacement, unmarked....... 200.00

Bon Bon, 7" h, 6" w, Venetian scene, multicolored landscape, dec rim, satin lining missing...............................1,200.00

Box, cov

3" d, double Shell, white, peach shells, blue, gray, and peach flowers 235.00

3" d, hexagon, orig lining, sgd "Nakara," Cohen 126 ..... 485.00

3" d, 2-1/2" h, swirl, white ground, small pink floral enamel, orig clasp, no lining, unmarked..............................165.00

3" d, 3-1/4" h, Rococo, soft blue ground, pink apple blossoms with green leaves on lid, no lining, repaired hinge, mkd "Wavecrest"...................................150.00

3-1/2" d, 3-1/4" h, hexagonal, pale mauve, applied white flowers and yellow centers, orig clasp and lining, minor wear to some applied petals 650.00

3" d, 4-1/2" h, Elephant's Foot mold, white shading to tan ground, transfer and enameled tiny pink roses, green leaves, four tiny nicks on cover, one small flake, orig lining worn, unmarked......................................400.00

3-3/4" d, 3" h, blown-out asters, round base, ivory and pink top, shaded green and pink base, small burst bubble on lid, good metal trim, orig base lining, mkd "Nakara" 500.00

4" d, blown-out pansy dec, cream ground blue and lavender flowers 650.00

4" d, blown-out shell, pin round, hp forget-me-not, lining replaced, mkd 400.00

4" d, Helmschmeid Swirl, paper label 275.00

4" d, Shell, blue, ftd 325.00

4" d, 3" h, hexagonal, mottled bright pink ground, six pale blue enameled flowers on lid, orig trim and clasp, no lining, mkd "Kelva" 550.00

4-1/4" d, bright blue ground, pink and white flowers, emb shell pattern, hinged...............................425.00

4-1/4" d, 3" h, Belle Ware, round, smooth finish, pale blue and pink ground, pink roses and buds, orig metal fittings and clasp, mkd "Belle Ware"..............................200.00

4-1/4" d, 3-1/2" h, Bishop's Hat shape, brown-orange ground, pink flowers on lid, no lining, stamped "Nakara" 340.00

4-1/4" d, 4" h, Bishop's Hat shape, solid blue ground shading to ivory, enameled bead work and pink and white apple blossoms with green leaves on cov, metal mountings, no lining, clasp possibly restored, mkd "Nakara" 400.00

4-1/2" d, 2-3/4" h, round, mottled blue ground, three large pink flowers, green leaves on lid, plated metal trim, worn clasp, orig worn lining, mkd "Kelva" 350.00

4-1/2" d, 2-3/4" h, round swirl base and lid, pink shading to white, blue and white forget-me-nots, green and gray leaves, some wear to lid dec, unmarked 115.00

4-1/2" d, 3" h, round, blue and white ground, swirled, wild flowers on lid, unmarked 225.00

4-3/4" d, 2-3/4" h, blown-out aster lid, pink floral dec, floral garland encircles base, remnants of orig lining.....985.00

5" d, 3" h, decorated crystal, holly leaves and berries dec, irid interior, sgd "C. F. Monroe" 300.00

5" d, 3-1/4" h, shaded yellow and butterscotch ground, white beaded dec and scene of three Kate Greenaway figures having tea, excellent metal trim, no lining, mkd "Nakara" 600.00

5" d, 4" h, peach shaded to butterscotch ground, enameled cross on lid, white dot dec, four pale blue flowers, ftd, metal mounts, minor bead wear, replaced lining, mkd "Nakara" 450.00

5" d, 5-3/4" h, egg crate, white ground interspersed with irregular panels surrounded by lavender enamel, heavily dec with whit and tan daisies and forget-me-nots, tan stems and leaves, ornate metal fittings and clasp, orig lining, unmarked 1,000.00

5-1/8" l, 3" h, oval, pale yellow ground shading to white, blue, gray, and white daisies and buds on lid, orig clasp, partial orig lining, mkd "Wavecrest" 325.00

5-1/4" l, oval, hp lilies, red Kelva mark 650.00

5-1/4" d, 3-3/4" h, Bishop's Hat, butterscotch and yellow shaded to white solid ground, thirteen blue, gray, white, and magenta azalea flowers and buds, good metal fittings and clasp, no lining, mkd "Nakara"..............450.00

5-1/2" d, Baroque Shell, pink daisies in medallion, enamel beading, lined, mkd 675.00

5-1/2" d, 3-1/4" h, crystal, Helmschmeid Swirl, pale translucent green, enameled leaves, ribbons, large raised flower on cov..225.00

5-1/2" d, 3-1/2" h, Bishop's Hat shape, gray-blue ground, pink and purple floral dec, orig lining, stamped "C.F.M. Co. Nakara"....................................425.00

6" d, courting couple, sgd "Nakara" 1,050.00

6" d, 3-1/2" h, round, mottled blue ground, six pink, yellow, and pale green Shasta daisies, worn orig lining in lid only clasp missing, mkd "Kelva"....................................350.00

6" d, 3-1/2" h, round, mottled green ground, seven large pink and white flowers, green and yellow centers, good metal trim and clasp, plating slightly worn, no lining, mkd "Kelva"....................................400.00

6" d, 3-1/2" h, round, scenic, peach colored ground, lavender panels, courting couple scene on lid, blue floral dec on base, orig clasp, replaced lining, mkd "Nakara" 1,000.00

6" d, 4-1/2" h, swirl, white satin ground, beige lily of the valleys enamel dec, green leaves, brown highlights, orig clasp, orig lining, three small burst bubbles, unmarked............. 225.00

6-1/4" d, Swirl, pink ground, hp forget-me-nots, orig lining, mkd..675.00

6-1/2" d, 4-1/4" h, Swirl pattern, crystal, holly leaves and berries dec, irid int., mkd "C. F. Monroe" 700.00

6-1/2" d, 4-1/2" h, Bishop's Hat, shaded green to pale pink round, large central pink and white rose with bud on top, surrounded by pale green frame, white beading, pale green and white beading on base, some wear to beading, tiny chip on top edge, no lining, no clasp, mkd "Nakara" 650.00

6-1/2" d, 4-1/2" h, octagonal, soft mint green ground, darker green overlaid shadow flowers, white beading, pink and white azalea flowers on lid, orig clasp, partial orig lining, mkd "Wavecrest"..700.00

6-3/4" d, 5-1/4" h, egg crate, glossy chocolate brown shaded to beige and rust ground, heavily enameled white and green lupine flowers, fancy ormolu trim with clasp and feet, unmarked 1,100.00

7" d, 3-3/4" h, Baroque Shell, glossy forest green ground, heavy overall gold spatter dec, top cartouche of Gibson-type girl portrait, fancy Victorian dress, beaded hat outlined in lavender enamel, good metal, trim, and clasp, no lining, mkd "Wavecrest" 1,000.00

7" d, 4" h, round, irid crystal, holly dec, Cohen, page 51 ......750.00

7" d, 4" h, shaded green, peach, light burgundy, yellow shaded ground, small enameled white flowers outlined in lavender with gold raised scroll work, pale blue top cartouche with nine storks in flight, shades of white, gray, and black, red beaks and feet, orig work lining, small burst bottom near bottom rim......3,700.00

7" d, 4" h, swirl, glossy dark green ground, pink and white roses with green leaves, which dotting, outlined in lavender enamel, no lining, unmarked......700.00

7-1/4" d, 3-3/4" h, Baroque Shell, raised pink-gold rococo shells, fancy Arabic pale turquoise dec, opaque white ground, lace-like network of hundreds of precisely placed raised white enamel beads, shiny metal work, satin lining missing 1,450.00

8" d, 3-3/4" h, strong mottled green ground, large enameled pink, white, and yellow poppies on bas and lid, orig trim and clasp, no lining, mkd "Kelva" 600.00

8" d, 4" h, Burmese colored ground shading from pink to yellow, large enameled pale blue and white flowers, minor bead wear, good metal trim and clasp, partial orig lining, mkd "Nakara" 1,000.00

8" l, 4-1/2" w, 3-1/2" h, oval, shaded tan to white ground, small blue and white asters, orig lining, mkd "Wavecrest"......850.00

Cake Box, cov, 3-1/2" h, 7-1/2" d, glossy dark green ground, pink enameled florals on base, six large blown-out flowers on lid in soft pink and white, yellow centers, lavender enamel trim, orig trim and clasp, mkd "Wavecrest"......2,150.00

Cigar Band Box, 3-3/4" d, 2-1/2" h, crystal ground, cigar bands with various dec, missing glass liner over orig paper liner, replaced royal blue cloth lining......1,250.00

Cigar Holder, 3-3/4" h, 4" d, white ground, blue forget-me-nots, yellow leaves, beaded centers, metal handled rim, metal base ftd base, unmarked 250.00

Cologne Bottle, 5-3/4" h, 2-1/8" w, glossy white ground, transfer dec of pink flowers, green and brown leaves, unmarked 650.00

Comb and Brush Holder, 4-1/2" h, 9" at widest point, white ground shading to pink, blue and purple enameled aster type flowers, mkd "Wavecrest," minor wear to floral dec on top panel 2,100.00

Collars and Cuff Box

7" d, 7-1/2" h, white shading to tan ground, ornate raised scroll work, "Collars & Cuffs" in pink and gold enamel, lid dec of dark and light pink chrysanthemum flowers, small pink daisies and leaves, sgd "Wavecrest"......1,100.00

8" d, pink and white florals, sgd "Nakara," clasp missing, Cohen 145......1,200.00

8" d, 3-3/4" h, pale green shading to gray and pink, cover cartouche with full length portrait of Queen Louise in red and white robe surrounded by white dotting and apple blossoms, flowers to continue to base, metal trim and clasp, replaced lining, unmarked Nakara......2,100.00

8" d, 6-1/4" h, Swirl pattern base and lid, shaded white to soft pink, enameled gray and green leaves, pink and white forget me not flowers, metal bottom, metal feet, trim, and clasp, no lining 700.00

8" d, 6-3/4" h, Spindrift, soft pink ground shading to white, ornate lavender and pink pansy dec, green shaded leaves, metal fittings with orig clasp, orig peach satin lining......2,500.00

Clock, 14" h, 7" w, ornate metal case, bottom glass panel of two cherubs wrapped in blue and red cloth, identical clock face plate and save Wavecrest finial with blue and gray floral dec, non-working Waterbury Clock, orig key 1,950.00

Cracker Jar, cov

7-1/4" h, 5" w, swirl shape, satin finish blank, shades from white to powder blue, white beading in panels, enameled white and gray pond lilies with tiny pink blossoms, green leaves, fancy silver plated metal trim, ornate twisted handle, unmarked 400.00

7-3/4" h, 5-1/2" w, white satin ground shading to yellow and peach, overall quarter moon dec, yellow, pink, and gray accented with brown and peach enameling, white dotting, one small rubbed int. spot, unmarked 200.00

10-1/2" h, 6" d, barrel shape, green-blue ground, yellow emb crests, hp yellow and brown wild roses, leaves, and stems, silver-plated cover and handle 675.00

11-1/4" h, 5" w, square, four sides with blown-out dec, pink roses and buds, leaves, medium blue ground, emb metal hardware, sgd "Wave Crest" in pink banner......675.00

Creamer and Sugar, cov

3-1/4" h x 3-1/4" w creamer, 3" h x 4" sugar, Swirl, white ground, blue and white enameled forget-me-nots on stems, leaves, silver plated trim on both, unmarked......350.00

3-3/8" h creamer, 5-1/2" h cov sugar, Helmschmeid Swirls, line of white enamel dots separates which upper portion of eight swirls from pastel-tan lower section, rose garland, single-petaled pink blossoms, shiny silver plated rims, handle, and cov......750.00

Dresser Box, 4" l, 4-3/4" w, sq, clear frosted box, shell type pattern, lavender enameled flowers, green leaves, brass fittings and clasp, mkd......175.00

Ewer

14-1/2" h, fishing scene, unmarked......110.00

16" h, blue ground, melon ribbed, courting scene, unmarked, pr......250.00

Ferner, 7" d, 2-1/2" h, pale blue, swirled, yellow flowers, unmarked 150.00

Flask, 6" h, 3" w at shoulder, white ground, hand painted blue flowers and green leaves, brown stems, minor wear to dec, unmarked 150.00

Frame, 6-1/2" h

Embossed, soft yellow ground, hp pink roses, ormolu rim, mkd......500.00

Puffy, cream ground, pink wild roses, mkd......475.00

Glove Box, cov, 9-1/2" l, 5-3/4" w, 5-1/2" h, white shaded to yellow ground, central dec of two large enameled pink, ivory, and white roses, green and pink leaf trim, ormolu feet, orig worn lining, orig locking device 1,550.00

Humidor

3-3/4" h, 2-7/8" w, powder blue ground, small pink and white enameled florals, "Cigarettes" written in lavender enamel, rare transfer scene of Niagara Falls and floral enamel on top, orig clasp, mkd "Wavecrest"......900.00

4-3/4" h, 3-3/4" w, white satin ground, orange swags, tiny pink roses, "Tobacco" enameled in black, brass trim, unmarked 400.00

5" h, 3-1/2" w, pale green ground, enamel dec on front, back, and lid, small blue forget-me-nots with white beading, green leaves, "Tobacco" enameled in purple on front, good trim, orig clasp, mkd "Wavecrest" 450.00

5" h, 3-1/2" w, round, mottled green ground, eleven orange poppies and buds, "Cigars" enameled in purple on front, clasp missing, mkd "Kelva"....................................500.00

5" h, 4-1/2" w, "The Old Sport," glossy white, russet and brown ground, transfer dec of bulldog and mug, monogrammed silver plated lid with two figural pipes, unmarked 450.00

5" h, 6-1/2" w, egg crate, glossy white ground, all over profuse floral and leaf dec, white enamel with russet, lavender, green, and gray, pink enameled "Cigars" on lid, removable pate and clasp missing, unmarked......650.00

5-1/2" h, soft green and pink florals, mkd "Nakara" 975.00

5-1/2" h, 6" w, inverted bear shaped body shading dark to light green, whimsical owl perched on tree branch, orig brass lid, mkd "Nakara" 1,300.00

5-1/2" h, 6-1/4" w, transfer portrait of Indian chief in head dress, white enameled bead work, shaded green to tan ground, orig brass lid, some wear to beading, mkd "Nakara" 1,500.00

5-3/4" h, 6-1/4" w, green ground shades to pin, seven enameled pink, white, and pale green flowers, word "Tobacco" enameled in lavender and gold, mkd "Nakara" 900.00

5-3/4" h, 6-1/2" w, solid blue shading to ivory ground, seven pink and white chrysanthemum flowers, int. shelf for sponge, clasp missing, mkd "Nakara"................1,300.00

6" h, 4-1/4" w, blown-out shell lid, pink shaded to white ground, all over blue and lavender daisies with white enamel and green and gray leaves, "Cigars" on front, mkd "Wavecrest"..850.00

6" h, 5" w, blown-out mold, brilliant glossy cobalt blue ground, blown out floral lid, all over dec of pink chrysanthemums, green leaves, lavender enamel highlights and word "Cigars," minor wear to purple enamel scroll work, no key, mkd "Wavecrest" 1,650.00

6-1/4" h, 4-1/4" w, barrel-shaped opaque body, shading yellow to russet ground, portrait of monk smoking cigar, pipe on reverse, dec both transfer printed and hand painted, some wear to dec, loose fitting cover, unmarked Nakara ... 350.00

8-3/4" h, blue body, single-petaled pink rose, pink "Cigar" signature, pewter collar, bail, and lid, flame-shaped finial, sgd "Kelva"...685.00

Jar, cov, 5" h, 6" w, melon ribbed, swirl and "Souvenir" on lid, off-white ground, blue and rust daisy-type flowers, white lettering on lid, unmarked......................................325.00

Jewel Stand, 4" d, 3" h, green and white ground, scroll design, pink floral dec, unmarked..90.00

Jewel Tray, 3-1/2" d, egg crate 145.00

Lamp

Boudoir, 7" h, 3-1/4" h x 2-1/2" w glass stem, blue shaded to white glass stem with pink and gray enamel forget-me-not dec, wear to brass plating and cord, unmarked, pr 500.00

Table, 31" h, 9" h x 9" w shade with glossy white shaded to beige ground, large pink and blue chrysanthemum dec, green leaves surrounded by lavender enamel scrolls and dots, white beaded top rim, heavily emb brass font and base, ornate reticulated scroll work and lions heads and human faces on foot, font and base connected by green onyx stem, has been electrified, but not drilled 950.00

Letter Holder, 5-1/2" l, 4" h, puffy, metal top rim, white ground with pink, lavender, and blue flowers, white enameled centers, minor wear to white beading, int. burst bubble, unmarked 200.00

Memo File, 7" h, 3-1/8" w, eight-sided white body, small blue for-

get-me-not enamel dec, orig brass finish figures, unmarked 450.00

Mustard Jar, cov

Burmese shaded ground, yellow to pink with gray, yellow, white, and green daisies, green leaves, hinged cover with slot for spoon, mkd "Nakara" 350.00

Green ground, floral dec, matching spoon, unmarked.... 140.00

White ground shaded to yellow, three colored fern dec, unmarked 100.00

Paperweight, 3-1/4" d, 1-1/4" h, white octagonal weight, metal fittings, small blue forget-me-nots and leaves, unmarked, brass fittings show wear...600.00

Perfume Bottle

4-1/2" h, 3-1/2" w, white ground, pink transfer roses, small yellow flower, cloth bulb cover worn, unmarked 275.00

4-3/4" h, white satin ground, blue, and pink enameled flowers, green leaves, metal fitting, no bulb, mkd "Wavecrest" 225.00

Pickle Castor, 5-1/2" h, white ground, floral dec, fork holder on both sides of SP holder, unmarked 150.00

Pin Cushion, 1-1/2" h, 4" w, white shading to green ground, rococo mold, small pink and purple daisies, orig metal trim, brown velvet cushion, mkd "Wavecrest"...............200.00

Pin Dish, open

3-1/2" d, 1-1/2" h, pink and white, swirled, floral dec, unmarked 35.00

3-3/4" d, Sunbonnet Baby, mkd 250.00

4-1/4" d, 2" h, pink and white, egg-crate mold, blue violets dec, mkd 80.00

5" d, 1-1/2" h, white, scrolls, pink floral dec, marked 80.00

Pin Tray, ftd, 5" , 4-1/2" w, molded opal glass, pale pink and green flowers, brass ormolu base with handle and leaves, sgd "Wavecrest"...600.00

Plaque, hanging

8" w, 10" h, satin ground, shaded pale pink to white, pink and russet nasturtium flowers, green, blue, and russet leaves, numerous small buds, 16" h x 9" orig frame, orig back and chips...3,000.00

8" x 10-1/2", landscape with trees, rocks, and mountains in background, green border, orig fancy metal frame, mkd "C. F. Monroe" 5,000.00

Plate, 7" d, reticulated border, pond lily dec, shaded pale blue ground 750.00

Playing Card Holder, 4" w, 1-1/4" d, 2-1/2" h, satin finish background shades from white to pale blue, pink roses dec, small edge chip covered by metal rim, mkd "Wavecrest," Cohen, pg. 74 middle..300.00

Ring Box, cov, 2-1/2" d, 2-1/4" h

Shaded green ground, portrait on cover of Victorian lady, worn orig lining, mkd "Nakara"..........................1,000.00

White ground, pink flowers with green leaves on lid, dec worn, mkd "Wavecrest" 175.00

Salt and Pepper Shakers, pr

Cylinder, glossy white and beige ground, pink, brown, and green aster type dec, orig screw-on pewter caps with agitators, 4" h, 1-1/2" w, unmarked...............................80.00

Shape No. 6, blue and white ground, fox and hound dec 75.00

Square, glossy white and pink ground, blue aster dec, 2-3/4" h, 1-1/4" w, damage to one metal cov, unmarked 200.00

Square, swirling panels of yellow, tan, and blue, blue and lavender forget-me-nots, orig pewter lids, 2-1/4" h, 1-3/4" h, unmarked 150.00

Swirled, light yellow ground, floral dec, unmarked 75.00

Tulip, brown and white ground, birds and floral dec 60.00

Salt, open, 1-1/8" h, 3" w, pale green ground, small pink and

Salt shaker, Erie Twist, satin, hand painted floral dec, two pc pewter top, sgd "C. F. Monroe Co.," $85.00.

white enameled flowers, white beaded rim, sgd
"Nakara" 325.00

Sugar Bowl, cov
  Glossy shaded tan to white ground, transfer dec of blue bird
    sitting on fence entwined with blue flowers, silver plated
    bail and lid, 2" h, 4" w, unmarked 100.00
  Swirl, hp white and blue florals, mkd 375.00

Sugar Shaker
  3" h, Helmschmeid Swirl, cream ground, blue and lavender
    violets, mkd 425.00
  3" h, 3-1/4" d, 8 Helmschmied Swirls, creamy pink ground,
    hp Johnny Jump-Up sprigs, SP metal cov with emb blos-
    soms and leaves 585.00
  5" h, 2-3/4" w, teepee shape, glossy white ground, blue dai-
    sies, green, and gray leaves, brass plated lid 125.00

Sweetmeat Jar, open
  1-3/4" h, 4" w, handled, six-sided base, painted Burmese shad-
    ing from yellow to pink, blue enamel flowers, white enam-
    eled scroll work, fancy brass plated rim and bail handle,
    minute wear to enamel dots, mkd "Nakara" 200.00
  3-3/4" h, 7" w, Belle Ware, textured crystalline finish, white
    and pale pink ground, pink roses and buds, wear to silver
    plated trim, mkd "Belle Ware" 350.00

Syrup Pitcher, Helmschmied Swirl, ivory colored body, blue and
    white floral dec, smoky-gray leafy branches, SP lid and
    collar..485.00

Toothpick Holder, 2" d, 2-1/8" h, straight sided, solid white, pink
    apple blossoms, green leaves, gold trim around top,
    white beaded edge, unmarked 300.00

Tray
  4" w, 4-1/2" h, pale blue and white ground, pink and yellow
    blossoms, white enamel dottings, orig beveled mirror, re-
    placed lining, mkd "Wavecrest" 500.00
  5" w, 1-7/8" h, mottled orange ground, purple violet dec, gold
    finished fancy metal trim, replaced lining, mkd
    "Kelva"..250.00
  6" w, 2-1/4" h, round, shaded green ground, pink, white, and
    yellow chrysanthemums, small burst bubble on int. rim,
    minor int. scratching, mkd "Nakara" 150.00

Trinket Dish, 1-1/2" x 5", blue and red flowers 175.00

Urn, 15-1/2" h, 4-1/2" w, baluster shape, center shades from ivo-
    ry to pale blue, heavily dec in brown, tan, green, pink, and
    white phlox-type flowers and tiny brown ferns, ornate emb
    brass finish base with gargoyle heads, ornate spouts and
    handles with emb heads and phoenix-type bird, un-
    marked, pr..600.00

Vase
  4" h, 4" w, bulbous, mottled pale blue and white ground, front
    panel of three pink flowers with white beading outlined in
    purple, white beaded rim, mkd "Belle Ware" 450.00
  4-3/4" h, 3-1/4" w, two handles, shaded white to pale green
    body, orange daisies on front and back, gold finish metal
    mounts, mkd "Wavecrest" 300.00
  5" h, 1-3/4" w, pale blue ground, white oval panels, small pink
    flowers and green leaves, ormolu foot and rim, un-
    marked 300.00
  6-1/8" h, 2-1/2" w, white ground, small enamel pink and blue
    flowers outlined in purple, bright metal trim,
    unmarked 200.00
  6-1/8" h, 3-1/4" w, pale white ground, front and back panels
    of blue forget-me-nots framed by lavender enamels, met-
    al mountings, unmarked.......................................300.00
  8" h, 3" w, mottled pink ground, nine blue, white, and gray flow-
    ers with white enameled centers, pink beaded top rim, plain
    glass base, mkd "Kelva," price for matched pr.........800.00
  8" h, 3-1/2" w, dark green mottled ground, seven pink and
    yellow lilies, buff trim at base, plain brass rim, mkd
    "Kelva"...350.00
  8-1/2" h, baluster form, opal, mottled blue ground, pink blos-
    soms, gold scrolls, silver plated foot, red "Kelva Trade/Mark"
    on base 490.00
  9-3/4" h, 3" w at shoulder, fancy emb mold, front and back
    with soft pink and blue pansies, white dotting, top beaded
    rim, small enclosed bubble on base, unmarked 250.00
  10" h, pale pink accents on white, pink and orange chrysan-
    themums, enameled foliage, beaded white top 600.00
  12" h, deep green ground, pink and purple poppy dec, mkd "C.
    F. Monroe Kelva," presently mounted as lamp.........225.00
  12" h, 7-1/2" w, dark green mottled ground, five central roses
    surrounded by smaller flowers and buds, metal mounts,
    unmarked Kelva 2,500.00
  12-1/2" h, 4-1/4" w, yellow shaded to russet ground, three
    large lavender and white iris blossoms, round top, flaring
    to six sided base resting on four metal feet, unmarked
    Nakara 900.00

Watch Box, cov, 3-3/4" w, 2-1/2" h, round, soft blue ground, cov
    dec with two cupids framed by panels with white beading,
    clasp missing, partial orig lining, mkd "Nakara" 400.00

Whisk Broom Holder, shaded white to ivory ground, enameled
    pink, lavender, blue, and butterscotch pansies with white
    enamel beading, outlined in lavender enamel, ormolu
    trim, orig satin lining 2,100.00

Whisk broom holder, pink and purple flowers, black trademark, $1,600. Photo courtesy of Gene Harris Antique Auction Center, Inc.

WEBB, THOMAS & SONS

History: Thomas Webb & Sons was established in 1837 in Stourbridge, England. The company probably is best known for its very beautiful English cameo glass. However, many other types of colored art glass were produced, including enameled, iridescent, heavily ornamented, and cased.

References: Victor Arwas, *Glass Art Nouveau to Art Deco*, Rizzoli International Publications, Inc., 1977; Ray and Lee Grover, *English Cameo Glass,* Crown Publishers, Inc., 1980; Charles R. Hajdamach, *British Glass, 1800-1914*, Antique Collectors' Club, 1991; Albert C. Revi, *Nineteenth Century Glass*, reprint, Schiffer Publishing, 1981.

Basket
   6" d, 5-1/2" h, Mat So No-Ke, crimped-in rose Bowl form, four applied crystal handles, eight trailing crystal leaves and flowers, three applied ball crystal feet, applied crystal raspberry, English registration number RD15353 .... 400.00
   8" l, 6-1/2" h, diamond quilted patterned body, vaseline opalescent shading to pink, petal edge, twisted pink handle, c1890...265.00
Beverage Set, 11-3/4" h x 6" w pitcher, four 3-3/4" tumblers, pale cream ext., brilliant cranberry cased int., large cranberry loop handle, white, yellow, and magenta roses and leaves dec 875.00
Bottle, 5-1/4" h, cameo, round cylindrical vial, yellow ground, white overlay, cameo cut and carved leafy spray of blossoms, two flying insects, double linear borders, hallmarked silver cov 800.00
Bowl
   3" w, 2-1/2" h, tricorn, shaded brown satin, gold prunus blossoms and butterfly dec, creamy int., gold trim.......345.00
   5-1/2" w, 5" h, tricorn, Rainbow MOP satin, deep pink, yellow, blue, and white, applied thorn feet, raspberry prunt, sgd "Patent"...1,500.00
   5-3/4" d, 4-1/2" h, avocado green, sapphire blue stripes, mica flakes, crystal applied fancy drippings on sides, applied crystal rigaree around top edge, applied clear feet, clear berry pontil 235.00
   10" d, 3-3/4" h, deep rose shading to pink to white ground, diamond quilted patterned body, MOP satin, box pleated top, applied solid frosted base 775.00
Bride's Basket, 10" d, diamond quilted patterned body, MOP satin, pink ground, ruffled edge, metal base, sgd........400.00
Cologne Bottle, 6" h, cameo, spherical, clear frosted body, overlaid white and red, carved blossoms, buds, leafy stems, and butterfly, linear pattern, hallmarked silver dec, molded and chased blossoms dec.....................3,200.00
Compote, 6-1/2" d, 2" h, Alexandrite, ruffled rim, honeycomb molded Bowl, shaded brilliant blue-purple to pink to amber, applied amber pedestal and foot 2,000.00
Cream Pitcher
   3-1/4" h, sepia to pale tan ground, heavy gold burnished prunus blossoms, butterfly on back, gold rim and base, clear glass handle with brushed gold 385.00
   3-3/4" h, 2-1/2" d, bulbous, round mouth, brown satin, cream lining, applied frosted handle................................210.00
Cup and Saucer, 3-1/2" d cup, 4-7/8" d saucer, Alexandrite, moiré ridged, molded handless cup, shading from blue to pink to yellow...1,200.00
Ewer, 9" h, 4" d, satin, deep green shading to off-white, gold enameled leaves and branches, 3 naturalistic applies, applied ivory handle, long spout, numbered base 425.00
Flower Holder, 12-1/2" l, 8-3/4" w, gold irid glass foot, brass

leaves and branches, four irid gold ribbed flower shaped vases 550.00
Jar, cov, 5" d, blue, diamond quilted patterned body, MOP satin, berries dec, SP hallmarked collar, lid, and bail handle.. 475.00
Perfume Bottle, 4-1/4" h, undulating body, yellow overlaid in white, cut and carved as swimming dolphin, inscribed registry mark, "Rd. 18100," rim and cap missing 4,950.00
Pitcher, 8-3/4" h, 8-1/2" w, deep rose to pale pink peachblow type satin glass body, creamy white int., white and yellow enamel floral dec, green leaves, gold stems, applied frosted loop handle 200.00
Rose Bowl
   2-3/4" h, 3-1/2" d, deep rose, ground pontil, shiny signature "Patent"..385.00
   3-3/4" d, blue swirled MOP satin, green satin glass leaf shaped base 250.00
   6-1/4" d, 5-1/4" h, brown shading to yellow to cream satin, creamy white int., box pleated top, sic crimps 350.00
Salt, master, frosted, Adam and Eve, butterfly signature 80.00
Scent Bottle, 1-1/4" h, 4-1/4" l, lay down, gold prunus blossoms, green shaded to yellow satin ground, hallmarked sterling silver domed monogrammed cap 425.00
Toothpick Holder, Alexandrite, ruffled edge................ 1,100.00
Tray, 12" l, clamshell, shaded pink over white, enameled butterfly and floral, acid script sgd "Webb" 300.00
Vase
   3-1/2" h, 5-1/2" w, pocket type, Flower and Acorn pattern, bridal white, MOP satin,, gold flowers and leaves 650.00
   4-1/4" h, Alexandrite, white body, optic honeycomb dec, gentle flare from shoulder to short neck, pie crusted sapphire blue crimped rim 1,250.00
   4-3/4" h, White Burmese, creamy-white body, all over rosy glow int., sepia-colored Oriental motif drawings, floral branch sweeps across, two small panels in center, one with cottage scene, other with bird in flight, line drawing of two happy birds on reverse, sepia line accents at rim and base 485.00
   5" h, 6" w, 18" circumference, shaded blue, sky blue to pale white cream, applied crystal edge, enameled gold and yellow dec of flowers, leaves, and buds, full butterfly, entire surface acid-cut in basketweave design 425.00
   5-1/4" h, 3-1/2" d, opaque ivory, cut leaves and berries, brown staining, circular cameo mark on base "Simulated Ivory English Cameo Glass," hallmarked silver rim and frosted ball feet..625.00

Vase, bulbous lobes, diamond quilted patterned satin body, mother of pearl int., shaded blue ground, 5-7/8" h, $175.

6-1/2" h, heat reactive amber to rose, cream lining, white overlay, cameo cut wild geraniums and grasses, top rim possibly ground, unsigned................................1,200.00

6-7/8" h, peachblow, acid finish, deep cream lining, shaded rose to cream, heavy gold daisies and leaves, large gold dragonfly on back 675.00

7" h

Cased, deep ruby over white, gold Art Deco thistle, propeller trademark 385.00

Gourd-shaped body, butterscotch yellow shaded to turquoise blue, cased to opal white, outer layer etched and carved as five-petaled rose on front, ornamental grasses on back, linear borders above and below 1,955.00

4" d, satin, robin's egg blue, leaves, berries, and vines dec, flowing gold and scroll design, white lining 450.00

5" w, basketweave patterned body, MOP satin, bulbous base shading from deep blue to pale blue, creamy lining 750.00

7-1/4" h

4" w at shoulder, Rainbow MOP satin, pink, yellow, blue, and white, diamond quilted patterned body, flaring top, broad shoulder, tapered body, glossy white int., sgd "Patent" 1,250.00

Japonesque, pale oval heat reactive body, white Burmese to pink at top, overall delicate oriental sepia scenes 345.00

7-1/2" h, 5-5/8" d, shaded orange overlay, off-white lining, gold flowers and fern-like leaves, gold butterfly on back, applied bronze-colored glass handles 255.00

8" h, 4" w, satin, pink and white stripes, fancy frilly top, bulbous base, unlined...425.00

8-1/2" h

Cased, pink shading to white, enameled floral swags and gold scrolling, three ball feet, acid script sgd "Webb" 175.00

4" w, cased, deep peach pink ext., creamy white lining, dec with spring flowers, blue, pink and white daisies, enameled gold, leaf and branch, pulled down tops with blue and gold enameled dec, pr 200.00

9" h, white opaque over yellow wash, enameled florals and scrolls, acid black letter sgd "Webb".....................250.00

10" h, 4" w, satin, pulled down edges, deep rose shading to pink, creamy lining, ruffled top, dome foot, pr 550.00

10-1/2" h

Gourd shape, satin, bright yellow shading to pale yellow, creamy white lining, bleed-through in pontil 285.00

4" w, bulbous, gold floral prunus blossoms, leaves, branches, pine needles, and insect, satin ground shaded brown to gold, creamy white lining, Jules Barbe dec..450.00

12-1/4" h, colorless oval body, all over etched surface, raised enameled iris flowers, frosted mallard duck poised for flight, base inscribed "Thomas Webb & Corbett Ltd/Stourbridge England" 700.00

Vase, cameo, narrow neck, bulbous base, cameo cut white chrysanthemum blossoms and foliage, peach ground, sgd with dragonfly, 7-1/4" h, $900. Photo courtesy of Freeman\Fine Arts of Philadelphia, Inc.

20" h, 7" w, banjo shape, bright yellow-green ground, pink and white azalea dec, green and white leaves, gold highlights, allover small enameled flowers on neck, painted and enameled collar, dome foot, two applied thorn handles, slight roughness to handles 895.00

Wine, 5-1/4" h, cranberry cut to clear, fine overlay, faceted teardrop stems, elaborate star bases, three stamped "Webb," set of six 600.00

WESTMORELAND GLASS COMPANY

c1910

History: The Westmoreland Glass Company was founded in October 1899 at Grapeville, Pennsylvania. From the beginning, Westmoreland made handcrafted high-quality glassware. During the early years the company processed mustard, baking powder, and condiments to fill its containers. During World War I candy-filled glass novelties were popular.

Although Westmoreland is famous for its milk glass, other types of glass products were also produced. During the 1920s, Westmoreland made reproductions and decorated wares. Color and tableware appeared in the 1930s; but, as with other companies, 1935 saw production return primarily to crystal. From the 1940s to the 1960s, black, ruby, and amber objects were made.

In May 1982 the factory closed. Reorganization brought a reopening in July 1982, but the Grapeville plant closed again in 1984.

Collectors should become familiar with the many lines of tableware produced. English Hobnail, made from the 1920s to the 1960s, is popular. Colonial designs were used frequently, and accessories with dolphin pedestals are distinctive.

The trademark, an intertwined "W" and "G," was imprinted on glass beginning in 1949. After January 1983, the full name, "Westmoreland," was marked on all glass products. Early molds were reintroduced. Numbered, signed, dated "Limited Editions" were offered.

References: Tom and Neila Bredehoft, *Fifty Years of Collectible Glass, 1920-1970*, Antique Trader Books, 1997; Lorraine Kovar, *Westmoreland Glass*, Vols. I and II, The Glass Press, 1991; Hazel Marie Weatherman, *Colored Glassware of the Depression Era, Book 2*, Glassbooks, Inc., 1982; Chas West Wilson, *Westmoreland Glass*, Collector Books, 1996.

Periodical: The Original Westmoreland Collector Newsletter, P.O. Box 143, North Liberty, IA 52317-0143.

Collectors' Clubs: National Westmoreland Glass Collectors Club, P.O. Box 372, Westmoreland City, PA 15692; Westmoreland Glass Collectors Club, 2712 Glenwood, Independence, 64052; Westmoreland Glass Society, 4809 420th St. SE, Iowa City, IA 52240.

Museum: Westmoreland Glass Museum, Port Vue, PA.

Miscellaneous

Animal, covered dish type, white milk glass

Camel, kneeling...75.00

Cat, blue eyes 75.00

October 1967 Keep

CHINA GLASS

& Tablewares

Line your shelves with 22 kt. gold . . . decorated Milk Glass by WESTMORE-LAND. These interest-stimulating milk glass items will add variety and sales appeal to your WESTMORELAND display.

Take advantage of this golden opportunity — order now through your WESTMORELAND representative.

WESTMORELAND GLASS COMPANY, GRAPEVILLE, PENNA.

Ad, showing decorated milk glass, all with 22 kt gold dec. China Glass & Tablewares, October 1967.

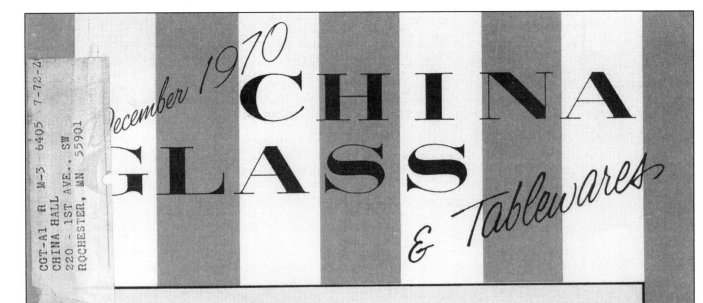

December 1970

CHINA GLASS & Tablewares

It's Time To Order Westmoreland's

ANNUAL NEW ITEM ASSORTMENT

Starting Jan. 1, 1971—Ending March 31, 1971

FREE ITEMS

Mint
Moonstone—Blue

Compote, Crimp,
Moonstone—Crystal

Westmoreland's special assortment of brand new items has proven so popular that we've made it an annual event. This colorful display of choice pieces of handcrafted Westmoreland will create profitable sales for you like magic.

59-PIECE SELECTION

$150.80 YOUR COST

RETAIL VALUE $313.05

$162.25 YOUR PROFIT

TWO FREE ITEMS WITH EACH ASSORTMENT—VALUE $11.45
(Shown at left)

First Come—First Served

Westmoreland
GLASS COMPANY
Grapeville, Pennsylvania 15634

Ad, Moonstone compotes, ruffled and scalloped. China Glass & Tablewares, December 1970.

Chick on eggs, iridized 85.00
Fox, brown eyes, lacy base 75.00
Rooster, standing 50.00
Swan, raised wing 115.00
Basket, Pansy, white milk glass 20.00
Bowl, crimped sailor edge, crystal 30.00
Branch for Wrens, white milk glass 25.00
Butter Dish, cov, Flute, red 35.00
Candlesticks, pr Ring & Petal 22.00
Candy Dish, cov
　Argonaut Shell, ruby, orig label 40.00
　Beaded Bouquet, blue milk glass 35.00
　Wakefield, crystal, low 45.00
Child's Mug, chick, #603, dec, orig label 30.00
Children's Dishes
　Creamer, File & Fan, ruby carnival 20.00
　Pitcher, Flute, cobalt blue, white floral dec 40.00
　Sugar, cov, File & Fan, ruby carnival 30.00
　Table Set, File & Fan, cov butter, creamer, cov sugar, milk
　　glass 45.00
　Tumbler, Flute, green, white floral dec 15.00
Compote
　Colonial, dark blue mist, tall, handle 30.00
　Sawtooth, Golden Sunset, 9" h, 12" w, orig label 75.00
Cruet, Colonial, 2 oz, blue 75.00
Pansy Basket, milk glass 25.00
Picnic Basket, cov, milk glass 30.00
Plate, 10-1/4" d, dinner, #1800 Daisy Decal, dark blue mist,
　scalloped edge 45.00
Punch Cup, Fruits, milk glass 6.00
Punch Set, Fruits, milk glass, 12 pc set 150.00
Slipper, figural, almond milk glass 20.00
Vase, 7" h, horn-shape, Lotus, #9 ....35.00
ater Set, 1776 Colonial, amber, flat water pitcher, six goblets,
　price for 7 pc set 70.00
Wedding Bowl, cov, 10" d, ruby stained 40.00

Patterns

American Hobnail, Pattern #77, white milk glass
Ashtray, 4-1/2" d, round 6.50
Bon Bon, cov 25.00
Candleholders, pr, 5" h 30.00
Compote, 6" h, ftd 20.00
Creamer and Sugar 22.00
Mayonnaise, bell rim, ftd 20.00
Puff Box, cov 25.00
Rose Bowl, cupped, ftd 20.00
Beaded Edge, Pattern #22, white milk glass
Berry Bowl, hand painted fruit center 8.00
Cup, red apple 13.00
Nappy, 5" d, hand painted fruit dec 12.00
Plate
　6" d 5.00
　7" d, salad
　　Fruit center, hand painted 13.00
　　Goldfinch center 13.00
　　Red edge 10.00
　10-1/2" d, dinner 20.00
Beaded Grape, Pattern #1884, white milk glass
Ashtray
　4" d 12.00
　5" d 15.00
Bowl, cov
　4" d, ftd 16.00
　5" d, flared 55.00
　7" d, ftd 35.00

Bowl, open, 9" w, sq, ftd 55.00
Candlesticks, pr 22.50
Candy Dish, cov, 9" d, ftd 40.00
Compote, open, ftd
　7" sq 17.00
　9" sq 30.00
Honey, cov, 5" d, roses and garland dec 45.00
Puff Box, cov, sq 40.00
Sugar
　Individual size 10.00
　Table size 15.00
Bramble/Maple Leaf, Pattern #1928, white milk glass
Bowl, 4-1/2" d, round, ftd 25.00
Compote, crimped, ftd 25.00
Creamer 10.00
Rose Bowl, 4-1/2" d, ftd 25.00
Sugar 10.00
Della Robbia, Pattern #1058. Made in crystal and crystal with
　hand applied stained dec
Candlesticks, pr, light luster 32.00
Compote
　3-1/4" d, stained dark luster colors 35.00
　6" d, stained 25.00
Creamer and Sugar, stained 25.00
Cup and Saucer, crystal 15.00
Dish, heart shape, handle, stained 70.00
Goblet, 8 oz, stained 40.00
Nappy, heart shaped, handle, 8", stained 35.00
Punch Set, cupped punch Bowl, 19" d liner, ladle, ten cups,
　stained dark luster colors 675.00
Salad Plate, dark stain 22.00
Salt and Pepper Shakers, pr, stained 70.00
Sherbet, 10-3/4" h, light stain 26.00
Torte Plate, 14" d, light stain 125.00
Tumbler, flat, dark stain, 8 oz 28.00
Dolphin
Bowl, 8-1/2" d, oval, ftd, milk glass 25.00
Candlesticks, pr
　4" h, cobalt blue 95.00
　4" h, milk glass 25.00
　9" h, milk glass 45.00
Compote, open, ftd
　8" d, milk glass 45.00
　8" d, 7" h, amber 70.00
Console Set, pr 9" h candlesticks, 11" d console Bowl,
　amber 180.00
Lamp, #1049/1, amber 145.00
English Hobnail
Creamer, crystal 8.00
Cruet, large, white milk glass 20.00
Goblet, round ftd, crystal 10.00
Nappy, 4" d, white milk glass 5.00
Plate, 8" d, crystal 10.00
Salt and Pepper Shakers, pr, barrel shape, white milk
　glass 25.00
Sherbet, sq ftd, crystal 8.00
Sugar, sq ftd, crystal 8.00
Wine, 2 oz, ftd, crystal 10.00
Old Quilt, Pattern #500, white milk glass
Bowl
　5" d, ftd, flared 30.00
　6" d, ftd, bell shape 32.00
　7-1/2" d, ftd 35.00
Box, cov, sq 25.00
Butter Dish, cov, 1/4 lb, milk glass 28.00
Candlesticks, pr, milk glass 16.00

February 1962

CHINA GLASS & Tablewares

Westmoreland's Handmade "Golden Sunset" Crystal

The lacy loveliness of Westmoreland's "Princess Feather" Reproductions finds full expression in Westmoreland's golden-hued GOLDEN SUNSET Crystal . . . Available in complete dinner and luncheon services as well as in many exquisite individual gift items—all are authentic reproductions.

Westmoreland's GOLDEN SUNSET Crystal is handmade in five popular patterns: "Beaded Grape", "Ball and Swirl", "English Hobnail", "Sawtooth", and "Princess Feather". Eighty-three exquisite items are now available. Every item in the best Westmoreland tradition of the late 1800's.

WESTMORELAND GLASS COMPANY GRAPEVILLE, PA.

Ad, showing Princess Feather tablewares, complete table service, 83 items available. China Glass & Tablewares, February 1962.

Candy Dish, cov, 4-1/2" d, ftd 25.00
Celery, ftd...20.00
Cheese, cov 52.00
Compote, open, ftd, 7" d, bell shape Bowl 26.00
Creamer
    Large 38.00
    Small 10.00
Cruet, stopper 30.00
Fruit Bowl, 9" d, ftd, crimped, #43.......................45.00
Goblet..48.00
Honey, cov, 5" d 20.00
Iced Tea Tumbler, flat, 11 oz 20.00
Juice Tumbler...6.00
Nappy, 5-1/2" d, bell shape 25.00
Pitcher 40.00
Salt and Pepper Shakers, pr 25.00
Spooner, 6-1/2" h..28.00
Sweetmeat, cov, 6" h, ftd.....................................30.00
Sugar
    Large 28.00
    Small 10.00
Vase, 7" h, ftd, fan 20.00
Wine 25.00

Paneled Grape, Pattern #1881, white milk glass, limited production in other colors.
Appetizer Canapé Set.......................................80.00
Ashtray, sq, large 18.50
Basket, 6-1/2" l, oval...30.00
Bowl, open
    9" d, 6" h, ftd 45.00
    9-1/2" d, lip 100.00
    9-1/2" d, scalloped 125.00
    10-1/2" d, ftd 100.00
    11" l, oval, lipped, skirted pedestal base 110.00
Butter Dish, cov, 1/4 lb....................................30.00
Cake Salver, skirted 85.00
Candelabra, 3-lite...245.00
Candlesticks, pr, 4" h 30.00
Candlesticks, pr
    3-lite..285.00
    4" h 25.00
Candy Dish, cov, 8" d, 3 legs, crimped 35.00
Cheese Dish, cov...60.00
Chip and Dip Set...25.00
Chocolate Box, cov, round...............................50.00
Compote, cov, 7" d Golden Sunset...................40.00
Compote, open, ftd
    6" d, crimped 40.00
    7" d, orig label 20.00
    9" d, clear foot 75.00
Creamer, 6-1/2 oz, orig label 16.00
Creamer and Sugar on Tray, individual size.......27.00
Creamer and Sugar, ice blue............................65.00
Cruet, stopper 30.00
Cup and Saucer 25.00
Decanter...200.00
Epergne, 8-1/2" h vase. 12" d lip Bowl 185.00
Flower Pot...50.00
Fruit Cocktail 20.00
Fruit Cocktail Underplate 9.00
Goblet, 8 oz..18.00
Gravy Boat and Underplate 70.00
Iced Tea Tumbler, 12 oz 25.00
Jardiniere, 6-1/2" h, ftd....................................42.00
Jelly, cov 30.00
Juice Pitcher, pint...40.00

Mayonnaise, 3 pc...28.00
Pitcher
    7-3/4" h 45.00
    8-1/2" h 35.00
Planter
    4-3/4" x 8-3/4" 45.00
    5" x 9" 48.00
Plate
    6-1/2" d, salad 25.00
    8-1/2" d, luncheon 27.50
    10" d, dinner 40.00
Puff Box, cov...30.00
Punch Bowl Base...115.00
Punch Cup 15.00
Punch Set, red hooks and ladle, 13" d, 15 pc set.......595.00
Rose Bowl, 4" d, ftd 30.00
Salt and Pepper Shakers, pr, ftd.........................25.00
Sauce Boat and Underplate.................................70.00
Saucer...8.50
Sherbet, ftd..16.00
Spoon Holder, cov...40.00
Toilet Bottle, orig stopper, 5 oz 45.00
Toothpick Holder..35.00
Tray
    9" l, oval 75.00
    13-1/2" l, oval 75.00
Tumbler, flat 12.50
Tumbler, 12 oz 20.00
Vase
    6" h, ftd, bell-shape 15.00
    9" h, ftd, bell-shape 40.00
    10" h, bud, orig label 30.00
    15" h, swung-type 20.00
    18" h, bud 50.00
Wine, 2 oz..22.50
Princess Feather
Bowl, 5-1/4" d, rolled edge, crystal 15.00
Goblet, 6 pc set..150.00
Plate, 8" d, crystal 15.00
Wine, 2 oz, crystal...12.00
Roses and Bows
Compote, cov, 7" d, green 65.00
Honey, cov, Beaded Grape 45.00
Vase, 9" h, bud 30.00
Vegetable Bowl, cov..75.00
Wedding Bowl, large, "Best Wishes" dec 75.00
Waterford
Cake Salver, ruby stained 75.00
Candy Dish, cov, ruby stained, 9" d...................35.00
Comport, 7" d, ruby stained 45.00
Goblet, ruby stained..15.00
Urn, cov, ruby stained..95.00

WHIMSIES

History: During lunch or after completing their regular work schedule, glassworkers occasionally spent time creating unusual glass objects known as whimsies, e.g. candy-striped canes, darners, hats, paperweights, pipes, and witch balls. Whimsies were taken home and given as gifts to family and friends.

Because of their uniqueness and infinite variety, whimsies can rarely be attributed to a specific glass house or glassworker. Whimsies were created wherever glass was made, from New Jersey to Ohio and westward. Some have suggested that style and color can be used to pinpoint region or factory, but no one has yet developed an identification key that is adequate.

Glass canes are among the most collectible types of whimsies. These range in length from very short (under one foot) to ten feet or more. They come in both hollow and solid form. Hollow canes can have a bulb-type handle or the rarer C- or L-shaped handle. Canes are found in many fascinating colors, with the candy striped being a regular favorite with collectors. Many canes are also filled with various colored powders, gold and white being the most common and silver being harder to find. Sometimes they were even used as candy containers.

References: Gary Baker et al., *Wheeling Glass 1829-1939*, Oglebay Institute, 1994, distributed by Antique Publications; Joyce E. Blake, *Glasshouse Whimsies*, published by author, 1984; Joyce E. Blake and Dale Murschell, *Glasshouse Whimsies: An Enhanced Reference*, published by authors, 1989; Kenneth Wilson, *American Glass 1760-1930: The Toledo Museum of Art, Volume I, Volume II,* Hudson Hills Press and The Toledo Museum of Art, 1994.

Collectors' Club: Whimsey Club, 20 William St., Dansville, KY 14437.

Bird Drinking Font, 4-1/2" h, blown molded, applied cobalt blue ball top and rim 200.00
Bird Feeder, 5-1/4" h, bottle green, emb bird and "Don't Forget To Feed Me" 150.00
Bracelet
  2" to 3" d, Lutz type, clear, multicolored twists and spirals, gold 85.00
  3" d, solid glass, varied colored stripes 65.00
Buttonhook
  5" to 10" l, plain
    Bottle green..35.00
    Colorless...25.00
  7" h, bottle green, elaborately twisted body, amber ends...75.00
Cane
  29" l, solid, aqua, round end, white threads, curved handle, 1860-80 ....165.00
  30" l, solid, colorless, looped end, white rod center ...150.00
  36-3/4" l, 1" w at widest point, white opal spiral with red and blue applied colors, crystal body, family attribution to Boston and Sandwich Glass Co............................625.00
  39" l, core swirl of red, white, and blue 135.00
  46-1/2" l, aqua, spiraled, mid 19th C............................175.00
  48" l, blown, hollow, large ball on end, colorless, red, white, and blue threadings, 1860-80 ....350.00
  48" l, cobalt blue, shepherd's crook handle................265.00
  50" l, blown, hollow, cranberry, white twist, 1860-80.......175.00
  50" l, solid, green-aqua, sq, twisted end and handle, 1860-80...160.00
  52" l, blown, hollow, colorless, deep red, clambroth, light blue, and medium blue twists, 1860-80 ....200.00
  60" l, bottle green, finely twisted, curved handle 150.00
Darner
  5" l, amber head, applied colorless handle 200.00
  6" l, Aurene, gold, Steuben 300.00
  7" l, white ground, blue Nailsea loopings..................165.00
  7-1/2" l, spatter glass, pink, green, blue, and yellow splotches, c1920 ....175.00
  7-1/2" l, white, red Nailsea looping..........................250.00
Egg, hollow, milk glass, various colored splotches
  2" h 65.00

4-1/2" h 85.00
Fly Catcher, 7" h, removable dome top, colorless, 19th C....250.00
Hat, free blown
  1-1/2" h, milk glass, c1910 ....50.00
  1-1/2" h, 4" d, amber, attributed to Keene, c1860.......165.00
  1-3/4" h, 3-3/8" d, light citron, inward rolled rim, pontil scar, attributed to New York state glass house, 1830-50 ......375.00
  2-1/4" h, blown three mold, over pattern mold vertical ribbing, colorless, 24 ribs, folded rim, pontil scar, attributed to Boston and Sandwich Glass Works, Sandwich, MA, 1820-40, 3/4" manufacturer's fissure in pontil scar 150.00
Horn
  8-1/2" l, French horn type, candy stripes 300.00
  10" l, trumpet type, red, white, yellow, purple, and green candy stripes...175.00
Ladle, 10" l, hollow, gold powder filled, colored splotches, curved handles...65.00
Mallet Style Hammer, 8" l, colorless, red, and blue splotches on head, c1920 ....85.00
Pen
  Elaborate, green, finely twisted applied bird finial........85.00
  Simple design, amber, colorless nib, 7" l.....................35.00
Pen Holder, 3" h, 3-1/2" d paperweight base, blown spatter glass, cobalt blue, red, and white solid round sphere, pulled into six coils to hold pen...........................175.00
Pipe
  7" h, standing on three legs, spatter style dec...........100.00
  20" l, spatter, large Bowl, English...............................250.00
  26" l, Nailsea type, opaque white ground, pink loopings, three separate pcs, Bowl, stem, and connector, c1870.....200.00
  36" l, long twisted stem, small hollow Bowl, aqua, America, c1900...120.00
Potichomanie Ball, 12" d, blown, aqua, paper cut-outs of flowers, etc., matching 24" h stand, attributed to Lancaster NY 600.00
Powder Horn
  6-1/2" h, twenty-eight vertical ribs, olive amber, applied ring and lip, pontil scar, New England, 1790-1830 ....1,500.00
  11" h, Nailsea type, ftd, colorless ground, blue and white loopings, tooled ground lip, pontil scar, mid 19th C.........500.00
  12" l, colorless, white Nailsea loopings, raspberry colored drape type striping, early Pittsburgh, 1930-50.......350.00
Rolling Pin
  14" l, black or deep olive green, white dec, early Keene or Stoddard...150.00
  15" l, Nailsea type, cobalt blue ground, white loopings ...165.00
Shoe, 5-1/2" l, Button and Daisy pattern, toboggan form, emb snow shoes, ice blue crystal 45.00
Sword, colorless, colored spirals in handle, attributed to Sandwich Glass Works, late 19th C, pr 400.00

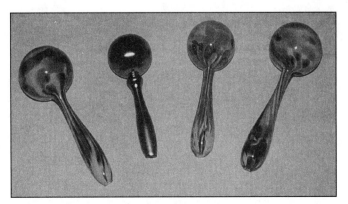

Darners, left: red, and green spatter on white ground, $90; right: blue irid, $115.

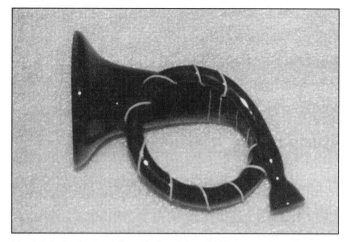

Horn, black glass, white spiral striping, $300.

Witch Ball, matching stand
    3-1/2" d, freeblown, attributed to Boston and Sandwich Glass Works, 1850-80, rose and green loops on white milk glass background, ground moth, smooth base, witch ball only 375.00
    4" d, amber ground, white loopings, matching 4-3/4" h ribbed baluster form holder 500.00
    8" h, tortoiseshell glass ball, attached to amber glass stem and foot 200.00
    9-1/2" h, free blown, deep sapphire blue, pontil scar, attributed to South Jersey, mid 19th C 1,200.00
    12-1/4" h, golden amber, hollow feet, tooled lip, pontil scar, attributed to Whitney Glassworks, Glassboro, NJ, mid 19th C 500.00
    16" h, Nailsea type, colorless, white loopings, pontil scar, attributed to Pittsburgh or New Jersey glasshouse, 1840-60..1,250.00

INDEX

C

D

G

T

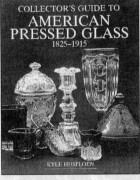